Management Accounting

Information for managing and creating value

Southern African Edition

Southern African Edition

Management Accounting

Information for managing and creating value

Carlos Correia,
Kim Langfield-Smith,
Helen Thorne &
Ronald W. Hilton

The McGraw·Hill Companies

London Boston Burr Ridge, IL Dubuque, IA Madison, WI New York San Francisco
St. Louis Bangkok Bogotá Caracas Kuala Lumpur Lisbon Madrid Mexico City
Milan Montreal New Delhi Santiago Seoul Singapore Sydney Taipei Toronto

Management Accounting, Information for Managing and Creating Value
Southern African Edition
Carlos Correia, Kim Langfield-Smith, Helen Thorne & Ronald W. Hilton
ISBN–13 978–0–07–711690–3
ISBN–10 0–07–711690–9

Published by McGraw-Hill Education
Shoppenhangers Road
Maidenhead
Berkshire
SL6 2QL
Telephone: 44 (0) 1628 502 500
Fax: 44 (0) 1628 770 224
Website: www.mcgraw-hill.co.uk

British Library Cataloguing in Publication Data
A catalogue record for this book is available from the British Library

Library of Congress Cataloging in Publication Data
The Library of Congress data for this book has been applied for from the Library of Congress

Senior Acquisitions Editor: Mark Kavanagh
Development Editor: Karen Harlow
Marketing Manager: Vanessa Boddington
Senior Production Editor: James Bishop

Typeset by Fakenham Photosetting Ltd, Fakenham, Norfolk
Printed and bound in Finland by WS Bookwell

ISBN–13 978–0–07––711690–3
ISBN–10 0–07–711690–9

The McGraw·Hill Companies

Contents in Brief

Contents in Full

Preface

Changes in the competitive landscape and a globalising world economy have had major effects on the theory and practice of management accounting. In the last two decades, there have been significant changes in thinking about the role of management accounting in organisations. Once it was sufficient to describe management accounting as being concerned with providing information for planning and control and for decision making. However, the role of management accounting has evolved and it is now concerned with the theories and practices that enable the effective use of organisational resources, to support managers in enhancing customer and shareholder value. Understanding how to design and implement contemporary cost management techniques or performance measurement systems requires an intimate knowledge of the nature of the business, its markets, its corporate strategies and its people. Over the last two decades, the practice of management accounting has developed to become more a part of the process of management and less a part of the practice of accounting.

Unlike financial accounting, there are no accounting standards or legally enforceable practices and few widely publicised debates over appropriate accounting practice. Management accounting takes place within organisations and can be quite specific to each business. Also, to understand the nature of management accounting practice we need to understand the broader aspects of business practice, across a range of areas including strategy, marketing, human resource management, operations management and organisational behaviour.

This book is aimed at students undertaking an introductory or intermediate course in Management Accounting. The book may also be used in Certificate in the Theory of Accounting (CTA) equivalent courses. The book includes an extensive bank of questions from professional examinations including CMA, ACCA, and CIMA and includes many of the questions from the Qualifying Examination (QE) set by the Southern African Institute of Chartered Accountants (SAICA) in recent years. Due to the integrated nature of many of the SAICA questions and some of the CIMA and ACCA questions, we have included these questions in a separate chapter and have included an index to assist lecturers to select questions from this chapter. Questions in each chapter are graded in terms of theory, short questions, longer problems and case studies.

The book includes many real world examples of management accounting applied by Southern African companies and the public sector which offers students an insight into how theory is applied in practice.

Whilst the book is based on the US text, Managerial Accounting, by Ronald Hilton, and the Australian adaptation by Kim Langfield-Smith and Helen Thorne, the Southern African adaptation includes information that is relevant to the Southern African economy and uses real life examples from Southern African companies. The use of QE questions set by SAICA also makes the book more relevant for Southern African students.

Carlos Correia

Guided Tour

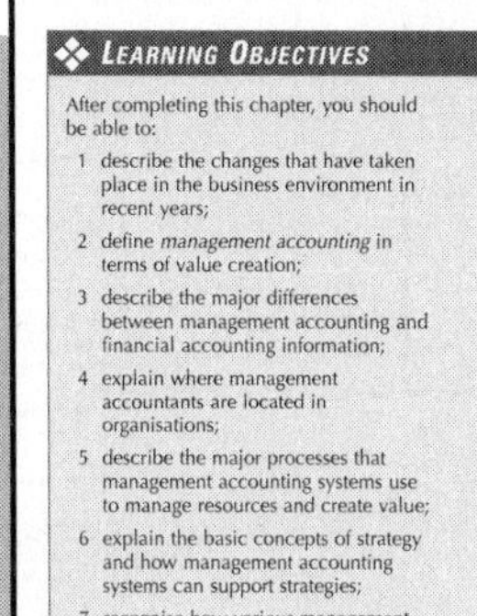
LEARNING OBJECTIVES

After completing this chapter, you should be able to:

1 describe the changes that have taken place in the business environment in recent years;
2 define *management accounting* in terms of value creation;
3 describe the major differences between management accounting and financial accounting information;
4 explain where management accountants are located in organisations;
5 describe the major processes that management accounting systems use to manage resources and create value;
6 explain the basic concepts of strategy and how management accounting systems can support strategies;
7 recognise how various management

Learning Objectives

Every chapter opens with a showcase of the chapter's learning objectives. These highlight what you should be able to do after you have finishing reading that chapter.

ance of the overall group that includes mo
development), incremental income from inno
and so on, thus providing an overview of perfo
and growth.

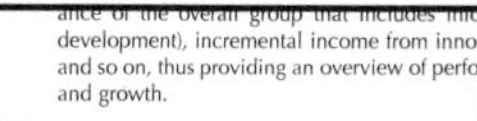
L.O. 3 **Differences between management ac accounting information**

It should be clear from the above discussion quite different to the external reporting focus o ment accounting and financial accounting inf
Financial accounting is concerned with p parties outside the organisation. The balanc reports distributed by Pick 'n Pay and BHP Bill from a financial accounting system. Users of f prospective shareholders, lenders, investment agencies. In contrast, management accounting is, managers).
Financial accounting reports are based on ifiability. Management accounting informatio standards or regulations, so the content and de mined by managers' needs. The nature of m future-oriented. Relevance and timeliness are ability.
There is clearly some overlap between m accounting information, because both dra

Key Terms

Key terms are in bold in the text where they first appear and defined in a full glossary at the end of the book.

REAL LIFE: THE VALUE OF MANAGEMENT ACCOU

Alcoa is one of the world's major aluminium p selected across a range of refineries and min managers were so swamped with information th subordinate managers.
The interviews unearthed several other prob mation. For example, many managers, both seni of the differences between budgeted and actua managers were aware of the inevitable fluctua during the year, which undermined the value

'Real Life' Features

Theory is one thing – but what happens in reality? These short case studies provide examples of management and management accounting in action in South Africa.

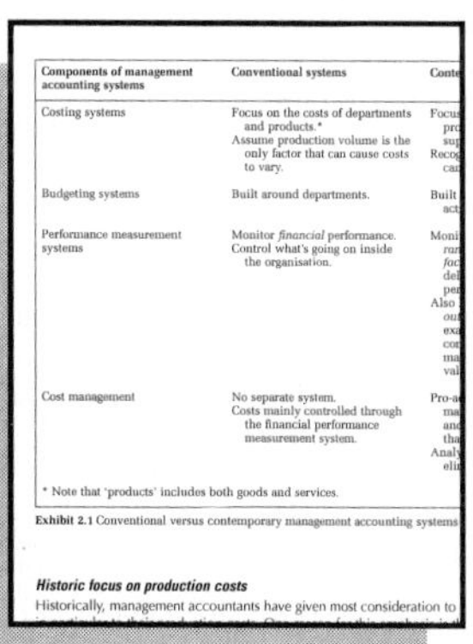

Components of management accounting systems	Conventional systems	Conte
Costing systems	Focus on the costs of departments and products.* Assume production volume is the only factor that can cause costs to vary.	Focu pr su Reco ca
Budgeting systems	Built around departments.	Built act
Performance measurement systems	Monitor *financial* performance. Control what's going on inside the organisation.	Moni ru foc de pe Also ou ex co mu va
Cost management	No separate system. Costs mainly controlled through the financial performance measurement system.	Pro-a ma an th Analy eli

* Note that 'products' includes both goods and services.

Exhibit 2.1 Conventional versus contemporary management accounting systems

Historic focus on production costs

Historically, management accountants have given most consideration to

Exhibits

These diagrammatic overviews of concepts, flow charts, examples of documents and worked examples add another dimension to the topics covered and help to reinforce learning.

Summary

- Product costing is the process of accumula
the firm's products. Product costs are requi
reports. They are also a vital input to maki
for the organisation. For example, manage
decisions such as product mix and pricing
may also use product cost information for
- Different measures of product costs are ap
costing systems assign only production co
for external accounting reports. However,
include upstream and downstream costs. M
product costs in order to make decisions,
future costs.
- One of the most difficult tasks in product c
Most conventional costing systems calcula
which is based on estimates of overhead c
allocated to products according to their co
Underapplied or overapplied overhead is c
goods sold.
- A range of different product costing system
characteristics of the products produced a

Summary

The chapter summary is presented in bullet-point form for easy reading and revision, and links back to the learning objectives.

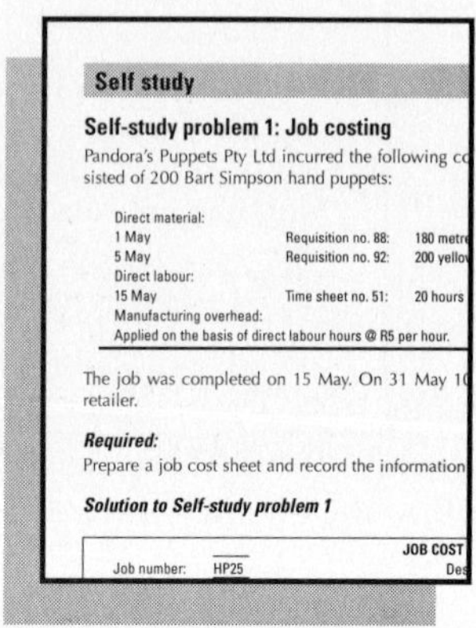

Self study

Self-study problem 1: Job costing

Pandora's Puppets Pty Ltd incurred the following c
sisted of 200 Bart Simpson hand puppets:

Direct material:		
1 May	Requisition no. 88:	180 metr
5 May	Requisition no. 92:	200 yello
Direct labour:		
15 May	Time sheet no. 51:	20 hours
Manufacturing overhead:		
Applied on the basis of direct labour hours @ R5 per hour.		

The job was completed on 15 May. On 31 May 1
retailer.

Required:
Prepare a job cost sheet and record the information

Solution to Self-study problem 1

JOB COST
Job number: HP25 Des

Self-Study Problems and Solutions

These problems provide the perfect opportunity to better understand and revise key topics and techniques covered in the chapter.

Cybersearch

1 Find a website that contains an organisation's
(a) Do these statements correspond with the
why.
(b) What type of management accounting
managers assess whether these objective
2 Find the annual report of a South African
financial information that is provided. Do y
management decisions? Explain your answer.

Cybersearch

Broaden your knowledge of chapter topics by undertaking Cybersearch assignments. These assignments ask you to search the Internet to help you to build a deeper and up-to-date understanding of management accounting concepts, systems and terminology as currently used in organisations and other industry contexts.

Questions

1.1 Select an organisation with which you are
that have taken place in its business envir
1.2 Examine the definition of management a
what is meant by *customer value* and *sha*
1.3 Consider two different products you are f
value as a customer.
1.4 What is meant by *resource management*
cerned with non-financial resources?
1.5 Briefly explain the key differences between f
1.6 Explain the key differences between cost a
1.7 'Some accounting information that is pro
business is of limited use for manageme
accounting procedures, or accounting sta
an example to illustrate this issue.
1.8 Where in an organisation would you expe

End of Chapter Assessment Material

Extensive end of chapter assessment material consisting of questions, problems, exercises and cases helps you to understand and apply knowledge and techniques to fully test your level of learning.

Technology to enhance learning and teaching

*Visit **www.mcgraw-hill.co.uk/textbooks/correia** today*

Online Learning Centre (OLC)

Lecturers adopting this textbook can access supporting resources to assist with their teaching by logging onto the supporting Online Learning Centre website.

Resources available are:

- Solutions to questions in the book
- PowerPoint slides.

Details of this online content are correct at the time of going to press and may be subject to change. Please refer to the website for up-to-date information.

Custom Publishing Solutions: Let us help make our content your solution

At McGraw-Hill Education our aim is to help the lecturer find the most suitable content for their needs and the most appropriate way to deliver the content to their students. Our **custom publishing solutions** offer the ideal combination of content delivered in the way which suits lecturer and students the best.

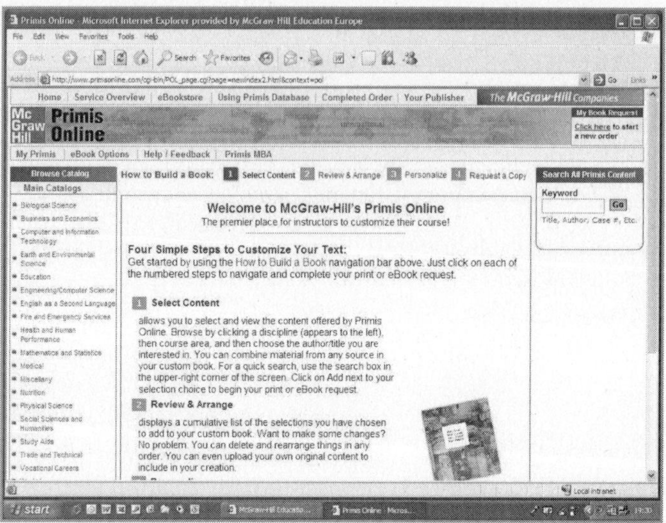

The idea behind our custom publishing programme is that via a database of over two million pages called Primis, *www.primisonline.com,* the lecturer can select just the material they wish to deliver to their students:

Lecturers can select chapters from:

- textbooks
- professional books
- case books – Harvard Articles, Insead, Ivey, Darden, Thunderbird and BusinessWeek
- Taking Sides – debate materials

Across the following imprints:

- McGraw-Hill Education
- Open University Press
- Harvard Business School Press
- US and European material

There is also the option to include material authored by lecturers in the custom product – this does not necessarily have to be in English.

We will take care of everything from start to finish in the process of developing and delivering a custom product to ensure that lecturers and students receive exactly the material needed in the most suitable way.

With a **custom publishing solution**, students enjoy the best selection of material deemed to be the most suitable for learning everything they need for their courses – something of real value to support their learning. Teachers are able to use exactly the material they want, in the way they want, to support their teaching on the course.

Please contact *your local McGraw-Hill representative* with any questions or alternatively contact Warren Eels e: *warren_eels@mcgraw-hill.com.*

Acknowledgements

Publisher's Acknowledgements

Our thanks go to the following reviewers for their comments at various stages in the text's development:

Anet Smit, *Potchefstroom Business School, North West University*
Kevin Freeman, *Nelson Mandela Metropolitan University*
Cecilia Beukes, *University of South Africa*
Max Mackenzie, *Wits Business School, University of Witwatersrand*
Colin Smith, *University of Cape Town*
Percy Phatshwane, *University of Botswana*

We'd also like to extend our thanks to the companies who kindly granted us permission to reproduce their logos. This includes:
Steers
City Lodge Hotel Group
Kulula.com
FIFA
Capitec Bank
Tongaat Hulett Sugar
Massmart Holdings Ltd
Gold Fields Ltd
PriceWaterhouseCoopers
Barloworld
Anglo Gold Ashanti Plc
ATM Solutions

Authors' Acknowledgements

We would like to thank Colin Smith for his significant contribution to Chapter 23 as well as his advice and insights drawn from many years of lecturing in Management Accounting.

About the Authors

CARLOS CORREIA, *BCom (Hons), MCom (Cape Town), CA (South Africa)*

Carlos Correia is Associate Professor and Convenor of the Masters in Financial Management programme at the University of Cape Town. Carlos has published in the financial press and in peer-reviewed research publications and was three times awarded the Standard Bank Prize (first or runner-up prize) for outstanding research published in the *SA Journal of Accounting Research* (formerly *De Ratione*). He is co-author of the textbook, *Financial Management* and the Australian textbook, *Corporate Financial Management.* He has presented papers at a number of international and national conferences. He has consulted widely and areas of specialisation include capital budgeting, performance evaluation, valuations and cost of capital.

KIM LANGFIELD-SMITH

Kim is Professor of Management Accounting in the Department of Accounting and Finance at Monash University, Australia. Prior appointments were at La Trobe University; The University of Melbourne; University of Tasmania; and University of Technology, Sydney. Kim has a BEc from the University of Sydney in accounting, a MEc from Macquarie University, a PhD from Monash University and is a fellow of CPA Australia.

HELEN THORNE

Helen is Professor of Management and Head of the International Graduate School of Business at the University of South Australia. Previously she has held appointments in the Graduate School of Management and the Commerce Department at the University of Adelaide. She has a BEc and DipAcc from Flinders University, and a PhD from The University of Adelaide.

About the Authors

PART 1
Introduction to Management Accounting

Part Contents

The first part of this book introduces management accounting, its purpose and basic concepts.

In Chapter 1 management accounting is defined as processes and techniques that are focused on the effective use of organisational resources to support managers in their task of enhancing both customer value and shareholder value. We outline the recent changes in the business environment that have influenced the development of management practices and management accounting systems, and management accounting is distinguished from financial accounting.

The processes and techniques of management accounting that are used to enhance value include systems to support the formulation and implementation of strategy; process improvement and cost management techniques to help develop and manage a firm's competitive advantage; planning and control systems to help managers manage resources; and estimates of the cost of products and services to support strategic and operational decisions.

In this first chapter we also consider the design of a management accounting system, including an awareness of the behavioural implications of management accounting information, and the costs and benefits of designing, producing and using management accounting information. A case study of Steers, one of South Africa's leading burger franchises, is used to illustrate many of the management accounting concepts.

Chapter 2 introduces some of the basic concepts and terminology used in management accounting. Management accounting systems often include costing, budgeting and performance measurement systems. Contemporary management accounting systems may also include cost management systems, which focus on the identification and elimination of wasteful activities.

Much of this chapter focuses on the different ways in which costs can be classified and reported to managers. These classifications include variable and fixed costs, direct and indirect costs, and controllable and uncontrollable costs. We use the concept of the value chain to explore the various cost classifications, paying particular attention to the classification of manufacturing costs as direct material, direct labour and manufacturing overhead costs. The essential message in this chapter is that costs can be classified in different ways to meet the different information needs of managers.

Management Accounting: Information for Managing Resources and Creating Value

Learning Objectives

After completing this chapter, you should be able to:

1 describe the changes that have taken place in the business environment in recent years;

2 define *management accounting* in terms of value creation;

3 describe the major differences between management accounting and financial accounting information;

4 explain where management accountants are located in organisations;

5 describe the major processes that management accounting systems use to manage resources and create value;

6 explain the basic concepts of strategy and how management accounting systems can support strategies;

7 recognise how various management accounting techniques have been developed to support a firm's competitive advantage;

8 explain how planning and control mechanisms can be used to support resource management;

9 explain how costing systems can provide information to support a range of operational and strategic decisions;

10 describe the behavioural issues and the cost–benefit trade-offs that need to be considered in the design of management accounting systems;

11 identify the organisational responses and management accounting responses to changes in the business environment;

12 after studying the appendix, describe how the focus of management accounting has evolved; and

13 after studying the appendix, discuss the professional qualifications that are relevant to becoming an accountant, and the ethical standards to which accountants must adhere.

Introduction

We all deal with many different types of organisations as part of our daily lives. Manufacturers, retailers, service providers, not-for-profit organisations and government enterprises provide us with a vast array of goods and services. These organisations seem very different, but they have three things in common. First, every organisation should have a stated purpose and objectives. For example, a police department may state that its purpose is to make the community a safer place in which to live. The specific objectives of an organisation flow from its purpose. In the case of the police department, the objectives may be to reduce the crime rate by 50 per cent and decrease the number of road fatalities by 30 per cent within the next five years. The objectives of organisations generally focus on adding value from the perspective of major stakeholders—in particular, owners and customers.

Second, in pursuing objectives managers need to make many decisions, and for this they need information. The information needs of managers extend across financial, production, marketing, legal and environmental areas. Generally, the larger the organisation, the more complex are its operations, and the greater is management's need for information. In the police department, senior officers will need information to assess progress towards objectives. Relevant information could include crime statistics for each quarter of the year, explanations of why crime rates may be meeting or exceeding targets, and details of the strategies put into place to reduce crime.

Finally, to help achieve the organisation's objectives, managers need to manage their resources effectively and efficiently. Resource management can involve using resources more effectively (that is, achieving better outcomes) and using resources more efficiently (that is, using fewer resources to achieve an objective). In the police department, management will need to know the cost of new crime-reduction programs that have been put in place.

Management accounting information helps to satisfy the information needs of managers so that they can manage resources effectively and add value for customers and the organisation as a whole.

Throughout this book we use case studies to bring management accounting principles and concepts to life. This chapter is based on the story of South Africa's well-known burger specialists, Steers, but before we move to the Steers story, let's explore the business environment in which management accounting has evolved and operates.

South African organisations in the 21st century

L.O. 1

Throughout the 1990s many South African organisations became exposed to global competition for the first time. South African companies could no longer ignore the activities of companies operating in Asia, Europe and the US. From the early 1990s, import tariffs, quotas and restrictions were gradually reduced or eliminated. Many overseas companies became direct competitors for South African businesses. For example, decreasing tariffs affected the South African textile and clothing sectors in a profound way with many textile and clothing manufacturers being forced to close down their operations. Even South African automotive manufacturers, such as General Motors, VW and Toyota, as well as their local suppliers were affected, although in a more positive way. High-quality motor vehicles manufactured overseas were imported into the domestic markets at competitive prices, to compete directly with locally produced cars. South African automotive component suppliers also found that they were competing directly with overseas suppliers, as Toyota and the other South African car manufacturers began to source their supplies globally. However, at the same time, South African automotive manufacturers and component suppliers have been successful in exporting to Europe and the USA. The South African government provides incentives in terms of the Motor Industry Development Programme although the pricing of motor vehicles in South Africa is being investigated by the competition authorities. However, the motor industry in South Africa remains one of the country's success stories and represents about one-third of the country's manufacturing base. Textile and clothing manufacturers have not been able to withstand global competition and we have seen the demise of many clothing manufacturers as retailers increasingly source merchandise from China.

Changes in the regulatory environment have affected many different industries. Deregulation of the telecommunications industry in the 1990s saw a variety of companies, such as MTN and Vodacom, enter the market as indirect competitors to Telkom, a business that once held a monopoly in the telecommunications market in South Africa. Although Telkom retains a monopoly over fixed-line telephony services, a new competitor to Telkom should start operations in the near future. In the airline sector, such airlines as Nationwide and 1Time have emerged to challenge the two dominant domestic airlines, South African Airways (SAA) and Comair (BA). Comair successfully launched a low-cost airline, called kulula.com, and SAA responded by introducing its own low-cost provider, Mango. In the 1990s, many former public utilities and government bodies were commercialised, or corporatised. Some public enterprises also found themselves competing directly with private companies. The process of corporatisation and privatisation of the public sector has continued into the new century. For example, we have seen the privatisation of parts of Transnet (ex. sale of the V&A), Telkom and the introduction of toll roads, which represents a partial privatisation of the road system. Many public hospitals and local government councils now operate as commercial businesses. There have also been major changes in the regulation of labour markets, which have significant implications for the competitiveness of businesses.

Over the past few decades we have seen a shift from South Africa as a primary producer and exporter of mineral resources to its becoming also a service-based economy. Growth areas in the service sector include tourism and 'knowledge-based' industries, such as software programming and business process outsourcing. Demand from China has given a renewed impetus to the role of resources and there has been increasing consolidation in the retail and banking sectors. In the banking sector there are really only four banking groups – Standard Bank, ABSA, First Rand and Nedcor. Perhaps we can also include Investec. Globalisation has affected the banking sector, as ABSA is now part of Barclays plc, a UK-based banking group.

South African businesses, in common with their overseas counterparts, operate in an environment that is subject to rapid and unpredictable change. Customers make increasingly strong demands on businesses for specific product requirements. The rise of the Internet and e-commerce has challenged the traditional modes of business operation, and the increase in outsourcing and a greater reliance on various forms of business networks and relationships has led to the emergence of virtual organisations. The Internet, for example, has changed banking in South Africa fundamentally, while information technology has affected all industries. For example, inventory control has been improved by the use of bar codes.

The changing environment has provided both opportunities and threats for South African organisations. Companies have had to evolve and adapt to find better ways to compete. New organisational structures, strategies and management philosophies have been adopted to enable organisations to be more responsive to customer needs and better able to make quick and informed decisions within global markets.

It is little wonder that the practice of managing businesses effectively in the 21st century is very different from even five years ago. In addition, the focus of management accounting has had to keep pace with the information needs of contemporary organisations. In the appendix to this chapter there is a detailed account of the changing focus of management accounting over the past few decades.

Steers: A South African success story

Steers, part of the Famous Brands retail franchise group,[1] is an incredible South African success story, with more than 450 restaurants selling over 30 million flame grilled burgers per year. Steers was the brainchild of George Halamandaris who, in the 1960s, decided to introduce the American concept of fast-food catering to South Africa. Steers is one of South Africa's leading burger franchises in the country and the company prides itself on providing consistent quality, cleanliness and great service.

The company describes its brand values as follows:

> The three pillars of the Steers brand are: Innovation, value for money and being the flame grilled burger specialists. Steers remains the market leader by offering the widest range of classic and gourmet burgers using a unique flame grilled process. It also offers the best value for money: a lot more for a little more — offering the consumer more quality and more satisfaction.

Steers opened its first fast-food store in Jeppe in 1970 and the Steers franchising concept was launched in 1983. Since then its franchising and retail operations have continued to grow and develop. The Steers story is one of growth driven by energy, enthusiasm and commitment. In 2004 Steers achieved sales turnover of R700 million from its South African stores and in 2008, Steers achieved a turnover of over R1 Billion. While South Africa has always been its primary market, Steers has not escaped the influences of globalisation, described earlier. During the 1990s Steers began expanding into Africa and now has restaurants in Kenya, Malawi, Mozambique, Namibia, Senegal, Sudan, Swaziland, Tanzania, Zambia and Zimbabwe.

In 1994 Steers Holdings (now known as Famous Brands) was listed on the JSE Securities Exchange. The group expanded and now includes the following brands: Steers, Wimpy, Debonairs Pizza, FishAways, Brazilian and House of Coffees. Steers has pursued growth and profitability strategies, leveraging off Steers' position in the fast-food sector, as well as diversifying into other activities such as sauce and spice production, operating bakeries and butcheries. The sauces and other products are also marketed through the supermarket chains. The franchise network under the Famous Brands banner consists of over 1500 restaurants located in South Africa on the African continent and in the UK as Wimpy.

Steers and the Famous Brands group provide a rich setting to explore the information needs of managers and the nature of management accounting.

L.O. 2 What is management accounting?

Management accounting refers to the processes and techniques that focus on the effective and efficient use of organisational resources, to support managers in their tasks of enhancing both customer value and shareholder value. Let's look more closely at this definition.

Value creation is a central focus for contemporary managers and can refer to both customer value and shareholder value. Customers have always been a key concern for organisations. However, it is only in recent years that managers have come to recognise explicitly that understanding **customer value**—the value that a customer places on particular features of a product—and satisfying customers is critical to achieving increased sales and market share, and therefore to achieving shareholder value.

Shareholder value is also a key focus for managers and involves improving the worth of the business from the shareholders', or owners', perspective. So what is important to shareholders? Shareholders are usually interested in increased profitability, increased share price, and dividends, and management is charged with the responsibility of delivering this.

However, increasing customer value comes at a cost and, at times, managers may need to make trade-offs between undertaking actions that increase customer value, and actions that increase shareholder value. For example, more seating at Steers' outlets may enhance customer value, and by increasing sales also enhance shareholder value. On the other hand, the push towards bigger sites with seating comes at a cost—which may have a detrimental effect on the potential to grow shareholder value. Where there is a conflict between increasing customer value and increasing shareholder value, shareholder value is likely to be given priority as this is the key strategic objective for most organisations. (Alternative objectives and priorities can be expected in not-for-profit organisations.) Resolving this conflict is not always straightforward. For example, increasing customer value may decrease shareholder value in the short run as costs also increase, but may increase shareholder value in the longer run, as market share increases.

To enhance customer value or shareholder value, managers need to understand what drives value. That is, they need to understand and make decisions about the activities or aspects of their business that lead to improvements in customer value or shareholder value. How important is seating. Do most Steers' customers want to 'eat in' or 'take away' their burgers? Later in this book we will learn about management accounting processes and techniques that may be used to assist managers to identify and manage those drivers, and to make decisions. Important decisions for managers include which products to produce or services to offer, what prices should be set, what equipment should be purchased and so on.

The effective and efficient use of resources is essential to creating both customer and shareholder value, and management accounting provides information to assist managers to perform this role. Effectiveness focuses managers on the successful achievement of an objective, whereas efficiency focuses managers on achieving the objective with the least possible consumption of resources. **Resources** can be defined broadly to include not only the financial resources of the organisation, but also non-financial resources such as information, work processes, employees, committed customers and suppliers. Non-financial resources determine the capabilities and competencies of the organisation, which allow it to survive and prosper in an increasingly turbulent global environment.

We will see in later chapters that there are a variety of management accounting techniques and skills that can be used to manage resources in order to achieve increased customer and shareholder value.

Management accounting systems

A **management accounting system** is an information system that produces the information required by managers to manage resources and to create value. It forms part of an organisation's wider management information systems. Management accounting information can be provided on a regular basis and can include estimates of the costs of producing goods and services, information for planning and controlling operations, and information for measuring performance. Management accounting systems also provide information on an *ad hoc* basis, to satisfy the short-term and long-term decision-making needs of management. The management accounting system may not be able to provide all of the information to satisfy managers' decision-making needs; sometimes information also needs to be obtained from other sources, including those outside the organisation. For example, the costing system at the Steers butchery provides regular reports on the cost of beef patties produced. Steers processes 3360 tons of beef patties per year. However, from time to time Steers managers may need information about the prices from other manufacturers, which are both competitors of Steers and potential suppliers to franchisees. Indeed, as franchising law requires the franchise system to ensure fair trading, Steers management needs to be sure that the price of Steers' own beef patties is competitive in the market.

Management accounting information

The focus of management accounting is on the needs of managers within the organisation. Because accounting standards apply only to external financial reports, there is great flexibility in deciding the type of information that should be generated for managers. As managers' information needs vary, and as the nature of the resources that they manage also varies, the type of management accounting information required will also need to vary. Other factors that cause management accounting systems to differ include differences in production or service technologies, organisational structure and organisational size, the external environment in which the organisation competes, and the levels of sophistication of computer systems. These aspects can affect managers' needs for, and the supply of, information, and will be an important influence on the design of a management accounting system. For example, when George Halamandaris set up the first Steers store in 1970, the cash register provided daily sales information, and recording payments to his small staff and purchases was straightforward. Now, with more than 350 stores located across South Africa and the rest of Africa and its own butchery, bakery and sauce and spice production facility, the information needs of Steers managers across the organisation are far more complex. Stores still collect daily sales information, but now this information can be analysed at the head office, in real time, to produce a wide range of reports about sales by store, region and product line.

Finally, it should be noted that management accounting information is relevant to managers from the top of the organisation through to managers in operational areas of a business. Senior managers need information that provides them with an overview of the entire organisation, whereas middle managers require more detailed information about their areas of responsibility. Also, operational managers will need information to help them manage their specific operations on a day-to-day basis, to help ensure that their performance targets are met. (**Operational managers** are managers who have responsibility for activities in the manufacturing areas of manufacturing firms, or for the areas that directly provide services to customers in service firms.)

Steers requires management accounting information reports on its value drivers. Different reports are prepared for different levels of management. The business has a separate division that works directly with franchisees on individual store reports. One critical measure of franchisees' performance is the rent-to-sales ratio. As well as informing store managers, this information and other forms of business intelligence are reported at head office, where trends in products, revenue, costs and the broader business model are tracked. Business analysts also collect and monitor a range of workforce and new product development indicators, as well as stock and distribution information. These reports are tailored to meet the needs of particular managers. For example, workforce reports are developed for the human resources manager, supply and distribution reports go to the logistics manager, and so on. Top management at head office receives a monthly scorecard on the performance of the overall group that includes information about the workforce (including employee development), incremental income from innovation, trends in unit sales and average transactions, and so on, thus providing an overview of performance in the Steers' key areas of people, innovation and growth.

L.O. 3 Differences between management accounting and financial accounting information

It should be clear from the above discussions that the orientation of management accounting is quite different to the external reporting focus of financial accounting. Exhibit 1.1 contrasts management accounting and financial accounting information.

Financial accounting is concerned with preparing and reporting accounting information for parties outside the organisation. The balance sheets and income statements within the annual reports distributed by Pick 'n Pay and BHP Billiton to their shareholders are examples of the output from a financial accounting system. Users of financial accounting information include current and prospective shareholders, lenders, investment analysts, unions, consumer groups and government agencies. In contrast, management accounting focuses on satisfying the needs of internal users (that is, managers).

Financial accounting reports are based on past information that emphasises objectivity and verifiability. Management accounting information and reporting are not constrained by accounting standards or regulations, so the content and design of management accounting information is determined by managers' needs. The nature of management accounting information is current and future-oriented. Relevance and timeliness are considered more important than objectivity and reliability.

There is clearly some overlap between management accounting information and financial accounting information, because both draw data from an organisation's transaction-based accounting system. However, to manage the wider resources of the organisation, management accounting also draws on data from many other sources, both internal and external to the organisation. These may include data from operations (production) systems, personnel systems and customer information systems, as well as market-share data and competitor costs from external bureaux. Also, the level of detail and the frequency of reporting of management accounting information is greater than for financial accounting.

	Management accounting	Financial accounting
Users of information	Internal: managers and employees at all levels.	External: shareholders, creditors, banks, stock exchange, trade unions, government agencies.
Regulations	No accounting standards or external rules are imposed. Information is generated to satisfy managers' information needs.	Accountants preparing reports must comply with accounting standards. Incorporated bodies must comply with applicable accounting standards and requirements of the *Companies Act*.
Source of data	Both financial and non-financial data drawn from many sources—the core accounting system; physical and operational data from production systems; market, customer and economic data from databases external to the organisation.	Financial data almost exclusively drawn from the organisation's core transaction-based accounting system.
Nature of the information	Historic, current and future-oriented; subjective; relevant; timely; supplied at various levels of detail to suit managers' specific needs.	Historic; objective; auditable; reliable; not timely; not always relevant; highly aggregated.

Exhibit 1.1 Management accounting versus financial accounting

One part of a firm's accounting system that is common to both financial accounting and management accounting is the costing system. The **costing system** (or **cost accounting system**) estimates the cost of goods and services, as well as the cost of organisational units, such as departments. Managers may need information about product costs for a range of strategic and operational purposes including setting prices, controlling operations and making decisions about the continuation of a particular product. These are management accounting uses. However, product cost data are also used to value inventory on a manufacturer's balance sheet and cost of goods sold on the income statement, which are financial accounting uses.

Management accounting is broader than just the preparation and reporting of financial information. Management accounting also includes analyses of non-financial resources, including manufacturing and sales performance data, and a range of techniques for managing costs and other organisational resources. Exhibit 1.2, which is drawn from a number of job advertisements, illustrates the diverse role of the management accountant and highlights the broad range of information provided to managers.

Management accountants within organisations

L.O. 4

To appreciate the management accountant's role in an organisation, we need to understand how organisations are structured and where the accounting staff may be located. However, the structures of organisations vary considerably and frequently change. Many large South African businesses are structured with a corporate head office and a series of operating divisions. These divisions may relate to different geographical locations of the company. Alternatively, they may focus on different product markets—Famous Brands has separate divisions for its franchising, food services and corporate services. Organisational structures often identify significant functions, especially at the corporate level. For example, the organisational structure of the Standard Bank includes units for domestic and international banking. Domestic banking is further divided into Retail banking and Corporate and Investment banking.

Working closely with the Financial Controller, your primary focus will be the provision of management accounting services to senior management teams, to enable the decision-making process and support them in the long-term planning process. You will also oversee product costing, review company finance procedures, management of general ledger and ensure legal compliance in respect of corporation tax and VAT.

* * *

Key duties will include variance analysis, cost investigations, budgeting, forecasting, balance sheet reconciliations and working cross functionally with operational managers. Candidates must be excellent communicators as this role will involve raising the profile of finance within operational areas of the business. The ability to influence and challenge decision-making is therefore key.

* * *

Reporting into the Finance Director, you will be responsible for overseeing the preparation of monthly management accounts, forecasting and budgeting, reviewing operational accounts procedures and analysis of P&L, as well as working with the commercial team on *ad hoc* projects. Good system and communication skills are a must, including a good knowledge of Excel and reporting packages.

* * *

Principal duties will include supporting the Finance Director in commercial projects and strategy, preparing monthly management accounts, preparing group sales and gross margin reports, managing inter-company accounts, quarterly forecasting, tax analysis and *ad hoc* project work. Good communication skills are essential.

Exhibit 1.2 The diverse role of the management accountant

The accounting function

Most large South African organisations have a 'finance function', which is the group of staff who undertake a variety of accounting activities. As you will note from Exhibit 1.2, within the finance function the senior accountant may have a variety of titles, including financial controller, finance director, financial analyst, business analyst, general manager of accounting and group accountant. (Indeed, the 'Real life' below indicates more creative titles such as strategic resource manager and e-commerce strategist!) The financial controller is usually responsible for both management accounting and financial accounting activities. As the organisation's most senior management accountant, the controller acts as an adviser to managers. Moreover, most financial controllers influence resource management decisions across all management levels and functional areas of the enterprise. In the 21st century, financial controllers are usually important members of the senior management team. In recent years, former accountants have served as chief executives in companies such as Bidvest and Old Mutual.

In some businesses accounting staff may be found in each operating division, as well as at the corporate level. Accounting staff are increasingly being located close to the operations of the business. This allows them to work more closely with operations managers and other employees.

In some organisations, accountants are clearly designated as either management accountants or financial accountants. In other businesses the distinction may be blurred, with many accountants being responsible for both functions. However, it should also be noted that the various processes and techniques that we describe as 'management accounting' increasingly involve managers in other areas of a business, and are not solely the domain of the accountants. For example, the design and operation of performance measurement systems, an important aspect of management accounting, may involve managers in the human resource-management area. A new costing system may be designed, and perhaps even initiated, by production engineers.

Clearly, management accountants have an important role to play in co-ordinating many aspects of the management accounting system, and as a part of the management team. However, we should not necessarily assume that they are the sole custodians of management accounting information across every organisation! In the appendix to this chapter you may read about the changes that have taken place in the positioning of management accounting in organisations over the past few decades.

The 'Real life' section outlines some of the changing skills and roles of accountants in organisations.

REAL LIFE: THE NEW GENERATION OF ACCOUNTANTS

A recent survey by international consultant Robert Half International of 1400 chief financial officers (CFOs) highlighted the sweeping changes that are taking place in the accounting and finance profession and in the necessary skills and competencies of accountants within organisations. For example, 82 per cent of CFOs indicated that their accounting departments had become more involved with their company's technology initiatives in the past five years, and 49 per cent had become involved in e-commerce projects in the past three years.

The mandatory skills for accountants were identified as:

Source: Williams (2001)

- *Technical.* An understanding of new applications and software, including wireless technologies.
- *Communication.* Strong written and verbal skills, including the ability to explain financial information in non-financial terms.
- *Interpersonal.* Persuasion, diplomacy, negotiation, coaching and team-building skills, to enable accountants to relate to colleagues from many different backgrounds and professions.
- *Managerial.* Expertise in the areas of management, marketing and operations, to allow accountants to understand the areas and function of the business.

The survey also revealed the many different job titles that now apply to senior accounting positions. These include financial manager, financial analyst, financial specialist, strategic resource manager, consultant, e-commerce strategist, asset manager and assurance services provider.

Management accounting processes and techniques

L.O. 5

So far in this chapter we have explained that management accounting is focused on the effective management of resources to support managers in their quest for improved customer value and shareholder value. But what are the processes and techniques that management accounting uses to achieve this?

Management accounting:

- supports the organisation's formulation and implementation of strategy;
- contributes to improving the organisation's competitive advantage in terms of quality, delivery, time, flexibility, innovation and cost, through modern process improvement and cost management techniques;

- provides information to help manage resources, through systems for planning (such as budgets) and control (such as performance measures); and
- provides estimates of the costs of the organisation's output (goods and services), to support both the strategic and operational decision needs of managers.

Let's look at examples of each of these areas.

Management accounting and strategy

L.O. 6

In many organisations in the 21st century management accountants play an important strategic role by contributing to the organisation's *formulation and implementation of strategy* and by helping managers *improve the organisation's competitive advantage.*

To make sense of this role we introduce some basic strategy concepts:

- mission statement
- vision
- objectives
- strategies.

Let's define each of these terms.

Many organisations prepare a **mission statement** that defines the purpose and boundaries of the organisation (Johnson & Scholes, 1999; Viljoen & Dann, 2000). Mission statements tend to change very infrequently.

Steers does not have a specific mission statement, but the statement of strategic intent of Steers parent company, Famous Brands, is set out on the company's website, www.famousbrands.co.za.

> It is the Group's intention to remain the leading marketer and developer of branded franchised QSR (Quick Service Restaurant) concepts on the African continent. Famous Brands Limited will continue to dominate the QSR industry through strong brands such as Steers, Wimpy, Debonairs Pizza, House of Coffees and Brazilian, as well as through other brands that may be acquired or established during the coming years.

The group is specific about how it will achieve its strategic intent:

> To ensure we maintain and grow our dominant position in the market, unwavering attention is focused on the cornerstones of the group's brand portfolio: affordability (value for money), accessibility (situated within arms' reach of desire), and appeal (high quality innovative offerings). At the forefront of our strategy is to establish the concept of quick service and casual dining restaurants as a way of life.

A **vision** is the desired future state or aspiration of an organisation (Johnson and Scholes, 1999). The vision of Unitrans Ltd, one of South Africa's leading transportation, distribution and logistics companies, is to be 'a customer-centric international provider of diversified services, delivering sustainable profit growth'. The vision is often used by senior management to focus the attention and energies of staff throughout the organisation.

Steers has acted on its vision is to grow its business by creating owner-operated franchised stores. Steers provides support to its franchisees in relation to site selection, training, operations and marketing. In return Steers earns an initial fee, an advertising royalty of 5 per cent of turnover and a franchise royalty of 5 per cent of turnover. Steers even indicates what a standard Steers store owner can earn, as shown in Exhibit 1.3 (from its website), although this return is not guaranteed, as many factors will determine the returns earned by individual stores.

While not all organisations specify a mission statement and vision, they all have some form of objectives. **Objectives** (or **goals**) are specific statements of what the organisation aims to achieve,

Exhibit 1.3 Business plan for a standard Steers store

Source: www.steers.co.za (August 2006)

INCOME STATEMENT		Year 1	%	Year 2	Year 3	Year 4	Year 5
Sales		**2 034 618**	**100.00%**	**2 339 811**	**2 690 783**	**3 094 400**	**3 558 560**
Less cost of sales		813 847	40.00%	935 924	1 076 313	1 237 760	1 423 424
Gross Margin		**1 220 771**	**60.00%**	**1 403 887**	**1 614 470**	**1 856 640**	**2 135 136**
Expenses		**804 653**	**39.55%**	**925 351**	**1 064 154**	**1 223 777**	**1 407 343**
Accounting & Audit fees		10 200	0.50%	11 730	13 490	15 513	17 840
Bank charges		20 346	1.00%	23 398	26 908	30 944	35 585
Credit card fees		12 208	0.60%	14 039	16 145	18 567	21 352
Cleaning		10 173	0.50%	11 699	13 454	15 472	17 793
Electricity		50 865	2.50%	58 495	67 269	77 359	88 963
Gas		17 294	0.85%	19 888	22 871	26 302	30 247
Insurance		12 938	0.64%	14 879	17 111	19 677	22 629
Phone & Fax		7 200	0.35%	8 280	9 522	10 950	12 593
Printing & Stationery		7 121	0.35%	8 189	9 418	10 830	12 455
Operating costs		9 000	0.44%	10 350	11 903	13 688	15 741
Rent		156 000	7.67%	179 400	206 310	237 257	272 845
Repairs & Maintenance		7 200	0.35%	8 280	9 522	10 950	12 593
Royalties		101 731	5.00%	116 991	134 539	154 720	177 928
Royalties – Advertising		101 731	5.00%	116 991	134 539	154 720	177 928
RSC Levies		6 307	0.31%	7 253	8 341	9 592	11 031
Salaries / Wages		151 200	7.43%	173 880	199 962	229 956	264 450
UIF		2 419	0.12%	2 782	3 199	3 679	4 231
Uniforms		3 600	0.18%	4 140	4 761	5 475	6 296
Staff food		15 120	0.74%	17 388	19 996	22 996	26 445
Security + cash collection		12 000	0.59%	13 800	15 870	18 251	20 988
Owners salaries		84 000	4.13%	96 600	111 090	127 754	146 917
Other		6 000	0.29%	6 900	7 935	9 125	10 494
N/I before interest & depr		**416 118**	**20.45%**	**478 536**	**550 316**	**632 864**	**727 793**
Depreciation		180 000		180 000	180 000	180 000	180 000
N/I before interest		**236 118**	**11.61%**	**298 536**	**370 316**	**452 864**	**547 793**
Interest on loan		50 239		41 377	31 390	20 137	7 457
N/I before taxation		**185 879**	**9.14%**	**257 159**	**338 926**	**432 727**	**540 336**
Taxation	30.0%	55 764		77 148	101 678	129 818	162 101
N/I after taxation		**130 115**	**6.40%**	**180 011**	**237 248**	**302 909**	**378 235**
CASHFLOW							
N/I before interest & depr		**416 118**		**478 536**	**550 316**	**632 864**	**727 793**
Loan repayment		120 120		120 120	120 120	120 120	120 120
Net Income for Reinvestment		**295 998**		**358 416**	**430 196**	**512 744**	**607 673**

Source: www.steers.co.za (August 2006)

often quantified and relating to a specific period of time. Many organisations focus their objectives around some of the following:

- profitability
- growth
- cost minimisation
- product leadership
- innovation
- product quality
- quality of service
- community service
- employee welfare
- environmental responsibility.

Unitrans Ltd set out its corporate objectives as follows:

- Revenue growth
- Headline earnings growth
- Growth in the international component of the group's businesses
- Reposition Freight and Logistics as a supply chain service provider
- Expand in the commuter bus transport market
- Growth in the group's car rental operations
- Expand Motors' retail footprint
- Increase return on shareholders' funds.

Organisational strategies

The **strategies** of an organisation specify the direction that the organisation intends to take over the long term, to meet its mission and achieve its objectives (based on Johnson and Scholes, 1999). The strategies will focus on ways to manage the organisation's resources to create value for customers and shareholders.

In *formulating an organisation's strategies*, major decisions include:

- In what business will we operate?
- How should we compete in that business?
- What systems and structures should we have in place to support our strategies?

The first decision involves formulating corporate strategy. **Corporate strategy** involves making choices about the types of businesses in which the organisation as a whole will operate. This includes decisions about what businesses to divest or acquire, and how best to structure and finance the company. In publicly listed companies the choice of corporate strategy is heavily influenced by expectations of major shareholders and the share market.

The decision by Steers to diversify business activities by, for example, acquiring Debonairs Pizza and Wimpy is an example of a change in corporate strategy to become a leader in the Quick Service Restaurant sector rather than to remain focused on flame-grilled burgers. The second type of decision involves business strategy. **Business** (or **competitive**) **strategy** is concerned with the way that a business competes within its chosen market. For example, Famous Brands operates its fast food divisions on a competing basis. If an organisation consists of several different business units, each with its own distinct market, then there will be a competitive strategy developed for each unit.

The third question is concerned with **strategy implementation**, which involves planning and managing the implementation of strategies. This can include introducing new structures and systems, such as setting up new business units, implementing new production processes, implementing new software packages, developing new marketing approaches, and introducing innovative human resource management policies.

In implementing its strategies, Steers has recognised the importance of getting the experience right, and will also focus on the selection of franchisees that will result in owner-operated stores as this together with other factors is seen as critical to the success of the brand.

A closer look at business strategy

To create shareholder value a business must develop and manage its sources of competitive advantage. A well-known model for thinking about competitive advantage was developed by Michael Porter of Harvard University. **Competitive advantage** refers to advantages that a business may have over another, which are difficult to imitate. Porter suggests that a firm can gain a sustainable competitive advantage through adopting a business strategy of cost leadership or product differentiation.

When a firm is a low-cost producer, this allows the business to sell its goods or services at a lower price than competitors (**cost leadership**). Alternatively, firms may derive competitive advantage by offering goods or services that have characteristics that are superior to those offered by competitors (**product differentiation**). Forms of product differentiation include superior quality, customer service, delivery performance and product features such as innovation. Within the one industry there may be successful cost leaders and successful differentiators. Many firms will develop a business strategy that emphasises both cost leadership and some form of differentiation. However, a firm may choose to place greater emphasis on either type of competitive strategy.

Businesses that choose to place a greater emphasis on cost leadership may achieve this in several ways, such as through economies of scale in production, superior process technology, tight cost control and cost minimisation in areas such as marketing, production, research and development, and customer service.

In South Africa examples of businesses that compete primarily on the basis of cost include Mr Price, Fruit & Veg, Shoprite, and Massmart. In these businesses attention is also paid to aspects of differentiation, such as customer service and quality, but it is the firm's cost performance that provides the basis for competitive advantage. However, for Woolworths Food, the focus is on quality rather than on price.

When a differentiation strategy is followed, the emphasis is on creating some characteristic of the good or service that is perceived by customers as unique. Successful differentiators are able to set selling prices that more than offset the cost of the added product features that are valued by customers. Differentiation may be on the basis of a number of characteristics such as high-quality products (Mercedes Benz), strong brand image (Coca-Cola, Rayban), superior customer service (Standard Bank) and product innovation (Nokia, Motorola). Many firms pursue a combination of differentiation strategies (for example, the Edgars department stores focus on quality and superior customer service).

The emphasis at Steers is on value-for-money experiences and customer service rather than on price. The overall experience is the key. The company's credo is 'real food made real good' and the company is committed to using the best ingredients and ensuring that all food is freshly prepared in each restaurant.

Management accounting: contributing to strategy

Management accountants should tailor information to support the formulation and implementation of their organisation's strategies.

Strategic planning

Strategic planning is the term given to long-term planning, usually undertaken by senior managers, with a three- to five-year timeframe. Strategic planning involves making *corporate strategy* decisions about the types of businesses and markets in which the organisation operates, and business (or competitive) strategy decisions about how the business is to compete within its particular markets. Strategic planning draws on a wide range of management accounting information from the costing, budgeting and performance measurement systems, as well as information from special studies internal and external to the organisation.

Implementing strategies

Once strategies have been formulated, managers at all levels of the organisation share the responsibility for implementing them. Management accountants can play an important role in this process using the planning and control systems described below. Long-term plans need to be linked to the budgeting system, to produce annual budgets that support the organisation's strategies. Likewise, performance measurement systems can be used to compare actual outcomes to budgets and other targets that focus on the organisation's strategic objectives.

Management accounting: contributing to competitive advantage

L.O. 7 Well-managed organisations focus their objectives and strategies on building and maintaining sources of competitive advantage. To be an effective contributor to strategy, the management accounting information should be shaped around the organisation's sources of competitive advantage. If a firm competes primarily on the basis of low cost, its management accounting information should focus on product costs and tight cost control. If a firm follows a differentiation strategy, the focus should be on performance around the sources of differentiation such as quality, delivery, time, flexibility and innovation. For example, the management accounting reports at Steers monitor costs, but they also provide a lot of information about product and process innovation, and about people—a key driver of customer service (and ultimately of quality and innovation).

With an increasing emphasis on strategy in organisations, several such strategic management accounting techniques have evolved since the 1990s. These include performance measurement systems that focus directly on aspects of business strategy, and techniques for improving the organisation's competitive advantage through modern process improvement and cost management, with an emphasis on reducing costs while also enhancing customer value.

Planning and control

L.O. 8 Planning and control systems are a vital element of management accounting. As part of strategy implementation, organisations need to put in place plans to set the direction of the organisation, and control systems to ensure that operations are proceeding according to plan. Planning and control systems provide the framework for effective resource management to generate customer and shareholder value.

Planning

Planning is a broad concept that is concerned with formulating the direction for future operations. Plans are necessary so an organisation can consider and specify all of the resources that will be needed in the future—whether financial or non-financial. Planning activities occur at many levels within an organisation. As described above, many organisations develop strategic plans that normally involve a three- to five-year timeframe. However, most organisations also prepare short-term or operational plans, called budgets. A **budget** is an example of a plan that summarises the financial consequences of an organisation's operating activities for a specified future time period, usually one year.

To examine the nature of planning, let's consider the planning processes at Steers during the 1990s. McDonald's, a multinational fast food giant, began setting up stores across South Africa with significant advertising, resulting even in long queues for the initial stores. Although the Steers experience was very different to that of McDonald's, it seemed that consumers were affected at least temporarily by the allure of McDonald's, which also offered burgers at a lower cost. Nonetheless, the strength of the Steers brand, great site selection, a focus on value for money, freshly prepared food and flame-grilled burgers enabled the company to withstand the competition from McDonald's, and the sales revenue of Famous Brands has grown from R292 million in 2003 to close to R900 million in 2007.

The repositioning of Steers and the creation of Famous Brands was a huge undertaking, which required detailed planning, supported by extensive information. The group needed estimates of the resources required to develop and produce new products, new store designs, new marketing campaigns, and so on. Planning for such an operation entails more than formulating resource budgets: it also includes formulating detailed schedules and time-lines for its implementation, and selecting performance measures and targets to assess its success. Much of this information was future-oriented and financial in nature, and management accounting assisted in providing and analysing this data. This future orientation is a particular characteristic of management accounting information that distinguishes it from financial accounting information. Non-financial information was also important in formulating and evaluating these plans, and the inclusion of non-financial information is another distinguishing feature of management accounting information.

Implementing plans: information for decisions

Almost every organisation has some sort of plans, whether detailed budgets or something less formal, and managers are responsible for implementing these plans (and sometimes for adapting them to take account of unplanned circumstances). Planning, implementing plans and controlling requires managers to make many decisions; and to make decisions, managers need information.

Many decisions made by managers occur frequently, so information to support these decisions, such as budgets, performance reports and product costs, is prepared on a regular basis. However, management accounting information is also needed to support non-routine decisions. For example, in making decisions about the development and implementation of their project, the Steers leadership team relied on information drawn from regular management accounting reports, such as sales performance and product and store costs. However, the project also required a lot of additional information that was not available from routine management accounting reports, such as estimates of the costs of new store designs, costs of new product lines, estimated uptake of new ideas by franchisees, and so on.

Management accounting systems are designed to produce frequently required information (often for control purposes), but need to be flexible enough to generate some of the information that is needed for decisions that occur very infrequently, or only once.

Controlling

Effective resource management must also include systems for control. **Control** involves putting in place mechanisms to ensure that operations proceed according to plan and that objectives are achieved. There is sometimes confusion between the terms 'planning' and 'control', probably because of their interdependence. Plans will not be effective unless there is some way of ensuring that they are achieved. This is the role of control and control systems. **Control systems** are the systems and procedures that provide regular information to assist with control.

Exhibit 1.4 describes the various components of planning and control, and how they relate. In providing information for control, an aim of management accounting systems is to motivate employees to act in the interests of the organisation. This can be achieved by setting targets and then measuring the performance of managers and business units against those targets.

Thus, the control function is an important aspect of management accounting, as it directly assists in managing the use of resources in order to achieve plans for creating value.

Let's evaluate the implementation of a family-image concept for an ice-cream company's stores in order to illustrate the nature of control. During the planning stage, targets are set for the number of stores converting to the new image, as well as for store growth (measured in sales

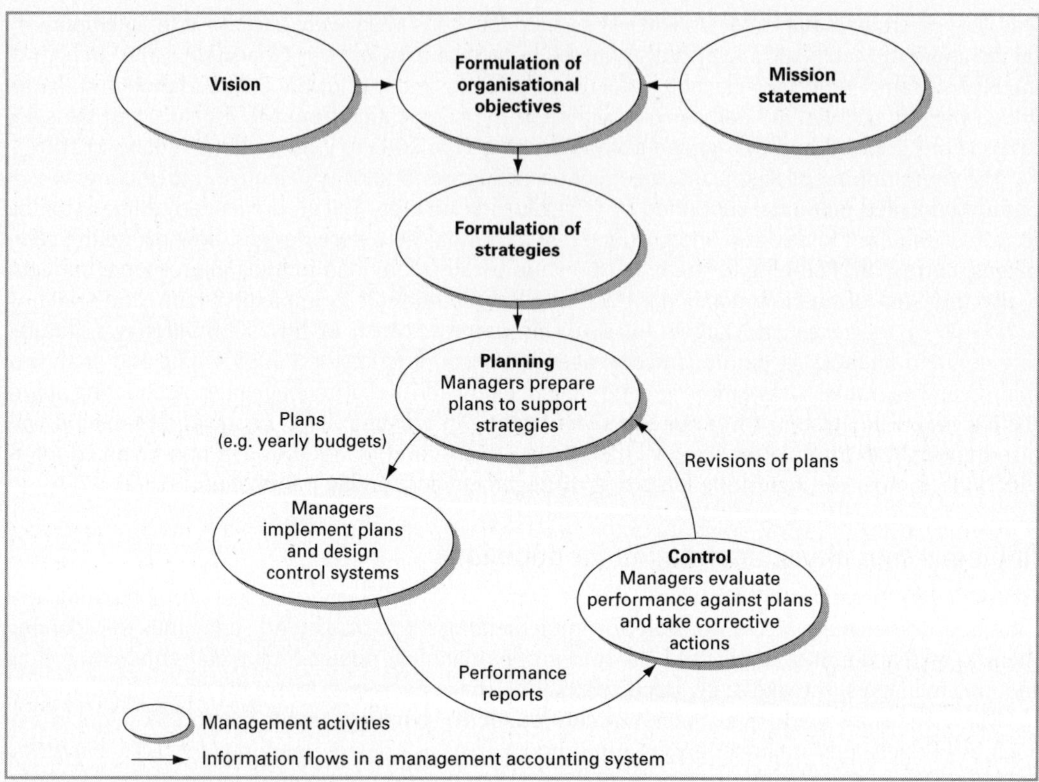

Exhibit 1.4 Planning and control systems

Rands), customer counts and average transaction value. Targets are also set to monitor the development of new products and various 'people skills', as well as movements in product mix expected with the new concept. For example, if an ice-cream retailer shifts to a more adult positioning, then soft-serve sales would be expected to become less important. The management accounting system at a company will need to produce reports that compare these targets (and many others) with actual performance. When actual performance moves away from the targets, the reasons need to be investigated and actions need to be taken to correct any problems. In this way, management are able to exercise a degree of *control* over the operations underlying the implementation of their new concept.

Costing goods and services

L.O. 9

Estimates of the cost of producing goods and services are often needed to support a range of operational and strategic decisions that confront managers. In manufacturing firms, and in some service firms, routine systems are established to estimate the cost of goods and services. Sometimes this forms a part of the financial accounting system. However, sometimes costs that are estimated for management decisions are produced outside of the financial accounting framework. Why is this so?

Financial data within an organisation's primary accounting system is usually prepared for external reporting purposes. Thus, it is governed by traditional accounting conventions ('generally accepted accounting principles' or GAAP) and legally enforceable accounting standards. However, the costing information produced by the financial accounting system may not be adequate for managers' decisions. For example, let's consider decisions that require an estimate of the cost of producing a product. Products that are costed for financial reporting purposes – for example, to value inventory or cost of goods sold – consist of manufacturing costs only. Many managers believe that for some decisions, such as whether or not to continue to produce a product, product costs should also include other product-related costs, such as marketing and customer support. Managers will also require information about the future revenues and costs of the product. However, future costs do not form part of the primary accounting systems of a business. (These issues will be discussed further in Chapter 4.)

Some managers also believe that the simplistic methods used to value products for external reporting purposes are too inaccurate to be used for managers' decisions. Thus, in the 1990s, some companies began to use activity-based costing (ABC) systems to provide more accurate estimates of product costs for use in managers' decision-making. These costing systems are described in Chapter 8.

Some important considerations in the design of management accounting systems

L.O. 10

Several important considerations influence the choice and design of management accounting systems. We will introduce these issues briefly here, and they will be considered further throughout the text.

Behavioural issues

When designing and implementing management accounting systems, we need to be conscious of the ways in which information impacts on individual behaviour. There may be expected and unexpected outcomes of management accounting systems. The reactions of both individuals and groups of individuals to management accounting information will significantly affect the activities and decisions within an organisation. For example, at Steers the accounting staff need to consider how franchisee sales staff might behave if made accountable for a very tight cost budget. Will they reduce customer satisfaction by reducing serve sizes? How much detail should be included in the reports to franchisees, and how often should they receive this information? If too much detail is provided, will they be overloaded with information and distracted from the main points? Understanding the behavioural implications of management accounting information is a real challenge for the Steers accounting team, given the potential impact on staff within the Steers corporate team, who are employees, and their franchisees, who are external to the business.

Motivating managers and other employees

We have seen that organisations have objectives or goals. However, organisations are made up of people who have goals of their own. The goals of individuals are diverse, and they do not always match those of the organisation. A key purpose of the management accounting system is to motivate managers and other employees to direct their efforts towards achieving the organisation's goals. One way of achieving this is through the design of tools such as budgeting and performance measurement. In management accounting, performance measurement systems are a key source of information for motivation. One means of motivating people to commit to the organisation's goals is to measure their performance in achieving performance targets. Such performance can be used as the basis for providing rewards. Rewards may include positive feedback (such as words of congratulation from the manager), promotions, bonuses and pay rises. For example, many large companies base the salaries of senior executives, in part, on achieving profit targets. In this way managers are encouraged to take actions that maximise the company's objectives. A growing trend in South African companies is to involve employees at all levels of the business in employee share plans. Many South African companies have employee share schemes in place. One reason for these schemes is to encourage all employees to identify more closely with their company and its goals.

REAL LIFE: WHAT INFORMATION SHOULD MANAGEMENT ACCOUNTANTS SUPPLY?

A survey of North American managers examined the type of information that managers used in their day-to-day activities and for performance evaluation. Accounting information was found useful for performance evaluation, but inadequate for the management and control of operational tasks. Many managers had given up using accounting reports and had developed their own systems. The authors recommended that:

1. *Management accountants should help in the provision of physical unit data to managers.* This includes daily information on physical measures for operational control, such as the number of units produced, number of units rejected, time lost to injuries, rescheduled shipments, quantity variances and units in inventory. Unlike financial measures, these are items that production managers can actually control.
2. *Management accountants should play a major role in ensuring effective interdepartmental communication between sales and production.* The information flows between sales and production are irregular and often undertaken on an informal basis.
3. *Management accountants should redefine their roles to include managing the development and implementation of information systems.* The traditional role of management accountants, as the primary providers of information within businesses, has slipped away. The scope of accounting information is regarded as too limited by many managers, and it often arrives too late to be of use for control or decision-making purposes.

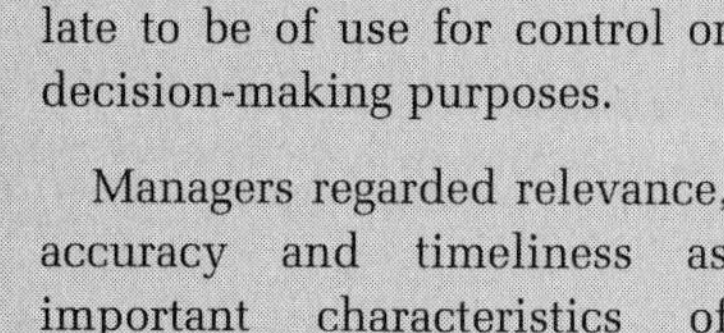

Managers regarded relevance, accuracy and timeliness as important characteristics of information. However, much accounting information provided to managers did not rank highly on these criteria, because some management accountants were tied to financial models of reporting. To regain their role as primary information providers, management accountants need to become more directly involved in the operation of data-collection and reporting systems, and move closer to the managers they are serving.

Source: McKinnon & Bruns (1992, 1993)

A company may use a sophisticated planning and control system that extends beyond financial budgets and performance measurement. For example, the performance of each member of a company's leadership team may be measured by a number of key performance indicators (KPIs), and their remuneration is linked to KPI achievement. Both short-term and long-term objectives may be rewarded, with long-term incentives based on three-year plans. There may also be franchisee reward programs, operating in an environment of continual performance reporting to the franchisee community.

Costs and benefits of information

Information is a commodity, much like wheat or wool. Like other goods, information can be produced, purchased and consumed. It can be of high or low quality, timely or late, appropriate for its intended use or totally irrelevant. The generation and provision of information entails both costs and benefits. The costs of providing management accounting information to managers include the salary cost of accounting personnel, the cost of purchasing and operating computers, the cost of the time spent by managers to read, understand and use the information, and the cost of gathering, processing and storing information.

The benefits include improved decisions, more effective planning, greater efficiency of operations at lower costs, better control, and improved customer and shareholder value.

Thus, there are both costs and benefits that need to be assessed when considering whether to provide particular information. However, some accountants, eager to show that they have not overlooked anything, provide too much information. When managers receive more information than they can use effectively, information overload occurs. Struggling to process large amounts of information, managers may be unable to recognise the most important facts. In deciding how much and what type of information to provide, management accountants should consider human information-processing limitations.

The Alcoa case, in the 'Real life', describes a situation in which the costs of information provided by the management accountant seemed to outweigh its benefits. And this is not an isolated example. A survey of 720 Australian organisations, from both private and public sectors, identified monthly reports of less than 10 pages as 'best practice' in management reporting. Yet 80 per cent of respondents exceeded this target, with 30 per cent producing reports of 30 pages or more each month. The report noted that a number of accountants seemed to:

> ... have a 'communicable' disease ... [that] manifests itself in reports growing in the number of pages, print size becoming squint size and report formats not designed to aid the manager [to] locate key information ... Busy executives want their reports to be concise. Best practice is to give them fast, brief reports that highlight the matters worthy of their attention and requiring action.

We will reinforce the need to trade off the costs and benefits of management accounting information throughout this text. Of course, a difficulty with this principle is that, while we can quantify the costs of providing information, the mainly intangible benefits of improved information cannot be determined with accuracy.

Management accounting responses to the changing business environment

L.O. 11

At the start of this chapter, we outlined some of the recent changes that have taken place in the business environment leading into the 21st century. Exhibit 1.5 provides a summary of key changes in the business environment, changes that have taken place within organisations to allow them to compete effectively, and new management accounting techniques that have been developed to support managers' changing needs.

To improve shareholder value, firms need to increase their competitiveness. By the 1990s, many firms realised that they needed to improve product or service quality, delivery responsiveness, cost performance, and ultimately market share and profits. This led to organisations adopting some of the new management structures, systems and practices listed in Exhibit 1.5. Throughout the following chapters we will refer to conventional and contemporary management accounting

REAL LIFE: THE VALUE OF MANAGEMENT ACCOUNTING INFORMATION AT ALCOA

Alcoa is one of the world's major aluminium producers. Interviews with a sample of managers selected across a range of refineries and mining sites in Western Australia found that senior managers were so swamped with information that the analysis of cost reports was delegated to subordinate managers.

The interviews unearthed several other problems with the management accounting information. For example, many managers, both senior and junior, considered the monthly reports of the differences between budgeted and actual results to be 'pointless' for control. Senior managers were aware of the inevitable fluctuations in production processes that occurred during the year, which undermined the value of the variance reports. Junior managers considered that the budgets were unrealistic and provided no constraint on their spending. Managers in the mine sites also viewed the routine management accounting reports as 'largely superfluous' for decision-making purposes. These managers regarded information from online systems, or the informal reports that the mine managers generated themselves, as much more valuable.

Courtesy of Alcoa World Alumina
Source: Smith (1994)

The evidence suggested a need for the Alcoa management accounting team to evaluate the costs and benefits of the information they provided to their managers. Indeed, the interviews were part of a total quality management program in the accounting function at Alcoa that addressed this issue.

approaches. Conventional approaches include budgeting systems, costing systems and financial performance measurement systems. These systems have been in wide use for many decades. Contemporary approaches are more recent developments, and some of these newer techniques are identified in Exhibit 1.5. For example, activity-based costing, a more accurate method for determining the costs of goods, services, customers, projects and activities within organisations, as well as for budgeting, is described in Chapters 7 and 8, and revisited in Chapters 11, 15, 16, 18 and 19. Chapter 12 introduces economic value added, a measure of shareholder value. New approaches to measuring performance are explored in Chapter 14. Chapter 15 presents new methods of cost management and time management. These include activity-based management, business process re-engineering and target costing. In Chapter 16, we describe new techniques for managing customers and suppliers, and in Chapter 17 we explore recent developments in management accounting for the environment and social responsibility. Of course, even in chapters that focus primarily on more traditional management accounting techniques, contemporary adaptations and developments are also described.

Changes in the business environment →	Organisational responses: structures, systems and practices →	Management accounting responses (chapter in which discussed)
■ Increased global competitiveness ■ Deregulation of the service sector—banks, communications, utilities ■ Privatisation/ commercialization of public service providers ■ Reduced tariffs on imports ■ Growth of the service sector	■ Flatter organisational structures ■ Employee empowerment ■ Team-based structures ■ Computerised production systems ■ ERP systems ■ e-commerce technologies ■ Real-time reporting systems ■ Supply chain management ■ Increased focus on key sources of customer value, such as quality, delivery and innovation ■ Increased focus on continuous improvement ■ Environmental management systems	■ Activity-based cost systems (Chapter 8, and revisited in 15, 16, 18 and 19) ■ Activity-based budgeting systems (Chapters 9 and 11) ■ Measures of shareholder value (Chapter 12) ■ Performance measurement systems such as balanced scorecards, and benchmarking (Chapter 14) ■ Cost management systems: activity-based management, business process re-engineering, managing throughput, life cycle management and target costing (Chapter 15) ■ Time management (Chapter 15) ■ Customer profitability analysis (Chapter 16) ■ Supplier cost analysis (Chapter 16) ■ Information to support environmental and social responsibility (Chapter 17)

Exhibit 1.5 Key influences on management accounting systems

The 1990s have passed, and we are now well into the 21st century. However, introducing change in organisations can be a difficult and slow process. Some South African organisations are yet to implement many of the organisational changes and new management accounting techniques, whilst many others are in the midst of implementing change.

A range of contemporary management accounting techniques have been developed in recent years to support the adoption of a range of new organisation structures, systems and practices, which are a response to changes in the business environment. As we move through the chapters of this book we will learn about both traditional and more contemporary management accounting techniques.

Summary

Management accounting refers to the processes and techniques that are focused on the effective use of organisational resources, to support managers in their tasks of enhancing both customer value and shareholder value. Key points include:

- By the 1990s South African companies had been exposed to increased competitiveness and rapid and unpredictable change.
- Management accounting can be distinguished from financial accounting. Financial accounting focuses on preparing and reporting accounting information for external parties, deals with past information, is regulated by International Financial Reporting Standards, and emphasises objectivity and verifiability. Management accounting draws data from wider sources than the transaction-based accounting system, is not subject to external regulations, considers current and future information, and emphasises relevance to managers.

- Management accountants in organisations may be located in accounting departments or closer to the aspects of the business that they support, such as the manufacturing operations areas. In some organisations, management accounting activities are also performed by managers from other functional areas of the business.
- The processes and techniques that are used by management accounting to improve value include:
  - systems to support the formulation and implementation of strategy
  - process improvement and cost management techniques to help develop and manage the firm's competitive advantage
  - information to help managers manage their resources through planning and control systems
  - estimates of the cost of products to support strategic and operational decisions.
- The objectives of an organisation flow from the vision and mission statement, and strategies are developed to achieve these objectives. Management accounting provides information to support the development and evaluation of strategies, and strategy implementation.
- Management accounting may contribute to activities that seek to improve the organisation's performance in terms of quality, delivery, time, flexibility, innovation and cost, through modern process improvement and cost management techniques.
- Planning and control systems are part of strategy implementation and assist in improving the management of resources. Planning systems set the direction of the organisation, while control systems help to ensure that operations are proceeding according to plan.
- Costing systems provide information about the costs of goods and services, which is important in a range of operational and strategic decisions.
- Some important considerations in the design of a management accounting system include an awareness of the behavioural implications of management accounting information, and of the costs and benefits of designing, producing and using management accounting information.

References

Famous Brands website: www.famousbrands.co.za

Famous Brands: 2005 annual financial statements

IFAC 2002, *Competency Profiles for Management Accounting Practice and Practitioners*, study no. 12, January, Financial and Management Accounting Committee, International Federation of Accountants, New York.

Johnson, G & Scholes, K 1999, *Exploring Corporate Strategy*, 5th edn, Prentice Hall Europe, Hemel Hempstead, England.

McKinnon, SM & Bruns, WJ 1992, *The Information Mosaic*, Harvard Business School Press, Boston, MA.

McKinnon, SM & Bruns, WJ 1993, 'What production managers really want to know . . . management accountants are failing to tell them', *Management Accounting* (US), January, pp. 29–35.

Viljoen, J & Dann, S 2000, *Strategic Management*, 3rd edn, Longman, Sydney.

Smith, M 1994, 'Improving management accounting reporting practices: a total quality management approach (Part 2)', *Journal of Cost Management*, Spring, pp. 49–56.

Steers web site: www.steers.co.za

Williams, K 2001, 'Are you the next-generation accountant?', *Strategic Finance*, July, pp. 17, 75.

Cybersearch

1 Find a website that contains an organisation's mission statement and objectives.
   (a) Do these statements correspond with the definitions in this chapter? If not, explain why.
   (b) What type of management accounting information could be collected to help managers assess whether these objectives are being achieved?
2 Find the annual report of a South African company on the Internet. Consider the financial information that is provided. Do you consider this information suitable for management decisions? Explain your answer.

Appendix to Chapter 1

Evolution and change in management accounting

L.O. 12 The area of activity that we now call management accounting has developed over the past 50 years. Exhibit 1.6 summarises changes in the focus of management accounting since the 1950s. Prior to the 1950s the focus was on cost accounting, primarily for inventory valuation, and financial control, and the emphasis was on the management accountant as a scorekeeper for management. *Cost accounting,* rather than management accounting, was the name given to this area of accounting.

	The focus of management accounting	Management accounting technologies	The positioning of management accounting within organisations
Prior to 1950			
	Cost		
	Cost determination and financial control	Budgeting and cost accounting	Technical activity
1965 ⇒	**Profitability**		
	Provision of information for planning and control	Decision analysis and responsibility accounting	A staff function, reporting to management
1985 ⇒	**Waste reduction**		
	Reduction of waste through strategic cost management	Process analysis and contemporary cost management	Team-based activity
1995 ⇒	**Resource management and value creation**		
	Creation of value through strategic resource management—the effective and efficient use of all resources	Analysis of drivers of customer value, shareholder value and organisational innovation	Part of the management process
2000s	?	?	?
Source: IFAC (2002)			

Exhibit 1.6 The changing focus of management accounting

Between 1950 and 1965 the term *management accounting* began to be used, and referred to the provision of information to management for planning and control. This area of accounting now included investment appraisal, decision analysis and responsibility accounting, as well as the established techniques of budgeting, and planning and control. From the mid-1980s, the focus of management accounting moved to waste reduction, and new techniques involving process analysis and cost management were added to the existing range of management accounting techniques. From the mid-1990s, the focus of management accounting started to shift towards the broader techniques of resource management, and focused on the creation of customer value and shareholder value through the effective use of resources.

In the 21st century management accounting has not abandoned the concepts of cost accounting and financial control, nor the provision of information for planning and control. These objectives now form part of the broader function of resource management. Management accounting still involves many of the techniques that were developed in past decades, such as budgets and basic product costing principles, but these are now supplemented by modern technologies that better assist managers in value creation. (We wait to see what new developments will arise in the 21st century!) As you read this book, you will become familiar with many of the terms used in Exhibit 1.6.

Notice that in Exhibit 1.6, with each of the changes in focus, there was a repositioning of management accounting within organisations (IFAC, 2002). Prior to the 1950s cost accounting was simply a technical activity. From the mid-1960s, management accounting emerged as a *staff function,* providing support to *line management.* **Staff management** are managers who support the activities of an organisation as a whole, and are only indirectly involved in the operations of a business. **Line management** are managers who are directly involved in the core activities of the business. In the 1980s, with the emergence of new process improvement technologies and waste reduction, management accounting often became a part of team-based activities. Management accountants played a role in decision-making teams and key aspects of management accounting came to be practised across the organisation. From the mid-1990s the domain of management accounting started to become a dimension of the management process. While in many organisations the management accounting responsibilities were clearly the responsibility of the accounting specialists, in other organisations a broader range of managers, such as marketing managers and engineers, became more involved in the production and analysis of management accounting information.

Given the major changes that have taken place in the business environment described earlier in this chapter, it is not surprising that there have been significant changes in the focus and positioning of management accounting. However, it is important to note that in some organisations management accounting may not yet be focused on resource management, and may rely on more traditional tools than some of the more contemporary technologies discussed above. In general, however, we can assume that as managers' information needs change, management accounting systems should continue to evolve to satisfy those needs better.

Management accountants play an important role in many enterprises. As a member of the management team, they need to be in touch with the heartbeat of the organisation. In most businesses, management accountants interact frequently with sales personnel, finance specialists, production people, and managers at all levels. To perform their duties effectively, management accountants must be knowledgeable, not only in accounting but in other major business disciplines. Strong oral and written communication skills are also becoming increasingly important for success as a management accountant.

Professional accounting organisations

L.O. 13

In South Africa, many management and financial accountants are members of the South African Institute of Chartered Accountants (SAICA). There are also South African management accountants who are members of US or UK management accounting bodies. These are the Institute of Management Accountants (IMA) and the Chartered Institute of Management Accountants (CIMA).

SAICA is the most prominent South African professional accounting body and the chartered accountant designation CA (SA) is highly respected in South Africa and internationally. There are over 24 000 chartered accountants in the country, many of whom work in the management accounting field. A South African chartered accountant will have a CTA or equivalent degree which represents at least four years of study at a tertiary institution. Members are required to write and pass Part I and Part II of the Qualifying Examination. Further, members will have completed a three-year training contract with a firm of chartered accountants in public practice or with an approved training organisation in commerce and industry. Thereafter, members are required to undertake continuing professional development. The CA (SA) qualification is designed for all types of accountants, whether they are corporate treasurers, auditors, financial accountants or management accountants.

There are also specialist qualifications that may be completed by chartered accountants in many different areas, one of which is management accounting. To qualify as a management accounting specialist, a CA will usually complete a postgraduate course in management accounting, as well as have experience in the area.

In the past, most members of The South African Institute of Chartered Accountants were employed in public practice. However, since the 1990s more than 50 per cent of members have been employed in commerce and industry, and many in the management accounting area.

The Chartered Institute of Management Accountants (CIMA) is an international professional accounting body with over 155 000 members and students which is based in the United Kingdom. The focus is on accounting services for business. Members have the right to use the title of Chartered Management Accountant. Members have to complete three levels of qualification and have three years of relevant industry experience. The focus of the CIMA qualification is Management Accounting although students will undertake modules in Financial Management, Taxation, Auditing and Financial Accounting.

ACCA (the Association of Chartered Certified Accountants) is probably the largest international accountancy body with 110 000 members in 170 countries. ACCA has 260 000 students worldwide. In order to obtain the ACCA professional qualification members are required to complete three levels of qualification and obtain supervised, relevant practical experience. ACCA's headquarters is in London and there are over 50 000 ACCA members in the UK alone.

Advantages of professional membership

The qualifications offered by the professional bodies provide employers with a level of assurance of the competence and skills of the accountant. Membership of a professional accounting body allows accountants to keep up to date with developments in their field. They can participate in conferences, seminars and specialist discussion groups, and gain valuable contact with other management accountants working in various organisations.

Professional ethics

The professional accounting associations offer support to members troubled by ethical issues. As professionals, management accountants have an obligation to themselves, their colleagues and their organisation to adhere to high standards of ethical conduct. In recognition of this obligation, the SAICA and CIMA professional accounting bodies have issued ethical standards in a code of conduct for their members. SAICA has determined that skills and integrity are the pre-eminent professional attributes of chartered accountants in South Africa. The Code of Professional Conduct of SAICA is consistent in all material respects with the Code of Ethics for Professional Accountants issued by the International Federation of Accountants (IFAC).The fundamental principles of the South African Institute of Chartered Accountants Code of Professional Conduct are as follows:[2]

A professional accountant is required to comply with the following fundamental principles:

Integrity

A professional accountant should be straightforward and honest in all professional and business relationships.

Objectivity

A professional accountant should not allow bias, conflict of interest or undue influence of others to override professional or business judgements.

Professional Competence and Due Care

A professional accountant has a continuing duty to maintain professional knowledge and skill at the level required to ensure that a client or employer receives competent professional service based on current developments in practice, legislation and techniques. A professional accountant should act diligently and in accordance with applicable technical and professional standards when providing professional services.

Confidentiality

A professional accountant should respect the confidentiality of information acquired as a result of professional and business relationships and should not disclose any such information to third parties without proper and specific authority unless there is a legal or professional right or duty to disclose. Confidential information acquired as a result of professional and business relationships should not be used for the personal advantage of the professional accountant or third parties.

Professional Behaviour

A professional accountant should comply with relevant laws and regulations and should avoid any action that discredits the profession.

Each of these principles is discussed in greater detail in the Code and readers should visit the SAICA website, www.saica.co.za for the complete Code of Professional Conduct.

CIMA requires that its members uphold the highest standards of ethical behaviour. CIMA revised its Code of Ethics for Professional Accountants in 2006 and the fundamental principles of the Code are based on the Code of Ethics issued by IFAC. This means that CIMA and SAICA's Code of Ethics are very close in relation to the fundamental principles of each Code. CIMA provides extensive guidance to its members and provides online support to members facing difficult ethical issues. Readers should refer to CIMA's website, www.cimaglobal.com for the complete Code which sets out the fundamental principles, detailed guidance to members, threats and possible safeguards.

ACCA's Code of Ethics and Conduct is in line with the Code issued by the IFAC and this represents a principles-based approach to setting ethical standards. Readers should visit ACCA's website, www.accaglobal.com, for more information about ACCA and its Code of Ethics and Conduct.

Questions

?

1.1 Select an organisation with which you are familiar, and outline some of the main changes that have taken place in its business environment in recent years.

1.2 Examine the definition of management accounting provided in this chapter, and explain what is meant by *customer value* and *shareholder value*.

1.3 Consider two different products you are familiar with, and describe the aspects that you value as a customer.

1.4 What is meant by *resource management*? Why should management accounting be concerned with non-financial resources?

1.5 Briefly explain the key differences between financial accounting and management accounting.

1.6 Explain the key differences between cost accounting and management accounting.

1.7 'Some accounting information that is produced by the financial accounting system of a business is of limited use for management accounting purposes. This is because of the accounting procedures, or accounting standards, that are used in its preparation.' Provide an example to illustrate this issue.

1.8 Where in an organisation would you expect to find management accountants?

1.9 'We don't have an accountant in our organisation but we do have a financial controller. His job is to control the finances.' Discuss.

1.10 Explain the relationship between an organisation's mission statement, vision and strategies. Select a well-known company to illustrate your answer.

1.11 Formulate a mission statement and vision for each of these organisations: The Surf Lifesaving Association of South Africa, Subway sandwich chain, and a university.

1.12 For the three organisations listed in the previous question, formulate some objectives that each organisation might wish to achieve over the next 12 months.

1.13 Explain the differences between corporate strategy and business strategy.

1.14 Give examples of how management accounting information could assist in managing resources in a winery.

1.15 Explain why senior managers, middle managers and operations managers require different types of management accounting information.

1.16 What types of management accounting information might assist management in a business that followed a differentiation strategy based on innovation?

1.17 What types of management accounting information might assist management in a business that followed a cost leadership strategy?

1.18 'Our management accounting system measures costs. Nothing else matters here as our strategy is based on cost leadership.' Discuss.

1.19 Do you think that a management accountant can play an important role in a not-for-profit organisation? Choose a specific not-for-profit organisation with which you are familiar to explain your answer.

1.20 'Planning systems and control systems are two unrelated parts of a management accounting system.' Discuss.

1.21 How do planning and control systems relate to strategies?

1.22 How might managers' behavioural characteristics affect the way they use information? How can management accountants take this into account when designing management accounting systems?

1.23 Explain how specific aspects of management accounting systems may be used to motivate employees and managers.

1.24 Explain how costs and benefits are relevant to the design of management accounting systems.

1.25 (appendix) Briefly describe changes in the focus of management accounting that have occurred since the 1950s.

1.26 (appendix) Explain what is meant by each of the following ethical standards for accountants: *competence, confidentiality, integrity* and *objectivity.*

1.27 (appendix) What do you think it means to be a professional? In your view, are management accountants professionals? Explain.

Exercises

E1.28 The nature of management accounting systems

Classify each of the following statements as true or false. In each case, provide reasons to explain your answer.

1 Management accounting is more concerned with physical information than with financial information.
2 Management accounting systems need to be flexible enough to provide information for financial statements.
3 Management accounting systems may draw on data that are internal and external to the organisation.
4 Management accounting systems are concerned with customer service.
5 Management accounting systems need to produce information that is reliable, objective and relevant to managers' needs.

E1.29 The nature of management accounting

Complete each of the following statements by selecting the best answer.

1 Management accounting:
   (a) often involves predicting future outcomes
   (b) is based on objective, verifiable information
   (c) emphasises the importance of accuracy
   (d) is based on financial information only
   (e) none of the above
2 Management accounting:
   (a) has changed very little since the 1950s
   (b) is tailored to the needs of the managers
   (c) involves aggregate rather than detailed analysis

(d) is another name for cost accounting
(e) none of the above

3 Management accounting:
(a) often causes information overload for managers
(b) is not relevant to strategy decisions
(c) is an exact science
(d) can have a major influence on the behaviour of employees
(e) none of the above

E1.30 Differences between management accounting and financial accounting

Which of the following roles belongs to:
(a) management accounting
(b) financial accounting
(c) cost accounting
(d) none of the above?

1 Preparing a balance sheet.
2 Preparing a profit forecast by product line.
3 Estimating the depreciation expense for a factory's equipment.
4 Monitoring the effects of a quality improvement program.
5 Estimating the cost of goods produced.
6 Estimating the cost of a prototype for a new product being developed.
7 Preparing a sales forecast.
8 Monitoring the effects of a waste reduction program.
9 Preparing a report on customer satisfaction.
10 Preparing an income statement.

E1.31 Management accounting information

Give an example of management accounting information that could be used by a manager to make each of the following decisions. Remember to consider non-financial information where relevant.

1 The manager of a discount department store is deciding how many security personnel to employ to reduce shoplifting.
2 A local council is deciding whether to build an extension to the council library.
3 The manager of a rental car agency is deciding whether to add luxury cars to the rental car fleet.
4 The production manager in a car manufacturing plant is deciding whether to have routine maintenance performed on a machine weekly or every two weeks.

E1.32 Major influences on management accounting

Classify each of the following statements as true or false. In each case, provide reasons to explain your answer.

1 The growth of the service sector in South Africa has led to the widespread development of new management accounting techniques.
2 As hierarchical organisational structures give way to team-based structures, management accountants need to learn how to provide their services to employees at all levels of the organisation.
3 Management accounting has only a limited role to play in developing measures of customer service.
4 Advances in information technology have changed the way that many businesses conduct their operations, and the way that management accountants supply information to managers.

E1.33 Management accounting information

Identify management accounting information that could assist managers in making each of the following decisions. Remember to consider non-financial information where relevant.

1 A marketing manager is considering whether or not to launch a new product.
2 A travel company is considering whether it should increase its staff numbers by one third.
3 A production team leader is considering whether an important customer order should be produced next week, or during overtime hours tonight.
4 A fruit-picking company is considering purchasing a new cherry-picking machine.

E1.34 Evolution of management accounting (appendix)

Complete each of the following statements by selecting the best answer.

1 Most of the costing and budgeting techniques used in the 20th century were developed:
   (a) before 1950
   (b) between 1950 and 1965
   (c) between 1965 and 1985
   (d) between 1985 and 1995
2 The term *management accounting* began to be used because:
   (a) costing systems became more sophisticated
   (b) the role expanded to include information for planning and control
   (c) accountants were moved into managerial roles
   (d) the role focused on scorekeeping for management
3 From the mid 1980s to the mid 1990s, management accountants:
   (a) became more interested in waste reduction because of the emphasis on the environment
   (b) made detailed inventory valuation as their primary focus
   (c) added process analysis and cost management to their techniques
   (d) introduced the concept of responsibility accounting to their organisations
4 From 1995 onwards, management accounting:
   (a) added a customer focus because managers were sick of hearing about costs
   (b) added a shareholder perspective to ensure consistency with financial accounting reports
   (c) introduced the concept of investment appraisal to satisfy investor concerns
   (d) recognised the importance of both customer and shareholder value
5 Over time the management accountant has increasingly become:
   (a) a technical adviser
   (b) a staff role, supporting line managers
   (c) a part of the management team, providing strategic advice
   (d) an expert on financial accounting reports

Problems

P1.35 Designing a new management accounting system

You have just been appointed as the new management accountant for Coronet Casino, a major new entertainment complex. The casino consists of 30 restaurants, most of which are managed by the casino, 20 shops (which are leased to tenants), 4 cinemas, 6 gaming rooms and 500 bedrooms. The new complex will not open for another nine months. You are a little uncertain as to what your role will be in this new business, as consultants have been engaged to design the new management accounting systems. You thought that as a management accountant you would be responsible for developing the new systems!

Required:

1 Write a report to senior management explaining how you, as the management accountant, may contribute to the design and operation of the new management accounting systems for the casino.

2 Outline the types of management accounting information that you believe senior managers may require on a regular basis (say, weekly and monthly) to manage the operations of the casino. Consider both financial and non-financial information.

3 The casino plans to invest in the latest computer technology to run various aspects of the business, including the management information systems. Discuss the opportunities that this may present for the way in which you supply weekly and monthly reports to managers.

P1.36 Role of the divisional accountant

A divisional manager is responsible for each division of Inland Products Ltd. Each divisional accountant (appointed by the chief accountant) manages the division's accounting system and provides an analysis of financial information for the divisional manager. The divisional manager evaluates the performance of the divisional accountant and makes recommendations for salary increases and promotions. However, the final responsibility for promotion and salary increases rests with the chief accountant.

Each of Inland's divisions is responsible for product design, sales, pricing, operating expenses and profit. However, corporate management exercises tight control over divisional financial operations. For example, all capital expenditures above a modest amount must be approved by corporate management. The method of financial reporting from the division to corporate headquarters provides further evidence of the degree of financial control. The divisional manager and the divisional accountant submit to corporate headquarters separate and independent commentaries on the financial results of the division. Corporate management states that the divisional accountant is there to provide an independent view of the division's operations, not as a spy.

Required:

1 Discuss the arrangements for management reporting at Inland Products Ltd.

2 Inland Products' dual reporting system for divisions may create problems for the divisional accountant.

(a) Identify and discuss the factors that make the divisional accountant's role difficult in this type of situation.

(b) Discuss the potential effect of the dual reporting relationship on the motivation of the divisional accountant.

(CMA, adapted)

P1.37 Information for management

Joe Murphy retired a few years ago at the age of 48, having built up a substantial retirement portfolio through a range of entrepreneurial activities. He moved to the Drakensberg to follow his dream of a peaceful mountain life. However, after a few months Murphy became restless and opened a ski equipment store. This single store soon grew into a chain of four outlets spread from the Drakensberg to the Lesotho highlands. Visitors who were not aware of the limited skiing the mountains offered were enthralled to try it out. As Murphy put it, 'I can't believe how fast we've expanded. It's basically been uncontrolled growth—growth that has occurred in spite of what we've done.'

Although business was profitable, the chain did have its share of problems. Sales tended to be seasonal, with a slowdown once the snow had disappeared. Murphy therefore added fishing and camping equipment to his product line. The need to finance required inventories, which seemed to be bulging and left cash balances at very low levels, occasionally giving rise to short-term bank loans.

Part of Murphy's business focused on skiing trips, which were arranged through local ski lodges, and included ski hire, lessons and lift passes. Reports from the company's financial accounting system seemed to indicate that this part of the business was losing money because of increasing costs, but Murphy could not be sure. 'The traditional income statement is not too useful in assessing the problem,' he noted. 'Also, my gut feeling is that we are not dealing with the best suppliers in terms of quality, delivery reliability and prices.' Additional complications were caused by an increasingly competitive marketplace, with many former customers now buying equipment through the Internet.

Murphy was not sure what to do. The company's accountant was very good at keeping the books and preparing the financial statements and tax return, but she did not understand the way the business really worked.

Required:

1 Describe the types of information that Murphy needs to run his business more effectively.
2 Murphy approaches the accountant to seek her help in gathering and analysing this information, but she responds: 'You must be joking—I'm an accountant. My job is to look after the money side of the business!' Do you agree with this statement?
3 What actions would you recommend that Murphy takes?

P1.38 Management accounting information for resource management

You have just been appointed as the management accountant for Wild Surf, a surfing equipment company. This company employs a team of 12 designers who design surfboards, skis, T-shirts and board shorts. These products are manufactured by independent companies. Wild Surf then sells the products to the public through six sales outlets located at popular surfing beaches, and to major department and sporting equipment stores.

Required:

1 Identify the specific types of management accounting information that may be needed by the following employees, on a monthly basis, to help them control operations:
   (a) the manager of each retail outlet
   (b) the manager of the design team
   (c) the marketing manager responsible for planning advertising campaigns and identifying customer needs
   (d) the manager who manages and renegotiates contracts with the outside manufacturers
2 The managing director of Wild Surf is interested in developing more sophisticated planning systems, but has some doubts over the value of undertaking strategic planning. Prepare a report outlining the importance of planning systems. In your report, consider the interrelationships between the objectives of the company, its strategies and short-term planning systems. Explain how management accounting information may assist in improving the planning function of the company.

P1.39 Behavioural issues; ethics (appendix)

Janet Kaniva is the head of the sales department for a large book distributor. She manages a team of five salespeople, including her close friend, Ima Lyer. Each salesperson is responsible for particular product lines and is entitled to receive an annual salary bonus provided that he or she exceeds the profit forecast for his/her product group by more than 10 per cent. Profit for each product group is estimated by deducting from sales revenue the cost of the books sold, plus a charge for corporate overheads. Corporate overheads are charged as a percentage of sales revenue, using a complex formula based on different percentages of revenue for different product lines; and salespeople can never make any sense of their annual overhead charge.

As the year end approaches, Lyer, who sells religious and philosophical texts, learns from the accountant, Stanley Riteous, that she will not receive a bonus, as she will not achieve her annual profit forecast. She is feeling very frustrated, as she has heard that the rest of the sales team will come in more than 20 per cent above their forecast.

Lyer approaches Riteous, suggesting that an accounting entry is made to move some of the overhead charges to the other salespeople, who, after all, will still earn their bonus. Riteous refuses on the grounds that he is a CA, but he is subsequently instructed by Kaniva to make this journal entry.

Required:

1 Discuss the behavioural implications of the bonus system.
2 What relevance does Riteous' CA status have to this situation?
3 How should Riteous respond to Kaniva's instruction to move overhead charges from Lyer to the other salespeople?

P1.40 Disclosure of confidential information; ethics (appendix)

Smart Worx Ltd, a developer and distributor of business applications software, has been in business for five years. The company's main products include programs used for sales management, billing and accounting for mail order shopping businesses. Smart Worx's sales have increased steadily to the current level of R15 million per year, and the company has 250 employees.

Erin McFail joined Smart Worx approximately one year ago as accounting manager. McFail's duties include supervision of the company's accounting operations and preparation of the company's financial statements. McFail has noticed that, in the past six months, Smart Worx's sales have ceased to rise and have actually declined in the two most recent months. This unexpected downturn has resulted in cash shortages. Compounding these problems, Smart Worx has had to postpone the introduction of a new product line because of delays in documentation preparation.

Smart Worx contracts most of its printing requirements to Web Graphics, a small company owned by Rob Rodent. Rodent has dedicated a major portion of his printing capacity to Smart Worx's requirements, because Smart Worx's contracts represent approximately 50 per cent of Web Graphics' business. Erin McFail has known Rodent for many years—as a matter of fact, she learned of Smart Worx's need for an accounting manager through Rodent.

While preparing Smart Worx's most recent financial statements, McFail became concerned about the company's ability to maintain steady payments to its suppliers. She estimated that payments to all vendors, normally made within 30 days, could exceed 75 days. McFail is particularly concerned about payments to Web Graphics. She knows that Smart Worx has recently placed a large order with Web Graphics for printing the new product documentation, and that Web Graphics will soon be placing an order for the special paper required for Smart Worx's documentation. McFail is considering telling Rodent about Smart Worx's cash problems, although she is aware that a delay in the printing of the documentation would jeopardise Smart Worx's new product.

Required:

1 Describe Erin McFail's ethical responsibilities in this situation.
2 Independent of your answer to requirement 1, assume that Erin McFail learns that Rob Rodent of Web Graphics has decided to postpone the special paper order required for Smart Worx's printing job; McFail believes that Rodent must have heard rumours about Smart Worx's financial problems from some other source, because she has not talked to Rodent. Should Erin McFail tell the appropriate Smart Worx officials that Rodent has postponed the paper order? Explain your answer.
3 Independent of your answers to the first two requirements, assume that Rob Rodent has decided to postpone the special paper order because he has learned of Smart Worx's financial problems from some source other than McFail. In addition, McFail realises that Jim Grason, Smart Worx's purchasing manager, knows of her friendship with Rob Rodent. Now McFail is concerned that Grason may suspect she told Rodent of Smart Worx's financial problems when Grason finds out Rodent has postponed the order. Describe the steps that Erin McFail should take to resolve this situation.

(CMA, adapted)

Cases

C1.41 Objectives, strategy and management accounting systems

At a recent meeting, the marketing manager of Cakes R Us, Ralph Slick, stated that the company should expand its product offerings, or there may be no future for the company. Specifically he believes that there are untapped markets for gourmet pies. The managing director is uncertain; he states: 'I really don't think that we can afford to invest time and money into fads. We sell cakes, we are not a gourmet caterer!' Ralph points out that it is these new items that customers are asking for, so it makes sense from a strategic point of view to develop these products. However, the managing director is still uncertain: 'I have no idea whether we are going to make a profit this year, and cash is always tight. We don't need strategies, I prefer to just sell good products.'

Cakes R Us operates a series of bakeries in Durban that specialise in supplying a range of cakes to restaurants and coffee shops. Major products include chocolate cakes, scones, éclairs and custard tarts. Until last year, sales levels were fairly stable. However, sales have been decreasing for the last 18 months. Ralph Slick is worried, and has visited major customers to find out the reasons for their decreasing sales orders. The comments of the owner of one of the most popular Durban coffee shops sum up the general response: 'Ralph, your style of cakes is old-fashioned. They are not what people want any more. Our customers prefer lighter, tastier food. They want variety, and are willing to pay more for high quality innovative creations.'

Ralph understands why the managing director is resisting his plea to be more innovative with products—the bakery has been producing the same line of cakes for 30 years. Ralph also knows that there has never been any formal planning undertaken within the company, or consideration of objectives or strategies.

Required:

1 Ralph Slick has asked for your help. As the new management accountant, prepare a report for the managing director outlining the advantages of implementing processes to determine organisational objectives, strategies and planning systems.
2 Consider the nature of the control system that you could design to report on monthly performance. What types of information do you think may be of interest to Ralph and the managing director? Consider both financial and non-financial data.

C1.42 Management accounting and ethical issues (appendix)

James Van Rooyen lives in Harding, and has recently joined the staff of his community hospital as the financial controller. He has lived in this town for most of his life, plays for the town's bowls club, attends church on a regular basis and is an active member of the Hospital Foundation. The Foundation runs a number of very successful fundraising events each year, such as charity auctions, trivia nights and an annual ball, a highlight of the Harding social calendar. The hospital is funded primarily through the public health system, but also depends on funds raised by the Foundation. James is a very experienced accountant, approaching retirement age. Although the salary for this position is considerably lower than for his last job, he has become passionate about the value of this hospital and wants to 'give back' to his community.

Hospitals operate in a high-risk environment because of their responsibility for human life and the potential for litigation in the case of error. During his first three months in the new role James completes a risk-management audit, identifying the likelihood of particular risks and assessing the systems for managing them. The audit covers processes in the areas of quality, occupational health and safety, and financial management. It uncovers some potential problems in the quality area, particularly around the identification and recording processes for patient mismanagement. The major risks in the occupational health and safety area relate to back injuries for nursing staff handling patients, and the processes for disposing of hazardous wastes. He is relieved that a review by the hospital's senior accountant, Craig Stevens, finds no significant problems of the financial management system.

Amalie Lester, the daughter of one of James's closest friends at the bowls club, is the treasurer of the Foundation. At the Foundation's most recent annual ball James noticed that Amalie spent most of the evening in Craig's arms. According to James's wife, who is the local gossip, Craig had become involved with Amalie when he completed an internal audit of the Foundation's books. She is appalled by this behaviour, as Craig's mother, who is part of her crochet group, has no idea that this is happening, and Craig's wife is due to have their baby in just a few weeks. Amalie owns a small business, located on the outskirts of Harding, that sells a range of funky clothes and accessories. The rumour around town is that Amalie's business is not doing well and that she owes a substantial amount to her landlord.

Although Harding is a fairly close-knit community, until now James has always been very careful to keep his work and social interests separate. However, given his accounting experience, James wonders whether he may be able to help Amalie solve her business problems or at least exit from the business without any further losses. He is convinced that her outskirts location is all wrong, as fashion businesses depend on a high volume of pedestrian traffic. However, her father tells James that there is no need to worry, as recently she seems to be doing much better. She has been able to pay all overdue rent and buy a 'new' car, a bright red mini, which her father describes as a relic from the 1960s! Although very relieved, Amalie's father is unable to explain the cause of this dramatic turnaround, other than to attribute it to good luck combined with good management.

A couple of days later James has a chance to think over this conversation. From experience he knows that 'good luck' is rarely an underlying factor in business turnarounds and, anyway, what miracle can have occurred to enlighten Amalie's previously lacklustre approach to management? He becomes increasingly concerned. Over the last few months, the Foundation has been through a very successful period of fundraising. Although Craig's recent internal audit and review of the hospital's financial management system had shown no cause for concern 'something is not right here', he laments to his wife over dinner that evening. A lively discussion on the possible influences of infatuation follows and next morning James leaves for work very early.

It does not take long for James to discover that in her role as treasurer, Amalie has been stealing Foundation funds. When confronted, Craig initially denies any knowledge of this situation but later admits to his involvement. He appeals to James to show sympathy, if not for Amalie's sake, then to protect her father, one of James's closest friends. Craig reminds him that, in a place like Harding, word will spread rapidly, ruining the lives of Amalie and her family as well as causing considerable distress to Craig's pregnant wife.

Required:

1 Review the accounting professional code of ethical conduct set out in the appendix to this chapter. Which of the standards are relevant to this case from Craig Stevens' perspective?
2 Which of the standards are relevant to this case from James Van Rooyen's perspective?
3 What actions would you advise James to take, given the ethical code of conduct of the accounting profession?

Endnotes

1 A franchise is the granting of a licence by one person (the franchisor) to another (the franchisee) for a fee, which entitles the franchisee to sell the physical product under the trade name of the franchisor. The franchisor usually retains control over the nature of the product being sold, including the way the product is marketed. Please go to www.steers.co.za for more information.

2 The summary is adapted from the *Code of Professional Conduct*, SAICA. Copyright SAICA. Reproduced with the permission of SAICA. The rules of ethical conduct of CIMA and ACCA are similar to those of SAICA.

CHAPTER

Management Accounting: Cost Terms and Concepts

❖ Learning Objectives

After completing this chapter, you should be able to:

1 describe the components of conventional and contemporary management accounting systems;

2 explain why management accountants focus particularly on costs;

3 explain what is meant by *different costs for different purposes*;

4 classify costs according to their behaviour—that is, as variable or fixed;

5 classify costs as direct or indirect;

6 classify costs as controllable or uncontrollable;

7 classify costs according to the segments of the value chain;

8 analyse costs using the classifications commonly used in manufacturing businesses;

9 explain the different definitions of product cost used in external accounting reports and for decision making; and

10 describe the cost flows in a manufacturing business and prepare a schedule of cost of goods manufactured, a schedule of cost of goods sold and an income statement for a manufacturer.[1]

Introduction

To be effective, organisations should focus on managing their resources to create value for their customers and shareholders (or owners). Understanding and managing costs is vital to this process. Managers need to plan future costs, monitor current costs and, most important, manage costs by focusing on their underlying causes. Effective cost management is essential to businesses that pursue a cost-leadership strategy, but will enhance shareholder wealth in any organisation.

Some organisations do not have shareholders but are 'owned' by government or not-for-profit bodies, such as churches and charities. Consider for example the St John's Ambulance Foundation, the Aids Foundation of South Africa, the Aids Consortium, the SPCA, the Nelson Mandela Children's Fund, CIDA or the Catholic Church's Nazareth House. These organisations focus on customer or client value rather than on the creation of wealth. However, resource management, and in particular cost management, remains an important consideration. In both profit and not-for-profit entities, costs are a vital source of information for managers, and most of the material in this chapter therefore focuses on costs, particularly the common accounting concepts used to accumulate, analyse and manage costs.[2]

Management accounting information

L.O. 1

In Chapter 1 we described how organisations are managed and we considered the information needs of managers. From this we can identify common components of management accounting systems.

Components of a management accounting system

Management accounting systems are tailored to an organisation's needs but they often include the following:

- a **costing system** that estimates the *cost of goods and services*, as well as the *cost of organisational units*, such as departments;
- a **budgeting system** that is used to prepare a detailed plan, which shows the financial consequences of the organisation's operating activities, for a specific future time period. The system estimates planned *revenues* and *costs*;
- a **performance measurement system** that measures performance by comparing actual results with some target;
- a **cost management system** that focuses on improving the organisation's cost effectiveness through understanding and managing the real causes of costs.

Management accountants also provide information from a variety of other sources to help managers with non-routine planning and decision-making.

Conventional versus contemporary approaches to management accounting

We also learned in Chapter 1 that major new approaches in management accounting have developed since the 1980s, in response to dramatic changes in the business environment. Costing, budgeting and performance measurement systems are common to both conventional and these more contemporary management accounting systems, although there are substantial differences between the old and the new. Cost management systems tend to be identified with contemporary systems.

Costing systems

Conventional costing systems estimate the costs of organisational units, such as departments, and of products (that is, goods and services). In analysing costs they assume that production volume is the only factor that can cause costs to change.

Contemporary costing systems are much more detailed. They estimate the cost of the individual activities performed in the organisation and use this information to cost goods and services, customers, organisational units or other items. Contemporary costing recognises that production volume can cause costs to change, but so can a range of other factors. These systems are called *activity-based costing systems.*

Budgeting systems

Conventional budgeting systems estimate planned revenues and costs for organisational units such as departments. Department budgets are aggregated to obtain a budget for the overall organisation. *Contemporary* approaches to budgeting, called *activity-based budgeting,* are much more detailed and, as the name would suggest, are built around activities.

Performance measurement systems

Conventional performance measurement systems provide measures of financial performance. They focus largely on controlling costs, by reporting differences between budgeted and actual costs. They monitor performance within the organisation.

Contemporary performance measurement systems provide measures of performance across a whole range of **critical success factors**, such as quality, delivery and innovation, as well as financial performance. In addition to reporting on internal performance, they look at what is happening outside the organisation – for example, by monitoring the performance of competitors and the satisfaction of customers. New approaches to performance measurement include strategically focused performance-measurement systems such as the balanced scorecard, benchmarking and activity-based performance measures. They focus on managing sources of customer value and shareholder wealth.

Cost management systems

Conventional performance measurement systems provide information to help managers control costs, by focusing on differences between actual costs and planned (that is, budgeted) costs. *Contemporary* approaches are far more proactive in providing information to manage resources. Systems are developed not only to control costs but to reduce them. Wasteful activities are identified and eliminated, and costs are analysed to identify their real 'root' causes. The causes rather than the costs are managed. Contemporary approaches to cost management include activity-based management, customer profitability analysis, supplier cost analysis, business process re-engineering, life-cycle management and target costing.

Exhibit 2.1 summarises the differences between conventional and contemporary management accounting systems. You need to have a knowledge of conventional management accounting systems, as they are still used in many organisations. You also need a knowledge of the contemporary approaches, which are becoming more common, especially within organisations that are responding to the pressures of the current business environment. These new approaches, as well as conventional costing, budgeting and performance measurement systems, are described in more detail in later chapters.

Emphasis on costs

L.O. 2

An examination of the components of both conventional and contemporary management accounting systems reveals that costs are an important source of information for managers. The systems include information about product costs, the costs of departments and activities, as well as both budgeted and actual costs. Contemporary management accounting systems also provide information about the causes of costs. Let's consider why management accountants pay so much attention to costs.

Components of management accounting systems	Conventional systems	Contemporary systems
Costing systems	Focus on the costs of departments and products.* Assume production volume is the only factor that can cause costs to vary.	Focus on the costs of activities, products, customers and suppliers. Recognise that a range of factors can cause costs to vary.
Budgeting systems	Built around departments.	Built around departments and activities.
Performance measurement systems	Monitor *financial* performance. Control what's going on inside the organisation.	Monitor performance *across a range of critical success factors*, such as quality and delivery, not just financial performance. Also look at what's happening *outside* the organisation, for example at customers and competitors. Support the management of both customer value and shareholder wealth.
Cost management	No separate system. Costs mainly controlled through the financial performance measurement system.	Pro-active approaches to managing resources systems and reducing costs, rather than just controlling them. Analyse real causes of costs and eliminate wasteful activities.

* Note that 'products' includes both goods and services.

Exhibit 2.1 Conventional versus contemporary management accounting systems

Historic focus on production costs

Historically, management accountants have given most consideration to manufacturing businesses, in particular to their production costs. One reason for this emphasis is the need to value inventory (at production cost) and to determine cost of goods sold for external reporting. However, the focus of conventional management accounting systems on manufacturing costs should not be viewed simply as the result of the pressures of external financial reporting requirements. Many of the techniques used in conventional management accounting had evolved in manufacturing businesses by the mid-1920s, and, at that time, the preoccupation with manufacturing costs made sense. The costs occurring outside the manufacturing area of these businesses were relatively insignificant compared with the costs in the production areas. In the current business environment, these costs have tended to increase relative to production costs, and management accountants have become much more interested in costs incurred right across the organisation. For example, in a software company such as Microsoft, production costs can be very low, while the costs of research and development, design, marketing and customer service can be very high. To focus attention only on production costs would ignore the other more significant costs of the products.

Ready availability of cost data

We learned in Chapter 1 that *management accounting* was once called *cost accounting*. The new name recognises that managers need a broad range of information for managing resources to create customer value and shareholder wealth. However, accounting systems are a prime source of data for management accountants. When costs are incurred as a result of external transactions, they are recorded in the accounting system. For example, when raw materials are purchased by a manufacturer, the costs of the raw material are recorded in the general ledger as inventory. The additional costs of converting the raw material into products are also recorded. Thus the accounting system, especially for a manufacturer, provides a wealth of basic data about costs.

Importance of cost information

Costs have a vital role to play in helping managers to manage resources effectively to create customer value and shareholder wealth. For example, in planning the routes and flight schedules of South African Airways (SAA), managers must consider aircraft fuel costs, salaries of flight crews and airport landing fees. To manage the costs of producing personal computers, IBM's accountants must carefully measure and keep track of the costs of research and development, production and customer service. All organisations incur costs, and managers need information to understand and manage them. Many short-term and long-term decisions require an understanding of costs.

The role of non-financial information

Conventional management accounting systems focus primarily on financial information, particularly costs. However, throughout the business, non-financial and qualitative information is also needed to help make decisions and to manage the various sources of customer value and shareholder wealth. If you are managing a hospital, costs and revenues are important for decision-making, but non-financial information on the number of beds occupied, patient waiting lists, the number of patients admitted for various medical and surgical procedures and the quality of patient care is also important. If the strategy of your business is focused on improving customer service, you may need regular non-financial information on the numbers of customer complaints, deliveries to customers on time and defective products returned by customers, as well as the results of customer satisfaction surveys. Contemporary management accounting places a much greater emphasis on non-financial information.[3]

Cost classifications: different classifications for different purposes

L.O. 3

Given the emphasis on costs, an important first step in management accounting is to understand the different ways that costs can be classified, analysed and reported.

Before management accountants can classify costs, they need to *consider how managers will use the information.* Different cost concepts and classifications are used for different purposes. For example, some cost concepts are relevant to cost management, as managers need to understand and manage the level of resources used to create customer value and shareholder wealth. Some are relevant to product costing, as managers need to determine product profitability and make informed decisions about which products to produce. Some are relevant to planning, as managers need to predict the costs of future operations, while some are relevant to reporting the results of current activities.

The same cost can be classified in a number of ways, depending on the intended use of the cost information. For example, to determine the *profitability* of producing cheese at a Dairy Belle cheese factory, it is useful to classify costs by whether or not they relate to the production of cheese. However, to *assess the performance of the production manager* we need to be able to classify the same costs according to whether or not they can be managed, or controlled, by the manager. Understanding the different cost concepts and classifications enables the management accountant to provide relevant cost information to the managers who need it. The 'Real life' from the Frame Textile Group (overleaf) illustrates the importance of understanding and managing costs.

We introduce now some common ways in which costs can be classified. Exhibit 2.2 summarises these cost classifications, the basis of classification and the way these various classifications are used by management accountants. This gives you an overview of the many different cost concepts used in this book. In this chapter, we focus on traceability, the value chain and manufacturing cost classifications. In Chapter 3 we describe cost behaviour in detail, and controllability is considered in Chapter 12.

REAL LIFE: SURVIVING GLOBALISATION: THE IMPORTANCE OF UNDERSTANDING AND MANAGING COSTS

The South African Textile industry has experienced severe competition directly from the import of textiles but also indirectly from the import of clothing and apparel which reduces the demand for textiles by local clothing manufacturers. It is estimated that 430 million units of apparel were imported in 2006. Employment levels in the clothing sector fell dramatically from 150 000 in 1996 to 80 000 in 2006. The role of imports from China has played a critical role and there has been a shift by the major retailers such as Edgars, Woolworths and Mr Price to sourcing clothing products from China.

Many textile and clothing firms have failed but a number have survived by focusing on niche activities, investing in advanced technologies and new equipment, focusing on reducing costs and achieving working capital efficiencies. Some clothing manufacturers have relocated to such countries as Lesotho in order to reduce their wage costs. The major retailers, of course, have been able to increase their margins by sourcing a significant share of their products from China.

The Frame Textile Group, which is part of the Seardel Group, has survived challenging times by reducing the investment in working capital, repositioning spinning mills, achieving productivity gains (with some falls in employment levels), training, improving quality, offering customers flexibility and focusing on cost management. Although it has experienced tough trading conditions and experienced a fall in sales turnover in 2006, the company was able to achieve an increase in operating income due to achieving enhanced operating efficiencies and productivity gains, and managing costs. Yet the return on tangible assets for the textile operations was only 5 per cent in 2006. Further, Seardel's net book value per share was close to R15.00 in 2006 and the share price at year end was R7.00 although it had been only R3.60 in 2005.

The implementation of quotas on Chinese imports in terms of the South African/China Import Limitation Arrangement in late 2006, as well as a lower Rand exchange rate, should result in lower imports and higher margins for local manufacturers such as the Frame Group. Longer-term initiatives include setting up clusters of manufacturers to benchmark against best international practice in terms of quality and cost management. This will involve the participation of the major retailers. Further, textile and clothing manufacturers will focus on maximising the speed of resupply, offering customers greater flexibility and reducing the lead time between ordering and supply, and will continue to focus on cost reduction and achieving productivity gains. In this way the Seardel Group is planning to survive and grow its margins despite experiencing an unprecedented level of competition from Chinese imports.

Source: Seardel Annual Report, 2006

What are costs?

Costs are resources given up to achieve a particular objective. In accounting they are usually measured in monetary terms—which, in South Africa, means in Rands. Although you may have studied accounting before, *cost* may be a new term. In financial accounting we refer to assets and expenses, but not to costs. Generally, costs are incurred to obtain future benefits.

If the benefits extend beyond the current accounting period, the costs are recorded as **assets**. As the benefits are used, the costs are no longer regarded as assets, but are expensed. Where benefits from a cost are confined to the current period, the cost is recorded as an expense rather than an asset. An **expense** is the cost that is used up in the generation of revenue.

Basis of classification	Cost classifications	Used to:
Behaviour (see Chapter 3)	Variable Unit level Engineered Fixed Committed Discretionary	Plan (budget) costs Control costs Make decisions
Traceability	Direct Indirect	Estimate the cost of goods and services Estimate the cost of organisational units, such as departments or activities
Controllability (see Chapter 12)	Controllable Uncontrollable	Measure managers' performance Control costs
Value chain	Upstream: Research and development Design Supply Manufacturing/production Downstream: Marketing Distribution Customer service	Analyse cost structures and identify strategies Measure performance Control/manage costs
Manufacturing/product costs	Direct material Direct labour Manufacturing overhead	Estimate the cost of products Estimate the cost of goods sold for the income statement, and inventory for the balance sheet
Timing of the expense	Product Period	Prepare income statement and balance sheet

Exhibit 2.2 Common cost classifications in management accounting

For example, KWV would regard all the *costs* of manufacturing its wine as an *asset,* inventory. When the wine is sold, the cost of producing the wine is classified as cost of goods sold expense. This *expense* is matched against the sales revenue of that wine to produce a profit (or loss). In comparison, the salary of the winery's sales manager does not generate any future benefit and is treated as an expense as it is incurred.

Classifying costs according to their behaviour

L.O. 4

Management accountants can help managers to understand the way costs behave as the *level of activity* in the business changes. The **level of activity** refers to the level of work performed in the organisation. Activity can be expressed in many different ways, including units produced, kilometres driven, lines printed and hours worked. Understanding cost behaviour is useful for planning and managing costs, particularly product costs. Two common cost behaviour classifications are variable and fixed costs. A **variable cost** changes in total, in direct proportion to a change in the level of activity. An example is the electricity used to manufacture a product, which may increase in proportion to the number of units of products manufactured. A **fixed cost** remains unchanged in total despite changes in the level of activity. For example, the cost of rent of a manufacturing plant will remain the same no matter what the level of production. These concepts are explained in greater detail in Chapter 3.

Direct and indirect costs

L.O. 5 One of the important functions of management accounting is to measure the costs of cost objects. A **cost object** is simply an item for which management wants a separate measure of costs. Most management accounting systems include some form of costing system to measure the costs of specific cost objects. Products, projects, contracts and departments or work centres are common cost objects in conventional costing systems. Cost objects of contemporary costing systems often include activities and customers, as well as products.

Costs can be classified as *direct* or *indirect*, depending on whether they can be traced to cost objects. A **direct cost** is a cost that can be identified with, or traced to, a particular cost object in an economic manner. Generally, there is a physically observable relationship between the cost (or the resource that it reflects) and the cost object. Consider, for example, this book as a cost object. The cost of paper is a direct cost of this book. In contrast, an **indirect cost** is a cost that cannot be identified with, or traced to, the cost object in an economic manner. The salary of the managing editor of McGraw-Hill South Africa is an indirect cost of this book. She oversees the editing of all books and it is not easy to identify her time with any one book.

Indirect costs cause difficulties in estimating the costs of cost objects. Since we cannot trace them to specific cost objects, we have to find some way to apportion (allocate) them. As your study of management accounting progresses, you will observe that cost allocation is a complex and troublesome area! We discuss the classification of direct and indirect product costs in more detail later in this chapter.

Direct and indirect costs of responsibility centres

In most organisations the costing system is set up to measure the costs of individual managers' areas of responsibility, such as departments, work centres or activity centres. In management accounting, we call the areas of the business where managers are held accountable for activities and performance **responsibility centres**. Assigning costs to units such as departments is part of **responsibility accounting**, which assigns responsibility to individual managers to run particular areas of the organisation and then holds the managers accountable for their area's performance. This provides useful information for cost control to department managers, as well as to their superiors, which helps to manage costs right across the business. (Responsibility accounting is discussed in Chapter 12.)

A cost that can be traced to a particular department, or responsibility centre, is called a *direct cost* of the department. The salary of a radiographer is a direct cost of the X-ray department at Vincent Pallotti Hospital in Cape Town. The costs of national advertising for the Gold Reef City complex are *direct costs* of the marketing department.

The salary of a plant manager at the pharmaceutical manufacturer Aspen is an *indirect cost* of each of the plant's production departments. While the manager's duties are important to the smooth functioning of each of the production departments, there is no precise way of tracing part of his or her salary to each department.

Direct and indirect costs of products

The direct and indirect cost classifications are also relevant to product costing. Manufacturing costs that can be traced to products in an economic manner are **direct product costs**. These include direct material and direct labour. The cost of sugar used in the production of Pepsi is a direct material cost, and the wage paid to an operator on the bottling line is a direct labour cost.

Indirect product costs are the manufacturing costs that cannot be traced to products in an economic manner. As discussed later in this chapter, these costs are called 'manufacturing overhead'. The wage paid to the forklift driver who moves the sugar around the Pioneer Foods' (Pepsi) plant is an indirect cost and part of manufacturing overhead. (We discuss the classification of product costs in more detail later in this chapter.)

Direct or indirect, what is the cost object?

Whether a cost is direct or indirect depends entirely on the nature of the cost object—do we need to know the cost of a department? A product? A project? An entire company? A given cost can be a direct cost of one cost object and an indirect cost of another cost object. For example, the advertising costs that are a *direct cost* of the marketing department at Gold Reef City are *indirect costs* of each of the departments that provide services to tourists, such as the Hotel, the Theme Park, the Gold Museum and the Casino. The salary of the plant manager at Aspen Ltd is an *indirect cost* of each of the plant's production departments but is a *direct cost* of the whole plant.

REAL LIFE: CLASSIFYING COSTS IN SOUTH AFRICA'S HOTEL INDUSTRY

Most international hotels in South Africa use a cost classification system based on the US 'Uniform System of Accounts for Hotels'. This system distinguishes between direct and indirect costs, controllable and uncontrollable costs, and fixed and variable costs, and provides an interesting example of the role these classifications can play in the management process.

The two major 'production' departments in most hotels are the rooms department and the food and beverage department. In a typical hotel in South Africa direct costs for the rooms department account for 30 to 40 per cent of rooms' revenue. In contrast, the direct costs of the food and beverage department average 70 to 95 per cent of its revenue. The overall cost structure of a hotel depends on the ratio of rooms revenue to food and beverage revenue. On average, hotels tend to have direct expenses of 50 to 65 per cent of revenue, and indirect expenses of 20 to 25 per cent. An additional 5 to 10 per cent of revenue is absorbed by property and owners' costs.

One way to influence profit is to manage the yield on accommodation through careful pricing. There is a trade-off between room rates and occupancy—as the room rate goes down, the occupancy level goes up. However, in setting room rates the hotel manager must consider cost behaviour: which costs are variable costs of providing accommodation, such as room-cleaning costs, and which are committed costs, such as council rates, premises costs and insurance costs. Room rates must be set so that they cover at least the variable cost per room per day.

The only costs for which department managers are held responsible are direct costs. Other costs are not allocated to departments as they are not controllable by these department managers. The average profit levels are around 60 to 70 per cent for room departments and 5 to 30 per cent for food and beverage departments. A manager's performance is compared with results in the previous period and with industry averages. A food and beverage manager would not be expected to earn the same rate of profit as a rooms' manager.

The system identifies the variable costs of the two major products: rooms and food and beverages. The variable costs per room tend to be low, whereas the variable costs per food and beverage service tend to be high. This means that the extra profit that can be earned from each extra night of accommodation sold is high. The key to improving profitability is, therefore, maximising room sales. However, how do we maximise revenue and occupancy without reducing prices for all the rooms in the hotel? Firstly, the room rate could change throughout the day or night depending on occupancy levels. Secondly, advertising on the Internet means that other customers will not see the rate being offered, enabling the hotel to achieve pricing differentiation without losing the higher paying customers.

Hotels are increasingly looking at ways of reducing costs particularly in relation to energy conservation and ensuring that hotels are environmentally friendly. Hotels tend to be energy intensive and there has been a significant increase in energy costs. Hotels are increasingly taking measures to both reduce costs and support the environment by reducing energy use. Let's look at the City Lodge Group in relation to maximising occupancy rates and measuring and controlling the cost per room in relation to energy use.

The City Lodge group of hotels consists of the Courtyard Hotel, City Lodge, Road Lodge, and Town Lodge hotel chains. The group has grown to over 38 hotels offering a total of over 4200 rooms. The hotels are situated in all the major areas of South Africa.

The company's revenue has grown from R150m in 1999 to R510m in 2007. The company achieved an impressive occupancy level of 82 per cent in 2007. The maximization of occupancy is critical to profitability, and City Lodge has seen an increase in operating profit from R59.5m in 1999 to R254m in 2007. As City Lodge is geared mainly to the business traveller, resulting in lower occupancy levels over weekends and at certain times of the year, achieving an average occupancy level of 82 per cent is remarkable. How does City Lodge do it? Apart from its level of service, City Lodge uses the Internet for booking rooms and also to achieve price differentiation. For example, City Lodge introduced its Bid2Stay online facility whereby customers can bid for rooms. The following is an extract from the company's annual financial statements:

Bid2Stay

The only thing better than staying with us, is staying with us at a fraction of the price. You get to decide how much you want to pay for a room by making a bid when you access our internet auction site. In five easy steps you can get up to 50% discount on a Courtyard Hotel, City Lodge or Town Lodge room.

Costs and sustainability are also important. The company is focused on reducing its energy consumption and water use on a per room-occupied basis. Energy consumption in hotels is driven by hot water boilers, air-conditioning units and laundry equipment. The company disclosed its cost of energy and water use per room as follows for the 2005 financial year:

	Energy		Water	
	kVA per occupied room	Cost per occupied room	Kl per occupied room	Cost per occupied room
Courtyard	72.04	R 11.81	0.76	R 5.80
City Lodge	31.78	7.91	0.46	2.70
Town Lodge	34.33	8.96	0.41	4.52
Road Lodge	13.76	5.67	0.36	2.52

The company has taken measures to contain costs such as heating water in off-peak periods, offering guests the choice of using the same towels and linen for the duration of their stay rather than incurring daily laundering costs, replacing lighting and instituting automatic switch-offs of air-conditioners during the day. It is important for City Lodge to be able to determine each cost. The appropriate classification of costs helps the hotel industry to understand and manage its costs and profitability.

Controllable and uncontrollable costs

L.O. 6

Performance evaluation can be enhanced by classifying responsibility centre costs, such as department costs, as either *controllable* by the manager or *uncontrollable*. Ideally, when evaluating performance, managers should be held responsible only for costs they can control. If a manager can control or significantly influence the level of a cost, then that cost is classified as a **controllable cost** of that manager. Costs that a manager cannot influence significantly are classified as **uncontrollable costs**.

However, few costs are completely under the control of any individual. In classifying costs as controllable or uncontrollable, management accountants generally focus on a manager's ability to *influence*, rather than *control*, costs. Exhibit 2.3 lists several cost items, along with their typical classification as controllable or uncontrollable. For example, a manager of a Steers restaurant can probably control (or influence) the quantity of food used in the restaurant but may not be able to influence the price charged by suppliers. A City Lodge hotel manager can influence energy use but cannot control the price of electricity. Also, some costs are controllable in the long term but not in the short term. For example, the long-term costs associated with computing equipment leased by the Cape Town City Council are controllable when the 10-year lease is negotiated. In the short term, during the lease period, the rental costs are not controllable.

The classification of costs as controllable or uncontrollable is relevant to both conventional and contemporary management accounting systems.

Cost item	Manager	Classification
Cost of raw material used to produce circuit boards in a Hewlett-Packard factory	Supervisor of the production department for circuit boards	Controllable (quantity is controllable, but the price probably is not)
Cost of food used in a Steers restaurant	Restaurant manager	Controllable (quantity is controllable, but the price probably is not)
Cost of national advertising campaign for the Imperial car-rental company	Manager of the Imperial rental agency at Oliver Tambo airport	Uncontrollable (under the control of head office marketing manager)
Cost of national accounting and data-processing operations for the Standard Bank	Manager of the Standard Bank branch in Kimberley, Northern Cape	Uncontrollable (under the control of head office managers)

Exhibit 2.3 Controllable and uncontrollable costs

Costs across the value chain

L.O. 7

The value chain (see Exhibit 2.4) provides a useful framework for examining the areas where costs are incurred within a business. The **value chain** is a set of linked processes or activities that begins with acquiring resources and ends with providing (and supporting) goods and services that customers value.

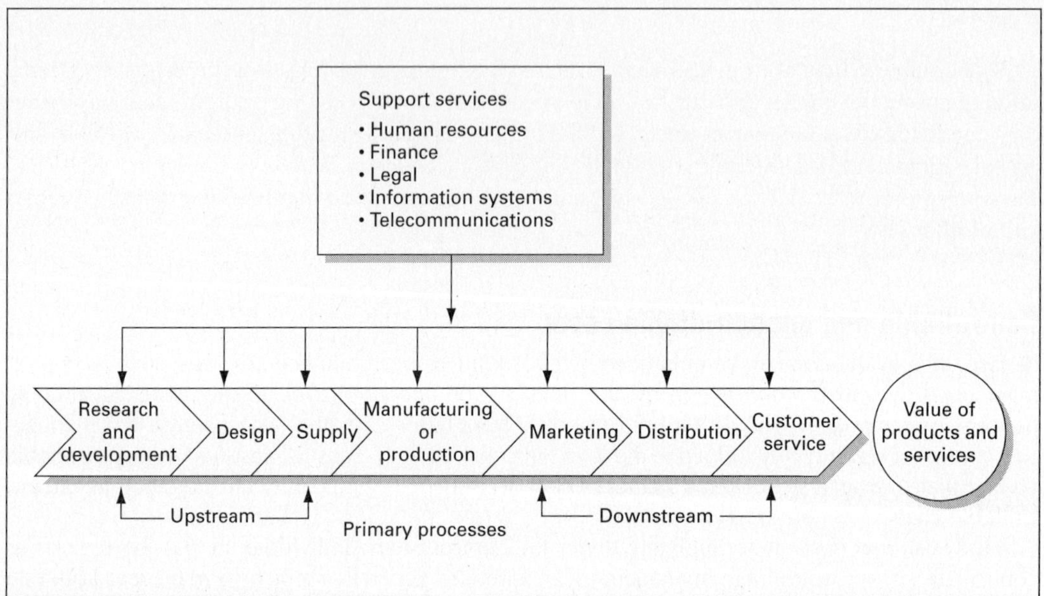

Exhibit 2.4 The value chain

Management accountants can use various cost classifications within the upstream, downstream and manufacturing areas to help them assign costs to products, and to provide other information to help manage resources effectively in order to create value. For example, by focusing on the costs of each primary process, management can consider how to reduce costs and can make decisions about whether to outsource aspects of the organisation. The 'Real life' on page 52 demonstrates the importance of managing costs and taking a value chain perspective.

Upstream costs

Research and development (or **R & D**) **costs** include all the costs involved in developing new products or processes. The costs of running laboratories, building prototypes of new products and testing new products and processes are all classified as research and development costs. These costs are becoming increasingly important as global competition increases, and product innovation is one source of competitive advantage. **Design costs** include all the costs associated with designing a product, as well as the costs of designing the processes that will be used to produce the new product. **Supply costs** refer to the costs of sourcing and managing incoming parts, assemblies and supplies. (Supply costs are discussed in more detail in Chapter 16.)

Production costs

Production costs include the costs incurred to collect and assemble the resources used to produce a product. In a manufacturing business these costs are often referred to as *manufacturing costs* or *factory costs*. Manufacturing costs are discussed in more detail below, and we explore the cost concepts relevant to service organisations in Chapter 6.

Downstream costs

Marketing costs refer to the costs of selling products, such as salaries, commissions and travel costs of sales personnel, and the costs of advertising and promotion. **Distribution costs** cover the costs of storing, handling and shipping finished products. **Customer service costs** include all the costs of serving customers, such as the costs of answering customer inquiries, after-sales service and warranty claims.

Manufacturing costs

L.O. 8

In a manufacturing business, the production costs are often referred to as **manufacturing costs**. They include all costs incurred within the factory area, whereas costs incurred outside the manufacturing area (that is, in upstream and downstream areas) are sometimes described as **non-manufacturing costs**.[4] Manufacturing costs are usually divided into three categories: *direct material, direct labour* and *manufacturing overhead* (or *indirect manufacturing costs*). This classification, as direct or indirect costs, assumes that products are the relevant cost objects. Indeed, one of the major reasons for analysing and classifying manufacturing costs is to determine the cost of products. In conventional product costing systems that focus on estimating product costs for external financial reporting, only manufacturing costs are considered to be product costs. As we will see in a later section, broader definitions of product cost are used by many businesses for managerial decision-making.

Direct material

Raw material that is:

- consumed in the manufacturing process;
- physically incorporated into the finished product; and
- can be traced to products conveniently

is called **direct material**. Examples include the cost of hoses used in a Defy dishwasher and the cost of paper used in *SL* magazine. Materials that become an integral part of the finished product but are insignificant in cost are often classified as *indirect material* (and also classified as *manufacturing overhead*). For example, materials such as glue or paint may be so inexpensive that on cost–benefit grounds it may not be worthwhile setting up a system to trace their cost directly to specific products.

Direct labour

The cost of salaries and wages and labour on-costs for personnel who work directly on the manufactured product is usually classified as **direct labour**. Examples include the wages of personnel who assemble notebook computers, and the wages of production workers who operate the sewing machines at a Levi Strauss jeans factory. These costs tend to be variable costs, as they vary with the level of production.

Labour on-costs are the additional labour-related costs that businesses have to incur to employ personnel, such as payroll tax, workers' compensation insurance, and employer contributions to pension funds.[5] Where labour on-costs relate to direct labour employees, they should be classified as part of direct labour costs, as they are as much a part of the cost of labour as are employees' regular wages. Interestingly, this treatment of labour on-costs is not always observed in practice, as some companies classify these on-costs as manufacturing overhead.

Sometimes contractual arrangements and union agreements may mean that labour is a *committed cost* that does not vary with the level of production. In this situation, it may not always be possible to trace labour costs directly to specific products, in which case these costs will be classified as indirect product costs.

REAL LIFE: MANAGING COSTS ACROSS THE VALUE CHAIN: THE ASIAN EXPERIENCE 

Multinational companies have always sought to manage costs by locating their operations to take advantage of relatively cheap resources. For example, over recent years most major multinational companies have established operations in China because of the relatively low labour costs.

Kenwood, the Japanese audio electronics manufacturer, set up production of its portable MiniDisc (MD) players in Johor Bahru, Malaysia, because of the effects on competitiveness of the high value of the yen and relatively high labour costs in Japan. However, when Kenwood sought to reduce MD costs further, its next move was not to China, but back to Japan. With a lower foreign exchange rate, the higher skills and productivity of Japanese labour, and a reduced need for re-exporting, this move resulted in a saving in costs across the value chain of 10 per cent, reduced lead times from two weeks to one to two days and inventory levels from 18 to three days. While an assembly line in Johor Bahru required 22 employees, the same work could be done by only four employees in Japan, using a cell production method. This method also enabled Kenwood to reduce the space required for the assembly process. The cell method, where employees work on a range of tasks in small production teams rather than on a single task as part of a large assembly line, ensures the flexibility to produce in small production lots, quickly, in order to meet customer demand more effectively. Moreover, the increase in sales once manufacturing returned to Japan indicated that customers placed significant value on the 'made in Japan' label.

While there is no doubt that the low cost of labour in China is attractive to manufacturers, the Kenwood story is not an isolated case in Japan, particularly for high-precision manufacturing. Seiko Epson decided to shift the production of its inkjet printers from China and the Philippines back to Japan, where the ink heads are manufactured. Likewise, Canon decided to limit production of digital cameras and copiers in China to the local market. Production for other markets will be located in Japan, where automation will be used to offset relatively higher labour costs. Canon has identified that costs across the value chain from development through to production and distribution can be managed more efficiently and effectively in Japan. According to Canon president, Mr Fujio Mitarai:

That can only be achieved by producing in Japan, where our development division is located. If labour costs go up, we only need to reduce costs through automation. The technology of production is limitless; as long as we try hard we can retain production in Japan.

Apart from more effective cost management and more flexibility to meet customer demand, the drive in Japan to retain high technology manufacturing operations also reflects a concern to retain the country's competitive advantage in this area.

Source: Kwan Wen Kin (2004)

Manufacturing overhead

All other costs of manufacturing are classified as **manufacturing overhead**, sometimes called **indirect manufacturing costs** or **factory burden costs**. Manufacturing overhead covers all manufacturing costs other than direct material and direct labour costs. It includes the cost of **indirect materials** and **indirect labour**, which covers any material and labour, used in production, that is not classified as *direct*. Manufacturing overhead also includes the costs of depreciation and insurance of the factory and manufacturing equipment, utilities such as electricity, as well as the costs of manufacturing support departments. **Support departments** (or **service departments**) are departments that do not work directly on producing products but are necessary for the manufacturing process to occur. Examples include equipment maintenance departments and production scheduling departments.

Manufacturing overhead costs also usually include *overtime premiums* and the cost of *idle time*. An **overtime premium** is the extra wages paid to an employee who works beyond normal working hours. Suppose an electronics technician who assembles compact disc players earns R40 per hour. The technician works 48 hours during a week instead of the normal working week of 40 hours. The overtime pay scale is time and a half, or 150 per cent of the regular wage. The technician's pay for the week is classified as follows:

Direct labour cost (R40 × 48 hours)	R1920
Overhead (overtime premium: 50% × R40 × 8 hours)	160
Total wages paid	R2080

Only the extra wage of R20 per hour (50% × R40) is classified as overtime premium. The regular wage of R40 per hour is treated as direct labour, even for the eight hours worked during overtime. The overtime premium is classified as manufacturing overhead, rather than being treated as a direct labour cost of the particular product that is produced during the overtime hours. This is because the overtime was caused by all the production scheduled during the day, not that particular product.

Idle time is time that is not spent productively by an employee due to such events as equipment breakdowns or new set-ups of production runs. The cost of an employee's idle time is classified as manufacturing overhead, relating to all the products produced rather than being associated with a particular product.

Conversion and prime costs

Direct labour costs and manufacturing overhead are often combined and called **conversion costs**, since they are the costs of 'converting' raw material into finished products. The costs of direct material and direct labour are often combined and called **prime costs**, as they are the major costs that can be directly associated with the product.

Contemporary costing in manufacturing businesses

Contemporary approaches to costing, such as activity-based costing, generally analyse costs in much more detail than do conventional costing systems. Instead of being classified as direct or indirect product costs, labour costs are often analysed as part of activity costs. Likewise, upstream and downstream costs may be classified and analysed within an activity framework.

Composition of manufacturing costs: the South African experience

The composition of manufacturing costs varies from one business to another depending on the industry, the nature of the product and the production processes. Generally, direct material is the largest cost, accounting for approximately one-half to three-quarters of total manufacturing costs. Of the remaining costs, in most businesses manufacturing overhead costs tend to be higher than direct labour costs, although the extent of this difference is influenced by the degree of automation.

Product costs

L.O. 9

One question managers often ask is: 'How much does it cost to make this product or to provide this service?' Managers need estimates of product costs to assess product profitability, to decide whether to make the product in-house or to outsource it and (sometimes) to set product prices, as well as to value inventory and cost of goods sold in the balance sheet and income statement. The problem is that managers need different measures of product cost for different purposes.

Product costs for financial accounting reports

For financial accounting reports (that is, the balance sheet and the income statement), a **product cost** is a cost assigned to goods that were either manufactured or purchased for resale. The product cost is regarded as part of the asset, inventory, until the goods are sold. When the goods are sold, the product cost is transferred from the inventory account to **cost of goods sold**, an expense account. Exhibit 2.5 illustrates the relationship between *product costs* and *cost of goods sold expense.*

The content of product costs used for financial reporting is defined in the international accounting standard, IAS 2 Inventories.[6] In brief, the product cost of inventory acquired for resale, by a retailer or wholesaler, consists of the purchase cost plus the cost of delivering the goods from the supplier. The product cost of manufactured inventory consists of manufacturing costs only—that is, the direct material, direct labour and a portion of manufacturing overhead costs. For example, the labour cost of a production employee at a Lucky Star pilchards cannery is part of the product cost of the cans of pilchards manufactured.

Another term used for product cost is **inventoriable cost** (or **inventoried cost**), since a product cost is stored as the cost of inventory until the goods are sold. The concept of product cost, which is used by retailers, wholesalers and manufacturers, is also used by other producers of inventoriable goods. Agricultural firms, timber companies and mining firms are examples of non-manufacturers that produce inventoriable goods. Apples, timber, coal and other goods are inventoried at their product cost until they are sold. Generally, service costs are not inventoried because services tend to be consumed as they are produced.

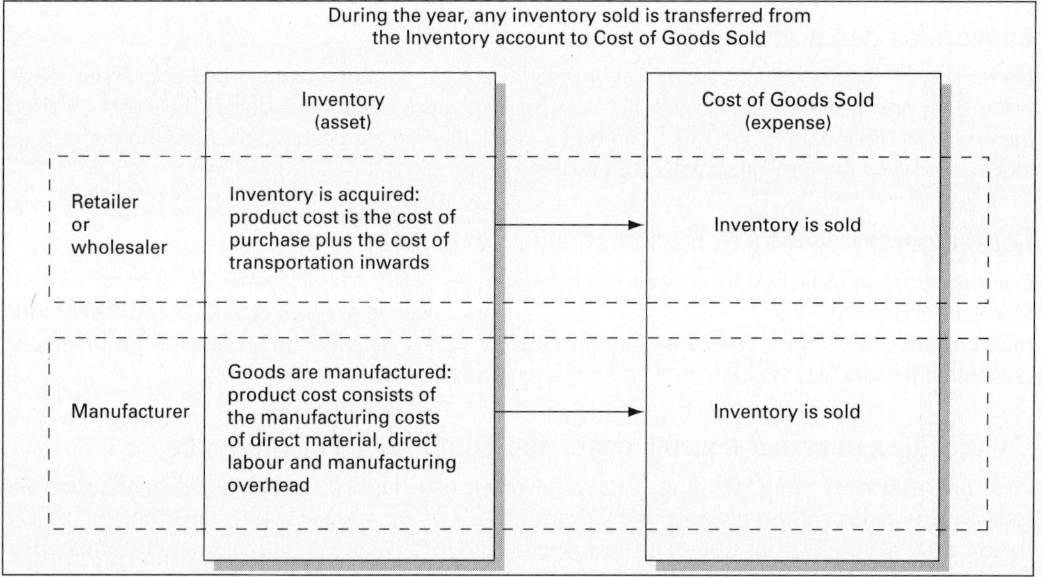

Exhibit 2.5 Product costs and cost of goods sold

Period costs

All costs that are not product costs are called **period costs**. These costs are expensed in the accounting period in which they are incurred rather than being attached to units of purchased or produced goods. Examples of period costs are salaries of sales personnel, advertising expenditures, depreciation of office equipment (but not depreciation of manufacturing equipment) and the salaries of top management. In the income statement, period costs are generally classified as either

REAL LIFE: SUGAR FARMERS ALSO NEED TO ANALYSE THEIR PRODUCTION COSTS

We have considered costs in manufacturing businesses, but primary producers also need to analyse and manage their costs effectively. The critical success factor for sugar growers in South Africa is to analyse and manage their production costs. Sugar farmers need to control labour costs, the costs of fertilizer and fuel as well as the cost of transporting the sugar cane to the mill. They also need to pay more attention to budgeting and forward planning. This is particularly relevant for small-scale cane growers and emerging farmers such as Mr. Gumede.

Sugar farmers measure costs in terms of Rand per ton cane, Rand per ton sucrose and Rand cost per hectare.

The SA Cane Growers Association ('Canegrowers') undertakes surveys of large-scale cane growers. For dryland producers, the division of production costs in 2005 was as illustrated in Exhibit 2.6.

Small-scale growers have until 2005 only earned a very small margin above the cost of harvesting. The low sugar price until 2005 resulted in many growers experiencing losses when capital costs, establishment and financing costs are taken into account. Further, the world sugar price has been highly volatile. This resulted in cane growers becoming increasingly focused on cost management. During 2005/2006 there was a significant improvement in the world price of sugar.

Why would the sugar industry indirectly welcome an increase in the cost of fuel, which is a major input cost? The price of sugar is increasingly underpinned by the growing demand for ethanol which is produced from sugar cane. Although the cost of fuel is a significant input cost, it is also true that the increased cost of fuel has added impetus to the use of sugar cane to produce fuel ethanol thereby supporting the world sugar price.

Source: www.sacanegrowers.co.za

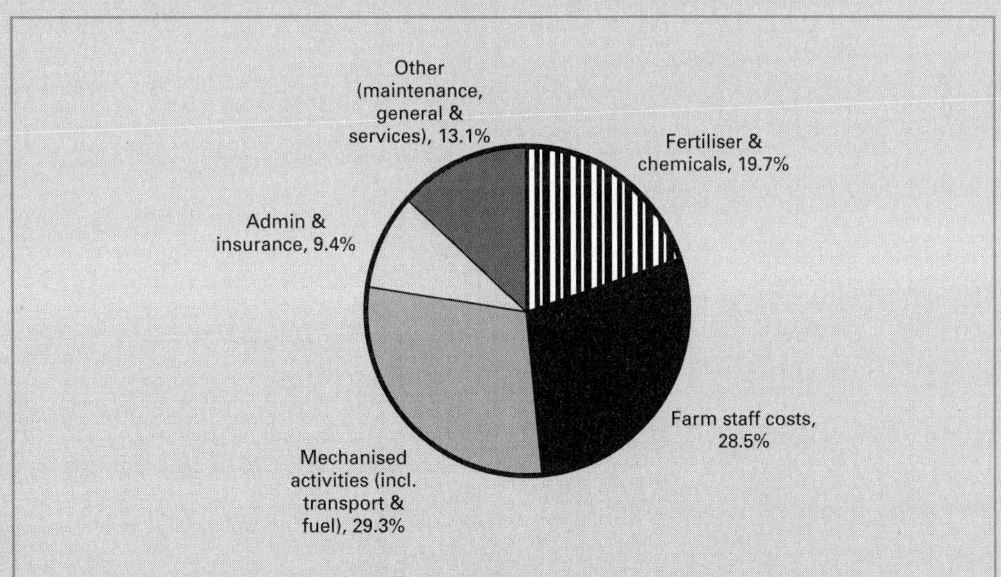

Exhibit 2.6 Production costs of sugar cane growers in South Africa

selling or administrative expenses. **Selling expenses** usually include the costs of selling goods or services *and* the costs of distribution. **Administrative expenses** refer to the costs of running the business as a whole, and include the costs of senior management as well as a range of (non-manufacturing) support services.

In most service firms there is no inventory, so all costs are treated as period costs.

Product costs for decision-making

While inventory valuations for financial accounting reports are limited to manufacturing costs, managers often need a wider definition of product cost for decision-making. For example, in setting a product's price, managers may need an estimate of all the costs associated with developing, producing and selling the product. The different measures of product cost relevant to different decisions are discussed in Chapter 4.

The mining industry is a particularly important source of products in South Africa, and, as the 'Real life' opposite shows, information about the costs of mineral products, such as gold, is essential for effective management in these industries.

Cost flows in a manufacturing business

L.O. 10

Direct material, direct labour and manufacturing overhead are the three types of production costs incurred by manufacturers. Most manufacturers have costing systems to keep track of the flow of these costs from the time production begins until the finished products are sold. There are four steps in the flow of costs in manufacturing.

1. When raw material is purchased, its cost is added to **raw material inventory**, an account which records the cost of all major materials purchased for manufacturing.
2. As direct material is consumed in production, its cost is removed from raw material and added to **work in process inventory**, an account which records the cost of manufactured products that are only partially completed at balance date. Similarly, the costs of direct labour and manufacturing overhead are accumulated in work in process inventory.
3. When products are finished, their costs are transferred from work in process inventory to **finished goods inventory**, an account which records the cost of manufactured goods that are complete and ready for sale. The costs are then 'stored' in finished goods until the products are sold.
4. When products are sold, the costs of those products are transferred from finished goods inventory to the cost of goods sold account, which is an expense during the period when the sale is made.

Exhibit 2.7 details these cost flows and their impact on the financial statements of a manufacturing business. You will notice that, as production costs move through the raw material, work in process and finished goods inventories, they are classified as assets and appear in the balance sheet. When finished goods are sold, the product costs move to the expense account, cost of goods sold, and are deducted from sales revenue to estimate the gross profit, which appears in the income statement. Period costs, relating to the expenses incurred in upstream and downstream areas of the value chain, are deducted from the gross profit to estimate net profit.[7] The detailed procedures and ledger accounts used to keep track of product costs are covered in Chapter 4.

Costing systems are used to track direct material, direct labour and manufacturing overhead costs through the various ledger accounts, to produce the financial accounting statements. These same systems enable the calculation of the costs of individual products, which may help managers to make decisions about issues such as product prices and product mix.

REAL LIFE: THERE'S GOLD, BUT AT WHAT COST?

South Africa has had a long and successful history in mining gold, and there is still plenty of gold to mine. However, the importance of assigning costs to cost objects becomes apparent in assessing the future of the gold industry. A key figure is the estimated production cost per ounce of gold. When the price fell to $250 per ounce in the late 1990s, a number of South African goldmines appeared unviable. Based on this price, only a few mines were covering costs, and this led to increasing consolidation in the sector.

Yet the cost per ounce has continued to rise. Let's look at the cost of producing gold at the three Gold Fields mines, Driefontein, Kloof and Beatrix.

Total cash cost US$/oz	2002	2003	2004	2005	2006
Driefontein	158	202	311	330	355
Kloof	179	215	341	379	421
Beatrix	173	229	356	406	409

These figures were based on cash costs, with no allowance made for depreciation and other charges. The rise in the gold price to about $1 000/oz at the time of writing has offered relief but the strong Rand in the period 2003 to 2005 impacted negatively on revenue. The fall in the Rand to about R8.00 per US Dollar at the time of writing has assisted the gold mines to deal with rising cost pressures. Yet what happens if costs carry on increasing at these rates and the gold price stagnates? Ultimately it is important for mining companies not only to estimate the cost of gold but to manage these costs tightly.

One of the reasons for the increasing costs relates to the depth of the South African mines and falling grades or yields. For example, the yield of gold from the Driefontein mine has fallen to 5.2 grams per ton of ore milled. Imagine processing one ton of ore to extract 5 grams of gold.

The cost of developing new mines is significant and there are few new mines on the horizon in the South African gold mining industry although there are a few significant extensions planned. The cost of the relatively new South Deep gold mine, owned by Gold Fields, is over R4 billion. The shaft goes down some 3 km into the earth. Imagine mining at depths which is akin to three inverted Table Mountains deep into the earth and imagine going down this shaft every day. The challenges that this presents to the mining companies is immense and the courage of the gold miners is remarkable.

Source: Gold Fields Annual Report 2006

Manufacturers often prepare a **schedule of cost of goods manufactured** and a **schedule of cost of goods sold** to summarise the flow of manufacturing costs during an accounting period and link this information to financial accounting statements. Unlike the financial statements, these schedules are not reported externally. Exhibit 2.8 shows these two schedules, together with an income statement, for a manufacturer called Ringo Instruments. The arrows that link the three statements explain the relationship between the *cost of goods sold* and the *cost of goods manufactured.* Notice that the cost of goods manufactured is calculated using the following formula:

$$\text{Cost of goods manufactured} = \text{beginning work in process} + \text{total manufacturing costs} - \text{ending work in process}$$

This represents the cost of goods that are completed (and moved from work in process into finished goods) during the period.

You will also note that cost of goods sold is calculated using this formula:

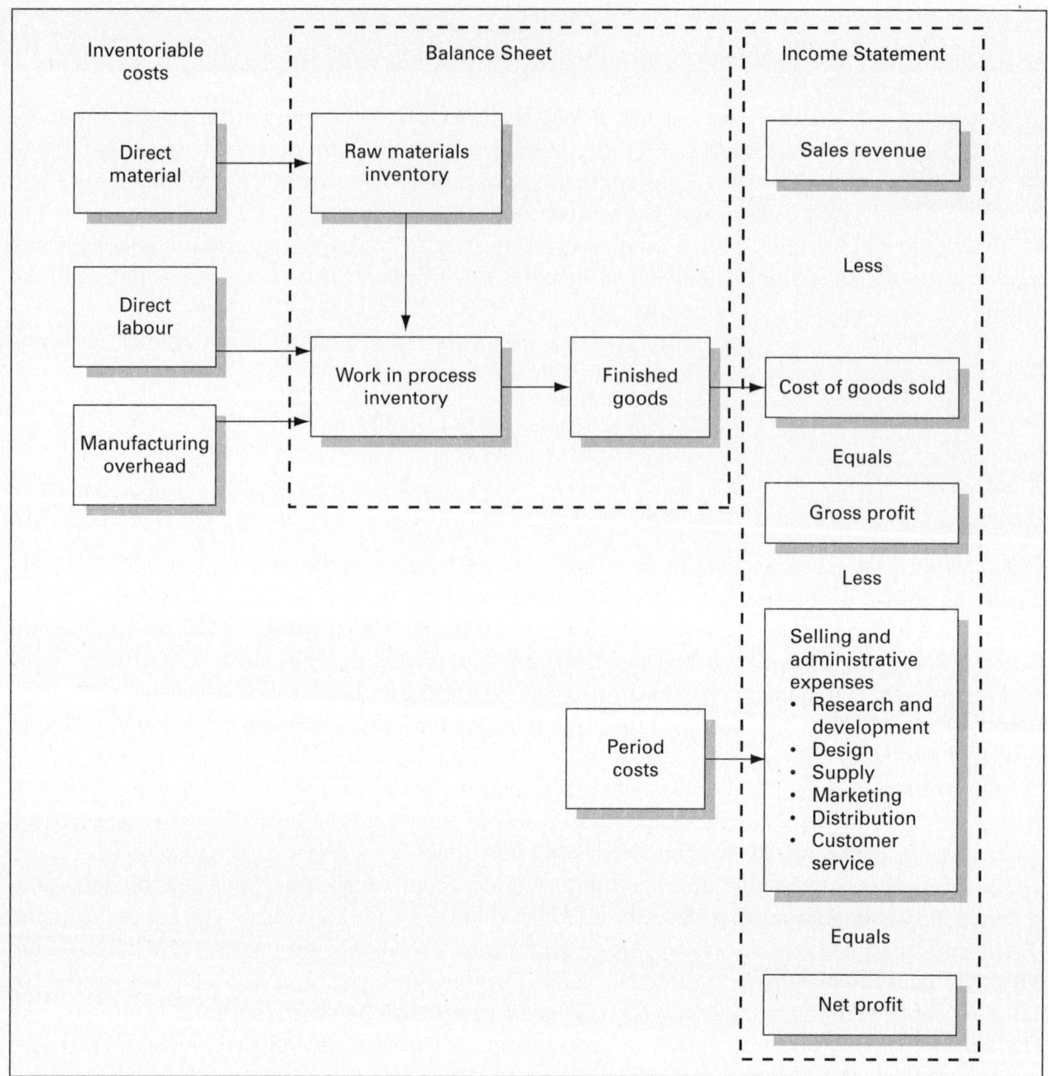

Exhibit 2.7 Cost flows and financial statements: manufacturer

Cost of goods sold	=	beginning finished foods	+	cost of goods manufactured	−	ending finished goods

This represents the cost of goods that are removed from finished goods and sold during the period. We return to these statements in Chapter 4.

Ringo Instruments **Schedule of Cost of Goods Manufactured for the year ended 31 December 20X6 (figures in 000s)**		
Direct material:		
Raw material inventory, 1 January	R10 000	
Add Purchases of raw material	100 000	
Raw material available for use	110 000	
Deduct Raw material inventory, 31 December	5 000	
Raw material used		R105 000
Direct labour		200 000
Manufacturing overhead:		
Indirect material	R8 000	
Indirect labour	17 000	
Depreciation on factory	50 000	
Depreciation on equipment	20 000	
Electricity	15 000	
Insurance	5 000	
Total manufacturing overhead		115 000
Total manufacturing costs		420 000
Work in process inventory, 1 January		25 000
Subtotal		445 000
Deduct Work in process inventory, 31 December		30 000
Cost of goods manufactured		R415 000

Schedule of Cost of Goods Sold for the year ended 31 December 20X6 (figures in 000s)	
Finished goods inventory, 1 January	R80 000
Add Cost of goods manufactured	415 000
Cost of goods available for sale	495 000
Finished goods inventory, 31 December	70 000
Cost of goods sold	R425 000

Income Statement for the year ended 31 December 20X6 (figures in 000s)	
Sales revenue	R700 000
Less Cost of goods sold	425 000
Gross profit	275 000
Selling and administrative expenses	175 000
Profit before taxes	100 000
Income tax expense	30 000
Net profit	R70 000

Exhibit 2.8 Manufacturing cost schedules

Summary

In this chapter we introduced some of the concepts and terminology used in management accounting. Key points include:

- Management accounting systems often include costing, budgeting and performance measurement systems. Contemporary management accounting systems also include cost management systems, which focus on the identification and elimination of wasteful activities.
- Management accounting systems focus on information about costs partially for historical reasons; and partially because of the ready availability of cost data in the accounting system; but primarily because understanding and managing costs is critical to managing resources to create value for customers and wealth for shareholders.

- Management accounting provides regular reports on product costs, the costs of organisational units such as departments and divisions, planned costs and actual costs, as well as information for cost management.
- Costs are the resources that we give up to achieve a particular objective. Yet the word 'cost' can have a variety of meanings in different situations, and it is useful to classify costs in different ways for different purposes.
- Costs may be classified according to their cost behaviour to provide management with useful information for planning and managing costs.
- Direct and indirect costs refer to the ability to trace costs to various cost objects, such as activities, departments, products, projects or customers.
- A cost may be classified as 'controllable' or 'uncontrollable' to describe the extent to which a manager can influence it. This may be useful for evaluating the performance of a responsibility centre or a manager.
- The value chain provides a useful framework for describing the costs that occur in different areas of a business—namely, research and development, design, supply, production, marketing, distribution and customer service.
- Production costs in a manufacturing business are called manufacturing costs and can be divided into direct material, direct labour and manufacturing overhead costs.
- The classification of costs as product costs is important. Product costs provide the basis for estimating the value of inventory and cost of goods sold for external accounting reports. The accounting standards confine these product costs to manufacturing costs. Managers often find more comprehensive estimates of product costs useful for making decisions on such things as which products to produce and what prices to set.
- Manufacturers have product costing systems to keep track of the flow of the manufacturing costs from the time production begins until the finished products are sold. They often prepare a schedule of cost of goods manufactured and a schedule of cost of goods sold to summarise the flow of manufacturing costs during an accounting period. These schedules link the information from the product costing system to the financial accounting reports.

In Chapter 3 we will explore techniques for analysing cost behaviour. Chapters 4, 5, 6, 7 and 8 will look at the various approaches and issues associated with estimating the costs of the goods and services that organisations produce.

References

Kwan WK 2004, 'It's back to Japan for high precision goods', *The Straits Times*, Singapore, 10 March, p. 6.

Annual Reports: City Lodge (2005, 2006, 2007), Gold Fields (2006), Seardel (2006).

Websites: www.sacanegrowers.co.za

Self study

Self-study problem: Cost classifications

Several costs incurred by Gauteng Golf Equipment Pty Ltd are listed below. For each cost, indicate which of the following classifications best describe the cost. More than one classification may apply to the same cost item. (For example, a cost may be both a period cost *and* a marketing cost.)

Cost classifications:

Period versus product cost
(a) period
(b) product

Product cost
(c) manufacturing
(d) direct material
(e) direct labour
(f) manufacturing overhead

Value chain
(g) product design
(h) marketing
(i) distribution
(j) customer service

Cost items:

1 Metal used in golf clubs.
2 Salary of plant manager.
3 Cost of electricity used to air-condition the factory.
4 Commissions paid to sales personnel.
5 Wages paid to employees who assemble golf bags.
6 Salary of engineer who is working on a prototype of a new solar-powered golf cart.
7 Depreciation on the word-processing equipment used by the managing director's secretary.
8 Wages paid to staff answering complaints from dissatisfied customers.
9 Cost of material used to develop new product packaging.
10 Maintenance cost of vehicles used to deliver products to customers.

Solution to Self-study problem

1 b, c, d
2 b, c, f
3 b, c, f
4 a
5 b, c, e
6 a, g
7 a
8 a, j

9 a, g
10 a, i

Cybersearch

1 Look for websites that discuss how product costs are used in particular decisions.
   (a) How are the product costs defined on that website?
   (b) Explain what the costs are used for.

2 Find two websites that discuss direct labour costs.
   (a) What have you learned about direct labour costs from your search?
   (b) Are the costs described in these websites direct costs of products or of organisational units such as departments or divisions?

3 Locate websites that include the terms *value chain* and *cost.*
   (a) What is the definition of a value chain as defined in this chapter?
   (b) Explain how the term is used on at least two websites.
   (c) How can this concept help managers?

4 In Exhibit 2.7 we showed research and development (R & D) costs as period costs. Refer to www.iasplus.com to explain when R & D costs may be treated as an asset rather than as a period cost. Look for IAS 39.

Questions

?

2.1 Describe the key components of *conventional* management accounting systems. How do these differ for *contemporary* management accounting systems?

2.2 Why do management accounting systems pay so much attention to costs?

2.3 Why do conventional management accounting systems pay so much attention to manufacturing costs? Do you think this is appropriate in today's business environment?

2.4 What is meant by the phrase, 'different costs for different purposes'?

2.5 Give four examples to illustrate how the managers of the City of Johannesburg could use cost information in planning and controlling costs.

2.6 Conventional management accounting systems classify costs as *fixed* and *variable*. Define these terms and provide three examples of each.

2.7 What are *cost objects*? Give four examples of cost objects, explaining why managers might be interested in knowing their cost.

2.8 What is a *direct cost*? What is an *indirect cost*? Explain the relevance of the phrase 'in an economic manner' in our definitions of direct and indirect costs.

2.9 Identify three cost objects and give two examples of direct and indirect costs for each of these cost objects.

2.10 List three costs that are likely to be controllable by an airport manager. List three costs that are likely to be uncontrollable by the manager.

2.11 Describe each segment of the value chain and explain why information about costs in the various segments of the value chain can be useful to managers.

2.12 Describe the three main components of product cost. Select a product with which you are familiar and provide examples of costs that would be classified under each of these three cost components.

2.13 Why are the costs of idle time and overtime premiums treated as manufacturing overhead?

2.14 Distinguish between *product* and *period* costs and give three examples of each.

2.15 Refer to the value chain in Exhibit 2.4. Consider a manufacturer of jeans and give two examples of costs for each segment of the company's value chain. Which of these costs would be included in an estimate of the cost of the jeans on hand at the end of the year, as shown in the company's balance sheet?

2.16 Why are product costs also called *inventoriable costs*?

2.17 Outline the four major steps in the flow of costs through a manufacturing company.

2.18 In a manufacturing context, explain how product costs can be classified as an asset, and then as an expense. What are the underlying principles behind this accounting treatment?

2.19 In your own words, explain the difference between *cost of goods manufactured* and *cost of goods sold*.

Exercises

E2.20 Classifying costs of support department; direct, indirect, controllable and uncontrollable costs

For each of the following costs, indicate:

(a) whether the amount is a direct or indirect cost of the equipment maintenance department

(b) whether each cost is at least partially controllable by the department supervisor

Costs:

1 Cost of depreciation on the building space occupied by the maintenance department.
2 Idle time of maintenance department employees.
3 Cost of plant manager's salary, which is allocated to the maintenance department.
4 Cost of property taxes and council rates allocated to the maintenance department.
5 Cost of electricity used in the maintenance department.

E2.21 Classifying costs; value chain: manufacturer

Igloo Icicle Company produces and sells ice-cream. Classify the costs listed below, using these value chain classifications:

(a) research and development
(b) product design
(c) supply
(d) manufacturing
(e) marketing
(f) distribution
(g) customer service

Costs:

1 The cost of cream and sugar used to make the ice-cream.
2 Electricity. The cold room that stores the completed ice-cream accounts for most of the electricity consumed.
3 The cost of fuel for delivery trucks.
4 The wages paid to staff who mix the ingredients to make the ice-cream.
5 The wages paid to the manager's mother who works part-time in the kitchen developing recipes for new ice-cream flavours, based on 'family secrets' handed down by her mother!
6 The cost of advertising in the food trade magazines.

E2.22 Idle time: manufacturer

A foundry employee worked a normal 40-hour week, but four hours were idle due to a small fire in the plant. The employee earns R56 per hour.

Required:

1 Calculate the employee's total wages for the week.
2 How much of this amount is a direct labour cost? How much is overhead? Why?
3 Under what circumstances would the normal weekly wage for this employee be treated as an indirect labour cost?

E2.23 Overtime cost: manufacturer

A loom operator in a textile factory earns R25 per hour, and R30 for each overtime hour. The operator worked 45 hours during the first week of May, instead of the usual 40 hours.

Required:

1. Calculate the loom operator's total wages for the week.
2. Calculate the operator's total overtime premium for the week.
3. How much of the operator's total wages for the week is direct labour cost? How much is overhead? Explain why.
4. Under what circumstances would the normal hourly rate be treated as an indirect labour cost?

E2.24 Cost of goods manufactured and sold

For each case below, find the missing amount:

	Case A	Case B	Case C
Beginning inventory of finished goods	R24 000	?	R3 500
Cost of goods manufactured during period	190 000	R419 000	?
Ending inventory of finished goods	16 000	98 000	10 500
Cost of goods sold	?	405 000	152 000

Required:

1. Calculate the missing data in the above table.
2. Explain the components of *cost of goods manufactured.*

E2.25 Schedules of cost of goods manufactured and sold; income statement: manufacturer

Pretoria Aluminium Company, a manufacturer of recyclable soft drink cans, had the following inventory balances at the beginning and end of 20X7:

Inventory account	1 January 20X7	31 December 20X7
Raw material	R600 000	R700 000
Work in process	1 200 000	1 150 000
Finished goods	1 500 000	1 650 000

During 20X7 the company purchased R2 500 000 of raw material and spent R4 000 000 on direct labour. Manufacturing overhead costs were as follows:

Indirect materials	R 100 000
Indirect labour	250 000
Depreciation on plant and equipment	1 000 000
Electricity	250 000
Other	300 000

Sales revenue was R 11 105 000 for the year. Selling and administrative expenses for the year amounted to R1 100 000. The firm's tax rate is 29 per cent.

Required:

1. Prepare a schedule of cost of goods manufactured.
2. Prepare a schedule of cost of goods sold.
3. Prepare an income statement.

Problems

P2.26 Product cost classification: manufacturer

The following cost data for 20X6 relate to Heartstrings Pty Ltd, a greetings card manufacturer:

Direct material used in production	R10 500 000
Advertising expense	495 000
Depreciation on factory building	575 000
Direct labour: wages	2 425 000
Cost of finished goods inventory at year-end	575 000
Indirect labour: wages	700 000
Production supervisor's salary	225 000
Support department costs*	500 000
Direct labour: labour on-costs	475 000
Indirect labour: labour on-costs	150 000
Labour on-costs for production supervisor	45 000
Total overtime premiums paid	275 000
Cost of idle time: production employees	200 000
Administrative costs	750 000
Rental of office space for sales personnel	75 000
Sales commissions	25 000
Product promotion expenses	50 000

*All support services are provided to manufacturing departments.

Required:
Calculate each of the following costs for 20X6:
1 Total prime costs.
2 Total manufacturing overhead costs.
3 Total conversion costs.
4 Total product costs (for external reporting purposes).
5 Total period costs.

P2.27 Classifying costs: manufacturer

Classify the costs below for the Donut King Company, a manufacturer of donuts, as:
(a) direct material
(b) direct labour
(c) manufacturing overhead
(d) selling and administrative expenses
(e) other (if other, explain)

Costs:
1 Flour
2 Depreciation on cooking vats
3 Cooking oil
4 Sugar
5 Wages of a donut cook
6 Repair of a cooking vat
7 Packaging for donuts
8 Cartons for shipping donuts
9 Accountant's salary
10 Production manager's salary
11 Advertising
12 Oil for the factory conveyor system
13 Fuel for the delivery truck used to ship donuts to customers.

P2.28 Classifying costs; value chain: manufacturer

1 Classify each of the costs in Problem 2.27 using the value chain classifications:
(a) research and development (b) product design (c) supply (d) manufacturing (e) marketing (f) distribution (g) customer service

2 Do you think these costs cover the complete value chain for the Donut King Company? Explain your answer.

P2.29 Classifying costs; product versus period; components of product cost

Indicate, for each of the costs listed below, whether it is:

(a) a product cost
(b) a period cost
(c) a conversion cost
(d) a prime cost
(e) a direct material cost
(f) a direct labour cost
(g) manufacturing overhead

More than one classification may apply to each item.

Costs:

1 Cost incurred by a department store chain to transport goods purchased for resale to its stores.
2 Cost of grapes purchased by a winery.
3 Depreciation on pizza ovens in a pizza restaurant.
4 Wages of aircraft mechanics employed by an airline.
5 Wages of drill-press operators in a manufacturing plant.
6 Cost of food in a TV dinner.
7 Salary of a plant manager in a computer production facility.
8 Wages of security personnel in a department store.
9 Cost of electricity and gas in a manufacturing facility.
10 Depreciation of computers used in a sales department.
11 Depreciation of computers used to control production equipment.

P2.30 Direct and indirect labour: manufacturer

KwaZulu Cutlery manufactures kitchen knives. One of the employees, whose job is to cut out wooden knife handles, worked 45 hours during a week in January. The employee earns R36 per hour for a 40-hour week. For additional hours the employee is paid an overtime rate of R48 per hour. The employee's time was spent as follows:

Regular duties involving cutting out knife handles	38 hours
General shop clean-up duties	6 hours
Idle time due to power failure	1 hour

Required:

1 Calculate the total cost of the employee's wages during the week described above.
2 Determine the portion of this cost to be classified in each of the following categories:
   (a) direct labour
   (b) manufacturing overhead (idle time)
   (c) manufacturing overhead (overtime premium)
   (d) manufacturing overhead (indirect labour)
3 Under what circumstances would the normal wage of this employee be treated as an indirect cost?

P2.31 Incomplete data: manufacturing costs

Determine the missing amounts in each of the following independent cases:

Figures in thousands

	Case A	Case B	Case C
Beginning inventory, raw material	R20 000	R15 000	?
Ending inventory, raw material	?	30 000	R90 000
Purchases of raw material	85 000	?	100 000
Direct material used	95 000	?	70 000
Direct labour	100 000	125 000	?
Manufacturing overhead	?	160 000	250 000
Total manufacturing costs	345 000	340 000	520 000
Beginning inventory, work in process	20 000	?	35 000
Ending inventory, work in process	35 000	5 000	?
Cost of goods manufactured	?	350 000	525 000
Beginning inventory, finished goods	40 000	?	50 000
Cost of goods available for sale	?	370 000	?
Ending inventory, finished goods	?	25 000	?
Cost of goods sold	330 000	?	545 000
Sales	?	480 000	?
Gross profit	170 000	?	255 000
Selling and administrative expenses	75 000	?	?
Profit before taxes	?	90 000	150 000
Income tax expense	45 000	?	40 000
Net profit	?	55 000	?

P2.32 Classifying costs according to value chain: boat builder

Southwoods is a medium-sized boat-building firm that builds a range of cruising yachts. Apply value chain and other classifications to the costs listed below. (More than one classification may be appropriate for each cost item.) What role might this approach to cost classification play in the management process?

Cost classifications:

(a) research and development
(b) design
(c) supply
(d) production
(e) marketing
(f) distribution
(g) customer service
(h) direct material
(i) direct labour
(j) manufacturing overhead

Costs:

1 The salary of the naval architect who designs the boats.
2 The salary of the financial and administration manager.
3 The cost of fibreglass used in making the boat hulls.
4 The wages of the employees who paint the hulls.
5 The cost of the sails purchased from a sailmaker.
6 The costs of advertising in yachting magazines.
7 Depreciation on equipment used in building and painting the hulls.
8 The cost of preprinted stationery used in the administration and sales office.
9 The salaries of the sales staff.
10 Depreciation on office computing equipment.

P2.33 Fixed and variable costs; forecasting: manufacturer

Egoli Electronics (Pty) Ltd incurred the following costs during the year just ended. The company sold all the products it manufactured during the year.

Direct materials	R3 000 000
Direct labour	2 200 000
Manufacturing overhead:	
Electricity	140 000
Depreciation on plant and equipment	230 000
Insurance	160 000
Supervisory salaries	300 000
Council rates and land taxes	210 000
Selling expenses:	
Advertising	195 000
Sales commissions	90 000
Administrative expenses:	
Salaries of top management and staff	372 000
Office supplies	40 000
Depreciation on building and equipment	80 000

During this period, the company operated at about half its capacity due to a slowdown in the economy. Prospects for next year are slightly better, with the marketing manager forecasting a 15 per cent growth in sales over the year just ended.

Required:
Categorise each of the costs listed above according to whether it is most likely to be variable or fixed, in relation to production volume. Forecast the amount for each of the costs listed above for the next year.

P2.34 Cost classifications by cost behaviour and value chain: manufacturer
Outer Banks Shirt Shop manufactures T-shirts and decorates them with customised designs for retail sale on the premises. Several costs incurred by the company are listed below. For each cost listed below, indicate which of the following classifications best describes the cost. More than one classification may apply to the same cost item.

Cost classifications:
(a) variable
(b) fixed
(c) research and development
(d) design
(e) supply
(f) manufacturing
(i) direct labour (ii) direct material (iii) manufacturing overhead
(g) marketing
(h) distribution
(i) customer service

Costs:
1 Cost of a new sign in front of the retail T-shirt shop.
2 Wages of the employee who repairs the firm's sewing machines.
3 Cost of fabric used in the T-shirts.
4 Wages of the shirtmakers.
5 Cost of electricity used in the sewing department.
6 Wages of the T-shirt designers and painters.
7 Wages of the sales personnel.
8 Depreciation on the sewing machines.
9 Rent on the building. Part of the building's first floor is used to make and paint T-shirts. Part of it is used for a retail sales shop. The second floor is used for administrative offices and storage of raw material and finished goods.

10 Cost of daily advertisements in the local media.
11 Wages of the designers who experiment with new fabrics, paints and T-shirt designs.
12 Cost of hiring a pilot to fly along the beach pulling a banner advertising the shop.
13 Salary of the owner's secretary.
14 Cost of repairing the gas furnace.
15 Cost of insurance for the production employees.

P2.35 Schedules of cost of goods manufactured and sold; income statement

The following data refer to The Bread Bakehouse for the year 20X6:

Work in process inventory, 31 December 20X5	R 810 000
Selling and administrative salaries	1 380 000
Insurance on factory equipment	360 000
Work in process inventory, 31 December 20X6	830 000
Finished goods inventory, 31 December 20X5	1 400 000
Indirect material used	490 000
Depreciation in factory equipment	210 000
Raw material inventory, 31 December 20X5	1 010 000
Property taxes for factory	240 000
Finished goods inventory, 31 December 20X6	1 540 000
Purchases of raw material in 20X6	3 900 000
Electricity for factory	600 000
Electricity for sales and adminstrative offices	250 000
Other selling and adminstrative expenses	400 000
Indirect labour cost incurred	2 900 000
Depreciation on factory building	380 000
Depreciation on cars used by sales personnel	120 000
Direct labour cost incurred	7 900 000
Raw material inventory, 31 December 20X6	1 100 000
Rental for warehouse space to store raw material	310 000
Rental of space for managing director's office	170 000
Sales revenue	20 580 000
Income tax expenses	510 000

Required:

1 Prepare The Bread Bakehouse's schedule of cost of goods manufactured for 20X6.
2 Prepare the company's schedule of cost of goods sold for 20X6.
3 Prepare the company's income statement for 20X6.

P2.36 Schedules of cost of goods manufactured and sold; income statement

The following data refer to Primrose CC for the year 20X7:

Sales revenue	R2 105 000
Raw material inventory, 31 December 20X6	89 000
Purchases of raw material in 20X7	731 000
Raw material inventory, 31 December 20X7	59 000
Direct labour cost incurred	474 000
Selling and administrative expenses	269 000
Indirect labour cost incurred	150 000
Council rates	90 000
Depreciation on factory building	125 000
Income tax expense	25 000
Indirect material used	45 000
Depreciation on factory equipment	60 000
Insurance on factory and equipment	40 000

Electricity for factory	70 000
Work in process inventory, 31 December 20X6	0
Work in process inventory, 31 December 20X7	40 000
Finished goods inventory, 31 December 20X6	35 000
Finished goods inventory, 31 December 20X7	40 000

Required:

1 Prepare Primrose Manufacturing's schedule of cost of goods manufactured for 20X7.
2 Prepare Primrose Manufacturing's schedule of cost of goods sold for 20X7.
3 Prepare Primrose Manufacturing's income statement for 20X7.

P2.37 Interpreting the schedule of cost of goods manufactured

Refer to the schedule of cost of goods manufactured prepared in Problem 2.36.

Required:

1 How much of the manufacturing costs incurred during 20X7 remain in work in process inventory on 31 December 20X7?
2 Suppose Primrose Manufacturing had increased its production in 20X7 by 20 per cent. Would the direct material cost shown on the schedule have been larger or the same? Why?
3 Answer the same question as in requirement 2 for depreciation on the factory building.
4 Suppose that only half of the R60 000 in depreciation on equipment was related to factory machinery, and the other half was related to selling and administrative equipment. How would this have changed the schedule of cost of goods manufactured?

Cases

C2.38 Cost classifications; schedules of cost of goods manufactured and sold; income statement; product costs: manufacturer

Central Tap Company (CTC) is a manufacturer of taps and fittings for the plumbing trade, located in Durban. The company was established by Ken Hall in 1951, with a workforce of 10, to meet the needs of the postwar housing boom. Its product range was fairly limited but the company had an excellent reputation for quality.

Nowadays, CTC manufactures an extensive range of high-quality brass and chrome taps. The company is managed by Ken's son, Michael, and employs 20 people. It has annual sales averaging approximately R10 million. Although it has been consistently profitable, CTC has experienced increasing pressure from competitors since the early 1990s. The company uses a cost-plus approach to pricing but is having to reduce its mark-up constantly in order to maintain market share.

Both Ken and Michael qualified as engineers. The business is small and has never been able to employ an accountant. Instead, a bookkeeper calculates monthly profit as sales revenue minus expenses. Prices are based on rough estimates of cost of direct material and direct labour inputs plus a 50 per cent mark-up.

With the decline in profit and constant pressure on prices, Michael began to feel uneasy about the way costs and profits were calculated. The results for the month just ended were:

Sales		R980 000
Less Expenses:		
Materials purchased	R300 000	
Factory wages—production line	250 000	
Production supervisor's salary	35 000	
Rent	80 000	
Council rates	5 000	
Sales staff	110 000	
Advertising	18 000	
Equipment depreciation	25 000	
Electricity	12 000	
Manager's salary	80 000	
Truck lease	10 000	
Total expenses		925 000
Net profit		55 000

Additional information:

- There was virtually no beginning inventory of raw material, work in process and finished goods.
- At the end of the month, 10 per cent of the materials purchased remained on hand, work in process amounted to 20 per cent of the manufacturing costs incurred during the month, and finished goods inventories were negligible.
- The factory occupies 80 per cent of the premises, the sales area 15 per cent and administration 5 per cent.
- Most of the equipment is used for manufacturing, with only 5 per cent of the book value being used for sales and administrative functions.
- Almost all of the electricity is consumed in the factory.
- The truck is used to deliver finished goods to customers.
- Michael Hall spends about one-half of his time on factory management, one-third in the sales area and the rest on administration.

Required:

Michael Hall asks you to review the results for the month and evaluate the company's approach to estimating product costs. In doing so, you should:

1 Comment on the cost classifications used in CTC's income statement.
2 Estimate the cost of goods manufactured and sold.
3 Prepare a revised income statement for the month.
4 Explain the differences between your income statement and the one above.
5 If possible, suggest a more useful format for analysing costs than that used in your revised income statement.
6 Evaluate the usefulness of product costs based on direct materials and direct labour.
7 Make recommendations for change.

C2.39 Cost classifications; schedules of cost of goods manufactured and sold; income statement: manufacturer

On 1 January 20X7 John Brown set up Valleyview Playgyms Company to manufacture and sell children's outdoor playgyms. He was an engineer by profession but he understood the importance of accounting information and kept his accounting records meticulously throughout the year. At the end of the year he prepared the following income statement for the year:

Sales		R4 500 000
Less Operating expenses:		
Purchases of raw material	R2 000 000	
Purchases of factory supplies	100 000	
Wages for factory employees who work directly on the playgyms	750 000	
Wages for other factory employees	100 000	
Manager's salary	400 000	
Office staff salaries	100 000	
Sales staff salaries	220 000	
Advertising	50 000	
Administrative expenses	80 000	
Cleaning costs	50 000	
Rent	250 000	
Electricity	45 000	
Purchases of factory equipment	1 400 000	
Purchases of office equipment	100 000	
Purchases of sales vehicles	150 000	
Total operating expenses		5 795 000
Net loss		−1 345 000

Although disappointed, Brown was not surprised. He knew that expenses were higher than sales because, throughout the year, he had been unable to generate a cash surplus. His bank overdraft had blown out and his bank manager has asked him to present his financial statements for 20X7 to the bank.

Required:

You are the bank's accountant and the bank manager has asked you to:

1 Review the performance of Valleyview Playgyms in 20X7 and make a recommendation as to whether Brown's overdraft facility should be cancelled.
2 Prepare a report for Brown explaining the errors he made in his income statement.

To perform this analysis you will need to recast Brown's income statement. The following information may be useful:

- The factory occupies 80 per cent of the rented building, the sales area 15 per cent and the administration area 5 per cent.
- All the company's fixed assets are estimated to have a useful life of five years and no salvage value at the end of their life.
- Brown spends 50 per cent of his time as factory manager and spends the remaining time equally on sales and general administration.
- Electricity costs are consumed almost entirely by the factory.
- At 31 December 20X7, the following inventories existed:

Raw material	R200 000
Work in process	400 000
Finished goods	515 000

Endnotes

1 In this text we use the term 'income statement' instead of 'profit and loss statement' or 'statement of financial performance' and the term 'balance sheet' instead of 'statement of financial position'.

2 The economic concepts of relevant costs for decision-making are described separately in the chapters in Part 4: Information for creating value.

3 See, for example, the new performance measurement systems described in Chapter 14 and the information used for cost management described in Chapter 15.

4 In practice, some businesses call non-manufacturing costs *overhead costs,* but this can lead to confusion with the term *manufacturing overhead.* This issue is discussed further in Chapter 7.

5 In South Africa, *labour on-costs* can be distinguished from *fringe benefits.* The term *fringe benefits* is increasingly being used to describe benefits that employees receive in addition to their wages, and is often associated with managers' salary packages. For example, a manager's salary package may include the use of a company car, payment of private school fees for children and membership of the local golf club.

6 The appendix to Chapter 4 summarises the key requirements of the International Financial Reporting accounting standard for inventory valuation.

7 This issue is discussed further in Chapter 8.

PART 2
Costs and Costing Systems

Part Contents

In this section we examine some cost concepts in more detail and describe various costing systems. Management accountants use costing systems to accumulate the costs of cost objects. Cost objects are simply the 'things' that managers want 'costed'. The costing systems used by most organisations usually have at least two cost objects: products (or services) and responsibility centres, such as departments. The primary focus of this section is on using costing systems to accumulate product and service costs. Estimates of product and service costs provide vital information for managers in their drive to manage resources more effectively and enhance shareholder value. For example, managers can use estimates of product and service costs to assess product profitability and to make a range of decisions about product mix, and sometimes about product price. Managers also use product and service costs to plan and control costs. We discuss costing for responsibility centres in Part 3, which deals with information for managing resources.

In Chapter 3 we explore the concept of cost drivers, which are factors or activities that cause costs. The chapter also examines cost behaviour and cost estimation. Understanding cost behaviour involves examining the relationship between a cost and the level of activity or cost driver. The chapter uses the Tasty Bread Company to illustrate a number of cost behaviour patterns including variable, fixed, step-fixed, semivariable and curvilinear costs. Cost estimation describes the process of determining how a particular cost behaves. Approaches to cost estimation include managerial judgement, the engineering method, and various quantitative methods such as the high–low method and regression analysis.

The remaining chapters in this part of the book focus primarily on product costing. Product costing is a vital part of the management accounting system. In Chapter 4 we recognise that different measures of product cost may be appropriate for different purposes. We describe the general principles for assigning the manufacturing costs, direct material, direct labour and manufacturing overhead to products. The costs are moved into work-in-process inventory at the start of production; from work-in-process inventory to finished-goods inventory as the products are completed; and from finished goods inventory to cost of goods sold when the products are sold.

The features of costing systems vary from one business to the next. One cause of variation is the nature of the production process and the product produced. Two basic sets of procedures are used: job costing and process costing.

Job costing is used where goods are produced in distinct batches and there are significant differences between the batches. Job costing would be used when firms manufacture aircraft, ships and furniture, for example. In job costing, the costing system is designed to assign costs to each job. In the second part of Chapter 4 we illustrate job costing with a case from real life.

Process costing is used by companies that produce a single product (or a small range of very similar products) in large quantities. Thus, in production environments where petrol, processed food, tobacco and chemicals are produced, process costing may be used. In these systems there is no need to trace costs to individual products, because each unit of product is identical. In process costing, the costing system accumulates all the production costs over the accounting period and then averages these costs over the number of units produced during the period. We introduce process costing in the later part of Chapter 4.

Process costing becomes more complex when there is beginning or ending work in process on hand. In this situation two approaches may be used: the weighted average and first-in, first-out (FIFO) methods. In Chapter 5 we use an illustration to explore both of these approaches. Also, in practice, job costing and process costing procedures represent the two extremes of costing systems. Many businesses operate in an environment that requires a combination of job- and process-costing features. These systems are called 'hybrid costing systems'. In Chapter 5, we extend the process-costing example to illustrate a particular hybrid costing system known as 'operation costing'.

Many organisations produce services rather than products. Estimates of service costs will enable managers to assess service profitability and to make a range of decisions about service mix, and sometimes about product price. In Chapter 6 we identify the types of costs incurred in service firms and consider how the product-costing principles described in Chapters 4 and 5 can be adapted to estimate the cost of services in some organisations.

One of the most difficult issues in product costing is how to allocate overhead costs to products. We explore this issue in Chapter 7, where we begin by outlining some general principles for allocating indirect costs to cost objects. We then use the Delta Controls case study to describe three different approaches to allocating overhead costs to products: a plant-wide overhead rate, departmental rates and activity-based costing. We also describe how to allocate indirect costs to responsibility centres. In particular, we present three approaches to allocating support department costs to production departments: the direct, step-down and reciprocal methods.

The costing systems described in Chapters 4, 5, 6 and 7 are conventional costing systems, based on principles and practices developed in the early part of last century. They are still used widely. However, there have been significant changes to the business environment—particularly to cost and product structures—since then. In Chapter 8 we discuss some of the weaknesses inherent in these conventional costing systems because of their failure to adapt to the changing business environment. Activity-based costing (ABC) has been the major response to the inadequacies of conventional costing systems. ABC can be used to improve the accuracy of product costs and to provide invaluable information to manage resources. We introduce activity-based costing briefly in Chapter 7, and in Chapter 8 we provide a more detailed description and evaluation of activity-based product costing. (We extend this case in Chapter 15 to illustrate the application of activity-based costing to cost management, and in Chapter 16 we consider how activity-based costing can be used to estimate and manage customer and supplier costs.)

Cost Behaviour, Cost Drivers and Cost Estimation

❖ Learning Objectives

After completing this chapter, you should be able to:

1. explain the relationships between cost estimation, cost behaviour and cost prediction;
2. explain the concept of cost drivers, including volume-based and non-volume-based cost drivers;
3. describe the unit, batch, product and facility level hierarchy of costs and cost drivers;
4. describe the different roles that cost driver analysis can play in management accounting;
5. define and analyse the behaviour of the following types of costs: variable, fixed, step-fixed, semivariable (or mixed) and curvilinear;
6. explain the importance of the relevant range when using a cost behaviour pattern for cost prediction;
7. define and provide examples of engineered, committed and discretionary costs;
8. describe the following approaches to cost estimation: managerial judgement (including account classification), the engineering method, and quantitative analysis (including high–low, and simple and multiple regression);
9. determine cost functions using the high–low method and regression analysis;
10. explain some of the issues that arise in estimating cost functions in practice, including data collection problems, learning curve effects, and cost–benefit evaluations;
11. after studying the appendix, use Microsoft Excel® to estimate and evaluate a regression equation; and
12. after studying the appendix, describe the impact of learning curve effects on the estimation of cost behaviour.

Introduction

Managers in almost any organisation need to know how costs will be affected by changes in the organisation's activities. You will recall from Chapter 2 that understanding cost behaviour involves examining the relationship between a cost and the level of activity. Managers need to know what activities drive or cause the major costs within their business.

Knowledge about cost behaviours can help managers to manage resources more effectively. To plan operations and prepare budgets, managers at Distell use their knowledge of cost behaviour and predictions about future activity levels. To control the costs of providing services to the community, local government councils need to know the costs they would incur at various levels of activity, so that they can then compare actual costs to these planned costs. In addition, the councils can actively manage and reduce costs by managing the major cost drivers.

Information about cost behaviour can also help managers as they decide how to enhance customer value and shareholder wealth. In deciding whether to add a new intensive-care unit, a hospital's administrators need to predict the cost of operating the new unit at various levels of patient demand. In deciding which products to produce at BMW South Africa, or which investment services to offer at Investec, managers need reliable estimates of product costs. In each of these situations, a good understanding of cost drivers and cost behaviour can enhance a manager's ability to manage resources effectively and create value.

L.O. 1

What are cost behaviour, cost estimation and cost prediction?

Cost behaviour is the relationship between a cost and the level of activity or cost driver. How does an accountant determine the cost behaviour of a particular cost item? This is called **cost estimation**, and can be accomplished in many ways. One way is to analyse historical data involving costs and different activity levels.

Estimates of cost behaviour provide the basis for predicting future costs. **Cost prediction** is a forecast of a cost at a particular level of activity. For example, in preparing its annual budget, the South African Film Corporation predicts studio costs on the basis of the production hours expected for the coming year. The corporate services manager identifies the number of films to be produced and the anticipated length of each production, which is influenced by the filming, sound-mixing and editing requirements.

Exhibit 3.1 summarises the relationship between cost behaviour, cost estimation and cost prediction.

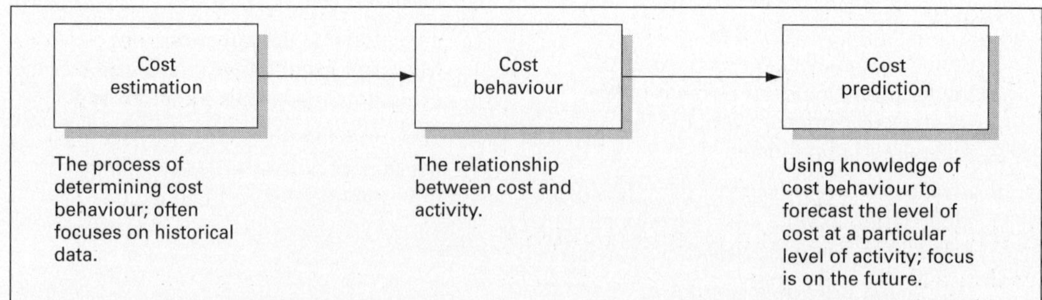

Exhibit 3.1 The relationship between cost behaviour, cost estimation and cost prediction

In this chapter we will consider the different types of cost drivers and cost behaviour patterns and describe several techniques for estimating costs. Some of these cost behaviour patterns were introduced briefly in Chapter 2.

Cost behaviour, cost estimation and cost prediction at Tasty Bread Company

Our discussion of cost behaviour will focus on a business called Tasty Bread Company, which operates a bakery and a chain of six crusty bread shops in Johannesburg. Each shop sells a variety of crusty breads and rolls. All the company's products are baked daily in a centrally located bakery. The company leases several small delivery trucks to transport goods to its shops. In peak sales periods there may be several deliveries to each shop daily. The owner believes that the use of a central bakery is more cost-efficient than establishing a bakery in each shop.

The accountant of Tasty Bread, Jack Dlamini, has begun a preliminary study of the company's cost behaviour. At this stage he has selected only a few costs for his study. At a later date he hopes to include all the costs incurred by the business, and to use this information to predict accurate costs for the annual budgeting process. Listed below are the costs he has selected:

- *direct material*: costs of the ingredients for wholemeal bread rolls;
- *premises cost*: bakery and shop leasing costs; council rates; land taxes; depreciation and insurance on the bakery building and shops;
- *delivery truck costs*: payments under lease contracts; cost of petrol, oil, tyres and maintenance;
- *electricity costs*: costs of electrical power consumption; and
- *shop managers' salaries*: salaries and on-costs of managers and assistant managers for the shops.

Jack Dlamini has realised that each of these costs may exhibit different behaviours and be driven by a range of activities. His first step will be to identify specific cost drivers for each cost.

Cost drivers

L.O. 2

Cost driver is a term that is used to describe activities or factors that drive (or cause) costs.[1] For example, the number of cars resprayed by Welkom Auto Works is the cost driver for the cost of paint used in the business. The number of batches of paintbrushes produced at Rokset Industries in Durban drives the cost of setting up the machines that make the brushes. The number of board meetings may drive the corporate administration costs at the Pick 'n Pay headquarters in Cape Town.

How does Tasty Bread's accountant, Jack Dlamini, work out what drives each cost? To identify a cost driver, he needs to think about the causes of costs. He must also consider the extent to which the cost varies in accordance with the cost driver. The *higher* the correlation between the cost and the cost driver, the *more accurate* will be the description and understanding of cost behaviour.

Exhibit 3.2 (below) shows the possible cost drivers that Jack has identified for the selected costs of Tasty Bread. A quick glance at Exhibit 3.2 should convince you that understanding and estimating cost behaviour can be difficult, as there are so many different cost drivers or factors that cause costs to be incurred. To keep complexity manageable, Jack Dlamini needs to make some simplifying assumptions.

A simple view of cost drivers and cost behaviour

Until recently, in estimating cost behaviour most accountants assumed that production (or sales) volume is the only cost driver. Using this approach they classified costs according to how they varied with production (or sales) volume. As described in Chapter 2, variable costs vary, in total, in proportion to the volume of production; and fixed costs remain unchanged as production volume increases or decreases. There are a number of measures of production volume, such as units produced, direct labour hours worked, direct labour cost and machine hours worked, but the underlying assumption is that production volume causes costs. Each of these measures is an example of a **volume-based cost driver**, which assumes that costs are driven, or caused, by the

Cost	Possible cost drivers
Direct material costs (wholemeal rolls)	Number of rolls produced Weight of ingredients used
Premises costs	Location of bakery and shops Lease terms Replacement value of buildings
Delivery costs	Number of deliveries Litres of fuel used Number of shops Location of shops Quality of shop unloading facilities
Electricity costs	Number of batches baked Number of kilowatt hours consumed Energy efficiency of equipment
Shop managers' salaries	Number of shops Shop trading hours Hours worked by managers

Exhibit 3.2 Costs and cost drivers at Tasty Bread

volume of production (or sales). Tasty Bread's direct material cost for wholemeal rolls is likely to be driven by production volume. We would expect that the greater the number of rolls produced, the greater will be the cost of the ingredients.

In analysing cost-behaviour patterns, some accountants recognised that not all costs vary in proportion to, or are fixed with respect to, production volume. While maintaining production volume as the only cost driver, they have recognised a range of other cost behaviour patterns, such as semi-variable, step-fixed and curvilinear costs, which are described later in this chapter.

A more realistic view of cost drivers and cost behaviour

More recent approaches to cost behaviour recognise that, while some costs are caused by production volume, there may be other important cost drivers. For example, the cost of operating delivery trucks at Tasty Bread is likely to be driven by the number of deliveries rather than the number of loaves and rolls produced. Deliveries made at different times of the day, to different shops, are likely to carry different volumes of bread. Similarly, electricity costs are likely to be driven by the number of production batches baked, not the number of loaves and rolls produced. Small batches will use as much electricity as large batches. Cost drivers that are not directly related to production volume are called **non-volume-based cost drivers.**

A contemporary view of costs and cost drivers

L.O. 3 Activity-based costing is a contemporary approach to costing that has made major advances in analysing cost behaviour by classifying costs and cost drivers into four distinct levels:

- unit
- batch
- product, and
- facility

Costs are assigned to **activities** that describe the work done in the business. **Unit level costs** relate to activities that are performed for each unit produced, such as the direct material costs at Tasty Bread. These costs require the conventional volume-based cost drivers.

Batch level costs relate to activities that are performed for a group of product units, such as a production batch or a delivery load. The electricity costs or delivery costs at Tasty Bread are examples of batch level costs. These costs require cost drivers such as the number of batches or number of loads. Since the number of units contained in a batch or load can vary, there is no direct relationship between production volume and batch level costs.

Product level (or **product-sustaining**) **costs** relate to activities that are performed for specific products or product families and include the costs of researching, designing and supporting products. For example, the cost of developing a new product line, such as fruit buns, would be a product level cost at Tasty Bread. The number of products may be the cost driver for product-sustaining costs.[2]

Facility level (or **facility-sustaining**) **costs** are costs that are incurred to run the business but are not caused by any particular product. An example is the premises cost at Tasty Bread. In the short term, this cost has no obvious cost driver.

We discuss the hierarchy of activity costs and cost drivers further when we look at activity-based costing in Chapter 8. In the meantime, the 'Real life' example (below) provides an interesting example of this concept.

Selecting the best cost drivers

Notice that Jack Dlamini, Tasty Bread's accountant, has identified more than one cost driver for each cost (Exhibit 3.2). How do they differ? And which one should the accountant choose for estimating cost behaviour?

Inputs or outputs?

For some costs, Jack Dlamini has identified both inputs and outputs as cost drivers. The cost drivers for direct material include two measures of production volume: an *output* measure, the number of bread rolls, and an *input* measure, the weight of ingredients used. Likewise, for the electricity cost, the number of batches baked is an *output* measure and the number of kilowatt hours consumed is an *input* measure. And for the delivery costs, the number of deliveries is an output measure and the number of litres of fuel is an input measure.

In choosing between input and output cost drivers for estimating cost behaviour and predicting costs, we should apply the cost–benefit principle. To predict costs accurately, we need a *strong correlation* between the cost and cost driver, but we also want a cost driver that is easy to measure. Unfortunately, in many organisations cost drivers are often selected for convenience reasons, not for their ability to predict costs accurately.

How detailed should the analysis be?

Jack Dlamini has improved the accuracy of the cost-behaviour analysis by disaggregating the total costs of the business into smaller cost categories and searching for the most appropriate driver for each cost. The level of disaggregation involves another cost–benefit trade-off. As the number of cost categories increases, the accuracy of the resulting information will increase. However, with more cost drivers, the costs of gathering and analysing information about costs and cost drivers will also increase.

The long or short term?

The Tasty Bread example also illustrates that the nature of cost behaviour and cost drivers can change over time. Costs that appear fixed in the short term (say, during one year) may vary in the long term. For example, the premises cost at Tasty Bread, such as the lease payments for the bakery and shops, the council rates and service levies, does not vary with the volume of production in the short term. However, in the longer term, the company may need to increase production to such an extent that it needs to move to a bigger bakery, or lease a second bakery, and open more retail outlets. *In the longer term* the premises cost will vary because the level of production has increased.

In identifying cost drivers and cost behaviour, the accountant needs to be clear about the timeframe for the analysis, which will depend on his reasons for analysing the cost behaviour. In this

REAL LIFE: COST DRIVERS IN THE SOUTH AFRICAN AUTOMOTIVE SECTOR 

The South African automotive industry sector is the 'bedrock of South Africa's manufacturing base' according to the DTI (Department of Trade and Industry) and the sector employs over 300 000 people. However, the industry is facing consolidation and there are competitive pressures being placed on component suppliers. Further, there has been a significant increase in product complexity. This means that pricing pressures will require that firms have to be accurate about costing their products.

Major automotive firms have implemented cost-management systems. Cost drivers in the automotive sector are recognised at five different levels: unit, batch, product, administration and facility. A range of cost drivers have been identified. A number of costing systems assumed that the volume-based measure, direct labour hours, was the cost driver for overhead costs. However, with the very large number of very different products and components that companies are producing, requiring varying amounts of production effort, it has become clear that direct labour is not an accurate cost driver. In an Australian study it was found that other factors were found to drive costs, including product complexity, machine cycle time, the number of parts shipped, product weight, containers of material handled, direct material cost and cycle time. Cost drivers are normally identified by conducting interviews with production managers and shop level employees to determine the percentage of time spent on various activities. Engineering studies of the manufacturing process are also used to determine cost drivers. In South Africa, Metair is a leading supplier of automotive products to original equipment manufacturers (OEMs) such as BMW, Ford, VW and Toyota. The company's subsidiaries manufacture auto components such as cooling systems, wiring harnesses, front-end modules, springs, shock absorbers, lighting, signalling devices and batteries. The chairman states in the company's 2005 annual report that 'new business won was at lower margins due to the need to meet globally benchmarked prices. Additional costs were incurred during the launch of technically more complex products. The group relied increasingly on the introduction of lean manufacturing systems to contain costs.' The launch of new products resulted in higher costs, and the managing director of the Smiths Plastics subsidiary, Kenneth Lello, referred to the learning curve effect on costs when he stated, ' the tremendous learning curve experienced during 2005 will show benefits in 2006. Pricing pressure remains intense but will be offset by the increased volume and efficiency improvements' (refer to the appendix on the effects of the learning curve on costs). The Hella subsidiary experienced higher costs. This was due to the production of new headlights which resulted in high scrap levels. However, the company managed to improve labour efficiency, and manufactured components in-house to reduce costs. For the battery division, the higher lead price was a concern as the company is not able to adequately pass on increased input costs to the OEMs owing to competitive pressures.

example, Jack Dlamini is interested in predicting costs for the budget, so a short-term perspective is appropriate.

Cost drivers for cost estimation or cost management?

L.O. 4 Recent developments in management accounting have emphasised the importance of analysing cost drivers to reduce costs and manage resources more effectively. Businesses can manage costs by managing their drivers. The primary focus of this chapter is to identify cost drivers that we can use to understand cost behaviour so that we can estimate cost functions and predict future costs. But are the cost drivers that we use to predict costs also useful for cost management? For example, in Exhibit 3.2 the cost drivers identified for direct material costs of Tasty Bread's wholemeal rolls were the number of rolls produced and the weight of ingredients. Tasty Bread could reduce its material costs by reducing the number of rolls produced, but sales revenue would reduce too! Alternatively, the baker could cut down the amount of flour used, but the quality of the rolls is likely to be affected. Thus, while these cost drivers are useful for understanding cost behaviour and predicting future costs, they are not very useful for cost management.

Effective cost management requires the identification of **root cause cost drivers**, which are the basic factors that cause costs to be incurred. In identifying root cause cost drivers it is necessary to extend the search beyond the cost drivers used for cost estimation and seek out the 'true' causes of costs. The cost driver 'weight of ingredients' provides a hint for managing costs, but Jack Dlamini needs to dig deep to identify the factors that influence the weight of ingredients used during production. Is there any wastage of ingredients? If so, is it caused by poor quality or inefficiency during the production process? Also, Tasty Bread could reduce electricity costs by reducing the kilowatt hours of electricity consumed. To do this the company would need to understand what really causes electricity consumption. Perhaps the existing ovens are energy inefficient. At Tasty Bread inexperienced truck drivers may be a major cause of delivery costs: in particular, maintenance, tyres and fuel consumption. Inefficient design of unloading facilities at the shops may be another major cause of delivery costs.

We revisit the issue of cost drivers for cost management in Chapter 15. In the meantime, the 'Real lifes' overleaf, describing the saga of I&J and the success of Comair, illustrate the vital importance of identifying and managing root cause cost drivers.

Cost drivers for cost estimation at Tasty Bread

Jack Dlamini, the accountant at Tasty Bread, wants to identify cost drivers for five cost categories so that he can estimate cost behaviour and predict future costs. Exhibit 3.2 summarised his initial thoughts on the factors that cause these costs. Next he must assess the costs and benefits of each driver, taking into account:

- the reasons for analysing cost behaviour: to provide estimates of cost behaviour for cost prediction;
- the timeframe for analysing the cost behaviour: short term, as costs will be predicted for the budget period (that is, the coming year);
- the availability of data on cost drivers; and
- any other uses for the information on cost behaviour.

Eventually Jack has some information that he can use to assess the cost and benefits of each cost driver. He feels a little uncertain and would like more time to build a clearer picture of all the costs and benefits associated with the various drivers. However, as is often the case, his resources are limited and he must trust his judgement. In any case, in estimating the cost behaviours, the appropriateness of the drivers will be tested by analysing the relationship between past costs and their selected cost driver. These are the cost drivers that he chooses:

- *direct material costs for wholemeal rolls*: the number of wholemeal rolls produced;
- *premises cost*: no cost driver in the short term;
- *delivery truck costs*: the number of deliveries;
- *electricity cost*: the number of batches of products baked; and
- *shop managers' salaries*: the number of shop trading hours.

Jack Dlamini is now ready to consider the cost behaviour patterns for each cost.

REAL LIFE: SEARCHING FOR SOLUTIONS AT I&J: UNDERSTANDING AND MANAGING COSTS

Irvin & Johnson, majority owned by AVI, is a key player in the South African fishing industry and operates fishing vessels, processing facilities and markets products around the world. However, the company experienced a significant fall in operating profit from R84 million in 2005 to R5.9 million in 2006. Further, the slide in operating profitability had occurred over a few years as the operating profit only a few years ago in 2003 was R235 million. Sales revenue in 2006 was R1.4 billion and this has been relatively constant. The CEO of AVI, Simon Crutchley, stated in the 2006 annual report that 'we need to adjust the (I&J) business and look at the cost base and we have initiatives across the board'. The operating profit margin fell from 14 per cent in 2003 to 0.4 per cent in 2006. So, why did this happen? A number of factors came together in creating a worst case scenario:

- Low catch rates required the company to increase the fishing effort and number of days at sea. This resulted in an increase in the cost per ton of fish landed.
- There was reduction in I&J's hake quota of close to 10 per cent in 2006.
- There was a reduction in the efficiency of fish processing plants due to lower volumes, erratic supply and an unfavourable size mix (mainly due to the preponderance of smaller fish).
- There was an increase in the cost of fuel due to the increased fishing effort by the trawlers as well as the general increase in the price of oil.
- The prevalence of small fish in catches resulted in higher processing costs and also a reduction in the sales of premium margin products.

Further, the company was not helped by a strong Rand in the 2006 financial year which reduced export revenues. The management team is focused on turning things around and the company is undertaking a number of measures to reduce its cost base and restore profitability. The company is restructuring its South African operations to reflect the reduced quota situation. The company reduced its workforce by 440 people and the former I&J Head Office building has been sold. I&J is evaluating all non-core activities and the company is planning to exit small operations with limited potential for future returns. The company is planning to focus on optimising its sales mix and to rationalise its processed products. Further, the company is planning to replace a number of vessels to ensure a greater level of fuel efficiency. Despite a better understanding of costs and cost drivers, I&J remains vulnerable to costs that are not controllable by the company such as the cost of fuel and the size of fish being caught in its nets. However, improving the fuel efficiency of vessels employed and extending the depth of fishing operations may have a favourable effect on fish size.

REAL LIFE: COST BEHAVIOUR AND COST MANAGEMENT AT COMAIR

Comair operates British Airways and kulula.com in South Africa. Unlike SAA the company cannot call on the State to provide support in challenging times. Comair is listed on the JSE Securities Exchange and the management team has undertaken intensive programs to lower cost and increase profits in an environment of high fuel costs. The key is about understanding the cost behaviour of the business. The airline business has high fixed costs, and, with the discounted fares that have occurred since the late 1990s, the passenger yields have been low. Passenger yield is measured by revenue per passenger-kilometre (RPK). Airline profits are dependent on those passenger yields—it has been estimated that a 1 cent move in the average RPK can shift an airline's profit significantly. At the beginning of an economic recovery, when more airline seats are filled, profits soar; during a recession, profits plummet.

In the last few years Comair has maintained its record of tight cost management while increasing capacity and the numbers of passengers flying British Airways and kulula.com. In the year ending 30 June 2006 the company earned a record operating before-tax profit of R133 million, up 20 per cent on the previous year. In 2002 the operating profit of Comair was only R12 million. The dramatic fall in the Rand exchange rate in 2002 and high interest rates impacted negatively on revenue and the profitability of Comair. In 2005–6, the company has had to deal with significant increases in the cost of jet fuel. This has placed many airlines under financial strain and a number have added fuel surcharges to airline ticket prices.

How did BA and kulula.com perform so well? Comair focused on filling planes, and implemented systems to ensure tight control of the costs of labour and retail distribution, with the adoption of smarter work practices. In short, the company's understanding of cost behaviour and cost drivers contributed to its excellent record of cost management. Furthermore, the company is undertaking a fleet replacement policy to ensure it acquires newer planes that are much more fuel efficient. Other initiatives include improvements in labour productivity, and process improvements, fleet simplification (which leads to cost savings in maintenance and fuel), and encouragement of online sales, particularly for kulula.com. The following is an extract from the joint CEOs' overview in the 2006 annual report,

Comair increased headline earnings per share by 8% to 20 cents per share despite an operating cost escalation of R149 million arising from the increased price of fuel. We have focused our efforts this year on growing our revenue base while further reducing our controllable costs, aided by our fleet replacement programme whereby we continue to introduce more modern and cost efficient aircraft. The market continued to grow strongly during the year on the back of the fast growing middle class in South Africa as well as a buoyant economy. Our growth in passenger volumes to over 3 million customers exceeded the market growth and resulted in record turnover as well as record occupancy levels.

To achieve profitability in the airline sector, an understanding of cost drivers and the management of cost drivers is of vital importance.

Cost behaviour patterns

L.O. 5

Cost behaviour is the relationship between a cost and the level of activity or cost driver. In Chapter 2 we introduced the concept of variable and fixed costs. Here we use Tasty Bread's experience to extend your understanding of cost behaviour patterns by examining:

- variable costs;
- fixed costs;
- step-fixed costs;
- semivariable costs; and
- curvilinear costs.

Variable costs

A **variable cost** changes, *in total*, in direct proportion to a change in activity. If the level of activity increases by 20 per cent, total variable cost also increases by 20 per cent. For example, the cost of fuel used by a delivery truck will increase by approximately 20 per cent if the distance driven increases by 20 per cent. In this example the level of activity is kilometres. Under conventional costing systems, we think of variable costs as varying in relation to some measure of production volume, such as units of output, machine hours or direct labour hours. However, in analysing cost behaviour, we need not be restricted by this. The relevant cost driver may be volume-based or non-volume-based.

Tasty Bread's direct material cost for each of its products is a variable cost. For example, as the company produces more wholemeal bread rolls, the total cost of the ingredients for this product increases in direct proportion to the number of items produced. Therefore, the activity that drives direct material cost is the number of wholemeal rolls produced. (In this example, as all products are sold the day they are baked, sales volume equals production volume.)

The graph in Exhibit 3.3 displays Tasty Bread's direct material cost for wholemeal rolls. As the graph shows, total variable cost increases in proportion to the number of wholemeal rolls produced. When production volume triples, for example from 50 000 rolls to 150 000 rolls, total direct material costs triple, from R5000 to R15 000. However, the variable cost per unit remains the same despite the number of rolls produced. The direct material cost incurred is constant at R0.10 per roll. The table in Exhibit 3.3 illustrates this point.

The variable cost per unit is also the slope of the cost line. We can express all linear cost functions in the form:

$$Y = a + bX$$

where Y = total cost
a = fixed cost component (the intercept on the vertical axis)
b = variable cost per unit of activity (the slope of the line)
X = the level of activity

Cost functions are equations that are often used to describe cost behaviours. In this case there is no fixed cost component, so a (the intercept on the vertical axis) drops out of the equation, and the cost function for the direct material cost of wholemeal rolls is:

Total monthly direct material cost for wholemeal rolls
= R0.10 × the number of wholemeal rolls produced in a month

To summarise, *total variable costs increase in direct proportion to changes in the level of activity, but the variable cost per unit remains constant.*

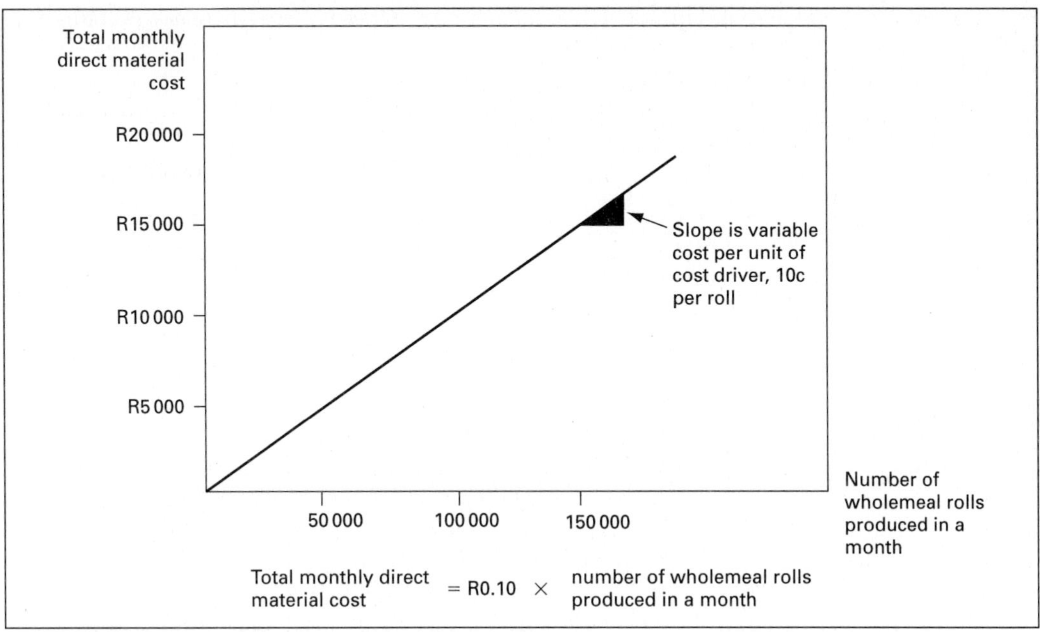

Quantity of cost driver	Direct material cost per unit	Total direct material cost
50 000	R0.10	R5 000
100 000	R0.10	R10 000
150 000	R0.10	R15 000

Exhibit 3.3 Variable cost: direct material cost for wholemeal rolls, Tasty Bread Company

Fixed costs

In Chapter 2 we also introduced the concept of a *fixed cost,* which remains unchanged *in total* as the level of activity varies. If the level of activity increases or decreases by 20 per cent, total fixed cost remains the same. Examples of fixed costs include depreciation of plant and equipment at a Plascon Paint factory, the cost of council rates for the Southern Sun hotel, and the rent paid by the Standard Bank to lease its premises. In these examples, the total cost remains constant despite increases or decreases in the level of activity.

At Tasty Bread the premises cost, which includes bakery and shop lease costs, council rates and land taxes, and depreciation and insurance on buildings, is an example of a fixed cost. Remember we said that the premises cost may change as production volume changes over the longer term, as new or bigger buildings can be leased, but in the short term this cost has no obvious cost driver.

Exhibit 3.4 illustrates the nature of fixed costs. Jack Dlamini, the accountant at Tasty Bread, has placed the number of bakery items produced on the horizontal axis. However, as he was unable to find any short-term cost driver, he could place any activity on the horizontal axis without changing the cost. The total cost is not affected by the number of products produced, nor the number of customers, nor any other activity that Jack might think of. More recent approaches to cost analysis, such as activity-based costing, would track these costs to activities and search for cost drivers for at least some of these so-called fixed costs. Using activity-based approaches, it is possible to find a cost driver for most costs, and very few costs remain 'fixed'.[3]

Exhibit 3.4 shows that the total monthly premises cost is R15 000, whatever the level of activity. For example, when the level of production doubles from 60 000 to 120 000 units, total fixed cost remains constant at R15 000. However, when the fixed cost is expressed as a fixed cost per unit, the amount does change as the level of activity varies. The company's monthly premises cost per bakery item is R0.25 when 60 000 items are produced, but this unit cost declines to R0.125 when 120 000 items are produced. We should note *that a fixed cost does not really behave in a 'per unit' fashion*. Unit fixed cost will decline steadily as the number of bakery items increases, but this does not reflect the actual behaviour of fixed costs.

The cost function for Exhibit 3.4 is:

Total monthly premises cost = R15 000

To summarise, *as activity increases, total fixed costs do not change, but unit fixed cost declines.*

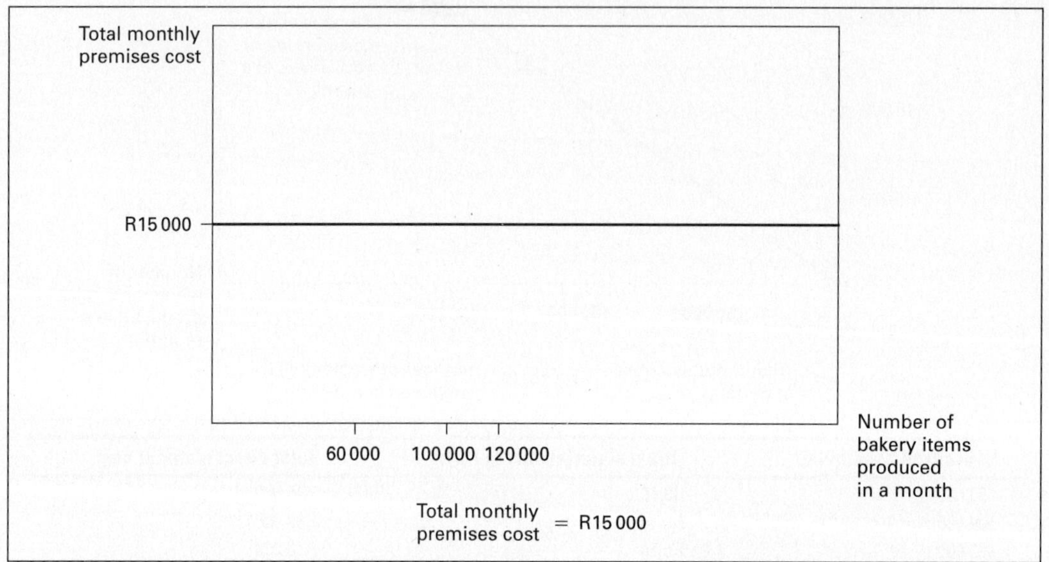

Quantity of cost driver	Premises cost per unit	Total monthly premises cost
60 000	R0.25	R15 000
100 000	R0.15	R15 000
120 000	R0.125	R15 000

Exhibit 3.4 Fixed cost: premises cost, Tasty Bread Company

Making decisions based on unit costs and total costs

When looking at the behaviour of variable and fixed costs, we calculated both the total costs and the unit costs for different levels of activity. As you will see in subsequent chapters, in management accounting a thorough understanding of the behaviour of both total costs and unit costs is vital. When making decisions, managers must be particularly careful about how they interpret unit costs. It is essential that the unit fixed costs are separated from unit variable costs, as changes in the levels of activities will affect the total variable costs but not the total fixed costs.

Expressing fixed cost on a per unit basis is often undertaken for use in product costing, but is of limited use for management decision-making, as this does not reflect the way the cost actually behaves.

Step-fixed costs

Some costs remain fixed over a wide range of activity levels but jump to a different amount for levels outside that range. These are called **step-fixed costs.**[4] The salaries and on-costs paid to Tasty Bread's shop managers are a step-fixed cost. The cost of Tasty Bread's shop managers' salaries is graphed in Exhibit 3.5.

As Exhibit 3.5 shows, when the opening hours for the shops are 160 hours or less per month, the cost of managers' salaries is R40 000 per month. A shop manager can manage each shop alone. When opening hours increase during spring and summer, the total opening hours will range between 160 and 240 hours per month. In this situation each shop will employ the full-time manager (for 8 a.m. to 4 p.m. weekdays) and a salaried part-time manager for the late afternoons and Saturday. The cost of managers' salaries rises to R60 000 per month. In December, each shop extends its opening hours into the evening, so that an additional part-time assistant manager is employed. The total cost is then R78 000 per month.

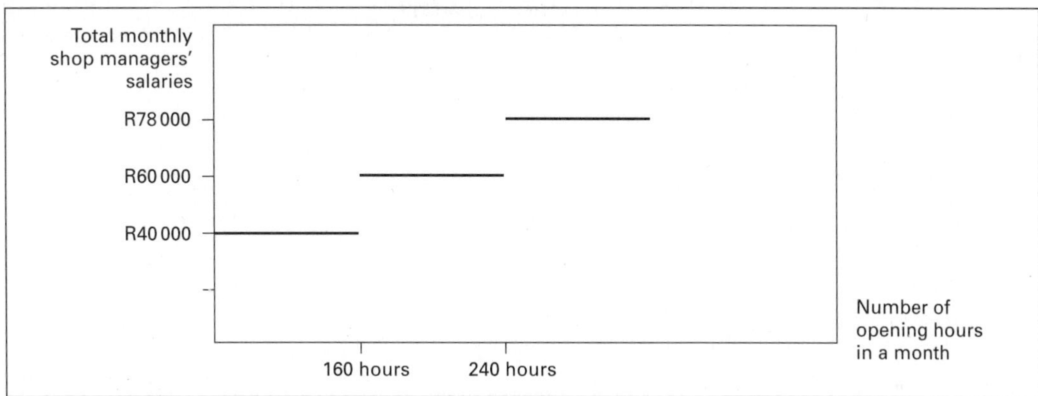

Exhibit 3.5 Step-fixed cost: shop managers' salaries, Tasty Bread Company

Semivariable cost

A **semivariable** (or **mixed**) **cost** has both fixed and variable components. The cost of operating delivery trucks is a semivariable cost for Tasty Bread. These costs are graphed in Exhibit 3.6. As the graph shows, the company's delivery truck costs have two components. The fixed cost component is R3000 per month, which is the monthly payment made under the lease contract for the delivery trucks. The monthly lease payments are constant, regardless of any changes in the number of deliveries made. The variable cost component consists of the costs of petrol, oil, routine maintenance and tyres; these costs vary with the number of deliveries per month. Jack Dlamini estimates that the variable component of the cost of operating delivery trucks is R10 per delivery. The distance between the fixed cost line (dashed line) and the total cost line in Exhibit 3.6 is the amount of variable cost. For example, at 100 deliveries per month, the total variable cost component is R1000 and the total cost is R4000. The slope of the total cost line is the variable cost per unit of activity.

The cost function in Exhibit 3.6 can be expressed as:

Total monthly cost of operating delivery trucks
= R3000 + (R10 × number of deliveries in a month)

Curvilinear cost

The graphs of all the cost behaviour patterns examined so far consist of either straight lines or several broken straight lines. A **curvilinear cost** behaviour pattern has a curved line. Tasty Bread's electricity cost, depicted as the solid curve in Exhibit 3.7, is a curvilinear cost. The relevant activity, or cost driver, is the number of batches baked. For low levels of activity, this cost exhibits decreasing marginal costs. A **marginal cost** is the cost of producing one additional unit, in this case the next batch. In the graph in Exhibit 3.7, the marginal electricity cost of producing the next batch declines as the number of batches increases from zero to 1000 per month. For more than 1000 batches per month, the graph in Exhibit 3.7 exhibits increasing marginal costs.

Tasty Bread's electricity cost is curvilinear as a result of the company's pattern of electricity usage in the bakery. If the demand in a particular month is less than 1000 batches, the goods can be produced entirely in the modernised section of the bakery. This section uses recently purchased ovens, which are relatively energy-efficient. As long as the bakery operates only the modernised section, the electricity cost per batch declines as production increases.

When Tasty Bread's sales exceed 1000 batches per month, the older section of the bakery must also be used. This section has much older cooking equipment that is less energy-efficient. As a

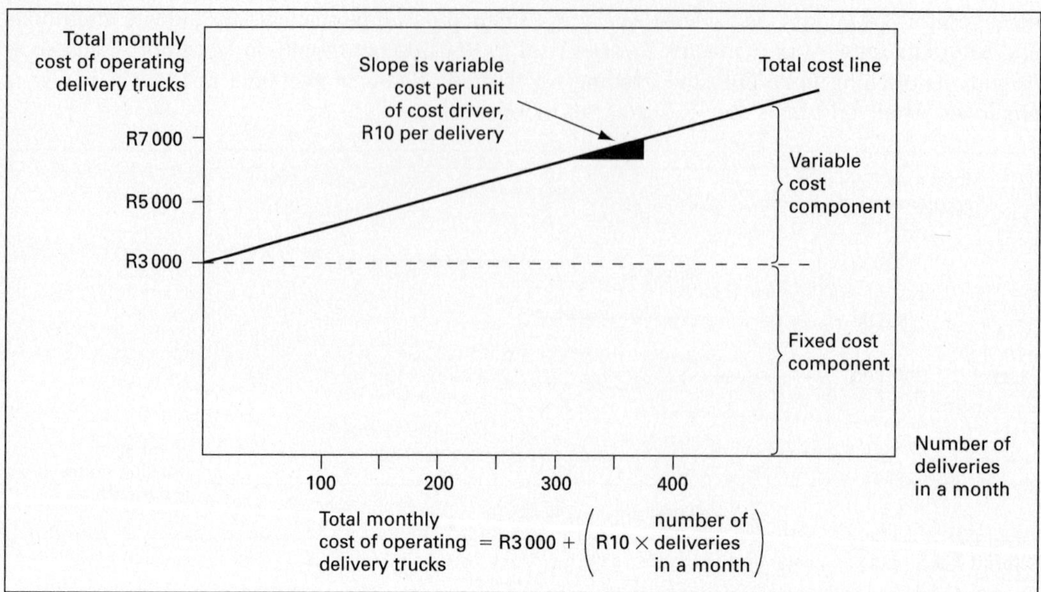

Exhibit 3.6 Semivariable cost: cost of operating delivery trucks, Tasty Bread Company

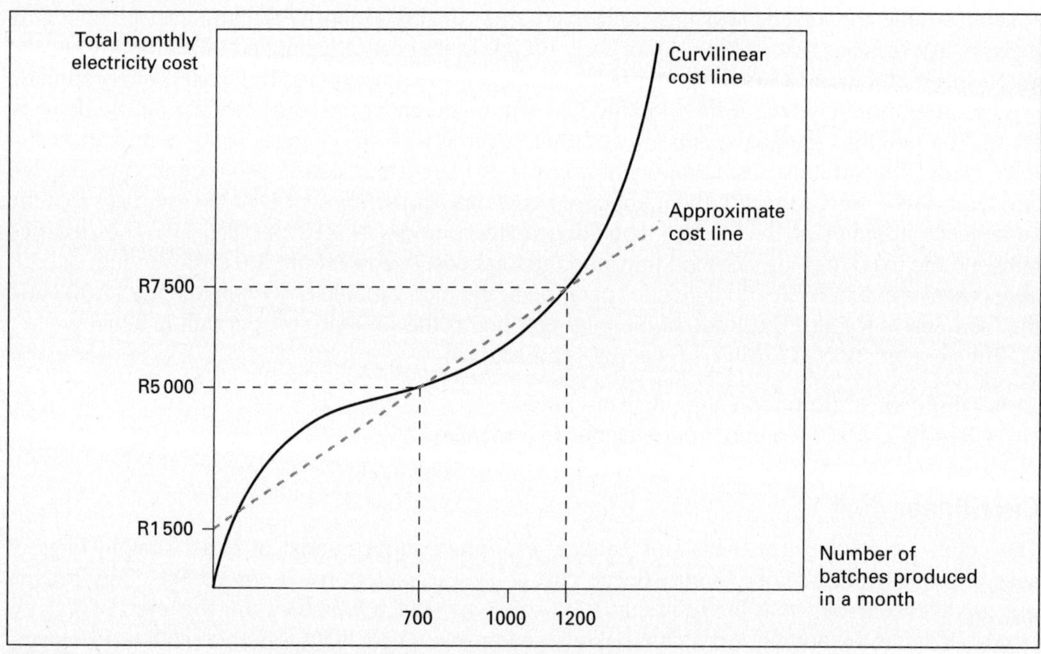

Exhibit 3.7 Curvilinear cost: electricity cost, Tasty Bread Company

result, the marginal electricity cost per batch rises as monthly activity increases in the range above 1000 batches per month. (Jack was right—the energy efficiency of the ovens is a root cause cost driver for electricity costs!)

Approximating a curvilinear cost with a semivariable cost function

The straight, dashed line in Exhibit 3.7 may be used to approximate Tasty Bread's electricity cost, provided that monthly production does not go below 700 batches or above 1200 batches. This straight line graph has a slope of R5, which represents a unit variable cost of R5 per batch. The line intersects the vertical axis of the graph at R1500, which represents a fixed-cost component of R1500 per month.

The semivariable cost function for electricity is:

Total monthly cost of electricity
= R1500 + (R5 × number of batches produced in a month)

Accountants often use a semivariable cost behaviour pattern to approximate a curvilinear cost.

Cost behaviour and the relevant range

L.O. 6

When analysing cost behaviour, it is important that the accountant identifies the **relevant range**, which is the range of activity over which a particular cost behaviour pattern can be assumed to be valid. In our example, the relevant range for the electricity costs is 700 to 1200 batches. Outside the relevant range the cost behaviour pattern may not hold. Below 700 batches and above 1200 batches, the cost function for electricity is curvilinear rather than semivariable.

Consider the variable direct material costs in Exhibit 3.3. If monthly production volume of wholemeal rolls rose to an extreme level, say 200 000 rolls per month, the direct material cost per unit might decrease. This may be due to the bakery taking advantage of purchase discounts offered by suppliers for large orders of direct materials.

Thus, the relevant range is implicit in the estimation of many cost behaviours. We should be cautious in assuming that variable and fixed costs will always exhibit consistent cost behaviours, especially when there are dramatic changes in the levels of activities of the business.

Engineered, committed and discretionary costs

L.O. 7

When management estimates costs for budgeting or planning purposes it is often useful to distinguish between engineered, committed and discretionary costs.

An **engineered cost** bears a defined physical relationship to the level of output. The direct material at Tasty Bread is an engineered cost, as there is a known quantity of direct material that must be used for each bread product. Thus, if we know the level of output, we can easily predict total material cost.

Fixed costs are sometimes described as either *committed* or *discretionary*. A **committed cost** results from an organisation's ownership or use of premises and its basic organisation structure. Council rates, depreciation on buildings and equipment, cost of renting buildings or equipment, and the salaries of management are examples of committed costs. Also, in many organisations employees' labour cost is a committed cost and cannot be changed easily because of contractual obligations or the regulatory environment. It is very difficult to change committed costs in the short term, and therefore committed costs do not exhibit simple causal relationships with the level of activity.

A **discretionary cost** arises from a *management decision* to spend a particular amount of money for some purpose; and, like committed costs, discretionary costs do not exhibit simple causal relationships with any level of activity. Examples of discretionary costs include amounts spent on research and development, advertising and promotion, management development programs, and contributions to charitable organisations.

The distinction between committed and discretionary costs is an important one. Management usually incurs committed costs by making relatively major decisions. These include decisions to build a new production facility, lease a fleet of vehicles, or add more managers to oversee a new division of the business. Such decisions will generally influence costs over a long period. In contrast, discretionary costs can be changed in the short run much more easily. Management can be flexible about expenditures for advertising and promotion, employee training, or research and development. This does not imply that such programs are unimportant, but simply that management can alter them over time. For example, the management of a manufacturing firm may plan to spend R10 million on research and development in the current year (a discretionary cost), but decide

REAL LIFE: COST BEHAVIOUR IN SOUTH AFRICAN COMPANIES

We have talked about the cost behaviour patterns at Tasty Bread Company, but do managers consider cost behaviour patterns in the real world? The evidence suggests that they do. For example, in Chapter 2 we described the cost classification systems used by most hotels, which included the identification of variable costs (room housekeeping costs, guest supplies and laundry) and fixed costs (insurance, rent, rates and council levies).

In a manufacturing context, around 80 per cent of respondents to a survey of Australia's largest manufacturers identified a range of manufacturing costs, including production labour, set-up labour, supervision, building occupancy and depreciation, as variable, fixed or semivariable. Responses varied from one industry to another, although most respondents classified production labour costs as variable or semivariable, and building occupancy and depreciation costs as fixed.

In South Africa, a survey undertaken by Oberholzer and Ziemerink (O&Z) in 2004 of manufacturing firms in the Vaal triangle, found that on average 40 per cent of costs were classified as fixed and 60 per cent of costs were classified as variable. The study analysed why firms classified costs into fixed and variable components and compared their results with other studies in South Africa, USA, Japan and Australia. In Australia and the UK cost classification was of primary importance for determining and fixing the price of products. South Africa offers contrasting views based on the two surveys conducted in the country.

	O&Z Survey	South Africa*	Australia*	Japan*	UK*
Price fixing	4	1	1	5	1
Decreasing costs	6	2	6	3	5
Profit planning	2	3	3	1	2
Cost–benefit analysis	5	4	4	6	5
Cost–volume–profit analysis	1	5	4	4	4
Budgets	3	6	2	2	3

*See Horngren, Foster, Datar and Uliana, 1999

In interpreting these results we must remember that the management accounting systems for large businesses, such as those included in most surveys, are likely to be more sophisticated than those in small-sized to medium-sized firms. We should also bear in mind that response rates to surveys are low.

In a study by Waweru, Hoque and Uliana (2004), of four retail companies, it was found that there had been significant changes in management accounting practices. The study found that companies had adopted contemporary management accounting practices, and increasingly made use of activity-based costing for cost allocation.

It is clear that managers will be effective in managing resources to create value only if they understand cost behaviour. How could they build and interpret budgets or estimate costs for making decisions without some understanding of cost behaviour?

halfway through the year to reduce this expenditure to R6 million because of an anticipated economic downturn.

Whether a particular cost is committed or discretionary differs between organisations. In some organisations, spending on research and development may be regarded as *committed,* not discretionary, as the firm may have a strong core value of investing in future product development.

Shifting cost structures in modern business environments

Conventional costing systems use production volume as the cost driver. Costs are classified as fixed or variable relative to the level of production. However, many businesses are finding that an increasing share of their costs no longer vary directly with the volume of production. Why?

One reason is that, as organisations become more automated, they tend to rely more on equipment and less on direct labour when producing their products. Unlike labour costs, equipment costs, such as depreciation, maintenance and insurance, do not vary with the volume of production. In the electronics industry, for example, small electronic components were once placed onto circuit boards, wired and soldered by hand. Now, pick-and-place robots and auto-insertion machines place electronic components on circuit boards with incredible speed and precision. Wash-and-dry machines eliminate contaminants and wave-solder machines solder the connections. A large part of the manufacturing process is computerised, and much of the labour force is now regarded as indirect labour, being involved in computer programming and maintenance rather than direct production activities. Many service organisations have also replaced most of their clerical and data processing functions through IT developments. Depreciation, maintenance and upgrades for the computerised equipment and the IT infrastructure are regarded as committed fixed costs, as are the costs of the labour force.

In addition, in many industries, labour unions negotiate enterprise agreements that result in a relatively stable workforce. Management is less able to adjust the numbers of employees when activity levels change.

Thus, changes in the commercial environment can have a major impact on cost behaviour. It is vital that management accountants who work in these modern environments are fully aware of the impact of these changes on cost estimation. More recent costing systems, such as activity-based costing, use both production volume and non-volume cost drivers. At Tasty Bread, some of the costs, such as direct material, are driven by the volume of production; others, such as electricity and delivery costs, are driven by the number of batches and the number of deliveries.

Cost behaviours in different industries

We have explained a variety of cost behaviours for the Tasty Bread Company. The same range of cost behaviours may be found in other industries, although these will vary in line with the different activities that the business undertakes. We should be cautious in assuming that a cost that is fixed in one company is necessarily fixed in another. As described in Chapter 18, at a theatre company, theatre rent may be a variable cost if rent is charged to the company based on the number of people occupying seats during each performance of a play. Also, for each play, direct labour is considered fixed because the director, actors and production staff are paid a fixed amount for the run of a particular play. These two cost behaviours are the opposite of those experienced by many businesses.

In contrast to conventional costing, activity-based costing identifies a range of cost drivers. Identifying and costing activities and using the unit–batch–product–facility cost hierarchy will improve the understanding of cost behaviour and the accuracy of cost prediction in any industry. The relevant question for the management accountant is whether the benefits of more accurate information outweigh the costs of using a more sophisticated approach.

Using cost behaviour patterns to predict costs

How can Jack Dlamini, Tasty Bread's accountant, use the cost-behaviour patterns identified in the cost study to help in the budgeting process or in management decisions? First, a forecast of each level of activity must be made for each month of the budget year. For example, management may expect Tasty Bread's production for June to include production of 800 batches (40 000 wholemeal rolls), 144 deliveries and 180 shop trading hours. Second, a cost prediction is made for each of the firm's cost items. The following cost predictions are based on the cost behaviours described earlier:

Cost item	Rate	June activity	Budgeted cost for June
Direct materials	R0.10 per unit	40 000 units	R4 000
Premises cost	Fixed cost		15 000
Delivery trucks	R3000 + R10 per delivery	144 deliveries	4 440
Electricity	R1500 + R5 per batch	800 batches	5 500
Managers' salaries	Step-fixed cost	180 hours	60 000

In this example we have focused on only a few costs of the business. You will realise from the descriptions of budgeting systems in Chapter 9 that the preparation of a complete budget involves considerably more analysis and detailed planning than is shown here. However, an analysis of cost behaviour is the basis for forecasting (predicting) costs for budgets. Budgets, in turn, provide the framework for controlling costs.

An analysis of cost behaviour is also used to identify cost drivers for overhead costs to estimate product costs (see Chapter 7) and for cost-volume profit (CVP) analysis, which is discussed in Chapter 18. A thorough understanding of cost behaviour is also necessary to provide cost information for a range of management decisions, including pricing decisions (see Chapters 19 and 20).

Cost estimation

L.O. 8

In an earlier section, we used the Tasty Bread Company to demonstrate a variety of cost behaviour patterns. But how would the accountant at Tasty Bread actually *identify* the specific cost behaviour pattern for each cost? Cost estimation is the process of determining how a particular cost behaves. We will use the Tasty Bread Company to examine three approaches to cost estimation:

- managerial judgment;
- the engineering approach; and
- quantitative analysis.

Using managerial judgement to estimate costs

In some businesses, managers estimate costs using their experience rather than any formal analysis. For example, they may make intuitive estimates of costs based on their knowledge of the company. Or sometimes managers may view the financial statements or the balances of accounts in the general ledger and classify cost items as fixed, variable or semivariable (mixed) costs. This approach to cost estimation is called the **account classification method** (also called **account analysis**). For example, when going through the ledger, it may be obvious to Jack Dlamini, Tasty Bread's accountant, that total direct material cost is a variable cost that varies with production volume. Likewise, premises costs are fixed, and the electricity cost is semivariable, as part of the cost varies with the number of batches and part is fixed.

Once the costs have been classified, the accountant can estimate future costs by examining past costs and identifying any other factors that may affect costs in the future. For example, Jack Dlamini knows from experience that council rates are a fixed cost. He can identify the cost of council rates for the past year. The local council may have recently advised ratepayers of a 15 per cent cost increase in the next year. With this information, Jack can estimate the council rates for next year. When estimating variable costs, Jack also needs information about the planned level of activity or cost driver.

The reliability of cost estimates based on managerial judgement depends on the ability of the manager. Good managers can make good estimates. You will notice that even the more objective methods of estimating costs, described below, require managerial judgement, for example to assess the validity of data and cost estimates.

The engineering approach to estimating costs

The **engineering method** of cost estimation is the study of the processes that result in the incurrence of a cost. **Engineering studies** identify the relationships that should exist between inputs and outputs. At Tasty Bread, for example, the accountant could instigate a study to identify how much material should be used to produce a wholemeal roll and how much it should cost. As discussed in Chapter 10, this method is often used to set standard costs for direct material and direct labour, particularly for new products.

Industrial engineers may conduct **time and motion studies** (also called **task analysis** or **work measurement**), in which employees are observed as they undertake work tasks. The steps required to perform the tasks are recorded, as are the times. Cost behaviours are then estimated based on this analysis.

In service businesses, such as banks, insurance companies and many government enterprises, task analysis is particularly useful for determining cost behaviour. The task analysis focuses on factors such as the steps required to perform the service, the time needed to complete each step, the number and type of employees required, and the materials or other inputs needed. In these service firms, there are no 'scientific' methods for formulating the costs of the product: that is, there are no technical product specifications.

Engineering studies are time-consuming and expensive. However, in rapidly evolving high-technology industries, such as genetic engineering, superconductivity and electronics, past data are often irrelevant to estimating costs. Also, when new products are introduced there are no historic cost data to rely upon. The engineering approach is likely to be most cost-effective where there is a direct relationship between inputs and outputs—that is, for direct material and direct labour costs.

The accuracy of engineering studies

Do engineering studies, particularly those based on task analysis, which dissects actual work, produce accurate data? There is some doubt as to whether employees will 'act naturally' when they know they are being observed. Where task analysis is used to develop performance standards, it is easy to understand that employees might purposely slow operations or use a generous amount of material during the task analysis.

For a particular manufacturer of suits, video recording of work practices was used, as time and motion studies using the old-fashioned method of 'clipboards and stopwatch' were found to be ineffective. Why? 'The workers played a battle of wits to create the slowest work-rate possible for the calculations.'

Activity-based costing and the engineering approach

Over recent years, methodologies have developed, as part of activity-based costing, to analyse the cost of activities. In some ways, these procedures are similar to engineering studies, especially task analysis. For example, in task analysis, processes are broken into tasks, and product costs are based, at least in part, on estimates of the costs of the tasks used by the product. In activity-based costing, activities are identified and costed, and product costs are built up from the costs of activities used by the product. A key difference between the two methods is that engineering methods such as task analysis, especially in the manufacturing environment, tend to be confined to analysing and estimating costs of direct operations. One of the major advances of activity-based costing is the analysis of indirect (or overhead) activities and costs.

Estimating costs using quantitative analysis

A third approach to estimating costs is to formally analyse past data to identify the relationship between cost and activities. For example, to estimate electricity costs, Jack Dlamini, Tasty Bread's **L.O. 9** accountant, could examine the relationship between monthly electricity costs and the number of batches produced over the past year, as Jack believes that the number of batches cooked in the bakery ovens is a major cause (or driver) of electricity costs. In addition, he believes that electricity costs may also be influenced by the number of customers served, as electricity consumption increases each time a shop door is opened or closed because of the air-conditioning. Examining the relationship between past costs and activity levels is useful in stable environments, but it is not appropriate in rapidly changing circumstances because past data will provide a poor basis for estimating current or future cost behaviour.

We will describe two methods of quantitative analysis: the high–low method and regression analysis.

When an analyst has no clear idea about the behaviour of a cost item, it is helpful to plot recent observations of the cost at various levels of activity. The resulting **scatter diagram** helps the analyst to visualise the relationship between cost and the level of activity. Jack has identified the company's monthly electricity costs last year, as well as the number of batches produced and customers served. These appear in Exhibit 3.8. He decides to begin his analysis by exploring the relationship between electricity costs and the number of batches produced.

The scatter diagram of these data is shown in Exhibit 3.9. A glance at the data points suggests that Tasty Bread's electricity cost is a semivariable cost within the range of activity experienced over the last year. Note that the scatter diagram provides no information about the cost relationship outside this range of activity. You will recall from the discussion of Tasty Bread's electricity cost that Jack Dlamini believed the cost behaviour to be curvilinear over the entire range of activity (see Exhibit 3.7), but that a semivariable function could be used to describe the cost behaviour when monthly production varied between 700 and 1200 batches.

A scatter diagram also allows an experienced cost analyst to spot **outliers** in the data; these are data points that fall far away from the other points in the scatter diagram. Suppose, for example, that the data point for January had been R7500 for 750 batches. Exhibit 3.9 reveals that such a data point would be way out of line with the rest of the data. Jack would discover the reasons behind this observation. It could be that the data point is an error. Perhaps an electricity bill was misread, or possibly the invoice itself was incorrect. Another possibility is that the cost observation is correct but there were unusual circumstances. Perhaps Auckland experienced a cold spell during January that required the company's shops to turn on their heating. An outlier can result from many factors. If the outlier is the result of an error or of very unusual circumstances, the data point should be ignored in the cost analysis.

Month	Electricity cost for month	Number of batches produced per month	Number of customers served per month
January	R5 100	750	600
February	5 300	780	680
March	5 650	800	710
April	6 300	920	750
May	6 400	980	760
June	6 700	1 080	780
July	7 035	1 180	790
August	7 000	1 120	740
September	6 200	950	730
October	6 100	900	710
November	5 600	850	700
December	5 900	900	680

Exhibit 3.8 Electricity costs and activity levels, Tasty Bread Company

High–low method

The high–low method is a simple way to estimate cost functions. In the **high–low method**, the cost function is calculated using only two data points. The observations with the highest and lowest

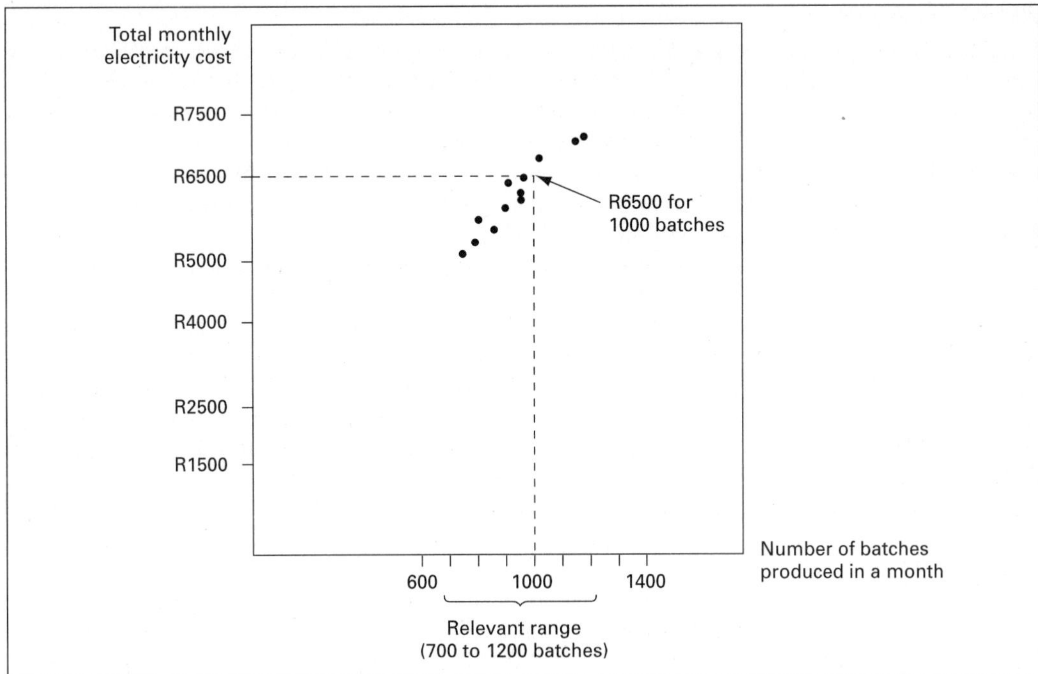

Exhibit 3.9 Scatter diagram: electricity cost, Tasty Bread Company

levels of activity are used to calculate the variable cost and fixed cost components. We will continue looking at Tasty Bread's electricity cost behaviour, and the activity 'number of batches'.

$$\text{Variable cost of electricity per batch} = \frac{\text{difference in cost levels}}{\text{difference in activity levels}}$$

$$= \frac{\text{R}7035 - \text{R}5100}{1180 - 750}$$

$$= \frac{\text{R}1935}{430}$$

$$= \text{R}4.50 \text{ per batch produced}$$

Now we can calculate the total variable cost at either the highest or lowest activity level. At the lowest level of activity of 750 batches, the total variable cost is R3375 (R4.50 × 750). Subtracting the total variable cost from the total cost for the 750 batches (R5100), we obtain the fixed cost estimate of R1725 (R5100−R3375). Notice that the highest and lowest activity levels (that is, the number of batches) are used in this analysis. These two points may not necessarily coincide with the highest and lowest cost levels in the sample data. Thus, using the high–low method:

Monthly cost of electricity = R1725 + (R4.50 × number of batches produced in a month)

Evaluation of the high–low method

We do not recommend the high–low method for estimating cost functions, as only two data points are used to estimate the cost behaviour; the remainder of the data points are ignored. We have no assurance that the cost function drawn using the high–low method accurately represents the cost behaviour within the relevant range.

Regression analysis

We can improve the objectivity and accuracy of cost estimation by using statistical techniques. The most common of these methods is called **regression analysis**, which can be used to estimate the relationship between a dependent variable (cost) and independent variables (cost drivers). To understand this method, examine Exhibit 3.10 which repeats the scatter diagram of Tasty Bread's electricity cost data. At this stage, the number of batches produced remains the focus of the analysis. The exhibit also includes a cost line, called the *least squares regression line,* which has been estimated using regression analysis.

Regression analysis utilises all of the data points to determine the line of best fit. The objective is to estimate the line of best fit by making the deviations between the cost line and the data points as small as possible. To do this, the cost line is positioned to *minimise the sum of the squared deviations* between the line and the data points. The inset to Exhibit 3.10 depicts this graphically. Note that the deviations between the cost line and the data points are measured *vertically* on the graph rather than perpendicular to the line.

A least squares regression line possesses some very desirable properties for making cost predictions and drawing inferences about the estimated relationship between cost and activity levels. As always, the regression estimate of the cost behaviour should be restricted to the relevant range.

Equation form of the regression line

As with the preceding methods, the regression line shown in Exhibit 3.10 may be represented by the equation:

$$Y = a + bX$$

where Y = total cost

a = fixed cost component (the intercept on the vertical axis)

b = variable cost per unit (the slope of the line)

X = the quantity of activity (cost driver)

In regression analysis, X is called the **independent variable**, since it is the variable that is used to estimate the **dependent variable**, and Y is called the dependent variable, since it is caused by, or can be estimated using, the independent variable.

Estimating the regression equation

The regression line for Tasty Bread's electricity cost is shown below in equation form:

$$Y = \text{R}1920 + \text{R}4.48X$$

where Y = the estimated electricity cost for one month

X = the number of batches produced (activity) for one month

Within the relevant range of activity, the regression estimate of the fixed cost component is R1920 per month, and the regression estimate of the variable cost component is R4.48 per batch.

How were the components of this equation estimated? Estimating regression equations is fairly simple using software packages such as Microsoft Excel® or SPSS. The procedure that Jack Dlamini followed for calculating a regression equation, using an Excel® spreadsheet, is described in the appendix to this chapter.

Evaluation of regression analysis

We have a different cost function for electricity, compared with that derived using the high–low method. The cost function developed using regression analysis would usually be considered more accurate. Regression analysis makes use of all available data, and the regression line has statistical properties that allow us to make cost predictions and draw inferences about the relationship between cost and activity (or cost driver) levels.

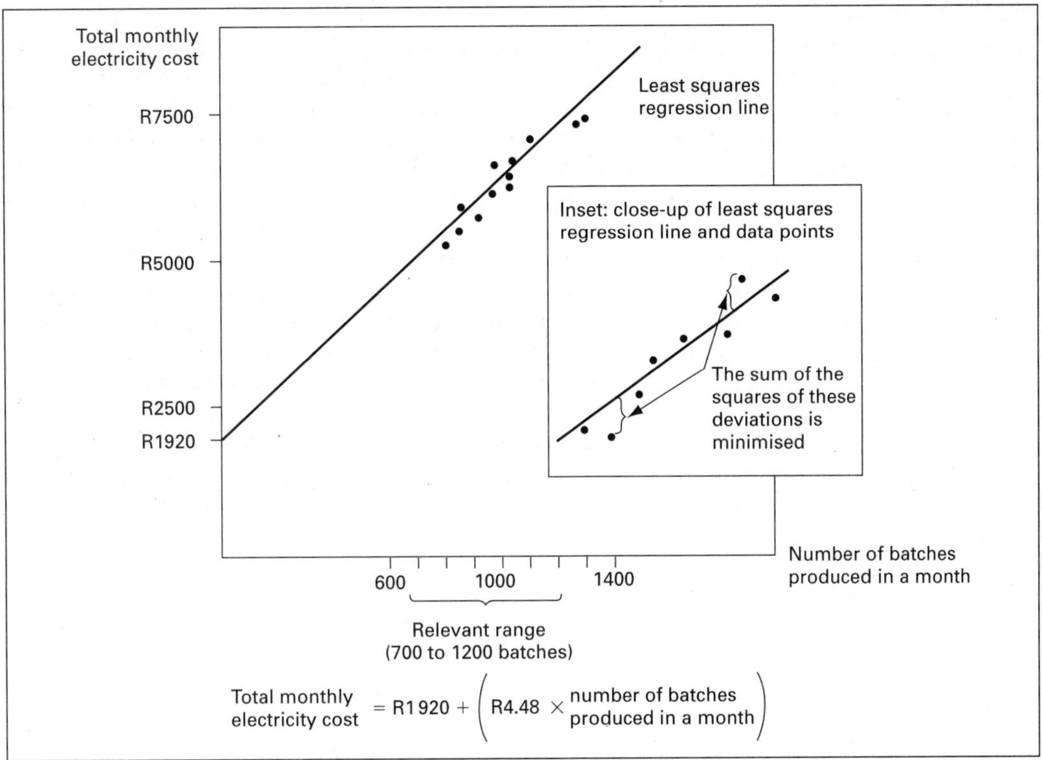

Exhibit 3.10 Least squares regression method: electricity cost, Tasty Bread Company

Evaluating a particular regression line

We have discussed the benefits of regression analysis. How does a cost analyst evaluate a particular regression line based on a specific set of data? Several criteria may be used, including:

1. *Economic plausibility*. Does the regression line make economic sense? Is it reasonable? If not, we might have chosen the wrong cost driver or have errors in our data. It could be that fundamental assumptions that underlie the regression method have been violated.[5]
2. *Goodness of fit*. How well does the line fit the data points? Statistical methods can be used to answer this question. The goodness of fit for Tasty Bread's regression line may be measured by the **coefficient of determination**, commonly called R^2. This measures the proportion of the change in the dependent variable that is explained by the change in the independent variable. The higher the R^2, the better the regression line fits the data. In cost estimation, the higher the R^2, the more confident the cost analyst can be about making cost predictions based on the estimated cost behaviour. The R^2 is routinely produced as part of the output of regression analysis. The R^2 for the regression equation in Exhibit 3.10 is 0.949.[6] This means that 94.9 per cent of the variation in electricity cost can be explained by the change in the number of batches. Jack Dlamini, the accountant, is pleased with this result, as it means that only 5.1 per cent of the variation in electricity cost is unexplained.

There are other statistics that also should be examined before the regression equation can be used with confidence. These statistics are described in the appendix.[7]

Multiple regression

In the quantitative methods we have discussed so far, we have used a single independent variable (a single activity or cost driver). However, there may be two or more independent variables that are important predictors of cost behaviour.

To illustrate, we will continue our analysis of Tasty Bread's electricity costs. The company uses electricity for two primary purposes: operating the cooking equipment, such as the ovens, and heating and cooling the bakery and shops. The cost of electricity for food production varies with the number of batches produced. However, the cost of electricity for the shop air-conditioning is related more closely to the number of customers than to the number of batches produced. A shop's electricity consumption increases each time the shop door is opened, resulting in loss of cool or warm air. Two customers purchasing a dozen bread rolls cause greater total electricity costs than one customer causes when buying two dozen bread rolls.

Suppose that Jack Dlamini wants to estimate a cost behaviour function for electricity cost based on both the number of batches produced and the number of customers. **Multiple regression**, which may be used for this purpose, is a statistical method that estimates a linear relationship between one dependent variable and two or more independent variables. In Tasty Bread's case, the following regression equation would be estimated:

$$Y = a + b_1X_1 + b_2X_2$$

where Y = the estimated electricity cost for one month
X_1 = the number of batches produced in one month
X_2 = the number of customers served in one month

In this equation, a is the regression estimate of the fixed cost component, b_1 is the regression estimate of the variable electricity cost per batch produced, and b_2 is the regression estimate of the variable electricity cost per customer served. The multiple regression equation will enable Jack Dlamini, Tasty Bread's accountant, to make more accurate cost predictions than could be made with the simple regression method discussed previously, as **simple regression** relies on only one independent variable to explain the behaviour of the dependent variable. Using the data in Exhibit 3.8, for all three variables, Jack again used Excel® to estimate the regression equation. This time there were two independent variables: the number of batches and the number of customers. The new regression equation is:

$$Y = \text{R}792.80 + \text{R}3.65X_1 + \text{R}2.65X_2$$

where Y = the estimated electricity cost for one month
X_1 = the number of batches produced in one month
X_2 = the number of customers served in one month

Note that this regression line cannot be drawn easily on a graph, as it would require a three-dimensional diagram to reflect the relationships between the dependent variable and the two independent variables.

The R^2 for this new regression equation is 0.96, which is an improvement on the prior regression equation. This tells Jack that he can more accurately predict electricity cost by taking into account both the number of batches and the number of customers.

Of course, there are likely to be other costs that Jack will wish to estimate using more than two activities, to attain greater levels of accuracy. He will need to determine whether the inclusion of extra variables is justified, by comparing the costs of collecting such data with the benefits that would be obtained from the greater level of accuracy in cost prediction.

Practical issues in cost estimation

L.O. 10

We have described some of the methods that Jack Dlamini could use to estimate the behaviour of the five costs included in his preliminary study of cost behaviour. However, there may be a number of practical issues to be considered in estimating cost behaviour.

Data collection problems

Regardless of the method used, the resulting cost estimates will only be as good as the data on which they are based. The collection of data for cost estimation requires skill and experience. Several problems frequently complicate this process:

1. *Missing data.* Misplaced source documents or failure to record a transaction accurately can result in missing data. What if a fuel account has mistakenly been charged to administrative expenses, rather than to delivery costs?
2. *Outliers.* We have discussed these extreme observations of cost/activity relationships. As outliers may represent highly unusual circumstances, they may be eliminated from the analysis. Of course, if the extreme observations are a result of errors, then these need to be corrected or eliminated from the analysis.
3. *Mismatched time periods.* The units of time for which the dependent and independent variables are measured may not match. For example, at Tasty Bread, the number of batches is recorded daily but electricity costs are recorded monthly. A common solution is to aggregate the production data to obtain monthly totals.
4. *Trade-offs in choosing the time period.* In choosing the period of analysis, often there is a trade-off between the number of observations and their reliability as predictors of future cost behaviour:
   - Increasing the number of observations increases the accuracy of cost functions.
   - However, we want the cost functions to describe current or future cost relationships. By extending the period of analysis further into the past to include more observations, the costs will not be current and work practices and technology may have changed during that period.
5. *Allocated fixed costs.* Fixed costs are sometimes allocated on a per unit basis. For example, fixed manufacturing overhead costs such as the production manager's salary may be allocated to units of production. This is a common characteristic of conventional product costing systems. As a result, such costs may appear to be variable in the cost records, but in practice they do not behave in a variable manner. The cost analyst needs to distinguish carefully between fixed and variable costs.
6. *Inflation.* During periods of inflation, historical cost data may not reflect future cost behaviour. One solution is to use historical data from a period of low inflation and then adjust with the current inflation rate. In recent years this has been less of a problem as the rate of inflation has remained relatively low.

Effect of learning on cost behaviour

At Tasty Bread, Jack Dlamini has noticed that, following the introduction of a new product, the product's labour time per unit tends to decrease. In the early stages, the reduction in labour times is dramatic. As the product 'settles in', the rate of improvement seems to slow. This effect, known as the **learning curve effect**, should be taken into account in estimating labour costs for relatively new products or production processes. The learning curve effect is described in more detail in the appendix to this chapter.

Cost behaviour, cost estimation and activity-based costing

We have already observed the similarity between task analysis and activity-based costing in estimating cost functions, particularly for direct costs such as material and labour. But are the conventional concepts of cost behaviour and cost estimation relevant to activity-based costing? Conventional management accounting systems classify costs as fixed or variable with respect to the volume of production. Variable costs are driven by the volume of production and fixed costs are not. More complex cost behaviour patterns, such as curvilinear and semivariable costs, are also recognised. These patterns are also represented as linear cost functions, with fixed and variable components, within the relevant range.

In an activity-based system, costs are assigned to activities. Activity costs that are driven by the volume of production are called *unit level costs*. The remaining costs, which would be classified as fixed in a conventional system, are classified as *batch level*, *product level* or *facility level costs*.[8] Cost drivers are identified for both batch level costs and product level costs but not for facility level costs. In costing products, activity-based systems assume that unit, batch and product level costs vary proportionally with their cost driver. These activity costs are variable costs, with respect to their particular cost driver. As in conventional costing systems, in activity-based costing we need to identify these 'variable' cost functions, calculate their slope (that is, the activity cost per unit of cost driver) and assess their goodness of fit. Understanding cost behaviour and estimating cost functions is just as important in activity-based systems as in conventional systems.

The accuracy of cost functions in business

Knowledge of cost behaviour is important to ensure that the best information is provided for managing resources to create customer and shareholder value. However, in some businesses in South Africa and elsewhere, accounting staff formulate budgets and develop cost information for management decisions with only an approximate understanding of how costs behave. Even in developing activity-based systems, some accountants ignore the basic principles in identifying and verifying cost functions.

Why might some businesses rely more on gut feeling than on objective techniques in describing cost behaviours? There are several possible explanations:

- The accountants responsible for cost analysis may not have enough time or knowledge to use appropriate quantitative techniques.
- The data required to estimate reliable cost functions may not exist.
- There may be low priority given to cost behaviour and cost estimation within the business.
- Cost estimates may be considered 'accurate enough' for the firm's needs. Cost behaviour classifications are often made to allow products to be costed. For external reporting of product costs, minor inaccuracies in inventory values that result from using only approximations of cost behaviours may be unimportant.

With the current sophistication of information systems, readily available computer software packages and recent advances in our understanding of cost behaviour, there are few reasons why more accurate cost behaviour functions cannot be developed within organisations. It may reflect a cost–benefit decision.

Assumptions underlying cost estimation

All cost functions are based on simplifying assumptions. The two most important assumptions are that:

1. Cost behaviour depends on one activity (or in the case of multiple regression, a few independent variables). In reality, however, costs are affected by a host of factors including the weather, the mood of employees, and the quality of the raw materials used.
2. Cost behaviours are linear (straight lines) within the relevant range.

The accountant must consider, on a case-by-case basis, whether these assumptions are reasonable.

Operating leverage, risk and cost behaviour

A company with a high level of fixed costs will have a higher operating risk than a company whose costs are mainly variable. The ratio of fixed costs to variable costs indicates the firm's level of operating leverage. What this means is that a firm with a high ratio of fixed costs may experience a 10 per cent increase in sales and a 30 per cent increase in operating profit. However, in a recession a fall in sales of 20 per cent may result in a 60 per cent fall in operating profit. What should the company do if it is expecting a fall in sales? First, the company should move from fixed costs to variable costs by undertaking actions such as outsourcing, cost-plus pricing, adopting remuneration plans that include bonuses for out-performance, entering into flexible contracts and leasing assets if possible on a pay-per-use basis or otherwise lease assets with favourable cancellation clauses. For example, a hospital may lease a CT scanner on a pay-per-use basis, rather than spend say R5 million on the purchase of a new scanner. This reduces the risk to the hospital if demand is less than expected. We saw in the 'real life' case of Comair that airlines have a high fixed-cost-ratio and it is critical for airlines to fill planes and have planes spend a greater amount of time in the air. However, airlines often enter into operating leases which may offer them a favourable cancellation clause in case demand for particular routes falls. The leasing companies have international operations and are better placed to lease planes to other airlines that are experiencing higher than expected demand.

Costs and benefits of accurate cost information

We have used the Tasty Bread Company to describe a variety of cost estimation methods ranging from managerial judgement to sophisticated techniques involving regression analysis. Which of these methods is best? The accountant must decide when it is important to use a more sophisticated, and more costly, cost estimation method, and when it is acceptable to use a simpler approach. In general, the more sophisticated methods will yield more accurate cost estimates than will the simpler ones. While it is easy to estimate the costs of estimating cost functions, it is more difficult to assess the benefits that can flow from better budgeting and planning, and from improved information for decision-making.

With an understanding of cost behaviour and cost estimation techniques, Tasty Bread's accountant can derive a cost function that describes the behaviour of each of the company's major costs. From there, he can use the cost functions, combined with estimates of future levels of activity, to budget the company's major costs. He can also use the cost estimates when making important decisions such as which equipment to replace or which products to make.

Summary

In this chapter we considered the relationship between cost behaviour, cost estimation and cost prediction, and described various approaches to identifying cost behaviour and estimating costs. Key points include:

- *Cost behaviour* refers to the relationship between a cost and the level of activity or cost driver. Cost estimation is the process of determining the cost behaviour of a particular cost item, and cost prediction uses a knowledge of a cost's behaviour to forecast the level of cost at a particular level of activity.
- The term *cost driver* is used to describe an activity or factor that causes a cost to be incurred. Conventional management accounting systems use various measures of production volume as cost drivers to analyse cost behaviour. These cost drivers are called *volume-based cost drivers.* More recent approaches recognise that some cost drivers are not directly related to production volume. These cost drivers are called *non-volume-based cost drivers.*

- Activity-based costing is a contemporary approach to costing that recognises a hierarchy of costs and cost drivers: unit, batch, product and facility levels. While unit level cost drivers measure production volume, the cost drivers for batch and product level costs are non-volume-based. There are no obvious cost drivers for facility level costs.
- Understanding a firm's cost behaviour can enable managers to anticipate changes in cost when the organisation's operations change. Cost predictions that are based on cost behaviour patterns facilitate planning and control, and this can help managers to manage resources more effectively and add value to their organisation. However, effective cost management requires an understanding of root cause cost drivers, which are the *underlying* factors that cause costs to be incurred.
- A variety of cost behaviours exist; they range from simple variable and fixed costs to more complicated semivariable and curvilinear costs.
- Cost predictions based on an analysis of cost behaviour should be confined to the relevant range, which is the range of activity over which a cost function is expected to remain valid.
- In predicting costs it is useful to recognise that some costs can be classified as engineered costs, where they bear a physical relationship to output. Fixed costs can be classified as committed or discretionary.
- Several approaches can be used to estimate costs. These include managerial judgement, the engineering method and various quantitative techniques. Engineering approaches to cost estimation are based on a detailed analysis of the process in which the costs are incurred.
- Quantitative techniques are based on an analysis of past cost data observed at a variety of activity levels and include the high–low and regression methods.
- In practice, analysing cost behaviour can be fraught with difficulties. For example, how do we ensure reliable data? What effect will increasing experience have on labour costs? How do we analyse cost behaviour in an activity-based costing environment? How do we assess the costs and benefits of the various approaches to estimating cost behaviour? And how well met are the assumptions underlying the cost functions? As in the selection of any accounting technique, the choice of a cost estimation method involves a trade-off of costs and benefits. More accurate estimation methods provide better information, but they are often more costly to use.

As you explore other topics in this book, you will discover that understanding and analysing cost behaviour is an essential skill for the management accountant. It can help to estimate the costs of goods and services, it provides a framework for predicting future costs (that is, budgeting) and reporting financial performance, and it is fundamental to cost volume profit analysis and to analysing costs for a range of tactical decisions.

In the next few chapters, we will continue our study of costs by identifying the various approaches to estimating the costs of goods and services.

References

Berenson, ML, Levine, DM & Krehbie, TK 2001, *Basic Business Statistics: Concepts and Applications,* 8th edn, Prentice Hall, Upper Saddle River, NJ.

Hair, JF, Anderson, RE, Tatham, RL & Black, WC 1998, *Multivariate Data Analysis,* 5th edn, Prentice Hall International, Upper Saddle River, NJ.

Horngren, CT, Foster, G, Datar, SM and Uliana, E 1999, *Cost accounting in South Africa: a managerial perspective,* Prentice Hall, Cape Town.

Joye, MP & Blayney, PJ 1990, *Cost Management Accounting Practices in Australian Manufacturing Companies: Survey Results,* University of Sydney.

Waweru, NM, Hoque, Z and Uliana, E 2004, 'Management accounting change in South Africa: Case studies from retail services', *Accounting, Auditing & Accountability Journal,* Vol. 17, No. 5

Annual Reports: Metair (2005), AVI (2006), Comair (2006)

Self study

Self-study problem 1: Using and interpreting regression analysis

Bongani Hardware Pty Ltd operates retail stores in the western suburbs of Johannesburg. Data on the company's maintenance costs for its buildings and furnishings are presented below:

Month	Maintenance cost	Sales revenue	Store opening hours
January	R53 000	R600 000	240
February	55 000	700 000	240
March	47 000	550 000	200
April	51 000	650 000	220
May	45 000	500 000	200
June	49 000	610 000	210

(a) Use regression analysis to estimate the cost function for the firm's maintenance costs, using sales revenue as the cost driver.
(b) Use multiple regression analysis to estimate the cost function for the firm's maintenance costs, using both sales revenue and store opening hours as the cost drivers.
(c) Which of the two equations provides the best predictor of maintenance costs?

Solution to Self-study problem 1

(a) The regression equation is of the form:

$$Y = a + bX$$

Using the regression function in a Microsoft Excel® spreadsheet, the regression formula is as follows:

Maintenance cost = R21 456 + R0.047 × sales revenue

(b) The regression equation is of the form:

$$Y = a + b_1X_1 + b_2X_2$$

Using an Excel® spreadsheet, the new regression formula is as follows:

Maintenance cost = R7958 + R0.021 × sales revenue + R134.44 × store opening hours

Thus, the monthly maintenance cost can be estimated as a fixed component of R7958, plus the variable components of R0.021 per Rand of sales revenue and R134.44 multiplied by the total monthly store opening hours.

(c) The R^2 for the first equation is 0.81, which indicates that sales revenue can be used to predict 81 per cent of the variation in maintenance cost. In the second equation, R^2 is 0.99, which indicates that by including the second independent variable, store opening hours, monthly maintenance costs can be more accurately predicted.

After reading the appendix to this chapter you will realise that, as the sample size is small, the adjusted R^2 should be compared. In this question the adjusted R^2 are 0.76 for part (a) and 0.99 for part (b). (These measures are still very acceptable.)

Both equations are significant, indicated by the F-statistics and by the p-values of 0.015 and 0.0007 respectively. In addition, each coefficient in the two equations is statistically significant. (These concepts are explained in the appendix.)

Thus, we can say that the two equations provide strong models for predicting maintenance cost, with the equation in part (b) providing the better solution.

Self-study problem 2: Estimating variable and fixed costs

The Wilderness is a weekly newspaper sold throughout South Africa and Namibia. The following costs were incurred by its publisher during a week when circulation was 100 000 newspapers: total variable costs, R40 000; total fixed costs, R66 000. Predict the total and per unit variable and fixed costs for circulations of 110 000 and 120 000 newspapers.

Solution to Self-study problem 2

	Circulation	
	110 000 newspapers	**120 000 newspapers**
Variable cost per unit	R40 000 ÷ 100 000 = R0.40	R40 000 ÷ 100 000 = R0.40
Total variable cost	110 000 × R0.40 = R44 000	120 000 × R0.40 = R48 000
Total fixed cost	R66 000	R66 000
Fixed cost per unit	R66 000 ÷ 110 000 = R0.60	R66 000 ÷ 120 000 = R0.55

Cybersearch

1 Find websites that include the term *cost driver.*
   (a) Find specific examples of cost drivers.
   (b) Select three appropriate websites and determine whether the concept discussed relates to cost behaviour or cost management.
2 What are variable costs?
   (a) Select two websites that describe organisations that use the variable cost classification.
   (b) Give examples of the variable costs described for each organisation and suggest possible cost drivers.
3 In this chapter we have introduced the concept of batch level costs.
   (a) Find websites that include the term *batch level costs.*
   (b) What did you learn about batch level costs from this search?
   (c) Describe any organisations that identify batch level costs and give examples of the types of batch level costs you have encountered in your search.

Appendix to Chapter 3

Part 1: Using Excel® to formulate a regression equation

L.O. 11

While regression estimates can be calculated manually,[9] the usual procedure is to rely on a software package such as Microsoft Excel® or SPSS. Using the data in Exhibit 3.8, the step-by-step procedures for calculating the regression equation will be explained.

Estimating the regression equation with Excel®

1 Type the data for the dependent variable and the independent variable(s) in separate columns on the worksheet. Include the name of the data in the first row of each column.

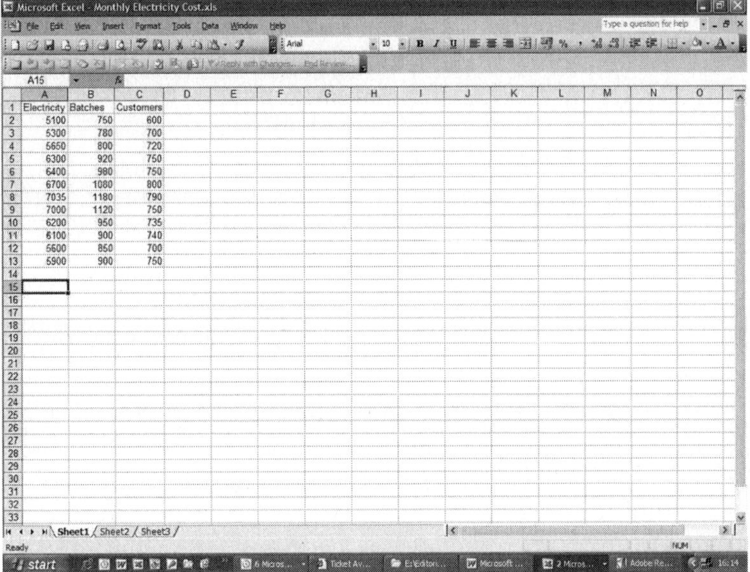

Electricity	Batches	Customers
5100	750	600
5300	780	700
5650	800	720
6300	920	750
6400	980	750
6700	1080	800
7035	1180	790
7000	1120	750
6200	950	735
6100	900	740
5600	850	700
5900	900	750

2 From the menu at the top of the screen, **select** *Tools/Data Analysis/Regression.*[10]

3 **Click** on *Input Y Range* and then **highlight** the cells that contain data for the dependent variable. **Click** on the box *Input X Range* and **highlight** the data for the independent variable(s). Note that more than one independent variable can be included, by simply highlighting all of the cells that contain the data for the independent variables. It is a good idea to include the column headings in the *Y* and *X* range, so that the regression output will identify the name of each variable. **Check** the label box, to indicate that the first row in each column is a label, rather than numeric data.

To run the regression, **click** OK.

4 The output will now appear on another sheet of your spreadsheet.

How do we interpret the statistics in this output?

Evaluating the regression equation

The coefficients for the regression equation are in the lower panel of the output. The constant, or intercept, is 792.80, and the coefficients for the two independent variables are 3.65 for number of

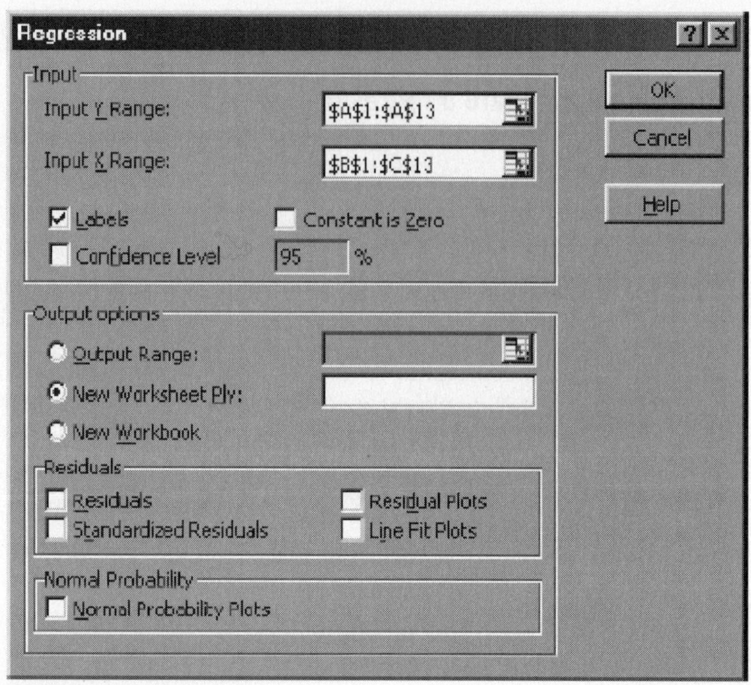

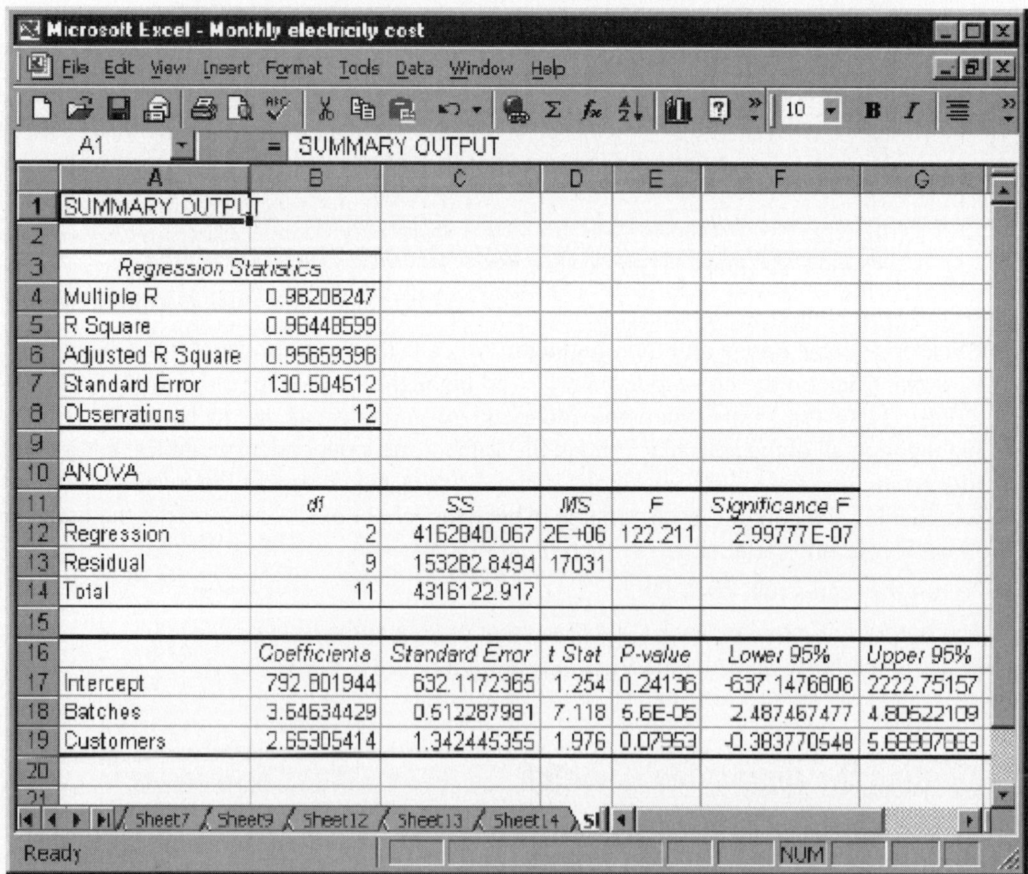

SUMMARY OUTPUT

Regression Statistics	
Multiple R	0.98208247
R Square	0.96448599
Adjusted R Square	0.95659398
Standard Error	130.504512
Observations	12

ANOVA

	df	*SS*	*MS*	*F*	*Significance F*
Regression	2	4162840.067	2E+06	122.211	2.99777E-07
Residual	9	153282.8494	17031		
Total	11	4316122.917			

	Coefficients	*Standard Error*	*t Stat*	*P-value*	*Lower 95%*	*Upper 95%*
Intercept	792.801944	632.1172365	1.254	0.24136	-637.1476806	2222.75157
Batches	3.64634429	0.612287981	7.118	5.6E-05	2.487467477	4.80522109
Customers	2.65305414	1.342445355	1.976	0.07953	-0.383770548	5.68987083

batches, and 2.65 for the number of customers. Thus, the regression equation can be expressed as follows:

$$Y = R792.80 + R3.65X_1 + R2.65X_2$$

where Y = the estimated electricity cost for one month
X_1 = the number of batches produced in one month
X_2 = the number of customers served in one month

The R^2 for the equation is 0.96, which means that 96 per cent of the variation of the monthly electricity cost can be explained by the variation in the numbers of batches and numbers of customers.

But what do the other statistics shown on this regression output mean? We should not use the results of any regression analysis without considering some of the statistics that may qualify how the regression equation can be used. Let's look at some of the more important statistics.

First, we need to consider whether our regression model represents a predictive model for all cases of monthly electricity cost for Tasty Bread, or whether the model is specific to cost behaviour in the particular months that we have selected. The first test is to consider the statistical significance of the regression model, by examining the ***F*-statistic**. The *F*-statistic tests the significance of the regression equation as a whole, by testing the likelihood that the relationships in the regression equation have occurred by chance. This significance is measured by the associated *p*-value. The ***p*-value** is used to test the significance of a result—that is, to assess that the result is not due to random factors. A *p*-value of 0.05 or less is usually considered to be significant. In the regression output above, the *F*-statistic equals 122.21 and is significant at $p < 0.0001$, which means that there is less than a 0.01 per cent probability that the relationships in the equation have occurred by chance. The usual benchmark for determining significance is for the probability to be less than 5 per cent ($p < 0.05$). This means that in the regression equation for electricity cost, we can be fairly confident that relationships are unlikely to have occurred by chance.

We should also consider the number of independent variables, relative to the sample size. Standard rules of thumb indicate that there should be between 5 and 20 observations per independent variable (this rule varies depending on which statistics expert is consulted). In the regression analysis, there are only 12 observations and two independent variables, which is clearly on the borderline for an acceptable sample size. In these situations the R^2 may be inflated. An **adjusted R^2** can be used to compensate for the small sample size. In this example, the adjusted R^2 is lower, at 0.956. However, this result is still very acceptable.

Another test is to consider the **standard error of the coefficient** to indicate to what degree the estimated value of each coefficient is likely to have been affected by random factors. This test is needed whenever a sample of observations (as opposed to the population of observations) is selected for the analysis. The larger the sample, the less concerned we are about the sample representing the population. In this case we need to assess whether changes in each of the independent variables result in significant changes in electricity cost for Tasty Bread. The standard error for each coefficient is assessed for significance. We do this by examining the ***t*-statistic** and associated *p*-value for each coefficient. The *t*-statistic indicates the significance of each individual independent variable in the regression equation, by testing whether each independent variable individually explains the some of the variance in the dependent variable. A *t*-test of less than 0.05 is usually considered significant. In the regression results reported above, the coefficient for the number of batches is significant ($p <$ 0.0001).[11] Note, however, that the coefficient for the number of customers is only significant at 7.96 per cent. This means that we should be a little cautious about assuming that the coefficient of the number of customers is truly representative of the relationships that may exist generally between electricity cost and number of customers at Tasty Bread (there is a 7.96 per cent chance that the coefficient is a result of random factors). There are other statistics that can be considered when interpreting the output from a regression analysis, but these are beyond the scope of this book.

While it is valuable to understand the meaning of the various statistics associated with regression analysis, when using regression analysis for cost estimation, we must remember that the results are only as good as the data on which the analysis is based. If the activities that are assumed to be the independent variables are not plausible cost drivers, and if the data collected are not accurate, then the relationships captured in the regression equation will not be useful.

Part 2: The learning curve effect

L.O. 12

In many production processes, production efficiency increases with experience. For example, it has been observed that as *cumulative* production output increases, the average labour time required per unit declines. A graphical expression of this phenomenon is called a **learning curve**. Exhibit 3.11 provides an example of an '80 per cent' learning curve. It also displays the total labour time and average labour time per unit for various levels of cumulative output. An 80 per cent learning curve means that when output X is doubled to $2X$, the *cumulative average time per unit* for $2X$ is 80 per cent of the *cumulative average time per unit* for X. In Exhibit 3.11, when *cumulative* output doubles from 5 to 10 units, the *cumulative* average labour time per unit for the 10 units (80 hours) is 80 per cent of the cumulative average labour time for the first 5 units (100 hours). Note that we are using *cumulative* output and *cumulative* average labour times. The first 5 units require a total labour time of 500 hours, at an average time of 100 hours each. The next 5 units require 300 hours (800−500 hours), at an average labour time of 60 hours each. However, added together, this cumulative output of 10 units requires 800 hours, at a cumulative average labour time of 80 hours each.[12]

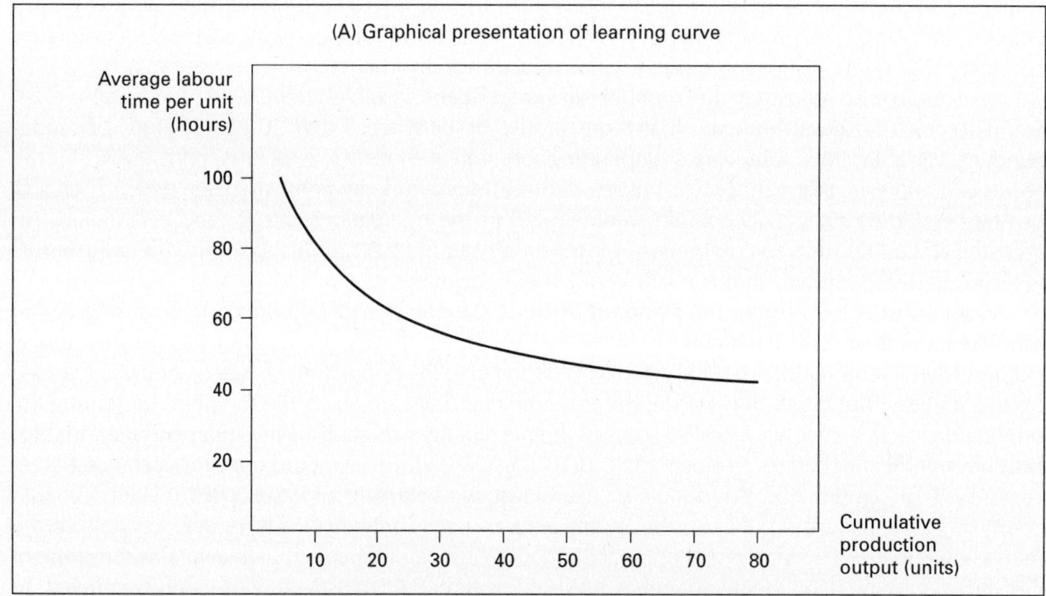

(B) Tabular presentation of learning curve

Cumulative output (in units)	Average labour time per unit (hours)	Total labour time (hours)
5	100.00	500.0
10	80.00	800.0
20	64.00	1 280.0
40	51.20	2 048.0
80	40.96	3 276.8

Exhibit 3.11 Learning curve

The learning curve effect means that labour costs are unlikely to have a linear relationship with the volume of production. As the number of units produced increases, the total labour cost will increase but at a decreasing rate. As a manufacturer gains experience with producing a product, estimates of the cost of direct labour should be adjusted downwards to take this learning effect into account. This is especially important early in the life of a product, when the learning curve is relatively steep. As more experience is gained, the learning curve flattens out and the relationship between labour costs and production volume may be approximately linear. When relatively new products are to be produced, Tasty Bread's accountant needs to build the learning curve effect into estimates of the relationship between labour costs and production volume.

Learning curves have been used extensively in industries such as aircraft production, shipbuilding and electronics to help predict manufacturing labour costs. In our 'Real life' example, Metair, the South African auto component supplier referred to the production of new components and the efficiency gains expected from the learning curve effect as the company continues with production of the same units in the following year. The principles of the learning curve have also been extended to other areas of the value chain, particularly the downstream areas such as selling, distribution and customer support. An **experience curve** is used to show how product costs, which include costs from across the value chain, decrease as units of output increase.

It is important to understand the effects of learning or experience on cost behaviour. Predictions that take account of the effects of experience are relevant to scheduling production, budgeting, setting product prices, and other management decisions.

Questions

?

3.1 Describe the role that an understanding of cost behaviour patterns can play in supporting effective resource management and enhancing shareholder value.

3.2 Define the following terms and explain the relationship between them: *cost estimation*, *cost behaviour* and *cost prediction*.

3.3 What is a *cost driver*? What role do cost drivers play in identifying cost behaviour patterns?

3.4 What types of cost drivers are used in conventional management accounting systems when costs are classified as fixed or variable? What types of cost drivers are used in more recent approaches, such as in activity-based costing?

3.5 Define *unit level*, *batch level*, *product level* and *facility level* costs and cost drivers. Provide three examples of costs, and their cost drivers, at each level.

3.6 Suggest an appropriate cost driver for each of the following costs:
(a) cleaning costs in a residential hotel
(b) administration costs in a hospital
(c) the cost of electricity in a computer sales store
(d) the cost of spare parts in a computer repair service
(e) the cost of professional wages in a public accounting firm

3.7 Draw a simple graph of each of the following types of cost behaviour patterns:
(a) variable
(b) fixed
(c) step-fixed
(d) semivariable
(e) curvilinear

3.8 'In the long term, all costs are variable.' Discuss.

3.9 Explain the impact of an increase in the level of cost driver on:
(a) total variable cost
(b) variable cost per unit

3.10 Describe the impact of an increase in activity on:
(a) total fixed cost
(b) fixed cost per unit of activity

3.11 Explain the meaning of an *engineered cost*; give three examples; and for each cost provide a cost driver.

3.12 Distinguish between *committed costs* and *discretionary costs*. Explain how this classification can help with planning and managing costs.

3.13 You are the management accountant for Southern Cape Tyres and have identified a linear relationship between the total direct material cost and the quantity of rubber used in production. Provide answers to the following questions, including reasons to explain your answer.
(a) Is this cost a variable cost or a semivariable cost?
(b) Is this cost a unit level cost or a batch level cost?
(c) Is the quantity of rubber a useful cost driver for cost management?

3.14 A cost analyst showed the general manager a graph that portrayed the firm's electricity cost as semivariable. The general manager looked at the graph and said: 'This fixed-cost component doesn't look right to me. If we shut down the plant for six months, we wouldn't incur half those costs.' If you were the cost analyst, how would you respond?

3.15 What is an *outlier*? List some possible causes of outliers. How should outliers be handled in cost estimation?

3.16 Explain the cost estimation problem caused by allocated costs.

3.17 What is the chief drawback of the high–low method of cost estimation? What problem could an outlier cause if the high–low method were used?

3.18 Use an equation to express a simple regression line. Interpret each term in the context of a cost function. Explain the meaning of the term *least squares* in the least squares regression method of cost estimation.

3.19 Explain how multiple regression can be used to estimate a cost function. Select an example of a cost and two cost drivers that could form a multiple regression equation.

3.20 Briefly describe two methods that can be used to evaluate a particular regression line.

3.21 Describe some of the problems often encountered when collecting data for cost estimation.

3.22 Some businesses use only approximations when estimating cost functions. What are some possible reasons for this?

3.23 'Classifying costs according to their behaviour is old hat. Our business is going to introduce activity-based costing and we won't have to worry about cost drivers, cost behaviour or estimating cost functions.' Discuss.

3.24 (appendix) What is meant by the term *learning curve*? Explain its role in cost estimation. How does a learning curve differ from an experience curve?

Exercises

E3.25 Cost drivers: manufacturer

Eastern Cape Automotive Industries Ltd manufactures seats and seat slides for the South African motor vehicle industry. Below is a list of some of the major costs incurred by the company:

(a) steel used in the manufacture of seats and seat slides
(b) wages paid to employees who produce seats and seat slides
(c) wages paid to employees who set up machinery for each production run
(d) salaries paid to design engineers who develop new seats and seat slides
(e) salaries paid to the chief executive officer who oversees the development, production and marketing of Eastern Cape Automotive Industries' products

Required:

1 For each cost, suggest a possible cost driver that could be used to estimate cost functions and predict cost behaviour.
2 Can we use the unit–batch–product–facility hierarchy to analyse these costs? Where possible, classify each cost as unit, batch, product or facility level.
3 Having identified cost drivers, describe the cost behaviour pattern that you would expect for each cost, giving your reasons.

E3.26 Cost drivers: service firm

Bank North is a regional bank offering deposit and withdrawal services, as well as a range of loan and investment products and retirement planning services. Branch offices have a full-time staff of four: a branch manager, a loans manager, a manager of investment products and a teller supervisor. Tellers are employed on a casual basis and can be called in for a minimum of two hours. Most customers make deposits through the branch tellers, and withdrawals through automatic teller machines, which are controlled through a data-processing department located at head office. The investment manager provides initial advice to customers on the range of investment and retirement-planning products, although most significant customers are referred to head office for specialist advice.

Required:

1 Prepare a list of five major costs likely to be incurred by Bank North branches.
2 For each cost, suggest a possible cost driver that could be used to estimate cost functions and predict cost behaviour.
3 Having identified these cost drivers, describe the cost behaviour pattern that you would expect for each cost, giving your reasons.

E3.27 Variable and fixed costs; graphical and tabular analyses: manufacturer

Smithfield Sheet Metal Pty Ltd incurs a variable cost of R60 per kilogram for raw material, and fixed costs of R100 000 per month, to produce a special alloy used in manufacturing aircraft.

Required:

1 Draw a graph of the firm's raw material cost, showing the total cost at the following production levels: 10 000 units, 20 000 units and 30 000 units.
2 Prepare a table that shows the unit cost and total cost of raw material at the following production levels: 10 000 units, 20 000 units and 30 000 units.
3 Draw a graph of the company's fixed production cost showing the total cost at the following production levels: 10 000 units, 20 000 units and 30 000 units.
4 Prepare a table that shows the unit cost and the total cost for the firm's fixed production costs at the following production levels: 10 000 units, 20 000 units and 30 000 units.

E3.28 Fixed and variable costs; missing data: service firm

Mag Mufflers Ltd specialises in replacing mufflers on cars. The company has a conventional management accounting system that classifies costs as variable or fixed with respect to the number of muffler replacements. The following table shows the costs during a month if 600 mufflers are replaced.

	Number of muffler replacements		
	500	**600**	**700**
Total costs:			
Fixed costs	(a)	R168 000	(b)
Variable costs	(c)	120 000	(d)
Total costs	(e)	288 000	(f)
Cost per muffler replacement:			
Fixed costs	(g)	(h)	(i)
Variable cost	(j)	(k)	(l)
Total cost per muffler replacement	(m)	(n)	(o)

Required:

Fill in the missing amounts labelled (a) to (o) in the table.

E3.29 Graphing cost behaviour patterns: hospital

Draw a graph of the cost behaviour for each of the following costs incurred by the Northern Johannesburg Medical Centre. The hospital measures costs on a monthly basis and uses patient-days as the cost driver. Label both axes and the cost line in each graph.

1 The cost of salaries and on-costs for the administrative staff total R36 000 per month.
2 The cost of food varies in proportion to the number of patient-days provided. In January, the hospital provided 3000 patient-days of care, and food costs amounted to R72 000.
3 The hospital's laboratory costs include two components:
   (a) R120 000 per month for salaries of personnel and depreciation on equipment
   (b) R30 per patient-day for chemicals and other materials used in performing the tests
4 The cost of utilities depends on how many wards the hospital needs to use during a particular month. During months with less than 2000 patient-days of care, two wards are used, resulting in utility costs of R30 000. During months with more than 2000 patient-days of care, three wards are used, and utility costs total R45 000.
5 Many of the hospital's nurses are part-time employees. As a result, the hours of nursing care provided can be easily adjusted to the amount required at any particular time. The cost of wages and on-costs for nurses is approximately R7500 for each block of 200 patient-days of care provided during a month. For example, nursing costs total R7500 for 1 to 200 patient-days, R15 000 for 201 to 400 patient-days, R22 500 for 401 to 600 patient-days, and so forth.

E3.30 Behaviour of fixed and variable costs: not-for-profit organisation

3EDU is an independent, not-for-profit television station run by a major university. The station's broadcast hours vary during the year, depending on whether it is semester time or holiday time. The station uses a conventional costing system that classifies costs as fixed or variable with respect to the number of broadcast-hours. The station's production crew and supervisory costs are as follows for July and September:

Cost item	Cost behaviour	Cost amount	Broadcast hours during month
Production crew:	Variable		
July		R26 650	410
September		44 200	680
Supervisory employees:	Fixed		
July		30 000	410
September		30 000	680

Required:

1 Calculate the cost per broadcast-hour during July and September for each of these cost items.
2 What will be the total amount incurred for each of these costs during December, when the station's activity will be 440 broadcast-hours?
3 What will be the cost per broadcast-hour in December for each of the cost items?

E3.31 Approximating a curvilinear cost: service firm

The behaviour of the annual repair and maintenance cost for the Polokwane Bus Company is shown by the solid line in the following graph. The dashed line depicts a semivariable cost approximation of the company's repair and maintenance cost.

Required:

1 What is the actual (curvilinear) and estimated (semivariable) cost shown by the graph for each of the following activity levels?
   (a) 20 000 kilometres
   (b) 40 000 kilometres
   (c) 60 000 kilometres
   (d) 80 000 kilometres
2 How good an approximation does the semivariable cost pattern provide if the company's expected level of activity falls between 40 000 and 60 000 kilometres per month? What if the expected range of activity is 20 000 to 90 000 kilometres per month?

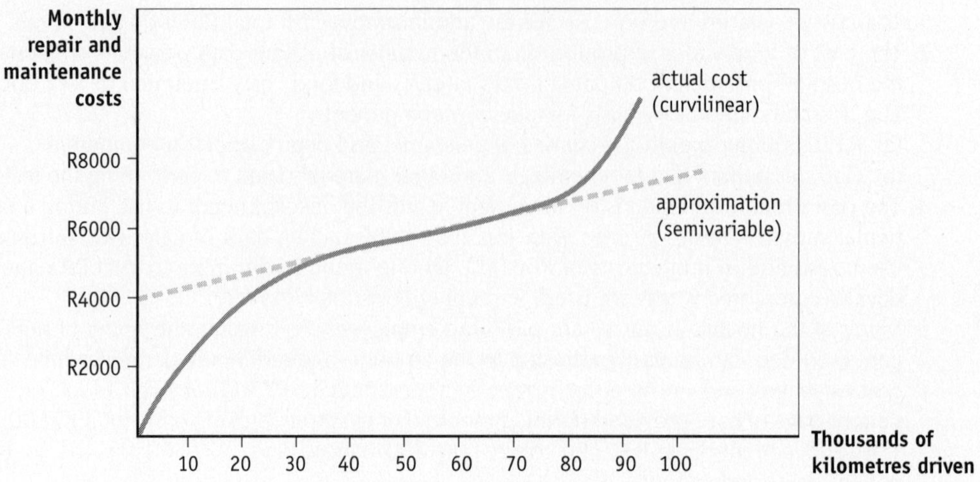

E3.32 Estimating cost behaviour; high–low method: manufacturer

Bill Lee is a highly successful vegetable grower who has formed his own processing and canning company, Lee's Fine Foods. The recently hired accountant for the firm, Alice Pillay, is about to use the high–low method to estimate the firm's energy cost behaviour. The following costs were incurred during the past 12 months:

Month	Kilograms of vegetables canned	Electricity (R)
January	105 000	70 200
February	63 000	66 300
March	66 000	66 000
April	72 000	67 350
May	90 000	68 700
June	96 000	70 050
July	120 000	84 000
August	90 000	68 400
September	90 000	69 000
October	84 000	68 100
November	123 000	72 300
December	117 000	74 850

Required:

1 Use the high–low method to estimate the company's electricity cost behaviour and express it in equation form.

2 Predict the electricity cost for a month in which 78 000 kilograms of food are canned.

E3.33 Estimating cost behaviour; regression analysis: manufacturer

Refer to the data in Exercise 3.32.

Required:

1 Use regression analysis to estimate the company's electricity cost behaviour.

2 Provide an assessment of the explanatory power of this equation.

E3.34 Estimating cost behaviour; high–low method: hospital

South Coast Regional Hospital has incurred the following costs in its diagnostic blood laboratory over the past year:

Month	Number of blood tests completed	Cost (R)
January	6 100	90 000
February	5 300	87 000
March	4 900	76 200
April	4 800	78 100
May	5 050	80 700
June	3 050	61 000
July	4 500	74 500
August	7 100	99 000
September	6 200	95 600
October	4 700	74 800
November	5 900	89 000
December	6 000	91 000

Required:

1 Plot the above data in a scatter diagram. Assign cost to the vertical axis and the number of blood tests completed to the horizontal axis.

2 Estimate the monthly fixed cost and the variable cost per blood test using the high–low method.

E3.35 Estimating cost behaviour; regression analysis: hospital

Refer to the data in Exercise 3.34.

Required:

1 Use regression analysis to estimate the hospital's blood laboratory cost behaviour.

2 Provide an assessment of the explanatory power of this equation.

E3.36 Regression analysis: service firm

Ikapa Bus Tours has incurred the following bus maintenance costs over the last half of the year:

Month	Kilometres travelled by tour buses	Cost (R)
July	12 700	11 700
August	15 000	12 000
September	22 000	12 500
October	8 000	11 000
November	10 500	11 400
December	12 600	11 600

Required:

1 Use regression analysis to estimate the variable cost per tour-kilometre travelled and the fixed cost per month.

2 Develop a formula to express the cost behaviour exhibited by the company's maintenance cost.

3 Predict the level of maintenance cost that would be incurred during a month when 20 000 tour-kilometres are driven.

E3.37 Average costs; learning curve effects (appendix): manufacturer

Peter Marais makes customised mooring covers for boats. Each mooring cover is hand-sewn to fit a particular boat. If covers are made for two or more identical boats, each successive cover generally requires less time to make. Marais has been approached by a local boat dealer to make mooring covers for all the boats sold by the dealer. Marais has developed the following cost schedule for mooring covers made to fit five-metre outboard powerboats.

Number of mooring covers made	Total cost of covers (R)
1	450
2	850
3	1 210
4	1 540
5	1 850

Required:

1 Calculate the average cost per unit if:
   (a) 2 mooring covers are made
   (b) 4 mooring covers are made
   (c) 5 mooring covers are made

2 Explain why the average cost changes as the number of covers made increases.

E3.38 Learning curve; high technology (appendix): manufacturer

Weathereye Ltd manufactures weather satellites. The final assembly and testing of the satellites is a largely manual operation involving dozens of highly-trained electronics technicians. The following learning curve has been estimated for the firm's newest satellite model, which is about to enter production.

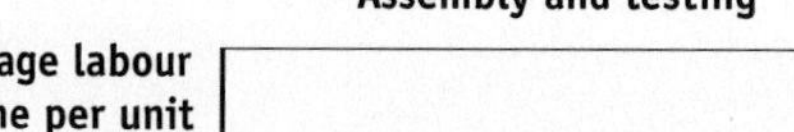

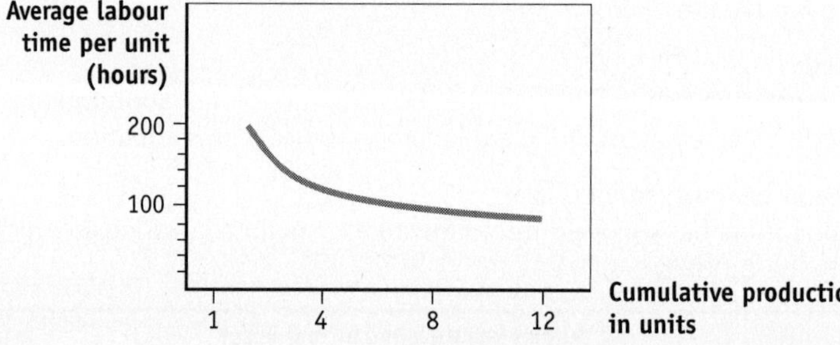

Required:

1 What will be the *average* labour time required to assemble and test each satellite when the company has produced four satellites? Eight satellites?

2 What will be the *total* labour time required to assemble and test all satellites produced if the firm manufactures only four satellites? Eight satellites?

3 How can the learning curve be used in the company's budgeting process? In setting cost standards?

E3.39 Estimating cost behaviour using multiple methods: retailer

Garden Route Markets, a chain of small convenience grocery stores, has store hours that fluctuate from month to month as the tourist trade varies. The electricity costs for one of the company's stores are listed below for the past six months:

Month	Total hours of operation	Total electricity cost (R)
January	550	3 240
February	600	3 400
March	700	3 800
April	500	3 200
May	450	2 700
June	400	2 600

Required:

1 Use the high–low method to estimate the cost behaviour for the store's electricity costs. Express the cost behaviour in formula form ($Y = a + bX$). What is the variable electricity cost per hour of operation?

2 Use regression analysis to estimate the cost behaviour for the store's electricity costs. Express the cost behaviour in equation form. What is the variable electricity cost per hour of operation?
3 During July, the store will be open 470 hours. Predict the store's total electricity cost for July using each of the cost estimation methods employed in requirements 1 and 2.

E3.40 Regression analysis: airline

Recent monthly costs of providing inboard flight service incurred by African Star Airlines are shown below:

Month	Thousands of passengers	Cost of inboard flight service (in R'000)
April	16	540
May	17	540
June	16	570
July	18	600
August	15	540
September	17	570

Required:

1 Use regression analysis to estimate the cost behaviour of the airline's inboard flight service. Express the relationship in equation form. (*Hint*: When interpreting the regression, remember that the data are given in thousands.)
2 Evaluate the regression equation.

Problems

P3.41 Cost drivers: service firm

The Mary Ellen Hospice provides services for terminally ill patients and their families. The hospice provides an accommodation unit for up to six patients and a support service for outpatients. In preparing next year's budget, the accountant is analysing the behaviour of the hospice's major costs, listed below, and seeking possible cost drivers.

(a) The salary of the administrator who manages the hospice and assists in the accommodation unit.
(b) The salaries of the domiciliary support staff who are employed on a casual basis to visit patients at home.
(c) The salary of the physiotherapist who visits the hospice each week to run a three-hour exercise clinic available to accommodation patients and outpatients.
(d) The salary of the anaesthetist who visits the hospice each week to develop and monitor pain management programs for patients.
(e) The lease payments on the two cars used by the domiciliary support staff.
(f) The cost of petrol used by the domestic support cars.
(g) Depreciation costs on pain relief medication pumps. These pumps are used within the accommodation unit, and are hired to outpatients on a weekly basis. Pumps are purchased as required and depreciated using a straight line method.
(h) The rent paid for the hospice buildings.
(i) The salaries of the nurses who work in the accommodation unit. One nurse is rostered for each shift and there are three shifts per day.
(j) The cost of the cleaning contract for the hospice, which results in a set payment each month.

Required:

1 For each cost, suggest two possible cost drivers, giving your reasons.

2 Can we use the unit–batch–product–facility hierarchy to analyse these costs? Where possible, classify each cost as unit, batch, product or facility level.

P3.42 Cost drivers: manufacturer

Soweto Press Pty Ltd produces a number of products, including a weekly paper called the *Soweto Times*, business cards to customers' specifications, and pre-printed stationery. In preparing next year's budget the accountant is analysing the behaviour of the company's major costs, listed below, and seeking possible cost drivers.

(a) The cost of paper used in the *Times*. Each week's edition comprises 40 pages.

(b) The cost of card used in business cards.

(c) The salary of the *Times*' editor.

(d) The depreciation on the printing presses. The cost of presses is depreciated on the basis of units of production.

(e) The cost of the lease on the company's building.

(f) The cost of setting up the presses.

(g) The cost of the leasing and the running of the delivery trucks, which deliver the *Times* to wholesale customers each week. Business cards and pre-printed stationery are picked up by customers.

(h) The salary of the company manager.

(i) The cost of the graphic artist who designs customers' business cards. This person is not an employee of Soweto Press but is paid a set amount per card design.

(j) The cost of an external marketing consultant who seeks advertising for the *Times*. This person is paid a percentage of advertising revenue.

Required:

1 For each cost, suggest two possible cost drivers, giving your reasons.

2 Can we use the unit–batch–product–facility hierarchy to analyse these costs? Where possible, classify each cost as unit, batch, product or facility level.

P3.43 Cost drivers: school

The Yamaha School of Music has hired you as a consultant to help in analysing the behaviour of, and budgeting, the school's costs. The school conducts music classes after school hours, and on Saturdays. You plan to use the account classification method of cost estimation to classify each of the following costs as variable, fixed or semivariable. However, before classifying the costs, you must sort out cost drivers.

Required:

Choose cost drivers for each of the following costs:

1 Repairs on musical instruments. The school employs a full-time repair technician. Repair jobs that are beyond the technician's capability are taken to a local musical instrument dealer for repairs.

2 Fee charged by a local public accounting firm to audit the school's accounting records. This fee is based on an estimate of the time taken for the audit, which, in turn, is influenced by the school's number of transactions for the year.

3 Salaries and on-costs of the school's full-time administrative staff.

4 Cost of buying books, sheet music and other academic materials that are supplied to each student by the school.

5 Salaries and on-costs of the school's full-time teachers.

6 Wages of the school's part-time assistant recital instructors. These employees are hired on a casual basis. For each student enrolled in the school's music programs, four hours of assistant instructor time are needed per week.

7 Straight-line depreciation on the school's musical instruments. Most students own their own instruments. The school holds a bank of instruments used largely by the full-time teachers.

8 Rent for the building in which the school operates.
9 Electricity for the school. The school pays a fixed monthly charge plus R0.10 per kilowatt hour of electricity.

P3.44 Cost behaviour patterns in a variety of settings

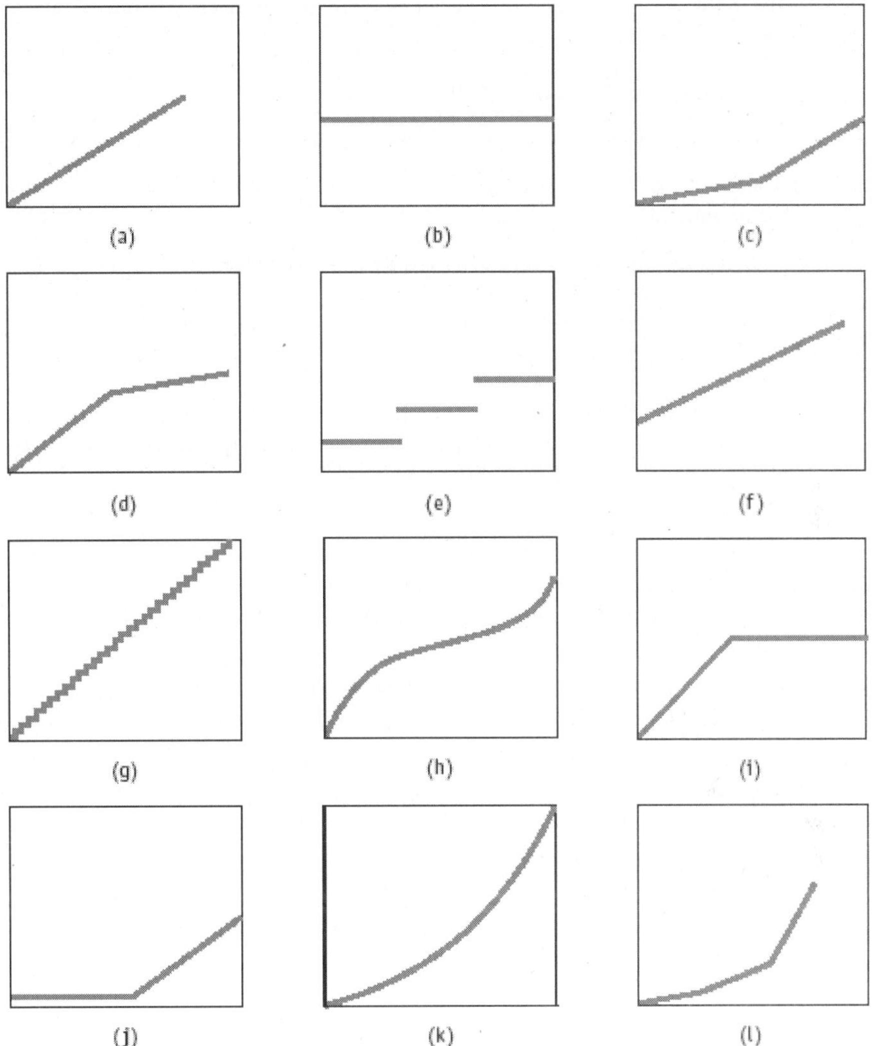

For each of the following cost items (1 through 11), choose the graph (a) through (l) that best represents it:

1 The cost of electricity at a university. For low student enrolments, electricity costs increase with enrolment, but at a decreasing rate. For large student enrolments, electricity costs increase at an increasing rate.
2 The cost of telephone service, which is based on the number of message units per month. The charge is R0.79 per message unit, for up to 650 message units. Additional message units (above 650) are free.
3 The cost of outsourcing diagnostic blood testing by a hospital. The hospital pays an independent lab a fee of R1000 per month plus R3 for each test done.

4 The salary costs of the shift supervisors at a truck depot. Each shift is eight hours. The depot operates with one, two, or three shifts at various times of the year.
5 The salaries of the security personnel at a factory. The security guards are on duty around the clock.
6 The wages of waiters in a restaurant. The employees are part-time workers, who can be called upon for as little as two hours at a time.
7 The cost of electricity during peak-demand periods is based on the following schedule:

Up to 10 000 kilowatt-hours (kWh)	R0.90 per kWh
Above 10 000 kilowatt-hours	R1.12 per kWh

The price schedule is designed to discourage overuse of electricity during periods of peak demand.

8 The cost of sheet metal used to manufacture automobiles.
9 The cost of chartering a private airplane. The cost is R4100 per hour for the first three hours of a flight. Then the charge drops to R3050 per hour.
10 Under a licensing agreement with an Indonesian import/export company, your firm has begun shipping machine tools to several countries. The terms of the agreement call for an annual licensing fee of R95 000 to be paid to the Indonesian import company if total exports are under R4 500 000. For sales in excess of R4 500 000, an additional licensing fee of 9 per cent of sales is due.
11 Your winery exports wine to several Indian Ocean islands. In one island, you must pay a tariff for every case of wine brought into the country. The tariff schedule is the following:

0 to 6000 cases per year	R11 per case
6001 to 12 000 cases per year	R14 per case
Above 12 000 cases per year	R19 per case

P3.45 Cost behaviour; engineered cost; committed and discretionary costs: manufacturer

Racy Rugs designs and manufactures funky floor rugs and decorates them with customised designs. For each cost listed below:

(a) Indicate whether it is variable or fixed.
(b) If the cost is variable, indicate whether it is an engineered cost. Explain why.
(c) If the cost is fixed, indicate whether it is committed or discretionary. Explain why.

Costs:

1 Cost of a new company advertising sign placed in front of the factory.
2 Wages of the employee who maintains the weaving machines.
3 Cost of the wool that is used to manufacture the rugs.
4 Salary of the managing director.
5 Cost of electricity used in the sewing department.
6 Wages of the staff who package the finished rugs.
7 Salaries of the marketing staff.
8 Depreciation on the sewing machines, calculated using the straight line method.
9 Rent on the factory building.
10 Cost of daily advertisements in the local newspapers.
11 Wages of the rug designers who experiment with new fabrics and designs.
12 Cost of car hire to take the managing director to important meetings.
13 Cost of the yearly staff Christmas party.
14 Cost of repairing the gas furnace.
15 Cost of workers' compensation insurance paid for the production employees.
16 Wages of the production employees who weave the rugs.

P3.46 Multiple regression analysis: service firm

Speedy Copy Centre operates a chain of photocopy centres near several major universities. The firm's accountant is accumulating data to be used in preparing its annual budget for the coming year. The cost behaviour pattern of the firm's equipment maintenance costs must be determined. Data regarding number of photocopies, maintenance hours and costs for last year are as follows:

Month	Number of photocopies	Hours of maintenance service	Maintenance costs
January	80 000	525	R4 710
February	68 000	505	4 310
March	69 000	310	2 990
April	64 000	495	4 200
May	90 000	315	3 000
June	85 000	485	4 215
July	55 000	315	2 950
August	85 000	405	3 680
September	62 000	475	4 100
October	82 000	345	3 250
November	60 000	350	3 260
December	70 000	335	3 015
Total	870 000	4860	R43 680
Average	72 500	405	R3 640

Required:

1 Use multiple regression analysis to estimate the behaviour of Speedy Copy Centre's maintenance costs.
2 Calculate R^2 and interpret this statistic.
3 Calculate the total variable cost and the fixed cost per maintenance hour at 500 hours of maintenance and 85 000 photocopies. Explain the problems that might occur when using fixed cost per hour in decisions.

(CMA, adapted)

P3.47 Interpreting regression analysis in cost estimation: catering company

Samuel Buthelezi owns a catering company that prepares banquets and parties for business functions throughout the year. Buthelezi's business is seasonal, with a heavy schedule during the summer months and the year-end holidays. During peak periods there are extra costs. However, even during non-peak periods Buthelezi must work more to cover his expenses. One of the major events that Buthelezi's customers request is a cocktail party. He offers a standard cocktail party and has developed the following cost structure on a per-person basis:

Food and beverages	28.00
Labour (0.6 hours @ R22 per hour)	13.20
Overhead (0.6 hours @ R28 per hour)	16.80
Total cost per person	58.00

When bidding on cocktail parties, Buthelezi adds a 15 per cent mark-up to this cost structure as a profit margin. Buthelezi is quite certain about his estimates of the prime costs but is not as comfortable with the overhead estimate. This estimate was based on the actual data for the past 12 months presented in the following table. These data indicate that overhead expenses vary with the direct labour hours expended. The R28 per hour overhead estimate was determined by dividing total overhead expended for the 12 months (R1.61 million) by total labour hours (57 600) and rounding to the nearest Rand.

Month	Labour hours	Overhead costs (R)
January	2 800	118 000
February	2 500	110 000
March	3 000	120 000
April	4 500	134 000
May	4 200	128 000
June	6 500	148 000
July	5 500	142 000
August	7 000	150 000
September	7 500	154 000
October	4 500	136 000
November	3 100	124 000
December	6 500	146 000

Buthelezi recently attended a meeting of the local chamber of commerce and heard a business consultant discuss regression analysis and its business applications. After the meeting, Buthelezi decided to do a regression analysis of the overhead data he had collected. The following results were obtained:

Intercept (*a*)	96 000
Coefficient (*b*)	8

Required:

1 Explain the difference between the overhead rate originally estimated by Buthelezi and the overhead rate developed from the regression method.
2 Using data from the regression analysis, determine the variable cost per person for a cocktail party.
3 Buthelezi has been asked to prepare a bid for a 250-person cocktail party to be given next month. Determine the minimum bid price that Buthelezi should be willing to submit.
4 What other factors should Buthelezi consider in developing the bid price for the cocktail party?

(CMA, adapted)

P3.48 Evaluation of cost estimation models: retailer

Motomation Pty Ltd plans to acquire several retail automotive parts stores as part of its expansion program. Motomation carries out an extensive review of possible acquisitions prior to making any decision to approach a specific company. Projections of future financial performance are one of the aspects of such a review. One form of projection relies heavily on using past performance (normally 10 prior years) to estimate future performance.

Currently, Motomation is conducting a review of Atlas Auto Parts, a regional chain of retail automotive parts stores. Among the financial data to be projected for Atlas is the future rental cost for its stores. The schedule below presents the rent and revenues (both in millions of Rands) for the past 10 years.

Year	Revenues (Rm)	Annual rent expense (Rm)
1	22	1.00
2	24	1.15
3	36	1.40
4	27	1.10
5	43	1.55
6	33	1.25
7	45	1.65
8	48	1.60
9	61	1.80
10	60	1.95

The following three methods were trialled for estimating future rental expense:

Method A
A regression analysis using time as the independent variable was performed. The resulting formula is as follows:

Rental expense = 0.93 + 0.0936 T

where T = the year

Method B
The annual rental expense was related to annual revenues, using regression analysis. The formula for predicting rental expense in this case is as follows:

Rental expense = 0.5597 + 0.02219 X

where X is equal to revenues divided by 1 000 000 (for example, X for Year 10 is 60).

Method C
Rental expense was calculated as a percentage of revenues using the average for the 10-year period.

Required:
1 Calculate for each of the three methods the rental expense estimate for Atlas Auto Parts for the next year, assuming the projected revenue will be the same as the Year 10 revenue (that is, R60 million).
2 Discuss the advantages and disadvantages of each of the three methods for estimating the rental expense for Atlas Auto Parts.
3 Identify one method from A, B or C that you would recommend Motomation to use in order to estimate rental expense. Explain why you selected this method, using the two criteria for evaluating regression equations outlined in the chapter.

(CMA, adapted)

P3.49 Task analysis; cost estimation with different methods: wholesaler
Saldanha Marine Supply is a wholesaler for a large variety of boating and fishing equipment. The company's accountant has recently completed a cost study of the firm's material-handling department, in which he used task analysis to quantify the department's activity. The cost driver used in the study was the number of hundreds of kilograms of equipment unloaded or loaded at the company's loading dock. The accountant compiled the following data:

Month	Cost driver (100 kg of equipment)	Material Handling Department costs (R)
January	1 800	117 000
February	1 600	113 000
March	1 300	112 500
April	1 000	102 000
May	2 200	111 000
June	2 400	125 500
July	2 000	120 000
August	1 800	114 000
September	2 600	121 200
October	1 100	110 500
November	1 200	113 500
December	1 400	113 500

Required:
1 Draw a scatter diagram of the cost data for the Material Handling Department.
2 Estimate the Material Handling Department's cost behaviour using the high–low method. Use an equation to express the results of this estimation method.

3 Estimate the variable and fixed components of the department's cost-behaviour pattern using regression analysis.
4 Write a brief memo to the company's managing director explaining why the cost estimates developed in requirements 2 and 3 differ.
5 Predict the company's material handling costs for a month when 230 000 kilograms of equipment is recorded. Use each of your cost equations to make the prediction. Which prediction would you prefer to use? Why?

P3.50 Comparing regression and high–low estimates: manufacturer

The accountant of Athlone Electronics Company believes that the identification of the variable and fixed components of the firm's costs will enable the firm to make better planning and control decisions. Among the costs the accountant is concerned about is the behaviour of indirect materials cost. She believes that machine hours are a cost driver for indirect materials costs.

A member of the accountant's staff has suggested that regression analysis be used to determine the cost behaviour of indirect materials. The following regression equation was developed from 40 pairs of observations:

S = R200 + R4 H

where S = total monthly costs of indirect materials

H = machine hours per month

Required:

1 Explain the meaning of '200' and '4' in the regression equation S = R200 + R4 H.
2 Calculate the estimated cost of indirect materials if 900 machine hours are to be used during a month.
3 To determine the validity of the cost estimate calculated in requirement 2, what questions would you ask the accountant about the data used for the regression?
4 Consider three other activities that could be used as cost drivers to predict the total monthly costs of indirect materials.

(CMA, adapted)

P3.51 Learning curve (appendix): manufacturer

Mzansi Fine Furniture manufactures high-quality furniture. During the past year, the company's design department developed a new product, a marble-topped dining table. This would be the first time that Mzansi would work with marble. The company's existing products were made of timber, sometimes in conjunction with glass. The design department selected a team of experienced tradespersons to manufacture a trial batch of 10 marble-topped tables. A task analysis of the processes used to produce this batch of tables indicated the following direct inputs and average costs per table:

Direct material	R900
Direct labour	600

The average hourly labour rate for the team of tradespersons was R60 per hour.

Required:

Assuming an '80 per cent learning curve':

1 Estimate how many direct labour hours will be required to produce a second batch of 10 marble-topped dining tables.
2 What is the direct labour cost per table for this second batch?
3 Will the last table produced in the second batch take the same amount of direct labour time as did the first table in the batch? Why?
4 Assume that after completing and selling these first two batches Mzansi receives an order from a wholesaler for a batch of 60 tables. How many direct labour hours will be required to produce this batch of tables?

5 What is the direct labour cost per table for the order from the wholesaler?
6 Mzansi uses a 'cost plus margin' approach to pricing its products. What implications does the learning curve effect have for the price of the marble-topped dining table?

Cases

C3.52 Multiple regression: hospital

'I don't understand this cost report at all,' exclaimed Jeff Mahoney, the newly-appointed administrator of Nguni General Hospital. 'Our administrative costs in the new paediatrics clinic are all over the map. One month the report shows R24 900, and the next month it's R48 300. What's going on?'

Mahoney's question was posed to Megan Smit, the hospital's accountant. 'The main problem is that the clinic has experienced some widely varying patient loads in its first year of operation. There seems to be some confusion in the public's mind about what services we offer in the clinic. When do they come to the clinic? When do they go to the outpatients' department? That sort of thing. As the patient load has varied, we've frequently changed our clinic administrative staffing. Also, we have found that the number of emergency procedures varies each month and emergency procedures cause additional staff costs.'

Mahoney continued to puzzle over the report. 'Could you pull some data together, Megan, so we can see how this cost behaves over a range of patient loads and over various emergency procedure loads?'

'You'll have it this afternoon,' Smit responded. Later that morning, she gathered the following data:

Month	Number of emergency procedures	Patient load	Adminstrative cost (R)
January	10	900	33 600
February	11	1 100	36 600
March	5	400	18 300
April	10	800	34 200
May	12	1 200	39 300
June	14	1 400	47 700
July	8	700	27 000
August	7	500	24 000
September	12	1 000	36 000
October	12	1 200	41 700
November	8	800	30 900
December	16	1 500	54 300

Smit does not believe that the first year's widely fluctuating patient load will be experienced again in the future. She has estimated that the clinic's relevant range of monthly activity in the future will be 600 to 1200 patients.

Required:

1 Use regression analysis to estimate how patient load predicts administrative cost.
2 Use multiple regression to estimate how both activities—patient load and the number of emergency procedures—predict administrative cost.
3 Does the inclusion of the additional cost driver of 'emergency procedures' improve the model? Explain your answer.

4 How confident should Smit be about the two cost models that she has developed? Explain your answer.

C3.53 Interpreting regression analysis; activity-based costing: service firm

Grassmere Pty Ltd provides commercial landscaping services. Linda Radebe, the firm's owner, wants to develop cost estimates that she can use to prepare bids on jobs. After analysing the firm's costs, Radebe has developed the following preliminary cost estimates for each 1000 square metres of landscaping:

Cost estimate per 1000 sq. metres	R
Direct materials	780
Direct labour (5 direct labour hours @ R22 per hour)	110
Overhead (@ R36 per direct labour hour)	180
Total cost per 1000 square metres	1070

Radebe is quite certain about the estimates for direct materials and direct labour, but she is not as comfortable with the overhead estimate. As indirect costs, overhead costs cannot be traced directly to landscaping. Instead, Radebe has used a common method of estimating an overhead rate per direct labour hour. However, the estimate for overhead is based on the overhead costs that were incurred during the past 12 months, as presented in the schedule below. The estimate of R36 per direct labour hour was determined by dividing the total overhead costs for the 12 month period (R2 592 000) by the total direct labour hours (72 000).

Month	Total overhead (R)	Regular direct labour hours	Overtime direct labour hours*	Total direct labour hours
January	216 000	5 820	380	6 200
February	188 000	4 760	40	4 800
March	192 000	4 420	80	4 500
April	224 000	5 180	420	5 600
May	228 000	6 060	940	7 000
June	260 000	6 480	1 520	8 000
July	256 000	6 760	1 240	8 000
August	224 000	6 100	700	6 800
September	212 000	5 520	80	5 600
October	188 000	5 540	60	5 600
November	188 000	4 240	60	4 300
December	216 000	5 120	480	5 600
Total	2 592 000	66 000	6 000	72 000

*The overtime premium is 50 per cent of the direct labour wage rate

Radebe believes that overhead is affected by total monthly direct labour hours. She decided to perform a regression analysis of overhead (*OH*) on total direct labour hours (*DLH*). The following regression formula was obtained:

$OH = R104\,805 + R18.53DLH$

Required:

1 The overhead rate developed from the regression analysis is different from Linda Radebe's preliminary estimate of R36 per direct labour hour. Explain the difference in the two overhead rates.

2 Using the overhead formula that was derived from the regression analysis, determine a total variable cost estimate for each 1000 square metres of landscaping.

3 Linda Radebe has been asked to submit a bid on a landscaping project for Cape Town City Council consisting of 50 000 square metres. Radebe estimates that 30 per cent of the direct labour hours required for the project will be on overtime. Calculate the variable costs per

1000 metres of landscaping that should be included in any bid that Radebe would submit on this project. Use the overhead formula derived from the regression analysis.

4 Should Grassmere rely on the overhead formula derived from the regression analysis as the basis for the variable overhead component of its cost estimate? Explain your answer.

5 After attending a seminar on activity-based costing, Radebe decided on a further analysis of Grassmere's activities and costs. She discovered that a more accurate portrayal of the firm's cost behaviour could be achieved by dividing overhead into three separate cost pools—administration, seeding and individual planting—each with its own cost driver. A separate regression equation was estimated for each overhead cost pool, with the following results:

Administration OH_1 = R40 000 + R8.30DLH

where DLH denotes direct labour hours

Seeding OH_2 = R36 400 + R27.20STS

where STS denotes the number of square metres of turf seeded (in thousands)

Planting OH_3 = R32 000 + R11.80PL

where PL denotes the number of individual plantings (such as trees and shrubs)

Assume that 5 direct labour hours are needed to landscape each 1000 square metres, regardless of the specific planting material that is used.

(a) Suppose the landscaping project for the city will involve seeding all 50 000 square metres of turf and planting 70 trees and shrubs. Calculate the variable overhead cost that Radebe should include in the bid.

(b) Recalculate the variable overhead cost for the city's landscaping project, assuming that half of the 50 000 square metre landscaping area will be seeded and there will be 230 individual plantings.

(c) Explain why the costs differ in requirements (a) and (b).

C3.54 Multiple regression: service firm (continuation of Case 3.53)

After attending a seminar on activity-based costing, Radebe decided to undertake a more sophisticated analysis of Grassmere's costs. After discussions with some of the landscapers who work within the firm, Radebe came to the conclusion that there were three possible cost drivers that could be used to predict total overhead cost—direct labour hours (*DLH*), the number of square metres of turf seeded (*STS*), and the number of individual trees and shrubs planted (*TSP*).

Radebe has access to the additional data below:

Month	Square metres of turf	No. of individual plantings
January	48 000	50
February	44 000	30
March	44 000	40
April	51 000	65
May	53 000	35
June	55 000	50
July	60 000	60
August	50 000	16
September	52 000	40
October	45 000	37
November	46 000	40
December	51 000	60

Required:

Refer to the data in the previous case, as well as the additional data above.

1 Use the data for the three cost drivers to formulate a single multiple regression equation to predict total overhead cost.

2 Does the new cost model provide a more accurate estimate of total overhead cost compared to the equation formulated in the prior case? Explain your answer.
3 Consider which cost drivers should be included in the regression equation to provide the more accurate cost model. Explain your choice.

Endnotes

1 Not all organisations use the term 'cost driver'. Another commonly used term is 'cost allocation base'.

2 Alternatively, specific features of individual products, such as product design features, may drive these costs.

3 Remember, in activity-based costing, costs with no obvious cost driver are called 'facility level costs' (see Chapter 8).

4 Step-variable costs may also be defined. These are variable costs that vary in small steps, rather than increasing continuously. As long as the steps are small, step-variable costs can be approximated as variable costs.

5 Regression analysis is based on a series of assumptions, for example that the cost function is linear. Another assumption is that the distribution of the residuals around the regression line should approximate a normal distribution. Details of these assumptions can be found in statistics books such as Berenson, Levine & Krehbie (2001) or Hair, Anderson, Tatham & Black (1998).

6 The process for calculating R^2 using Excel® is explained in the appendix.

7 We have only scratched the surface of regression analysis as a tool for cost estimation. For an expanded discussion of ordinary least squares regression, see any statistics textbook, such as those cited in endnote 5.

8 In fact, in addition to the fixed costs, some of the variable costs in a conventional system may not really vary proportionally with production volume and may be more accurately classified as batch level, or possibly product level, costs.

9 See any standard statistics book, such as Berenson, Levine & Krehbie (2001) or Hair, Anderson, Tatham & Black (1998).

10 If you do not have *Data Analysis* on the *Tools* menu, **click** *Add-ins* on the *Tools* menu, **select** *Analysis ToolPak*, and **click** *OK*.

11 In the Excel regression results, a t statistic above 2 (for larger samples) will indicate that the coefficient is significant. Due to the limited sample size for our regression, a t statistic above approximately 2.20 would indicate that the coefficient is statistically significant.

12 This particular model of the learning curve, in which the cumulative average time per unit decreases by a constant percentage each time the cumulative quantity of output doubles, is known as the *cumulative average time learning model*. This is not the only model of learning curve effects, and an appropriate model can be selected only after careful consideration of the behaviour of labour usage as output increases.

CHAPTER 04 Product Costing Systems

❖ LEARNING OBJECTIVES

After completing this chapter, you should be able to:

1. explain the role of product costing systems;
2. describe why managers need different measures of product costs for different purposes;
3. outline the flow of costs through the manufacturing accounts used in product costing;
4. use basic techniques to allocate manufacturing overhead costs to products;
5. distinguish between job costing and process costing and understand in which situations job costing or process costing may be the most appropriate costing system;
6. estimate product costs using a job costing system;
7. describe the procedures and source documents used in a job costing system;
8. prepare journal entries to record the costs of direct labour, direct material and manufacturing overhead in a job costing system;
9. prepare a schedule of cost of goods manufactured and a schedule of cost of goods sold, and understand the relationship between these reports and external accounting reports;
10. estimate product costs using a basic process costing system;
11. prepare journal entries to record the costs of direct labour, direct material and manufacturing overhead in a basic process costing system;
12. after studying the appendix, explain how inventories must be valued for external financial reporting; and
13. after studying the appendix, prorate underapplied or overapplied overhead to various inventory accounts.

Introduction

Information about product costs is vital for managers in making decisions that create value for the business. It may also be important in planning, controlling and, more generally, managing resources. Managers at the South African Revenue Service may ask: 'What does it cost us to produce the "Tax Pack"? Is there a less expensive way of informing taxpayers about how to fill out their income tax returns?' The marketing manager at Toshiba may ask: 'What does it cost to produce the Tecra Notebook? Can we price it competitively and still make a profit?' The production manager at Samsung may ask: 'What has it cost to produce the D900 model of mobile phone this year? How does this compare with the planned cost for this product? What do we estimate our production costs to be next year?' The financial manager at BMW South Africa may wish to continuously monitor the cost of producing a 320i and if required to ensure that suppliers reduce the cost of components supplied to BMW. The financial accountant at Texas Instruments may ask: 'What was the cost of our inventory of calculators at the end of the year and what was the cost of goods sold during the year?'

In this chapter we begin our study of costing systems. Management accountants use costing systems to determine the costs of cost objects. Remember, cost objects are simply the things that managers want 'costed'. The costing systems used by most organisations have at least two cost objects: products (goods or services), and responsibility centres such as departments. In this chapter and the next we focus on costing products, and in Chapter 6 we consider how to estimate the cost of services. In Chapters 12 and 13 we explore the role that costing systems can play in performance reporting and responsibility accounting.

We begin this chapter by recognising that the elements included in a product cost should depend on the way the information is to be used. For example, a product cost used for long-term pricing will need to cover costs right across the value chain, whereas in the short term a business may be willing to accept orders that cover only production and downstream costs. We describe the flow of costs through the product costing system and outline the basic principles for allocating manufacturing overhead costs to products. As you work your way through this chapter, you will notice that the features of a product costing system depend on the nature of the production environment. There are two basic approaches: one called job costing, which focuses on estimating the cost of each job produced, and the other called process costing, which estimates a product's cost by focusing on the average cost of the production processes used to produce a product. We illustrate job costing with an example from Williams Elevators, and process costing using the example of Spritz soft drinks. In practice, many businesses operate in an environment that requires a combination of job and process costing features, but we will not explore this issue until Chapter 5.

L.O. 1

Product costing

A **product costing system** accumulates product-related costs and uses a series of procedures to assign them to the organisation's final products. Product-related costs include the costs incurred during the production process, called **production costs**. In some organisations, upstream costs of research and development, product design and supply, and downstream costs of marketing, distribution and customer service are also regarded as product-related. As Exhibit 4.1 shows, product costs are the output of the product costing system.

Different product costs for different purposes

L.O. 2

In Chapter 2 we explained that different concepts of product cost are appropriate for different purposes. While inventory valuations for external accounting reports are limited to manufacturing costs, managers often need a wider definition of product cost for decision-making. Exhibit 4.2 illustrates the different measures of product cost relevant to some common management decisions. External accounting reports require products (that is, inventory) to be valued at manufacturing cost. However, in making long-term decisions about products, such as which products to produce and

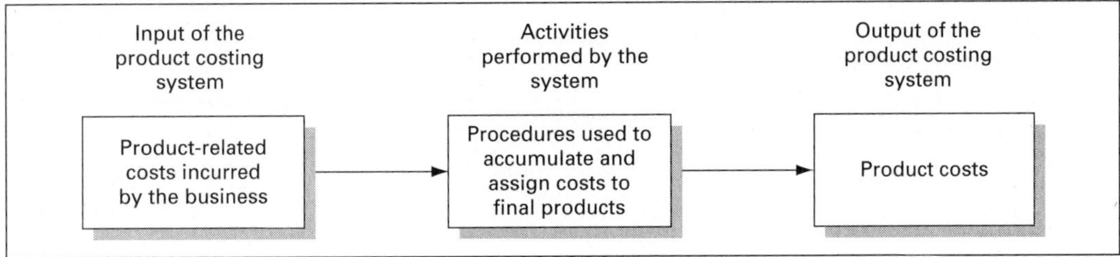

Exhibit 4.1 The product costing system

what price to set, managers need a complete picture of all the costs associated with the product. In the shorter term, particularly for existing products, the manager may ignore research and development and design costs, since they have already been incurred. In this case, the relevant product cost will include the manufacturing, marketing, distribution and customer service costs associated with the product. The two 'Real life' examples on the following pages illustrate the importance of product cost information across very different industries. One focuses on costing scholarly journals and the other on costing defence contracts.

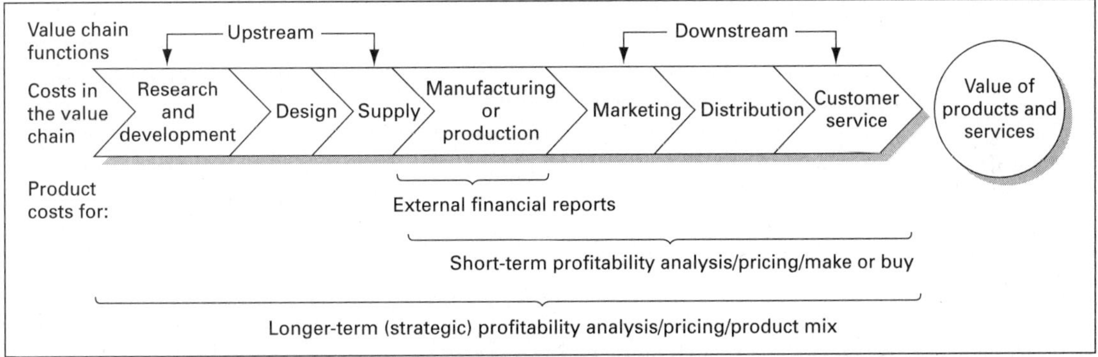

Exhibit 4.2 Relevance of product cost measures to management decisions

REAL LIFE: THE COST OF SCHOLARLY JOURNALS

As students, you may have spent many hours in your university library, reading articles from a range of scholarly journals. But did you know that the price that universities pay for journal subscriptions has increased by 730 per cent since the mid-1970s? This rise in prices has been caused by increases in the production and distribution costs of journals, and decreases in the number of personal subscriptions. (The prices of scholarly journals produced overseas and purchased in South Africa were also seriously affected by the decline in the value of the South African Rand in the 1990s and in 2001–2.) There are now some doubts over the continued economic viability of printed journals, and suggestions that electronic journals may be the solution to this problem. But there is some debate over the costs of electronic journals. The founder of *Psycoloquy*, one of the first electronic journals, claims that electronic publishing costs 70 per cent less than printed journals, as only two major costs remain: peer review and editing. Moreover, while the costs of printing are expected to rise over time, the costs of information technology are expected to decrease. However, others claim that editing and peer review are expensive processes and that there are also administrative and marketing costs for electronic publishing.

The library and computer centre staff of Tilburg University and Utrecht University in the Netherlands, supported by PricewaterhouseCoopers, set up a research project to establish the cost of publishing the *Electronic Journal of Comparative Law*. A general costing model was developed to estimate the direct and indirect costs of publishing an electronic journal. The model included 'creation of material' (such as authors, editors and reviewers), 'publications' (for example editing, training and marketing), 'facilities' (computers and networks), 'general overhead' (buildings and management), and user costs (personal computers and Internet connections).

The model was used to estimate the cost of publishing the *Electronic Journal of Comparative Law*. Indirect costs were found to be relatively low. The major direct costs included website design and development costs, website programming costs and organisation maintenance costs for the electronic journal. 'Creation' costs were relatively low because authors and reviewers were not paid. The project team estimated that this electronic journal is likely to cost less than one half, and possibly as little as one quarter, of the cost of printed journals in the same field.

As the cost of scholarly journals has increased by about 10 per cent per year, university libraries have responded by purchasing fewer books and have been reducing the number of subscriptions to journal titles. It is interesting to note that academics produce the research which the commercial publishers then sell back to the universities increasingly in the form of bundles of printed journal titles and online subscriptions. Most journal titles are highly specialised and go by such titles as the *Journal of Comparative Neurology*. As libraries reduce subscriptions and the total number of subscribers to a journal falls, this means that the fixed cost component of a journal's total costs increases. Miller indicates that 60 per cent of scientific journals have fewer than 2500 subscribers and this means that fixed costs dominate the total cost of producing most journals. He further states, quoting research by Tenopir and King, that in the USA, 'the total cost per average journal subscription ranges from $70 for a journal with 10 000 subscribers to $775 for a journal with only 500 subscribers.' Miller refers to Tenopir and King's study that the average journal will have fixed costs of $400 000 per year (about R2.8 million) but according to Miller, the fixed cost of publishing an electronic journal is only $100 000 (about R700 000). Increasingly, professional non-profit societies of scientists are publishing journals at a significantly lower cost. The general product-costing model provides an important decision tool for managers in any organisation involved in, or contemplating, the publication of electronic journals.

Source: Miller, Lee N. (2000) 'Will Electronic Publishing Reduce the Cost of Scholarly Scientific Journals?', *Psycoloquy*: 11, 93

In addition to using product cost information to value inventory and for short-term and strategic decision-making, managers often use product costs for planning and controlling costs, and sometimes for claiming costs under cost reimbursement contracts. In these situations managers may focus primarily on production costs, although the scope of the analysis can be extended to include product-related costs from other areas of the value chain.

Although different product costs are appropriate for different types of decisions, sometimes management accountants provide only the product costs that are required for external reporting purposes. For example, in many small to medium-sized businesses there is only one accountant to perform both the financial and management accounting functions. Where resources are stretched, the financial accounting function, which is essential to meet external reporting and income tax requirements, may be given priority. In these firms, managers are deprived of valuable information for effective decision-making.

Current costs or future costs?

In establishing product costs the management accountant must consider whether to use current costs, as recorded in the general ledger, or estimates of future costs.[1] The appropriate timeframe depends on the way in which managers use the product cost information. Product costs used for

REAL LIFE: WHAT IS THE COST OF STADIUMS FOR THE 2010 FIFA WORLD CUP™

South Africa is hosting the 2010 FIFA World Cup™. This is the first time that the FIFA World Cup™ is to be hosted on the African continent and the event is expected to attract about 500 000 visitors to this country. The cumulative number of viewers is expected to be over 25 billion. When South Africa won the bid to host the FIFA World Cup™ in 2004, the expected cost of the event was just over R2 billion but this has increased to an expected cost of over R9 billion due to the construction of new stadiums rather than utilising the rugby stadiums as per the original bid. The cost of the new Green Point Stadium in Cape Town is expected to be between R2.3 and R3.3 billion but this has now been revised to R2.49 billion owing to changing specifications. We have used a figure of R2.8 billion in line with projections. What will the new stadiums cost in total and on a per seat basis?

	Cape Town	Durban	Nelspruit	Port Elizabeth	Johannesburg
Stadium	Green Point	King Senzangakhona	Mbombela	Nelson Mandela	Soccer City FNB (upgrade)
Projected cost	R2 800 000 000	R1 700 000 000	R1 100 000 000	R1 100 000 000	R1 300 000 000
No. of seats	68 000	70 000	45 000	45 000	94 700
Cost per seat	R41 176	R24 286	R24 444	R24 444	R13 728
US$ per seat	$5564.39	$3281.85	$3303.30	$3303.30	$1855.08

The cost of the Green Point stadium is significantly higher on a per seat basis than the other stadiums. Its cost is comparable to the cost of the Allianz stadium in Munich which is the home of two clubs: Bayern Munich and TSV 1860 München. The stadium's facade changes colour depending on who is playing.

How do these costs compare to other stadiums? The Allianz stadium in Munich cost about R40 000 per seat. The Beijing stadium cost about R23 000 per seat while the Arsenal Emirates stadium cost about R25 500 per seat. Wembley has incurred cost over-runs and will finally cost about – wait for it – R120 000 per seat. Think about that when you are watching the FA Cup Final. Each spectator is sitting on a seat that effectively cost R120 000.

We need to consider that attendances at domestic soccer matches are low and government will wish to ensure that the stadiums do not become 'white elephants' after the FIFA World Cup™. Sustainability is important as the experience of Korea and Japan has not been without problems in relation to sustainability. The cost of any stadium is not only its construction cost. There will be the ongoing costs of maintenance after the event. In Japan and Korea, the ongoing maintenance costs of the stadiums built for the 2002 FIFA World Cup™ have become an issue. The cost of annual maintenance for one of the stadiums in Japan is R20 million per year.

The ongoing benefits of improved facilities, infrastructure, new roads, and new transportation systems such as the Gautrain will add impetus to the South African economy. People will argue that a developing country should rather spend its money on housing. Others will say that hosting the FIFA World Cup™ is the stuff that dreams are made of and that there is more to life than simply analysing costs.

making decisions should reflect expectations about future costs, as managers make decisions about what to do in the future, not the past! For example, selling prices may be set to cover the expected costs of making a product in the future. Current costs may provide a reliable indicator of future costs, but they may also need to be adjusted for expectations about inflation, competitors' actions and so on. When used for planning, costs should also reflect the costs expected in the future. In contrast, product costs used for inventory valuation or cost reimbursement will be based on current costs, which are objective and verifiable.

How often do managers need product cost information?

There is one more characteristic that varies: the frequency with which managers require estimates of product costs. Estimates of product costs for long-term decisions will be required infrequently—when strategic plans are being developed or revised. Even short-term decisions about products may be made irregularly. In contrast, product costs for control and for inventory valuation are required regularly, possibly monthly. Likewise, managers may choose to monitor product profitability on a regular basis.

To summarise, managers use product cost information in many different ways. Depending on how managers intend to use this information, product costs may differ over:

- the range of costs included;
- whether current costs or future costs are included; and
- how frequently the information is required.

Designing product-costing systems

What does all this mean for the management accountant?

- In designing a product costing system, the management accountant must identify managers' needs.
- All product cost information may not come from one product costing system. For example, the product costing system may be set up to provide inventory valuations. It may be expanded to include some upstream and downstream costs. However, to use this information for decision-making, the management accountant will have to assess its relevance to the future. Some businesses set up a separate system for estimating future product costs, especially for quoting and tendering for jobs; others use special studies to develop product costs for decision-making, particularly for longer-term decisions. In Chapter 15 we describe an approach to product costing, called *life cycle costing,* which provides useful information for making longer-term decisions about products.
- As always, in deciding what information to provide and how to provide it, the management accountant must make a careful assessment of the costs and benefits of providing the various estimates of product cost.

Product costing in practice

Most businesses need some information about product costs. The range of costs included within a product costing system varies from one organisation to another. The more upstream and downstream costs covered by the system, the more comprehensive will be the picture of product costs. In practice, many businesses, particularly small to medium-sized manufacturing businesses, confine their product costing systems to manufacturing costs. These costing systems produce the inventory valuations for external reporting required by South African and international accounting standards. Any additional product-related costs must be identified through special studies. Often, smaller businesses do not have the resources for special studies, and managers may rely on product costs developed for external reporting for making a whole range of decisions. This does not seem ideal, although it must reflect management's assessment of the costs and benefits of obtaining more relevant product cost information! The inadequacy of product costing in small businesses is acknowledged in the following 'Real life'.

REAL LIFE: PRODUCT COSTING IN SMALL BUSINESS

The Department of Trade and Industry (DTI) has formed the Small Enterprise Development Agency (seda) to promote and support small business in South Africa. Seda produces fact sheets to assist entrepreneurs. The following are extracts from fact sheets that focus on product costs:

Itemise the equipment involved, as you will have to cost each item for your financial plan. Describe how long this equipment generally lasts and how much maintenance it requires;

Describe the materials and components that you will consume in the manufacturing process, and estimate what is used in each product. This could range from square metres of wooden board to litres of paint or grams of glue. This will lay the foundation for forecasting your unit cost in your financial plan;

If you produce goods to order, then you will have a deadline to meet and you can organise the production of that batch of goods like a project, giving attention to:

Scheduling – draw up a timetable highlighting the times at which the various phases of the job can be started and when they must be completed;

Estimating the amount of materials, the number of employees, and all the associated costs;

Controlling costs as the project proceeds, ensuring that there is no significant over-spending;

Controlling the purchase and utilisation of materials in line with the project estimates.

Source: www.seda.org.za

As pricing may be driven by product costs, this makes it critical that a small business enterprise should accurately estimate its costs in order to ensure that it remains profitable. Undercharging by small business enterprises is often a problem due to firms understating the costs of producing and marketing a product.

Flow of costs in manufacturing businesses

L.O. 3

Product costing systems will differ from one business to the next. Let's begin by considering the flow of costs in a manufacturing business that uses its product costing system to value inventory. Remember, this is the purpose of the product costing system in many businesses, particularly small businesses.

Assigning manufacturing costs to products

When used for inventory valuation, product costing systems assign manufacturing costs to products, as required by the International Financial Reporting standards. (The requirements of the International Financial Reporting standard for inventory valuation are summarised in Part 1 of the appendix to this chapter.) **Manufacturing costs** consist of direct material, direct labour and manufacturing overhead. The system involves several manufacturing ledger accounts:

- As raw materials are purchased, they are charged (debited) to the **raw material inventory** account.
- As production takes place, all manufacturing costs are charged (debited) to the **work in process inventory** account. Work in process is partially completed inventory. For example, as raw materials are used in production, the cost of those materials is transferred

from the raw material inventory account to the work in process inventory account. Direct labour and manufacturing overhead costs are accounted for in a similar fashion.

- When products are completed, their product costs are transferred from work in process inventory to the **finished goods inventory**.
- When products are sold, the product cost of the inventory is transferred from finished goods to **cost of goods sold expense**.
- Finally, cost of goods sold is closed to the **profit and loss account** at the end of the accounting period, along with all other expenses and revenues of the period.

Exhibit 4.3 depicts the flow of costs through the manufacturing accounts.

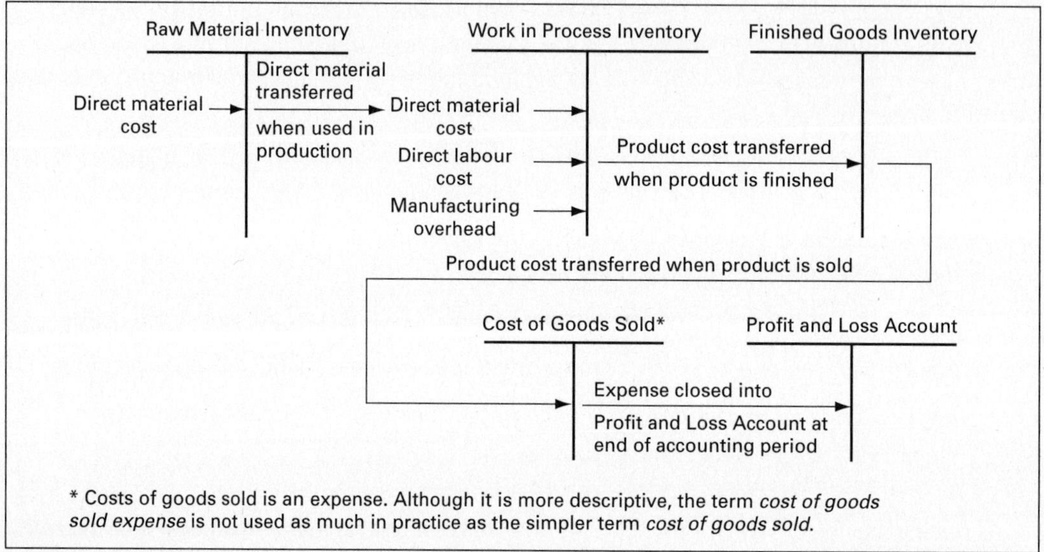

Exhibit 4.3 Flow of costs through manufacturing accounts

Example of manufacturing cost flows

Suppose that Bradley Paper Pty Ltd incurred the following manufacturing costs during the past year:

Direct material purchased	R45 million
Direct material used in production	30 million
Direct labour	20 million
Manufacturing overhead	40 million

During this period, products costing R60 million were finished, and products costing R25 million were sold for R32 million. Exhibit 4.4 shows the flow of costs through Bradley Paper's manufacturing accounts and the effect of the firm's product costs on its balance sheet and income statement.

Assigning upstream and downstream costs

Accounting standards require that, when valuing inventory, upstream costs (such as development, design and supply costs) and downstream costs (such as marketing, distribution and customer service costs) are expensed in the period in which they are incurred. However, some businesses extend their product costing system to include any product-related upstream and downstream costs to support managers' decision needs better. Including these costs gives managers a more comprehensive picture of the costs caused by products and, therefore, better information to support decisions such as those concerning which products to produce and what prices to set. For example,

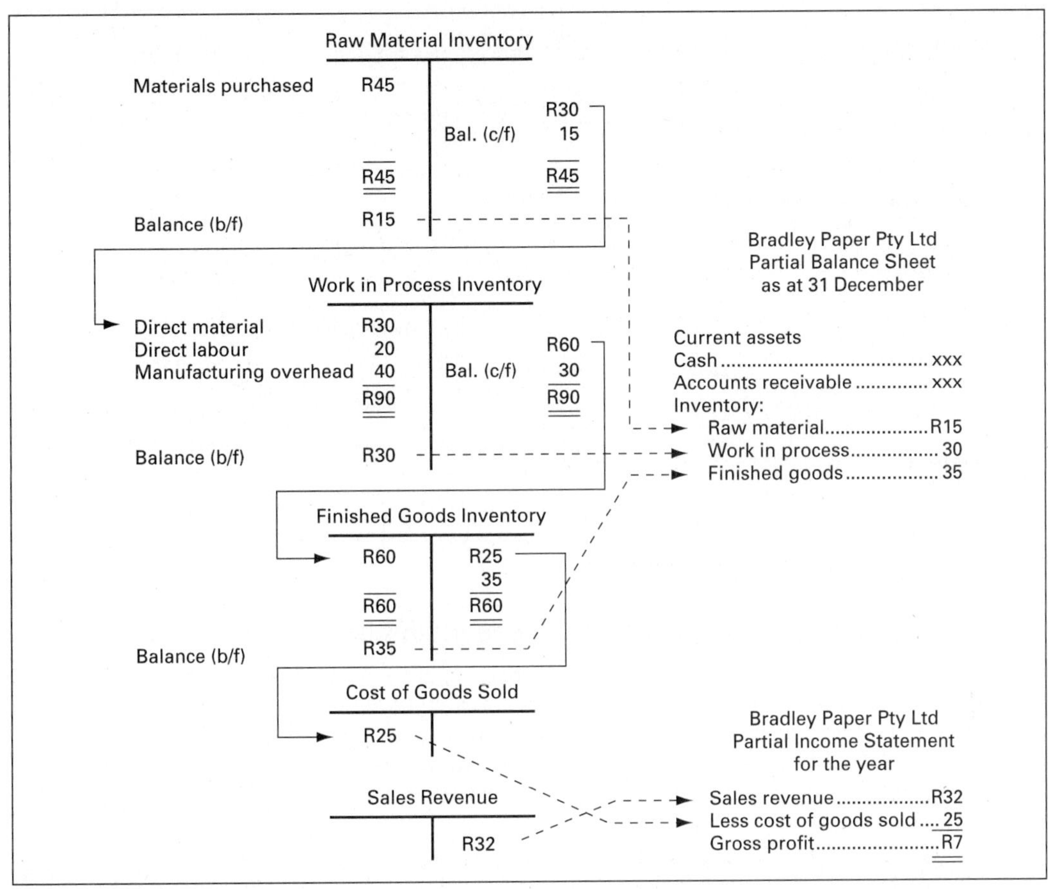

Exhibit 4.4 Example of manufacturing cost flows for Bradley Paper Pty Ltd (figures in millions)

ABI, the bottler of the Coca-Cola range of soft drinks in South Africa, tracks marketing costs to individual product lines, such as Coke, Sprite, Powerade, Appletizer, Valpre and Fanta. The company, which is part of the SABMiller group, can then assess the profitability of each product line and make decisions about which products to produce and promote. The 'Real life' overleaf on SABMiller provides another example of this broader approach to product costing.

Allocating overhead costs to products

L.O. 4

In estimating the cost of a product, we need to identify the cost of the resources used by the product. Some of these resources, such as direct material and direct labour, are consumed *directly* by products, and their costs can be *traced directly* to each product. In contrast, overhead costs, such as the cost of production supervisors and factory insurance, are essential to production but do not have any observable relationship with the product. These are *indirect* costs of products, which cannot be traced; instead they must be allocated. The major difficulty in costing both goods and services is how to allocate overhead costs. Exhibit 4.5 outlines the way in which direct and indirect costs are traced and allocated to products. Below, we give a brief outline of the procedures for allocating overhead costs to products in conventional costing systems. Activity-based costing has been proposed as an alternative approach for assigning overhead costs to products. We discuss overhead issues in more detail in Chapter 7, and activity-based costing in Chapter 8.

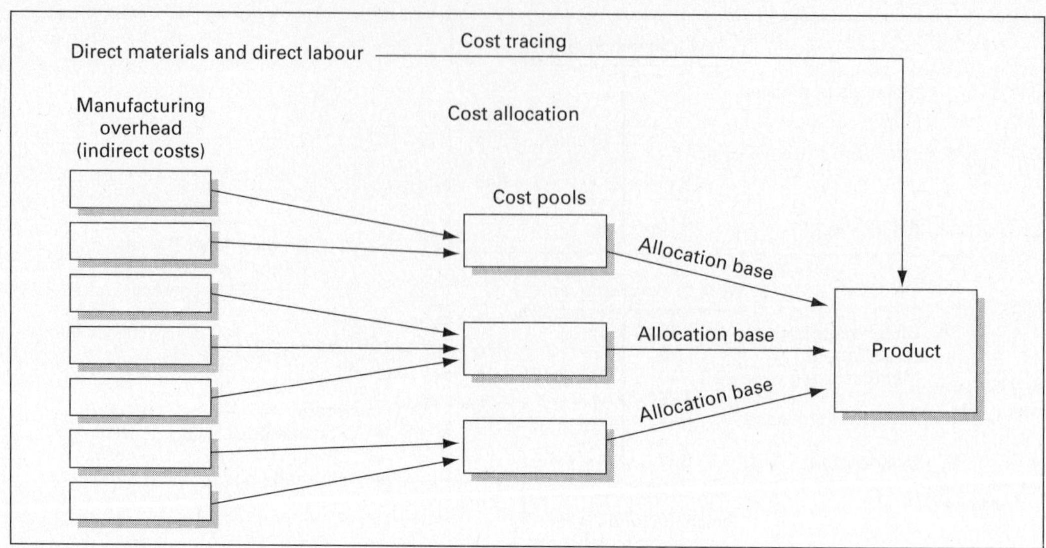

Exhibit 4.5 Direct and indirect costs of products

The process of allocating overhead costs to products

Manufacturing overhead consists of a heterogeneous pool of indirect production costs such as indirect material, indirect labour, electricity and gas costs, equipment depreciation, insurance and council rates paid for the factory. These costs bear no obvious relationship to individual units of product, but they must be incurred for production to take place.

As manufacturing overhead costs are *indirect* costs, we need to take an *indirect* route to assign them to products. This involves three steps:

1. *Identifying the overhead cost driver*—that is, a factor or activity that causes overhead costs to be incurred. Conventional costing systems assume that overhead costs are caused by the volume of production. Common overhead cost drivers include measures of production *output*, such as the number of units produced, or measures of production *input*, such as the number of direct labour hours or machine hours worked.
2. *Calculating a* **predetermined** (or **budgeted**) **overhead rate** *per unit of cost driver*. This is equal to the budgeted overhead divided by the budgeted level of cost driver, for the coming year. For example, if the budgeted overhead for the coming year is R10 000 000, and it is expected that 200 000 direct labour hours will be worked in the coming year, then the budgeted overhead rate will be R50 per direct labour hour (R10 000 000 ÷ 200 000 direct labour hours).
3. *Applying manufacturing overhead costs to products* at the budgeted (or predetermined) overhead rate multiplied by the quantity of cost driver consumed by the product. Thus, if producing a product required 10 direct labour hours, then the amount of overhead applied to the product would be R500 (R50 per direct labour hour × 10 direct labour hours).

Accounting for manufacturing overhead

Exhibit 4.6 summarises the flow of manufacturing overhead costs through the accounting system. The left side (debit side) of the manufacturing overhead account accumulates **actual manufacturing overhead** costs as they are incurred throughout the accounting period. The actual costs incurred for indirect material, indirect labour and other indirect manufacturing items are recorded as debits to the account. The right side (credit side) of the manufacturing overhead account records overhead applied to work in process inventory. **Applied manufacturing overhead** is the predetermined over-

REAL LIFE: PRODUCT COSTS AT SABMILLER

SABMiller is a leading global brewer and the company has expanded from South Africa to operate breweries in major markets in the world. The company owns some of the world's leading brands including Castle, Miller, Black Label, Peroni, Bavaria and Pilsner Urquell. The costs of making beer include inputs such as hops, malted grains, water and yeast. The brewing costs will include energy costs, cost of materials such as aluminium, and packaging. Factory overheads are significant because of the capital intensive nature of the industry. Then there are administrative costs and distribution costs. Marketing costs are important to support the company's brands. In the 2006 annual report SABMiller reported that it had experienced significant increases in energy and aluminium costs, yet it expected the following trends in the underlying upstream and downstream costs of the company:

Component	Direction	Drivers
Brewing costs	↘	Improved scale, commodity volatility
Packaging costs	→	Improved scale, higher costs for premium brands
Admin overheads	↓	Integration, scale and efficiency improvements
Marketing	↗	Increased brand building, in-market spend
Sales and distribution	↑	Personnel, systems to enable market penetration

The company states in relation to Miller, its US subsidiary;

Miller continued to extract operational efficiencies in its breweries and realise cost savings on brewing materials, waste reduction and procurement. These gains were more than offset by significantly higher aluminium, fuel and energy costs, resulting in an increase in domestic costs of goods sold per hectolitre slightly below the US Consumer Price Index.

The company is focused on reducing energy costs and the Ibhayi brewery in Port Elizabeth, for example, experienced cost savings of 10 per cent. The company is also moving to recycling packaging and waste material produced by the brewing process and wishes to reduce its use of water. About 5 litres of water are required to make one litre of beer. The company also wishes as part of this commitment to reduce its 'carbon footprint'.

Source: SABMiller 2006 annual report and media briefing by Tony van Kralingen, Managing Director SAB Ltd, 14 July 2006

head rate multiplied by the quantity of cost driver consumed by products worked on during the period.[2]

Disposing of underapplied or overapplied overhead

Because we apply overhead to products using a predetermined rate, we would expect that in some months manufacturing overhead will be **overapplied** (in other words, the overhead applied to production is greater than the actual overhead costs incurred) and in other months it will be **underapplied** (overhead applied is less than actual overhead costs incurred). Over the whole year we would expect these differences to disappear. However, this is not always the case. Sometimes we will either underestimate or overestimate the predetermined overhead rate.

At the end of the accounting period, the accountant has two alternatives for disposing of underapplied or overapplied overhead:

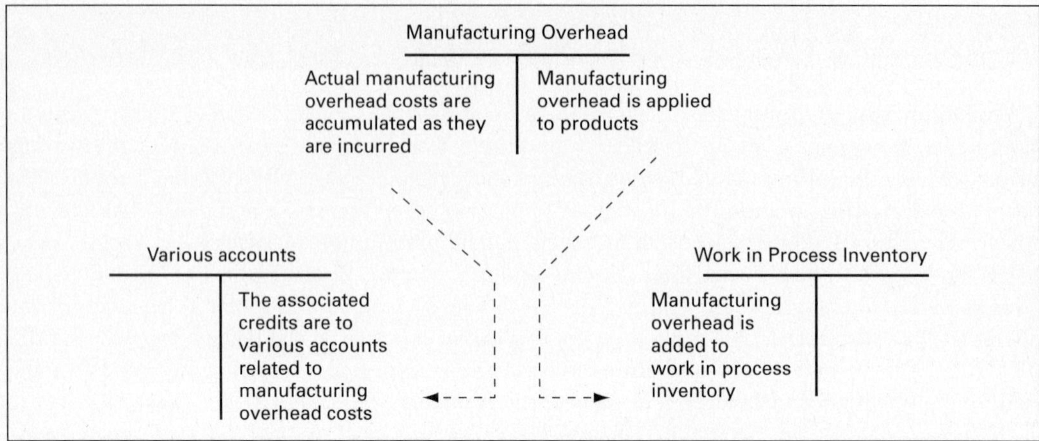

Exhibit 4.6 Manufacturing Overhead Account

1 *Close the underapplied or overapplied overhead to cost of goods sold.* This is the most common approach. It is simple, and it is appropriate when the amount of underapplied or overapplied overhead is small.
2 *Prorate (distribute proportionately) the underapplied or overapplied overhead to cost of goods sold, work in process inventory and finished goods inventory.* **Proration** is more accurate as it recognises that underestimating or overestimating the predetermined overhead rate affects not only cost of goods sold, but also work in process inventory and finished goods inventory. Applied overhead passes through each of these accounts. Therefore, all three accounts are affected by any inaccuracy in the predetermined overhead rate. This method is appropriate when the amount of underapplied or overapplied overhead is significant. The appendix to this chapter outlines the method for prorating underapplied or overapplied overhead.

When should we close the manufacturing overhead account?

Once we dispose of underapplied or overapplied overhead, the manufacturing overhead account will have a zero balance; that is, we close the account. Most firms close underapplied or overapplied overhead *at the end of the year only*. If underapplied or overapplied overhead is closed *at the end of each month*, the effects of monthly fluctuations in overhead costs and cost driver volumes are shifted to cost of goods sold. Yet over the year many of these fluctuations are likely to average out. Thus, underapplied or overapplied overhead should be considered only for the whole year, not at the end of each month.

We illustrate the accounting for overhead in a manufacturing business with the Williams Elevators case later in this chapter.

Types of product costing systems

L.O. 5

The detailed accounting procedures used in product costing systems depend on the nature of the production environment. The costing procedures used by businesses that produce individual products, where each product differs from the next, are not appropriate for businesses that mass-produce one or two major product lines. Instead, two basic sets of procedures are used: job costing and process costing. In practice, job costing and process costing represent the two extremes of a continuum, as shown in Exhibit 4.7. Many businesses operate in an environment that requires a combination of job and process costing features.

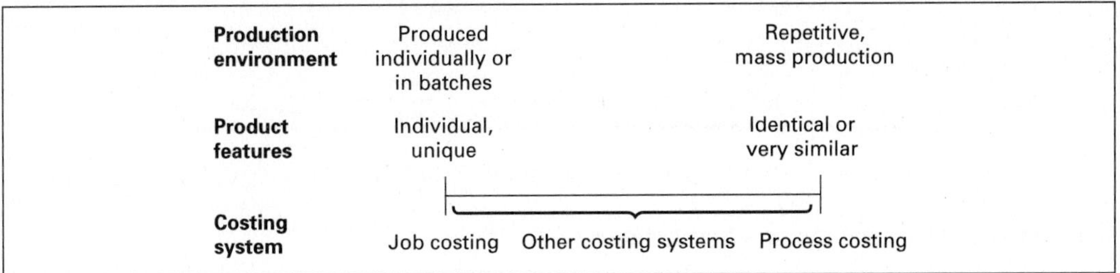

Exhibit 4.7 Continuum of conventional costing systems

Job costing systems

Businesses use **job costing** when they produce products in distinct batches and there are significant differences between those batches. Manufacturers that use job costing include printers, furniture manufacturers and machinery and equipment manufacturers. Given that service outputs often differ from one client or customer to the next, job costing is appropriate for many service firms. For example, plumbers, electricians, law firms, consulting engineers and public accountants could use a job costing system. (Service costing is covered in Chapter 6.)

In job costing, each distinct batch of production is called a **job** or **job order**. Each job is different, so the costing procedures are designed to assign costs to each individual job. The cost of the job is then averaged over the number of units produced in the job to obtain an average cost per unit. For example, suppose that QuikPrint worked on many printing jobs during October, and the following costs were assigned to two of the jobs:

	Job A27 (1000 brochures)	Job B39 (100 wedding invitations)
Direct material	R1000	R400
Direct labour	1250	500
Manufacturing overhead	250	100
Total manufacturing cost	2500	1000

The cost per brochure is R2.50 (R2500 ÷ 1000 brochures), and the cost per wedding invitation is R10.00 (R1000 ÷ 100 invitations).

Process costing systems

Process costing is used by companies that produce a single product (or a small range of very similar products) in large quantities. Manufacturers that produce petrol, processed food, chemicals and plastics are among those likely to use process costing. Process costing can be used in service firms where services are repetitive: for example, in routine processing of cheques by a bank, or the handling of licence applications by a government department. These businesses have repetitive production environments, where production consists of a number of processes that are performed repetitively. Each unit of product passes through identical (or very similar) production processes. In a repetitive production environment, in which a large number of very similar units are produced, there is no need to assign the production costs specifically to each individual unit produced. An average cost for all units produced provides a reasonably accurate estimate of the product cost—after all, one unit of product is the same as the next.

Thus, a **process costing system** involves two main steps:

1 estimating the costs of the production process; and
2 calculating an average cost per unit by dividing the cost of the process by the number of units produced.

For example, the output of Technology Park Company for the month of November was 40 000 microchips, and the following manufacturing costs were incurred:

Direct material	R10 000
Direct labour	20 000
Manufacturing overhead	30 000
Total manufacturing cost	R60 000

The cost per microchip is R1.50 (total manufacturing cost of R60 000 ÷ 40 000 units produced).

The flow of costs in process costing systems

The microchip example, above, aggregates the production costs for the entire company. In many process costing businesses, products undergo a number of separate processes, undertaken by different production departments. In this situation, the process costing system accumulates costs by department. The costs of products that have completed processing in the first department are transferred into, and become part of, the costs of the second department, and so on. Costs are transferred from one department to the next at an average unit cost for the department, as each unit of product is virtually identical to the next. Exhibit 4.8 compares the flow of costs:

- where the entire production process is completed within one department;
- where the production occurs in two sequential processes, completed by two production departments.

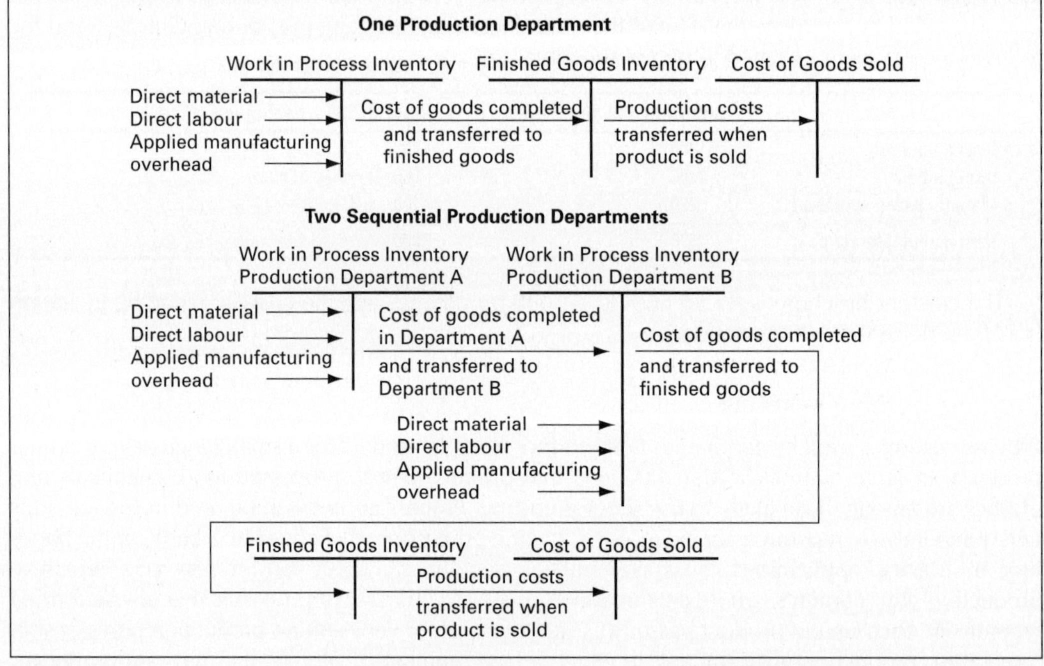

Exhibit 4.8 Flow of costs in process costing systems

When direct material is purchased, it is added to the raw material inventory account. Once production begins, direct material, direct labour and manufacturing overhead costs are added to a work in process inventory account. As goods are finished, costs are transferred to finished goods inventory. During the period when goods are sold, the product costs are transferred to cost of goods sold. (This approach is described below, using Spritz as an example.)

For two-stage production processes, when goods are finished in the first production department, A, costs accumulated in the work in process inventory account for that department are transferred to the work in process inventory account for Production Department B. (We explore this situation in Chapter 5.)

You will notice that the flow of costs through the manufacturing accounts is similar for manufacturers, whether they use job costing or process costing (see, for example, Exhibit 4.3). The key difference is that, with multiprocesses, there are separate work-in-process accounts for each production department.

Summary: job versus process costing

The distinction between job costing and process costing hinges on the nature of the product and, therefore, on the type of production process:

- Job costing systems assign costs to distinct production jobs that are significantly different. An average cost per unit of product is then calculated for each job.
- Process costing systems assign costs to one or more production processes. Because all units are identical or very similar, average costs for each unit of product are calculated by dividing the process costs by the number of units produced.
- Many businesses produce products with some unique features and some common processes. These businesses use costing systems that have both job and process costing features.

Exhibit 4.9 summarises the key differences between job and process costing. This exhibit assumes that only the production costs (direct material, direct labour and manufacturing overhead costs) are assigned to products. However, both job costing and process costing can be extended to assign upstream and downstream costs to products. In this chapter we describe job costing, using Williams Elevators, and introduce process costing, using Spritz soft drinks. In Chapter 5 we explore process costing for Spritz in more depth and introduce operation costing as an example of a costing system with both job and process costing features.

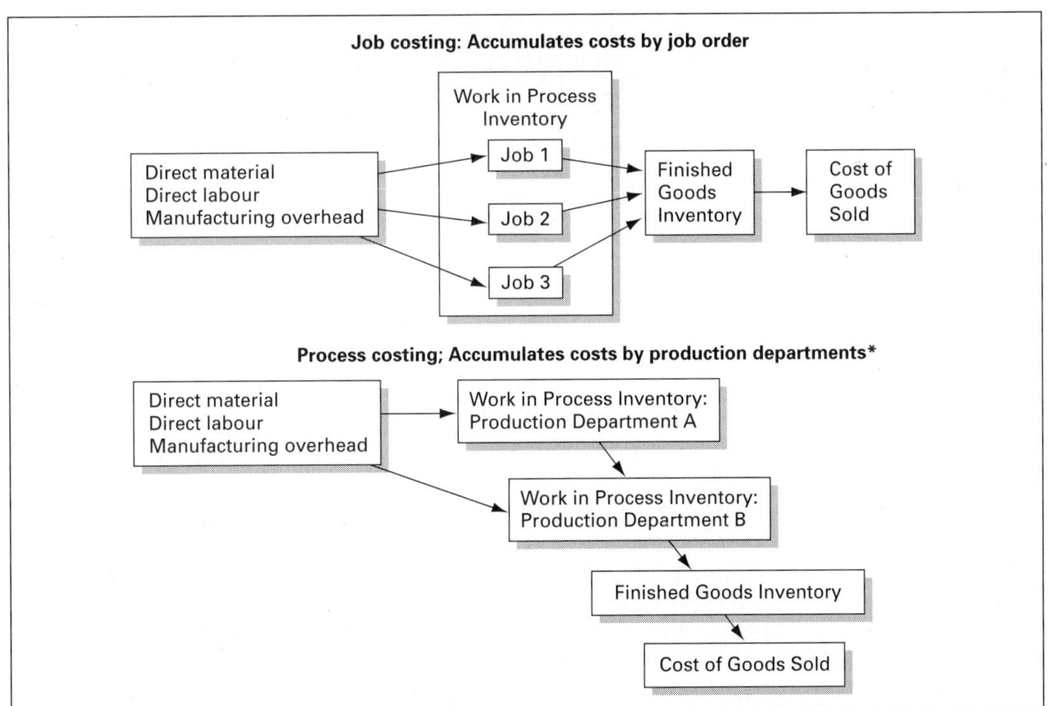

*In a process costing environment there may be one or more production departments (or production processes).

Exhibit 4.9 Comparison of job costing and process costing

Job costing: Williams Elevators

L.O. 6 Williams Elevators Ltd produces lifts to individual customer specifications, often for the European market. The range of possible performance characteristics of lifts is vast, varying from relatively simple lifts for buildings of three or four storeys, to banks of lifts for high-rise towers. Earlier in this chapter we explained that although accounting standards require inventory valuations to include only manufacturing costs, some businesses include upstream and downstream costs as part of product costs. At Williams Elevators the costing system assigns only manufacturing costs—that is, direct material, direct labour and manufacturing overhead—to products.

To understand the nature of the job costing system at Williams Elevators, we need to understand how a lift is produced. Lifts are produced in three production departments:

- the *Structural Department,* which produces the aluminium 'cars' that transport lift passengers, and also the lift doors;
- the *Electrical Department,* which works on the 'controllers'—the 'brains' of the lifts; and
- the *Mechanical Department,* which works on the motors that power the lifts.

The job costing system

L.O. 7, 8 To illustrate job costing we will focus on the operations and accounting entries of Williams Elevators during November. During this period, the company worked on two production jobs:

- job number FS12: two lifts for a four-storey building; and
- job number MS16: a bank of three lifts for a multi-storey building.

The job numbers designate these as the *twelfth 'four-storey lift' job* (FS12) and the *sixteenth 'multi-storey lift' job* (MS16) undertaken during the year. Job FS12 had started three months earlier and was completed during November. Job MS16 was a new job that began in November.

The costs incurred on job number FS12 *prior* to the beginning of November are as follows:

Job no. FS12			
Direct materials:			
07 Aug	Aluminium sheet metal	R200 000	
31 Aug	Steel cable	70 000	
15 Oct	Motors and generator sets	150 000	
			420 000
Direct labour			176 000
Manufacturing overhead			160 000
Total cost as at 31 October			756 000

These costs have been classified in the accounting system as work in process inventory, and are recorded on the *job cost sheet* for FS12. This is illustrated in Exhibit 4.10. Note that the job cost sheet for job number FS12 shows the entire cost for the completed job. At the beginning of November the job was incomplete.

A **job cost sheet** shows details of the costs of the direct material, direct labour and manufacturing overhead used to complete the job. These reports are usually generated by a computer software package, and the layout of the report may vary. Each job will have its own separate job cost sheet. You will notice that there are three sections on the job cost sheet to accumulate the costs of direct material, direct labour and manufacturing overhead assigned to the job. The other two sections are used to record the total cost and average unit cost for the job, and to detail when the units of product are delivered to the customer.

JOB COST SHEET					
Job number:	FS12		Description:	2 four-storey lifts	
Date started:	07-Aug		Date completed:	22-Nov	
			Number of units completed:		2
Direct Material					
Date	**Req. no.**	**Description**	**Quantity**	**Cost/unit**	**Cost**
07-Aug	498	Aluminium sheet (m^2)	2,000	R 100	R 200,000
31-Aug	499	Cable (m)	500	140	70,000
15-Oct	500	Motor and generator	2	75,000	150,000
14-Nov	502	Control panels	2	25,000	50,000
14-Nov	502	Counterweights	2	10,000	20,000
Total					R 490,000
Direct Labour					
Date	**Time sheet no.**	**Description**	**Hours**	**Rate**	**Cost**
August– October	Various	Various employees	1,600	R 110	R 176,000
November	Various	Various employees	600	110	66,000
Total					R 242,000
Manufacturing Overhead					
Date	**Cost driver**		**Quantity**	**Application rate**	**Cost**
August– October	Direct labour hours		1,600	R 100	R 160,000
November	Direct labour hours		600	100	60,000
Total					R 220,000
Cost Summary					
Cost item				**Amount**	
Total direct material				R 490,000	
Total direct labour				R 242,000	
Total manufacturing overhead				R 220,000	
Total cost				R 952,000	
Unit cost				R 476,000	
Delivery Summary					
Date	**Units shipped**	**Units remaining in inventory**		**Cost balance**	
30-Nov	1	1		R 476,000	

Exhibit 4.10 Job cost sheet, Williams Elevators Ltd

The procedures used to accumulate the costs of direct material, direct labour and manufacturing overhead for a job are discussed next.

Purchase of material

Williams Elevators uses an ERP system,[3] which includes a computerised inventory management module that compares the items listed on the *bill of materials* for a job with current inventory, and prepares purchase orders for items not in stock. A **bill of materials** lists all the materials needed for the job.

During November the following items were purchased:

Description	Quantity	Price	Total
Aluminium sheet metal (square metres)	3000	R100	R300 000
Cable (metres)	4000	140	560 000
Motors and generator sets	3	75 000	225 000
Control panels	5	25 000	125 000
Counterweights	5	10 000	50 000
			R1 260 000

The purchases are recorded in the accounting system with the following journal entry:

(1) Raw material inventory	R1 260 000	
Accounts payable		R1 260 000

The posting of this and all subsequent journal entries to the ledger are shown in Exhibit 4.13 on p. 155.

Transferring direct material to jobs

In manufacturing systems, when raw materials are needed for the production process they are transferred from the warehouse to the production department. In most manufacturing firms a material requisition form is completed by manufacturing personnel and presented to the warehouse staff. A copy of the **material requisition form** is sent to the accounting department. There it is used to transfer the cost of the requisitioned material from the raw material inventory account to the work-in-process inventory account, and to enter the direct material cost on the job cost sheet for the production job in process. A document such as the material requisition form, which is used as the basis for an accounting entry, is called a **source document**.

In many factories, material requisitions are entered directly into a computer by production employees. The requisition is automatically transmitted to terminals in the warehouse and the accounting department. Such automation reduces the flow of paperwork, minimises clerical errors, and speeds up the product costing process.

Exhibit 4.11 contains the two material requisition forms that were filed during November at Williams Elevators. If you look back to Exhibit 4.10, you will see the direct materials that were requisitioned for job number FS12 included in the job cost sheet. The same types of information would be detailed on a separate job cost sheet for job number MS16.

Material requisition no.: 501

Job no. to be charged: MS16 — Date: 1 November

Item	Quantity	Unit cost	Amount
Aluminium sheet metal (square metres)	3000	100	300 000
Cable (metres)	4000	140	560 000
Motor and generator set	3	75 000	225 000
			R1 085 000

Material requisition no.: 502

Job no. to be charged: FS12 — Date: 14 November

Item	Quantity	Unit cost	Amount
Control panel	2	25 000	50 000
Counterweights	2	10 000	20 000
			R70 000

Exhibit 4.11 Material acquisition forms, Williams Elevators Ltd

The following journal entry records the release of the raw materials to production:

(2) Work in process inventory	R1 155 000	
Raw material inventory		R1 155 000

Use of indirect material

On 15 November, a further material requisition was filed:

Requisition number 503: 500 soldering rods, @ R5 per rod, for a total cost of R2 500

Soldering rods are used in the production of all types of lifts manufactured by Williams Elevators. Since the cost incurred is small, no attempt is made to trace the cost of the rods to specific jobs. Instead, soldering rods are considered an indirect material and their cost is included in manufacturing overhead. The company accumulates all manufacturing overhead costs in the manufacturing overhead account. All actual overhead costs are recorded by debiting this account. The account is debited when indirect materials are requisitioned, when indirect labour costs are incurred, when electricity bills are paid, when depreciation is recorded on manufacturing equipment, and so forth. The journal entry made to record the usage of soldering rods is as follows:

(3) Manufacturing overhead	R2 500	
Manufacturing supplies inventory[4]		R2 500

No entry is made on the job cost sheets for the usage of soldering rods, since their cost is part of overhead, not traceable directly to individual production jobs. Instead, overhead is applied to jobs using a predetermined rate, as shown in journal entry (7) on page 153.

Charging direct labour to jobs

In a job costing system, direct labour costs are assigned to jobs using time sheets filled out by employees. A **time sheet** records the amount of time an employee spends on each production job. The time sheet is used to add direct labour costs to work in process inventory and to the job cost sheets for the various jobs in process, and as the basis for paying employee wages. Time sheets may be completed daily or weekly.

The production employees at Williams Elevators complete time sheets each day. Exhibit 4.12 shows a time sheet for employee A. Berry for 22 November. You can see that Berry spent 4 1/2 hours on job number FS12 and a total of 4 hours on job number MS16. This direct labour will be charged to these jobs. Of the 4 hours spent on job MS16, 1 1/2 were worked as overtime. Note that the format of time sheets can vary, depending on the computer software that is used to generate the report. As explained in Chapter 2, the overtime premium relating to this will be classified as manufacturing overhead. Berry also spent half an hour on shop clean-up duties. This time will be classified by the accounting department as indirect labour, and its cost will be included in manufacturing overhead.

Employee name: A. Berry   Date: 22 November
Employee no.: 4510
Department: Electrical

Job no.	Start	Stop	Ordinary hours	Overtime hours
FS12	7.30	12.00	4½	–
MS16	1.00	3.30	2½	–
Clean-up	3.30	4.00	½	–
MS16	4.00	5.30	–	1½

Exhibit 4.12 Time sheet, Williams Elevators Ltd

You will notice on the job cost sheet in Exhibit 4.10 that direct labour is a summary of many time sheets for various employees who worked on that particular job during November. In practice, there would be numerous entries made on different dates at a variety of wage rates for different employees, across the three production departments—Structural, Electrical and Mechanical. The information on the time sheets is also used for accounting entries and the processing of wages.

At the end of November, the accounting department used the time sheets filed during the month to determine the following direct labour costs for each job:

Direct labour: Job no. FS12 (600 hours)	R66 000
Direct labour: Job no. MS16 (3500 hours)	385 000
Total direct labour	R451 000

The journal entry made to record these costs is as follows:

(4) Work in process inventory	R451 000	
Wages payable		R451 000

Accounting for indirect labour

The analysis of all the time sheets for November revealed that a total of R70 000 of wages could be classified as indirect labour. This cost comprised the production supervisors' salaries and the wages of various employees who spent some of their time on maintenance and general clean-up duties, and overtime premiums paid during November. The following journal entry is made to add indirect labour costs to manufacturing overhead:

(5) Manufacturing overhead	R70 000	
Wages payable		R70 000

These data are not recorded on the job cost sheets because indirect labour costs are part of overhead not traceable to any particular job.

In practice, journal entries (4) and (5) are usually combined into one compound entry as follows:

Work in process inventory	R451 000	
Manufacturing overhead	70 000	
Wages payable		R521 000

Accounting for manufacturing overhead costs

In addition to the indirect material and indirect labour costs, the following manufacturing overhead costs were incurred during November:

Manufacturing overhead:	
Rent on factory building	R110 000
Depreciation on equipment	175 000
Electricity	20 000
Council rates	10 000
Insurance on factory building and equipment	25 000
Total	R340 000

The following journal entry is made on 30 November to record these costs:

(6) Manufacturing overhead	R340 000	
Prepaid rent		R110 000
Accumulated depreciation: equipment		175 000
Accounts payable (electricity and council rates)		30 000
Prepaid insurance		25 000

Once again, no entry is made on any job cost sheet, since manufacturing overhead costs are not traceable to any particular job. Instead, overhead is applied to jobs using a predetermined rate, as below.

Application of manufacturing overhead to production

Various manufacturing overhead costs were incurred during November, and these costs were accumulated by debiting the manufacturing overhead account. However, no manufacturing overhead costs have yet been charged to work in process inventory or recorded on the job cost sheets. The application of overhead to the firm's products is based on a predetermined overhead rate.

This rate was calculated by the accounting department prior to the beginning of the year as follows:

$$\text{Predetermined overhead rate} = \frac{\text{budgeted total manufacturing overhead for coming year}}{\text{budgeted total direct labour hours for coming year}}$$

$$= \frac{\text{R5 000 000}}{\text{50 000 direct labour hours}}$$

$$= \text{R100 per direct labour hour}$$

The total manufacturing overhead applied to work in process inventory during November is calculated as follows:

	Direct labour hours		Predetermined overhead rate		Manufacturing overhead applied
Job no. FS12	600	×	R100	=	60 000
Job no. MS16	3500	×	R100	=	350 000
Total manufacturing overhead applied					R410 000

The following journal entry is made to add applied manufacturing overhead to work in process inventory:

(7) Work in process inventory	R410 000	
Manufacturing overhead		R410 000

The manufacturing overhead applied to job number FS12 is entered on the job cost sheet in Exhibit 4.10.

Selling and administrative costs

During November, Williams Elevators incurred selling and administrative costs as follows:

Rental of sales and administrative offices	R25 000
Salaries of sales personnel	20 000
Salaries of management	40 000
Advertising	5 000
Office supplies used	1 500
Total	R91 500

Since these are not manufacturing costs, they are not added to work in process inventory.

At Williams, selling and administrative costs are not included in product costs. They are treated as expenses of the accounting period. The following journal entry is made:

(8) Selling and administrative expenses	R91 500	
Prepaid rent		R25 000
Wages payable		60 000
Accounts payable (advertising)		5 000
Office supplies inventory		1 500

Completion of a production job

Job number FS12 was completed during November, whereas job number MS16 remained in process. As the job cost sheet in Exhibit 4.10 indicates, the total cost of job number FS12 was R952 000. The following journal entry records the transfer of these job costs from work in process inventory to finished goods inventory:

(9) Finished goods inventory	R952 000	
Work in process inventory		R952 000

Sale of goods

The customer requires the delivery of one lift to the site of the partially-completed four-storey building on 25 November, and the other on 10 December. An invoice for R1 000 000 for the first of the two lifts was submitted to the building's owner on 25 November. The cost of each lift was R476 000 as shown in the job cost sheet in Exhibit 4.10. The following journal entries are made:

(10) Accounts receivable	R1 000 000	
Sales revenue		R1 000 000
(11) Cost of goods sold	R476 000	
Finished goods inventory		R476 000

You will notice that all the journal entries have been posted to ledger accounts, as shown in Exhibit 4.13.

Underapplied and overapplied overhead

During November, Williams Elevators incurred total actual manufacturing overhead costs as follows:

Manufacturing overhead:	
Indirect material	R2 500
Indirect labour	70 000
Rent on factory building	110 000
Depreciation on equipment	175 000
Electricity	20 000
Council rates	10 000
Insurance on factory building and equipment	25 000
Total	R412 500

However, only R410 000 of overhead was applied to work in process inventory. The amount by which actual overhead exceeds applied overhead, called *underapplied overhead*, is calculated as follows:

Actual manufacturing overhead*	R412 500
Applied manufacturing overhead	410 000
Underapplied overhead	R2 500

* Note that this is the sum of debit entries in the manufacturing overhead account: R2500 + R70 000 + R340 000 = R412 500 (see Exhibit 4.13).

Accounts Receivable*

	Debit		Credit	
Bal	250 000			
(10)†	1 000 000			

Accounts Payable*

	Debit		Credit	
		Bal	200 000	
			1 260 000	(1)
			30 000	(6)
			5 000	(8)

Prepaid Insurance

	Debit		Credit	
Bal	50 000		25 000	(6)
		Bal (c/f)	25 000	
	50 000		50 000	

Wages Payable*

	Debit		Credit	
		Bal	75 000	
			451 000	(4)
			70 000	(5)
			60 000	(8)

Prepaid Rent

	Debit		Credit	
Bal	200 000		110 000	(6)
			25 000	(8)
		Bal (c/f)	65 000	
	200 000		200 000	

Office Supplies Inventory

	Debit		Credit	
Bal	2 500		1 500	(8)
		Bal (c/f)	1 000	
	2 500		2 500	

Manufacturing Supplies Inventory

	Debit		Credit	
Bal	25 000		2 500	(3)
		Bal (c/f)	22 500	
	25 000		25 000	

Accumulated Depreciation Equipment

	Debit		Credit	
		Bal	1 000 000	
			175 000	(6)

Raw Material Inventory

	Debit		Credit	
Bal	150 000		1 155 000	(2)
(1)	1 260 000	Bal (c/f)	255 000	
	1 410 000		1 410 000	

Manufacturing Overhead

	Debit		Credit	
(3)	2 500		410 000	(7)
(5)	70 000		2 500	(12)
(6)	340 000			
	412 500		412 500	

Work in Process Inventory

	Debit		Credit	
Bal	756 000		952 000	(9)
(2)	1 155 000			
(4)	451 000			
(7)	410 000	Bal (c/f)	1 820 000	
	2 772 000		2 772 000	

Cost of Goods Sold

	Debit		Credit	
(11)	476 000			
(12)	2 500			

Finished Goods Inventory

	Debit		Credit	
Bal	50 000		476 000	(11)
(9)	952 000	Bal (c/f)	526 000	
	1 002 000		1 002 000	

Selling and Administrative Expenses

	Debit		Credit	
(8)	91 500			

Sales Revenue

	Debit		Credit	
			1 000 000	(10)

*The balances of these accounts are not calculated, as they are likely to include further entries for the month.

†The numbers in brackets link the ledger entries to the associated journal entries.

Exhibit 4.13 Ledger accounts for November, Williams Elevators Ltd

Disposition of underapplied or overapplied overhead

At the end of an accounting period, Williams Elevators closes its underapplied or overapplied overhead into cost of goods sold. The journal entry is as follows:

(12) Cost of goods sold	R2500	
Manufacturing overhead		R2500

This entry, which is posted in Exhibit 4.13, brings the balance in the manufacturing overhead account to zero. The account is then clear to accumulate manufacturing overhead costs incurred in the next accounting period. Journal entry (12) has the effect of increasing cost of goods sold expense. This reflects the fact that the cost of the units sold had been underestimated due to the slightly underestimated predetermined overhead rate. (Although we have shown the journal entry for November, most businesses make this entry at the end of the year rather than monthly.)

Some businesses choose to prorate their underapplied or overapplied overhead, particularly if it is a significant amount. The appendix at the end of the chapter shows how to prorate the underapplied overhead of Williams Elevators.

Schedule of cost of goods manufactured

L.O. 9 Exhibit 4.14 summarises the November transactions for Williams in a **schedule of cost of goods manufactured**. The schedule details the cost of direct materials, direct labour and manufacturing overhead applied to work in process during November and shows the changes to the work in process inventory. The **cost of goods manufactured**, shown in the last line of the schedule, is R952 000. This is the amount transferred from the work in process inventory to finished goods inventory during November, as recorded in journal entry (9) on page 154.

You will notice that the schedule lists the actual manufacturing costs incurred during November, R412 500, and then adjusts these by the amount of underapplied overhead, R2500, to show the amount of overhead applied to work in process, R410 000. It is important to remember that, in estimating total manufacturing costs for the month, applied overhead, not actual overhead, is added to direct material and direct labour costs.

Schedule of cost of goods sold

L.O. 9 A **schedule of cost of goods sold** for Williams Elevators is shown in Exhibit 4.15. This schedule shows the November cost of goods sold and details changes in the finished goods inventory during the month. Exhibit 4.16 shows the company's income statement for November.

Product costing and the balance sheet

We have focused on the effects of the product costing system on cost of goods sold and, therefore, on the income statement. However, you will notice from Exhibit 4.13 that the product costing system also affects account balances in the balance sheet. At the end of November the product costing system provides Williams Elevators with an estimate of the cost of partially completed lifts (that is, work in process inventory), and the cost of lifts completed but not sold (that is, finished goods inventory). It also provides an estimate of the cost of the raw material on hand at the end of November (that is, the raw material inventory). Exhibit 4.17 shows a partial balance sheet for Williams Elevators, at 30 November.

Sequence of events in job costing

The flowchart in Exhibit 4.18 summarises the sequence of activities performed by the job costing system. The role of the various documents used in job costing is also emphasised in the flowchart.

Williams Elevators Ltd Schedule of Cost of Goods Manufactured for the month of November		
Direct material:		
Raw material inventory, 1 November	R150 000	
Add November purchases of raw material	1 260 000	
Raw material available for use	1 410 000	
Deduct Raw material inventory, 30 November	255 000	
Raw material used		1 155 000
Direct labour		451 000
Manufacturing overhead:		
Indirect material	2 500	
Indirect labour	70 000	
Rent on factory building	110 000	
Depreciation on factory equipment	175 000	
Electricity	20 000	
Council rates	10 000	
Insurance	25 000	
Total actual manufacturing overhead	412 500	
Deduct Underapplied overhead	2 500	
Overhead applied to work in process		410 000 *
Total manufacturing costs		2 016 000
Add Work in process inventory, 1 November		756 000
Manufacturing costs to account for		2 772 000
Deduct Work in process inventory, 30 November		1 820 000
Cost of goods manufactured		R952 000

*The schedule of cost of goods manufactured lists the manufacturing costs applied to work in process. Therefore, the underapplied overhead, R2500, must be deducted from the total actual overhead to arrive at the amount of the overhead applied to work in process during November. If there had been overapplied overhead, the balance would have been added to total actual manufacturing overhead.

Exhibit 4.14 Schedule of Cost of Goods Manufactured, Williams Elevators Ltd

Williams Elevators Ltd Schedule of Cost of Goods Sold for the month of November	
Finished goods inventory, 1 November	R50 000
Add Cost of goods manufactured*	952 000
Cost of goods available for sale	1 002 000
Deduct Finished goods inventory, 30 November	526 000
Cost of goods sold	476 000
Add Underapplied overhead†	2 500
Cost of goods sold (adjusted for underapplied overhead)	R478 500

* The cost of goods manufactured is obtained from the schedule of cost of goods manufactured in Exhibit 4.14.

† The company closes underapplied or overapplied overhead into cost of goods sold. Hence the R2500 balance in underapplied overhead is added to cost of goods sold for the month.

Exhibit 4.15 Cost of Goods Sold Report, Williams Elevators Ltd

Responsibility accounting at Williams Elevators

Williams Elevators also uses its costing system to provide information for control. The direct material, direct labour and manufacturing overhead costs are assigned to the three production departments (Structural, Electrical and Mechanical) as well as to jobs. The costs incurred in each department are compared with planned or budgeted costs, and the manager of each department is held responsible for any variances.

Williams Elevators Ltd Income Statement for the month of November	
Sales revenue	R1 000 000
Less Cost of goods sold*	478 500
Gross margin	521 500
Selling and administrative expenses	91 500
Profit before taxes	430 000
Income tax expense	130 000
Net profit	R300 000

* The cost of goods sold is obtained from the schedule of cost of goods sold in Exhibit 4.15.

Exhibit 4.16 Income Statement, Williams Elevators Ltd

Williams Elevators Ltd Partial Balance Sheet at 30 November		
Current assets:		
Cash		Rx xxx
Accounts receivable*		x xxx
Inventories:		
Office supplies inventory	1 000	
Manufacturing supplies	22 500	
Raw material	255 000	
Work in process	1 820 000	
Finished goods	526 000	
		2 624 500
Prepaid insurance		25 000
Prepaid rent		65 000
Other current assets		x xxx
Total current assets		Rx xxx

* It is not possible to use the balance of the ledger account for accounts receivable shown in Exhibit 4.13, as this account is likely to include further entries for payments received during November.

Exhibit 4.17 Partial Balance Sheet, Williams Elevators Ltd

Process costing: Spritz

L.O. 10

Spritz is a popular fruit-flavoured soft drink produced by Lloyd Products. It is made in a variety of flavours including lemon, orange, peach, strawberry and mixed berry, using natural fruit concentrates, and is targeted at the adolescent market. At Williams Elevators each lift (or batch of lifts) differs from the next, and job costing is required to estimate the cost of the lifts. In contrast, the Spritz production environment is highly repetitive, involving mass production of a range of almost identical products. As discussed earlier in the chapter, process costing is appropriate under these circumstances.

The production processes for Spritz

The production of a bottle of Spritz can be divided into two processes, as illustrated in Exhibit 4.19. In the Mixing Department the fruit concentrate, sucrose and purified water are introduced at the beginning of the process and mixed in a large tank. The output of the Mixing Department is measured in litres of mixture produced. The mixture is then pumped to the Finishing Department where it is carbonated, bottled, labelled and packed into cartons.[5] The carbonate and bottles are added at the beginning of the finishing process and the labels and packaging at the end of the process. The

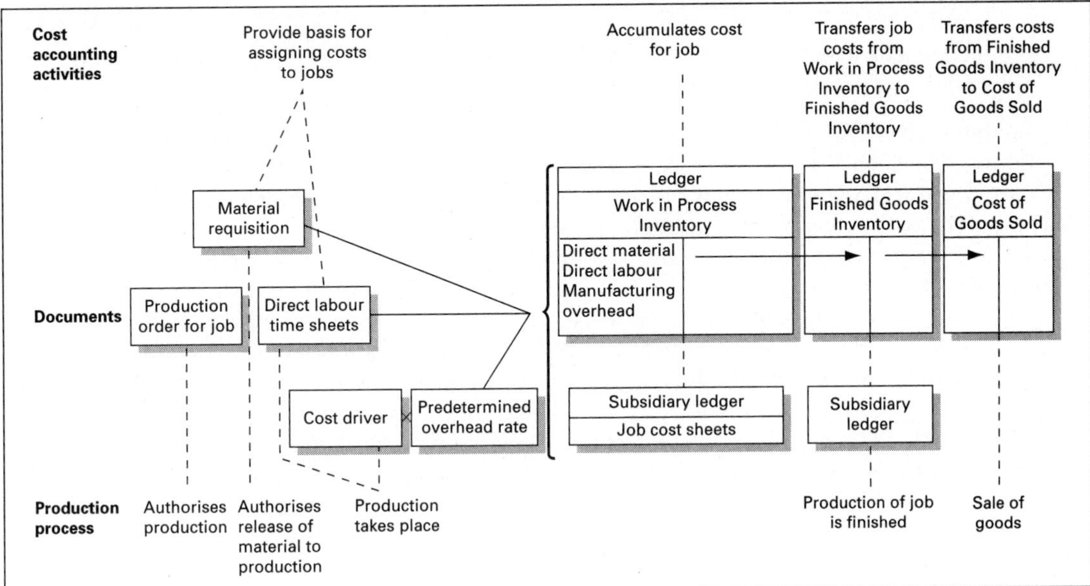

Exhibit 4.18 Summary of event sequence in a job costing system

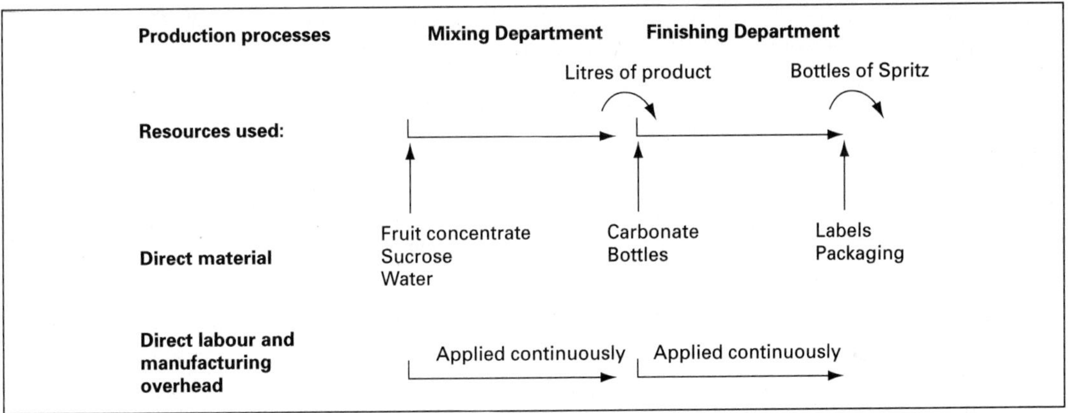

Exhibit 4.19 Production processes in the Mixing and Finishing departments, Spritz

output of the Finishing Department is measured in bottles ready for sale to customers. In both departments, direct labour and manufacturing overhead resources are used uniformly throughout the process.

A costing system for Spritz

In establishing a costing system for Spritz, management identified three major information needs. First, they needed to know the cost per bottle of Spritz to help them set the price. Second, they needed an estimate of product cost to value inventories and the cost of goods sold for external accounting reports. And third, they needed a costing system that would help them control costs.

Earlier in this chapter we recognised that product costs for pricing may include product-related downstream costs such as selling, distribution and customer support costs. For longer-term pricing, it is also useful to include upstream costs such as design and development costs. In its current stage of development, the costing system at Spritz measures production costs only—that is, direct material, direct labour and manufacturing overhead.

The approach to process costing depends on a number of factors, including:

- the existence of work in process inventory at the end of the accounting period; and
- the degree to which the products are identical in their consumption of direct material and specific production processes.

In this chapter we will describe a process costing system where there are no work-in-process inventories at the end of the accounting period and the products are identical in their consumption of direct material and production processes. This scenario describes the situation at Spritz well. The nature of the production process for Spritz means that there is no work in process (partially completed bottles of Spritz) at the end of the accounting period. At the end of each day the line is shut down and all equipment is cleaned. Any material still in the mixing tank is discarded. This means that the only units of inventory on hand are the finished goods (bottles of Spritz that have been labelled and packed). Also, although there are different Spritz flavours, each of these 'products' goes through identical mixing and finishing processes. Each product receives the same input of water, sucrose, carbonation, bottle, labels and lid. The different flavours use different fruit concentrates but the cost of the concentrates does not vary much from one flavour to the next.

In Chapter 5 we will expand our study of process costing to consider how we cost products when there is ending work-in-process inventory, and different material inputs at different stages of production and differing production processes.

Cost information for Spritz

Exhibit 4.20 describes the production and cost data for the month of April.[6] The cost per bottle of Spritz, R4.355, can be calculated simply as the total manufacturing costs, R5 226 020, divided by the number of bottles produced, 1 200 000 bottles.

		Mixing Department	Finishing Department	Total cost
Direct materials:				
Purified water		R47 500		R47 500
Fruit concentrate		1 600 000		1 600 000
Liquid sucrose		879 500		879 500
Carbon dioxide			335 620	335 620
Bottles			510 000	510 000
Labels			270 000	270 000
Packaging			260 000	260 000
Total direct material	a	2 527 000	1 375 620	3 902 620
Conversion costs:				
Direct labour		154 400	122 000	276 400
Manufacturing overhead*		553 000	494 000	1 047 000
Total conversion cost	b	707 400	616 000	1 323 400
Total production cost	a+b	3 234 400	1 991 620	5 226 020
		Litres	Bottles	
Units produced		390 000	1 200 000	
Cost per bottle			R.4.355 (R5 226 020/1.2m)	

* Manufacturing overhead is applied at the predetermined rates of 141.795 cents per litre produced in the Mixing Department and 41.1667 cents per bottle in the Finishing Department.

Exhibit 4.20 Process costing with no work in process inventories, Spritz, April

Journal entries for process costing

L.O. 11 The journal entries to record the production costs for the month are:

(1) Work in process inventory: Mixing Department	R 3 234 400	
Raw material inventory		R 2 527 000
Wages payable		154 400
Manufacturing overhead		553 000

—to add the costs of direct material, direct labour and manufacturing overhead to work in process inventory in the Mixing Department.

(2) Work in process inventory: Finishing Department	R3 234 400	
Work in process: Mixing Department		R3 234 400

—to add the cost of the litres of mixture transferred from the Mixing Department to the Finishing Department.

(3) Work in process inventory: Finishing Department	R1 991 620	
Raw material inventory		R1 375 620
Wages payable		122 000
Manufacturing overhead		494 000

—to add the costs of direct material, direct labour and manufacturing overhead to work in process inventory in the Finishing Department.

(4) Finished goods inventory:	R5 226 020	
Work in process: Finishing Department		R5 226 020

—to record the cost of bottles of Spritz transferred from the Finishing Department to finished goods inventory.

In the general ledger, the production costs are transferred through work in process accounts for the Mixing Department and the Finishing Department to the finished goods inventory. Yet there are no work-in-process inventories at the end of the accounting period. Some businesses in this situation transfer production costs directly into the finished goods account instead of using work in process accounts. After all, by the end of the accounting period all production inputs end up in finished goods, as there are no partially completed goods (that is, work in process) on hand. We did not need this breakdown of costs by departments to calculate the cost per bottle of Spritz of 433.5 cents. We simply divided the total production costs by the number of bottles produced in the month.

So why do we track production costs to production departments? There are two reasons. First, it provides information for control. Department managers can be held responsible for the costs incurred in their area. The second reason is to deal with the complications that arise when work in process inventories exist at the end of the accounting period, a situation that we will examine in Chapter 5.

Evaluation of process costing

This form of process costing offers a simple way to estimate product costs and provide information for control. It is appropriate for businesses that produce a single product or a range of very similar products and have no work in process inventories.

There are some businesses that fit this description. Oil refineries produce litres of fuel. Beverage companies often produce a range of different-flavoured drinks that each cost the same to produce. Businesses that complete production at the end of each day have no work-in-process inventories. Also, businesses that use a just-in-time (JIT) approach to inventory management have negligible work-in-process inventories. (As discussed in Chapter 16, under the JIT philosophy all inventories, including work-in-process, are kept to a minimum.) This form of process costing can also be used when work in process inventory levels and costs are reasonably stable from one period to the next. Under these circumstances, the effects of beginning and ending work-in-process inventories are not significant.

Summary

- Product costing is the process of accumulating product-related costs and assigning them to the firm's products. Product costs are required to value inventory for external accounting reports. They are also a vital input to making decisions that enhance the creation of wealth for the organisation. For example, managers may use product costs to support short-term decisions such as product mix and pricing, and for longer-term, strategic decisions. They may also use product cost information for planning costs and for managing resources.
- Different measures of product costs are appropriate for different purposes. Many product costing systems assign only production costs. This approach is useful for valuing inventory for external accounting reports. However, product costs for decision-making may also include upstream and downstream costs. Managers need information about expected future product costs in order to make decisions, although current costs can provide a guide to future costs.
- One of the most difficult tasks in product costing is allocating overhead costs to products. Most conventional costing systems calculate a predetermined (or budgeted) overhead rate, which is based on estimates of overhead costs and cost driver volume. Overhead costs are allocated to products according to their consumption of the overhead cost driver. Underapplied or overapplied overhead is usually closed, at the end of the year, to cost of goods sold.
- A range of different product costing systems is used by businesses, depending on the characteristics of the products produced and the production environment. Process costing and job costing are two common product costing systems. Process costing is used by companies that produce identical or very similar products in very large quantities. Job costing is used by firms that produce a range of dissimilar products.
- In job costing, the direct material and direct labour costs are traced to specific batches of production, called *jobs* or *job orders*. Manufacturing overhead is applied to production jobs using a predetermined overhead rate. In process costing, the manufacturing costs are assigned to processes, usually represented by departments. Product costs are then estimated using an average cost per unit of product for each department through which the product passes. Both of these systems can be expanded to assign upstream and downstream costs to products; this gives managers a more comprehensive picture of product costs for assessing product profitability and making product-related decisions.

References

Alfred, L 2006, 'SA's R9bn World Cup Bid', *Sunday Times*, 24 November.

Bergstrom, CT and Bergstrom, TC 2006, 'The economics of ecology journals', *Font. Ecol. Environ.*, 4(9), pp 488–95

Bot, M 1998, 'The cost of publishing an electronic journal: a general model and case study', *D-Lib Magazine*, November.

Van Orsdel, LC and Born, K 2006, 'Journals in the time of Google', *Library Journal*, 15 April.

Self study

Self-study problem 1: Job costing

Pandora's Puppets Pty Ltd incurred the following costs to produce job number HP25, which consisted of 200 Bart Simpson hand puppets:

Direct material:		
1 May	Requisition no. 88:	180 metres of fabric @ R2.10 per metre
5 May	Requisition no. 92:	200 yellow plastic 'crowns' @ R0.40 each
Direct labour:		
15 May	Time sheet no. 51:	20 hours @ R15 per hour
Manufacturing overhead:		
Applied on the basis of direct labour hours @ R5 per hour.		

The job was completed on 15 May. On 31 May, 100 of the puppets were shipped to a local toy retailer.

Required:

Prepare a job cost sheet and record the information given above. (Use Exhibit 4.10 as a guide.)

Solution to Self-study problem 1

JOB COST SHEET

Job number:	HP25	Description:	Bart Simpson hand puppets
Date started:	1 May	Date completed:	15 May
		Number of units completed:	200

Direct Material

Date	Requisition no.	Description	Quantity	Unit price	Cost
1 May	88	Fabric	180	R2.10	R378
5 May	92	Crowns	200	0.40	80
					R458

Direct Labour

Date	Time sheet number	Hours	Rate	Cost
15 May	51	20	R15	R300

Manufacturing Overhead

Date	Cost driver	Quantity	Application rate	Cost
15 May	Direct labour hours	20	R5	R100

Cost Summary

Cost item	Amount
Total direct material	R458
Total direct labour	300
Total manufacturing overhead	100
Total cost	R858
Unit cost	R4.29

Delivery Summary

Date	Units shipped	Units remaining in inventory	Cost balance
31 May	100	100	R429*

* 100 remaining in inventory × R4.29 = R429

Self-study problem 2: Process costing

Pharmasyrup Ltd produces a syrup for treating coughs and colds, in 250 ml bottles. Production takes place in two departments: Mixing and Bottling. The manufacturing costs for each department for April were:

	Mixing	Bottling
Direct materials	R17 000	R5 000
Direct labour	5 000	1 000
Manufacturing overhead	10 000	2 000

In July the output of the Mixing Department was 1250 litres and the output of the Bottling Department was 5000 bottles. There were no work-in-process inventories.

Required:

1 What is the cost per bottle of cough syrup for April?

2 Prepare the journal entries to record the production costs for April. Assume that the costs of the two production departments are charged to separate work in process inventory accounts.

Solution to Self-study problem 2

1

	Mixing Department	Bottling Department	Total cost
Direct materials	R17 000	R5 000	R22 000
Direct labour	5 000	1 000	6 000
Manufacturing overhead	10 000	2 000	12 000
Total production cost	R32 000	R8 000	R40 000
Units produced	1250 litres	5000 bottles	
Cost per bottle		R8 (R40 000 ÷ 5000 bottles)	

2

The journal entries to record the production costs for the month are:

(1) Work in process inventory: Mixing Department	R32 000	
Raw material inventory		R17 000
Wages payable		5 000
Manufacturing overhead		10 000

—to add the costs of direct material, direct labour and manufacturing overhead to work in process inventory in the Mixing Department.

(2) Work in process inventory: Bottling Department	R32 000	
Work in process: Mixing Department		R32 000

—to add the cost of the litres of mixture transferred from the Mixing Department to the Bottling Department.

(3) Work in process inventory: Bottling Department	R8000	
Raw material inventory		R5000
Wages payable		1000
Manufacturing overhead		2000

—to add the costs of direct material, direct labour and manufacturing overhead to work in process inventory in the Bottling Department.

(4) Finished goods inventory:	R40 000	
Work in process: Bottling Department		R40 000

—*to record the cost of bottles of cough syrup transferred from the Bottling Department to finished goods inventory.*

Cybersearch

1 Find some websites advertising product costing software. Find examples of software that provides product cost information for:

(a) pricing

(b) assessing product profitability

(c) planning costs

(d) controlling costs

(e) inventory valuation

2 Find, using the Internet, examples of firms that you believe would use:

(a) job costing

(b) process costing

In each case, identify the features of the products and production environment that would require job or process costing.

3 After reading Part 1 of the appendix to this chapter, visit the Deloitte website www.iasplus.com for more information on accounting standards and review the information on accounting for inventories.

(a) How are inventories measured under IAS 2?

(b) Describe the standard's approach to allocating overhead costs to products.

(c) In what circumstances does the standard recommend that non-production costs be included as part of the cost of inventories?

Appendix to Chapter 4

Part 1: Product costing standards

L.O. 12 Product costs are required for external accounting reports, such as the balance sheet and income statement, which are used by people outside the organisation. To ensure objectivity and consistency, financial accounting reports are governed by accounting standards. *International Accounting Standard 2: Inventories* (IAS 2) prescribes the measurement of inventories. This standard requires inventories to be measured at the *lower of cost or net realisable value.* **Net realisable value** is the estimated selling price in the ordinary course of business less the estimated costs of completion and the estimated cost necessary to make the sales. Businesses aim to sell inventories at a profit, so in most circumstances net realisable value will be greater than cost, and inventories will be recorded at cost. For not-for-profit entities inventory held for distribution is to be valued at the lower of cost and current replacement cost.

Under IAS 2, the cost of inventories is to consist of:

- the cost of purchase (including purchase price, import duties, transportation and handling costs) less any trade discounts and rebates;
- the cost of conversion into finished products (such as direct labour, and should include an allocation of fixed and variable production overhead costs); and
- any other costs in bringing the inventories to their present location.

The cost should exclude the cost of abnormal wastage, storage, administration and selling cost.

The carrying amount of inventories is recorded as an expense in the same period that the inventories are sold and the associated revenue is recognised. IAS 2 does not apply to work-in-process occurring from construction contracts, financial instruments and agricultural, forest and other biological assets.

Part 2: Prorating underapplied or overapplied overhead

L.O. 13 In this chapter we used Williams Elevators to illustrate job costing. Williams Elevators closed its underapplied and overapplied overhead to cost of goods sold. If the company had prorated its underapplied or overapplied overhead, it would have been spread across work in process inventory, finished goods inventory and cost of goods sold. The amount of the current period's applied overhead remaining in each account is the basis for the proration procedure. The amounts of applied overhead remaining in the three accounts on 30 November are determined in Exhibit 4.21.

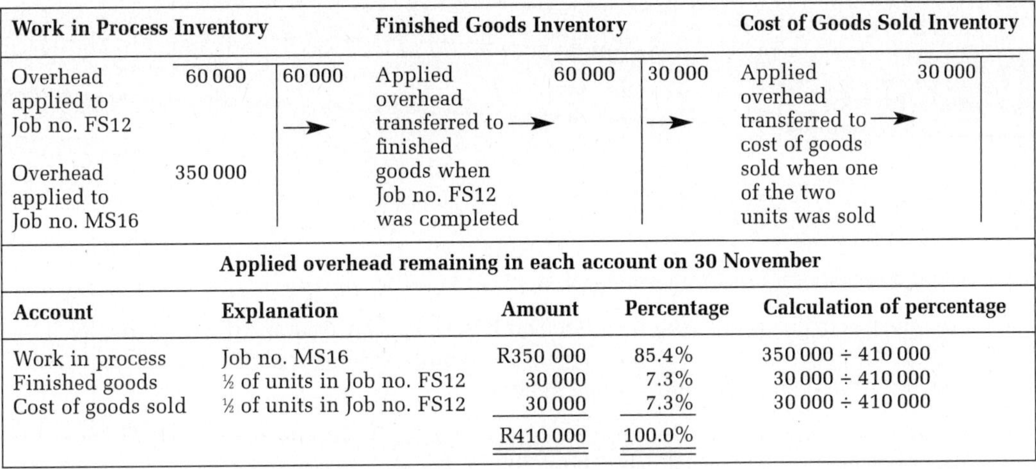

Applied overhead remaining in each account on 30 November

Account	Explanation	Amount	Percentage	Calculation of percentage
Work in process	Job no. MS16	R350 000	85.4%	350 000 ÷ 410 000
Finished goods	½ of units in Job no. FS12	30 000	7.3%	30 000 ÷ 410 000
Cost of goods sold	½ of units in Job no. FS12	30 000	7.3%	30 000 ÷ 410 000
		R410 000	100.0%	

Exhibit 4.21 Proration of underapplied overhead, Williams Elevators Ltd

Using the percentages calculated in Exhibit 4.21, the proration of Williams Elevators' underapplied overhead would have been as follows:

Account	Underapplied overhead	×	Percentage	=	Amount to be added to the account
Work in process	R2 500	×	85.4%	=	R2 135.00
Finished goods	2 500	×	7.3%	=	182.50
Cost of goods sold	2 500	×	7.3%	=	182.50
Total underapplied overhead prorated					R2 500.00

Questions

?

4.1 What are *cost objects?* What role do they play in costing systems?

4.2 Identify the major purposes of product costing. For each purpose discuss whether information about current or future product costs is required. What implication does your answer have for developing a product costing system?

4.3 Identify the major purposes of product costing. For each purpose discuss which costs (production, upstream or downstream) should be included. Explain.

4.4 Identify the major purposes of product costing. For each purpose discuss the frequency with which management would usually require this information. What implication does your answer have for developing a product costing system?

4.5 'We don't need a product costing system. We are a small manufacturer with a just-in-time approach so that our inventories are minimal. We have no influence over product price; whatever the big fellows do, we follow. Anyway, our accountant only comes in on Fridays and she is already far too busy to bother with a product costing system.'
Is this a reasonable attitude? Explain why.

4.6 Describe the flow of costs through a product costing system used to value inventory. What special ledger accounts are involved, and how are they used?

4.7 Applying manufacturing overhead to products involves three steps. Describe each step.

4.8 What are the causes of overapplied or underapplied overhead?

4.9 Briefly describe two ways of disposing of overapplied or underapplied overhead at the end of an accounting period.

4.10 When should underapplied or overapplied overhead be closed? Explain your answer.

4.11 When manufacturing overhead is underapplied, we close it by debiting (adding) it to cost of goods sold. Yet in Exhibit 4.14, in estimating the cost of goods manufactured, underapplied overhead is subtracted, not added! Explain why.

4.12 Explain the difference between *job costing* and *process costing.* Give three examples (other than those in the chapter) of businesses that you think would use:
(a) a job costing system
(b) a process costing system
Explain your choices.

4.13 Describe the two main steps involved in process costing.

4.14 Describe the flow of costs through the manufacturing accounts in a process costing system where:
(a) there is a single production department
(b) there are two or more production departments

4.15 'There is no such thing as a job costing system or a process costing system. In the "real world" most businesses use a costing system that has some elements of job costing and some elements of process costing.' Discuss.

4.16 What are the purposes of the following documents:
(a) job cost sheet
(b) material requisition form
(c) labour time sheet?

4.17 Explain the meaning of the following terms in the schedule of cost of goods manufactured:
(a) total manufacturing costs
(b) manufacturing costs to account for
(c) cost of goods manufactured

4.18 Process costing is a product costing system, yet the focus is on the costs of processes or production departments. Explain why.

4.19 Refer to the Spritz example of process costing in the chapter. Explain why the production costs for each department are added together to obtain an estimate of the cost per bottle of Spritz, yet the journal entries record the costs in each production department separately.

4.20 In this chapter we describe a simple approach to process costing, which can be used by businesses with no beginning or ending work in process inventories. Evaluate this approach to product costing and give three examples of the types of businesses where it may be appropriate.

4.21 (appendix, Part 1) Describe how inventories are measured under International Accounting Standard IAS 2 *Inventories*.

4.22 (appendix, Part 2) Describe one advantage and one disadvantage of prorating overapplied or underapplied overhead.

Exercises

E4.23 Job cost sheet: manufacturer

Cuddly Toys Pty Ltd incurred the following costs to produce job number TB78, which consisted of 1000 teddy bears that could walk, talk and play cards:

Direct material:		
1 April	Requisition no. 101:	400 metres of fabric @ R2.40 per metre
5 April	Requisition no. 108:	500 cubic metres of stuffing @ R0.90 per cubic metre
Direct labour:		
15 April	Time sheet no. 72:	500 hours @ R36 per hour
Manufacturing overhead:		
Applied on the basis of direct labour hours @ R8 per hour.		

On 30 April, 700 of the bears were shipped to a local toy shop.

Required:
1 Prepare a job cost sheet and record the information given above. (Use Exhibit 4.10 as a guide.)
2 How might the managers at Cuddly Toys use this information?

E4.24 Schedule of cost of goods manufactured

PopSnaps Cereal Company incurred the following actual costs during 20X6:

Direct material used	R4 125 000
Direct labour	1 800 000
Manufacturing overhead	3 780 000

The firm's predetermined overhead rate is 210 per cent of direct labour cost. The inventory balances, on 1 January 20X6, were as follows:

Raw material	R450 000
Work in process	585 000
Finished goods	630 000

Each of these inventory balances was 10 per cent higher at the end of the year.

Required:

1 Prepare a schedule of cost of goods manufactured for 20X6.
2 What was the cost of goods sold for the year?

E4.25 Manufacturing cost flows

Pierre's Sporting Equipment Pty Ltd incurred the following costs during the year:

Direct material	R2 262 000
Direct labour	4 212 000
Manufacturing overhead applied	234 000

Products costing R1 200 000 were finished, and products costing R1 320 000 were sold for R1 950 000. The balances in the firm's inventory accounts at the beginning of the year were as follows:

Raw materials	R2 951 000
Work in process	234 000
Finished goods	390 000

Required:

1 Prepare ledger accounts to show the flow of costs through the company's manufacturing accounts during the year.
2 Prepare a partial balance sheet and a partial income statement to reflect the information given above.

E4.26 Manufacturing cost flows

Selected data concerning the past year's operations of the Blaster Sound Company are presented below:

	Inventories		
	Beginning	Ending	
Raw material	R1 420 000	R1 620 000	
Work in process	1 600 000	600 000	
Finished goods	1 800 000	2 200 000	
Other data:			
Direct materials used			6 520 000
Total manufacturing costs charged to production during the year (includes direct material, direct labour, and manufacturing overhead applied at a rate of 60% of direct labour cost)			13 720 000
Cost of goods available for sale			16 520 000
Selling and administrative expenses			630 000

Required:

1 What was the cost of raw materials purchased during the year?
2 What was the direct labour cost charged to production during the year?
3 What was the cost of goods manufactured during the year?
4 What was the cost of goods sold during the year?

(CMA, adapted)

E4.27 Overapplied or underapplied overhead: manufacturer

The following information relates to Gloworm Glass Works for 20X6:

Budgeted direct labour cost	77 000 hours @ R17 per hour
Actual direct labour cost	79 000 hours @ R18 per hour
Budgeted manufacturing overhead	R993 300
Actual manufacturing overhead:	
Depreciation	R225 000
Property taxes	19 000
Indirect labour	79 000
Supervisory salaries	210 000
Electricity	58 000
Insurance	32 000
Factory rent	295 000
Indirect material (see data below)	79 000
Indirect material:	
Beginning inventory, 31 December 20X5	R46 000
Purchases during 20X6	95 000
Ending inventory, 31 December 20X6	62 000

Required:

1 Calculate the firm's predetermined overhead rate, which was based on direct labour hours.
2 Calculate the overapplied or underapplied overhead for 20X6.
3 Prepare a journal entry to close the manufacturing overhead account to cost of goods sold.
4 What caused the overapplied or underapplied overhead?

E4.28 Basic journal entries in job costing: manufacturer

Jigsaw Educational Products started and finished job number B67 during June. The job required R13 800 of direct material and 40 hours of direct labour at R51 per hour. The predetermined overhead rate is R15 per direct labour hour.

Required:

Prepare journal entries to record the incurrence of production costs and the completion of job number B67.

E4.29 Manufacturing overhead: furniture manufacturer

The following data relate to Fine Furniture Pty Ltd for the year just ended:

Actual manufacturing overhead	R680 000
Budgeted machine hours	20 000
Budgeted direct labour hours	40 000
Budgeted direct labour rate	R28
Budgeted manufacturing overhead	R728 000
Actual machine hours	22 000
Actual direct labour hours	36 000
Actual direct labour rate	R30

Required:

1 Calculate the company's predetermined overhead rate using each of the following cost drivers:
(a) machine hours
(b) direct labour hours
(c) direct labour Rands

2 Calculate the overapplied or underapplied overhead for the year using each of the cost drivers listed above.

3 Which cost driver seems to be the most appropriate? Explain.

4 Prepare a journal entry to charge the total manufacturing overhead cost for the year to work in process inventory.

E4.30 Process costing; no work in process: manufacturer

Stanmore CC produces hospital-grade disinfectant, called Super Clean, in two-litre containers. Production takes place in two departments: Mixing and Packing. The manufacturing costs for each department for July were:

	Mixing	Packing
Direct materials	R50 000	R10 000
Direct labour	24 000	8 000
Manufacturing overhead	14 400	4 800

In July the company produced 140 000 litres of Super Clean mixture, which was packed into 70 000 containers.

Required:

1 What is the cost per container for Super Clean?

2 Prepare the journal entries to record the production costs for July. Assume that the costs of the two production departments are charged to separate work in process inventory accounts.

E4.31 Process costing; no work in process: brewer

South Brew Ltd, a brewing company, produces its primary product, South Bay Draught, in 300 ml cans. Production takes place in two departments: Mixing and Bottling. The manufacturing costs for each department for August were:

	Mixing	Bottling
Direct materials	R1 125 000	R180 000
Direct labour	150 000	60 000
Manufacturing overhead	225 000	90 000

In August the company produced 150 000 litres of South Bay Draught, which was canned into 500 000 cans. There were no work-in-process inventories.

Required:

1 What is the cost per can for South Bay Draught?

2 Prepare the journal entries to record the production costs for August. Assume that the costs of the two production departments are charged to separate work in process inventory accounts.

3 Evaluate this approach to product costing.

E4.32 Proration of underapplied overhead (appendix): manufacturer

Leura Confectionery incurred R1 670 000 of manufacturing overhead costs during the past year. However, only R1 450 000 of overhead was applied to production. At the conclusion of the year, the following amounts of the applied overhead remained in the various manufacturing accounts:

Work in process inventory	R290 000
Finished goods inventory	507 500
Cost of goods sold	652 500

Required:

1 Explain whether the company has overapplied or underapplied its overhead to production.

2 Prepare a journal entry to close off the balance in the manufacturing overhead account and prorate the balance to the three manufacturing accounts.

3 What would be the effect on profit if the alternative method of closing off overhead were used?

Problems

P4.33 Job costing; journal entries

Southern Fashions, which uses a job costing system, had two jobs in process at the start of the year: job number 101 (R1 680 000) and job number 102 (R1 070 000). The following information is available:

(a) The company applies manufacturing overhead on the basis of machine hours. Budgeted overhead and machine activity for the year were anticipated to be R16.8 million and 32 000 hours, respectively.

(b) The company worked on four jobs during the first quarter. Direct materials used, direct labour incurred, and machine hours consumed were as shown in the table below.

Job no.	Direct material	Direct labour	Machine hours
101	R420 000	R700 000	24 000
102		440 000	14 000
103	880 000	1 300 000	40 000
104	300 000	176 000	10 000

(c) Manufacturing overhead during the first quarter included charges for depreciation (R680 000), indirect labour (R1 200 000), indirect materials used (R100 000), and other factory costs (R2 790 000).

(d) Southern Fashions completed job number 101 and job no 102. Job number 102 was sold on credit, producing a profit of R 694 000 for the firm.

Required:

1 Determine the company's predetermined overhead application rate.

2 Prepare journal entries for the first quarter to record the following (Note: Use summary entries where appropriate by combining individual job data):
   (a) the issue of direct material to production and the direct labour incurred
   (b) the manufacturing overhead incurred during the quarter
   (c) the application of manufacturing overhead to production
   (d) the completion of job numbers 101 and 102
   (e) the sale of job number 102

3 Determine the cost of the jobs still in production as of March 31.

4 Did the finished goods inventory increase or decrease during the first quarter? By how much?

P4.34 Predetermined overhead rate; journal entries

Seaspray Ltd manufactures outboard motors and an assortment of other marine equipment. The company uses a job costing system and manufacturing overhead is applied on the basis of machine hours. Estimated manufacturing overhead for the year is R15 202 000, and management expect that 69 100 machine hours will be used.

The following events occurred in April:

(a) The firm purchased marine propellers from Peninsula Marine Corporation for R82 400 on credit.
(b) A requisition was filed by the Gauge Department supervisor for 280 kilograms of clear plastic. The material was purchased for R7.00 per kilogram.
(c) The Motor Testing Department supervisor requisitioned 320 metres of electrical wire, which is considered an indirect material. The wire was purchased for R1.00 per metre.
(d) An electric utility bill of R9 000 was paid in cash.
(e) Direct labour costs incurred in April were R735 000.
(f) April's insurance cost was R21 000 for insurance on the cars driven by sales personnel. The policy had been prepaid in March.
(g) Metal tubing costing R28 000 was purchased on credit.
(h) A cash payment of R18 500 was made on outstanding accounts payable.
(i) Indirect labour costs of R190 000 were incurred during April.
(j) Depreciation on equipment for April amounted to R85 000.
(k) Job number G22, consisting of 60 tachometers, was finished during April. The total cost of the job was R12 000.
(l) During April, 6500 machine hours were used.
(m) Sales on account for April amounted to R1 810 000. The cost of goods sold in April was R1 425 000.

Required:

1 Calculate the company's predetermined overhead rate for the year.
2 Prepare journal entries to record the events listed above.

P4.35 Basic job costing; journal entries; ledger accounts; job cost card

Quality Boxes CC manufactures fine, handcrafted wooden jewellery boxes. The firm uses a job costing system, and manufacturing overhead is applied on the basis of direct labour hours. Estimated manufacturing overhead for the current year is R240 000. The firm employs 10 trainee carpenters, who are regarded as direct labour. Each of these employees is expected to work 2000 hours during the year.

At the beginning of October 20X5 the inventory balances were as follows:

- Raw material: 5000 metres of wood at R11 per metre, R55 000.
- Work in process: job number G60, R3700, consisting of direct material R500, direct labour, R2000 and manufacturing overhead R1200.
- Finished goods: job number B50, R12 000.

The following events occurred during October 20X5:

(a) The firm purchased 3000 metres of wood at R11 per metre.
(b) The following raw materials were transferred to production:
  - job number G60: 1000 metres of wood
  - job number C81: 5000 metres of wood
(c) Five litres of glue were purchased in October and issued to production. The glue cost R20 per litre. Glue is treated as an indirect material.
(d) Depreciation on the factory equipment for October was R8000.
(e) R400 electricity bill for the manufacturing plant was paid in cash.
(f) Time sheets showed the following use of labour:
  - job number G60: 100 hours of direct labour
  - job number C81: 700 hours of direct labour

  The carpenters (direct labour) earn R20 per hour.

(g) The October council rates bill of R910 for the manufacturing plant was received but not yet paid in cash.
(h) The firm employs labourers who perform various tasks such as material handling and shop clean-up. Their wages for October amounted to R2500.
(i) Job number G60, which was started in July, was finished in October. Job number C81 was incomplete at the end of October.
(j) Job number B50 was sold in October for R15000.

Required:

1 Provide journal entries to record the events listed above for October 20X5.
2 Post journal entries to the following inventory ledger accounts:
   (a) raw material
   (b) work in process
   (c) finished goods
   and determine closing balances.
3 Prepare a job cost card for job number G60.

P4.36 Manufacturing cost flows; analysis of ledger accounts

Pronto Pizza Company produces microwaveable pizzas. The following accounts appeared in Pronto's ledger as at 31 December 20X6:

Raw Material Inventory

1/1/X6 Bal.	29 400		?
	?	31/12 Bal. (c/f)	50 400
	?		?
1/1/X7 Bal.(b/f)	50 400		

Accounts Payable

	191 100	1/1/X6 Bal.	3 500
31/12 Bal.(c/f)	1 400		?
	192 500		192 500
		1/1/X7 Bal. (b/f)	1 400

Work in Process Inventory

1/1/X6 Bal.	23 800		
Direct material	?		?
Direct labour	?	31/12 Bal. (c/f)	26 600
Manufacturing overhead	?		
	?		?
1/1/X7 Bal. (b/f)	26 600		

Finished Goods Inventory

1/1/X6 Bal.	16 800		?
	?	31/12 Bal. (c/f)	28 000
	?		?
1/1/X7 Bal. (b/f)	28 000		

Cost of Goods Sold

	994 000		

Manufacturing Overhead

	?		?

Sales Revenue

			?

Wages Payable

	205 800	1/1/X6 Bal.	2 800
31/12/ Bal. (c/f)	7 000		?
	212 800		212 800
		1/1/X7 Bal. (b/f)	7 000

Accounts Receivable

1/1/X6 Bal.	15 400		1 128 400
	?	31/12 Bal. (c/f)	21 000
	1 149 400		1 149 400
1/1/X7 Bal. (b/f)	21 000		

Additional information

- Accounts payable is used only for direct material purchases.
- Underapplied overhead of R3500 for the year has not yet been closed to cost of goods sold.
- Wages payable is used only for direct labour wages.
- All sales are on credit.

Required:

Complete the ledger accounts by calculating the amounts indicated by a question mark.

P4.37 Flow of manufacturing costs; incomplete data

Woodgrain Company manufactures furniture. Due to a fire in the administrative offices, the accounting records for November were partially destroyed. You have been able to piece together the information below from the ledger:

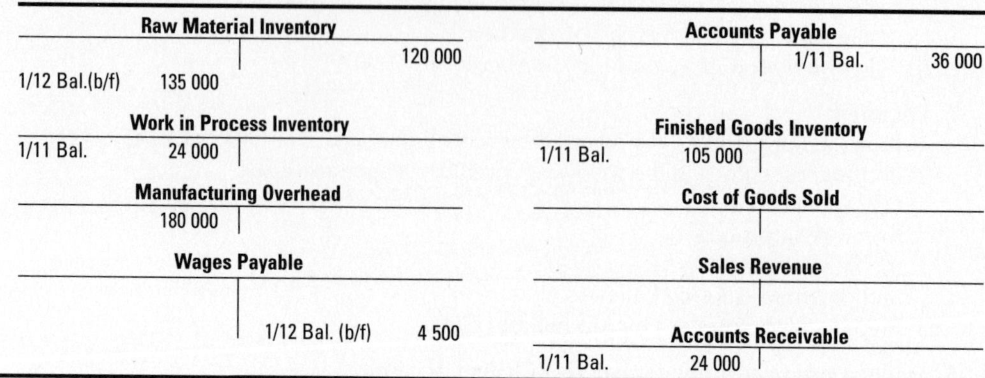

Raw Material Inventory

			120 000
1/12 Bal.(b/f)	135 000		

Work in Process Inventory

1/11 Bal.	24 000		

Manufacturing Overhead

	180 000		

Wages Payable

		1/12 Bal. (b/f)	4 500

Accounts Payable

		1/11 Bal.	36 000

Finished Goods Inventory

1/11 Bal.	105 000		

Cost of Goods Sold

Sales Revenue

Accounts Receivable

1/11 Bal.	24 000		

By examining various source documents and interviewing several employees, you have been able to gather the following additional information:

- Collections of accounts receivable during November amounted to R615 000.
- Sales revenue in November was 120 per cent of cost of goods sold. All sales are on account.
- Overhead is applied using an annual predetermined overhead rate based on direct labour hours.
- The budgeted overhead for the current year is R2 160 000.
- Budgeted direct labour cost for the current year is R2 880 000. The direct labour rate is R20 per hour.
- The accounts payable balance on 30 November was R3000. Only purchases of raw material are credited to accounts payable. A payment of R243 000 was made on 15 November.
- November's cost of goods sold amounted to R540 000.
- The 30 November balance in finished goods inventory was R15 000.
- Payments of R238 500 were made to direct labour employees during November. The 31 October balance in the wages payable account was R3000.
- The actual manufacturing overhead for November was R180 000.
- An analysis of the furniture still in process on 30 November revealed that, so far, these items have required 1500 hours of direct labour and R61 500 of direct material.

Required:

1 Calculate the following amounts:
   (a) sales revenue for November
   (b) the 30 November balance in accounts receivable
   (c) cost of raw material purchased during November
   (d) the 30 November balance in work in process inventory
   (e) direct labour added to work in process during November
   (f) applied overhead for November
   (g) cost of goods completed during November
   (h) raw materials used during November
   (i) the 31 October balance in raw material inventory
   (j) overapplied or underapplied overhead for November

2 Complete the ledger accounts given in the problem.

P4.38 Cost of goods manufactured; overapplied or underapplied overhead; journal entries

Cool Cooking Tools Ltd, manufacturer of gourmet cooking utensils, uses job costing. Manufacturing overhead is applied to production at a predetermined overhead rate of 150 per cent of direct labour cost. Any overapplied or underapplied manufacturing overhead is closed to cost of goods sold at the end of each month. Additional information follows:

- Job SR22, consisting of ceramic spoon rests, was the only job in process on 31 January, with accumulated costs as follows:

Direct material	R40 000
Direct labour	20 000
Applied manufacturing overhead	30 000
Total	90 000

- Jobs BS67, TR29 and GT108 were started during February.
- Direct materials requisitions during February totalled R260 000.
- Direct labour cost of R200 000 was incurred during February.
- Manufacturing overhead incurred in February was R320 000.
- The only job still in process on 28 February was job number GT108, with costs of R28 000 for direct material and R18 000 for direct labour.

Required:

1 Calculate the cost of goods manufactured for February.
2 Calculate the amount of overapplied or underapplied overhead to be closed to cost of goods sold on 28 February.
3 Prepare journal entries to record the events described in requirements 1 and 2.

(CPA, adapted)

P4.39 Cost of goods manufactured; prime and conversion costs

Vancol Crisps Ltd's cost of goods sold for March was R345 000. The 31 March work-in-process inventory was 90 per cent of the 1 March work-in-process inventory. Manufacturing overhead applied was 50 per cent of direct labour cost. Other information relating to Vancol Crisps' inventories and production for the month of March is as follows:

Beginning inventories, 1 March:	
Direct material	R17 000
Work in process	40 000
Finished goods	102 000
Purchases of direct material during March	113 000
Ending inventories, 31 March:	
Direct material	26 000
Work in process	?
Finished goods	105 000

Required:

1 Prepare a schedule of cost of goods manufactured for the month of March.
2 Prepare a schedule to calculate the prime costs (direct material and direct labour) incurred during March.
3 Prepare a schedule to calculate the conversion costs (direct labour and manufacturing overhead) charged to work in process during March.

(CPA, adapted)

P4.40 Ethical issues; underapplication of manufacturing overhead: manufacturer

Tom Savin has recently been hired as a cost accountant by Offset Press Pty Ltd, a company that produces a line of offset printing presses and lithograph machines. During his first few months on the job, Savin discovered that Offset has been underapplying factory overhead to the work in process account, while overstating expenses through the general and administrative account. This practice has been going on since the start of the company, which is in its sixth year of operation. The effect in each year has been favourable, having a material impact on the company's tax position. No internal audit function exists at Offset, and the external auditors have not yet discovered the underapplied factory overhead.

Prior to the sixth-year audit, Savin pointed out the practice and its effect to Mary Brown, the accounting manager, and asked her to let him make the necessary adjustments. Brown directed him not to make the adjustments but to wait until the external auditors had completed their work and see what they uncovered.

The sixth-year audit has now been completed, and the external auditors have once again failed to discover the underapplication of factory overhead. Savin again asks Brown if he can make the required adjustments and again is told not to make them. Savin, however, believes that the adjustments should be made and that the external auditors should be informed of the situation.

Since there are no established policies at Offset Press for resolving ethical conflicts, Savin is considering one of the following three courses of action:

1 Follow Brown's directive and do nothing further.
2 Attempt to convince Brown that she should make the proper adjustments, and advise the external auditors of her actions.
3 Tell the Audit Committee about the problem and give them the appropriate accounting data.

Required:

1 For each of the three courses of action that Tom Savin is considering, explain whether or not the action is appropriate. (*Hint:* Refer to the ethical issues discussed in Chapter 1.)
2 Independent of your answer to requirement 1, assume that Tom Savin again approaches Mary Brown to make the necessary adjustments and is unsuccessful. Describe the steps that Tom Savin should take to resolve this situation.

(CPA, adapted)

P4.41 Schedule of cost of goods manufactured

Norton Industries, a manufacturer of cable for the construction industry, closes its books and prepares financial statements at the end of each month. The schedule of cost of goods sold for April follows:

Norton Industries for the month ended 30 April (in R'000s)	
Inventory of finished goods, 31 March	R50
Add Cost of goods manufactured	790
Cost of goods available for sale	840
Less Inventory of finished goods, 30 April	247
Unadjusted cost of goods sold	593
Add Underapplied manufacturing overhead	25
Cost of goods sold (adjusted for underapplied overhead)	R618

Norton has a policy of selling its oldest inventory first. The actual cost of direct materials and direct labour is used to value the inventories. However, manufacturing overhead is applied to production and charged to inventory at a predetermined rate of R4000 per tonne of cable manufactured.

The preclosing trial balance as at 31 May is as follows:

Norton Industries Preclosing Trial Balance 31 May (in R'000s)		
Account	**Debit**	**Credit**
Cash and marketable securities	R54	
Accounts and notes receivable	210	
Direct materials inventory (30 April)	28	
Work in process inventory (30 April)	150	
Finished goods inventory (30 April)	247	
Property, plant and equipment (net)	1140	
Accounts and taxes payable		R70
Bonds payable		600
Ordinary shares		100
Retained earnings		930
Sales		1 488
Sales discounts	20	
Interest revenue		2
Purchases of direct material	525	
Direct labour	260	
Indirect labour	90	
Office salaries	122	
Sales salaries	66	
Utilities	135	
Rent	9	
Property taxes	60	
Insurance	20	
Depreciation	54	
Total	R3 190	R3 190

Additional information:

- 80 per cent of the utilities cost is related to the manufacture of cable; the remaining 20 per cent is related to the sales and administrative functions in the office building.
- All the rent is for the office building.
- The property taxes are assessed on the manufacturing plant.
- 60 per cent of the insurance is related to the manufacture of cable; the remaining 40 per cent is related to the sales and administrative functions in the office building.
- Depreciation expense includes the following:

Manufacturing plant	R20 000
Manufacturing equipment	30 000
Office equipment	4 000
Total	R54 000

- Norton manufactured 78.25 tonnes of cable during May. The inventory balances at 31 May are as follows:

Direct material	R23 000
Work in process	220 000
Finished goods	175 000

Required:

1 Prepare a schedule of cost of goods manufactured for Norton Industries for May. Norton Industries closes all underapplied or overapplied manufacturing overhead to cost of goods sold at the end of each month.

2 Describe an alternative treatment for closing underapplied or overapplied manufacturing overhead.

3 Explain the problems that arise with closing overhead accounts at the end of each month.

(CMA, adapted)

P4.42 Process costing; journal entries: manufacturer

Eliminator Ltd produces a weed-killing spray, in 250-ml bottles. Production takes place through three departments: Mixing, then Bottling and finally Packaging. The manufacturing costs for each department for April were:

	Mixing	Bottling	Packaging
Direct materials	R86 000	R30 000	10 000
Direct labour	33 600	15 800	8 600
Manufacturing overhead	39 000	4 000	1 800

In April the output of the Mixing Department was 5000 litres, the output of the Bottling Department was 20 000 spray pump bottles, and the output of the Packaging Department was 20 000 packed spray pump bottles. There were no work-in-process inventories.

Required:

1 What is the cost per litre of weed-killing solution produced by the Mixing Department for April?
2 What is the cost per filled spray pump bottle produced by the Bottling Department for April (including the cost of the solution produced in the Mixing Department)?
3 What is the cost per packed spray pump bottle produced by the Packaging Department for April (including the cost of the filled bottles produced in the Bottling Department)?
4 What information do you obtain from estimating the cost per packed spray pump bottle, using Steps 1 to 3 above, that is not available from the method described in the chapter?
5 Prepare the journal entries to record the production costs for April. Assume that the costs of the three production departments are charged to separate work in process inventory accounts.
6 Which approach would you recommend? Explain your answer.

P4.43 Proration of overapplied or underapplied overhead (appendix): manufacturer

African Jewellery Pty Ltd allocates manufacturing overhead to work in process on the basis of machine hours. On 1 January 20X7, there were no balances in work in process or finished goods inventories. The following estimates were included in the 20X7 budget:

Total estimated manufacturing overhead	R2 350 000
Total estimated machine hours	470 000

During January, the firm worked on the following production jobs:

A79:	1000 machine hours
N08:	2500 machine hours
P82:	500 machine hours

During January, job numbers A79 and N08 were completed, and job number A79 was sold. The actual manufacturing overhead incurred during January was R260 000.

Required:

1 Calculate the company's predetermined overhead rate for 20X7.
2 How much manufacturing overhead was applied to production during January 20X7?
3 Calculate the overapplied or underapplied overhead for January 20X7.
4 Prepare a journal entry to close the balance calculated in requirement 3 to cost of goods sold.

5 Prepare a journal entry to prorate the balance calculated in requirement 3 between the work in process inventory, finished goods inventory, and cost of goods sold accounts.

Cases

C4.44 Comprehensive job costing problem: manufacturer

Brass Design Ltd manufactures brass musical instruments. The company uses a job costing system, in which manufacturing overhead is applied on the basis of direct labour hours. The company's budget for the current year included the following predictions:

Budgeted total manufacturing overhead	R4 620 000
Budgeted total direct labour hours	21 000

During March, the firm began two production jobs:

- Job number T81, consisting of 76 trombones.
- Job number C40, consisting of 110 cornets.

The events of March are described below:

- 1000 square metres of rolled brass sheet metal were purchased for R60 000 on account.
- 400 kilograms of brass tubing were purchased on account for R52 000.
- The following requisitions were filed on 5 March:
  - Requisition number 112: 260 square metres of brass sheet metal (for job number T81) @ R55 per square metre
  - Requisition number 113: 1100 kilograms of brass tubing (for job number C40) @ R90 per kilogram
  - Requisition number 114: 10 litres of valve lubricant @ R120 per litre

  All brass used in production is treated as direct material. Valve lubricant is an indirect material.
- An analysis of labour time sheets revealed the following labour usage for March:
  - Direct labour: job number T81, 850 hours @ R200 per hour
  - Direct labour: job number C40, 950 hours @ R200 per hour
  - Indirect labour: general factory clean-up, R45 000
  - Indirect labour: factory supervisory salaries, R96 000
- Depreciation of the factory building and equipment during March amounted to R130 000.
- Rent paid in cash for warehouse space used during March was R13 400.
- Electricity costs incurred during March amounted to R24 000. The invoices for these costs were received, but the bills were not paid in March.
- March council rates and property taxes on the factory were paid in cash, R23 700.
- The insurance cost covering factory operations for the month of March was R29 000.
- The insurance policy had been prepaid.
- The costs of salaries and on-costs for sales and administrative personnel paid in cash during March amounted to R75 000.
- Depreciation on administrative office equipment and space amounted to R45 000.
- Other selling and administrative expenses paid in cash during March amounted to R11 500.
- Job number T81 was completed during March.
- Half the trombones in job number T81 were sold on account during March for R7200 each.

The 1 March balances in selected accounts are as follows:

Cash	R110 000
Accounts receivable	200 000
Prepaid insurance	60 000
Raw material inventory	1 500 000
Manufacturing supplies inventory	6 000
Work in process inventory	890 000
Finished goods inventory	2 230 000
Accumulated depreciation: buildings and equipment	990 000
Accounts payable	145 000
Wages payable	85 000

Required:

1 Calculate the company's predetermined overhead rate for the current year.
2 Complete the job cost sheet below for job number T81.
3 Prepare journal entries to record the events of March.
4 Set up ledger accounts, and post the journal entries made in requirement 2.
5 Calculate the overapplied or underapplied overhead for March. Prepare a journal entry to close this balance into cost of goods sold.
6 Prepare a schedule of cost of goods manufactured for March.
7 Prepare a schedule of cost of goods sold for March.
8 Prepare an income statement for March.

JOB COST SHEET				
Job number: T81		Description: ________		
Date started: ________		Date completed: ________		
________		Number of units completed: ________		
		Direct Material		
Date	**Requisition number**	**Quantity**	**Unit price**	**Cost**
		Direct Labour		
Dates	**Time sheet numbers**	**Hours**	**Rate**	**Cost**
8/3 to 12/3	308 to 312			
		Manufacturing Overhead		
Dates	**Cost driver**	**Quantity**	**Application rate**	**Cost**
8/3 to 12/3				
		Cost Summary		
Cost item			**Amount**	
Total direct material				
Total direct labour				
Total manufacturing overhead				
Total cost				
Unit cost				
		Delivery Summary		
Date	**Units shipped**	**Units remaining in inventory**	**Cost balance**	

C4.45 Interpreting information from a job costing system: manufacturer

Constructo Ltd is a manufacturer of furnishings for children. The company uses a job costing system. Constructo's work in process inventory on 30 November consisted of the following jobs:

Job no.	Items	Units	Accumulated cost
CBS102	Cribs	20 000	R4 500 000
PLP086	Playpens	15 000	2 100 000
DRS114	Dressers	25 000	1 250 000
Total			7 850 000

The company's finished goods inventory consisted of five items:

Item	Quantity	Unit cost	Accumulated cost
Cribs	7 500	R320.00	R2 400 000
Strollers	13 000	115.00	1 495 000
Carriages	11 200	510.00	5 712 000
Dressers	21 000	275.00	5 775 000
Playpens	19 400	175.00	3 395 000
Total			18 777 000

Constructo applies manufacturing overhead on the basis of direct labour hours. The company's overhead budget for the year totals R22 500 000, and the company plans to use 600 000 direct labour hours during this period. Through the first 11 months of the year, a total of 555 000 direct labour hours were worked, and total overhead amounted to R21 367 500. At the end of November, the balance in Constructo's raw material inventory account, which includes both raw materials and purchased parts, was R3 340 000. Additions to inventory and requisitions from inventory during December included the following:

	Raw material	Purchased parts
Purchases	1 210 000	1 980 000
Requisitions:		
Job no. CBS102	255 000	520 000
Job no. PLP086	15 000	54 000
Job no. DRS114	620 000	435 000
Job no. STR077 (10 000 strollers)	310 000	405 000
Job no. CRG098 (5000 carriages)	325 000	935 000

During December, Constructo's factory payroll consisted of the following:

Job no. CBS102	12 000 hours	R612 000
Job no. PLP086	4 400 hours	216 000
Job no. DRS114	19 500 hours	1 002 500
Job no. STR077	3 500 hours	150 000
Job no. CRG098	34 000 hours	690 000
Indirect labour	3 000 hours	147 000
Supervision		288 000
Total		3 105 500

The following list shows the jobs that were completed and the unit sales for December:

	Production		Sales	
Job no.	Items	Quantity completed	Items	Quantity shipped
CBS102	Cribs	20 000	Cribs	17 500
PLP086	Playpens	15 000	Playpens	21 000
STR077	Strollers	10 000	Strollers	14 000
CRG098	Carriages	5 000	Dressers	18 000
			Carriages	6 000

Assume that the units produced first are sold first.

Required:

1 Explain when it is appropriate for a company to use a job costing system.
2 Calculate the Rand balance in Constructo's work in process inventory account as at 31 December.
3 Calculate the Rand amount related to the playpens in Constructo's finished goods inventory account as at 31 December.

(CMA, adapted)

C4.46 Cost flows in a job costing system; schedule of cost of goods manufactured; automation: manufacturer

Optic Vision Pty Ltd, a manufacturer of fibre-optic communications equipment, uses a job costing system. Since the production process is heavily automated, manufacturing overhead is applied on the basis of machine hours using a predetermined overhead rate. The current annual rate of R30 per machine hour is based on estimated manufacturing overhead costs of R2 400 000 and an estimated cost driver level of 80 000 machine hours.

Operations for the current year have been completed, and all the accounting entries have been made for the year except the application of manufacturing overhead to the jobs worked on during December, the transfer of costs from work in process to finished goods for the jobs completed in December, and the transfer of costs from finished goods to cost of goods sold for the jobs that have been sold during December. Summarised data as at 30 November, and for December, are presented in the following table. Job numbers T11–007, N11–013 and N11–015 were completed during December. All completed jobs except job number N11–013 had been turned over to customers by the close of business on 31 December.

Work in Process: December activity

Job no.	Balance 30 November	Direct material	Direct labour	Machine hours
T11-007	R174 000	R3 000	9000	300
N11-013	110 000	8 000	24 000	1 000
N11-015	0	51 200	53 400	1 400
D12-002	0	75 800	40 000	2 500
D12-003	0	52 000	33 600	800
Totals	R284 000	R190 000	R160 000	6 000

Operating activity	Activity to 30 November	December activity
Actual manufacturing overhead incurred:		
Indirect material	R250 000	R18 000
Indirect labour	690 000	60 000
Utilities	490 000	44 000
Depreciation	770 000	70 000
Total overhead	R2 200 000	R192 000
Other items:		
Raw material purchases*	R1 930 000	R 196 000
Direct labour cost	R 1 690 000	R 160 000
Machine hours	73 000	6 000
Account balances at beginning 1 January:		
Raw material inventory*		R 210 000
Work in process inventory		120 000
Finished goods inventory		250 000

* Raw material purchases and raw material inventory consist of both direct and indirect materials. The balance of the raw material inventory account as at 31 December is R170 000.

Required:

1 How much manufacturing overhead would Optic Vision have applied to jobs to 30 November?
2 How much manufacturing overhead would be applied to jobs by Optic Vision during December?
3 Determine the amount by which the manufacturing overhead is overapplied or underapplied as at 31 December.
4 Determine the balance in Optic Vision's finished goods inventory account on 31 December.
5 Prepare a schedule of cost of goods manufactured for Optic Vision Pty Ltd for the year. (*Hint:* In calculating the cost of direct material used, remember that Optic Vision includes both direct and indirect material in its raw material inventory account.)

(CMA, adapted)

Endnotes

1 Note that the term 'current costs' refers to actual costs incurred as distinct from the financial accounting concept of current costs.

2 The manufacturing overhead account is not an asset account or an expense account; it is a temporary account that enables us to accumulate the manufacturing overhead expense on the debit side and to apply manufacturing overhead on the credit side.

3 An ERP (enterprise resource planning) system is an integrated software package that spans a range of functional areas of a business. This is discussed in more detail in Chapter 16.

4 While some businesses use the raw material inventory account for both their direct and indirect materials, others choose to separate the indirect materials as supplies inventory.

5 In fact there are three clearly defined processes at the Spritz factory: the mixing process; the carbonation and bottling process; and the labelling and packing process. However, to keep this example simple, we have combined the last two processes into a single Finishing Department.

6 In order to protect Spritz's competitive stance, the cost and production data are fictitious.

Process Costing and Operation Costing

❖ Learning Objectives

After completing this chapter, you should be able to:

1 describe the principles of process costing where work in process (WIP) inventories are involved;

2 assign total production costs for a department to completed units and WIP inventory using the weighted average method of process costing;

3 assign total production costs for a department to completed units and WIP inventory using the FIFO method of process costing;

4 account for the costs of normal and abnormal spoilage under the weighted average method of process costing;

5 assign total production costs for a department to completed units and WIP inventory under an operation costing system;

6 recognise and explain important issues that influence the design of process costing and operation costing, including the use of standard costs and predetermined conversion costs, the relevance of process costing for responsibility accounting, the choice of cost drivers, and determining the degree of completion; and

7 after studying the appendix, calculate product costs and prepare journal entries to record the flow of costs in a process costing system with sequential production departments.

Introduction

In Chapter 4 we explained how important it is for managers to have information about product costs, both to help them manage resources effectively and to make decisions that create customer value and shareholder wealth. Managers use estimates of product costs to assess product profitability and make decisions about product mix, make outsourcing decisions, set product prices, plan future costs, control current costs, calculate the cost of goods sold for the income statement, and value inventory for the balance sheet. Some of this information comes from costing systems, and some comes from special costing studies. Costing systems must be designed to meet the information needs of managers and suit the production environment in which the business operates.

Job costing and process costing represent the two extremes of a continuum of conventional product costing systems. In Chapter 4 we described job costing at Williams Elevators, a company that produces lifts. This type of product costing system is used when relatively small numbers of products are produced in distinct batches or job orders, and these products differ significantly from each other. Job costing systems accumulate the costs of each job.

We also introduced process costing at Spritz, the soft drink manufacturer in Chapter 4. You will remember that process costing is used by businesses that mass-produce one product or a small range of almost identical products. Production in these businesses involves a number of processes that are performed repetitively. Each unit of product passes through identical (or very similar) production processes. The process costing system accumulates the cost of each process and these costs are averaged across all units produced to give an average cost per unit of product. Businesses that use process costing include oil refineries, food processors and manufacturers of tobacco, chemicals and paper. They may also include producers of repetitive services, such as banks (with the routine processing of cheques) or the South African Post Office (with the delivery of standard letters).

In practice, many businesses operate in an environment that requires a combination of job costing and process costing features. These systems are called *hybrid costing systems*.

In this chapter we continue our study of process costing by exploring how we assign production costs where there are work-in-process inventories and spoilage. Later in the chapter we describe operation costing, a hybrid costing system used in repetitive production environments.

Process costing at Spritz

You will remember from Chapter 4 that Spritz is a popular fruit-flavoured soft drink produced for the adolescent market, made in a variety of flavours including lemon, orange, peach, strawberry and mixed berry, using natural fruit concentrates. The production of a bottle of Spritz can be divided into two processes. In the Mixing Department the fruit concentrate, sucrose and purified water are introduced at the beginning of the process and mixed in a large tank. The output of the Mixing Department is measured in litres of mixture produced. The mixture is then pumped to the Finishing Department where it is carbonated, bottled, labelled and packed into cartons.[1] The carbonate and bottles are added at the beginning of the finishing process and the labels and packaging at the end of the process. The output of the Finishing Department is measured in bottles ready for sale to customers. In both departments, direct labour and manufacturing overhead resources are used uniformly throughout the process.

In Chapter 4 we described process costing at Spritz, where the business produces a high volume of identical products and there are no work-in-process inventories. You will remember that the **process costing system** involves two main steps:

- first, estimating the costs of the production process; and
- second, calculating an average cost per unit by dividing the cost of the process by the number of units produced.

We will now extend the Spritz illustration to consider the effects of work in process inventories on process costing.

Process costing with work-in-process inventories

L.O. 1

Let's focus on the Mixing Department and consider what would happen if, at the beginning and end of the month, there was some mixture that had not been completed and transferred to the Finishing Department. When there are partially completed units on hand (work in process inventory) at the beginning or end of the period, we must change the way we allocate production costs. Production costs will relate to:

- units started in the previous period (beginning work in process) and completed in the current period;
- units started and completed during the period; and
- units that are incomplete at the end of the period (ending work in process).

The effects of ending work in process inventory

To illustrate the effects of ending work in process inventory, once again we will focus on production during the month of April. You may remember from Chapter 4 that 390 000 litres of mixture were produced in April, which resulted in the production of 1 200 000 bottles of Spritz. Assume that there were 10 000 partially completed litres in the Mixing Department at the end of April (in addition to the 390 000 litres completed and transferred to the Finishing Department). What effect do these partially completed units have on the calculation of the cost per litre of the Spritz mixture? The answer lies in the concept of equivalent units.

Equivalent units: a key concept

Where partially completed units (work in process inventories) exist at the beginning or end of the accounting period, they need to be converted into **equivalent units**. The term equivalent units refers to the amount of production inputs that have been applied to the **physical units** in production. In this example, if the 10 000 litres in the Mixing Department at the end of April were half-completed, we could say that they represented 5000 equivalent units. In other words, those 10 000 litres have received the same amount of production inputs as 5000 litres of the completed mixture.

The problem with this calculation is that it assumes that all the production inputs are used uniformly throughout the mixing process. We know that this is not true for Spritz: material is added at the beginning of the mixing process, and direct labour and overhead costs are added uniformly throughout the process. In fact, in most businesses that use process costing, material and labour and overhead costs are incurred at different stages of the production process. Direct material is usually placed into production at one or more discrete points in the process. In contrast, direct labour and manufacturing overhead, called **conversion costs**, are usually incurred continually throughout the process.[2] When an accounting period ends, the partially completed goods that remain in process are generally at different stages of completion with respect to material and conversion.

Calculation of equivalent units

If the mixing process were only 50 per cent complete for the 10 000 litres on hand at the end of the last day of April, the partially completed units (work in process inventory) would be:

- 100 per cent complete for direct material, as the fruit concentrate, sucrose and water are added at the beginning of the mixing process;
- 50 per cent complete for conversion costs, as conversion occurs uniformly across the production process.

We can convert the 10 000 litres on hand in the Mixing Department at the end of April into *equivalent units*. Direct materials are incorporated at the beginning of the production process.

When the process is 50 per cent complete, 100 per cent of the direct material costs for the process have been incurred, so the 10 000 litres represent 10 000 equivalent units of direct material. This number is calculated as follows:

10 000 partially completed physical units in process	×	100% complete with respect to direct materials	=	10 000 equivalent units of direct material

The term *equivalent units* is also used to measure the amount of conversion costs represented by the partially completed goods. Each litre is 50 per cent complete with respect to conversion (direct labour and manufacturing overhead). Equivalent units for conversion are calculated as follows:

10 000 partially completed physical units in process	×	50% complete with respect to conversion	=	5000 equivalent units of conversion

The most important feature of process costing is that equivalent units must be used to calculate unit costs whenever work in process exists. We need to calculate equivalent units separately for the inputs (direct material and conversion) whenever these inputs enter the production process at different stages.

The effects of beginning and ending work-in-process inventories

Having explained the concept of equivalent units, we will now consider the effects of work in process inventories at the beginning and end of the accounting period. Exhibit 5.1 presents a summary of the production and costs for the Mixing Department for April, assuming that there were 20 000 litres of mixture in the work in process inventory at the beginning of April and 10 000 litres at the end of April. You will notice that there are two sets of costs:

1 *The costs of 1 April work in process.* These are the direct material and conversion costs incurred during March and assigned to the 20 000 litres of partially completed mixture remaining in process at the end of March. Exhibit 5.1 indicates that the balance of the Mixing Department's work in process inventory account on 1 April was R296 350.

2 *The costs incurred by the Mixing Department during April.* The direct material, direct labour and manufacturing overhead costs incurred by the Mixing Department during April were:

Direct material	R2 527 000
Conversion costs:	
Direct labour	154 400
Manufacturing overhead	553 000 *
	3 234 400

*Manufacturing overhead is applied at the predetermined rate of 141.795 cents per litre in the Mixing Department.

The journal entry to add these costs to work in process inventory is:

Work in process inventory: Mixing Department	3 234 400	
Raw material inventory		2 527 000
Wages payable		154 400
Manufacturing overhead		553 000

The four steps for process costing

Our ultimate aim is to estimate the cost of Spritz transferred into finished goods during April and the cost of any work in process inventories for the Mixing and Finishing Departments at the end of April. At this stage, however, we have confined our focus to the Mixing Department. The aim, therefore, is to calculate the cost of:

Work in process, 1 April: 20 000 litres			
Direct material: 100% complete		R273 000 *	
Conversion: 10% complete		23 350	
Balance in work in process,1 April		296 350	
Physical flow of units			
Units in work in process inventory, 1 April		20 000	litres
Units started during April		380 000	litres
Units completed during April and transferred to Finishing Department		390 000	litres
Units in work in process inventory, 30 April		10 000	litres
Direct material: 100% complete			
Conversion: 50% complete			
Costs incurred during April			
Direct material		R2 527 000	
Conversion:			
Direct labour	154 400		
Manufacturing overhead	553 000	707 400	
Total production costs incurred during April		3 234 400	

* These costs were incurred during March.

Exhibit 5.1 Process costing with work in process inventories, Spritz Mixing Department, April

- the 390 000 litres of mixture transferred into the Finishing Department; and
- the 10 000 litres of partially completed mixture that remains in the Mixing Department at the end of April.

To do this we need to work through four steps:

Step one	Analyse the physical flow of units.
Step two	Calculate the equivalent units (for direct material and conversion).
Step three	Calculate the unit costs (that is, the cost per equivalent unit for direct material conversion).
Step four	Analyse the total costs (to determine the cost to be removed from work in process and transferred either to the next production department or to finished goods).

In process costing it is necessary to make some assumptions about the physical flow of inventory. The accounting standard for recording inventory, IAS 2 Inventories,[3] allows two alternative sets of assumptions, described as:

- the weighted average method; and
- the first in, first out (FIFO) method.

We will now describe these methods using the Spritz illustration.

Process costing using the weighted average method

L.O. 2

We will begin by using the weighted average method to analyse the Mixing Department's costs. The **weighted average method** averages the cost of opening work in process inventory with current production costs to determine the cost of completed production and closing work in process.

Step one: Analyse the physical flow of units, weighted average method

The first step is to prepare a table summarising the physical flow of production units during April. The table is included in Exhibit 5.2 and reflects the following inventory formula:

physical units in beginning work in process + physical units started − physical units completed and transferred out = physical units in ending work in process

Step two: Calculate the equivalent units, weighted average method

The second step is to calculate the equivalent units of direct material and conversion. A table of equivalent units, also included in Exhibit 5.2, is based on the table of physical flows prepared in Step one. The 390 000 litres transferred out of the Mixing Department were 100 per cent complete. Thus they represent 390 000 equivalent units for both direct material and conversion. As explained on page 190, the 10 000 litres in the ending work in process inventory represent 10 000 equivalent units of direct material and 5000 equivalent units of conversion.

	Physical units	Percentage of completion with respect to conversion	Equivalent units	
			Direct material	**Conversion**
Work in process, 1 April	20 000	10%		
Units started in April	380 000			
Total units to account for	400 000			
Units completed and transferred out during April	390 000	100%	390 000	390 000
Work in process, 30 April	10 000	50%	10 000	5 000
Total units accounted for	400 000			
Total equivalent units			400 000	395 000

Exhibit 5.2 Steps one and two: Analysis of physical units and calculation of equivalent units, including spoiled units, Spritz Mixing Department (weighted average method)

As Exhibit 5.2 indicates, the total number of equivalent units is calculated as follows:

Equivalent units completed and transferred out + equivalent units in ending work in process = total equivalent units

You will notice from this formula (and from Exhibit 5.2) that the equivalent units reflected in beginning work in process inventory are not identified separately. They are simply included in the units completed and transferred out. *This is the key feature of the weighted average method.*

Step three: Calculate the unit costs, weighted average method

The third step, calculating the cost per equivalent unit for both direct material and conversion, is shown in Exhibit 5.3. The cost per equivalent unit for direct material is calculated by dividing the total direct material cost by the total equivalent units (from Exhibit 5.2). Note that the total direct material cost includes the cost of the beginning work in process and the cost incurred during April. A similar procedure is used for conversion costs. *Note that under the weighted average method, the cost per equivalent unit is based on the total costs incurred, including the cost of beginning work in process.*

Does the inclusion of the costs in beginning work in process mean that double-counting is taking place? No: we need to take account of the costs from the previous period in beginning inventory, as we have included the work done on this beginning inventory in estimating the equivalent units. If the production manager is going to claim credit for this amount of 'work' or 'effort' in the current period, then he or she must accept the costs of what was done in the previous period also being brought into the current period.

	Direct material	Conversion	Total
Work in process, 1 April (from Exhibit 5.1)	273 000	23 350	296 350
Costs incurred during April (from Exhibit 5.1)	2 527 000	707 400	3 234 400
Total costs to account for	2 800 000	730 750	3 530 750
Equivalent units (from Exhibit 5.2)	400 000	395 000	
Cost per equivalent unit	R7.00	R1.85	R8.85
	↑	↑	↑
	2 800 000 / 400 000	730 750 / 395 000	R7.00 + R1.85

Exhibit 5.3 Step three: Calculation of unit costs, Spritz Mixing Department (weighted average method)

Step four: Analyse the total costs, weighted average method

Now we can determine the total cost of the litres of mixture transferred out of the Mixing Department's work in process inventory account and into the Finishing Department's work in process inventory account. Exhibit 5.4 provides the required calculations. At the bottom of Exhibit 5.4, a check is made to ensure that the total costs of R3 530 750 have been fully accounted for in the cost of goods completed and transferred out, and in the work in process inventory.

The calculations in Exhibit 5.4 are used as the basis for the following journal entry to transfer the cost of goods completed and transferred to the Finishing Department:

Work in process inventory: Finishing Department	R3 451 500	
Work in process inventory: Mixing Department		R3 451 500

	Direct material	Conversion	Total
Cost per equivalent unit	R7.00	R1.85	R8.85
Cost of goods completed and transferred out of the Mixing Department during April:			
{No. of units transferred out} × {total cost per equivalent unit}	390 000 × R8.85		R3 451 500
Cost remaining in 30 April:			
Work in Process Inventory in Mixing Department			
Direct material:			
{Number of equivalent units of direct material} × {cost per equivalent unit of direct material}	10 000 × R7.00		R70 000
Conversion:			
{Number of equivalent units of conversion} × {cost per equivalent unit of conversion}		5 000 × R1.85	R9 250
Total cost of 30 April work in process			R79 250
Check: Cost of goods completed and transferred out			R3 451 500
Cost of 30 April work in process			R79 250
Total costs accounted for			R3 530 750

Exhibit 5.4 Step 4: Analysis of total costs, Spritz Mixing Department (weighted average method)

Exhibit 5.5 shows the Mixing Department's work in process inventory account at 30 April. The closing balance in the account agrees with the cost of the closing work in process inventory calculated in Exhibit 5.4.

Work in Process Inventory Mixing Department					
1 April	Balance	296 350	30 April	Cost of goods completed and transferred out of Mixing Department	3 451 500
	April cost of direct material, direct labour and applied manufacturing overhead	3 234 400	30 April	Balance (c/f)	79 250
		3 530 750			3 530 750
1 May	Balance (b/f)	79 250			

Exhibit 5.5 Work in Process, Spritz Mixing Department (weighted average method)

Departmental production report

We have now completed all four steps necessary to prepare a departmental production report for the Mixing Department. This is a key document in a typical process costing system, prepared for each production department at the end of every accounting period. This report replaces the job cost sheet used to accumulate costs by jobs in a job costing system. The **departmental production report** summarises the flow of production quantities through the department, and shows the amount of production cost transferred out of the department's work in process inventory account during the period. Its format varies from one organisation to another. Some businesses choose to include all the details from Exhibits 5.2, 5.3 and 5.4 in their production report. Others use a more summarised format, possibly similar to the report displayed in Exhibit 5.6.

	Direct material	Conversion	Total
Costs:			
Work in process 1 April	R273 000	R23 350	R296 350
Costs incurred during April	2 527 000	707 400	3 234 400
	2 800 000	730 750	3 530 750
Equivalent units of production (litres)	400 000	395 000	
Cost per equivalent unit	R7.00	R1.85	R8.85
Cost of units completed and transferred out (390 000 litres)			3 451 500
Cost of work in process, 30 April:			
Direct material (10 000 equivalent units)	70 000		
Conversion (5000 equivalent units)		9 250	
Total work in process			79 250
Total costs accounted for			3 530 750

Exhibit 5.6 Production Report, Spritz Mixing Department (weighted average method), April

Why is this process costing method called the 'weighted average method'?

Under weighted average process costing, the costs of beginning work in process inventory and the equivalent units of work done on it are included in the calculation of the cost per equivalent unit. The resulting cost is a weighted average of some of the costs incurred prior to the current month and all the costs incurred during the current month.

Subsequent production departments

The production of Spritz requires two sequential production operations: mixing and finishing. Although the process costing procedures for the Finishing Department will be similar to those illustrated for the Mixing Department, there is one additional complication: the cost of goods completed and transferred out of the Mixing Department must remain attached to the partially completed product units as they undergo further processing in the Finishing Department. Process costing procedures for subsequent production departments are covered in the appendix at the end of this chapter.

Process costing using the FIFO method

L.O. 3

We will now illustrate the **first in, first out** (or **FIFO**) **method** of process costing, using the data for the Mixing Department for April (Exhibit 5.1). Under FIFO, it is assumed that the oldest inventory is processed and completed first, before new inventory is commenced. Unlike the weighted average method, the FIFO method does not average the costs of beginning work in process with the costs of the current period. As the illustration will show, the costs from each period are treated separately.

Step one: Analyse the physical flow of units, FIFO method

The physical flow of units is unaffected by the process costing method used. Therefore, Step one is identical under the weighted average and FIFO methods (see Exhibit 5.2).

Step two: Calculate the equivalent units, FIFO method

A table of equivalent units, under FIFO process costing, is presented in Exhibit 5.7. It is identical to the table prepared under the weighted average method except for one important difference: under the FIFO method, the equivalent units of direct material and conversion represented by the 1 April work in process inventory are subtracted in the last row of the table to determine the new equivalent units of production in April only. The 20 000 physical units in the 1 April work in process have all their materials, so they represent 20 000 equivalent units of direct material. However, these units are only 10 per cent complete with respect to conversion, so they represent only 2000 equivalent units of conversion (20 000 physical units × 10 per cent complete).

			Equivalent units	
	Physical units	Percentage of completion with respect to conversion	Direct material	Conversion
Work in process, 1 April	20 000	10%		
Units started in April	380 000			
Total units to account for	400 000			
Units completed and transferred out during April	390 000	100%	390 000	390 000
Work in process, 30 April	10 000	50%	10 000	5 000
Total units accounted for	400 000			
Total equivalent units			400 000	395 000
Less equivalent units of work in 1 April work in process			20 000	2 000
New equivalent units of production in April only			380 000	393 000

Exhibit 5.7 Steps one and two: Analysis of physical units and calculation of equivalent units, Spritz Mixing Department (FIFO method)

Step three: Calculate the unit costs, FIFO method

The calculation of unit costs is presented in Exhibit 5.8. The cost per equivalent unit for direct material is calculated by dividing the direct material cost incurred during April only by the new equivalent units of direct material added during April only. The same procedure is used for conversion costs. Note that the costs for direct material and conversion assigned to the beginning inventory are not included in this calculation.

	Direct material	Conversion	Total
Work in process, 1 April (from Exhibit 5.1)	These costs were incurred during March. They are not included in the unit cost calculation for April		R296 350
Costs incurred during April (from Exhibit 5.1)	2 527 000	707 400	3 234 400
Total costs to account for			3 530 750
Equivalent units for April only (from Exhibit 5.7)	380 000	393 000	
Cost per equivalent unit	R6.65	R1.80	R8.45
	↑	↑	↑
	2 527 000 / 380 000	707 400 / 393 000	R6.65 + R1.80

Exhibit 5.8 Step three: Calculation of unit costs, Spritz Mixing Department (FIFO method)

Step four: Analyse the total costs, FIFO method

To complete the process costing procedure, we determine the total cost to be transferred out of the Mixing Department's work in process inventory account and into the Finishing Department's work in process inventory account. Exhibit 5.9 presents this analysis of total costs.

Calculating the cost of goods completed and transferred out is more complicated under the FIFO method than under the weighted average method. FIFO (first in, first out) assumes that the units in the 1 April work in process inventory are completed and transferred out first. The costs assigned to the 1 April work in process are not mixed with those incurred during April. The 20 000 units in the 1 April work in process are 10 per cent complete, so 90 per cent of the conversion remains to be done. Therefore, 18 000 equivalent units of conversion are applied during April to complete the 1 April work in process. These equivalent units of conversion cost R1.80 per unit, since they are accomplished during April. The remaining 370 000 units completed and transferred out of the Mixing Department during April were started and finished during April. Thus, these 370 000 units cost R8.45 each during April. (The calculation of the unit costs of R1.80 for conversion and R8.45 for the total inputs is shown in Exhibit 5.8.)

The calculations in Exhibit 5.9 are used as the basis for the following journal entry to transfer the cost of goods completed and transferred out to the Finishing Department:

Work in process inventory: Finishing Department	R3 455 250	
Work in process inventory: Mixing Department		R3 455 250

Exhibit 5.10 shows the Mixing Department's work in process inventory account at 30 April. The closing balance in the account agrees with the cost of the closing work in process inventory calculated in Exhibit 5.9. Note that the 30 April balance in the Mixing Department's work in process inventory account differs under the FIFO and weighted average methods of process costing.

Departmental production report, FIFO method

The tables presented in Exhibits 5.7 to 5.9 can now be combined to form a production report for the Mixing Department. This report, displayed in Exhibit 5.11, provides a convenient summary of the FIFO process costing method.

Comparison of weighted average and FIFO methods

The key difference between the weighted average and FIFO methods lies in the treatment of the beginning work in process inventory. Under the weighted average method, the costs of begin-

	Direct materials	Conversion	Total
Cost per equivalent unit	R6.65	R1.80	R8.45
Cost of goods completed and transferred from Mixing Department to Finishing during April:			
1 Cost of 1 April work in process which is transferred out first			R296 350
2 Cost incurred to complete 1 April work in process:			
Direct material: complete	0		0
Conversion:			
{No. of equivalent units of conversion} × {cost per equivalent unit of conversion}		20 000 × 90% × R1.80	R32 400
3 Cost incurred to produce units that were started and completed during April:			
(No. of units) × (total cost per equivalent unit)	370 000* × R8.45		R3 126 500
Total cost of goods completed and transferred out			R3 455 250
Cost remaining in 30 April work in process:			
Direct material:			
{No. of equivalent units of direct material} × {cost per equivalent unit of direct material}	10 000 × R6.65		R66 500
Conversion:			
{No. of equivalent units of conversion} × {cost per equivalent unit of conversion}		5000 × R1.80	R9 000
Total cost of 30 April work in process			R75 500
Check: Cost of goods completed and transferred out			R3 455 250
Cost of 30 April work in process			R75 500
Total costs accounted for			R3 530 750

* Units started and completed during April: 390 000 completed and transferred out minus 20 000 units from 1 April work in process.

Exhibit 5.9 Step four: Analysis of total costs, Spritz Mixing Department (FIFO method)

Work in Process Inventory Mixing Department					
1 April	Balance	296 350	30 April	Cost of goods completed and transferrred out of Mixing Department	3 455 250
	April cost of direct material, direct labour and applied manufacturing overhead	3 234 400	30 April	Balance (c/f)	75 500
		3 530 750			3 530 750
1 May	Balance (b/f)	75 500			

Exhibit 5.10 Work in Process, Spritz Mixing Department (FIFO method)

ning work in process inventory and the equivalent units of work done on it are included in the calculation of the cost per equivalent unit. The resulting cost is a weighted average of some of the costs incurred prior to the current month and all the costs incurred during the current month. In contrast, under the FIFO method, the costs per equivalent unit are based only on the costs incurred during the current month divided by the equivalent units of work done in the current month.

In practice, the weighted average method of process costing is used more widely than the FIFO method, probably because it is simpler. In an inflationary environment, it also offers tax advantages in relation to the FIFO method.

With no work in process, the difference between the weighted average and FIFO methods disappears. This difference is caused solely by differences in the treatment of beginning work in process inventory.

	Direct material	Conversion	Total
Work in process, 1 April	These costs were incurred during March. They are not included in the unit cost calculation for April		R296 350
Costs incurred during April	2 527 000	707 400	3 234 400
			3 530 750
Equivalent units of production (litres)	380 000	393 000	
Cost per equivalent unit	R6.65	R1.80	R8.45
Costs of units completed and transferred out:			
Cost in 1 April work in process			296 350
Cost to finish 1 April work in process:			
Direct material (0 equivalent units)			0
Conversion (18 000 equivalent units)			32 400
Cost to produce units started and completed during April (370 000 litres)			3 126 500
Total cost of units completed and transferred out			3 455 250
Cost of work in process, 30 April:			
Direct material (10 000 equivalent units)	R66 500		
Conversion (5000 equivalent units)		R9 000	
Total work in process			75 500
Total costs accounted for			3 530 750

Exhibit 5.11 Production Report, Spritz Mixing Department (FIFO method), April

Evaluation of process costing with beginning or ending work in process inventories

This form of process costing is appropriate for businesses producing identical or very similar products and with beginning or ending work in process inventories. No doubt, many businesses fit this description. However, this approach is complex to use. It requires estimates of the degree of completion (for direct materials and conversion costs) for work in process in each department at the end of the period.

Some businesses use the simplified form of process costing described in Chapter 4, even though they have some levels of work in process inventory. Why? Because the more sophisticated methods, with their fiddly assessments of the percentages of completion and detailed calculations of equivalent units, are too complex. For these businesses the costs of using more sophisticated process costing methods outweigh their benefits. By ignoring beginning and ending work in process inventories, their product costs will be distorted; but if these inventories are not large compared with the overall level of production, or are reasonably stable, the distortions may not be significant.

L.O. 4

Process costing and spoilage

In our earlier examples, we have assumed that every litre and bottle of Spritz is of good quality. Unfortunately, this is most unlikely. In almost all businesses, mistakes are made, defective outputs are produced and resources are wasted. The cost of these defective products and wasted resources that cannot be recovered by rework or recycling is called **spoilage**. In Chapter 15 we recognise that activities associated with defective production are non-value-added. And in Chapter 16, we explore the approaches that businesses use to manage quality and minimise defective production. Let's now look at how we can measure the costs of spoilage, which can help managers to focus on the costs associated with poor quality.

Calculating spoilage costs

So far we have identified two forms of output from the production process: the units completed and transferred out and the unfinished units remaining in work in process. When spoilage occurs there are three forms of output:

- the units completed and transferred out;
- the spoiled units; and
- the unfinished units remaining in work in process.

To estimate the costs of the spoiled units we need to work through the same four steps for process costing described above, but include all forms of output. Let's return to the Mixing Department at Spritz and assume that 39 500 of the 390 000 litres of mixture produced during April were spoiled. The spoilage occurred because of contamination to one of the mixing vats, which was discovered at the first quality inspection when the mixing process was 25 per cent complete.

Step one: Analyse the physical flow of units, including spoiled units

The first step is to prepare a table summarising the physical flow of production units, including spoiled units during April. The table is included in Exhibit 5.12 and reflects the following inventory formula:

Physical units in beginning work in process	+	physical units started	−	physical units completed and transferred out	−	physical units spoiled	=	physical units in ending work in process

Note that the physical units calculation in Exhibit 5.12 is almost identical to that in Exhibit 5.2, except for the additional item of units spoiled.

	Physical units	Percentage of completion with respect to conversion	Equivalent units	
			Direct material	Conversion
Work in process, 1 April	20 000	10%		
Units started in April	380 000			
Total units to account for	400 000			
Units completed and transferred out during April	350 500	100%	350 500	350 500
Units spoiled during April	39 500	25%	39 500	9 875
Work in process, 30 April	10 000	50%	10 000	5 000
Total units accounted for	400 000			
Total equivalent units			400 000	365 375

Exhibit 5.12 Steps one and two: Analysis of physical units and calculation of equivalent units, including spoiled units, Spritz Mixing Department (weighted average method)

Step two: Calculate the equivalent units, including spoiled units

The second step is to calculate the equivalent units of direct material and conversion. A table of equivalent units is also included in Exhibit 5.12. Note that the 39 500 spoiled litres were complete with respect to material but only 25 per cent complete for conversion costs (that is, 9875 equivalent units).

You will notice that the equivalent units reflected in beginning work in process inventory are not identified separately. This is because we have chosen to demonstrate the effects of spoilage using the weighted average method.

Step three: Calculate the unit costs, including spoiled units

The third step, calculating the cost per equivalent unit for both direct material and conversion, is shown in Exhibit 5.13.

	Direct material	Conversion	Total
Work in process, 1 April (from Exhibit 5.1)	273 000	23 350	296 350
Costs incurred during April (from Exhibit 5.1)	2 527 000	707 400	3 234 400
Total costs to account for	2 800 000	730 750	3 530 750
Equivalent units (from Exhibit 5.12)	400 000	365 375	
Cost per equivalent unit	R7.00	R2.00	R9.00
	↑	↑	↑
	2 800 000 / 400 000	730 750 / 365 375	R7.00 + R2.00

Exhibit 5.13 Step three: Calculation of unit costs, including spoiled units, Spritz Mixing Department (weighted average method)

Step four: Analyse the total costs, including spoilage

Now we can determine the cost of:

- the 350 500 litres of mixture transferred out of the Mixing Department's work-in-process inventory account and into the Finishing Department's work-in-process inventory account;
- the 39 500 litres of contaminated mixture; and
- the 10 000 litres of partially completed mixture remaining in the Mixing Department as work-in-process inventory.

Exhibit 5.14 provides the required calculations. At the bottom of Exhibit 5.14, a check is made to ensure that the total costs of R3 530 750 have been fully accounted for in the cost of goods completed and transferred out, spoiled units and in the work in process inventory.

Accounting for spoilage

Exhibit 5.14 indicates that the 39 500 litres of contaminated mixture cost R296 250. But how do we record this information in the accounting system? This depends on whether the spoilage is considered *normal* or *abnormal*.

Normal spoilage is the spoilage that is considered to be inherent in the production process and that occurs even under efficient operating conditions. This spoilage is a necessary part of the production process, which is unavoidable, and, therefore, its cost is treated as part of the cost of the good units completed and transferred out.[4] As discussed below, the spoilage in the Mixing Department is likely to be abnormal spoilage; however, if the spoilage were considered to be normal, the costs would be included as part of the cost of the units completed and transferred into the next department as shown in the following journal entry:

Work-in-process inventory: Finishing Department	R3 450 750*	
Work-in-process inventory: Mixing Department		R3 450 750

*Being the cost of good units completed and transferred out (R3 154 500) and spoiled units (R296 250).

Why do we bother to calculate the costs of normal spoilage if we then include these costs as part of the cost of the units completed and transferred to the next department? Estimating the cost of spoilage highlights the cost of wasted resources in the Mixing Department for the month of April, which provides useful information for the manager of the Mixing Department at Spritz, his supe-

	Direct materials	Conversion	Total
Cost per equivalent unit	R7.00	R2.00	R9.00
Cost of goods completed and transferred out of Mixing Department during April:			
{No. of units transferred out} × {total cost per equivalent unit}	350 500 × R9.00		R3 154 500
Cost of spoiled units in Mixing Department			
Direct material:			
{No. of equivalent units of direct material} × {cost per equivalent unit of direct material}	39 500 × R7.00		R276 500
Conversion:			
{No. of equivalent units of conversion} × {cost per equivalent unit of conversion}		9 875 × R2.00	R19 750
			R296 250
Cost remaining in 30 April work in process inventory in Mixing Department:			
Direct material:			
{No. of equivalent units of direct material} × {cost per equivalent unit of direct material}	10 000 × R7.00		R70 000
Conversion			
(No. of equivalent units of conversion) × (cost per equivalent unit of conversion)		5 000 × R2.00	R10 000
Total cost of 30 April work in process			R80 000
Check: Cost of goods completed and transferred out			R3 154 500
Cost of spoiled units			R296 250
Cost of 30 April work in process			R80 000
Total costs accounted for			R3 530 750

Exhibit 5.14 Step four: Analysis of total costs, including spoilage, Spritz Mixing Department (weighted average method)

riors and the quality manager, to help them focus their attention on the cost of wasted resources. (Note that in Chapter 10, the practice of incorporating normal allowances for spoilage in standard product costs is discouraged as, from a cost control perspective, it may encourage an attitude that it is 'OK' to expect a certain amount of wastage. To avoid this problem, normal spoilage needs to be strictly limited to defects that cannot be avoided, under efficient operating conditions.)

In contrast, **abnormal spoilage** is spoilage that should not occur under efficient operating conditions. Given that contamination in the Mixing Department at Spritz occurs only when employees ignore standard sterilising procedures, this spoilage is abnormal. The costs of abnormal spoilage are expensed in the current period, as shown in the following journal entry:

Work in process inventory: Finishing Department	R3 154 500	
Loss on abnormal spoilage	R296 250	
Work in process inventory: Mixing Department		R3 450 750

Spoilage under FIFO

Exhibits 5.12 to 5.14 use the weighted average costing approach to estimate the cost of spoilage. To use a FIFO approach we would need to identify separately:

- the units that are spoiled from work done on the April 1 work in process inventory; and
- the units that are started and spoiled during April.

In conclusion, measuring the costs of spoilage can help managers to track the costs of wasted resources. However, modern approaches to cost management and quality management, as discussed in Chapters 15 and 16, focus on continuous improvement and actively strive to eliminate all wastage.

Operation costing

L.O. 5

The process costing methods described above are appropriate only for businesses that mass-produce a single product or a limited range of very similar products. Many businesses with repetitive production processes produce a narrow range of products that differ in some significant aspects. We will now look at a form of costing that can be used for these products.

Businesses can use repetitive production processes to produce product lines that differ because they require:

- different material inputs; or
- different combinations of specific production processes.

This type of production environment is described as **batch manufacturing processes**, as individual product lines are produced in large batches, each requiring a specific combination of direct materials and a specific sequence of production processes. Large-scale clothes manufacturers, food processors, and chemical and plastic producers are likely to use batch manufacturing processes. For example, in manufacturing jeans, the Levi Strauss Company uses a number of repetitive processes such as cutting, stitching, adding buttons, inserting zips, and labelling. Different product lines use different materials. Loose-fit styles are made of soft cotton denim, whereas stretch styles use a stretch denim fabric. Different product lines may also use some production processes but not others. All product lines require cutting and stitching but some have a button fly and will pass through the button department, while others have a zip fly and will pass through the zip department.

Although these businesses use repetitive processes, they cannot use the process costing systems described above. Why not? Because despite the repetitive processes, different products may use different materials and a different combination of processes, and therefore have different costs. They could use a job costing system, as described in Chapter 4, and carefully assign costs to each production batch, but, as the production processes are repetitive, this level of detail is not required. The conversion costs of each process – that is, the direct labour and manufacturing overhead costs of each process – will be the same for each unit processed, but the combination of processes required to produce each product may differ. The materials costs of each product may also differ. A better solution is to use a **hybrid costing system**, which has features of both job costing and process costing. You may remember the continuum of costing systems, introduced in Chapter 4, with job costing at one end and process costing at the other. Hybrid costing systems fit in between these two extremes, as shown in Exhibit 5.15. Many businesses use hybrid costing systems.

Production environment	Produced individually or in batches	Large batches, some individual inputs, some repetitive processes	Repetitive, mass production
Product features	Individual, unique	Some unique features, some common features	Identical or very similar
Costing system	Job costing	Hybrid costing	Process costing

Exhibit 5.15 Continuum of costing systems

Operation costing for batch manufacturing processes

Operation costing, which is used to estimate product costs in a batch manufacturing environment:

- assigns direct material costs to *individual batches* – a *job costing* approach;
- accumulates conversion costs by *department* (or *operation* or *process*). These costs are allocated to all units passing through the department – a *process costing* approach.

The main features of operation costing are illustrated in Exhibit 5.16. Notice that the product in Batch 1 passes sequentially through operations in production departments A and B, whereas the product in Batch 2 passes directly from Department A to Finished Goods. It does not require the operation in Department B. Direct material costs are traced directly to each batch of goods, but conversion costs are applied on a departmental basis. As in process costing, direct labour and manufacturing overhead are often combined into a single cost category, called conversion costs, rather than identified separately. Moreover, under operation costing, conversion costs are often applied to products using a predetermined application rate. This predetermined rate is based on budgeted conversion costs, as follows:

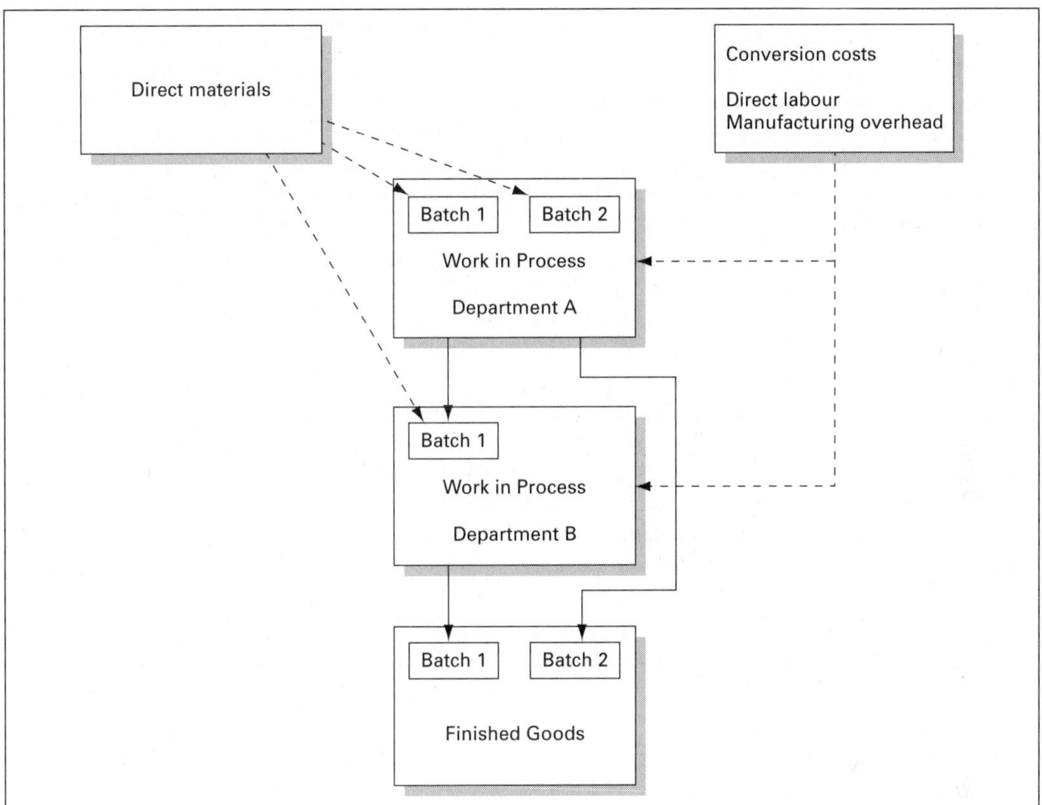

Exhibit 5.16 Operation costing

$$\text{Predetermined rate for conversion costs} = \frac{\text{budgeted conversion costs (i.e. direct labour and manufacturing overhead)}}{\text{budgeted level of cost driver}}$$

You may have noticed that the concept of a predetermined rate for conversion costs is similar in some ways to the predetermined manufacturing overhead rate described in Chapter 4.

'Operation costing' or 'process costing'?

In practice the term 'operation costing' is not widely used, even though these systems are probably more prevalent than pure process costing systems. (Very few businesses mass-produce only one product line or a small range of virtually identical products.) Instead, these systems are often described mistakenly as 'process costing systems', presumably because of their focus on repetitive processes.[5]

Operation costing for Spritz

As an illustration of operation costing, we will extend our example of Spritz soft drinks. Spritz is produced in a range of different flavours, which effectively represent different product lines, but process costing is appropriate because the material costs of each flavour are very similar. From a costing perspective, all products are virtually identical. They travel through the same conversion processes and consume direct material resources that cost the same amount per bottle.

Now let's assume that this is no longer the case. Changes in the availability of the fruits used to make the fruit concentrates have caused the suppliers to charge different prices for different flavours. The concentrates made from fruits in limited supply, such as strawberries and peaches, are much more expensive than the concentrates made from more common fruits, such as lemons and oranges. In addition, Spritz's management has decided to tap into the children's market. After leaving the Finishing Department, the children's drinks will go to a special packaging area where stickers and posters will be added to make the product more appealing to children.

From a costing perspective Spritz now has a range of product lines. The direct material costs will depend on the flavour of the drink and whether it is produced for children or for the normal adolescent market. With respect to conversion costs, all products will pass through the identical mixing and finishing operations, but only the children's drinks will go through the additional packaging process. To cost its products, Spritz needs to accumulate the costs of direct material used by each batch and the average conversion cost of each operation through which the batch passes. Conversion costs do not need to be traced separately to each batch because the same process is performed on each bottle that passes through a given operation, regardless of the identity of its batch.

As discussed earlier, in operation costing, conversion costs are often applied using a predetermined application rate. We will assume that Spritz decides to base its operation costing system on predetermined application rates for conversion costs, which have been determined as follows:

Operation	Annual budgeted conversion costs	Annual budgeted production (units)	Predetermined application rate (per unit)
Mixing	R8 100 000	18 000 000	R0.45 per bottle*
Finishing	R9 000 000	18 000 000	R0.50 per bottle
Special packaging	R125 000	500 000	R0.25 per bottle

*The output from the mixing operation is measured in litres but is converted to a cost per bottle to simplify this example.

Let's look at costing two batches under this system:

- Batch AS12 of 20 000 bottles of strawberry drink produced for the adolescent market; and
- Batch KO7 of 10 000 bottles of orange drink produced for the children's market.

The production requirements for these two batches are:

	Batch AS12 Adolescent Strawberry	Batch KO7 Children's Orange
Direct material	1 Strawberry fruit 2 All other mixing materials 3 All finishing materials	1 Orange fruit 2 All other mixing materials 3 All finishing materials 4 Stickers and posters
Conversion	1 Mixing 2 Finishing	1 Mixing 2 Finishing 3 Special packaging

The cost per bottle is calculated in Exhibit 5.17. Notice that each bottle of Spritz receives the same conversion costs in the Mixing and Finishing departments, since these operations are identical for the two products. The Children's Orange goes through an additional packaging operation where the stickers and posters are added. The direct material costs and packaging costs differ for the products. The strawberry concentrate is more expensive than the orange concentrate, but the direct material cost per bottle of Children's Orange is actually higher because of the cost of the stickers and posters. The total cost of R132 000, divided into the product costs, is shown below:

	No. of bottles	Cost	Total
Adolescent Strawberry (No. of bottles × cost)	20 000	4.20	84 000
Children's Orange (No. of bottles × cost)	10 000	4.80	48 000
Total			R132 000

Costs		
Direct material costs:		
Batch AS12: 20 000 bottles Adolescent Strawberry		
Strawberry concentrate	15 000	
Other materials used in the Mixing Department	27 500	
Materials used in the Finishing Department	22 500	
		R65 000
Batch KO7: 10 000 bottles of Children's Orange		
Orange concentrate	6 000	
Other materials used in the Mixing Department	13 750	
Materials used in the Finishing Department	11 250	
Materials used in the Special Packaging Department	5 000	
		R36 000
Conversion costs applied:		
Mixing (30 000 bottles)	13 500	
Finishing (30 000 bottles)	15 000	
Special Packaging (10 000 bottles)	2 500	
		R31 000
Total costs		R132 000

	AS12 Adolescent Strawberry	KO7 Children's Orange
Costs per unit		
Direct material:		
Batch AS12 (65 000 ÷ 20 000)	R3.25	
Batch KO7 (36 000 ÷ 10 000)		R3.60
Conversion:		
Mixing	R0.45	R0.45
Finishing	R0.50	R0.50
Special Packaging		R0.25
Total costs per unit	R4.20	R4.80

Exhibit 5.17 Operation costing, Spritz

The first entry is made to record the requisition of raw material by the Mixing Department when batch AS12 is entered into production:

(1) Work-in-process inventory: Mixing Department	R42 500*	
Raw material inventory		R42 500

* Strawberry concentrate R15 000 and other materials R27 500.

The next entry is made to record the requisition of raw material by the Mixing Department when batch KO7 is entered into production:

(2) Work-in-process inventory: Mixing Department	R19 750*	
Raw material inventory		R19 750

* Orange concentrate R6000 and other materials R13 750

Conversion costs are applied in the Mixing Department with the following journal entry:

(3) Work-in-process inventory: Mixing Department	R13 500	
Applied conversion costs		13 500

Finally, this next entry records the transfer of the strawberry and orange mixture to the Finishing Department:

(4) Work in process inventory: Finishing Department	R75 750*	
Work in process inventory: Mixing Department		R75 750

* Direct materials for strawberry drinks R42 500, direct materials for Children's Orange drinks R19 750, and conversion costs for Mixing Department R13 500

Corresponding entries are made for the transactions in the subsequent departments, Finishing and Special Packaging.

Work in process inventories and operation costing

This example does not involve work in process inventory. If partially completed batches existed at the beginning or end of the accounting period, the direct material costs would be traced directly to the batch. Equivalent units would have to be calculated for each operation in order to apply conversion costs to the batches transferred out and to those remaining on hand.

Evaluation of operation costing

Job costing and process costing represent two extremes on the continuum of costing systems. Many businesses, particularly small businesses, operate in a job costing environment in which each product or job differs from the next. Likewise, many businesses, particularly large businesses, produce high volumes of product using repetitive production processes. Most businesses using repetitive production processes produce a range of product lines and require some form of hybrid costing system. Operation costing is a hybrid costing system that meets the needs of high-volume batch manufacturers who produce a small range of similar products using repetitive production processes. It is likely that many businesses use versions of operation costing, although they may refer to their system as process costing rather than operation costing.

Other issues in process costing

L.O. 6

Several other issues related to process costing (and operation costing) are worth discussing.

Process and operation costing using standard costs

So far in this book we have assumed that product costs are measured using actual direct material costs, actual direct labour costs and predetermined overhead costs. However, as we will see in later chapters, many companies use standard costs to measure product costs. **Standard costs** are budgeted costs, based on estimates of the cost of material, labour and overhead resources that *should be used* to make one unit of product. In standard process costing or standard operation costing, equivalent units are estimated for work done in the current period (as in FIFO), and the cost per equivalent unit is based on the standard cost per unit. A process costing environment is well suited to standard costing, as setting standards for one (or a few) mass-produced products is much simpler than in a job costing environment where each job is unique. Variances between actual and budgeted costs provide useful information for control. Standard costing is discussed further in Chapters 10 and 11.

Process costing, operation costing and responsibility accounting

Process costing and operation costing are consistent with the concepts of responsibility accounting. Costs are accumulated by processes (or operations) that are usually performed in separate departments. Department managers can be held responsible for the department's costs and for the output produced. The cost per equivalent unit provides a measure of production efficiency. Standard costs, in particular, provide good information for cost control and performance evaluation. In monitoring the cost per equivalent unit, FIFO provides more useful information than does the weighted average method because FIFO isolates current costs. When current and prior period costs are averaged, a departmental manager's current performance is less clear.

REAL LIFE: WHAT IS THE PROCESS OF MAKING BOTTLES?

In our example of Spritz we looked at manufacturing soft drinks. One of the inputs will be bottles. It is helpful to understand the concept of process costing if we understand the underlying manufacturing process. We will describe the process of manufacturing glass bottles used for soft drinks, wine and other products. Consol Ltd is the leading glass container manufacturer in South Africa.

The making of glass bottles follows a set of processes such as melting, forming, inspection, decoration and palletising. Glass is made by melting sand, soda ash and limestone in furnaces. Recycled glass (cullet) is also an input and for Consol it is about 50 per cent of the raw materials used to make glass containers. Raw materials are stored in silos and transported to batch mixers and then transported to the furnaces. Materials are continuously fed into the furnace which converts the materials into molten glass at temperatures of over 1500°C. After refining at 1200°C the molten glass is sent to the individual bottle-making machines. Molten glass enters feeders where streams of glass are cut into pieces required to make individual bottles. These 'gobs' of molten glass shoot out of the feeders continuously and are fed into moulds. We would expect that a mould is used to shape the bottle. However, how is the inside created? We cannot use a mould for the inside. How would we get the inside mould out through the small neck? We do use something to mould the inside of each bottle and that something is . . . air. A bottle is formed in two stages. In the first stage, the gob of molten glass is pushed into a blank mould to form the neck of the bottle and a long very narrow hole (cavity) is blown by using compressed air in the centre of the parison (the name of the shape at this stage). This is then transferred to the main mould which results in the final shape of each bottle. Air is forced under high pressure into the narrow cavity to expand the glass against the sides of the mould to create the final shape. The next question you may have is: how do we get the bottle out of the mould with its shape intact? It means that the mould is made of two equal parts which open after forming the bottle, enabling the bottle to get out. This is why, if you go to any bottle and you feel on the outside, you will notice a very slightly raised line. This is where the two parts of the mould come together. Newly formed bottles are coated with tin oxide and then enter the lehr in which each bottle is cooled from 600°C to 100°C. Bottles are then inspected and a stress simulator applies pressure on the outside to break bottles that are structurally weak. Machines check each bottle for glass thickness, detection of cracks, neck openings and so on. Camera equipment and computer systems are also employed to check each bottle visually. Defective bottles are recycled and become cullet. Bottles may then be labelled in terms of customer requirements. Finally, the bottles are shrink-wrapped and placed into pallets. In terms of costing we would expect that different bottles would require different moulds and production would occur in batches. As this is a highly automated process, we would expect that overhead costs relating to furnaces and specialised plant and equipment would form a large component of

unit costs. There would be material costs and inventory of materials but we would expect that work in process inventories would be relatively low due to the nature of the production process. Direct labour would be a small component of product cost due to the highly automated processes required to manufacture glass containers.

Source: www.consol.co.za

Predetermined overhead and conversion costs

In the process costing examples in this chapter, the costing system applied manufacturing overhead using a *predetermined* (budgeted) overhead rate. And in the operation costing example, the operation costing system applied *predetermined* conversion (direct labour and overhead) costs.

Predetermined rates smooth out the effects of fluctuations in actual costs and cost driver volumes from one month to the next. Process costing and operation costing environments involve stable, repetitive production processes. Labour and overhead costs and cost driver volumes may not fluctuate much over time, and, under these circumstances, actual costs may be used instead of predetermined costs. However, where costs and cost driver volumes are unstable, predetermined overhead (and sometimes conversion) costs are preferred.

When predetermined costs are used, there may be overapplied or underapplied costs at the end of the period. This amount is either closed into cost of goods sold or prorated, as explained in Chapter 4.

Cost drivers for process or operation costing

Where predetermined rates are used, it is necessary to identify a cost driver. In process costing and operation costing, predetermined rates are usually calculated for separate departments (that is, processes or operations). The department's volume of output is often a suitable cost driver because each unit of product undergoes the same process, using similar amounts of production resources such as labour and overhead.

Some businesses use inputs, such as machine hours or labour hours, as cost drivers. This approach is useful in operation costing where different products make different use of a particular process. For example, in a mixing process, some products may require more mixing than others. It would not be appropriate to use a cost per litre for this mixing process, as some products need more mixing per litre, but we could use the cost per machine hour. We discuss the choice of cost drivers further in Chapter 7.

Determining the percentage of completion

Where work in process inventory exists, it is necessary to estimate the *percentage of completion* for each cost element. As materials are usually added to the units of product at a few discrete points, estimating the percentage of completion for direct materials is relatively straightforward. It is much more difficult to estimate the percentage of completion for direct labour and overhead costs, because these costs tend to be incurred at numerous points throughout the production process. It is especially difficult to estimate the degree of completion where there are a large number of physical units at various stages of completion. Often it is feasible to make only a rough estimate, and, as discussed previously, many businesses ignore work in process inventories altogether.

Many businesses assume that direct labour drives overhead costs, which enables labour and overhead costs to be combined as conversion costs. In addition, it is common to assume that conversion takes place uniformly across the production process. In fact, there is no reason to expect this, and when this assumption is not valid, the resultant product cost will be distorted. Where overhead resources are consumed in a different pattern from direct labour, the two costs should not be combined as conversion costs. Instead, equivalent units should be calculated for direct labour and manufacturing overhead as separate cost elements. There will now be three cost elements: direct material, direct labour and manufacturing overhead. Perhaps the practice of combining conversion costs reflects managers' assessments of the costs and benefits of a simpler but less accurate costing system.

Process and operation costing in service firms

Although we have illustrated process costing and operation costing using a manufacturing example, the same procedures can be used to cost services. Most service businesses tend to produce *heterogeneous* outputs, while process costing is appropriate only for *homogeneous* outputs. However, there may be some routine repetitive or similar services that can be costed using process costing or operation costing procedures. Examples include the processing of licence applications by a government department and the processing of cheques by a bank. In these situations there will be no work in process inventory, so process costing will be very simple. Service costing is considered in more detail in Chapter 6.

Summary

In Chapter 4 we introduced process costing as a product costing system suited to businesses that mass-produce one product or a small range of almost identical products. In this chapter we extend our description of process costing to include the effects of work in process inventories and spoilage and to consider the differences between the weighted average and FIFO methods of process costing. We also introduce operation costing, which is a product costing system suited to businesses that use repetitive production processes to produce products requiring specific combinations of materials and these processes. Key points include:

- Under process costing, when products are completed, the costs assigned to them are transferred either to finished goods inventory or to the next production department's work-in-process inventory account. Where work-in-process inventories exist at the beginning or end of the accounting period, it is necessary to calculate the cost per equivalent unit. An equivalent unit is a measure of the amount of production input that has been applied to physical units during production.
- The key document in a process costing system is the departmental production report, rather than the job cost sheet used in job costing. There are four steps in preparing a departmental production report:
  - *Step one* Analyse the physical flow of units.
  - *Step two* Calculate the equivalent units.
  - *Step three* Calculate the cost per equivalent unit.
  - *Step four* Analyse the total costs of the department into the cost of units completed and transferred out and the cost of partially completed units (work in process) on hand at the end of the accounting period.
- Two methods of process costing are the weighted average method and the FIFO method. In practice, the weighted average method is more widely used.

- In the weighted average method, the cost per equivalent unit is a weighted average of costs from prior periods assigned to the beginning work in process inventory and the costs incurred during the current period.
- In the FIFO method, the cost per equivalent unit includes costs from the current period only.

- It is also possible to use process costing to estimate the costs of spoilage. Normal spoilage is inherent in the production process and occurs even under efficient operating conditions. Its cost is treated as part of the cost of good units completed and transferred out. In contrast, abnormal spoilage is the spoilage that should not occur under efficient operating conditions and its cost is expensed in the current period. Measuring the costs of spoilage can help managers to track the costs of wasted resources.
- Job costing and process costing represent the polar extremes of the continuum of conventional product costing systems. Operation costing is a hybrid of these two methods. It is designed for repetitive production processes in which the direct material differs significantly between product lines and where the combination of repetitive processes used to produce individual products may differ. Direct material costs are accumulated by batches of products using job costing methods. Conversion costs are accumulated by production departments (or operations) and are assigned to product units by process costing methods.
- There are a number of issues that influence the design of process and operation costing systems. These include the use of standard costs and predetermined conversion costs, the relevance of process costing for responsibility accounting, the choice of cost drivers, and the difficulty in estimating the degree of completion for work in process.

The purpose of process costing and operation costing systems is the same as that of a job costing system – to accumulate costs and assign these costs to units of product. Product costs are needed to help managers manage resources and make decisions that create value, as well as for reporting to various outside organisations. Chapters 4 and 5 have focused on costing systems that are used to estimate the cost of outputs produced by manufacturing businesses. In Chapter 6 we will continue our study of costing systems by exploring approaches to estimating the cost of outputs produced by service organisations.

References

Hoque, Z, Uliana, E and Waweru, NM 2005, 'A survey of management accounting practices in South Africa', *International Journal of Accounting, Auditing and Performance Evaluation*, 2(3): 226–263

Joye, MP & Blayney, PJ 1990, *Cost and Management Accounting Practices in Australian Manufacturing Companies: Survey Results*, Accounting and Finance Foundation, University of Sydney.

Self study

Self-study problem 1: Process costing – weighted average costs

The following data have been compiled for Pacific Enterprises Ltd for the month of June. Conversion occurs uniformly throughout the production process.

Work in process, 1 June – 10 000 units:	
Direct material (100% complete)	R220 000
Conversion (20% complete)	45 000
Balance in work in process, 1 June	R265 000
Units started during June	100 000
Units completed during June and transferred out to finished goods inventory	80 000
Work in process, 30 June:	
Direct material (100% complete)	
Conversion (33⅓% complete)	
Costs incurred during June:	
Direct material	R1 980 000
Conversion costs:	
Direct labour	528 000
Applied manufacturing overhead	1 056 000
Total conversion costs	R1 584 000

Required:

Prepare schedules to accomplish each of the following process costing steps for the month of June. Use the weighted average method of process costing.

1 Analysis of physical flow of units.
2 Calculation of equivalent units.
3 Calculation of unit costs.
4 Analysis of total costs.

Solution to Self-study problem 1

1

	Physical units
Work in process, 1 June	10 000
Units started during June	100 000
Total units to account for	110 000
Units completed and transferred out during June	80 000
Work in process, 30 June	30 000
Total units accounted for	110 000

2

	Physical units	Percentage of completion with respect to conversion	Equivalent units	
			Direct material	Conversion
Work in process, 1 June	10 000	20%		
Units started during June	100 000			
Total units to account for	110 000			
Units completed and transferred out during June	80 000	100%	80 000	80 000
Work in process, 30 June	30 000	33⅓%	30 000	10 000
Total units accounted for	110 000			
Total equivalent units			110 000	90 000

3

	Direct material	Conversion	Total
Work in process, 1 June	R220 000	R45 000	R265 000
Costs incurred during June	1 980 000	1 584 000	3 564 000
Total costs to account for	R2 200 000	R1 629 000	R3 829 000
Equivalent units	110 000	90 000	
Cost per equivalent unit	R20.00	R18.10	R38.10

4

Cost of goods completed and transferred out during June:		
{Number of units transferred out} × {total cost per equivalent unit}	80 000 × R38.10	R3 048 000
Cost remaining in 30 June work in process inventory:		
Direct material:		
{Number of equivalent units of direct material} × {cost per equivalent unit of direct material}	30 000 × R20.00	R600 000
Conversion:		
{Number of equivalent units of conversion)} × {cost per equivalent unit of conversion}	10 000 × R18.10	181 000
Total cost of 30 June work in process inventory		R781 000
Check: Cost of goods completed and transferred out		R3 048 000
Cost of 30 June work in process inventory		R781 000
Total costs accounted for		R3 829 000

Self-study problem 2: Process costing – FIFO

Refer to the data for Pacific Enterprises given in Self-study problem 1 above. Complete the same requirements, but use the FIFO method of process costing.

Solution to Self-study problem 2

1

	Physical units
Work in process, 1 June	10 000
Units started during June	100 000
Total units to account for	110 000
Units completed and transferred out during June	80 000
Work in process, 30 June	30 000
Total units accounted for	110 000

2

	Physical units	Percentage of completion with respect to conversion	Equivalent units	
			Direct material	Conversion
Work in process, 1 June	10 000	20%		
Units started during June	100 000			
Total units to account for	110 000			
Units completed and transferred out during June	80 000	100%	80 000	80 000
Work in process, 30 June	30 000	33⅓%	30 000	10 000
Total units accounted for	110 000			
Total equivalent units			110 000	90 000
Less equivalent units represented in 1 June work in process			10 000	2000
New equivalent units accomplished in June only			100 000	88 000

3

	Direct material	Conversion	Total
Work in process, 1 June	These costs were incurred before June. They are not included in the unit cost calculation for June		R265 000
Costs incurred during June	R1 980 000	R1 584 000	R3 564 000
			R3 829 000
Equivalent units of production (litres)	100 000	88 000	
Cost per equivalent unit	R19.80	R18.00	R37.80

4

Cost of goods completed and transferred out during June:		
Cost of 1 June work in process inventory, which is transferred out first		R265 000
Cost incurred to finish the 1 June work in process inventory:		
{Number of units} × {percentage of conversion remaining} × {cost per equivalent unit of conversion}	10 000 × 0.80 × R18.00	R144 000
Cost incurred to produce units that were both started and completed during June:		
(Number of units) × (total cost per equivalent unit)	70 000* × R37.80	R2 646 000
Total cost of goods completed and transferred out		R3 055 000

* Units started and completed during June: 80 000 units completed and transferred out minus 10 000 units in the 1 June work in process inventory.

Cost remaining in 30 June work in process inventory:		
Direct material:		
{Number of equivalent units of direct material} × {direct material cost per equivalent unit}	30 000 × R19.80	R594 000
Conversion:		
{Number of equivalent units of conversion} × {conversion cost per equivalent unit}	10 000 × R18.00	180 000
Total cost of 30 June work in process inventory		R774 000
Check: Cost of goods completed and transferred out		R3 055 000
Cost of 30 June work in process inventory		R774 000
Total costs accounted for		R3 829 000

Cybersearch

1 Several company websites contain 'virtual factory tours' of their production facilities. Using the search term *virtual factory tour,* find a company web page that has this information and answer the following questions:

   (a) What is (are) the product(s) produced?
   (b) Describe the stages in the production process.
   (c) Would you recommend job costing, process costing, or some form of hybrid costing? Explain your answer.

A good site is www.manufacturing.stanford.edu at which you can watch online videos of manufacturing processes.

Find websites with examples of product costing software.

   (d) Does this software support process costing? (*Hint*: Do not expect that the term *process costing* will necessarily be used. You may need to study the specific features of the software.)
   (e) If so, does the software undertake process costing using similar concepts to those presented in the chapter? Explain.
   (f) Do you think that this software would provide accurate product costs for a company with a repetitive production process environment? Explain your answer.

Appendix to Chapter 5

Process costing in sequential production departments

L.O. 7

In manufacturing operations with sequential production departments, the costs assigned to the units transferred out of one department remain assigned to those units as they enter the next department. In our process costing illustration for Spritz, the soft drink mixture is transferred out of the Mixing Department to the Finishing Department. There the mixture is carbonated, bottled, labelled and packed in cartons. The carbonate and bottles are introduced at (or very near) the beginning of the finishing process. The remaining direct materials, that is, labels and cartons, are used at the end of the process in the Finishing Department.

The flow of costs for the goods completed and transferred out of the Mixing Department is shown in Exhibit 5.18.

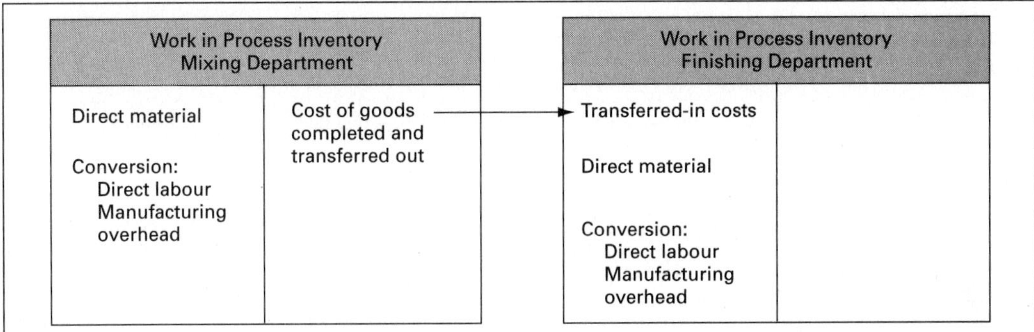

Exhibit 5.18 Moving costs of work in process to a subsequent department

As the ledger accounts show, the Mixing Department has two cost elements: direct material costs and conversion costs. However, the Finishing Department has three cost elements: direct material costs, conversion costs and transferred-in costs. **Transferred-in costs** are the costs assigned to the units transferred from the Mixing Department to the Finishing Department. Transferred-in costs are conceptually similar to direct material costs. The only difference is that direct material costs relate to raw materials, whereas transferred-in costs relate to partially completed products.

Exhibit 5.19 presents the basic data for our illustration of process costing in the Finishing Department. The 1 April work in process inventory in the Department consists of 20 000 bottles that received some work in the Finishing Department during March but were not completed. The R132 100 of transferred-in costs in the 1 April work in process inventory are costs that were transferred into the Finishing Department's work in process inventory account during March. Note that any partially completed bottles of drink in the Finishing Department must have received their transferred-in input or they would not have been transferred from the Mixing Department. The 1 April work in process inventory has received carbonate and bottles, as these materials are added at the beginning of the finishing process. The other direct materials, labels and cartons, have not been added, as these are not introduced until the end of the finishing process.

Exhibit 5.19 shows that 1 220 000 bottles were started during April. Where the same unit of output is used in all departments, the number of units started in the current department will be equal to the number of units transferred out from the previous department. In the Spritz illustration, this is not the case. The Mixing Department produces litres of mixture, whereas the Finishing Department produces bottles of Spritz (refer to Exhibit 5.1, which shows that 390 000 litres were completed and transferred out of the Mixing Department during April). The Finishing Department completed 1 200 000 bottles of drink during April and transferred them to finished goods inventory. This left 40 000 bottles in the Finishing Department's 30 April work in process inventory.

Exhibit 5.19 shows that the costs incurred in the Finishing Department during April were R1 375 620 for direct material, R122 000 for direct labour, and R494 000 for applied manufacturing

Work in process, 1 April 20 000 bottles:	
Transferred-in: 100% complete	R132 100
Direct material: 60% complete*	31 980
Conversion: 20% complete	14 360
Balance work in process, 1 April†	R178 440
Units started during April‡	1 220 000 bottles
Units completed during April and transferred to finished goods	1 200 000 bottles
Work in process, 30 April:	
Transferred-in: 100% complete	40 000 bottles
Direct material: 60% complete	
Conversion: 90% complete	
Cost incurred during April:	
Transferred-in from Mixing Department; depends on whether weighted average (R3 451 500) or FIFO (R3 455 250) used	
Direct material	R1 375 620
Conversion costs:	
Direct labour	R122 000
Applied manufacturing overhead	494 000
Total conversion costs	R616 000

* Carbonate and bottles account for 60% of the direct material costs of the Finishing Department. Labels and cartons account for the other 40%.

† These costs were incurred during March.

‡ These will be equal to the units transferred out from the previous department, except where, as in this example, the output from the previous department is a different unit of measurement (e.g. litres, not bottles).

Exhibit 5.19 Basic data for illustration, Spritz Finishing Department

overhead. The following journal entry is made during April to add the costs of direct material, direct labour and manufacturing overhead to work in process inventory in the Finishing Department:

Work in process inventory: Finishing Department	R1 991 620	
Raw material inventory		R1 375 620
Wages payable		122 000
Manufacturing overhead		494 000

The April transferred-in cost in the Finishing Department is the cost of goods completed and transferred out of the Mixing Department. The amount of this cost depends on whether the weighted average or FIFO process costing method is used in the Mixing Department. The journal entries for transferring these costs from the work in process account for the Mixing Department to the work in process account for the Finishing Department are shown on pages 193 and 196. As in the Mixing Department, the weighted average and FIFO methods produce different results.

Weighted average method in subsequent departments

Exhibit 5.20 presents a detailed production report for the Finishing Department, using weighted average process costing. Steps one to four are identified in the exhibit. The process costing procedures used for the Finishing Department are identical to those used for the Mixing Department, except for two important differences. First, while there were only two cost elements (direct material and conversion) in the Mixing Department, there are three cost elements in the Finishing Department. In each of the four steps in Exhibit 5.20, transferred-in costs are listed, together with direct material and conversion, as a separate cost element. Second, in the Mixing Department it was assumed that all direct materials were added at the beginning of the process. In the Finishing Department, 60 per cent of the direct material cost is incurred at the beginning of the process and the remaining 40 per cent at the end of the process. This means that the percentage of completion column must be expanded to include direct materials as well as conversion costs.

Step one		Step two				
		Percentage of completion with respect to:		Equivalent units		
	Physical units	Direct material	Conversion	Transferred in	Direct material	Conversion
Work in process, 1 April	20 000	60%	20%			
Units transferred in during April	1 220 000					
Total units to account for	1 240 000					
Units completed and transferred out during April	1 200 000			1 200 000	1 200 000	1 200 000
Work in process, 30 April	40 000	60%	90%	40 000	24 000	36 000
Total units accounted for	1 240 000					
Total equivalent units				1 240 000	1 224 000	1 236 000

Step three

	Transferred-in	Direct material	Conversion	Total
Work in process, 1 April (from Exhibit 5.19)	R132 100	R31 980	R14 360	R178 440
Costs incurred during April (from Exhibits 5.6 and 5.19)	3 451 500	1 375 620	616 000	R5 443 120
	3 583 600	1 407 600	630 360	5 621 560
Equivalent units	1 240 000	1 224 000	1 236 000	
Cost per equivalent unit	R2.89	R1.15	R0.51	R4.55
	↑	↑	↑	
	3 583 600 / 1 240 000	1 407 600 / 1 224 000	630 360 / 1 236 000	

Step four

Cost of goods completed and transferred out {Number of units transferred out} × {total cost per equivalent unit}	1 200 000 × R4.55	R5 460 000
Cost remaining in 30 April work in process:		
Transferred in: {Number of equivalent units of transferred-in costs} × {cost per equivalent unit of transferred-in costs}	40 000 × R2.89	R115 600
Direct material: {Number of equivalent units of direct material costs} × {cost per equivalent unit of direct material cost}	24 000 × R1.15	R27 600
Conversion: {Number of equivalent units of conversion costs} × {cost per equivalent unit of conversion costs}	36 000 × R0.51	R18 360
Total cost of 30 April work in process		R161 560
Check: Cost of goods completed and transferred out		R5 460 000
Cost of 30 April work in process inventory		161 560
		R5 621 560

Exhibit 5.20 Process costing in sequential department, Spritz Finishing Department (weighted average method)

The analysis of the physical flow of units (Step one in Exhibit 5.20) is like the analysis for the Mixing Department. But now focus on Step two: in calculating equivalent units, we add a 'transferred-in' column. Both the 1 200 000 units completed and transferred out of the Finishing Department and the 40 000 units in 30 April work in process inventory are 100 per cent complete as to transferred-in inputs. Thus the number of equivalent units is the same as the number of physical units. The calculation yields a total of 1 240 000 equivalent units of transferred-in inputs for April. The calculation of equivalent units of direct material and conversion in Step two are determined as described earlier for the Mixing Department.

Costs per equivalent unit are calculated in Step three. Since we are using the weighted average method, the transferred-in costs in the 1 April work in process inventory are added to the April transferred-in costs before dividing by the equivalent units. Direct material and conversion costs are handled like those for the Mixing Department.

The analysis of total costs is completed in Step four. The 1 200 000 units completed and transferred out of the Finishing Department are assigned a total weighted average cost per unit of R4.55. This unit cost includes the transferred-in cost per equivalent unit of R2.89 calculated in Step three. The total cost of the units completed and transferred out is R5 460 000. The following journal entry is made to transfer the cost of the units completed to the finished goods inventory account:

Finished goods inventory	R5 460 000	
Work in process inventory: Finishing Department		R5 460 000

The cost remaining in the work in process inventory on 30 April consists of three cost elements: transferred-in costs, direct material costs and conversion costs.

FIFO method in subsequent departments

The FIFO process costing for the Finishing Department is very similar to the FIFO process costing for the Mixing Department described in the chapter. The only differences are the inclusion of the transferred-in costs as an additional cost element, and the addition of some direct material at the end of the process.

Summary of transferred-in costs

When manufacturing is done in sequential production departments, the cost assigned to the units completed in each department is transferred to the next department's work-in-process inventory account. This cost is called the *transferred-in cost,* and it is handled as a distinct cost element in the process costing calculations. In this way, the final cost of the product is built up cumulatively as the product progresses through the production sequence.

Questions

5.1 Explain the primary differences between job costing, process costing and operation costing.

5.2 List five types of products for which process costing would be an appropriate product-costing system. What is the key characteristic of these products that makes process costing a good choice?

5.3 List three non-manufacturing businesses in which process costing could be used. (For example, a public accounting firm could use process costing to accumulate the costs of processing clients' tax returns.)

5.4 How can process costing and operation costing be used for responsibility accounting purposes?

5.5 Define the term *equivalent unit,* and explain how the concept is used in process costing. When is it sensible to ignore the concept of equivalent units in process costing?

5.6 Explain how the equivalent units for direct material and conversion costs in Exhibit 5.2 were calculated. Why are there more equivalent units for direct material than for direct labour?

5.7 Explain how the direct material, conversion and total cost per equivalent unit shown in Exhibit 5.3 were calculated.

5.8 Explain how the cost of goods completed and transferred out and the work-in-process inventory on 30 April, shown in Exhibit 5.4, were calculated.

5.9 List and briefly describe the purpose of each of the four process costing steps.

5.10 Show the journal entry for entering direct material costs into the work-in-process inventory account for the first department in a sequential production process. Show the journal entry for recording the transfer of partially completed goods from the first to the second department in the sequence.

5.11 Explain how the calculation of equivalent units differs between the weighted average and FIFO methods of process costing, by referring to Exhibits 5.2 and 5.7.

5.12 Explain how the calculation of cost per equivalent unit differs between the weighted average and FIFO methods of process costing, by referring to Exhibits 5.3 and 5.8.

5.13 Explain the reasoning underlying the name of the weighted average method of process costing.

5.14 How are the costs of the beginning work in process inventory treated differently under the weighted average and FIFO methods?

5.15 Identify the key differences between departmental production reports prepared under weighted average and FIFO assumptions, by referring to Exhibits 5.6 and 5.11.

5.16 Why is it useful to identify the costs of spoiled units separately in process costing?

5.17 Explain the terms *normal spoilage* and *abnormal spoilage*. How does the accounting for these two types of spoilage differ under process costing?

5.18 How would the process costing calculations differ from those illustrated in the chapter if overhead costs were used in the production process in a different pattern to direct labour costs?

5.19 Why might the FIFO method of process costing be more effective than the weighted average method from a performance evaluation standpoint?

5.20 Process costing is a product costing system. What are the key pieces of information provided by the process costing system, and how might managers use this information?

5.21 Explain the concept of *operation costing*. How does it differ from process costing or job costing? Describe the product features and production environments suited to operation costing.

5.22 Explain why determining the percentage of completion is vital in estimating product costs. Do we need to determine the percentage of completion in an operation costing system? Explain.

5.23 JIT inventory and production management systems are becoming more common. What are the implications of the JIT approach for process costing?

5.24 (appendix) What are *transferred-in costs*? Describe two examples of products and sequential production processes to illustrate your answer.

5.25 (appendix) A food-processing company has two sequential production departments: mixing and cooking. The cost of the 1 January 20X6 work in process in the cooking department is as follows:

Direct material	R400 000
Conversion	100 000
Transferred-in costs	900 000

During what time period and in what department were the R900 000 costs listed above incurred? Explain your answer.

Exercises

E5.26 Physical flow of units: manufacturer

In each case below, fill in the missing amount:

1	Work in process, 1 June	10 000 kg
	Units started during June	?
	Units completed during June	16 000 kg
	Work in process, 30 June	3 000 kg
2	Work in process, 1 April	12 000 m
	Units started in April	22 000 m
	Units completed during April	21 500 m
	Work in process, 30 April	?
3	Work in process, 1 January	50 000 L
	Units started during the year	67 000 L
	Units completed during the year	?
	Work in process, 31 December	45 000 L

E5.27 Equivalent units; FIFO and weighted average: manufacturer

Glass Creations Ltd manufactures decorative glass bowls. The firm employs a process costing system for its manufacturing operations. All direct materials are added at the beginning of the process, and conversion costs are incurred uniformly throughout the process. The company's production quantity schedule for November follows:

Units	
Work in process on 1 November (60% complete as to conversion)	2000
Units started during November	3500
Total units to account for	5500
Units from beginning work in process, which were completed and transferred out during November	2000
Units started and completed during November	1800
Work in process on 30 November (20% complete as to conversion)	1700
Total units accounted for	5500

Required:
Calculate each of the following amounts:

1 Equivalent units of direct material during November. Use the FIFO method.
2 Equivalent units of conversion during November. Use the FIFO method.
3 Equivalent units of direct material during November. Use the weighted average method.
4 Equivalent units of conversion during November. Use the weighted average method.

(CMA, adapted)

E5.28 Physical flow and equivalent units; weighted average and FIFO: manufacturer
Country Life Corporation produces breakfast cereal. In the year just completed the following results were recorded:

		Percentage of completion	
	Units	Direct material	Conversion
Work in process, 1 January	20 000 kg	80%	60%
Work in process, 31 December	15 000 kg	70%	30%

During the year the company started 120 000 kilograms of material in production.

Required:
1 Prepare a schedule analysing the physical flow of units and calculating the equivalent units of both direct material and conversion. Use weighted average process costing.
2 Repeat requirement 1 using the FIFO method.

E5.29 Physical flow and equivalent units; weighted average: manufacturer
The Gauteng plant of Healthy Life Styles produces low-fat salad dressing. The following data relate to the year just ended:

		Percentage of completion	
	Units	Direct material	Conversion
Work in process, 1 January	30 000 litres	70%	50%
Work in process, 31 December	25 000 litres	75%	20%

During the year the company started 140 000 litres of material in production.

Required:
Prepare a schedule analysing the physical flow of units and calculating the equivalent units of both direct material and conversion for the year. Use weighted average process costing.

E5.30 Cost per equivalent unit; weighted average
Sakhisizwe Glass Company manufactures window glass for automobiles. The following data relate to the Plate Glass Department :

Work in process, 1 February:	
Direct material	R43 200
Conversion	40 300
Costs incurred during February:	
Direct material	R135 000
Conversion	190 000

The equivalent units of activity for February were as follows: 16 500 equivalent units of direct material, and 47 000 equivalent units of conversion activity.

Required:
Calculate the cost per equivalent unit, for both direct material and conversion during February. Use weighted average process costing.

E5.31 Cost per equivalent unit; weighted average and FIFO: timber mill
Williamstown Timber Pty Ltd grows, harvests and processes timber for use in the building industry. The following data relate to the company's sawmill during November:

Work in process, 1 November:	
Direct material	R650 000
Conversion	1 800 000
Costs incurred during November:	
Direct material	R4 250 000
Conversion	6 900 000

The equivalent units for November were as follows:

	Weighted average	FIFO
Direct material	7000	4 250
Conversion	1740	1 000

Required:
1 Calculate the cost per equivalent unit, for both direct material and conversion, during November. Use weighted average process costing.
2 Repeat requirement 1 using the FIFO method.

E5.32 Weighted average cost and FIFO: manufacturer
The data below relate to Setsoto Packaging Ltd, a manufacturer of small cardboard boxes:

Work in process, 1 February:	10 000 units*
Direct material	R10 900
Conversion	28 950
Costs incurred during February:	
Direct material	R112 700
Conversion	160 200

*Complete as to direct material; 35% complete as to conversion.

The equivalent units for February were as follows:

	Weighted average	FIFO
Direct material	103 000	98 000
Conversion	97 000	93 000

During February, 89 000 units were completed and transferred out.

Required:
1 Calculate each of the following amounts using weighted average process costing:

(a) cost of goods completed during February
(b) cost of the 28 February work in process inventory

2 Repeat requirement 1 using the FIFO method.

E5.33 Weighted average cost and FIFO: manufacturer

Sheridan Textiles Ltd manufactures natural fabrics for the clothing industry. The following data relate to the Weaving Department for the month of September:

	Weighted average	FIFO
Total equivalent units of direct material	60 000	40 000
Total equivalent units of conversion	52 000	44 000
Units completed and transferred out during September	50 000	50 000

The cost data for September were as follows:

Work in process 1 September:	
Direct material	R940 000
Conversion	444 000
Costs incurred during September:	
Direct material	R1 640 000
Conversion	2 728 000

There were 20 000 units in process in the Weaving Department on 1 September (100 per cent complete as to direct material and 40 per cent complete as to conversion).

Required:

1 Calculate each of the following amounts using weighted average process costing:
(a) cost of goods completed and transferred out of the Weaving Department during September
(b) cost of the 30 September work in process inventory in the Weaving Department

2 Repeat requirement 1 using the FIFO method.

E5.34 Weighted average versus FIFO; journal entry: manufacturer

On 1 January the Moulding Department of Pipes and Fittings Ltd had no work in process inventory due to the implementation of a just-in-time inventory system. On 31 January the following journal entry was made to record the cost of goods completed and transferred out of the Moulding Department:

Finished goods inventory	R2 140 000	
Work in process inventory: Moulding Department		R2 140 000
The company uses weighted average process costing.		

Required:

What would the amount have been in the journal entry above if Pipes and Fittings had used the FIFO method of process costing? Explain why.

E5.35 Operation costing: manufacturer

AllSports Ltd produces sporting equipment in a number of plants across South Africa. The Durban Division's production for November consisted of Batch P25 (2000 professional soccer balls) and Batch S33 (4000 scholastic soccer balls). Professional soccer balls have genuine leather exteriors and are packaged in an attractive cardboard box. Scholastic soccer balls use imitation leather and are sold without special packaging. Both products go through identical preparation and finishing operations. Each batch was started and finished during November, and there was no beginning or ending work in process. Costs incurred were as follows:

Direct material:
Batch P25, R420 000, including R25 000 for packaging material
Batch S33, R450 000
Conversion costs:
Preparation Department, predetermined rate of R75 per unit
Finishing Department, predetermined rate of R60 per unit
Packaging Department, predetermined rate of R5 per unit

Required:

1 Draw a diagram depicting the Division's batch manufacturing process. Refer to Exhibit 5.16 for guidance.
2 Calculate the November product cost for each type of soccer ball.
3 Prepare journal entries to record the cost flows during November.

E5.36 Physical flow and equivalent units including spoilage: manufacturer

Dry Babies Corporation produces disposable nappies. In the year just completed the following results were recorded:

	Units	Percentage of completion with respect to conversion
Work in process, 1 January	20 000	60%
Work in process, 31 December	15 000	40%

During the year 120 000 nappies were started in production. Of these, 10 000 were rejected at the quality inspection process, which occurred two-thirds of the way through the production process. All materials are added at the beginning of the production process and conversion costs are incurred uniformly throughout the process.

Required:

1 Prepare a schedule analysing the physical flow of units and calculating the equivalent units of both direct material and conversion. Use weighted average process costing.
2 How would your approach differ using the FIFO method?

E5.37 Cost flows in process costing; journal entries (appendix): manufacturer

Pallet Pavers manufactures concrete paving bricks. The processing takes place in two sequential departments. The following cost data relate to the month of October:

	Pouring Department	Finishing Department
Direct material entered into production	R140 000	R50 000
Direct labour	680 000	560 000
Applied manufacturing overhead	1 360 000	840 000
Cost of goods completed and transferred out	1 800 000 *	800 000 †

* Cost of goods transferred to Finishing Department.
† Cost of goods transferred to finished goods.

Required:

Prepare journal entries to record the following events:

1 Incurrence of costs for direct material and direct labour, and application of manufacturing overhead in the Pouring Department.
2 Transfer of goods from the Pouring Department to the Finishing Department.
3 Incurrence of costs for direct material and direct labour, and application of manufacturing overhead in the Finishing Department.
4 Transfer of goods from the Finishing Department to finished goods inventory.

Problems

P5.38 Partial production report; journal entries; FIFO method: manufacturer

Umzimkhulu Chemicals Ltd accumulates costs for its single product using FIFO process costing. Direct material is added at the beginning of the production process, and conversion occurs uniformly throughout the process. A partially completed production report for the month of May follows.

Production Report for May (FIFO method)

	Physical units	Percentage of completion with respect to conversion	Equivalent units: Direct material	Equivalent units: Conversion
Work in process, 1 May	25 000	40%		
Units started during May	30 000			
Total units to account for	55 000			
Units completed and transferred out during May	35 000		?	?
Work in process, 31 May	20 000	80%	?	?
Total units accounted for	55 000			

	Direct material	Conversion	Total
Work in process, 1 May	R143 000	R474 700	R617 700
Costs incurred during May	165 000	2 009 000	2 174 000
Total costs to account for	R308 000	R2 483 700	R2 791 700
Costs per equivalent unit	R5.50	R49.00	R54.50

Required:

1 Prepare a schedule of equivalent units for Umzimkhulu Chemicals.
2 Show how the costs per equivalent unit were determined in the production report above.
3 Calculate the cost of goods completed and transferred out during May.
4 Calculate the cost remaining in the work in process inventory on 31 May.
5 Prepare a journal entry to record the transfer of the cost of goods completed and transferred out during May.
6 How would the production report above be different if the company used weighted average process costing?

P5.39 Weighted average process costing; journal entries: manufacturer

Refer to the data for Umzimkhulu Chemicals Ltd given in Problem 5.38.

Required:

1 Complete each of the following process costing steps using weighted average process costing:
   (a) calculation of equivalent units
   (b) calculation of unit costs
   (c) analysis of total costs
2 Prepare a journal entry to record the transfer of the cost of goods completed and transferred out during May.

P5.40 Weighted average process costing: manufacturer

The following data relate to the Gariep Flour Milling Company for the month of October:

Work in process, 1 October (in units)	?
Units started during October	70 000
Total units to account for	80 000
Units completed and transferred out during October	?
Work in process, 31 October (in units)	5000
Total equivalent units: Direct material	80 000
Total equivalent units: Conversion	?
Work in process, 1 October: Direct Material	R112 000
Work in process, 1 October: Conversion	?
Costs incurred during October: Direct material	?
Costs incurred during October: Conversion	900 000
Work in process, 1 October: Total cost	142 225
Total costs incurred during October	1 500 000
Total costs to account for	1 642 225
Costs per equivalent unit: Direct material	8.90
Cost per equivalent unit: Conversion	?
Total cost per equivalent unit	20.75
Cost of goods complete and transferred out during October	?
Cost remaining in ending work in process inventory: Direct material	?
Cost remaining in ending work in process inventory: Conversion	41 475
Total cost of 31 October work in process	85 975

Additional information:

- Direct material is added at the beginning of the production process, and conversion activity occurs uniformly throughout the process.
- Gariep uses weighted average process costing.
- The 1 October work in process was 15 per cent complete as to conversion.
- The 31 October work in process was 70 per cent complete as to conversion.

Required:
Calculate the missing amounts, and prepare the firm's October production report.

P5.41 Weighted average process costing: manufacturer

Tintinara Titanium Ltd manufactures a highly specialised titanium sheathing material. The following data have been compiled for the month of June. Conversion activity occurs uniformly throughout the production process.

Work in process, 1 June–40 000 units	
Direct material: 100% complete	R110 500
Conversion: 38% complete	22 375
Balance in work in process, 1 June	R132 875
Units started during June	190 000
Units completed during June and transferred to finished goods inventory	180 000
Work in process, 30 June:	
Direct material: 100% complete	
Conversion: 55% complete	
Costs incurred during June:	
Direct material	R430 000
Conversion costs:	
Direct labour	R128 000
Applied manufacturing overheads	192 000
Total conversion costs	R320 000

Required:
Prepare schedules to accomplish each of the following process costing steps for the month of June. Use the weighted average method of process costing.

1 Analysis of physical flow of units.
2 Calculation of equivalent units.
3 Calculation of unit costs.
4 Analysis of total costs.

P5.42 Determination of production costs; analysis of equivalent units: manufacturer

Dellkana Company assembles various components used in the computer industry. The company's major product, a disk drive, is the result of assembling three parts: JR1163, JY1065 and DC0766. The following information related to the activities of April:

Beginning work in process inventory: 3000 units, 80% complete as to conversion; cost, R293 940 (direct material, R230 000; conversion, R63 940)
Production started: 27 000 units
Production completed: 26 000 units
Ending work in process inventory: 4000 units, 45% complete as to conversion
Direct material used: JR1163, R225 000; JY1065, R710 000; DC0766, R455 000
Hourly wage of direct labourers, R21; total direct labour payroll, R134 274
Overhead application rate: R69 per direct labour hour

All parts are introduced at the beginning of the manufacturing process; conversion cost is incurred uniformly throughout production.

Required:

Using weighted average process costing:
1 Calculate the total cost of direct material and conversion during April.
2 Determine the cost of goods completed during the month.
3 Determine the cost of the work in process inventory on 30 April.
4 With regard to the ending work in process inventory:
   (a) how much direct material cost would be added to these units in May?
   (b) what percentage of conversion would be performed on these units in May?
5 Assume that the disk drive required the addition of another part (TH55) at the 75 per cent stage of completion. How many equivalent units with respect to part TH55 would be represented in April's ending work in process inventory?

P5.43 Analysis of work in process inventory account; T-accounts: manufacturer

Lawncraft Ltd manufactures lawn furniture using an assembly-line process. All direct materials are introduced at the start of the process, and conversion cost is incurred evenly throughout manufacturing. An examination of the company's work in process inventory account for June revealed the following selected information:

Debit side:
  1 June balance: 200 units, 25% complete as to conversion, cost R180 000*
  Production started: 800 units
  Direct material used during June: R430 000
  June conversion cost: R300 000
Credit side:
  Production completed: 600 units

* Supplementary records revealed direct material cost of R120 000 and conversion cost of R60 000.

Discussions with manufacturing staff revealed that the ending work in process was 75 per cent complete with respect to conversion costs.

Required:

Using weighted average process costing:
1 Determine the number of units in the 30 June work in process inventory.

2 Calculate the cost of goods completed during June and prepare the appropriate journal entry to record completed production.
3 Determine the cost of the 30 June work in process inventory.
4 Briefly explain the meaning of equivalent units. Why are equivalent units needed to properly allocate costs between completed production and production in process?

P5.44 Missing data; FIFO; production report: manufacturer

The following data relate to the Bending Department of Footscray Metals Ltd for August:

Unit data	
Work in process, 1 August (in units)	?
Units started during August	?
Total units to account for	?
Units completed and transferred out during August	105 000
Work in process, 31 August (in units)	75 000
Total equivalent units: Direct material	?
Total equivalent units: Conversion	?
New equivalent units accomplished in August: Direct material	120 000
New equivalent units accomplished in August: Conversion	?
Cost data	
Work in process, 1 August: Direct material	R456 000
Work in process, 1 August: Conversion	?
Costs incurred during August: Direct material	918 000
Costs incurred during August: Conversion	?
Work in process, 1 August: Total cost	?
Total costs incurred during August	2 240 100
Total costs to account for	2 900 100
Cost per equivalent unit: Direct material	?
Cost per equivalent unit: Conversion	?
Total cost per equivalent unit	?
Cost of goods completed and transferred out during August	?
Cost remaining in ending work in process inventory:	
Direct material	?
Conversion	?
Total cost of 31 August work in process	?

Additional information:

- Direct material is added at the beginning of the production process, and conversion occurs uniformly throughout the process.
- Footscray Metals uses FIFO process costing.
- The 1 August work in process was 30 per cent complete as to conversion.
- The 31 August work in process was 40 per cent complete as to conversion.

Required:

Calculate the missing amounts (marked '?') and prepare the August production report for the Bending Department.

P5.45 Process costing in a public accounting firm

Mason and Company, a public accounting firm, is engaged in the preparation of income tax returns for individuals. The firm uses the weighted average method of process costing for internal reporting. The following information pertains to the month of February:

Number of returns in process, 1 February (20% complete)	300
Number of returns started in February	900
Number of returns in process, 28 February (75% complete)	400
Returns in process, 1 February:	
Labour	R17 500
Overhead	R20 000
Labour, 1 February to 28 February (4500 hours)	R450 000
Overhead, 1 February to 28 February	R255 000

Required:

1 Calculate the following amounts for labour and for overhead:
   (a) equivalent units
   (b) cost per equivalent unit

2 Calculate the cost of returns in process as at 28 February.

(CMA, adapted)

P5.46 Process costing with spoilage; journal entries: manufacturer

Regency Park Plastics Ltd accumulates costs for its single product using weighted average process costing. Direct material is added at the beginning of the production process, and conversion occurs uniformly throughout the process. All spoilage is detected at the quality inspection point, which occurs after production is 25 per cent complete. Below is a partially completed production report for the month of September:

Production Report for September

	Physical units	Percentage of completion with respect to conversion	Equivalent units: Direct material	Equivalent units: Conversion
Work in process, 1 September	50 000	60%		
Units started during September	100 000			
Total units to account for	150 000			
Units completed and transferred out during September	110 000		?	?
Units spoiled during production	30 000		?	?
Work in process, 30 September	10 000	80%	?	?
Total units accounted for	150 000			

	Direct material	Conversion	Total
Work in process, 1 September	R58 500	R24 000	R82 500
Costs incurred during September	114 000	76 400	190 400
Total costs to account for	R172 500	R100 400	R272 900

Required:

1 Prepare a schedule of equivalent units for Regency Park Plastics.

2 Calculate the costs per equivalent unit.

3 Calculate the cost of goods completed and transferred out during September.

4 Calculate the cost of spoiled units during September.

5 Calculate the cost remaining in the work in process inventory on 30 September.

6 Prepare a journal entry to record the transfer of the cost of goods completed and transferred out during September, assuming:
   (a) the spoiled units represent normal spoilage
   (b) the spoiled units represent abnormal spoilage

7 How would the production report above be different if the company used FIFO process costing?

P5.47 Operation costing; unit costs; journal entries: manufacturer

Goulbourn Industries Ltd manufactures a variety of plastic products, including a series of moulded chairs. The three models of moulded chairs, which are all variations of the same design, are Standard (can be stacked), Deluxe (with arms) and Executive (with arms and padding). The company uses batch manufacturing and has an operation costing system. The production process includes an extrusion operation and subsequent operations to form, trim and finish the chairs. Plastic sheets are produced by the extrusion operation, some of which are sold directly to other manufacturers. During the forming operation, the remaining plastic sheets are moulded into chair seats and the legs are added; the Standard model is sold after this operation. During the trimming operation, the arms are added to the Deluxe and Executive models and the chair edges are smoothed. Only the Executive model enters the finishing operation where the padding is added. All the units produced complete the same steps within each operation. The May production run had a total manufacturing cost of R1 347 000. The units of production and direct material costs incurred were as follows:

	Units of production	Extrusion materials	Forming materials	Trimming materials	Finishing materials
Plastic sheets	10 000	R90 000			
Standard model	12 000	108 000	R36 000		
Deluxe model	6 000	54 000	18 000	R13 500	
Executive model	4 000	36 000	12 000	9 000	R18 000
Total	32 000	R288 000	R66 000	R22 500	R18 000

Manufacturing costs applied during the month of May were as follows:

	Extrusion operation	Forming operation	Trimming operation	Finishing operation
Direct labour	R228 000	R90 000	R45 000	R27 000
Manufacturing overhead	360 000	108 000	58 500	36 000

Required:

1 For each product produced by Goulbourn Industries during the month of May, determine:
(a) the unit cost
(b) the total cost
Be sure to account for all costs incurred during the month.
2 Prepare journal entries to record the flow of production costs during May.
3 Independent of your answer to requirements 1 and 2, assume that 1000 units of the Deluxe model remained in work in process at the end of the month. These units were 100 per cent complete as to raw material and 60 per cent complete in the trimming operation. Determine the value of the 1000 units of the Deluxe model in Goulbourn Industries' work-in-process inventory at the end of May. (There was no work-in-process inventory on 1 May.)

(CMA, adapted)

P5.48 Operation costing: manufacturer

Wilkey Ltd manufactures a variety of glass windows in its Polokwane plant. In Department A, clear glass sheets are produced, and some of these sheets are sold as finished goods. Other sheets made in Department A have metallic oxides added to them in Department B to form coloured glass sheets. Some of these coloured sheets are sold, while others are moved to Department C for etching and are then sold. The company uses operation costing. Wilkey's production costs, applied to products in May, are given in the following table. There was no beginning or ending inventory of work in process for May.

Cost category	Department A	Department B	Department C
Direct material	R450 000	R72 000	R0
Direct labour	38 000	22 000	38 000
Manufacturing overhead	230 000	68 000	73 500

Products	Units	Department A Direct material	Department B Direct material
Clear glass, sold after Department A	11 000	R247 500	R0
Unetched coloured glass, sold after Department B	4 000	90 000	32 000
Etched coloured glass, sold after Department C	5 000	112 500	40 000
		R450 000	R72 000

Each sheet of glass requires the same steps within each operation.

Required:

Calculate each of the following amounts:

1 The conversion cost per unit in Department A.
2 The conversion cost per unit in Department B.
3 The cost of a clear glass sheet.
4 The cost of an unetched coloured glass sheet.
5 The cost of an etched, coloured glass sheet.

(*Roland Minch*)

P5.49 Operation costing; unit costs; cost flow; journal entries

Orbital Industries Ltd manufactures a variety of materials and equipment for the aerospace industry. A team of R & D engineers in the firm's Technology Park plant has developed a new material that will be useful for a variety of purposes in orbiting satellites and spacecraft. Trade-named Ceralam, the material combines some of the best properties of both ceramics and laminated plastics. Ceralam is already being used for a variety of housing in satellites produced in three different countries. Ceralam sheets are produced in an operation called rolling, in which the various materials are rolled together to form a multilayer laminate. Orbital Industries sells many of these Ceralam sheets just after the rolling operation to aerospace firms world-wide. However, Orbital also processes many of the Ceralam sheets further in the Technology Park plant. After rolling, the sheets are sent to the moulding operation, where they are formed into various shapes used to house a variety of instruments. After moulding, the sheets are sent to the punching operation, where holes are punched in the moulded sheets to accommodate protruding instruments, electrical conduits and so forth. Some of the moulded and punched sheets are then sold. The remaining units are sent to the dipping operation, in which the moulded sheets are dipped in a special chemical mixture to give them a reflective surface.

During the month of November, the following products were manufactured at the Technology Park plant (the direct material costs are also shown):

	Units	Direct material used in Ceralam sheets	Direct material used in dipping
Ceralam sheets (sold after the rolling operation)	6 000	R960 000	
Non-reflective housings (sold after the punching operation)	2 500	400 000	
Reflective housings (sold after the dipping operation)	1 500	240 000	R60 000
Total	10 000	R1 600 000	R60 000

	Rolling	Moulding	Punching	Dipping
Direct material	R1 600 000	0	0	R60 000
Direct labour	600 000	R224 000	R256 000	90 000
Manufacturing overhead	900 000	336 000	384 000	135 000
Total	R3 100 000	R560 000	R640 000	R285 000

Orbital Industries uses operation costing for its Ceralam operations at the Technology Park plant. (There were no inventories of work in process or finished goods on 1 November or 30 November.)

Required:

1 Prepare a table that includes the following information for each of the four operations:
   (a) total conversion costs
   (b) units manufactured
   (c) conversion cost per unit
2 Prepare a second table that includes the following information for each product (that is, rolled Ceralam sheets, non-reflective Ceralam housings and reflective Ceralam housings):
   (a) total manufacturing costs
   (b) units manufactured
   (c) total cost per unit
3 Prepare journal entries to record the flow of all manufacturing costs through the Technology Park plant's Ceralam operations during November. (Ignore the journal entries to record sales revenue.)

P5.50 Process costing; operation costing: manufacturer

Camata Paint Ltd manufactures domestic house paint in two processes: mixing and packaging. The company has several products that consume the same basic materials (at a cost of R18 per litre) and undergo similar processes. The following data relate to the two production departments for May:

	Mixing	Packaging
Direct labour	R180 000	R240 000
Manufacturing overhead	R210 000	R90 000
Litres produced	100 000	100 000

Products	Processing hours in Mixing Department	Processing hours in Packaging Department	Litres of finished product
Sheen	6000	4000	70 000
Glamour	2000	3800	20 000
Glow	2000	3200	10 000

Required:

1 Calculate the conversion cost per litre for each department, and use these rates to determine the total production cost per litre for the three products.
2 The engineers have advised you that the method of allocating cost as a rate per litre may not result in accurate product costs. For example, Glow requires more processing time in the mixing department than do the other two products to achieve its high gloss finish, but this is not reflected in the product costs. The engineers believe that applying conversion cost as a rate per process hour may result in a more accurate allocation of cost to the three products.

   Recalculate the total production cost per litre for the three products, applying conversion cost as a rate per process hour.

3 Consider the costs calculated in requirements 1 and 2. Explain why they are different. Does it matter which product costs you use?

P5.51 Transferred-in costs; no work in process (appendix): manufacturer

Woolly Ltd of Bloemfontein designs and manufactures woollen coats, which are in high demand in the cold highveld winters. The company uses a process costing system to cost products because it produces only two basic styles through two production departments – the Cutting and Sewing departments. It is company policy to complete all units of product by month-end. During July, one style of coat was manufactured – the Woolly Warmer. The following data relate to that month:

	1 July	31 July
Raw material	R40 000	R25 000
Work in process	0	0
Finished goods	10 000	5 000

Production data	Cutting Department	Sewing Department
Direct material	R60 000	R5 000
Direct labour	R25 000	R60 000
Direct labour hours (DLH)	1250	2 400
Machine hours (MH)	900	400
Budgeted overhead	R30 000	R16 000
Budgeted cost driver	10 000 MH	2 000 DLH

Required:

1 Determine the unit cost per coat in July. There were 5000 units produced in July.

2 Prepare the journal entries to record the production costs for July. Assume that the costs of the two production departments are charged to separate work-in-process inventory accounts.

3 Given the company policy of no work-in-process inventory at month-end, why would the company include departmental work in process accounts in its general ledger?

P5.52 Transferred-in costs; weighted average method (appendix): manufacturer

Autofab Ltd uses a process costing system. A unit of product passes through three departments – Moulding, Assembly and Finishing – before it is completed. The following production took place in the Finishing Department during May:

	Units
Work in process inventory, 1 May	700
Units transferred in from Assembly Department	7 000
Units transferred out to finished goods inventory	5 950

Raw material is added at the beginning of processing in the Finishing Department. The work-in-process inventory was 60 per cent complete as to conversion on 1 May, and 30 per cent complete as to conversion on 31 May.

Autofab Ltd uses the weighted average method of process costing. The equivalent units and costs per equivalent unit of production for each cost element for the Finishing Department are shown below:

	Equivalent units	Cost per equivalent unit
Transferred-in costs	7 700	R6.00
Raw material	7 700	3.00
Conversion cost	6 475	7.00
Total		R16.00

Required:

1 Calculate the following amounts:
   (a) cost of units transferred to finished goods inventory during May
   (b) cost of the Finishing Department's work in process inventory on 31 May

2 The total costs of prior departments included in the work-in-process inventory of the Finishing Department on 1 May amounted to R14 500. Prepare the journal entry to record the transfer of the goods from the Assembly Department to the Finishing Department during May.

(CMA, adapted)

P5.53 FIFO process costing; sequential departments; two types of direct material; ethics (appendix): manufacturer

Wood Glow Manufacturing Company produces a wood-refinishing kit that sells for R17.95. The final processing of the kits occurs in the Packaging Department. A quilted wrap is applied at the beginning of the packaging process. A compartmentalised outside box, printed with instructions and the company's name and logo, is added when units are 60 per cent through the process. Conversion costs, consisting of direct labour and applied overhead, occur evenly throughout the packaging process. Conversion activities after the addition of the box involve package sealing, testing for leakage, and final inspection. The following data relate to the activities of the Packaging Department during the month of October:

- Beginning work in process inventory was 10 000 units, 40 per cent complete as to conversion.
- 40 000 units were transferred to Packaging during October.
- There were 10 000 units in ending work in process, 80 per cent complete as to conversion.
- The Packaging Department's October costs were as follows:

Quilted wrap	R80 000
Outside boxes	50 000
Direct labour	22 000
Applied overhead (R3 per direct labour Rand)	66 000

- The costs transferred in from prior processing were R3 per unit. The cost of goods sold for the month was R240 000, and the ending finished goods inventory valuation was R84 000.
- Wood Glow uses the FIFO method for inventory valuation and for process costing.

Wood Glow's accountant, Mark Brandon, has been asked to analyse the activities of the Packaging Department for the month of October.

Required:

1 Prepare a schedule of equivalent units for October in the Packaging Department. (Hint: You will need two columns for direct material – wrap and boxes.)

2 Determine the cost per equivalent unit of the October production.

3 Wood Glow's production manager, Michael Drake, has been under pressure from the company chairman to reduce the cost of conversion in the Packaging Department. Although Drake has initiated various changes in the process to try to bring the cost down, he has been unsuccessful. Now Drake is faced with an early November meeting with the chairman, at which Drake will have to discuss the packaging cost and explain his failed attempts. Drake has approached Mark Brandon, Wood Glow's accountant and a close friend, with the following request:

Mark, I've got to show some cost reduction in the Packaging Department. Even a little bit will help me get through next week's meeting. Then I can work on the problem without the chairman breathing down my neck. I want you to do me a favour. Let's call October's ending inventory 95 per cent complete instead of 80 per cent. This will increase the number of equivalent units and lower the unit costs.

By how much would Drake's proposal lower the kit's unit cost? What should Brandon do?
(CMA, adapted)

Cases

C5.54 Equivalent units; unit costs; evaluation of weighted average and FIFO: manufacturer
Pillay Paints (Pty) Ltd, which manufactures quality paint sold at competitive prices, uses a single production department. Production begins with the blending of various chemicals, which are added at the beginning of the process, and ends with the canning of the paint. Canning occurs when the mixture reaches the 90 per cent stage of completion. The litre cans are then transferred to the Shipping Department for crating and shipment. Labour and overhead are added continually throughout the process. Manufacturing overhead is applied on the basis of direct labour hours at the rate of R15 per hour.

Prior to May, when a change in the process was implemented, work in process inventories were insignificant. The change in the process enables greater production but has resulted in significant amounts of work in process for the first time. The company has always used the weighted average method to determine equivalent units of production and unit costs. Now, production management are considering changing from the weighted average method to the first in, first out method. The following data relate to actual production during the month of May:

	Costs for May
Work in process inventory, 1 May (4000 litres; 25% complete):	
Direct material (chemicals)	R228 000
Direct labour (R50 per hour)	31 250
Manufacturing overhead	9 375
Costs incurred in May:	
Direct material (chemicals)	1 142 000
Direct material (cans)	35 000
Direct labour (R50 per hour)	175 000
Manufacturing overhead	52 500

Production data for May	Litres
Work in process inventory, 1 May (25% completion)	4 000
Started in May	21 000
Sent to Shipping Department	20 000
Work in process inventory, 31 May (80% complete)	5 000

Required:

1 Prepare a schedule of equivalent units for each cost element for the month of May using:
   (a) the weighted average method
   (b) the first in, first out (FIFO) method
2 Calculate the cost (to the nearest cent) per equivalent unit for each cost element for the month of May using:
   (a) the weighted average method
   (b) the first in, first out (FIFO) method

3 Discuss the advantages and disadvantages of the weighted average method versus the first in, first out method.

(CMA, adapted)

C5.55 Weighted average process costing: manufacturer

Leather Products Ltd manufactures high-quality branded leather goods. The company's profits have declined during the past nine months. In an attempt to isolate the causes of poor profit performance, management is investigating the manufacturing operations of each of its products.

One of the company's main products is fine leather belts. The belts are produced in a single, continuous process in the Port Elizabeth plant. During the process, leather strips are sewn, punched and dyed. The belts then enter a final finishing stage to conclude the process. Labour and overhead are applied continually during the manufacturing process. All materials are introduced at the beginning of the process. The firm uses the weighted average method to calculate its unit costs.

The leather belts produced at the Port Elizabeth plant are sold wholesale for R229.50 each. Management want to compare the current manufacturing costs per unit with the market prices for leather belts. Top management has asked the Port Elizabeth plant accountant to submit data on the cost of manufacturing the leather belts for the month of October. These cost data will be used to determine whether modifications in the production process should be initiated or whether an increase in the selling price of the belts is justified. The cost per belt used for planning and control is R115.00.

The work-in-process inventory consisted of 500 partially completed units on 1 October. The belts were 30 per cent complete as to conversion. The costs included in the inventory on 1 October were as follows:

Leather strips	R16 500
Buckles	3 500
Conversion costs	25 000
Total	45 000

During October, 8000 leather strips were placed into production. A total of 8100 leather belts were completed. The work in process inventory on 31 October consisted of 400 belts that were 40 per cent complete as to conversion.

The costs charged to production during October were as follows:

Leather strips	R410 000
Buckles	80 000
Conversion costs	553 200
Total	1 043 200

Required:

1 In order to provide cost data on the manufacture of leather belts in the Port Elizabeth plant to the top management of Leather Products Ltd, calculate the following amounts for the month of October:
   (a) the equivalent units for material and conversion
   (b) the cost per equivalent unit for material and conversion
   (c) the assignment of production costs to the 31 October work in process inventory and to goods transferred out
   (d) the weighted average unit cost of the leather belts completed and transferred to finished goods

2 Comment on the cost per belt of R115.00 which the company has used for planning and control.

(CMA, adapted)

C5.56 Sequential production departments; FIFO method; JIT (appendix): manufacturer
Home and Garden Products Ltd manufactures a plant nutrient known as Garden Pride. The manufacturing process begins in the Grading Department when raw materials are started in process. Upon completion of processing in the Grading Department, the output is transferred to the Saturating Department for the final phase of production. Here, the product is saturated with water and then dried again. There is no weight gain in the process, and the water is virtually cost-free.

Home and Garden Products has recently adopted a JIT production approach, and work in process inventories have been reduced substantially. The following information about work in process inventories is available for the month of November:

	1 November		30 November quantity (kg)
	Quantity (kg)	**Cost**	
Grading Department	–	–	–
Saturating Department	1 600	R17 600*	2 000

* Includes R3750 in Saturating Department conversion costs.

The work-in-process inventory in the Saturating Department is estimated to be 50 per cent complete both at the beginning and end of November. Costs of production for November are as follows:

	Materials used	Conversion
Grading Department	R265 680	R86 400
Saturating Department	–	85 920

The material produced in the Grading Department weighed 36 000 kilograms. The firm uses the FIFO method of process costing.

Required:
Prepare production reports for both the Grading and Saturating Departments for the month of November. Show supporting calculations. The answer should include the following:

1 Equivalent units of production (in kilograms).
2 Total manufacturing costs.
3 Cost per equivalent unit (kilograms).
4 Cost of ending work in process inventory.
5 Cost of goods completed and transferred out.

(CMA, adapted)

C5.57 Sequential production departments; weighted average method; JIT (appendix): manufacturer
Refer to the data given in Case 5.56. Complete the same requirements, assuming that Home and Garden Products Ltd uses weighted average process costing. In calculating unit costs, round your answer to four decimal places. (Hint: How does the firm's movement towards JIT simplify your work for the Grading Department?)

Endnotes

1 As explained in Chapter 4, in fact there are three clearly defined production processes at the Spritz factory: the mixing process, the carbonation and bottling process, and the labelling and packing process. However, to keep this example simple, we have combined the last two processes into a single Finishing Department.

2 The assumption that direct labour and manufacturing overhead costs are incurred uniformly throughout the production process is quite common. It simplifies the process costing task, as it enables labour and manufacturing overhead costs to be combined. The modifications required where direct labour and manufacturing overhead costs are incurred at different stages of the production process are discussed later in the chapter.

3 This standard is described in the appendix to Chapter 4.

4 In our example, the units in ending work in process inventory, which are 50 per cent complete, have also passed the quality inspection point, which occurred 25 per cent of the way through the production process. Strictly speaking, therefore, the cost of normal spoilage in this example should be prorated between the units completed and transferred out and the units in ending work in process inventory, as all units have been inspected and the spoilage relates to both completed and partially completed units. However, most businesses attribute the cost of normal spoilage to good units completed and transferred out rather than prorate the cost, except when the cost of ending work in process is relatively large.

5 For example, in a survey of Australia's 2000 largest manufacturers (Joye and Blayney, 1990), the majority of respondents identified their costing systems as job costing or process costing. Operation costing was not mentioned in their report, even though many of these manufacturers are likely to be using some form of operation costing rather than pure process costing. In South Africa, which is a developing country, we would expect that labour-intensive industries would dominate the economic landscape. However, South Africa also has many highly capital-intensive industries which will generally use some form of process costing. A survey by Hoque, Z., Uliana, E. and Waweru, N.M. (2005) depicts the management accounting practices of South African companies.

Service Costing

LEARNING OBJECTIVES

After completing this chapter, you should be able to:

1 describe the features of service organisations and explain how they differ from manufacturers;

2 apply cost classifications, such as fixed and variable costs, direct and indirect costs and controllable and uncontrollable costs, to analyse costs in service organisations;

3 describe the value chain of service organisations, explaining the relevance of various upstream, downstream and production functions;

4 describe the value chain of retailers and wholesalers;

5 use the service firm continuum to describe the production environments of various types of service entities, ranging from professional service firms to service shops and mass service businesses;

6 identify whether job, process or hybrid costing is most appropriate for the various types of service entities;

7 estimate service costs in a job costing environment;

8 explain the concepts of billable hours, charge out rates and realisation, and their use in estimating service costs, prices and profits;

9 estimate service costs in a process costing environment;

10 demonstrate how to estimate service costs in a hybrid costing environment;

11 assess when a service entity should implement service costing by considering the costs and benefits of information about service costs;

12 describe how overhead is accounted for in service costing; and

13 estimate the costs of the goods (and services) provided by retailers and wholesalers.

Introduction

In Chapter 4 we explained that product costs can be a vital source of information for managers in their quest to enhance shareholder value and manage resources, especially in the increasingly competitive contemporary business environment. And in Chapters 4 and 5 we described various approaches to estimating the costs of goods produced by manufacturers. Yet, in South Africa, as in most advanced economies, the service sector is larger than manufacturing and the effects of globalisation, deregulation and rapid technological advances challenge service organisations as well as manufacturers. In this environment, information about service costs can be just as important to managers as information about product costs. For example, in estimating the charge for its management consulting services, PricewaterhouseCoopers needs to know the cost of providing consulting advice. In deciding whether to add a rubbish-recycling service, managers at the City of Durban need an estimate of the cost of the proposed service and the revenues from recycled materials. A manager at the University of Johannesburg can make a better decision about whether to introduce a new course if the cost of providing similar courses at other universities is known.

As discussed in Chapter 1, costing systems have evolved in a manufacturing environment. Some management accounting textbooks argue that the costing systems used in manufacturing can also be used in service organisations. However, there are important differences between manufacturing and service organisations that must be recognised in determining the relevance of cost information and the approach to costing services.

What are service organisations?

L.O. 1

The distinguishing features of **service organisations** are that they deliver help, utility or care; provide an experience, information or other intellectual content; and the majority of the value is intangible rather than residing in any physical products.

In South Africa and overseas, service organisations dominate the economy. It has been stated by the Governor of the Reserve Bank that the services sector in the 1960s contributed around 52 per cent to Gross Domestic Product and this had grown to about 64 per cent in 2007. Service organisations are common in the private sector. The next time you walk to your local shopping centre, see how many service businesses you can spot. You will find lawyers, accountants, doctors, banks, hairdressers, hotels, gyms, cafés and car-repair workshops. The financial services sector, which includes banks and insurance companies, is a significant provider of services such as bank and cheque account services, financing, life insurance policies and auto insurance. There are firms providing logistical services such as distribution and transport. There are firms providing security services to companies as well as individuals. In addition, the public sector consists of a vast array of organisations that provide services at the national, provincial and local government levels. For example, the South African Revenue Service provides services to taxpayers across the nation; the department of education provides a range of teaching and administrative services; and local governments provide services that range from building approvals to libraries and care programs for the elderly. There is also a range of not-for-profit organisations that provide services, like the Red Cross Society, the Salvation Army and World Vision. The service sector in South Africa covers a vast array of business activity spread across many different industries, including electricity, water and gas; construction; wholesale trade; retail trade; accommodation, cafés and restaurants; transport and storage; communication services; finance and insurance; property and business services; government administration and defence; education; health and community services; cultural and recreational services; and personal and other services.

Differences between service and manufacturing businesses

There are four major differences between manufacturing and most service businesses (Fitzgerald et al., 1991):

- *Most service outputs are intangible.* Manufacturers produce goods but service outputs tend to be performances rather than physical objects. For example, consider a travel company that offers a range of tours to Europe. When you book and travel on a particular tour you will receive brochures, airline tickets and accommodation vouchers. But this is not the product. The product is the 'experience' of the tour.
- *Service outputs are often heterogeneous.* Many manufacturers produce a limited range of repetitive products. Even where a manufacturer produces a diverse product range, these products tend to involve common features or processes. Service outputs are often heterogeneous. Even the same services provided within a business may differ, depending on the person who serves you! (The tour company may tailor a variety of individual tours to suit each of its clients. Very few will be the same: different airlines, different itineraries, and different lengths of time.)
- *Often, services are consumed as they are produced.* Manufacturers produce goods which are stored, as inventory, until they are sold, whereas services are often consumed as they are produced. (As you experience your tour, you 'consume' the tour as it is provided, although memories are an important part of the experience.)
- *Services are perishable and cannot be stored.* While goods produced by manufacturers can be stored as inventory, services are perishable. (The travel company does not store an 'inventory' of unused tours.)

However, some services do entail some physical, or tangible, aspects. For example, when you purchase accommodation from a hotel, the 'package' includes a room, with a minibar stocked with beverages, and meals available through room service; but the primary value of hotel accommodation rests in the service, from the friendliness at reception to the efficiency of the porter, the comfort of the bed, the cleanliness of the room, and so on. And, as discussed later in this chapter, the costs of some services are stored in the accounting system as 'work-in-process inventory' – for example, when a lawyer works on a case over a number of months the costs may be accumulated until the case is resolved.

Where do merchandisers fit?

Merchandising businesses, such as retailers and wholesalers, purchase goods to sell to customers without any further conversion processes. **Retailers** sell goods directly to the public. **Wholesalers** sell goods to other businesses for use in their production processes or for resale to the public. In addition to purchasing goods to sell to customers, merchandisers also provide a range of services to support the sales transaction, although the extent of this service component varies from one business to the next. In some businesses, the goods provided are the primary source of customer value, while in others, intangible aspects of the transaction, such as the service provided by the sales staff and after sales support, are also important. For example, in purchasing a pair of board shorts, you are likely to receive considerably more service from the sales staff at a small boutique than at Makro. Customer service is a key source of competitive advantage for the boutique, whereas Makro competes more on price.

Retail and wholesale businesses are included in the service sector, but they do not fit comfortably within the definition and distinguishing features described above. They provide tangible goods that can be stored. Also, depending on their competitive strategy, the physical product may be the primary source of value. As you work your way through this chapter, you will notice that we often need to qualify comments we make about service organisations when we consider retailers and wholesalers. As Tito Mboweni, the governor of the South African Reserve Bank, stated, 'We still have to feed ourselves from agricultural activities . . . food does not come from Pick 'n Pay but from agriculture! Sometimes people forget this' (South Africa: Land of hope and opportunity: Remarks by Mr T.T. Mboweni, Governor of the South African Reserve Bank, at an ANC breakfast meeting, Johannesburg, 22 June 2005).

Services are produced outside the service sector too

Service production is not confined to service organisations. In the modern business environment, characterised by increasing customer expectations, the value chain for most businesses includes a customer services segment. This includes firms that manufacture products. The significance of customer service will depend on the business's competitive strategy. For example, Toshiba may differentiate itself in the market for home computers by offering a very high level of after-sales service. Moreover, the other upstream and downstream segments of the value chain also produce services. Information about the costs of the services produced across the value chain can be useful to managers. For example, the cost of its distribution services is a critical input to a manufacturer's decision about whether to outsource this function. The approaches to service costing described in this chapter are relevant to services produced across all sectors of the economy, not just within service organisations.

Challenges to service organisations in the contemporary business environment

The dramatic changes to the contemporary business environment described in Chapter 1 have had profound implications, both for service organisations and for service activities within organisations. Many service businesses compete on the basis of their intellectual property, and advances in information and communication technologies have changed the way knowledge is managed. For example, the taxation services offered by accounting firms have broadened significantly since the introduction of Value Added Tax and Capital Gains Tax. Also, in marketing, sophisticated approaches to customer relationship management (CRM) have led to a much more systematic and focused approach to servicing customers in many businesses. Advances in e-commerce have had a huge impact on the management of both suppliers and customers, with the development of business-to-business (B2B) and business-to-consumer (B2C) transactions supported by electronic data interchange (EDI). (We consider these changes in more detail in Chapter 16.) In addition, many organisations have outsourced services because of the demands of keeping pace with technology or to reduce costs. This has led to the emergence of new services entities, sometimes located in other countries. Examples include the outsourcing of IT services to specialist IT firms, and customer inquiry services to call centres. Modern information and communications technologies have enabled countries with relatively low labour costs, such as India, to become significant providers of these services. (Outsourcing is discussed in Chapter 19.)

Cost classifications in service organisations

L.O. 2

Exhibit 6.1 lists some cost classifications that are relevant to service organisations. Cost traceability is discussed in Chapter 2 and cost behaviour in Chapter 3. You may wish to revisit that material now. For more information about cost classifications based on controllability, please turn to Chapter 12. (You may remember that Chapter 2 also described various cost classifications relevant to inventory valuation and to timing of expenses. These classifications are not relevant to most services entities, as they do not produce inventory and all expenses are charged against profit as they are incurred.)

The value chain in service firms

L.O. 3 Management accountants can use the value chain to help to assign costs to products, and to provide other information to help managers to manage resources and create value. The **value chain** is a set of linked processes or activities that begins with acquiring resources and ends with providing (and supporting) goods and services that customers value. In Chapter 2 we described cost classifications for the upstream, downstream and production areas of a manufacturing business, but what does the value chain for a service firm look like?

Basis of classification	Cost classifications	Used to:
Behaviour	Variable Fixed Committed Discretionary	Plan (budget) costs Control costs Make decisions
Traceability	Direct/indirect	Cost services Cost organisational units, such as departments or activities
Controllability	Controllable/uncontrollable	Measure performance Control costs

Exhibit 6.1 Costs classifications for service entities

Upstream activities and costs

Exhibit 6.2 illustrates the value chain for a 'typical' service organisation. It is difficult to generalise about the relevance of upstream activities in a service firm, because of the enormous variety of service entities. Large-scale service providers, such as banks, insurance companies and airlines, undertake **research and development activities** to identify potential new services or service production processes. However, smaller service firms are less likely to be involved in such activities. The existence of **design activities**, which involve the design of new services and service production processes, also depends on the nature of the service. In some organisations, such as medical and legal practices, the service production process involves considerable discretion rather than conforming to a specific design. However, in others, such as bus and rail companies, there is more scope for design. (You will notice that the supply segment, included in the value chain for a manufacturer, does not exist in a service firm. This is because supply activities normally relate to the management and receipt of incoming parts, assemblies and supplies, which are not significant in most service entities, where labour is the main input.)

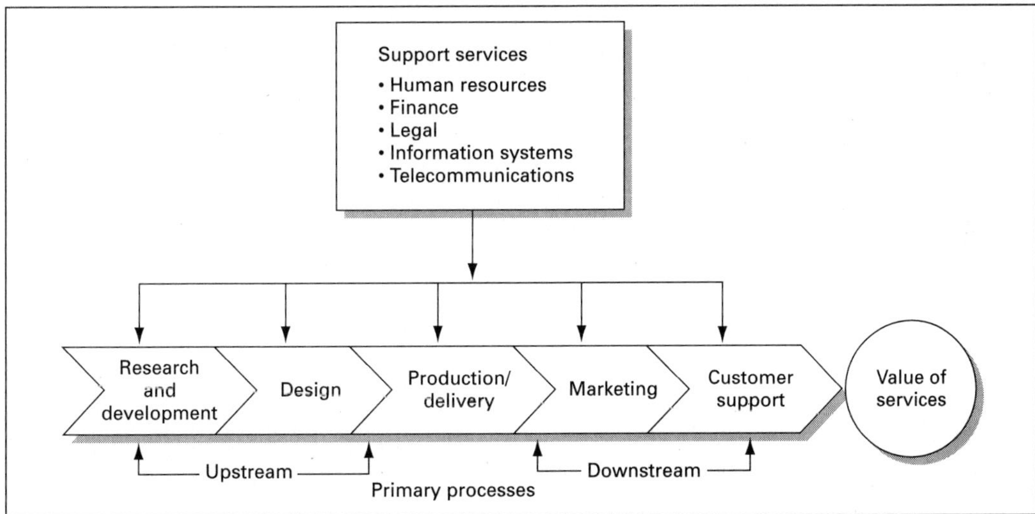

Exhibit 6.2 The value chain in a service firm

Downstream activities and costs

The downstream area of the value chain for most service organisations is likely to involve **marketing activities**, which focus on selling the services produced; advertising and promotion; and **customer support activities**, which occur after the production/delivery processes and include customer inquiry lines and ongoing information for customers about the service that they have purchased.[1] If you have studied Chapter 2, you will notice some differences between the downstream activities of manufacturing and service organisations. The distribution segment in the manufacturer's value chain is not relevant, as most services are 'delivered' to customers as they are produced. And it is more useful to identify customer support activities for service organisations rather than the customer services segment identified for manufacturers as, in a service organisation, customer service is also delivered throughout the production delivery processes.

Production and delivery activities and costs

The value chain framework in Exhibit 6.2 identifies the **production and delivery** segment, which covers the activities undertaken to produce and deliver the services. Because in most service organisations services are consumed as they are produced, production and delivery occur simultaneously. Producing a service is effectively the same as delivering a service.

In many businesses, production activities account for a major part of their total costs. Let's compare the cost of producing a service with the cost of producing a tangible product.

In manufacturing firms, under a conventional product costing system, production costs are generally classified as direct material, direct labour and manufacturing overhead. Direct material and direct labour costs can be traced directly to the product, whereas manufacturing overhead is an indirect cost. The cost classifications used in manufacturing companies may be useful in estimating service costs. Consider the cost of transportation services in an airline company such as Comair (operator of British Airways and Kulula.com in South Africa). Direct material would include jet fuel, and food and beverages. Direct labour would include the salaries of the flight crew. And overhead costs would include depreciation of the aircraft and of baggage-handling equipment, plus insurance and airport landing fees.

However, the differences between manufacturing businesses and service entities may mean that some modification to these cost classifications is required. For example:

- In many service firms, direct labour costs dominate, and all other costs are classified as indirect or overhead costs. The direct material classification is often not used, as material costs are relatively insignificant and might more easily be included in overhead as 'indirect material'.
- Costs in upstream or downstream areas may also be included as overhead costs, as costing of services is not influenced by accounting standards. This issue is explored in more detail later in this chapter.

The cost classifications used in service costing, the approach to estimating service costs, and, indeed, the relevance of service cost information vary with the type of services produced and the service production environment. These issues are explored in the material that follows.

The 'Real life' example below shows how the classification and analysis of costs can help managers in service industries.

The value chain for retailers and wholesalers

L.O. 4 As we explained earlier, merchandising firms, such as retailers and wholesalers, differ from most other service entities because of their focus on providing tangible products to their customers.

Upstream activities and costs

Exhibit 6.3 illustrates the value chain for a 'typical' large merchandising organisation. As with other service organisations, it is difficult to generalise because of the wide range of retail and wholesale businesses. The research and development and design activities found in some other service entities are unlikely to be relevant in merchandisers. Instead, the value chain commences with the **purchasing activities**, which involve the acquisition and management of goods purchased for resale. (You may have noticed the similarity between this segment and the supply segment included in the value chain for a manufacturer.)

REAL LIFE: SERVICE COSTS AT A PRIVATE HOSPITAL

A public hospital may be funded for the cost of expected inputs, such as salaries, based on past expenditure on inputs. A private hospital, however, needs to price its services according to the output (services) it produces. To manage its business effectively, a hospital needs to measure its output.

A hospital is required to identify a number of different cost objects. 'The treated patient' is the final 'product', but each treated patient may receive a range of different services, such as a laboratory test, an X-ray, an operation and a number of drugs. The costing system identifies the cost of each of these services and traces them to the patient. Costs need also to be aggregated for the hospital's responsibility centres, such as divisions and clinical units. This provides the managers of these centres and their superiors with important information for effective resource management.

There are challenges about how output statistics are measured and the reliability of the cost data. For example, the funding for the neonatal babies is an issue as these babies may stay in hospital for months, and may require one-to-one nursing care. As most private hospitals are required to set prices and recover costs, service costing is of vital importance in the private health sector.

The Netcare Group is listed on the JSE and operates the largest private hospital group in South Africa with 68 hospitals, over 9000 beds and 358 operating theatres. The group also operates in the UK. In total, the group manages 120 private hospitals and clinics, which are equipped with over 11 700 beds. In 2006 the group's revenue amounted to almost R12 billion and the group made a profit of almost R1.6 billion. In the hospital sector an important indicator of output is patient days, and in 2006 the group recorded over 1.6 million patient days for its South African operations. The average length of stay was 3.23 days.

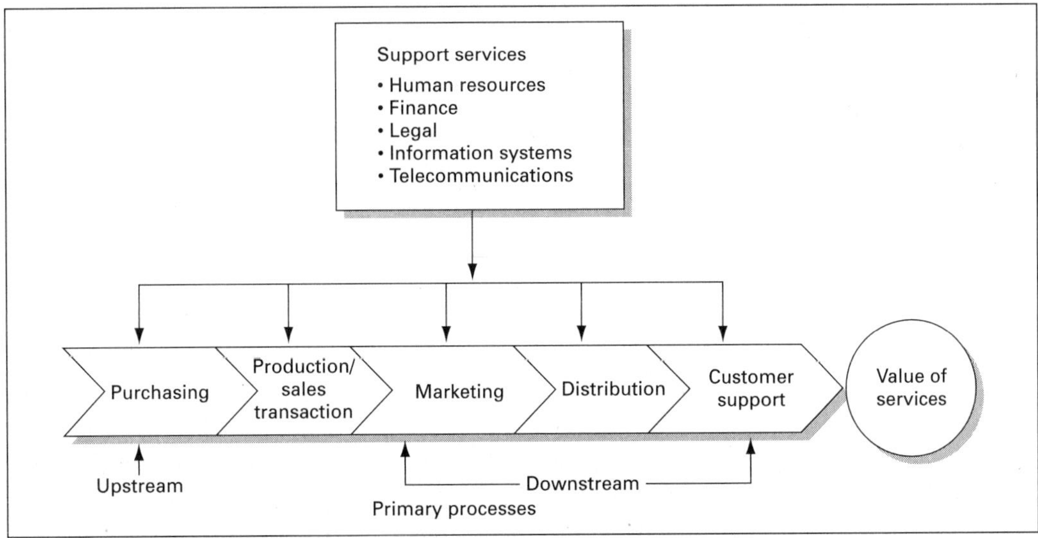

Exhibit 6.3 The value chain in a merchandising firm

Production activities and costs

In a merchandising business, production activities primarily involve the sales transaction, where the sales staff sells goods to customers. As discussed earlier, depending on the competitive strategy of the business, there may also be a substantial element of customer service involved in this transaction. Also, in a retail business, distribution usually occurs as part of this transaction, as customers receive their goods at the point of sale.

Downstream activities and costs

As in many other service organisations, marketing activities are an important function for many retailers and wholesalers. Some retail businesses, such as supermarkets and department stores, offer a distribution (home delivery) service. Likewise, the value chain of wholesale businesses will include a distribution segment, and customer support activities can play an important part in merchandise businesses in providing after-sales support to customers.

Estimating service costs

In Chapter 4 we discovered that costing systems must be tailored to fit an organisation's production environment. How can we identify service costing principles and practices, given such a vast array of service entities?

Service production environments

L.O. 5 Although the range of service organisations that operate in our economy is vast, it is possible to distinguish three different types: professional services, service shops and mass services, depending on the production environment (Fitzgerald et al., 1991). Exhibit 6.4 summarises the key differences among these three types of service entities.

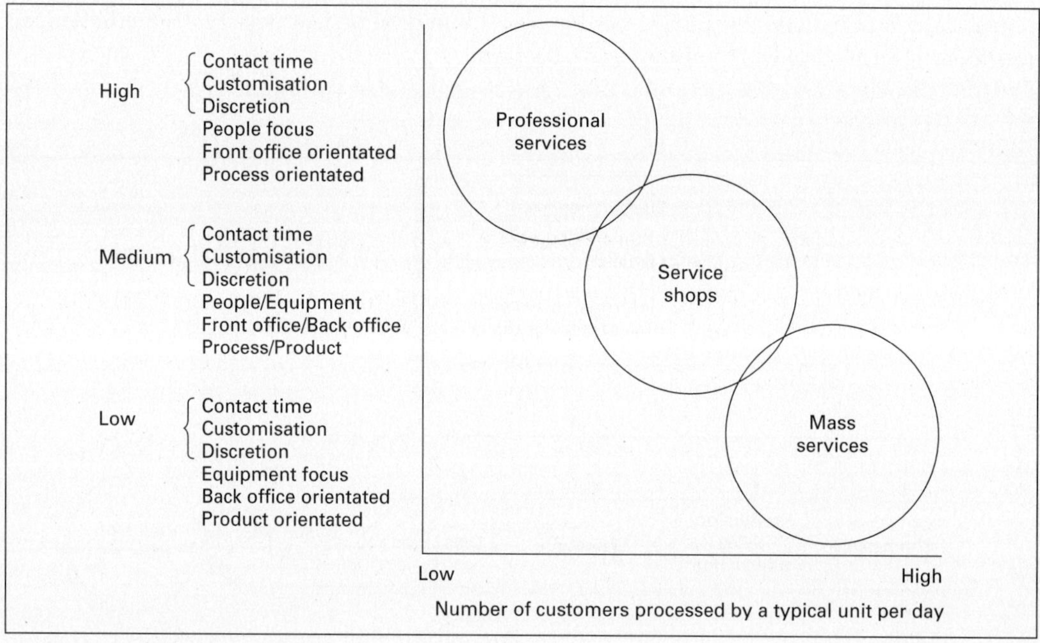

Exhibit 6.4 Types of service entities

Professional services

Professional services firms are staffed by professional staff who provide individual services to customers. These firms tend to serve relatively few customers, despite often having large numbers of staff. This is because staff spend a lot of time producing and delivering the service to the customer – 'serving' each customer – and often adapting the service to meet individual needs. The **front office** part of the production process, where staff interact directly with customers, is more important than the **back office**, where the customer is not present. The service production process primarily involves people rather than equipment and, because emphasis is often placed on how the service is delivered rather than what is delivered (the 'product'), staff are given a lot of discretion over how they deal with customers.

Examples of professional service firms include medical, legal, accounting, management consulting and architectural businesses, and customers tend to be referred to using value terms, such as 'patients' or 'clients'. While many professional service firms may be quite small, consisting of several professional partners and a supporting staff, they can also be large. Consider, for example, the multinational accounting firms, such as Deloitte and PricewaterhouseCoopers, with hundreds of partners, thousands of staff, and substantial operations across South Africa.

Mass services

In contrast to professional services, **mass services entities** serve many customers, with each one requiring limited staff time and little customisation. Staff are mainly non-professional. The service process often involves equipment, and the focus is on *what* is delivered rather than how. Most of the value is created in back-office functions, while front-office staff, who deal directly with the customer, have limited scope to change the service that is provided. Mass service entities often provide facilities rather than customised services. Consider, for example, providers of passenger transport such as bus and rail entities. Equipment, such as trains or buses, ticket vending machines and ticket scanners, is an essential part of the service. Passengers decide their destination from the set range of services that are offered. Ticketing staff may advise them on possible routes and fares but cannot customise services by providing passengers with a special train or bus destination to meet their requirements. Staff may include engineers, accountants and legal advisers, but also a large contingent of semi-skilled and unskilled employees such as drivers, ticket inspectors and security guards, as well as a range of administrative and clerical employees. Other examples of mass service entities include airline companies, post offices, electricity suppliers, telecommunications companies, and various public service organisations such as the motor registration departments that issue drivers' licences and vehicle registration certificates.

Service shops

Service shops process more customers than professional firms but fewer than mass service entities. Staff have less customer contact than professional firms but more than mass service providers. Likewise, they fit between professional and mass service entities in terms of the degree of customisation, staff discretion and the involvement of front-office and back-office functions and equipment. Examples of service shops include hotel chains, banks, cafés and restaurants, and car repair workshops.

A continuum of service firm types

Given the vast array of service organisations, not every entity will fit neatly into one of the three categories described above. You will find that there is some overlap among the various service types, as some service entities will exhibit a mixture of mass and shop features, or a mixture of shop and professional features. Indeed, it is more useful to consider this classification as a continuum, with the vast array of service firms displaying varying combinations of the features of professional firms, service shops and mass service entities.

You may be wondering where retailers and wholesalers fit in this continuum. Depending on their scale of operations and emphasis on customer service, they may exhibit features of mass service entities or service shops. For example, in large supermarkets very large numbers of customers are served; and there is a lack of customisation, high reliance on repetitive processes, and the extensive use of equipment for storing and managing inventory and for selling goods. In contrast, small fashion boutiques serve far fewer customers and make relatively little use of equipment, and their sales staff have substantial contact with each individual customer, with considerable room for discretion in the sales process.

A continuum of costing systems for service entities

L.O. 6 In Chapter 4 we discovered that the features of product costing systems also fit along a continuum, depending on the types of products produced and the production environment. At one extreme, each product (or batch of products) is different from the next and **job costing** is used to estimate product costs, by assigning costs to each job. At the other extreme, companies produce a single product (or a small range of very similar products) in large quantities and use **process costing** to estimate product costs by estimating the average cost per unit processed. In practice, many businesses produce products with some unique features and some common processes and require a **hybrid costing system** with a combination of job and process costing features.

Exhibit 6.5 assesses the relevance of these costing systems to the production environments of our continuum of service entities.

Job costing systems for professional service firms

Few professionals would consider their firm environment as being similar to a manufacturer operating in a job environment! There are obvious differences, ranging from the appearance of the workplace to the qualifications of the workforce, as well as many aspects of the production process. Unlike the manufacturer, most professional service firms use little material and equipment, and produce no inventories. However, as shown in Exhibit 6.5, there is common ground from a costing perspective.

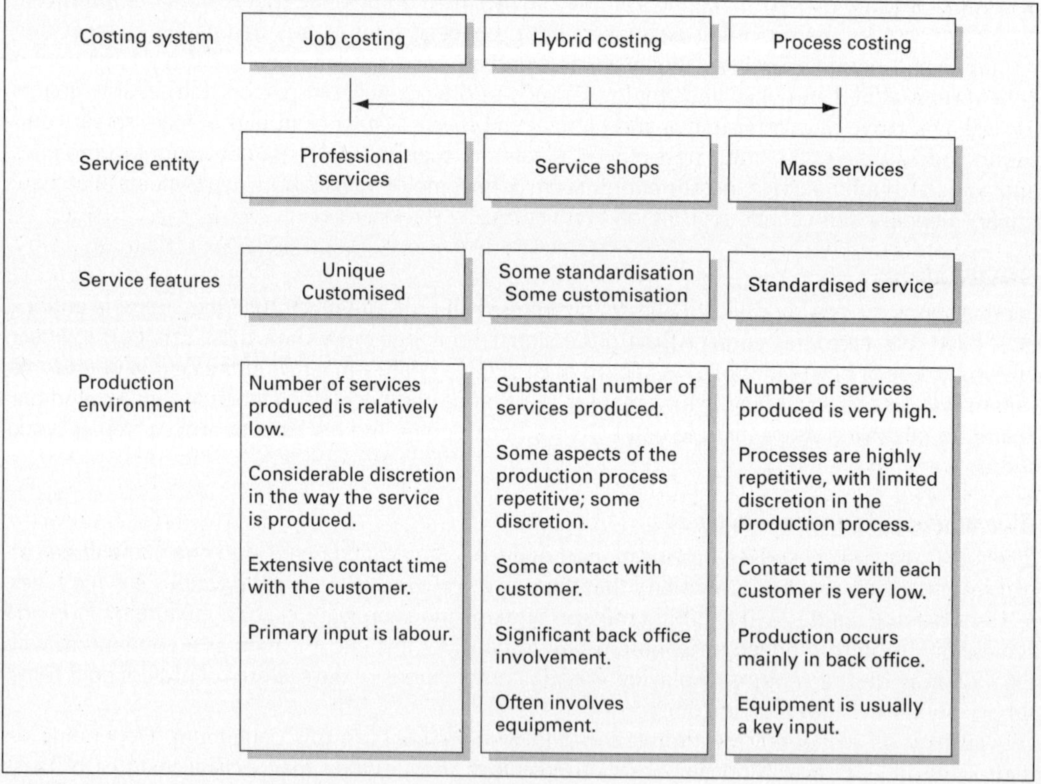

Exhibit 6.5 Job, process and hybrid costing in service entities

Professional service firms deal with relatively few clients, which means that a detailed system such as job costing is feasible. The production process for each client is unique, which means that reliable estimates of the service costs can only be obtained by assigning the costs of resources to each individual service (or job). The primary input is labour. Much of the labour involves direct contact with the client and its cost can be traced directly to individual services in an economically feasible manner. Although these firms often have significant IT costs, indirect costs tend to be relatively insignificant when compared to direct labour costs. The next time you receive an account from your lawyer or accountant, remember that the price may have been based on an estimate of the cost of the services provided, in turn derived from some form of job costing – although, as described later in this chapter, many professional service firms use a variation of this approach based on *job billing* rather than job costing.

Process costing systems for (some) mass services

At the other extreme of the costing continuum, process costing systems can be used to estimate the cost of services produced by some mass service entities. As shown in Exhibit 6.5, in a 'pure' mass service environment, services are produced in very large quantities, which mean that tracking costs to each service is not feasible. Moreover, production processes are repetitive, with little or no customisation or room for discretion, which indicates that one service consumes much the same resources as the next, with no need to track costs to each service. Contact with customers is low, with much of the production occurring in back-office functions. Although labour costs remain substantial, the low level of contact with customers implies that a substantial part of the labour costs is indirect. The service outputs often involve the provision of facilities, where equipment is a major input, adding substantially to the level of indirect costs. Although indirect to services, often these costs can be tracked directly to production processes. In this environment of totally standardised service production, the cost of the services can be estimated economically and reliably by averaging the production process costs over the number of services produced – that is, by using a process costing system.

Process costing for mass services: a word of warning

Process costing assumes that each unit of output involves the same production processes, consuming the same resources. This may be approximately true in a manufacturing environment – for example, where one bottle of soft drink is the same as the next. However, it is less likely in a mass service environment where, despite *some* standardisation, each service 'experience' depends on the requirements of the customer. How often have we queued to check in our luggage at the airport, to find the queue at the next check-in counter moves twice as fast? Why? Because someone's bag is overweight, or someone needs to check the details of their connecting flight, or someone wants to sit next to a friend, and so on! The point is that, although there are many mass service entities, very few of them are likely to obtain reliable estimates of the costs of individual types of services using process costing. The greater the scope for discretion in the service provision, the less accurate will be the service cost based on process costing.

The Independent Electoral Commission's cost per voter, determined in the 'Real life' below, is an example of where average costs are estimated under process costing. Other examples are the cost per passenger transported by bus companies and the cost per customer processed by bank tellers. Information about the cost of these services is important for making decisions to create value and manage costs, but how reliable are the estimates of these costs? Wherever there are variations in the production processes, service costs based on process costing should be interpreted with caution.

Hybrid costing systems for service shops and (other) mass services

Service shops fit between professional and mass service entities but cover such a wide range of production environments that it is difficult to generalise about their costing systems. The level of direct labour costs is lower than in professional firms, and indirect costs are higher. However, some firms, such as computer maintenance businesses and car repair workshops, are suited to job costing. Each service is unique, although possibly involving some standardised processes; and direct labour (and often direct material) costs are substantial and easily traceable to specific jobs.

As we move to the right along the service type continuum occupied by service shops, we find that a larger number of services are produced and production processes become more standardised. For example, in hotels the preparation of rooms is relatively repetitive, although there may also

REAL LIFE: COSTS AT THE INDEPENDENT ELECTORAL COMMISSION (IEC)

In 2004 South Africa celebrated 10 years of democracy and held a national election which was convincingly won by the African National Congress (ANC). In 2006 South Africa held local government elections, again won by the ANC. The Independent Electoral Commission is responsible for managing national, provincial and municipal elections and it is tasked with ensuring that elections are free and fair.

The number of registered voters for the 2006 municipal elections amounted to just over 21 million. The IEC was allocated over R944 million in 2006 in order to manage its operations and finance the electoral process. Staff remuneration for permanent and temporary personnel, travelling, communication expenses, printing, IT, advertising and professional services are significant cost categories for the IEC. The total expenditure of the IEC in 2006 amounted to R923.25 million. This amounts to about R44 per registered voter.

How does this compare to other countries? Australia has 12.961 million registered voters and in 2004, the commission incurred costs of A$111 million. This works out to about A$8.56 per voter. If we use an exchange rate of R5.50 = A$1, the Rand cost would be R47 per voter. Of course, this was stated in 2004 as compared to 2006 for South Africa, but we can see that the cost of the IEC *per voter* is reasonably close to the cost of the Australian Electoral Commission per voter.

The Australian Electoral Commission (AEC) also estimates the cost per voter for each federal election, presumably to give some indication of the effectiveness of resource management at the AEC. In 2004 this cost was $5.79. Election costs include the costs of advertising, ballot papers, polling booth staff and equipment, certified lists of electors, postal voting, and computer and corporate administration resources. The costs per voter are likely to differ significantly from one electorate to the next, depending on the number of voters, the size and remoteness of the electorate, the number of polling booths and the number of postal votes.

Decisions on how to manage resources effectively at the IEC are more likely to have been based on a detailed analysis of individual cost classifications, than on broad averages of the cost per voter.

Source: Independent Electoral Commission of South Africa and the Australian Electoral Commission.

be considerable customisation of meals, room service and tour services. The large number of services would make job costing unwieldy. In addition, even if job costing could be used, the high level of indirect costs that needs to be allocated to individual types of services may undermine the accuracy of the service costs. On the other hand, the elements of customisation and discretion in the production process make process costing unreliable. Some sort of hybrid costing system is required, but the greater the variation within the service production processes, the more complex such a system would become.

Further still along the continuum of service types we enter the realm of mass service organisations. As discussed above, these types of organisations may also produce services that involve some variation in production processes because of room for discretion by employees to meet customers' requirements. Where the variability is substantial, these organisations also require some form of hybrid costing systems to ensure accurate service costs.

Costing for retailers and wholesalers

Although it is possible to classify retailers and wholesalers within the service type continuum described above, their costing systems differ because of the need to assess the costs of merchandise purchased for resale. Costing for merchandisers is considered separately, later in the chapter.

Activity-based costing for services

Although service entities tend to be characterised by high labour costs, many of which can be traced directly to services, all service businesses incur some indirect (or overhead) costs. Overhead costs cannot be traced easily to services; instead, they are allocated using cost drivers. As we explain in Chapter 7, it can be difficult to find suitable cost drivers because of the vast array of overhead costs. Overhead costs are likely to increase, relative to direct costs, as we move along the service type continuum, from professional service firms towards mass service entities (although it may be possible to trace some of these costs to processes and then to services). The greater the proportion of overhead costs, the greater is the potential for inaccuracy in estimating service costs.

Activity-based costing, which is described in more detail in Chapter 8, can be used to provide more accurate estimates of the overhead costs of products and services. Under an activity-based approach, broad classifications such as direct labour and overhead may be replaced by more detailed analysis within an activity framework. In fact, service firms are an ideal environment for the implementation of activity-based costing. If management wants accurate costs of services, a more sophisticated understanding of activities and their cost drivers is required due to the high proportion of indirect costs. Although the case study in Chapter 8 has a manufacturing focus, the concepts and principles described also apply in service organisations. Certainly a wide range of service organisations in South Africa have adopted activity-based costing; and in Chapter 8 you will find numerous examples of service entities that have used activity-based costing to estimate the cost of their services, including universities, hospitals, banks and various local government bodies.

Costing services at a bank

We will focus on a bank to explore the various types of service costing systems. A bank such as ABSA provides retail financial products and services through its own distribution outlets and branch network. In terms of number of customers, the balance between front and back office functions, and the degree of customisation of many of its products, a bank is primarily a service shop. For example, a bank offers a range of loan 'products', generally with standard terms, such as interest rates and underlying security requirements, but staff have some discretion over the establishment fees and repayment periods. Although it is a service shop, a bank also offers professional services, such as investment advice delivered by highly qualified investment advisers and tailored to the needs of individual clients after extensive consultation. At the other end of the spectrum, some of a bank's services, such as its ATM (Automatic Teller Machine) services, are mass services involving standardised procedures with no customisation or room for discretion in the service production process. Thus, a bank is an ideal entity for us to explore the range of costing systems, as it could adopt a job costing approach for professional services such as investment advice, a process costing approach to cost mass services such as ATM services, and a hybrid costing system for its 'shop' services such as loan products.

We will now use a case study of a bank and, although we will use financial data which does not apply to any specific South African bank, the information offers a realistic depiction of the operations and costs that would be incurred in the real world.

Job costing for investment advice

The Investment Advisory Department operates from XYZ Bank's head office.[2] The department's staff consists of: L.O. 7

- the department manager;
- a team of investment advisers who work directly with clients, and who specialise in one of four market segments: corporate, personal, retirement planning and retiree;
- a research team that monitors the financial services market, develops new investment products and trains the investment advisers; and
- a secretarial pool, providing reception, word processing and filing support.

The department accesses other support services, such as Information Technology (IT), Human Resources (HR), Finance and Marketing, from a range of corporate services provided by the Head Office.

Let's look at an example of how the Bank provides investment advice to a customer. After 25 years of loyal service, John Donovan accepted an early-retirement package from his employer, a multinational manufacturer located in Cape Town's northern suburbs. He received a substantial retirement package and approached the Bank for investment advice. Donovan was assigned to Stephanie Thwala, the investment adviser for retirees, who met with Donovan to appraise his circumstances. After this initial meeting Thwala arranged for Donovan and herself to meet with Graham Van Wyk, the Bank's retirement planning adviser, to determine how best to manage the large investment in the retirement fund that Donovan had accumulated during his working life. She then developed three possible investment strategies. One focused on equity investments in the South African and international share markets, another was built around a series of fixed-interest investments, and a third was based on a mixture of residential and commercial property investments throughout South Africa. Thwala met with Donovan several times to finalise his investment strategy, which he decided to base on equity investments. Donovan then became a client of the Bank's equity investment service, which worked with him to implement this strategy.

Exhibit 6.6 sets out the Investment Advisory Department's costs for the year. You will notice that providing investment advice consumes two types of resources:

- **professional labour costs**, which are the salaries of the investment advisers who provide the advice directly to Donovan; and
- indirect or **overhead costs**, which are the costs of supporting the investment advisers that cannot be traced directly to individual services.

Costs	Actual	Budgeted	Classification
Wages and salaries:*			
Investment advisers	R4 100 000	R4 000 000	Professional labour
Other employees	525 000	490 000	Overhead
Phone, fax and data	91 000	90 000	Overhead
Electricity	12 500	12 500	Overhead
Stationery and supplies	22 500	22 500	Overhead
Rent†	139 000	125 000	Overhead
Corporate resources‡	275 000	260 000	Overhead
Total	R5 165 000	R5 000 000	

* Includes labour on-costs.

† Allocated per square metre.

‡ Includes a charge for IT, HR, Finance, Legal and Marketing support, allocated based on the number of employees.

Exhibit 6.6 Investment Advisory Department costs

But how can we use this information to estimate the cost of the investment advice provided to John Donovan?

The cost of professional labour

The Bank's investment advisers are required to maintain a database that records the amount of time they spend on each client's case, both in face-to-face meetings and in follow-up activity. Although professional labour is usually paid an annual salary, hourly rates (also shown on the cost sheet) can be estimated for investment advisers by dividing the annual salary plus labour on-costs by the number of **billable hours** available to service clients each year.

The calculation of Thwala's hourly rate of R450 per billable hour is shown in Exhibit 6.7.

Annual salary, Thwala		390 000.00	
Labour on-costs (payroll tax, employer's pension contribution and workers' compensation insurance)		109 500.00	
Total annual salary cost	a		R499 500.00
Billable hours:			
Total annual hours (52 weeks × 37.5 hours)		1 950	
Less annual leave and public holidays and allowance for sick leave (8 weeks × 37.5 hours)		−300	
Less non-billable time (time not available for client work, including time spent on professional development, department meetings and idle time)		−540	
Total billable hours	b		1 110
Hourly labour cost (total annual salary cost divided by billable hours)	a/b		**R450.00**

Exhibit 6.7 Estimating hourly labour costs for professional labour

The amount of time that each adviser spent on the client's case and their hourly rate can be entered into a client cost sheet, as shown in Exhibit 6.8.

The overhead costs

The overhead costs incurred by the Investment Advisory Department include the salaries and wages of the department manager, research team and secretarial pool, as well as the cost of telecommunications, electricity, supplies, rent and corporate resources. (The Bank could trace the costs of stationery and supplies and selected phone calls and faxes directly to individual clients, but this is not worthwhile as it would involve a lot of work and the tracing of such insignificant costs would make little difference to the overall accuracy of the costs of each service.)

In Chapter 4 you learned how manufacturing businesses can use a predetermined rate to allocate (or apply) manufacturing overhead costs to products. Service entities may use a similar approach, by estimating a single overhead rate for their entire business, or a separate overhead for each production department. Given that investment advisory services are produced completely within the Investment Advisory Department, service costs will be more accurate using a departmental overhead rate rather than a business-wide rate.[3] Exhibit 6.8 shows that the cost of investment advice provided to Donovan includes overhead costs of R2535. This overhead cost has been calculated using the following three steps:

1 *Identifying the overhead cost driver* – that is, a factor or activity that causes overhead costs to be incurred. Conventional costing systems assume that overhead costs are caused by the volume of production. Common overhead cost drivers include measures of production output, such as the number of services produced, or measures of production input, such as the number of professional labour hours worked. The Bank assumes that the indirect resources are consumed in the Investment Advisory Department largely because of expenditure on professional labour. This seems a reasonable assumption, as the more hours an investment adviser works (and therefore the higher the expenditure on professional labour), the greater will be the need for word processing, filing, phone calls, faxes and so on. Conventional costing systems also assume that overhead costs vary in

Client number	234	Client manager	Stephanie Thwala			
Client name	John Donovan	Service provided	Retiree investment advice			
Date started	4 February	Date completed	31 March			
		PROFESSIONAL LABOUR				
Date	**Database reference**	**Description**	**Person**	**Hours**	**Rate**	**Cost**
4 Feb	02–21	Initial meeting with Donovan	Thwala	2.50	450.00	1 125.00
14 Feb	02–29	Retirement advice meeting with Donovan	Van Wyk Thwala	1.20 1.20	500.00 450.00	600.00 540.00
17–21 Feb	02–35	Development of investment strategies for Donovan	Thwala	13.00	450.00	5 850.00
28 Feb	02–47	Presentation of investment strategies to Donovan	Thwala	2.00	450.00	900.00
14 Mar	02–58	Review of strategies with Donovan	Thwala	1.50	450.00	675.00
31 Mar	02–77	Finalisation of investment strategy with Donovan	Thwala	1.00	450.00	450.00
				22.40		R10 140.00
		Total per person	Thwala	21.20	450.00	9 540.00
		Total per person	Van Wyk	1.20	500.00	600.00
Total cost of professional labour				22.40		R10 140.00

		OVERHEAD		
Date	**Cost Driver**	**Quantity**	**Rate**	**Cost**
04–28 Feb	Professional labour cost	9 015.00 R0.25 per R1	0.25	2 253.75
01–31 Mar	Professional labour cost	1 125.00 R0.25 per R1	0.25	281.25
		10 140 00		R2 535.00

	COST SUMMARY	
	Cost category	**Cost**
	Total Professional labour cost	10 140.00
	Total overhead cost	2 535.00
	Total cost	R12 675.99

Exhibit 6.8 Client cost sheet: investment advice

direct proportion with the level of cost driver. For example, if expenditure on professional labour doubles, then consumption of indirect resources will also double. This assumption may be more difficult to satisfy, and where it is not met service costs will be unreliable.

2 *Calculating a* **predetermined** *(or* **budgeted***)* **overhead rate** *per unit of cost driver*. This is equal to the budgeted overhead divided by the budgeted level of cost driver, for the coming year. Exhibit 6.6 shows that the budgeted overhead for the Investment Advisory Department for the year is the sum of all costs other than professional labour, which amounts to R1 000 000, and it is expected that R4 000 000 will be spent on professional labour. Thus the budgeted overhead rate will be 25 cents per Rand spent on professional labour (R1m of overhead costs ÷ R4m expenditure of professional labour).

3 *Applying overhead costs to services* at the budgeted (or predetermined) overhead rate multiplied by the quantity of cost driver consumed by the service. Exhibit 6.8 shows that the investment advice to Donovan consumed professional labour costing R10 140. Thus overhead of R2 535 (R0.25 × R10 140) is included in the cost of the service.

The *principal difference* between the overhead rates of service organisations and manufacturers is the range of costs included. In most manufacturing businesses the overhead rate includes only manufacturing overhead. This is because the International Accounting Standard, IAS 2 *Inventories*, in most situations specifies that product costs used for external reporting purposes should include manufacturing costs only. In most service businesses there are no inventories, as services are consumed as they are produced. Individual service costs are not disclosed separately in external reports, but may be used within a firm to support managers to create value and manage resources. In service costing, therefore, the overhead rate usually includes the cost of all upstream and downstream resources that support the service production. For example, in the Investment Advisory Department, the Bank classifies all costs other than professional labour as overhead. No distinction is made between indirect production costs and other indirect costs, such as IT, administration and marketing costs.

As in manufacturing businesses, using a predetermined overhead rate will result in underapplied overhead when the actual overhead costs exceed the overhead costs applied to services, and overapplied overhead when the overhead costs applied to services exceed the actual overhead costs incurred. Methods for accounting for overhead are discussed later in this chapter.

Why estimate the cost of investment advisory services?

The Bank could benefit from understanding the cost of its investment advisory services in the following ways:

- *As a basis for setting fees.* For example, the Bank may decide to charge fees for its investment advice based on the estimated cost of providing the advice plus a profit margin. However, as discussed below, many professional service firms use a billing system rather than a costing system for charging clients.
- *To assess the profitability of each service.* For example, the Bank may compare the costs and revenues associated with its various services, to consider strategies for increasing profitability and shareholder value.
- *To determine which services to promote, refine or withdraw.* For example, having determined the profitability of its various services, the Bank may be able to identify the appropriate mix of services to offer in order to maximise profits, given the available resources.
- *To control costs.* For example, the Bank may compare the cost of individual advisers providing advice, in order to assess the relative performance of each investment adviser. (Note, however, that the customisation of each service may make this difficult.)

Some professional service firms focus on billing rather than costing

L.O. 8

Many professional service firms, especially accounting, legal, engineering and management consulting firms, develop billing systems that accumulate client charges for services rather than using costing systems. A **billing system** estimates the fees to be charged to the client for the service, based on **chargeout rates per billable hour** for the various categories of labour that have been consumed in providing the service. Ideally, a chargeout rate is set to cover the cost of labour and overheads, *and* a profit margin. In practice, however, many firms do not estimate their chargeout rates using this cost-based approach. Instead, they use market-based rates – tending, for example, to match competitors' rates or use rates recommended by their professional association.

Exhibits 6.9 and 6.10 illustrate a cost-based approach to estimating fees chargeable for the investment advice provided to retiree John Donovan at the Bank. Exhibit 6.9 shows that the chargeout rate per billable hour for a retiree adviser such as Stephanie Thwala is R731.25. This rate is based on:

1 an hourly labour cost of R450 (which you will notice coincides with Thwala's hourly rate estimated in Exhibit 6.7);

2 overhead costs for the Investment Advisory Department, also calculated previously, and estimated to be 25 cents per Rand of professional labour costs; and

3 the Bank's required profit margin (which in this case is assumed to be 30 per cent of costs).

Total annual salary cost (including on-costs), retiree adviser	a	499 500.00		
Estimated annual billable hours for retiree adviser	b	1 110		
Salary cost per billable hour, retiree adviser	a/b			450.00
Estimated overhead cost (25 cents per R1 professional labour costs)			0.25	112.50
Total estimated labour and overhead cost per billable hour				562.50
Required proft margin (30% of cost)			0.30	168.75
Chargeout rate per billable hour, retiree adviser				731.25

Exhibit 6.9 Estimating hourly chargeout rate for a retiree adviser

Exhibit 6.10 shows that the charges for the service provided to John Donovan total R16 477.50, based on hours of advice received (as shown in Exhibit 6.8). You will notice that the chargeout rate for Van Wyk, who is a retirement planning adviser, is higher than for Thwala. A billing system may also include a charge for other traceable costs, such as phone, fax and postage, which may or may not be marked up by the firm's required profit margin. (You may recognise similarities between this approach and the time and material pricing described in Chapter 20.) However, these costs are not included for Donovan, as they are not significant in the Investment Advisory Service.

Client number	234	Client manager	Stephanie Thwala			
Client name	John Donovan	Service provided	Retiree investment advice			
Date started	4 February	Date completed	31 March			
		Billable work				
Date	**Database reference**	**Description**	**Person**	**Hours**	**Rate**	**Cost**
4 Feb	02–21	Initial meeting with Donovan	Thwala	2.50	731.25	1828.13
14 Feb	02–29	Retirement advice meeting with Donovan	Van Wyk	1.20	812.50	975.00
			Thwala	1.20	731.25	877.50
17–21 Feb	02–35	Development of investment strategies for Donovan	Thwala	13.00	731.25	9506.25
28 Feb	02–47	Presentation of investment strategies to Donovan	Thwala	2.00	731.25	1462.50
14 Mar	02–58	Review of strategies with Donovan	Thwala	1.50	731.25	1096.88
31 Mar	02–77	Finalisation of investment strategy with Donovan	Thwala	1.00	731.25	731.25
				22.40		R16 477.50
		Total per person	Thwala	21.20	731.25	15 502.50
		Total per person	Van Wyk	1.20	812.50	975.00
Total billable charges (covering professional labour and overhead costs and profit margin)				22.40		R16 477.50
		Breakdown of client charges				
		Cost category				**Cost**
		Total Professional labour cost				10 140.00
		Total overhead				2535.00
		Total cost				12 675.00
		Required profit margin				3802.50
		Total billable charges				R16 477.50

Exhibit 6.10 Client billing sheet: investment advice

The lower part of Exhibit 6.10 illustrates that the charges for Donovan are made up of estimated costs of labour and overhead amounting to R12 675 and the required profit margin of R3 802.50.

This information is not normally included in a billing system but is shown to help you understand the composition of the client charges.

If the Bank were to charge clients for investment advice, it might choose to use a billing system rather than a costing system, to provide an ongoing estimate of charges for each client. A billing system also enables a professional services firm to monitor current earnings on partially completed jobs by accumulating the billable charges for all clients.

In most professional service firms, a senior manager will review proposed client charges, based on chargeout rates, in the light of current market conditions and adjust the final fee if necessary. A **realisation rate** can be estimated, which is equal to the final fee charged to the client as a percentage of the billing system fee based on the firm's chargeout rates. For example, if the senior manager of the investment advisory services reduced the charges to Donovan to R15 000, rather than the R16 477.50 estimated by the billing system, the realisation rate for this service would be 91 per cent (that is, R15000/R16477.50 × 100). This provides a measure of profitability, as a realisation rate below 100 per cent indicates that the firm has been unable to earn its required profit margin. In this example, the Bank has earned a profit of R2325 (that is, R15000 − R12675), which is R1477.50 below the required profit margin of R3802.50. Realisation rates can also be used to monitor the profitability of the entire business, by comparing the total fees invoiced to clients per accounting period with the amount based on chargeout rates and accumulated in the billing system. The extent of the write down of billable fees indicates the extent to which the firm has failed to achieve its required profit margin.

How do accounting firms determine charge-out fees? What are the principles underlying the hourly rate charged by accountants to clients? An accounting firm will set a charge-out hourly rate which covers overheads (rent, communications, and secretarial salaries), salaries of employee accountants and includes an adjustment for profit.

Another important component relates to the level of experience and expertise required for each task. A partner should not do what could be done by a junior employee accountant on a lower charge-out rate. The billing rate is linked to the level of expertise and experience required for each task. Another factor relates to efficiency. The number of hours taken should be the minimum required to adequately undertake the task. The accounting firm will try and ensure that all hours worked by its employee accountants are billable hours.

Clients are aware when firms try to maximise billable hours which are not required in terms of the work undertaken for the client. Increasingly accounting firms are being obliged to tender for the work of large companies and this may require accounting firms to reduce billable hours and/or billing rates indirectly in order to win the audit or consulting services contracts from such companies. It may be important that firms are billed during the term of any contract so that clients are aware of how fees are built up over the course of any assignment. There are time recording and billing computer programs that enable firms to offer a high level of detail regarding the fees charged for each assignment.

The 'Real life' below reflects the billing system used by the Auditor General of South Africa when using the services of accounting firms.

REAL LIFE: THE BILLING SYSTEM USED BY CHARTERED ACCOUNTANTS FOR AUDITS DONE ON BEHALF OF THE AUDITOR-GENERAL

The Auditor-General is the auditor of government. This involves auditing the financial statements and financial management of national government as well as provincial, local government and selected public entities. Terence Nombembe, the current Auditor-General, states that, 'public sector audits go beyond merely expressing an opinion on the financial statements. When we audit the public sector, we also comment on the effectiveness of key management processes and give feedback on compliance with laws and regulations. This qualitative approach enables public sector managers better to understand the financial impact of the identified prob-

lems and assists in helping them to prioritise the corrective actions. This is how we add value and help improve public sector financial management and our contribution to service delivery.'

Although the Auditor-General employs about 300 staff members and undertakes the majority of the audit assignments relating to government entities, his department does also make use of the services of private accounting firms. Charge-out rates are agreed with the South African Institute of Chartered Accountants (SAICA). These charge-out rates are based on the remuneration levels of employees of the private accounting firms. The South African Institute of Chartered Accountants publishes a guideline on fees for audits done on behalf of the Auditor-General. The following are extracts from the guideline published in November 2006.

- Rates are calculated by dividing the monthly earnings by recoverable hours and multiplying by a factor of 2.75 (2005: 2.70) to accommodate overhead costs. The recoverable hours have been revised owing to the impact of the training requirements.
- Fees should be based on the time spent on audits. Time records should be kept for individual staff or grades of staff and should indicate the actual time spent on the audit.
- Members are reminded that invoices to the Auditor-General must be accompanied by a schedule setting out the monthly earnings category for each employee, the associated rate and number of hours charged in respect of that invoice.
- Members are exhorted to review their audit approaches to ensure that up to date techniques are used so as to reduce to a minimum the time spent on audits.

The rate for partners is R1321 per hour while the maximum rate for specialists is R1387 per hour. For employees, the charge-out rates are based on monthly remuneration levels, For example, employees earning a monthly remuneration of R17 000 would be charged out at a rate of R417 per hour, while an employee earning R30 000 per month, would be charged out at a rate of R786 per hour. For the year ending March 2008, these rates have been increased by 4 per cent.

It is interesting to determine the available hours in a year. We need to adjust for weekends, public holidays, annual leave and sick leave. This may result in 1760 available hours for the year calculated as follows:

Days in year		365
Weekends		−104
Public holidays		−11
Annual leave		−22
Sick leave		−8
Available days		220
Hours per day	×	8
Available hours		1760

In an accounting firm, employees will be required to undertake training as well as administrative and internal management tasks which will mean that the billable or recoverable number of hours will be less than 1760 hours per year. Let's go back to the Auditor-General rate of R786 per hour for an employee earning R360 000 per year (R30 000 per month). If we divide this hourly rate by the factor of 2.75, we get to a rate of R285.82 per hour which relates to the cost of an employee accountant earning R360 000 per year. To get to this hourly cost rate we need to divide R360 000 by about 1260 hours. This means that only 1260 hours are recoverable out of a total available number of 1760 hours.

Process costing for ATM services

L.O. 9

John Donovan not only uses XYZ Bank for investment advice, he has both his home loan and a savings account with the Bank. Although Donovan occasionally uses the Bank's teller services to access his savings account, he normally uses the ATM facility at his local bank branch. As a mass service, the Bank can use process costing to estimate the cost of ATM transactions, which involve the following processes:

- the provision of ATM service facilities that accept deposits and issue cash, involving costs for site leases, hardware maintenance, electricity, data transmission to and from the front-end processor, servicing to ensure adequate stocks of cash (which is performed by an external contractor), and consumables such as receipt and journal rolls;
- initial transaction processing by the front-end processor, which involves costs for hardware and software maintenance, data transmission to and from the Bank's mainframe system (or to other financial institutions) and the salaries of development, technical and support staff; and
- back-end processing of the transactions by the Bank's mainframe system, which involves costs for hardware and software maintenance and the salaries of development, technical and support staff.

The costs of these three processes for the year are listed in Exhibit 6.11. You will notice that there are few, if any, direct costs (that is, costs that can be traced directly to an ATM transaction) apart from the consumables used when the customer accesses the ATM. Although there are substantial labour costs for development, technical and support staff, these are not direct costs of ATM transactions, as this labour does not work directly on each ATM transaction. Instead it performs back-office support and development functions. It is also interesting to note that, as a capital-intensive service facility, equipment is a key input to each of the three processes and, therefore, equipment-related costs such as depreciation and insurance are significant.

Cost		ATM service	Front-end processing	Back-end processing*	Total costs
Site leases		1 225 000			
Hardware maintenance		2 100 000	1 925 000	1 470 000	
Software maintenance			1 225 000	980 000	
Equipment depreciation		1 470 000	507 500	840 000	
Equipment insurance		280 000	192 500	280 000	
Electricity		665 000			
Data transmission		343 000	280 000		
Servicing		2 555 000			
Consumables		717 500			
Salaries for development, technical and support staff			1 540 000	1 365 000	
Corporate costs†		262 500	322 000	402 500	
Total costs	a	9 618 000	5 992 000	5 337 500	20 947 500
Number of transactions processed	b	13 540 723	13 540 723	13 540 723	13 540 723
Cost per transaction	a/b	R0.71030	R0.44252	R0.39418	R1.54700

* Mainframe costs are allocated between ATM and non-ATM transactions, based on the number of transactions processed.

† Includes a charge for IT, HR, Finance, Legal and Marketing support, allocated based on the number of employees.

Exhibit 6.11 Costs of ATM processes

During the year, the Bank processed 13 540 723 ATM transactions. In Chapters 4 and 5 we explained that the approach to process costing depends on whether or not the business holds work in process inventories. Most service entities do not produce inventories, as services are consumed as they are produced. This is certainly true for ATM transactions. Therefore, there are no complications, such as the degree of completion, to consider. The cost per ATM transaction (R1.547) can be estimated simply by adding up the costs of the three processes (R20 947 500) and dividing this sum by the number of transactions produced (13 540 723). Of course, XYZ Bank could use a more detailed approach to its process costing by estimating the cost per transaction for each process, as shown in the last four lines of Exhibit 6.11.[4] If collected over time, this information would enable the Bank to assess the efficiency of each of the three processes.

Why estimate the cost of ATM services?

It is common for banks to charge a fee per ATM transaction, or for all transactional activity above a certain monthly limit. If the Bank used this approach, knowing the cost per transaction would enable it to set fees to cover costs, or at least to assess the profit or loss associated with each transaction. In addition, if the Bank is approached by other entities to provide ATM services on their behalf, the cost per transaction will be a vital input in the pricing of those services. Furthermore, the cost per ATM transaction, particularly if it is broken down into processes, provides information for control, as managers will be able to monitor changes over time and benchmark against other ATM service providers.

Note that the cost per unit calculated above must be used with caution. While some of the costs included in Exhibit 6.11, such as electricity, data transmission and consumables, would be incurred for each transaction, others, such as site leases, software maintenance, staff salaries and corporate costs, would not behave on a per unit basis. The cost of R1.547 per transaction is valid only for the particular volume of activities or output used to determine the unit cost. If the volume of transactions were to increase (or decrease) beyond 13 540 723, total costs would not increase (or decrease) at the rate of R1.547 per transaction. For many decisions about its ATM services, such as whether to outsource, the Bank should be careful to focus on the total costs of ATM services rather than the cost per transaction.

Hybrid costing for other bank services

L.O. 10 There are very few examples of 'pure' mass services at the Bank. While there are a number of services that involve standardised procedures – for example opening accounts, issuing credit cards, and processing deposits and withdrawals – there is some room for discretion in the service delivery. Using process costing to estimate the cost of these services will not provide a reliable estimate of the cost of each unit of service produced. The Bank also produces some services (for example various lending products) that involve customised features tailored to individual clients' needs combined with standardised processes. To estimate the costs of these services the Bank would need to develop a costing system that:

- assigns the costs of the customised elements directly to the service;
- averages the costs of the standardised processes across all of the services that use these production processes; and
- accumulates the costs of each service by adding together the specific costs of the customised features with the average costs of the standardised processes.

If you have studied Chapter 5 you will recognise the similarities between this approach and operation costing.

Given the wide range of services offered by the Bank, costing services using this approach is likely to become incredibly complex.

Which costs should be included in the Bank's service costs?

In Chapter 4 we explained that the accounting standards limit inventory costs to manufacturing costs, although managers often find it useful to adjust these product costs by including product-related upstream and downstream costs. As inventory valuation is not an issue in most service organisations, the management accountant is free to decide which costs to include. Service costs are estimated to support managers in their quest to manage resources and create value rather than to meet external reporting requirements. You will notice in the examples above that upstream costs, such as the salaries of the research team that designs and develops investment products, and downstream costs, such as the marketing costs included in the charge for corporate costs, are included in the overhead costs applied to investment products. Likewise, the costs of ATM transactions include upstream costs, such as the salaries of the development staff, and downstream costs, such as the data transmission costs involved in 'distributing' the services to ATMs, as well as the marketing costs embodied in the corporate costs.

Does the Bank need more than one costing system?

We have used examples from XYZ Bank to describe the different approaches to costing professional services, mass services and shop services. Does this mean that to cost its services the Bank needs to implement a costing system that uses job costing to estimate the cost of some services, process costing to estimate the cost of other services, and a hybrid approach for costing still others? Yes it does! If the Bank wished to estimate the cost of each of its services then it would need a very extensive costing system. However, unlike manufacturing businesses, which must value inventories for external reporting purposes, service entities are not required to estimate the cost of their output. After considering the costs and benefits of obtaining and using this information, the Bank may decide to cost some services but not others.

The range of services produced by many service entities, particularly smaller firms, is narrower than the Bank's, and it may be possible to have a single costing model such as job costing. However, every organisation should consider the associated costs and benefits before deciding whether to estimate service costs and, if so, which approach to take.

When should firms estimate their service costs?

L.O. 11

Manufacturing businesses are required to estimate product costs to value inventory and the cost of goods sold. In contrast, service entities estimate the costs of the services solely to help managers to create shareholder value and manage resources. As there is no external reporting requirement to estimate service costs, service entities should only estimate the costs of particular services when the benefits from this information exceed the costs of obtaining and using this information. Three factors influence the costs and benefits associated with service costing:

1 the complexity of the costing system;

2 the accuracy of the service cost information; and

3 the relevance of service cost information to managing resources and creating value.

The complexity of the costing system

The complexity of the costing system depends on the production environment and the nature of the service produced. Professional service firms tend to produce a relatively low volume of services, and direct costs – in particular, direct labour costs – usually predominate. In this environment, a simple job costing system can be used.

Mass service providers produce a large volume of services. With high levels of equipment-related costs and low levels of front office labour, many of their costs tend to be indirect to services but may be traceable to processes. The calculation of service costs is relatively simple, based on the average cost of the production processes.

It is difficult to generalise about approaches to costing for the wide range of service entities between professional service firms and mass service entities. As discussed earlier, these systems will vary from relatively simple and accurate job costing systems to more complex hybrid costing systems, depending on the production environment and the extent of overhead costs.

The accuracy of the service cost information

As we move from left to right along the service-type continuum in Exhibit 6.5, a service entity's costs tend to become more overhead intensive, reflecting the increased involvement of back office functions and of equipment and facilities in the production processes. Overhead costs cannot be traced directly to services; therefore, service cost information in service shops is likely to be less accurate than in professional firms, and the service cost information in mass service entities is likely to be less accurate than for service shops. When each service is identical or very similar to the next, such as with ATM transactions (see the 'Real life' below), and when the indirect costs can be traced to specific processes, process costing can provide reasonably accurate service costs. However, very few service entities produce identical services day after day.

The relevance of service costs to managing resources and creating value

Managers can use service costs to:

- assess service profitability;
- decide which services to produce;
- set service prices (fees); and
- plan and control costs.

Assessing service profitability and supporting service mix decisions

Knowledge of individual service costs enables firms to assess the profitability of their various services, so that they can focus on the services that earn the highest profit. This is true for firms across the service-type continuum. There are many firms, particularly smaller entities, that have gone out of business because they did not understand the costs and profitability of their various services.

Setting service prices

The relevance of service cost information for pricing depends on a firm's competitive environment. As is discussed in Chapter 20, in many industries price is determined by the market, although the cost per unit of a product usually sets a lower limit for prices. In other industries, firms base prices on costs plus a profit margin. It is common for professional services firms, including accountants, lawyers, management consultants and consulting engineers, to set their fees based on direct costs plus a margin to cover overhead and generate a profit. Where there are significant direct material costs, the costing system may identify labour and material costs separately, and may distinguish labour-related overhead costs from those associated with materials. This enables the firm to implement 'time and material pricing', where the service price includes separate charges for labour and material. Time and material pricing is described in Chapter 20.

Even when prices are set totally by market forces or by regulation, it may be useful to know the cost of providing those services. For example, in an accounting firm some services may be offered at a price below cost to encourage a new customer to use the firm's services, or as a strategy to build up a clientele or reputation in emerging areas of the business.

Planning and controlling costs

Information about service costs can be used to plan resource requirements and monitor efficiency. For example, it is common for businesses that produce major services, often called *projects*, to use information from the job costing system to monitor actual costs and compare them to project budgets.

REAL LIFE: ATM FEES

'That's where the money is,' Willie Sutton replied on why he robbed banks. It is true that banks are subject to significant levels of fraud and are required to spend millions on security. Yet some customers have been asking whether banks are not robbing clients by charging high fees. When in November 2006 the *Pretoria News*, headed an article with 'Daylight robbery at your local ATM', they were intimating that it was the banks that were guilty of robbery.

Banks are major service providers and an important service they provide relates to offering customers access to Automated Teller Machines (ATMs) so that clients can obtain balances, make transfers and cash withdrawals. Banks charge a fee each time a customer uses an ATM and this fee is increased by SASwitch fees and carriage fees if customers do not use their own bank's ATM. The high level of fees charged by banks has attracted public attention and the Competition Commission is currently investigating the level of fees and competition in the sector.

It is difficult to obtain estimates of what an ATM transaction costs a bank, but a survey in the USA a few years ago estimated that the average cost of an ATM transaction was $0.27 to a bank which equates to about R2.10 at the exchange rate at the time of writing. However, we cannot simply use an estimate from USA banks and apply this to South Africa and we would expect that the cost would probably be somewhat lower in this country.

It is interesting that Capitec Bank, a new retail bank registered in 2001, is charging significantly lower fees than the major banks. Capitec has indicated that an ATM withdrawal from a Capitec ATM in 2007 will cost R2.00 as compared to an average ATM fee of R6.00 for other banks. The average ATM fee for the other banks is indicated by Capitec at www.capitec.co.za. However, depending on the bank's product that a customer may have, then an average withdrawal, for example, at ABSA would cost R3.10. If a Capitec customer makes a withdrawal from another bank's ATM, then the charge is R6.50. The cost of a transfer at a Capitec account will cost R2.00 in 2007, while a transfer at an ABSA ATM will cost R3.10.

ATM fees are an issue for consumer groups in other countries such as the USA and Canada, as these fees are regarded as too high in relation to the cost of providing ATM services. Capitec in its submission to the Competition Commission in October 2006, states that:

After implementing a new system the volumes are normally low. The price has to be set at a level to attract clients to use our services. Prices are therefore not quantifiable by pure costing, but rather subjective based on the objective of the price. Only once a system has reached reasonable volumes and has a predictable behaviour can costing become more specific.

It is interesting that service costing often is based on the direct cost of such a service plus a factor to cover overheads and a profit margin. Is the profit margin too high on ATM fees? This goes to the heart of whether there is sufficient competition in South Africa's banking sector to ensure that banks charge low fees.

Where services are produced in much larger quantities and involve lower costs per service, and where there is room for variability in the service production processes, planning and control is probably better achieved by managing the costs of responsibility centres rather than service costs. (Responsibility accounting is discussed in Chapter 12.)

Strategic considerations

The relevance of service costs for pricing, assessing profitability, making service mix decisions and planning and controlling costs ultimately depends on an entity's strategies and competitive environment. For example, cost leaders are more likely to need information about their service costs. This is especially true where competition is tight and competitors have a good grasp of their own service costs. Also, as demonstrated in the medical practice 'Real life' below, some service firms have little say over prices or service mix. And others, particularly in the public sector and not-for-profit environment, may not charge for their services at all!

REAL LIFE: THE COSTS AND BENEFITS OF SERVICE COSTS AT SMALL MEDICAL PRACTICES

A small medical practice usually offers a wide range of services, primarily in the area of diagnosis and first-line treatment. A medical practice's accounting system may be used solely for billing patients and there is often no system for estimating the cost of services. The medical partners may not know what it costs to treat an ear infection or to remove a skin lesion. This does not necessarily mean that such practices are poorly managed. Medical practices may base service prices on guidelines set by the Medical Schemes or the ethical tariff (a maximum rate) set by the Health Professions Council of South Africa (HPCSA) for medical practitioners. This means that there may be no need for cost-based pricing.

There may be little point in assessing individual service profitability, since medical partners have no say over service mix. As general practitioners, they are not able to service only those patients requiring the removal of skin lesions or those patients with fractured bones! For planning and controlling costs, it makes more sense to focus on the number of patients and the number of consulting sessions as key cost drivers, rather than service costs. All services are consumed as produced, so there is no requirement to value inventory.

There may be little to be gained from costing services at small medical practices. Information about service costs can play an important role in the management of a business, but before developing a service costing system it is vital to weigh up both the costs and the benefits. However, the growth of managed healthcare and the employment of medical doctors at such practices may result in a focus on the time taken per patient and on the specialisation of medical doctors in order to maximise productivity. Companies such as Discovery that offer medical insurance to clients will be highly focused on managing service costs, as revenues are based on set fees. Therefore, companies like Discovery will monitor the costs of services rendered to members and will endeavour to reduce the incidence of medical claims by monitoring claims experience as well as offering incentives for members to lead healthy lives by promoting gym membership.

Firms are most likely to estimate their service costs when ...

Exhibit 6.12 summarises the factors that are likely to influence the decision to implement a service costing system. It shows that professional service firms operating in a competitive environment that allows cost-plus pricing are most likely to implement a service costing system. Service shops operating in a cost-plus pricing environment may also implement a service costing system, especially where they produce relatively few services and their indirect costs are relatively low. Service costing systems in a mass services environment will be simple but are likely to be inaccurate because of the high level of indirect costs and/or some degree of variability in production processes. Therefore, mass service entities are unlikely to implement service costing, except where it is essential to support their strategies and competitive environment. In these circumstances, it may be appropriate to implement an activity-based costing system to obtain more accurate estimates of the indirect costs of products. Service costing has little to offer all three types of service organisations for planning and control because the customisation of most services means that there is no clearly identifiable relationship between the service outputs produced and the inputs required to produce them.

	Professional services	Service shops	Mass services
Complexity of costing system	Low	High	Low
Accuracy of estimated service costs	High	Medium	Low*
Relevance for:			
Assessing service profitability/service mix	High	High	High
Pricing	Depends on competitive environment	Depends on competitive environment	Depends on competitive environment
Planning and controlling costs	Low	Low	Low

* Except in rare circumstances where the firm produces identical services for each customer.

Exhibit 6.12 Factors affecting the decision to implement service costing

Costing some services but not others

So far we have talked about firms implementing costing systems to cost all of their services. However, with no inventory and therefore no requirement to cost services, firms can choose to estimate the cost of just some of their services. For example, a bank may not have a comprehensive service costing system, but may choose to estimate the cost of its various lending products. This information would enable it to assess the profitability of each product and develop the most profitable product mix. Costing individual services also makes sense in the public sector where there is pressure to outsource some services.

In addition, information about service costs is required primarily to support management decisions. To be effective, much of this information needs to reflect future costs and may be required only infrequently. Rather than producing this information routinely, via a comprehensive costing system based on the general ledger accounts, managers' needs may be met more effectively with occasional service costing studies.

Service costing in practice

It is difficult to generalise about service costing systems because of the vast range of service entities, and there is little documented evidence of service costing practices. However, our own experience suggests that, apart from some professional service firms and service shops operating in a job environment, many South African service entities produce limited, if any, information about their service costs. Instead, their costing systems tend to focus on estimating the costs of responsibility centres, such as departments, for planning and control.

Exhibit 6.12 helps to explain why many South African service firms do not have service costing systems. Applying our theme of costs versus benefits, management must perceive that the benefits from a service costing system would be less than the costs. In addition, many service firms are small, with limited accounting resources, and may not have the knowledge or time to cost services.

Flow of costs in service firms

In Chapter 4 we described the flow of product costs through the accounting system, which enabled manufacturing businesses to estimate the cost of inventories to be included in the balance sheet and the cost of goods sold to be included in the income statement. In service firms there is no inventory to value, so the influence of external reporting requirements for accumulating inventory costs is not relevant. Where service costing systems do exist, they are created to meet management's needs rather than financial accounting requirements. Although these systems draw on the accounting system to estimate and report service costs, in most cases the service costs are not accumulated in the general ledger. There is no inventory to record in the balance sheet, and in most cases costs are shown as line item operating expenses, rather than accumulated in a separate cost of sales account, in the income statement. Exhibit 6.13 sets out an example of the income statement for XYZ Bank.

XYZ Bank Ltd Income Statement for the year ended 30 June 20X6	
Operating revenue:	
Interest revenue on loans to customers	R135 446 000
Other interest revenue	56 864 500
Other operating revenue	8 894 500
	201 205 000
Less operating expenses:	
Interest expense on deposits	69 748 000
Other interest expense	9 709 500
Doubtful debts expense	9 539 500
Employee wages and benefits	58 621 000
Building occupancy	6 903 500
General administrative	9 865 000
Other	811 000
	165 197 500
Operating profit	36 007 500
Other expenses (net)	633 000
Profit before income taxes	35 374 500
Income tax expense	10 602 500
Net profit	R24 772 000

Exhibit 6.13 Income Statement

Accounting for overhead costs

L.O. 12 In Chapter 4 we explained that overhead costs are normally allocated to products using a predetermined (budgeted) overhead rate. At the end of the accounting period it is necessary to adjust the cost of goods sold for the difference between the actual overhead costs incurred and the overhead costs that have been applied to products – that is, for underapplied or overapplied overhead. But what happens when budgeted overhead rates are used in service costing? As most service costing systems are not fully integrated into the accounting system, there will be no requirement to adjust the service costs for underapplied or overapplied overhead. However, it would still be necessary to monitor the accuracy of overhead costs applied to services, as service costs may be a key input to managers' decisions and consistent and significant under- or over-application of overhead would indicate under- or overstated service costs. (If the service costing system is integrated with the accounting system, then, at the end of the accounting period, the cost of sales must be adjusted for underapplied or overapplied overhead and you should review the material in Chapter 4 for a description of the necessary accounting entries.)

Can we have work in process in a service firm?

So far we have assumed that service organisations do not produce inventories, as services are consumed as they are produced. However, some service entities do need to account for work in process at the end of the accounting period to determine profits for external reporting purposes. For example, a legal firm may work on a case over several months or even years. Likewise projects in engineering, management consulting and accounting practices can extend over many months. (Indeed, a report from the billing system is actually a WIP, or work in process report.) Although this work in process is not inventory in a physical sense, where fees have not been charged for these services, the accounting standard, IAS 2 *Inventories*, requires their costs to be carried forward. According to IAS 2, costs of work in process should usually be confined to production costs. They may not include any upstream or downstream costs.[5]

Costing in retail and wholesale businesses

L.O. 13

Although retail and wholesale businesses are included in the service sector, they differ from other service entities as there are two distinct components to their output:

- the tangible goods that they sell to customers;[6] and
- the range of services that they provide to customers.

Costing the goods sold by retailers and wholesalers

Under international financial reporting standards, merchandisers are required to estimate the cost of inventories purchased for resale. This information is necessary to estimate the value of the asset, inventory, in the balance sheet and the cost of goods sold (or cost of sales) in the income statement, as shown in Exhibit 6.14.

According to IAS 2 *Inventories*, the cost of inventories purchased for resale should include:

- the purchase price of the merchandise;
- any import duties and other taxes related to the purchase price;
- costs of conversion (including fixed and variable manufacturing overheads);
- the cost of transportation into the business and handling; and
- any other costs directly attributable to acquiring the inventory; less
- any deductions for trade discounts, rebates and other similar items.

Smashes Electrical Stores Ltd Income Statement for the year ended 30 June 20X7		
Sales		R705 680 000
Cost of sales		380 110 000
Gross profit		R325 570 000
Less Other expenses:		
Operating, general selling and administrative expenses	R120 311 000	
Interest expense	5 270 000	
		125 581 000
Profit before income taxes		199 989 000
Income tax expense		59 990 000
Net profit		R139 999 000

Smashes Electrical Stores Ltd Partial Balance Sheet at 30 June 20X7	
Current assets:	
Cash	R5 640 000
Accounts receivable	24 195 000
Inventories	104 875 000
Prepaid expenses	2 515 000
Other	730 000
Total current assets	R137 955 000

Exhibit 6.14 Financial statements for a typical merchandising business

These costs are recorded in the general ledger account for inventory. However, at the end of the accounting period, for most organisations, the inventory must be valued in the balance sheet at the lower of cost and **net realisable value**. In IAS 2, net realisable value is defined as the estimated selling price less the estimated costs of completion and the estimated costs necessary to make the sale. For not-for-profit entities inventory is valued at the lower of cost and **current replacement cost**. Current replacement cost is the cost that the entity would incur to acquire the asset on the reporting date.

The cost of goods sold is also recorded in the general ledger. Some merchandising businesses use computerised inventory management systems to record the cost of inventory received and the cost of inventory sold. In other businesses the cost of goods sold is estimated as:

Cost of goods sold = cost of beginning inventory + purchases − cost of ending inventory

Exhibit 6.14 illustrates the financial statements for a typical merchandising business, Smashes Electrical Stores, a national chain of retailers of electrical and white goods.

Understanding the costs of goods, a management perspective

Although prepared primarily for external reporting purposes, information about the costs of goods enables retail and wholesale managers to assess the profitability of sales and, if disaggregated, provides useful information about the profitability of various product lines and responsibility centres. For example, Musica may estimate the cost and profitability of CDs versus DVDs. Or a company such as Woolworths may estimate the cost and profitability of departments that sell food, clothing, home wares, and so on. Similarly, if sufficiently disaggregated, information about the costs of individual products or product lines may be used for pricing. Your local service station may price oil at the cost it pays per four-litre container (including inwards freight) plus a margin to cover other costs and profits. When using cost information to manage resources and create value, rather than for external reporting, in some circumstances managers may require a more comprehensive estimate of the cost of goods, which includes any product-related costs from the upstream and downstream areas of the value chain.

Costing the services provided to customers

In addition to the goods that they sell, retailers and wholesalers provide a range of services to customers during the sales transaction and at other points of the value chain. As discussed above, the extent of these services will depend on a business's strategy. For external reporting purposes the accounting standards require these costs to be treated as period costs – that is, they are expensed in the current period. As shown in Exhibit 6.14, these costs tend to be aggregated into major categories that are often based on the chart of accounts used in the business' accounting system.

Regardless of the external reporting requirements, understanding the costs of these services can help retail and wholesale businesses to manage resources and create value more effectively. But how do we estimate their costs? It may be possible to estimate the costs of repetitive services, such as the cost of checkout services in a supermarket, using the process costing approach described earlier in this chapter. The costs of non-repetitive services can only be estimated reliably with a more detailed approach such as activity-based costing (which is described in Chapter 8). In Chapter 16 we describe how some businesses accumulate these costs by customer to identify the costs of serving individual customers or groups of customers. As the costs of these services are not required for external reporting purposes, they are usually estimated outside of the general ledger system.

Summary

In Chapters 4 and 5 we describe how to estimate the cost of goods produced by manufacturers. In this chapter we consider how and when to estimate the costs of services. The service sector is a vital part of the South African economy. Key points include:

- The distinguishing features of a service organisation are that it delivers help, utility or care; it provides an experience, information or other intellectual content; and the majority of the value is intangible rather than residing in any physical products.
- In contrast to manufacturing, most service outputs are intangible, heterogeneous, consumed as they are produced, and are perishable and cannot be stored.
- The common cost classifications introduced in Chapter 2, such as fixed and variable costs, direct and indirect costs and controllable and uncontrollable costs, can be used to analyse costs in service entities.
- The value chain in a service organisation is likely to differ from the more general model described in Chapter 2. The major activities for a typical large service organisation are likely to be research and development, design, production/delivery, marketing and customer support. The value chain for a typical large merchandiser includes purchasing, production/sales transaction, marketing and customer support activities. Some merchandisers, such as wholesalers and large supermarkets and department stores, also include distribution activities in their value chains.
- There is a vast array of service organisations, and these can be classified along a continuum, based on their production environment, with professional service firms at one extreme, mass services entities at the other and, in between, a wide range of service shops.
- In estimating service costs in professional service firms, the production environment is well suited to job costing, with the major costs being professional (direct) labour and overhead. Overhead may include a wide range of upstream and downstream costs, as well as indirect production costs.
- Rather than using a service costing system, many professional service firms operate a client billing system, which accumulates the amounts that the client is to be charged for the service rather than the costs of the service.
- Process costing can be used to estimate the costs of mass services, although this approach assumes that each service is identical. Any variation in service production processes will undermine the accuracy of this cost information.
- Between these two extremes it is difficult to generalise about a suitable costing system. Job costing will be suited to service shops operating in a job environment. And hybrid costing systems, with both job and process costing features, will be suited to service production processes that involve some jobbing aspects and some repetitive processes, although these systems are likely to be cumbersome.
- While manufacturers are required to estimate the cost of their products to meet external accounting requirements, service costs are produced solely to support managers in their quest to manage resources and create value. In general:
  - professional service firms operating in a competitive environment are most likely to implement a service costing system/client billing system;
  - service shops operating in a cost-plus pricing environment may also implement a service costing system, especially where they produce relatively few services and their indirect costs are relatively low; and
  - mass service entities are unlikely to implement service costing, except where it is essential to support their strategies and competitive environment. In these circumstances, it may be

appropriate to implement an activity-based costing system to obtain more accurate estimates of the indirect costs of services.

- The relevance of service costing for planning and control depends on the extent that there is a clearly identifiable relationship between inputs and outputs. Generally, customisation makes this relationship more difficult to identify, although project management systems can be useful in planning and controlling costs of major services.
- Where service costs are based on predetermined overhead rates, the amount of under- or overapplied overhead at the end of each accounting period should be monitored, as consistent and significant under- or overapplication of overhead would indicate under- or overstated service costs. However, because most service costing systems are not fully integrated into the accounting system, there will be no need to formally adjust for under- or overapplied overhead at the end of the accounting period.
- In retail and wholesale businesses there are two types of output to be costed: the goods sold and the services provided to customers. Accounting standards provide a reasonable basis for estimating the aggregate cost of the goods sold to customers, although this information may need to be disaggregated, or enhanced, to be useful to managers within the business. The costs of the services provided to customers can be estimated using a process costing approach, if they are repetitive. If not, a more detailed approach, such as activity-based costing, may be required.

Obtaining accurate estimates of the indirect (or overhead) cost of goods and services can be difficult. In Chapter 7 we explore this issue further and in Chapter 8 we describe activity-based costing, which can be used to improve the accuracy of the estimated costs of goods and services.

References

Fitzgerald, L, Jonston, R, Brignall, S, Silvestro, R & Voss, C 1991, *Performance Measurements in Service Businesses*, The Chartered Institute of Management Accountants, London.

Self study

Self-study problem 1: Job costing for services

Engineering Experts Pty Ltd offers a range of engineering services. The company's service costing system estimates the cost of each engineering job by accumulating costs of the professional labour that works on the job plus a charge for overhead.

The professional labour is charged to jobs using the following rates:

	Cost of labour	Chargeout rate for billing system
Engineer's assistant	R60.00 per hour	R250.00 per hour
Graduate engineer	300.00 per hour	1200.00 per hour
Senior engineer	700.00 per hour	2400.00 per hour

The predetermined overhead rate is based on professional labour costs, which are budgeted to be R1.6 million for the current year.

The estimated overhead costs for the current year are budgeted to be:

Management salaries	950 000
Salaries of clerical and reception staff	600 000
Depreciation on IT hardware and software	750 000
Stationery	70 000
Telecommunications	55 000
Insurance	314 250
Depreciation on office fixtures and fittings	37 500
Rent	307 500
Electricity	81 750
Council rates	34 000
Total	3 200 000

During the month of May the company provided three services, which consumed the following quantities of professional labour (in hours):

Client	Engineer's assistant	Graduate engineer	Senior engineer
Smith and Sons	25	100	15
Jones and Partners	10	120	20
The Business Centre	35	90	10

Required:

1 Calculate the predetermined overhead rate to be used at Engineering Experts.

2 Calculate the cost of the three services.

3 Assume that Engineering Experts uses a billing system with the chargeout rates shown above. Calculate the client fees for each of the three services.

Solution to Self-study problem 1

1

$$\text{Predetermined overhead rate} = \frac{\text{total budgeted overhead costs}}{\text{total budgeted quantity of cost driver}}$$

$$= \frac{3\,200\,000}{1\,600\,000}$$

$$= 200\%$$

[or R2.00 per professional labour Rand]

2 Costing system:

Client service	Engineer's assistant	Graduate engineer	Senior engineer	Total professional labour	Overhead	Total cost of each service
Smith and Sons	25 × R60 = R1 500	100 × R300 = R30 000	15 × R700 = R10 500	R42 000	R84 000	R126 000
Jones & Partners	10 × R60 = R600	120 × R300 = R36 000	20 × R700 = R14 000	R50 600	R101 200	R151 800
Business Centre	35 × R60 = R2 100	90 × R300 = R27 000	10 × R700 = R7 000	R36 100	R72 200	R108 300

3 Billing system:

Client service	Engineer's assistant	Graduate engineer	Senior engineer	Total client fee for each service
Smith and Sons	25 × R250 = R6 250	100 × R1200 = R120 000	15 × R2 400 = R36 000	R162 250
Jones & Partners	10 × R250 = R2 500	120 × R1200 = R144 000	20 × R2 400 = R48 000	R194 500
Business Centre	35 × R250 = R8 750	90 × R1200 = R108 000	10 × R2 400 = R24 000	R140 750

Self-study problem 2: Process costing for services

CThru Radiology Services is a major provider of radiological services in Bloemfontein, in the Free State. Despite the variety of patients seen at CThru, the radiological services involve the same three processes:

- The patient is booked in at reception and the referral from his or her doctor is processed.
- The X-rays of the patient are taken by the radiographer.
- The X-rays are developed, checked and then emailed to the radiologist for a clinical assessment. The originals of the X-ray are then posted to the patient.

The costs of these three processes for the year just ended are listed below.

Cost	Reception	X-ray taken	X-ray developed and despatched
Staff salaries	R240 000	R705 000	R180 000
Equipment depreciation	123 000	1 965 000	720 000
Equipment insurance	18 000	375 000	150 000
Telephone	27 000	0	0
Data processing and transmission	25 500	0	156 000
Postage	4 500	0	48 000
Developing and other consumables	12 000	105 000	186 000

During the year, CThru processed 15 000 radiology patients.

Required:

1 Calculate the cost per patient for each process.

2 Calculate the total cost per radiology patient.

3 We usually use job costing to estimate the cost of professional services. Why is it possible to use process costing in this case?

Solution to Self-study problem 2

1 and 2

Cost	Reception	X-ray taken	X-ray developed and despatched	Total
Staff salaries	R240 000	R705 000	R180 000	R1 125 000
Equipment depreciation	123 000	1 965 000	720 000	2 808 000
Equipment insurance	18 000	375 000	150 000	543 000
Telephone	27 000	0	0	27 000
Data processing and transmission	25 500	0	156 000	181 500
Postage	4 500	0	48 000	52 500
Developing and other consumables	12 000	105 000	186 000	303 000
Total cost of each process	R450 000	R3 150 000	R1 440 000	R5 040 000
Number of patients processed	15 000	15 000	15 000	15 000
Cost per process per patient	R30.00	R210.00	R96.00	R336.00

3 Although these services are provided by professional labour, the processes are repetitive, with each patient consuming identical or a very similar amount of resources. In these circumstances, there is no need to use job costing to specifically assign costs to each patient who is X-rayed. Instead, we can estimate the average cost per patient X-rayed using a process costing approach.

Cybersearch

1 Use the search term *service costing* to find websites of industries or organisations that estimate service costs. Identify possible reasons for estimating service costs in these industries.

2 Search the Internet to find organisations that implement service costing systems.

(a) What are the key features of the costing systems described?

(b) Why do you think that service costing is useful in these particular organisations, and not others?

Questions

?

6.1 What are the distinguishing features of service organisations? Consider the extent to which these features are present in three of the 14 industries included in the service sector, according to government classifications.

6.2 Identify two service organisations and two manufacturing businesses and compare and contrast the nature of their outputs.

6.3 Do *retail* and *wholesale* businesses provide services or goods to customers? Discuss.

6.4 'In setting up costing systems we need to be very careful to distinguish between manufacturing firms and service entities. Manufacturers produce goods but not services.' Discuss.

6.5 Universities are service organisations. Think of an example of a fixed cost and a variable cost within a university, specifying the cost driver for the variable cost. How might the university's management use this information?

6.6 Your local hotel is a service entity. Give two examples each of the hotel's direct and indirect costs, specifying the cost object. How might the hotel's management use this information?

6.7 What is a *value chain*? Select any major service organisation with which you are familiar, and describe the segments that you think would be included in its value chain. You should give a brief explanation of the role of each segment in the organisation.

6.8 Compare and contrast the value chain of a typical manufacturer, described in Chapter 2, with the value chain for a typical service organisation.

6.9 Compare and contrast the value chain of a typical retailer or wholesaler with the value chain of a typical service organisation.

6.10 In estimating the costs of products, manufacturers usually identify direct material, direct labour and manufacturing overhead costs. What modifications may be made to these classifications in estimating service costs?

6.11 Identify the key features of:
(a) professional service firms
(b) service shops
(c) mass service entities
and give three examples of each of these types of service organisations.

6.12 Describe the service costing system that is most appropriate for:
(a) professional service firms
(b) service shops
(c) mass service entities

6.13 What type of service entities are likely to use a client billing system rather than a service costing system? Give three examples.

6.14 What are the key differences between a service costing system and a client billing system?

6.15 Describe the problems that can arise in using process costing to estimate the cost of the services produced in mass service entities.

6.16 Consider the costs across the various segments of the value chain of a software developer. Which of these costs should be included in the cost of the firm's software products? Explain your answer.

6.17 The managing director of African Life Home Interiors, an interior design firm, asked the accountant to consider developing a service costing system. The accountant responded: 'We're a service business. All our costs are period costs that have to be expensed in the period in which they have been incurred. We don't need product costing.'

The managing director is furious. (He's never heard of period costs!) He asks you to evaluate the accountant's response and to prepare a clear explanation of how service costing could help him manage the business.

6.18 How can estimates of service costs help managers to manage resources and create value?

6.19 Do service costs provide a useful basis for planning and controlling costs? Explain.

6.20 Describe the three factors that influence the costs and benefits associated with service costing. How are these factors affected by the type of service firm?

6.21 Given the information included in this chapter, do you believe that most service organisations in South Africa would estimate the costs of:
(a) their responsibility centres, such as departments
(b) the services that they produce?
Explain your answer.

6.22 Explain why there is no need to separately aggregate and record service costs in the accounting ledger. Does this mean that service costs are never accumulated in the general ledger?

6.23 'Despite the use of predetermined overhead rates in estimating service costs, there is no need to consider underapplied or overapplied overhead.' Discuss.

6.24 Identify three service firms that are likely to produce work in process inventory, and explain how the costs of work in process are recorded in the accounting system.

Exercises

E6.25 Classifying costs; direct costs: hotel restaurant

Indicate whether each of the following costs is a direct cost of the restaurant in a hotel:
(a) cost of food served
(b) chef's salary and labour on-costs
(c) part of the cost of maintaining the grounds around the hotel, which is allocated to the restaurant
(d) part of the cost of advertising the hotel, which is allocated to the restaurant

E6.26 Classifying costs; controllable costs: hospital

Which of the following costs are likely to be controllable by the director of nursing in a hospital:
(a) cost of medication administered

(b) cost of overtime paid to nurses due to scheduling errors
(c) cost of depreciation of hospital beds?

E6.27 Classifying costs; value chain: telecommunications organisation

Consider a major telecommunications business such as Telkom. Classify the costs listed below using the following value chain classifications:

(a) research and development
(b) design
(c) production/delivery
(d) marketing
(e) customer support

Costs:

1 The salaries of the technicians who install new phone and data lines.
2 The salaries of the scientists and engineers who develop new services.
3 The cost of cables used to connect new services.
4 The salaries paid to sales staff.
5 The salaries of staff who deal with customer complaints.
6 The cost of fuel for vans used by technicians who install new services.
7 The cost of advertising in the newspapers.
8 The salaries of the technicians who resolve service problems.
9 The cost of fuel for vans used by technicians who resolve service problems.

E6.28 Classifying costs; value chain: bank

Classify the costs listed below, using the following value chain classifications, for a major bank:

(a) research and development
(b) design
(c) production/delivery
(d) marketing
(e) customer support

Costs:

1 The salaries of the tellers who process deposits and withdrawals.
2 The salaries of the finance staff who develop new services.
3 The cost of the IT equipment used by the tellers.
4 The cost of the mainframe computer, which processes all deposits and withdrawals.
5 The cost of the automatic teller machines (ATMs).
6 The salaries paid to the staff who service the ATMs.
7 The salaries of staff who deal with customer complaints.
8 The salaries of the head office team that monitors new trends in the banking industry.
9 The cost of advertising in the newspapers.

E6.29 Classifying costs; value chain: retailer

Ndebele General Store is a major independent supermarket located in Soweto. Classify the costs listed below, using these value chain classifications:

(a) purchasing
(b) production/sales
(c) marketing
(d) distribution
(e) customer support

Costs:

1 The wages paid to the purchasing manager.
2 The wages paid to the staff who operate the service desk. The service desk assists customers to locate items in the store and resolves customer complaints.

3 Electricity. The fridges and freezers that store cold goods in the shop account for most of the electricity consumed.
4 The cost of plastic bags supplied to customers with sales.
5 The wages paid to check-out assistants.
6 The wages paid to the supermarket manager.
7 The cost of advertising in the local paper, *The Soweto Sun*.

E6.30 Service firm types

Classify the following organisations as professional service firms, mass service entities or service shops. In each case, explain the reasons for your classification.

1 A motor registration department that processes applications and payments for drivers' licences and vehicle registration.
2 A medical practice staffed by five doctors who specialise in the treatment of skin conditions.
3 A bank.
4 A motor vehicle repair workshop that employs three mechanics.
5 An airline company.

E6.31 Job costing and pricing: interior decorating firm

Design Arts Associates is an interior decorating firm located in Cape Town's northern suburbs. The following costs were incurred in the firm's contract to redecorate the local council offices:

Direct material	R14 000
Professional labour	30 000

The firm's budget for the year included the following estimates:

Budgeted overhead	R2 000 000
Budgeted professional labour	1 250 000

Required:

1 Calculate the total cost of the firm's contract to redecorate the council offices. Overhead is applied to contracts using a predetermined overhead rate, calculated annually, based on the professional labour cost. Materials are charged directly to each contract.
2 Use the total cost to calculate a service fee, assuming that the company adds a 40 per cent profit margin to total cost.

E6.32 Job billing: interior decorating firm (continuation of Exercise 6.31)

Refer to the information for Exercise 6.31.

1 Calculate the fee charged to redecorate the council offices, assuming that the firm uses a chargeout rate of R900 per professional labour hour (which includes a profit margin of 40 per cent) and 120 hours are worked on this contract. Materials are charged to the client at cost.
2 Explain the key differences between this approach to estimating service fees and the method described in Exercise 6.31.
3 Which method would you recommend for estimating client fees? Explain your answer.

E6.33 Job costing: hairdressing salon

Creatif Cutz is an up-market hairdressing firm. When the manager, B. Sharp, bought the business he adopted the pricing structure used by the previous owner. He has now employed you to estimate the cost of the various services provided in his salon so that he can use a cost-based pricing system. After examining the cost structure of the business and the vast range of services supplied, you decide to use a job costing system that, for each service, will measure the cost of the hairdressers' time (that is, direct labour) and apply overheads using a predetermined rate based on direct labour hours.

Estimated overhead costs for the next year are:

Cutting scissors	R15 000
Combs and brushes	7 500
Shampoos, conditioners and gels	5 000
Laundry costs	5 500
Salon cleaning	2 600
Insurance	6 000
Depreciation on equipment	1 750
Rent	12 500
Electricity	6 750
Council rates	7 400
Total overhead costs	R70 000

Creatif Cutz employs three hairdressers who are expected to work a total of 5000 hours in the coming year. To test the system, you observe and cost three services that took the following amounts of hairdressing time:

Product	Time
Complex cut and colour	90 minutes
Shampoo, cut and blow dry	45 minutes
Simple cut	20 minutes

Required:

1 Calculate the predetermined overhead rate to be used at Creatif Cutz.

2 Calculate the cost of the three services and their recommended prices if Creatif Cutz sets prices at cost plus a 20 per cent mark-up. Hairdressers are paid an average hourly rate of R100.

3 When you present your findings to B. Sharp he rejects them, claiming, 'This is ridiculous. If I charged that much for a complex cut and colour, my clients would go elsewhere!' What would you reply?

E6.34 Job costing and billing: IT consultant

IT Mania Pty Ltd offers a range of IT consulting services. The company's service costing system estimates the cost of each consulting job by accumulating costs of the professional labour that works on the job plus a charge for overhead.

The cost of professional labour is charged to jobs using the following three rates:

IT trainee	R100	per hour
IT graduate	R250	per hour
IT senior consultant	R750	per hour

The predetermined overhead rate is based on professional labour costs, which are budgeted to be R2 212 000 for the current year.

The estimated overhead costs for the current year are budgeted to be:

Management salaries	R2 450 000
Salaries of clerical and reception staff	950 000
Depreciation on IT hardware and software	800 000
Stationery	75 000
Telecommunications	105 000
Insurance	600 000
Depreciation on office fixtures and fittings	37 500
Rent	302 500
Electricity	131 750
Council rates	78 250

During the month of May the company provided three services, which consumed the following quantities of professional labour (in hours):

Client	IT Trainee	IT Graduate	Senior consultant
Smith and Sons	50	100	15
Jones and Partners	20	140	10
The Business Centre	70	80	20

Required:

1 Calculate the predetermined overhead rate to be used at IT Mania.
2 Calculate the cost of the three services.
3 How might the management of IT Mania use this information?
4 How would IT Mania's approach differ if the firm used a billing rather than a costing system?

E6.35 Job costing and job billing: health resort

Healthy Alternatives is a health resort that offers a range of programs for health-conscious managers. Managers who participate are provided with a tailored program, consisting of a series of activities. A job costing system is used to calculate the cost of each program.

The manager of Healthy Alternatives has designed the following programs for managers at the local water authority:

Program A: Health check, 2-hour mountain hike, 30-minute yoga class, 15-minute massage
Program B: Health check, 1-hour gym workout, 30-minute massage
Program C: Health check, 2-hour mountain hike, 60-minute yoga class, 2-hour gym workout
Program D: 1-hour gym workout, 30-minute yoga class, 2-hour mountain hike

The following labour costs and overheads apply:

Employee	Labour cost per hour	Overhead applied per hour	Chargeout rates per hour
Mountain hike leader	R80	R240	R384
Massage therapist	R160	R400	R672
Personal trainer (for gym workout)	R160	R800	R1 152
Yoga class leader	R80	R480	R672
Medical doctor (for 30-minute health check)	R400	R720	R1 344

Required:

1 Determine the total cost of each of the programs.
2 How might the resort managers use these total costs?
3 Explain why there is a different overhead rate for each class of labour.
4 Calculate the price of each program using the chargeout rates.

E6.36 Job costing: car repair business

Bodge Auto Company is a car repair workshop specialising in luxury European vehicles. The company estimates the costs of repair services by recording the labour time spent on the vehicle, the cost of spare parts used on the repair job and allocating overhead at the rate of 40 per cent of labour cost. Overheads include the wages of the receptionist and secretarial staff, as well as the costs of accommodation and depreciation of a wide range of expensive technical equipment.

In the last week, the company has completed two repair jobs: an engine replacement and a complete overhaul of a vehicle's braking system. The engine replacement involved extensive use of equipment, while the brake overhaul was largely a manual process. The direct costs assigned to the two jobs were as follows:

	Engine replacement	Brake overhaul
Mechanic's time	R2 500	R2 750
Spare parts	R4 000	R 450

Required:

1 Estimate the cost of each job.

2 Do you think that the costing system provides a reliable estimate of the costs of the resources used during the two jobs? Explain your answer.

E6.37 Process costing: airport check-ins

Airport Services Ltd operates the check-in facilities at domestic and international terminals throughout South Africa. During the month of April the following costs were incurred as passengers were processed by the Check-in Department at Cape Town's Airport:

	International terminal	Domestic terminal
Costs:		
Managers' and supervisors' salaries	R600 000	R900 000
Check-in staff salaries	450 000	1 500 000
Depreciation on baggage handling equipment	978 000	1 920 000
Boarding passes, baggage tags and other consumables	30 000	84 000
Depreciation on computer hardware and software	300 000	1 020 000
Equipment insurance	30 000	78 000
Rent (allocated per square metre)	60 000	240 000
Electricity	72 000	198 000
Number of passengers processed	70 000	220 000

Required:

1 Calculate the cost per check-in at the international and domestic terminal.

2 Why does the cost per check-in differ between the two terminals?

3 Do these costs provide a reliable estimate of the costs incurred to check in each passenger at the international and domestic terminals? Explain your answer.

4 How might the management of Airport Services Ltd use this information?

E6.38 Process costing: book order agency

All Texts and Stationery Ltd (ATS) is a major provider of texts and stationery to secondary schools throughout the Eastern Cape. Students submit their order to ATS through their school at the beginning of the year. ATS fills the order in three stages:

- The order is received from the school and entered into the ATS inventory order system.
- The books and stationery required to fill the order are drawn from inventory, packed and despatched to the student.
- Payment is received from the student and processed.

The costs of these three processes in the year just ended are listed below:

Cost	Receipt of order	Pack and despatch order	Receipt of payment
Staff salaries	200 000	500 000	240 000
Equipment depreciation	1 680 000	580 000	960 000
Equipment insurance	320 000	220 000	320 000
Telephone	16 000	12 000	8 000
Data processing	30 000	8 000	48 000
Postage	0	620 000	0
Consumables	12 000	140 000	8 000

During the year, ATS processed 22 000 student orders.

Required:

1 Calculate the cost per order for each process.
2 Calculate the total cost per order.
3 Does the total cost per order provide a reliable estimate of the costs incurred to process each order? Explain your answer.

E6.39 When to use service costing

Classify each of the following statements as true or false. In each case, provide reasons to explain your answer.

1 An estimate of the cost of individual services is necessary for external reporting purposes.
2 Professional service firms may calculate service costs to assist in pricing.
3 Service costing is worthwhile only in businesses that have high levels of overheads.
4 Activity-based costing may provide a useful way to cost services in professional service firms.
5 Conventional product costing methods will provide more accurate product costs for services, compared to goods.

Problems

P6.40 Overtime premiums and labour on-costs: service firm

Skysouth Airways operates commuter flights between Bloemfontein, Johannesburg and Durban. Because of a political convention being held in Bloemfontein, the airline added several extra flights during a two-week period. Additional cabin crews were hired on a temporary basis. However, rather than hiring additional flight attendants, the airline used its current attendants on overtime. Monica Buthelezi worked the following schedule on 10 August. All Buthelezi's flights on that day were extra flights that the airline would not normally fly.

- Regular time: 2 round-trip flights between Bloemfontein and Johannesburg (8 hours)
- Overtime: 1 round-trip flight between Bloemfontein and Durban (3 hours)

Buthelezi earns R120 per hour plus time and a half for overtime. Labour on-costs cost the airline R30 per hour for any hour worked, regardless of whether it is a regular or overtime hour.

Required:

1 Calculate the direct cost of compensating Buthelezi for her services on the round trip from Bloemfontein to Johannesburg.
2 Calculate the indirect cost of Buthelezi's service.
3 How should the cost calculated in requirement 2 be treated for cost accounting purposes?

P6.41 Classifying costs; direct and indirect, variable and fixed: consulting engineers

B.K. Scheepers and Associates is a firm of consulting engineers that specialises in environmental impact statements. These projects involve assessing the potential impact of proposed developments on the environment. In most cases, the assessment requires soil samples to be taken by engineering staff and analysed by an external laboratory service. The firm's costing system traces direct costs to projects. All remaining costs are allocated to projects using an indirect cost rate based on consulting hours worked.

Required:

Classify each of the costs listed below as:

(a) a direct cost of projects
(b) an indirect cost of projects
(c) a variable cost (assuming the number of projects is the cost driver)
(d) a fixed cost (in relation to the number of projects)
(e) a committed cost
(f) a discretionary cost

Costs:

1 Salaries paid to engineering staff.
2 Cost of drill bits used to take soil samples. Each bit has a life of more than 1000 samples. Usually only a few samples are required for each project.
3 Cost of soil analysis.
4 Cost of advertising the firm's services in the Yellow Pages directory.
5 Office lease costs. Terms of the lease fix this payment for a three-year period.
6 Computer and other equipment depreciation (straight line basis).
7 Computer and other equipment insurance.
8 Telephone expenses. The quarterly Telkom account itemises individual calls.
9 Stationery and other supplies.
10 Salaries paid to the firm's administrator, who oversees the allocation of engineers and support services to individual projects.

P6.42 Classifying costs; direct and indirect, variable and fixed, controllable and uncontrollable, period and product: retailer

The Massmart group owns the Makro chain of discount department stores. The Makro store in Wonderboom consists of several departments. The revenues and costs for each department are recorded separately, and department managers are held responsible for these results. Peter Smith manages the Menswear Department.

Required:

Classify each of the costs listed below as:

(a) a direct cost of the Menswear Department
(b) an indirect cost of the Menswear Department
(c) a variable cost (assuming the number of items sold is the cost driver)
(d) a fixed cost (in relation to the number of items sold)
(e) a committed cost
(f) a discretionary cost
(g) a controllable cost for Peter Smith
(h) an uncontrollable cost for Peter Smith
(i) a product cost
(j) a period cost

More than one classification may apply to each item.

Costs:

1 The salary of the manager of the Wonderboom Makro store.
2 The salaries of the sales staff working in the Menswear Department.
3 The cost of advertising men's shirts in a national marketing brochure produced by the Makro head office in Johannesburg.

4 The rent paid by the Wonderboom store, which is allocated to individual departments on the basis of floor area.
5 The cost of shirts sold in Menswear.
6 The wages of store security staff, allocated to departments on the basis of sales revenue.
7 The cost of obsolete stock written off or written down at the end of each year. Obsolescence is caused by changing customer tastes.
8 The cost of the computerised inventory management system that is administered by the Johannesburg head office.
9 The cost of staff bonuses paid on the basis of sales revenue achieved.
10 The cost of stock stolen from the Menswear Department.

P6.43 Classifying costs according to value chain: accounting firm

Sonn & Brits is a medium-sized accounting firm that provides services in the areas of audit, taxation and investment advice. Apply value chain and other classifications to the costs listed below. (More than one classification may be appropriate for each cost item.) What role might this approach to cost classification play in the management process?

Cost classifications:

(a) research and development
(b) design
(c) production/delivery
(d) marketing
(e) customer support
(f) fixed costs
(g) variable costs (identify cost driver)
(h) professional labour
(i) overheads

Costs:

1 The salaries of staff who work directly on audit assignments.
2 The salary of the financial planning consultant who provides investment advice to retirees.
3 The salary of a research assistant who investigates and develops new financial planning products.
4 The salary of the receptionist.
5 The costs of advertising financial planning products.
6 The cost of telephone calls. These relate primarily to follow-up calls to taxation clients.
7 Depreciation on photocopiers used in the provision of all services.
8 The cost of pre-printed stationery used in the preparation of taxation returns.
9 The salaries of staff who are directly involved in the preparation of taxation returns.
10 Depreciation on office computing equipment used in the provision of all services.

P6.44 Classifying costs; direct, indirect, controllable, uncontrollable: service firm

Several costs incurred by Water's Edge Hotel and Restaurant are listed below. The kitchen is one of the work areas within the food and beverage department. For each cost listed below, indicate which of the following classifications best describes the cost. More than one classification may apply to the same cost item.

Cost classifications:

(a) direct cost of the food and beverage department
(b) indirect cost of the food and beverage department
(c) controllable by the kitchen manager
(d) uncontrollable by the kitchen manager
(e) controllable by the hotel's general manager
(f) uncontrollable by the hotel's general manager

Costs:

1 The cost of food used in the kitchen.

2 The cost of general advertising by the hotel, which is allocated to the food and beverage department.
3 The cost of space (depreciation) occupied by the kitchen.
4 The cost of space (depreciation) occupied by the reception area, which is allocated to the food and beverage department.
5 The wages earned by table service personnel.
6 The salary of the kitchen manager.
7 The cost of dishes broken by kitchen employees.
8 The cost of leasing a computer used for room reservations, payroll and general hotel accounting, which is allocated to the food and beverage department.
9 The salary of the general manager of the hotel, which is allocated to the food and beverage department.
10 The wages of the hotel's maintenance employees, who spent 11 hours repairing the dishwasher in the kitchen.

P6.45 Cost classifications; variable and fixed, direct and indirect, controllable and uncontrollable: government department

The South African National Parks (SANParks) is responsible for maintaining the country's national parks, stocking the lakes and rivers with fish and generally overseeing the protection of the environment. Several costs incurred by SANParks are listed below. For each cost, indicate which of the following classifications best describe the cost. More than one classification may apply to the same cost item.

Cost classifications:

(a) variable
(b) fixed
(c) committed
(d) discretionary
(e) controllable by the SANParks director
(f) uncontrollable by the SANParks director
(g) direct cost of SANParks
(h) indirect cost of SANParks
(i) direct cost of providing a particular service
(j) indirect cost of providing a particular service

Costs:

1 Cost of the fish, purchased from private hatcheries, which are used to stock public waters.
2 Cost of live-trapping and moving hippos, which are creating a nuisance in recreational lakes and rivers.
3 The SANParks director's salary.
4 Cost of containing naturally caused veldfires that are threatening private property.
5 Cost of the vehicles used by SanPark's rangers. Each ranger station is provided with a vehicle.
6 Cost of producing literature that describes SanPark's role in environmental protection. This literature is mailed free, upon request, to schools, state governments, local councils, libraries and members of the public.
7 Cost of operating the government's computer services department, a portion of which is allocated to SANParks.
8 Cost of administrative supplies used in the SanPark's head office.
9 Cost of providing a telephone number (calls to be paid by SANParks) for members of the public to report environmental problems.
10 The cost of replacing batteries in equipment used to monitor the effects of droughts on lakes in national parks.

11 Cost of a ranger's wages when the ranger is giving a talk about environmental protection to primary school children.
12 Cost of direct mailing, to one million households, a brochure explaining the benefits of voluntarily recycling cans and bottles.
13 Cost of producing a TV show to teach people how to minimise property damage from veldfires by developing and maintaining 'fire-safe' gardens.

P6.46 Job costing: medical practice

Healthaware is a large medical practice in Durban owned by Dr Pillay, a medical entrepreneur, and staffed by salaried doctors. Until recently the practice had been managed by Pillay's son, Jay. However, Dr Pillay became concerned about his son's financial management and appointed a qualified accountant, Joseph Naledi, as practice manager. Naledi was amazed by the lack of information about the costs of the services provided for patients. He immediately implemented a service costing system that required the doctors to keep detailed records of the time they spent on each medical procedure. Each service cost included:

- professional labour costs, based on the doctor's time multiplied by the doctor's average salary rate of R360 per hour; and
- practice overhead costs, based on a predetermined overhead rate of 400 per cent of professional labour costs.

The predetermined overhead rate was based on the budget for the next year and estimated using the following formula:

$$\text{Overhead rate} = \frac{\text{total budgeted practice costs} - \text{budgeted medical salaries}}{\text{budgeted medical salaries}}$$

At a practice meeting, Naledi presented the following estimates of service costs and profits:

	Cost	Fee	Profit
Standard consultation	R90	R120	R30
Pregnancy test	90	240	150
Blood test	90	330	240

As each of these services required the same amount of time, Naledi recommended that the doctors should focus on blood tests rather than on standard consultations or pregnancy tests.

Required:

1 Identify and explain the differences between Healthaware's overhead rate and overhead rates usually used in manufacturing firms.
2 Discuss the costs and benefits of the service cost information provided by Naledi.
3 Do you agree with Naledi's advice?

P6.47 Job costing; future versus current costs: engineering firm

Westwoods Engineers is a firm of consulting engineers. The business provides two main services: the design and support services for civil engineering projects, such as the building of bridges and roads, and environmental assessments for planned and existing developments. Westwoods is preparing a tender for a project involving the extension of the main runway at George Airport. An initial feasibility study recommended extending the western boundary of the airport by either shifting the major arterial road on the western boundary, or building an underpass for the road beneath the extended runway. The tender involves assessing the economic and environmental feasibility of each alternative.

Westwoods' tender manager is responsible for preparing tender bids. She estimates tender costs by identifying all costs that are likely to be directly associated with the project. To obtain the final tender bid, the total professional (engineering and scientist) labour costs are marked up by 75 per cent, and all other costs are marked up by 50 per cent. These margins are intended to cover any indirect costs plus provide the required profit margin on the project.

The tender manager estimated the following direct costs for the airport project:

	Input	Costs
Civil engineers	100 hours	R70 000
Environmental scientists	80 hours	50 000
Support labour	100 hours	30 000
Travel	500 km	2 500
Computer time	40 hours	10 000
Photocopying, phone, fax		1 250

Required:

1 Estimate the tender bid for the project.

2 Estimate the profit on the project if the bid is successful and all costs are incurred as planned.

3 Once a project has begun, Westwoods will use a costing system that tracks all direct costs to projects. If the airport bid is successful, how would managers at Westwoods use this information?

4 Do you think there is likely to be any link between the costing system used to account for existing projects and the system that the tender manager uses to prepare bids for potential projects? Explain.

P6.48 Service costing: hospital; department cost allocation

Southern Clinic is a private hospital in Cape Town. The hospital is a not-for-profit organisation, and currently bills its patients at R1500 per day. This rate was set at the beginning of the year to cover the costs of running the hospital, based on the expected level of activity. The costs at this activity level have been estimated at:

Medical staff	R15 000 000
Nursing staff	20 000 000
Overhead:	
Patient records	2 500 000
Radiology	4 000 000
Kitchen	6 000 000
Other overhead	5 000 000

The expected level of activity in the hospital is measured in patient-days, and was estimated as follows:

	Patient-days	Number of patients
Surgical Ward	10 000	1 000
Maternity Ward	5 000	1 000
General Ward	20 000	3 000

It is expected that the medical and nursing staff will work 100 000 hours and 250 000 hours respectively during the year, and that their time will be spent as follows:

	Surgical Ward	Maternity Ward	General Ward	Total staff hours
Medical staff hours	50 000	10 000	40 000	100 000
Nursing staff hours	120 000	10 000	120 000	250 000

The billing system had been well accepted within the local community. However, one day, on being discharged from the Maternity Ward, a patient lodged a complaint over the fee. She claimed that as a maternity patient she should have been charged less than a surgical patient, as she required less care from both the medical and nursing staff. Also, unlike surgical patients, maternity patients rarely require radiology support or special meals from the kitchen. A subsequent review of the medical, nursing and support services required by patients in the Maternity and Surgical wards substantiated her claims.

Required:

1 Show how the billing rate of R1500 per patient-day was set.

2 Estimate separate billing rates for each of the three wards, assuming that medical and nursing staff costs are allocated to the three wards using staff hours, and all other overhead costs are allocated using patient-days as the cost driver.

3 When the departmental billing rates are discussed at the next board meeting, the treasurer opposes them, claiming that they do not address all of the issues raised by the maternity patient. Do you agree? What is the problem?

4 Assume that the review indicates the following cost drivers should be used to allocate overhead costs to each ward:

Overhead cost	Cost driver
Patient records	The number of patients
Radiology	Medical staff hours spent in the Surgical and General wards
Kitchen	Nursing staff hours
Other overhead	Nursing staff hours

Now estimate the billing rates for the Surgical, Maternity and General wards.

5 Which approach would you recommend? Explain your answer.

6 Can you suggest further improvements to Southern Clinic's costing/billing system?

P6.49 Process costing: university enrolments

The university is exploring the possibility of outsourcing part or all of its enrolment function. This function involves three separate processes:

- Validation, where the new student's secondary school results are sighted and the University's offer of enrolment is validated.
- Student records, where the student's study program details for the current year are entered into the student record system.
- Fees collection, where students pay their academic fees.

The annual costs of these three processes are:

Cost	Validation	Student records	Fees collection
Staff salaries	R240 000	R160 000	R140 000
IT and other equipment depreciation	40 000	100 000	80 000
Equipment insurance	4 000	8 400	8 000
Telephone	4 400	13 200	8 000
Data processing	25 200	80 000	20 800
Postage	0	4 000	26 000
Consumables	12 000	140 000	36 000
Electricity	4 800	9 600	8 800

The university processes 14 000 student enrolments per year.

Required:

1 Calculate the cost per student enrolment for each process.

2 Calculate the total cost per student enrolment.

3 Does the total cost per student enrolment provide a reliable estimate of the costs incurred to process *each enrolment*? Explain your answer.

4 Apart from informing its outsourcing decision, how might the university's management use this information?

5 Would you recommend estimating service costs for all major student services in the university? Explain your answer.

P6.50 Estimating service costs; ethical issues: accounting firm

Callaghan, Moroka and Associates is a firm of chartered accountants specialising in the preparation of financial statements and income tax returns for medical practitioners. By specialising, the firm has been able to build up expertise in the accounting for medical practices, as well as charge a healthy fee because of its in-depth knowledge in the area. Among the firm's clients are Dr Watson and Dr Holmes, two general practitioners from rural practices of approximately the same size and business structure.

Watson and Holmes were at medical school together but had not kept in touch. Recently they bumped into each other at the South African Medical Practitioners Association's Christmas party. During the evening, the conversation turned to financial statements, and then to tax returns. Watson and Holmes were amazed to find that they paid significantly different amounts to have their financial statements and tax returns prepared. They use the same accountants and have the same billing system, roughly the same number of patients and even the same number of staff.

The next day Watson, who last year paid nearly 50 per cent more than Holmes, challenged the managing partner, C.J. Callaghan, over the charges. Callaghan assured Watson that the firm uses a very accurate costing system that tracks costs for five different categories of professional labour to individual clients. Professional labour costs are marked up by 150 per cent to cover other costs and generate a profit. He promises to investigate the problem.

The following are the records for Watson and Holmes for last year:

	Rate per hour	Watson	Holmes
Senior partner	R1 050	R2 100	R525
Partner	875	1 750	875
Manager	560	560	560
Supervisor	350	700	1 050
Graduate	210	105	630
Total cost of labour		5 215	3 640
Mark-up (covering overhead costs and a profit margin)	150%	7 823	5 460
Total charge to client		R13 038	R9 100

Callaghan investigated both jobs and found that they had involved similar work but that Watson's job had used more senior staff because, at the time, junior staff were tied up on other projects, including completing Holmes' tax return! Both projects had also made similar use of resources other than professional labour.

Required:

1 Does the costing system used by Callaghan, Moroka and Associates provide a reliable estimate of:
   (a) the professional labour costs?
   (b) the cost of other resources used in preparing clients' tax returns?
2 Does the costing system provide a reasonable basis for estimating the charges to clients? Explain.
3 How could Callaghan, Moroka and Associates improve their costing/charge-out system?
4 If you were C.J. Callaghan, how would you respond to Watson's query?

P6.51 Estimating costs in a retail business

Auto Spares Pty Ltd is a retail business that sells car parts to customers who maintain their own cars. The company began business on 1 January 20X7 and the acquisition of the inventory of car parts during the year involved the following amounts:

The purchase price of the merchandise	R2 725 000
Value Added Tax (VAT) on the purchase of merchandise	381 500
The cost of inwards freight on the merchandise (excl. VAT)	50 000
Trade discounts on the merchandise (excl. VAT)	225 000

In addition to the cost of merchandise, the company incurred the following costs (excl. VAT) during 20X7:

	Cost
Staff salaries:	
Purchasing staff	R200 000
Sales staff	525 000
Delivery driver (part-time)	75 000
Rent	150 000
Equipment depreciation and insurance	25 000
Telephone	16 500
Computer software and hardware depreciation (inventory management system)	75 000
Data transfer (EDI order system)	30 000
Stationery and other consumables	15 000
Electricity	24 000

Required:

1 Estimate the cost of inventory purchased during 20X7.
2 Prepare an income statement for the company for 20X7 assuming that, in pricing goods for sale, the company adds a mark-up of 80 per cent on costs and that 90 per cent of the value of the inventory purchased during 20X7 was sold.
3 Suggest three ways in which the company could refine its costing system to provide more useful information for managing its resources and creating value for its owners.

Note: All revenue and expenses reported in the income statement should be exclusive of Value Added Tax (VAT) as all VAT charged on sales (outputs) is payable to the SA Revenue Service and all VAT paid on expenses (inputs) is claimable by the company from the SA Revenue Service. For example, if we paid R114 for stationery, which includes VAT, then we would put through the following journal entry:

Stationery	R100	
VAT	14	
Bank		R114

Cases

C6.52 Job costing; department overhead cost allocation: tour operator

African Adventure Holidays is a small travel company that offers a series of holiday packages aimed at families, seniors and corporate groups. The owner, John Makhabane, is preparing for the annual meeting with the company's bank and is concerned about the loss that the business sustained in the past year. He has examined the profits for each of the three departments of the business – family, seniors and corporate – and it seems that the corporate department is the source of the problem.

John has asked you to assist him to look more closely at the three packages offered by the corporate department to see which holiday packages are yielding profits and which are not. The three packages are to Namibia, Mozambique and Zambia. The sales and direct costs of each of the corporate packages for last year are as follows:

	Namibia Adventure	Mozambique Discovery	Zambia Orienteering
Number of packages sold	10	20	10
Number of people per package	5	6	8
Revenue per person	R36 000	R24 000	R28 000
Direct cost per package:			
Tour leader	10 000	24 000	18 000
Tour assistant	4000	6000	12 000
Air travel	56 000	60 000	64 000
Accommodation	30 000	52 000	48 000
Equipment hire	8000	0	18 000
Meals	36 000	30 000	16 000

To calculate the profitability of each package, a proportion of the overhead costs of running the corporate department needs to be allocated to the three packages. Jack has suggested that these costs could be allocated to each package in proportion to actual sales revenue. For last year these overhead costs were as follows:

Salaries	R400 000
Phone	12 000
Depreciation on equipment	10 000
Utilities	4000
Rent	30 000
Other department costs	4000
Total	460 000

Required:

1 Calculate the profit per package and the total profitability of each of the three corporate packages.
2 Compare the profitability of the three corporate packages.
3 Do you consider that the allocation of department overhead to packages using actual sales revenue is appropriate? Can you suggest a better method?
4 Suggest what actions the company could take in regard to the three corporate packages.

C6.53 Job costing using client cost sheet; fraud investigation: accounting firm

Spicer and Dlamini is a large accounting firm that specialises in fraud investigation. In May 20X7, Jackson Moselane, the general manager of Jazz Industries, approached John House, a partner of Spicer and Dlamini, to discuss a problem that has arisen in one of his warehouses. Moselane is not sure whether fraud is involved or not, but over the past year there have been a series of unexplained inventory shortages, and he has heard rumours of some warehouse staff selling supplies for cash to friends, at greatly reduced prices. Moselane would like Spicer and Dlamini to conduct an investigation to see if there is any evidence of misappropriation. This matter is urgent and Moselane would like a final report within the next two weeks.

John House agrees to undertake the investigation. He will oversee the project, Christine Ndlulu will manage the project and Graeme Smith will assist. The following labour rates apply:

John House	Partner	R1500
Christine Ndlulu	Manager	1000
Graeme Smith	Investigator	600

At the end of each week, every employee of Spicer and Dlamini completes a time sheet online, to account for each hour of their day. The following extracts are taken from time sheets for the three staff involved in the investigation. The Jazz Industries case has been assigned the code 4506B:

John House			
Date	**Case**	**Detail**	**Time**
1 May 20X7	4506B	Initial meeting with Moselane	1 hour
	3547A	Delivery of final report	2 hours
	4508F	Initial meeting with Abox Ltd	1 hour
	4506B	Briefing meeting with CN and GS	1 hour
3 May 20X7	4506B	Review of investigation plan	2 hours
	4508F	Assessment of review	1 hour
	2408D	Report recommendations	1 hour
	78432S	Briefing to police	1 hour
	4540D	Meeting with lawyers	2 hours
10 May 20X7	4506B	Discussion of final report with CN and GS	3 hours
11 May 20X7	4506B	Delivery of final report	2 hours

Christine Ndlulu			
Date	**Case**	**Detail**	**Time**
1 May 20X7	4506B	Initial meeting with Moselane	1 hour
	4506B	Briefing meeting with JH and GS	1 hour
2 May 20X7	4506B	Review of investigation plan with GS	2 hours
	6592F	Delivery of final report	4 hours
3 May 20X7	4506B	On-site review of inventory ordering systems	5 hours
	4506B	Interviews with suppliers	3 hours
6 May 20X7	4506B	Consultation with GS	2 hours
	4506B	Interview of key managers	3 hours
	4508F	Review of transactions	3 hours
9 May 20X7	4506B	Meeting with GM to review report	2 hours
	4508F	Computer audit of master files	6 hours
10 May 20X7	4506B	Discussion of final report with JH and GS	3 hours

Graeme Smith			
Date	**Case**	**Detail**	**Time**
1 May 20X7	4506B	Briefing meeting with JH and CN	1 hour
2 May 20X7	4506B	Preparation of investigation plan	6 hours
	4506B	Review of investigation plan with CN	2 hours
3 May 20X7	4506B	Initial interviews with warehouse staff	4 hours
	4506B	Documentation of ordering procedures	4 hours
6 May 20X7	4506B	Consultation with CN	2 hours
		Character checks of key employees	4 hours
		Checking of supplier history	2 hours
7 May 20X7	4506B	Checking of supplier history	2 hours
	4506B	Random check of inventory and supplier transactions	6 hours
8 May 20X7	4506B	Preparation of draft report	8 hours
9 May 20X7	4506B	Meeting with CN to review report	2 hours
	4506B	Edit report	3 hours
10 May 20X7	4506B	Discussion of final report with JH and CN	3 hours

Spicer and Dlamini calculate a predetermined overhead rate to cover support staff salaries, office rent, utilities and telecommunication costs, marketing costs, and other costs of running the firm. Professional labour costs make up about 75 per cent of the firm's total operating costs. The estimated overhead cost for 20X7 is R40 million.

Required:

1 Calculate the predetermined overhead rate per rand of professional labour.
2 Explain how the firm can justify using a single overhead rate to cost each labour rate and each case.
3 Use the information in the time sheets to prepare a client cost sheet for the Jazz Industries investigation, similar to that in Exhibit 6.8.

4 Determine the total cost of the investigation.
5 Spicer and Dlamini operate in a very competitive market and cannot always charge clients prices sufficient to cover the full cost of undertaking a case. In the light of this information:
   (a) Why would Spicer and Dlamini require staff to fill in detailed time sheets?
   (b) What use could the partners make of the client cost sheet, and the total cost of the case?
   (c) How could John House justify undertaking the investigation of Jazz Industries for a loss?
6 If Spicer and Dlamini introduced a client billing system, in what ways would it differ from their costing system described above?
7 Would you recommend that Spicer and Dlamini use a client costing system, a client billing system, or both? Explain your answer.

C6.54 Job costing, process costing and hybrid costing: backpacker lodges

Happy Wanderer Ltd owns a chain of backpacker lodges located throughout South Africa. The company's profits have declined over the past year. In an attempt to isolate the causes of poor profit performance, the company has recently introduced a costing system to estimate the cost of its major services at each lodge. The company intends to use this information to review the service pricing structure and assess the profitability of its various service lines at each lodge.

JBay Lodge is one of the busiest lodges in the Happy Wanderer chain. One of its main products is the provision of accommodation, which involves three main processes: reception, room maintenance and the collection of payments for accommodation. The Lodge charges backpackers R200 per day for single bedrooms. (Double rooms are not available!)

Another major product is the provision of evening meals, which involve a variety of ingredients and two major processes: kitchen service (cooking and clean-up) and table service. The price of the evening meals varies between R25 and R75, depending on the menu items selected.

A third product is the provision of a range of one-day and half-day tours. The Lodge hires guides and provides equipment and transportation for a range of activities such as surfing, waterskiing, canyoning, canoeing and mountain trekking. Lunches, purchased from the local bakery, are also provided. Tour prices vary considerably, depending on the activities included.

In the past year, the Lodge provided accommodation to 2400 backpackers, who stayed an average of 5 nights each, purchased 8000 evening meals, 300 one-day tours and 400 half-day tours. The following data relate to the JBay Lodge for the past year:

	Accommodation		
Cost	**Reception**	**Room maintenance**	**Collection of accommodation payments**
Staff salaries	R250 000	R375 000	R300 000
Equipment depreciation and insurance	30 000	725 000	20 000
Electricity	15 000	225 000	12 500
Telephone	20 000	0	10 000
Building lease*	6 000	150 000	4 500
Linen	0	24 000	0
Consumables	15 000	175 000	10 000

*Allocated per square metre.

	Evening meals	
Cost	**Kitchen service**	**Restaurant/table service**
Staff salaries	R250 000	R150 000
Equipment depreciation and insurance	100 000	125 000
Electricity	75 000	20 000
Telephone	5 500	4 500
Building lease*	9 500	20 500

*Allocated per square metre.

Tours	
Cost	
Tour guides	R1000 per day
Equipment depreciation	R100 000 per annum
Tour van depreciation	R25 000 per annum
Fuel and van maintenance	R50 000 per annum
Public liability insurance	R75 000 per annum
Picnic lunches	R60 per person per day
Other expenses	R30 000 per annum

Required:

1 Use process costing to estimate:
   (a) the cost per person of the accommodation reception process
   (b) the cost per day of the room maintenance process. Occupied rooms are maintained (that is, vacuumed and dusted) each day
   (c) the cost per accommodation payment processed
   (d) the total cost per person per day of accommodation, on average, assuming a five-day stay

2 Assess the profitability of the accommodation service per person per day and in total.

3 Assume that the same kitchen and restaurant processes are used for each customer. Use a hybrid costing approach to estimate the cost of the following evening meals:

Meal	Cost of ingredients per meal
Roast	R17.50
Spaghetti bolognaise	R13.75
Vegetarian burgers	R15.75
Fish fillets	R22.50

4 Given the information about the costs of the kitchen and restaurant processes, do you believe that the evening meal service is profitable? Explain your answer.

5 Describe the approach that you would take to estimating the cost of each tour.

6 Given the information about the costs of the tours, do you believe that the tour service is profitable? Explain your answer.

7 What recommendations would you make to the management of the JBay Lodge to improve the profitability of their business?

8 How might the management of Happy Wanderer Ltd use this information?

Endnotes

1 Although the value chain shows production activities preceding marketing activities, in some service organisations services are marketed at the same time that they are produced (and delivered).

2 The examples of the XYZ Bank's costs included in this chapter are fictitious.

3 The use of departmental overhead rates is described in Chapter 7, which includes an explanation of the accounting for services provided to production departments by support departments. However, in this example we have assumed that all overhead costs, apart from the corporate costs, can be traced directly to the Investment Advisory Department. The corporate costs are allocated to each department on the basis of the number of employees working in the department.

4 You may have noticed that this approach differs from the process costing for manufacturers described in the appendix to Chapter 5, in which the cost of each process included transferred-in costs from prior processes. This cumulative approach was required to estimate the cost of work in process at the end of each stage of production, in the general ledger. In a service environment, such as a bank, there is no inventory to value and the inclusion of transferred-in costs of prior processes would undermine the usefulness of the cost per process as an indicator of efficiency.

5 Under IAS 2, for not-for-profit entities, the work-in-process of services that are to be provided to clients for no consideration or a nominal consideration are not valued.

6 Tangible goods may also be included in the output of other service organisations, but in merchandising businesses these goods are such a significant part of the transaction that they become a key focus of the costing system.

CHAPTER 07

A Closer Look at Overhead Costs

Learning Objectives

After completing this chapter, you should be able to:

1. explain the nature of overhead costs and other indirect costs;
2. describe the general principles for allocating indirect costs to cost objects;
3. allocate overhead costs to products, using a plantwide rate;
4. use the two-stage allocation process used to estimate departmental overhead rates and allocate overhead costs to products;
5. use activity-based costing principles to assign overheads to products;
6. recognise the costs and benefits of choosing alternative approaches to assigning overhead costs to products;
7. explain the relevant issues in estimating overhead rates, including identifying cost drivers, choosing volume-based and non-volume-based cost drivers, and deciding between budgeted and actual overhead rates;
8. explain the effect of alternative capacity measures on overhead rates;
9. discuss the general principles and reasons for allocating indirect costs to responsibility centres;
10. allocate support department costs to production departments using the direct method, the step-down method and the reciprocal services method; and
11. after studying the appendix, understand and evaluate variable and absorption costing and prepare profit reports using both approaches.

Introduction

Managers need to know the costs of goods and services, to help them assess product profitability, make decisions about product mix and, sometimes, set prices. In addition, manufacturers must value inventories. Managers also need to know the costs of responsibility centres, such as departments, to help them manage resources within their work areas. Some costs can be traced to products or responsibility centres, but others are indirect and must be allocated.

In this chapter we describe some general principles for allocating indirect costs to cost objects, such as products or departments. Indirect costs of products are often called 'overhead costs'. You may remember that in Chapter 4 we allocated overhead costs to products using a single plantwide overhead rate. In this chapter we explore some more accurate ways for allocating overhead costs to products. We also describe approaches to allocating indirect costs to responsibility centres, such as departments.

In studying this chapter you will notice that it can be very difficult to obtain reliable estimates of the indirect costs of products and responsibility centres. However, in many organisations, indirect costs are increasing relative to direct costs, so understanding these costs is vital to managing resources and creating value.

L.O. 1

What are overhead costs?

Overhead costs generally refer to indirect product costs, although many businesses also describe the indirect costs of *responsibility centres* as *overheads*. (You may remember from Chapter 2, that responsibility centres are areas of the business for which individual managers are responsible, such as work areas, departments, plants and divisions.) The various interpretations of overhead costs can be summarised in Exhibit 7.1.

Product costing perspective			Responsibility centre perspective
Indirect manufacturing costs (manufacturing overhead)	*OR*	All indirect costs (manufacturing overhead and non-manufacturing costs)	Indirect costs of responsibility centres

Exhibit 7.1 Common views of overhead costs

Indirect product costs

From a product costing perspective, overheads may refer to all costs other than direct costs. In manufacturing businesses, however, it is helpful to distinguish between indirect costs within the manufacturing area, called *manufacturing overhead,* and other indirect costs, particularly when valuing inventory for external reporting purposes.[1] To avoid confusion, we use the term *non-manufacturing costs* to describe costs incurred outside the manufacturing area of a business's value chain.

Manufacturing overhead costs

Manufacturing overhead costs (sometimes called **factory burden costs** or **indirect manufacturing costs**) are all manufacturing costs other than direct material and direct labour. They include:

- production costs that are incurred for a variety of products and cannot be traced to individual products (for example the costs of occupying, maintaining and managing a production facility);
- production costs that could be traced to individual products, but it is not worth the trouble (for example the costs of glue used in furniture manufacture); and
- production costs that could be traced to an individual product but are more appropriately treated as a cost of all output (for example overtime premiums and the costs of idle time).[2]

Manufacturing overhead includes depreciation and insurance of the factory and manufacturing equipment, utility costs such as electricity, as well as the costs of manufacturing support departments. **Support** (or **service**) **departments** are departments that do not work directly on producing products but are necessary for the manufacturing process to occur. For example, the Maintenance Department in a motor vehicle plant does not make cars, but if it did not exist the production process would stop when equipment broke down. Manufacturing overhead also includes **indirect materials** and **indirect labour**, which cover any material and labour used in production that is not classified as 'direct'. Indeed, manufacturing overhead is made up of a large number of different costs, which vary from one business to the next depending on the nature of the production processes.

Non-manufacturing costs

Non-manufacturing costs are all costs incurred outside the manufacturing area. They include upstream costs, such as research and development, design and supply costs; and downstream costs, such as marketing, distribution and customer service costs. Accounting standards require inventory to be valued at manufacturing cost for external financial accounting purposes, but managers may require more comprehensive estimates of product costs for making product-related decisions. Thus, the management accountant may also assign these indirect costs to products.

Overhead costs in service firms

The costing systems in most service organisations assign costs to responsibility centres but not to services. Where service costs are estimated, the term 'overhead costs' is often used to describe all costs other than direct costs. There is no need to distinguish overhead in production areas from other indirect costs, as service inventories do not exist and the accounting standard for inventory valuation is not relevant.

Indirect responsibility centre costs

Some businesses refer to the indirect costs of responsibility centres, such as departments or divisions, as overhead costs. However, to avoid confusion, in this book *we describe these costs as 'indirect costs' rather than 'overhead costs'*.

Allocating indirect costs: some general principles

L.O. 2

Later in the chapter we describe a number of specific approaches to allocating indirect costs to products and responsibility centres. Let's begin, however, by considering some general principles for allocating costs.

Using cost pools

In Chapter 2 we introduced the concept of cost objects, and direct and indirect costs. You may remember that a **cost object** is an item that is assigned a separate measure of cost. For example, cost objects in an international chain of hotels might include hotels, hotel departments and specific guest services. To estimate their cost, the management accountant assigns costs to the cost objects. Cost assignment can take two forms: tracing or allocation. **Direct costs** can be *traced* directly to cost objects. **Indirect costs** cannot be traced to cost objects; instead they are *allocated*.

The management accountant often uses cost pools to simplify the allocation process. A **cost pool** is a collection of costs that are to be allocated to cost objects. In the example of an international hotel chain, all computing costs may be pooled together. Costs may be pooled if they have a common allocation base. The number of computer terminals, or the amount of computer processing time, may be used as an allocation base for computing costs in the hotel chain. The general process of allocating costs in a cost pool to cost objects is called **cost allocation**. The principles for estimating the cost of a cost object, and the role of cost allocation, are illustrated in Exhibit 7.2.

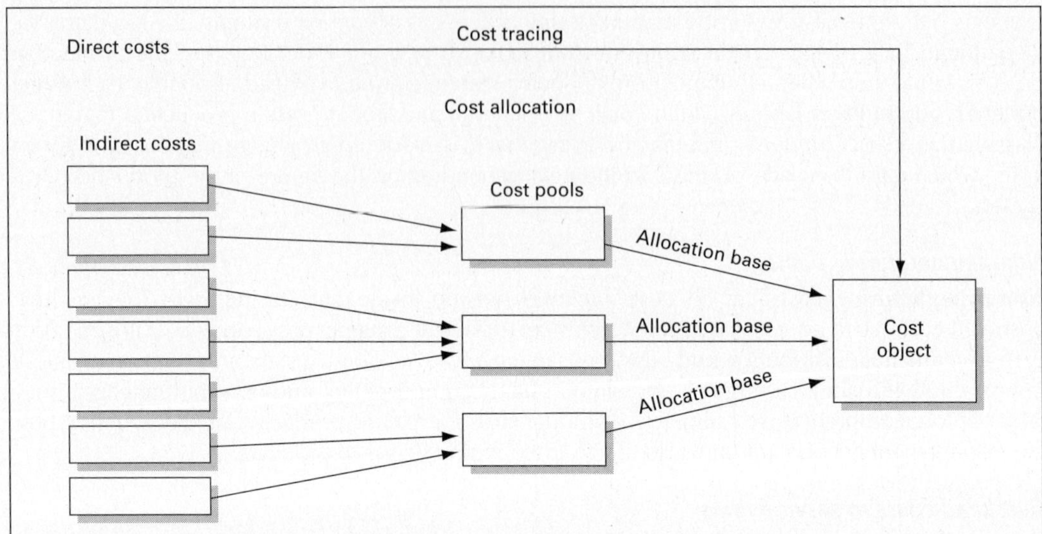

Exhibit 7.2 Estimating the cost of a cost object

Determining cost allocation bases

To allocate indirect costs to cost objects, the management accountant needs to choose a cost allocation base for each cost pool. A **cost allocation base** is some factor or variable that allows us to allocate costs in a cost pool to cost objects. Ideally, the allocation base should be selected on cause-and-effect grounds; that is, it should be a *cost driver.* A **cost driver** is an activity or factor that causes costs to be incurred. For example, in allocating overhead costs to products, machine hours may be an appropriate cost driver if overhead costs are largely machine-related and tend to increase proportionately with increases in machine time. And in allocating indirect costs to departments, the number of square metres of floor space occupied by each department may be an appropriate allocation basis for an occupancy cost pool, which includes the costs of rent, cleaning and electricity. The number of square metres is used as the allocation base, although the causal relationship is imperfect. It is assumed that the greater the floor space occupied by a department, the more rent,

Costs (or cost pools)	Allocation base (or cost driver)
Allocations to products	
Manufacturing overhead	Units of output
	Input measures, for example direct labour hours, machine hours, direct material cost
Allocations to responsibility centres	
Administration costs	Number of employees in centre
Occupancy costs	Floor area of centre
Marketing costs	Sales revenue generated by the centre
Information technology costs	Number of computer terminals in the centre
	Computer processing time in the centre
Human resources costs	Number of employees in the centre
Material-handling costs	Number of kilograms of material used in the centre

Exhibit 7.3 Allocation bases for indirect costs

cleaning and electricity resources are used. Ideally costs should increase or decrease in direct proportion to the allocation base (or cost driver); if this is not possible, at least there should be a reasonably strong correlation between the costs and the allocation base chosen. Exhibit 7.3

describes some common cause-and-effect allocation bases or cost drivers used for allocating indirect costs to products and responsibility centres.

Allocating overhead costs to products

Reliable product costs are important to a range of decisions, such as which products to produce and what prices to charge, as well as for valuing inventory. Direct costs are easily traced to products, but including indirect costs that are in some way related to the product can provide a more complete picture of product cost. The real issue is how to allocate indirect (overhead) costs to obtain a reliable estimate of a product's cost.

Let's examine some specific approaches for allocating overhead costs to products. Remember, overhead consists of a heterogeneous pool of indirect costs. We want to include them in product costs but they cannot be traced directly. We can use three different approaches to solve this problem:

1 a plantwide overhead rate;

2 departmental overhead rates; or

3 activity-based costing.

We will use Delta Controls Ltd to illustrate these three approaches.

Delta Controls Ltd manufactures two types of sophisticated control valves used in the food-processing industry. Valve A has been Delta's main product for 15 years. It is used to control the flow of milk in various food-processing operations, such as the production of biscuits. Valve B, introduced more recently, is a more complex, specialty valve used to control the flow of thicker foods such as pastes and sauces. Production takes place in the Machining Department, where the major components are produced using a series of cutting, stamping and grinding machines, and in the Assembly Department, where the valves are assembled from the components and packed. In addition there are three other departments that support the manufacturing process: Equipment Maintenance, Material Handling and Quality Control. The basic cost and production data for Delta Controls are given in Exhibit 7.4.

Allocating overheads using a plantwide rate

L.O. 3

Delta Controls Ltd wants to know the costs of producing the two valves. The actual prime (or direct) costs of Valves A and B are R199 and R216 per unit respectively, but what is their manufacturing overhead cost? One way of allocating the manufacturing overhead costs to the products is to use a plantwide overhead rate. This involves three steps:

1 *Identifying the overhead cost driver* – that is, a factor or activity that causes overhead costs to be incurred. Selection of cost drivers is discussed on pages 306–7. At this stage we will assume that direct labour hours is the appropriate cost driver at Delta Controls.

2 *Calculating an overhead rate per unit of cost driver.* This is usually a predetermined (or budgeted) rate, determined on a yearly basis. For a **plantwide overhead rate** we combine all manufacturing overhead costs into a single cost pool and relate it to the amount of cost driver for the entire production plant. The total budgeted overhead at Delta Controls is R945 000, and it is expected that 105 000 direct labour hours will be worked in the coming year. Therefore the plantwide manufacturing overhead rate will be:

$$\text{Predetermined manufacturing overhead rate} = \frac{\text{budgeted manufacturing overhead}}{\text{budgeted level of cost driver}}$$

$$= \frac{\text{R945 000}}{\text{105 000 direct labour hours}}$$

$$= \text{R9 per direct labour hour}$$

	Valve A	Valve B	
Actual prime costs per unit			
Direct material	R140	R150	
Direct labour:*			
Machining Department	29	36	
Assembly Department	30	30	
Total prime costs per unit	R199	R216	
Budgeted production data			**Total**
Annual production	30 000 units	5000 units	
Machine time in Machining Department	30 000 MH	15 000 MH	45 000 MH
Direct labour hours in:			
Machining Department	43 500 DLH	9000 DLH	52 500 DLH
Assembly Department	45 000 DLH	7500 DLH	52 500 DLH
Total direct labour hours	88 500 DLH	16 500 DLH	105 000 DLH
Budgeted manufacturing overhead costs†			
Machining Department			R630 000
Assembly Department			315 000
Total budgeted overhead			R945 000

* Valve A required 1.45 direct labour hours in the Machining Department and 1.5 direct labour hours in the Assembly Department. Valve B required 1.8 direct labour hours in the Machining Department and 1.5 direct labour hours in the Assembly Department. Direct labour cost R20 per hour.

† Department overhead costs include allocated support department costs.

Exhibit 7.4 Cost and production data, Delta Controls Ltd

3 *Applying manufacturing overhead costs to products,* based on the predetermined overhead rate and the product's consumption of the cost driver. Valve A required 2.95 direct labour hours (1.45 hours in the Machining Department and 1.5 hours in the Assembly Department).

Valve B required 3.3 direct labour hours (1.8 hours in the Machining Department and 1.5 hours in the Assembly Department). Thus the manufacturing overhead allocated to valves A and B is:

$$\text{Applied overhead} = \begin{array}{c}\text{predetermined}\\ \text{overhead rate}\end{array} \times \begin{array}{c}\text{quantity of cost driver}\\ \text{consumed by the product}\end{array}$$

$$\text{Overhead applied to Valve A} = \text{R9} \times 2.95 \text{ direct labour hours}$$
$$= \text{R26.55}$$
$$\text{Overhead applied to Valve B} = \text{R9} \times 3.3 \text{ direct labour hours}$$
$$= \text{R29.70}$$

Notice that in allocating overhead costs to products we use the term 'applying' rather than 'allocating' costs. You may recognise this approach to applying overhead costs to products. It was described in Chapter 3 and was used to apply overhead costs to products in the Williams Elevators case.

While the focus of Tongaat Sugar was to achieve a reduction in overheads (see 'Real life' below), other companies will take actions to increase their overhead costs if this is required to grow revenues. For example, CashBuild reported the following in 2005:

> Some of these adjustments during the past year include extended trading hours (seven days a week) and free local deliveries. The latter initiative has meant a considerable increase in overheads, but has undoubtedly led to an increase in volumes particularly cement and bricks.

REAL LIFE: REDUCING FIXED OVERHEADS AT TONGAAT HULETT SUGAR

The sugar industry experienced a significant improvement in profitability levels in 2005 and 2006. This was due to increased production and higher world prices. The growing use of sugar cane for ethanol production was also a factor. Tongaat has sugar plantations and mills in Southern Africa. However, 2003 and 2004 were very tough years and the industry outlook for sugar then was poor due to the effects of droughts and a very weak international sugar price. Tongaat Sugar focused on reducing overheads in difficult times. The group had high overhead costs due to low capacity utilisation and a costly head office structure. The company undertook the following actions to reduce its fixed overheads:

- Sugar head office closure and downsizing of the head office function
- Downsizing of centralised services
- Elimination of Maputo office costs
- Sale of buildings, including London office
- South African milling operations reorganised from five mill structures into two regional business units
- Operating and service functions rationalised
- New refining technology installed to achieve cost savings.

The company has the capacity to produce 1.5 million tons of sugar, compared to the 1.228 million tons produced in 2006. Higher sugar production will result in higher capacity utilisation and lower fixed costs per unit.

If high overheads are caused by unutilised capacity, this does also mean that the company may increase production quickly in reaction to increases in demand without incurring high capital expenditure costs and without losing market share. The cement industry in South Africa was facing a different situation in 2007. Cement production capacity was fully utilised and companies started importing cement, often at a loss, to meet demand while they increased local production capacity by spending billions of rands on new kilns and mining facilities.

Allocating overheads using departmental rates

L.O. 4

The plantwide overhead rate for Delta Controls assumes that direct labour hours worked are the sole cause (that is, driver) of manufacturing overhead costs. However, the causes of manufacturing overhead costs may vary from one production department to another. For example, in the Assembly Department, where the production process is labour-intensive, direct labour may be the cost driver. On the other hand, in the Machining Department, where the production process is machine-intensive, machine hours may be the cost driver. Delta Controls can improve the accuracy of its product costs by using **departmental overhead rates**, which are based on the estimated overhead cost divided by the level of cost driver for each department.

Two-stage cost allocation for departmental overhead rates

Exhibit 7.5 illustrates the **two-stage cost allocation process** used to allocate overhead costs to products via departments. Note the two stages:

- Stage one, where overhead costs are assigned to production departments; and
- Stage two, where overhead costs are applied to the products.[3]

This two-stage process of cost allocation is examined below.

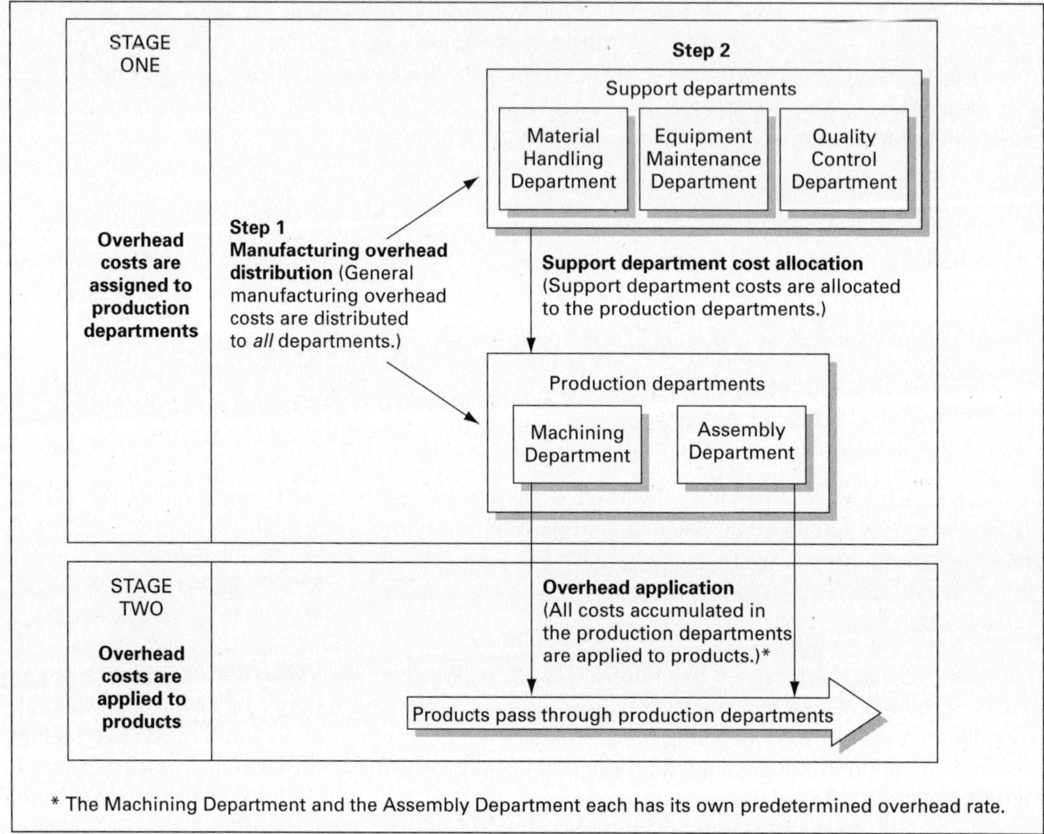

Exhibit 7.5 Developing departmental overhead rates using two-stage allocation

Stage one

In the first stage, all manufacturing overhead costs are assigned to the firm's production departments. This often involves two steps:

1 First, all manufacturing overhead costs are distributed to departments. This step is called **cost distribution**. Cost distribution may involve both tracing and allocating costs. Remember, manufacturing overhead costs are indirect product costs, but some of them may be the direct costs of departments. For example, the costs related to machinery, such as depreciation, are part of manufacturing overhead but they can be traced directly to the departments in which the machines are housed. In the cost distribution step, manufacturing overhead costs are assigned to both production and support departments. **Production departments**, such as the Machining and Assembly departments at Delta Controls, work directly on the product. In contrast, support (or service) departments do not work directly on the firm's products but are necessary for production to take place. For example, at Delta Controls there are three support departments: Material Handling,

Equipment Maintenance and Quality Control. All the costs of support departments are classified as manufacturing overhead because they relate to the manufacturing function but cannot be traced directly to products.

2 Second, all support department costs are reassigned to the production departments. This step is called **support department cost allocation**. Support department costs must be reassigned to production departments because, in Stage two, overhead is applied to products using overhead rates for each production department. Support department cost allocation is described in more detail on pages 311–20.

At the end of Stage one, all manufacturing overhead costs have been assigned to production departments. The overhead costs for Delta Controls' production departments, Machining and Assembly, shown in Exhibit 7.4, include allocated support department costs. We examine this allocation process later.

Stage two

In the second stage, manufacturing overhead rates are calculated for each production department. Note that each department has its own cost driver. For example, Delta Controls has selected machine hours as the cost driver for its Machining Department and direct labour hours for its Assembly Department. The departmental overhead rates are:

$$\text{Predetermined manufacturing overhead rate, Machining Department} = \frac{\text{budgeted manufacturing overhead Machining Department}}{\text{budgeted level of cost driver in Machining Department}}$$

$$= \frac{\text{R630 000}}{\text{45 000 machine hours}}$$

$$= \text{R14 per machine hour}$$

$$\text{Predetermined manufacturing overhead rate, Assembly Department} = \frac{\text{budgeted manufacturing overhead Assembly Department}}{\text{budgeted level of cost driver in Assembly Department}}$$

$$= \frac{\text{R315 000}}{\text{52 500 direct labour hours}}$$

$$= \text{R6 per direct labour hour}$$

The manufacturing overhead costs accumulated in each production department are then applied to the products using these rates and the products' consumption of cost drivers in each production department. This approach applies manufacturing overhead costs of R23 per unit to Valve A and R51 per unit to Valve B, as shown in Exhibit 7.6. Valve A, which spent considerably less time in the more overhead-expensive Machining Department than did Valve B, is now assigned a lower overhead cost than it was when a plantwide overhead rate was used. In contrast, Valve B's assigned overhead cost has increased.

Applied overhead per unit:	**Valve A**		**Valve B**	
Machining Department	1 machine hour* × R14	= R14	3 machine hours* × R14	= R42
Assembly Department	1.5 direct labour hours† × R6	= R9	1.5 direct labour hours† × R6	= R9
Total overhead applied		**R23**		**R51**

*Based on actual machine time.
†As shown in Exhibit 7.4.

Exhibit 7.6 Applying overhead costs using departmental rates, Delta Controls

Allocating overheads using activity-based costing

L.O. 5 Manufacturing overhead costs comprise a large array of cost items that, in reality, are likely to have a range of different cost drivers. One recently developed solution to this problem is to use an **activity-based costing (ABC) system** to allocate overhead costs to products. As described in Chapter 8, there are a number of approaches to activity-based product costing. Exhibit 7.7 describes an ABC system for allocating manufacturing overhead costs to products. You will observe that it uses a two-stage allocation process similar to that used for departmental overhead rates. In Stage one, overhead costs are assigned to cost pools representing overhead activities rather than departments. **Activities** describe the work done in the business. In Stage two, activity costs are assigned from each activity to products using an overhead rate based on the cost per unit of activity driver. An **activity driver** is a cost driver used to estimate the cost of an activity consumed by the cost object.

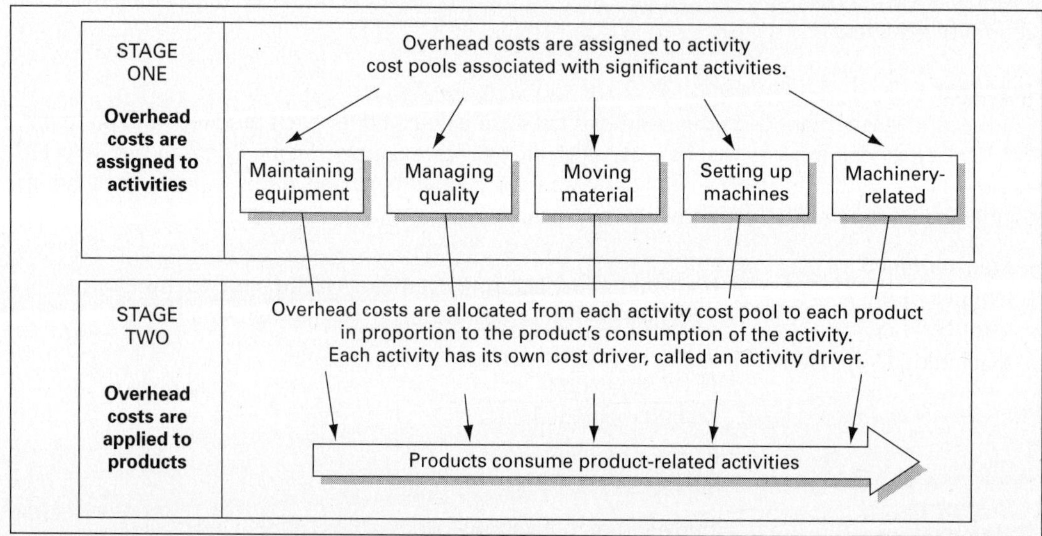

Exhibit 7.7 Activity-based costing for assigning overhead costs to products

Assume that Delta's accountants have established activity cost pools and activity drivers in Stage one of the ABC method, as shown in panel A of Exhibit 7.8.[4] These can be used to calculate the **cost per unit of activity driver** for each activity, which is the total cost of an activity divided by the quantity of its activity driver, and is sometimes called the *cost pool rate*. In Stage two of the ABC method, the amount of each activity driver consumed by each product is estimated. The overhead cost of each product is estimated based on the quantities of activity drivers consumed by each product multiplied by the costs per unit of activity driver, as shown in panel B of Exhibit 7.8. The ABC system assigns overhead costs of R504 000 (or R16.80 per unit) to Valve A and R441 000 (or R88.20 per unit) to Valve B. Valve A, a high-volume and relatively simple product, is considerably less expensive to produce than is Valve B, a low-volume and relatively complex product.

Activity-based costing compared with the two-stage cost allocation process

Under the conventional two-stage cost allocation process used to calculate departmental rates, the allocation bases used are ideally determined by causal relationships. However, in the second stage the number of allocation bases (cost drivers) is limited to one per department, and all cost drivers are measures of production volume. This means that the system does not recognise the wide range of cost drivers and cost behaviours related to various overhead cost items.

Activity-based costing is also based on a two-stage cost allocation process, but rather than focusing on the costs of departments, the emphasis is on the cost of activities. Activity-based costing improves the accuracy of product costs because of:

- the identification of a large number of activity cost pools; and

- the selection of an appropriate cost driver for each activity, called an 'activity driver'. As discussed below, activity drivers may be related to production volume or some other factor.

(A) Cost per unit of activity driver

Activity	Activity cost	Quantity of activity driver	Cost per unit of activity driver
Setting up machines	R6000	120 setups	R50 per setup
Maintaining equipment	210 000	7000 engineering hours	R30 per engineering hour
Moving material	22 000	220 000 kg of material	R0.10 per kg
Managing quality	32 000	800 inspections	R40 per inspection
Machinery-related costs	675 000	45 000 machine hours (MH)	R15 per machine hour (MH)
Total	R945 000		

(B) Activity-based costs of valves

Activity (cost per unit of activity driver)	Valve A	Quantity of activity driver	Valve B	Quantity of activity driver
Setting up machines (R50 per setup)	R1 000	(20 setups)	R5 000	(100 setups)
Maintaining equipment (R30 per hour)	30 000	(1000 hours)	180 000	(6000 hours)
Moving material (R0.10 per kg)	17 000	(170 000 kg)	5 000	(50 000 kg)
Managing quality (R40 per inspection)	6 000	(150 inspections)	26 000	(650 inspections)
Machinery-related (R15 per MH)	450 000	(30 000 MH)	225 000	(15 000 MH)
Total overhead applied	R504 000*		R441 000*	
Units produced	30 000		5 000	
Applied overhead per unit	R16.80		R88.20	

* Total applied overhead = R504 000 + R441 000 = R945 000

Exhibit 7.8 Activity-based costing at Delta Controls Ltd

Evaluating the alternatives for allocating overheads

L.O. 6

As you can see in Exhibit 7.9, by recognising a range of activities and identifying how each product uses those overhead resources, activity-based costing yields the most accurate product cost for each valve. Notice that both the plantwide and departmental overhead costing systems *significantly overcost* the high-volume and relatively simple Valve A, and *undercost* the low-volume, more complex Valve B. This is a common problem with conventional approaches to product costing and is discussed further in Chapter 8.

	Valve A		Valve B	
	Cost per unit	Product cost*	Cost per unit	Product cost*
Direct material per unit	R140		R150	
Direct labour per unit	59		66	
Manufacturing overhead per unit:				
Plantwide rate	R26.55	R225.55	R29.70	R245.70
Departmental rates	23.00	222.00	51.00	267.00
Activity-based costing rate	16.80	215.80	88.20	304.50

* Product cost = Direct material + Direct labour + Manufacturing overhead

Exhibit 7.9 Product costing using three methods of overhead allocation

The theme of costs versus benefits arises with respect to using a plantwide overhead rate, departmental overhead rates or activity-based costing. A product costing system using multiple cost drivers and overhead rates is more complicated and more costly to use than a product costing system with a single plantwide rate. However, the product costing information that results is more accurate and more useful for decision-making. Weighing these costs and benefits is part of the management accountant's job in designing a product costing system.

More and more businesses are moving towards using an increased range of cost drivers to improve the accuracy of their product costing systems. ABC systems are coming into greater use as managers see the strategic importance of having more accurate product cost information to help them create shareholder value more effectively.

L.O. 7

Issues in estimating overhead rates

In allocating overhead costs to products, whether using plantwide, departmental or activity rates, the management accountant needs to decide what allocation bases or cost drivers to use, whether to use budgeted or actual data, and over what period overhead rates should be set. In setting plantwide and departmental rates, it is also necessary to decide whether to use separate rates for fixed and variable overhead costs. Let's consider each of these issues.

Identifying overhead cost drivers

Identifying appropriate cost drivers is the key to allocating overhead costs to products accurately. You may recall that we described the general principles for identifying cost drivers in Chapter 3, when we analysed cost behaviour at the Tasty Bread Company. To find an overhead cost driver, the management accountant needs to ask three questions:

1 What is the major factor that causes manufacturing overhead costs to be incurred for this plant, department or activity?

2 To what extent does the overhead cost vary in proportion with this cost driver?

3 How easy is it to measure this cost driver?

Manufacturing overhead includes a variety of indirect manufacturing costs that vary greatly in their relationship to the production process. In practice, it is difficult to identify one factor that is the sole or predominant cause of manufacturing overhead costs, particularly at the plant or department level. However, there should be a strong correlation between the incurrence of overhead costs and the use of the cost driver, even if the driver chosen is not the sole cause of most of the costs.

Volume-based cost drivers

Conventional costing systems assume that overhead costs vary proportionally with production volume and use only volume-based cost drivers. **Volume-based cost drivers** are a measure of, or proxy for, the volume of production. Some common volume-based cost drivers include:

1 *Output (that is, the number of units produced).* If a business produces only one product, the number of units produced is the simplest measure of production volume. However, if the business produces more than one product, different products are likely to consume different amounts of overhead resources and output should not be used as the cost driver.

2 *Inputs.* To overcome the problem of heterogeneous outputs, management accountants use inputs, which are homogeneous, as measures of production volume. Examples include:

(a) *Direct labour hours or direct labour costs.* Many businesses choose direct labour hours worked or direct labour costs as a manufacturing overhead cost driver. This assumes that as direct labour hours are worked they cause overhead costs to be incurred. In some cases this will be true. (For example, in a custom-made furniture factory, the more labour time spent on sawing, sanding and assembling furniture, the higher the costs of electricity, saw blades, sandpaper, glue and cleaning rags.)

(b) *Machine hours.* As businesses increase their level of automation, their use of direct labour decreases. Under these circumstances, management accountants may choose machine hours as the overhead cost driver. In doing so, they are assuming that the more machine hours worked, the higher the level of overhead costs. Sometimes this will be true; for example, a greater number of machine hours is likely to imply more maintenance costs and more machine-related consumables such as oil, grease and cleaning compounds.

(c) *Direct material quantities or costs.* Some businesses require large amounts of material handling; where this is the major source of overhead costs, it may make sense to use some measure of material – either costs or quantities – as the overhead cost driver.

Selecting a cost driver that is common to all products

If a single volume-based cost driver is used, it should be an input that is common to all of the firm's products. If, for example, all products require direct labour but only some products require machine time, then direct labour hours would be a preferable cost driver. If machine hours were used, products not requiring machine time would not be allocated any overhead cost!

Problems with cost drivers measured in rands

Cost drivers that are measured in rands, such as direct labour cost or material cost, are appealing because they are already recorded in the accounting system. However, they should be avoided as they are subject to price level changes and tend to fluctuate more than physical measures.

Non-volume-based cost drivers

Management accountants know that some manufacturing overhead costs vary with production volume (that is, they are variable), and some do not (they are fixed). Yet, in using volume-based cost drivers to allocate overhead costs to products, they treat fixed overhead as though it is variable (that is, volume-driven). In many businesses overhead has become a major cost, and a large part of it is not volume-driven but is caused by factors such as product diversity and production complexity. Major distortions to product costs occur in these circumstances.

Activity-based costing, which uses both volume-based and non-volume-based cost drivers, evolved in response to this problem. As described in Chapter 3, the activity-based hierarchy of costs and cost drivers has four distinct levels: unit, batch, product and facility. Unit level costs have volume-based cost drivers, but batch, product and facility level costs are not driven by production volume. For batch and product level costs it is possible to identify **non-volume-based cost drivers**, which are cost drivers that are not directly related to production volume. Facility level costs have no identifiable cost driver. These issues are discussed in more detail in Chapter 8.

Distinguishing between fixed and variable overhead

Some businesses find it useful to distinguish between fixed overhead costs, which do not change as production volume changes, and variable overhead costs, which vary with production volume. The identification of the fixed and variable elements helps managers to understand the behaviour of overhead costs, supports product-related decisions and is useful for planning and control. Two approaches to product costing make this distinction: dual overhead rates and variable costing.

Dual overhead rates

This approach involves calculating separate rates for fixed and variable overhead costs. However, we need to identify a cost driver for fixed overhead costs, to estimate the fixed overhead rate. These costs have no cost driver, as they have been classified as fixed! As long as volume-based cost drivers are used to allocate both fixed and variable overhead costs to products, calculating dual overhead rates will not improve the accuracy of the product costs. Indeed if a common cost driver is used, such as direct labour hours, the dual overhead rates will make no difference to the final estimate of product costs. (This issue is not a concern for activity-based costing, which identifies 'fixed costs' as facility level costs or seeks out non-volume-based cost drivers for costs that do not vary directly with production volume.)

Variable costing

Under a variable costing system the variable costs – that is, direct material, direct labour and variable manufacturing overhead costs – are included in product cost. Fixed manufacturing costs are expensed in the period in which they are incurred. With its focus on cost behaviour, variable costing is particularly useful for short-term decision making and for planning and control. However, variable product costs do not comply with International Financial Reporting Standards and, therefore, cannot be used for inventory valuation in external financial reports. Variable costing is discussed in more detail in the appendix to this chapter.

Budgeted or actual overhead data?

Generally, budgeted overhead costs and amounts of cost driver are used to calculate overhead rates. The accountant uses *budgeted costs* (that is, planned costs) so that the overhead rate can be determined *prior to the commencement of the current year*. If actual overhead costs were used, the overhead rate could not be calculated until after the end of the year, and managers would not be able to estimate what each product cost was until the year had finished! For product costing information to be useful, it must be provided to managers on a timely basis.

A product costing system could use an **actual overhead rate** (based on the actual manufacturing overhead cost and the actual amount of cost driver for the year) instead of a *predetermined overhead rate*. The result would be more accurate because *actual* costs would be applied to products, rather than an *estimate*; however, the product costing information would be untimely.[5] A trade-off exists between accuracy and timeliness. Management accountants must weigh the costs and benefits of these choices. When designing product costing systems, accountants generally recommend predetermined overhead rates.

Actual costing versus normal costing

When direct material and direct labour are added to work-in-process inventory at their actual amounts, but *overhead is applied to work-in-process inventory using a predetermined overhead rate*, then the product costing system is called **normal costing**. This approach takes its name from the use of an overhead rate that is normalised over a fairly long time period. A few companies use an **actual costing** system, in which direct material and direct labour are added to work in process at their actual amounts, and *overhead is applied to work in process using an actual overhead rate* calculated at the end of each accounting period. Note that although an actual overhead rate is used, the overhead assigned to each product is still an allocated amount. Overhead costs, which are by definition indirect costs, cannot be traced to individual products. The key difference between actual and normal costing is explained as follows:

- In an *actual costing system*, manufacturing overhead is applied to work-in-process inventory based on the actual overhead rate (calculated at the end of the period) × the actual amount of cost driver used during the period.
- In a *normal costing system*, manufacturing overhead is applied to work in process inventory based on the predetermined overhead rate × the actual amount of cost driver used during the period.

Over what period should overhead rates be set?

Generally, yearly overhead rates are used. Monthly rates are likely to change from one month to the next due to fluctuations in the level of overhead costs or in the amount of cost driver. For example, seasonal factors can cause monthly overhead costs to differ; electricity for air-conditioning the factory may be used only in the summer months. Fluctuations in the amount of cost driver may be caused by variations in the number of workdays in a month, as well as by seasonal factors. Monthly overhead rates would cause the cost of a given product to vary from one month to the next, which could give misleading signals for product pricing and other decisions about products.

By using relatively long periods to calculate the overhead rate, management accountants smooth out the fluctuations in the overhead rate. An overhead rate calculated in this fashion is called a **normalised overhead rate**. Most businesses choose a period of one year, as this corresponds with their annual budgeting process, although, as discussed below, some businesses set their overhead rates over their normal business cycle, which may extend over two or more years.

Estimating the amount of cost driver: the effects of capacity

L.O. 8

In estimating overhead rates, the management accountant needs to estimate the quantity of cost driver, called the **denominator volume**. As discussed above, budgeted rather than actual data are usually used. However, the denominator volume can be based on expected use or expected supply.

Based on expected use of cost driver

The simplest approach to estimating overhead rates, which is used by many businesses, is to estimate the budgeted volume of cost driver for the coming year, often referred to as the **budget** (or **master budget**) **volume**. A longer-term measure is based on **normal volume**, which is the volume of production that will satisfy average customer demand over the normal business cycle (which may span several years, taking account of seasonal, cyclical and trend factors). The normal volume can differ from the budget volume when a business experiences peaks and troughs in demand for its products, and these peaks and troughs extend beyond the budget period.

Based on expected supply of cost driver

An alternative approach to estimating the denominator volume is to estimate the amount of cost driver available, based on production capacity. Two different measures may be used: theoretical capacity or practical capacity. **Theoretical capacity** is the maximum level of production that can be achieved in a specified period, assuming that the plant runs at peak efficiency all day, every day, without ever stopping. **Practical capacity** is the plant's theoretical capacity adjusted for normal downtime, including holidays, maintenance and the normal level of machine breakdowns and idle time. It assumes that the business operates at the maximum level that its resources allow under normal, efficient operating conditions.

The measure of denominator volume will affect the overhead rate and, therefore, product cost. Using capacity measures as denominator volumes results in lower overhead rates and product costs. High levels of excess capacity will be reflected in high levels of underapplied overhead. Normal volume or budget volume will be lower than practical capacity and will result in higher overhead rates and product costs, and less underapplied overhead. For external reporting purposes, international accounting standards require a denominator volume based on the company's 'normal operating capacity', after considering practical capacity, budgeted activity for the ensuing year, and current and past levels of activity. This seems to coincide most closely with normal volume. Although mandatory only for external reporting purposes, this requirement may have some influence over the selection of denominator volumes for internal purposes.

The issue of cost driver volumes and the implications of capacity for activity-based costing are considered further in Chapter 8.

Allocating indirect costs to responsibility centres

L.O. 9

Let's now consider the allocation of indirect costs to responsibility centres. In large businesses there may be several levels of cost allocation:

- *At the corporate level.* Some head office costs are allocated to business units (operating subsidiaries or divisions).
- *Within business units.* Administrative costs of business units may be allocated to operating units.
- *In the manufacturing plant.* Indirect manufacturing costs may be allocated to the production departments.

Reasons for allocating indirect costs to responsibility centres

There are three main reasons for allocating indirect costs to responsibility centres:

1. *To help managers understand the economic effects of their decisions.* Allocating costs to responsibility centres helps the managers of the responsibility centres to be more aware of the effect of their actions on the organisation's costs. For example, allocating some of a hotel's electricity costs to its Recreational Department will assist the manager of that department to be more conscious of the economic effects of his or her actions. The amount of electricity charged to the Recreational Department will increase if the manager raises the temperature in the heated swimming pools, or makes greater use of the floodlights on the tennis courts.
2. *To encourage a particular pattern of resource usage.* Organisations may allocate costs to encourage desired behaviour. For example, some head offices allocate part of their interest costs to individual responsibility centres, based on the centres' usage of scarce funds. This encourages managers to manage their spending more effectively. On the other hand, some costs may not be allocated in order to encourage a greater use of a service. For example, if corporate management want to encourage their divisions to seek advice from the new cost management team, they may not charge divisions for using the service during the first year.
3. *To support the product costing system.* Some product costing systems assign overhead costs using departmental overhead rates. Before these rates can be calculated, it is necessary to allocate indirect costs to production departments. This process involves support department cost allocation, which is described later in this chapter.

Principles for allocating indirect costs to responsibility centres

The general principles for allocating indirect costs to cost objects, described earlier, apply here. Direct costs can be traced to responsibility centres, but indirect costs must be allocated using cost pools and appropriate allocation bases. Ideally, the allocation bases will be cost drivers, where there is a clear and direct relationship between the amount of cost driver and the level of cost.

Where cost drivers cannot be determined, some organisations use other criteria. Costs may be allocated to departments according to the benefits received. It may be felt, for example, that a company-wide advertising campaign provides more benefit to the retail departments of a company than to the administrative departments, and so the retail departments are allocated a greater share of the cost of the campaign.

Cost allocation may also be guided by the centre's ability to bear the additional costs. For example, corporate managers' salaries may be allocated to operating divisions based on the relative sizes of the divisions' sales or profits. The division with the largest profits would receive the largest share of the senior managers' salaries as it is more able to absorb those costs than is a division with low profits.

Using allocation bases that are not cost drivers needs to be handled with extreme caution. If the purpose of the cost allocation is to obtain a reliable estimate of product costs or to help managers understand the economic effects of decisions, then cost drivers should be used as allocation bases.

If the purpose is to encourage a particular pattern of resource usage, then other allocation bases may be appropriate. The World Vision 'Real life' below provides an example of the role of cost drivers in allocating costs.

Using budgeted, not actual, allocation data

In allocating indirect costs to responsibility centres, it is better to use budgeted amounts of the relevant allocation bases and budgeted costs for two main reasons:

1 to minimise the possibility that the activities of one department will affect the costs allocated to other departments; and

2 to provide better information for managers to plan and control their use of indirect resources.

Minimising the effects of one department on the performance of another

Using actual amounts of *allocation base* or actual *costs* can cause the activities of one department to impact on the results of other departments. This may cause problems because the costs may be used to evaluate the performance of the department or its manager, and managers should not be held accountable for costs over which they have no control.

If *actual amounts of allocation base* are used to allocate costs, the use of the allocation base by one department will affect the costs allocated to other departments. Consider the example of allocating the costs of a computer department in a bank to the departments that use its services, using the actual amount of computer processing time as the allocation base. Assume that during the year, the Tellers' Department reduced its use of processing time, while there were no changes in the other departments. The costs allocated to the Tellers' Department would decrease but the fixed costs of the Computer Department would not change. Each of the other departments would be allocated a larger share of fixed costs even though their usage of computer processing had not changed and even though their managers had no control over these costs. This problem is best addressed by allocating fixed costs separately from variable costs, using longer-term estimates of allocation bases.

If *actual amounts of cost* are allocated from a department, the efficiencies or inefficiencies of that department will affect the results of other departments. For example, if allocations were based on actual costs and the actual cost of the Computer Department rose above the budgeted amount, then the amount allocated to each user department would increase. These increased costs are not controllable by the managers of the user departments. Also, if budgeted rates are used there is an incentive for the Computer Department to manage its costs carefully, because if its costs exceed budget it does not have the flexibility to charge those cost increases to user departments.

Providing better information for planning

Knowing the budgeted rates in advance allows the user departments to plan their activities with greater certainty. For example, if the managers of the user departments in the bank know that the Computer Department costs are to be allocated at a budgeted rate per minute of processing time, then they can manage allocated computer costs by carefully controlling their use of computer time.

Allocating support department costs

L.O. 10

A common situation where the management accountant allocates indirect costs to responsibility centres is the allocation of support department costs to user departments. This process informs user department managers of the costs of the services provided by the support departments, which helps them to plan and control their use of services. The same process can be used to allocate support department costs to production departments to calculate departmental overhead rates for product costing.

REAL LIFE: DIRECT AND INDIRECT COSTS AT WORLD VISION

World Vision is a not-for-profit organisation that seeks donations to fund humanitarian aid throughout the developing world. According to the Group Executive, fundraising organisations should apply certain principles in accounting for donated monies. These include the following:

- All donations are spent in accordance with the message given to donors.
- If donors restrict how their donations are to be used, that they are used only in accordance with the specified purposes.
- Only reasonable deductions (for expenses) are made from those donations for administration.

To comply with these principles, World Vision must closely monitor the costs of its programs. Its costing system uses three separate categories of costs: direct costs, indirect costs and overhead or corporate costs. The direct costs are the costs that can be traced directly to individual programs, such as the wages of field staff working on particular projects. The indirect costs are the joint costs of fundraising, such as the costs of advertising sponsorship programs. The corporate costs are the other costs incurred by World Vision, such as the costs of information technology (IT) functions performed by head office staff. These costs are allocated to individual programs based on estimates of the use of corporate resources. Accounting staff try to identify cost drivers for corporate costs to provide 'a rational and objective method for cost allocation'. For example, they allocate IT costs on the basis of staff time, CPU usage, pages printed, transactions input and disk space used for storage.

World Vision understands that 'accurate costings are necessary if organisations are to have integrity with their members, donors and service recipients'. The appropriate selection of cost pools and cost drivers provides the foundation for obtaining these costings.

Source: Alley (1996)

Support department costs and services at Delta Controls

We will continue with the example of Delta Controls Ltd to illustrate support department cost allocation. At this stage you may find it useful to return to Exhibit 7.5, which illustrates the two-stage process used to allocate overhead costs to products via departmental rates. Stage one involves two steps: first, overhead costs are distributed to all departments, and then the support department costs are allocated to production departments. At the end of Stage one, we obtain estimates of the overhead cost for each production department. In Stage two, overhead costs are applied to products using the departmental overhead rates. In calculating departmental overhead rates at Delta Controls, we said that the budgeted overhead costs of R630 000 for Machining and R315 000 for Assembly, shown in Exhibit 7.4, included an allocation of the costs of the company's three support departments: Material Handling, Equipment Maintenance and Quality Control. Let's now consider how these support department costs were allocated to the production departments.

Provision of services by the support departments

Exhibit 7.10 (below) describes the relationships between the three support departments and two production departments at Delta Controls Ltd. Notice that the Quality Control Department and the Material Handling Department provide services to each other. When this situation occurs, we say the two support departments provide **reciprocal services**. Exhibit 7.11 gives specific details about the provision of services to each user department.

Equipment Maintenance

The services of the Equipment Maintenance Department are consumed only by the Machining and Assembly departments. Annual maintenance hours is the allocation base used to estimate that 30

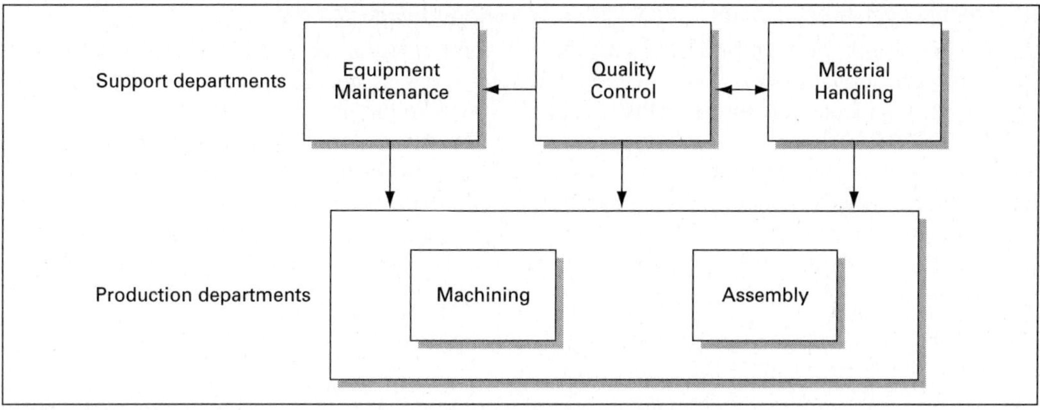

Exhibit 7.10 Support departments and production departments, Delta Controls Ltd

	User departments				
	Support departments			Production departments	
Service provider (allocation base)	**Equipment Maintenance**	**Quality Control**	**Material Handling**	**Machining**	**Assembly**
Equipment Maintenance (annual maintenance hours)	–	–	–	30%	70%
Quality Control (number of employees)	5%	–	20%	25%	50%
Material Handling (size of department, m²)	–	5%	–	35%	60%

Exhibit 7.11 Provision of services by support departments, Delta Controls Ltd

per cent of the Equipment Maintenance Department's services are consumed by Machining and 70 per cent by Assembly.

Quality Control

Delta Controls has a total quality management program that encompasses the entire organisation. The overall program is managed by the Quality Control Department, which serves each of the company's other departments, including the other two support departments and also the two production departments. The allocation base used to determine the proportions of the Quality Control Department's services consumed by the four user departments is the number of employees in those departments. For example, 5 per cent of the plant's employees (excluding those in the Quality Control Department) work in the Equipment Maintenance Department. The number of employees in the department is considered an appropriate allocation base, since the larger the number of employees, the greater the resources required to set up and maintain quality management projects in that department.

Material Handling

This support department provides services only to the Quality Control, Machining and Assembly departments. (The service to the Quality Control Department consists mainly of moving defective products to special testing and rework stations within the Quality Control Department.) *Departmental size,* measured in square metres, is the allocation base used to determine the proportion of material-handling services consumed by each user department, as each department has its own store and most of the material handling involves movement within departments. For example, 5 per cent of the plant's floor space (excluding that occupied by Equipment Maintenance, which is not served by Material Handling, and Material Handling itself) is devoted to the Quality Control Department.

Manufacturing overhead costs in production and support departments

Exhibit 7.12 shows the total budgeted cost of each support department, which is to be allocated among the user departments, and budgeted overhead costs for the two production departments. (These costs have been distributed to the five departments in the first step of Stage one, illustrated in Exhibit 7.5.) To estimate the total budgeted overhead costs of the two production departments, we need to allocate the support department costs to these production departments (shown as Step two for Stage one in Exhibit 7.5). (Remember that support department costs are manufacturing overhead costs, as they cannot be traced directly to final products.) There are three methods of support department cost allocation: the direct method, the step-down method and the reciprocal method.

Support departments:	
Equipment Maintenance	R100 000
Quality Control	60 000
Material Handling	190 000
	R350 000
Production departments:	
Machining	R510 000
Assembly	85 000
	R595 000
Total overhead costs	**R945 000**

Exhibit 7.12 Budgeted department costs, Delta Controls Ltd

The direct method for allocating support department costs

Under the **direct method**, each support department's costs are allocated among the production departments that consume part of the support department's output. This method ignores the fact that some support departments provide services to other support departments. Thus, although Delta Controls' Quality Control Department provides services to the two other support departments, none of its costs is allocated to those departments. Exhibit 7.13 presents Delta Controls' support department cost allocations under the direct method.

	Support departments			**Production departments**	
	Quality Control	**Material Handling**	**Equipment Maintenance**	**Machining**	**Assembly**
Costs distributed*	R60 000	R190 000	R100 000	R510 000	R85 000
Allocation of Quality Control Department costs	(R60 000)	→	→	20 000 (25/75)	40 000 (50/75)
Allocation of Material Handling Department costs		(R190 000)	→	70 000 (35/95)	120 000 (60/95)
Allocation of Equipment Maintenance Department costs			(R100 000) →	30 000 (3/10)	70 000 (7/10)
Total allocated costs				R120 000	R230 000
Total budgeted overhead cost of production departments				R630 000	R315 000

* Cost distribution is Step one of Stage one of the two-stage cost allocation process (see Exhibit 7.5).

Exhibit 7.13 Direct method of support department cost allocation, Delta Controls Ltd

Notice that the proportion of each support department's costs allocated to each production department is determined by the *relative proportion* of the support department's output consumed by *each production department*. For example, a glance at Exhibit 7.11 shows that the Quality Control Department provides 25 per cent of its services to Machining and 50 per cent to Assembly. Summing these two percentages yields 75 per cent: 25/75 is the fraction of Quality Control's cost allocated to Machining, and 50/75 is the fraction allocated to Assembly.

Overhead costs allocated to products under the direct method

The total budgeted overhead cost of the production departments, R630 000 for Machining and R315 000 for Assembly, is determined by adding the allocated support department costs to the overhead costs distributed to production departments. (You will notice that these two estimates match the budgeted overhead costs for the Machining and Assembly departments shown in Exhibit 7.4.) This completes Stage one of the two-stage process for allocating overhead costs to products, described in Exhibit 7.5. As described earlier in the chapter, in Stage two the total budgeted overhead costs for the two production departments are used to estimate departmental overhead rates of R14 per machine hour for the Machining Department and R6 per direct labour hour for the Assembly Department. Overhead applied to Delta Controls' two products, Valve A and Valve B, based on the departmental overhead rates multiplied by the products' consumption of overhead cost driver in each department, is estimated to be R23 and R51 respectively (see Exhibit 7.6).

The step-down method for allocating support department costs

Delta Controls chose the direct method because it is simple. However, the direct method ignores the provision of services by one support department to another support department. This shortcoming could be partially overcome by using the **step-down method**, where first we choose a sequence in which to allocate the support departments' costs. Usually, the support department that serves the largest number of other support departments is allocated first. The support departments are ordered in this manner, with the last support department being the one that serves the smallest number of other support departments.[6] Then we allocate each support department's costs among the production departments and all the other support departments that follow it in the sequence. Note that the total costs eventually allocated to each production department will differ depending on the sequence chosen.

The step-down method is best explained by extending our Delta Controls illustration. Delta Controls' Quality Control Department serves two other support departments: Equipment Maintenance and Material Handling. The Material Handling Department serves only one other support department: Quality Control. Finally, the Equipment Maintenance Department serves no other support departments. Thus, Delta Controls' sequence of allocation of support departments' costs is Quality Control, then Material Handling and finally Equipment Maintenance.

Following this sequence, each support department's costs are allocated to the other departments, as shown in Exhibit 7.14.

Cost allocated from this support department ⟶	To these departments
Quality Control	Material Handling Equipment Maintenance Machining Assembly
Material Handling	Machining Assembly
Equipment Maintenance	Machining Assembly

Exhibit 7.14 Allocation sequence: step-down method

Under the step-down method, we cannot recognise the full set of support relationships that exists. For example, we cannot recognise that the Material Handling Department provides services to the Quality Control Department, because the costs of the Quality Control Department were allocated first.

Exhibit 7.15 presents the results of applying the step-down method at Delta Controls. First, the Quality Control Department's R60 000 cost is allocated among the four departments using its services. Second, the cost of the Material Handling Department is allocated. The total cost to be allocated is the department's original R190 000 plus the R12 000 allocated from the Quality Control

Department. The new total of R202 000 is allocated to the Machining and Assembly departments according to the relative proportions in which these two departments use the services of the Material Handling Department. Finally, the Equipment Maintenance Department's cost is allocated. If you look carefully at Exhibit 7.15 you will understand why this is called the step-down method: when the departments are listed in their chosen sequence, the costs allocated to the support departments 'step down' the page.

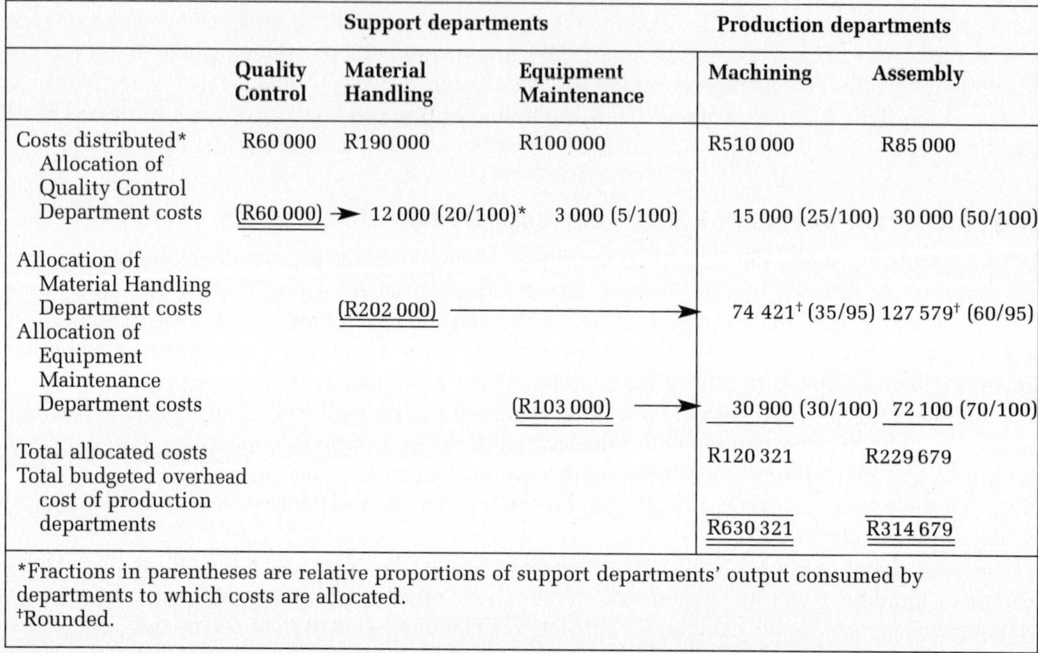

	Support departments			**Production departments**	
	Quality Control	**Material Handling**	**Equipment Maintenance**	**Machining**	**Assembly**
Costs distributed*	R60 000	R190 000	R100 000	R510 000	R85 000
Allocation of Quality Control Department costs	(R60 000) →	12 000 (20/100)*	3 000 (5/100)	15 000 (25/100)	30 000 (50/100)
Allocation of Material Handling Department costs		(R202 000) →		74 421† (35/95)	127 579† (60/95)
Allocation of Equipment Maintenance Department costs			(R103 000) →	30 900 (30/100)	72 100 (70/100)
Total allocated costs				R120 321	R229 679
Total budgeted overhead cost of production departments				R630 321	R314 679

*Fractions in parentheses are relative proportions of support departments' output consumed by departments to which costs are allocated.
†Rounded.

Exhibit 7.15 Step-down method of support department cost allocation, Delta Controls Ltd

Overhead costs allocated to products under the step-down method

Under the step-down method, the total budgeted overhead cost for the Machining and Assembly departments is R630 321 and R314 679 respectively. This would result in overhead rates of R14.0071 per machine hour for the Machining Department (R630 321 ÷ 45 000 machine hours) and R5.9939 per direct labour hour for the Assembly Department (R314 679 ÷ 52 500 direct labour hours). These rates are very similar to the rates obtained using the direct method (R14 and R6 respectively), and have virtually no impact on the estimated overhead cost of Valves A and B. Delta Controls' decision to use the simpler direct method makes sense in this case.

The reciprocal services method for allocating support department costs

Under the reciprocal services method, we account fully for the provision of services between support departments. We can recognise that the Material Handling Department and the Quality Control Department serve each other and thus have more accurate support department cost allocation.

The relationships between Delta Controls' three support departments are shown in Exhibit 7.16.

The first step in the technique is to specify a set of equations that express the relationships

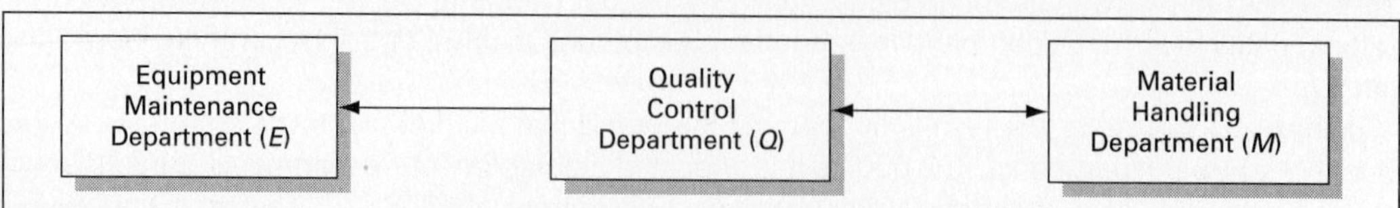

Exhibit 7.16 Allocating support department costs using the reciprocal method, Delta Controls Ltd

between the departments. The following equations, which express these relationships for Delta Controls, are based on the information in Exhibits 7.11 and 7.12.

$$E = R100\,000 + 0.05Q \quad \textbf{(1)}$$
$$Q = R60\,000 + 0.05M \quad \textbf{(2)}$$
$$M = R190\,000 + 0.20Q \quad \textbf{(3)}$$

where E = the total cost of the Equipment Maintenance Department
Q = the total cost of the Quality Control Department
M = the total cost of the Material Handling Department

Equation (1) indicates that the *total cost* of operating the Equipment Maintenance Department (E) is R100 000 plus 5 per cent of the total cost of operating the Quality Control Department (Q). The R100 000 comes from Exhibit 7.12 and is the total cost traceable to the Equipment Maintenance Department. We add to this amount 5 per cent of the total cost of operating the Quality Control Department. Why? Because Exhibit 7.11 tells us that the Equipment Maintenance Department uses 5 per cent of the Quality Control Department's services. Similar explanations underlie equations (2) and (3).

The second step in the reciprocal services method is to solve the simultaneous equations. Let's begin by substituting the expression for M from equation (3) into equation (2), and solving for Q as follows:

$$Q = R60\,000 + 0.05\ (R190\,000 + 0.20Q)$$
$$Q = R60\,000 + R9500 + 0.01Q$$
$$0.99Q = R69\,500$$
$$Q = R70\,202 \text{ (rounded)}$$

Then we substitute the value for Q just obtained into equation (3), and solve for M as follows:

$$M = R190\,000 + 0.20Q$$
$$M = R190\,000 + (0.20 \times R70\,202)$$
$$M = R204\,040 \text{ (rounded)}$$

Now we can solve for E by substituting the value for Q into equation (1) as follows:

$$E = R100\,000 + 0.05Q$$
$$E = R100\,000 + (0.05 \times R70\,202)$$
$$E = R103\,510 \text{ (rounded)}$$

Thus, we have determined that Q = R70 202, M = R204 040 and E = R103 510.

The final step in the reciprocal services method is to allocate the total cost of operating each support department (E, Q and M) to the various departments that use its services. For example, we will allocate the total cost of operating the Quality Control Department (Q) among all four of Delta Controls' other departments because they all use Quality Control's services. This allocation is made in proportion to the use of Quality Control's services by the other departments, as given in Exhibit 7.11. The allocations are shown in Exhibit 7.17. Focus on the second row of numbers, which refers to the Quality Control Department. The R70 202 shown in parentheses in the Quality Control column is that department's total cost, as calculated using the simultaneous equations. This R70 202 total cost is allocated as follows:

- 20 per cent (or R14 040) to Material Handling, because that department uses 20 per cent of Quality Control's services;
- 5 per cent (or R3510) to Equipment Maintenance, because that department uses 5 per cent of Quality Control's services;
- 25 per cent (or R17 551) to Machining, because that department uses 25 per cent of Quality Control's services;

- 50 per cent (or R35 101) to Assembly, because that department uses 50 per cent of Quality Control's services.

	Support departments			Production departments	
	Quality Control	Material Handling	Equipment Maintenance	Machining	Assembly
Costs distributed	R60 000	R190 000	R100 000	R510 000	R85 000
Allocation of Quality Control Department costs	(R70 202) →	14 040* (0.20)	3 510*(0.05)	17 551* (0.25)	35 101 (0.50)
Allocation of Material Handling Department costs	10 202 (0.05)[†] ←	(R204 040) →	–	71 414 (0.35)	122 424 (0.60)
Allocation of Equipment Maintenance Department costs	–	–	(R103 510) →	31 053 (0.30)	72 457 (0.70)
Total allocated costs				R120 018	R229 982
Total budgeted overhead cost of production departments				R630 018	R314 982

*Rounded.

[†]Percentages in parentheses are relative proportions of the support departments' output consumed by departments to which costs are allocated (from Exhibit 7.11).

Exhibit 7.17 Reciprocal services method of support department cost allocation, Delta Controls Ltd

A similar explanation underlies the Material Handling row and the Equipment Maintenance row in Exhibit 7.17. The total support department costs allocated to Delta Controls' two production departments are as follows: R120 018 to Machining and R229 982 to Assembly. Notice that these two amounts add up to R350 000, which is the total of the original traceable costs for the three support departments. Thus, all support department costs have been fully allocated.

Overhead costs allocated to products under the reciprocal method

Under the reciprocal method, the total budgeted overhead cost for the Machining and Assembly departments is R630 018 and R314 982 respectively. This would result in overhead rates of R14.0004 per machine hour for the Machining Department (R630 018 ÷ 45 000 machine hours) and R5.9996 per direct labour hour for the Assembly Department (R314 982 ÷ 52 500). These rates are very similar to the rates obtained using the direct method and have virtually no impact on the estimated overhead cost of valves A and B. The reciprocal services method is more accurate than the direct and step-down methods because it accounts fully for reciprocal services. However, if you compare the allocations under the reciprocal method to the direct and step-down allocations in the chapter, you will notice that the difference is not large. At Delta Controls, the decision to use the direct method, which is simple and results in only minor inaccuracies, makes sense.

Which support department cost allocation method is the best?

You will note that, in the Delta Controls case, the direct, step-down and reciprocal methods of support department cost allocation gave slightly different total overhead costs and overhead rates for each production department. This was due to the different recognition that each method gives to support relationships. The direct method does not recognise any relationships that exist between support departments, while the step-down method gives only partial recognition to these relationships. The reciprocal method recognises *all* support relationships. Does this imply that the reciprocal method is the best and the direct method is the worst? Not necessarily. *The choice of method is simply one of costs versus benefits.* At Delta Controls the more complex methods made little difference to costs eventually allocated. In other situations, where there are stronger reciprocal relationships between support departments, the benefits are likely to be greater.

The choice of allocation bases is also a cost versus benefits decision. In the Delta Controls example, the cost allocations were made using various allocation bases, including departmental size, number of employees and number of maintenance hours. However, these allocation bases are not accurate cost drivers – there are no strong causal relationships between the costs being allocated and the chosen allocation bases. For example, the cost of running the Material Handling Department is unlikely to decrease in direct proportion to decreases in the size (area in square metres) of the various user departments. While we may prefer the allocation bases to be *cost drivers*, these do not always exist. However, if cost drivers are not used, the potential for arbitrary and inaccurate cost allocations increases.

While we can take care in selecting cost drivers, many would argue that the conventional cost allocation methods described in this chapter are of little value because of the arbitrary nature of the allocation bases and methods that are often used. It is for these reasons that activity-based costing systems have developed.

Other issues in allocating support department costs

A number of the general principles for allocating indirect costs to departments, described earlier in the chapter, are relevant to allocating support department costs to production departments. For example, budgeted rather than actual costs should be allocated, planned levels of allocation bases or cost drivers should be used, and it is better to use a dual allocation approach where fixed and variable costs are allocated separately.

Allocating support department costs in a service organisation

Delta Controls is a manufacturing business, and the aim of the illustration was to allocate its support department costs to its production departments, so that departmental overhead rates could be estimated in order to allocate the company's manufacturing overhead costs to its two products, Valves A and B. In manufacturing businesses, only manufacturing costs are included as part of the costs of products for valuing inventory for external reporting. This means that only the costs of manufacturing support departments should be allocated to production departments. The International accounting standard, IAS 2 *Inventories*, does not allow upstream and downstream costs to be allocated to products. In a service business, however, inventories are not produced and we do not need to distinguish between production and non-production areas when determining the costs of service outputs.

Cost allocation in modern manufacturing environments

Changes in manufacturing technology may cause changes in cost allocation practices. For example, the extent of allocations is diminished in some advanced manufacturing systems because more costs are directly traceable to product lines and products. In a flexible manufacturing system (FMS), most operations on individual products are performed within one defined work area, called an FMS cell. Even machine maintenance is done largely by the FMS cell operators rather than by a separate maintenance department. Inspection is often performed by FMS cell operators, thereby eliminating the need for a separate inspection department. In this environment more costs become directly traceable to both responsibility centres and products, so the need for allocation of indirect costs declines.

On the other hand, in the modern manufacturing environment we often find that manufacturing overhead accounts for an increasing proportion of total manufacturing costs. The greater investment in machinery results in high depreciation, machine maintenance and other machine-related costs, and a decrease in the amount of direct labour that is used. Thus, there are more costs that are not directly traceable to products. In this situation it becomes critical for overheads to be allocated accurately.

Summary

As we have discussed in earlier chapters, managers need to know the costs of goods and services to help them make decisions that will enhance the organisation's wealth. They also need to know the costs of responsibility centres, such as departments, to help them manage resources in their work areas. Some costs can be traced directly to products or responsibility centres, but others are indirect and must be allocated. In this chapter we described some general principles for allocating indirect costs to both products and responsibility centres. Key points include:

- Most businesses use the term 'overhead costs' to describe a range of indirect costs. However, there is some confusion in practice as to whether the term applies to indirect product costs or the indirect costs of responsibility centres, such as departments and business units. In this chapter we use the term 'indirect costs' to describe costs that cannot be traced to cost objects, either products or responsibility centres. In addition, we use the term 'manufacturing overhead' to describe indirect product costs; and 'non-manufacturing costs' to describe upstream and downstream costs.
- Indirect costs can be allocated to cost objects by assigning costs to cost pools and using allocation bases to allocate cost pools to cost objects. Ideally, an allocation base should be a cost driver – that is, it should cause the costs in the cost pool to be incurred.
- Three approaches to allocating manufacturing overhead costs to products are to use a plantwide overhead rate, departmental overhead rates or activity-based costing.
  - Under the plantwide approach, a single overhead rate is calculated for the entire production area.
  - Under the departmental approach, a separate overhead rate is calculated for each production department.
  - Under activity-based costing, a separate rate is calculated for each major overhead activity.
- As the number of overhead rates increases, the accuracy of the product costing system is likely to increase, but the complexity and cost of the system are also likely to increase. In designing a product costing system, the management accountant must weigh up these costs and benefits.
- In setting overhead rates the management accountant also needs to:
  - Select appropriate overhead cost drivers by considering the causes of the overhead costs and the ease with which these cost drivers can be measured. In conventional product costing systems the cost drivers will be volume-based, but activity-based costing will also include non-volume-based cost drivers.
  - Decide whether to use dual overhead rates – that is, separate rates for variable and fixed overhead costs. Some businesses use a variable costing system, where product costs include direct material, direct labour and variable manufacturing overhead. Fixed manufacturing is expensed rather than inventoried. Variable costing is examined in more detail in the appendix to this chapter.
  - Decide whether to use actual or predetermined (that is, budgeted) overhead rates, and over what period overhead rates should be set. Budgeted annual rates result in more timely and stable product costs.

  - Decide what measure of production capacity to use in identifying the estimated level of cost driver (called the denominator volume) to set budgeted overhead rates. Options include the budget volume, the normal volume, practical capacity and theoretical capacity.
- Managers also need to know the costs of responsibility centres, such as divisions, plants and departments, to help them manage their resources. The general principles for allocating indirect costs, described above, can be used to estimate the indirect costs of responsibility centres.
- Businesses allocate support department costs to production departments to make them aware of the costs of the services provided by the support departments. Support department cost allocation also provides estimates of the manufacturing overhead costs of production departments for calculating departmental overhead rates for product costing. Three approaches to allocating support department costs are the direct, step-down and reciprocal methods.

You will notice that it can be very difficult to obtain reliable estimates of the indirect costs of products and responsibility centres. However, in many organisations indirect costs are increasing relative to direct costs, so understanding these costs is vital.

In Chapter 8 we will consider some of the problems that businesses may encounter when they use conventional product costing systems, based on plantwide or departmental overhead rates, and explore activity-based costing in more detail.

References

Alley, EB 1996, 'The role of the management accountant in a non-profit organisation', Australian Society of CPAs, National Management Accounting Conference, Sydney, May.

Tongaat Hulett Annual Report, 2005 and 2006.

Self study

Self-study problem 1: Allocating support department costs using the direct method

Boris Morris Laboratories tests soil samples for mining companies and various government departments. The firm has two production departments: the Mineral Analysis Department and the Hydrological Analysis Department. The firm also has two support departments: the Engineering Department and the Computing Services Department. The usage of these two support departments' output for the year was as follows:

	Provider of service	
User of service	**Engineering**	**Computing Services**
Engineering	–	20%
Computing Services	–	–
Mineral Analysis	60%	30%
Hydrological Analysis	40%	50%

The budgeted costs in the two support departments for the year were as follows:

Engineering	R600 000
Computing Services	240 000

The budgeted overhead costs, prior to the allocation of support department costs, and the amounts of cost driver in the two production departments for the year were as follows:

	Overhead costs	Cost driver
Mineral Analysis	R180 000	30 000 direct labour hours
Hydrological Analysis	300 000	60 000 machine hours

Required:

1 Use the direct method to allocate the budgeted costs of the Engineering Department and the Computing Services Department to the Mineral Analysis and the Hydrological Analysis departments.

2 Determine departmental overhead rates, and estimate the total overhead costs (after the allocation of the support department costs) of tests performed on two samples during May:

- Test number 132, which required 3 direct labour hours in the Mineral Analysis Department and 2 machine hours in the Hydrological Analysis Department.
- Test number 133, which required 4.5 direct labour hours in the Mineral Analysis Department and 7 machine hours in the Hydrological Analysis Department.

Solution to Self-study problem 1

1 Allocation of support department costs:

	Support departments		Production departments	
	Computing Services	Engineering	Mineral Analysis	Hydrological Analysis
Costs distributed	R240 000	R600 000	R180 000	R300 000
Allocation of Computing Services costs	(240 000)		90 000 (3/8)	150 000 (5/8)
Allocation of Engineering costs		(600 000)	360 000 (6/10)	240 000 (4/10)
Total cost allocated to each department			R450 000	R390 000
Total budgeted overhead costs			R630 000	R690 000

2 Estimation of the departmental overhead rates and costs of the two tests:

	Mineral Analysis Department	Hydrological Analysis Department
Predetermined overhead rates	R630 000 / 30 000 direct labour hours = R21 per direct labour hour	R690 000 / 60 000 machine hours = R11.50 per machine hour

	Overhead cost of:	
	Test no. 132	Test no. 133
Mineral Analysis	R63.00 (R21 × 3 hours)	R94.50 (R21 × 4.5 hours)
Hydrological Analysis	23.00 (R11.50 × 2 hours)	80.50 (R11.50 × 7 hours)
	R86.00	R175.00

Self-study problem 2: The step-down method for allocating support department costs

Refer to the data given in Self-study problem 1.

Required:

1 Use the step-down method to allocate the support departments' costs to the Mineral Analysis and Hydrological Analysis departments.

2 Estimate the total overhead costs (after the allocation of the support departments' costs) of test number 132 and test number 133.

Solution to Self-study problem 2

1 Allocation of the support departments' costs:

	Support departments		Production departments	
	Computing Services	Engineering	Mineral Analysis	Hydrological Analysis
Costs distributed	R240 000	R600 000	R180 000	R300 000
Allocation of Computing Services costs	(240 000)	48 000 (2/10)	72 000 (3/10)	120 000 (5/10)
Allocation of Engineering costs		(648 000)	388 800 (6/10)	259 200 (4/10)
Total cost allocated to each department			R460 800	R379 200
Total budgeted overhead costs			R640 800	R679 200

* Allocated first because Computing Services provides service to Engineering, but not vice versa.

2 Estimation of the departmental overhead rates and costs of the two tests:

	Mineral Analysis Department	**Hydrological Analysis Department**
Predetermined overhead rates	R640 800 / 30 000 direct labour hours = R21.36 per direct labour hour	R679 200 / 60 000 machine hours = R11.32 per machine hour
	Overhead cost of:	
	Test no. 132	**Test no. 133**
Mineral Analysis	R64.08 (R21.36 × 3 hours)	R96.12 (R21.36 × 4.5 hours)
Hydrological Analysis	22.64 (R11.32 × 2 hours)	79.24 (R11.32 × 7 hours)
	R86.72	R175.36

Cybersearch

1 Find websites that contain the term *overhead costs*.
   (a) Provide five examples of the types of overhead costs described.
   (b) Are the overheads that you have selected examples of indirect product costs? If so, identify the product to which they relate.
   (c) Or are the overheads indirect costs of responsibility centres? If so, identify the responsibility centre to which they relate.

2 Look for websites with the term *overhead charges*.
   (a) Can you find any examples of indirect costs that are allocated to responsibility centres?
   (b) Describe the purposes of allocating these indirect costs to responsibility centres. (*Hint*: Refer to the material in the chapter on 'reasons for allocating indirect costs to responsibility centres'.)
   (c) Can you find any examples of overhead costs that are applied to products or services?

3 Go to the website of an organisation that allocates its support department costs (*Hint*: Use the term *support department cost allocation*).
   (a) Describe the approach used for allocating these costs.
   (b) What is the reason for the cost allocation?

Appendix to Chapter 7

Variable costing and absorption costing

L.O. 11

In this chapter (and in Chapters 4 and 5), we assumed that all manufacturing overhead is applied to products, regardless of whether it is fixed or variable. This approach is known as **absorption costing**, as it includes (or absorbs) fixed manufacturing overhead as a part of product cost. An alternative approach, **variable costing**, excludes fixed manufacturing overhead from product cost. Both these product costing systems assign direct material, direct labour and variable manufacturing overhead costs to products in exactly the same way, using the manufacturing accounts described in earlier chapters, but they differ in their treatment of fixed manufacturing overhead. This means that, for the one accounting period, the two costing systems report different product costs and, in many cases, different profits.

In most situations, the international accounting standard, IAS2 *Inventories*, requires inventory to be valued at absorption cost for external reporting. Therefore, the main reason for preparing *variable product costs* is for internal management reports.

Fixed manufacturing overhead: the key

The distinction between variable and absorption costing is summarised in Exhibit 7.18. Notice that the distinction involves the timing with which fixed manufacturing overhead becomes an expense. Eventually, fixed overhead is expensed under both product costing systems. Under variable costing, however, fixed overhead is expensed immediately, as it is incurred. Under absorption costing, fixed overhead is inventoried until the manufactured goods are sold.

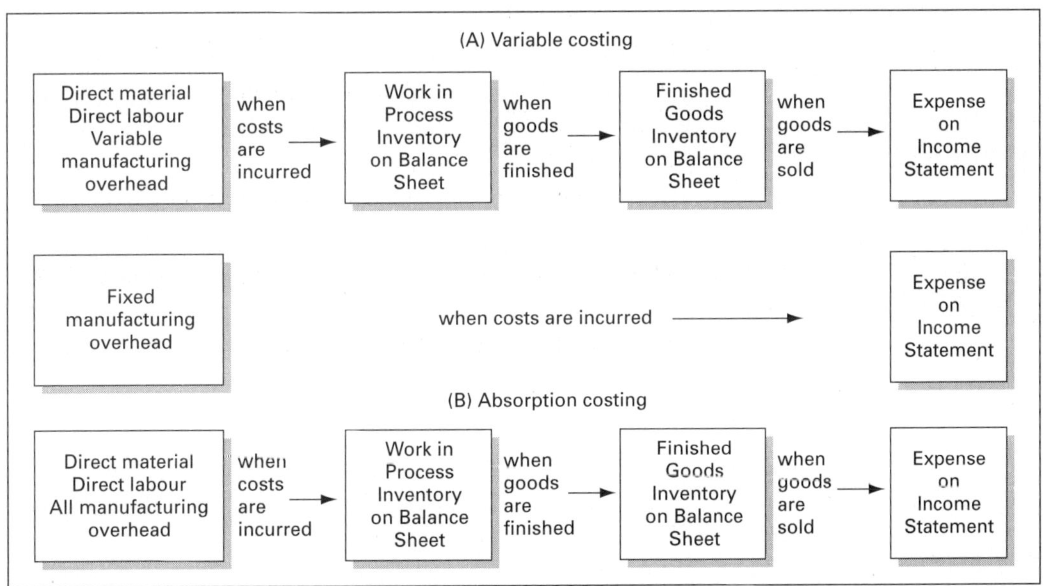

Exhibit 7.18 Variable costing versus absorption costing

Product costs under variable and absorption costing

We will use Luxury Furniture Company to illustrate the differences between variable and absorption costing, focusing on one of the company's major products, a three-cushioned leather lounge.

Variable product cost

Product costs calculated using a variable costing system include:

- direct material;
- direct labour; and
- variable manufacturing overhead costs.

Exhibit 7.19 shows that the variable cost of the leather lounge is R1450.

	Variable product cost	Absorption product cost
Direct material	R810	R810
Direct labour	480	480
Variable manufacturing overhead*	160	160
Variable product cost	R1 450	
Fixed manufacturing overhead†		240
Absorption product cost		R1 690

*The company uses a predetermined variable overhead rate of 33⅓% of direct labour cost.

†The predetermined fixed overhead rate is based on the following:

$$\text{Predetermined fixed overhead} = \frac{\text{budgeted annual fixed overhead}}{\text{budgeted direct labour cost}}$$

$$= \frac{\text{R2 880 000}}{\text{R5 760 000}}$$

$$= 50\% \text{ of direct labour cost}$$

Exhibit 7.19 Cost of the leather lounge

In previous chapters we have treated manufacturing overhead as a single cost classification, but when variable costing is used it is necessary to distinguish between variable and fixed manufacturing overhead. **Variable manufacturing overhead costs** are indirect manufacturing costs that vary in proportion to the level of production (or volume of overhead cost driver). Examples include indirect materials, some indirect labour, utilities costs such as electricity and water, and telephone costs. **Fixed manufacturing overhead costs** are also indirect manufacturing costs but they do not vary with the level of production. These costs include items such as factory managers' salaries, factory rent, council rates, depreciation on machinery, and insurance on the factory building and equipment.

Absorption product cost

How would the cost of the leather lounge have differed if the company had used absorption costing? Product costs calculated using an absorption costing system include:

- direct material;
- direct labour; and
- both variable and fixed manufacturing overhead costs.

Exhibit 7.19 shows that the absorption cost of the lounge is R1690. Comparing this cost with the variable product cost, you will note that the only difference is that the absorption cost includes fixed manufacturing overhead of R240, which is not included in the variable product cost.[7]

Calculating profit under variable and absorption costing

A product cost under variable costing will always be lower than its counterpart under absorption costing. But what does this mean for profit? The difference between variable and absorption costing profits depends on the relationship between the volume of sales and the volume of production. We can illustrate this by extending the Luxury Furniture Company example.

The company has a wide range of products but, to highlight the differences between variable and absorption costing, we will assume that the leather lounge is the company's only product. Exhibit 7.20 sets out sales and production data for April, May and June. (We will assume that, in each month, budgeted manufacturing overhead is equal to the applied manufacturing overhead so that the distraction of underapplied or overapplied overhead is avoided.)

	April	May	June
A. Production and inventory data (in units)			
Planned production	1 000	1 000	1 000
Beginning inventory, finished goods	0	0	100
Actual production	1 000	1 000	1 000
Sales	1 000	900	1 100
Ending inventory, finished goods	0	100	0
B. Additional cost data (in R)			
Actual fixed manufacturing overhead	R240 000	R240 000	R240 000
Actual selling and administrative expenses:			
Fixed	R100 000	R100 000	R100 000
Variable (per unit)	R200	R200	R200
C. Sales price (per unit)	R3 000	R3 000	R3 000

Exhibit 7.20 Luxury Furniture Company: production, sales and additional cost data

Profit under variable costing

The profit for April, May and June under variable costing is shown in panel A of Exhibit 7.21. Notice that the format of this statement is different from the income statement with which we are familiar. Businesses that use variable costing prepare a profit report called a **contribution margin** (or **contribution** or **variable costing**) statement that separates fixed and variable costs, and calculates a contribution margin. Notice that the **total contribution margin** is equal to sales revenue less the **variable cost of goods sold** and the variable selling and administrative expenses. The fixed expenses deducted below the contribution margin include both fixed manufacturing overhead and fixed selling and administrative expenses. (Contribution margin statements are discussed further in Chapters 12 and 18.)

These differences are highlighted in Exhibit 7.21. Notice first that the manufacturing expenses subtracted from sales revenue each month include only the variable costs, which amount to R1450 per unit. Second, fixed manufacturing overhead is subtracted as a lump sum period expense at the bottom of each month's contribution margin statement.

Profit under absorption costing

Now examine the profit under absorption costing in panel B of Exhibit 7.21. You will be familiar with this format as it is the one that has been used so far in this book.

How do absorption costing profit reports differ from the variable costing contribution margin statements? First, notice that the cost of goods sold expense for each month is determined by multiplying the month's sales by the absorption manufacturing cost per unit, R1690, which includes the predetermined fixed manufacturing overhead cost of R240 per unit. Second, note that the only period expenses are the selling and administrative expenses. Unlike the variable costing contribution statement, there is no deduction of fixed manufacturing overhead costs as a lump sum period

Panel A: Profit under variable costing (R'000)			
	April	**May**	**June**
Sales revenue (@ R3000 per unit)	R3 000	R2 700	R3 300
Less Variable expenses:			
Variable cost of goods sold (@ R1450 per unit):			
Beginning inventory	0	0	145
Add Current production costs	1 450	1 450	1 450
	1 450	1 450	1 595
Less Ending inventory	0	145	0
Variable cost of goods sold	1 450	1 305	1 595
Variable selling and administration expenses	200	180	220
Total variable expenses	1 650	1 485	1 815
Contribution margin	R1 350	R1 215	R1 485
Less Fixed expenses:			
Fixed manufacturing overhead	240	240	240
Fixed selling and administrative expenses	100	100	100
Operating profit	R 1 010	R875	R1 145
Panel B: Profit under absorption costing (R'000)			
	April	**May**	**June**
Sales revenue	R3 000	R2 700	R3 300
Less Cost of goods sold (@ R1690 per unit):			
Beginning inventory	0	0	169
Add Current production costs	1 690	1 690	1 690
	1 690	1 690	1 859
Less Ending inventory	0	169	0
Cost of goods sold	1 690	1 521	1 859
Gross margin	R1 310	R1 179	R1 441
Less Selling and administrative expenses:			
Variable	200	180	220
Fixed	100	100	100
Operating profit	R1 010	R899	R1 121

Exhibit 7.21 Luxury Furniture Company's profit under variable costing and absorption costing

expense in the lower part of the absorption costing statement, as fixed manufacturing overhead costs are included in cost of goods sold.

Reconciling profit under variable and absorption costing

Examination of Exhibit 7.21 reveals that the profits reported under absorption and variable costing are sometimes different. Let's work out why these differences occur.

No change in inventory

In April there is no change in inventory over the course of the month, because actual production and sales are the same. Think about the implications of the stable inventory level for the treatment of fixed manufacturing overhead. Under variable costing, the R240 000 of fixed manufacturing overhead incurred during April is an expense in April. Under absorption costing, however, fixed manufacturing overhead is applied to production at the predetermined rate of R240 per unit. Since all the 1000 units produced in April were sold in April, all the fixed manufacturing overhead cost flowed through into cost of goods sold. Thus, R240 000 of fixed manufacturing overhead was expensed in April, also under absorption costing.

The April column of Exhibit 7.22 reconciles the April profit reported under variable and absorption costing. The reconciliation focuses on the two places in the profit statements where differences occur between variable and absorption costing. These differences correspond to the differences highlighted by the shaded areas in Exhibit 7.21.

Increase in inventory

In May inventory increased from zero on 1 May to 100 units on 31 May because production exceeded sales. Under variable costing, the R240 000 of fixed overhead cost incurred in May is expensed, just as it was in April. Under absorption costing, however, only a portion of the fixed manufacturing overhead cost incurred in May is expensed in May. Since the fixed overhead is inventoried under absorption costing, some of this cost remains in inventory at the end of May.

The May column of Exhibit 7.22 reconciles the May profit reported under variable and absorption costing. As before, the reconciliation focuses on the two places in the profit statements where differences occur between absorption and variable costing.

	April	May	June
Cost of goods sold under absorption costing (R'000)	R1 690	R1 521	R1 859
Variable cost of goods sold	1 450	1 305	1 595
Difference in cost of goods sold*	R240	R216	R264
Fixed manufacturing overhead as a period expense under variable costing	240	240	240
Total differences between the two methods	R0	R(24)	R24
Profit under variable costing	R1 010	R875	R1 145
Profit under absorption costing	1 010	899	1 121
Difference between the two estimates of profit	R0	R(24)	R24

*This is due to the inclusion of fixed manufacturing overhead in absorption cost of goods sold but not in variable cost of goods sold.

Exhibit 7.22 Reconciling profit under variable and absorption costing, Luxury Furniture Company (in R'000)

Decrease in inventory

In June, inventory decreased from 100 units to zero, as sales exceeded production. As in April and May, under variable costing, the R240 000 of fixed manufacturing overhead incurred in June is expensed in June. Under absorption costing, however, more than R240 000 of fixed overhead is expensed in June. Why? Because some of the fixed overhead incurred during May, which was inventoried then, is now expensed in June as the goods are sold.

A short cut to reconciling profit

When inventory increases or decreases, reported profit differs under absorption and variable costing. This results from the fixed overhead that is inventoried under absorption costing but is expensed immediately under variable costing. The following formula may be used to calculate the difference in the amount of fixed overhead expensed in a given time period under the two product costing methods:

$$\text{Difference in fixed overhead expensed under absorption and variable costing} = \text{change in inventory (in units)} \times \text{predetermined fixed overhead rate per unit}$$

As the following table shows, this difference in the amount of fixed overhead expensed explains the difference in profit under absorption and variable costing.

Month	Change in inventory (in units)		Predetermined fixed overhead rate (per unit)		Difference in fixed overhead expensed		Absorption costing profit minus variable costing profit
April	0	×	R240	=	0	=	0
May	100 increase	×	R240	=	R24 000	=	R24 000
June	100 decrease	×	R240	=	(R24 000)	=	(R24 000)

Variable versus absorption costing

The international accounting standard, IAS 2 *Inventories*, requires that for external financial reporting, absorption costing is used to value inventory; but which approach is most useful for managers? As discussed in later chapters, variable costing provides information that is useful for planning costs and for a range of common tactical decisions that managers face. Moreover, absorption product costs include unitised fixed overhead, which can lead to erroneous decisions, especially in the short term, because fixed costs do not change in the short term. In addition, absorption costing can encourage managers to improve their profit performance by simply building up inventories: fixed overhead costs are carried forward as inventory rather than expensed during the current period.

However, in the longer term a business must cover its fixed costs too, and many managers prefer to use absorption costing data, particularly in cost-based pricing decisions. Also, in the modern business environment fixed costs are increasing and variable costs provide only a partial picture of product cost. Finally, it may be difficult to classify all costs as fixed or variable and absorption costing does fit in with external reporting requirements.

Questions

?

7.1 What are *manufacturing overhead costs*? Give three examples.

7.2 What are *cost objects, cost pools* and *allocation bases*? What role do they play in cost allocation? What is the difference between *cost allocation bases* and *cost drivers*?

7.3 In estimating the cost of a cost object, how are direct costs and indirect costs assigned to the cost object? Choose a cost object and give two examples of direct and indirect costs for that cost object.

7.4 Define the term *cost allocation base*. Can you think of a sensible allocation base for assigning advertising costs to the various attractions in a large theme park?

7.5 Describe the process of two-stage cost allocation in the development of departmental overhead rates, using the terms *overhead cost distribution, support department cost allocation* and *overhead application*.

7.6 Distinguish between a *support department* and a *production department*. Give an example of a production department in a bank and a support department in a restaurant chain.

7.7 Explain the difference between activity-based costing for manufacturing overhead and a conventional costing system that uses departmental overhead rates.

7.8 Describe some costs and benefits of using (a) departmental overhead rates and (b) activity based costing, for product costing.

7.9 What is meant by the term *cost driver*? What is a *volume-based cost driver*?

7.10 Describe the commonly used volume-based overhead cost drivers and explain when they are appropriate.

7.11 When a single, volume-based cost driver is used to apply manufacturing overhead, what is the management accountant's primary objective in selecting the cost driver?

7.12 What is a *non-volume-based cost driver*? What problems can arise in product costing systems that use only volume-based cost drivers?

7.13 Explain the difference between *actual costing* and *normal costing*. Describe the benefits of using a predetermined overhead rate instead of an actual overhead rate.

7.14 Describe an important cost benefit issue involving accuracy versus timeliness in accounting for overhead.

7.15 What do we mean by the *denominator volume*? Describe four possible denominator volumes and outline the likely effects of each one on product cost.

7.16 Why do management accountants allocate indirect costs to responsibility centres?

7.17 Should actual or budgeted support department costs be allocated? Why?

7.18 Explain the term *reciprocal services* and give examples of the reciprocal services offered by the various support departments within a university.

7.19 Explain briefly the main differences between the *direct, step-down* and *reciprocal services* methods of support department cost allocation.

7.20 How do we determine the sequence of allocation of support departments in the step-down method? How are 'ties' handled?

7.21 Explain how simultaneous equations can be used to allocate the costs of reciprocal services to support departments.

7.22 (appendix) What is the key difference between *variable* and *absorption* costing?

7.23 (appendix) What are the major differences between a *contribution margin statement* and an *absorption costing profit report*?

7.24 (appendix) When will profits reported under variable and absorption costing differ? How can we reconcile the profits reported under the two approaches?

7.25 (appendix) Would you recommend variable costing or absorption costing as a source of information for managers? Explain your answer.

Exercises

E7.26 Predetermined plantwide overhead rate: printing firm

The following annual data relate to Zelda Printing Pty Ltd:

Budgeted machine hours	10 000
Budgeted direct labour hours	20 000
Budgeted direct labour cost	R1 120 000
Budgeted manufacturing overhead	R2 912 000

During the month of May the firm worked on three products – business cards, wedding invitations and promotion flyers – using the following inputs:

	Business cards	Wedding invitations	Promotion flyers
Actual machine hours	600	300	200
Actual direct labour hours	800	600	400

Actual manufacturing overhead costs for May were R260 000 and the actual direct labour rate was R60 per hour.

Required:

Assume that the firm uses machine hours as its overhead cost driver:

1 Calculate the firm's predetermined plantwide overhead rate.
2 Estimate the overhead costs of each of the three products.
3 Compare the actual overhead cost to the amount of overhead applied to the three products in May.

E7.27 Predetermined plantwide overhead rate; alternative cost drivers (continuation of Exercise 7.26)

Repeat the requirements for Exercise 7.26, assuming that Zelda uses:

(a) direct labour hours (b) direct labour rands

as overhead cost drivers. In hindsight, which cost driver seems to be the most appropriate: machine hours, direct labour rands or direct labour hours? Explain your answer.

E7.28 Departmental overhead rates: manufacturer

Hawke's Leatherworks, which manufactures saddles and other leather goods, has three departments. The Assembly Department manufactures various leather products, such as belts, purses and saddlebags, using an automated production process. The Saddle Department produces handmade saddles and uses very little machinery. The Tanning Department produces leather. The tanning process requires little in the way of labour or machinery, but it does require space and process time. Due to the different production processes in the three departments, the company uses three different cost drivers for the application of manufacturing overhead. The cost drivers and overhead rates are as follows:

	Cost driver	Predetermined overhead rate
Tanning Department	Square metres of leather	R4 per square metre
Assembly Department	Machine time	R11 per machine hour
Saddle Department	Direct labour hours	R5 per direct labour hour

The company's deluxe saddle and accessory set consists of a handmade saddle, two saddlebags, a belt and a vest, all coordinated to match. The entire set uses 110 square metres of leather from the Tanning Department, 4 machine hours in the Assembly Department, and 45 direct labour hours in the Saddle Department.

Required:

Estimate the amount of overhead that will be applied to a deluxe saddle and accessory set.

E7.29 Cost drivers for different businesses

1 Imagine that you are the financial controller of a company that produces handmade glassware. Choose a cost driver that could be used to allocate manufacturing overhead to products. Explain your choice.
2 You have now changed jobs and you work for a microchip manufacturer that uses a highly automated production process. Choose a cost driver that could be used to allocate manufacturing overhead to products. Explain your choice.
3 Consider your two responses above and explain why they are different.

E7.30 Two-stage allocation process: hospital

Look at Exhibit 7.5, which outlines the steps used in the two-stage allocation process. Use your imagination to provide an example of each of these steps for a hospital. The final cost object is a patient-day of hospital care. This is one day of care for one patient.

In developing your answer, identify the various departments of a hospital by asking the following questions: Which departments deal directly with patients (that is, are 'production' departments)? Which departments are support departments and do not deal directly with patients? Which support department costs should be allocated to the 'production' departments, and hence to a patient-day of hospital care?

E7.31 Plantwide and departmental overhead rates: manufacturer

Modack Ltd produces two types of computer printers, a laser model and an inkjet model, which pass through two production departments, Fabrication and Assembly. The following data relate to 20x7:

	Fabrication	Assembly
Budgeted overhead	R1 800 000	R900 000
Expected activity (in direct labour hours)	15 000	60 000
Expected activity (in machine hours)	30 000	8 250

Actual overhead costs for the year were R3 million.

	Laser	Inkjet
Units produced	7500	75 000
Prime costs (material and labour)	R600 000	R4 500 000
Direct labour hours used:		
Fabrication	1000	14 000
Assembly	20 000	48 000
Machine hours used:		
Fabrication	10 000	20 000
Assembly	1 000	8 000

Required:

1 Calculate the predetermined overhead rate based on direct labour hours.
2 Calculate the per unit cost of the laser and inkjet printers, based on a plantwide overhead rate assuming that direct labour hours is the cost driver.
3 Calculate predetermined departmental overhead rates, assuming that machine hours is the cost driver in Fabrication and direct labour hours is the cost driver in Assembly.
4 Calculate the per unit cost of the laser and inkjet printers, based on the departmental overhead rates.
5 Estimate the amount of underapplied or overapplied overhead using:
(a) plantwide overhead rate (b) the departmental overhead rates
6 Which approach is best for Modack: a plantwide overhead rate or departmental overhead rates? Why?

E7.32 Cost drivers in activity-based costing: service firms

The activity-based costing examples in this chapter describe how to assign manufacturing overhead costs to activities and then to products. ABC systems can identify all activities, not just manufacturing overhead activities. Also, ABC is not confined to manufacturers: service firms can use it too.

For each of the following businesses, list five key activities that are likely to be important in the provision of the firm's service. (Remember, these activities do not have to be overhead activities.) For each activity, suggest an appropriate cost driver to use in assigning costs from the activity cost pool to the services provided.

1 A bank. 4 A hotel.
2 A hospital. 5 An airline.
3 A restaurant. 6 A fitness club.

E7.33 Normal costing; alternative denominator volumes: engineering firm

Thomas Pty Ltd is a defence engineering business. Contracts are costed using a normal job costing system, with a plantwide overhead rate based on practical capacity. I.M. Rite, the firm's accountant, has recommended a switch from practical capacity to the budgeted volume of cost driver for the coming year. Rite believes that the volume of production for the current year will be well below the practical capacity. He is worried that by the end of the year there will be a significant difference between actual and applied overhead.

The marketing manager, U.R. Slick, is strongly opposed to the proposed change in denominator volume. Most of the company's business is obtained by tendering for contracts on a cost-plus basis. Tenders are based on the estimated cost for the job plus a 40 per cent mark-up.

The normal business cycle for Thomas Pty Ltd tends to fluctuate over two years. At its peak the company operates almost at practical capacity. Predictions for the coming year are based on the expected trough in the cycle.

Required:

1 If the firm continues to use practical capacity as its denominator volume for the coming year, what will be the effect on underapplied or overapplied overhead at the end of the coming year? What will be the effect on job costs and tender quotes during the year?

2 Why would Slick oppose the change of denominator volume from practical capacity to the budgeted volume for the coming year?
3 If the company used normal volume as its denominator volume, what would be the effect on underapplied or overapplied overhead at the end of the coming year and at the end of the next year? What will be the effect on job costs and tender quotes over each of the next two years?

E7.34 Cost allocation in a university

PMB University has three faculties: Arts, Sciences and Business. The university's finance manager is trying to decide how to allocate the costs of the Student Enrolment Department, the Library and the Computer Services Department. The finance manager has compiled the following data for next year:

Faculty	Budgeted enrolment	Budgeted teaching hours	Planned number of courses requiring computer access
Arts	1000	30 000	12
Sciences	800	28 000	24
Business	700	22 000	24

Department	Annual cost
Student Enrolment	R1 800 000
Library	4 500 000
Computer Services	6 400 000

Required:

1 For each department, choose an allocation base and distribute the departmental costs to the university's three faculties. Justify your choice of an allocation base.
2 Would you have preferred a different allocation base from those available using the data compiled by the finance manager? Explain your answer.

E7.35 Direct method of support department cost allocation: bank

Bisho Bank has two support departments: the Human Resources Department and the Computing Department. The bank also has two departments that service customers directly: the Deposit Department and the Loan Department. The usage of the two support departments' output in 20X5 is as follows:

	Provider of service	
User of service	Human Resources	Computing
Human Resources	–	15%
Computing	10%	–
Deposit	60%	50%
Loan	30%	35%

The budgeted costs in the two support departments in 20X5 were as follows:

Human Resources	R459 000
Computing	688 500

Required:

Use the direct method to allocate the budgeted costs of the Human Resources and Computing departments to the Deposit and Loan departments.

E7.36 Step-down method of support department cost allocation: bank

Refer to the data given in Exercise 7.35.

Required:
Use the step-down method to allocate the budgeted costs of the Human Resources and Computing departments to the Deposit and Loan departments. Bisho Bank allocates the costs of the Human Resources Department first.

E7.37 Reciprocal services method of support department cost allocation: bank
Refer to the data given in Exercise 7.35.

Required:
Use the reciprocal services method to allocate the budgeted costs of the Human Resources and Computing departments to the Deposit and Loan departments.

E7.38 Variable and absorption costing (appendix)
Higgins Ltd began operations on 1 January, and achieved the following results for the year:

Sales	24 000 units
Selling price	R15 per unit
Manufacturing costs:	
Direct material	R4 per unit
Direct labour	R2 per unit
Variable overhead	R3 per unit
Fixed manufacturing overhead	R100 000
Selling and administrative costs:	
Variable	R1 per unit sold
Fixed	R10 000
Production	25 000 units

Required:
1 Prepare an absorption costing profit statement for Higgins Ltd.
2 Prepare a variable costing contribution margin statement for Higgins Ltd.
3 Reconcile the differences between the profits under the two statements by:
(a) identifying the areas where the profit statements differ; and
(b) using the short-cut method.

Problems

P7.39 Predetermined plantwide overhead rate; different time periods; pricing: manufacturer
Futhi Electronics Ltd calculates its predetermined overhead rate on a quarterly basis. The following estimates were made for next year:

	Estimated manufacturing	Estimated direct labour hours overhead	Quarterly predetermined overhead rate (per direct labour hour)
First quarter	R100 000	25 000	?
Second quarter	80 000	16 000	?
Third quarter	50 000	12 500	?
Fourth quarter	70 000	14 000	?
Total	R300 000	67 500	

The firm's main product, part number B40, requires R100 of direct material and 20 hours of direct labour per unit. The labour rate is R30 per hour.

Required:

1 Calculate the firm's quarterly predetermined overhead rate for each quarter of next year.
2 Determine the cost of one unit of part number B40 if it is manufactured:
(a) in January (b) in April.
3 Suppose the company's pricing policy calls for a 10 per cent mark-up on cost. Calculate the price to be charged for a unit of part number B40 if it is produced:
(a) in January (b) in April.
4 Calculate the company's predetermined overhead rate for next year if the rate is calculated annually.
5 Based on your answer to requirement 4, what is the cost of a unit of part number B40 if it is manufactured:
(a) in January (b) in April?
6 What is the price of a unit of part number B40 if the predetermined overhead rate is calculated annually?
7 Which approach would you recommend to management – quarterly overhead rates or an annual rate? Explain your answer.

P7.40 Departmental overhead rates and activity-based costing: manufacturer

Quality Pool Accessory Ltd manufactures a variety of accessory equipment for swimming pools. For many years the company has used a conventional product costing system with direct labour hours as the only cost driver for overhead application. The firm is organised into five departments, listed below with the key activities performed by each:

- Production Support Department (purchasing, receiving, inventory control, material handling, engineering, quality control, shipping).
- Machinery Department (equipment maintenance, equipment setup).
- Cutting Department (cutting out metal and other parts to be used in various products).
- Fabrication Department (forming and trimming operations on various parts and components).
- Assembly Department (assembly of final products).

The pool accessory industry has recently experienced a significant increase in the level of competition, largely from overseas companies. As a result, Quality Pool Accessory's profits have been squeezed. In response, the firm has moved to increase production efficiency and altered its accounting system to get a more accurate picture of its product costs. The aim is to enable management to price products more competitively. The most significant change in the accounting system is the introduction of departmental overhead rates. The cost drivers used in the three production departments are the following:

- Cutting (machine hours).
- Fabrication (number of parts processed).
- Assembly (direct labour hours).

So far, the new accounting system seems to be effective. Management feel that the reported product costs are more in line with their intuition about what various products cost to manufacture. The accounting manager, however, is considering further improvement in the accounting system through the introduction of activity-based costing.

Required:

1 Draw three diagrams to depict the three different product costing systems discussed in the above description:
(a) the firm's former system, which uses a plantwide overhead rate
(b) the current system, which uses three departmental overhead rates
(c) the contemplated system, which will use activity-based costing to assign manufacturing overhead costs to products

(*Hint*: Refer to Exhibits 7.5 and 7.7. Make sure to show in your diagrams the roles of the predetermined overhead rates, departments, cost distribution, support department cost allocation, cost application, two-stage cost allocation, activity cost pools, activity drivers and products.)

2 For the activity-based costing system, suggest the activity cost pools and activity drivers that could be used.

P7.41 Plantwide versus departmental overhead rates; product pricing: manufacturer

Gauteng Telecommunications Ltd manufactures two different fax machines for the business market. Cost estimates for the two models for the year 20X6 are as follows:

	Basic system	Advanced system
Direct material	R450	R900
Direct labour (20 hours @ R16 per hour)	320	320
Manufacturing overhead*	420	420
Total	R1 190	R1 640

* The predetermined overhead rate is R21 per direct labour hour.

Each model of fax machine requires 20 hours of direct labour. The basic system requires 5 hours in Department A and 15 hours in Department B. The advanced system requires 15 hours in Department A and 5 hours in Department B. The budgeted overhead costs in these two production departments are as follows:

	Department A	Department B
Variable cost	R17 per direct labour hour	R5 per direct labour hour
Fixed cost	R210 000	R210 000

The firm's management expects to operate at a level of 21 000 direct labour hours in each production department during 20X6.

Required:

1 Show how the company's predetermined overhead rate was determined.
2 If the firm prices each model of fax machine at 10 per cent over its cost, what will be the price of each model?
3 Suppose the company were to use predetermined departmental overhead rates. Calculate the rate for each of the two production departments.
4 Calculate the product cost of each model, using the departmental overhead rates calculated in requirement 3.
5 Calculate the price to be charged for each model, assuming the company continues to price each product at 10 per cent above cost. Use the revised product costs calculated in requirement 4.
6 Write a memo to the managing director of Gauteng Telecommunications making a recommendation as to whether the firm should use a plantwide overhead rate or departmental rates. Consider the potential implications of the overhead rates and the firm's pricing policy. How might these considerations affect the firm's ability to compete in the marketplace?

P7.42 Activity-based costing calculations (continuation of Problem 7.41)

Refer to the data given in the preceding problem for Gauteng Telecommunications. The company has implemented an activity-based costing system for its manufacturing overhead costs with the following activity cost pools and cost drivers:

Activity	Activity cost	Total	Activity drivers	
			Basic system product line	Advanced system product line
Machine setup	R102 000	200 setups	45 setups	155 setups
Material receiving	80 000	80 000 kg	30 000 kg	50 000 kg
Inspection	80 000	1600 inspections	690 inspections	910 inspections
Machinery-related	480 000	60 000 MH*	20 000 MH	40 000 MH
Engineering	140 000	7000 EH†	2800 EH	4200 EH
Total overhead	R882 000			

* MH = machine hours.
† EH = engineering hours.

Aurora plans to produce 1000 units of each model of fax machine.

Required:

1 For each activity, calculate the cost per unit of activity driver (for example, the cost per setup).
2 Determine, under activity-based costing, the total overhead to be assigned to each product line.
3 Calculate, under activity-based costing, the overhead assigned per unit of each type of fax machine.
4 Prepare a table comparing the total product cost assigned to each type of fax machine using a plantwide overhead rate, departmental overhead rates, and activity-based costing. (This requirement relies on the solution to Problem 7.41.)

P7.43 Plantwide versus departmental overhead rates; actual and normal costing: manufacturer
Countdown Ltd manufactures sheet music stands in two separate departments: Cutting and Welding. The following data relate to 20X7:

	Cutting Department	Welding Department	Total plant
Budgeted manufacturing overhead	R40 000	R80 000	R120 000
Actual manufacturing overhead	R36 000	R72 000	R108 000
Budgeted machine hours	16 000	64 000	80 000
Actual machine hours	18 000	60 000	78 000
Budgeted direct labour hours	20 000	10 000	30 000
Actual direct labour hours	19 600	7 800	27 400

One of Countdown's major products, the A Frame, has the following production requirements:

	Product: A Frame		
	Cutting Department	Welding Department	Total plant
Machine hours	2.5	4	6.5
Direct labour hours	4	1	5

Required:

1 Calculate the manufacturing overhead cost of the A Frame using:
  (a) a predetermined plantwide rate based on direct labour hours
  (b) a predetermined plantwide rate based on machine hours
  (c) predetermined departmental rates based on direct labour hours for the Cutting Department and on machine hours for the Welding Department

  Which of these three estimates of overhead cost is likely to be the most accurate? Explain.
2 Calculate the manufacturing overhead cost of the A Frame, using an actual costing system and departmental overhead rates based on labour hours for Cutting and on machine

hours for Welding. Explain why cost drivers must be used with actual costing as well as with normal costing.

3 Which estimate of overhead costs is likely to be more accurate – that based on predetermined departmental rates or that based on actual departmental rates? Explain.

P7.44 Overhead application using a predetermined overhead rate; practical capacity versus normal volume: manufacturer

Dianne Peterson, the accountant for Tshwane Teddy Bears Ltd, is in the process of analysing the company's overhead costs for November 20X6. She has gathered the following data for the month:

■ Labour:	
Direct labour hours:	
Job no. 77: Small teddy bears	3 500
Job no. 78: Large teddy bears	3 000
Job no. 79: Small soccer teddy bears	2 000
Labour costs:	
Direct labour wages	R510 000
Indirect labour wages (4000 hours)	150 000
Supervisory salaries	60 000
■ Inventories, 1 November:	
Direct material and supplies	R105 000
Work in process (Job no. 77)	540 000
Finished goods	1 125 000
■ Purchases of direct material and supplies:	
Direct material	R1 350 000
Supplies (indirect material)	150 000
■ Direct material and supplies requisitioned for production:	
Job no. 77	R450 000
Job no. 78	375 000
Job no. 79	255 000
Supplies (indirect material)	120 000
Total	R1 200 000
■ Production equipment costs:	
Power	R41 000
Repairs and maintenance	15 000
Depreciation	15 000
Other	10 000
Total	R81 000
■ Other costs:	
Building occupancy costs (heat, light, depreciation etc.):	
Factory facilities	R64 000
Sales offices	16 000
Administrative offices	10 000
Total	R90 000

The job costing system used by the firm uses direct labour hours as the overhead cost driver. In November 20X5, Peterson had prepared the following budget for direct labour and manufacturing overhead costs for the year 20X6. The plant is capable of operating at 140 000 direct labour hours per year. However, Peterson estimates that the normal usage is 120 000 hours in an average year.

	Manufacturing overhead budget	
Direct labour hours	**Variable**	**Fixed**
100 000	R3 250 000	R2 160 000
120 000	3 900 000	2 160 000
140 000	4 560 000	2 160 000

During November the following jobs were completed:

- Job number 77: Small teddy bears.
- Job number 78: Large teddy bears.

Required:

1 Calculate the predetermined overhead rate for 20X6 using (a) practical capacity, and (b) normal volume as denominator volumes.
2 Calculate the total cost of job number 77, using both overhead rates.
3 Calculate the amount of manufacturing overhead applied to job number 79 during November 20X6, using both overhead rates.
4 What was the total amount of manufacturing overhead applied during November 20X6, using both overhead rates?
5 Calculate the actual manufacturing overhead incurred during November 20X6.
6 Calculate the overapplied or underapplied overhead for November 20X6, using both overhead rates. Explain the differences.
7 Which of these denominator volumes is likely to result in accurate estimates of product costs? Explain.

(*CMA, adapted*)

P7.45 Cost distribution using allocation bases: hospital

Maling General Hospital is a not-for-profit organisation, supported by patient billings, the state health funds and private donations. The hospital's organisation is as follows:

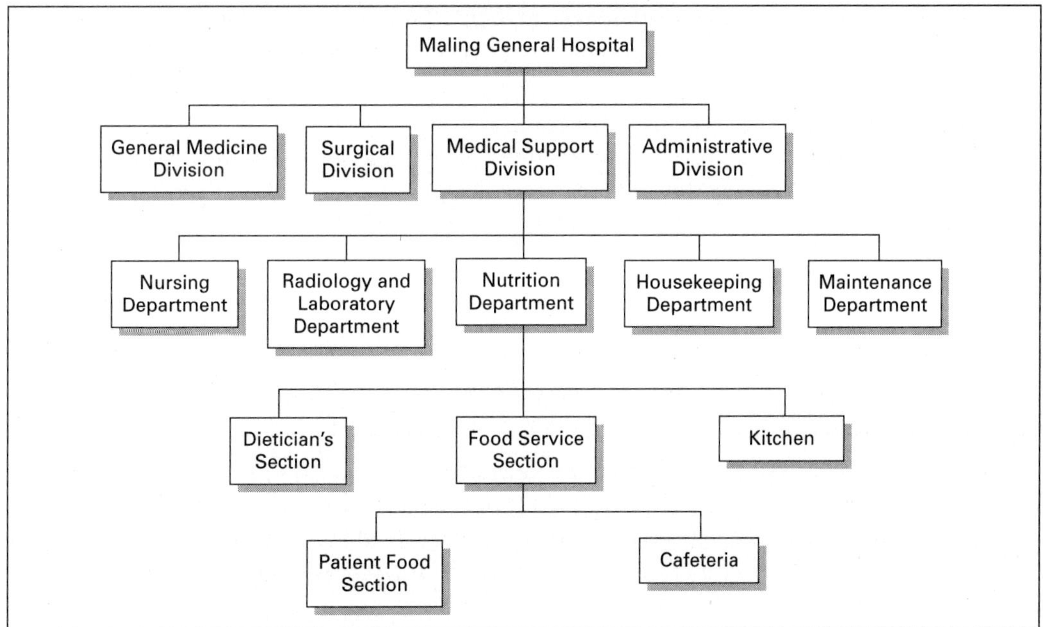

The following table shows the cost allocation bases used to distribute various costs among the hospital's divisions:

Cost pool	Cost items	Cost allocation base	Annual cost
Facilities	Building depreciation Equipment depreciation Insurance	Square metres of space	R1 900 000
Utilities	Electricity Waste disposal Water and sewer Telephone Heat	Cubic metres of space	R240 000
General administration	Administrator Administrative staff Office supplies	Budgeted number of employees	R2 200 000
Community outreach	Public education School physical exams	Budgeted rands of patient billings	R400 000

Shown below are the amounts of each cost allocation base associated with each division:

	Square metres	Cubic metres	Number of employees	Patient billings R'000
General Medicine Division	15 000	135 000	60	R20 000
Surgical Division	8 000	100 000	40	12 500
Medical Support Division	9 000	90 000	40	7 500
Administrative Division	8 000	75 000	10	0
Total	40 000	400 000	150	R40 000

Required:

1 Prepare a table that distributes to the hospital's divisions each of the costs listed in the first table given in this problem.

2 Comment on the appropriateness of patient billings as the basis for distributing community outreach costs to the hospital's divisions. Can you suggest a better allocation base?

3 Is there any value in allocating utilities costs to the divisions? What purposes could such an allocation process serve?

P7.46 Support department cost allocation: manufacturer

Mabaso Instrument Company manufactures gauges for the construction industry. The company has two production departments: Machinery and Finishing. There are also three support departments: Human Resources (HR), Maintenance and Design. The budgeted overhead costs for the year for each department are as follows:

HR	R250 000
Maintenance	230 000
Design	350 000
Machining	800 000
Finishing	400 000

The budgeted machine hours for the Machining Department are 30 000, and the budgeted direct labour hours for the Finishing Department are 10 000. These activities are used to allocate manufacturing overhead costs to products in the two departments.

The usage of the support departments' output for the year is as follows

Provision of Service Output (hours of service)			
	Provider of the service		
User of the service	**HR**	**Maintenance**	**Design**
HR	–	–	–
Maintenance	1 500	–	–
Design	1 500	1 500	–
Machining	4 000	3 500	4 500
Finishing	5 000	4 000	1 500
Total	12 000	9 000	6 000

Required:

1 Use the direct method to allocate support cost to production departments, and determine the predetermined manufacturing overhead rates for the two production departments.

2 Explain the sequence that should be used to allocate the support department costs to production departments using the step-down method.

3 Use the step-down method to allocate support costs to production departments, and determine the predetermined manufacturing overhead rates for the two production departments.

P7.47 Support department cost allocation; departmental overhead rates; product costing: manufacturer

Kevin Ltd is developing departmental overhead rates based on machine hours for its Moulding Department and direct labour hours for its Assembly Department. The Moulding Department has 20 machines, each of which runs 2000 hours per year. The Assembly Department employs 80 people. Each person in the Assembly Department works 2000 hours per year. The production-related overhead costs distributed to the Moulding and Assembly departments are budgeted at R4.0 million and R6.4 million respectively. Two support departments, Repairs and Engineering, directly support the two production departments, Moulding and Assembly. These support departments have budgeted costs of R960 000 and R5.0 million respectively. The production departments' overhead rates cannot be determined until the support departments' costs are allocated. The following schedule reflects the use of the Repairs Department's and Engineering Department's output by the various departments.

	User department			
Support department	**Repairs**	**Engineering**	**Moulding**	**Assembly**
Repairs (repair hours)	0	1000	1000	8000
Engineering (kilowatt hours)	240 000	0	840 000	120 000

Required:

1 (a) Calculate the overhead rates per machine hour for the Moulding Department and per direct labour hour for the Assembly Department. Use the direct method to allocate support department costs.

(b) Estimate the overhead cost of a 'doodad', which is produced using 3 machine hours in the Moulding Department and 5 labour hours in the Assembly Department.

2 (a) Calculate the overhead rates per machine hour for the Moulding Department and per direct labour hour for the Assembly Department. Use the step-down method to allocate support department costs. Allocate the Repair Department's costs first.

(b Now estimate the overhead cost of the doodad.

P7.48 Reciprocal service method; departmental overhead rates; product costing: manufacturer

Refer to the data given in Problem 7.47 for Kevin Ltd.

Required:

1 (a) Calculate the overhead rates per machine hour for the Moulding Department and per direct labour hour for the Assembly Department. Use the reciprocal services method to allocate support department costs.
(b) Now estimate the overhead cost of the doodad.

2 Which of the three methods of support department cost allocation results in the most accurate overhead rates and product costs? Why?

P7.49 Absorption versus variable costing (appendix): manufacturer

Slim and Trim Ltd produces frozen yoghurt, a low-fat dairy dessert. The product is sold in five-litre containers and had the following price and variable costs per unit in 20X8:

Sales price	R30
Direct material	10
Direct labour	4
Variable overhead	6

Budgeted fixed overhead in 20X8 was R600 000, which was equal to actual fixed overhead. Actual production was 150 000 five-litre containers, which was equal to the budgeted level of production, but only 125 000 containers were sold. Slim and Trim incurred the following selling and administrative expenses:

Fixed	R100 000
Variable	R2 per container sold

Required:

1 Calculate the cost per unit under variable and absorption costing.

2 Prepare profit reports for 20X8 using:
(a) absorption costing
(b) variable costing

3 Reconcile the profit reported under the two methods by listing the two key areas where the profit reports differ.

4 Reconcile the profit reported under the two methods using the short-cut method.

P7.50 Normal costing; profit under absorption and variable costing (appendix): manufacturer

Furry Pillows Pty Ltd's planned production for 20X7 was 10 000 units. This production level was achieved, but only 9000 units were sold at R400 each. Other data are as follows:

Direct materials used	R800 000
Direct labour incurred	400 000
Fixed manufacturing overhead (actual and planned)	500 000
Variable manufacturing overhead (actual and planned)	240 000
Fixed selling and administrative expenses	600 000
Variable selling and administrative expenses	90 000
Finished goods inventory, 1 January 20X7	None

The company uses normal costing. There were no work-in-process inventories at the beginning or end of the year.

Required:

1 Prepare a profit report for Furry Pillows for 20X7 using:
(a) absorption costing
(b) variable costing

2 Which costing method, absorption costing or variable costing, shows a higher operating profit for 20X7? Why?

3 What would be Furry Pillows' finished goods inventory cost on 31 December 20X7, under:
   (a) variable costing
   (b) absorption costing?
4 Which costing method, variable or absorption, would you recommend to Furry Pillows' management? Explain.

(CPA, adapted)

Cases

C7.51 Support department cost allocation; plantwide versus departmental overhead rates; product costing; cost drivers: manufacturer

Travel Smart Pty Ltd manufactures a complete line of fibreglass attaché cases and suitcases. The firm has three manufacturing departments: Moulding, Component and Assembly. There are also two support departments: Power and Maintenance. The sides of the cases are manufactured in the Moulding Department. The frames, hinges and locks are manufactured in the Component Department. The cases are completed in the Assembly Department. Varying amounts of materials and time are required to manufacture each type of case.

Travel Smart has always used a plantwide overhead rate. Direct labour hours are used to assign overhead to products. The predetermined overhead rate is calculated by dividing the company's total estimated overhead by the total estimated direct labour hours to be worked in the three manufacturing departments.

Jennifer Mason, manager of cost accounting, has recommended that Travel Smart use departmental overhead rates. The planned operating costs and expected levels of activity for the coming year have been developed by Mason and are presented by department in the following schedules. (All numbers are in thousands.)

	Manufacturing departments (numbers in thousands)		
	Moulding	**Component**	**Assembly**
Departmental activity measures:			
Direct labour hours	500	2 000	1 500
Machine hours	875	125	0
Departmental costs:			
Direct material	R24 800	R60 000	R2500
Direct labour	7000	40 000	24 000
Manufacturing overhead	42 000	32 400	45 200
Total departmental costs	R73 800	R132 400	R71 700

	Use of support departments (numbers in thousands)		
	Moulding	**Component**	**Assembly**
Maintenance:			
Estimated usage in labour hours for the coming year	90	25	10
Power (in kilowatt hours):			
Estimated usage for the coming year	360	320	120

	Support departments (numbers in thousands)	
	Power	Maintenance
Departmental activity measures:		
Estimated usage for the coming year	800 kWh	125 labour hours
Departmental costs:		
Materials and supplies (variable)	R10 000	R3000
Variable labour	2800	4500
Fixed overhead	24 000	500
Total support department costs	R36 800	R8000

Required:

1 (a) Calculate the plantwide overhead rate for Travel Smart for the coming year using the same method as used in the past.

(b) Estimate the overhead cost of an Elite attaché case that requires 4 direct labour hours and 5 machine hours in the Moulding Department, 3 direct labour hours in the Component Department and 2 direct labour hours in the Assembly Department.

2 Jennifer Mason has been asked to develop departmental overhead rates for comparison with the plantwide rate. The following steps are to be followed in developing the departmental rates:

(a) Allocate the total Maintenance Department costs to the three manufacturing departments, using the direct method.

(b) Allocate the Power Department costs to the three manufacturing departments, using the direct method.

(c) Calculate departmental overhead rates for the three manufacturing departments, using a machine hour cost driver for the Moulding Department and a direct labour hour cost driver for the Component and Assembly departments.

3 Estimate the overhead cost of the Elite attaché case using the departmental overhead rates.

4 Should Travel Smart use a plantwide rate or departmental rates to assign overhead to products? Explain your answer.

(*CMA, adapted*)

C7.52 Plantwide and departmental overhead rates for decision-making: manufacturer

Top Plating Ltd plates metal products to individual customers' specifications. Most of the company's work is obtained through the tender process, where the company responds to an invitation to submit a competitive bid. Over the last few months Top Plating has been very quiet, and the managing director, B.R. Khawula, is concerned that the business will fail if it does not improve its success rate with tenders. The company has two production departments, Preparation and Coating, and the production requirements for individual jobs can differ significantly. Some jobs require extensive preparation, with minimal coating; others require little preparation but multiple coats.

The following table describes the results of the five bids that the company submitted last month. (The numbers in brackets after losses indicate where the company was ranked in the bid process.)

Job no.	Direct labour hours in Preparation	Direct labour hours in Coating	Estimated direct labour hours	Overhead cost of bid	Won/lost
1	12 000	3000	15 000	R41 250	Lost (5th)
2	3 000	12 000	15 000	41 250	Won
3	15 000	0	15 000	41 250	Lost (3rd)
4	0	15 000	15 000	41 250	Won
5	7500	7500	15 000	41 250	Lost (2nd)

The pattern of resource usage implied in the above table has persisted now for several months.

The company uses a predetermined plantwide overhead rate based on practical capacity in direct labour hours. The budgeted overhead for the year for the Preparation Department is R540 000 (R180 000 fixed and R360 000 variable), and for the Coating Department it is R1 440 000 (R360 000 fixed and R1 080 000 variable). Each department has a monthly practical capacity of 30 000 direct labour hours.

Required:
Write a report to B.R. Khawula identifying a possible cause of this situation. Develop an alternative bidding scheme to overcome this problem. Support your analysis with a comparison of the suggested and existing bidding schemes.

Endnotes

1 Under the international accounting standard, IAS 2 *Inventories*, only manufacturing costs may be included in inventory valuations; other costs must be expensed when they are incurred.

2 As discussed in Chapter 2, overtime premiums and the costs of idle time should be treated as overhead costs if they are caused by the general level of production rather than an individual product.

3 Although there are really three distinct steps in this process (cost distribution, support department cost allocation and overhead application), it is described as a two-stage process because of the two cost objects – production departments for Stage one and products for Stage two.

4 You may wonder how the activity costs in Exhibit 7.8 are calculated. They include the costs of the activities performed in three support departments (Equipment Maintenance, Material Handling and Quality Control) and the costs of overhead activities performed within the two production departments (Machining and Assembly). For example, the activity 'Managing quality' includes the cost of the Quality Control Department and the cost of product inspections within the Machining and Assembly departments.

5 Timeliness could be improved by using *monthly* actual overhead rates, but, as discussed later, these rates may be unstable over time.

6 If a tie occurs, where two or more support departments serve the same number of other support departments, then the support department with the largest overhead budget can be allocated first.

7 The absorption cost in Exhibit 7.19 shows the variable and fixed overhead costs separately to highlight the difference between variable and absorption costing. However, with absorption costing, there is no need to distinguish between variable and fixed overheads, so an overall manufacturing overhead rate can be used.

Activity-Based Costing

❖ Learning Objectives

After completing this chapter, you should be able to:

1. explain the problems associated with conventional costing systems, resulting from a failure to adapt to the changing business environment;
2. recognise common indicators of an outdated product costing system;
3. describe both the costing view and the activity-management view of the activity-based costing (ABC) model;
4. evaluate the costs and benefits associated with some of the different approaches to activity-based costing, which include different subsets of costs;
5. use the activity-based model to measure the costs of activities, and assign activity costs to products;
6. explain the differences between product costs prepared under activity-based costing and those prepared under conventional costing systems;
7. recognise what types of organisations can gain the greatest benefits from activity-based costing;
8. identify the impediments to implementing activity-based costing;
9. outline various design issues to be considered when implementing activity-based costing, including budgeted versus actual costs, implementation of activity-based costing as a 'project' and the inclusion of other cost objects;
10. explain the implications of excess capacity for estimating the cost of activities;
11. appreciate the importance of 'behavioural issues' in implementing activity-based costing;
12. delineate the limitations of activity-based costing in providing accurate product costs;
13. describe the difficulties of implementing activity-based costing in service organisations; and
14. after studying the appendix, use a relatively simple version of activity-based costing to allocate overhead costs to products.

Introduction

A revolution is transforming manufacturing industries. Not since the mid-19th century have changes been as sweeping and dramatic as they are today. The growth of global markets for both production inputs and for products with an increasing emphasis on customer satisfaction, the breakneck pace of technological innovation, and startling advances in computerised systems have resulted in a new playing field for manufacturers around the world. Some manufacturers have emerged as world-class producers, while others have fallen by the wayside.

The service sector, which includes businesses such as consulting firms, banks and transportation companies, has also been through a period of dramatic change. Spectacular advances in information and communication technologies have altered the service environment. Competition has increased. Customers are demanding a greater diversity of services, more flexibility and better quality. As in the manufacturing sector, some service enterprises have adapted; others have failed.

As we discussed in Chapter 1, managers in many organisations have responded to the changing business environment by adopting new management structures and practices. Concepts such as team-based structures, employee empowerment, enterprise resource planning systems, real-time reporting and continuous improvement have gained widespread acceptance. What has happened to management accounting during this period of change? Gradually, management accountants have become aware of the deficiencies in conventional approaches and a number of techniques have developed that are more suited to the changing needs of businesses, to help them create value for both their owners and their customers. Many of these techniques are still not widely used in practice. However, it is important for you to understand them because they are likely to gain popularity as more managers and management accountants become aware of the limitations of conventional management accounting systems. These new approaches will help to provide the information that managers need to make their businesses world-class.

We begin this chapter by identifying some of the problems with conventional costing systems. Activity-based costing has been one of the most significant responses to these problems. We introduced activity-based costing in Chapter 7 when we looked at alternative methods for allocating overhead costs to products at Delta Controls. However, there are several different approaches to activity-based costing that suit particular cost structures and problems that businesses face. In this chapter we look at an implementation of activity-based costing at a company, Mason & Cox, to explain the principles of activity-based costing and to describe a common approach to activity-based costing that provides useful information for cost management as well as product costing.[1]

The focus in this chapter is on using activity-based costing to assign costs to products. The role that activity-based costing (ABC) can play in managing resources is discussed in Chapter 15, where the concept is extended to incorporate activity-based management, and in Chapter 16, where ABC is applied to the management of customers and suppliers. The broader implications of activity-based costing for making decisions to create value are dealt with throughout Part 4 of this book.

Problems with conventional product costing systems

L.O. 1

Most South African businesses use conventional costing systems. However, since the early 1980s these systems have been widely criticised for failing to provide accurate product costs to inform management decisions. Activity-based costing has evolved as an alternative approach. Let's begin our study of activity-based costing by reviewing the key features of, and problems with, conventional costing systems.

Features of conventional product costing systems

Although **conventional product costing systems** vary from one business to another, they usually include the following features:

- Direct material and direct labour costs are traced to products.
- Manufacturing overhead costs are allocated to products using a predetermined overhead rate for the whole plant (or one for each production department).
- The manufacturing overhead rate is calculated using some measure of production volume – that is, using a volume-based cost driver.
- Non-manufacturing costs are not assigned to products.

In selecting an overhead cost driver we should ask: 'What causes, or drives, these manufacturing overhead costs?' There needs to be a strong correlation between the overhead costs and the cost driver to ensure that product costs are accurate – that is, that product costs do measure the cost of resources used to produce the product. However, most conventional costing systems *assume* that manufacturing overhead is driven by the volume of production, which is measured by output measures such as the number of units produced, or, more commonly, by input measures such as the number of direct labour hours worked, the direct labour cost, the number of machine hours worked or some measure of material inputs. Conventional product costing systems tend to aggregate the overhead costs into very large cost pools, sometimes with a separate cost pool for each department, but often with just one cost pool for the whole plant. Chapter 7 describes several conventional methods for allocating overhead costs to products.

Failure to adapt to the changing business environment

It is generally believed that the principles and practices of conventional costing systems were developed by the mid-1920s (Kaplan, 1984; Johnson & Kaplan, 1987). Chapter 1 describes the dramatic changes in the business environment since the 1980s. In many businesses, these changes have led to changes in the number of products, the types of production processes and the composition of costs, which are no longer compatible with assumptions underlying conventional approaches to product costing. The 'Real life' on page 354 indicates that by the late 1980s, managers were being frustrated by problems with conventional product costs. But what causes these problems?

Increasing levels of non-volume-driven manufacturing overhead costs

Conventional costing systems allocate manufacturing overhead costs to products, using volume-based cost drivers. However, fixed manufacturing overhead costs do not vary with production volume, although some of them do vary with other factors. That is, fixed overhead may be *non-volume driven.* Also, it is assumed that variable overhead costs vary *in proportion* to production volume. However, it is unlikely that a single cost driver (or even one cost driver in each production department) can explain the behaviour of all variable overhead costs, and while some of these costs may increase or decrease with production volume, they do not vary in proportion to volume change. In the past these problems have not always caused major distortions to product costs because non-volume-driven manufacturing overhead costs have been relatively insignificant. But is this still the case?

In the USA, overhead costs represented about 15 per cent of product costs in the early 1960s. Yet by the late 1990s, overheads represented close to 35 per cent of a product's manufacturing cost. Direct labour has fallen dramatically from about 25 per cent to 10 per cent of a product's cost. Cooper and Kaplan also reported that labour cost as a proportion of total product cost had fallen and overhead costs had risen. In South Africa, direct labour represents a large proportion of a product's cost and this is true for all developing countries.

Exhibit 8.1 presents the cost allocation methods used by South African companies. This is from a survey undertaken by Waweru, Hoque and Uliana (2005).

A survey of Australian manufacturers in 1995 found that manufacturing overhead costs accounted for 20 per cent of manufacturing costs, and the majority of respondents indicated that overhead had increased as a proportion of product cost over the previous five years (Booth & Giacobbe, 1997).[2]

Method	Percentage	Rank
Machine/labour hours	24%	2
Activities performed	37%	1
Labour costs	9%	4
Material costs	5%	6
Units of output	15%	3
Others	10%	5
	100%	

Exhibit 8.1 Cost allocation methods used by South African companies

Costs are increasingly driven by non-volume-related factors such as set-ups, the number of suppliers and the range of products assembled. However, based on a survey commissioned by KPMG of 400 leading companies around the world in 2007, we have started to see a greater increase in variable costs relative to overhead costs. In South Africa, increasing automation will invariably lead to overheads and non-volume activities becoming a greater driver of costs.

Increasing proportions of non-manufacturing costs

Conventional product costing usually excludes non-manufacturing costs. However, many non-manufacturing costs can be related directly to products, and these costs have become a more significant proportion of total costs in many organisations. In today's environment of high technology, increased research and development, increased levels of customer support and substantial marketing costs, manufacturing overhead and non-manufacturing costs may account for a large proportion of a manufacturing entity's costs.

Causes of changes in costs

Although not clear-cut, the evidence does suggest that manufacturing overhead costs are increasing and becoming more non-volume-driven, and the proportion of non-manufacturing costs that are incurred to develop, support and promote products is becoming more substantial. What has caused these changes?

- Growing automation has certainly increased manufacturing overhead costs, relative to direct labour costs. Moreover, more machines imply more *non-volume-driven* overhead costs are incurred, such as depreciation, insurance and setups.
- Greater **product diversity** has caused increased production complexity and this has led to increased demand for manufacturing overhead support, such as production scheduling, material handling and production setups. The costs of many of these support functions do not vary in proportion to production volume. More product diversity has also increased costs in non-manufacturing areas such as research and development, product design, distribution and after-sales service.
- Increased customer demands for improved service and quality have resulted in increased manufacturing overhead and non-manufacturing costs (many of them not being driven by production volume).
- Many organisations are investing more resources in downstream areas such as customer service and marketing. The increase in customer service costs reflects an increasing emphasis on customer support. Increased marketing expenditure is also occurring as many firms engage in increased product promotion and advertising to position their products in the more aggressive market place.

Volume-based cost drivers do not drive many of the above costs, and therefore they are inappropriate to use in costing products. Yet, as discussed in Chapter 7, volume-based cost drivers are commonly used in South African firms. Also, the wisdom of omitting, from product costs for management decision-making purposes, non-manufacturing costs that are product-related can be queried given their increased significance.

Changing product structures

The conventional approach to product costing did not cause too many problems when businesses produced a limited range of products. However, to remain competitive many businesses have increased the number of different products they produce. Apart from its effects on the cost structure, product diversity causes cost distortions because conventional costing systems are not good at recognising different overhead consumption patterns for different products.

Indicators of problems with a product costing system

Conventional approaches to product costing are likely to result in inaccurate product costs when: **L.O. 2**

- the proportion of direct labour costs decreases;
- the proportion of manufacturing overhead costs increases;
- the proportion of manufacturing overhead costs not related directly to production volume increases;
- non-manufacturing costs that are product-related become substantial; and
- product diversity increases.

Firms often experience these types of changes in the modern business environment, but how do they know when they need a new product costing system? Exhibit 8.2 outlines common indicators of an outdated product costing system.

Indicator	Probable cause
Production managers want to drop products that the costing system claims are profitable.	These products use more production resources than is indicated by their product cost.
Profit margins on individual products are difficult to explain. For example, a product has a higher than expected cost, and lower margin.	The product costing system is distorting the product's costs.
Products that are difficult to make have high profit margins.	The costing system understates the costs of making these products.
Manufacturing and marketing managers develop their own 'private' systems for estimating product costs.	Managers have lost faith in the 'official' product costing system.
The management accountant spends a lot of time on special product costing studies.	The costing system does not provide reliable information for product-related decisions.
There are no competitors for products that the costing system claims are profitable.	The costing system is understating the costs of these products.
Competitors' prices appear unrealistically low.	The costing system is overstating the costs of these products.
Customers are not deterred by price increases.	The costing system is understating the costs of these products. Competitors already charge higher prices.
At year-end, actual overhead far exceeds overhead applied to products.	Applying overhead to products, using the overhead application rate, understates the overhead resources consumed. Product costs are understated.
The company consistently wins bids for products that are difficult to produce and loses bids for simple products.	The costing system is understating the costs of complex products and overstating the costs of simple products.
Source: adapted from Cooper (1989)	

Exhibit 8.2 Indicators of an outdated costing system

When inaccurate product cost information is used by managers to make decisions, the effect on the business may be profound. The 'Real life' overleaf provides some examples of firms that have had this unhappy experience.

Problems with costing in service businesses

In Chapter 6 we noted the increasing size and importance of the service sector. There are also problems with conventional costing systems in service enterprises. Many businesses do not estimate the costs of individual services, but those that do have tended to use business-wide volume-based overhead rates. As in the manufacturing sector, overhead costs have become increasingly important and increasingly non-volume driven.

In the service sector, customers are demanding a more diverse range of higher-quality services. Consider, for example, housing loans. There was once very little difference between the terms and conditions of housing loans offered by the various banks but, since the late 1980s, the range of housing loan packages has grown exponentially. Banks are seeking to differentiate their products by offering different establishment fees, different terms and flexible repayment plans. Moreover, the range of non-bank lenders in the housing market has increased dramatically. There is fierce competition over interest rates. These forces have had the same impact as in manufacturing: increased product diversity and increased overhead costs. Each of these products is part of a carefully devised marketing strategy, supported by detailed cost analysis. However, customer demands for service diversity and quality add to the level of non-volume-driven overhead costs and cast doubt on the accuracy of service costs derived from conventional costing systems. Clearly accurate costing can provide important information to assist those banks to achieve their strategies.

REAL LIFE: COST SYSTEMS HAVE GONE AWRY!

In 1992 Stewart Lamond observed the following fundamental changes to the business environment: the development of the global marketplace, an increased customer focus on quality, increased price sensitivity, the effects of deregulation, and the 'technological explosion'. In his experience, 'Companies today have many questions to which they need answers, though usually they must seek answers from increasingly moribund traditional cost systems'. More than a decade later, these changes and outdated costing systems continue to present major challenges in many businesses.

Lamond noted a range of information needs not satisfied by current costing systems, including accurate estimates of the costs and profitability of goods and services. He described the experience of three Australian companies, Parke Davis, ICI Film Products and Comalco Rolled Products, in their search for better costing information. Each of these companies had identified a need for better product costing, in particular for better ways to allocate overhead.

Management at Parke Davis was concerned about the company's increasing level of overhead costs and its arbitrary allocation of overhead to products, which resulted in the costs of some products being understated and others overstated. ICI was troubled by product costs that were inconsistent with operations managers' views of actual costs. Products that the operations managers felt were unprofitable were reported in 'a favourable light' in the current costing system. Comalco's management faced the same sorts of problems. Their product costing system lacked credibility with managers and resulted in decisions that were inconsistent with the company's manufacturing strategy.

In many businesses, accurate product costs are essential to enable managers to make informed decisions, and relying on inaccurate costs may adversely impact on an organisation's competitiveness.

Source: Lamond (1992)

Activity-based costing

Activity-based costing (ABC) may be used to overcome the problems with conventional product costing systems. Let's evaluate how activity-based costing could be implemented at a foundry, such as Mason & Cox. This foundry produces moulded metal equipment, called 'castings', for a wide range of local industries including mining, sugar refining, cement manufacture, and general engineering and process companies. It also produces for export markets. The company's major product lines include the 'Hensley' line of digging equipment, used in mining; the 'Canron' range of mining products; and custom-made castings.

Production processes at Mason & Cox

To understand Mason & Cox's costing system, you need to be familiar with its production processes. Casting usually involves six main steps:

1 Product designs, called 'patterns', are drawn.
2 Moulds are built, based on the patterns.
3 The metal is melted and poured into the moulds.
4 When the metal has set, the castings are knocked out of their moulds and sent for finishing.
5 In finishing, the castings are smoothed using a shot-blast machine. Any high spots are ground down, and hollow spots are welded up.
6 Finally, the casting is heated.

Problems with the conventional costing system at Mason & Cox

Mason & Cox's management became concerned about their product costing. The company used a conventional costing system. However, there were a number of managers at Mason & Cox who were sure that their product costs were inaccurate.

The product costs did not make sense to production managers

Joe Costello, the manufacturing manager, had no faith in the current system and selected two products to prove his point. Mason & Cox manufactures two types of 7.5 kg 'teeth' for digging up ground in the mining industry. The Hensley Tooth is one of their best sellers. It is made in batches of 250 and the company sells about 25 000 each year. The other type, a Custom Cast Tooth, is made specifically for copper mines. It is made to order in batches of 50 about ten times a year. As shown in Exhibit 8.3, the existing conventional product costing system estimated that both these castings cost the same to produce – R177.70. Their direct costs were the same, because they used the same basic direct labour operations and the same direct materials. Manufacturing overhead was applied on direct labour hours, so they both had the same amount of applied overhead.

Yet Costello was certain that the Hensley Tooth could not cost the same as the Custom Cast Tooth. Many overhead services are provided for individual batches and, as the Custom Cast Tooth is made in much smaller batches, Costello felt that its overhead cost *per unit* should be higher. Also, the Hensley Tooth is simple to make, while custom-made products are generally more complex. For these reasons, each Custom Cast Tooth requires a lot more overhead support, yet none of this showed up in its conventional product cost. This was not an isolated case. Costello was sure that the conventional product costing system was overstating the cost of the company's popular products, the high-volume lines, and understating the cost of the minor products, the low-volume lines.

Product profit margins were difficult to explain

The marketing people at Mason & Cox were also perplexed. The company set its prices at the conventional product cost plus some 'mark-up', but the marketing manager, Danny Harris, could not

7.5 kg Hensley Tooth		
Direct material (metal and sand)		R60.00
Direct labour:		
Moulding (4 minutes @ R1.65 per minute)	6.60	
Metal melting (6 minutes @ R1.85 per minute)	11.10	
Finishing (20 minutes @ R1.50 per minute)	30.00	47.70
Manufacturing overhead:		
(0.5 direct labour hours @ R140 per hour)*		70.00
Product cost (DM, DL and MOH)		177.70
7.5 kg Custom Cast Tooth		
Direct material (metal and sand)		R60.00
Direct labour:		
Moulding (4 minutes @ R1.65 per minute)	6.60	
Metal melting (6 minutes @ R1.85 per minute)	11.10	
Finishing (20 minutes @ R1.50 per minute)	30.00	47.70
Manufacturing overhead:		
(0.5 direct labour hours @ R140 per hour)*		70.00
Product cost (DM. DL and MOH)		177.70
*Manufacturing overhead rate = budgeted manufacturing overhead/budgeted direct labour hours		
Budgeted manufacturing overhead	a	R24 400 000
Budgeted direct labour hours	b	174 285
Manufacturing overhead rate per direct labour hour	a/b	R140

Exhibit 8.3 Conventional product costs at Mason & Cox

make any sense of these prices. To compete in the marketplace, Harris found he had to cut the price of the high-volume lines like the Hensley Tooth. But with speciality products like the Custom Cast Tooth, a low-volume line, they seemed able to charge well above the cost-based price.

Company profits were being eroded

Roy Kidman, the managing director, was also far from pleased because company profit was not meeting monthly targets. The price cuts on the high-volume lines increased sales volume but eroded total sales revenue. The better-than-expected prices on the speciality products did not offset the poor performance of the high-volume lines.

Causes of the problems with the conventional costing system

Eventually, Costello and Harris tackled the accounting manager, Olivia Buthelezi, who recognised these problems as classic indicators of an outdated costing system. Mason & Cox's costing system was developed in the 1920s and had changed little since then, despite:

- the product range becoming far more diverse;
- manufacturing overhead increasing significantly, relative to direct costs, and becoming more non-volume driven; and
- non-manufacturing costs, which were product-related, increasing, relative to manufacturing costs.

Using a volume-based cost driver

Mason & Cox's product costing system used direct labour hours, a measure of production volume, as a cost driver to apply manufacturing overhead costs to products. Yet an analysis of the company's manufacturing processes indicated that a significant part of the overhead costs was caused by factors other than production volume. For example, some of the overhead costs, such as set-up costs, are incurred for each production batch regardless of the number of castings in the batch. Others, such as factory rent, are incurred each month regardless of the number of castings produced. Still others are caused by product complexity.

Outdated costing systems imply distorted product costs

What did this mean for the product costs at Mason & Cox? Earlier in this chapter we warned that conventional costing systems are not suited to businesses where product diversity has increased and cost structures have become more overhead-intensive, and where a higher proportion of the overhead costs are fixed costs. Under these circumstances, the costs of high-volume, relatively simple products produced in large batches are likely to be overstated, and the costs of low-volume, speciality products produced in small batches are likely to be understated. Indeed, this seemed to be happening with the Hensley Tooth and the Custom Cast Tooth.

In addition, Olivia Buthelezi was concerned about the non-manufacturing costs. She felt that product-related costs were not confined to the manufacturing area but were spread right across the value chain. Over time, non-manufacturing costs, both upstream and downstream, had grown. Many of them, such as product design and development costs and advertising costs, *were* related to particular products and were used disproportionately by different products. Yet, as shown in Exhibit 8.4, like many other conventional costing systems, the Mason & Cox system did not assign these costs to products. Instead, all non-manufacturing costs were expensed in the period in which they were incurred. How could management make rational decisions about which products to produce, and what prices to set, if these product-related costs were ignored?

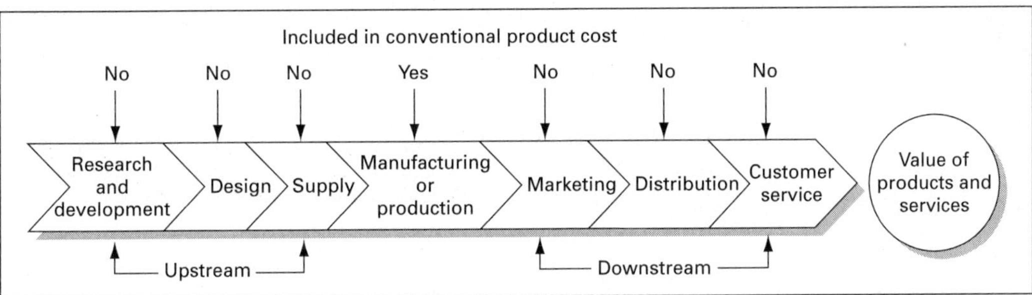

Exhibit 8.4 The value chain and conventional product costing

The solution: Activity-based costing

Buthelezi had heard about activity-based costing, which has the potential to overcome many of the problems that occur with conventional costing systems. **Activity-based costing (ABC)** is a methodology that can be used to measure both the cost of cost objects *and* the performance of activities. It evolved in the mid-1980s to improve the allocation of manufacturing overhead costs to products, but it soon became apparent that activity-based costing systems could be expanded to include non-manufacturing costs.

From the early 1990s many companies, and even public sector corporations, have come to realise that activities that form the basis of activity-based costing are more than mechanisms for costing products. They can be used to analyse the profitability of major customers and they provide a logical framework for managing the business through the identification and analysis of key activity characteristics such as root cause cost drivers and performance measures. We consider this broader role for activity-based costing in Chapters 15 and 16.

An activity-based costing model

L.O. 3

In learning about activity-based product costing, Buthelezi felt overwhelmed by the many new terms she encountered.[3] The model shown in Exhibit 8.5 helped her to come to grips with the mechanics of activity-based costing.

The model shows that activity-based costing can be used for two purposes: costing and activity management.

Costing view

The vertical, costing view shows how activity-based costing can be used to estimate the cost of products.

REAL LIFE: ABC AT THE SOUTH AFRICAN POST OFFICE, STANDARD BANK AND MEDSCHEME

A survey of finance staff members found that implementation of ABC at the South African Post Office was mainly seen as positive. The main benefits of ABC for the Post Office related to a better allocation of overhead costs, the breakdown in barriers between functional areas, an improvement in cost control, a better design of services and products and product and services mix as well as improving the budgeting process.

However, the survey recorded a number of significantly negative effects such as the high cost of implementing ABC, a lack of software packages, lack of knowledge of data requirements, resistance to change, difficulty in gathering data on cost drivers and the lack of top management support. Active support by top management has been identified in other studies as the critical factor in ensuring the successful implementation of ABC.

In a submission to the Competition Commission Enquiry into Competition in the Banking Sector, Standard Bank indicated that although the bank does employ ABC, pricing decisions were not based on the cost of each transaction. In the submission, Standard Bank states:

Even though we engage in limited activity based costing, we do not apportion all costs across each and every product (of which there are over 1000), each and every transaction type (over 40) and each and every channel utilised (around 10). Therefore we do not record costs down to an individual transaction level. To do so would be an investment decision for which the business case in terms of value to our customers and to our shareholders is not sufficient. It would be misleading to place undue reliance on costing information for pricing decisions. Furthermore, the vast majority of our costs (our capital, our computer systems, our branches and ATM networks, our staff in the distribution network and our head-office expenses) are fixed.

According to the Standard Bank, using ABC for measuring the cost of each transaction reflects an investment decision for which it cannot yet make a business case.

Medscheme is a leading South African medical scheme administrator and was one of the first companies in health care to adopt activity- based costing. The company has identified more than 1400 activities and 278 cost drivers. This has allowed the company to accurately determine product costs and product and customer profitability. Accurate pricing has led to an increase in new business. The company adopted ABC due to competitive pressures in the sector. PricewaterhouseCoopers were appointed as consultants and top management were committed to the adoption of ABC. A technical committee set out the cost drivers for each activity. The company initially used the general ledger to determine account categories. ABC has indicated to management which areas of the business are unprofitable and this has enabled management to focus their attention on making these areas profitable over a period of time.

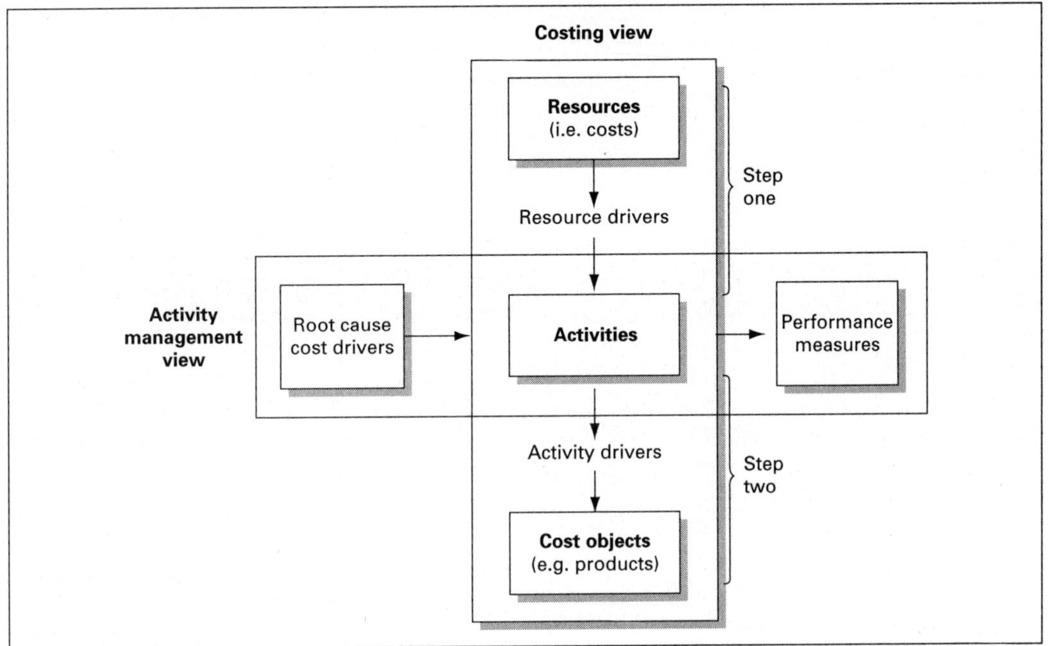

Exhibit 8.5 An activity-based costing model
Source: Turney (1991)[4]

Step one: Measuring the costs of activities

The first step is to measure the cost of the resources used to undertake each activity. An activity is a unit of work performed within the organisation – that is, activities are the 'things that are done' within the business. Common activities in the manufacturing area of Mason & Cox include 'Set up machine', 'Operate machine', 'Move material' and 'Inspect parts'. To determine the total cost of each type of activity, *resource drivers* are used to assign costs to separate cost pools for each activity. The costs of the resources are already recorded in the existing accounting system and include items such as wages, supplies and utilities costs. **Resource drivers** are cost drivers used to estimate the cost of resources consumed by an activity. Remember, **cost drivers** are factors or activities that cause costs. For example, factory area may be a cost driver for factory cleaning costs – the bigger the factory, the higher the costs of cleaning.

Step two: Assigning activity costs to products

The outcome of Step one is a list of the activities performed in the business, and total activity costs. The second step is to calculate the cost per activity and to assign these activity costs to cost objects using *activity drivers*. An **activity driver** is a cost driver used to estimate the cost of an activity consumed by the cost object. For example, the number of set-ups might drive the cost of the activity 'Set up machine'. The more times the machine has to be set up, the higher the total cost of the set-up activity. A product that uses two set-ups will be assigned twice as much in set-up costs as a product that uses only one set-up. A **cost object** is any item for which management wants a separate measure of cost. Products, services, customers, suppliers, contracts and projects are examples of cost objects. In Chapter 16 we describe how activity-based costing can be used to estimate the costs associated with customers and suppliers. At Mason & Cox, the activity-based system was used to estimate the costs of the products. Step two produces a total cost for each product that consists of a list of the activities used by the product and their costs.

Activity management view

The horizontal, activity management view shows how activity-based information can be used to monitor and control what is happening in a business. In addition to analysing activity costs, the activity management view provides information about the root causes of activities, their value to customers, and various measures of their performance. This can provide an effective way of managing (or controlling) costs, as well as managing other sources of customer value such as quality and timely delivery. Mason & Cox actually used activity-based costing to cost products and to manage activities, but at this stage we will focus on the product costing. In Chapter 15 we will look at how Mason & Cox also used their activity-based system for activity management.

REAL LIFE: IDENTIFYING AND MEASURING ACTIVITIES AT UNISA

The University of South Africa experienced significant budget deficits in the 1990s. A reduction in government subsidies, pressure to contain student fees and higher operating costs meant that the university was forced to take drastic action. This led the university to evaluate its financial management system so that it would be able to manage its resources in a more optimal way. The university appointed Deloitte to evaluate its finances. Deloitte indicated that the cause of the university's financial crisis related to the absence of strategic financial management. A key cornerstone was the introduction of an activity-based costing model and, to ensure a buy-in from senior staff members, the university undertook 63 seminars to explain the workings of ABC. The costing model looked at the cost per faculty, the cost per course and cost per activity. Professor Pityana, the Principal and Vice-Chancellor stated that:

... to date we have costed and mapped almost 10 000 activities. This has allowed us to effect a much more focused and targeted financial strategy. We are able to determine quite accurately, what any particular activity is likely to cost, and plan accordingly.

The adoption of ABC at UNISA has had a significantly positive impact on the university's financial position and has led to a reversal of the budget deficits experienced in prior years. UNISA is currently advising other universities in South Africa on how to adopt ABC in education.

Source: Pityana (2005)

The nature of the cost drivers

By now you will have noticed that ABC uses cost drivers in three different ways: cost drivers called *resource drivers* are used to assign costs to activities; cost drivers called *activity drivers* are used to assign activity costs to cost objects; and, as Exhibit 8.5 shows, cost drivers called *root cause cost drivers* are used for activity management. They are called **root cause cost drivers** because they describe the primary reason that the activity is performed. Different names are used for each of these cost drivers because they each play a different role in activity-based costing.

L.O. 4

Initial decisions about ABC at Mason & Cox

The starting point for any ABC implementation is to identify the problem that needs to be addressed. Buthelezi identified the main problem that the company was facing as distorted product costs. She assessed three possible activity-based approaches that could be used to tackle this problem:

- a simple activity-based product costing system, which allocates manufacturing overhead costs to products;

- an activity-based product costing system for indirect costs, which allocates manufacturing overhead costs and non-manufacturing costs to products;
- a comprehensive activity-based system for allocating all costs (except direct material) to products and for activity management.

The report she prepared for Kidman is shown in Exhibit 8.6. It demonstrates that the more inclusive the system, the greater are both the costs and the benefits.

To: Roy Kidman, Managing Director
From: Olivia Buthelezi, Accounting Manager
RE: Evaluation of activity-based costing

I have had a look at activity-based costing. This is a tricky area because there are a number of different approaches that we could use. Since we have a serious problem with product costing, I have evaluated the simplest approach to activity-based product costing and then looked at two refinements. I have summarised my findings in the accompanying table.

		Evaluation	
ABC approach	**Costs included**	**Benefits**	**Costs**
1 Simple activity-based product costing system*	Manufacturing overhead	Product costs more accurate than existing system.	More complex than existing system because more thorough analysis of manufacturing overhead.
2 Activity-based product costing system for indirect costs	Manufacturing overhead and non-manufacturing costs	Product costs more accurate than simple ABC system as it covers wider range of costs.	More complex than simple ABC system because wider range of costs analysed.
3 A comprehensive ABC system for product costing and activity management	All costs, except direct material costs	Accurate product costs as full range of costs covered. Improved management of costs and performance in other strategic areas.	More complex than including just indirect costs because an even wider range of costs is analysed and the costs are analysed in more detail.

* This approach is described in Chapter 7 and the appendix to this chapter.

Exhibit 8.6 Evaluation of activity-based costing for Mason & Cox

In Chapter 7 we described three approaches to allocating *manufacturing overhead costs* to products. It is useful to think of each of these approaches as part of a continuum of costing systems, with both the accuracy of product costs and the complexity of the costing system increasing as we move along the continuum.

- The simplest and least accurate approach is to use a *plantwide overhead rate*, where all manufacturing overhead costs are accumulated in a single cost pool and allocated to products using a single volume-based cost driver.
- *Departmental overhead rates* are more accurate than a plantwide rate, but also more complex as manufacturing overhead costs are accumulated into a separate cost pool for each production department, and each cost pool has its own volume-based cost driver.
- *Activity-based costing* further increases the accuracy and complexity of allocating manufacturing overhead costs to products. Manufacturing overheads are accumulated in a separate cost pool for each activity, and each activity has its volume- *or* non-volume-based cost driver.

Now in this chapter we have introduced two refinements to activity-based costing that expand the possible range of costs to include:

- non-manufacturing overheads; and
- direct labour costs.

While Buthelezi and Kidman could not predict the actual levels of costs and benefits identified in Exhibit 8.6, they felt intuitively that, at Mason & Cox, the best solution was to adopt an ABC system that could be used firstly for product costing, and then at a later stage for activity cost management. Thus, a comprehensive ABC system would be implemented. This would involve higher costs in designing, implementing and maintaining the system, but would provide more accurate product costs and improved information for cost management.

Which costs should be included in the ABC system?

Although activity management is not discussed until Chapter 15, it is important to understand that the decision to include activity management in its ABC system influenced the range of costs analysed by Mason & Cox. Direct labour, manufacturing overhead and non-manufacturing costs were analysed so that management could obtain useful information for *managing activities* right across the business. Also, the system was built around a long and detailed list of activities. If a simple product costing system had been chosen instead, the structure would have looked quite different. It would have covered manufacturing overhead costs only, and would have been based on a relatively short list of broadly defined overhead activities. You have encountered this simpler approach to ABC in the Delta Controls case study in Chapter 7, and it is described in more detail in the appendix to this chapter. Ultimately, the range of costs included in an activity-based system depends on its purpose, which, in turn, depends on the needs of the organisation.

Direct material costs were not included in the Mason & Cox ABC system. As in most organisations, the Mason & Cox's existing accounting system provided accurate estimates of direct material costs, so Buthelezi saw no real benefit in putting them through the activity-based system.

L.O. 5

Using the ABC model for product costing at Mason & Cox

In the activity-based costing model described in Exhibit 8.5, the costing view is used to cost products. There are two steps: measuring the cost of activities and assigning activity costs to cost objects or products. We will describe how Buthelezi worked through these two steps by analysing the costs and activities for the year just completed.

Step one: Measuring the costs of activities

In the first step, the costs of resources are assigned to activities. This process can be simplified by using activity centres: costs are assigned to activity centres and then to activities.[5]

Assigning costs to activity centres

Buthelezi began by dividing the company into activity centres. An **activity centre** consists of a work area in which the activities have a common purpose. The types of activity centres vary from one organisation to another. At Mason & Cox, there were nine activity centres: Corporate Management, Administration, Sales and Dispatch, Factory Management, Metal Melting, Moulding, Finishing, Pattern Design, and Maintenance.

Next, Buthelezi assigned costs to each activity centre using resource drivers. The costs included all direct labour, manufacturing overhead and non-manufacturing costs for the past year and totalled R55.65 million. They were drawn directly from the general ledger accounts. Where costs were of a similar nature and driven by the same resource driver, Buthelezi combined them into a single cost category to simplify the allocation process. For example, rent, insurance, council rates and cleaning costs were combined as 'building costs'. This approach enabled Buthelezi to reduce the relatively large number of general ledger accounts to six cost categories: Wages, Depreciation, Consumables, Energy, Building costs and Other costs.

You will remember that a *resource driver* is a cost driver used to estimate the cost of resources used by an activity. It can also be used to estimate the cost of the resources used by an activity centre. Resource drivers often include the sorts of cost allocation bases used to assign indirect costs to responsibility centres, as described in Chapter 7, such as floor area, number of employees and various measures of direct inputs used. Some costs can be traced directly to activity centres rather than allocated, for example the wages of the people who work in a particular activity centre.

Exhibit 8.7 overleaf shows how Buthelezi assigned the costs to the nine activity centres, and the resource drivers used. Let's look at the costs of the Administration Centre. She identified the employees who worked in the Administration Centre and, using payroll records, estimated their wages and related on-costs at R4 000 000. She prepared a list of the equipment in the Administration Centre and identified depreciation expenses of R200 000 for that equipment. She reviewed the order forms for consumables and compiled a list of the orders from Administration; they totalled R250 000. She measured the floor space occupied by the Administration Centre and allocated building costs of R50 000 on that basis. Finally, she spread the 'Other costs' in proportion to the number of employees working in each centre, and Administration was assigned R35 000. Exhibit 8.7 shows only the costs assigned to the Administration Centre, but exactly the same procedures were used to assign costs to the other eight centres.

Identifying and costing the activities performed in each activity centre

Once the activity centres had been costed, Buthelezi needed to assign the activity centre costs to activities. She interviewed representatives from each activity centre to identify activities and their resource drivers. While some activities may be common to most organisations, many of them will be specific to individual businesses.

Let's look at the method that Buthelezi used for developing the cost pool for the activity 'Process receivables' in the Administration Centre. This is illustrated in Exhibit 8.8 on page 365. The wages assigned to Administration in Exhibit 8.7 were R4 000 000. The interviewees from Administration estimated that the employees within the centre spent 10 per cent of their time processing receivables, so 10 per cent of the wages cost (R400 000) was assigned to 'Process receivables'. The depreciation costs for the Administration Centre were R200 000, which related to the Centre's 10 computer terminals. One of the terminals was used exclusively and another was used about half of the time to process receivables, so 15 per cent of the *depreciation* costs (R30 000) were assigned to the activity 'Process receivables'. To understand how the remaining costs were assigned to the activity 'Process receivables', review the costs assigned to the Administration Centre and the resource drivers shown for each cost in Exhibit 8.8. While we describe 'Process receivables' as an activity, some businesses refer to activities as cost pools, reflecting the fact that a number of costs have been pooled to estimate the cost of an activity.

Exhibit 8.8 shows the costs of only one activity, 'Process receivables', in one activity centre, Administration. However, the same procedures were used to cost the other activities in the Administration Centre and in the eight other centres.

Once the interviews were complete, Buthelezi was able to compile a list of all the activities performed at Mason & Cox and their estimated cost. The costed activities became the basic building blocks for the product costing system.

Step two: Assigning activity costs to products

According to the model shown in Exhibit 8.5, the second step of activity-based product costing is to assign activity costs to products. This involves estimating the cost per unit of activity driver for each activity, and then preparing a bill of activities for each product.

Calculating the cost per unit of activity driver

When interviewees identified activities in the previous step, they also identified activity drivers for each activity. You will remember that an *activity driver* is a cost driver used to estimate the cost of

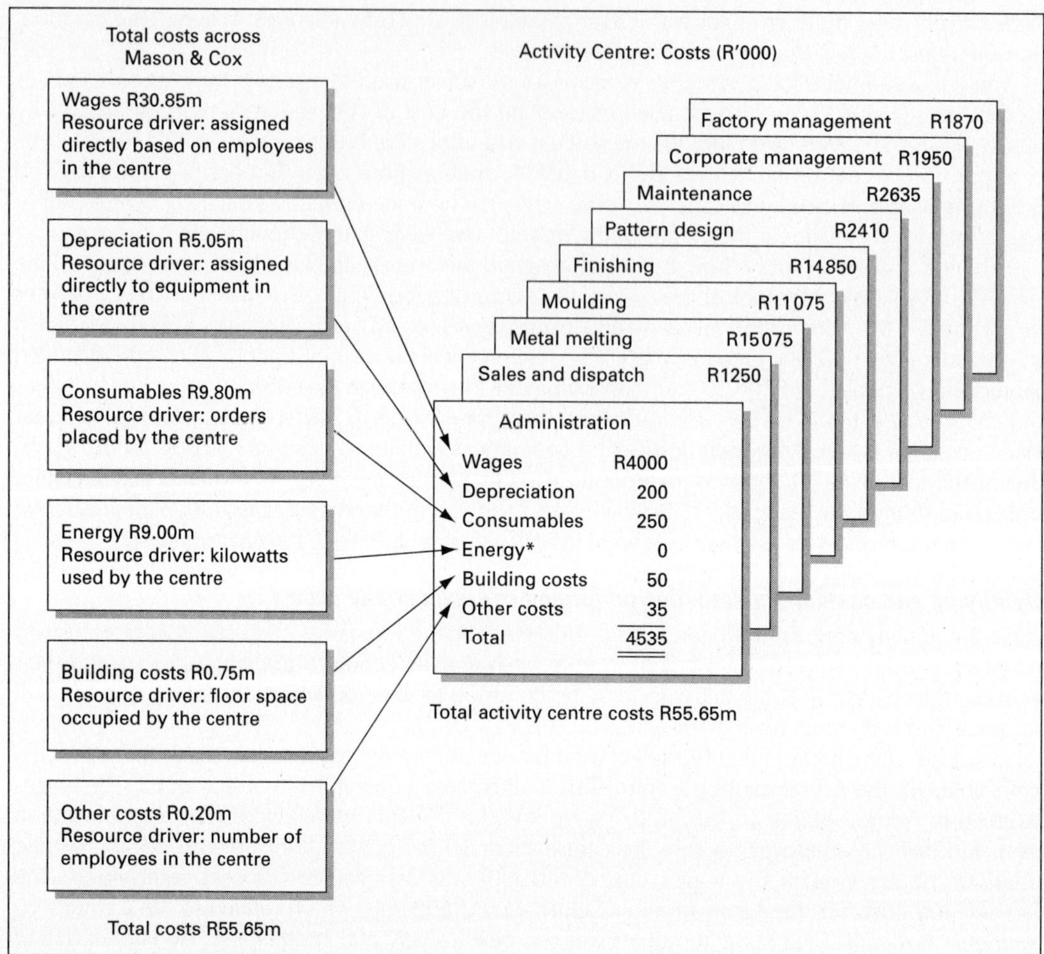

* Energy used by Administration Centre was minimal.

Exhibit 8.7 Assigning costs of resources to activity centres at Mason & Cox

an activity consumed by the cost object – in this case, products. For example, the 'number of invoices processed' is an activity driver for the activity 'Process receivables'. It can be used to assign the cost of the activity 'Process receivables' to all the products that involve receivables. In selecting an activity driver, there must be a linear relationship between the activity costs and the activity driver, otherwise the cost of the cost object will be distorted. For example, when we select the number of invoices as the activity driver, we are saying that twice as many resources are used to process two invoices as are used to process one invoice.

Buthelezi obtained estimates of the quantity of activity driver for each activity for the past year so that she could calculate the **cost per unit of activity driver**. Some businesses use the term *cost pool rate* to describe the cost per unit of activity driver, reflecting the fact that an activity is a cost pool.[6] The activities, costs and activity drivers are shown in Exhibit 8.9.

A careful examination of Exhibit 8.9 shows that there are three main types of activity driver:

1 *Physical volume*, such as the number of kilograms for the activity 'Pour metal'.
2 The *number of transactions*, such as the number of set-ups for the activity 'Set up heat treat furnace'.
3 *Time duration*, such as the number of man-hours for the activity 'Make CT moulds'.

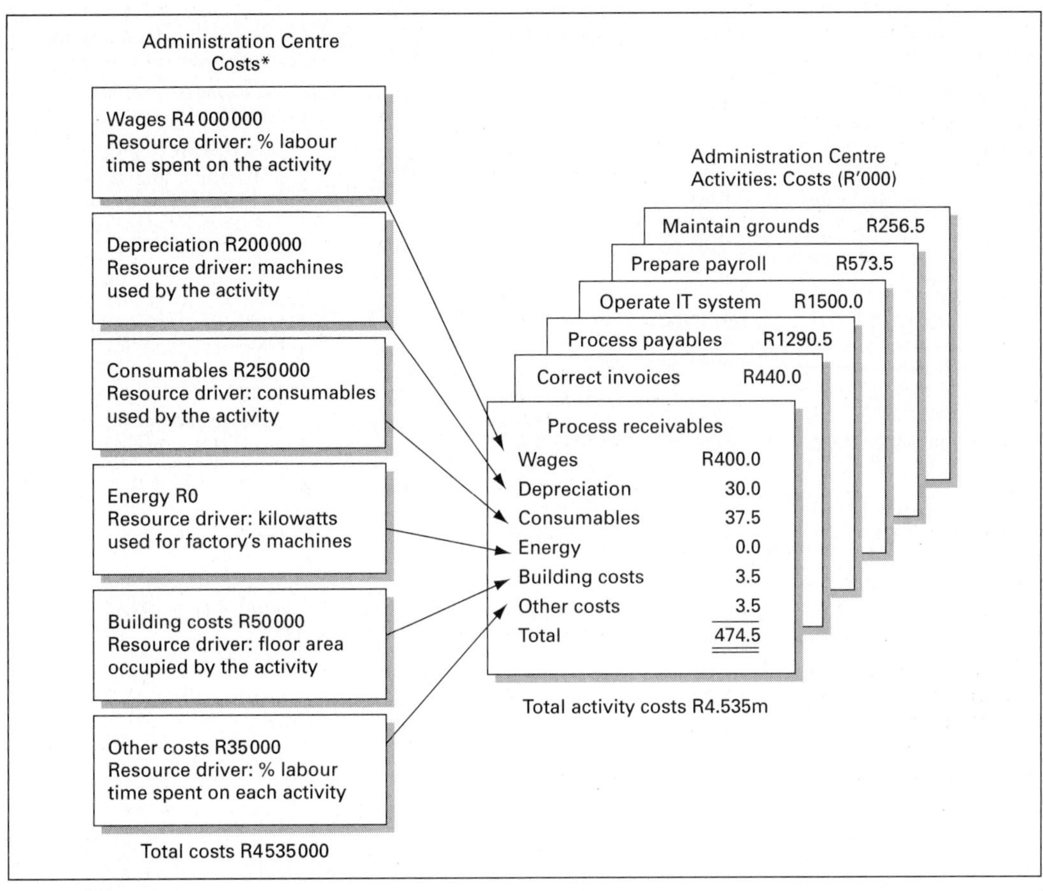

* See Exhibit 8.7.

Exhibit 8.8 Assigning activity centre costs to activities at Mason & Cox

In addition, the costs of some activities, such as 'Design method' and 'Rework pattern', relate to specific products and can be assigned directly to those products.

Preparing a bill of activities for each product

Next, Buthelezi prepared a **bill of activities** for each major product, which identified the activities, the cost per unit of activity driver, the quantity of activity drivers consumed and, therefore, the cost of the activities consumed by the product. The bills of activities for the Hensley Tooth and the Custom Cast Tooth are shown in Exhibit 8.10.

The activity-based product costs

The activity-based product costs for the Hensley Tooth and the Custom Cast Tooth are shown in Exhibit 8.10. The Hensley Tooth now has an estimated cost of **R168.54** per unit. The direct material cost, which was drawn from the conventional costing system, remains at R60.00 per unit. The remaining R108.54 reflects the estimated cost of all the activities consumed in designing, producing and selling one Hensley Tooth. The Custom Cast Tooth now has an estimated cost of **R363.73** per unit, of which R60.00 is the direct material cost and R303.73 is the cost of activities.

Where did Buthelezi get these numbers from, and what do they mean? Let's focus on the cost of the Hensley Tooth. Over the year, the Hensley Tooth is produced in 100 batches of 250 units to meet the required annual volume of 25 000 units. Exhibit 8.10 shows the cost of producing the annual volume of 25 000 units. For each activity, the annual cost is the cost per unit of activity driver, multiplied by the quantity of activity drivers consumed in producing and selling the Hensley

Activity centres and activities	Activity cost	Activity driver	Quantity of activity driver	Cost per unit of activity driver
Corporate management				
Manage business (CEO)	R500 000	None available		Facility activity
Manage business (Board)	1 000 000	None available		Facility activity
Prepare annual accounts	175 000	None available		Facility activity
Produce annual report	275 000	None available		Facility activity
	1 950 000			
Administration*				
Process receivables	474 500	No. of invoices	5 000	R 94.90
Correct invoices	440 000	No. of invoices corrected	1 000	440.00
Process payables	1 290 500	No. of purchase orders	2 500	516.20
Operate IT system	1 500 000	No. of minutes CPU time	100 000	15.00
Prepare payroll	573 500	No. of payslips	3 380	169.67
Maintain grounds	256 500	None available		Facility activity
	4 535 000			
Sales and dispatch				
Process sales order	1 250 000	No. of sales orders	4 000	312.50
Factory management				
Program production	1 305 500	No. of production runs	1 200	1 087.92
Manage plant	564 500	No. of production man-hours	61 000	9.25
	1 870 000			
Metal melting				
Pour metal	15 075 000	No. of kilograms	7 500 000	2.01
Moulding				
Make CT moulds	4 075 000	No. of man-hours	13 500	301.85
Make job moulds	3 900 000	No. of man-hours	12 500	312.00
Make cores	875 000	No. of man-hours	3 000	291.67
Move material	1 225 000	No. of moves	10 000	122.50
Inspect moulds	1 000 000	No. of moulds inspected	65 000	15.38
	11 075 000			
Finishing				
Oxy cut casting	721 250	No. of man-hours	3 000	240.42
Grind castings	2 007 500	No. of man-hours	16 000	125.47
Weld defects	1 390 000	No. of man-hours	13 000	106.92
Operate shot blast machine	3 662 500	No. of loads	3 200	1 144.53
Set up heat treat furnace	2 135 000	No. of setups	4 000	533.75
Operate heat treat furnace	3 260 000	No. of kilogram-hours	5 400 000	0.60
Expedite castings	1 082 500	No. of expedited batches	800	1 353.13
Inspect castings	591 250	No. of castings inspected	10 000	59.13
	14 850 000			
Pattern design				
Design method	1 250 000	Direct assignment†		
Issue pattern	625 000	No. of pattern issues	1 200	520.83
Rework pattern	535 000	Direct assignment†		
	2 410 000			
Maintenance				
Repair shot blast machine	875 000	No. of loads	3 200	273.44
Repair heat treat furnace	925 000	No. of kilogram-hours	5 400 000	0.17
Preventative maintenance	835 000	No. of man-hours	10 000	83.50
	2 635 000			
TOTAL COSTS	**R55 650 000**			

* See Exhibit 8.8.

† The costs of the activities 'Design method' and 'Rework pattern' are assigned directly to individual products based on their consumption of these activities.

Exhibit 8.9 Activities and activity costs per unit of activity driver, Mason & Cox

7.5 kg Hensley Tooth: Bill of activities					
Activity level	**Activity**	**Cost/unit of actvity driver**	**Annual quantity of activity driver consumed**	**Annual cost**	**Cost per unit of product**
Unit	Prepare payroll*	R169.67	600	R101 802	
Unit	Make CT moulds	301.85	1 500	452 775	
Unit	Pour metal	2.01	187 500	376 875	
Unit	Weld defects	106.92	3 500	374 220	
Unit	Operate heat treat furnace	0.60	1 125 000	675 000	
Batch	Process payables*	516.20	200	103 240	
Batch	Operate IT system*	15.00	2 150	32 250	
Batch	Process sales order*	312.50	300	93 750	
Batch	Program production	1 087.92	100	108 792	
Batch	Issue pattern*	520.83	100	52 083	
Batch	Move material	122.50	1 000	122 500	
Batch	Operate shot blast machine	1 144.53	100	114 453	
Batch	Set up heat treat furnace	533.75	100	53 375	
Product	Design method*†			6 250	
Facility	Manage plant	9.25	5 000	46 250	
Total activity cost (annual and per unit)‡			25 000	R2 713 615	108.54
Direct material cost/unit					60.00
TOTAL PRODUCT COST/UNIT					**R168.54**

7.5 kg Custom Cast Tooth: Bill of activities					
Activity level	**Activity**	**Cost/unit of actvity driver**	**Annual quantity of activity driver consumed**	**Annual cost**	**Cost per unit of product**
Unit	Prepare payroll*	R169.67	15	R2 545	
Unit	Make job moulds	312.00	30	9 360	
Unit	Inspect moulds	15.38	500	7 690	
Unit	Pour metal	2.01	3 750	7 538	
Unit	Weld defects	106.92	70	7 484	
Unit	Operate heat treat furnace	0.60	22 500	13 500	
Unit	Inspect castings	59.13	500	29 565	
Batch	Process payables*	516.20	15	7 743	
Batch	Operate IT system*	15.00	112	1 680	
Batch	Process sales order*	312.50	10	3 125	
Batch	Program production	1087.92	10	10 879	
Batch	Issue pattern*	520.83	10	5 208	
Batch	Move material	122.50	100	12 250	
Batch	Operate shot blast machine	1144.53	10	11 445	
Batch	Set up heat treat furnace	533.75	10	5 338	
Batch	Expediate castings	1353.13	5	6 766	
Product	Design method*†			8 825	
Facility	Manage plant	9.25	100	925	
Total activity cost (annual and per unit)§			500	R151 866	303.73
Direct material cost/unit					60.00
TOTAL PRODUCE COST/UNIT					**R363.73**

* Non-manufacturing activity.
† Design costs are assigned directly to products.
‡ Annual cost is based on 100 batches of 250 units; unit cost is based on annual volume of 25 000 units.
§ Annual cost is based on 10 batches of 50 units; unit cost is based on annual volume of 500 units.

Exhibit 8.10 Activity-based product costs, Mason & Cox

Tooth over the year.[7] The unit cost is the annual cost divided by the number of units, 25 000, produced over the year.

As you examine Exhibit 8.10 you may notice that the quantity of activity drivers consumed by a product depends on whether the activity is performed for each unit, batch, or entire product line. (You may remember that we introduced the concept of unit, batch, product and facility level activities in Chapter 3, when discussing cost drivers.) For example, the activities 'Program production' and 'Set up heat treat furnace' are **batch level activities**, as they are performed for each batch of castings. In contrast, activities such as 'Inspect moulds', 'Inspect castings' and 'Pour metal' are **unit level activities**, as they must be performed for each casting (production unit) produced. The third type of activity identified in Exhibit 8.10 is a **product level** (or **product-sustaining**) **activity**, which is an activity performed to enable the design, production and sale of an entire product line. At Mason & Cox, the activity 'Design method', which refers to designing a product and its production processes, is a product level activity. The costs of some product level activities vary with the number of products produced, but others may be assigned directly to individual products. There is a fourth type of activity, a **facility level** (or **facility-sustaining**) **activity**, which is an activity required to run the business. Facility level activities reflect the costs of providing the overall environment for producing and selling products. Since facility level activities are not caused by any particular product and can only be allocated to products in some arbitrary manner, it can be argued that they should not be included in the product cost. However, it seems that the allocation of facility level costs to products does occur in practice (Cooper, 1990). In Exhibit 8.9 all the activities in the Corporate Management Centre, plus the activity 'Maintain grounds' in the Administration Centre, are facility level activities. Hence no activity drivers are identified. The activity 'Manage plant' is also a facility level cost, but Buthelezi has decided to allocate the costs of this activity to products. She wishes to include all manufacturing activities in product costs, and, in her view, the man-hours worked in the production plant provide a reasonable basis for allocating this cost.

Activity-based versus conventional product costs

L.O. 6

To demonstrate the impact of the new activity-based system, Buthelezi chose to compare the activity-based cost of the 7.5 kg Hensley Tooth and the 7.5 kg Custom Cast Tooth to their cost under the existing, conventional product costing system. As mentioned earlier, under the current conventional costing system these products had identical product costs, but this did not seem to make sense to the managers.

When comparing activity-based product costs with conventional product costs, we must be careful to compare 'like with like'. For example, the conventional product costs calculated earlier in this chapter included manufacturing costs only, but at Mason & Cox, the activity-based product costs include both the manufacturing and non-manufacturing costs that were related to the product. The non-manufacturing costs are denoted by an asterisk in Exhibit 8.10. If these costs are removed, we find that the manufacturing cost is R152.97 for the Hensley Tooth and R305.48 for the Custom Cast Tooth.

Remember that Costello was sure that the existing system overstated the manufacturing cost of the high-volume product line, the Hensley Tooth, and understated the cost of the low-volume product line, the Custom Cast Tooth. Exhibit 8.11 shows that he was right. The conventional cost for the Hensley Tooth is 16 per cent higher than its activity-based cost, and the conventional cost of the Custom Cast Tooth is 42 per cent lower than its activity-based cost. What caused these differences? How do we know that the activity-based cost is more accurate?

Causes of differences between ABC and conventional product costs

The existing system assumed that the two products had the same manufacturing overhead cost because they consumed the same amount of direct labour. In fact, the Hensley Tooth has a *much lower manufacturing overhead cost*, for two reasons. First, the conventional system assumed that

	Hensley Tooth	Custom Cast Tooth
Conventional product cost	R177.70	R177.70
Activity-based manufacturing product cost	152.97	305.48
Difference	16% overstated	42% understated
Total activity-based product cost*	168.54	363.73

*Total product cost, which includes product-related non-manufacturing costs, is not available from the conventional costing system

Exhibit 8.11 Comparison of conventional and activity-based product costs at Mason & Cox

all manufacturing overhead costs were driven by the volume of production – that is, that they were unit level costs. But, as shown in Exhibit 8.10, a number of the overhead costs were batch level costs rather than unit level costs. Hensley Tooth batches are large, so there is a relatively low level of consumption of batch activities *per unit* produced. Second, the Hensley Tooth is a simple product to make. It does not require a large amount of overhead support. The level of overhead support is lower than the average level of support assumed in the average plantwide overhead rate. The Custom Cast Tooth has a *much higher manufacturing cost* than that estimated by the conventional system. As shown in Exhibit 8.10, it has a number of batch activities, and batch sizes are small. This means a relatively high consumption of batch level costs *per unit.* The Custom Cast Tooth is also complex to make and requires a higher than average level of overhead support activities.

In the activity-based system, the inclusion of non-manufacturing costs increases the cost of the Hensley Tooth by R15.57 and of the Custom Cast Tooth by R58.25. Both products use the same types of non-manufacturing support activities, but the non-manufacturing costs have a more dramatic effect on the Custom Cast Tooth. This is because a number of these activities are batch level activities, and the small batch size results in a relatively high cost per unit. Mason & Cox's management can use this total cost information to assess product profitability and review product prices (or to consider how activities and costs can be managed more effectively, as we will see in Chapter 15).

ABC at Mason & Cox: trial or triumph?

Once the activity-based system was established, Kidman and Buthelezi decided to review its costs and benefits. Implementing activity-based costing had consumed a lot of Buthelezi's time and a lot of management and interviewee time. The activity-based system was more complex than the existing costing system and would require a considerable amount of ongoing effort and costs to maintain the accuracy of the information used within the system.

The new system had not been in place for long, but Kidman could already see some benefits. Product costs now reflected more accurately the cost of the resources used in producing and selling the product. They made sense to both the production and marketing people. Under ABC, the company's 'cost-plus' pricing now seemed to be in line with competitors' prices and customer expectations. Also, it was possible to make more reliable estimates of product profitability, which provided a sound basis for decisions about product mix and product promotion. It was early days, but already sales revenue and profits looked more favourable.

Under the conventional costing system, many product costs had been distorted and the 'cost-plus' prices were not being accepted by customers. It was frightening to think that management may have used this unreliable costing information to decide which products to produce and promote. They may also have discontinued some high-volume products because they appeared unprofitable when, in fact, they were not. Or perhaps they had promoted some low-volume products that appeared profitable, when they were losers rather than winners!

The important point is that these problems are not confined to Mason & Cox. They are likely to occur in many businesses. Kidman had heard that a number of progressive South African businesses had implemented activity-based costing in some of their business units. Now he understood why!

REAL LIFE: ACTIVITY-BASED COSTING AT BARLOWORLD

Barloworld is a leading industrial brand management company. The company's brands include Caterpillar, Avis and Hyster.

The company adopted a Value-Based Management (VBM) program in early 2000 and evaluated all projects by comparing project returns to the company's real weighted average cost of capital of 8 per cent. Integral to achieving higher returns has also been the company's move to a system of activity-based costing. A number of years ago, the CEO indicated in the annual report that:

As mentioned last year, the VBM process has led us to place a greater emphasis on the quality of business we do and, as a result, we have improved our margins in many areas. The roll-out of activity-based costing (ABC) across the business units is assisting in our identification of the true costs associated with each aspect of our business.

The company refocused its attention on profitable operations, rationalised the steel tube business and exited unprofitable operations. The company also outsourced certain non-strategic activities.

Barloworld has achieved significant returns for its shareholders in the years up to 2007 and this is partly due to the adoption of Value-Based Management and activity-based costing.

The ABC decision

In many businesses product diversity has increased and cost structures have become more overhead-intensive and less volume-driven. Under these circumstances, conventional costing systems are likely to overstate the costs of high-volume simple products produced in large batches, and understate the costs of low-volume customised products produced in small batches. Where product costs are an essential part of the strategic decision-making, planning and control processes, these businesses are likely to experience considerable difficulty because of the inadequate information from their conventional costing systems, and to reap substantial benefits from implementing activity-based costing. However, many of these businesses do not use ABC. The decision of whether or not to implement ABC should be based on a careful assessment of the costs and benefits.

When to use ABC

L.O. 7 The benefits from ABC will be greatest where:

- overhead costs are a significant portion of total costs, and a large part of overhead is not directly related to production volume;
- the business has a diverse product range, and individual products' use of support resources differs from their use of volume-based cost drivers;
- production activity involves diverse batch sizes and product complexity;

- the proportion of product-related costs incurred outside of manufacturing is increasing relative to manufacturing costs;
- there are likely to be high 'costs' associated with making inappropriate decisions based on inaccurate product costs (this is most likely in a highly competitive environment where product cost is a key input to strategic decision-making and where competitors have accurate product cost information);
- the cost of designing, implementing and maintaining the ABC system is likely to be relatively low due to sophisticated IT support.

Impediments to introducing ABC

L.O. 8

While the benefits from ABC can be significant, the take-up rate has been relatively slow. Some firms believe that their existing costing is adequate – and it may be, if they have low overheads and limited product diversity. In other firms ABC would significantly improve the accuracy of product costing, but it has not been adopted. Why not? Perhaps these firms:

- remain unaware of ABC;
- are uncertain about the potential benefits from ABC;
- understand the need for change but are concerned about the extensive resource requirements to implement ABC; or
- are constrained by powerful behavioural factors that cause resistance to change. (This issue is explored later in the chapter.)

We should not view the decision to stick with an existing costing system as irrational. In many cases it is likely to reflect an assessment, formal or informal, of the perceived costs and benefits of ABC. The 'Real life' below, on ABC in South African manufacturing companies, discusses these issues further.

Other activity-based costing issues

L.O. 9

The Mason & Cox case provides a comprehensive description of activity-based costing, but there are a number of additional issues that must be considered, including the variations in the types of ABC systems, the implications of excess capacity, behavioural issues and limitations of ABC.

Variations in types of ABC

There is not one ABC system but many. ABC can be used for product costing, activity management, or both. Product costing systems may be confined to the analysis of manufacturing overhead, or they may include product-related non-manufacturing costs and direct labour costs too. But there are other sources of variation, such as whether:

- actual (past) or budgeted costs are analysed;
- the implementation is a one-off project or an ongoing system;
- cost objects other than products are included.

Budgeted or actual costs

The ABC implementation at Mason & Cox analysed the prior year's costs. However, it's not 'What did this product cost?' but 'What will this product cost?' that is relevant to making strategic decisions such as deciding which products to produce and what prices to charge. Budgeted costs provide more timely and relevant information for such decisions. In a *stable* environment, past costs can be reliable indicators of future costs. In a *rapidly changing* environment, past costs are less

REAL LIFE: ABC IN SOUTH AFRICAN, UK AND AUSTRALIAN COMPANIES

A survey of South African companies found that 32 per cent of responding companies had adopted ABC and a further 17 per cent were intending to introduce ABC, while only 8.5 per cent had decided against adopting ABC. Other companies had given some consideration and 23.4 per cent of companies had no discussions on the introduction of ABC. It was found that 13.3 per cent of the companies using ABC used between 1 and 5 cost drivers, 60 per cent of the companies used between 6 and 10 cost drivers, while 26.7 per cent of the companies used between 11 and 20 cost drivers. In the UK, a study by Burns in 1999 reported that 31 per cent of companies had adopted ABC.

A survey of Australian manufacturers in the mid-1990s found that only 12 per cent of respondents had adopted ABC, 29 per cent were currently evaluating it, 45 per cent had never formally considered adopting it, and 14 per cent had considered and rejected it.

The firms that had adopted ABC perceived their overhead costs to be high and important. Interestingly, the survey results indicated little actual difference between the level of overhead costs of adopters and of other respondents, although adopters' views of the increases in overhead costs over the previous five years were stronger than for other respondents. Other reasons for adopting ABC included a large number of product lines, and problems with their old costing system. Adopters were seeking more accurate product costs, better allocation of overhead, and better information for cost control and cost management. Almost all adopters had achieved their objectives, and adopters were unanimous in their view that the introduction of ABC had been successful.

Although the adoption rate was low, one-third of the firms that had never formally considered ABC expected to do so, largely within the next two years. Also, almost half of the firms currently *evaluating* ABC considered it probable that they would adopt ABC, mainly within the next year. And almost one-third of those firms that had considered ABC and rejected it, indicated that they would probably reconsider ABC, mostly within the next year. However, a survey of Australia's CPAs in 2000 ranked ABC as 22nd in importance from a list of 33 tools and techniques, suggesting relatively little increase in enthusiasm for activity-based approaches over the mid to late 1990s.

Another recent survey found ABC adoption rates among *very large* manufacturing firms in Australia to be 56 per cent. While this rate appears high, larger firms are more likely than small firms to have access to resources and expertise to experiment with ABC systems. Also, in some cases, ABC may have been used as an *ad hoc* special costing project rather than as a fully implemented costing system. In the same survey, managers indicated only low levels of benefits had been gained from ABC, although they intended to place increased emphasis on ABC in the future. In the South African survey, the responding companies tended to be large listed companies and the adoption of ABC in small companies remains elusive.

Sources: Waweru, Hoque and Uliana (2005), Burns et al. (1999), Booth & Giacobbe (1997); Chenhall & Langfield-Smith (1998); CPA Australia (2000)

relevant, but it may be very difficult to predict future costs and activities accurately. (You may remember that Delta Controls, in Chapter 7, developed budgeted activity costs to estimate the costs of its two valves.) Some businesses analyse past costs as a starting point for their ABC system, and later move to budgeted costs. Others simply analyse past costs as a one-off exercise.

ABC project or ABC system?

Not all businesses implement ABC as an ongoing costing system; some adopt a project approach instead. However, the choice is not whether ABC is either a project or an ongoing system: these choices can be viewed as ends of a continuum. Where strategic plans are developed or reviewed relatively infrequently, a business may not require accurate estimates of product costs on a day-by-day basis. They may simply determine activity-based product costs as an occasional special project to better understand the relative costs of their products.

Other cost objects

In the Mason & Cox case study, we have focused on using activity-based costing to estimate product costs. However, the cost assignment dimension of ABC can be used to assign costs to any chosen cost object. For example, as described in Chapter 16, some businesses use ABC to estimate the costs of using particular suppliers, and some businesses identify the costs of producing products *and* servicing particular customers. These ABC models include product-related cost drivers (that is, unit, batch and product level cost drivers) and customer-related cost drivers. We describe customer-related activities and cost drivers in Chapter 16, and in Chapter 18 we explore the profit model for a business that recognises both product-related and customer-related activities and cost drivers.

Implications of excess capacity

L.O. 10

ABC estimates the cost of resources *used* to perform activities to produce and sell products. Conventional financial statements, such as the income statement, focus on the cost of the resources *supplied*. Some resources, such as direct material, energy sources and some forms of labour, are supplied as they are used. However, other resources, such as plant, equipment and supervision, are supplied in advance. These resources are called **committed resources**. Where activity costs are based on budgeted costs, *the committed resources supplied will not necessarily equal the resources used* because of unused capacity (that is, *underutilised* activities). In estimating and reporting profit under an ABC system, therefore, it is necessary to include the cost of unused capacity, when budgeted costs have been used (Cooper & Kaplan, 1992). At Mason & Cox, the ABC system was used to assign actual costs, including committed costs, to products at year-end, so this issue did not arise. The 'Real life' on art.com below describes an ABC system that included the identification of costs of unused capacity.

Behavioural issues in implementing activity-based costing

L.O. 11

ABC involves major changes in the ways in which data are collected and analysed and the business is managed. In many organisations, any change is perceived as threatening and is therefore likely to be resisted. To succeed, the introduction of activity-based costing must be accompanied by a change management plan that is carefully constructed to take account of the extent of change required and the personalities involved. The design and implementation of ABC requires far more involvement of *non-accounting* staff than that of a conventional costing system. Consider the amount of involvement of operational employees from across the business in the development of the ABC system at Mason & Cox. Developing an effective ABC system requires the cooperation and expertise of many people – not just accountants!

There is no single formula for managing change, although there is some evidence to suggest that the process will be most effective where a 'bottom up' approach rather than a 'top down' approach is used. With a 'bottom up' approach, instead of viewing the activity-based system as a financial system imposed by top management, employees would be encouraged to consider ABC as a tool that *they* own, to help *them* manage *their* work. Developing a sense of ownership requires a high degree of participation in the development and implementation of the new system across all levels of the organisational hierarchy. Management must be seen to be totally committed to the activity-based project, but also willing to let employees play a major role in developing and using the system. Evidence from the US indicates that organisational and behavioural issues can have a major effect on the success of activity based costing (Shields, 1995).

REAL LIFE: THE COST OF UNUSED CAPACITY AT ART.COM

The e-retailer art.com sells prints and framed print art. Timely and accurate cost information is particularly important for e-businesses because their competitive environment tends to be very fluid. Activities for art.com include 'service customers', 'web site optimisation', 'merchandise inventory selection and management', 'purchasing and receiving', 'customer acquisition and retention – revenue share marketing', 'customer acquisition and retention – paid for marketing', 'sustain information system', 'sustain business – administration', 'sustain business – production', 'sustain business – executive', 'maintain facility – administration' and 'maintain facility – production'. A major problem facing dot.com companies is the difficulty in predicting demand and, therefore, in matching resources supplied with resources used. At art.com, in addition to estimating the cost of each order, the ABC system was used to estimate the Rand value of unused resources in total, by activity and by product line. According to art.com, 'unless a Rand value is attached to used and unused capacity, it won't gain management's attention'.

Source: Zeller, Kublank & Makris (2001)

Limitations of activity-based costing

L.O. 12 While ABC has the potential to improve the accuracy of product costs, it is important to understand its limitations:

- *Facility level costs*. Some proponents of ABC recommend that virtually all costs, including facility costs, be assigned to products. However, facility level activities bear no obvious relationship to products. (In the Mason & Cox case, the costs of 'Manage plant' were the only facility level costs assigned to products.) If facility level costs are assigned to products, the allocation basis must be arbitrary. The higher the proportion of allocated facility costs, the greater the arbitrary element of the product costs. Of course a business must cover its facility level costs to make a profit but, in the profit statement, it is better to deduct them after estimating the product-related profit margin rather than including them in the product costs.
- *Use of average costs*. Activity-based estimates of the cost per unit of product, such as the costs of the Hensley Tooth and the Custom Cast Tooth in Exhibit 8.10, are *average costs*. Unit level costs *are* incurred for each unit of product, but batch level, product level and any allocated facility level costs must be divided by the number of units produced to estimate the cost per unit of product. It is important that managers understand this. Many product-related decisions are better based on either unit level costs in the short term or *total* product costs in the longer term, rather than looking at the average cost *per unit* of product.
- *Complexity*. When ABC is set up as an ongoing costing system, it involves more detailed recording and analysis than for conventional costing systems. If the company is changing rapidly, the data in the activity-based system must be updated frequently to avoid the production of outdated, irrelevant information. This can be expensive. The level of complexity increases dramatically when the system is used for activity management as well as for product costing, because activity management requires a more extensive and detailed analysis of costs and activities. This issue is dealt with further in Chapter 15.

Despite these limitations, there are many examples of businesses, both in South Africa and abroad, that have implemented ABC, such as the organisations described in the 'Real life' below and in other 'Real life' features spread throughout this chapter.

REAL LIFE: ACTIVITY-BASED COSTING ABROAD

So far we have cited mainly the experiences of South African businesses that use activity-based costing, but there are also numerous examples of successful ABC implementations from abroad. For example, in the US, the United Methodist Publishing House (UMPH) implemented an activity-based system to obtain more reliable estimates of its product costs than those available from its conventional costing system, and to generate information about the profitability of various sales channels. UMPH is a not-for-profit religious organisation, with 1000 employees and annual sales of approximately $US112 million. It sells its products in many different ways: through the Internet, a toll-free phone catalogue, 70 retail stores, and a range of wholesalers. The organisation was able to use activity-based information to make strategic decisions about what products to offer through which sales channels.

Environmental activities, such as preventing adverse effects on the environment, disposing of waste in an environmentally friendly manner, detecting activities and remedying outcomes that are environmentally damaging, and meeting regulatory requirements for environmental reporting, are becoming an increasing cost for many businesses. A chemical processing business in the US developed an Environmental Activity Cost Analysis (EACA) to measure its environmental costs and to attribute them to both business functions and products. (Environmental issues in management accounting are considered in more detail in Chapter 17.)

In a major project, the multinational Dow Chemical Company implemented ABC across its operations throughout the world. Dow uses its SAP system to track activities and their costs, and to cost products, internal services and customer orders. The information at Dow is used both for product costing and for activity-based management.

Sources: Forsythe, Bunch & Burton (1999); Quarles & Stratton (1998); Damitio, Hayes & Kintzele (2000)

REAL LIFE: ACTIVITY-BASED COSTING IN LOCAL GOVERNMENT

The National Treasury of South Africa has introduced legislation in terms of the Municipal Finance Management Act (MFMA) which will lead municipalities to introduce activity-based costing to determine the costs of services.

Buffalo City is a major municipality which encompasses the towns of East London, King William's Town and Bisho. The Buffalo City Municipal Council is responsible for over 900 000 residents and the municipality wished to determine the cost of providing each service. The implementation of ABC had been defined as a strategic priority in the city's 5-year Strategic Plan. Buffalo City states in its uniform tariff policy document that:

The annual tariffs per service should be compared to the activity-based costing results, to view the profitability per service and level of cross subsidization. The goal should be to, where possible, provide a cost-reflective service charge

In the municipality's 2006 to 2008 operating budget, the adoption of activity-based costing is crucial for the setting of tariffs. The following are extracts from the operating budget.

A major initiative which supports the reliability of the Budgets has been the implementation of Activity-Based Costing / Management in tariff setting and calculation of inter-departmental charges.

In relation to refuse removal, Buffalo City stated that:

Tariffs have been based on cost and surplus financial modelling, under-pinned by activity-based costing methodology.

In relation to electricity services, Buffalo City stated that:

Future percentage increases will no longer be requested on a 'global percentage' increase basis, but on activity-based costing results, per consumer type, per voltage level, per time of use.

Buffalo City was the first municipality in South Africa to adopt activity-based costing and activity-based management and the city used the Metify ABM system. Management ran seminars and presentations to all employees on the workings of ABC. Buffalo City focused on the 10 most expensive services and the city was able to determine the cost of each activity. This enabled the city to compare the cost of each service to the tariff charged to the public and the city plans to realign tariffs to the costs of providing services. In relation to health care, the city now knows for example the costs of treating an HIV patient, an infant and a TB patient. This enables the city to budget and forecast more accurately what the future health care costs will be.

The City of Johannesburg is currently introducing activity-based costing, which is part of the city's Integrated Development Plan. The Executive Mayor, Amos Masondo, indicated in his State of the City address in 2006 that:

In this term of office, we will ensure that the following is achieved: Implementation of an Activity-Based Costing methodology, which will drive the allocation of resources for the City and its Municipality-Owned Entities.

The Gauteng Treasury in its Budget Statement for 2006/7 reported that an activity-based costing pilot project was undertaken in the Department of Sports, Recreation, Arts and Culture. The Budget Statement stated that the project resulted in:

- Installation of SAS ABM software
- Interview of managers and validation of activities
- Restructuring of the general ledger and reallocation of general ledger costs to cost centres
- Costing and validation of activities
- Construction of an ABC budget.

Activity-based costing has been introduced by the ANC national government, yet the DA, not to be outdone, indicated in its approach to local government that:

The DA will ensure that before any outsourcing or privatisation takes place, an activity-based costing exercise is undertaken. This will allow a local council to determine accurately the competitiveness of the services they provide and the viability of outsourcing.

Who would have thought that the ANC and the DA would be vying to be the first to implement an activity-based costing system for local government? Politics is coming into the arena of management accounting!

Activity-based costing in service organisations

L.O. 13

Activity-based costing can help to overcome the problems of inaccurate conventional costing in service businesses, although three factors make it more difficult to implement than in manufacturing:

1 Service businesses often have a higher level of facility costs than do most manufacturers, so fewer costs may be included in the ABC system.

2 It is often difficult to identify individual activities, because they are non-repetitive. An activity may be repeated, but in a different way for each client.

3 The non-repetitive production environment may also make it difficult to identify service outputs.

Consider the services provided by your local doctor. Two patients may be booked in for the removal of skin lesions. One skin lesion is a small sunspot that can be removed by burning it with dry ice. The second lesion is much larger and deeper and has to be cut out. Is there one product, 'The removal of a skin lesion', or are there two products, 'Burning off skin lesions' and 'Cutting out skin lesions'? To cut out the skin lesion, the doctor has to administer a local anaesthetic. Is this part of the product 'Cutting out skin lesions', or a separate product, 'Administering local anaesthetic'? What appears to be a basic product may actually disguise a whole range of different products.

Now what if both patients had sunspots which required the same basic activities of drawing up the dry ice, burning the lesion and dressing the wound, but the burning of one lesion turned out to be much more difficult and time consuming than burning the other? Both services require the same basic activities, but they have very different costs. Is 'Burning the lesion' one activity, or should there be one activity for 'Burning simple lesions' and another for 'Burning more difficult lesions'?

Despite these problems, activity-based costing has been used in a number of major South African service businesses including the South African Post Office, Standard Bank, ABSA and at a number of municipalities. The ABC experiences of some of these organisations have been outlined earlier. The 'Real life' below describes ABC in universities.

REAL LIFE: ABC FOR EDUCATION INSTITUTIONS: AN INTERNATIONAL PERSPECTIVE

In a prior 'real life', we have referred to the implementation of the ABC model at the University of South Africa (UNISA). It is interesting to evaluate the adoption of ABC by universities in Australia, the UK and the USA.

In Australia, the federal government's Department of Education, Training and Youth Affairs (DETYA) has been active in promoting activity-based costing within universities. In 1998 DETYA commissioned the multinational accounting firm, Ernst & Young, to develop an activity-based costing methodology for Australian higher education institutions. The study identified a range of activities, such as 'teaching', 'conducting research', 'undertaking professional development' and 'developing a new subject', and corresponding activity drivers, such as 'number of teaching hours', 'number of research hours', 'number of training days' and 'number of new subjects developed'. These activities could be used to estimate the cost of courses and programs, as well as the cost of research.

Despite its evolution in the US, very few of the more than 3000 colleges and universities in the US have introduced ABC. The conventional costing systems in these institutions tend to allocate all overhead costs using a single volume-based cost driver. They fail to recognise the cost implications of students who take courses outside of their major study area and they assume that all courses consume the same overhead activities in the same proportions. Clearly, some programs are likely to be cross-subsidising others. Professors at the University of Texas applied ABC to a

department in a large business school, in a study funded by PricewaterhouseCoopers. It was claimed that this study provided information that was 'more useful for virtually all decisions that faculty and administrators are likely to make'.

Several universities in the UK have used ABC for both costing and cost management. After introducing ABC, one university discovered that some of its graduate programs cost more than three times the tuition fees that they raised and, in another university, teaching departments actively competed for floor space, until activity-based charges for accommodation were introduced!

Courtesy of Getty Images

Sources: Ernst & Young (1998); Ernst & Young (2000); Tatikonda & Tatikonda (2001)

Summary

Product costs are needed to help managers manage resources and make decisions that create value, as well as for reporting to various outside organisations. In Chapters 4, 5 and 6 we described conventional approaches to estimating the costs of goods and services. In this chapter we identified the problems that may occur with conventional product costing systems and described activity-based product costing, which has been developed to overcome these problems. Key points include:

- Conventional product costing systems allocate overhead costs to products using one (or sometimes several) broad volume-based overhead rates. They also tend to ignore non-manufacturing costs. Yet, in many businesses a large part of overhead is now caused by such factors as product diversity and production complexity, rather than by production volume, and non-manufacturing costs are becoming more substantial. In these situations, the conventional approach to product costing is likely to distort product costs.
- There are a number of common indicators of an outdated costing system, as described in Exhibit 8.2.
- Activity-based costing (ABC) has been the major response to the problems encountered with conventional costing systems. The ABC model has two dimensions. The costing view assigns resources to the activities that consume them and then to products on the basis of the activities that the products consume. The activity management view provides information about the root causes of activities and their value to customers, and various measures of their performance.
- The range of costs assigned by the activity-based system depends on the purpose of the system. An ABC system can be used to assign manufacturing overhead costs to products, or manufacturing overhead and product-related non-manufacturing costs, or direct labour costs, in addition to manufacturing overhead and non-manufacturing costs. This third approach to activity-based costing was illustrated in this chapter, using the Mason & Cox case, and is discussed further in Chapter 15.
- The activity-based product costing involves two main steps:

– measuring the costs of activities; and

– assigning activity costs to products.

Each of these steps is described in the chapter using the Mason & Cox example.

- A comparison of activity-based and conventional product costs indicates that, in businesses that are overhead intensive and have a diverse product range, conventional product costing systems tend to overstate the cost of simple products that are made in large quantities and understate the costs of complex products made in small quantities.
- Activity-based costing is likely to benefit businesses with significant levels of non-volume driven overhead costs, a diverse product range (involving diverse batch sizes and differing degrees of production complexity) and substantial non-manufacturing costs, and where product cost information is important and IT resources are good.
- Organisations may not use ABC because of a lack of awareness or concerns about the potential benefits, finding appropriate cost drivers and the level of resources required.
- There are a range of design issues to be considered in implementing activity-based costing, including whether to use budgeted or actual costs, whether to develop an ongoing costing system or a project approach, and which cost objects should be included.
- In estimating and reporting profit under an activity-based system, where activity costs are based on budgeted costs, the cost of unused capacity should be recognised, because of the difference between the costs of resources used (identified under ABC) and the cost of resources supplied.
- Activity-based costing, particularly as an ongoing system, can involve significant organisational change and the ABC implementation should consider and actively manage resistance to change.
- Although more accurate than conventional product costing, ABC also has some limitations. Facility level costs should not be assigned to products, as they have no obvious cost drivers; average batch, product and facility level costs per unit can undermine product-related decisions; and ABC is more complex than conventional product costing.
- Activity-based costing can be useful in service organisations but can be more difficult to implement because of high facility-level costs, non-repetitive activities and difficulties in identifying and measuring service outputs.
- As discussed in the appendix, where activity-based costing is used solely to assign manufacturing overheads to products, it is possible to develop a simple system with relatively few major overhead activities and cost drivers.

We will return to activity-based costing in Chapters 15 and 16, where we examine its role in cost management.

References

Booth, P & Giacobbe, F 1997, 'Activity-based costing in Australian manufacturing firms: key survey findings', *Issues Report 5*, CPA Australia Management Accounting Centre of Excellence, March, p. 2.

Brimson, JA 1991, *Activity Accounting*, John Wiley & Sons, New York.

Burns, J, Ezzamel, M and Scapens, RW 1999, 'Management accounting change in the UK', *Management Accounting*, Vol. 77, No. 3, pp. 28–30.

Chenhall, RH & Langfield-Smith, K 1998, 'Adoption and benefits of management accounting practices: an Australian study', *Management Accounting Research*, vol. 8, no. 3, pp. 1–20.

Cooper, R 1989, 'You need a new cost system when . . .', *Harvard Business Review*, January/February, pp. 77–82.

Cooper, R 1990, 'Cost classification in unit-based and activity-based manufacturing cost systems', *Journal of Cost Management*, Fall, pp. 4–14.

Cooper, R & Kaplan, RS 1992, 'Activity-based systems: measuring the cost of resource usage', *Accounting Horizons*, September, pp. 1–13.

CPA Australia 2000, *Management Practice Trends 2000*, Report of Strategic Business Management Centre of Excellence.

Damitio, JW, Hayes, GW & Kintzele, PL 2000, 'Integrating ABC and ABM at Dow Chemical', *Management Accounting Quarterly*, Winter.

Ernst & Young 1998, *Costing Methodology for Use in Australian Higher Education Institutions.*

Ernst & Young 2000, *ABC Pilot Study at The University of Newcastle.*

Forsythe, R, Bunch, JA & Burton, EJ 1999, 'Implementing ABC and the balanced scorecard at a publishing house', *Management Accounting Quarterly*, Fall.

Johnson, HT & Kaplan, RS 1987, *Relevance Lost: The Rise and Fall of Management Accounting*, Harvard Business School Publishing, Boston, MA.

Kaplan, RS 1984, 'The evolution of management accounting', *The Accounting Review*, July, pp. 390–418.

KPMG 2007 Rethinking Cost Structures – Creating a sustainable cost advantage

Lamond, S 1992, 'Activity-based management: an Australian perspective', *Journal of Cost Management*, Summer, pp. 42–6.

O'Guin, M 1991, *The Complete Guide to Activity Based Costing*, Prentice Hall, New York.

Pityana, NB 2005, Address to the UNISA seminar on Activity-Based Costing for Organisations and Higher Education Institutions, 30–31 August 2005.

Quarles, R & Stratton, A 1998, 'A case study using ABC to quantify environmental costs in plant operations', *Journal of Cost Management*, September/October, vol. 12, no. 5, pp. 23–31.

Raffish, N & Turney, PBB (eds) 1991, 'Glossary of activity-based management', *Journal of Cost Management*, Fall, pp. 53–63.

Shields, M 1995, 'An empirical analysis of firms' implementation experiences with activity-based costing', *Journal of Management Accounting Research*, vol. 7, Fall, pp. 148–66.

Tatikonda, LU & Tatikonda, RJ 2001, 'Activity-based costing for higher education institutions', *Management Accounting Quarterly*, Winter.

Turney, PBB 1991, *Common Cents: The ABC Performance Breakthrough*, Cost Technology Inc., Beaverton, OR.

Waweru, NM, Hoque, Z and Uliana, E 2005, 'A survey of management accounting practices in South Africa', *Int. J. Accounting, Auditing and Performance Evaluation*, Vol. 2, No. 3.

Zeller, TL, Kublank, DR & Makris, PG 2001, 'How art.com uses ABC to succeed', *Strategic Finance*, March, pp. 24–31.

Self study

Self-study problem: activity-based costing

Barbara Higgins is the manager of Inhouse Training, a company that provides in-house management development training courses. The company offers two basic training packages: two-day short courses covering topics such as leadership skills, managing change and learning organisations, and five-day courses in areas such as strategic management, total quality management and developing performance measurement systems.

At the end of 20X5, Higgins reviewed the company's total costs with a view to setting prices for 20X6. During 20X5, the company ran 50 two-day courses, with an average of 50 participants, and 30 five-day courses, with an average of 30 participants. Total costs amounted to R2 088 000. Higgins decided to base prices for 20X6 on the cost per day for 20X5 plus a 20 per cent profit margin.

Before setting these prices, Higgins bumped into a friend who was a management consultant. He suggested that activity-based costing would provide a more accurate estimate of the cost of the two types of courses. With his help, Higgins identified the following activities and costs for 20X5:

Activity	Activity cost	Activity driver	Quantity of activity driver
Advertise courses	120 000	Number of courses	80
Enrol participants	51 000	Number of participants	3 400
Hire presenters	1 125 000	Number of days	250
Hire premises	75 000	Number of days	250
Hire audiovisual equipment	187 500	Number of days	250
Produce handouts	102 000	Number of participants	3 400
Provide lunches	427 500	Number of person-days	9 500
Total cost	R2 088 000		

Required:

1 Estimate the costs of a two-day course and a five-day course, using the 'average cost per day' approach.

2 Estimate the cost of a two-day course and a five-day course, using activity-based costing.

3 Which cost out of those estimated in requirements 1 and 2 do you think would provide a more reliable basis for cost-plus pricing? Explain your answer.

Solution to Self-study problem

1 Cost per course based on average cost per day:

$$\text{Total number of days on which courses were run} = (50 \times 2) + (30 \times 5) = 250 \text{ days}$$

$$\text{Total cost} = \text{R2 088 000}$$

$$\text{Cost per day} = \frac{\text{R2 088 000}}{\text{250 days}}$$

$$= \text{R8 352 per day}$$

$$\text{Cost of two-day course} = \text{R8352} \times 2 = \text{R16 704}$$

$$\text{Cost of five-day course} = \text{R8352} \times 5 = \text{R41 760}$$

2 Cost per course based on activity-based costing:

Two-day course

Activity driver	Cost per unit of activity driver	Quantity of activity driver	Activity cost
Advertise courses	R1500/course	1 course	R 1 500
Enrol participants	R15/participant	50 participants	750
Hire presenters	R4500/day	2 days	9 000
Hire premises	R300/day	2 days	600
Hire equipment	R750/day	2 days	1 500
Produce handouts	R30/participant	50 participants	1 500
Provide lunches	R45/person-day	100 person-days	4 500
Total costs			R19 350

Five-day course

Activity driver	Cost per unit of activity driver	Quantity of activity driver	Activity cost
Advertise courses	R1500/course	1 course	R 1 500
Enrol participants	R15/participant	30 participants	450
Hire presenters	R4500/day	5 days	22 500
Hire premises	R300/day	5 days	1 500
Hire equipment	R750/day	5 days	3 750
Produce handouts	R30/participant	30 participants	900
Provide lunches	R45/person-day	150 person-days	6 750
Total costs			R37 350

You will notice that we have omitted the step shown in Exhibit 8.10, in which annual activity costs were calculated for products and these costs were divided by the number of units produced over the year. For Inhouse Training, we have sufficient information to identify directly the consumption of activities for each unit of product (that is, each course).

3 The activity-based costing system provides a more accurate estimate of cost. The average cost assumes that the cost of courses varies proportionately with the number of days. While this is true for some costs (such as the costs of presenters, premises and equipment hire), other costs are incurred for each course (such as advertising costs), or for each participant (such as the costs of enrolling participants and providing them with handouts).

Cybersearch

1 Look for websites of consulting firms that offer activity-based costing services or software packages.
   (a) Are the concepts of activity-based product costing consistent with those described in the chapter? If not, describe any differences.
   (b) What benefits do the software consultants suggest may be expected from activity-based product costing? Do you consider the proposed benefits to be realistic? Explain your answer.
   (c) Do the software consultants suggest that activity-based product costing is appropriate for all organisations? If so, do you agree? Explain your answer.
2 Find a website with an example of an organisation that uses activity-based product costing.
   (a) Compare their approach with that described in the chapter.
   (b) Outline the advantages that activity-based product costing has provided for the organisation.
3 Locate websites with examples of universities that have implemented activity-based costing.
   (a) Describe the benefits from ABC that universities have experienced in estimating the costs of their courses and programs.
   (b) Can you find any evidence of resistance to the move to ABC in these universities?

Appendix to Chapter 8

Activity-based costing: an alternative approach

L.O. 14 From the discussion in this chapter, you will be aware that there are many variations of activity-based costing. Management assesses the problems that their business is facing, and an ABC system is designed to tackle those problems. The approach used at Mason & Cox is common in practice because many businesses need more accurate product costs and better information for activity management. However, the inclusion of the activity management view, in addition to the product costing view, makes the ABC system more complex. Some businesses choose a simpler version of ABC to meet their product costing needs. This type of ABC assigns only indirect costs (often only manufacturing overhead costs) to products. We introduced this approach to activity-based costing in the Delta Controls case in Chapter 7. Now we will look at it in more detail and consider how it differs from the activity-based costing system described in this chapter.

Simplifying activity-based product costing

Let's assume that the only serious problem facing Mason & Cox was distorted product costs. The distortions were caused by the inappropriate allocation of manufacturing overhead. Remember, Mason & Cox used a plantwide overhead rate based on direct labour hours. There were no major difficulties with the conventional approach to tracing direct material and direct labour costs to products. The solution to this problem is to develop an ABC system to assign the manufacturing overhead costs to activities and then to products. This is the simple activity-based product costing system that was described in the chapter (see Exhibit 8.6).

The activity-based costing model in Exhibit 8.5 can be used to describe this simple activity-based product costing system. However, this ABC system is confined to the vertical costing view and analyses only manufacturing overhead costs and manufacturing overhead activities. Thus, the two steps for the costing view become:

- Step one: Measure the costs of the *manufacturing overhead* activities.
- Step two: Assign the costs of the manufacturing overhead activities to the products.

The ABC system at Mason & Cox, which we described in the chapter, assigned R55.65 million to activities. These costs included direct labour costs (R21.1m), manufacturing overhead (R24.4m) and non-manufacturing costs (R10.15m). Direct material costs were not included as they were traced to products using the conventional approach. What happens to these costs in the simple activity-based product costing model? The direct material costs are still traced using the conventional approach and so are the R21.1 million direct labour costs. With direct costs, the conventional tracing should be reasonably accurate. The direct labour costs were included in the ABC system described in the chapter to enhance the activity management view, not to improve the product costing. The R10.15 million of non-manufacturing costs are expensed as they are incurred. These were included previously for activity management and also to provide a more complete measure of product cost. (The simple ABC system could be expanded to include these costs if management believed that their omission seriously distorted the product costs.)[8] Thus, at Mason & Cox, the simple ABC system would assign the R24.4 million manufacturing overhead costs, first to activities and then to products. Let's look at these two steps.

Step one: Measuring the cost of overhead activities

As in the more complex system, the first step in simple activity-based product costing is to identify the activities and measure their costs. Let's suppose that there were five manufacturing overhead activities at Mason & Cox: a machine-related activity, a set-up activity, a material-handling activity, an engineering activity and a facility activity.

Exhibit 8.12 shows the allocation of the R24.4 million of manufacturing overhead costs to the five major activities. Note that the activities are classified as unit level, batch level, product level and facility level, just as the detailed activities were in the chapter. The machine-related activity is a unit level activity since every product unit (casting) requires machine time. The setup and material-handling activities are classified as batch level activities because these activities must be performed for batches of castings. The engineering activity is classified as a product level activity because it is needed to support an entire product line, but is not always performed every time a new casting or batch of castings is produced. The facility level activity covers the costs that support the entire production process – plant management salaries, and some plant maintenance and insurance costs.

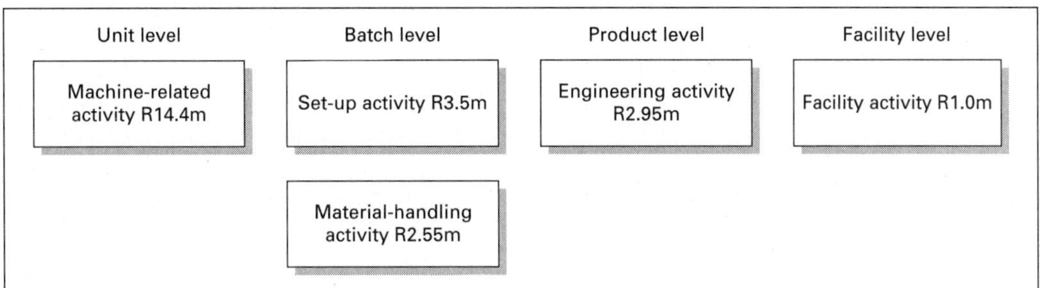

Exhibit 8.12 Measuring the cost of overhead activities at Mason & Cox

The procedure for assigning the manufacturing overhead costs to the activities is similar to the procedure for measuring activity costs described earlier in this chapter. The accounts that make up the R24.4 million are reviewed and, where they are of a similar nature and driven by the same resource driver, they are combined into cost categories. Resource drivers are used to assign the costs in each category to activities. For example, the machine-related costs would include machinery depreciation costs, consumables used by machines and the energy costs of operating the machinery. The set-up costs would include wages of employees involved in setting up machinery, consumables used during set-ups, and the costs of other resources used during set-ups. In the chapter, activity centres were used as an intermediate step to accumulate costs before assigning them to activities. Activity centres can also be used in this way in a simple product costing system.

In reality, there are more than five manufacturing overhead activities at Mason & Cox. The five major activities identified above are made up of a number of smaller activities that have been aggregated into larger activity cost pools. Activities can be aggregated in this way if they are at the same level (that is, unit, batch or product) and use the same activity driver. As discussed in the chapter, reducing the number of activities helps to keep down the complexity and cost of the system. Detailed activities are not required because the system is to be used only for product costing, not for activity management.

Step two: Assigning the activity costs to products

The second step is to assign the costs of the overhead activities to the products that consume them, based on the costs per unit of activity driver, sometimes called **cost pool rates**. You will notice that the costing procedures are very similar to those described in this chapter. Once the activity cost pools have been estimated, the costs are divided by the annual quantity of activity driver to obtain the cost per unit of activity driver for each activity. Let's assume that, in the Mason & Cox case, activity drivers could be measured for machine-related costs (machine hours), set-up costs (number of production runs), material handling (metres of material moved) and engineering (the number of engineering hours). This is shown in Exhibit 8.13. You will notice that we have not calculated a cost per unit of activity driver for facility level costs, and they have not been apportioned to product lines. As discussed in the chapter, facility costs are not attributable to any particular product lines and it would be misleading to assign them to products.

Activity	Activity cost (Rm)	Quantity of activity drivers	Cost per unit of activity driver
Machine-related*	14.40	100 000	R144.00
Set-up	3.50	4 000	875.00
Material handling	2.55	17 000	150.00
Engineering	2.95	59 000	50.00

* Activity drivers were:
- machine-related: number of machine hours
- set-up: number of production runs
- material handling: number of metres moved
- engineering: number of engineering hours

Exhibit 8.13 Calculating the activity cost rates at Mason & Cox

To estimate the overhead cost of a product, it is necessary to estimate the amount of each overhead activity consumed by the product. This is illustrated in Exhibit 8.14, which shows the cost of the manufacturing overhead activities consumed by our old favourites, the 7.5 kg Hensley Tooth and the 7.5 kg Custom Cast Tooth. The costs of the activities are calculated by multiplying the cost per unit of activity driver by the quantity of activity driver consumed by each product. Exhibit 8.14 also includes the cost of direct material and direct labour to give the manufacturing cost of each product. The cost of the Hensley Tooth, at R147.60, is similar to the ABC manufacturing product cost given in the chapter of R152.97 (see Exhibit 8.11). However, the difference between the cost of the Custom Cast Tooth from the simple ABC system (R269.60) and manufacturing product cost from the more comprehensive system described in the chapter (R305.48) is more significant.

		7.5kg Hensley Tooth		Custom Cast Tooth	
Activity	**Cost per unit of activity driver**	**Quantity of activity driver**	**Activity cost**	**Quantity of activity driver**	**Activity cost**
Machine-related	R144.00 per machine hour	2 500	R360 000	50	R7 200
Set-up	R875.00 per set-up	100	87 500	10	8 750
Material handling	R150.00 per metre	1 000	150 000	100	15 000
Engineering	R50.00 per engineering hour	8 000	400 000	1 000	50 000
Total costs			R997 500		R80 950
Number of units produced					
7.5 kg Hensley Tooth			25 000		
Custom Cast Tooth					500
Overhead cost per unit			39.90		161.90
Direct material*			60.00		60.00
Direct labour*			47.70		47.70
Product cost per unit			R147.60		R269.60

*From Exhibit 8.1

Exhibit 8.14 Product costs based on the simple ABC system at Mason & Cox

Evaluating the simple activity-based product costing system

The simple ABC approach can be compared to the conventional approaches to product costing and to the more comprehensive approaches to activity-based costing described in this chapter.

Simple ABC compared to conventional product costing

Simple activity-based product costing can be viewed as a refinement to the conventional approaches to estimating product costs, which were described in Chapter 7. Exhibit 8.15 shows that it differs from the conventional approaches only in its treatment of manufacturing overhead. As we move from a plantwide rate to departmental rates and then to the simple ABC manufacturing overhead rates, the level of disaggregation of manufacturing overhead increases, enabling better identification of cost drivers; and, as a result, the accuracy of the allocation of the manufacturing overhead costs to products also increases.

Product costing approach	Costs traced directly to products	Costs allocated to products	Overhead cost driver(s) (activity driver(s))	Overhead allocation basis (cost per unit of activity driver)
Conventional approach: Plantwide rate	Direct material Direct labour	Manufacturing overhead	One volume-based cost driver for the entire plant	One rate for the whole plant
Conventional approach: Departmental rates	Direct material Direct labour	Manufacturing overhead	One volume-based cost driver for each production department	One rate for each production department
Simple ABC	Direct material Direct labour	Manufacturing overhead	One cost driver, either volume-based or non-volume-based for each overhead activity	One rate for each manufacturing overhead activity

Exhibit 8.15 Comparing conventional and simple ABC approaches to estimating product costs

Simple ABC compared to more comprehensive activity-based costing models

Exhibit 8.6 in the chapter evaluated the various approaches to activity-based costing and concluded that the more comprehensive activity-based costing systems result in more accurate product costs because they include a wider range of costs. In Mason & Cox's case, there was a significant difference in the *manufacturing* cost of the Custom Cast Tooth (but not the Hensley Tooth) under the two approaches. Using an ABC system with a large number of detailed activities may not greatly improve the accuracy of the product costing over the simple ABC system based on relatively few manufacturing overhead activities. However, the comprehensive ABC system described in the chapter does offer two advantages. First, it includes non-manufacturing costs in product costs, although the simple system could be expanded to accommodate non-manufacturing activities. Second, and much more importantly, the ABC system described in the chapter provides lots of useful information for activity management. The value of this information is explained in Chapter 15. The issue of which system is appropriate can be resolved only in the light of the needs of each business.

Questions

?

8.1 Conventional costing systems apply manufacturing overhead costs to products using a volume-based cost driver such as direct labour hours. What do we mean by the term *volume-based cost driver?* What problems can arise with this approach to product costing when used in a modern manufacturing environment?

8.2 Describe the common indicators of an outdated product costing system.

8.3 Which types of businesses are most likely to experience product costing problems with conventional costing systems? (*Hint:* Think about the composition of costs, and product diversity.) Why?

8.4 What types of products are likely to have distorted product costs under a conventional costing system? Will this be true for all businesses or only for some? Explain your answers.

8.5 How are non-manufacturing costs treated under conventional costing systems? Is this approach useful for management?

8.6 Describe the two dimensions of the activity-based costing model shown in Exhibit 8.5. Using the terms *resources, activity* and *resource driver,* explain how costs are assigned to activities.

8.7 Using the terms *activity costs, activity drivers* and *cost per unit of activity driver* explain how the costs of the Hensley Tooth have been calculated in Exhibit 8.10.

8.8 Explain the three different ways in which the term *cost driver* is used in activity-based costing.

8.9 There is not just one approach to activity-based costing: there are many. Describe some of the major areas of difference between the various approaches to activity-based costing systems.

8.10 Outline the three major approaches to activity-based product costing discussed in the chapter and describe their costs and benefits. What are the major differences between each of these approaches and conventional product costing systems?

8.11 What factors would you consider in deciding whether a business needs to implement activity-based costing; and, if so, what is the most appropriate approach to adopt?

8.12 Explain why an activity-based costing system might include direct labour and non-manufacturing costs, as well as manufacturing overhead costs.

8.13 Describe the role of activity centres when assigning costs to activities.

8.14 Explain how cost categories can be used to simplify the assignment of costs to activities. Give three examples of cost categories that a manufacturing business might find useful and describe the costs that might be included in each category.

8.15 Activities may be classified as *unit level, batch level, product level* or *facility level.* Define each of these terms and give an example of each of these four types of activities. How do customer related activities affect this classification?

8.16 How is the unit, batch, product and facility level classification relevant to product costing?

8.17 Describe the three main types of activity driver found in activity-based costing and give two examples of each type of driver.

8.18 What factors should be considered in deciding whether to aggregate individual activities into larger homogeneous 'activity cost pools' and in deciding how many cost pools to use?

8.19 What causes conventional product costing systems to report lower product costs than those reported by activity-based costing systems for low-volume, small-batch, speciality product lines?

8.20 Describe the circumstances in which the benefits from ABC will be greatest.

8.21 What factors may impede the introduction of ABC?

8.22 What are the implications of excess capacity when activity-based costing is used to report on the profitability of a firm?

8.23 The success (or failure) of activity-based costing is determined by the reactions of the people who develop and use the system. Discuss.

8.24 Describe the limitations of activity-based costing.

8.25 Can activity-based costing be used in service businesses? If so, are there any special problems that are likely to arise?

8.26 (appendix) Compare the simple ABC system described in this chapter with the conventional approaches to product costing that use either a plantwide manufacturing overhead rate or departmental overhead rates.

Exercises

E8.27 Assigning costs to activity centres: manufacturer

Silverwater Ltd manufactures DVD players and has decided to develop an activity-based product costing system to assign labour and overhead costs to products. The table below lists Silverwater's costs during 20X5 and the resource drivers to be used to assign these costs to activity centres.

Silverwater Ltd
Labour and Overhead Costs, 20X5

	Total cost	Resource driver	Total amount of resource driver
Wages	R6 000 000	Head count	100 employees
Building costs	2 000 000	Floor area	10 000 square metres
Energy	3 000 000	Kilowatt hours	250 000 kilowatt hours
Other	500 000	Head count	100 employees
Total labour and overhead costs	R11 500 000		

Required:

1 Calculate the costs assigned to the Assembly Centre given its usage of resource drivers during 20X5, as follows:

Number of employees	20
Floor area	1000 square metres
Power used	10 000 kilowatt hours

2 The costs listed above are not individual costs but a series of costs grouped together into cost categories such as wages, building costs and so on. Explain why Silverwater combined the costs from its general ledger into cost categories. Under what conditions is it appropriate to combine costs into cost categories? Give three examples of the types of costs likely to be included in each category.

3 What is meant by the term *resource driver*? Can you suggest a better basis for assigning 'Wages' to activity centres?

E8.28 Assigning activity centre costs to activities: manufacturer

Ludux Ltd manufactures paints for artists and uses an activity-based product costing system. The table below lists the labour and overhead costs of the Mixing Centre for 20X7, and their resource drivers.

Ludux Ltd
Mixing Centre
Costs and Resources Drivers

	Total cost	Resource driver	Amount of resource driver consumed by the centre
Wages	400 000	Head count	5 people
Energy	320 000	Kilowatt hours	10 000 kilowatt hours
Depreciation	80 000	Machine hours	5000 machine hours
Other	40 000	Head count	5 people
Total cost	R840 000		

Required:

1 Complete the following table to calculate the cost of the activity 'Load mixer' for 20X7. This activity is performed in the Mixing Centre.

Ludux Ltd
Activity: Load mixer

Cost category	Mixing centre cost	Amount of resource driver used to load mixer	Cost of activity 'Load mixer'
Wages	400 000	5% of total labour time in Mixing centre	?
Energy	320 000	500 kilowatt hours	?
Depreciation	80 000	100 machine hours	?
Other	40 000	5% of total labour time in Mixing centre	?
Total cost	R840 000		

2 Why would Ludux use an activity-based product costing system that assigns labour as well as overhead costs to activities?

3 How would the management accountant obtain details of the activities performed and the quantity of resource drivers used by the activities in the Mixing Centre?

E8.29 Calculating the cost per unit of activity driver: manufacturer

Letsema Ltd manufactures delicious shortbread biscuits in a variety of shapes and sizes. The following is a list of activities, costs, and quantities of activity drivers for the Mixing Centre for 20X6:

Letsema Ltd
Mixing Centre
Activities and costs

Activity	Activity cost	Activity driver	Quantity of activity driver
Weigh ingredients	R6 000	No. of batches	400 batches
Load mixing machine	9 200	No. of batches	400 batches
Operate mixing machine	51 200	No. of machine hours	3200 machine hours
Unload mixing machine	8 000	No. of batches	400 batches
Press biscuits onto trays	20 000	No. of biscuits	500 000 biscuits
Move trays to ovens	6 400	No. of loads	2000 loads
Total cost	R100 800		

Required:

1 Calculate the cost per unit of activity driver for each activity in the Mixing Centre.
2 Explain how these costs are used to calculate the cost of the range of shortbread products produced by Letsema Ltd.
3 Classify each activity in the Mixing Centre as facility, product, batch or unit level. Give your reasons for each classification.
4 Suggest alternative activity drivers for each of the activities.

E8.30 Assigning activity costs to products: manufacturer

Loud Ltd manufactures compact disc players and uses an activity-based product costing system that assigns labour and overhead costs. Below is an incomplete bill of activities for the high-volume product, CD Standard.

Loud Ltd
Bill of activities: CD Standard

Activity	Cost per unit of activity driver	Annual quantity of activity drivers used by the product
Process payables	R60 per purchase order	400 purchase orders
Program production	R225 per production schedule	100 schedules
Process sales order	R75 per sales order	300 sales orders
Issue materials	R120 per issue	100 issues
Set up solder machine	R158 per setup	100 setups
Solder circuit boards	R15 per solder joint	40 000 solder joints
Insert motor	R30 per player	5000 players
Assemble player	R18 per player	5000 players
Design player	Directly assigned cost of R12 000 for model CD Standard	

Required:

1 Complete the bill of activities and estimate the total activity cost of the CD Standard player, calculated on an annual and per unit basis, assuming the annual production is 5000 units. (You may find it useful to refer to Exhibit 8.10.)
2 If the direct material cost of a CD Standard player is R45 per unit, what is the total unit cost of the product?
3 Explain the treatment of the costs of the activity 'Design player'.

E8.31 Activity-based costing and inventory valuation: manufacturer

Refer to the data in Exercise 8.30. Would the product cost calculated using the activity-based costing system be allowed as a basis for valuing inventory under international accounting standards? Explain your answer. (The inventory valuation requirements of the International Accounting Standards are described in the appendix to Chapter 4.)

E8.32 Classifying activities as unit, batch, product or facility level costs: manufacturer

Refer to the data in Exercise 8.30. For each activity, indicate whether it represents a unit, batch, product or facility level activity. In each case, explain your answer.

E8.33 Classification of activities: winery

Seneca Falls Winery is a small, family-run operation in the Caledon area. The winery produces two varieties of wine: Riesling and Chardonnay. Among the activities engaged in by the winery are the following:

1 Pruning: At the end of a growing season, the vines are pruned, which helps prepare them for the next harvest.
2 Tying: The vines are tied onto wires to help protect them from the cold. (This also occurs at the end of the season.)
3 Hilling: Dirt is piled up around the roots to help protect them from frost.
4 Conditioning: After the snow melts in the spring, dirt is levelled back from the roots.
5 Untying: The vines are untied from the wires to allow them freedom to grow during the spring and summer months.
6 Chemical spraying: The vines are sprayed in the spring to protect them from disease and insects.
7 Harvesting: All of the grapes of both varieties are picked by hand to minimise damage.
8 Stemming and crushing: Batches of grapes are hand-loaded into a machine, which gently removes the stems and mildly crushes them.
9 Pressing: After removal from the stemmer/crusher, the juice runs freely from the grapes.
10 Filtering: The grapes are crushed mechanically to render more juice from them.
11 Fermentation: The Riesling grape juice is placed in stainless steel tanks for fermentation. The Chardonnay grape juice undergoes a two-stage fermentation process in oak barrels.
12 Ageing: The Riesling wines are aged in the stainless steel tanks for approximately a year. The Chardonnays are aged in the oak barrels for about two years.
13 Bottling: A machine bottles the wine and corks the bottles.
14 Labelling: Each bottle is manually labelled with the name of the vintner, vintage and variety.
15 Packing: The bottles are manually packed in 12-bottle cases.
16 Case labelling: The cases are hand-stamped with the same information that the bottles received.
17 Shipping: The wine is shipped to wine distributors and retailers, mainly in Cape Town and Johannesburg. Generally, about 100 cases are shipped at a time.
18 Maintenance on buildings: This is done during the slow winter months.
19 Maintenance on equipment: This is done when needed, and on a routine basis for preventative maintenance.

Required:

Classify each of the activities listed as a unit, batch, product-sustaining or facility level activity.

E8.34 Comparison of activity-based and conventional product costs: manufacturer

Fantastique Fashions Ltd has switched from a conventional product costing system to an activity-based product costing system to assign manufacturing overhead costs to products. The table below shows the cost per unit for two products under the two costing systems:

Costing system	Product A	Product B
Conventional	R36.00	R25.00
ABC	R30.00	R45.00

Required:

1 Describe the most likely features of products A and B by replacing the question marks (?) in the following table with 'Yes' or 'No'.

Product feature	Product A	Product B
High-volume product line	?	?
Low-volume product line	?	?
Produced in small batches	?	?
Produced in large batches	?	?
Simple to produce	?	?
Complex to produce	?	?

2 Explain your answers to requirement 1.

E8.35 Volume-based cost driver versus ABC: manufacturer

Precision Lens Company manufactures sophisticated lenses and mirrors used in large optical telescopes. The company is now preparing its annual profit plan. As part of its analysis of the profitability of individual products, the management accountant estimates the amount of overhead that should be allocated to the individual product lines from the following information:

	Mirrors	Lenses
Units produced	30	30
Material handling (number of moves) per product line	4	16
Direct labour hours per unit	250	250

The total budgeted material handling cost is R900 000.

Required:

1 Calculate the material handling costs allocated to one mirror under a costing system that allocates overhead on the basis of direct labour hours.

2 Calculate the material handling costs allocated to one lens under a costing system that allocates overhead on the basis of direct labour hours.

3 Calculate the material handling costs allocated to one mirror under activity-based costing. The activity driver for the material handling activity is the number of material moves.

4 Calculate the material handling costs allocated to one lens under activity-based costing.

(CMA, adapted)

E8.36 Distortion of product costs: manufacturer

Wheelco Pty Ltd manufactures car and truck wheels. The company produces four basic, high volume wheels used by manufacturers of cars and bakkies. Wheelco also has two specialty wheel lines. These are fancy, complicated wheels used in expensive sports cars.

Lately, Wheelco's profits have been declining. Foreign competitors have been undercutting Wheelco's prices in three of its four major product lines, and Wheelco's sales volume and market share have declined. In contrast, Wheelco's speciality wheels have been selling steadily, although in relatively small numbers, in spite of three recent price increases. At a recent staff meeting, Wheelco's managing director made the following remarks:

Our profits are going down the tube. It costs us R290 to manufacture our A22 wheel. That's our best seller, with a volume last year of 170 000 units, but our chief competitor is selling basically the same wheel for R270. I don't see how they can do it. I think it's just one more example of foreign dumping. I'm going to write to my local MP about it!

Thank goodness for our speciality wheels. We must get our salespeople to push those wheels more and more. Take the D52 model, for example. It's a complicated thing to make and we don't sell many, but look at the profit margin. Those wheels cost us R490 to make, and we're selling them for R1050 each.

Required:

What do you think is behind the problems faced by Wheelco? Comment on the managing director's remarks. Do you think his strategy is a good one? What do you recommend, and why?

E8.37 Key features of activity-based costing: manufacturer

Refer to the description of Wheelco Ltd in Exercise 8.36. Suppose the firm's managing director has decided to implement an activity-based costing system.

Required:

1 List and briefly describe the key features that Wheelco's new product costing system should include.
2 What impact will the new system be likely to have on the company's situation?
3 What strategic options are likely to be considered once the results of the new costing system are examined?

E8.38 Activity-based costing: service firm

Roy Mtini, the manager of Outdoor Adventures, uses activity-based costing to calculate the cost of the company's adventure walking trips. The company offers two basic trips: a two-day walk along the southern part of the Nkomazi Trail and a five-day trip to the Drakensberg. The activities and costs relevant to the walking trips are as follows:

Activity	Activity driver	Cost per unit of activity driver
Advertise trips	No. of trips	R750 per trip
Obtain National Park permit	Destination	R1500 per group permit issued
Use equipment	No. of person-days	R300 per person per day
Insure participants	No. of people	R75 per person
Cook meals	No. of person-days	R375 per person per day
Guide walkers	Distance walked	R105 per kilometre

The Nkomazi Trail trip caters for 8 people, does not enter the uKhahlamba Drakensberg National Park and covers a walking distance of 50 kilometres. The uKhahlamba Drakensberg trip caters for 15 people, is based in the National Park, and covers 100 kilometres.

Required:

1 Calculate the total cost of each trip, the cost per person for each trip, and the cost per day for each trip, using the activity-based costing system.
2 Before introducing activity-based costing, Roy had estimated the average cost of all trips at R975 per person per day. (This was based on the previous year's costs, adjusted for any expected changes.) Explain how the activity-based system results in more accurate service cost estimates.

E8.39 Activity-based costing; identifying activities and activity drivers: university

Your university has decided to adopt an activity-based costing system to estimate the cost of the various courses taught at the university.

Required:

1 Identify the major activities performed by the staff in the department that teaches the accounting courses.
2 Suggest possible activity drivers for each activity.
3 Prepare a bill of activities that could be used to estimate the total cost of the management accounting subject that you are currently studying.
4 Do the terms unit level, batch level, product level or facility level activities have any relevance in this example? Explain.

5 In estimating the cost of the management accounting subject, how would you account for materials? Explain your answer.

E8.40 Cost drivers and activity costs in a simple activity-based product costing system (appendix): manufacturer

Digitech Ltd manufactures a computer security component in its Durban plant. The following costs are budgeted for 20X6:

Insurance, plant	R780 000
Electricity, machinery	156 000
Electricity, light	78 000
Engineering design	793 000
Depreciation, plant	910 000
Depreciation, machinery	1 820 000
Custodial wages, plant	52 000
Equipment maintenance, wages	195 000
Equipment maintenance, parts	39 000
Set-up wages	52 000
Inspection	39 000
Property taxes	156 000
Natural gas, heating	39 000
Raw materials and components	3 835 000

Required:

1 Suggest possible activities for Digitech and identify which costs would be assigned to each activity.

2 For each activity, suggest an activity driver that could be used to assign activity costs to products.

E8.41 Categorising activity costs: manufacturer

Refer to the information given in the preceding exercise. For each of the activity costs identified, indicate whether it represents a unit level, batch level, product-sustaining level or facility level activity.

E8.42 Activity-based costing; quality control costs: manufacturer

Rainbow Spray Paints Pty Ltd has used a conventional cost accounting system to apply quality control costs uniformly to all products at a rate of 16 per cent of direct labour cost. Monthly direct labour cost for the enamel paint line is R98 000. In an attempt to distribute quality control costs more equitably, Rainbow is considering activity-based costing. The following data relate to monthly quality control costs for the enamel paint line:

Activity	Activity driver	Cost per unit of activity driver	Quantity of activity driver for enamel paint
Incoming material inspection	Type of material	R23 per type	24 types
In-process inspection	Number of units	R0.28 per unit	35 000 units
Product certification	Per order	R144 per order	50 orders

Required:

1 Calculate the monthly quality control cost to be assigned to the enamel paint line under each of the following approaches:

(a) conventional system which assigns overhead on the basis of direct labour costs

(b) activity-based costing

2 Does the conventional product costing system overcost or undercost the enamel paint line with respect to quality-control costs? By what amount and why?

(CMA, adapted)

Problems

P8.43 Calculating activity-based product costs; identifying non-manufacturing costs: manufacturer
Hassiem and Sons manufactures components for the computer industry. The company uses an activity-based costing system to assign labour, manufacturing overhead and non-manufacturing costs to products. Below is a partially completed bill of activities for one of the company's products, Switch 3901.

Switch 3901		
Activity	**Cost per unit of activity driver**	**Annual quantity of activity driver**
Prepare purchase order	R43 per purchase order	50 purchase orders
Process payables	R27 per invoice received	50 invoices
Prepare payroll	R10 per payslip	300 payslips
Process sales orders	R33 per sales order	500 sales orders
Pack and dispatch	R17 per sales order	500 sales orders
Program solder robots	R153 per program	200 programs
Solder circuits	R2 per solder joint	72 000 solder joints
Assemble circuit boards	R5 per board	15 000 boards
Wire in switch	R14 per switch	5000 switches
Insert fuse	R10 per fuse	5000 fuses
Test switch	R4 per switch	5000 switches
Design switch	R5000 for model 3901	

These annual costs relate to an annual production level of 5000 switches. The direct material cost per switch is R20.

Required:

1 Calculate the total cost per unit for Switch 3901.
2 Calculate the manufacturing cost per unit for Switch 3901. (*Hint:* Include only those activities that relate to manufacturing.)
3 Discuss the role that product costs that include both manufacturing and non-manufacturing costs can play in management decision-making.

P8.44 Calculating activity costs: winery
The management of Van Der Spuy Wines Pty Ltd is contemplating the introduction of an activity-based costing system and has just conducted an activity-based costing exercise in its bottling plant. The costs of the plant, summarised into cost categories for the year, are as follows:

Bottling Plant costs			
	Total cost	**Resource driver**	**Total amount of resource driver**
Wages	R2 000 000	No. of employees	40 employees
Building costs	200 000	Floor area	50 000 square metres
Machinery costs	900 000	Machine hours	90 000 machine hours
Energy costs	1 200 000	Kilowatt hours	600 000 kilowatt hours
Other	45 000	Machine hours	90 000 machine hours
	R4 345 000		

Four activity centres have been identified in the plant, with the following resource driver consumption patterns:

Bottling Plant activity centres Resource drivers				
Activity centre	**No. of employees**	**Floor area (m²)**	**Machine hours**	**Kilowatt hours**
Filling	20	15 000	40 000	250 000
Corking	10	5 000	15 000	100 000
Labelling	4	10 000	10 000	50 000
Packing	6	20 000	25 000	200 000
Total	40	50 000	90 000	600 000

The work in the Labelling Centre has been broken down into the following five activities. Their use of resource drivers is also shown.

Labelling Centre activities Resource drivers				
Activity	**No. of employees**	**Floor area (m²)**	**Machine hours**	**Kilowatt hours**
Set up front label machines	0.5	–	–	–
Operate front label machines	1.0	3 000	7 000	30 000
Set up back label machines	0.5	–	–	–
Operate back label machines	1.0	2 000	3 000	20 000
Inspect labelled bottles	1.0	5 000	–	–
Total	4.0	10 000	10 000	50 000

Required:

1 Calculate the cost of each activity centre.
2 Calculate the cost of the activities performed in the Labelling Centre.
3 Why would Van Der Spuy contemplate using an activity-based product costing system?
4 What are the limitations of activity-based product costing?

P8.45 Activity-based costing: service

Robert Mothibi is the manager of a firm, QuikTax, which specialises in the preparation of income tax returns. The firm offers two basic products: the preparation of income tax returns for wage and salary earners and the preparation of income tax returns for small businesses. Any clients requiring more complex services are referred to Robert's brother Roger, who is a partner in a large firm of chartered accountants.

The processing of wage and salary tax returns is quite straightforward, and the firm uses a software package to process data and print the return. A software package is also used to prepare returns for small businesses, although more information is required, particularly about business expenses.

Robert has only recently joined QuikTax and he is concerned about the firm's pricing policy, which sets a flat fee of R400 per return for wage and salary clients and R2000 for small businesses. He decides to use activity-based costing to estimate the costs of providing each of these services.

At the end of the year, Robert reviewed the company's total costs and activities, resulting in the following list:

Activity	Activity cost	Activity driver	Quantity of activity driver
Interview salaried client	R400 000	No. of wage and salary clients	8 000
Interview business client	500 000	No. of business clients	2 000
Obtain missing data	4 000 000	No. of follow-up calls	8 000
Input data	800 000	No. of data entries	400 000
Print return	600 000	No. of returns	10 000
Verify return with client	1 200 000	No. of hours	6 000
Rectify errors	600 000	No. of errors	6 000
Submit return	200 000	No. of returns	10 000
Total costs	R8 300 000		

In identifying the activities required for each type of return, Robert noted the following:

- Clients are interviewed only once per return.
- All follow-up calls to obtain missing data relate to business returns; on average, each business tax return requires four follow-up calls.
- Processing a wage and salary tax return requires 20 data entries, whereas a business return requires 120 data entries.
- On average, it takes 22.5 minutes to verify a wage and salary tax return, whereas it takes one and a half hours to verify a business return.
- All errors relate to business returns; on average, there are 3 errors per business return.

Required:

1 Use activity-based costing to estimate the cost of preparing:
   (a) a wage and salary tax return; and
   (b) a business tax return.

2 In the light of your answers to requirement 1, evaluate the firm's pricing policy.

P8.46 Activity-based costing; analysis of operations: service firm

Viljoen and Govender perform consulting services related to e-commerce consulting and information systems in Durban. The firm, which bills R700 per hour for services performed, is in a very tight local labour market and is having difficulty finding quality staff. The labour cost per hour paid by Viljoen and Govender for professional staff time is R250. Selected information follows:

- Billable hours to clients for the year totalled 6000, consisting of: information systems services, 3600; e-commerce consulting, 2400.
- Administrative cost of R1 908 800 was (and continues to be) allocated to both consulting services based on billable hours. These costs consist of staff support, R1 035 000; in-house computing, R725 000; and miscellaneous office charges, R148 800.

A recent analysis of staff support costs found a correlation with the number of clients served. In-house computing and miscellaneous office charges varied directly with the number of computer hours logged and number of client transactions, respectively. The following table shows the number of clients, computer hours and client transactions for the e-commerce and information systems consulting services:

	e-commerce consulting	Information systems consulting	Total
Number of clients	60	240	300
Number of computer hours	2 100	2 900	5 000
Number of client transactions	720	480	1 200

Required:

1 Activity-based costing (ABC) is said to result in improved costing accuracy when compared with conventional costing procedures. Briefly explain how this improved accuracy is attained.

2 Assume that the firm uses conventional costing procedures, allocating total costs on the basis of billable hours. Determine the profitability of the firm's e-commerce and information systems consulting services, expressing your answer both in Rands and as a percentage of activity revenue.
3 Repeat requirement 2, using activity-based costing.
4 Stephen Viljoen, one of the firm's partners, doesn't care where his professionals spend their time because, as he notes, 'Many clients have come to expect both services and we need both to stay in business. Also, information systems and e-commerce professionals are paid the same hourly rate.' Should Viljoen's attitude change? Explain.
5 Is an aggressive expansion of either consulting service desirable? Briefly discuss.

P8.47 Estimating activity-based product costs; problems with conventional costing systems: manufacturer

Sunsafe Optics Ltd manufactures lenses for sunglasses. Although the company manufactures a range of lenses that vary in size and shape, these products can be grouped into three basic product lines: coloured plastic lenses, lenses that absorb ultraviolet radiation, and lenses that provide both sun protection and the correction of optical defects.

All three products undergo the same injection moulding process where a plastic substance is injected between two glass dies. When the plastic is set, the lenses are removed from the dies, which, if possible, are re-used for subsequent batches. The coloured plastic lenses and the UV-absorbing lenses are high-volume lines produced in large batches. These two products are simple to make and are similar in many ways, except that the material used for the UV-absorbing lenses is much more expensive than the material used for the coloured plastic lenses. The optical lenses are a low-volume line, produced in small batches. These lenses are complex to make. They require specially ground optical dies and careful inspection at several points during production.

Currently, the company uses a conventional costing system and applies overhead on the basis of direct labour cost. This system was developed many years ago when the company's production processes were labour-intensive and overhead costs were relatively insignificant. However, over time, the production environment has become more automated, overhead costs have increased significantly and many of the overhead costs bear no direct relationship to the volume of production in general, or to the direct labour cost in particular.

The company's management accountant believes that the current costing system no longer fits Sunsafe's production environment and has set up a special costing study to analyse the labour and overhead costs for the year that has just finished. The study identified the activities and costs shown below:

Sunsafe Optics Ltd

Activity	Actvity cost	Annual quantity of activity driver
Prepare purchase order	R250 000	2 000 purchase orders
Process payables	200 000	2 000 invoices
Prepare payroll	300 000	4 000 payslips
Process sales orders	900 000	15 000 sales orders
Move finished goods	6 000 000	15 000 sales orders
Pack and dispatch	2 400 000	15 000 sales orders
Produce basic dies	1 800 000	60 000 dies
Produce optical dies	2 000 000	20 000 dies
Inspect dies	600 000	20 000 dies
Clean injection moulders	6 000 000	1 000 batches
Program injection moulders	3 600 000	1 000 batches
Move material	8 000 000	1 000 batches
Operate injection moulders	28 000 000	40 000 machine hours
Remove dies	960 000	4 800 000 lenses
Inspect lens	900 000	50 000 lenses
Design lens	900 000	Assigned directly to products

These annual costs relate to an annual production level of 2.5 million coloured plastic lenses, 2.25 million UV-absorbing lenses and 50 000 optical lenses. The direct material costs for each product are as follows:

Coloured plastic	R20 per lens
UV-absorbing	R40 per lens
Optical	R40 per lens

The management accountant estimates that the activity consumption of the three product lines during the year was:

Sunsafe Optics Ltd
Quantity of activity driver used by each product line

Activity	Activity driver	Coloured plastic	UV-absorbing	Optical
Prepare purchase order	No. of purchase orders	1 000	900	100
Process payables	No. of invoices	1 000	900	100
Prepare payroll	No. of payslips	2 000	1 800	200
Process sales orders	No. of sales orders	6 950	8 000	50
Move finished goods	No. of sales orders	6 950	8 000	50
Pack and dispatch	No. of sales orders	6 950	8 000	50
Produce basic dies	No. of dies	30 000	30 000	–
Produce optical dies	No. of dies	–	–	20 000
Inspect dies	No. of dies	–	–	20 000
Clean injection moulders	No. of batches	500	450	50
Program injection moulders	No. of batches	500	450	50
Move material	No. of batches	500	450	50
Operate injection moulders	No. of machine hours	20 000	18 000	2 000
Remove dies	No. of lenses	2 500 000	2 250 000	50 000
Inspect lens	No. of lenses	–	–	50 000
Design lens	Assigned directly to products	R300 000	R500 000	R100 000

Required:

1 Estimate the per unit cost of each of the three products (rounded to three decimal places).

2 Do you expect these costs to be higher than or lower than the product costs estimated under the existing conventional costing system? Explain your answer.

P8.48 Activity-based costing: service organization

The SA Welfare Council has the responsibility for distributing government grants to fund support services for mentally handicapped people. The director is concerned that grants be distributed on an equitable basis, and asks Sue Mkoloti, the Council's management accountant, to estimate the cost of providing institutional care to clients with mental disabilities. Mkoloti decides to use activity-based costing in one of the state's larger institutions, Greenfields, to obtain an initial estimate of the costs of the services provided.

Working with a project team at Greenfields, she identifies the major activities and costs for next year (listed below).

Greenfields Activities performed		
Activity	**Cost (in R'000s)**	**Annual volume of activity drivers**
Cook meals	R1 000	100 000 meals
Transport clients (internal)	400	4 000 hours of assistance
Transport clients (external)	900	6 000 hours of assistance
Clean rooms	200	20 000 rooms cleaned
Bath clients	288	16 000 baths given
Dress clients	60	10 000 clients dressed
Administer medication	240	75 000 doses administered
Provide occupational therapy	180	600 classes
Provide physiotherapy	500	5 000 hours of physiotherapy
Run sheltered workshop	300	200 days of operation

Although the needs of the individual clients vary tremendously, the project team identifies three major service types: high-dependency support, low-dependency support and outpatient support. High-dependency and low-dependency clients live at Greenfields, while outpatients attend the centre on a daily basis. The average number of activities required to support each of the three types of clients each day is estimated as follows:

Greenfields Activities consumed per client per day			
Activity	**High-dependency**	**Low-dependency**	**Outpatient**
Cook meals	3	3	1
Internal transport	4	0	0
External transport	3	2	1
Clean room	2	1	0
Bath client	1	0	0
Dress client	1	0	0
Administer medication	4	1	1
Provide occupational therapy*	1	2	2
Provide physiotherapy	4	2	1
Run sheltered workshop†	0	1	1

* Occupational therapy classes are attended by an average of 10 clients.

† The sheltered workshop is used by an average of 20 clients per day.

Required:

1 Calculate the cost per unit of activity driver for each of the activities identified by the project team.

2 Calculate the daily cost of supporting:
  (a) a high-dependency client
  (b) a low-dependency client
  (c) an outpatient client

3 Review the list of activities and suggest some major activities that may have been overlooked by the project team.

4 Do you think activity-based costing is useful in this situation? Explain your answer.

P8.49 Activity-based costing; product decisions: manufacturer

Leribe Electronics Company manufactures two small-screen television models, the Novelle which has been produced for 10 years and sells for R910, and the Zodiac, a new model introduced in early 20X5, which sells for R1160. Based on the following income statement for 20X6, a decision has been made to concentrate Leribe marketing resources on the Zodiac model and to begin to phase out the Novelle model.

Leribe Electronics Company
Income Statement
for the year ended 31 December 20X6

	Zodiac	Novelle	Total
Sales	R4 640 000	R20 020 000	R24 660 000
Cost of goods sold	3 232 000	13 024 000	16 256 000
Gross margin	R1 408 000	R6 996 000	R8 404 000
Selling and administrative expenses	980 000	5 700 000	6 680 000
Net profit	R428 000	R1 296 000	R1 724 000
Units produced and sold	4 000	22 000	
Net profit per unit sold	R107.00	R58.91*	

* Rounded.

The unit costs for the Zodiac and Novelle models are as follows:

	Zodiac	Novelle
Direct material	R655	R363
Direct labour:		
Zodiac (3.5 hr × R14)	49	
Novelle (1.5 hr × R14)		21
Manufacturing overhead*	104	208
Cost per unit	R808	R592

* Manufacturing overhead was applied on the basis of machine hours at a predetermined rate of R26 per hour.

Leribe Electronics Company's financial controller is advocating the use of activity-based costing, and has gathered the following information about the company's manufacturing overhead costs for 20X6:

		Quantity of activity drivers consumed		
Activity (activity driver)	**Activity costs**	**Zodiac**	**Novelle**	**Total**
Soldering (number of solder joints)	R880 000	400 000	1 200 000	1 600 000
Shipments (number of shipments)	836 000	3 800	15 200	19 000
Quality control (number of inspections)	1 170 000	21 060	56 940	78 000
Purchase orders (number of orders)	1 110 000	105 450	79 550	185 000
Machine power (machine hours)	47 500	15 200	174 800	190 000
Machine set-ups (number of setups)	948 500	4 500	4 985	9 485
Total activity costs	R4 992 000			

Required:

1 Briefly explain how an activity-based costing system operates.
2 Using activity-based costing, determine if Leribe Electronics should continue to emphasise the Zodiac model and phase out the Novelle model.

(CMA, adapted)

P8.50 Activity-based costing for overhead versus conventional costing systems (appendix): manufacturer

Wilmington Office Equipment (Pty) Ltd is a small company that manufactures two types of compact filing cabinets – Deluxe and Executive – and applies manufacturing overhead to all units at the rate of R80 per machine hour. Production information follows.

	Deluxe	Executive
Direct material cost	R40	R65
Direct labour cost	25	25
Budgeted volume (units)	16 000	30 000

The management accountant, who is studying activity-based costing, has determined that the firm's overhead can be identified with three activities: manufacturing set-ups, machine processing and product shipping. Data on the number of set-ups, machine hours and outgoing shipments, which are the activities' three respective cost drivers, follow:

	Deluxe	Executive	Total
Set-ups	100	60	160
Machine hours	32 000	45 000	77 000
Outgoing shipments	200	150	350

The firm's total overhead of R6 160 000 is subdivided as follows: manufacturing set-ups, R1 344 000; machine processing, R3 696 000; and product shipping, R1 120 000.

Required:

1 Calculate the unit manufacturing cost of Deluxe and Executive filing cabinets by using the company's current overhead costing procedures.

2 Calculate the unit manufacturing cost of Deluxe and Executive filing cabinets by using activity-based costing.

3 Is the cost of the Deluxe filing cabinet overstated or understated (that is, distorted) by the use of machine hours to allocate total manufacturing overhead to production? By how much?

4 Calculate the aggregate amount by which the Deluxe cabinet line is under-costed by the company's current conventional overhead costing procedures. Then calculate the aggregate amount by which the conventional system over-costs the Executive cabinet line.

5 Assume that the current selling price of a Deluxe filing cabinet is R270 and the marketing manager is contemplating a R30 discount to stimulate sales. Is this discount advisable? Briefly discuss.

P8.51 Activity cost pools; cost drivers (appendix): manufacturer

The accountant for Halifax Supply Ltd has estimated the following activity cost pools and activity drivers for the coming year:

Activity	Budgeted overhead cost	Activity driver	Budgeted level for activity driver	Cost per unit of activity driver
Machine set-ups	R2 000 000	No. of set-ups	100	R20 000 per set-up
Material handling	1 000 000	Weight of raw material	50 000 kg	R20 per kg
Hazardous waste control	500 000	Weight of hazardous chemicals used	10 000 kg	R50 per kg
Quality control	750 000	No. of inspections	1000	R750 per inspection
Other overhead costs	2 000 000	Machine hours	20 000	R100 per machine hour
Total	R6 250 000			

An order for 1000 boxes of film development chemicals has the following production requirements:

Machine set-ups	4 set-ups
Raw material	10 000 kg
Hazardous materials	2000 kg
Inspections	10 inspections
Machine hours	500 machine hours

Required:

1 Calculate the total overhead that should be assigned to the order for development chemicals.

2 What is the overhead cost per box of chemicals?

3 If Halifax Photographic Supply Ltd were to use a plantwide predetermined overhead rate based on machine hours, calculate the rate per hour.

4 Under the approach in requirement 3, how much overhead would be assigned to the order for development chemicals:
(a) in total
(b) per box of chemicals?

5 Explain why these two product costing systems result in such widely differing costs. Which system do you recommend? Why?

6 Calculate the unit cost of a production order for 100 specially coated plates used in film development. In addition to direct material costing R1 200 per plate and direct labour costing R400 per plate, the order requires the following:

Machine set-ups	2 set-ups
Raw material	800 kg
Hazardous materials	300 kg
Inspections	3 inspections
Machine hours	50 machine hours

Cases

C8.52 Activity-based costing; forecasting; ethics: manufacturer

Peninsula Air Industries (PAI) manufactures parts for small aircraft. Over the past decade, PAI's management has met its goal of reducing its reliance on government contract work to 50 per cent of total sales. PAI is now equally reliant on commercial sales and government contracts.

Traditionally, the costs of the Material Handling Department have been allocated to direct material as a percentage of direct material Rand value. This was adequate when the majority of the manufacturing was homogeneous and related to government contracts. Recently, however, government auditors have rejected some proposals, stating that 'the amount of Material Handling Department costs allocated to these proposals is disproportionate to the total effort involved'.

Kara Lindley, the newly hired cost accounting manager, was asked by the manager of PAI's Government Contracts Unit, Paul Anderson, to find a more equitable method of allocating the Material Handling Department costs to the user departments. Her review has revealed the following information:

- The majority of the direct material purchases for government contracts are high-Rand, low-volume purchases, while commercial materials represent low-Rand, high-volume purchases.

- Administrative departments such as Marketing, Finance and Administration, Human Resources and Maintenance also use the services of the Material Handling Department on a limited basis but have never been charged in the past for material handling costs.
- One purchasing manager with a direct phone line is assigned exclusively to purchasing high-Rand, low-volume material for government contracts on an annual salary of R540 000. Employee on-costs are estimated to be 20 per cent of the annual salary. The annual costs of the dedicated phone line are R42 000.
- The components of the Material Handling Department's budget for 20X7, as proposed by Lindley's predecessor, are as follows.

Payroll	R2 700 000
Employee on-costs	540 000
Telephone	570 000
Other utilities	330 000
Materials and supplies	90 000
Depreciation	90 000
Direct material budget:	
Government contracts	30 090 000
Commercial products	13 110 000

Lindley has estimated the number of purchase orders to be processed in 20X7 as follows:

Government contracts*	120 000
Commercial production	234 000
Marketing	2 700
Finance and Administration	4 050
Human Resources	750
Maintenance	1 500
Total	**363 000**

* Exclusive of high-Rand, low-volume materials.

Lindley has recommended to Anderson that material handling costs should be allocated on a per purchase order basis. Anderson realises that the company has been allocating to government contracts more material handling costs than can be justified. However, the implication of Lindley's analysis could be a decrease in his unit's earnings and, consequently, a cut in his annual bonus. Anderson told Lindley to 'adjust' her numbers and modify her recommendation so that the results will be more favourable to the Government Contracts Unit.

Being new in her position, Lindley is not sure how to proceed. She feels ambivalent about Anderson's instructions and suspects his motivation may not be in the best interest of PAI. To complicate matters for Lindley, the company's new managing director has asked her to prepare a three-year forecast of the Government Contracts Unit's results, and she believes that the newly recommended allocation method would provide the most accurate data. However, this would put her in direct opposition to Anderson's directives.

Lindley has assembled the following data to project the material handling costs over the next three years:

- The number of purchase orders increases 5 per cent per year.
- The ratio of government purchase orders to total purchase orders remains at 33 per cent.
- Total direct material costs increase 2.5 per cent per year.
- Material handling costs remain the same percentage of direct material costs.
- Direct government costs (payroll, employee on-costs, and direct phone line) remain constant.
- In addition, she has assumed that the cost of government material in the future will be 70 per cent of total material.

Required:

1 Calculate the material handling rate that would have been used by Kara Lindley's predecessor at Peninsula Air Industries.

2 (a) Calculate the revised material handling costs to be allocated on a per purchase order basis.

(b) Discuss why purchase orders might be a more reliable cost driver than the Rand amount of direct material.

3 Calculate the difference due to the change to the new method of allocating material handling costs to government contracts.

4 Prepare a forecast of the cumulative Rand impact over a three-year period from 20X7 through 20X9 of Kara Lindley's recommended change for allocating Material Handling Department costs to the Government Contracts Unit. Round all calculations to the nearest whole number.

5 Referring to the standards of ethical conduct for accountants described in Chapter 1:

(a) Discuss why Kara Lindley has an ethical conflict.

(b) Identify several steps that Lindley could take to resolve the ethical conflict.

(CMA, adapted)

C8.53 Activity-based costing; conventional costing: manufacturer

Cravings for Cakes Pty Ltd manufactures a wide range of delicious cakes and pastries. At the annual Christmas party, the company's owner, I.M. Craving, treated his employees to a nostalgic review of the firm's history. He told them:

Twenty years ago we had only three product lines – pies, finger buns and chocolate cakes. We were flat out producing large volumes of each product, using very simple machinery and a lot of hard work.

My, how things have changed! We still make and sell a lot of pies and chocolate cakes, but we also produce a wide range of low-volume lines, such as danish pastries, donuts and vanilla slices. I hear you sighing, and no wonder; these low-volume products are a pain in the neck. They are complex to produce and their short production runs involve a lot of extra machinery setups and material handling. But the accountants tell me that these speciality lines have wonderful profit margins, so we must not complain.

Craving then outlined the dramatic changes that had occurred within the business over the past 20 years. In the factory he had seen the introduction of computer-controlled mixing machines and ovens that replaced a lot of the direct labour operations, and an increased emphasis on quality and delivery performance. Indeed, right across the business, more and more effort had been placed on keeping the customer happy.

However, his speech cast a gloomy shadow across the Christmas festivities when he warned:

Despite all this progress, the company seems to be struggling. Our profits are declining, and if things don't improve over the next few months, this may be our last Christmas together. To survive we must all work very hard. We must focus on increasing sales, particularly of our high-margin specialty products.

The company's management accountant, Ursula B. Bright, had become concerned about the conventional product costing system at Cravings for Cakes. The manufacturing people were also sure that the costing system was distorting product costs.

Required:

1 Describe the changes in cost structure that are likely to have occurred at Cravings for Cakes over the last 20 years, and explain their causes.

2 Do you think that the existing costing system understates or overstates the cost of:

(a) a chocolate cake

(b) a danish pastry?

Explain your answers.

3 Explain how activity-based costing could overcome the deficiencies inherent in the existing costing system.

4 What factors should U.B. Bright consider when deciding whether to use:
   (a) a simple activity-based costing system to assign manufacturing overhead to products
   (b) an activity-based system that includes both manufacturing overhead and non-manufacturing costs
   (c) a comprehensive activity-based system that includes all product-related costs except direct material?

C8.54 Estimating activity costs; assigning costs to activity centres: manufacturer

Refer to Case 8.53. Assume that U.B. Bright decided to implement an activity-based costing system that included all costs except direct material. She identifies the following costs, by cost category, for the past year and selects the following resource drivers:

Cravings for Cakes
Costs and resource drivers

Cost category	Cost	Resource driver
Wages	R3 000 000	Number of employees
Building costs	800 000	Floor space
Depreciation	1 000 000	Machine hours
Consumables	500 000	Orders placed by centre
Energy	4 000 000	Kilowatt hours used
Other	200 000	Number of employees
Total	R9 500 000	

Next, Bright divides the company into the following activity centres:

Product Development	Baking
Sales and Dispatch	Packing and Warehousing
Mixing Pastries and Batters	Administration
Filling Pies and Danishes	Corporate Management

The resource driver usage by each activity centre, for the various cost categories, is set out below.

Cravings for Cakes
Resource drivers consumed by activity centres
Cost categories (resource drivers)

Activity centres	Wages (employees)	Building (m^2)	Depreciation (machine hours)	Consumables (orders)	Energy (kilowatt hours)	Other (employees)
Product development	5	200	–	10	–	5
Sales and dispatch	10	500	–	15	–	10
Mixing	15	500	1 000	50	10 000	15
Filling	20	1 000	3 000	100	10 000	20
Baking	15	500	5 000	100	200 000	15
Packing	20	1 000	500	150	30 000	20
Administration	10	1 000	500	50	–	10
Corporate management	5	300	–	25	–	5
Total quantity of resource drivers across all activity centres	100	5 000	10 000	500	250 000	100

Required:

1 Assign the costs to the activity centres using the resource driver consumption patterns shown above.

2 Why did U.B. Bright use cost categories in her analysis?

3 Explain how she would have identified the cost categories, and give two examples of the costs likely to be included in each category.

4 U.B. Bright used the number of employees as the resource driver for wages. Can you suggest a more accurate basis for assigning wage costs to activity centres?

5 Can you suggest a more accurate basis than machine hours for assigning depreciation costs to activity centres?

C8.55 Estimating activity costs; assigning activity centre costs to activities: manufacturer

Refer to Cases 8.53 and 8.54. Notwithstanding your answers so far, assume the following costs and resource drivers for the Mixing Centre:

Cravings for Cakes
Mixing Centre: Costs and resource drivers

	Costs	Resource drivers
Wages	R450 000	Percentage of labour time
Building costs	80 000	Floor space occupied
Depreciation	100 000	Machine hours
Consumables	50 000	Percentage of labour time
Energy	160 000	Kilowatt hours
Other	30 000	Percentage of labour time
Total	870 000	

U.B. Bright has identified the following activities that take place in the Mixing Centre, and estimates that they use the following percentage of labour time and floor space:

Cravings for Cakes
Mixing Centre:
Activities and resource drivers used

Activity	Percentage of labour time	Percentage of floor space
Set up scales	20	5
Weigh ingredients	10	5
Load mixers	25	10
Operate mixers	30	50
Clean mixers	10	20
Move mixture to filling	5	10
Total	100%	100%

The only activity that makes significant use of machinery (and therefore depreciation and energy) is 'Operate mixers'.

Required:

1 Calculate the cost of each activity performed in the Mixing Centre.

2 Explain how U.B. Bright would have collected the information necessary to identify the activities and their resource driver consumption.

3 What steps can U.B. Bright take to ensure that this information is reliable?

4 Classify each activity as unit, batch, product or facility level.

C8.56 Assigning activity costs to products; benefits, costs and limitations of ABC: manufacturer

Refer to Cases 8.53 to 8.55. After much hard work, U.B. Bright produces a list of the activities performed at Cravings for Cakes and their annual costs. In addition, Bright identifies an activity driver for each activity and the annual quantity of each activity driver. A partial list of activity costs and quantities of activity drivers is shown below.

Cravings for Cakes
List of activities

Activity	Activity cost	Activity driver	Annual quantity of activity driver
Prepare annual accounts	R50 000	None available	
Process receivables	150 000	No. of invoices	5 000 invoices
Process payables	250 000	No. of purchase orders	2 500 purchase orders
Program production	280 000	No. of production schedules	1 000 schedules
Process sales order	400 000	No. of sales orders	4 000 sales orders
Dispatch sales order	300 000	No. of dispatches	2 500 dispatches
Develop and test products	120 000	Assigned directly to products	
Load mixers	140 500	No. of batches	1 000 batches
Operate mixers	459 000	No. of kilograms	200 000 kilograms
Clean mixers	69 000	No. of batches	1 000 batches
Move mixture to filling	34 500	No. of kilograms	200 000 kilograms
Clean trays	200 000	No. of trays	16 000 trays
Fill trays	160 000	No. of cakes/pastries	800 000 cakes/pastries
Move to baking	80 000	No. of trays	16 000 trays
Set up ovens	500 000	No. of batches	1 000 batches
Bake cakes/pastries	1 300 000	No. of batches	1 000 batches
Move to packing	400 000	No. of trays	16 000 trays
Pack cakes/pastries	800 000	No. of cakes/pastries	800 000 cakes/pastries
Inspect pastries	25 000	No. of pastries	50 000 pastries

Required:

1 Calculate the cost per unit of activity driver for the activities listed above. (Work to four decimal places.)

2 Use the following information to prepare a bill of activities and determine the cost per unit for:

(a) the chocolate cake

(b) the danish pastry

Chocolate cake (batch size 1000; annual volume 100 000)

Activities consumed	Annual quantity of activity driver
Process receivables	500 invoices
Process payables	200 purchase orders
Program production	100 production schedules
Process sales order	400 sales orders
Load mixers	100 batches
Operate mixers	30 000 kg
Clean mixers	100 batches
Move mixture to filling	30 000 kg
Clean trays	2 000 trays
Fill trays	100 000 cakes
Move to baking	2 000 trays
Set up ovens	100 batches
Bake cakes/pastries	100 batches
Move to packing	2 000 trays
Pack cakes/pastries	100 000 cakes
Dispatch sales order	500 sales orders
Develop and test product	R6 000 assigned directly to this product

Danish Pastry (batch size 200; annual volume 10 000)	
Activities consumed	**Annual quantity of activity driver**
Process receivables	150 invoices
Process payables	100 purchase orders
Program production	50 production schedules
Process sales order	100 sales orders
Load mixers	50 batches
Operate mixers	4000 kg
Clean mixers	50 batches
Move mixture to filling	4000 kg
Clean trays	400 trays
Fill trays	10 000 pastries
Move to baking	400 trays
Set up ovens	50 batches
Bake cakes/pastries	50 batches
Inspect pastries	10 000 pastries
Move to packing	400 trays
Pack cakes/pastries	10 000 pastries
Dispatch sales order	150 sales orders
Develop and test product	R24 000 assigned directly to this product

3 What other costs must be added to calculate the product cost for chocolate cakes and danish pastries?

4 Why is the cost per danish pastry much higher than the cost per chocolate cake? Would this difference be reflected in the conventional costing system? Explain your answers.

5 U.B. Bright, as management accountant for Cravings for Cakes Pty Ltd, has recommended the introduction of an activity-based costing system to improve the accuracy of the company's product costs. Bright is filled with enthusiasm, but the company's owner, I.M. Craving, is more cautious:

All these new-fangled systems, with fancy names. Five years ago it was JIT, or was it MRP? Two years ago, TQM, and now it's ABC or is it ABM? I'm not keen – ABC sounds complex and expensive. Your report outlines the benefits of ABC but it can't be all positive. I know every cloud has a silver lining, but I also know every silver lining has a cloud. Rewrite your report – but this time describe the costs of ABC and its limitations, as well as the benefits.

Prepare a report for Craving that outlines the benefits, costs and limitations of activity-based costing. (To set your report in the appropriate business context, you should refer to the information given in Case 8.53.)

C8.57 Conventional versus simple activity-based costing systems (appendix); strategic cost analysis: manufacturer

Gigabyte Ltd manufactures three products for the calculator industry:

- Gismos (product G): annual sales, 8000 units.
- Thingamajigs (product T): annual sales, 15 000 units.
- Whatchamacallits (product W): annual sales, 4000 units.

The company uses a conventional, volume-based product costing system with manufacturing overhead applied on the basis of direct labour Rands. The product costs have been calculated as follows:

	Product G	Product T	Product W
Raw material	R105.00	R157.50	R52.50
Direct labour	48.00 (2.4 hr × R20)	36.00 (1.8 hr × R20)	24.00 (1.2 hr × R20)
Manufacturing overhead*	420.00 (R48 × 875%)	315.00 (R36 × 875%)	210.00 (R24 × 875%)
Total product cost	R573.00	R508.50	R286.50

*Calculation of predetermined overhead rate:

Manufacturing overhead budget:

Machinery	R3 675 000
Machine set-up	15 750
Inspection	1 575 000
Material handling	2 625 000
Engineering	1 034 250
Total	R8 925 000

Direct labour budget (based on budgeted annual sales):

Product G:	(8000 × R48.00)	R384 000
Product T:	(15 000 × R36.00)	540 000
Product W:	(4000 × R24.00)	96 000
Total		R1 020 000

$$\text{Predetermined overhead rate} = \frac{\text{Budgeted overhead}}{\text{Budgeted direct labour}} = 875\%$$

Gigabyte's pricing method has been to set a budgeted price equal to 150 per cent of full product cost. However, only the thingamajigs have been selling at their budgeted price. The budgeted and actual current prices for all three products are the following:

	Product G	Product T	Product W
Product cost	R573.00	R508.50	R286.50
Budgeted price	859.50	762.75	429.75
Actual current selling price	639.00	762.75	600.00

Gigabyte has been forced to lower the price of gismos in order to get orders. In contrast, Gigabyte has raised the price of whatchamacallits several times, but there has been no apparent loss of sales. Gigabyte has been under increasing pressure to reduce the price even further on gismos. In contrast, Gigabyte's competitors do not seem to be interested in the market for whatchamacallits. Gigabyte apparently has this market to itself.

Required:

1 Is product G the company's least profitable product?
2 Is product W a profitable product for Gigabyte Ltd?
3 Comment on the reactions of Gigabyte's competitors to the firm's pricing strategy. What dangers does Gigabyte face?
4 Gigabyte's financial controller, Nan O'Second, recently attended a conference at which activity-based costing systems were discussed. She became convinced that such a system would help Gigabyte's management to understand its product costs better. She obtained top management's approval to design an activity-based costing system, and an ABC project team was formed. In Stage one of the ABC project, each of the overhead items listed in the overhead budget was placed into its own activity cost pool. Then an activity driver was identified for each activity cost pool. Finally, the ABC project team compiled data showing the percentage of each activity driver that was consumed by each of Gigabyte's product lines. These data are summarised as follows:

Activity cost pool	Activity driver	Product G	Product T	Product W
Machinery	Machine hours	24%	50%	26%
Machine set-up	Number of set-ups	22%	30%	48%
Inspection	Number of inspections	16%	44%	40%
Material handling	Raw material costs	25%	69%	6%
Engineering	Number of change orders	35%	10%	55%

Show how the financial controller determined the percentages given above for raw material costs. (Round to the nearest whole per cent.)

5 Develop product costs for the three products on the basis of a simple activity-based costing system. (Round to the nearest cent.)

6 Calculate a budgeted price for each product, using Gigabyte's pricing formula. Compare the new budgeted prices with the current actual selling prices and previously reported product costs.

7 Refer to the new budgeted prices for Gigabyte's three products, based on the new activity-based costing system. Write a memo to the company's managing director commenting on the situation Gigabyte has been facing regarding the market for its products and the actions of its competitors. Discuss the strategic options available to management. What do you recommend, and why?

8 Refer to the product costs developed in requirement 5. Prepare a table showing how Gigabyte's conventional, volume-based product costing system distorts the product costs of gismos, thingamajigs and whatchamacallits.

Endnotes

1 The Mason & Cox story is based on fact. However, the characters are fictional, the analysis has been simplified, and the numbers have been altered to protect the company's competitive stance.

2 More recent information about the extent of overhead costs in manufacturing businesses is not available. However, the increasing emphasis on computer integrated automation and the associated reduction in direct labour suggests that, in many businesses, manufacturing overheads are likely to be a significant cost.

3 The terminology used in this section is based on Raffish & Turney (1991) and Turney (1991).

4 Adapted from p. 96 of *Common Cents: The ABC Performance Breakthrough* by Dr Peter B.B. Turney, president and CEO of Cost Technology Inc., a management consulting firm specialising in ABC/ABM implementations, Cost Technology Inc., Beaverton, Oregon, 1991. Reprinted by permission of the publisher. All rights reserved.

5 Activity centres receive inconsistent treatment in the literature. Brimson (1991) and O'Guin (1991) use them in this manner. In contrast, Turney (1991) uses activity centres to aggregate activities within processes or functions for reporting purposes.

6 Because each product may consume a large number of activities, some ABC systems include an intermediate step where individual activities are combined into larger homogeneous 'activity cost pools'. The aim is to reduce the complexity of the costing system by reducing the number of 'activities' and therefore the number of activity drivers. To be aggregated into a larger cost pool, activities must share a common activity driver. Buthelezi chose not to use these larger 'activity cost pools'.

7 The only exception is the activity 'Design method'. The cost of this activity is assigned directly to products and then spread over the expected life of the product.

8 In this chapter we described this approach as the activity-based product costing system for indirect costs (see Exhibit 8.6). It is not illustrated here, but the procedures for costing the non-manufacturing activities are similar to the procedures for costing the manufacturing overhead activities.

PART 3
Information for Managing Resources

Part Contents

Part 3 of this book examines the role of management accounting in generating information for managing resources.

Chapter 9 explains budgeting systems and emphasises the importance of viewing budgeting within the wider strategic planning processes of a business. Budgets should also be considered as a major tool for managing resources. Budgets have many purposes, including planning, facilitating communication and co-ordination, allocating resources, controlling profit and operations, evaluating performance and providing incentives. Behavioural aspects must also be considered when formulating and using a budget. A case study of budgeting at a building company provides the focus for the discussion.

In Chapters 10 and 11, the case study of a "rough wear" clothing manufacturer is used to explain the principles of standard costing. The calculation of variances can help to determine the reasons for differences between actual costs and budgeted costs. The control process involves investigating significant variances, and taking corrective actions if required. An important control aspect of standard costing systems is assigning responsibility for certain variances to particular managers and departments.

Chapter 11 explains the use of flexible budgets and overhead variances as control tools. It should be noted that standard costing and variance analysis may provide only limited assistance in cost control, particularly in modern manufacturing environments. Contemporary methods for managing costs, which also consider how to manage costs to enhance customer value, are described in Chapter 15.

Financial performance reports and the use of transfer prices are examined in Chapter 12. Many organisations structure their businesses into responsibility centres – cost centres, revenue centres, profit centres and investment centres; and financial performance reports and measures should be selected to match the particular type of responsibility centre. An issue that is relevant in evaluating the financial performance of profit and investment centres is the use of transfer pricing. The appropriate transfer price will encourage divisional managers to make supply and selling decisions that enhance the overall performance of the organisation.

In Chapter 13 measures for evaluating the financial performance of investment centres are presented. Return on investment, residual income and shareholder value methods are outlined, as are the advantages and disadvantages of using such techniques. Various forms of individual reward systems are examined, in particular performance-based pay. The principles in this chapter are explained by using an example from a producer of aluminium.

Contemporary approaches to measuring and managing performance are covered in Chapter 14. The use of non-financial measures and benchmarking processes are discussed, as are strategic approaches such as the balanced scorecard. The performance measurement system at an auto manufacturer provides the case study for this chapter. An important theme of Chapters 13 and 14 is designing performance measurement and reward systems to provide incentives for managers (and other employees) to identify with and commit themselves to the organisation's objectives.

Contemporary approaches to managing costs and time are explained in Chapter 15. The Mason & Cox case discussed in Chapter 8 is reintroduced as an example of activity-based management (ABM). ABM uses information from activity-based costing to improve cost management as well as customer value. Other techniques discussed include life cycle management, business process re-engineering, target costing, and time-based management.

In Chapter 16 we consider contemporary techniques for managing suppliers, customers and quality as part of supply-chain management. E-commerce contributions to supplier and customer management are emphasised; activity-based approaches to analysing supplier and customer costs are demonstrated; and methods for evaluating performance in the areas of supply, customers and quality are outlined. Contemporary and conventional approaches to managing inventory are also included in this chapter.

Environmental and social management accounting is the topic of Chapter 17. A consistent theme in this book is that management accounting focuses on supporting managers within the organisation in their quest to enhance both shareholder and customer value. However, organisations increasingly are recognising the broader information needs of a wider range of stakeholders. In this chapter we consider how management accounting can provide information to help organisations manage environmental and social performance, which can benefit the organisation as well as the community and society. The tools and techniques that can be used in environmental accounting are outlined; and various ways in which environmental cost and impacts can be incorporated into management decisions, including capital expenditure decisions, are explained. Performance measurement systems that include environmental and social indicators are outlined, and examples of real life forms of environmental and social reporting are provided.

CHAPTER

Budgeting Systems

Learning Objectives

After completing this chapter, you should be able to:

1 understand how the budgeting process fits into the wider strategic planning processes of an organisation;

2 explain the five major purposes of the budgeting process;

3 understand how budgets are developed and used in responsibility accounting systems;

4 understand the various components that make up an annual budget;

5 discuss the importance of assumptions and predictions in budgeting;

6 describe the similarities and differences in the operating budgets prepared by manufacturers, retailers and wholesalers, and service firms;

7 complete the major budgeting schedules for a service organisation;

8 describe a typical organisation's process of budget administration;

9 discuss the behavioural consequences of budgets: participative budgeting, budgetary slack and budget difficulty;

10 understand zero-base budgeting and program budgeting; and

11 after studying the appendix, complete the major budgeting schedules for a manufacturing organisation.

Introduction

Developing a budget is a critical step in planning any activity. This is true for businesses, for government enterprises and for individuals. We must all budget to meet our daily expenses and to plan for major expenditures such as buying a car or taking a holiday. Similarly, private and government businesses of all types must make financial plans to provide information for managers to assist them in managing resources and creating value. Budgets may be used to control routine operations, to plan for major expenditures and to assist with financing decisions.

L.O. 1

Strategic planning and budgeting systems

In Chapter 1 we discussed managers' needs for information to help them manage resources and create value. This information is often future-oriented, and one way of developing and presenting such information is to prepare a budget. A **budget** is a detailed plan that shows the financial consequences of an organisation's operating activities for a specific future time period. A budget acts as a financial model that summarises future operations and it is usually viewed as a core component of an organisation's planning and control system. (Planning and control systems were described in Chapter 1.)

Strategic planning is the term given to the long-term planning usually undertaken by senior managers. Strategic planning involves making decisions about the types of businesses and markets that an organisation operates in, and about how those businesses and activities will be financed. This is termed **corporate strategy**. For example, the senior management of a large multinational corporation such as BHP Billiton may make decisions about acquiring certain companies, selling existing businesses, moving operations into Asia or restructuring its South African operations. These types of decisions have very long-term implications and require large financial resources.

Strategies need to be developed to determine how a business will compete within its particular markets. Individual firms will have a **business** (or **competitive**) **strategy**, as will each business unit within a larger company. For example, a business (division) within SABMiller may choose to compete by being a low-cost producer, while another business within SABMiller may compete by having a constantly changing range of innovative products.

While strategic planning can involve a horizon of three or more years, the budgeting process is short-term planning, often for a one-year period. The financial implications of strategic plans are estimated in broad terms, while the budgeting process is more detailed. The strategies adopted by senior management have direct implications for the formulation of budgets. For example, if the strategies include the development of a new product range, or establishing new overseas branch offices, then the annual budget must include these new operations.

L.O. 2

Purposes of budgeting

The procedures and activities that are undertaken to develop the budget are called the **budgeting process**. The budgeting process can serve five primary purposes. It should be noted that not all purposes are served by all budgeting systems. For example, in some small businesses, planning and resource allocation may be the only intended purposes of the budgeting system.

1. *Planning*. The most obvious purpose of a budget is to quantify a plan of action. The budgeting process forces the individuals within a business to plan. For example, in formulating a quarterly budget for a five-star hotel, the hotel manager, the reservations manager and the food and beverage manager must work together to plan the staffing and supplies needed to meet anticipated demand for the hotel's services.

2. *Facilitating communication and co-ordination.* For a business to plan operations effectively there must be good communication and coordination between all managers. The budgeting process provides a formal mechanism to enable this to take place. For example, to plan pricing structures and the number of ticket sales, the sales manager for Kulula.com or Mango airlines must know the flight schedules developed by the airline's route manager. The budgeting process pulls together the plans of each manager in an organisation.
3. *Allocating resources.* Generally, a firm's resources are limited, and budgets provide one way of allocating resources among competing uses. A large retailer, such as the Shoprite group, would use the budgeting process to consider the many alternative uses that could be made of its limited resources. For example, managers running the company's supermarkets would be competing for resources against managers operating its super stores and speciality stores such as OK Furniture and House and Home. The budgeting process provides a forum for evaluating alternative uses of those limited resources.
4. *Controlling profit and operations.* The budget can serve as a benchmark to allow a comparison against actual financial results at all levels of a business. For example, within a sales department, actual sales against budgeted sales may be reported on a weekly basis to help sales staff exercise some control over total sales. In addition, the budgeted costs of a customer service department may be compared with actual costs each month to point to areas where there needs to be greater cost control. As part of the budgeting process, standard costs are often developed for major production inputs (such as direct materials used in production) or activities. These ideal costs provide benchmarks to help managers control financial resources. (In Chapters 8 and 10, standard costs for control are outlined.)

   At CIG Gas Cylinders, in the 1990s, the operations staff were organised into work teams (Chenhall & Langfield-Smith, 2003). These teams develop and manage their own work schedules and cost budgets. This is an innovative way of allowing production workers a more active role in controlling costs and operations.
5. *Evaluating performance and providing incentives.* Comparing actual results with budgeted results also helps managers to evaluate the performance of individuals, departments, divisions or the entire company. Since budgets are used to evaluate performance, they can also be used to provide incentives for people to perform well. For example, hotel managers of a hotel chain may participate in a profit-sharing scheme that provides them with incentives to meet or exceed their budgeted profit goals. However, budgeting does not always provide an effective tool to assist in planning and control, as illustrated in the 'Real life' below.

Responsibility accounting

L.O. 3

Budgets are usually developed along responsibility accounting lines. **Responsibility accounting** is the term used to describe the practice of holding managers responsible for the activities and performance of their area of the business. For example, a particular manager might be held responsible for the activities and results of an accounting department, the personnel department or a production department. A senior manager might be responsible for a complete business unit, which may include many departments. The budget can be used as a benchmark to measure the performance of people and departments.

As part of the budgeting process, the managers of various departments or other sections of a business are often required to develop their own budget estimates for the costs, revenue or profits of their areas. These same managers are then held responsible for meeting budget targets when actual operations commence.

Responsibility centres

A responsibility accounting system is built around a framework of responsibility centres. A responsibility centre is a sub-unit in an organisation (for example, a department or a division) whose manager is held accountable for the sub-unit's activities and performance. There are four common types of responsibility centres: cost centres, revenue centres, profit centres and investment centres. (These centres are described in greater detail in Chapter 12.)

REAL LIFE: WARNING – BUDGETING MAY BE A WEALTH HAZARD!

The formulation of a budget does not always provide a solution to the planning and control needs of a business, as the following discussion indicates.

Budgets are used in businesses for a variety of purposes. However, the budgeting process does not cease once budgets are approved. In small businesses, budgets are often formulated primarily to satisfy banks and other financiers. These budgets may not be a reliable management tool for use within the business unless they are kept up to date during the year. A reliance on budgets that fail to take into account major changes may lead to significant problems for a business.

It is very common for finance executives to develop budgets using spreadsheet software such as Excel, which provides a quick and convenient way of keeping budget schedules up to date through the budget period as budget assumptions change. However, failing to detect even minor errors in the embedded formulas in spreadsheets can lead to serious cash flow problems. Typically, spreadsheet applications do not incorporate any double-checking mechanisms to uncover errors. In addition, it is common for people to place undue faith in the accuracy of printed output of spreadsheet programs, just because they are produced by computer software.

Some companies develop their budgets from the chart of accounts. However, this may limit the value of the budgets, as they may not always take into account operational and business planning viewpoints. Business planning needs to be dynamic and linked to strategic plans; and it should include not only financial but also key non-financial indicators, such as sales per customer and number of repeat customers.

Some experts have suggested that the practice of budgeting is a constraint on creativity, and the time and energy spent on budget formulation is better spent elsewhere. A European consortium of 20 large companies investigated life without budgets and found that as much as 20 per cent of management time is freed up once the budgeting process is eliminated, as the politics and gaming which seems to be necessarily associated with the budgeting process also disappears. Does this mean that such companies operate with no plans? Successful European companies like Volvo and Ericsson replace budgets with sophisticated performance measurement tools, which operating units use to monitor performance through forecasting and reporting strategically driven performance indicators. A key aspect of such models is the creation of self-governing business units where clear boundaries and values are devolved to business unit teams, and where targets assess performance relative to competitors. Those same targets may allow for flexibility and 'exit routes' if business conditions change.

Courtesy of Volvo Car

Sources: Thomas (1998); Anon (1999); Hope & Fraser (2000)

The type of responsibility centre determines the types of financial results for which a manager is held accountable. For example, managers of cost centres are held responsible for the costs of running that unit, and managers of profit centres are accountable for profits generated in their unit.[1] Chapters 10 and 11 examine conventional methods for controlling costs in cost centres, and Chapter 13 considers the financial control of profit centres and investment centres.

The annual budget: a planning tool

L.O. 4

The **annual budget** (sometimes called the **master budget**) is a comprehensive set of budgets that covers all aspects of a firm's activities. The annual budget consists of many separate interdependent budgets. Exhibit 9.1 describes these interrelationships.

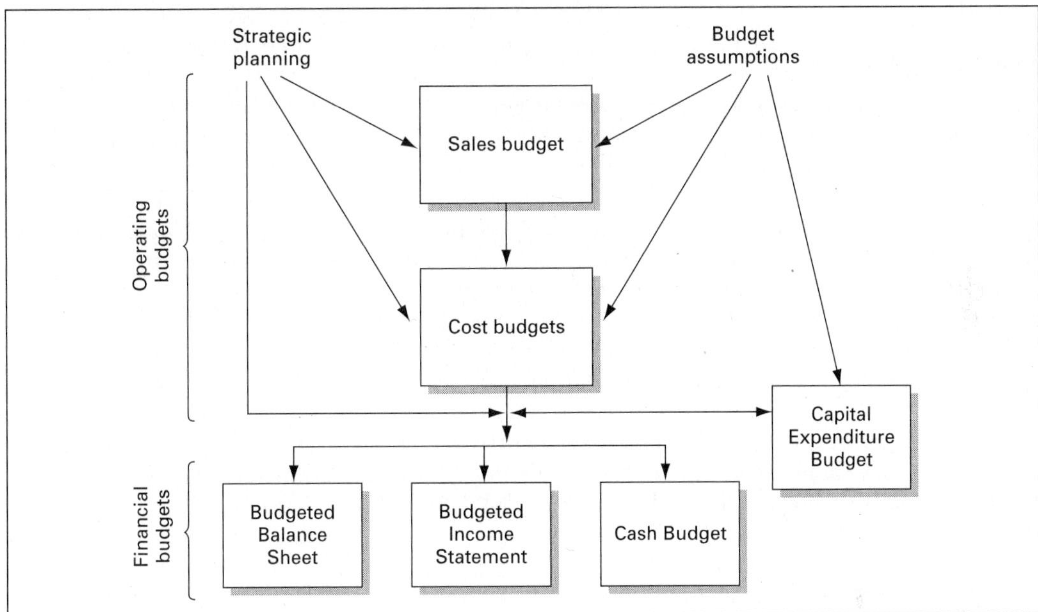

Exhibit 9.1 Components of the annual budget

The sales budget and the various cost budgets are often termed the **operating budgets**. The **financial budgets** consist of the budgeted income statement, the budgeted balance sheet, the cash budget and the capital expenditure budget.

Budgets are developed for specific time periods. The budgeting process usually covers a year's operations but may sometimes be prepared for a quarter of a year or for a month. **Rolling** (or **continuous**) **budgets** are budgets that are continually updated by periodically adding a new time period, such as a quarter, and dropping the period just completed.

The level of detail involved in developing the annual budget will vary. In large businesses, very comprehensive and formal budgeting procedures may be used and the development of the annual budget may take several months. In smaller businesses, the process is often less formal and less detailed. The descriptions of the budgeting process that follow are more common to large businesses, but the principles also apply to smaller firms.

Strategic plans and budget assumptions

L.O. 5

The starting point in the budgeting process is for managers to understand the strategy of the organisation and to formulate the budget in the light of strategic plans. For example, a company may have decided to enter new product markets or withdraw from others, or to place greater emphasis on achieving a higher level of customer service. These decisions have implications for many of the budgeted operations. If a higher level of customer service is the new focus of strategic plans, then the budget may include expenditure to fund customer service training courses for staff and to conduct surveys of customer satisfaction.

In estimating the budget, various assumptions must be made about the competitive and economic environment for the coming year. These assumptions include new competitors entering the market, forecasts of material prices, wage rate increases, market growth, government legislation and changes in interest rates.

The operating budgets

L.O. 6 The operating budgets include the sales budget, based on forecast sales for goods and services, and a series of cost budgets that specify how operations will be carried out to meet the forecast sales demand.

The sales budget

Most budgeting processes begin with the **sales budget**, which is a detailed summary of the estimated sales units and revenues from the organisation's products for the budget year, based on the sales forecast. **Sales forecasting** involves estimating which products will be sold, and in what quantities. For example, airlines forecast the number of passengers who will fly on each of their routes, and the average air fares. Banks forecast the number and Rand amount of the personal loans and home mortgages that they will provide in the coming year. Hotels estimate the number of rooms that will be occupied during various seasons. Manufacturing and retail businesses forecast sales of their goods. Sales estimates must be made at the start of the budgeting process as many other budget components depend on these estimates. For example, once the estimated sales volume is known, the required production volume and the total costs of production for the budget year can be estimated.

Most managers would agree that sales forecasting is a critical step in the budgeting process, and that it is very difficult to do accurately. Some large firms have market research staff to co-ordinate the company's sales forecasting efforts. Accurate forecasting of sales is so important to the budgeting process that managers at all levels of the business may participate in the forecasting.

Major factors that are considered when forecasting sales will differ, depending on the industry and the nature of the firm, but will include the following:

1 Internal factors

- Past sales levels and trends for the company.
- New products planned by the company.
- The intended pricing policy of the company.
- Planned advertising and product promotion.

2 External factors

- General economic trends. (Is the economy growing? How fast is it growing? Is a recession or economic slowdown expected?) If the Rand is expected to depreciate, then this may promote wine exports. Increasing interest rates may result in reduced demand by customers for wine.
- Economic trends that directly relate to the company's industry. (In the wine industry, for example, is consumers' disposable income likely to increase, with the subsequent possibility of an increased demand for wine?)
- Other factors expected to affect sales in the industry. (For example, will the growing emphasis on healthier lifestyles increase the demand for red wine as compared to beer?)
- Consolidation of buyers. (For example, increasingly wine is being sold through the

supermarket chains such as Pick 'n Pay, Shoprite/Checkers and Spar. This means that the buyers will have a significant amount of pricing power relative to the large number of wine makers).

- Political and legal events. (For example, will increases due to duties on wine affect demand for the product?)
- Expected activities of competitors and customers.

The typical starting point in forecasting sales for the budget year is to consider the sales achieved in the current year, and then to assess the effect of other factors listed above. Elaborate computer models may be built to incorporate systematically all the available information. Statistical methods, such as regression analysis and probability distributions for sales, may be used. (Regression analysis was described in Chapter 3.) A great deal of effort generally goes into the sales forecast since it is such a critical step in the budgeting process.

The cost budgets

Following the sales budget, a firm develops a series of **cost budgets** that detail the cost of operations that will be carried out to support the forecast demand for its goods or services. The types of budgets that are prepared will depend on the nature of the business – that is, whether it is a manufacturing, service, retail or wholesale firm.

Manufacturing firms

A manufacturing firm develops a **production budget**, which shows the number of units of products to be manufactured. This is based on the forecast sales, adjusted for planned inventory levels. Based on the production budget, a manufacturer develops cost budgets for the direct materials, direct labour and overhead that will be required in the production process. The cost budgets for a manufacturing firm are illustrated in Exhibit 9.2.

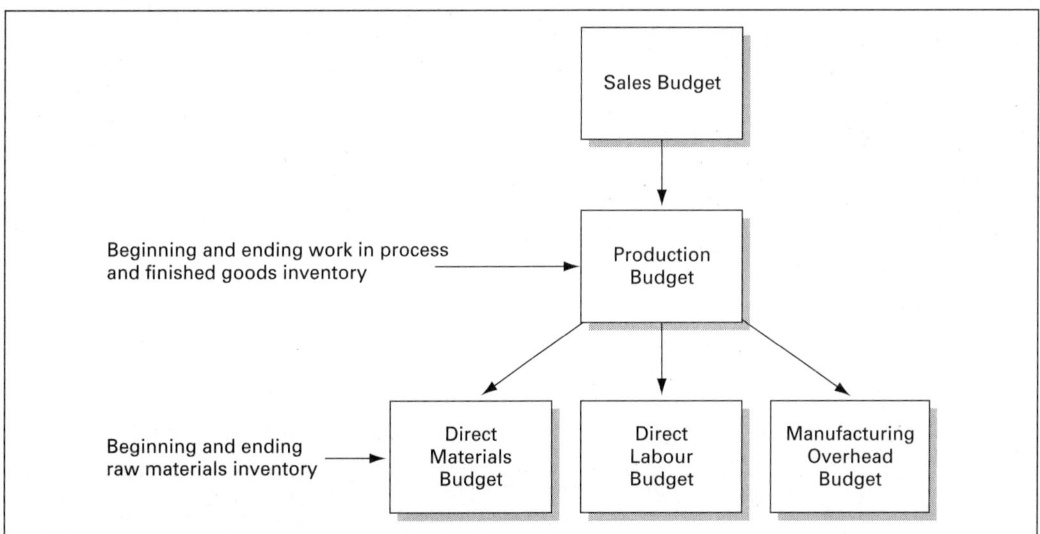

Exhibit 9.2 Detail of operating budgets for a manufacturing business

Budgets are also developed for selling and administrative expenses. These comprise the costs of running support departments such as accounting and human resources, costs relating to senior management, and cost budgets for the sales, advertising and marketing functions. The appendix to this chapter contains an example that shows how the various operating budgets of a manufacturing company fit together.

Retail and wholesale businesses

For a retail business, such as a department store or supermarket, or for a wholesale business, the cost budgets are similar to those of a manufacturing firm. However, rather than preparing a production budget for goods, a retailer or wholesaler develops a **purchases budget** to determine the quantity and cost of goods that it needs to purchase for resale. Planned levels of finished goods inventories will be taken into account in the purchases budget.

Budgets for selling expenses will include the wages paid to sales staff (for example, to sales assistants and checkout operators) and overheads that relate to the other selling activities of the retail or wholesale operations. Budgets for administrative expenses will be similar to those of a manufacturing firm.

Service firms

Using the sales budget for its services, a service firm develops a set of budgets that show how the demand for those services will be met. An airline, for example, would prepare the following budgets:

- a budget of planned kilometres to be flown;
- material budgets for aircraft spare parts, aircraft fuel and in-flight food;
- labour budgets for flight crews and maintenance personnel; and
- an overhead budget – service firms are characterised by large selling and administrative budgets.

The financial budgets

Once the operating budgets are complete, the financial budgets can be prepared.

The cash budget

All types of businesses prepare a cash budget. The **cash budget** shows detailed expected cash receipts and planned cash payments. Most cash receipts result from selling goods or services. Cash payments will relate to planned payments for all purchases to be made throughout the budget year, including major asset purchases, which are identified from the capital expenditure budget. A **capital expenditure budget** is a plan for the acquisition of long-term assets, such as buildings, plant and equipment. (Capital budgeting techniques are covered in depth in Chapters 21 and 22.)

In addition, large cash inflows, for example from borrowings or from the sale of assets, will be included in the cash budget as cash receipts.

By considering the timing of all cash receipts and cash payments, the cash budget will reveal when the firm will have cash shortages throughout the budget year, and when there will be cash surpluses available for short-term investment. The cash budget allows the business to plan how and when it will acquire its financial resources.

The budgeted income statement and balance sheet

The final output of the budgeting process, as shown in Exhibit 9.1, includes a **budgeted income statement** that shows the expected revenues and planned expenses of the firm during the budget period, and a **budgeted balance sheet**, which sets out the expected financial position at the end of the budget period. These budgeted financial statements show the complete financial results of the planned operations for the budget period. In many businesses, these statements are formulated not just for the year's operations, but for each quarter and month of the year. Similarly, the component budgets are also broken down into shorter time periods. This allows for more detailed and accurate planning and for ongoing cost control to take place.

Budgets in not-for-profit organisations and government agencies

The annual budget for a not-for-profit organisation includes many of the components shown in Exhibit 9.1. However, there are some important differences. Many not-for-profit organisations provide services free of charge, so there is no sales budget. Nevertheless, such firms do begin their budgeting process with a budget that shows the level of services to be provided. For example, the budget for the City of Johannesburg would show the planned levels of the various public services it provides, and the cost budgets would be formulated to support these levels of services. Not-for-profit organisations also prepare budgets that show their anticipated funding. In a local government council, these funds would include the rates and taxes charged to residents and businesses, central government funding, and any special government funding such as grants for various job creation projects.

Budgeting at AVJ Ltd

L.O. 7

To illustrate the steps involved in developing a budget, the budgeting process used at AVJ Ltd will be described.[2] AVJ is a building company that focuses on building low-cost residential houses, land development and pre-planned housing estates for the lower end of the market.

AVJ operates in Western Cape, the Eastern Cape and Kwazulu-Natal. Financial reporting and budgeting within the group focuses on provincial divisions and product lines. The product lines are residential housing, land, home improvements, housing projects and kit homes. Not all product lines are offered in each province. The head office is located in Cape Town and each province has a manager and administrative staff. Exhibit 9.3 shows the organisational structure for AVJ and the Western Cape Division. Each division can be regarded as a profit centre, with various component revenue and cost centres. These include the sales department and building department respectively.

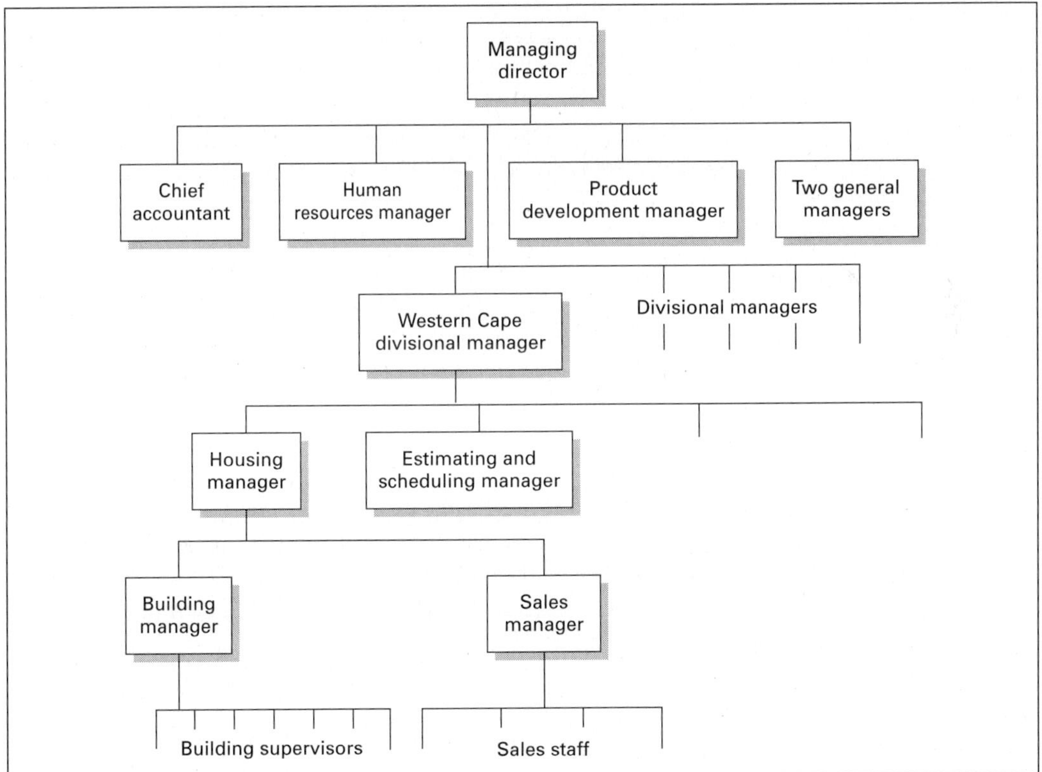

Exhibit 9.3 Organisational chart, AVJ

The annual budgeting process at AVJ commences in February each year and is completed before the end of June, ready for the beginning of the new financial year on 1 July. The steps that take place

REAL LIFE: BUDGETING AT SOUTH AFRICAN COMPANIES

Robor is a supplier of stainless steel and cold-rolled steel tube and pipe and other value-added products. The company concluded a R480 million management-led buyout from its former holding company, Barloworld.

In January 2007, Robor reported that it was budgeting to increase production of stainless steel tubes by 25 per cent in 2007. This was caused by increased demand from such sectors as construction and the automotive industry as well as the food and beverage industry. In relation to the company's budgeting process, this would mean that Robor would need to estimate and budget for increased requirements for materials, labour and energy costs as well as costs relating to increasing capacity such as relocating to a new factory, refurbishing mills and investing in new plant and equipment. Budgeted revenue and costs for the next year would include both volume and price increases.

Idu Software is a South African company that produced a leading financial budgeting and forecasting application, called Idu-Concept, which is used by over 40 listed companies including Old Mutual, and New Clicks.

At Old Mutual, the collation of annual budgets used to take months. According to Kevin Cilliers, a financial manager at Old Mutual, the implementation of Idu-Budgets has simplified the budget process and has reduced significantly the time taken to prepare budgets. All supporting data is available online which enables reviewers to analyse the composition of each budget and the person preparing the budget does not need to do any workings on a separate spreadsheet.

The Web-based financial budgeting and reporting tool has been adopted across more than 800 cost centres in Old Mutual's Retail division. According to Cilliers, 'Receiving figures and consolidations in real-time means cost centre managers spend more time looking at numbers that are relevant, and less time trying to manage the process and consolidate figures. The application is simple and easy to use, even for non-financially astute users.'

The University of South Africa (UNISA) has implemented Idu-Concept for undertaking its budgeting process. UNISA has over 200 000 students and assets of over R2 billion. Budgeting for a large educational institution such as UNISA is complex and budgets need to include estimates of student intakes, government subsidy collections, student fee collections, future salaries and human resource costs, administrative and property costs. Further, collections are lumpy while costs are incurred over the whole year and budgets are a critical component of management's ability to deliver services and ensure financial sustainability. As human resources are the major cost component of a university, UNISA wishes to determine the total cost to the university of each staff member.

New Clicks has also adopted Idu-Concept for its budgeting process and according to the financial accountant, Roy Williams, this enabled the company to reduce its budget cycle from 5 to 6 months to 3 weeks. The system has also enabled the company to report back to cost centres monthly budget versus actual results and monthly forecasted expenditure and has enabled the company to achieve cost savings as well as time savings.

in the budget process at AVJ will be explained, using the year ending 30 June 20X8 budget for residential housing for the Western Cape Division as an example.

How the company operates

To gain insight into AVJ's budgeting system, it is important to understand how the houses are built and the responsibilities and duties of the key managers in the Western Cape Division.

The sales staff are directly involved in selling contract houses to clients. These houses are selected from AVJ's range of house designs. Once a customer has paid a deposit, the sales manager supervises the preparation of the building contract and the housing plans, arranges finance for the home buyer, if required, and obtains local council approval for the plans. The project then becomes the responsibility of the building manager. The building manager assigns a building supervisor to the housing project. The supervisor engages subcontractors and supervises all work done on the house. AVJ does not employ construction workers directly to work on the housing sites but engages subcontractors, such as plumbers, builders, bricklayers and plasterers, as they are required.

It takes 10 to 15 weeks to build a house. The estimating and scheduling team in the Western Cape office plays a key role in ordering materials as they are needed and in maintaining price files and records of the quantities of material used on each house.

Strategic planning and budget assumptions

The annual budget for AVJ is guided by the strategic plan. The strategic planning process sets the direction for the company for the next five years. During strategic planning, decisions are made concerning which markets the company will compete in and the types of products that will be offered. Financing issues are also considered. The senior managers from the head office and in each province are involved in strategic planning, and industry analysts are brought in to give advice on medium-term and long-term projections for the housing industry.

As a basis for the strategic plans, both the anticipated size of the housing market and AVJ's market share must be estimated for the next five years. The housing market is cyclical and the demand for houses is heavily influenced by economic considerations such as the level of consumer confidence. AVJ's market share over the five-year period will be affected by projections of the supply and demand for land and housing and by the estimated number of building commencements. The accountants at AVJ play an important role in the strategic planning process by advising on future profit margins, allowing the financial impact of alternative strategies to be assessed. The strategies for the company are reviewed and updated about every 18 months.

Overview of budgeting at AVJ

AVJ has a number of operating divisions located throughout the three provinces. Therefore, like many large companies, the budgeting process is lengthy and must be tightly co-ordinated. The budgeting timetable for the year ending 30 June 20X8 was distributed to all managers within AVJ in January 20X7. The major stages in the preparation of the budget were as follows:

1 In mid-February 20X7, instructions and underlying budget assumptions were sent to the divisions in each province. These included economic assumptions about the likely interest rates and the number of housing commencements for that province. The provincial managers decided what products they would offer in the coming year, and the budgeting process began with the sales budget.

2 At the end of March, each division sent its preliminary budget to the head office Budget Committee for review and approval. It consisted of a budgeted income statement and a budgeted balance sheet. The Budget Committee recommended that amendments be made to most of the budgets, which were then returned to the divisional managers.

3 By the end of April, the amended divisional budgets were resubmitted to the Budget Committee for approval. Once approved, they were consolidated with the head office administrative budgets to form the budgeted income statement and budgeted balance sheet for the company.

4 The consolidated budget for AVJ was reviewed by the Budget Committee and submitted to the Board of Directors. Some minor amendments took place before the annual budget was finalised at the end of June 20X7, ready for the budget year that commenced on 1 July 20X7. The budgeting process for the year ending 30 June 20X8 commenced with the sales budget. A series of budgets for variable building and variable selling expenses were estimated, based on the estimated level of sales activity. Budgets for building overheads and for administrative, selling and finance expenses were then formulated. These operating budgets were summarised to form the budgeted income statement. The cash budgets and budgeted balance sheet were estimated to complete the process. Note that AVJ uses a contribution margin format in the budgeted income statement, which classifies costs according to cost behaviour (variable or fixed) rather than according to function (production and non-production).

The sales budget

Each provincial management team determined its budgeted sales revenue by estimating sales volume and selling price. The Western Cape sales manager estimated the sales volume for the budget by considering the forecast number of housing approvals for the industry for each region in the Western Cape (provided by head office) and the market share that AVJ would achieve in each region during the budget year.

The first step in estimating the sales budget was to consider the size of the market in the current financial year, and the number of sales contracts signed by AVJ during that year. However, at this stage, only sales results for the first eight months of the financial year ending 30 June 20X7 were known, and the sales for the remaining months of March to June had to be estimated. This information was used to estimate AVJ's market share for the year ending 30 June 20X7. Panel A of Exhibit 9.4 shows that for the year, the total number of Western Cape housing approvals was estimated to be 27 000, of which AVJ's share was estimated to be 1080, or 4 per cent.

The industry reports that were supplied to the Western Cape sales manager suggested that the housing market would improve in the budget year, as the Western Cape's economy improved and mortgage interest rates remained at reasonable levels. AVJ expected to increase its share of the market from 4.0 per cent to 4.2 per cent because of the increased marketing and promotional activities planned. These expectations were built into the budgeted sales volume as shown in panel B of Exhibit 9.4. The final column in panel B of Exhibit 9.4 shows the change in market share that the Western Cape sales manager assumed for the budget year. When the sales budgets are reviewed by the Budget Committee it is important that the sales manager can justify his or her predicted market share increase.

The second step in estimating the sales budget was to estimate the average contract price (selling price) for houses for the budget year. Consideration was given to the proportion of customers that would be 'first-home buyers' and those that would be 'move-up buyers'.[3] Customers in the first category buy cheaper houses than do those in the second category. In Exhibit 9.5 it can be seen that the average selling price for the budget year was estimated to be R220 000. This was based on 75 per cent of sales being to first-time buyers and the remainder to move-up buyers. Therefore, the total sales revenue was budgeted at R258 720 000 (R220 000 × 1176 contracts).

The cost budgets

AVJ Ltd is not a manufacturing company in the conventional sense, as it does not prepare separate budgets for direct materials or direct labour. However, it does prepare budgets for the variable

(A) Latest forecast year ending 30 June 20X7			
Regions	**Total housing approvals for Western Cape**	**Contracts signed by AVJ**	**Market share (%)**
Cape Town	18 500	800	4.3%
West Coast	2 000	125	6.2%
Boland	2 500	50	2.0%
South Coast	3 000	95	3.2%
Other	1 000	10	1.0%
Total	27 000	1080	4.0%*

*[1080/27000]

(B) Budget year ending 30 June 20X8				
Regions	**Total housing approvals for Western Cape**	**Contracts signed by AVJ**	**Market share (%)**	**Percentage change in market share**
Cape Town	19 500	900	4.6%	0.3%
West Coast	3 000	180	6.0%	−0.2%
Boland	2 000	50	2.5%	0.5%
South Coast	2 500	36	1.4%	−1.8%
Other	1 000	10	1.0%	0.0%
Total	28 000	1176	4.2%	0.2%

Exhibit 9.4 Budgeted sales volumes for year ending 30 June 20X8, AVJ Western Cape

House buyer	Percentage of contracts signed	Average sales value per house	Weighted average selling value
First-time buyer	75%	R 200 000	R150 000
Move-up buyer	25%	280 000	70 000
	100%		R220 000*

*Calculated as (R200 000 × 0.75) + (R280 000 × 0.25) = R220 000

Exhibit 9.5 Calculation of budgeted average selling price, AVJ Western Cape

building costs and for building overheads. The operating budgets for a manufacturing company are described in the appendix to the chapter.

Estimating the variable costs

To calculate the variable building expenses, estimates were made of the cost of direct materials (such as timber, mortar, bricks) and the cost of subcontractors. AVJ subcontracts all the work on building sites to independent trades-people. The direct costs of constructing a building were regarded as variable with respect to sales revenue, which from experience was a fairly constant 80 per cent of sales revenue. Thus, for the year ending 30 June 20X8, the total variable cost of building projects was budgeted at R206 976 000 (sales revenue of R258 720 000 × 0.80).

Another variable expense was sales commission. Besides their fixed salary, sales staff receive a commission of 1 per cent of gross sales for every housing contract they sell. The sales commission was calculated as R2 587 000 (R258 720 000 × 0.01, rounded to the nearest thousand Rands).

These expenses are shown in the budgeted income statement in Exhibit 9.6.[4]

	R'000s	R'000s
Sales revenue		258 720
Variable building expenses	206 976	
Variable sales commission	2 587	209 563
Contribution margin		49 157
Building overheads:		
Supervisors' salaries	3 120	
Motor vehicle expenses	810	
Contract drafting	148	4 078
Selling expenses:		
Sales salaries	4 550	
Motor vehicle expenses	1 000	
Advertising	1 500	7 050
Administrative expenses:		
Salaries	5 600	
Motor vehicle expenses	840	
Rent	1 500	
Depreciation on office equipment	680	
Office expenses	775	9 395
Finance expenses:		
Interest on head office loan	180	
Interest on bank overdraft	444	
Bad and doubtful debts	110	734
Net profit		27 900

Exhibit 9.6 Budgeted Income Statement for year ending 30 June 20X8, AVJ Western Cape

Estimating the building overheads

The overheads of building houses consisted of the salaries of building supervisors, supervisors' motor vehicle expenses (for example, petrol and leasing expenses) and the cost of drafting house plans. While these costs would be fixed for the budget year, each was estimated by considering the expected sales volume and anticipated price rises. Over a year, one building supervisor can manage about 80 houses.

Therefore, as the Western Cape operation estimated 1176 housing contracts for the budget year, 15 building supervisors would be needed. It was assumed that the company would pay supervisors a salary of R160 000 per year. Payroll taxes, employer superannuation contributions, provisions for annual and long-service leave and workers' compensation insurance would increase the cost of salaries by 30 per cent. Thus, the total cost of the building supervisors' salaries was estimated as:

Supervisors' salaries = (R160 000 + 30%) × 15
= R3 120 000

The Western Cape Division planned to lease and maintain 15 motor vehicles for the supervisors to use. Based on experience and assumptions about price movements, it was estimated that each motor vehicle would cost an average of R28 000 per year to lease and insure, R6000 in repairs and maintenance, and R20 000 in petrol. Thus the motor vehicle expenses amounted to:

(R28 000 + R6000 + R20 000) × 15 = R810 000

Contract drafting of housing plans was regarded as a building overhead, as plans were not usually created for each individual house contract. The estimated cost of drafting was R148 000.

Budgeting for fixed selling, administrative and finance expenses

The fixed selling, administrative and finance expenses were carefully estimated by managers in the Western Cape office. The fixed selling expenses consisted of sales salaries, motor vehicle expenses and advertising expenses.

It was estimated that, in the budget year, the 25 sales staff would be paid fixed salaries of R140 000, in addition to their sales commissions. Therefore, allowing for labour on-costs of 30 per cent, total sales salaries amounted to:

(R140 000 + 30%) × 25 = R4 550 000

Sales staff drive their own motor vehicles, but are reimbursed for expenses such as the cost of petrol. The motor vehicle expenses for the sales staff were estimated as R1 000 000, or R40 000 per salesperson per year.

The sales manager estimated the advertising expenses by considering the cost of regular newspaper advertisements and any planned promotions that would involve television commercials, newspaper advertisements or promotional brochures. These were estimated as R1 500 000 for the year.

Administrative expenses included administrative salaries, motor vehicle expenses for administrative staff, rent, office expenses and depreciation. To estimate the cost of administrative salaries, the Western Cape divisional manager considered the likely staffing levels in the budget year, and any changes in salary levels. The total cost of administrative salaries was estimated as R5 600 000. The cost of motor vehicles driven by senior managers was estimated as R840 000. This consisted of the cost of leasing, motor vehicle maintenance and petrol. The rent of the Western Cape office was contracted with the building owners and would be R1 500 000 for the year. Depreciation of office equipment and fittings amounted to R680 000, and office expenses were estimated as R775 000. The company's average bank overdraft balance over the year is expected to be R3.7 million and the interest rate is 12%. This will result in an expected interest charge of R444 000 for the year.

Interest expenses were also charged to the Western Cape Division by the AVJ head office. Like most large companies, the management of cash and the financing of operations is a centralised activity, undertaken by specialists in the head office. Each division was charged interest for its use of cash throughout the year. For the budget year this charge was based on a notional interest rate of 9 per cent. This was calculated as follows:

Interest charge = average balance × notional interest rate per annum
= R2 000 000 × 0.09
= R180 000

AVJ has a very low incidence of bad and doubtful debts. For the year ending 30 June 20X8 they were estimated at R110 000.

The budgeted income statement

Exhibit 9.6 contains a summary of the budgeted income statement for the Western Cape Division of AVJ. As discussed in Chapters 6 and 18 this statement is often called a ***contribution margin statement*** rather than an income statement as it highlights the total contribution margin generated from building and selling houses. The fixed expenses are classified as building overheads, selling expenses, administrative expenses and finance expenses. There is no income taxation expense included in the profit calculation. In common with many divisionalised companies, the cost of income taxation is considered to be outside the control of the divisions and is accounted for in the final consolidation of the company budgets.

When the budgeted income statement was submitted to the head office to be reviewed by the Budget Review Committee, monthly income statements were also provided. This would allow the budget to be used for monthly performance reports during 20X8. In preparing the monthly profit statements, the provincial managers considered how sales volume and expenses would differ for each month. For example, in January there may be fewer sales contracts signed, and administrative expenses may be lower than in April. The classification of expenses as variable or fixed helped managers to estimate the level of expenses for various monthly sales volumes.

The budgeted balance sheet

The budgeted balance sheet was developed at the same time as the budgeted income statement, as the interrelationships between the profit and loss activities and balance sheet items must be considered. For example, the equity in the budgeted balance sheet increased by the amount of the budgeted profit. Also, the levels of inventories and debtors were dependent on the estimated sales for the year.

The budgeted balance sheet as at 30 June 20X8 is shown in Exhibit 9.7. The major balance sheet items of debtors, inventory and non-current assets will be explained in detail.

	R'000s	R'000s
Assets		
Non-current assets:		
Property plant and equipment	42 400	
Less Accumulated depreciation	11 496	30 904
Current assets:		
Petty cash		16
Debtors	26 863	
Less Provision for doubtful debts	269	26 594
Inventories:		
Raw materials	10 160	
Work in process	13 439	
Finished goods	4 587	28 186
Prepaid rent		225
Total assets		85 925
Equity and Liabilities		
Long-term liabilities:		
Loan from head office		1 180
Provision for employee benefits		1 200
Short-term liabilities:		
Trade creditors		9 336
Sub-contractors		23 700
Sundry creditors		420
Provision for employee benefits		600
Cash		688
Total liabilities		37 124
Equity*		
Share Capital and retained earnings		R48 801
Total shareholders' equity and liabilities		R85 925

*Equity of R48 801 includes the net profit for 20X8 of R27 900.

Exhibit 9.7 Budgeted Balance Sheet as at 30 June 20X8, AVJ Western Cape

Debtors

The estimated balance of the debtors (or accounts receivable) at 30 June 20X8 was calculated by considering the number of houses that would be under construction at year-end, the average estimated sales value of each contract, and the timing of progress payments set out in the house sale contracts. The amount owing from customers, R26 863 000, was an estimate of the amount of progress payments due from customers that would not be received by year-end.

The amount of doubtful debts is very low for AVJ, as most customers observe the contract terms. Experience has shown that only about 1 per cent of debtors are bad. At 30 June 20X8, the estimated provision for doubtful debts was R269 000 (R26 863 000 × 0.01, rounded to the nearest thousand Rands).

Inventories

For AVJ, there were three categories of inventory. The raw materials inventory (R10 160 000) referred to unused materials on building sites and in stock. The largest category of inventory was houses still under construction (R13 439 000). The estimated value of this work in process inventory was calculated by considering the various stages of completion of the houses that would be under construction at balance date, and the estimated costs to date. The cost of finished goods inventory (R4 587 000) related to display homes. Display homes are built to allow potential customers to inspect the latest styles of AVJ houses. There are only a few houses on display at any time, and they are usually sold within a year of construction at a reduced selling price.

Non-current assets and depreciation

The non-current assets of AVJ related to office equipment and fittings. The amount of depreciation charged to the accumulated depreciation for the year was increased by the depreciation expense (R680 000) charged in the budgeted income statement; this gave accumulated depreciation of R11 496 000.

The cash budget

Preparing a cash budget is an important component of any formal budgeting system. While a cash budget is necessary to obtain the cash balance for the budgeted balance sheet, it also plays an important role in helping the company to evaluate its finance needs. For example, if the cash budget showed that there would be a cash shortage during the budget year, this would lead the accountant to recommend that additional financing (such as a bank loan or overdraft facility) be arranged as part of the budget. The cash budget also forms the basis for detailed monthly or weekly cash planning and control. The cash budget for the Western Cape Division of AVJ is shown in Exhibit 9.8.

	R'000
Cash balance as at 1 July 20X7	−R6 593
Cash receipts:	
Payments from customers	245 766
Cash available	R239 173
Cash payments:	
Trade creditors	42 697
Subcontractors	168 803
Purchase of office equipment	3 660
Payments to employees	13 270
Sales commissions	2 587
Rent	1 507
Loan from head office repaid	1 640
Motor vehicle expenses	2 650
Advertising	1500
Interest on Head Office loan	180
Interest on overdraft	444
Contract drafting	148
Office expenses	775
Total payments	R239 861
Cash balance at 30 June 20X8	−688

Exhibit 9.8 Cash Budget for year ending 30 June 20X8, AVJ Western Cape

Cash receipts

To estimate the cash that would be received from customers, the accountant considered the balance of the debtors at the beginning and end of the year, the amount of bad debts that would be written off during the budget year, and the estimated level of sales. This calculation is shown in Exhibit 9.9.

Cash payments

Most of the estimated cash payments shown in Exhibit 9.8 were based on budgeted expenses, adjusted for any amounts unpaid (accrued) or prepaid at the beginning and end of the year. For example, the estimate of cash payments to trade creditors for materials is shown in Exhibit 9.10. Note that the amount of raw materials to be purchased for use in the construction of housing was calculated first. This amount was then adjusted for opening and closing trade creditor balances.

To estimate the amount of rent to be paid during the budget year, the rent expense was adjusted by the prepayment at the beginning and end of the year (see Exhibit 9.10). Although rent expense was estimated to be R1 500 000, a cash amount of R1 507 000 would be paid during the year.

Cash budgeting is widely used in many businesses to predict cash surpluses and cash shortfalls. Many companies produce cash budgets that track receipts and payments monthly, weekly or even daily. In these circumstances it is critical that the timing of cash receipts and payments is estimated with great accuracy.

	R'000s	
Amount owing from customers at 1 July 20X7	R14 000	
Estimated 20X8 sales revenue (see Income Statement)	258 720	
	272 720	
Less Bad debts to be written off during year*	91	
Less Amounts owing from customers, 30 June 20X8 (see Balance Sheet)	26 863	
Estimated cash received from customers	R245 766	
*The estimate of bad debts to be written off is calculated as follows:		R'000
Opening balance of provision for doubtful debts at 1 July 20X7		R250
Plus increase to provision in year ending 30 June 20X8 (see Income Statement)		110
		R360
Less Estimate of balance of provision for doubtful debts 30 June 20X8 (see Balance Sheet)		269
Estimate of amount to be written off during year		R91

Exhibit 9.9 Estimated cash receipts for year ending 30 June 20X8, AVJ Western Cape

Calculation of cash payments to trade creditors	
(1) Estimate of the amount of materials to be purchased during year ending 30 June 20X8	
	R'000s
Unused raw materials, 30 June 20X8 (see Balance Sheet)	10 160
Plus Materials used in construction	44 723
	54 883
Less Raw materials on hand, 1 July 20X7	10 100
Materials to be purchased during year ending 30 June 20X8	44 783
(2) Estimate of the payments to suppliers during year ending 30 June 20X8	
Balance owing to suppliers, 1 July 20X7	7 250
Plus Materials to be purchased (see Estimate (1) above)	44 783
	52 033
Less Balance owing to suppliers, 30 June 20X8 (see Balance Sheet)	9 086
Payments to suppliers during year ending 30 June 20X8	42 947
Calculation of rent payment	
Rent expense for year ending 30 June 20X8 (see Income Statement)	1500
Less Amount prepaid, 1 July 20X7	218
	1282
Plus Amount prepaid, 30 June 20X8 (see Balance Sheet)	225
Rent to be paid during year ending 30 June 20X8	1507

Exhibit 9.10 Estimated cash payments for year ending 30 June 20X8, AVJ Western Cape

The review process

At the end of March the Western Cape divisional manager submitted the budgeted income statement and balance sheet for the year ending 30 June 20X8 to the Budget Review Committee. The members of this committee were the managing director of AVJ, the divisional (provincial) managers, the chief accountant, and four other senior head office managers from areas such as human resource management and product development. From the wide membership of this committee, it is clear that budgeting is considered an important management tool within AVJ. The Committee will often ask the provincial divisions to amend some of their budget estimates in order to bring projections in line with head office expectations. In May, when all regional budgets were finalised, they were consolidated with the head office selling and administrative expense budgets and the head office balance sheet to form the final budgeted financial statements for the company.

The purposes of AVJ's budgeting system

In an earlier section, budgets were described as having many purposes. At AVJ, the budgeting process was designed primarily to satisfy management's needs for planning and performance evaluation. The annual operating and financial budgets allowed AVJ to anticipate and plan for a certain level of operations for the coming year. For example, working from the budgeted sales volume, the Western Cape Division of AVJ planned to employ 15 building supervisors and to have available sufficient administrative staff and other resources to support that level of sales. Another reason for preparing the budget was that, at the corporate level of AVJ, it was becoming increasingly important to provide banks and other lenders with detailed, accurate projections for the coming year. This was best achieved through the formal budgeting processes, which involved all areas of the company.

Detailed budgeted balance sheets were prepared for each month of the budget. This allowed the budget to be used as a benchmark to evaluate the actual monthly performance of each region and each product group during the budget year.

Budget administration

L.O. 8

In small businesses, the procedures used to gather information and construct a budget are usually informal. In contrast, larger businesses use formal processes to collect data and prepare the budget. A senior accounting manager is often responsible for the **budget administration**. This accountant devises the process by which budget data will be gathered, collects the information and prepares the final budget. To communicate budget procedures and deadlines to employees throughout the organisation, the accountant often develops and distributes a **budget manual,** which identifies who is responsible for providing various types of information, when the information is required, and what form that information is to take.

A **budget committee** consisting of key senior executives is often appointed to advise the accountant during the preparation of the budget. We saw in the AVJ situation that the Budget Committee had the task of accepting or recommending changes to the divisional budgets. The authority to give final approval to the budget usually belongs to the board of directors, or to the board of management in many non-profit organisations.

Behavioural consequences of budgeting

L.O. 9

An underlying theme stressed in this text is the behavioural impact of management accounting systems. Budgeting systems have many behavioural consequences. A budget affects virtually everyone in an organisation: those who prepare the budget, those who use the budget to facilitate decision-making, and those whose performance is evaluated using the budget. The human reactions to the budgeting process can have a considerable influence on an organisation's overall effectiveness and should be considered when the budgeting process is designed and implemented. Much study has been devoted to the behavioural effects of budgets. Here we will briefly consider three issues: participative budgeting, budgetary slack and budget difficulty.

Participative budgeting

The AVJ budget preparation process has many features in common with that of other large companies. You will have noticed that it was an iterative process, that is, there were many repetitive steps involved in gaining approval for the budgets. The process of gaining acceptance of the budget involved a lot of negotiation and subsequent revisions of budget estimates. This lengthy and time-consuming process, called **participative budgeting**, allows managers at all levels to develop their own initial estimates for budgeted sales, costs and so on.

Top-down budgeting describes the system where senior managers impose budget targets on more junior managers – there is little participation or consultation in the budget-setting process. Budgets may be set at the corporate level and then cascaded down to the various responsibility centres – profit centres and cost centres – throughout the organisation. This may be a cost-effective and timely way of setting budgets, but there are two major disadvantages. First, senior managers may have less knowledge of the local business environment than do those managers working directly in the particular responsibility centres. Budget targets may not embody this knowledge and may be unrealistic. Second, limited involvement in setting budget targets can result in a lack of commitment of middle and junior managers to achieving the company's goals.

The term **bottom-up budgeting** is used to describe the participative process in which people at the lower managerial and operational levels play an active role in setting their own budget. Budgets are collected at the lowest responsibility centres of the business and are consolidated and fed up to senior management. The budgeting process at AVJ operated in a bottom-up manner. Under this approach, we would still expect a certain amount of review and negotiation to take place before budgets are approved by senior managers. Participative budgeting can encourage coordination and communication between managers and a greater understanding and appreciation of the objectives and strategy of the wider organisation. Accuracy of the budget estimates may be enhanced because those people close to operations have the best knowledge of the likely sales in their region or the likely costs of running their responsibility centre.

It is generally believed that most people will perform better and try harder to achieve a budget goal if they have been consulted in setting that goal. Such participation can give employees the feeling that 'this is my budget', rather than the common feeling that 'this is the budget you imposed on me'.

While participative budgeting can be very effective, it also has shortcomings. Participative budgeting is expensive and time-consuming. Too much participation and discussion can lead to indecisiveness and delay. Also, when those involved in the budgeting process disagree in significant and irreconcilable ways, the process of participation may aggravate those differences. Finally, opportunities for padding the budget arise in participatory systems unless incentives for accurate projections are provided.

In recent years, greater levels of **employee empowerment** have become more common in many businesses. Employee empowerment is when employees develop greater levels of independence, allowing them to make day-to-day decisions and solve work-related problems. It implies that employees at all levels of the organisation may be given the authority to develop their own budgets and targets and to manage their own work areas. Employee empowerment is a wider concept than that of budgetary participation. It is based on the idea that employees will experience greater motivation and will improve their performance through this increased authority and responsibility. This idea is discussed further in Chapter 12.

Budgetary slack: padding the budget

In a participatory budgeting system, the information upon which a budget is based comes largely from people throughout the business. For example, the sales forecast relies on market research and analysis by market research staff, but it also incorporates the projections of sales personnel. If the evaluation of a regional sales manager's performance is based on whether his or her sales budget for the territory is exceeded, what incentive does this create for the sales manager when estimating the budgeted sales? The incentive is to provide a conservative, or low, sales estimate.

When a supervisor provides a departmental cost estimate to his or her manager for the budget, there is an incentive to overestimate costs. When the actual cost incurred in the department is found to be less than the inflated cost projection, the manager may believe that the supervisor has managed the department in a cost-effective way.

These illustrations are examples of **padding the budget**. Budget padding means underestimating revenue or overestimating costs. The difference between the revenue or cost projection that a person provides, and a realistic estimate of the revenue or cost, is called **budgetary slack**. For

REAL LIFE: BEST PRACTICE IN BUDGETING

A recent survey of South African listed companies revealed some current budgeting practices used by 52 South African companies and opinions as to what was considered best practice.

- Of the 52 responding companies, 51 (98 per cent) operate a formal budgeting system. This compares favourably with other countries.
- About 69 per cent of the responding companies use flexible budgeting and 31 per cent of the companies use fixed budgets. The use of flexible budgets is consistent with management accounting theory. South African companies make greater use of flexible budgets than companies in the UK. This may be due to a higher level of uncertainty in South Africa.
- About 59 per cent of the companies reported using zero-based budgeting techniques. This is consistent with the move towards zero-based budgeting techniques in order to overcome the disadvantages of incremental budgets.
- Companies mainly used subjective methods to forecast sales, with market research and statistical forecasting methods also being used. The use of subjective methods reflects the important role of managerial experience to forecast future sales.
- There is a very low use of activity-based budgeting methods by South African companies.
- Senior managers seem to have a greater degree of influence over budget authorisation.
- Control was rated as the most important aspect of budgeting, while motivation was ranked as the least important objective.

In a survey of Australian companies, it was found that:

- More than 25 per cent of companies devoted between four and six months to preparing their budgets. The longer period of time did not guarantee higher-quality budgets; rather, it increased the likelihood of an inflexible budget. The accountants responding to the survey considered that between two and three months was best practice, but how effectively the time is spent was regarded as more important.
- About 50 per cent of companies produce budget packages of 30 pages or more for the approval of senior management. The accountants who participated in the survey believed that best practice included the use of graphics, ratios and key performance indicators to communicate key budget data, and that the report should be limited to less than 20 pages.
- To provide a reality check against unduly optimistic forecasts, one in 20 accountants evaluated alternative scenarios as part of the budget package, and one in seven commented on threats and included contingency plans. The inclusion of these aspects was considered to be best practice in budgeting.
- The barriers to accountants achieving best practice in budgeting were found to include a lack of staff skills, inaccurate and late data, insufficient personal time to initiate changes, management indifference, and a lack of vision and capability of the accountants themselves.

Sources: Waweru, Hoque and Uliana (2005), Hood & Cohen (1997). Copyright CPA Australia. Reproduced with the permission of CPA Australia and acknowledgment of the authors.

example, if a plant manager believes that the annual electricity cost will be R180 000, but estimates a budget of R200 000, then the manager has built R20 000 of slack into the budget.

Why do people create budgetary slack? There are three primary reasons. First, people often believe that their performance will look better to their superiors if they can 'beat the budget'. Second, budgetary slack is often used to cope with uncertainty. A departmental supervisor may feel reasonably confident of the cost projections in the departmental budget, but may also feel that some unforeseen event during the budgetary period could result in unanticipated costs. (For example, an unexpected machine breakdown could occur.) One way of allowing for that unforeseen event is to pad the budget. If nothing goes wrong, the supervisor can beat the cost budget. If some unfortunate event does occur, the budgetary slack will absorb the impact of the event and the budget will still be met.

The third reason for padding budgets is that managers are competing for limited resources, and it is common for their initial budget requests to be cut by their manager or the budget review committee. Thus we have a vicious circle: budgetary projections are padded because they are likely to be cut, and they are cut because they are likely to be padded.

How does an organisation solve the problem of budgetary slack? First, it can avoid relying on the budget as a negative evaluative tool. If a departmental supervisor is harassed by his or her manager every time a budgeted cost projection, or a sales projection, is not achieved, the likely response will be to pad the budget. In contrast, if the supervisor is allowed some discretion to exceed the budgeted costs when necessary, there will be less of a tendency towards budgetary padding. Second, managers can be given incentives not only to achieve budgetary projections but also to provide accurate projections. This can be accomplished by asking managers to justify all or some of their projections and by rewarding managers who consistently provide accurate budget estimates.

Budget difficulty

One of the purposes of budgeting is to evaluate performance and motivate employees to direct their efforts towards organisational goals. This is achieved by allocating to employees the responsibility for achieving certain budget targets. But how can we ensure that employees are motivated to achieve those targets? This is a question that has occupied the time of many researchers, and while we do not have the precise answer, we can present some general principles.

It seems that for budgets to be motivational, employees must accept the budgets as their own. The situation in which the organisation's goals coincide with an individual's goals is called **goal congruence**. Achieving goal congruence is often considered one of the greatest challenges in managing large organisations. Budget acceptance is more likely when:

- targets are developed with the participation of employees;
- targets are considered achievable;
- there is frequent feedback on performance;
- employees are held responsible for activities that they believe are within their control; and
- achievement of targets is accompanied by rewards that are valued.

Many of these factors are considered in Chapter 13 where performance measures and rewards are discussed. Here, we will consider the issue of budget difficulty. The relationship between budget difficulty and an individual's performance is illustrated in Exhibit 9.11.

The diagram indicates that as the budget target increases, then performance will also increase, up to a certain point. At a relatively low level of budget difficulty, actual performance is likely to remain low, even though it may exceed the budget target. Budgets that are not challenging may be suitable when the prime purpose of budgeting is forecasting, but they do not motivate high performance. As the difficulty of the budget increases, the employees' performance may increase in an attempt to attain the higher targets. However, when the budget is regarded as too difficult, performance will decrease – it is too hard and the employee just gives up!

Optimal performance is likely to occur when a budget provides sufficient challenge and stretch but is still considered achievable. Of course, determining this level is very difficult. In addition, budgets that are set to challenge may not always reach their target, so they are not suitable in situations where accurate forecasting is the major concern. It may be difficult to develop a budget that satisfies simultaneously the purposes of forecasting and motivating performance.

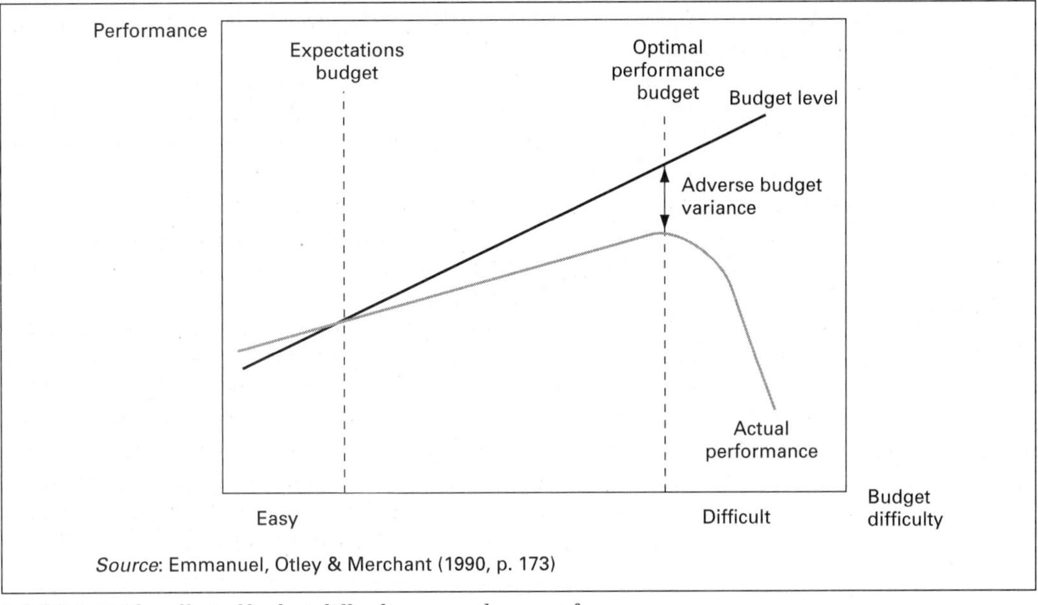

Source: Emmanuel, Otley & Merchant (1990, p. 173)

Exhibit 9.11 The effect of budget difficulty on employee performance

Zero-base budgeting

L.O. 10

Zero-base budgeting is a technique that was widely used in the 1970s and 1980s but is probably used to a lesser extent today. Under zero-base budgeting, the budget for virtually every activity in the organisation is initially set to zero. To receive an allocation of resources during the budgeting process, managers must justify each activity in terms of its continued usefulness to the business. This approach forces managers to rethink each phase of a firm's operations before requesting resources. Zero-base budgeting is designed to restrict the very common practice of projecting next year's budgeted costs by adding a percentage increase to the current year's costs. A firm's costs can easily escalate unless there are strong requirements for justification. However, zero-base budgeting can be a very expensive process, as it requires extensive in-depth analysis of activities, and so may be used only every three or four years.

Zero-base budgeting has been criticised as being too introspective. When managers focus on their own part of the business, they can overlook the interactions with other departments and the relevance of their operations to overall business objectives and strategies. Thus, zero-base budgeting may not be very useful in helping businesses to manage costs or improve their performance. It has also been claimed that it does not help in identifying areas of waste, redundant activities, communication barriers or opportunities for more effectively deploying resources to support business needs. In the modern business environment, there are more sophisticated techniques, such as value analysis, that allow businesses to consider the viability of activities in terms of whether they add value to the customer and, therefore, to the business. These methods will be discussed in Chapter 16.

Zero-base budgeting is used in the government sector in South Africa. For example, in the 2005/2006 financial year, the North West provincial government adopted a combination of zero-base budgeting and activity-based costing approaches. Traditional incremental budgeting was found to be inadequate as it did not assist the province in meeting budgetary pressures. Zero-based budgeting provides provinces with opportunities to:

- prioritise programs;
- calculate the cost of delivering programs from the bottom up;
- make sure that resources are used to achieve objectives;

- identify inefficiencies and opportunities for savings; and
- identify options for resourcing programs.

A recent Markinor survey rated the North West province (the 'Platinum Province') as the second best performing province in the country. The following is extract from the North West Province Budget Statement for 2005–6.

> The budget process is the most crucial instrument for translating government policies and priorities into public goods and services. The reform of the budget process has become imperative for the successful delivery of public services. The increased demand for public services, without a simultaneous increase in available funds, has compelled the provincial government to introduce an appropriate budgeting system to enhance the effective and efficient use of public funds. To overcome the historic budget shortcomings, the Provincial Government approved the introduction of 'Strategic Budgeting'. Strategic Budgeting is a combination of zero-based budgeting and activity-based budgeting while the advantages of performance budgeting is retained. Strategic Budgeting is aimed at releasing money in the budget process that could be used to fund provincial priorities and policies.
>
> *Source*: www.nwpg.gov.za

REAL LIFE: BUDGETING AT CAPE TOWN OPERA

For the Cape Town Opera Company, resources are limited and so budgeting is critical. In an interview, the manager of Cape Town Opera, Mr. Michael Williams, indicated that some of his responsibilities involve the management of monthly financial statements and cash flow management and setting annual company budgets. He states that 'finding the money' was one of the most stressful aspects of his job.

An accurate breakdown of budgeted costs for each project is necessary because each project is very different and costs can easily outstrip revenue from ticket sales. The company may be developing or staging a number of operas in any year and each project is accounted for separately. To manage the complexities, the budget is modelled on a spreadsheet package. This allows management to consider the detailed costs of all productions and to do 'what if' analyses. For example, it is possible to ascertain what would happen to profits if cost levels, ticket prices, ticket sales or any other budget assumptions or data were to change. A computer package allows such analyses to be undertaken very quickly, as all budget relationships can be stored as part of the model.

Cape Town Opera is one of many arts organisations that carefully prepare budgets. The budgets are used to help to manage the limited resources of these organisations, but detailed budgets are also required by the various arts funding bodies. To obtain funding from the National Lotteries organisation or from other government-based funding bodies, arts organisations must show that they can manage the financial aspects of their businesses and that they have carefully considered all of the financial implications of future operations. This normally takes the form of budgeted financial statements that extend several years into the future.

Source: www.capetownopera.co.za

Program budgeting

Program budgeting requires the various programs undertaken by the enterprise to be identified, program objectives to be developed and budgets to be prepared for each program. Program budgeting provides control through the development of quantitative and qualitative performance measures that derive from the program objectives.

In a program budgeting system, managers of government departments or enterprises are given discretion to manage the resources allocated to particular programs, and are required to meet the financial and non-financial objectives that are set for each program. The focus is on outputs and outcomes rather than on inputs.

Program budgeting was developed by the US Department of Defense in the 1960s and was extended to all federal departments and many state government bodies. Program budgeting can be distinguished from **line item budgeting**. Under line item budgeting, resources are allocated to line items (inputs) such as salaries, office supplies or telephone expenses. Under a line item budgeting system, there may be little consideration given to how budget performance relates to the objectives of the enterprise. For example, in a police department, a department manager might be evaluated on his or her ability to keep expenditure within budget limits, but this does not indicate whether the manager is achieving the department's objectives that relate to law enforcement.

REAL LIFE: BUDGETING FOR THE 2010 FIFA WORLD CUP IN SOUTH AFRICA

The awarding of the 2010 FIFA World Cup™ to South Africa required that the Bid Committee submit a budget of revenues and expenditure for the event. In the 2007–8 budget the government had indicated that it was budgeting the following amounts for the event in 2010. This represents only one component of budgeting for the FIFA World Cup™ in 2010 and shows the government's contribution to funding the event.

Government Budget for the 2010 FIFA World Cup™ Event in South Africa	Rm
Transport and supporting infrastructure	9000
Building and upgrading stadiums	8400
Safety and security (CCTV, control centres and 31 000 police for the event)	666
Preparation of Volunteers	25
Festivals and street football programme	17
Leaving a Legacy projects (sports club support)	337
Opening and closing ceremonies (arts & culture)	150

The cost of Information and Communication Technology is expected to be about R5 billion. The cities such as Port Elizabeth, Cape Town and Johannesburg are also contributing to the costs of hosting the FIFA World Cup in 2010™ and this expenditure forms part of their municipal budgets. The provinces have to budget for the emergency medical services to be provided at the event. Revenue will arise from the sale of TV rights, sponsorship and marketing and ticket sales. The major component of revenue from the sale of TV rights will accrue to FIFA and at the time of writing it was reported that FIFA had already received $3.2 billion from the sale of TV rights to the 2010 FIFA World Cup™. Estimating ticket revenue will take into account the seating capacity of each stadium as well as the ticket prices for each game.

Source: www.sa2010.gov.za

Budgeting for the 2000 Olympic Games in Sydney

In September 1993 the International Olympic Committee (IOC) announced that the 2000 Olympic Games would be held in Sydney. However, the successful bid was preceded by years of planning and budgeting. In May 1991 Sydney Olympic Bid Ltd was established with a $25 million budget, funded by the private and public sectors. The company was assisted by many commissions, committees and working groups, and drew on people from all sectors of society. An important element of the Olympic bid was the financial report. The task of the Finance Committee was to prepare the US$1 billion budget for the Games.

A computerised spreadsheet package was used to integrate the complex budget data and assumptions. The committee had to consider exchange rates, inflation and interest rates, as well as detailed costs and revenues for eight years into the future. Advice was obtained from many areas, including major banks, the New South Wales Treasury, and experts involved in accommodation, transport and medical services, and in the media. It was considered critical that the costing be accurate and, to help to achieve this aim, budget assumptions needed to be as realistic as possible. For example, any errors in exchange rates would have a major impact on the overall budget. Members of the bid team also consulted with the cities of Barcelona (1992 Games) and Atlanta (1996 Games) to review and check their budgets.

It was a massive task to budget for each of the 25 sports in the Games – the cost of holding each event, venue selection, spectator capacity and ticket revenue all had to be estimated on a day-by-day basis. The main source of revenue was from television rights and international and local sponsorships, and all of these had to be predicted. Because of the great uncertainty, contingency amounts were built into the budget.

The bid budget was submitted to the executive board of the bid company and to the New South Wales State Cabinet in November 1992, and became an important part of the three-volume, 550-page 'Bid Book' submitted to the IOC in February 1993. Despite careful planning, it was inevitable that the budget was revised many times before the staging of the Games. For example, in 1997 a revised budget was prepared which estimated that the Games would only break even, compared to the original predicted surplus. Revenue estimates were revised upwards in the light of favourable exchange movements and record contracts for international television rights – $2.4 billion, 30 per cent up on the original estimate. In addition, significant cost increases were estimated for the construction of the Olympic village. In February 2000 a $193 million shortfall in sponsorship and ticket revenue was announced, to be followed by the announcement of a balanced budget a month later when various opportunities for cost cutting were identified and additional stadium seats were 'found'. Further changes to the budget were made in the last few months leading up to the Games, as various unbudgeted costs emerged and budgeted revenues failed to materialise.

The complexity of staging the Olympic Games and the high levels of uncertainty attached to many of the sources of revenue and costs made accurate budgeting a difficult exercise. However, the massive expenditures involved in the venture made budgets an essential tool in managing the project.

Sources: Mace (1993); Aylmer (1996); Brenchley (1996); Condon (2000)

Summary

In this chapter we introduced budgeting systems, which are essential aspects of organisations' strategic planning systems. Key points include:

- A budget is a detailed plan that summarises the financial consequences of an organisation's operating activities for a specified time period. It is future-oriented and helps managers to manage resources and create value.
- The five major purposes of a budgeting system are:
  - planning;
  - facilitating communication and co-ordination;
  - allocating resources;
  - controlling profit and operations; and
  - evaluating performance and providing incentives.
- Budgets are typically developed along responsibility lines. That is, managers and employees of various responsibility centres may participate in developing budgets for their areas.
- The annual budget consists of a set of interdependent budgets. The sales budget drives the budgeting process. Based on the sales forecast, a series of cost budgets are prepared to plan the production or purchase of services or goods, and to outline the acquisition and use of material, labour and other resources. Finally, the overall financial implications of the budget schedules are summarised in the cash budget, the budgeted income statement and the budgeted balance sheet.
- Formal budget administration processes are often used to gather information and construct the budget. A budget manual may be developed, which is a set of instructions that communicates to all parties in the organisation the budget procedure and deadlines. A budget committee may be formed to advise the accountants in the preparation of the budget.
- Since budgets affect many people in an organisation, they can have significant behavioural implications. Allowing people to participate in setting their own budget targets may improve commitment to those targets, but can create the incentive to build budgetary slack into budget estimates. It is also important to consider the appropriate level of budget difficulty, to ensure that budgets are motivational and encourage high performance.
- Zero-base budgeting involves managers justifying each activity in terms of its continued usefulness to the business.
- Program budgeting requires that the various programs undertaken by the enterprise are identified, program objectives developed, and budgets prepared for each program. This provides control through the development of quantitative and qualitative performance measures that derive from the program objectives.

In Chapters 10 and 11 we will consider how standard costs, which derive from the budget, can be used to control costs.

References

Aylmer, S 1996, 'Cost blow-outs dampen Olympic budget news', *Business Sydney*, 9 December, p. 3.

Anon 1999, 'Rethinking life without budgets', *Business Review Weekly*, 16 July, p. 41.

Brenchley, F 1996, 'Games look to break even', *The Australian Financial Review*, 11 October, p. 19.

Chenhall, RH & Langfield-Smith, K 2003, 'Performance Measurement and Reward Systems, Trust and Strategic Change', *Journal of Management Accounting Research*, vol. 15, pp. 117–44.

Condon, T 2000, 'Final cost remains a mystery', *Business Review Weekly*, 24 March, pp. 62–3.

Emmanuel, C, Otley, D & Merchant, K 1990, *Accounting for Management Control*, 2nd edn, Chapman and Hall, London.

Hood, B & Cohen, B 1997, 'Budgeting: Seeking Best Practice', *The Australian Accountant*, February, pp. 38–9.

Hope, J & Fraser, R 2000, 'Beyond Budgeting', *Strategic Finance*, October, pp. 30–5.

Mace, J 1993, 'Countdown to Olympic gold', *Charter*, December, pp. 12–17.

North West Provincial Government, www.nwpg.gov.za

Thomas, T 1998, 'A bit of forward planning can help to prepare for stormy weather', *Business Review Weekly*, August 10, pp. 89–91.

Waweru, NM, Hoque, Z and Uliana, E 2005, 'A survey of management accounting practices in South Africa', *International Journal of Accounting, Auditing and Performance Evaluation*, Vol.2, No.3, 2005.

www.capetownopera.co.za

www.sa2010.gov.za

Self study

Self-study problem: Budgeting in a retailing company

The following information relates to Diana's Fashions, a small women's clothing retailer:

- Sales were budgeted at R54 000 for November 20X7 and R40 000 for December 20X7.
- Collections are expected to be 70 per cent in the month of sale and 30 per cent in the month following the sale.
- The gross margin is budgeted at 30 per cent of sales.
- Merchandise is purchased on credit and payable in the following month.
- 70 per cent of the merchandise is purchased in the month prior to the month of sale, and 30 per cent is purchased in the month of sale.
- Depreciation on shop fixtures and fittings is budgeted at R3600 per month.
- Other monthly expenses are budgeted at R4520.

The budgeted balance sheet at 31 October 20X7 is:

Assets:	
Cash	R4 400
Accounts receivable	15 200
Inventory	26 400
Fixtures and fittings*	174 000
Total assets	R220 000
Liabilities and owners' equity:	
Accounts payable	R20 000
Owners' equity	200 000
Total liabilities and owners' equity	R220 000

*Net of accumulated depreciation of R136 000.

Required:

1 Estimate the budgeted cash receipts for November 20X7.

2 Estimate the budgeted profit for November 20X7.

3 Estimate the budgeted accounts payable at 30 November 20X7.

4 Estimate the budgeted inventory at 30 November 20X7.

Solution to Self-study problem

1 Budgeted cash receipts for November 20X7:

From November	R 54 000 × 70% =	R37 800
From October (Accounts receivable)		15 200
		R53 000

2 Budgeted profit for November 20X7:

Sales		R54 000
Cost of goods sold*	70% of sales	37 800
Gross margin	30% of sales	16 200
Depreciation		3 600
Other expenses		4 520
Net profit		R8 080

*Gross margin is 30% of sales, so cost of goods sold must be 70%.

3 Budgeted accounts payable at 30 November 20X7:

Opening balance		R20 000
Purchases on credit:		
For November sales*	37 800 × 30% =	11 340
For December sales*	28 000 × 70% =	19 600
		50 940
Payments (from Accounts payable 31 October 20X7)		20 000
		R30 940

*Based on cost price not selling price.

4 Budgeted inventory at 30 November 20X7:

Opening inventory (31 October)		26 400
Plus Purchases (see part 3 above)		30 940
Cost of goods available for sale		57 340
Less Cost of goods sold	70% of sales =	37 800
Closing inventory (30 November)		R19 540

Cybersearch

1 The 'Real life' that appeared on page 418 of this chapter referred to 'life without budgets'.

(a) Outline the main arguments against budgeting that are provided by the 'beyond budgeting' group at www.beyondbudgeting.plus.com/BBRTweb4/index.htm

(b) Does this mean that companies should abandon their budgeting practices?

2 Find the website of a government organisation that has implemented program budgeting in your own country.

(a) What are the main features/components of the implementation?

(b) Briefly describe how the program budgeting example differs from the description of the AVJ budgeting system.

(c) Were there any other details of the implementation that you found of interest?

3 Locate websites that provide details of budgeting software.

(a) Briefly contrast the features of two packages from two different software providers, and consider the advantages that these packages provide, compared to manual budgeting systems.

(b) Do you think that there are any disadvantages associated with using these forms of software?

Appendix to Chapter 9

Budgeting in a manufacturing company

L.O. 11

The annual budget of a manufacturing company can entail a greater level of detail than that of a service firm or retail company. This is because of the different types of inventory and the detailed production costs that must be accounted for. The interrelationships between the various components of the operating budgets of a manufacturing company were shown in Exhibit 9.2. The example below explains how the components are developed.

Pillay Cleaners (Pty) Ltd produces two cleaning products and sells them to industrial cleaning businesses. The budget estimates for 20X6 are as follows:

Finished goods

Product	Sales volume (units)	Selling price	Required inventory at 30/6/X6 (units)	Balance inventory at 1/7/X5 (units)
Miracle	120 000	R85.00	1 000	2000 @ R45 = R90 000
Foamy	385 000	50.00	12 750	2750 @ R20 = R55 000

Direct material

Material	Cost per litre	Direct material per unit of finished product (litres) Miracle	Foamy	Required inventory at 30/6/X6 (litres)	Balance at 1/7/X5 (litres)
A	R1.50	6	3	30 000	20 000
B	1.00	4	1	5 000	4 250
C	3.00	2	2	3 000	5 500
D	2.50	6	0	5 000	8 000

Direct labour

Process	Direct labour hours per batch of finished product Miracle	Foamy	Cost per direct labour hour
Blending	3.0	1.2	
Packaging	0.3	0.2	
	3.3	1.4	
Batch size (units)	33	35	
Direct labour hours per unit	0.1	0.04	R25

The first step is to prepare a sales budget:

Sales Budget

Product	Sales volume	Selling price per unit	Budgeted sales revenue
Miracle	120 000	R85.00	R10 200 000
Foamy	385 000	45.00	17 325 000
Total			R27 525 000

The estimated sales volume for the year is used to prepare the production budget. The production budget provides us with an estimate of the quantity of the two products that need to be produced during 20X6.

	Production Budget	
	Miracle	Foamy
Budgeted sales (units)	120 000	385 000
Plus Required ending finished goods inventory	1 000	12 750
Finished goods required	121 000	397 750
Less Beginning finished goods inventory	2 000	2 750
Required production (units)	119 000	395 000

Once the required production has been determined, the direct materials and direct labour budgets can be developed.

Direct Material Budget

Material	Direct material used* in production (litres) Miracle	Total used Foamy	Direct material cost (litres)	Direct material used per litre	(R)†
A	714 000	1 185 000	R1 899 000	R1.50	R2 848 500
B	476 000	395 000	871 000	1.00	871 000
C	238 000	790 000	1 028 000	3.00	3 084 000
D	714 000	–	714 000	2.50	1 785 000
			R4 512 000		R8 588 500

*Direct materials used in production = direct material per unit of finished product × number of units produced; for example: Material A used in Miracle = 6 ×119 000 = 714 000 litres.

†The cost of direct materials used will be used in the cost of goods sold budget.

The total direct materials used in production can now be used within the direct material purchases budget.

Direct Material Purchases Budget

	A	B	C	D
Direct material required for production (litres)	1 899 000	871 000	1 028 000	714 000
Plus Ending inventory	30 000	5 000	3 000	5 000
Materials needed	1 929 000	876 000	1 031 000	719 000
Less Beginning inventory	20 000	4 250	5 500	8 000
Materials to be purchased	1 909 000	871 750	1 025 500	711 000

Direct Labour Budget

	Units produced	Direct labour hours per unit	Direct labour hours (DLH) required	Direct labour cost* @ R25 per DLH
Miracle	119 000	0.10	11 900	R297 500
Foamy	395 000	0.04	15 800	395 000
				R692 500

*Direct labour cost will be used in the cost of goods sold budget.

The manufacturing overhead budget has been estimated:

	Manufacturing Overhead Budget
Indirect labour	R371 502
Supplies	198 500
Electricity	400 569
Repairs and maintenance	746 823
Rates and insurance	300 599
Factory rental	1 200 000
Depreciation	1 400 600
Other	750 000
Total	R5 368 593

The management accountant of Pillay Cleaners uses conventional methods for allocating overhead to products. Manufacturing overheads are allocated to products using a predetermined rate based on the number of units produced. This is not thought to create large inaccuracies in product costs, as the two products undergo similar production processes.

$$\text{Predetermined overhead rate} = \frac{\text{total budgeted overhead}}{\text{total budgeted units produced}}$$

$$= \frac{\text{R5 368 593}}{(119\,000 + 395\,000)}$$

$$= \text{R10.44 per unit}$$

From the above budgets, the budgeted cost per unit can be calculated to allow the finished goods inventory to be costed and the cost of goods sold budget to be completed.

Budgeted cost per unit

	Miracle			Foamy		
Direct material	**Quantity**	**Cost**	**Unit cost**	**Quantity**	**Cost**	**Unit cost**
A	6	R1.50	R9.00	3	R1.50	R4.50
B	4	1.00	4.00	1	1.00	1.00
C	2	3.00	6.00	2	3.00	6.00
D	6	2.50	15.00	–		
Total material			R34.00			R11.50
Direct labour	0.10	25.00	2.50	0.04	25.00	1.00
Manufacturing overhead			10.44			10.44
Budgeted production cost per unit			R46.94			R22.94

Cost of Goods Sold Budget

Finished goods as at 1/7/X5:		
Miracle: 2000 @ R45	R90 000	
Foamy: 2750 @ R20	55 000	
		R145 000
Material used in production	R8 588 500	
Direct labour used in production	692 500	
Manufacturing overhead	5 368 593	
Total manufacturing costs		14 649 593*
		R14 794 593
Less Finished goods as at 30/6/X6:		
Miracle: 1000 @ R46.94	R46 940	
Foamy: 12 750 @ R22.94	292 485	
		339 425
Cost of goods sold		R14 455 168

*Total manufacturing costs can also be calculated as:
(119 000 units × R46.94) + (395 000 units × R22.94) = R14 647 160
The difference between this figure and the total manufacturing costs in the cost of goods sold budget is due to the manufacturing overhead rate being rounded to two decimal points in the unit product cost.

We can now complete the budgeted income statement. We will imagine that budgets for administrative and selling expenses have also been formulated.

Budgeted Income Statement for 20X6

Sales	R29 450 000
Less Cost of goods sold	14 455 168
Gross profit	R14 994 832
Selling and administrative expenses	12 400 500
Net profit	R2 594 332

If the budgeted balance sheet were also completed, some of the above data would be used. The profit from the income statement would be included as part of the shareholders' equity. The inventory balances as at 30 June 20X6 would be included in the current assets section of the balance sheet. Any amounts owing to direct material suppliers or to production workers at balance date would be listed as current liabilities.

Questions

9.1 Explain how a budget can be used to evaluate performance and provide incentives.

9.2 How can a budget facilitate communication and co-ordination?

9.3 Explain how strategic planning can influence the budgeting process. Provide an example from a specific industry to illustrate your answer.

9.4 Explain why predicting sales is one of the most important steps in the budgeting process.

9.5 Explain how responsibility accounting relates to the budgeting process.

9.6 Draw flowcharts, similar to those in Exhibits 9.1 and 9.2, to represent the budgeting process used for a bookshop that sells magazines, books and tickets to the local playhouse.

9.7 Give two examples of how general economic trends and international events may affect sales forecasting in the computer manufacturing industry.

9.8 Distinguish between *operating budgets* and *financial budgets*. Explain this within the context of formulating the annual budget for a medical centre.

9.9 Give three examples of how a high school could use a budget for planning purposes.

9.10 Describe the typical role of the accountant in the budgeting process.

9.11 What is the purpose of a *budget manual*?

9.12 How can a company's board of directors use the budget to influence the future direction of the business?

9.13 Explain why a cash budget is vital to any business.

9.14 Explain the concept of *zero-base budgeting*.

9.15 Explain what is meant by 'budget development follows an iterative process'.

9.16 Define the term *budgetary slack*, and briefly describe the problems it can cause.

9.17 How can an organisation reduce the problems caused by budgetary slack?

9.18 Why is *participative budgeting* often regarded as an effective management tool?

9.19 Discuss this comment by the manager of a small manufacturing company: 'Budgeting is a waste of time. I've been running this business for forty years. I don't need to plan.'

9.20 Explain the steps you would undertake to develop a budget to meet the costs of attending university as a full-time student.

9.21 What is *program budgeting*? How does it differ from line item budgeting?

9.22 How difficult should budget targets be before they cease to be motivational?

Exercises

E9.23 Cash budgeting

The following information is available from the financial records of Berwick (Pty) Ltd:

	Sales	Purchases
April	R180 000	R105 000
May	165 000	120 000
June	150 000	90 000
July	195 000	135 000

- Receipts from customers are normally 70 per cent in the month of sale, 20 per cent in the month following the sale, and 9 per cent in the second month following the sale. The balance is expected to be uncollectable.
- Berwick takes full advantage of the 2 per cent discount allowed on purchases paid for by the 10th day of the following month.
- Purchases for August are budgeted at R150 000, and sales for August are forecast at R165 000.
- Cash payments for expenses are expected to be R36 000 for the month of August.
- Berwick's cash balance on 1 August was R55 000.

Required:

Prepare a cash budget for Berwick for August that includes:

1 expected cash receipts during August;
2 expected cash payments during August;
3 expected cash balance on 31 August.

(CPA, adapted)

E9.24 Cash receipts: retailer

Classical Jazz (Pty) Ltd is a small retailer of musical instruments and has the following historical collection pattern for its credit sales:

- 70 per cent collected in the month of sale.
- 15 per cent collected in the first month after sale.
- 10 per cent collected in the second month after sale.
- 4 per cent collected in the third month after sale.
- 1 per cent uncollectable.

The credit sales have been budgeted for the last seven months of 20X6, as shown below:

June	R122 500
July	150 000
August	175 000
September	200 000
October	225 000
November	250 000
December	212 500

Required:

1 Calculate the estimated total cash receipts during October 20X6 from credit sales.
2 Calculate the estimated total cash receipts during the fourth quarter from credit sales during the fourth quarter.

(CMA, adapted)

E9.25 Professional services budget: dental practice

City Dental Associates is a dental practice in Durban. The firm's accountant is preparing the budget for next year. He projects a total of 48 000 patient visits evenly distributed throughout the year. Eighty per cent of the visits will be half-hour appointments, and the remainder will be one-hour visits. The average rates for professional dental services are R400 for half-hour appointments and R700 for one-hour visits. Ninety per cent of each month's professional service revenue is collected during the month when services are rendered, and the remainder is collected the month following service. Uncollectable billings are negligible. City's dentists earn R500 per hour.

Required:

1 Prepare a direct labour budget for the month of June.
2 Estimate the cash receipts during June.

E9.26 Budgeted financial statements: retailer

Pilot Office Supplies is a small retail store supplying stationery and other office supplies to small and medium businesses. Information about the store's operations is as follows:

- November 20X6 sales amounted to R400 000.
- Sales are budgeted at R440 000 for December 20X6 and R400 000 for January 20X7
- Receipts are expected to be 60 per cent in the month of sale and 38 per cent in the month following the sale. Two per cent of sales are expected to be uncollectable.
- The store's gross margin is 25 per cent of its sales revenue.
- A total of 80 per cent of the merchandise for resale is purchased in the month prior to the month of sale, and 20 per cent is purchased in the month of sale. Payment for merchandise is made in the month following the purchase.
- Other monthly expenses paid in cash amount to R45 200.
- Annual depreciation is R432 000.

Pilot's balance sheet as at 30 November 20X6 is shown below:

Pilot Office Supplies
Balance Sheet
30 November 20X6

Assets:	
Cash	R44 000
Accounts receivable (net of R7000 allowance for uncollectible accounts)	152 000
Inventory	280 000
Property, plant and equipment (net of R1 180 000 accumulated depreciation)	1 724 000
Total assets	R2 200 000
Liabilities and shareholders' equity:	
Accounts payable	R324 000
Ordinary shares	1 590 000
Retained earnings	286 000
Total liabilities and shareholders' equity	R2 200 000

Required:

Calculate the following amounts:

1 the budgeted cash receipts for December 20X6;
2 the budgeted profit (loss) before income taxes for December 20X6;
3 the projected balance in accounts payable on 31 December 20X6.

(CMA, adapted)

E9.27 Budgetary slack: bank

Tanya Van Wyk is the new accounts manager at Southpac Bank. She has just been asked to project how many new bank accounts she will generate during 20X6. The South African economy has been growing and the bank has experienced a 10 per cent increase in its number of bank accounts over each of the past five years. In 20X6 the bank had 10 000 accounts.

The new accounts manager is paid a salary plus a bonus of R500 for every new account she generates above the budgeted amount. Thus, if the annual budget calls for 500 new accounts, and 540 new accounts are obtained, Williams' bonus will be R20 000 (40 × R500).

Williams believes that the economy will continue to grow at the same rate in 20X6 as it has in recent years. She has decided to submit a budgetary projection of 700 new accounts for 20X6.

Required:

Your consulting firm has been hired by the managing director of the bank to make recommendations for improving its operations. Write a memorandum to the managing director defining and explaining the negative consequences of budgetary slack. Also discuss the bank's bonus system for the new accounts manager, and how the bonus program tends to encourage budgetary slack.

E9.28 Budgeted balance sheet and income statement; missing amounts: retailer

Fill in the missing amounts in the following schedules:

Accumulated depreciation, 31/12/20X5	R405 000
Depreciation expense during 20X6	75 000
Accumulated depreciation, 31/12/20X6	?
Retained earnings, 31/12/20X5	R1 537 500
Net profit for 20X6	300 000
Dividends paid in 20X6	0
Retained earnings, 31/12/20X6	?
Accounts receivable, 31/12/20X5	R1 700 000
Credit sales during 20X6	4 500 000
Collections of accounts receivable during 20X6	3 900 000
Accounts receivable, 31/12/20X6	?
Accounts payable, 31/12/20X5	R600 000
Purchases of goods and services on credit during 20X6	2 400 000
Payments of accounts payable during 20X6	?
Accounts payable, 31/12/20X6	800 000

	July	August	September
Sales*	R240 000	R180 000	?
Cash receipts:			
From cash sales	?	?	R135 000
From credit sales†	?	R102 000	?
Total cash receipts	?	?	?

*Half of each month's sales are on credit. June sales were R180 000.

†60 per cent of credit sales are collected in the month of the sales; 40 per cent are collected in the following month.

E9.29 Budgets in service firms: veterinary clinic

Paws and Claws is a veterinary clinic operating in the southern suburbs of Johannesburg. Recently John Tilley, the manager of the clinic, has been concerned about cash flow shortages, which arose quite unexpectedly in the last three months of 20X6. The clinic bank account went into overdraft and incurred interest charges. Tilley believes that the main source of the cash flow difficulties is a lack of attention to outstanding client accounts and the practice of purchasing expensive veterinary supplies in large quantities at irregular intervals. Tilley has asked you to help design a spreadsheet to help with planning for client consultations, purchases of supplies, cash shortages and cash surpluses in 20X7. The following data are available:

Revenue earned is as follows:

November 20X6	R80 000 (actual)
December 20X6	90 000 (actual)
January 20X7	30 000 (budget)
February 20X7	90 000 (budget)
March 20X7	80 000 (budget)

During 20X6 50 per cent of consultation revenue was collected in the month of the veterinary visit, 20 per cent in the following month, 20 per cent in the second month, and 10 per cent was not received. In 20X7, new credit policies are expected to result in collections of 60 per cent, 20 per cent, 10 per cent and 10 per cent respectively.

The cost of veterinary supplies was R30 000 in December and is budgeted as R50 000 in February. Half of the suppliers' accounts are paid in the month they are incurred and half in the following month. Salaries of R40 000 per month and other costs of R30 000 are paid in the month they are incurred.

Required:

1 Use a spreadsheet package to complete a cash budget for the first three months of 20X7, using the format below.

Cash Budget

	January	February	March
Opening cash balance	R(40 000)		
Cash received from consultations:			
Two months ago			
Last month			
Current month			
Total cash receipts			
Cash payment			
Supplies:			
Previous month purchases			
Current month purchases			
Salaries			
Other costs			
Total cash payments			
Closing cash balance			

2 What further steps could Tilley take to help ensure that the cash balance of the clinic remains positive? In your answer, consider ways in which budgeting may assist.

E9.30 Budgeting production and direct material purchases (appendix): manufacturer

Caterpillar Company prepares annual budgets. The following beginning and ending inventory levels (in units) are planned for next year. Four kilograms of direct material are required to produce each unit of finished product.

	1 January	31 December
Direct material	80 000	100 000
Work in process	20 000	20 000
Finished goods	160 000	100 000

Required:

1 If Caterpillar Company plans to sell 480 000 units during the year, calculate the number of units the firm would have to manufacture.

2 If 600 000 finished units are to be manufactured by Caterpillar Company during the year, determine the amount of direct material that needs to be purchased.

(CMA, adapted)

E9.31 Budgeting production and direct material purchases (appendix): manufacturer

Sparkle Ltd, a manufacturer of swimming pool chemicals, plans to sell 200 000 units of finished product in July 20X7. Management anticipates a growth rate in sales of 5 per cent per month. The desired monthly ending inventory in units of finished product is 80 per cent of the next month's estimated sales. There are 150 000 finished units in the inventory on 30 June 20X7. Each unit of finished product requires 4 kilograms of direct material at a cost of R1.20 per kilogram. There are 800 000 kilograms of direct material in the inventory on 30 June 20X7.

Required:

1 Calculate Sparkle's production requirements in units of finished product for the three-month period ending 30 September 20X7.

2 Independent of your answer to requirement 1, assume that the company plans to produce 600 000 units of finished product in the three-month period ending 30 September 20X7. The firm will have direct materials inventory at the end of the three-month period equal to 25 per cent of the direct material used during that period. Calculate the estimated cost of direct materials purchases for the three-month period ending 30 September 20X7.

(CMA, adapted)

Problems

P9.32 Sales and labour budgets: university

Southern Business University (SBU) is preparing its budget for the upcoming academic year. This is a specialised private university that charges fees for all degree courses. Currently, 12 000 students are enrolled on campus. However, the university is forecasting a 5 per cent growth in student numbers in the coming year, despite an increase in fees to R3000 per subject. The following additional information has been gathered from an examination of university records and conversations with university managers:

- SBU is planning to award scholarships to 180 students, which will cover their fees.
- The average class has 80 students, and the typical student takes 4 subjects per semester. SBU operates 2 semesters per year.
- The average academic staff salary is R350 000 per annum including on-costs.
- SBU's academic staff are evaluated on the basis of teaching, research, administration and professional/community service. Each of the academic staff teaches the equivalent of three subjects during the academic year.

Required:

1 Prepare a revenue budget for the upcoming academic year.

2 Determine the number of staff needed to cover classes.

3 Assume there is a shortage of full-time academic staff. List at least five actions that SBU might take to accommodate the growing student body.

4 You have been requested by the university's deputy vice chancellor (DVC) to construct budgets for other areas of operation (such as the library, grounds, cafeteria, and maintenance). The DVC noted: 'The most important resource of the university is its academic staff. Now that you know the number of staff needed, you can prepare the other budgets.

Academic staff are indeed the key driver – without them we don't operate.' Does the deputy vice chancellor really understand the linkages within the budgeting process? Explain.

P9.33 Cash budgeting: hospital

Alice Medical Centre provides a wide range of hospital services. The hospital's board of directors has recently authorised the following capital expenditures:

Neonatal care equipment	R900 000
CT scanner	800 000
X-ray equipment	650 000
Laboratory equipment	1 450 000
Total	R3 800 000

The expenditures are planned for 1 October 20X7, and the board wishes to know the amount of borrowing, if any, necessary on that date. Marc Kelly, the management accountant, has gathered the following information to be used in preparing an analysis of future cash flows:

- Billings for the first six months of 20X7, made in the month of service, are as follows:

Month	Actual amount
January	R4 400 000
February	4 400 000
March	4 500 000
April	4 500 000
May	5 000 000
June	5 000 000

- Eighty per cent of the hospital's billings are made to health funds and private health insurance companies. The remaining 20 per cent of billings are made directly to patients. Historical patterns of billing receipts are presented below:

	Health fund billings (%)	Direct patient billings (%)
During month of service	50	20
During month following service	20	40
During second month following service	20	30
Uncollectable	10	10

- Estimated billings for the last six months of 20X7 are listed below. The same billing and collection patterns that have been experienced during the first six months of 20X7 are expected to continue during the last six months of the year.

Month	Estimated amount
July	R4 500 000
August	5 000 000
September	5 500 000
October	5 700 000
November	5 800 000
December	5 500 000

- The purchases of the past three months and the planned purchases for the last six months of 20X7 are presented in the following schedule:

Month	Amount
April	R1 100 000
May	1 200 000
June	1 200 000
July	1 250 000
August	1 500 000
September	1 850 000
October	1 950 000
November	2 250 000
December	1 750 000

Additional information:

- All purchases are on credit, and accounts payable are paid in the month following the purchase.
- Salaries for each month during the remainder of 20X7 are expected to be R1 500 000 per month plus 20 per cent of that month's billings. Salaries are paid in the month of service.
- The hospital's monthly depreciation charges are R125 000.
- The Medical Centre incurs interest expense of R150 000 per month and makes interest payments of R450 000 on the last day of each quarter (31 March, 30 June, 30 September and 31 December).
- Investment income is expected to continue at the rate of R175 000 per month.
- The hospital has a cash balance of R300 000 on 1 July 20X7, and has a policy of maintaining a minimum end-of-month cash balance of 10 per cent of the current month's purchases.
- The hospital uses a calendar year reporting period.

Required:

1 Prepare a cash budget for the third quarter of 20X7 (July to September) that includes:
   (a) budgeted cash receipts by month;
   (b) budgeted cash payments by month.
2 Determine the amount of borrowing, if any, necessary on 1 October 20X7 in order to acquire the capital expenditure items totalling R3 800 000.

(CMA, adapted)

P9.34 Ethics; budgetary pressure; management bonuses: manufacturer

Belco Industries produces and distributes industrial chemicals. Belco's earnings increased sharply in 20X6, and bonuses were paid to the management staff for the first time in several years. Bonuses are based in part on the amount by which reported profit exceeds budgeted profit.

Jim Kern, the finance director, was pleased with Belco's 20X6 earnings and thought that the pressure to show financial results would ease. However, Ellen North, Belco's managing director, told Kern that she saw no reason why the 20X7 bonuses should not be double those of 20X6. As a result, Kern felt great pressure to increase reported profit well above the budgeted profit. This would assure increased bonuses.

Kern met with Bill Keller of Pristeel Ltd, which supplied most of the company's manufacturing supplies and small equipment. Kern and Keller have been close business contacts for many years. Kern asked Keller to invoice all Belco's purchases of perishable supplies as equipment. Kern told Keller that Belco's managing director had imposed stringent budget constraints on operating costs but not on capital expenditures. Keller agreed to do as Kern had asked.

Kern planned to capitalise the purchase of perishable supplies and include them with the equipment account on the balance sheet. This way, Kern could defer the full expense recognition for these items to later years. This would increase reported profits, leading to increased bonuses.

While analysing the second-quarter 20X7 financial statements, Gary Wood, Belco's accountant, noticed a large decrease in the cost of supplies compared with that of last year. Wood reviewed the supplies account and noticed that very few supplies had been purchased from Pristeel, a major source of supplies. However, there had been large purchases of equipment from Pristeel. Wood, who reports to Kern, immediately brought this to Kern's attention. Kern told Wood of North's high expectations and of the arrangement made with Bill Keller of Pristeel. Wood told Kern that his action was an improper accounting treatment for the supplies purchased from Pristeel. Wood requested that he be allowed to correct the accounts and urged that the arrangement with Pristeel be discontinued. Kern refused the request and told Wood not to become involved.

After clarifying the situation in a confidential discussion with an objective and qualified peer within Belco, Wood arranged to meet with North, Belco's managing director. At the meeting, Wood disclosed the arrangement Kern had made with Pristeel.

Required:

1 Explain why the use of alternative accounting methods to manipulate reported earnings is unethical.

2 Is Gary Wood, Belco's accountant, correct in saying that the supplies purchased from Pristeel were accounted for improperly? Explain your answer.

3 Discuss whether the actions of Gary Wood, Belco's accountant, were appropriate or inappropriate. In your answer refer to the code of ethical conduct discussed in Chapter 1.

(CMA, adapted)

P9.35 Budgeting, financial objectives: manufacturing company

Healthy Foods Ltd, a manufacturer of breakfast cereals and healthy snack bars, has experienced several years of steady growth in sales, profits, and dividends while maintaining a relatively low level of debt. The board of directors has adopted a long-term strategy to maximise the value of the shareholders' investment. To achieve this goal, the board of directors established the following financial objectives for the next five years:

- Increase sales by 12 per cent per year.
- Increase income before taxes by 15 per cent per year.
- Maintain long-term debt at a maximum of 16 per cent of assets.

These financial objectives have been attained for each of the past three years. At the beginning of last year the president of Healthy Foods, Andrea Adonis, added a fourth financial objective: maintaining cost of goods sold at a maximum of 70 per cent of sales. This goal was also attained last year. The company's budgeting process is to be directed towards attaining these goals in the forthcoming year. This is a difficult task as the economy is in the middle of a prolonged recession. In addition, the increased emphasis on eating healthy foods has driven up the price of ingredients used by the company at a much greater rate than the expected rate of inflation. John Winslow, cost accountant at Healthy Foods, has responsibility for preparation of the profit plan for next year. Winslow has assured Adonis that he can prepare a budget that will satisfy all of the financial objectives. Winslow will do this by overestimating the ending inventory and reclassifying fruit and grain inspection costs as administrative rather than manufacturing costs. The actual statements for last year and the budgeted statements for next year that Winslow prepared are as follows:

Healthy Foods Ltd
Income Statement

	Last year actual	Next year budgeted
Sales	R17 000 000	R18 955 000
Less Variable costs:		
Cost of goods sold	−10 200 000	−11 494 500
Selling and administrative	−1 800 000	−1 750 000
Contribution margin	5 000 000	5 710 500
Less Fixed costs:		
Manufacturing	−1 700 000	−1 895 500
Selling and administrative	−1 200 000	−1 400 000
Profit before taxes	R2 100 000	R2 415 000

Healthy Foods Ltd
Balance Sheet

	Last year actual	Next year budgeted
Assets:		
Cash	200 000	340 000
Accounts receivable	1 200 000	1 360 000
Inventory	6 000 000	7 300 000
Plant and equipment (net of accumulated depreciation)	32 600 000	32 000 000
Total	40 000 000	41 000 000
Liabilities:		
Accounts payable	2 200 000	2 440 000
Long-term debt	6 400 000	6 160 000
Shareholders' equity:		
Ordinary shares	8 000 000	8 000 000
Retained earnings	23 400 000	24 400 000
Total	40 000 000	41 000 000

The company paid dividends of R554 400 last year, and the expected tax rate for the coming year is 28 per cent.

Required

1 Describe how budgeting relates to a firm's strategic planning process.

2 Provide calculations to evaluate whether or not John Winslow's budget attains each of the financial objectives. Use the following format for your answer:
   (a) Objective
   (b) Attained/Not Attained
   (c) Calculations

3 Explain whether or not the adjustments contemplated by John Winslow are unethical.

(CMA adapted)

P9.36 Revised operating budget: consulting firm

The Clark Services, a division of General Service Industries operating in Kwazulu-Natal, offers consulting services to clients for a fee. The corporate management at General Service is pleased with the performance of the Clark Services for the first nine months of the current year and has recommended that the divisional manager of the Clark Services, Ahmed Omar, submit a revised budget for the remaining quarter, as the division has exceeded the budgeted operating profit for the year to date by 20 per cent. An unexpected increase in the number of billed hours over the original plan is the main reason for this increase in profit. The original operating budget for the first three quarters for the Clark Services is as follows:

The Clark Services 20X7 Operating Budget	First quarter	Second quarter	Third quarter	Nine months
Revenue				
Consulting fees:				
Management consulting	R945 000	R945 000	R945 000	R2 835 000
Computer system consulting	1 265 625	1 265 625	1 265 625	3 796 875
Total consulting fees	R2 210 625	R2 210 625	R2 210 625	R6 631 875
Other revenue	100 000	100 000	100 000	300 000
Total revenue	R2 310 625	R2 310 625	R2 310 625	R6 931 875
Expenses				
Consultant salary	R1 160 250	R1 160 250	R1 160 250	R3 480 750
Travel	136 875	136 875	136 875	410 625
General and administrative	300 000	300 000	300 000	900 000
Depreciation	120 000	120 000	120 000	360 000
Corporate allocation	150 000	150 000	150 000	450 000
Total expenses	R1 867 125	R1 867 125	R1 867 125	R5 601 375
Operating profit	R443 500	R443 500	R443 500	R1 330 500

Omar will take the following information into account in his revised budget for the fourth quarter:

- The division currently has 25 consultants on staff – 10 for management consulting and 15 for computer systems consulting. Three additional management consultants have been hired to start work at the beginning of the fourth quarter in order to meet the increased client demand.
- The hourly billing rate for consulting revenue will remain at R270 per hour for each management consultant and R225 per hour for each computer consultant. However, due to the increase in billed hours compared with the plan during the first nine months, the budgeted billed hours will be increased by an additional 50 hours for each consultant (new and old) in the fourth quarter.
- The budgeted annual salaries and actual annual salaries, paid monthly, are the same: R150 000 for a management consultant and R138 000 for a computer consultant. Corporate management has approved a merit increase of 10 per cent at the beginning of the fourth quarter for all 25 existing consultants, while the new consultants will be compensated at the planned rate.
- The planned salary expense in the original budget includes an allowance for employee on-costs and benefits amounting to 30 per cent of the annual salaries. However, the introduction of a corporate-wide bonus program will increase this amount to 40 per cent in the fourth quarter.
- The original plan assumes a fixed hourly rate for travel and other related expenses for each billing hour of consulting. These are expenses that are not reimbursed by the client, and the previously determined hourly rate has proven to be adequate to cover these costs.
- Other revenue, derived from temporary rentals and interest, is expected to be the same in the fourth quarter as in each of the previous quarters.
- General and administrative expenses have been favourable at 7 per cent below the plan; this 7 per cent saving on fourth-quarter expenses will be reflected in the revised plan.
- Depreciation of office equipment and personal computers will stay constant at the projected straight-line rate.

Due to the favourable performance during the first three quarters and the division's increased ability to absorb costs, the corporate management at General Service Industries has increased the corporate expense allocated to the Division by 50 per cent for the fourth quarter.

Required:

1 Prepare a revised operating budget for the fourth quarter for the Clark Services. This revised budget will be presented by Ahmed Omar to General Service Industries.

2 What factors might cause an organisation to prepare a revised operating budget?

(CMA, adapted)

P9.37 Production and direct labour budgets (appendix): manufacturer

Alpha Mann Ltd makes and sells computer carry bags. Willem Van Breda, the company accountant, is responsible for preparing the company's annual budget. In compiling the budget data for 20X6, Van Breda has learned that new automated production equipment will be installed on 1 March 20X6. This will reduce the direct labour per frame from 1 hour to 0.75 hour.

Labour-related costs include employer superannuation contributions of 9 per cent of employee wages, workers' compensation insurance of R1.00 per hour, and payroll tax equal to 7 per cent of employee wages. These 'on-costs' are treated as an additional direct labour cost. The accountant estimates that a wage increase for production workers of R10.00 per hour will take place on 1 April 20X6.

Management expects to have 16 000 bags on hand at 31 December 20X6, and has a policy of carrying an end-of-month inventory of 100 per cent of the following month's sales plus 50 per cent of the second following month's sales.

This and other data compiled by Van Breda are summarised in the following table:

	January	February	March	April	May
Direct labour hours per unit	1.00	1.00	0.75	0.75	0.75
Wage per direct labour hour	R80.00	R80.00	R80.00	R90.00	R90.00
Estimated unit sales	20 000	24 000	16 000	18 000	18 000
Sales price per unit	R250.00	R237.50	R237.50	R237.50	R237.50
Manufacturing overhead:					
Shipping and handling (per unit)	R15.00	R15.00	R15.00	R15.00	R15.00
Purchasing and material handling (per unit produced)	R22.50	R22.50	R22.50	R22.50	R22.50
Other (per direct labour hour)	R52.50	R52.50	R52.50	R52.50	R52.50

Required:

1 Prepare a production budget and a direct labour budget for Alpha Mann Ltd, by month and for the first quarter of 20X6. Both budgets may be combined in one schedule. The direct labour budget should include direct labour hours and show the detail for each direct labour cost category.

2 For each item used in the firm's production budget and direct labour budget, identify the other components of the annual budget that would also use these data.

3 Prepare a manufacturing overhead budget for each month and for the first quarter.

(CMA, adapted)

P9.38 Sales, production and purchases budgets (appendix): manufacturer

George Ltd manufactures and sells two different types of coils used in electric motors. In September 20X7, Jessica Mabena, the management accountant, compiled the following data for the 20X8 annual budget:

Use of direct material

	Amount used per unit	
Direct material	**Light coil**	**Heavy coil**
Sheet metal	4 kg	5 kg
Copper wire	2 kg	3 kg
Platform		1 unit

Raw material prices and inventory levels

Raw material	Anticipated purchase price	Expected inventories 1 January 20X8	Desired inventories 31 December 20X8
Sheet metal	R16	32 000 kg	36 000 kg
Copper wire	R10	29 000 kg	32 000 kg
Platform	R6	6000 units	7000 units

Direct labour requirements and rates

Product	Hours per unit	Rate per hour
Light coil	4	R15
Heavy coil	6	R20
Overhead is applied at the rate of R2 per direct labour hour.		

Finished goods inventories (in units)

Product	Expected 1 January 20X8	Desired 31 December 20X8
Light coil	20 000	25 000
Heavy coil	8000	9000

Sales forecast for 20X8

Product	Units	Price
Light coil	60 000	R130
Heavy coil	40 000	R190

Required:

Prepare the following budgets for 20X8:

1 Sales budget (in Rands).
2 Production budget (in units).
3 Direct material purchases budget (in quantities).
4 Direct material purchases budget (in Rands).
5 Direct labour budget (in Rands).
6 Budgeted finished goods inventory on 31 December 20X8 (in Rands).

(*CPA, adapted*)

P9.39 Direct labour, machine hour and production cost budgets (appendix): manufacturer

Bheka Company manufactures three products in a factory with four departments. Both labour and machine time are applied to the products as they pass through each department. The nature of the machines and labour skills is such that neither can be switched from one department to another.

Bheka's management is planning its production schedule for the next several months. The planning is complicated by labour shortages in the community, and some machines will be down several months for repairs. Information follows regarding (a) available machine and labour time by department, and (b) machine hours and direct labour hours required per unit of product. These data will remain valid for at least six months.

	Department			
Monthly capacity availability	**1**	**2**	**3**	**4**
Normal machine capacity (machine hours)	3500	3500	3000	3500
Capacity of machine being repaired (machine hours)	(500)	(400)	(300)	(200)
Available machine capacity (machine hours)	3000	3100	2700	3300
Labour capacity (direct labour hours)	4000	4500	3500	3000
Available labour (direct labour hours)	3700	4500	2750	2600

Labour and machine time requirements per unit of product					
Product	**Labour and machine time**	**Required time**			
401	Direct labour hours	2	3	3	1
	Machine hours	1	1	2	2
403	Direct labour hours	1	2	–	2
	Machine hours	1	1	–	2
405	Direct labour hours	2	2	2	1
	Machine hours	2	2	1	1

The sales manager believes that the monthly demand for the next six months will be as follows:

Product	Monthly sales volume in units
401	500
403	400
405	1000

Inventory levels are satisfactory and need not be increased or decreased during the next six months. The selling price and cost data that will be valid for the next six months are as follows:

	Product		
	401	**403**	**405**
Unit costs			
Direct material	R7	R13	R17
Direct labour:			
Department 1	24	12	24
Department 2	42	28	28
Department 3	48	–	32
Department 4	18	36	18
Variable overhead	54	40	50
Variable selling expenses	3	2	4
Unit selling price	R296	R223	R267

Required:

1 Calculate the monthly requirement for machine hours and direct labour hours for the production of products 401, 403 and 405 to determine whether the monthly sales demand for the three products can be met by the factory.

2 Prepare a schedule showing budgeted costs of direct material, direct labour and variable overhead. Assume the following production schedule:

Product	Planned production
401	250 units
403	400 units
405	1000 units

3 Demonstrate that the planned production levels given in requirement 2 are feasible in light of Bheka's labour and machine time shortages.
4 Identify some alternatives Bheka might consider so that it can supply its customers with all the product they demand.

(*CMA, adapted*)

P9.40 Participative budgeting: manufacturing

Kelly Manufacturing is a medium-sized company that manufactures and markets a range of products. The divisions of Kelly include Whitegoods, Kitchenware and Outdoor Furniture Divisions. The senior management team oversees the budgeting process, and includes the managing director, the financial controller, the manufacturing director and marketing director. Jack Kohler, the managing director for Kelly Manufacturing, recognises the importance of the budgetary process for planning, control, and motivation. He believes that a properly implemented process of participative budgeting and management by exception will motivate managers and their subordinates to improve productivity within their particular divisions. Based upon this philosophy, Jack has implemented the following budgetary procedures:

- A target sales revenue and target profit figure is determined by the senior management team and given to each divisional manager for the following budget year. Profit targets are based on targeted overall increases in returns to shareholders, and are assigned to divisions based on senior management's expectations of which divisions need to improve in the coming year. Target sales revenues are based on a percentage increase in the prior year's sales revenue for each division.
- Divisional managers develop their individual divisional budgets within the following constraints as directed by the company financial controller:
  - The target sales revenue and profit targets can only differ by 10 per cent, and this deviation must be clearly justified by the divisional manager.
  - All fixed commitments should be included in the budget. Fixed expenditures include such items as long-term supplier contracts and salaries.
  - All capital expenditure projects that are undertaken in divisions, at the direction of the senior management team, should be included in the divisional budgets.
  - An estimate of head office charges is provided to divisions for incorporation in their budget.
  - Divisional budgets need to specify all line items for expenditure.
- The final divisional budgets are approved by senior management, after careful scrutiny by the senior management team. Sometimes, as an incentive to motivate divisional managers, the estimated head office charges are increased, which has the effect of reducing budgeted divisional profits. Divisional managers are then asked to review their overall budgets, to find areas of cost savings to meet their profit targets.
- The final budget is used as the basis of control for a management-by-exception form of reporting. Excessive expenditures by each division are highlighted on a monthly basis. Divisional managers are expected to account for all expenditures over budget. Financial responsibility is an important factor in the overall performance evaluation of all managers. Jack Kohler believes that the policy of allowing the divisional managers to participate in the budget process and then holding them accountable for the final budget is essential, especially in times of limited resources. He further believes that the divisional managers will be motivated to increase the efficiency and effectiveness of their divisions because they have provided input into the initial budgetary process and are required to justify any unfavourable performance.

Required:

1 Discuss the advantages and limitations of participative budgeting.
2 Identify deficiencies in Kelly's budgetary process. Recommend how each identified deficiency can be corrected.

P9.41 Revising a budget based on new information (appendix): manufacturer

Wet Designs (Pty) Ltd manufactures and sells stylish bathroom basins. Janet Short, who is a budget analyst, co-ordinated the preparation of the annual budget for 20X6. The budget was based on the prior year's sales and production activity. The budgeted income statement and schedule of cost of goods manufactured and sold are as follows:

Wet Designs (Pty) Ltd
Budgeted Income Statement
for the year ending 31 December 20X6

	(R'000)	(R'000)
Sales revenue		R25 550
Cost of goods sold		16 565
Gross margin		8 985
Operating expenses:		
Marketing	R3 200	
General and administrative	2 000	5 200
Profit from operations before taxes		R3 785

Budgeted Schedule of Cost of Goods Manufactured and Sold
for the year ending 31 December 20X6

	(R'000)	(R'000)
Direct material:		
Raw material inventory, 1/1/20X6	R1 200	
Raw material purchased	11 400	
Raw material available for use	R12 600	
Raw material inventory, 31/12/20X6	1 480	
Direct material used		R11 120
Direct labour		980
Manufacturing overhead:		
Indirect material	1 112	
Other overhead	2 800	3 912
Cost of goods manufactured*		R16 012
Finished goods inventory, 1/1/20X6		930
Cost of goods available for sale		R16 942
Finished goods inventory, 31/12/20X6		377
Cost of goods sold		R16 565

*No work in process inventory is anticipated at the beginning or end of 20X6.

On 18 April 20X6, Short met with Peter Marker, the finance director, to discuss the first quarter's results. After their discussion, Marker directed Short to incorporate the following changes to the budget assumptions in revised budgeted statements:

- The estimated production in units for the year should be revised from 140 000 to 160 000 units, with the balance of production being scheduled in equal segments over the last nine months of the year. The actual first quarter's production was 25 000 units. There will be no work in process inventories.
- The planned finished goods inventory of 3300 units at the end of the year remains unchanged and will be valued at the average manufacturing cost for the year. The finished goods inventory of 9300 units on 1 January 20X6 had dropped to 9000 units by 31 March 20X6.
- Due to a new labour agreement, the labour rate will increase by 8 per cent, effective 1 October 20X6, the beginning of the fourth quarter, instead of the previously anticipated effective date of 1 January 20X7.
- The assumptions remain unchanged for raw material inventory: 16 000 units for the beginning inventory and 18 500 units for the ending inventory. Raw material inventory is

valued on a first in, first out (FIFO) basis. During the first quarter, raw material for 27 500 units of output was purchased for R2 200 000. Although raw material will be purchased evenly for the last nine months, the cost of the raw material will increase by 5 per cent on 1 July 20X6.

- Indirect material costs will continue to be projected at 10 per cent of the cost of direct material used.
- Half of the other manufacturing overhead, and all the marketing and general and administrative expenses, are fixed. The remainder of the manufacturing overhead varies in proportion to the volume of production.

Required

1 Based on the revised data, calculate Wet Designs (Pty) Ltd's projected sales for 20X6 in: (a) Units (b) Rands

2 Prepare the revised budgeted schedule of cost of goods sold for 20X6. (Carry your calculation of the average cost per unit to the nearest cent. Round the finished goods inventory to the nearest Rand.)

(CMA, adapted)

P9.42 Production, materials, labour, and overhead budgets (appendix): manufacturer

The Durban Division of Reid Ltd produces an intricate component used in Reid's major product line. The divisional manager has been concerned recently by a lack of co-ordination between purchasing and production personnel and believes that a monthly budgeting system would be better than the present system.

Durban's divisional manager has decided to develop budget information for the third quarter of the current year as an experiment before the budget system is implemented for an entire year. In response to the divisional manager's request, the divisional accountant has accumulated the following data:

Sales

Sales to 30 June 20X6, the first six months of the current year, are 240 000 units. Actual sales in units for May and June, and estimated unit sales for the next four months, are as follows:

May (actual)	40 000
June (actual)	40 000
July (estimated)	50 000
August (estimated)	60 000
September (estimated)	70 000
October (estimated)	70 000

The Durban Division expects to sell 600 000 units during the year ending 31 December 20X6.

Direct material

Data regarding the materials used in the component are shown in the following schedule. The desired monthly ending inventory for all direct materials is an amount sufficient to produce the next month's estimated sales.

Direct material	Units of direct material per finished component	Cost per unit	Inventory level 30/6/20X6 (units)
No. 101	6	12.00	350 000
No. 211	4	18.00	300 000
No. 242	2	6.00	140 000

Direct labour

Each component must pass through three different processes to be completed. Data regarding direct labour follow:

Process	Direct labour hours per finished component	Cost per direct labour hour
Forming	0.400	R100.00
Assembly	1.000	80.00
Finishing	0.125	90.00

Manufacturing overhead

The division produced 270 000 components during the six-month period ending 30 June 20X6. The actual variable overhead costs incurred during this six-month period are given in the following schedule. The divisional accountant believes that the variable overhead costs will be incurred at the same rate per unit of output during the last six months of 20X6:

Supplies	R2 970 000
Electricity	1 350 000
Indirect labour	2 700 000
Other	405 000
Total variable overhead	R7 425 000

The fixed overhead costs incurred during the first six months of 20X6 amounted to R4 675 000. Fixed overhead costs are budgeted for the full year as follows:

Supervision	R3 000 000
Taxes	360 000
Depreciation	4 320 000
Other	1 620 000
Total fixed overhead	R9 300 000

Finished goods

The desired monthly ending inventory of completed components is 80 per cent of the next month's estimated sales. There are 50 000 finished units in inventory on 30 June 20X6.

Required:

1 Prepare a production budget in units for the Durban Division for the third quarter ending 30 September 20X6.

2 Independent of your answer to requirement 1, assume that the Durban Division plans to produce 180 000 units during the third quarter ending 30 September 20X6 and 600 000 units for the year ending 31 December 20X6.

(a) Prepare a direct material purchases budget, in units and Rands, for the third quarter ending 30 September 20X6.

(b) Prepare a direct labour budget, in hours and Rands, for the third quarter ending 30 September 20X6.

(c) Prepare a manufacturing overhead budget for the six-month period ending 31 December 20X6.

(CMA, adapted)

P9.43 Preparation of the annual budget (appendix): manufacturer

Athena Boxes manufactures two types of cardboard boxes used in shipping canned food, and fruit and vegetables. The canned food box (type C) and the perishable food box (type P) have the following material and labour requirements:

	Type of box	
	C	P
Direct material required per 100 boxes:		
Paperboard (R0.30 per kg)	30 kg	70 kg
Corrugating medium (R0.15 per kg)	20 kg	30 kg
Direct labour required per 100 boxes (R18 per hour)	0.25 hour	0.50 hour

The following manufacturing overhead costs are anticipated for 20X6. The predetermined overhead rate is based on a production volume of 4 950 000 units for each type of box. Manufacturing overhead is applied on the basis of direct labour hours.

Indirect materials	R157 500
Indirect labour	750 000
Utilities	375 000
Land tax and council rates	270 000
Insurance	240 000
Depreciation	435 000
Total	R2 227 500

The following inventory information is available:

	Inventory 1 January 20X6	Desired ending inventory 31 December 20X6
Finished goods:		
Box type C	100 000 boxes	50 000 boxes
Box type P	200 000 boxes	150 000 boxes
Direct materials:		
Paperboard	150 000 kg	50 000 kg
Corrugating medium	50 000 kg	100 000 kg

The sales forecast for 20X6 is as follows:

	Sales volume	Sales price
Box type C	5 000 000 boxes	R135.00 per hundred boxes
Box type P	5 000 000 boxes	R195.00 per hundred boxes

The following selling and administrative expenses are anticipated for 20X6:

Salaries of sales personnel	R600 000
Advertising	100 000
Management salaries	1 000 000
Clerical wages	350 000
Miscellaneous administrative expenses	50 000
Total	R2 100 000

Required:

Prepare an annual budget for Athena Boxes for 20X6. Assume an income tax rate of 28 per cent. Include the following schedules:

1 Sales budget.
2 Production budget (in units).
3 Direct material budget.
4 Direct labour budget.
5 Manufacturing overhead budget.
6 Selling and administrative expense budget.

7 Budgeted income statement. (*Hint*: To determine cost of goods sold, first calculate the manufacturing cost per unit for each type of box. Include applied manufacturing overhead in the cost.)

Cases

C9.44 Using budgets to evaluate business decisions: sports club

Hawthorn Leisure Works (HLW) offers tennis courts and other physical fitness facilities to its members. The club has 2000 members. Revenue is derived from annual membership fees and hourly court fees. The annual membership fees are:

Individual	R 225
Student	150
Family	500

Approximately half the members are 'family', and the remaining memberships are split equally between individuals and students. For 20X6 and 20X7, the hourly court fees are R40 and R60, depending on the season and the time of day (prime versus non-prime time). There are 10 courts at each club.

The peak tennis season runs from October to April (181 days). During this period, court usage averages 90 to 100 per cent of capacity during prime time (5–9 pm) and 50 to 60 per cent of capacity during the remaining hours (9 am–4 pm). Daily court usage during the off-season averages only 20 to 40 per cent of capacity, and is charged at R30 per hour. All of HLW's memberships expire at the end of September. A substantial amount of the cash receipts is collected during the early part of the tennis season due to the renewal of annual membership fees and heavy court usage. However, cash receipts are not as large in autumn and drop significantly in the winter months.

For the start of the new financial year on 1 October 20X6, HLW is considering introducing a new membership and fee structure in an attempt to improve its cash flow planning. Under the new membership plan, only an annual membership fee would be charged, rather than a membership fee plus hourly court fees. There would be two classes of membership, with annual fees as follows:

Individual	R 1500
Family	2500

The annual fee would be collected in advance at the time the membership application was completed. Members would be allowed to use the tennis courts as often as they wished during the year under the new plan. All future memberships would be sold under these new terms. A special promotional campaign would be instituted to attract new members and to encourage current members to remain with the club. The annual fees for individual and family memberships would be reduced to R1 250 and R2 250 respectively if members pay for their yearly memberships in advance during the two-month promotional campaign.

HLW's management estimates that 70 per cent of the current members will continue with the club, and student members would convert to individual membership. The most active members (45 per cent of the current members) would pay the yearly fee in advance and receive the special fee reduction, while the remaining members who continued would renew memberships in October. Those members who would not rejoin are not considered active (that is, they play five times or less during the year). Management estimates that the loss of members would be offset fully by new members within six months of instituting the new plan. These new members would pay a proportional amount of the yearly fee on joining. Furthermore, many of the new members would be individuals who would play during non-prime time. Management estimates that adequate court time will be available for all members under the new plan.

If the new membership plan is adopted, it would be instituted on 1 October 20X6 at the start of the tennis season. The special promotional campaign would be conducted during August and September.

Required:

Your consulting firm has been hired to help HLW to evaluate its new fee structure. Write a letter to the club's managing director dealing with the following issues:

1 Will HLW's new membership plan and fee structure improve its ability to plan its cash receipts? Explain your answer.
2 Estimate the effect on sales revenue resulting from the planned change in fee structure for the 12 months ending 30 September 20X7. State any assumptions that you need to make.
3 HLW should evaluate the new membership plan and fee structure completely before it decides to adopt or reject it.
   (a) Identify the key factors that HLW should consider in its evaluation.
   (b) Explain what type of financial analyses HLW should prepare in order to make a complete evaluation.
4 Explain how HLW's cash management practices might differ from the present if the new membership plan and fee structure are adopted.

(CMA, adapted)

C9.45 Comprehensive budget question: wholesaler

Universal Electric Company is a small, rapidly growing wholesaler of consumer electrical products. The firm's main product lines are small kitchen appliances and power tools. Marcia Wilcox, Universal's general manager of marketing, has recently completed a sales forecast. She believes that the company's sales during each of the months in the first quarter of 20X3 will increase by 10 per cent each month over the previous month's sales. Wilcox then expects sales to remain constant for several months. Universal's projected balance sheet as at 31 December 20X2 is as follows:

Cash	R350 000
Accounts receivable	2 700 000
Marketable securities	150 000
Inventory	1 540 000
Buildings and equipment (net of accumulated depreciation)	6 260 000
Total assets	R11 000 000
Accounts payable	R1 764 000
Bond interest payable	125 000
Property taxes payable	36 000
Bonds payable (10%, issued in 20X1, due in 20X9)	3 000 000
Share capital	5 000 000
Retained earnings	1 075 000
Total liabilities and shareholders' equity	R11 000 000

Jack Hanekom, the assistant accountant, is now preparing a monthly budget for the first quarter of 20X3. In the process, the following information has been accumulated:

- Projected sales for December 20X2 are R4 000 000. Credit sales typically are 75 per cent of total sales. Universal's credit experience indicates that 10 per cent of the credit sales are collected during the month of sale, and the remainder are collected during the following month.

- Universal's cost of goods sold generally runs at 70 per cent of sales. Inventory is purchased on account, and 40 per cent of each month's purchases are paid during the month of purchase. The remainder is paid during the following month. In order to have adequate stocks of inventory on hand, the firm attempts to have inventory at the end of each month equal to half of the next month's projected cost of goods sold.
- Hanekom has estimated that Universal's other monthly expenses will be as follows:

Sales salaries	R180 000
Advertising and promotion	190 000
Administrative salaries	210 000
Depreciation	250 000
Interest on bonds	25 000
Property taxes	9000

In addition, sales commissions run at the rate of 1 per cent of sales.

- Universal's managing director, Beth Davies-Lowry, has indicated that the firm should, just after the new year begins, invest R1250 000 in an automated inventory-handling system to control the movement of inventory in the firm's warehouse. To the extent possible, these equipment purchases would be financed from the firm's cash and marketable securities. Davies-Lowry believes that Universal needs to keep a minimum cash balance of R250 000. If necessary, the remainder of the equipment purchases would be financed using short-term credit from a local bank. The minimum period for such a loan is three months. Hanekom believes short-term interest rates will be 10 per cent per year at the time of the equipment purchases. If a loan is necessary, Davies-Lowry has decided it should be paid off by the end of the first quarter if possible.
- Universal's board of directors has indicated an intention to declare and pay dividends of R500 000 on the last day of each quarter.
- The interest on any short-term borrowing would be paid when the loan is repaid. Interest on Universal's bonds is paid semi-annually, on 31 January and 31 July, for the preceding six-month period.
- Property taxes are paid half-yearly on 28 February and 31 August for the preceding six-month period.

Required:

Prepare Universal's annual budget for the first quarter of 20X3 by completing the following schedules and statements:

1

Sales Budget

	20X2	20X3			
	December	January	February	March	1st quarter
Total sales					
Cash sales					
Credit sales					

2

Cash Receipts Budget				
	20X3			
	January	February	March	1st quarter
Cash sales				
Cash receipts from credit sales made during current month				
Cash receipts from credit sales made during preceding month				
Total cash receipts				

3

Purchases Budget					
	20X2	20X3			
	December	January	February	March	1st quarter
Budgeted cost of goods sold					
Add Desired ending inventory					
Total goods needed					
Less Expected beginning inventory					
Purchases					

4

Cash Payments Budget				
	20X3			
	January	February	March	1st quarter
Inventory purchases:				
Cash payments for purchases during the current month*				
Cash payments for purchases during the preceding month†				
Total cash payments for inventory purchases				
Other expenses:				
Sales salaries				
Advertising and promotion				
Administrative salaries				
Interest on bonds‡				
Property taxes‡				
Sales commissions				
Total cash payments for other expenses				
Total cash payments				

*40 per cent of the current month's purchases (schedule 3).
†60 per cent of the prior month's purchases (schedule 3).
‡Bond interest is paid every six months, on 31 January and 31 July. Property taxes are also paid every six months, on 28 February and 31 August.

5 Complete the first three lines of the summary cash budget. Then do the analysis of short-term financing needs in requirement 6, and then finish requirement 5.

Summary Cash Budget				
	20X3			
	January	February	March	1st quarter
Cash receipts (from schedule 2)				
Less Cash payments (from schedule 4)				
Change in cash balance during quarter due to operations				
Sale of marketable securities (2/1/20X3)				
Proceeds from bank loan (2/1/20X3)				
Purchase of equipment				
Repayment of bank loan (31/3/20X3)				
Interest on bank loan				
Payment of dividends				
Change in cash balance during 1st quarter				
Cash balance, 1/1/20X3				
Cash balance, 31/3/20X3				

6 Analysis of short-term financial needs:

Projected cash balance as at 31 December 20X2
Less Minimum cash balance
Cash available for equipment purchases
Projected proceeds from sale of marketable securities
Cash available
Less Cost of investment in equipment
Required short-term borrowing

7 Prepare Universal Electric's budgeted income statement for the first quarter. (Ignore income taxes.)

8 Prepare Universal Electric's budgeted statement of retained earnings for the first quarter of 20X3.

9 Prepare Universal Electric's budgeted balance sheet as at 31 March 20X3. (*Hint:* On 31 March 20X3, bond interest payable is R50 000 and property taxes payable are R9000.)

Endnotes

1 Note that managers of investment centres are held responsible for using the invested capital (assets) to generate profit.

2 AVJ Ltd is based on an actual company but the financial data are for illustrative purposes only and bear no resemblance to the actual financial data of the company.

3 Move-up buyers are those customers who have owned a house before, and now seek a more expensive house

4 While this schedule has been titled an income statement, it does not necessarily meet the disclosure requirements for external reporting as it is to be used for management reporting and analysis.

CHAPTER

Standard Costs for Control: Direct Material and Direct Labour

❖ Learning Objectives

After completing this chapter, you should be able to:

1. explain how standard costing can be used to help control costs and manage resources more effectively;
2. describe the historical cost analysis and engineering methods of setting standards;
3. understand how participation in standard setting, and the choice between perfection and practical standards, can impact on behaviour;
4. develop standard costs for direct material and direct labour;
5. calculate and interpret the direct material price and quantity variances, and the direct labour rate and efficiency variances;
6. explain several methods that can be used for assessing the significance of standard cost variances;
7. understand how to determine the causes of variances, and when to take corrective actions;
8. describe some behavioural effects of standard costing systems;
9. understand how control can be achieved through assigning responsibility for certain variances to particular managers;
10. explain how standard costs are used in product costing;
11. prepare journal entries to account for direct material and direct labour cost variances;
12. after studying the appendix, explain the meaning of the joint rate efficiency variance and the pure rate variance.

Introduction

Chapter 9 discussed how businesses prepare budgets for a variety of purposes: planning, facilitating communication and coordination, allocating resources, controlling profits and operations, and evaluating performance and providing incentives. In this chapter and in Chapter 11 we will examine one approach that managers can use for evaluating performance and controlling operations. This is using standard costs as a benchmark against which the actual financial results can be compared. Did the company make as much profit as anticipated in the budget? Were costs greater than or less than expected? Why were actual costs different from budgeted costs?

In this chapter we will focus on direct material and direct labour standards and cost variances, while in Chapter 11 we will consider the control of manufacturing overhead.

Controlling costs

L.O. 1

In Chapter 1 we encountered the terms control and control systems. We learned that businesses are 'in control' when operations proceed to plan and objectives are achieved. Control systems provide regular information to assist in control, which is an essential component of effective resource management.

What are the necessary requirements for control? All control systems have three basic parts:

- a predetermined or standard performance level;
- a measure of actual performance; and
- a comparison between standard performance and actual performance.

The thermostat of an air-conditioner is a familiar control system. First, a thermostat can be set at any desired level, establishing a predetermined or standard temperature. If you want the temperature in a room to be 22°C, you set the thermostat at the standard of 22°C. Second, the thermostat has a thermometer, which measures the actual temperature in the room. Third, the thermostat compares the preset or standard temperature with the actual room temperature. If the actual temperature rises above the preset or standard temperature, the thermostat activates the cooling mechanism to bring the temperature back to 22°C. The three features of a control system are depicted in Exhibit 10.1.

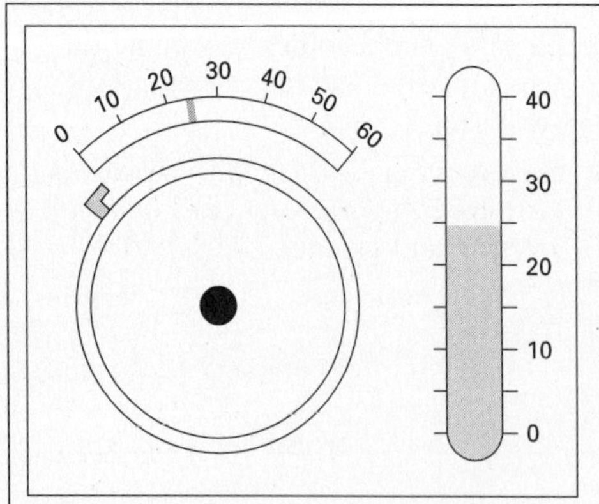

Exhibit 10.1 Control systems: a thermostat

Standard costing is a part of the budgetary control system that works like a thermostat. First, *a predetermined or standard cost is developed.* In essence, a **standard cost** is a budget for the production of one unit of product, either goods or services. It is the cost that serves as the benchmark in the budgetary control system. When the firm produces many units, the management accountant uses the standard unit cost to calculate the total standard or budgeted cost of production. For example, suppose the standard direct material cost for one unit of product is R5, and 100 units are manufactured. The total standard or budgeted direct material cost, given actual output of 100 units, is R500 (R5 × 100).

Second, the management accountant *measures the actual cost incurred* in the production process.

Third, the management accountant *compares the actual cost with the budgeted or standard cost.*

Any difference between the two is called a **standard cost variance**. Standard cost variances are used to evaluate actual performance and control costs. We can calculate standard cost variances for direct materials, direct labour and manufacturing overhead.[1] When standard cost variances are significant, the cause of the variance must be investigated. This may result in changes to actual operations to bring them back in line with standards (for example, retraining production workers or purchasing raw materials of the correct quality). Alternatively, management may need to reconsider whether the standards are appropriate benchmarks.

In this and the following chapter we will consider, in detail, conventional ways in which budgets and standard costs can be used to control costs. Standard costing has been used to control costs for many decades, and is still used in many organisations. However, as we will see in Chapter 15, since the mid-1990s more effective methods of cost management have been developed. These contemporary cost management techniques focus on identifying and controlling the activities that drive costs. Conventional uses of standard costs for control tend to focus on more aggregated analyses of actual spending, relative to standard. These conventional methods have been criticised as not relevant to today's fast-paced business environment. We will investigate these criticisms in Chapter 11.

Setting standards

Management accountants may use several methods for setting cost standards. These include the analysis of historical data, and engineering methods. Sometimes standards will be developed with the participation of those managers who are an integral part of the process, which can have an impact on commitment to achieving those standards. In addition, the use of perfection or practical standards can also have an impact on employee behaviour.

Analysis of historical data

L.O. 2

One guide to future costs is historical cost data. In a mature production process, where there is much production experience, historical costs can provide a good basis for predicting future costs. Some of the quantitative techniques that can be used to predict future costs were described in Chapter 3. The management accountant will often need to adjust predictions to reflect expected movements in price levels or technological changes in the production process. For example, the amount of rubber required to manufacture a particular type of tyre this year will probably be the same as it was last year, unless there has been a significant change in the manufacturing process. However, the price of rubber is likely to be different this year, and this must be reflected in the new standard cost of manufacturing a tyre.

Despite the relevance of historical cost data in setting cost standards, management accountants must guard against relying on them excessively. Even a seemingly minor change in the way a product is manufactured may make historical data irrelevant; and standards based on historical data will embody any inefficiencies of the past. Moreover, for new products there will be no historical cost data upon which to base standards.

Engineering methods

Another way to set cost standards is to use **engineering methods** to analyse the process of manufacturing a product or providing a service. The emphasis shifts from what the product *did* cost in the past to what it *should* cost in the future. When using this approach, the management accountant typically works with engineers who are familiar with the production process. Together they conduct studies to determine exactly how much direct material *should be required* and how machinery and direct labour *should be used* in the production process. **Time and motion studies** may be conducted to ascertain how long it should take workers to perform each step.

A combined approach

In practice, both historical cost analysis and engineering methods are used to set cost standards. For example, if the technology has changed for one step of the production process, the management accountant would work with engineers to set cost standards for the changed part of the production process. However, the accountant would probably rely on the less expensive method of analysing historical cost data to update the cost standards for the remainder of the production process.

Participation in setting standards

L.O. 3 While cost standards are often considered the domain of management accountants, standards should not be set by the management accountant alone. People will usually be more committed to meeting standards, and have greater confidence in their accuracy, if they are allowed to participate in setting them. Any managers who are an integral part of an operation or process should participate in the standard setting process. For example, engineering methods can be undertaken by a team of production engineers, production supervisors and management accountants. (The advantages and disadvantages of participative budgeting were discussed more fully in Chapter 9.)

Perfection versus practical standards: a behavioural issue

In Chapter 9 we discussed budget difficulty and its impact on employee motivation. This issue is also important when setting standard costs. Should standard costs be set so that actual costs come well within budget? Or should standards be made so challenging that they are rarely achieved? The answers to these questions *depend on the purpose* for which standards will be used and on assumptions about how *standards affect behaviour.*

Perfection standards

Perfection standards (also called **ideal standards** or **theoretical standards**) reflect the minimum attainable costs under nearly perfect operating conditions. Such standards assume peak efficiency, the lowest possible material and labour prices, the use of the best quality materials, and no disruptions in production due to problems such as machine breakdowns or power failures.

Some managers believe that perfection standards motivate employees to achieve the lowest cost possible. They claim that, since the standard is theoretically attainable, employees will be motivated to work as hard as possible to achieve it. Other managers and many psychologists disagree. They feel that perfection standards discourage employees from working hard since they are so unlikely to be achieved. Moreover, setting unrealistic and difficult standards may encourage employees to sacrifice product quality to achieve those lower costs. By purchasing low-quality raw materials or giving scant attention to manual production tasks, employees can decrease the production cost. However, this lower cost may be achieved at the expense of a higher rate of defective units. Thus the firm ultimately incurs higher costs, as defective products may be scrapped or returned by dissatisfied customers.

Practical standards

Standards that are challenging but are expected to be attained are called **practical** (or **attainable**) **standards.** These standards assume a production process that is as efficient as it is practical, under normal operating conditions. Practical standards factor in occurrences such as occasional machine breakdowns and normal amounts of raw material wastage. Attaining a practical standard keeps employees on their toes, without demanding miracles. Many organisational psychologists believe that practical standards result in greater motivation to achieve standards, and encourage more positive and productive employee attitudes, than do perfection standards.

In some companies, standard costs are determined by adding an amount (say 5 per cent) to costs to allow for idle time, wastage of material or normal spoilage. However, this practice is considered by many managers to provide the wrong signals to employees – that is, 'It's OK to have a certain level of inefficiency and waste'. It also means that cost variances will 'hide' the amount of wastage or spoilage that is built into the standard costs. Many manufacturing companies aim for *continuous improvement*, including improvements in work practices, standard costs and budget targets.

This implies that standards should be challenging and, once attained, can then be made more demanding. The use of static practical standards may not meet these needs, as they are not continually adjusted to provide that extra 'stretch'.

Techniques for eliminating waste and encouraging continuous improvement are discussed further in Chapter 15. Normal and abnormal spoilage were discussed in Chapter 4.

Benchmarking cost standards

In recent years it has become more common to formulate cost standards by comparing costs with those achieved by the better performing companies. Benchmarking of costs involves identifying companies that have the best cost performance, assessing their levels of cost, and identifying the cost performance gap that needs to be closed. This allows the company to identify areas where it needs to improve its cost performance to achieve greater competitiveness. Cost standards may be formulated to achieve external performance standards over the medium to long term. Clearly, it is difficult to benchmark costs against those of direct competitors. Some industry groups supply cost data to their members, while other firms may benchmark against other businesses within their wider company group. (Benchmarking is covered in more detail in Chapter 14.)

Use of standards by non-manufacturing organisations

Some service firms, including government enterprises, use standard costs in some form. For example, airlines set standards for fuel and maintenance costs. Standard costs may be used for budgeting and cost control in much the same way that manufacturers use standards. However, many service organisations are not suited to standard costing because the services they produce are non-repetitive. It is not feasible to set standards when one service differs from the next.

Developing standards at R.M. Williams

L.O. 4

To see how standards can be used to control costs and analyse performance, we will examine the systems used at R.M. Williams Pty Ltd,[2] a manufacturer of outdoor and hiking clothing and equipment.

The business specialised in producing saddlery, as well as hiking boots, pants, shirts, jackets and many other lines. Over the next few decades the company expanded through mail order catalogues, and the popular products came to be stocked by stores throughout South Africa. In the late 1980s the company opened a number of retail outlets, including shops in London, Munich and Stockholm.

The current range of products includes moleskin trousers, oilskin jackets, shirts, belts and hiking boots and thermal wear. The products are renowned for being hardwearing, comfortable and of a high standard. The business is proud of its heritage and traditional manufacturing techniques. While the products have been enhanced over the decades, the company does not use mass-production or high-tech machinery. There are many manual operations; for example, the famous Williams boots are hand-sewn. There are three production departments: Clothing, which produces oilskins, shirts and trousers; Craftware, producing plaited belts, saddlery and hardware; and Footwear.

To illustrate how R.M. Williams uses standards to control costs, we will examine how standards are developed and used in the manufacture of moleskin pants. Moleskins are popular hardwearing trousers that date from the earliest days of the company. They are manufactured in the Clothing Department through two processes. In the first process the cotton moleskin fabric is cut into the required pattern shapes. The second process is stitching, where the pants are sewn to shape, and a zipper, buttons and labels are added.

The accountant, Bill Sithole, develops standards for direct material and direct labour for each product. The standards are revised once a year to take account of changes in material prices and labour wage rates. There may also be changes in the quantities of materials used in each product, and in production times.

Direct material standards

In the manufacture of moleskins the materials used are cotton fabric, a zipper, buttons, labels and thread. The cotton fabric is regarded as direct material as it is a significant cost that can be traced directly to the product. The other materials – the zipper, buttons, labels and thread – are relatively inexpensive, and the cost of tracing their usage to each pair of pants would be great. Therefore, they are treated as indirect materials, part of manufacturing overhead.[3]

At R.M. Williams, the quantities needed to produce one unit of a product are determined by the product designer when the product is initially designed. In subsequent years these quantities are adjusted as workers become more efficient in using materials, or as production processes change. The standard quantity and price of direct materials for one pair of moleskins are as follows:

Standard material quantity	3.1 metres
Standard material price per metre	× R 25.00
Standard direct material cost per pair of moleskins	R 77.50

The standard price of fabric reflects all the costs incurred to acquire the material. The fabric is imported from the UK, and the standard price includes the cost of transportation to the plant. The prices of all materials are estimated by the purchasing manager as part of the budgeting process. The prices are based on the company ordering a *certain quality* of material in *specific order quantities* from a *specified supplier*. Thus any discounts for ordering material in economic quantities have been incorporated in the estimated price. The purchasing manager, Tariq Fataar, is in the best position to estimate future prices – he is familiar with the company's suppliers and has years of experience in this area.

To summarise, the **standard material quantity** is the total amount of direct material normally required to produce one unit of a product. The **standard material price** is the total delivered cost of that material, after subtracting any discounts.

Direct labour standards

The **standard direct labour quantity** is the number of labour hours normally needed to manufacture one unit of a product. The **standard labour rate** is the total hourly cost of wages, including 'on-costs'. These on-costs are the extra salary-related costs that all South African companies have to pay, and are usually treated as part of the cost of labour. They include a provision for annual and long service leave, workers' compensation insurance, UIF, payroll taxes and employer's pension contributions.

The standard time that it takes to produce each R.M. Williams product is determined by the company engineer, who uses *time and motion* techniques. That is, he observes the production workers as they produce each product, and records the average times for each process.[4] The accountant, Bill Sithole, then compares these average times with the times of the previous year to arrive at an accurate standard time for each product. The standard wage rates are determined by the accountant by considering the current wage rate and estimates of future wage rises for the coming year.

The standard quantity and standard rate for direct labour to make one pair of moleskins are as follows:

Standard quantity:	
Cutting process	0.10 hours
Stitching process	1.30 hours
Standard direct labour quantity per pair of moleskins	1.40 hours
Standard rate:	
Hourly wage rate	R30.00
On-costs (20% of gross wages)	6.00
Standard labour rate per hour	R36.00
Standard direct labour cost per pair of moleskins (1.40 DLH × R36 per hour)	R50.40

Standard costs given actual output

Let's assume that during September 20X6, R.M. Williams manufactured 2000 pairs of moleskins. The total standard or budgeted costs for direct material and direct labour are calculated as follows:

Direct material:	
Standard direct material cost per pair of moleskins	R77.50
Actual output	× 2000
Total standard direct material cost	R155 000

Direct labour:	
Direct labour cost per pair of moleskins	R50.40
Actual output	× 2000
Total standard direct labour cost	R100 800

Notice that the total standard cost for the direct material and direct labour inputs is based on the company's *actual output*. The company *should* incur costs of R155 000 for direct material and R100 800 for direct labour, given that it produced 2000 pairs of moleskins. The total standard costs for direct material and direct labour serve as the benchmarks against which to compare actual costs. This comparison then provides the basis for controlling direct material and direct labour costs.

Allowances for wastage, inefficiency or normal spoilage

Some accountants argue that, when developing standards for direct material and direct labour, allowances should be made for material wastage and labour inefficiency. For example, instead of the standard quantity of 3.1 metres of fabric, an allowance of 5 per cent may be added to account for material wastage due to error or production problems.[5] Such errors or production problems may result in 'normal spoilage', which is discarded. Therefore, the standard for cotton fabric would be 3.25 metres (3.1 metres × 1.05).

Similarly, an allowance for inefficiency in labour time, say 6 per cent, may be included in the standard for direct labour. These inefficiencies occur for many reasons, including process workers purposely working slowly, or where it takes longer to process poor-quality materials. The standard for direct labour quantity would be 1.48 hours (1.4 hours × 1.06).

However, these practices are becoming less common as many managers consider that wastage, allowances for inefficiency or normal spoilage should not be included in the standard cost. This is because it can send a message to operators and managers that a certain amount of wastage is an expected part of the production process. When allowances for wastage are not included within the standards for materials and labour, then any inefficiencies that occur are highlighted as unfavourable cost variances.

Calculating standard cost variances

L.O. 5

The actual costs for direct materials and direct labour for September 20X6 are shown in Exhibit 10.2. When we compare these actual costs with the total standard costs for the production of 2000 pairs of moleskins, we can see that R.M. Williams spent more than the budgeted amount for both direct material and direct labour. But why were these extra costs incurred? The calculation of standard cost variances helps to answer this question.

Direct material variances

What caused the company to spend more than anticipated on direct material? First, the cotton fabric was purchased for R25.40 per metre, rather than the standard price of R25.00 per metre. Second, the plant used more fabric than the standard amount. The amount of fabric actually used was 6500 metres instead of the standard amount of 6200 metres (2000 units × 3.1 metres per unit).

The management accountant can calculate a **direct material price variance** (sometimes called a **purchase price variance**) to show the effect of purchasing at a price that is different from the standard price. In addition, a **direct material quantity variance** (sometimes called a **direct material usage variance**) will show the effect of using a different quantity in production compared to standard (given the actual output).

Direct material purchased, actual cost:	
25 000 metres of fabric @ R25.40 per metre	R635 000
Direct material used, actual cost:	
6500 metres of fabric @ R25.40 per metre	R165 100
Direct labour, actual cost:	
2700 hours @ R38 per hour	R102 600

Exhibit 10.2 Actual costs for moleskin pants, R.M. Williams, September 20X6

Direct material price variance

The formula for the direct material price variance is as follows:

$$\text{Direct material price variance} = (PQ \times AP) - (PQ \times SP)$$
$$= PQ(AP - SP)$$

where PQ = quantity purchased
AP = actual price
SP = standard price

The direct material price variance for the moleskin fabric for September is therefore calculated as follows:

$$\text{Direct material price variance} = PQ(AP - SP)$$
$$= 25\,000(\text{R}25.40-\text{R}25.00)$$
$$= \text{R}10\,000 \text{ unfavourable}$$

The direct material price variance is unfavourable because the actual purchase price of fabric exceeded the standard price. Notice that the price variance is based on the quantity of material *purchased* (PQ), not the quantity actually used in production.

Direct material quantity variance

The following formula defines the direct material quantity variance:

$$\text{Direct material quantity variance} = (AQ \times SP) - (SQ \times SP)$$
$$= SP(AQ - SQ)$$

where SP = standard price
AQ = actual quantity used
SQ = standard quantity allowed, given actual output[6]

The direct material quantity variance for moleskin fabric for September is therefore calculated as follows:

Direct material quantity variance = $SP(AQ - SQ)$
= R25.00(6500−6200*)
= R7500 unfavourable

*SQ = 2000 units × 3.1 metres per unit

This variance is unfavourable because the actual quantity of direct material used in September exceeded the standard quantity allowed, given actual September output of 2000 pairs of moleskins. The quantity variance is based on the quantity of material actually used in production (AQ).

In Exhibit 10.3 an alternative format for calculating the direct material variances is presented.

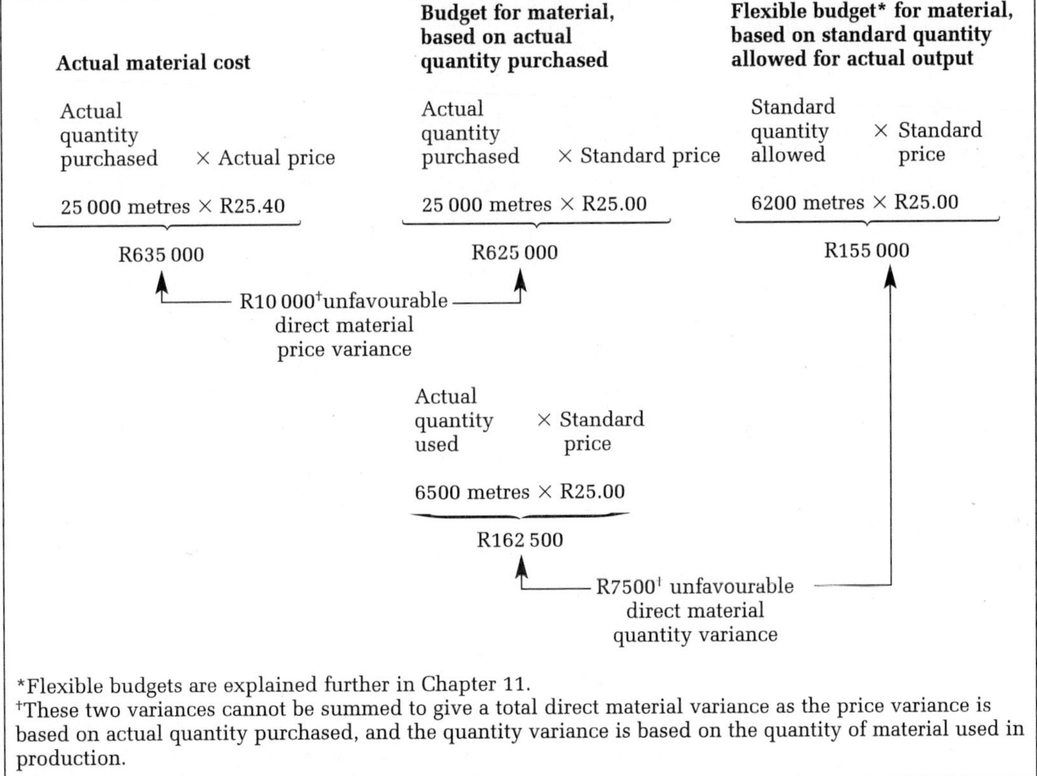

Exhibit 10.3 Direct material price and quantity variances, R.M. Williams

Basing the quantity variance on actual output

Notice that the *standard quantity of material* must be based on the *actual production output* for the quantity variance to be meaningful. For example, in preparing the operating budget for 20X6, R.M. Williams may have planned an output of 2500 pairs of moleskins for the month of September. However, it would not make any sense to compare standard or budgeted material usage at this level of output with the actual material usage at a different level of output (say 2000 pairs of moleskins). Everyone would expect less direct material to be used in the production of 2000 pairs of moleskins than in the production of 2500 pairs. The direct material quantity variance compares the two quantities shown in Exhibit 10.4.

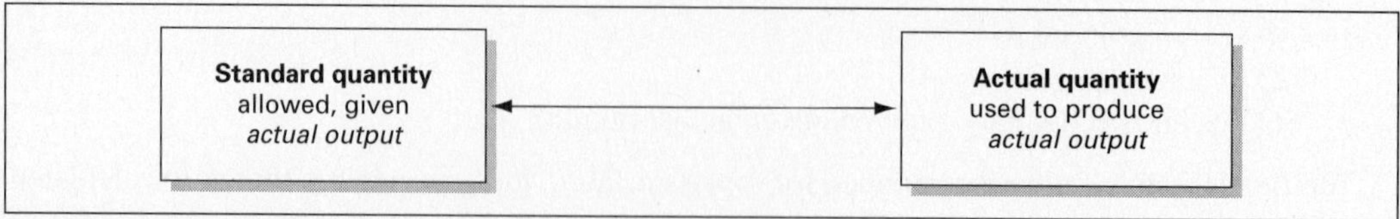

Exhibit 10.4 Comparisons used in direct material quantity variance

Calculating the price variance based on material used in production

In some companies, the direct material price variance is calculated using the quantity of materials *used in production* (*AQ*) rather than the quantity of material *purchased* (*PQ*). The price variance formula will change:

$$\text{Direct material price variance} = (AQ \times AP) - (AQ \times SP) = AQ(AP - SP)$$

Thus, for R.M. Williams, the price variance for moleskin fabric would be:

$$\begin{aligned}\text{Direct material price variance} &= AQ(AP - SP)\\ &= 6500(\text{R}25.40 - \text{R}25.00)\\ &= \text{R}2600 \text{ unfavourable}\end{aligned}$$

where *AQ* = actual quantity of material used in production.

This alternative method of calculating the price variance is not recommended, for two reasons. First, it delays recognition of the total price variance until the material is used in production. Only R2600 of the unfavourable variance is recognised in September. The remainder of the variance relating to the September material purchase will be recognised in later months when the material is used in production. This means that any corrections that need to be made to buying practices, such as renegotiating the price with the supplier, may occur some time after the particular September purchase took place. Second, the responsibility for the price variance lies with the purchasing department, not with the production department. It is the purchasing department that can directly influence the price. Therefore, it is more sensible to recognise the *total* direct material price variance close to the time at which the buying activity occurs, rather than waiting until the producing activities take place.

Direct labour variances

Why did R.M. Williams spend more than anticipated on direct labour during September? As with the analysis of direct material, there are two components to consider. Clearly, the company incurred a cost for labour: R38 per hour for direct labour instead of the standard amount of R36 per hour. However, there were fewer labour hours worked compared with standard. Only 2700 direct labour hours (DLH) were used, which is less than the standard quantity of 2800 hours, given actual output of 2000 pairs of moleskins (2000 pairs of moleskins × 1.4 DLH per unit). The accountant can analyse direct labour costs by calculating a **direct labour rate variance** to show the impact of paying a different labour rate compared to standard. A **direct labour efficiency variance** will indicate the cost implications of using a different number of direct labour hours, compared to standard (given the actual output).

Direct labour rate variance

The formula for the direct labour rate variance is as follows:

$$\text{Direct labour rate variance} = (AH \times AR) - (AH \times SR) = AH\,(AR - SR)$$

where *AH* = actual hours used
AR = actual rate per hour
SR = standard rate per hour

(Notice the similarity between this formula and the one used to calculate the material price variance. Both focus on prices – one on the price of material and the other on the 'price' of labour.)

The direct labour rate variance for September is therefore calculated as follows:

Direct labour rate variance = $AH(AR - SR)$
= 2700(R38−R36)
= R5400 unfavourable

This variance is unfavourable because the actual rate exceeded the standard rate during September.

Direct labour efficiency variance

The formula for the direct labour efficiency variance is as follows:

Direct labour efficiency variance = $(AH \times SR) - (SH \times SR)$
= $SR(AH - SH)$

where SH = standard hours allowed, given actual output[7]

(This formula is similar to that for the direct material quantity variance. Both focus on the quantity of resources used – one on material, one on labour.)

Therefore the direct labour efficiency variance for September is calculated as follows:

Direct labour efficiency variance = $SR(AH - SH)$
= R36(2700−2800*)
= R3600 favourable

*SH = 2000 units × 1.4 DLH per unit

This variance is favourable because the actual direct labour hours used in September were less than the standard hours allowed, given the actual September output of 2000 pairs of moleskins.

Notice that the direct labour rate and efficiency variances add up to the total direct labour variance. The total direct labour variance is the difference between the actual cost of labour (R102 600) and the standard cost of labour (R100 800) for the actual output of 2000 pairs of moleskins. However, the rate and efficiency variances have opposite signs, since one variance is unfavourable and the other is favourable.

Direct labour rate variance	R5400	unfavourable
Direct labour efficiency variance	3600	favourable
Direct labour variance	R1800	unfavourable

An analysis of the direct labour variances is presented in Exhibit 10.5.

Basing the efficiency variance on actual output

We noted in a previous section that for material quantity variances to be meaningful they must be based on the *quantity of material allowed for the actual output produced.* Similarly, the number of standard hours of direct labour allowed is based on the *actual production output.* It is not meaningful to compare standard or budgeted labour usage at one level of output with the actual hours used at a different level of output.

Multiple direct material and direct labour variances

In our example, R.M. Williams classified moleskin fabric as direct material, and the remaining materials (zipper, buttons, labels and thread) as indirect materials. However, we could have decided to classify the zipper, buttons, labels and thread as direct materials. Why would we choose to do this? Under a standard costing system, when a material is classified as direct material, standards for those materials are calculated as well as individual price and quantity variances. Thus we are able to maintain tighter control over price and quantity for each material.

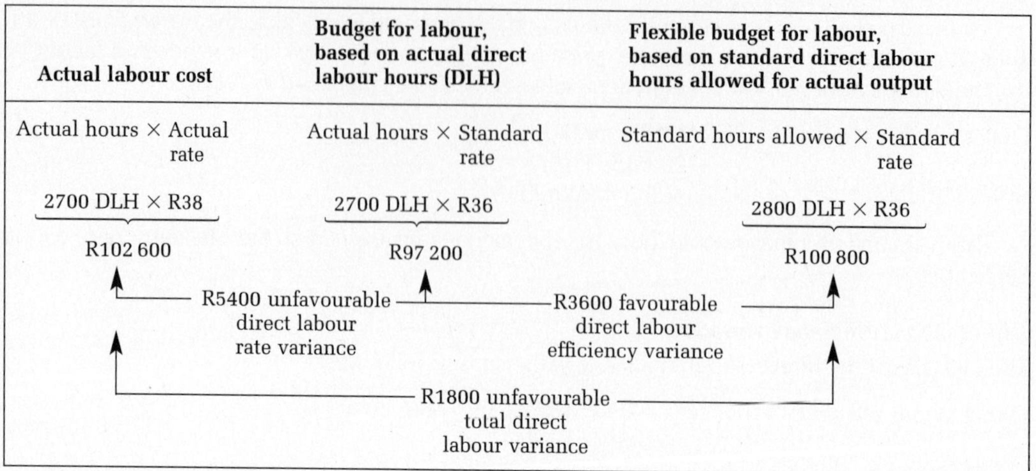

Exhibit 10.5 Direct labour rate and efficiency variances, R.M. Williams

Similarly, we may also have multiple direct labour rate and efficiency variances. This occurs when production employees are paid different wage rates to reflect different skills and qualifications. However, many firms limit the number of direct material and direct labour standards developed, as the cost of increased data collection and processing may exceed the benefits. While the zipper, buttons, labels and thread could be traced to the units of production, it would entail greater costs.

Investigating significant variances and taking corrective actions

Managers do not have time to look into the causes of every standard cost variance, so they need to determine which variances are significant enough to warrant investigation. This process of reporting and following up only significant cost variances is called **management by exception**. Significant cost variances may be investigated to determine their causes and corrective action can be taken when needed.

Which variances are significant?

L.O. 6 How does a manager know when to follow up on a standard cost variance and when to ignore it? These questions are difficult to answer because to some extent the answers form part of the skill of management. A manager applies judgement and experience in making guesses, pursuing hunches and relying on intuition to decide when a variance should be investigated. Nevertheless, there are guidelines and 'rules of thumb' that managers often apply.

Size of variance

The absolute size of a variance is one consideration. Managers are more likely to follow up large variances than small ones. The *relative size* of the variance compared with the standard is probably even more important. A manager is more likely to investigate a R20 000 material quantity variance that is 20 per cent of the standard direct material cost of R100 000, than a R50 000 labour efficiency variance that is only 2 per cent of the standard direct labour cost of R2 500 000. The relative size of the R20 000 material quantity variance (20 per cent) is greater than the relative size of the R50 000 labour efficiency variance (2 per cent). Therefore, management accountants often show the relative sizes of variances in their cost variance reports.

An example of a standard cost variance report for moleskins for R.M. Williams is shown in Exhibit 10.6. The managers at R.M. Williams may consider that the direct labour rate variance at 5.4 per cent of standard cost is more significant than the direct labour efficiency variance, which is 3.6 per cent of standard.

Managers may apply a rule of thumb that allows for both the absolute and the relative size of a variance; for example: 'Investigate variances that are either greater than R20 000 or greater than 10 per cent of standard cost'.

If the managers at R.M. Williams developed a rule of thumb to investigate variances that were greater than R8 000 or greater than 5 per cent of standard, then they would consider the direct material price variance and the direct labour rate variance.

	Amount	Percentage of standard cost
Direct material purchased:		
Standard cost, given actual quantity of material purchased	R625 000	
Direct material price variance	10 000 U*	1.6
Direct material used in production:		
Standard cost, given actual output	R155 000	
Direct material quantity variance	7 500 U	4.8
Direct labour:		
Standard cost, given actual output	R100 800	
Direct labour rate variance	5 400 U	5.4
Direct labour efficiency variance	3 600 F†	(3.6)

*U denotes an unfavourable variance.
†F denotes a favourable variance.

Exhibit 10.6 Cost variance report, R.M. Williams, September 20X6

Recurring variances

Another consideration in deciding when to investigate a variance is whether the variance occurs repeatedly or only infrequently. Suppose a manager uses the rule of thumb: 'Investigate all variances greater than R20 000 or greater than 10 per cent of standard cost', and the following direct material quantity variances occurred:

Month	Variance	Percentage of standard cost*
January	R6000 F†	6.0
February	6400 F	6.4
March	3600 F	3.6
April	6200 F	6.2

*The standard direct material cost is R100 000.
†F denotes a favourable variance.

A strict adherence to the rule of thumb indicates no investigation, since none of the monthly variances is greater than R20 000 or 10 per cent of standard cost. Nevertheless, the manager might investigate the variance after April, since it has recurred at a reasonably high level for several consecutive months. In this case the consistency of the variance, not its absolute or relative size, triggers an investigation.

Trends

A trend in a variance may also call for investigation. Suppose that a manager observes the following direct labour efficiency variances:

Month	Variance	Percentage of standard cost*
January	R200 U†	0.10
February	1 100 U	0.55
March	6 000 U	3.00
April	18 200 U	9.10

*The standard direct labour cost is R200 000.
†U denotes an unfavourable variance.

None of these variances is large enough to trigger an investigation if the manager uses the 'R20 000 or 10 per cent' rule of thumb. However, the four-month trend is a worry. An alert manager may follow up this trend to find out the causes before costs get out of hand.

Controllability

Another important consideration is the manager's view of the *controllability* of the cost item. A manager is more likely to investigate the variance for a cost that is *controllable* by someone in the organisation than a cost that is *uncontrollable*. For example, there may be little point in investigating a material price variance if the business has no control over the price. This could happen, for example, if the firm has a long-term contract with a supplier at a price determined by the international market. In contrast, the manager is likely to follow up on a variance that should be controllable, such as a direct labour efficiency variance or a direct material quantity variance.

Favourable variances

It is just as important to investigate significant favourable variances as it is to investigate significant unfavourable variances. For example, a favourable direct labour efficiency variance may indicate that employees have developed a more efficient way of doing a production task. By investigating the variance, management can learn about the improved method. It may be possible to use a similar approach elsewhere in the organisation.

A continuing favourable variance may also indicate that the standard for material or labour is too loose or inaccurate, and needs to be made more challenging.

A statistical approach to variance investigation

There are many reasons for standard cost variances. For example, an unfavourable direct labour efficiency variance could be caused by inexperienced employees, employee inefficiency, poor-quality raw materials, poorly maintained machinery, an intentional work slowdown due to employee grievances, or many other factors. In addition to these substantive reasons, there are purely random causes of variances. People are not machines, and they are not perfectly consistent in their work habits. *Random fluctuations* in direct labour efficiency variances can be caused by such factors as employee illnesses, or simply fatigue.

Ideally, managers should sort the randomly caused variances from those with substantive and controllable underlying causes. While it is impossible to accomplish this with 100 per cent accuracy, a statistical control chart can help. A **statistical control chart** plots standard cost variances across time and compares them with a statistically determined **critical value** that triggers an investigation. This critical value is usually determined by assuming that standard cost variances have a normal probability distribution with a mean of zero. The critical value is set at some multiple of the distribution's standard deviation. Variances greater than the critical value are investigated.[8]

Exhibit 10.7 shows a statistical control chart for the direct labour efficiency variance for R.M. Williams' production of moleskin pants for the first six months of 20X6. The critical value is one standard deviation from the mean. This was determined to be a variance of R3000. This chart indicates that only the May variance would have been investigated, as it is greater than R3000. The variances for the remaining five months would not be investigated. The assumption is that these minor variances are due to random causes and are not worth investigating, as this would be costly and there may be no problems to correct.

Determining the causes of variances

L.O. 7 We have discussed the process of *management by exception*, where only significant variances are reported to management and investigated. However, what do we mean by *variance investigation*, and what type of corrective actions can be taken after investigation?

Once variances are considered significant, managers need to find out the causes of those variances. It is not enough merely to calculate and report standard cost variances. The control process is not complete unless the causes of variances are identified and corrective actions are taken.

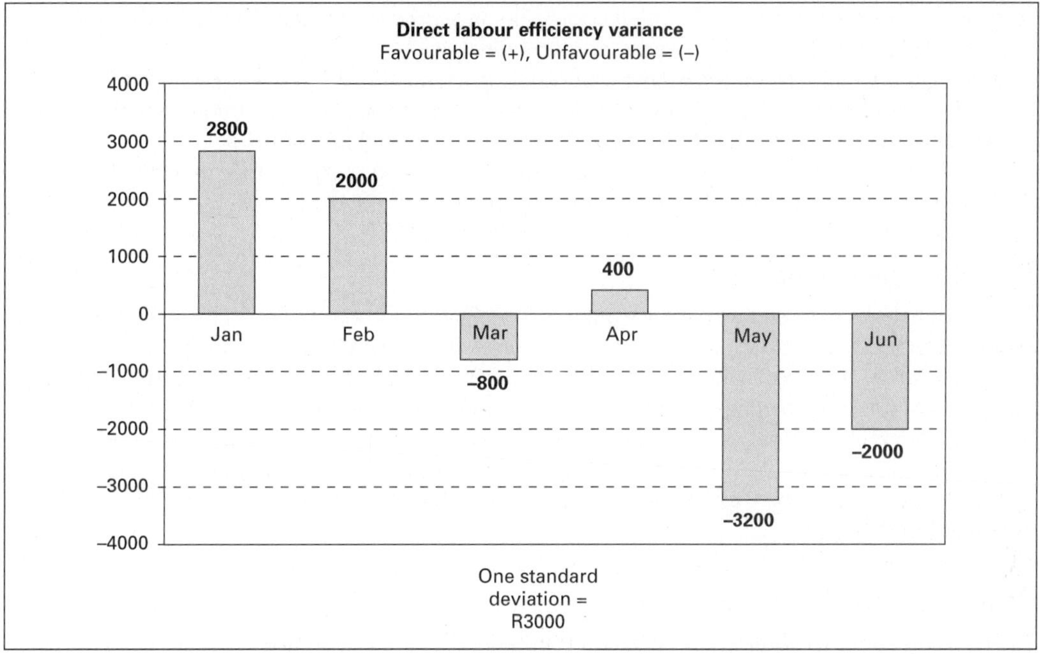

Exhibit 10.7 Statistical control chart for direct labour efficiency variance, R.M. Williams, January to June 20X6

Investigation may entail talking to managers and other employees who are familiar with the operations to find out the causes of the significant variances. Sometimes, managers or supervisors in charge of departments are required to provide written explanations for significant variances as part of their monthly variance reports. In these situations, the accountant may provide the monthly standard cost variances to departmental supervisors, who then prepare a report for management. This report may include the reasons for significant variances and the steps that have been taken, or will be taken, to correct operations (if corrections need to be made).

Variance investigation at R.M. Williams

At the beginning of October the accountant at R.M. Williams, Bill Sithole, visited the purchasing manager, Tariq Fataar, to ask him about the causes of the *direct material price variance*. You will remember that this variance arose because the moleskin fabric was purchased for R25.40 per metre instead of the standard price of R25.00 per metre. While the variance was only 1.6 per cent of standard, the price of moleskin fabric was contracted for in advance and price variances should not occur.

Tariq knew the cause immediately. When Tariq estimated the standard material prices for 20X6, he had assumed a material price of R25.00 per metre for purchases made from January to October, with a rise to R25.50 per metre in November. While the price rise had occurred two months earlier than anticipated, it was a lower price rise than expected. Tariq had contacted the supplier, who assured him that no further price rises would occur that year. Bill was satisfied that no further action needed to be taken on this item.

The *direct material quantity variance* was only 4.8 per cent of the standard. However, in the previous two months there had also been recurring, unfavourable, direct material quantity variances amounting to 4 per cent and 4.5 per cent. These all related to using too much moleskin fabric compared with standard. Bill Sithole called on the production supervisor of the Clothing Department,

Hannah Visser. Hannah was not at all sure why her department was using too much material to manufacture the moleskins. There were several possibilities: Were mistakes being made in the stitching processes, resulting in garments being secretly discarded? Were there clerical errors in recording how many pairs of pants were being produced? (This seemed unlikely.) Were some operators wasting material during the cutting stage? The answer was not clear, but Hannah intended to keep a close eye on this area during the next few weeks.

Although the *direct labour efficiency variance* was not significant, Bill was curious to know why it was a favourable variance. Hannah explained that the reason for the improvement in direct labour time was the increasing skills of the operators in the stitching process.[9]

Bill Sithole himself knew that the unfavourable direct labour rate variance was due to a rise in the award wage that had not been anticipated when he set the budget.

Taking corrective actions

Corrective actions may be taken after variance investigation to correct non-standard practices that are taking place. In our example, there were no corrective actions relating to the price of the moleskin fabric or to the direct labour wage rate, as these events could not be changed – they were outside the control of managers within the company. After a week of observing the production process, Hannah Visser introduced tighter control over procedures in the cutting area to detect any wastage of material that was occurring. No actions were needed regarding the favourable direct labour efficiency variance. However, Bill Sithole noted that the increased skills would be reflected in tighter standards next year.

Costs and benefits of investigation

The decision about whether to investigate a standard cost variance should consider costs and benefits. The costs of investigation include the time spent by employees investigating the problem. Other costs include disruption to the production process as the investigation is conducted and corrective actions taken to eliminate the cause of a variance.

The *benefits* of a variance investigation include reduced future production costs if the cause of an unfavourable variance is eliminated. Another potential benefit is the cost savings that can arise when the cause of a favourable variance is discovered and used to improve work practices.

Weighing these considerations requires the judgement of skilful and experienced managers. A key to this judgement is an intimate understanding of the organisation's production processes, and day-to-day contact with its operations.

Behavioural impact of standard costing

L.O. 8

Standard costing does not identify the causes of problems that may be occurring in the production processes, but it can indicate to managers the areas that should be investigated to help uncover problems. Standard costs, budgets and variances are also used to evaluate the performance of employees and departments. Comparing the performance of individuals with standards or budgets is often used to determine salary increases, bonuses and promotions, and this practice can profoundly influence behaviour.

For example, suppose that the manager of a hotel's Food and Beverage Department earns a bonus when food and beverage costs are below the budgeted amount, given actual sales volume. This reward structure may provide a powerful incentive for the manager to keep food and beverage costs under control. But such an incentive can result in either positive or negative consequences. The desire for the bonus may induce the manager to seek the most economical food suppliers and to watch more carefully for employee theft and waste. However, it could also persuade the manager to buy cheaper but less tender steaks for the restaurant, and to make smaller meals. This could ultimately result in lost patronage for the restaurant and the hotel. One aspect of skilful management is knowing how to use standards, budgets and variances to encourage the best performance from employees. Unfortunately, there are no simple answers or formulas for success in this area.

In South Africa, the practice of linking compensation schemes to the attaining of standards or budgets is increasing. There are examples of this occurring at middle management levels and at the production level. Performance measurement and reward systems are studied in more detail in Chapter 13.

REAL LIFE: PERFORMANCE-RELATED PAY AND THE DEVELOPMENT OF LABOUR STANDARDS AT A MEN'S SUIT MANUFACTURER

The Flair Group is a manufacturer of men's suits. It competes at the quality end of the suit market, and its growth and profitability are due to investment in the latest production technology and to harmonious employee relations. The production workers' pay was based on performance, using complex measurements of work difficulty. Labour standards were based on time and motion studies. Initially, these were developed using the old methods of 'clipboard and stopwatch', but this was not effective. The owner described the problems: 'The workers played a battle of wits to create the slowest work rate possible for the calculations.' Since 1984 the factory had used video recording to set the standard labour hours. This method was accepted as objective by both managers and production workers. The pay-by-results scheme was designed, implemented and maintained by a special work group.[10]

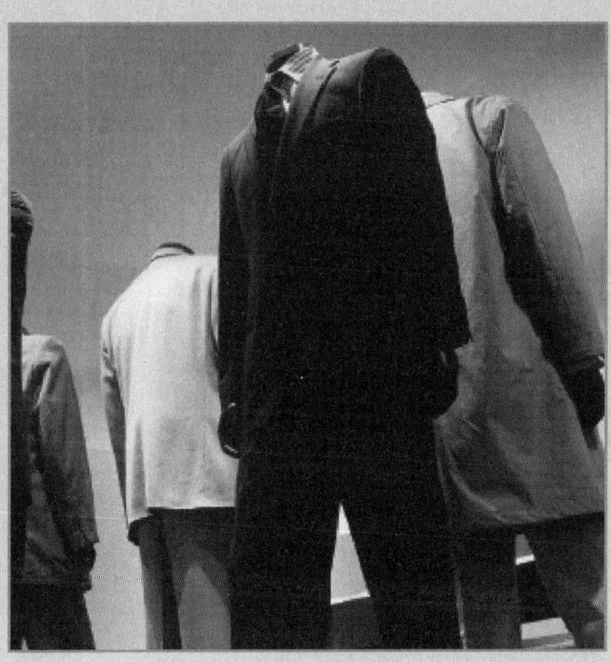

© Shania Shegedyn
Hugo Boss suits
Source: Thomas (1993)

Cost control through assigning responsibility

L.O. 9

Cost control is accomplished through the efforts of individual managers and employees in an organisation. By deciding which managers are in the best position to *influence or control* each standard cost variance, the management accountant can help the organisation to derive the greatest benefit from standard cost variance analysis.

Responsibility accounting was discussed in Chapter 9. Standard setting and variance reporting should follow responsibility accounting frameworks. It is important that those managers who are to be held responsible for achieving certain cost or efficiency standards can control these outcomes and that they are also involved in setting those standards. Who is responsible for the direct material price and quantity variances, or the direct labour rate and efficiency variances? Answering these questions is often difficult, because it is rare that any one person completely controls any event.

Nevertheless, it is often possible to identify the manager who is most able to influence a particular variance, even if he or she does not exercise complete control over the outcome.

Responsibility for variances

In general, we can isolate responsibility for certain variances to particular managers and departments.

Direct material price variance

The purchasing manager is generally in the best position to influence material price variances. Through skilful purchasing practices, an expert purchasing manager can obtain the best prices for purchased goods and services. To achieve this goal, the purchasing manager may buy materials in large quantities to gain discounts, negotiate purchase contracts, compare prices among suppliers, and use global sourcing.

Despite these skills, the purchasing manager is not in complete control of prices. The need to purchase component parts with precise engineering specifications, the frequent rush requests from production departments and worldwide shortages of critical materials all contribute to the challenges faced by the purchasing manager. If the direct material price variance is calculated at the time the material is used in production, then recognition of the full price variance is delayed. This makes it more difficult to take prompt corrective action.

Direct material quantity variance

Production managers or supervisors are usually in the best position to influence material quantity variances. Skilful supervision of production employees coupled with the careful use and handling of materials, contributes to minimal waste. Production engineers are also partially responsible for material quantity variances, since they decide the grade and technical specifications of materials and component parts. Sometimes, using a low-grade material may result in greater waste than using a high-grade material.

Direct labour rate variance

Direct labour rate variances generally result from using a mix of employees that is different from the mix anticipated when the standards were set. Wage rates differ among employees according to the employees' different skills. Using employees who are more highly skilled than a task requires can result in unfavourable direct labour rate variances. The production manager (or supervisor) is generally in the best position to influence the work schedules of employees.

Direct labour efficiency variance

Again, the production supervisor is usually most responsible for the efficient use of employee time. This may be achieved by creating a work environment that encourages employees to work towards production goals. Moreover, through designing effective work schedules the efficiency of employees can be maximised.

Interaction between variances

When there are *interactions* between variances it becomes difficult to assign responsibility for particular variances. To illustrate, consider the following example. In May 20X6 Tariq Fataar, the purchasing manager at R.M. Williams, obtained a special price on boot leather from a new supplier. This leather was to be used for the upper section of the boot. When the material was placed into production it was found to be of a different grade, and the production workers had difficulty using it. The leather was not as malleable as the standard boot leather, and it bent less easily during the formation of the boots. The company could have returned the material to the supplier but that would have interrupted production and kept the company from filling its orders on time. Since using the non-standard material would not affect the quality of the boots, the plant manager decided to keep the material and make the most of the situation.

The result was that the company incurred four interrelated variances during May. The material was less expensive than was the standard material, so the direct material price variance was favourable. However, the employees had difficulty using the material, which resulted in more waste than expected, and so the company incurred an unfavourable direct material quantity variance. Also, due to the difficulty in working with the leather, the employees worked more than the standard amount of time to form the boots. This resulted in an unfavourable direct labour efficiency variance. Finally, the production manager had to use employees who were more highly skilled to work with the non-standard material. Since these people earned relatively high wages, the direct labour rate variance was also unfavourable.

Such interactions between variances make it more difficult to assign responsibility for any particular variance.

Trade-offs between variances

Does the previous example mean that the decision to buy and use the non-standard material was a poor one? Not necessarily. Suppose the amounts of the variances were as follows:

R8 500	Favourable direct material price variance
(1 000)	Unfavourable direct material quantity variance
(2 000)	Unfavourable direct labour rate variance
(1 500)	Unfavourable direct labour efficiency variance
R4 000	Total favourable variance

The company saved R4000 in total due to the purchasing of a different grade of leather. Given that the quality of the product was not compromised, the plant manager acted wisely in deciding to keep the material. However, there could be other favourable implications of the decision. If the non-standard material was purchased because the standard material would be unavailable for some time, then other costs may have been avoided. These include customer dissatisfaction and the potential loss of sales that could have arisen if the company had not produced the product but had waited for the standard material.

It is important to note that an unfavourable variance does not necessarily indicate that a particular manager has made an incorrect decision. Consider the production manager who may have had no influence over those unfavourable variances that were supposedly 'under his control'. Similarly, a favourable variance does not always imply that a manager has acted in the company's best interests. In the above example, the purchasing manager's decision to buy a non-standard material could have been very costly for the company.

The overall favourable variance that resulted from the decision raises another issue for consideration: should the company now continue to purchase the 'new' material and adjust the material and labour standards to reflect the new specifications?

The message here is that we need to interpret variances cautiously. The reason for investigating significant variances is to help point to causes of variances and to find answers if possible. We should not necessarily assume that a favourable variance means that something desirable has occurred, or that an unfavourable variance means there is a problem. Also, the source of a variance may lie in a different area of the business from where the variance is being reported.

Standard costs for product costing

L.O. 10

Our discussion of standard costing so far has focused on its use in evaluating performance and controlling costs. However, many firms that use standard costs for control also use them for product costing. Recall from Chapter 4 that product costing is the process of accumulating product-related costs and assigning them to final products. Product costs are used for various purposes in both financial and management accounting.

As production takes place, product costs are added to the work in process inventory account. The flow of product costs through a firm's manufacturing accounts is outlined in Exhibit 10.8.

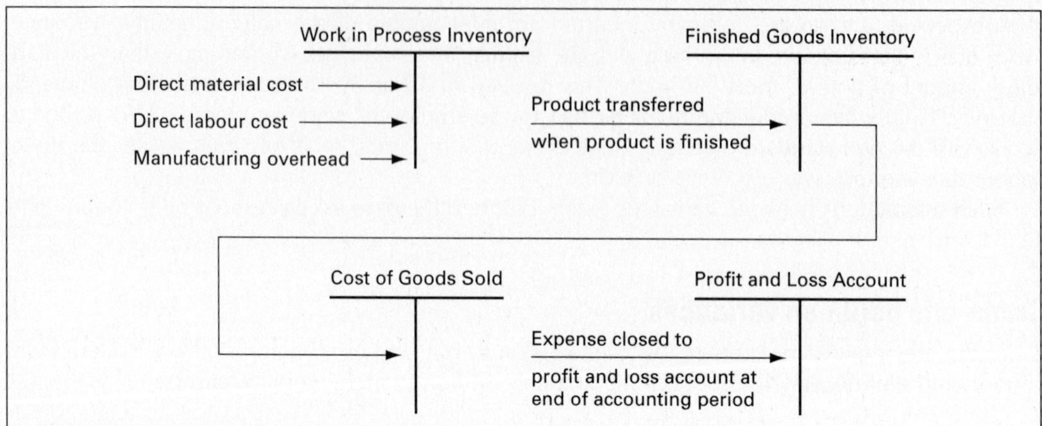

Exhibit 10.8 Flow of costs through manufacturing accounts

Different types of product costing systems can be distinguished by how the costs are measured. In Chapter 7, we described *actual* and *normal* costing systems. In these systems, the *actual* costs of direct material and direct labour are charged to work in process inventory. In a **standard costing system**, the *standard* costs of direct material and direct labour are recorded in work in process inventory.

Journal entries using standard costs

L.O. 11 To illustrate the use of standard costs in product costing, we will continue our illustration of R.M. Williams. In Exhibit 10.2 we saw that during September the company purchased R635 000 of direct materials. In addition, for 2000 pairs of moleskins the standard direct material cost was R155 000 (R77.50 × 2000). The following journal entries record these events and isolate the direct material price and quantity variances:

Raw material inventory: *PQ* × *SP*	R625 000	
Direct material price variance: *PQ* (*AP* − *SP*)	R10 000	
Accounts payable: *PQ* × *AP*		R635 000
To record the purchase of raw material and an unfavourable price variance.		
Work in process inventory: *SQ* × *SP*	R155 000	
Direct material quantity variance: *SP* (*AQ* − *SQ*)	R7 500	
Raw material inventory: *AQ* × *SP*		R162 500
To record the use of direct material in production and an unfavourable quantity variance.		

Notice that the material purchase is recorded in the raw material inventory account at its standard price – that is, 25 000 metres of cotton fabric at R25.00 per metre, which is R625 000.

The R155 000 debit entry to work in process inventory is also charged at the standard cost of the materials to production. The two variances are isolated in their own variance accounts. Since they are both unfavourable, they are represented by debit entries.

The following journal entry records the actual September cost of direct labour, as an addition to wages payable. The entry also adds the standard cost of direct labour to work in process inventory and isolates the direct labour variances.

Work in process inventory: *SH* × *SR*	R100 800	
Direct labour rate variance: *AH* (*AR* − *SR*)	R5 400	
Direct labour efficiency variance: *SR* (*AH* − *SH*)		R3 600
Wages payable: *AH* × *AR*		R102 600
To record the usage of direct labour and the direct labour variances for September.		

The standard cost of direct labour is R100 800 (2000 pairs of moleskins × R50.40 per unit). The total wages paid to production workers, R102 600, are credited to the wages payable liability account. Since the direct labour efficiency variance is favourable, it is recorded as a credit entry.

Disposition of variances

Variance accounts are closed at the end of the accounting period. Most companies close their variance accounts directly to cost of goods sold expense. The journal entry required to close the R.M.Williams' September variance accounts is as follows:

Cost of goods sold	R19 300	
Direct labour efficiency variance	R3 600	
Direct labour rate variance		R5 400
Direct material price variance		R10 000
Direct material quantity variance		R7 500

The increase of R19 300 in cost of goods sold is explained as follows:

	Unfavourable variance	Favourable variance	Net increase
Direct labour efficiency variance		3600	
Direct labour rate variance	5400		
Direct material price variance	10 000		
Direct material quantity variance	7500		
Total	22 900	3600	19 300

The unfavourable variances are the costs of operating inefficiently compared with the standards, thus causing cost of goods sold to be higher. The opposite is true for favourable variances.

An alternative method of variance disposition is to prorate variances between work in process inventory, finished goods inventory and cost of goods sold.[11] This accounting treatment spreads the additional costs among the inventories through which the manufacturing costs flow.

REAL LIFE: THE USE OF STANDARD COSTING IN SOUTH AFRICA

In a survey by Waweru et al. (2005) of 52 South African firms, it was found that 19 (36.5 per cent) respondents were currently using a standard costing system and 35 (67.3 per cent) respondents indicated that they had used standard costing within the last 10 years. This compares to the UK survey by Drury where it was found that 74 per cent of companies were using a standard costing system. In South Africa, most companies using standard costing will review their standards within three months. Companies were asked about the purposes of variance investigation and control was rated as extremely important while the use of standard costs for budgeting purposes was viewed as being of lesser importance. The authors argue that economic uncertainty and greater volatility in South Africa made the use of standard costing of less value than in the UK. Greater exchange rate volatility over the period of the survey may have certainly impacted on the value of using standard costs over this specific time. A more plausible reason for the difference may relate to the fact that the Drury survey was targeted at manufacturing firms while the South African survey also included service firms. In another survey, Jacobs found that 51 per cent of respondents used standard costing.

Cost flow under standard costing

In a standard costing system, *standard* costs are recorded in the raw material inventory and work in process inventory. Therefore, standard costs, rather than actual costs, flow through to the finished goods inventory and cost of goods sold.

REAL LIFE: USING STANDARD COSTS TO VALUE INVENTORY

In terms of the International Accounting Standard (IAS 2) companies may use standard costs to value inventory if these costs approximate actual cost. The following represent examples of South African companies that employ standard costs to value inventory:

Murray & Roberts

In certain business operations the standard cost method is used. The standard costs take into account normal levels of materials and supplies, labour, efficiency and capacity utilisation. These are regularly reviewed and, if necessary, revised in the light of current conditions. All abnormal variances are immediately expensed as overhead costs.

Highveld Steel

Finished goods, work-in-progress and consignment stock are valued at standard cost, which includes an appropriate apportionment of overheads. Standard cost approximates actual cost determined on the first-in, first-out ('FIFO') basis.

Foskor

Cost of production is calculated on a standard cost basis, which approximates to the actual cost and includes the production overheads. Production overheads are allocated on the basis of normal capacity.

Distell

Distell refers to the use of standard costs in the context of internal control systems of the group.

The systems of internal control are based on established organisational structures, together with written policies and procedures, and provide for suitably qualified employees, segregation of duties, clearly defined lines of authority and accountability. They also include standard cost and budgeting controls, and comprehensive management reporting.

In this chapter we have considered standard costs for direct material and direct labour. However, the system is not complete. We will discuss manufacturing overhead costs under a standard costing system in the next chapter.

Summary

In this chapter we considered the use of standard costs for controlling direct material and direct labour costs. Key points include:

- Organisational control systems provide information to assist in controlling operations, which is an essential part of effective resource management.
- A standard cost is a budgeted cost, based on an estimate of the cost of material, labour and overhead, and represents the resources that should be used to produce one unit of product. A standard cost variance can assist in cost control and is calculated as the difference between actual and standard cost.
- Standards can be developed by analysing historical data, or through the engineering method, which is a method for determining how much it should cost to manufacture the product.
- As discussed in Chapter 9, standards may be developed with the participation of managers who work in the relevant area. This can improve managers' commitment to the target.

- Standards may be based on perfection standards, which assume near-perfect operating conditions, or practical standards, which allow for downtime and wastage.
- Conventional standard cost variances that can be calculated include direct material price variances, direct material quantity variances, direct labour rate variances and direct labour efficiency variances.
- A key aspect of controlling costs is determining which cost variances should be investigated. Management by exception is used to decide which variances are significant and worthy of investigation. Managers can determine the significance of standard cost variances using judgement and experience, and rules of thumb. The absolute and relative sizes of variances, recurrence of variances, variance trends and controllability of variances are all considered in deciding whether variances warrant investigation. On investigation, corrective actions may be taken to bring actual operations into control.
- A variance reporting system forms part of a company's responsibility accounting system. Those managers or employees who are to be held responsible for certain variances should also participate in setting standards for their particular areas.
- The standard costing system can also be used to cost products within the financial accounting system.

The final aspect of controlling costs and operations through variances will be covered in Chapter 12, where we consider how standard costs and flexible budgets can be used to control manufacturing overhead.

References

Drury, C, Bround, S, Osbourne, P and Tayles, M (1993), 'A survey of management accounting practices in UK manufacturing companies', *The Association of Chartered Certified Accountants*, London.

Jacobs, L 2004, 'The impact of the changing practitioner requirements on management accounting education at South African universities', Doctorate of Commerce thesis, University of Pretoria, 2004.

Montgomery, DC 2000, *Introduction to Statistical Process Control*, 4th edn, John Wiley & Sons, New York.

Ryan, TP 2000, *Statistical Methods for Quality Improvement*, John Wiley & Sons, New York.

Thomas, T 1993, 'Manufacturing realist shows how to compete', *Business Review Weekly*, 15 January, pp. 48–50.

Waweru, NM, Hoque, Z and Uliana, E 2005, 'A survey of management accounting practices in South Africa', *Int. J. Accounting, Auditing and Performance Evaluation*, vol. 2, no. 3, 2005.

Distell, 2006 annual report

Foskor, 2006 annual report

Highveld Steel, 2006 annual report

Self study

Self-study problem: Standard costing systems

In November 20X6, R.M. Williams produced 5000 pairs of hiking boots. The standard costs for producing these boots are as follows:

Direct material:	
0.5 metre of leather type A @ R62.00 per metre	31.00
0.3 metre of leather type B @ R45.00 per metre	13.50
Standard direct material cost per unit	44.50
Direct labour:	
1 hour in the leather forming process @ R50.00 per hour	50.00
0.75 hour in the stitching process @ R40.00 per hour	30.00
Standard direct labour cost per unit	80.00

The following actual costs for direct material and direct labour were incurred during November:

- Purchased 10 000 metres of leather type A (for uppers) at R65.50 per metre.
- Purchased 13 000 metres of leather type B (for soles) at R42.65 per metre.
- Used 2560 metres of leather type A at R65.50 per metre.
- Used 1799 metres of leather type B at R42.65 per metre.
- Used 4400 hours of direct labour in leather forming at R50.20 per hour.
- Used 3700 hours in stitching at R43.00 per hour.

Required:
Calculate the direct material variances for each material, and the direct labour variances for each process:

1 using the variance formulas;

2 using the formats shown in Exhibits 10.3 and 10.6.

Solution to Self-study problem

1 Using variance formulas:

Leather type A	**Leather type B**
Direct material price variances:	
= *PQ*(*AP* – *SP*)	= *PQ*(*AP* – *SP*)
= 10 000(R65.50–62.00)	= 13 000(R42.65–R45.00)
= R35 000 U	= R30 550 F
Total direct material price variance = R4450 U	
Direct material quantity variances:	
= *SP*(*AQ* – *SQ*)	= *SP*(*AQ* – *SQ*)
= R62.00(2560 – 2500)	= R45.00(1799 – 1500)
= R3720 U	= R13 455 U
Total direct material quantity variance = R17 175 U	

Leather forming process	Stitching process
Direct labour rate variances:	
= *AH*(*AR* – *SR*)	= *AH*(*AR* – *SR*)
= 4400(R50.20 – R50.00)	= 3700(R43.00 – R40.00)
= R880 U	= R11100 U
Total direct labour rate variance = R11 980 U	
Direct labour efficiency variances:	
= *SR*(*AH* – *SH*)	= *SR*(*AH* – *SH*)
= R50(4400 – 5000)	= R40(3700 – 3750)
= R30 000 F	= R2000 F
Total labour efficiency variance = R32 000 F	

2 Using variance diagrams:

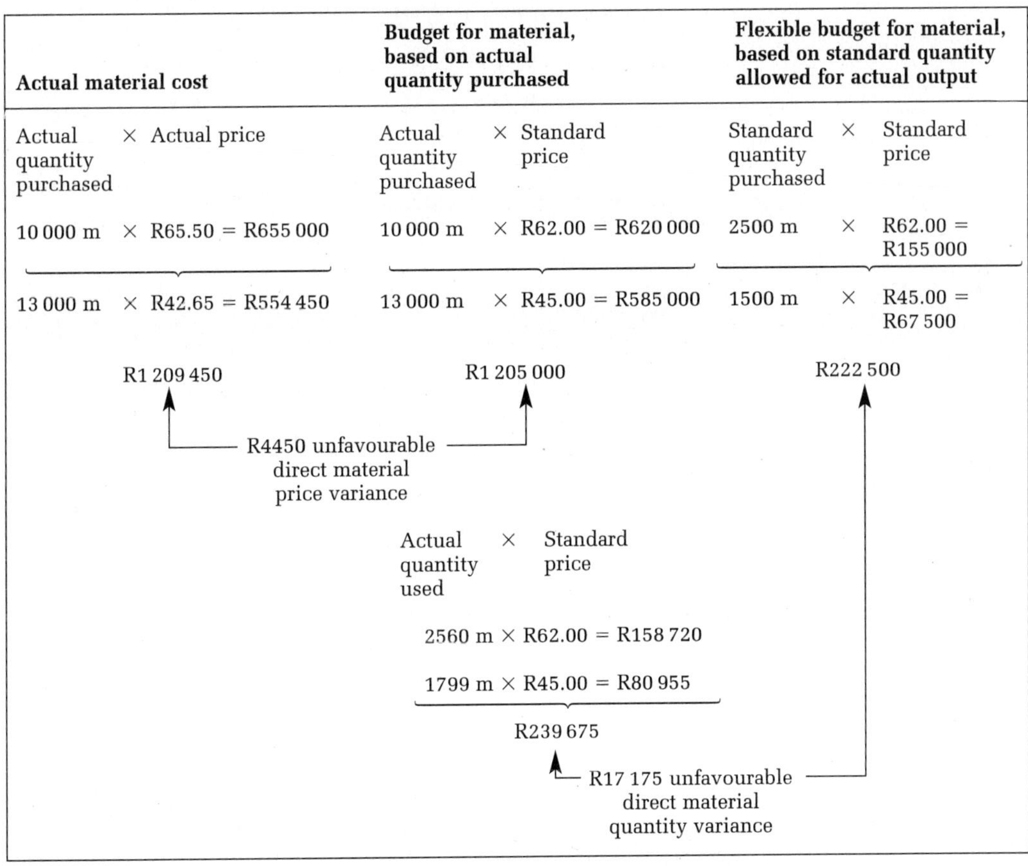

Exhibit 10.9 Direct material variances, R.M. Williams – boots (Self-study problem)

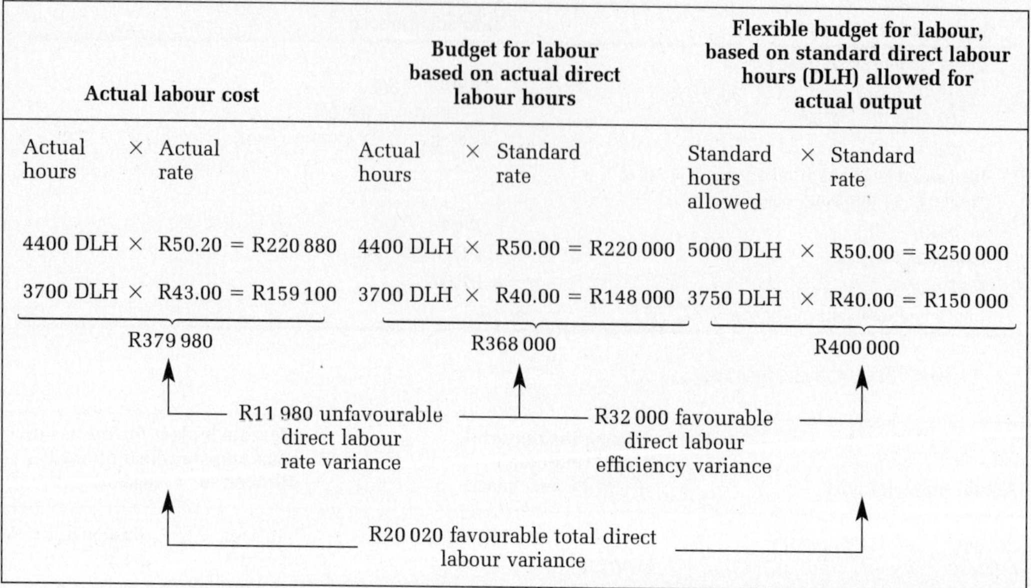

Exhibit 10.10 Direct labour variances, R.M. Williams – boots (Self-study problem)

Cybersearch

1 Find websites of organisations that report and analyse cost variances as part of their performance reports. Contrast the types of cost variances that you find with those described in the chapter.

2 Look for websites of organisations that are using statistical process control (SPC).

   (a) Within what industries do these organisations operate?

   (b) In what types of manufacturing processes was SPC used?

   (c) Why do you think that SPC is useful in these particular industries/processes, and not others?

Appendix to Chapter 10

Graphical analysis of variances

L.O. 12

A graphical analysis provides additional insight into the calculation and interpretation of variances. During December 20X6 the accountant at R.M. Williams recorded the following direct labour data in the Clothing Department:

Actual direct labour cost: 10 100 hours at R39 per hour
Standard direct labour cost: 10 000 hours at R36 per hour

Direct labour rate variance = $AH(AR - SR)$
= 10 100(R39−R36)
= R30 300 unfavourable

Direct labour efficiency variance = $SR(AH - SH)$
= R36(10 100–10 000)
= R3600 unfavourable

Exhibit 10.11 provides a graphical analysis of the December direct labour variances. The graph shows the direct labour rate per hour on the vertical axis, and the direct labour hours on the horizontal axis. Since a labour cost is found by multiplying the rate by the hours, the labour cost is depicted on the graph as an area. The white rectangle on the graph represents the standard cost of direct labour, given actual output (R360 000 = 10 000 hours × R36 per hour). The largest rectangle on the graph, which is enclosed by the exterior lines, represents the actual cost of direct labour used in December (R393 900 = 10 100 hours × R39 per hour). The difference between the largest rectangle and the white rectangle represents the total direct labour variance (R33 900 = R393 900−R360 000). This area is coloured on the graph to highlight the variance.

The total direct labour variance is divided into the rate variance and the efficiency variance. The rate variance, calculated as $AH(AR - SR)$, is represented on the graph by the medium grey and dark grey areas. The direct labour efficiency variance, calculated as $SR(AH - SH)$, is depicted on the graph as the light grey area. The areas representing the rate and efficiency variances add up to equal the total direct labour variance.

Joint rate efficiency variance

Note that the small dark rectangle in the upper right corner of the graph represents the product of the rate difference (R39−R36) and the difference in hours (10 100−10 000). This area represents the portion of the rate variance that is really the joint result of:

1 paying more than the standard rate; and
2 using more labour hours than the standard allowance.

Thus the rate variance, $AH(AR - SR)$, does not result only from deviations from the standard rate.

This problem in interpreting the rate variance could be avoided by calculating a **pure rate variance** and a **joint rate efficiency variance** as follows:

Pure rate variance = $SH(AR - SR)$
Joint rate efficiency variance = $(AH - SH) \times (AR - SR)$

Calculating these variances for R.M. Williams for December yields the following results:

Pure rate variance = 10 000(R39 − R36)
= R30 000 unfavourable
Joint rate efficiency variance = (10 100−10 000) × (R39−R36)
= R300 unfavourable

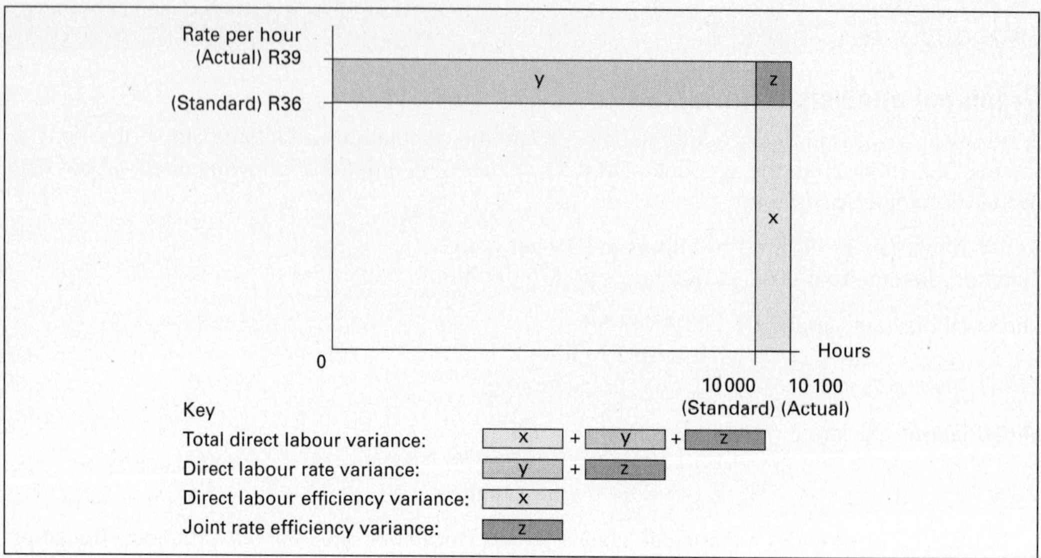

Exhibit 10.11 Graphical analysis of direct labour variances, R.M. Williams

Together these variances add up to the direct labour rate variance, as it is typically calculated. While this breakdown of the rate variance makes sense conceptually, it is used only rarely in practice.

Questions

10.1 What are the three parts of a control system? Use an example to explain how such a system works. (Do not use a thermostat or budget example.)

10.2 Explain what is meant by the term *management by exception*, and why it may be used.

10.3 Describe the two approaches to setting standards, and explain why you would choose to use one approach over the other.

10.4 Explain how benchmarking may relate to the formulation of standard costs.

10.5 Explain how a business can use standard costing for control.

10.6 Distinguish between *perfection standards* and *practical standards*. Which type of standard is likely to produce the best motivational effects?

10.7 Describe how an accounting firm might use standard costs.

10.8 How do responsibility accounting concepts relate to standard cost variance reporting?

10.9 Which managers should be involved in setting standard costs?

10.10 Explain how standard material prices and quantities can be determined.

10.11 List some of the possible causes of an unfavourable direct material price variance.

10.12 Explain which manager is usually in the best position to influence the direct material price variance.

10.13 List some of the possible causes of an unfavourable direct material quantity variance.

10.14 Explain which manager is usually in the best position to influence the direct material quantity variance.

10.15 Explain the two ways of calculating a direct material price variance. Which one is the best?

10.16 What is the meaning of the *direct labour rate variance*? What are some possible causes?

10.17 Explain which manager is generally in the best position to influence the direct labour rate variance.

10.18 What might an unfavourable direct labour efficiency variance indicate? What actions might be taken to correct this variance?

10.19 Explain which manager is generally in the best position to influence the direct labour efficiency variance.

10.20 What is a statistical control chart and how can it be used?

10.21 Describe the factors that managers often consider when assessing the significance of a variance.

10.22 Why do we need to assess the significance of variances? Why can't we just investigate all variances?

10.23 Comment on the following: 'Investigating variances is simple. We simply pick out the largest unfavourable variances and the rest look after themselves.'

10.24 What is meant by the expression *interaction between variances*?

10.25 Describe how, and why, standard costs are used for product costing.

10.26 (appendix) Explain the difference between the traditional direct labour rate variance and a pure rate variance.

10.27 (appendix) Explain the meaning of *the joint rate efficiency variance for direct labour.*

Exercises

E10.28 Calculating standards: manufacturer

Khumalo Hardwoods produces handcrafted coffee tables. A standard size table requires 10 metres of hardwood, of which 2 metres of scrap timber is normally left over. Hardwood costs R3 per metre, plus R1 per metre in transportation charges. It usually takes 4 direct labour hours to produce one table, and the hourly rate is R30. The company incurs on-costs of 24 per cent of wages, and this is regarded as part of the cost of labour.

Required:

1 Calculate the standard direct material cost of a coffee table.
2 Calculate the standard direct labour cost of a coffee table.

E10.29 Straightforward calculation of variances; variance diagrams: manufacturer

During June Gorgio Ltd's material purchases amounted to 6500 kilograms at a price of R7.40 per kg. Actual costs incurred in the production of 2000 units were as follows:

Direct labour	R118 035	(R18.30 per hour)
Direct material	31 820	(R7.40 per kg)

The standards for one unit of Gorgio's product are as follows:

Direct labour	Direct material
Quantity: 3 hours per unit	Quantity: 2 kg per unit
Rate: R18 per hour	Price: R7.20 per kg

Required:

1 Calculate the direct material price and quantity variances and the direct labour rate and efficiency variances. Indicate whether each variance is favourable or unfavourable.
2 Draw diagrams depicting the direct material and direct labour variances, similar to the diagrams in Exhibits 10.3 and 10.5.

E10.30 Cost variance investigation

The accountant for Lane and Company uses a statistical control chart to help management to decide when to investigate variances. The critical value is one standard deviation from the mean. The company incurred the following direct labour efficiency variances during the first six months of the year:

January	R 2500 F	April	R 9000 U
February	8000 U	May	10 500 U
March	7000 U	June	12 000 U

The standard direct labour cost during each of these months was R200 000. The accountant has estimated that the firm's monthly direct labour efficiency variances have a standard deviation of R9500.

Required:

1 (a) Draw a statistical control chart and plot the variance data given above.
  (b) Which variances should be investigated? Explain why.

2 Suppose that the accountant's rule of thumb is to investigate all variances equal to or greater than 5 per cent of standard cost. Which variances will be investigated?

3 Would you investigate any of the variances listed above other than those indicated by the rules discussed in requirements 1 and 2? Explain your answer.

E10.31 Straightforward calculation of variances; variance diagrams: manufacturer

Naran Plastic Company manufactures plastic buckets. A unit of production is a box of 4 buckets. The following standards have been set by the production engineering staff and the factory accountant:

Direct material	Direct labour
Quantity: 4 kg	Quantity: 0.25 hour
Price: R0.80 per kg	Rate: R20 per hour

Actual material purchases amounted to 240 000 kilograms at R0.81 per kilogram. Actual costs incurred in the production of 50 000 units were as follows:

Direct material	R170 100 for 210 000 kilograms
Direct labour	R273 000 for 13 000 hours

Required:

1 Use the variance formulas to calculate the direct material price and quantity variances and the direct labour rate and efficiency variances. Indicate whether each variance is favourable or unfavourable.

2 Use diagrams similar to those in Exhibits 10.3 and 10.5 to determine the direct material and direct labour variances.

E10.32 Journal entries under standard costing: manufacturer

Refer to the data in Exercise 10.31.

Required:

1 Prepare journal entries to:
  (a) record the purchase of direct material on credit
  (b) add direct material and direct labour cost to work in process inventory
  (c) record the direct material and direct labour variances
  (d) close these variances to cost of goods sold

2 Set up ledger accounts, and post the journal entries to the general ledger.

E10.33 Reconstructing standard cost information from partial data: manufacturer

Part of your company's accounting database was destroyed in the recent floods that spread through your town. You have been able to gather the following data from your files. Reconstruct the remaining information (where there is a question mark) using the available data. All the raw material purchased during the period was used in production.

	Direct material	Direct labour
Standard quantity per unit of output	?	?
Standard price or rate per unit of input	R16 per kg	?
Actual quantity used per unit of output	?	3.5 hours
Actual price or rate per unit of input	R14 per kg	R21 per hour
Actual output	20 000 units	20 000 units
Direct material price variance	R120 000 F	–
Direct material quantity variance	?	–
Total of direct material variances	R40 000 F	–
Direct labour rate variance	–	?
Direct labour efficiency variance	–	R200 000 F
Total of direct labour variances	–	R135 000 F

E10.34 Direct material and direct labour variances: service firm

Ralph Ltd is engaged in aerial spraying of vegetables. Operating costs are difficult to control, so standard costs and standard cost variances are reported. The following standards were developed for the 'maxi-protect' spraying service. This is one of the company's major products.

	Standard quantity	Standard price or rate	Standard cost
Direct material (insecticide)	8 kg	R17.50 per kg	R140.00
Direct labour	2 hours	R200 per hour	400.00
Total			R540.00

During May, Ralph purchased 160 000 kg of insecticide at a total cost of R3 040 000. The total wages for May were R50 000, 40 per cent of which was direct labour cost of the maxi-protect sprays. Ralph completed 40 maxi-protect sprays during May, using 400 kg of insecticide and 90 direct labour hours.

Required:

Calculate the following variances for May, and indicate whether each is favourable or unfavourable:

1 The direct material price variance.
2 The direct material quantity variance.
3 The direct labour rate variance.
4 The direct labour efficiency variance.

(*CMA, adapted*)

E10.35 Determining standard costs: service firm

You have just been appointed the cost accountant for a new company called Amazing Joy Flights. In its first few years the company will provide three types of scenic flights: 'Over and Around Cape Town', 'The Winelands', and 'The Surf Coast'. Each takes a different length of time, involves different flight crews and different food and (sometimes very expensive) beverages.

Required:

1 Explain the processes that you will undertake to develop standard costs for material and labour. Make sure that your answer is specific to the company and to the services that are being offered.
2 Outline how the company management would use these standard costs. Once again, make sure your answer is specific to the particular company.

E10.36 Determining standard material cost: manufacturer

Salie Valley Chemical Company manufactures industrial chemicals. The company plans to introduce a new chemical solution and needs to develop a standard product cost. The new chemical solution is made by combining a chemical compound (nyclyn) with a solution (salex), heating the mixture to boiling point, adding a second compound (protet), and bottling the resulting solution in 10-litre containers. The initial mix, which is 11 litres in volume, consists of 12 kilograms of nyclyn and 9.6 litres of salex. A 1 litre reduction in volume occurs during the boiling process. The solution is cooled slightly before 5 kilograms of protet are added. The protet evaporates, so it does not affect the total liquid volume.

The purchase prices of the raw materials used in the manufacture of this new chemical solution are as follows:

Nyclyn	R1.45 per kg
Salex	R1.80 per litre
Protet	R2.40 per kg

Required:

Determine the standard material cost of a 10-litre container of the new product.

(CMA, adapted)

E10.37 Joint rate efficiency variance; graphing variances (appendix): manufacturer

Refer to the data in Exercise 10.29. Calculate the pure rate variance and joint rate efficiency variance for direct labour. Draw a graph of the direct labour variances similar to the graph in Exhibit 10.11.

Problems

P10.38 Direct material and labour variances: manufacturer

During January Tasman Ltd produced 7800 valve units, and the accounting records indicated the following:

Direct material purchased	25 000 kg	@	R5.20 kg
Direct material used	23 100 kg		
Direct labour	40 100 hours	@	R36.00 per hour

The valve has the following standard prime costs:

Direct material	3 kg	@	R 5.00 per kg	R15.00
Direct labour hours	5 hours	@	R 34.00 per hour	170.00
Standard prime cost per unit				R185.00

Required:

1 Prepare a schedule of standard production costs for January.

2 For the month of January, calculate the following variances, indicating whether each is favourable or unfavourable:

(a) direct material price variance

(b) direct material quantity variance

(c) direct labour rate variance

(d) direct labour efficiency variance

(CPA, adapted)

P10.39 Direct material variances; journal entries: service firm

Home Assist Pty Ltd has been successful in gaining a major contract to prepare and deliver meals to elderly and disabled people who reside in Richmond. These operations were previously managed by the local council, and the services were outsourced by the council as a cost-saving measure. Home Assist tendered a low price, so it is very focused on cost control. The following standard prices have been established for some major food ingredients:

	Standard price
Lamb roast	R40.00 per kg
Fish fillets	R60.00 per kg
Chips	R30.00 per kg
Mixed veggies	R25.00 per kg

Home Assist purchases the prepared food frozen in 10-kilogram containers, and kitchen workers produce a range of standard meals. Two popular meals are the lamb dinner and the fish dinner. The standard quantities used in these two meals are as follows:

Lamb dinner		Fish dinner	
Lamb roast	200 g	Fish fillets	350 g
Mixed veggies	250 g	Chips	300 g
Chips	150 g		

During March, the company produced 500 lamb dinners and 800 fish dinners. Purchase and usage data for the major material ingredients during March are as follows:

	Purchases in March		
	Qty (kg)	Price per kg	Used in production (kg)
Lamb roast	250	R42.00	105
Fish fillets	170	R63.00	300
Chips	300	R25.00	320
Mixed veggies	200	R27.00	120

Required:

1 Calculate the total direct material quantity variance and price variances for March.

2 Prepare journal entries to record the purchase of material, use of material and incurrence of variances in March.

P10.40 Calculation of variance, analysis: service company

George Arendse runs a landscaping business in a wealthy suburb of Cape Town. He provides a high quality service and focuses on the design and installation of top-of-the-market landscaping plans that include fountains, trees, paving, lighting and exotic plants. However, his clients are continually requesting new services. Therefore, he has recently introduced a range of lawn maintenance services, including fertilisation.

The following data relate to the first year of his landscaping service, when he serviced 55 clients. Each client needs six applications of fertiliser during the year and was charged R200 for each application. For each client, two applications involve Grade A fertiliser, which contains a special ingredient for weed control. The remaining four applications are with Grade B fertiliser.

Based on prior knowledge of the operation and after advice from other landscapers, George estimated the following:

- Typical wage rate per employee: R45 per hour.
- Labour time per application of fertiliser: 40 minutes.
- Purchase price of fertiliser per kilogram: Grade A, R2.50; Grade B, R2.10.

- Fertiliser usage: 40 kilograms per application.

George purchased 5000 kilograms of Grade A fertiliser at R2.65 per kilogram and 10 000 kilograms of Grade B fertiliser at R2.00 per kilogram. Actual usage were 3700 and 7800 kilograms respectively.

A new part-time employee, Fred, was hired to spread the fertiliser. George found he had to pay Fred R57.50 per hour due to the very tight market for fertiliser specialists, and Fred worked a total of 165 hours over the year. Unfortunately, George's new service did not go smoothly, and customers' complaints were much higher than expected.

Required:

1 Calculate the direct material variances for each type of fertiliser.
2 Calculate direct labour variances.
3 Calculate the total actual cost of the new service. Was it a financial success?
4 Consider the variances that you calculated in requirements 1 and 2.
 (a) Was the new service a success from an overall cost-control perspective?
 (b) What seems to have happened that gave rise to customer complaints?
5 In view of the complaints, should the fertiliser service continue to be offered next year?

P10.41 Analysing performance and responsibility, calculating variances: manufacturing company

Suntex uses a standard costing system to assist in the evaluation of production operations. The company has had so many problems in recent months with suppliers and employees that they have hired a new production supervisor, Mark Harris. Mark has been working for the company now for five months and has brought the difficult situations under control.

The director of manufacturing recently commented: 'Harris has really done the trick. The change to the new material suppliers and Harris' team building skills and morale-boosting activities have really made a difference.'

These comments were made after a plant tour, where the director observed a very contented work force and a review of the monthly performance reports. Included in the report were the following variances: direct material R4620 favourable and R6175 favourable. These variances were considered outstanding as they are small and they are favourable. (Suntex's budgeted material and labour costs are usually about R350 000 in total for a similar period.)

Additional information:

- The company purchased and consumed 45 000 kilograms of direct material at R7.70 per kilogram, and paid R16.25 per hour for 20 900 direct labour hours of activity.
- Total units produced were 9500.
- A review of the company's standard cost records shows that each completed unit requires 4.2 kilograms of direct material at R8.80 per kilogram, and 2.6 direct labour hours at R14 per hour.

Required:

1 On the basis of the information contained in the performance report, should Suntex's management be concerned about its variances? Explain why.
2 Calculate the direct material and the direct labour variances.
3 Based on your answer to requirement 2, should Suntex's management be concerned about its variances? Explain why.
4 Are things going as smoothly as the director of manufacturing believes? Evaluate the company's variances and determine whether or not the change to a new supplier and Harris' team building and morale-boosting activities appear to be working.
5 Is it possible that some of the company's current problems are outside of Harris' control?

P10.42 Setting standards; responsibility for variances: publishing company

Associated Media Graphics (AMG) is a rapidly expanding company involved in the publication of teaching materials. Ralph Bekker, owner and manager of AMG, has made a concentrated effort to provide a quality product at a fair price, with delivery on the promised date. Bekker is finding it increasingly difficult to supervise the operations of AMG personally, and he is beginning to institute an organisational structure that will facilitate management control.

One recent change made was the transfer of control over departmental operations from Bekker to each departmental manager. However, the Quality Control Department still reports directly to Bekker, as do the Finance and Accounting departments. A materials manager was hired to purchase all raw materials and to oversee the material-handling (such as receiving and storage) and record-keeping functions. The materials manager is also responsible for maintaining an adequate inventory based on planned production levels.

The loss of personal control over the operations of AMG caused Bekker to look for a method of evaluating performance efficiently. Dave Cupido, a new management accountant, proposed the use of a standard costing system. Variances for material and labour could then be calculated and reported directly to Bekker.

Required:

1 Assume that Associated Media Graphics is going to implement a standard costing system and establish standards for materials and labour. For each of these cost components, identify and discuss:
   (a) which managers should be involved in setting the standards (consider each standard separately)
   (b) what types of information should be considered in establishing the standards
2 Describe the basis that is used to assign responsibility for variances to particular managers or departments under a standard costing system.

(CMA, adapted)

P10.43 Multiple direct labour variances: manufacturer

The accountant for Lovely Manufacturing Company compares each month's actual results with a monthly plan. The standard direct labour rates and the standard hours allowed, given the actual output in April, are shown in the following schedule:

	Standard direct labour rate per hour	Standard direct labour hours allowed, given April output
Labour class III	R48.00	1000
Labour class II	R42.00	1000
Labour class I	R30.00	1000

A new union contract negotiated in March resulted in actual wage rates that differed from the standard rates. The actual direct labour hours worked and the actual direct labour rates per hour experienced for the month of April were as shown below.

	Actual direct labour rate per hour	Actual direct labour hours
Labour class III	R51.60	1100
Labour class II	R45.00	1300
Labour class I	R32.40	750

Required:

1 Calculate the following variances for April, indicating whether each is favourable or unfavourable:
   (a) direct labour rate variance for each labour class
   (b) direct labour efficiency variance for each labour class
2 Discuss the advantages and disadvantages of a standard costing system in which the standard direct labour rates per hour are not changed during the year to reflect events such as a new labour contract.

(CMA, adapted)

P10.44 Development of standard costs: manufacturer

Gauteng Kitchen Products Ltd manufactures kitchen utensils in a number of divisions. Oswood Division is a small plant that manufactures wooden household items. Bert Rivkin, the division's management accountant, plans to implement a standard costing system. Rivkin has collected information from several people within the company that will assist him in developing standards.

One of Oswood's products is a wooden cutting board. Each cutting board requires 0.75 metre of timber and 12 minutes of direct labour time to prepare and cut the timber. The cutting boards are inspected after they are cut. Because the cutting boards are made of natural wood that has imperfections, one board is normally rejected for each five that are accepted. Four rubber foot pads are attached to each good cutting board. A total of 15 minutes is required to attach all four pads and to finish each cutting board. The timber for the cutting boards costs R15.00 per metre, and each foot pad costs R0.10. Direct labour is paid at the rate of R30 per hour.

Required:

1 Develop the standard cost for direct material and direct labour of one cutting board.
2 Explain the role of each of the following people in developing the standards:
   (a) purchasing manager
   (b) industrial engineer
   (c) management accountant

P10.45 Development of standard costs; ethics: manufacturer

Refer to the information in Problem 10.44.

Assume that Oswood's standard costing system has been in place for six months. Jack Smith, the purchasing manager, is about to place an order for wood to be used in Oswood's cutting boards. Smith has found a supplier who will supply the necessary wood at R14 per metre instead of the standard cost of R15. This is very appealing to Smith, since his annual bonus is influenced by any favourable price variances he is able to obtain. Smith is due to be transferred at the end of the year to another division, which manufactures metal kitchen utensils. The transfer is a promotion for Smith.

After further discussions with the potential supplier, Smith realised that the wood being offered would not be well suited for use in cutting boards. Although the wood would seem fine in the manufacturing process, and would result in an attractive product, it would not hold up well over time. This particular species of wood, after repeated cycles of getting wet and then drying out, would tend to crack. Smith figured that it would take about a year for the cutting boards to deteriorate, and then Oswood would be beset with customer complaints.

Smith mulled over the situation for a while and then decided to accept the new supplier's offer. The R14 price would help to get him a nice annual bonus, which would go towards the cost of his annual holiday. By the time the cutting boards cracked and customers started to complain, he would be long gone. Someone else could worry about the problem then, he reasoned. After all, he thought, people shouldn't expect a cutting board to last forever.

Several weeks later, when the invoice for the first shipment of wood came through, Bert Rivkin noticed the large, favourable price variance. When he ran into Smith on the golf course, Rivkin congratulated Smith on the purchase. The following conversation resulted:

Rivkin: That was quite a price break on that wood, Jack. How'd you swing it?
Smith: Hard negotiating, Bert. It's as simple as that.
Rivkin: Is it good wood? And how about the supplier, Jack? Will they deliver on time?
Smith: This supplier is very timely in their deliveries. I made sure of that.
Rivkin: How about the quality, Jack? Did you check into that?
Smith: Sure I did, Bert. Hey, what is this? An interrogation? I thought we were here to play golf.

Rivkin was left feeling puzzled and concerned by Smith's evasiveness. The next day Rivkin talked to the production manager, Amy Skosana, about his concerns. Later that day, Skosana raised the issue with Smith. After a lengthy and sometimes heated exchange, the story came out.

Required:

Discuss the ethical issues involved in this scenario:

1 Did the purchasing manager, Jack Smith, act ethically?
2 Did the accountant, Bert Rivkin, act ethically when he asked Smith about the quality of the wood?
3 Did Rivkin act ethically when he went to the production manager with his concerns?
4 What should Rivkin do now?

(CMA, adapted)

P10.46 Variances; process costing; journal entries: manufacturer

Pointer Ltd manufactures bodyboards. The standard cost for material and labour is R89.20 per board. This includes 8 kilograms of direct material at a standard cost of R5 per kilogram, and 6 hours of direct labour at R16.40 per hour. The following data pertains to November:

- Work in process inventory on 1 November: none
- Work in process inventory on 30 November: 800 units (75 per cent complete as to labour; material is issued at the beginning of processing)
- Units completed: 5600
- Purchases of materials: 50 000 kg for R249 250
- Total actual labour costs: R620 500
- Actual hours of labour: 36 500
- Direct material quantity variance: R1500 unfavourable

Required:

1 Calculate the following amounts, indicating whether each variance is favourable or unfavourable:
   (a) direct labour rate variance for November
   (b) direct labour efficiency variance for November
   (c) actual kilograms of material used in the production process during November
   (d) actual price paid per kilogram of direct material in November
   (e) total amounts of direct material cost and direct labour cost transferred to finished goods inventory during November
   (f) the total amount of direct material and direct labour cost in the ending balance of work in process inventory at the end of November

(Hint: You will need to calculate equivalent units for material and labour, so review Chapter 5.)

2 Prepare journal entries to record the following:
   (a) purchase of raw material
   (b) adding direct material to work in process inventory
   (c) adding direct labour to work in process inventory
   (d) recording of variances

(CMA, adapted)

P10.47 Development of standard costs: manufacturer

ColdKing is a small producer of fruit-flavoured frozen desserts. For many years, ColdKing's products have had strong regional sales on the basis of brand recognition. However, other companies have begun marketing similar products in the area, and price competition has become increasingly important. Ridwaan Khan, the company's accountant, is planning to implement a standard costing system for ColdKing and has gathered considerable information on production and material requirements for ColdKing's products. Khan believes that the use of standard costing will allow ColdKing to improve cost control and make better pricing decisions.

ColdKing's most popular product is raspberry sherbet. The sherbet is produced in 40-litre batches, and each batch requires 6 kilograms of good raspberries. The fresh raspberries are sorted by hand before entering the production process. Because of imperfections in the raspberries and normal spoilage, 1 kilogram of berries is discarded for every 4 kilograms of acceptable berries. Three minutes is the standard direct labour time for the sorting required to obtain 1 kilogram of acceptable raspberries. The acceptable raspberries are then blended with the other ingredients; blending requires 12 minutes of direct labour time per batch. After blending, the sherbet is packaged in 1-litre containers.

Khan has gathered the following information:

- ColdKing purchases raspberries at a cost of R3.20 per kilogram. All other ingredients cost a total of R0.60 per litre. Thirty-four litres of the other ingredients are required per batch.
- Direct labour is paid at the rate of R60 per hour.
- The total cost of material and labour required to package the sherbet is R1.52 per litre.

Required:

1 Develop the standard cost of direct material and direct labour required to produce and package a 40-litre batch of raspberry sherbet.

2 For those responsible for maintaining the standards, Ridwaan Khan is planning training in the use of variance analysis as part of the implementation of a standard costing system at ColdKing. Khan is particularly concerned with the causes of unfavourable variances.
   (a) Discuss the possible causes of unfavourable material price variances and identify the individual(s) who should be held responsible for these variances.
   (b) Discuss the possible causes of unfavourable labour efficiency variances and identify the individual(s) who should be held responsible for these variances.

(CMA, adapted)

P10.48 Direct labour variances, cost variance investigation: Coldpalm company

Coldpalm produces various personal care items including toothpaste. The following data relates to the company's liquid filling line during the first 10 months of a single year. The standard ratio of direct labour hours to machine hours is 4:1. The standard direct labour rate is R30.16.

	Units produced	Machine hours	Standard DLH	Actual DLH	Direct efficiency variance
January	50 478	165.5	662.00	374.00	R8 686
February	31 943	100.3	401.20	214.00	5 646
March	185 179	552.0	2 208.00	1 068.00	34 382
April	212 274	713.8	2 855.20	1 495.75	41 002
May	48 390	160.0	640.00	364.00	8 324
June	82 436	232.0	928.00	536.50	11 808
July	36 208	104.0	416.00	283.00	4 012
August	33 483	96.0	384.00	317.50	2 006
September	31 560	96.0	384.00	328.50	1 674
October	28 191	72.0	288.00	158.00	3 920

Required:

1 Show how the following amounts were calculated for the month of January:
   (a) standard direct labour hours
   (b) direct labour efficiency variance

2 Calculate the standard direct labour cost for each of the 10 months.

3 Suppose management investigates all variances in excess of 20 per cent of standard cost. Which variances will be investigated?

4 Draw a statistical control chart and plot the variance data.

5 Use the chart to outline which variances will be investigated.
6 The variances for March, April and June are much larger that the other. Suggest at least one reason for this.

P10.49 Responsibility for variances; behavioural effects: manufacturer

Madeleine Appliances manufactures washers and dryers on a single assembly line in its main factory. The market has deteriorated over the last five years and competition has made cost control very important. Management has been concerned about the material cost of both washers and dryers. There have been no model changes in the past two years, and economic conditions have allowed the company to negotiate price reductions for many key parts.

Madeleine uses a standard costing system. The price variance is the difference between the contract price and the standard price, multiplied by the actual quantity used. When a substitute part, rather than the regular part, is used in production, a price variance is calculated that is equal to the difference between the actual cost of the part used and the standard cost of the regular part. This variance is calculated at the time of substitution in the production process. The direct material quantity variance is the actual quantity used compared with the standard quantity allowed, with the difference multiplied by the standard price.

Roberta Ndlovu, the purchasing manager, claims that unfavourable price variances are misleading. Ndlovu says that her department has worked hard to obtain price concessions and purchase discounts from suppliers. In addition, Ndlovu has indicated that engineering changes have been made in several parts, increasing their prices. These price increases are not her department's responsibility. Ndlovu declares that price variances simply no longer measure the Purchasing Department's performance.

Jim Van Breda, the manufacturing manager, thinks that responsibility for the quantity variance should be shared. Van Breda states that the manufacturing employees cannot control quality arising from less expensive parts, substitutions of material to use up otherwise obsolete stock, or engineering changes that increase the quantity of materials used.

Required:

Discuss the appropriateness of Madeleine's current method of variance analysis for materials, and indicate whether the claims of Roberta Ndlovu and Jim Van Breda are valid.

(CMA, adapted)

P10.50 Standard costing; process costing; variances: manufacturer

Groen Ltd produces a special valve used in the burners of gas stoves. The firm uses the weighted average cost (WAC) process costing method for product costing. The costs entered into work in process inventory are standard costs, which are set annually. The standards for direct material and direct labour, which are based on one equivalent unit of production, are as follows:

Direct material per unit	1 kg @ R10 per kg
Direct labour per unit	2 hours @ R24 per hour

The following data relate to the month of April:

- The beginning inventory consisted of 2500 units, which were 100 per cent complete as to direct material and 40 per cent complete as to direct labour.
- An additional 10 000 units were started during the month.
- The ending inventory consisted of 2000 units, which were 100 per cent complete as to direct material and 40 per cent complete as to direct labour.
- Costs applicable to April production are as follows:

	Actual cost	Standard cost
Direct material purchased and used (11 000 kg)	R121 000	R100 000
Direct labour (25 000 hours actually worked)	625 000	494 400

Required:

1 For each element of prime production costs (direct material and direct labour), calculate the following for April:
   (a) equivalent units of production
   (b) cost per equivalent unit of production, at actual cost and at standard cost
   (*Hint*: It may be useful to study Chapter 5.)

2 Prepare a schedule that calculates the following April variances, indicating whether each variance is favourable or unfavourable:
   (a) direct material price variance
   (b) direct material quantity variance
   (c) direct labour rate variance
   (d) direct labour efficiency variance

(*CPA, adapted*)

P10.51 Investigating standard cost variances: manufacturer

Cooper Ltd manufactures agricultural machinery. At a recent staff meeting, the following direct labour variance report for the past year was presented by the management accountant:

Cooper Ltd
Direct Labour Variance Report

	Direct labour rate variance		Direct labour efficiency variance	
	Amount	Percentage of standard cost	Amount	Percentage of standard cost
January	R800 F	0.16	R5 000 U	1.00
February	4 900 F	0.98	7 500 U	1.50
March	100 U	0.02	9 700 U	1.94
April	2 000 U	0.40	12 800 U	2.56
May	3 800 F	0.76	20 100 U	4.02
June	3 900 F	0.78	17 000 U	3.40
July	4 200 F	0.84	28 500 U	5.70
August	5 100 F	1.02	38 000 U	7.60
September	4 800 F	0.96	37 000 U	7.40
October	5 700 F	1.14	42 000 U	8.40
November	4 200 F	0.84	60 000 U	12.00
December	4 300 F	0.86	52 000 U	10.40

Cooper Ltd's management accountant uses the following rule of thumb: investigate all variances equal to or greater than R30 000, or 6 per cent of standard cost.

Required:

1 Which variances would have been investigated during the year? (Indicate month and type of variance.)

2 What characteristics of the variance pattern shown in the report should draw the accountant's attention, regardless of the usual investigation rule? Explain. Given these considerations, which variances would you have investigated? Why?

3 Is it important to follow up on favourable variances, such as those shown in the report? Explain your answer.

4 The management accountant believes that the firm's direct labour rate variance has a normal probability distribution with a mean of zero and a standard deviation of R5000.

Prepare a statistical control chart, and plot the company's direct labour rate variances for the year. The critical value is one standard deviation. Which variances would have been investigated under this approach?

P10.52 Labour variances: hospital

Mountain View Hospital has adopted a standard costing system for evaluation and control of nursing labour. Diagnosis Related Groups (DRGs) are used as the output measure in the standard costing system. A DRG is a classification scheme for diseases, and hospitals are reimbursed by the government based on the number of patients that they treat in each DRG category. Mountain View Hospital has developed standard nursing times for the treatment of each DRG classification, and nursing labour hours are assumed to vary with the number of DRGs treated within a time period.

The nursing unit on the fourth floor treats patients with four DRG classifications. The unit is staffed with nursing sisters (NS), trainee nurses (TN) and aides. The standard nursing hours and salary rates are as follows:

DRG classification	NS (hours)	TN (hours)	Aides (hours)
1	6	4	5
2	26	16	10
3	10	5	4
4	12	7	10
Standard hourly rates	R48.00	R32.00	R24.00

For the month of May, the number of patients and hourly rates for the fourth floor nursing unit are as follows:

Actual number of patients	
DRG 1	250
DRG 2	90
DRG 3	240
DRG 4	140
Total	720

	NS	TN	Aides
Actual salary	R400 980	R141 040	R101 200
÷ Actual hours	8 150	4 300	4 400
Actual hourly rate	R49.20	R32.80	R23.00

The accountant for Mountain View Hospital calculated the following standard times for the fourth floor nursing unit for May:

		Standard hours per patient			Total standard hours		
DRG classification	Number of patients	NS	TN	Aides	NS	TN	Aides
1	250	6	4	5	1 500	1 000	1 250
2	90	26	16	10	2 340	1 440	900
3	240	10	5	4	2 400	1 200	960
4	140	12	7	10	1 680	980	1 400
Total					7 920	4 620	4 510

The hospital calculates labour variances for each reporting period by labour classification (NS, TN, Aide). The variances are used by nursing supervisors and hospital administrators to evaluate the performance of nursing labour. The variances are calculated as follows:

- A total nursing labour variance equal to the difference between the total actual nursing cost and the total standard nursing cost.
- A nursing labour efficiency variance, calculated as the sum of the efficiency variances across the three types of nursing labour.
- A nursing labour rate variance, calculated as the sum of the rate variances across the three types of nursing labour.

Required:

1 Calculate the hospital's nursing labour variances for May.

2 Comment on the nursing labour efficiency variance. Does this variance tell the whole story about nursing efficiency?

(*CMA, adapted*)

P10.53 Comprehensive problem on variance analysis: manufacturer

Elvis Ltd manufactures guitars. The company uses a standard job costing system in its two production departments. In the Construction Department, the wooden guitars are built by highly skilled craftworkers and are coated with several layers of lacquer. The units are then transferred to the Finishing Department, where the bridge of the guitar is attached and the strings are installed. The guitars are also tuned and inspected in the Finishing Department. The diagram below depicts the production process:

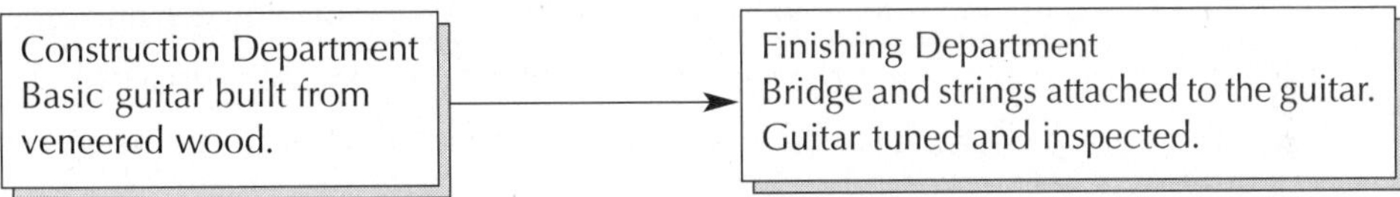

Each finished guitar contains 7 metres of veneered wood. In addition, 1 metre of wood is typically wasted in the production process. The veneered wood used in the guitars has a standard price of R60 per metre. The other parts needed to complete each guitar, such as the bridge and strings, cost R75 per guitar. The labour standards for a guitar are as follows:

Construction Department	6 hours of direct labour	@	R 100 per hour
Finishing Department	3 hours of direct labour	@	R 75 per hour

The following data relate to the month of July:

- There were no beginning or ending work in process inventories in either production department.
- There was no beginning finished goods inventory.
- Actual production was 750 guitars, and 450 guitars were sold for R1950 each.
- The company purchased 9000 metres of veneered wood at a price of R62.50 per metre.
- Actual usage of veneered wood was 6750 metres.
- Enough parts (bridges and strings) to finish 900 guitars were purchased at a cost of R67 500.
- The Construction Department used 4275 direct labour hours. The total direct labour cost in the Construction Department was R406 125.
- The Finishing Department used 2355 direct labour hours. The total direct labour cost in that department was R188 400.
- There were no direct material variances in the Finishing Department.

Required:

1 Prepare a schedule that calculates the standard costs of direct material and direct labour in each production department.

2 Prepare three exhibits that calculate the July direct material and direct labour variances in the Construction Department and the July direct labour variances in the Finishing Department. (*Hint*: Refer to Exhibits 10.3 and 10.5 for guidance.)

3 Prepare a standard cost variance report for July similar to that shown in Exhibit 10.6.

P10.54 Journal entries under standard costing: manufacturer

Refer to Problem 10.53.

Required:

1 Prepare journal entries to record all the events listed for Elvis Ltd during July. Specifically, these journal entries should reflect the following events:
   (a) purchase of direct material
   (b) use of direct material in production
   (c) incurrence of direct labour costs
   (d) incurrence of all variances
   (e) completion of 750 guitars
   (f) sale of 450 guitars
   (g) closing of all variance accounts to cost of goods sold

2 Draw ledger accounts, and post the journal entries prepared in requirement 1. Assume the beginning balance in all accounts is zero.

P10.55 Direct material and direct labour variances; graphical analysis of direct labour variance (appendix): manufacturer

During July, Nautilus Company manufactured 500 units of a special multilayer fabric called Zylex. The following information from the Zylex production department pertains to July:

Direct material purchased: 18 000 metres @ R1.38 per metre	R24 840
Direct material used: 9500 metres @ R1.38 per metre	13 110
Direct labour: 2100 hours @ R18.30 per hour	38 430

The standard prime costs for one unit of Zylex are as follows:

Direct materials: 20 metres @ R1.35 per metre	R27
Direct labour: 4 hours @ R17 per hour	68
Total standard prime cost per unit of output	R95

Required:

1 Calculate the following variances for the month of July, indicating whether each variance is favourable or unfavourable:
   (a) direct material price variance
   (b) direct material quantity variance
   (c) direct labour rate variance
   (d) direct labour efficiency variance

2 Draw a graph depicting Nautilus Company's direct labour variances for July. Include the joint rate efficiency variance in your graph. (Refer to Exhibit 10.11 for guidance.)

3 Provide an interpretation of the variances that are revealed in the graph.

(CMA, adapted)

Cases

C10.56 Direct material and direct labour variances; job costing; journal entries: manufacturer

Trend Setter Fashions manufactures one type of women's blouse, produced in jobs to fill each customer order. These blouses are supplied in boxes of six. Its customers are various department stores, and Trend Setter sews the label of each store onto the blouses.

During November, Trend Setter worked on three orders. The job cost records disclose the following data:

Job no.	Boxes in job	Total material used (metres)	Total hours worked
AB	2 000	48 200	5 960
CD	3 400	80 880	10 260
MN	2 400	57 650	5 780

The following additional information is available:

- Trend Setter purchased 190 000 metres of material during November at a cost of R638 400
- Direct labour during November amounted to R990 000. According to payroll records, production employees were paid R45 per hour.
- There was no work in process on 1 November. During November, jobs AB and CD were completed. All material was issued for job MN, which was 80 per cent complete as to direct labour.
- The standard costs for a box of 6 blouses are as follows:

Direct material	24 metres	@	R3.30	R79.20
Direct labour	3 hours	@	R44.10	R132.30
Manufacturing overhead	3 hours	@	R36.00	R108.00
Standard cost per box				R319.50

Required:

1 Prepare a schedule calculating the standard cost of jobs AB, CD and MN for November.

2 Calculate the following variances for November:
   (a) direct material price variance
   (b) direct material quantity variance for each job and in total
   (c) direct labour efficiency variance for each job and in total
   (d) direct labour rate variance for each job and in total
   Indicate whether each variance is favourable or unfavourable.

3 Prepare journal entries to record each of the following events:
   (a) purchase of material
   (b) incurrence of direct labour cost and direct labour variances for November
   (c) addition of direct material to work in process inventory, and direct material variances for November

4 Discuss possible causes for each of the variances that you calculated under requirement 2. Consider each variance separately. Also, consider possible interactions between variances.

(CPA, adapted)

C10.57 Missing data; variances; ledger accounts: manufacturer

MacGyver Corporation manufactures a product called Miracle Goo, which comes in handy for just about anything. The thick, tarry substance is sold in 6 litre drums. Two raw materials are used, referred to by people in the business as A and B. Two types of labour are also required: mixers (labour class I) and packers (labour class II).

You were recently hired by the managing director, Pete Thorn, to be the chief accountant. You soon learned that MacGyver uses a standard costing system. Variances are calculated and closed to cost of goods sold monthly. After your first month on the job, you gathered the necessary data to calculate the month's variances for direct material and direct labour. You had finished everything by 5 pm on the last day of the month, including the credit to cost of goods sold for the sum of the variances. You decided to take all your notes home to review them before your formal presentation to Mr Thorn first thing the next morning. As an afterthought, you grabbed a drum of Miracle Goo as well, thinking it could prove useful around the house.

You spent the evening studying the data for your report and were ready to call it a night. However, as you finished, the cat jumped onto the table and knocked over the Miracle Goo. The goo splattered everywhere and unfortunately obliterated most of your notes, and turned the cat an attractive shade of green! All that remains legible on your notes is the following information:

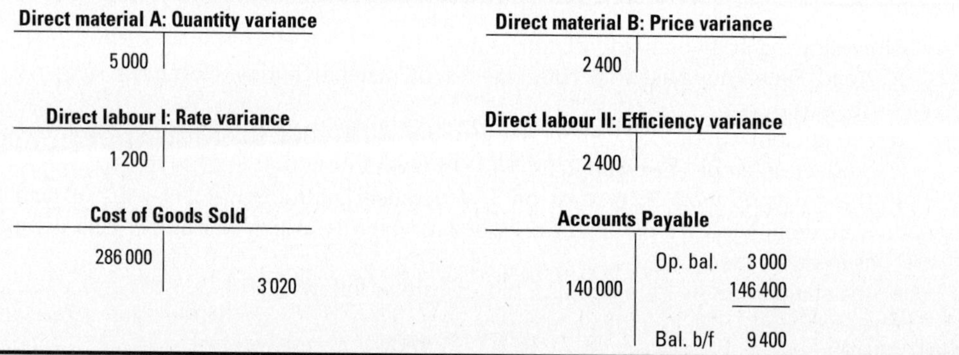

Other assorted data gleaned from your notes:

- The standards for each drum of Miracle Goo include 10 kilograms of material A at a standard price of R10 per kilogram.
- The standard cost of material B is R30 for each drum of Miracle Goo.
- Purchases of material A were 12 000 kilograms at R9.00 per kilogram.
- Given the actual output for the month, the standard quantity allowed of material A was 10 000 kilograms. The standard quantity allowed of material B was 5000 litres.
- Although 6000 litres of B were purchased, only 4800 litres were used.
- The standard wage rate for mixers is R30 per hour. The standard labour cost per drum of product for mixers is R60 per drum.
- The standards allow 4 hours of direct labour II (packers) per drum of Miracle Goo. The standard labour cost per drum of product for packers is R96 per drum. Packers were paid R23.80 per hour during the month.

You also remember two additional facts. There were no beginning or ending inventories of either work in process or finished goods for the month; and the increase in accounts payable relates to direct material purchases only.

Required:

Now you've got a major problem. Somehow you've got to reconstruct all the missing data in order to be ready for your meeting with Pete Thorn. (You also have to wash the cat.) You start by making the following list of the facts you want to be able to use in your presentation:

1 Actual output (in drums): ____________

2 Direct material:	Material A	Material B
(a) standard quantity per drum	________	________
(b) standard price	________	________
(c) standard cost per drum	________	________
(d) standard quantity allowed, given actual output	________	________
(e) actual quantity purchased	________	________
(f) actual price	________	________
(g) actual quantity used	________	________
(h) price variance	________	________
(i) quantity variance	________	________
3 Direct labour:	I (mixers)	II (packers)
(a) standard hours per drum	________	________
(b) standard rate per hour	________	________
(c) standard cost per drum	________	________
(d) standard quantity allowed, given actual output	________	________
(e) actual rate per hour	________	________
(f) actual hours	________	________
(g) rate variance	________	________
(h) efficiency variance	________	________
4 Total of all variances for the month:	________	________

Fill in the missing amounts in the list, using the available facts.

Endnotes

1 Cost variances can also be calculated for the non-manufacturing areas of the business, and in service firms.

2 Although this example is based on the standard costing system used at an actual company, the system has been simplified and all of the costs and employee names are fictitious.

3 This example is simplified as the company actually classifies fabric, buttons, thread and zipper as direct materials for greater control.

4 Note that labour costs are unlikely to have a linear relationship with the volume of production over time, due to the learning curve effect. This is discussed in the appendix to Chapter 3.

5 This should be distinguished from unavoidable scrap, which is already included in the standard material quantity. For example, in cutting out the moleskin pants, the standard quantity is 3.1 metres of fabric. There will be unavoidable material scraps as a result of the particular shapes of the pattern pieces that are cut from the piece of fabric.

6 SQ = actual output × standard quantity per unit of output.

7 SH = actual output × standard hours per unit of output.

8 For further discussion of statistical control charts, see Montgomery (2000) and Ryan (2000).

9 This is termed 'the learning curve effect', and is covered in the appendix to Chapter 3.

10 The production facility of this company has since closed indicating the effects of competition and globalisation. Tailored clothing is now sourced from offshore facilities.

11 The material price variance will be prorated across these three accounts and the raw material inventory.

Standard Costs for Control: Flexible Budgets and Manufacturing Overhead

❖ Learning Objectives

After completing this chapter, you should be able to:

1. distinguish between *static* and *flexible* budgets;
2. explain the advantages of a flexible budget for performance evaluation and control;
3. prepare a flexible overhead budget, using both a formula and a report format;
4. apply overheads to work in process under a standard costing system;
5. calculate and interpret the variable overhead spending and efficiency variances, and the fixed overhead budget and volume variances;
6. prepare an overhead cost performance report;
7. prepare journal entries to account for manufacturing overhead under standard costing;
8. apply flexible budgets in a non-manufacturing environment;
9. outline the criticisms and advantages of standard costing;
10. understand how activity-based budgeting provides a more accurate form of budgeting than does conventional budgeting; and
11. after studying the appendix, calculate and interpret the sales price and sales volume variances.

Introduction

In Chapter 10 we saw how conventional standard costing systems can be used to help control direct material and direct labour costs. In standard costing we prepare a 'flexible budget' based on the actual level of output produced. In this chapter we explain flexible budgets and consider how standard costing systems can be used to control manufacturing overhead costs.

Controlling manufacturing overheads is a challenge. Unlike direct materials and direct labour, manufacturing overheads are not directly traceable to individual products, and they consist of many different costs. Examples include the wages of factory supervisors, depreciation, electricity and factory rent. These costs may exhibit different relationships to production output. Some may be fixed with respect to the volume of production, while others may be variable. Also, many overhead costs vary with non-volume-related cost drivers, such as the number of batches and number of product lines.

A further problem for cost control is that, often, different individuals are responsible for different types of overhead costs. For many manufacturing (and non-manufacturing) companies, the relative proportion of overhead costs is growing, so it is becoming even more important to consider ways of controlling these costs. Standard costing systems provide one way of controlling overhead costs. More contemporary methods of cost management are presented in Chapter 15.

Flexible budgets

L.O. 1

Some companies use a flexible budget to control overhead costs. Flexible budgets resemble the budgets we studied in Chapter 10, with one important difference. A **flexible budget** is a detailed plan for controlling costs that is valid for a *range of levels of activity*. In contrast, **static budgets**, like the annual budgets described in Chapter 10, are prepared for *one specific planned level of activity*. For example, the operating budgets for AVJ were static budgets, as they were based on a single planned output of 1176 houses.

Let's return to the R.M. Williams example in Chapter 10, where we considered the production of moleskin pants. Suppose that, when the annual budget was prepared for 20X6, it was assumed that during September 2500 pairs of moleskins would be produced. The production budget for September (the static budget) would have consisted of the total planned costs of material and labour based on those 2500 units. However, production did not go to plan, and only 2000 pairs of moleskins were produced. How can the accountant detect whether too many resources were used when the budget was based on one volume and the actual costs were based on a different volume?

We recognised this problem in Chapter 10. When we calculated cost variances for direct materials and direct labour, we compared actual costs to *standard costs allowed for actual output produced.* That is, we adjusted the standard cost benchmark to reflect the actual volume of production.

Exhibit 11.1 contains budget data relating to the production of moleskins. (You may recognise the standard cost per unit from Chapter 10.) The flexible budget for moleskins for direct material and direct labour is based on three possible volumes of production. The flexible budget based on the actual production output of 2000 units is the appropriate benchmark to use for comparing the actual costs in September 20X6, not the static budget based on 2500 units. Thus, for direct labour we can analyse the cost performance:

Actual direct labour used (2700 hours × R38)[#]	R102 600
Standard labour costs, given actual production of 2000 units	100 800
Total direct labour variance	R1 800 U
Consisting of:[§]	
Direct labour rate variance	R5 400 U
Direct labour efficiency variance	R3 600 F

[#]The actual direct labour and direct material costs for moleskins for September 20X6 are taken from Exhibit 10.2.
[§]The labour and material variances were calculated in Chapter 10 (see Exhibit 10.5).

	Static budget for September	Flexible budget for September		
Production units	2 500	2 000	2 500	3 000
Direct materials @ R77.50 per unit	R193 750	R155 000	R193 750	R232 500
Direct labour @ R50.40 per unit	R126 000	R100 800	R126 000	R151 200
	Static budget: based on only one level of activity	*Flexible budgets* include several possible levels of activity		

Exhibit 11.1 Static and flexible budgets for moleskins, R.M. Williams

For direct materials, the reconciliation is a little different. You will remember that the direct material price variance is usually based on the *total units purchased,* not the quantity used in production. If the price variance were to be calculated just for the units that were transferred to production, it would be R2600 unfavourable. The total material variance relating to the production of moleskins for September is then:

Actual direct material used (6500 metres × R25.40)	R165 100
Standard material cost, given actual production of 2000 units (6200 metres R25.00)	155 000
Total direct material variance	R10 100 U
Consisting of:	
Direct material price variance (for materials used in production) [6500 metres × (R25.40−R25.00]	R2 600 U
Direct material quantity variance	R7 500 U

The term *flexible budget* is often restricted to the practice of *flexing* overhead costs to various levels of activity. However, a flexible budget can be prepared for any budgeted revenues and costs. For example, we can see that it can be used for calculating direct material and direct labour variances under standard costing.

Advantages of flexible budgets

Understanding the distinction between static and flexible budgets allows us to select the most appropriate benchmark for cost control. Here is an example for the variable overhead cost of electricity for R.M. Williams. **L.O. 2**

During the March quarter 20X7, R.M. Williams produced 280 pairs of women's boots in its Footwear Department. The firm used 720 machine hours and incurred electricity costs of R880. Does this reflect good or poor use of electricity?

The following data relate to the March quarter budget:

Budgeted production	320 pairs of boots
Standard machine hours	× 2.50 per unit
Total budgeted machine hours	800 machine hours

Variable overhead budget for electricity = R960 (800 machine hours × R1.20 per machine hour)

The accountant could use this static budget to make the following comparison:

Actual electricity cost	Budgeted electricity cost (static budget)	Cost variance
R880	R960	R80F

This comparison suggests that operating personnel maintained control over electricity costs during the March quarter, generating a favourable variance of R80.

However, in this analysis the accountant is comparing the electricity cost incurred at the *actual activity level* (280 units) with the budgeted electricity cost at the *planned activity level* (320 units). Since these activity levels are different, we would expect the electricity cost to be different.

A more sensible approach is to compare the actual electricity cost incurred with the cost that should be incurred when 280 units are manufactured. At this production level, 700 machine hours should be used (at 2.50 hours per unit). The flexible budget in Exhibit 11.2 shows that, for 700 machine hours, R840 of electricity cost should be incurred. Therefore, an analysis based on the flexible budget gives the following comparison:

Actual electricity cost	Budgeted electricity cost (flexible budget)	Cost variance
R880	R840	R40 U

Now the accountant's conclusion is different. The revised analysis indicates an unfavourable variance. Electricity cost was more than it should have been, given the actual level of output. As machine hours are driving the cost of electricity, one reason for this variance is that actual machine hours were 720, while standard machine hours allowed for actual output of 280 units were 700. (Another reason relates to differences between the actual and standard price of electricity.) The flexible budget provides the correct basis for comparing actual and expected costs, for the actual level of activity.

	Static budget	Flexible budget		
Activity (machine hours)	800	700	750	800
Budgeted electricity costs (machine hours × R1.20 per hour)	R960	R840	R900	R960

Exhibit 11.2 Static versus flexible budgets, R.M. Williams

Input measures and output measures

Why did we calculate the flexible budget for electricity cost using machine hours (an *input* measure) and not the number of units produced (an *output* measure)? For example, we could have formulated a flexible budget based on a standard electricity cost of R3.00 per unit (2.50 machine hours per unit × R1.20 per machine hour). When only a single product is manufactured, it makes no difference whether the flexible budget is based on input or output. In our example, the variances would have been the same. However, it does make a difference when there are multiple products all using different quantities of inputs (machine hours in this case).

Suppose the Footwear Department of R.M. Williams manufactured three different types of footwear during the June quarter 20X7: 150 pairs of walking boots, 50 pairs of children's boots and 200 pairs of mountain boots. The following standards were developed:

Product	Standard machine hours per unit
Walking boots	2.20
Children's boots	2.00
Mountain boots	2.60

During the June quarter, the total production output was 400 units. However, a flexible budget for electricity cost cannot be based on units of output when each product has different machine hour requirements. In this case, the flexible budget must be based on the input measure: machine hours. The standard number of machine hours allowed for the June quarter production is calculated as follows:

Product	Production units	Standard machine hours per unit	Total standard machine hours
Walking boots	150	2.20	330
Children's boots	50	2.00	100
Mountain boots	200	2.60	520
	400		950

Recall that electricity cost is estimated to be R1.20 per machine hour. Thus, the flexible budget cost of electricity for the June quarter is calculated as follows:

Standard machine hours allowed, given June output	950
Electricity cost per machine hour	× R1.20
Flexible budget for electricity cost	R1140

This flexible budget of R1 140 can now be used as the benchmark against which the actual cost of electricity for the June quarter 20X7 can be compared.

The important point is that *units of output* are not usually a meaningful measure of the level of activity in a multi-product firm, because it would require the addition of quantities of unlike products. To avoid this problem, output is measured in terms of the *standard quantity of input allowed, given actual output*. The flexible overhead budget is then based on this standard input measure – in this case, machine hours. In the following sections we will expand our study of flexible budgets by considering how a flexible budget may be formulated and used to control overhead costs in the Clothing Department of R.M. Williams.

Flexible overhead budget: R.M. Williams

L.O. 3

The accountant at R.M. Williams, Bill Sithole, estimates the manufacturing overhead costs as part of the yearly budgeting process. The starting point for estimating the manufacturing overhead budget is to consider the level of overheads incurred in the past year. Each fixed overhead item is considered separately and is adjusted to reflect any likely increases in price. Estimates of *variable overhead* must also reflect any likely changes in the prices of individual items, as well as changes in the volume of activity. By examining accounting records for the past few years, Bill Sithole has found that total variable overhead increases in proportion to total direct labour hours. Thus, direct labour hours is a suitable activity on which to base the flexible budget. Bill estimates that, for 20X6, variable overhead costs will be incurred in the Clothing Department at the rate of R6.00 per direct labour hour.

Separate manufacturing overhead budgets are formulated for each of the three production departments – Clothing, Craftware and Footwear – for the year and for each month.[1] These manufacturing overhead budgets are based on the planned level of activity; that is, they are *static budgets*. However, to assess monthly performance we need to construct *monthly flexible budgets*.

A monthly flexible manufacturing overhead budget for 20X6 for the Clothing Department is shown in Exhibit 11.3. This contains estimates of costs for several levels of activity. The overhead costs in the flexible budget are divided into variable costs and fixed costs. The total budgeted variable manufacturing overhead cost increases proportionately with increases in activity (that is, direct labour hours). The variable overhead is budgeted at R6 per direct labour hour. For example, for the flexible budget based on 4200 direct labour hours, the total variable overhead is R25 200 (R6 × 4200 direct labour hours). In contrast, the total budgeted fixed overhead does not change with increases in activity; it remains constant at R30 000 per month.

Monthly Manufacturing Overhead Budget for 20X6 Clothing Department				
	Direct labour hours			
	4000	**4200**	**4400**	**4600**
Variable overheads:				
Indirect materials	14 560	15 288	16 016	16 744
Electricity	5 840	6 132	6 424	6 716
Consumables	3 600	3 780	3 960	4 140
Total variable overhead	24 000	25 200	26 400	27 600
Fixed overheads:				
Supervisors' salaries	14 000	14 000	14 000	14 000
Factory rent	6 000	6 000	6 000	6 000
Council rates	1 200	1 200	1 200	1 200
Cleaning costs	3 600	3 600	3 600	3 600
Insurance	1 600	1 600	1 600	1 600
Depreciation of machinery	3 600	3 600	3 600	3 600
Total fixed overhead	30 000	30 000	30 000	30 000
Total manufacturing overheads	54 000	55 200	56 400	57 600

Exhibit 11.3 Flexible Manufacturing Budget, R.M. Williams

Formula flexible budget

The format used in Exhibit 11.3 is a **flexible budget report**. It shows a range of flexible overhead budgets at various levels of activity. A more general format for expressing a flexible budget is called a **formula flexible budget**. In this format, the accountant expresses the relationship between the activity level and the total budgeted overhead cost with the following formula:

Total budgeted cost = (budgeted variable overhead cost per unit of activity)
× (total activity units) + budgeted fixed overhead cost

This formula can be used to describe the annual budgeted overhead or to help construct the *monthly flexible budget*. The formula for R.M. Williams' monthly flexible overhead budget for the Clothing Department is as follows:

Total budgeted monthly overhead cost = (R6 × number of direct labour hours) + R30 000

To check the accuracy of the formula, we can calculate the total budgeted monthly overhead cost at each of the activity levels shown in Exhibit 11.3.

Activity (Direct labour hours)	Formula flexible overhead budget	Flexible budget for a month
4 000	R6 × 4 000 + R30 000 =	R54 000
4 200	R6 × 4 200 + R30 000 =	R55 200
4 400	R6 × 4 400 + R30 000 =	R56 400
4 600	R6 × 4 600 + R30 000 =	R57 600

The formula flexible budget is more general than the flexible budget report, as it allows the budgeted overhead costs to be calculated at any activity level. The flexible budgeted overhead cost can be used each month as a benchmark to compare against the actual overhead costs incurred.

Overhead application in a standard costing system

L.O. 4

Recall that *overhead application* refers to the methods of allocating overhead cost to products, and is recorded in the work in process inventory account. In a standard costing system, overhead is applied to inventory using the *standard overhead rate*, and is based on the *standard quantity of input allowed, given actual output.*

R.M. Williams calculates its predetermined or standard overhead rates annually. For each of the three production departments there are separate variable overhead and fixed overhead rates. In Exhibit 11.4 these rates are calculated for the Clothing Department for 20X6.

	Annual budgeted overhead for 20X6	Total budgeted activity for 20X6	Pre-determined overhead rate
Variable overhead	R270 000	45 000 DLH*	R6.00 per DLH
Fixed overhead	360 000§	45 000 DLH	R8.00 per DLH
Total overhead	R630 000		R14.00 per DLH

*DLH = direct labour hours.
§Monthly fixed overhead = R 360 000 ÷ 12 months = R 30 000 per month

Exhibit 11.4 Calculation of predetermined manufacturing overhead rates, R.M. Williams Clothing Department

Choice of activity

R.M. Williams' flexible overhead budget is based on direct labour hours. However, a variety of activities may be used. Machine hours, direct labour hours, direct labour cost and direct material cost are among the most common activities used to construct flexible budgets. However, to ensure an accurate flexible budget that can be used to control overhead costs, the activity chosen *should be a cost driver,* which is any activity or factor that causes costs to be incurred. Determining cost drivers requires an understanding of cost behaviour. Cost behaviour and cost estimation techniques are discussed in greater detail in Chapter 3. The selection of overhead cost drivers is discussed in Chapter 7.

Calculating overhead cost variances

L.O. 5

The flexible overhead budget provides a tool for controlling manufacturing overhead costs. At the end of each accounting period, the management accountant can use the flexible overhead budget to calculate the level of overhead cost that should have been incurred, given the actual level of activity. The accountant then compares the flexible overhead cost with the actual overhead cost incurred. Four separate overhead variances can be calculated, each of which conveys different information.

Although R.M. Williams uses standard overhead rates to cost products, it does not use standard cost variances to control overhead costs. Overhead is controlled by directly comparing actual versus budgeted expenditure for each major item of overhead cost. Many South African businesses use this same approach. However, we will use the R.M. Williams data to demonstrate standard cost overhead variance analysis.

Flexible overhead budget

R.M. Williams' monthly flexible overhead budget for the Clothing Department, displayed in Exhibit 11.3, shows budgeted variable and fixed manufacturing overhead costs for four levels of activity. During September 20X6, three products were manufactured in the Clothing Department, each having different standard direct labour hours:

Product	Actual production	Standard direct labour hours per unit	Total standard direct labour hours for actual output
Shirts	1 360	1.0	1 360
Moleskins	2 000	1.4	2 800
Coats	400	0.6	240
			4 400

From the 4400 direct labour hour column of Exhibit 11.3, we can see that the flexible budgeted overhead cost for September is as follows:

	Budgeted overhead cost for September
Variable overhead	R26 400
Fixed overhead	30 000
	R56 400

From the cost accounting records Bill Sithole, the accountant, learned that the following overhead costs were actually incurred during September:

	Actual cost for September
Variable overhead	R29 440
Fixed overhead	34 200
Total overhead	R63 640

The production supervisor's records show that 4600 *actual* direct labour hours were worked in September.

By comparing the actual overhead costs to the flexible budgets, we can calculate the overhead variances for the Clothing Department for September 20X6. The *total overhead variance* that we are trying to explain is R7240 – that is, the difference between the actual overhead (R63 640) and the budgeted overhead, based on the actual output (R56 400).

Variable overhead variances

The total variable overhead variance for September is calculated below:

Actual variable overhead	R29 440
Budgeted variable overhead	26 400
Total variable overhead variance	R3 040 U

What caused the company to spend R3040 more than budgeted on variable overhead? To begin to answer this question, we can calculate a **variable overhead spending variance** to indicate the overall cost impact of the difference between the actual and standard variable overhead rate, and a **variable overhead efficiency variance**, which shows the cost impact on variable overheads of the difference in actual and standard activity. We can use the format in Exhibit 11.5, or we can use formulas.

Variable overhead spending variance

The formula for the variable overhead spending variance is as follows:

$$\text{Variable overhead spending variance} = \text{actual variable overhead} - (AH \times SVR)$$

where AH = actual direct labour hours
SVR = standard variable overhead rate

The variable overhead spending variance for September is therefore calculated as follows:

$$\begin{aligned}\text{Variable overhead spending variance} &= \text{actual variable overhead} - (AH \times SVR)\\ &= \text{R29 440} - (4600 \times \text{R6})\\ &= \text{R29 440} - \text{R27 600}\\ &= \text{R1840 U}\end{aligned}$$

This variance is unfavourable because the actual variable overhead cost exceeded the expected amount, after adjusting for the actual number of direct labour hours used.

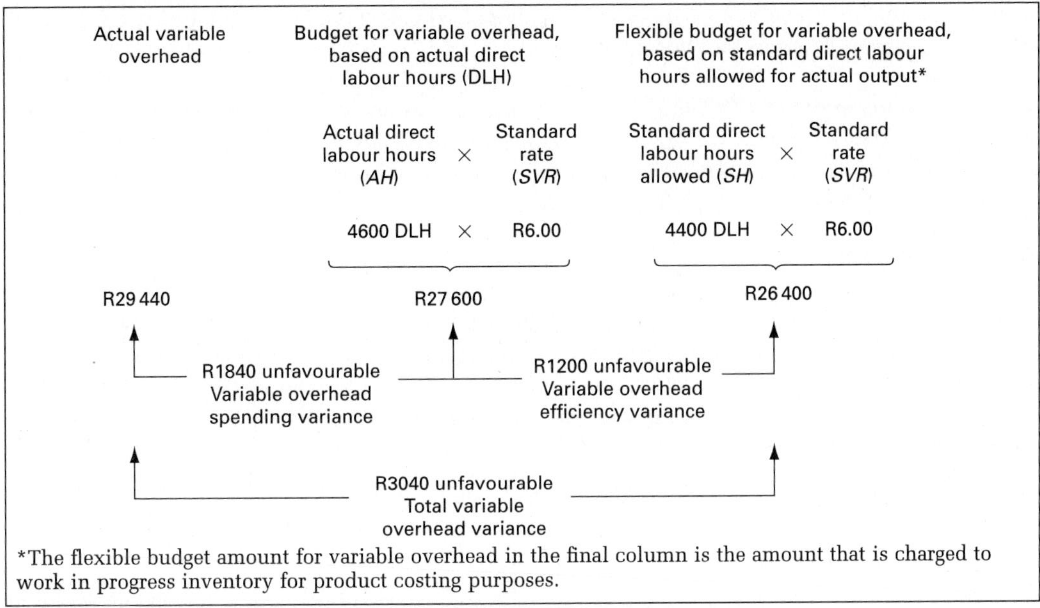

*The flexible budget amount for variable overhead in the final column is the amount that is charged to work in progress inventory for product costing purposes.

Exhibit 11.5 Variable overhead spending and efficiency variances, R.M. Williams

Variable overhead efficiency variance

The following formula defines the variable overhead efficiency variance:

$$\text{Variable overhead efficiency variance} = (AH \times SVR) - (SH \times SVR)$$
$$= SVR(AH - SH)$$

where SH = standard direct labour hours allowed, for actual output

The variable overhead efficiency variance for September is therefore calculated as follows:

$$\text{Variable overhead efficiency variance} = SVR(AH - SH)$$
$$= \text{R}6(4600 - 4400)$$
$$= \text{R}1200 \text{ U}$$

This variance is unfavourable because actual direct labour hours exceeded standard direct labour hours allowed, given actual output. Together, these two variances make up the total unfavourable variable overhead variance of R3040.

Interpreting variable overhead variances

What do the variable overhead variances mean? What information do they convey to management? The formulas for calculating the variable overhead variances resemble those used to calculate the direct labour variances. To see this resemblance, compare Exhibit 11.5 (variable overhead) with Exhibit 10.5 (direct labour). Despite these similarities, the interpretation of the variable overhead variances is quite different from that of the direct labour variances.

Efficiency variance

R.M. Williams' variable overhead efficiency variance did not result from using more of the variable overhead items, such as electricity and indirect material, than the standard amount allowed. Instead, this variance is the result of using *more direct labour hours* than the standard quantity, given actual output. Recall that the accountant assumed that variable overhead cost is driven by direct labour hours. Since 200 more direct labour hours than the standard quantity were used, management *should* expect that variable overhead costs will be greater. Thus, the variable overhead efficiency variance does not measure the efficient or inefficient usage of electricity, indirect material or other variable overhead items. This variance simply reflects the extra amount of variable overhead cost incurred that can be attributed to working more direct labour hours than the standard quantity allowed.

The variable overhead efficiency variance may provide control information to management about the cost effects of excessive or low use of the particular activity (in this example, direct labour hours). However, this information is useful only if the activity is an accurate cost driver, as then controlling the activity will help to control the cost.

Spending variance

An unfavourable spending variance simply means that the total actual cost of variable overhead is greater than expected, after adjusting for the actual quantity of labour hours used. An unfavourable spending variance can result from paying a higher than expected price per unit for variable overhead items. Alternatively, the variance could result from using more of the variable overhead items than expected.

Suppose, for example, that electricity was the only variable overhead cost item. An unfavourable variable overhead spending variance could result from paying a higher than expected *price* per kilowatt hour for electricity, or from using a greater *quantity* of electricity than expected, or from both.

Control of variable overhead

Since the variable overhead efficiency variance says nothing about efficient or inefficient usage of variable overhead, the *spending variance is the real control variance* for variable overhead. Individual spending variances can be calculated for each variable cost item to alert managers to variable overhead costs that are out of line with expectations.

Fixed overhead variances

To analyse performance regarding fixed overhead, the management accountant can calculate fixed overhead variances. Once again, variance formulas or the format in Exhibit 11.6 can be used.

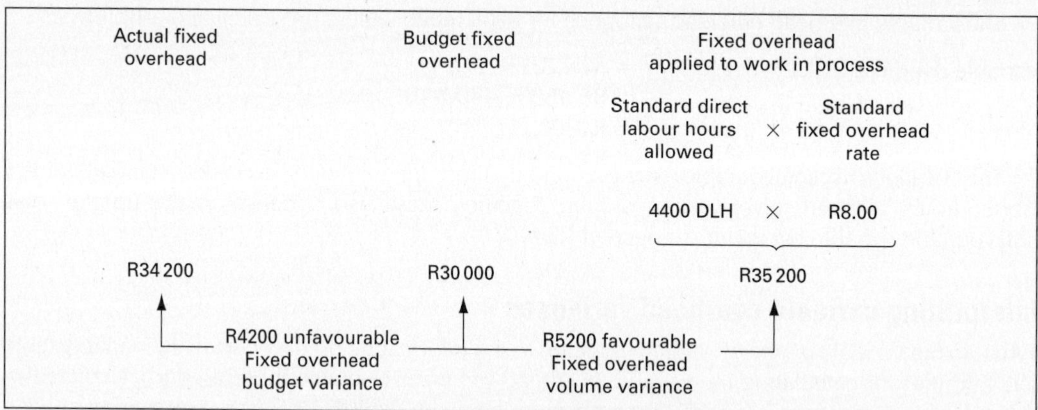

Exhibit 11.6 Fixed overhead budget and volume variances, R.M. Williams

Fixed overhead budget variance

The variance used by managers to control fixed overhead is called the **fixed overhead budget variance**. It is defined as follows:

Fixed overhead budget variance = actual fixed overhead – budget fixed overhead

R.M. Williams' fixed overhead budget variance for September is therefore calculated as follows:

Fixed overhead budget variance = actual fixed overhead – budgeted fixed overhead
= R34 200 – R30 000
= R4200 U

The fixed overhead budget variance is unfavourable because the managers in the Clothing Department spent more than the budgeted amount on fixed overhead. Notice that no activity level is used to determine budgeted fixed overhead, as fixed overhead is assumed not to be driven by any activity. That is, fixed costs remain unchanged in total, regardless of the level of activity (or cost driver). All four columns in the flexible budget (Exhibit 11.3) specify R30 000 as budgeted fixed overhead.

Fixed overhead volume variance

Although the fixed overhead budget variance has already explained the difference between actual and budgeted fixed overhead, a **fixed overhead volume variance** can also be calculated:

Fixed overhead volume variance = budgeted fixed overhead − applied fixed overhead

To calculate this variance we first have to calculate the applied fixed overhead. R.M. Williams' applied fixed overhead for September is the amount that is charged to work in process inventory. This is calculated as follows:

Applied fixed overhead = standard fixed overhead rate × standard hours allowed, for actual output
= R8 per DLH × 4400 DLH
= R35 200

The R8 predetermined fixed overhead rate was calculated in Exhibit 11.4. The 4400 standard direct labour hours allowed are based on actual September production. Thus, the fixed overhead volume variance is calculated as follows:

Fixed overhead volume variance = budgeted fixed overhead − applied fixed overhead
= R30 000−R35 200
= R5 200 F

A *favourable* volume variance indicates that the standard hours allowed for actual output are greater than the planned level of production – that is, actual output is greater than the level planned at the beginning of the year. An *unfavourable* volume variance indicates that the standard hours allowed are less than the planned level of production.

Interpreting fixed overhead variances

The fixed overhead budget variance is the real control variance for fixed overhead because it compares *actual* expenditure with budgeted fixed overhead costs. The volume variance is merely a way of reconciling the two different purposes of the costing system.

To satisfy the *control purpose*, the costing system assumes that fixed overhead will not change as activity varies. Therefore, budgeted fixed overhead is the same at all activity levels in the flexible budget. Budgeted fixed overhead is the basis for controlling fixed overhead because it provides the benchmark against which actual expenditures are compared.

For the *product costing purpose* of the costing system, budgeted fixed overhead for the year is divided by planned (budgeted) activity to obtain a predetermined (or standard) fixed overhead rate. For R.M. Williams, this rate is R8 per direct labour hour (annual budgeted fixed overhead of R360 000 ÷ budgeted activity of 45 000 direct labour hours).[2] This predetermined rate is then used to apply fixed overhead to work in process inventory. During any month in which the standard number of direct labour hours allowed, for the actual output, differs from the budgeted level of direct labour hours, there will be a volume variance. For R.M. Williams, the *average* budgeted activity for each month is 3750 direct labour hours (45 000 budgeted direct labour hours for the year ÷ 12).

Exhibit 11.7 illustrates this point graphically. In any month, budgeted fixed overhead is constant at R30 000 for all levels of activity. However, the total *applied* fixed overhead increases with activity, since fixed overhead is applied to work in process inventory at the rate of R8 per standard direct labour hour allowed. Notice that budgeted and applied fixed overhead are equal only if the number of standard hours allowed equals the average monthly planned activity level of 3750 direct labour hours. When this happens, there will be no fixed overhead volume variance. The company has a R5200 volume variance in September because the standard hours allowed, given actual output (4400 hours), and the average monthly planned hours are different. It is common to have a series of monthly favourable and unfavourable volume variances occurring throughout the year. For the full year, if the number of standard direct labour hours is equal to the total budgeted direct labour hours (45 000), then there would be no volume variance.

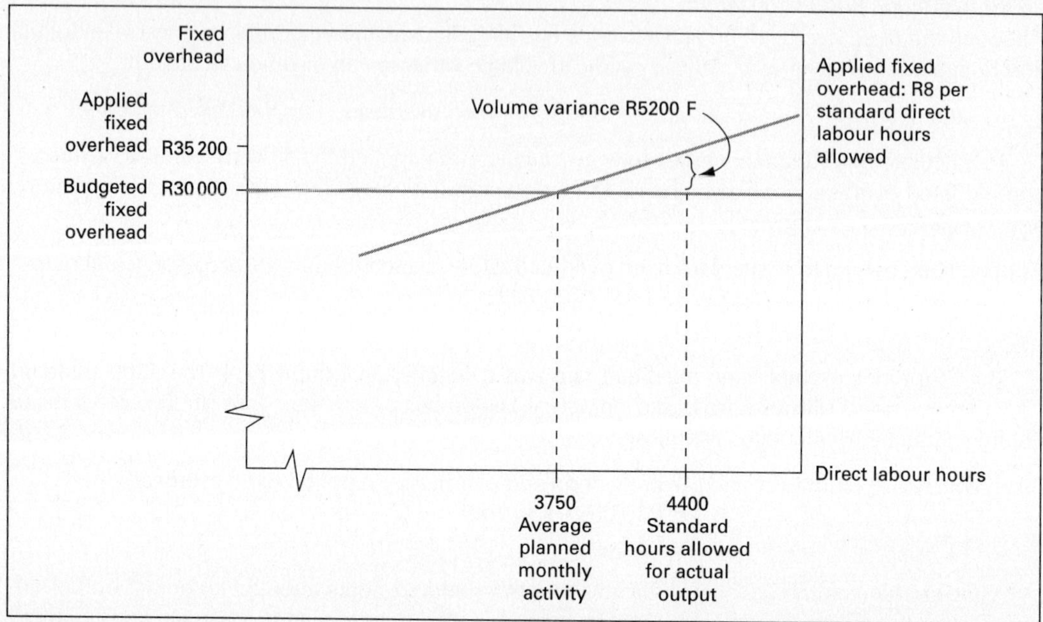

Exhibit 11.7 Budgeted versus applied fixed overhead, R.M. Williams

Capacity utilisation

A common, but faulty, interpretation of an unfavourable volume variance (where standard hours allowed for actual output are less than the average planned hours) is that it measures the cost of underutilising productive capacity. The reasoning behind this view is that the predetermined fixed overhead rate measures the cost of providing an hour of productive capacity. After all, the planned activity level used to calculate the predetermined fixed overhead rate is a measure of normal capacity utilisation. Moreover, fixed overhead costs, such as depreciation and factory rent, are costs incurred to create productive capacity. So if, for example, 3750 direct labour hours are planned, but actual output is such that only 3500 standard direct labour hours should have been worked, then capacity has been underutilised by 250 hours. Since each hour 'costs' R8, the cost of under-utilisation is R2000 (250 × R8), which is the volume variance.

The weakness in this interpretation of the volume variance is that it ignores the real cost of underutilising productive capacity. The real cost is the lost contribution margins on the products that are not produced when capacity is underutilised. In addition, the interpretation fails to recognise that underutilising capacity, and reducing inventory, may not be 'unfavourable'. It may be a wise managerial response when demand for a product is decreasing.

In summary, calculating the volume variance provides a way of reconciling the two purposes of costing systems: product costing and cost control. It has no implications for controlling costs. As we will see in a later section, the volume variance is required as a 'balancing item' to enable standard costs to be used for product costing purposes within the ledger system.

Four-way, three-way and two-way overhead variance analysis

Four variances were discussed in the preceding two sections: the variable overhead spending and efficiency variances, and the fixed overhead budget and volume variances. This is called a *four-way analysis*. Some managers prefer to combine the variable overhead spending and fixed overhead budget variances into a single combined spending variance. Since this presentation leaves only three separate variances, it is called a *three-way analysis*. Other managers prefer to combine the variable overhead spending, variable overhead efficiency and fixed overhead budget variances into a single combined budget variance. This leaves only two separate variances, so it is called a *two-way analysis*. Exhibit 11.8 displays the four-way, three-way and two-way variance analyses for R.M. Williams' September performance for the Clothing Department.

	Variable overhead spending variance	Fixed overhead budget variance	Variable overhead efficiency variance	Fixed overhead volume variance
Four-way analysis	R1 840 U	R4 200 U	R1 200 U	R5 200 F
	combined spending variance			
Three-way analysis	R6 040 U		R1 200 U	R5 200 F
	combined budget variance			
Two-way analysis	R7 240 U			R5 200 F
	underapplied overhead R2 040*			

*The underapplied overhead is the difference between the actual overhead incurred (R63 640) and overhead applied to work in process (R61 600).

Exhibit 11.8 Four-way, three-way and two-way overhead variance analysis, R.M. Williams

Overhead cost performance report

L.O. 6

There are many different formats that can be used to report variances. The focus of most variance reports is to highlight differences between actual and budgeted expenditure. We can explain these differences by considering the flexible budgets:

- a flexible budget based on the standard direct labour hours allowed for the actual output; and
- a flexible budget based on the actual direct labour hours worked.[3]

Using these flexible budgets, we can calculate the variable overhead spending and efficiency variances, and the fixed overhead budget variance for each overhead cost item in the flexible budget. An **overhead cost performance report** shows actual and budgeted costs, along with these itemised variances for *each overhead item*. The performance report, displayed in Exhibit 11.9, could be used by management to help exercise control over each of the overhead costs.

Notice that the performance report includes spending and efficiency variances only for the variable items, and a budget variance for the fixed items. The volume variance is not included as it has no implications for cost control. Upon receiving this report, a manager might investigate significant variances to determine underlying causes. Chapter 10 describes various methods for determining the significance of variances.

	1 Actual overhead	2 Flexible budget (4600 actual direct labour hours × standard rate)	3 Flexible budget (4400 standard direct labour hours allowed × standard rate)	4 Spending variance (column 1 − column 2)	5 Efficiency variance (column 2 − column 3)
Variable overheads:					
Indirect materials	18 000	16 744	16 016	1 256 U	728 U
Electricity	7 000	6 716	6 424	284 U	292 U
Consumables	4 440	4 140	3 960	300 U	180 U
Total variable overhead	R29 440	R27 600	R26 400	R1 840 U	R1 200 U
				Budget variance	
Fixed overheads:					
Supervisors' salaries	17 200	14 000	14 000	3 200 U	
Factory rent	5 800	6 000	6 000	−200 F	
Council rates	1 400	1 200	1 200	200 U	
Cleaning costs	4 600	3 600	3 600	1 000 U	
Insurance	1 600	1 600	1 600	0	
Depreciation of machinery	3 600	3 600	3 600	0	
Total fixed overhead	R34 200	R30 000	R30 000	R4 200 U	
Total manufacturing overheads	R63 640	R57 600	R56 400	R6 040 U	R1 200 U
Total variance between actual overhead and flexible budget		R7 240 U			

Exhibit 11.9 Overhead Cost Performance Report, R.M. Williams

Standard costs for product costing

L.O. 7

In a standard costing system, the standard costs are often used for product costing as well as for cost control. Therefore, the costs of direct material, direct labour and manufacturing overhead are all charged to work in process inventory at their standard costs, not actual costs.

Journal entries using standard costs

The journal entries required to record standard costs and variances for direct material and direct labour were explained in Chapter 10. Now we will complete the system by looking at how we account for manufacturing overhead under a standard costing system.[4] During September 20X6, actual manufacturing overhead costs incurred in the Clothing Department of R.M. Williams were R63 640. This consisted of R29 440 of variable overhead and R34 200 of fixed overhead. A summary journal entry to record these actual expenditures is as follows:

Manufacturing overhead	R 63 640	
Indirect materials inventory		R 22 440#
Electricity payable		7 000
Wages payable		17 200
Prepaid rent		5 800
Council rates payable		1 400
Cleaning costs		4 600
Prepaid insurance		1 600
Accumulated depreciation		3 600

#Includes consumables.

The credit amounts can be verified by examining column 1 of Exhibit 11.9. For example, indirect labour costs (wages payable) amounted to R17 200 for supervisors' salaries.

The *application* of manufacturing overhead to work in process is based on a predetermined (or standard) overhead rate of R14 per direct labour hour (total of the variable and fixed rates), and 4400 standard direct labour hours allowed, given actual output. In our journal entry we will also isolate each of the overhead variances:

Work in process inventory (4400 hours × R14)	R61 600	
Variable overhead spending variance	1 840	
Variable overhead efficiency variance	1 200	
Fixed overhead budget variance	4 200	
Manufacturing overhead		R63 640
Fixed overhead volume variance		5 200

In this journal entry, we have *applied* overhead to work in process inventory at the standard rate of R14 per direct labour hour allowed. We have also charged overhead variances to temporary ledger accounts. Unfavourable variances are debit entries, and the favourable volume variance is a credit entry. After this journal entry is posted to the ledger accounts, the manufacturing overhead account will have a zero balance. It was noted earlier that the fixed overhead volume variance has no implications for cost control. However, when we use standard costing for product costing, the volume variance allows us to account for all of the difference between actual overhead cost incurred and the overhead applied to production.

Disposition of variances

As explained in Chapter 10, variances are charged to temporary ledger accounts, and most companies close them directly to cost of goods sold at the end of each accounting period. If R.M. Williams were to close the variance accounts at the end of the month, a net difference of R2 040 would be charged to cost of goods sold:

Cost of goods sold	R2 040	
Fixed overhead volume variance	5 200	
Variable overhead spending variance		R1 840
Variable overhead efficiency variance		1 200
Fixed overhead budget variance		4 200

This amount of R2040 is the *underapplied overhead* for September. This means that the overhead applied to work in process inventory in September (R61 600) was R2040 less than the actual overhead cost incurred (R63 640). In a standard costing system, the total of the four overhead variances will always be equal to the overapplied or underapplied overhead for the accounting period.

Note that this journal entry would not usually be made at the end of the month, as underapplied or overapplied overhead is typically closed off to cost of goods sold annually. This is because the monthly amounts of underapplied and overapplied overhead are due in part to the seasonal (or lumpy) nature of many overhead costs. These monthly differences are assumed to even out by year-end.

An alternative accounting treatment to closing underapplied or overapplied overhead to cost of goods sold is to prorate underapplied or overapplied overhead among work in process inventory, finished goods inventory and cost of goods sold, as explained in Chapter 4. This treatment is appropriate where the amount of underapplied or overapplied overhead is substantial.

Flexible budgets in non-manufacturing organisations

L.O. 8

Non-manufacturing organisations also use flexible budgets to control overhead costs. For example, some airlines use air-kilometres flown, hotels may use occupancy rates, and restaurants can use customers served as the basis for their flexible overhead budgets.

As an illustration, Exhibit 11.10 displays the flexible overhead budget for Karoo Hospital. This hospital uses patient-days as the basis for its flexible overhead budget. The hospital administrator can use this budget for planning and for controlling overhead costs. Since a hospital does not produce inventoriable goods, there is no product costing role for its costing system.

Monthly Flexible Overhead Budget
Karoo Hospital

	Patient-days		
Budgeted cost	**10 000**	**12 500**	**15 000**
Variable costs:			
Electricity and gas	R10 000	R12 500	R15 000
Water and sewerage	1 600	2 000	2 400
Maintenance	6 000	7 500	9 000
Housekeeping	12 000	15 000	18 000
Medical supplies	14 000	17 500	21 000
Laundry	4 000	5 000	6 000
Billing and appointments	8 000	10 000	12 000
Total variable cost	R55 600	R69 500	R83 400
Fixed costs:			
Depreciation: building	6 000	6 000	6 000
Depreciation: equipment	12 000	12 000	12 000
Telephone	600	600	600
Nursing supervision	18 000	18 000	18 000
Administrative services	24 000	24 000	24 000
Total fixed cost	R60 600	R60 600	R60 600
Total overhead cost	R116 200	R130 100	R144 000

Exhibit 11.10 Flexible overhead budget for a hospital

An appraisal of standard costing systems

L.O. 9

Standard costing has been used in manufacturing companies for product costing and cost control for many decades. It has also spread to non-manufacturing firms. However, by the 1980s many changes had begun to take place in manufacturing companies. These included the growth of global competition, the introduction of new manufacturing practices such as JIT manufacturing, goals of continuous improvement, and the increasing focus on quality and customer service. These changes have brought into question the continuing relevance of conventional standard costing systems as a way of managing resources and creating value.

Criticisms of standard costing systems

Criticisms that can be made of the ability of conventional standard costing systems to help control costs within modern manufacturing environments include the following (Kaplan, 1990; Johnson, 1990; Bonsack, 1991; Malcolm, 1992):

1 *Variances are too aggregated and concentrate on the consequences rather than the causes of problems.* Conventional standard costing systems are based on the cost categories of direct material, direct labour and overhead. This can make it difficult to determine the cause of cost variances. Many managers require information about the cost performance of product lines, production batches or activities, and conventional standard costing systems do not provide this. An unfavourable direct labour efficiency variance may be a result of many different activities that are taking place on the factory floor, but is not sensitive enough to indicate the source of any particular problems. Is it taking longer to process a batch? Is the variance associated with any particular product line or production

batch? Do machine programs or settings need correcting? More focused measures, such as cycle time or batch-related measures, may provide answers to these questions. In Chapter 14, a range of different types of operational measures are discussed.

2 *Variance reports are produced too late to be useful.* In some businesses, monthly variance reports are prepared and presented to managers one or two weeks after month-end. But this is too late to determine or correct any problems. Even if monthly reports are produced promptly at the end of each month, this may still be too late to correct problems that occurred two or three weeks before! As a response, for years many managers have relied on their own more direct performance indicators to monitor their performance, and to correct problems closer to the time that they occur. For example, daily or even hourly measures of material usage, yield or cycle time can be used to monitor operations. Real time reporting, discussed in Chapter 12, also addresses this issue.

3 *Standard costing systems tend to focus too heavily on cost minimisation.* Standard cost variances are reported along responsibility accounting lines. This may provide incentives to decrease costs, but some actions taken to minimise costs may adversely affect other areas of strategic importance (such as product quality or customer service).

4 *Standard costing systems take a departmental perspective rather than a process perspective.* Modern approaches to cost management take a process perspective, which involves monitoring and managing links between departments as well as performance within departments. In contrast, conventional standard costing systems assign responsibility for cost variances to certain managers and functional departments. This can give rise to two problems. First, it may neglect opportunities for effective cost control, which may only become obvious when departmental boundaries are crossed and the interlinked activities that make up the organisation-wide value chain are recognised. This may reveal redundant and non-value-added activities that can be eliminated. In Chapter 15 we consider cost management techniques that take this process perspective. Second, assigning responsibility for variances to managers or departments may encourage managers to take actions to minimise costs in their own department at the expense of managers in other responsibility centres. For example, responsibility for the material price variance usually lies with the purchasing manager. To create favourable variances, cheap or low-quality material may be purchased, or materials may be purchased in excessive quantities to obtain quantity discounts. These actions will make the price variance appear more favourable, but may have adverse effects on other costs or aspects of the business, which are someone else's responsibility. Chapter 10 described an example of interactions between variances that can confound attempts at cost control and evaluating managers' responsibility.

5 *Standard costing systems place too much emphasis on the cost and efficiency of direct labour.* Direct labour is becoming a less important factor in production as many businesses increase their level of automation.

6 *Overhead variances, in particular, give limited information for cost control.* We stated earlier that the variable overhead spending variance and the fixed overhead budget variance can provide information for control. However, due to their high level of aggregation, their focus on total overhead items rather than on activities or processes, and the difficulty that many non-accounting managers have in interpreting these variances, they provide only a limited basis for controlling costs. As automation is increasing in many companies, there is a shift from variable costs towards greater fixed costs. Therefore, it is important that more effective ways of controlling overheads are found.

7 *Variance analysis does not explicitly encourage continuous improvement.* Many companies emphasise continuous improvement in all aspects of their business. With standards being set for periods of 6 to 12 months or longer, they can be criticised for not providing that extra stretch that is needed to encourage continuous cost improvement.
8 *Standard costs become outdated quickly because of shorter product life cycles.* In many industries, where there is a rapid turnover of new products, standards are relevant for only a very short time. However, setting standards more frequently to accommodate new products would make standard costing expensive to maintain.
9 *Standard costing systems are not defined broadly enough to capture the full costs of materials.* The standard costs of direct materials do not capture the full costs of purchasing inventory. The total cost of ownership of materials is the purchase price of materials, plus associated costs. These are the costs of ordering and paying; scheduling delivery, receiving, inspection, handling and storing; scrap, rework and obsolescence; and the production disruptions from incorrect delivery. This issue is explored further in Chapter 16.

Standard costing is very widely used for product costing. However, many companies have de-emphasised standard costing as a mechanism for cost control. More effective cost control techniques include the greater recognition of multiple cost drivers, and the use of activity analysis and operational performance measures. These techniques are discussed in Chapters 14 and 15.

Despite these criticisms, standard costing systems are still used in many South African companies (although some companies only focus on direct material and direct labour standards). The 'Real life' below illustrates how standard costing and variance analysis can be tailored to meet the needs of management better. Even without tailoring, standard costing systems offer a number of advantages.

Advantages of standard costing

Despite the criticisms outlined in the previous section, there are many positive outcomes of using standard costing.

1 Standard costs provide a *good basis for cost comparisons.* As discussed earlier, it would make no sense to compare budgeted costs at one (budgeted) activity level with actual costs incurred at a different (actual) activity level. Standard costs enable the management accountant to calculate the standard cost allowed, given actual output, which then serves as a sensible benchmark for comparing with the actual cost.
2 Calculation of standard costs and cost variances enables managers to use *management by exception* in order to concentrate on significant variances only. This approach conserves valuable management time.
3 Variances can provide a convenient basis for *performance evaluation and determining bonuses* for employees.
4 Participation in the setting of standards, assigning responsibility for certain variances and the use of variances for performance evaluation can have a *motivational effect* on employees.
5 The use of standard costs in product costing results in *more stable product costs* compared to actual product costs. These standard costs can be used for decisions such as pricing or setting product mix. Actual costs often fluctuate erratically, whereas standard costs are changed only periodically.
6 Standard costs can also be used for *external reporting.* The International Accounting Standard IAS 2 states that inventories can be valued at standard cost. However, those standard costs must approximate actual cost. Standard costs should be realistically attainable and reviewed regularly in the light of current conditions.

REAL LIFE: STANDARD COSTING IS ALIVE AND KICKING!

Parker Hannifin Corporation (PHC) is a manufacturer of tube and brass fittings in Michigan, USA. PHC has adapted its standard costing systems and variance analysis to target the problem areas in its business and to focus on continuous improvement. What are some of the features of its system?

- Variances are reported on an exception basis for individual product lines. If cost variances exceed 5 per cent of sales, each product line manager must provide an explanation for the variances and a plan of action to correct problems.
- The variances are reported the day after jobs are completed (rather than at month-end) so that a review can be undertaken while the job is fresh in everyone's mind.
- Corrective actions to control problems are more effective, due to the timely reporting of variances.
- Aggregate variance reports are run each week and at the end of each month, by product line and job, to enable further analysis of performance.
- Employees are trained and empowered to manage operations using variances. Meetings are held with production employees to explain variance performance and the importance of monitoring and acting on variances.
- New forms of cost variances that are generated include:
  - The standard run quantity variance – which shows the cost impact where the size of a batch is less than the optimal batch size.
  - Material substitution variance – to evaluate the feasibility of the use of alternative raw materials.
  - Method variance – to assess situations where different machines can be used for the same job.

So it may be premature to say that cost variance analysis is irrelevant – it is simply a case of modifying the system to meet the specific needs of managers.

Source: Johnsen & Sopariwala (2000)

Like any tool, a standard costing system can be misused. For example, when employees are criticised for every unfavourable cost variance, the positive motivational effects will vanish quickly. Moreover, if standards are not revised often enough, they will become inaccurate and the benefits of standard costing will therefore disappear.

Activity-based budgeting

L.O. 10

In our discussions of flexible budgeting and standard costing we have assumed that material, labour and overhead costs are driven by a single cost driver. For example, in the flexible budgets for R.M. Williams (see Exhibit 11.3) it was assumed that the variable overhead costs were driven by direct labour hours; all other overhead costs were treated as fixed. This approach is consistent with conventional volume-based product costing systems. However, in Chapter 3 we saw that an increasing number of businesses have refined their cost management systems to recognise multiple cost drivers, some of which are non-volume-related. If a company has adopted activity-based costing, then it makes sense to incorporate these more accurate cost drivers into activity-based flexible budgets.

How does an **activity-based budgeting (ABB)** *system differ from a conventional budgeting system?* Activity-based costing (ABC) is relatively new and there are no hard and fast rules on how activity-based systems can be used for budgeting. ABB uses the principles of ABC to estimate the firm's future demand for resources. However, in order to formulate the budget we need to 'reverse' the ABC system (Cooper & Slagmulder, 2000a). That is, rather than starting with an analysis of resources, calculating the cost of activities and then the cost of products, customers or other cost objects (see the vertical view of ABC in Exhibit 7.6), ABB works in reverse. Building an ABB parallels the way in which conventional budgets are formulated: we start with an analysis of the market, then forecast sales demand, which leads to estimating production activities and the required level of production and resources.

Exhibit 11.11 contrasts the structure of ABC and ABB. Under ABB, once sales volume and production volume have been estimated, the demand for activities can be determined. The type and quantity of activities consumed by each product (or other cost objects) would already be available as part of the activity-based costing system. The resources required to undertake the activities can then be calculated by multiplying the products by activity drivers to get the activities required, and then activities by resource drivers to get resources or costs. This process is illustrated in Exhibit 11.12 in a simplified form.

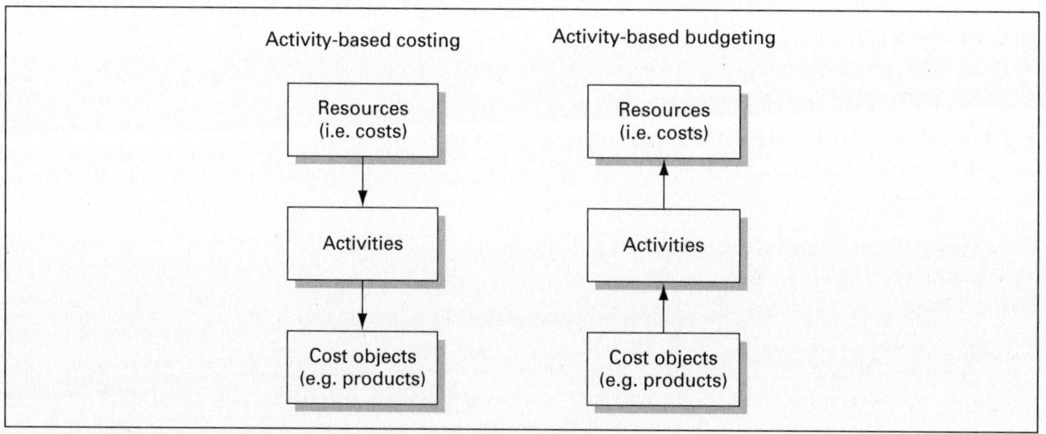

Source: adapted from Cooper & Slagmulder (2000a)

Exhibit 11.11 Activity-based costing versus activity-based budgeting

Inaccuracies in the ABB system

ABB can provide a more accurate method for forecasting future costs, and a more accurate benchmark against which to compare actual costs. However, the ABB process is not as simple as it sounds. Cooper and Slagmulder (2000a, 2000b) claim that estimating budgeted resources through the reversal process will be 'hopelessly inaccurate'! Why is this?

1 *Spending versus consumption of resources.* ABC systems model the way in which resources are consumed, not how they are acquired. Thus, the cost of unused capacity is not included in ABC product costs. (This was discussed briefly in Chapter 7.) When the reversal process is used for ABB, it is assumed that resources consumed equals resources acquired. In some cases, resources are purchased in fixed quantities (for example, equipment or salaried employees), while other resources are purchased on an 'as-needed' basis (such as hourly labour and minor materials). For example, if a company currently employs six salaried workers on the production line, and output is estimated to increase by 20 per cent in the ABB, using our ABC system we may predict that we need to employ 7.2 employees (6 + 20 per cent). This is clearly not possible, so the resources consumed (7.2 employees) will not equal the resources acquired (8 employees). We have unused

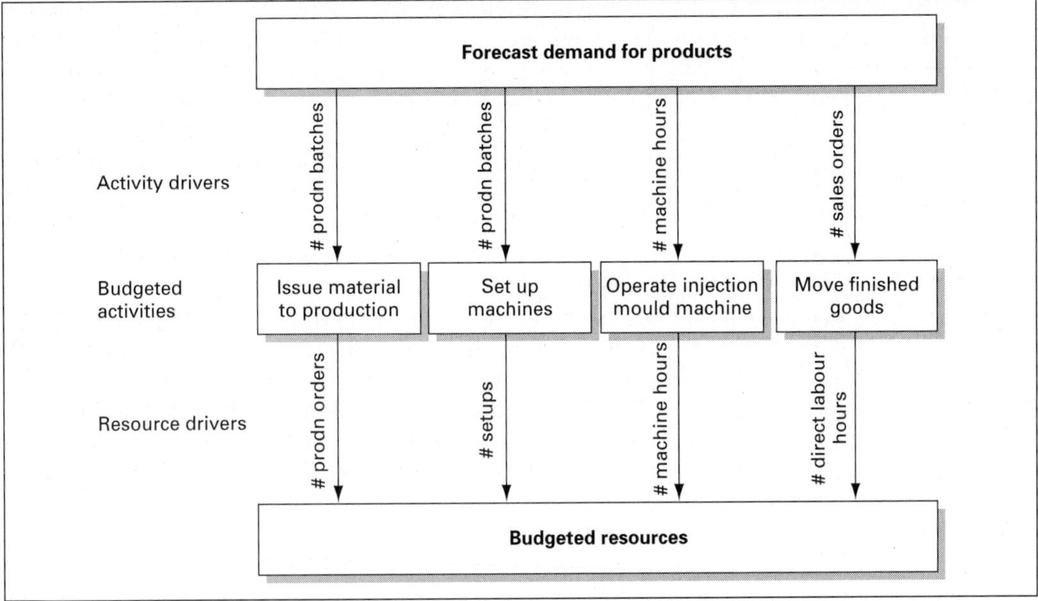

Exhibit 11.12 ABB: reversing the ABC system

capacity. Thus, by including the cost of the 7.2 employees in the ABB, the required resources are understated.

2 *Non-manufacturing activities.* As discussed in Chapter 8, the calculation of product costs under ABC may include the cost of activities that occur in non-manufacturing areas, such as human resources, customer service and information systems departments. Under ABB, if demand for products is predicted to increase by 20 per cent, the reversal system would assume that the number of activities that are consumed by products, and the cost of those activities, will increase by 20 per cent. However, the total cost of activities undertaken in the information systems department or customer service department, may increase by some other percentage – or not change at all – as a result of the 20 per cent increase in demand for product.

3 *Shared resources.* Under ABC, it is difficult to account for two or more activities consuming a common resource. For example, 4 leased forklift trucks may be used to move material between machines in the manufacture of three types of products for half of the time, and used to move delivered materials from delivery truck to warehouse for the remainder of the time. Thus, the ABC system would split half the cost of the lease between the three products, in proportion to the number of move activities that the forklift truck performs for each product. The other half of the lease would be assigned to warehousing activities. If production increases by 20 per cent, then the ABB system may predict that we need 2.4 forklift trucks in production and 2.4 forklift trucks in warehousing. We know that we cannot acquire part forklift trucks, so the system would estimate that 6 forklift trucks are required to be purchased in total, 3 in production and 3 in the warehouse. Clearly, only 5 forklift trucks are required.

4 *Information requirements.* The above examples are simplistic and you might be wondering why a company could not detect these inaccuracies within the ABB process. You need to remember that an ABC system may include hundreds of activities and cost drivers. The complexity of such a system may mean that inaccuracies are easily overlooked. Some of the problems can be avoided if a firm has an ABC/ABB system based on sophisticated

models that account for differences in resource consumption and resource acquisition and that recognise a number of cost objects. However, decisions about design, implementation and maintenance of such systems are governed by the costs of incorporating detail and sophistication versus the benefits of having budgets with greater levels of accuracy. ABB requires a greater level of detailed information than traditional budgeting. This includes information about how resources are consumed, and how both production and administrative activities increase or decrease in the light of production level changes.

Performance evaluation under ABB

To evaluate performance under an activity-based budgeting system, we need to compare actual activity costs to budgeted costs. The budgeted costs should be based on flexible budgets that show the budgeted cost of activities as the various cost drivers change. However, as each activity may have a different cost driver, it would be difficult to prepare an informative flexible budget report. There would need to be many columns to demonstrate the many different changes that might take place in the level of cost drivers. There may be many cost drivers, all of which could vary in different ways and at different levels of hierarchy – unit level, batch level, product level. For each specific activity we could develop a formula flexible budget, but this becomes very complex, particularly where the activity-based system covers all activities – manufacturing and non-manufacturing. Assigning actual costs to activities may also involve considerable complexity and inaccuracy.

The development of new budgeting techniques does not necessarily mean that we abandon well-established practices. Rather, under activity-based budgeting we could construct standards and develop flexible budgets that are more accurate benchmarks, compared with those formulated under conventional budgeting systems. Against this benefit, the additional costs of formulating activity-based budgets must also be considered. The large number of activities and planned levels of cost drivers that need to be estimated increases both the complexity of the budgeting system and the cost of data collection and maintenance of the various activity and cost databases. Even so, ABB can play a useful role in forcing managers to think about their costs and how those costs actually behave.

Summary

In this chapter we extended our discussion of the use of standard costs to control costs, by considering the use of flexible budgets and manufacturing overhead. It is far more difficult to control manufacturing overhead costs than direct material and direct labour costs. This is because manufacturing overhead consists of many different costs, which exhibit a variety of cost behaviours and relate to many different cost drivers. In addition, overhead costs cannot be traced easily to processes, products or services, and this makes it difficult to determine the source of cost overruns. Key points include:

- A flexible budget can be used to control manufacturing costs. The flexible overhead budget is based on a range of levels of activity. Machine hours and direct labour hours are commonly used measures of activity.
- A flexible budget formula can be used to determine the budgeted overhead, based on the actual level of activity, and thus provides a benchmark against which to compare the actual manufacturing overhead costs.
- Four types of overhead variances can be calculated: the variable overhead spending, variable overhead efficiency variances, the fixed overhead budget variance and fixed overhead volume variance. The usefulness of these variances for achieving effective cost control of manufacturing overheads can be questioned.

- Standard or predetermined overhead rates can be used for product costing under a standard costing system. The amount of overhead cost applied to work in process inventory is equal to the standard overhead rate multiplied by the standard quantity of the activity allowed, given actual output.
- While standard costing systems can offer a business many benefits, their continued relevance within the modern manufacturing environment has been questioned. Many organisations have de-emphasised or modified their standard costing systems to adopt more modern methods of controlling costs and evaluating performance.
- As an extension to activity-based costing, activity-based budgeting can be formulated using a variety of different cost drivers. Activity-based budgeting provides more accurate benchmarks than do flexible budgets calculated using only volume-based cost drivers.

In Chapters 10 and 11 we have considered conventional techniques for controlling costs. However, more effective methods of managing costs, through managing activities and the drivers of cost, are considered in Chapter 15.

References

Bonsack, RA 1991, 'Does activity based costing replace standard costing?', *Journal of Cost Management,* Winter, pp. 46–7.

Cooper, R & Slagmulder, R 2000a, 'Activity-based Budgeting – Part 1', *Strategic Finance,* September, pp. 85–6.

Cooper, R & Slagmulder, R 2000b, 'Activity-based Budgeting – Part 2', *Strategic Finance,* October, pp. 26–8.

Johnsen, D & Sopariwala, P 2000, 'Standard costing is alive and well at Parker Brass', *Management Accounting Quarterly,* Winter, pp. 13–20.

Johnson, HT 1990, 'Performance measurement for competitive excellence', in RS Kaplan (ed.), *Measures for Manufacturing Excellence,* Harvard Business School Press, Boston MA, pp. 61–90.

Kaplan, RS 1990, 'Limitations of cost accounting in advanced manufacturing environments', in RS Kaplan (ed.), *Measures for Manufacturing Excellence,* Harvard Business School Press, Boston MA, pp. 15–38.

Malcolm, RE 1992, 'Overhead control implications of activity costing', *Accounting Horizons,* December, pp. 69–78.

Self study

Self-study problem: Overhead variances

In November 20X6, the R.M. Williams Clothing Department worked 3900 direct labour hours and incurred the following manufacturing overhead costs:

Variable overhead	R 25 740
Fixed overhead	R 31 600

The production was as follows:

Product	Actual production	Standard direct labour hours per unit	Total standard direct labour hours for actual output
Shirts	1200	1.0	1200
Moleskins	1700	1.4	2380
Coats	200	0.6	120
			3700

R.M. Williams' monthly flexible overhead budget for November is the same as that given in Exhibit 11.3. The standard variable overhead rate of R6.00 per DLH and the fixed overhead rate of R8.00 per DLH are set out in Exhibit 11.4.

Calculate R.M. Williams' variable overhead variances and fixed overhead variances, using the formats shown in Exhibits 11.5 and 11.6.

Solution to Self-study problem

The solution to the Self-study problem is given in Exhibits 11.13 and 11.14.

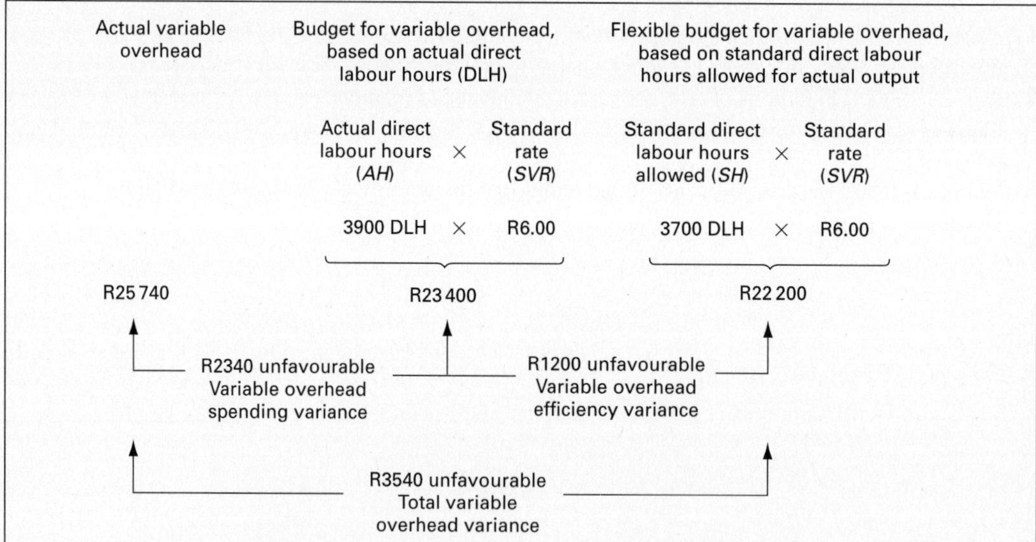

Exhibit 11.13 Variable overhead spending and efficiency variances (Self-study problem)

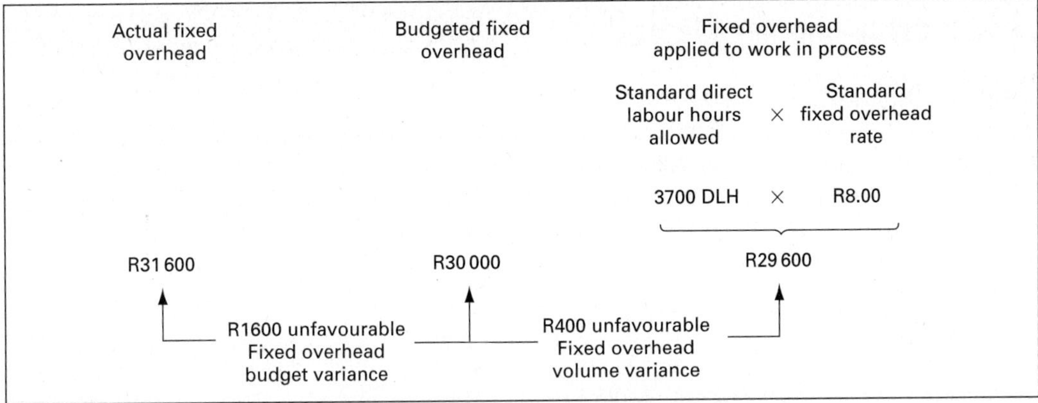

Exhibit 11.14 Fixed overhead budget and volume variances (Self-study problem)

Cybersearch

1 Find the website of an organisation that has implemented activity-based budgeting and see if you can answer the following questions:
   (a) What was the stated motivation for implementing ABB?
   (b) Were there any implementation problems?
   (c) Has ABB been a success?
   (d) Were there any other interesting details of the ABB implementation that you found?
2 Search the web for South African companies that use standard costs to value inventories.

Appendix to Chapter 11

Sales variances

L.O. 11 The variances discussed in Chapters 10 and 11 focus on production costs. However, we can also calculate variances to help management to analyse the firm's sales performance. To illustrate two sales variances, we will continue our discussion of R.M. Williams. The expected sales price and standard variable costs for a pair of moleskin pants are as follows:

Expected sales price	R200.00
Standard variable costs:	
Direct material	R77.50
Direct labour	50.40
Variable overhead (1.4 direct labour hours @ R6)	8.40
Total unit variable cost	R136.30

The difference between the sales price and the unit variable cost is called the **unit contribution margin**. R.M. Williams' unit contribution margin on moleskins is R63.70 per unit (R200−R136.30). This is the amount that the sale of one pair of moleskin pants contributes towards covering the fixed costs and making a profit.

During October 20X6, management at R.M. Williams expected to sell 1500 pairs of moleskins. Based on this sales forecast, the accountant calculated the following budgeted **total contribution margin**:

Budgeted sales revenue (1500 units × R200)	R300 000
Budgeted variable costs (1500 units × R136.30)	204 450
Budgeted total contribution margin (1500 units × R63.70)	R95 550

The actual results for October were as follows:

Actual sales volume	1600 units
Actual sales price	R 190.00
Actual unit variable cost	R 136.30

Using these results, R.M. Williams' total contribution margin for October is calculated as follows:

Actual sales revenue (1600 units × R190)	R304 000
Actual variable costs (1600 units × R136.30)	218 080
Actual total contribution margin (1600 units × R53.70)	R85 920

R.M. Williams' total contribution margin in October was R9630 less than the budgeted amount. What caused this variance? First, the company sold more moleskins than were budgeted for. This would increase the total contribution margin. Second, the sales price was lower than budgeted for, and this would cause the total contribution margin to decline. Two sales variances can be calculated to reflect these facts. These variances are defined below and are calculated for October:

Sales price variance = (actual sales price − budgeted sales price) × actual sales volume
= (R190−R200) × 1600
= 16 000 U

Sales volume variance = (actual sales volume − budgeted sales volume) × budgeted unit contribution margin
= (1600−1500) × R63.70
= R6370 F

Together, the **sales price variance** and the **sales volume variance** explain the R9630 variance between actual and budgeted total contribution margin:

Sales price variance	R16 000 U
Sales volume variance	R6 370 F
Variance between actual and budgeted total contrtibution margin	R9 630 U

You will notice in this example that budgeted variable costs per unit were equal to actual variable costs per unit. In practice, there would be both cost variances and sales variances.

Questions

?

11.1 Distinguish between *static* and *flexible* budgets and explain the advantages of using a flexible budget for control, compared with using a static budget.

11.2 Why are flexible overhead budgets often based on an *input* measure, such as machine hours or direct labour hours, rather than an *output* measure?

11.3 Explain the difference between the *formula* and the *report format* of the flexible budget.

11.4 Use ledger accounts to show how manufacturing overhead is added to work in process inventory when standard costing is used.

11.5 How has the increased level of automation in manufacturing affected overhead application?

11.6 Explain how you would interpret a *variable overhead spending variance.*

11.7 The only variable overhead cost at Lightening Cinema is electricity. Does an unfavourable variable overhead spending variance imply that the cinema paid more than the anticipated rate per kilowatt hour?

11.8 Explain the meaning of the *variable overhead efficiency variance.*

11.9 Distinguish between the *direct labour efficiency variance* and the *variable overhead efficiency variance* (assuming direct labour hours is the relevant activity).

11.10 Define the *fixed overhead budget variance,* and explain how it may assist managers to control costs.

11.11 What is the correct interpretation of the *fixed overhead volume variance*?

11.12 Describe a common but faulty interpretation of the fixed overhead volume variance. Why is this interpretation incorrect?

11.13 Draw a graph showing budgeted and applied fixed overhead, and indicate clearly an unfavourable volume variance.

11.14 Why would some managers prefer to use a two-way analysis or three-way analysis, compared to the four-way analysis that you have learned in this chapter?

11.15 What types of organisations may use flexible budgets for control?

11.16 Explain the difference between the *control purpose* and the *product costing purpose* of standard costing.

11.17 Why are fixed overhead costs sometimes called 'capacity-producing costs'?

11.18 Explain how an activity-based budget differs from a conventional flexible budget.

11.19 In your own words, explain two of the sources of inaccuracies in an ABB system.

11.20 Select three activities and three activity drivers that might be used under an activity-based budgeting system for a hospital.

11.21 Outline the criticisms of standard costing systems.

11.22 Describe the advantages of a standard costing system.

11.23 (appendix) Explain how the sales price variance and the sales volume variance can assist managers to control costs.

Exercises

E11.24 Straightforward calculation of overhead variances: manufacturer

The data below relate to Tokologo Napkin Company, a manufacturer of paper napkins:

Standard variable overhead rate	R18 per machine hour
Standard quantity of machine hours	2 hours per unit of output
Budgeted fixed overhead	R300 000
Budgeted output	25 000 units

Actual results for December are as follows:

Actual output	20 000 units
Actual variable overhead	R960 000
Actual fixed overhead	R291 000
Actual machine time	50 000 machine hours

Required:

Calculate the following variances, indicating whether each variance is favourable or unfavourable:

1 Variable overhead spending variance.
2 Variable overhead efficiency variance.
3 Fixed overhead budget variance.
4 Fixed overhead volume variance.

E11.25 Diagram of overhead variances: manufacturer

Refer to the data in Exercise 11.24.

Required:

Use diagrams similar to those in Exhibits 11.5 and 11.6 to calculate the variable overhead spending and efficiency variances, and the fixed overhead budget and volume variances.

E11.26 Constructing a flexible overhead budget: hospital

The chief accountant for Rainbow Community Hospital estimates that the hospital uses 25 kilowatt hours of electricity per patient-day, and that the cost of electricity will be R0.50 per kilowatt hour. The hospital also pays a fixed monthly charge of R10 000 to the electricity supplier to rent emergency back-up electricity generators.

Required:

Construct a flexible budget for the hospital's electricity costs using each of the following techniques:

1 A formula flexible budget.
2 A report form flexible budget for 30 000, 40 000 and 50 000 patient-days of activity. List variable and fixed electricity costs separately.

E11.27 Activity-based budgeting; cost drivers

Suggest three activities and a possible activity driver for each activity that might be used as part of an activity-based budgeting system in each of the following industries:

1 An insurance company.
2 An express parcel delivery service.
3 A restaurant.
4 A regional office of the South African Revenue Service Office.

E11.28 Straightforward calculation of overhead variances: manufacturer

Andromeda Glassware Pty Ltd has the following standards and flexible budget data:

Standard variable overhead rate	R6 per direct labour hour
Standard quantity of direct labour	2 hours per unit of output
Budgeted fixed overhead	R100 000
Budgeted output	25 000 units

Actual results for April are as follows:

Actual output	20 000 units
Actual variable overhead	R320 000
Actual fixed overhead	R97 000
Actual direct labour	50 000 hours

Required:

Use the variance formulas to calculate the following variances, indicating whether each variance is favourable or unfavourable:

1 Variable overhead spending variance.
2 Variable overhead efficiency variance.
3 Fixed overhead budget variance.
4 Fixed overhead volume variance.

E11.29 Diagram of overhead variances; graphing fixed overhead variances: manufacturer

Refer to the data in Exercise 11.28.

Required:

1 Use diagrams similar to those in Exhibits 11.5 and 11.6 to calculate the variable overhead spending and efficiency variances, and the fixed overhead budget and volume variances.
2 Draw a graph similar to the one in Exhibit 11.7 (fixed overhead) to depict the fixed overhead volume variance for Andromeda Glassware Pty Ltd.

E11.30 Journal entries for overhead: manufacturer

Refer to the data in Exercise 11.28.

Required:

Prepare journal entries for Andromeda Glassware Pty Ltd to:

1 Record the incurrence of actual variable overhead and actual fixed overhead.
2 Add variable and fixed overhead to work in process inventory.
3 Account for the overhead variances.

E11.31 Reconstruct missing information from partial data: manufacturer

You took your work home one evening, and your brother spilled his chocolate milkshake on the variance report you were preparing. Fortunately, you were able to reconstruct the obliterated information from the remaining data. Fill in the missing numbers below:

Actual variable overhead rate per machine hour	?
Actual machine hours per unit of output	?
Actual fixed overhead	?
Actual production in units	?
Standard variable overhead rate per machine hour	R8.00
Standard machine hours per unit of output	4 hours
Budgeted fixed overhead	R25 000
Budgeted production in units	12 500
Variable overhead spending variance	R36 000 U
Variable overhead efficiency variance	R96 000 F
Fixed overhead budget variance	R7500 U
Fixed overhead volume variance	?
Total actual overhead	R356 500
Total budgeted overhead (flexible budget)	?
Total budgeted overhead (static budget)	?
Total applied overhead	R408 000

E11.32 Overhead variances: manufacturer

Able Control Company is a manufacturer of electrical switches, and uses a standard costing system. The standard manufacturing overhead costs per switch are based on direct labour hours and are as follows:

Variable overhead (5 hours @ R24 per hour)	R120
Fixed overhead (5 hours @ R36 per hour)*	180
Total overhead	R300

*Based on capacity of 300 000 direct labour hours per month.

The following information is available for the month of October:

- 56 000 switches were produced, although 60 000 switches were budgeted.
- 275 000 direct labour hours were worked at a total cost of R7 650 000.
- Variable overhead costs were R7 020 000.
- Fixed overhead costs were R11 250 000.

Required:
Calculate the variable overhead spending and efficiency variances and the fixed overhead budget and volume variances for October. Indicate whether each variance is favourable or unfavourable.

(CMA, adapted)

E11.33 Sales variances (appendix): manufacturer

JBay Boogie is a small company based in Jeffreys Bay that manufactures boogie boards. The company's performance report for November is as follows:

	Actual	Budget
Boogie boards sold	6000	8000
Sales revenue	R240 000	R300 000
Variable costs	145 000	180 000
Contribution margin	R95 000	R120 000
Fixed costs	84 000	80 000
Operating profit	R11 000	R40 000

The company uses a flexible budget to analyse its performance and to measure the effect on operating profit of the various factors affecting the difference between budgeted and actual operating profit.

Required:

Calculate the sales price and sales volume variances for November, and indicate whether each is favourable or unfavourable.

(CMA, adapted)

E11.34 Sales variances (appendix): manufacturer

The data below relate to Aurora Electronics for the month of February:

	Static budget	Actual
Units sold	15 000	13 500
Sales revenue	R1 800 000	R1 552 500
Variable manufacturing cost	600 000	540 000
Fixed manufacturing cost	300 000	300 000
Variable selling and administrative expenses	150 000	135 000
Fixed selling and administrative expenses	150 000	150 000

Required:

Calculate the sales price and sales volume variances for February.

Problems

P11.35 Interpretation of variable overhead efficiency variance

You recently received the following note from the production supervisor of the company for which you work as the accountant:

I don't understand these crazy variable overhead efficiency variances. My employees are very careful in their use of electricity and manufacturing supplies, and we use very little indirect labour. What are we supposed to do?

Write a brief memo responding to the production supervisor's concern.

P11.36 Straightforward overhead variances: manufacturer

Tsolwana Paper Company manufactures paper for photocopiers. The company has developed standard overhead rates based on a monthly capacity of 180 000 direct labour hours as follows:

Standard costs per unit (one box of paper):	
Variable overhead (2 hours @ R6 per hour)	R12
Fixed overhead (2 hours @ R10 per hour)	20
Total	R32

During April, 45 000 units were budgeted for production; however, only 40 000 units were produced. The following data relate to April:

- Actual direct labour cost incurred was R1 567 500 for 82 500 actual hours of work.
- Actual overhead incurred totalled R1 371 500, of which R511 500 was variable and R860 000 was fixed.

Required:

Prepare two exhibits, similar to Exhibits 11.5 and 11.6 in the chapter, showing the following variances. State whether each variance is favourable or unfavourable.

1 Variable overhead spending variance.
2 Variable overhead efficiency variance.
3 Fixed overhead budget variance.
4 Fixed overhead volume variance.

(CMA, adapted)

P11.37 Graphing budgeted and applied overhead: recording studio

Countrytime Studios is a small recording studio in Knysna. The studio budgets and applies overhead costs on the basis of production time. Countrytime's accountant anticipates 10 000 hours of production time next year. The following overhead amounts have been budgeted for next year:

Variable overhead	R40 000
Fixed overhead	R90 000

Required:

1 Draw two graphs – one for variable overhead and one for fixed overhead. The variable on the horizontal axis of each graph should be production time, in hours, ranging from 5000 to 15 000 hours. The variable on the vertical axis of each graph should be overhead cost (variable or fixed). Each graph should include two lines – one for the flexible budget amount of overhead and one for applied overhead.
2 Write a brief memo to Countrytime Studios' general manager, explaining the graphs, so that she will understand the concepts of budgeted and applied overhead.

P11.38 Standard hours allowed; flexible budget; multiple products: insurance company

Ouseker Insurance Company uses a flexible overhead budget for its New Policy Department. The firm offers five types of policy, with the following standard hours allowed per policy for clerical processing:

Health	1 hour
Life	1.5 hours
Automobile	2 hours
Renter's	2 hours
Homeowner's	5 hours

The following numbers of insurance applications were processed during July:

Health	375
Life	300
Automobile	150
Renter's	600
Homeowner's	300

The accountant estimates that the variable overhead rate in the application processing department is R50 per hour, and that fixed overhead costs will amount to R30 000 per month.

Required:

1 Calculate the number of standard clerical hours allowed in July, given the number of applications processed.
2 Explain why the company's flexible budget should be based on the number of clerical hours allowed rather than on the number of applications processed.
3 Construct a formula flexible overhead budget for the company.
4 What is the flexible budget for total overhead cost in July?

P11.39 Overhead variances; journal entries; closing variance accounts: manufacturer

Bloem Instruments Company manufactures a control valve used in air-conditioning systems. The firm uses a standard costing system for product costing. The manufacturing overhead rate is based on a normal annual activity level of 600 000 machine hours. The company planned to produce 25 000 units each month during 20X6. The budgeted manufacturing overhead for 20X6 is as follows:

Variable	R18 000 000
Fixed	15 000 000
Total	R33 000 000

During November 20X6, the company produced 26 000 units and used 53 500 machine hours. Actual manufacturing overhead for the month was R1 300 000 fixed and R1 600 000 variable. The total manufacturing overhead applied during November was R2 860 000.

The standard cost of a control valve is as follows:

Direct material	R72.50
Direct labour (2 hours @ R55)	80.00
Manufacturing overhead (2 hours @ R55)	110.00
Total standard cost	R 262.50

Required:

1 Calculate the following variances for November, indicating whether each variance is favourable or unfavourable:
   (a) variable overhead spending variance
   (b) variable overhead efficiency variance
   (c) fixed overhead budget variance
   (d) fixed overhead volume variance

2 Prepare journal entries to add manufacturing overhead to work in process inventory, and record variances and actual overhead costs.

(CMA, adapted)

P11.40 Activity-based budgeting, cost drivers: manufacturer

Sandra Smit is the financial controller of Fluffy Clouds, which is a manufacturer of baby clothes. The company is considering implementing an activity-based budgeting system and Sandra has asked for your advice on how to proceed.

Required:

Write a report for Sandra that covers the following issues:

1 The advantages of ABB over conventional budgeting.
2 How activities and cost drivers could be selected.
3 The types of information that may need to be collected to maintain the system.

(*Hint:* You may need to review Chapter 8.)

P11.41 Overhead variances: manufacturer

Ugu Products developed its overhead application rate from the annual budget. The budget is based on an expected total output of 720 000 units requiring 3 600 000 machine hours. The company is able to schedule production uniformly throughout the year.

A total of 66 000 units requiring 315 000 machine hours were produced during May. Actual overhead costs for May amounted to R750 000. The actual costs, compared with those in the annual budget and the monthly budget, are as follows:

Annual Budget					
	Total amount	Per unit	Per machine hour	Monthly budget	Actual costs for May
Variable overhead:					
Indirect labour	R1 800 000	R2.50	R0.50	R150 000	R150 000
Supplies	2 448 000	3.40	0.68	204 000	222 000
Fixed overhead:					
Supervision	1 296 000	1.80	0.36	108 000	102 000
Utilities	1 080 000	1.50	0.30	90 000	108 000
Depreciation	2 016 000	2.80	0.56	168 000	168 000
Total	R8 640 000	R12.00	R2.40	R720 000	R750 000

Required:

1 Prepare a schedule showing the following amounts for Ugu Products for May:
  (a) applied overhead costs
  (b) variable overhead spending variance
  (c) fixed overhead budget variance
  (d) variable overhead efficiency variance
  (e) fixed overhead volume variance

  Be sure to indicate whether each variance is favourable or unfavourable.

2 Draw a graph to depict the variable overhead variances. There should be two lines – one for the flexible variable overhead budget and one for the applied overhead (see Problem 11.37, requirement 1).

(CMA, adapted)

P11.42 Overhead variances; journal entries: manufacturer

Singh Products Ltd uses a standard costing system. The firm estimates that it will operate its manufacturing facilities at 800 000 machine hours for the year. The estimate for total budgeted overhead is R2 000 000. The standard variable overhead rate is estimated to be R2 per machine hour or R6 per unit. The actual data for the year are presented below:

Actual units produced	250 000
Actual machine hours	764 000
Actual variable overhead	R1 701 000
Actual fixed overhead	R 392 000

Required:

1 Calculate the following variances. Indicate whether each is favourable or unfavourable.
  (a) variable overhead spending variance
  (b) variable overhead efficiency variance
  (c) fixed overhead budget variance
  (d) fixed overhead volume variance

2 Prepare journal entries to add manufacturing overhead to work in process inventory, and to record the variances and the actual overhead cost.

(CMA, adapted)

P11.43 Linking flexible budgets and variances: hospital

Waverley Hospital runs an outpatient clinic. Jenny Holtzhausen, the Hospital's CEO, is very concerned about cost control and has asked that performance reports be prepared that compare budgeted and actual amounts for the clinic. She wants these reports to focus on three problem areas: the cost of medical assistants, clinic supplies and lab tests. Past financial studies have shown that the cost of clinic supplies used is driven by the number of medical assistant labour hours worked. Lab tests are highly correlated with the number of patients served.

The following information is available for June:

- Lab tests: Actual lab tests cost R795 135 and averaged 3.3 tests per patient. Each patient is anticipated to have 3 lab tests at an average cost of R325 per test.
- Medical assistants: The standard wage rate is R70 per hour, and each assistant is expected to spend 30 minutes with a patient. Assistants worked 420 hours helping 790 patients, at an average pay rate of R77.50 per hour.
- Clinic supplies: The cost of clinic supplies is budgeted at R60 per direct labour hour, and the actual cost of supplies used was R22 875.

Required:

1 Prepare a report that shows the budgeted cost and the actual costs for the 790 patients that were seen by the clinic during June. Calculate the variance between these amounts and label these as favourable or unfavourable.

2 Based on your report prepared for requirement 1, determine whether Waverley Hospital has any significant problems with respect to the cost of clinic supplies and lab tests. Briefly discuss your findings.

3 Calculate the spending and efficiency variances for lab tests. Do you think that the hospital has any significant problems with the cost of lab tests? (*Hint*: In applying the overhead variance formulas, think of the number of tests as equivalent to the number of hours, and the cost per test as similar to the variable overhead rate.)

4 Compare the lab test variances calculated in requirement 1, a flexible budget variance, with the sum of the variances in requirement 3. Discuss your findings and explain the relationship between the flexible budget variances and the standard cost variances for variable overhead.

P11.44 Flexible budget; multiple cost drivers; performance report: software distributor

Mark Mogale, Managing Director of SoftGro Ltd, was looking forward to seeing the performance reports for the month of November because he knew the company's sales for the month had exceeded budget by a considerable margin. SoftGro, a distributor of educational software packages, had been growing steadily for approximately two years. Mogale's biggest challenge at this point was to ensure that the company did not lose control over costs during this growth period. When Mogale received the November reports, he was dismayed to see the large unfavourable variance in the company's Monthly Selling Expense Report:

SoftGro Ltd
Monthly Selling Expense Report
November

	Annual budget	November budget	November actual	November variance
Unit sales	2 000 000	280 000	310 000	30 000
Rand sales	R160 000 000	R22 400 000	R24 800 000	R2 400 000
Orders processed	54 000	6500	5800	−700
Sales personnel per month	90	90	96	−6
Advertising	R39 600 000	R3 300 000	R3 320 000	R20 000 U
Staff salaries	3 000 000	250 000	250 000	0
Sales salaries	2 592 000	216 000	230 800	14 800 U
Commissions	6 400 000	896 000	992 000	96 000 U
Daily travel allowance	3 564 000	297 000	325 200	28 200 U
Office expenses	8 160 000	680 000	716 800	36 800 U
Shipping expenses	13 500 000	1 805 000	1 953 000	148 000 U
Total expenses	76 816 000	7 444 000	7 787 800	343 800 U

Mogale called in the company's new accountant, Susan Petersen, to discuss the implications of the variances reported for November and to plan a strategy for improving performance. Petersen suggested that the reporting format that the company had been using might not be giving Mogale a true picture of the company's operations. She proposed that SoftGro implement flexible budgeting. Petersen offered to redo the Monthly Selling Expense Report for November, using flexible budgeting, so that Mogale could compare the two reports and see the advantages of flexible budgeting.

Petersen discovered the following information about the behaviour of SoftGro's selling expenses:

- The total compensation paid to the sales force consists of a monthly base salary and a commission; the commission varies with sales revenue.
- Sales office expense is a semivariable cost with the variable portion related to the number of orders processed. The fixed portion of office expense is R6 million annually and is incurred uniformly throughout the year.
- Subsequent to the adoption of the annual budget for the current year, SoftGro decided to open a new sales territory. As a consequence, approval was given to hire six additional salespeople effective 1 November. Petersen decided that these additional six people should be recognised in her revised budget.
- The payment of the daily travel allowance to the sales force, while a fixed amount per day, is variable with the number of sales personnel and the number of days spent travelling. SoftGro's original budget was based on an average sales force of 90 people throughout the year, with each salesperson travelling 15 days per month.
- The company's shipping expense is a semivariable cost with the variable portion, R6 per unit, dependent on the number of units sold. The fixed portion is incurred uniformly throughout the year.

Required:

1 Citing the benefits of flexible budgeting, explain why Susan Petersen would propose that SoftGro use flexible budgeting in this situation.

2 Prepare a revised Monthly Selling Expense Report for November that would permit Mark Mogale to evaluate more accurately SoftGro's control over selling expenses. The report should have a line for each selling expense item, showing the appropriate budgeted amount, the actual selling expense and the monthly Rand variance.

(*CMA, adapted*)

P11.45 Finding missing data; overhead accounting

For each of the following independent companies, fill in the missing information. The company budgets and applies manufacturing overhead costs on the basis of direct labour hours.

		Company A	Company B
1	Standard variable overhead rate	R7.50 per hour	?
2	Standard fixed overhead rate	? per hour	?
3	Total standard overhead rate	? per hour	R13.00 per hour
4	Flexible budget for variable overhead	R270 000	?
5	Flexible budget for fixed overhead	R630 000	?
6	Actual variable overhead	?	?
7	Actual fixed overhead	R621 000	?
8	Variable overhead spending variance	R16 650 U	R8 000 U
9	Variable overhead efficiency variance	?	R1 600 F
10	Fixed overhead budget variance	?	R4 320 U
11	Fixed overhead volume variance	?	R14 400 U
12	Under (or over) applied variable overhead	?	?
13	Under (or over) applied fixed overhead	?	?
14	Budgeted production (in units)	5 000 units	?
15	Standard direct labour hours per unit	6 hours	2 hours
16	Actual production (in units)	?	?
17	Standard direct labour hours allowed, given actual production	36 000 hours	6 400 hours
18	Actual direct labour hours	37 000 hours	6 000 hours
19	Applied variable overhead	?	?
20	Applied fixed overhead	?	?

P11.46 Review of Chapters 10 and 11; interactions between variances; flexible manufacturing system: manufacturer

Thaba Auto Parts Company manufactures replacement parts for car repairs. The company recently installed a flexible manufacturing system (FMS), which has significantly changed the production process. The installation of the new FMS was not anticipated when the current year's budget and cost structure were developed. The installation was hastened by several major breakdowns in the company's old production machinery.

The new system was very expensive, but management expects it to cut the labour time required by a substantial amount. Management also expects the new equipment to allow a reduction in direct material waste. On the negative side, the FMS requires a more highly skilled labour force to operate it than was needed for the company's old equipment.

The following cost variance report was prepared for the month of June, the first full month after the equipment was installed:

Thaba Auto Parts Company Cost Variance Report June	
Direct material:	
Standard cost	R6 024 500
Actual cost	5 987 000
Direct material price variance	1500 U
Direct material quantity variance	39 000 F
Direct labour:	
Standard cost	R3 930 000
Actual cost	3 838 000
Direct labour rate variance	48 000 U
Direct labour efficiency variance	140 000 F
Manufacturing overhead:	
Applied to work in process	R4 000 000
Actual cost	4 080 000
Variable overhead spending variance	80 000 U
Variable overhead efficiency variance	100 000 F
Fixed overhead budget variance	300 000 U
Fixed overhead volume variance	200 000 F

Required:

Comment on the possible interactions between the variances listed in the report. Which ones are likely to have been caused by the purchase of the new system? The company budgets and applies manufacturing overhead on the basis of direct labour hours. (Hint: You may find it helpful to review the discussion of variance interactions in Chapter 10.)

P11.47 Complete analysis of cost variances; review of Chapters 10 and 11: manufacturer

Chill Ltd produces cases of frozen food. During April, Chill produced 725 cases of food and incurred the following actual costs:

Variable overhead	R5 500
Fixed overhead	13 000
Actual direct labour cost (4000 direct labour hours)	75 600
Actual material cost (15 000 kg purchased and used)	33 000

Standard cost and annual budget information is as follows:

	Standard cost per case
Direct labour (5 hours @ R18)	R90.00
Direct material (20 kg @ R2)	40.00
Variable overhead (5 hours @ R1.50)	7.50
Fixed overhead (5 hours @ R3)	15.00
Total	R152.50

	Annual budget information
Variable overhead	R75 000
Fixed overhead	R150 000
Planned activity for year	50 000 direct labour hours

Required:

Prepare as complete an analysis of cost variances as is possible from the available data.

P11.48 Comprehensive problem on overhead accounting under standard costing: publisher

Reams Ltd prints textbooks. A monthly flexible overhead budget for the firm is as follows:

Reams Ltd
Monthly Flexible Overhead Budget

	Direct labour hours		
Budgeted costs	**1500**	**1750**	**2000**
Variable costs			
Indirect material:			
Glue	7 500	8 750	10 000
Tape	3 000	3 500	4 000
Miscellaneous supplies	30 000	35 000	40 000
Indirect labour	75 000	87 500	100 000
Utilities:			
Electricity	15 000	17 500	20 000
Natural gas	4 500	5 250	6 000
Total variable cost	135 000	157 500	180 000
Fixed costs			
Supervisory labour	125 000	125 000	125 000
Depreciation	34 000	34 000	34 000
Property taxes and insurance	41 000	41 000	41 000
Total fixed cost	200 000	200 000	200 000
Total overhead cost	335 000	357 500	380 000

The planned monthly production is 6400 books. The standard direct labour allowance is 0.25 hours per book. During February 20X7 Reams produced 8000 books and used 2100 direct labour hours. The actual overhead costs for the month were as follows:

Actual variable overhead	R195 300
Actual fixed overhead	376 000

Required:

1 Determine the formula flexible overhead budget for Reams.
2 Prepare a diagram, similar to that in Exhibit 11.5, to show Reams' variable overhead variances for February 20X7. Indicate whether each variance is favourable or unfavourable.
3 Draw a graph to depict Reams' variable overhead variances for February (see Problem 11.37, requirement 1).
4 Explain the meaning of each of the variances calculated in requirement 2.
5 Prepare a diagram, similar to that in Exhibit 11.6, to show Reams' fixed overhead variances for February 20X7.
6 Draw a graph, similar to that in Exhibit 11.7, to depict the company's applied and budgeted fixed overhead for February. Show the firm's February volume variance on the graph.
7 Interpret the variances calculated in requirement 5.
8 Prepare journal entries to record each of the following:
   (a) incurrence of February's actual overhead cost
   (b) overhead variance for the month
   (c) application of February's overhead cost to work in process inventory
9 Draw ledger accounts for all the accounts used in the journal entries of requirement 8. Then post the journal entries to the ledger accounts.

P11.49 Analysing sales performance using variances (appendix): manufacturer

Quoll Pen Company manufactures two lines of ballpoint pens: Super and Executive. Budgeted and actual contribution margin statements for 20X6 follow:

Quoll Pen Company
Budget and Actual Contribution Statements
for the year ended 31 December
(in '000s)

	Budget			Actual		
	Super	**Executive**	**Total**	**Super**	**Executive**	**Total**
Unit sales	150	100	250	130	130	260
Sales revenue	R9 000	R10 000	R19 000	R7 800	R12 350	R20 150
Variable expenses	4 500	7 500	12 000	3 900	9 750	13 650
Contribution margin	R4 500	R2 500	R7 000	R3 900	R2 600	R6 500
Fixed expenses:						
Manufacturing			2 000			1 900
Marketing			1 530			1 400
Administration			950			900
Total fixed expenses			R4 480			R4 200
Profit before taxes			R2 520			R2 300

Required:

1 The budgeted total volume of 250 000 units was based on the company's achieving a market share of 20 per cent. Actual industry volume reached 1 290 000 units. Calculate the portion of Quoll's increased volume due to improved market share.

2 Calculate the variance of actual contribution margin from budgeted contribution margin attributable to the sales price. Indicate whether the variance is favourable or unfavourable. (*Hint:* Add the sales price variances calculated for each product line.)
3 Calculate the variance of actual contribution margin from budgeted contribution margin attributable to unit variable cost changes. For each product, indicate whether the variance is favourable or unfavourable.
4 Provide a reconciliation that explains the source of differences between actual contribution margin and budgeted contribution margin. (*Hint:* List variances that explain the difference.)

(*CMA, adapted*)

P11.50 Sales variances and analysis (appendix): distributor

Tommee Tool Company distributes two types of home use power tools to hardware stores: a heavy-duty hand drill and a circular saw. The tools are purchased from a manufacturer that attaches the Tommee private label to the tools. The wholesale selling prices to the hardware stores are R1200 each for the drill and R600 each for the circular saw. The 20X6 budget and actual results are presented below. The budget was adopted in late 20X5 and was based on Tommee's estimated share of the market for the two tools.

Tommee Tool Company
Profit Statement
for the year ended 31 December 20X6
(in '000s)

	Hand drill		Circular saw		Total		
	Budget	**Actual**	**Budget**	**Actual**	**Budget**	**Actual**	**Variance**
Sales (units)	40	37	60	43	100	80	–20
Revenue	48 000	42 550	36 000	25 370	84 000	67 920	–16 080
Cost of goods sold	32 000	30 340	30 000	21 500	62 000	51 840	10 160
Gross margin	16 000	12 210	6 000	3 870	22 000	16 080	–5 920
Unallocated costs:							
Selling					5 000	5 000	0
Advertising					5 000	5 300	–300
Administration					2 000	2 030	–30
Income taxes (29%)					2 900	1 088	1 812
Total unallocated costs					14 900	13 418	1 482
Net profit					7 100	2 662	–4 438

During the first quarter of 20X6, management estimated that the total market for these tools would actually be 10 per cent below the original estimates. In an attempt to prevent unit sales from declining as much as industry projections, management implemented a marketing program. Included in the program were dealer discounts and increased direct advertising. The circular saw line was emphasised in this program.

Required:

1 Calculate the sales price and sales volume variances for each product line. Indicate whether each variance is favourable or unfavourable.
2 Discuss the apparent effect of Tommee Tool Company's special marketing program (dealer discounts and additional advertising) on the 20X6 operating results.

(*CMA, adapted*)

Cases

C11.51 Preparing and using a flexible budget report; ethical issues: tour company

Flaming Foliage Sky Tours is a small sightseeing tour company in Plettenberg that specialises in aerial tours of the Garden Route area. Until recently, the company had not had an accounting department. Routine bookkeeping tasks, such as billing, had been handled by a person who had little formal training in accounting. As the business began to grow, however, the owner recognised the need for more formal accounting procedures. Jacqueline Vermaak was recently hired as the new accountant, and she has the authority to hire an assistant.

During her first week on the job, Vermaak was given the performance report below. The report was prepared by Red Leif, the company's manager of Aircraft Operations, who was planning to present it to the owner the next morning.

'Look at these favourable variances for fuel and so forth,' Leif pointed out, as he showed the report to Vermaak. 'My operations people are really doing a great job.'

Later that day, Vermaak looked at the performance report more carefully. She immediately realised that it was improperly prepared and would be misleading to the company's owner.

Flaming Foliage Sky Tours
Performance Report
September

	Formula flexible budget (per air-km)	Actual (32 000 air-km)	Static budget (35 000 air-km)	Variance
Passenger revenue	R3.50	R112 000	R122 500	R10 500 U
Less Variable expenses:				
Fuel	0.50	17 000	17 500	500 F
Aircraft maintenance	0.75	23 500	26 250	2750 F
Flight crew salaries	0.40	13 100	14 000	900 F
Selling and administration	0.80	24 900	28 000	3100 F
Total variable expenses	2.45	78 500	85 750	7250 F
Contribution margin	R1.05	R33 500	R36 750	R3250 U
Less Fixed expenses (per month):				
Depreciation on aircraft	R2 900	R2 900	R2 900	R0
Landing fees	900	1 000	900	100 U
Supervisory salaries	9 000	8 600	9 000	400 F
Selling and administrative	11 000	12 400	11 000	1 400 U
Total fixed expenses	R23 800	R24 900	R23 800	R1 100 U
Net profit		R8 600	R12 950	R4 350 U

Required:

1 Prepare a flexible budget report for Flaming Foliage Sky Tours' expenses, based on the following activity levels:
   (a) 32 000 air-kilometres
   (b) 35 000 air-kilometres

(c) 38 000 air-kilometres.

2 In spite of several favourable expense variances shown in the report above, the company's September net profit was only about two-thirds of the expected level. Why?

3 Write a brief memo to the manager of Aircraft Operations explaining why the original variance report is misleading.

4 Prepare a revised expense variance report for September, based on the flexible budget prepared in requirement 1.

5 Jacqueline Vermaak presented the revised expense report to Red Leif, along with the memo explaining why the original performance report was misleading. Leif did not take it well. He complained of Vermaak's 'interference', and pointed out that the company had been doing just fine without her.

'I'm taking my report to the owner tomorrow,' Leif insisted. 'Yours just makes us look bad.' What are Vermaak's ethical obligations in this matter? What should she do?

C11.52 Integrative case on Chapters 10 and 11; drawing conclusions from missing data: manufacturer

Your next-door neighbour recently began a new job as assistant accountant for Marsh Pty Ltd. As her first assignment, your neighbour prepared a performance report for January. She is scheduled to present the report to management the next morning, so she has brought it home to review. As the two of you chat in the backyard, she casually shows you the report she has prepared. Unfortunately, your dog thinks the rolled-up report is a stick. The dog makes a flying leap and gets a firm grip on the report. After chasing the dog round the block, you manage to wrestle the report from its teeth. Needless to say, it is torn to bits. Only certain data are legible on the report:

Marsh Pty Ltd
Performance Report
January

	Direct material	Direct labour	Variable overhead	Fixed overhead
Standard cost allowed for actual output	? (? kg @ R18 per kg)	? (2 hours @ R21 per hour)		
Flexible overhead budget			?	R60 000
Actual cost	R283 500 (14 000 kg @ R20.25 per kg)	? (8800 hours @ ? per hour)	?	?
Direct material price variance	?			
Direct material quantity variance	R9000 U			
Direct labour rate variance		R13 200 U		
Direct labour efficiency variance		R4200 F		
Variable overhead spending variance			R3960 U	
Variable overhead efficiency variance			R1800 F	
Fixed overhead budget variance				R4875 U
Fixed overhead volume variance				?

In addition to the fragmentary data still legible on the performance report, your neighbour remembers the following facts:

- Planned production of Marsh's sole product was 500 units more than the actual production.
- All the direct material purchased in January was used in production.
- There were no beginning or ending inventories.
- Variable and fixed overhead are applied on the basis of direct labour hours. The fixed overhead rate is R6 per hour.

Required:

Feeling guilty, you have agreed to help your neighbour reconstruct the following information, which will be necessary for her presentation:

1 Planned production (in units).
2 Actual production (in units).
3 Actual fixed overhead.
4 Total standard direct labour hours allowed, given actual production.
5 Actual direct labour rate.
6 Standard variable overhead rate.
7 Actual variable overhead rate.
8 Standard direct material quantity per unit.
9 Direct material price variance.
10 Applied fixed overhead.
11 Fixed overhead volume variance.

C11.53 Comprehensive review of Chapters 10 and 11; variances; behavioural effects (appendix): manufacturer

Funtime Ltd manufactures an electronic device. Market saturation and technological innovations have caused pricing pressures that have resulted in declining profits. To stem the slide in profits until new products can be introduced, top management has turned its attention to both manufacturing economies and increased sales. Sales can be increased only if production increases. To realise these objectives, an incentive program has been developed to reward those production managers who contribute to an increase in the number of units produced and achieve cost reductions. In addition, a just-in-time purchasing program has been implemented, and raw materials are purchased on an as-needed basis.

The production managers have responded to the pressure to improve manufacturing performance in several ways that have resulted in an increased number of completed units over normal production levels. The electronic devices are put together by the Assembly Group, which requires parts from both the Printed Circuit Boards (PCB) and the Reading Heads (RH) groups. To attain increased production levels, the PCB and RH groups started to reject parts that previously would have been tested and modified to meet manufacturing standards. Preventive maintenance on machines used in the production of these parts has been postponed, with only emergency repair work being performed to keep production lines moving. The Maintenance Department is concerned that there will be serious breakdowns and unsafe operating conditions.

The more aggressive Assembly Group production supervisors have pressured maintenance personnel to attend to their machines at the expense of other groups. This has resulted in machine downtime in the PCB and RH groups which, when coupled with demands for accelerated parts delivery by the Assembly Group, has led to more frequent parts rejections and increased friction between departments. Funtime uses a standard costing system. The standard costs for electronic devices are as follows:

	Standard cost per unit Quantity	Cost	Total
Direct material:			
Housing unit	1 unit	R 100.00	R 100.00
Printed circuit boards	2 boards	75.00	150.00
Reading heads	4 heads	50.00	200.00
Direct labour:			
Assembly Group	2.0 hours	40.00	80.00
PCB Group	1.0 hour	45.00	45.00
RH Group	1.5 hours	50.00	75.00
Total	4.5 hours		
Variable overhead*		10.00	45.00
Total standard cost per unit			R695.00

*Applied on the basis of direct labour hours: 4.5 direct labour hours @ R10 per hour

Funtime prepares monthly performance reports based on standard costs. The following table shows the contribution report for May, when production and sales both reached 2200 units. The budgeted and actual unit sales price in May was the same, at R1000.

Funtime Ltd
Contribution Report
for the month ending 31 May

	Budgeted	Actual	Variance
Units	2000	2200	200 F
Revenue	R2 000 000	R2 200 000	R200 000 F
Variable costs:			
Direct material	900 000	1 102 000	202 000 U
Direct labour	400 000	467 300	67 300 U
Variable overhead	90 000	94 000	4000 U
Total variable costs	R1 390 000	R1 663 300	R273 300 U
Contribution margin	R610 000	R536 700	R73 300 U

Funtime's top management was surprised by the unfavourable contribution margin variance in spite of the increased sales in May. Jack Makhanya, cost accountant, was assigned to identify and report on the reasons for the unfavourable results as well as the individuals or groups responsible. After a thorough review of the data, Makhanya prepared the following usage report:

Funtime Ltd
Usage Report
for the month ending 31 May

Cost item	Actual quantity	Actual cost
Direct material:		
Housing units	2200 units	R220 000
Printed circuit boards	4700 boards	376 000
Reading heads	9200 heads	506 000
Direct labour:		
Assembly	3900 hours	156 000
Printed circuit boards	2400 hours	118 800
Reading heads	3500 hours	192 500
Total	9800 hours	
Variable overhead		94 000
Total variable cost		R1 663 300

Makhanya reported that the PCB and RH groups had supported the increased production levels but had experienced abnormal machine downtime, causing idle personnel. This required the use of overtime to keep up with the accelerated demand for parts. The idle time was charged to direct labour. Makhanya also reported that the production managers of these two groups had resorted to parts rejections, as opposed to the testing and modification procedures formerly applied. Makhanya determined that the Assembly Group had met management's objectives by increasing production while utilising lower than standard hours.

Required:

1 Calculate the following variances, and prepare an explanation of the R73 300 unfavourable variance between the budgeted and actual contribution margin during May. Assume that all raw material purchased during May was placed into production.
  (a) direct labour rate variance
  (b) direct labour efficiency variance
  (c) direct material price variance
  (d) direct material quantity variance
  (e) variable overhead spending variance
  (f) variable overhead efficiency variance
  (g) sales price variance
  (h) sales volume variance

2 (a) Identify and briefly explain the behavioural factors that might promote friction between the production managers, and between the production managers and the maintenance manager.
  (b) Evaluate Jack Makhanya's analysis of the unfavourable contribution results in terms of its completeness and its effect on the behaviour of the production groups.

(CMA, adapted)

C11.54 Review of Chapters 10 and 11: manufacturer

Vulamehlo Pump Company, a fuel pump manufacturer, is developing a budgeted contribution margin statement for the calendar year 20X7. The managing director is generally satisfied with the projected net profit for 20X6. However, next year he would like earnings to increase. Vulamehlo Pump Company uses a standard costing system. Inflation necessitates an annual revision in the standards. The standard manufacturing cost for 20X6 is R720 per fuel pump.

The company's management expects to sell 100 000 fuel pumps at R1100 each in the current year (20X6). Forecasts from the Sales Department are favourable, and management is projecting an annual increase of 10 per cent in unit sales in 20X7. This increase in sales is expected even though a R150 increase in the selling price will be implemented in 20X7. The selling price increase was absolutely essential to compensate for increased production costs and operating expenses. However, management is concerned that any additional sales price increase will prevent the desired growth in sales volume.

The following schedule represents the 20X7 standard quantities and rates for the material and labour to produce one fuel pump:

Brass	4 kg @ R 53.50 per kg	R 214.00
Steel alloy	5 kg @ R 31.60 per kg	158.00
Direct labour	4 hours @ R 70.00 per hour	280.00
Total prime costs		R 652.00

The material content of a fuel pump has been reduced slightly, without a decrease in the quality of the finished product. Improved labour productivity and an increase in automation have resulted in a decrease in the number of labour hours per unit from 4.4 to 4.0. However, significant increases in material prices and hourly labour rates more than offset any savings from reduced input quantities. The flexible overhead budget for 20X7 has not been completed yet. Preliminary estimates are as follows:

	Production level (units)		
Overhead cost	**100 000**	**110 000**	**120 000**
Supplies	R4 750 000	R5 225 000	R5 700 000
Indirect labour	5 300 000	5 830 000	6 360 000
Utilities	1 700 000	1 870 000	2 040 000
Maintenance	3 630 000	3 775 000	3 920 000
Property taxes and insurance	870 000	870 000	870 000
Depreciation	4 210 000	4 210 000	4 210 000
Total overhead	R20 460 000	R21 780 000	R23 100 000

The standard overhead rate is based on direct labour hours. The rate is developed by using the total overhead costs from the schedule above for the activity level closest to planned production. In developing the standards for manufacturing costs, the following two assumptions were made:

1 Brass is currently selling at R56.50 per kilogram. However, this price is historically high, and the purchasing manager expects the price to drop to the predetermined standard in 20X7.
2 Several new employees will be hired for the production line in 20X7. These employees will be unskilled. If basic training programs are not effective and improved labour productivity is not experienced, then the production time per unit of product will increase by 15 minutes over the 20X7 standards.

Vulamehlo Pump Company's management accepts the cost standards developed by the production and accounting departments. However, the managing director is concerned about the possible effect on net profit if the price of brass does not decrease or the labour efficiency does not improve as expected. Therefore, he has asked that a special report be prepared that shows the anticipated variances for 20X7, using the standards as developed but assuming the worst possible situation for material prices and labour efficiency.

Required:

Calculate the direct material, direct labour and variable overhead variances, assuming the worst possible scenario for 20X7. Then write a brief memo to the company managing director, commenting on the likelihood that Vulamehlo Pump Company's profit will increase in 20X7. Assume no change in the finished goods and raw material inventories in 20X7. (*Hint*: You can calculate the standard variable overhead rate by focusing on the budgeted level of overhead costs for the volumes 100 000, 110 000 and 120 000 units. Remember that the budgeted fixed overhead cost at these volumes will not change, so any difference in budgeted overhead costs must reflect a change in the budgeted variable overhead costs.)

(*CMA, adapted*)

Endnotes

1 See Chapter 7 for a description of how departmental overhead rates are calculated.

2 As shown in Exhibit 11.4.

3 Although not based on the standard quantity allowed, this is also a flexible budget.

4 The direct material and direct labour variances that were calculated in Chapter 10 related to the production of moleskin pants. However, the manufacturing overhead variances presented in this chapter relate to the entire Clothing Department, which includes the production of moleskins, shirts and coats.

CHAPTER 12

Financial Performance Reports and Transfer Pricing

Learning Objectives

After completing this chapter, you should be able to:

1. explain the benefits and costs of decentralisation;
2. define and provide examples of cost centres, revenue centres, profit centres and investment centres;
3. understand how shared services operations and teams can enhance competitiveness;
4. prepare segmented profit reports for divisionalised organisations;
5. explain the potential differences in information provided to evaluate sub-unit performance and managers' performance;
6. complete divisional financial performance reports taking into account allocated costs, common costs and variances;
7. understand how real-time reporting can enhance management decision making;
8. understand why divisionalised organisations have transfer pricing systems;
9. explain the various methods that can be used to determine transfer prices;
10. explain the general rule that can be used to set transfer prices;
11. determine appropriate transfer prices under a variety of scenarios; and
12. understand the nature of service level agreements.

Introduction

As an organisation grows in size and complexity, management needs to consider the degree of decentralisation required to allow the organisation to compete effectively. **Decentralisation** is the structuring of an organisation into smaller sub-units, such as divisions and departments, each of which is assigned particular operations and decision-making responsibilities. To ensure the effectiveness of these organisations, there must be a high level of **goal congruence** – that is, the managers of the various sub-units must be committed to achieving the goals of the organisation set by top management, while still satisfying their own personal goals.

One way in which an organisation can help to promote goal congruence is through the operation of a **responsibility accounting system**, which assigns responsibility to managers to run particular sub-units of the organisation. These managers then become accountable for the performance of their sub-units. Responsibility accounting helps an organisation to reap the advantages of decentralisation while minimising the costs. It involves using various tools and systems to measure the performance of people and sub-units. In Chapters 9 and 10 we learned that budgeting systems and standard costing systems operate within a responsibility accounting framework.

In this chapter, we will review the principles of responsibility accounting and consider the financial performance reports used in various types of responsibility centres. We will also consider the various methods that are used to price goods and services that are transferred between responsibility centres. These are called transfer prices. Since the transfer price impacts the profit of both the buying and selling units, it affects the reported performance of the responsibility centres.

Decentralisation

L.O. 1

Most medium and large organisations are decentralised – that is, managers of an organisation's divisions and departments are given a specified level of decision-making authority. A major issue that needs to be considered by senior management is: *What is the appropriate level of decentralisation?*

Benefits of decentralisation

As an organisation grows in size and complexity, decentralisation provides the only effective way to manage the business. Corporate managers do not have the time or the expertise to manage all aspects of the business directly. Decentralisation provides several advantages over centralised structures:

- Managers of the organisation's sub-units have better local information about their particular markets and operations that enables them to manage their area effectively. This advantage is particularly apparent where the sub-units are located in remote geographic locations, or where sub-units operate in different industries.
- Allowing managers decision-making autonomy provides managerial training for future higher-level managers. For example, the manager of a restaurant that is part of a restaurant chain, who demonstrates that she can manage her business skilfully, might be promoted to regional manager.
- Managers with decision-making authority may have greater motivation than do those who merely execute the decisions of others. Wider responsibilities can produce greater job satisfaction.
- Delegating some decisions to lower-level managers allows corporate-level managers to devote more time to strategic issues.
- Delegating decision-making to operational levels allows an organisation to react quickly to opportunities and problems as they arise.

Costs of decentralisation

Negative consequences can also result from decentralisation:

- Managers in a decentralised organisation may focus narrowly on their own sub-units' performance, rather than on the attainment of the organisation's overall goals. For example, the two discount stores Game and Makro may regard each other as competitors, even though they are both part of the Massmart group. Excessively high levels of competitiveness, where managers of one sub-unit are unwilling to share information with managers in a 'rival' sub-unit, may lead to gains for external competitors rather than advantages for the larger organisation.
- In a decentralised organisation, some tasks or services may be duplicated unnecessarily. For example, two departments in a decentralised university might each have their own mainframe computer when in fact one could serve both departments at a lower overall cost.

Obtaining goal congruence: a behavioural challenge

The biggest challenge in making a decentralised organisation function effectively is to obtain goal congruence among the organisation's autonomous managers. This is an important aspect of control.

However, goal congruence is difficult to achieve. Managers are often unaware of the effects of their decisions on the other sub-units of the organisation. Also, it is only natural for people to be more concerned with the performance of their own sub-units than with the effectiveness of the entire organisation.

To achieve goal congruence, the behaviour of managers throughout a decentralised organisation must be directed towards achieving organisational goals. One way of doing this is to develop performance measures and reward systems. Performance measures provide direction for managers of decentralised units, and are used by corporate management to evaluate the performance of a sub-unit and its manager. Reward systems are often tied to a manager's achievement against these performance measures and provide further incentives for managers to strive towards organisational goals. However, if the responsibility accounting system is not designed wisely, and the performance measures selected are inappropriate, undesirable behaviour can result.

Responsibility centres

L.O. 2

The basis of a responsibility accounting system is the designation of each sub-unit of the organisation as a particular type of **responsibility centre**. A responsibility centre is a sub-unit in an organisation where the manager is held accountable for the sub-unit's activities and performance. The characteristics of various types of responsibility centres are summarised in Exhibit 12.1.

Exhibit 12.2 contains an example of a decentralised organisation, Bay Hotels, which is organised along responsibility accounting lines. The two divisions are regarded as **investment centres**, and each of the hotels is a **profit centre**. These descriptions reflect the degree of financial decision-making authority that the head office managers have chosen to delegate to the managers running these divisions and hotels. For example, the division managers have the authority to manage all aspects of profits for their division, and to make decisions about acquiring and reducing the resources (assets) they require to run their division. If head office managers had chosen to *centralise* all decisions about asset acquisitions, then the divisions would reduce to profit centres. Most departments of the Durban Hotel are **cost centres**, as this reflects the financial responsibility given to each department manager. Note that the Food and Beverage Department is a profit centre, because the department manager is responsible both for generating revenue and for managing costs. If the manager were given responsibility for revenue alone (a **revenue centre**), there would be no incentive to manage costs wisely. Similarly, if the manager were held responsible only for managing costs, then there would be little incentive to improve revenue.

Type of responsibility centre	Examples	Financial responsibility	Financial performance measures
Investment centre	Subsidiary companies Divisions	Profit and invested capital (assets) used to generate profit in that centre	Return on investment (i.e. profit ÷ invested capital)
Profit centre	Subsidiary companies Divisions Production plants	Profit – all revenues and costs – of that centre	Some measure of profit
Revenue centre	Sales departments	Revenues of that department	Revenues
Cost centre	Administrative departments Production teams Production departments Production lines Process lines	Costs of running the department or area	Costs Detailed cost variances

Exhibit 12.1 Responsibility centres and financial performance

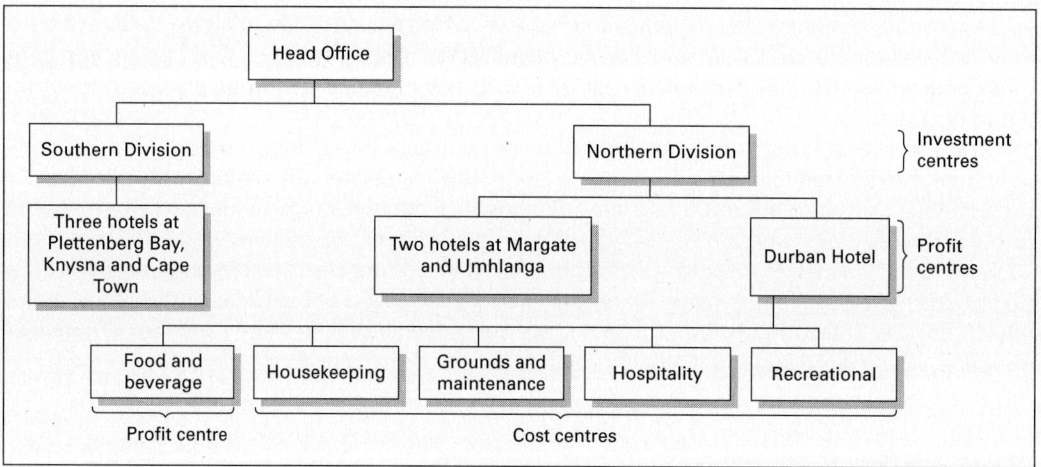

Exhibit 12.2 Organisation chart for the Bay Hotels Group

A key aspect of responsibility accounting is designing appropriate performance measures and performance reports for each type of responsibility centre. Exhibit 12.1 outlines the type of financial performance measures that match the responsibilities of the managers running each unit. These measures provide incentives for managers to exercise financial control over their segment of the organisation. However, many businesses evaluate the performance of sub-units using a broad range of performance measures. These include non-financial measures, such as customer satisfaction, safety performance and productivity, as well as financial measures. In this chapter we focus on the various reports for monitoring financial performance, and in Chapter 13 we consider other financial measures that are commonly used to evaluate performance. More comprehensive approaches to performance measurement, which include both financial and non-financial measures, are described in Chapter 14.

REAL LIFE: MASSMART AND PICK 'N PAY GROUP STRUCTURES

The Massmart Group is the third largest distributor of consumer goods in Africa, the leading retailer of general merchandise, liquor and home improvement equipment and supplies, and the leading wholesaler of basic foods. The group measures performance in relation to four major divisions which have strategic objectives in relation to market performance. The Massbuild division has the highest operating margin in the group but the Massdiscounters division consisting of Game and Dion provides the largest contribution to group profit. The group structure is as follows:

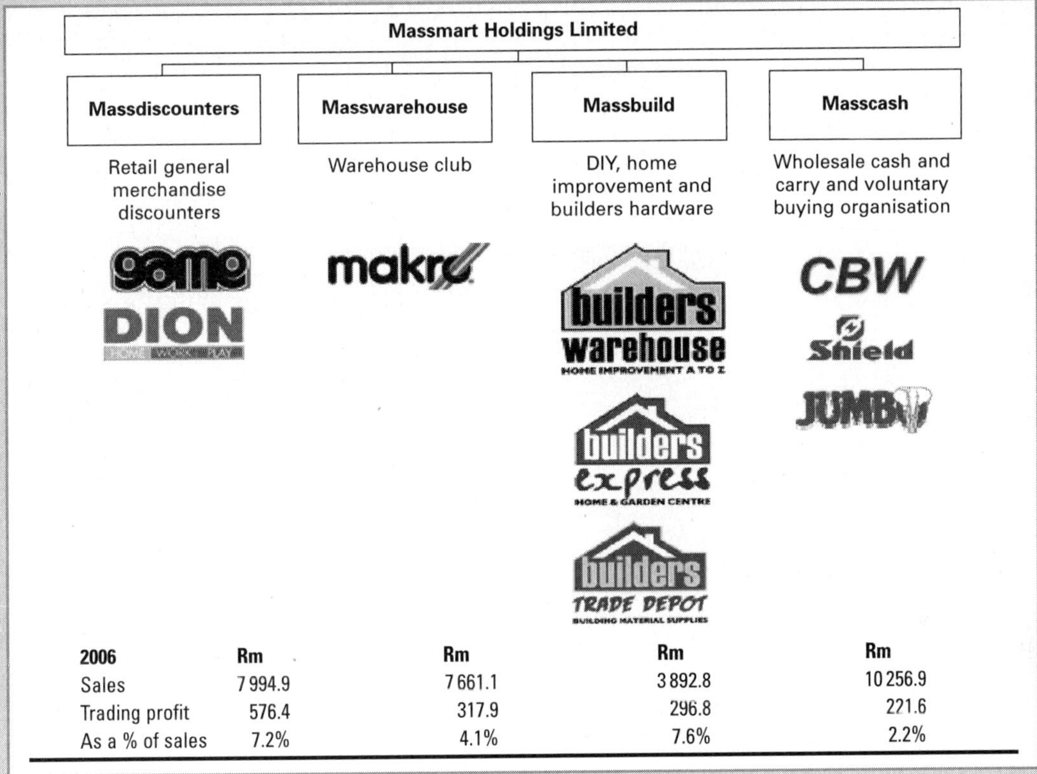

2006	Rm	Rm	Rm	Rm
Sales	7 994.9	7 661.1	3 892.8	10 256.9
Trading profit	576.4	317.9	296.8	221.6
As a % of sales	7.2%	4.1%	7.6%	2.2%

One of Pick 'n Pay's enduring principles is decentralisation of operations. This is seen as key to the success of the group as it offers management initiative and the ability to respond quickly to a changing business environment. In the group's 2006 annual report, it is reported that:

Group structure

The Group has a flat organisational structure. Overall responsibility lies with the Pick 'n Pay Stores Limited Board. Operational responsibility for the Group is vested in three divisions: the Retail Division, the Group Enterprises Division and Franklins Australia. Each division has its own management board, and Retail and Franklins have managing directors reporting directly to the CEO. This flat Group structure enables local operations to take ownership of decision-making and to assume individual responsibility for their actions and success. The structure encourages personal growth and achievement, ensuring that initiative is enabled, identified and rewarded.

Enduring principles of Pick 'n Pay

The Board has a responsibility to ensure that the CEO and management do not depart from the following enduring principles that were applied by Raymond Ackerman while building the Group and which ensure that the spirit of Pick 'n Pay remains intact:

- Consumer sovereignty
- Striving for a flat organisational structure
- Where appropriate, maximising decentralisation of authority to enable local control.

It is interesting that after consumer sovereignty, Pick 'n Pay has indicated that a flat organisational structure and decentralisation of authority are the key principles of the group.

Responsibility centres in practice

The titles given to responsibility centres vary considerably among South African businesses. For example, the term 'cost centre' is commonly used, whereas the term 'revenue centre' is less common. Also, while there are important differences between profit centres and investment centres, the latter term is not widely used in practice. Many managers use the term 'profit centre' to refer both to profit centres (as defined in this chapter) and to investment centres.

Another term that is used in practice to describe investment centres (and sometimes profit centres) is **strategic business unit** or **SBU**. In decentralised organisations, SBUs are usually regarded as 'independent businesses', having their own clearly defined strategies and markets.

REAL LIFE: COST CENTRE OR PROFIT CENTRE?

Administrative departments and service departments, which have no direct external revenue-generating responsibilities, are usually classified as cost centres. However, this is not always the case. Some businesses prefer to operate these departments as profit centres. Consider the following examples.

Construction and maintenance departments are typically regarded as cost centres. However, a company may change its construction and maintenance group from being a cost centre merely providing services to other areas of the business, to a profit centre. As a profit centre, the group may be permitted to bid for work outside the company and to generate revenue from internal customers.

Research and development (R & D) departments and engineering service departments are usually cost centres. Vision Systems Limited is a technology-based company. It manufactures and markets products that include video-based surveillance systems, fire-protection systems and automated laboratory equipment. The R & D Department and engineering departments operate as profit centres. The R & D area generates revenue from divisions within the company as well as major customers from all over the world.

Does it really matter if an area is identified as a cost centre or a profit centre?

When a department is classified as a cost centre, it can colour managers' perceptions of the value of that department. Some people even believe that it is 'dangerous' to classify some departments as cost centres. Let's consider information technology (IT) departments. When IT is regarded as a cost centre, managers outside the department may regard IT as a drain on resources and see it as a less important part of the business, compared to profit centres. Within the cost centre there is little incentive to pursue external revenue-generating activities, or new opportunities for customers inside the organisation, as cost centre managers are evaluated on their ability to manage costs. In addition, by regarding IT as a cost centre and evaluating performance on cost, the value-adding aspects of IT may be ignored. In a survey of Fortune 1000 companies by the US IT advisory company, Meta Group, 30 per cent of companies saw IT as a cost, 55 per cent were increasing their spending but did not see IT as an investment, 10 per cent saw spending on IT as a strategic move, and 5 per cent managed IT as an investment. Also, it was estimated that only 30 per cent of the world's largest companies had adopted a way of charging users for IT services. If IT is not regarded as an investment, spending on IT may be low and strategic opportunities may be lost. Such thinking is encouraged when IT is treated as a cost centre. These same issues may apply to other support areas of a business. Moving from a cost centre to a profit centre can encourage new ways of thinking and creativity.

How important is IT in South Africa? Let's view the case of Edcon which views its investment in IT as offering the company a significant competitive edge. The following is an extract from the financial director's report in Edcon's 2006 annual report:

Edcon's reliance on IT for its competitive advantage means that IT security, risk management and governance are key focus areas for IT. Another exciting and successful year has passed with excellent service delivery, improved security and risk management remaining a focus of the Group IT department. We delivered significant new functionality to the Group and improved cost-efficiencies, while implementing leading-edge technologies and enhancements to system architectures. The demands placed on IT support grew substantially across the Group: a net 175 new stores were equipped; active users of the Edcon Business Intelligence System rose from 700 users last year to 950; and SKU (Stock Keeping Units) and store combinations jumped to 300 million from 210 million last year. Generally, IT costs increase if transactions and other input parameters to systems grow; however we improved batch processing times for the Edcon financial services system by 50%; store file transmission times by up to 120% and system stability by up to 300%. All these performance improvements resulted in only a marginal increase in the cost to run, support and maintain the Edcon IT system.

Sources: Greenmeier (2001); Vision Systems Ltd (2001); Edcon (2006)

The emergence of responsibility accounting systems

How do businesses become decentralised? When an organisation is created, it is often small and decision-making is centralised. The chief executive can control operations without formal information and accounting systems. Managers can keep in touch with routine operations through close personal contact with employees.

As an organisation grows, however, its managers need more formal information systems, including management accounting information, to maintain control. Accounting systems are established to provide the framework for internal and external financial reports. Budgets become necessary to plan the organisation's activities. The organisation gains experience in producing its goods or services, and cost standards and operational performance measures may be established. But as the organisation grows it becomes too difficult to manage centrally, so the organisation begins to decentralise decision-making responsibility. Ultimately, a fully developed responsibility accounting system emerges. Cost centres, revenue centres, profit centres and investment centres are created, and performance measures and reports for each of these sub-units are developed.

An organisation's accounting and information systems adapt and increase in complexity as the organisation changes and grows.

New developments in organisational structuring

L.O. 3

The responsibility structures described above have been used in organisations for many decades. In recent years, the concept of shared services has emerged as an improved way of structuring and managing support services. Also, many organisations have moved towards flatter organisational structures and made greater use of teams.

Shared services

Shared services is the concentration of support services that are typically spread across a decentralised organisation, into a separate unit to service multiple internal customers. The aims are to reduce cost, to increase the quality of the services delivered and to enhance shareholder value. Shared services may focus on *non-strategic areas*, such as accounts payable, finance, human resource management and information technology. Shared services units are given a high level of autonomy and incentives to operate as if they were a stand-alone business.

Shared services units are usually set up as profit centres rather than as cost centres. As was explained in the 'Real life', classifying a department as a cost centre rather than as a profit centre can create disincentives for managers to seek value-adding opportunities. When shared services units are regarded as profit centres, they are encouraged to achieve break-even rather than to make profits (Schulman, Dunleavy, Harmer & Lusk, 1999). The prices that the shared services units charge to internal customers for their services should be high enough to recover costs, but not so high as to be a burden on their customers. This requires decisions on the price to be charged to business units, which is called a *transfer price*. Different methods for determining transfer pricing are discussed later in this chapter.

As a shared services unit has as its *core business* a particular support service, such as accounts payable or human resource management, and is encouraged to operate as a stand-alone business, managers in that unit have the opportunity to become experts in the field and to focus on achieving improved customer service, and greater efficiency and effectiveness.

Does this mean that decentralised organisations that implement shared services are moving to a centralised structure? Shared services are formed to capture the best aspects of centralisation and decentralisation. Exhibit 12.3 highlights the difference between shared service units and centralised service units. Improved productivity and service quality can be achieved in shared service units through the increased scale of operations, common systems and procedures, and the critical mass of specialised skills and technology.

Shared service units	Centralised service units
■ The focus is on the needs of internal customers, such as business units and divisions	■ Head office concerns dominate
■ The type and scope of services are negotiated and defined, based on customer needs	■ Services tend to be standardised, regardless of the needs of the business units being serviced
■ The location is chosen to best serve internal customers	■ Usually located at corporate headquarters
■ The unit has full responsibility for both the cost and the quality of services delivered	■ Support service managers have little accountability for quality and customer satisfaction
■ Usually structured as a profit centre, but often only required to achieve break-even	■ Structured as a cost centre, reporting to head office managers
■ Performance is assessed against *service level agreements* (SLAs)*, which outline the type of service to be provided to internal customers, the standard of the service in terms of specific performance measures and targets (including response times, quality, deadlines and prices)	■ Performance is judged against budget and corporate objectives

*SLAs are described later in this chapter.

Source: adapted from Institute of Management Accountants (2000, p. 5)

Exhibit 12.3 Shared service versus centralised services

Does the establishment of shared services units diminish the independence of autonomous business units? In some organisations, business units are not forced to use the shared services unit. They may provide their own services or enter into a contract with an outside provider. In other organisations, business units may be asked to use the shared services unit for a few years, and then make their decision about whether they will continue to use the unit or not.

What will stop a shared services unit from developing a centralised 'take-it-or-leave-it' attitude to the internal customers? This attitude is common in centralised support units, where business units do not have alternative external supply sources, and therefore there is little incentive for the centralised unit to worry about its performance. However, business units are not 'captive customers' and this creates an incentive for the shared services unit to focus on delivering a high level of service to internal customers. Also, monitoring and rewarding the performance of the shared services unit using measures such as internal customer satisfaction, productivity and break-even performance can motivate managers in the shared services unit to work at achieving high levels of performance.

Team-based structures

Over the past decade, some firms have moved away from hierarchical structures towards **flatter organisational structures** that involve fewer levels of management. These flatter structures promote the quicker flow of ideas up and down the organisation, and assist business units to respond more quickly to market opportunities. Within business units, **self-managed work teams** may be formed to manage all aspects of a particular process. In the production area, self-managed work teams may operate in place of individual production departments. The responsibilities of the teams may include production planning, ordering materials, liaising with suppliers and customers, completing all aspects of the production process, managing the cost budget and managing their own performance. In the administrative areas of a business unit, teams may be formed to more effectively manage some processes. For example, individual teams in the human resources department may be assigned responsibility for particular work areas of a business unit, and to manage all human resource aspects in that area, such as new employment, payroll processing, and training needs. Members of the team will be multi-skilled so that they can complete all the required tasks.

The implementation of self-managed teams is thought to promote employee satisfaction, improved customer satisfaction and improved productivity. Why is this? The creation of self-managed work teams involves placing decision-making responsibility, which once rested with middle management, with teams. Thus, decentralisation is pushed to the lower levels of the organisation. The additional responsibilities and higher levels of empowerment are thought to promote a high level of motivation among team members.

Clearly, management accountants have a role to play in designing information systems that will provide the necessary information and feedback to teams. In addition, management accountants may assist teams in interpreting information and designing performance measures to help them monitor their processes and performance (Chenhall & Langfield-Smith, 1998). However, as with any decisions to decentralise decision-making authority, there are trade-offs that must be made. The benefits and risks of implementing self-managed teams are described in Exhibit 12.4.

How do teams fit into the conventional responsibility accounting structures discussed earlier in this chapter? Self-managed work-based teams are formed within divisions or business units (profit centres or investment centres), and in situations where the teams manage their own cost budget they would be regarded as cost centres. However, it should be noted that due to the critical nature of the operations a team performs, non-financial performance measures – such as those that measure productivity, internal customer satisfaction, quality, wastage and delivery – may be considered more important in managing operations and in evaluating the performance of a team than cost measures. (Non-financial measures are discussed in Chapter 14.)

The benefits	The costs/risks
■ Improved response time to customer delivery needs	■ Increased cost of employee selection and training
■ Improved response time to recovery from equipment breakdown	■ Increased labour costs as team members' salaries increase
■ Improved job satisfaction and feelings of self-worth for team members	■ Disruption to operations in the transition from departments to teams
■ Enhanced enthusiasm for customer interactions among team members	■ Supervisors and middle managers have difficulty adjusting when their jobs change from direction to facilitation
■ Increased opportunities for team members to improve the quality of operations directly	■ Resource commitments are made by team members with less appreciation for the long-term impact of their decisions
■ Improved customer service	■ Resistance to change from employees who are asked to form teams and take on the added responsibilities
■ Increased goal congruence among team members	■ Increased stress among team members from the additional responsibility
Source: adapted from Hays (1996, p. 165)	

Exhibit 12.4 Trade-offs in the implementation of self-managed work teams

REAL LIFE: SHARED SERVICES TO ENHANCE CUSTOMER VALUE AND MANAGE COSTS

Early adopters of shared services units include Hewlett Packard, AT&T, BBC (London), McDonald's (Europe), IBM, Johnson & Johnson, General Electric and Lucent Technologies. In South Africa many organisations have also formed shared services units to manage common support services.

BHP Billiton Limited has structured its company to include a marketing group that services the entire company. The group is located in the Netherlands, Switzerland and Singapore. The marketing group provides shared services that include compliance, risk management, legal services, tax, financial services, human resources and information technology. There is also a shared services unit for transport and logistics. BHP Billiton sees the shared services model as providing better service to external customers through the facilitation of a common IT system, improved employee skills, improved information flow and improved speed and quality of decisions. Services such as risk management are an additional service provided to customers, to enhance the customer value of the physical products.

There are many organisations in South Africa that have consolidated such functions as IT, human resources, finance and debtors management into shared services units. A number of shared services units may move from being cost centres to being profit centres and may be spun off as independent entities. Arivia.kom is a state-owned Information and Communication Technology service provider to Transnet, SA Revenue Service, Airports Company of South Africa and Eskom. Arivia.kom employs more than 1500 people and the company provides IT services and human resource and supply-chain management services. The South African government is currently considering the sale of the company. If successful, this will mean that IT services will be provided by a company that is independent from its customers. In the public sector the consolidation of such services as invoicing, information technology and payroll management is expected to result in cost savings as well as improving the quality of government services. In a survey by Accenture of

143 senior government executives in 13 countries, including South Africa, it was reported by two-thirds of the government executives that they had implemented, or were in the process of implementing, a shared services model. Objectives indicated by the respondents included an improvement in efficiencies, achieving cost reductions and realising better levels of service.

Cost management has become a critical component of gold mining in South Africa. The Goldfields Group is one of the major gold mining companies in South Africa. Goldfields Ltd has stated that it wishes to 'generate business value through World Class Shared Services Centre operations'. Since the group created Goldfields Shared Services (GFSS) in 2003 to take responsibility of all repetitive common processes, Goldfields has stated that Shared Services has moved from being a cost centre to being a value generator. The company achieved savings of R22 million per year on the implementation of Shared Services and GFSS is expected to achieve annual savings of R320m per year. Inventory levels have been reduced by 30 per cent. The company has invested in systems, implemented improved standards for mining, metallurgical operations and engineering and has improved controls over materials usage. In terms of procurement, GFSS has implemented greater standardisation, strategic sourcing, and analysis of the total cost of ownership. The number of vendors and inventory items has been rationalised and GFSS has implemented world-class procurement practices. This includes consolidation of its bargaining power and a restructuring of its supplier relationships as well as creating a credible switching threat. GFSS has also installed a new payroll system.

Sources: BHP Billiton Ltd (2001); Schulman, Dunleavy, Harmer & Lusk (1999), Accenture (2005), GoldFields (2004), Arivia.kom (2006)

Financial performance reports

L.O. 4

Evaluating performance is a key aspect of managing and controlling a decentralised organisation. As organisations become larger, and greater decision-making authority is delegated to various sub-units, corporate management needs to develop methods for evaluating performance. In Exhibit 12.1 we described the types of financial measures commonly used to evaluate performance in various areas of a decentralised business. In this section, we consider the provision of regular financial performance reports. We will follow this by considering real-time reporting.

A **financial performance report** shows the key financial results *appropriate for the type of responsibility centre*. For example, the performance report of a cost centre may concentrate on budgeted and actual costs that relate to the operations of the cost centre. The financial reports of profit centres and investment centres will include a wider range of financial information, in line with the managers' specific responsibilities. Performance reports typically show the variance between budgeted and actual financial results.

Many organisations prepare **segmented profit statements**, which show the profits for major responsibility centres (divisions and departments) and for the entire organisation. Exhibit 12.5 contains a segmented profit statement for the Bay Hotels Group for the month of January 20X8. For simplicity, only profit statements for the two divisions and for the three hotels in the Northern Division are provided. (Budgets and variances are also omitted, although they will be covered in a later example.) Notice that the report highlights the *segment contribution margin*. This means that the report is in **contribution margin format**. Under the contribution margin format, costs are reported by cost behaviour (that is, the variable costs are reported separately from the fixed costs). This allows a total **contribution margin** to be reported, which is the difference between the sales revenue and variable costs. Managers often find it more useful to report costs by cost behaviour, as it then becomes easy to project how overall profit may change if production volume, or other cost driver, changes. The variable costing format for profit statements was described in the appendix to Chapter 7. The use of variable costs and contribution margins for decision-making is discussed in detail in Chapters 18, 19 and 20.

Performance of sub-units versus sub-unit managers

L.O. 5

In Exhibit 12.5 you will notice that we have distinguished between 'Profit margin controllable by segment manager' and 'Profit margin attributable to segment'. This helps us to distinguish between the performance of sub-unit managers and the sub-units themselves. In *evaluating the manager's performance*, only revenues and costs that the manager can *control or significantly influence* should be included in the profit measure. In contrast, when evaluating the *economic performance of a subunit* we focus on revenues and costs that are attributable to that sub-unit.

Note that some costs that are attributable to a sub-unit may be completely beyond the influence of the sub-unit manager. For example, land taxes on the Umhlanga Hotel are traceable to the hotel, but the hotel manager cannot influence them. To evaluate the Umhlanga Hotel correctly as an investment of the company's resources, the land taxes should be included in the hotel's costs. However, in evaluating the *hotel manager's performance* the land taxes should be excluded, since the manager has no control over them.

An important reason for considering business unit and managerial performance separately is to prevent penalising good managers who are asked to manage poorly performing divisions or departments. If managers are able to improve the performance of poorly performing business units, this should be reflected in the manager's performance. While the division may still have a poor performance, the manager may have performed well. Despite the importance of this difference, in many businesses this distinction is not recognised. Some senior managers take the view that, when a manager is given responsibility for a division or subsidiary, that manager is accountable for *all the profits of that sub-unit*, controllable or not. If unfavourable events occur that are beyond his or her control, then the manager must skilfully manage around those events.

Cost allocations in performance reports

L.O. 6

Preparing segmented profit statements may require costs to be allocated to determine the 'complete' financial performance of a responsibility centre, and to allow us to assess the performance of the unit manager. In Chapter 7, the practice of cost allocation was discussed.

Some costs incurred outside a sub-unit may relate to that sub-unit. These may include advertising or public relations activities undertaken by head office for the benefit of a specific division. Also, computing services may be controlled and operated centrally but be used directly by divisions and departments. Causal allocation bases may be used to charge the cost of these activities to the particular sub-unit that used the service.

More difficult decisions relate to **common costs**; these result from activities that are performed for the benefit of more than one responsibility centre. The salary of the managing director of Bay Hotels is a common cost. The managing director manages the entire company, works with the company's board of directors, develops strategic plans for the company, and helps to set policies and goals for the entire enterprise. Some of his time is spent on matters related specifically to individual hotels, but much of it is spent on tasks that are not directly attributable to any hotel. Since common costs are not clearly attributable to the activities of sub-units, any allocation can only be made on some highly arbitrary allocation basis. Arbitrary cost allocations will result in misleading sub-unit profit information and are better not attempted.

In Exhibit 12.5 there are three examples of common costs that have not been allocated to sub-units. First, R1 200 000 of common fixed expenses (in the left-hand column) have not been allocated from the head office to the company's two divisions. Included in this figure are salaries of the corporate management team.

	Bay Hotels	Segments of company		Segments of Northern Division			
		Southern Division	**Northern Division**	**Umhlanga**	**Durban**	**Margate**	**Not Allocated**
Sales revenue	R 25 000 000	R 16 000 000	R 9 000 000	R 4 500 000	R 1 500 000	R 3 000 000	0
Variable operating expenses:							
Personnel, electricity & water	8 209 000	5 104 000	3 105 000	1 555 000	500 000	1 050 000	0
Food, beverages and supplies	3 690 000	2 293 000	1 397 000	698 500	232 000	466 500	0
Other	830 000	580 000	250 000	125 000	40 000	85 000	0
Total	12 729 000	7 977 000	4 752 000	2 378 500	772 000	1 601 500	0
Segment contribution margin	12 271 000	8 023 000	4 248 000	2 121 500	728 000	1 398 500	0
Less Fixed expenses controllable by segment manager	2 400 000	1 680 000	720 000	320 000	80 000	240 000	80 000
Profit margin controllable by segment manager	9 871 000	6 343 000	3 528 000	1 801 500	648 000	1 158 500	−80 000
Less Fixed expenses traceable to segment, but controllable by others	3 750 000	2 500 000	1 250 000	130 000	40 000	80 000	1 000 000
Profit margin attributable to segment	6 121 000	3 843 000	2 278 000	1 671 500	608 000	1 078 500	−1 080 000
Less Common fixed expenses	1 200 000						
Profit before taxes	4 921 000						
Less Income tax expense	1 427 090						
Net profit	R 3 493 910						

Exhibit 12.5 Segmented profit statements for January 20X8, Bay Hotels Group

Second, R80 000 of controllable fixed expenses (in the right-hand column) incurred by the Northern Division have not been allocated to the division's three hotels. This R80 000 of fixed expense includes the cost of regional advertising and divisional office salaries. This procedure illustrates an important point. Costs that are attributable to sub-units at one level in an organisation may become common costs at a lower level in the organisation. Thus, the Northern Division's office advertising and salary costs are traceable to the Northern Division, but cannot be allocated fairly between the division's three hotels.

Third, the R1 million of fixed expenses controllable by others in the right-hand column is part of the Northern Division's R1.25 million fixed expenses controllable by others. The R1 million are costs of operating the Northern Division that are not controllable by the Northern Division manager. They could include property taxes and office rental. They cannot be easily allocated between the division's three hotels.[1]

A hierarchy of financial performance reports

Within many organisations, a *hierarchy* of regular financial performance reports is prepared. These reports start at the bottom of a business and build towards the top, in line with the organisational structure. All managers in the organisation receive a financial performance report for their own responsibility centre, in addition to the performance reports for the major sub-units at the next lower level (for which they are also responsible). For example, the general manager of the Northern Division of Bay Hotels would receive the financial report for his entire division, as well as the financial reports of the Umhlanga Hotel, Durban Hotel and the Margate Hotel. Similarly, the manager of the Durban Hotel would receive the reports for the entire hotel and for each of its departments: Grounds and Maintenance, Housekeeping, Recreational, Hospitality, and Food and Beverage. By using these reports, the hotel manager can evaluate the performance of each department of his hotel, as well as that of the entire hotel. This will help the manager to consider ways of improving the hotel's financial performance, motivating employees and planning future operations.

While the reports in Exhibit 12.5 indicate the relative contribution of the various divisions and departments to the profits of the Bay Hotels Group, better performance reports can be provided by reporting actual performance compared with budgeted performance.

Exhibit 12.6 presents financial performance reports for February 20X8 for some selected sub-units of the Bay Hotels Group. This exhibit is a summary of key financial information from sub-unit performance reports. In many businesses, each financial sub-unit would have a separate set of performance reports that include non-financial information as well as detailed financial information. However, in this example it is the linkages between the various sub-unit financial reports that are the focus. You will notice that there are separate columns for actual results, flexible budget, and variances, for both February and the year to date. The relationships between the performances of the various sub-units of the business will be explained.

In the Durban Hotel, the kitchen, together with two profit centres (Catering, and Restaurants) is part of the Food and Beverage Department. The kitchen is a cost centre headed by a chef who reports to the manager of the Food and Beverage Department. Thus, the various costs of the kitchen are presented at the base of Exhibit 12.6. The total cost of this cost centre then forms part of the profit performance of the Food and Beverage Department. (This is indicated by an arrow in the flexible budget column.) In turn, the profits of the Food and Beverage Department form part of the performance of the Durban Hotel, together with the other four departments. The profit of the Durban Hotel is then included as part of the profit performance of the Northern Division, which is then part of the overall profit performance of Bay Hotels. (Notice that, at the company level, there are head office costs that are attributable to the head office only.)

Budgets, variance analysis and responsibility accounting

You can see from the reports in Exhibit 12.6 that budgeting, variance analysis and responsibility accounting are closely interrelated. The flexible budget provides the benchmark against which

	Flexible Budget		Actual results		Variance†	
	February	Year to date	February	Year to date	February	Year to date
Company	4 972 000	9 903 600	4 943 200	9 864 200	−28 800 U	−39 400 U
Southern Division	3 680 000	7 535 000	3 694 000	7 537 000	14 000 F	2 000 F
Northern Division	2 452 000	4 728 600	2 449 200	4 727 200	−2 800 U	−1 400 U
Head Office	−1 160 000	−2 360 000	−1 200 000	−2 400 000	−40 000 U	−40 000 U
Total profit	4 972 000	9 903 600	4 943 200	9 864 200	−28 800 U	−39 400 U
Northern Division						
Umhlanga Hotel	1 210 000	2 340 000	1 212 000	2 348 000	2 000 F	8 000 F
Margate Hotel	420 000	1 100 000	410 000	1 086 000	−10 000 U	−14 000 U
Durban Hotel	822 000	1 288 600	827 200	1 293 200	5 200 F	4 600 F
Total profit	2 452 000	4 728 600	2 449 200	4 727 200	−2 800 U	−1 400 U
Durban Hotel						
Grounds & Maintenance	−9 000	−18 000	−8 800	−18 000	200 F	0
Housekeeping	−8 000	−18 000	−8 200	−18 000	−200 U	0
Recreational	8 000	17 000	8 200	17 600	200 F	600 F
Hospitality	560 000	969 600	568 000	975 600	8 000 F	6 000 F
Food and Beverage	271 000	338 000	268 000	336 000	−3 000 U	−2 000 U
Total profit	822 000	1 288 600	827 200	1 293 200	5 200 F	4 600 F
Food and Beverage Department						
Catering	120 000	252 000	121 000	253 000	1 000 F	1 000 F
Restaurant	357 000	519 600	352 000	517 600	−5 000 U	−2 000 U
Kitchen	−206 000	−433 600	−205 000	−434 600	1 000 F	−1 000 U
Total profit	271 000	338 000	268 000	336 000	−3 000 U	−2 000 U
Kitchen						
Kitchen and staff wages	−30 000	−47 600	−29 600	−47 800	400 F	−200 U
Food	−135 000	−284 000	−135 600	−284 200	−600 U	−200 U
Paper products	−10 000	−36 000	−9 000	−35 600	1 000 F	400 F
Variable overhead	−14 000	−30 000	−14 200	−30 800	−200 U	−800 U
Fixed overhead	−17 000	−36 000	−16 600	−36 200	400 F	−200 U
Total cost	−206 000	−433 600	−205 000	−434 600	1 000 F	−1 000 U

*F denotes favourable variance; U denotes unfavourable variance.

Exhibit 12.6 Performance reports for February 20X8, showing selected segments, Bay Hotels Group

actual revenues, expenses and profits are compared. As you saw in Chapter 11, it is important to use a flexible budget so that appropriate comparisons can be made. It would make no sense, for example, to compare the actual costs incurred in the Housekeeping Department at the Durban Hotel with budgeted costs that were based on a different level of hotel occupancy.

The performance reports in Exhibit 12.6 show variances between budgeted performance and actual performance. On more detailed performance reports, these variances are often broken down into smaller components to help management pinpoint responsibility and diagnose performance.

Inclusion of allocated costs

How are allocated costs treated in the performance reports in Exhibit 12.6? Exhibit 12.5 showed that several levels of profits can be reported, based on controllability and attributability. Some common costs were not allocated to sub-units, as they were not controllable or attributable to any sub-unit other than the corporate head office.

If management is using the performance reports to evaluate the *economic performance* of the sub-units, then the cost and profit reports in Exhibit 12.6 for the Kitchen or the Food and Beverage Department should include those financial results that are *attributable to the sub-units.* Thus, some allocated costs would be included. However, if the focus for performance reports is on evaluating the performance of the managers of each sub-unit, then *only* costs or profits that are *controllable by sub-unit managers* should be included. This will mean that fewer allocated costs are included. The extent to which allocated costs are included in sub-unit performance reports varies between companies, and really depends on what corporate managers consider relevant and which methods of reporting are cost-effective.

L.O. 7

Real-time reporting

In many organisations managers receive regular financial performance reports, as described in the above example. These reports may arrive between one and two weeks after the closing date – that is, after the end of the month. However, many managers require more timely reports and more frequent reporting. In some organisations, real-time reporting is available. **Real-time reporting** involves managers having access to up-to-date information whenever they require it. In some businesses, gaining a competitive advantage may rest on having the latest information on company performance so that it can be used to make quick decisions.

As many of the reports that managers require include accounting data, one problem in meeting the demand for real-time reporting relates to the difficulty of achieving a virtual close. The **virtual close** is the ability to close the accounting books at any time. Some firms have difficulty achieving a virtual close, as their computer systems are not sufficiently flexible to close accounts at any time other than at the standard reporting times (such as at the end of each month, quarter or year). A virtual close requires all business transactions to be immediately and continually posted to the ledger, and for aggregate data to be accessible in the form of a report. The 'Real life' below reports on leading companies that have achieved the virtual close in their businesses.

How can companies achieve a virtual close? The main issue is to *reduce the complexity* associated with the end-of-period closing of accounts, to speed up the reporting process. This is particularly a problem in multi-divisional organisations. The following issues are important in reducing complexity (Leahy, 2000; Caplan, 2001b):

- *Focus on critical performance data.* A real-time reporting system should focus on providing a top-level snapshot of performance, rather than including unnecessary detail. **Flash reports** are daily online reports of critical information, usually consisting of key financial and non-financial data. More detailed real-time reports may be provided weekly and monthly.
- *Implementing a single enterprise resource planning (ERP) system* that runs across all business units and which can easily consolidate and process financial data. This will help to achieve the necessary timelines. In companies where different accounting systems are used in different business units, and where not all of the processes are automated, achieving a shorter closing period is very difficult. These ERP systems will also allow for the automation of reports. ERP systems are explained in Chapter 16.
- *Re-engineer the reporting system.* The processes used to gather and process information will also need to be examined, in order to uncover any unnecessary activities that could be eliminated to improve efficiency. More information on re-engineering and process improvement can be found in Chapter 15.

REAL LIFE: ACHIEVING THE VIRTUAL CLOSE

Some companies use powerful Internet technologies to achieve virtual close and effective real-time reporting. These include large US companies such as Dell Computers, Federal Express, Cisco Systems, General Electric and Ford.

Managers at Dell Computers use information produced as part of the virtual close to make real-time decisions on resource allocation, and to forecast profit margins and growth rates of products. The real-time reporting systems include both financial and operational information.

Federal Express, the global transportation and logistics company, is able to produce reports quickly as a result of eliminating non-value-added activities and non-essential information from the reporting process. Its reports focus on what the company calls Service Quality Indicators (SQI), which consist of 12 critical performance indicators.

Cisco Systems claims to be able to produce consolidated financial statements and continually monitor critical business information on any given work day. Thus, managers at Cisco are able to access and analyse up-to-date revenue and profit margins based on product line, geographic region, business line or sales channel for the day, month, quarter and year to date, within a few hours. However, the CEO reported that it took eight years to put the technology and systems in place to allow the accounting systems to achieve virtual close.

General Electric (GE) created a new position of e-Finance Leader to manage the virtual close. The reporting systems at GE were inefficient due to the many varied financial and processing systems used throughout the global group, which were the legacy of acquisitions of other companies. The e-Finance Leader, Brian J. West, moved GE towards standard processes and cultural change. West explained: 'It requires a little bit of an iron fist from management. Let's not debate six ways of paying a bill. It's just paying a bill, and there is going to be one good way of doing it.' Finance employees had worked to a comfortable rhythm of weekly, monthly and quarterly reporting, and a major challenge was to break that system.

In 2001 Ford Motor Company began the overhaul of its finance systems, which had been developed just after World War II. The aim was to achieve the virtual close to allow managers to integrate financial analysis with operational and decision-making systems across the global company. In its early stages of development, common rules for analysis were implemented and real-time information on profitability by vehicle line and business unit became available. Such information is used by Ford managers to make decisions on where and when to market products worldwide and whether to offer rebates. A KPMG survey found that the median number of days to close the books had fallen from 10 to 7 days. However, the survey found that companies were taking longer to release the numbers due to concerns about the quality and accuracy of the financial reports.

What about South African companies? Are South African companies implementing systems that will enable them to minimise the time it takes to produce financial statements?

In order to move towards on-line, real-time reporting, companies will increasingly need to adopt Extensible Business Reporting Language (XBRL) to prepare financial statements. XBRL is a standard electronic language for preparing financial statements which is Internet based and which enables financial statements to become interactive. Analysts and investors are easily able to integrate data from financial statements into analytical and financial models without rekeying data. Each data point has an electronic tag.

The JSE Securities Exchange became the first major stock exchange in the world to use XBRL to present its financial statements. In May 2007 it was reported that the SEC would require companies to use the XBRL format to submit financial statements to the SEC. This would impact on South African subsidiaries of US companies as well as South African companies with secondary listings in the USA. At the time of writing, only the JSE Securities Exchange and

Alexander Forbes produced financial statements in XBRL. However, Linda de Beer stated that, 'The South African Institute of Chartered Accountants (SAICA) believes that XBRL will impact and simplify financial reporting in the future significantly.' XBRL South Africa was launched in 2006 in order to oversee the development of XBRL in South Africa. Microsoft software such as Excel supports XBRL.

Sources: Caplan (2001a), Leahy (2000), Pawling (2001), Kersnar (2002), Williams (2005), Linda de Beer (2006)

Transfer pricing

L.O. 8

In decentralised organisations goods and services are often transferred between investment centres and profit centres. The amount charged when one business unit sells goods or services to another business unit is called a transfer price.[2] **Transfer prices** are effectively *internal selling prices* used within a divisionalised organisation. However, the level of transfer price that is used is important – the transfer price is revenue for the supplying division and a cost of the buying division.

Why do organisations use transfer prices? The financial performance of an investment centre or profit centre is usually evaluated using some measure of profit. When goods and services are transferred between divisions, a transfer price will allow the selling division to record revenue to earn a profit on the transfer, to reflect the effort that it has expended in producing that product. The transfer price will allow the buying division to record the cost of the transfer of the product, which will be matched against the revenue when it eventually sells the product to the external market. In situations where there is a series of transfers of product between divisions, transfer prices will allow each division to show profits for their efforts – not just the final division that sells the completed product to the external market.

The use of transfer prices encourages each division to generate profits, and should encourage managers of units to manage their own unit as if it were a stand-alone business. Therefore, the transfer pricing system should operate in a way that does not undermine goal congruence or the decentralised managers' autonomy. Thus, a transfer pricing system should:

- result in divisional profits that are a reliable and accurate measure of divisional performance;
- reserve and encourage divisional autonomy; and
- encourage goal-congruent behaviour.

Who sets the transfer prices?

In a decentralised organisation, the managers of profit centres and investment centres usually have considerable autonomy in deciding whether to accept or reject orders for goods or services, and whether to source their materials and components, or services, from inside or outside the organisation. They may also have considerable autonomy over setting and accepting transfer prices.

Direct intervention by corporate management to establish transfer prices is usually considered to be inconsistent with the philosophy of decentralisation. Nevertheless, corporate management usually develops general policies to guide transfer pricing practices throughout the organisation. Occasionally, the transfer prices that are set by managers of business units may lead to decisions that are not in the best interests of the organisation as a whole. However, unless the impact is very large, corporate management may be reluctant to interfere if it could *undermine the autonomy of decentralised managers.*

Transfer pricing methods

L.O. 9

There are three general methods that can be used for determining transfer prices.

Market-based prices

Basing transfer prices on external market prices usually results in decisions that are consistent with responsibility accounting concepts and decentralisation philosophies. In addition, market-based transfer prices result in a reasonable estimate of the profit contribution of each business unit to overall company profit. If there are competitive external markets for a product, then market prices are generally the recommended transfer price. However, as we will see, using the market prices will not always encourage goal-congruent behaviour.

Cost-plus prices

Some transferred goods and services do not have reliable external market prices; for example, they may be intermediate products. **Intermediate products** have no market outside the company, and are processed further to become final products. In these situations the transfer price may be based on cost. Cost-based transfer prices may also be appropriate, even where there is a market price, when the supplying unit has excess capacity. The issue of excess capacity will be explained in a later section.

One approach to using cost-plus pricing is to set the transfer price equal to the *standard variable cost plus a mark-up*. The mark-up allows the supplying unit to show a contribution margin on the transferred goods or services, to reflect a return on the effort of producing the product. For example a mark-up of, say, 10 or 20 per cent may provide an incentive for the supplying business to produce and transfer products internally. An alternative is to set the transfer price equal to the *standard absorption cost* of the transferred good or service. (You may remember from Chapter 7 that absorption cost is equal to the product's variable cost plus an allocated portion of fixed overhead.) However, as illustrated in the next section, where there is no external market for a product, transfer prices based on absorption cost can lead to overpriced transfers and possibly dysfunctional decisions. Note that when using cost-based transfer prices, *standard costs* (predetermined or budgeted costs) rather than actual costs should be used. Basing transfer prices on actual costs allows an inefficient supplying business unit to pass excessive production costs on to the buying business unit within the transfer price. When standard costs are used in transfer pricing formulas, the supplying business unit is given an incentive to control its costs, since any actual cost inefficiencies cannot be passed on in the transfer price.

Negotiated prices

The managers of profit centres and investment centres may negotiate the price at which transfers will be made. The external market price may form the starting point for negotiations, and the incremental cost of producing and supplying the product to the buying division may form the lower bounds of the transfer price.

An important issue in considering the appropriate level of transfer price is whether or not the supplying division has *excess capacity*. In the examples that follow we will consider in more detail the three transfer pricing systems outlined above.

General transfer pricing rule

L.O. 10

There is a *general rule* for transfer pricing that can give some guidance as to the appropriate transfer price. The use of this general transfer rule will result in transfer prices that promote goal congruent behaviour.

$$\text{Transfer price} = \begin{array}{c}\text{additional outlay costs per unit}\\\text{incurred by supplying division}\end{array} + \begin{array}{c}\text{opportunity cost per unit}\\\text{to the supplying division}\end{array}$$

The general rule specifies the optimal transfer price as the sum of two cost components. The *first component* is the costs incurred by the supplying division to produce and supply the goods or services to be transferred. While this outlay cost is usually approximated as the variable cost of the product, it will also include any other costs that are incurred only as a result of the transfer, such as product design costs, and savings in selling and distribution costs that arise due to the transfer. The *second component* is the opportunity cost. This is any profit forgone by the supplying division resulting from its production capacity being used to produce and supply product for the internal buying business, rather than for its usual purpose.

The price set by the general formula generally represents a minimum transfer price, as the supplying division must receive at least the price calculated by the general formula to be as well off as if the goods or services were sold to the external customers. In the transfer pricing scenarios that follow, we will see that the general rule results in a transfer price that leads divisional managers to make goal-congruent decisions.[3]

L.O. 11

Transfer pricing under different scenarios

Clean Wash Ltd is a manufacturer of washing powders and soap. It is structured into a series of investment centres. The Industrial Division produces chemicals, including glycerol, which it sells to external customers as well as to other divisions. (Glycerol is a material used in the manufacture of soap and washing powders.) The Industrial Division has the capacity to produce 200 tonnes of glycerol per month. Currently, external customers purchase 140 tonnes of glycerol each month from the Industrial Division. Let's suppose that the variable manufacturing cost incurred by the Industrial Division to produce glycerol is R7000 per tonne. These costs include direct materials, direct labour and variable overhead. The Soap Division needs to purchase 30 tonnes of glycerol per month to use in the manufacture of soap. The Soap Division will incur further processing costs of R3500 per tonne to convert the 30 tonnes of glycerol into 30 tonnes of soap, which it can sell to the external market at R17 000 per tonne. Exhibit 12.7 illustrates the relationships between the various divisions of Clean Wash.

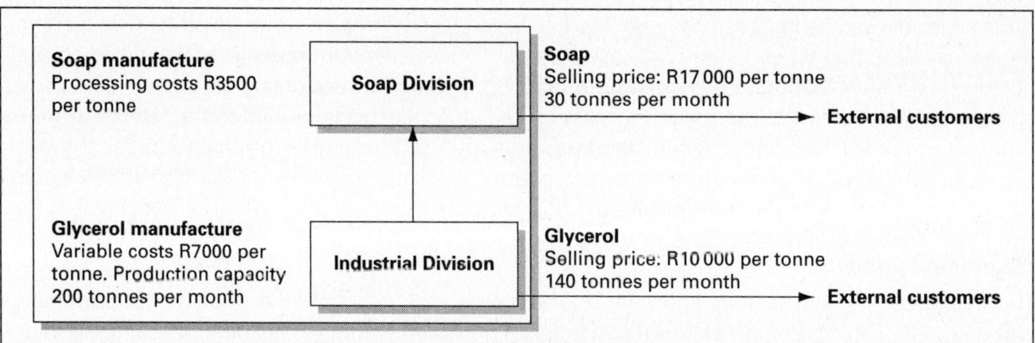

Exhibit 12.7 Transfer of glycerol between divisions, Clean Wash Ltd

Scenario 1: An external market, and excess capacity in the supplying division

Let's suppose the manager of the Industrial Division offers to transfer glycerol to the Soap Division at a market-based transfer price of R10 000 per tonne. Exhibit 12.8 shows the divisional and company profits that would result.

As in many decentralised companies, both divisions are able to buy and sell on the external market. However, the Industrial Division has *excess capacity*, and can only sell 140 tonnes to external customers. Therefore, the profit of R90 000 per month that it makes from producing and transferring the 30 tonnes to the Soap Division is additional profit that *it would not otherwise make.* In contrast, the Soap Division can purchase its glycerol from external suppliers at R10 000 per tonne, and be no worse or better off.

While the manager of the Industrial Division certainly has an incentive to produce and transfer the additional 30 tonnes to the Soap Division, the manager of the Soap Division may be unconcerned as to whether the glycerol is purchased from inside or outside the organisation. However,

Industrial Division		Soap Division	
Transfer price per tonne	R10 000	Sales price per tonne	R17 000
Variable costs	7 000	Transfer price	10 000
		Processing costs	3 500
Contribution margin on glycerol	3 000	Contribution margin on soap	3 500
Incremental profit per month if glycerol is transferred		Incremental profit if glycerol is purchased internally*	0
R3000 × 30 tonnes glycerol	R 90 000		
Company as a whole			
Incremental profit from the transfer of glycerol between divisions: R3000 × 30 tonnes			R 90 000

*The Soap Division will make R3500 per tonne whether it purchases glycerol from inside or outside the firm, and will thus make no additional profit if it is purchased internally.

Exhibit 12.8 Transfer of glycerol at market price of R10 000 per tonne, Clean Wash Ltd

the company as a whole would be better off by R90 000 per month if the transfer took place. (This represents the savings to the company of manufacturing glycerol for R7000, rather than purchasing it for R10 000.)

So the transfer is clearly in the interests of the overall organisation. But how can we encourage the transfer to take place in this decentralised environment?

The two divisions may be encouraged to negotiate a transfer price at a price *less than market* to provide an incentive to the Soap Division to purchase from the Industrial Division. The manager of the Industrial Division will be open to such negotiations, as if he or she insists on charging market price the Division may lose the internal sale (and the additional profits).

What would the general rule tell us is the appropriate transfer price?

$$\text{Transfer price} = \begin{array}{l}\text{additional outlay costs per unit}\\ \text{incurred by supplying division}\end{array} + \begin{array}{l}\text{opportunity cost per unit}\\ \text{to the supplying division}\end{array}$$
$$= \text{R7000} + \text{R0}$$
$$= \text{R7000}$$

The transfer to the Soap Division does not cause any opportunity cost to the Industrial Division, as the Industrial Division has excess capacity.

As the Industrial Division has excess capacity, any transfer price which is greater than the variable costs of producing and transferring the product (R7000), will yield incremental profits for the Industrial Division. And any price lower than R10 000 per tonne is attractive to the managers in the Soap Division.

So how will the managers of the two divisions arrive at the transfer price? In many organisations this decision will be left to the managers in the two divisions to sort out. However, some people believe that this can lead to problems:

- Negotiations can lead to divisiveness and competition between participating business unit managers, which can undermine the spirit of co-operation and unity that is desirable throughout any organisation. As divisional managers' performance and rewards are based on their divisional profits, they will have an incentive to maximise their own profit results through obtaining favourable transfer prices. However, remember that the selling division will want to maximise the transfer price, while the buying division will be trying to minimise the transfer price.
- Although negotiating skills are a valuable managerial attribute, they should not be the sole or dominant factor in evaluating a business unit manager. If, for example, the supplying unit's manager is a better negotiator than the buying unit's manager, then the supplying

unit's profit will be more favourable as a result, simply because of its manager's superior negotiating ability.

To overcome some of these problems, corporate management may set up a negotiating team to assist in transfer pricing negotiations and to help resolve transfer pricing disputes. Alternatively, corporate management may institute a transfer pricing policy stating that transfer prices should be based on market prices, less a discount of, say, 5 to 10 per cent.

Let's assume in the above example that the managers of the two divisions arrived at a transfer price of R9000 per tonne for glycerol. How will this affect the profits of the two divisions and the company as a whole? Exhibit 12.9 shows that the Industrial Division will show additional profits of R60 000 per month, and the Soap Division will be better off by R30 000 per month. Thus, the transfer will take place. Note that the total incremental profits for the company as a whole are the same as when the transfer price of R10 000 was used. This highlights an important aspect of transfer pricing systems. Whatever transfer price is used, the total company profits remain unchanged if the transfer takes place. However, the individual divisional profits will differ, and this can provide divisional managers with incentives to either proceed or stop the transfer. At the proposed price of R10 000 the transfer might not have gone ahead, and so no additional company profits would have been made.

Industrial Division		**Soap Division**	
Transfer price per tonne	R9 000	Sales price per tonne	R17 000
Variable costs	7 000	Transfer price	9 000
		Processing costs	3 500
Contribution margin per tonne on glycerol transferred internally	2 000	Contribution margin per tonne on soap if the internal transfer takes place	4 500
Incremental profit per month from the transfer R2000 × 30 tonnes	R 60 000	Incremental profit from the transfer (R4500 − R3500) × 30 tonnes	R30 000
		Company as a whole	
Incremental profit per month if the transfer takes place			R 90 000

Exhibit 12.9 Clean Wash Ltd: Transfer of glycerol at negotiated price of R9000 per tonne

Scenario 2: An external market and no excess capacity in the supplying division

In the above example the Industrial Division had sufficient spare capacity to produce and transfer 30 tonnes of glycerol to the Soap Division without forgoing any external sales. However, what if the external demand for glycerol was 200 tonnes a month? In this case, the Industrial Division has no excess capacity to satisfy the demands of the Soap Division. If the Industrial Division were to give up external sales to sell to the Soap Division, then it must account for an opportunity cost. This is the contribution margin (R3000) that will be lost as a result of giving up external sales in favour of the internal transfer. In this situation, the general rule will provide the following solution:

Transfer price = additional outlay costs per unit incurred by supplying division + opportunity cost per unit to the supplying division
= R7000 + R3000
= R10 000

Thus, if the Soap Division wants to obtain its glycerol from the Industrial Division, then it will need to pay the market price of R10 000. In this situation, the internal transfer may not take place, as neither division will be better off.

Scenario 3: External market price and limited capacity in the supplying division

Let's take this one step further. What if the external demand for glycerol was 190 tonnes per month? In this situation the Industrial Division would want to use its spare 10 tonnes of capacity, but it cannot supply the full 30 tonnes required by the Soap Division. One option might be to offer to sell only 10 tonnes to the Soap Division at the cost-plus price of at least R7000 per tonne (as in scenario 1), and for the Soap Division to obtain the remaining 20 tonnes from the external market. However, the manager of the Soap Division may not want to deal with two different suppliers. To provide the full 30 tonnes to the Soap Division, the manager of the Industrial Division needs to obtain a transfer price that compensates for the opportunity cost of losing 20 tonnes of sales to the external market. In this situation, as the opportunity cost will be based on one production volume and the outlay costs on another, it is easier to use total costs, rather than unit costs, in the general rule.

$$\begin{aligned}\text{Transfer price} &= \begin{matrix}\text{additional outlay costs incurred}\\ \text{by supplying division}\end{matrix} + \begin{matrix}\text{opportunity cost to the}\\ \text{supplying division}\end{matrix}\\ &= (\text{R}7000 \times 30 \text{ tonnes}) + (\text{R}3000 \times 20 \text{ tonnes})\\ &= \text{R}270\,000\end{aligned}$$

The minimum transfer price that would leave the Industrial Division no worse off if it transferred 30 tonnes to the Soap Division is R9000 per tonne (R270 000 ÷ 30 tonnes). In reality, the transfer price would be set between R9000 per tonne and the market price of R10 000. The Soap Division should be agreeable to the transfer at any price below R10 000.

Scenario 4: No external market and excess capacity in the supplying division

Suppose that the Industrial Division has excess capacity, and it has agreed to produce and supply 20 tonnes per month of G-grade glycerol (a product with no easily determined market price) to the Soap Division. G-grade glycerol is not readily available from any outside suppliers. Assume the Industrial Division has priced the product at the absorption cost of R10 400 per tonne, being variable costs of R6900 plus R3500 fixed overhead. The Soap Division will process the 20 tonnes of glycerol into 20 tonnes of G-grade soap at a cost of R2000 per tonne, and sell this to the external market for R11 000 per tonne. The Soap Division would reject the Industrial Division's transfer price of R10 400 per tonne, as it would result in a loss of R1400 per tonne (R11 000 less costs of R10 400 and R2000). Exhibit 12.10 summarises the relevant costs of this transaction.

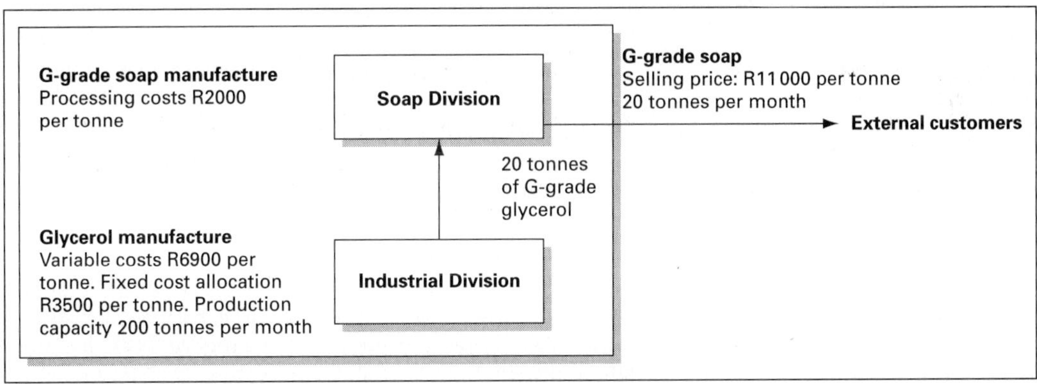

Exhibit 12.10 Clean Wash Limited: Transfer of intermediate product

The *total contribution margin* that the company as a whole will make from the G-grade glycerol being manufactured and sold as G-grade soap is R2100 per tonne (R11 000 − 6900 − 2000), so it is in the interests of the company for the transfer to take place. Thus, the managers of the two divisions need to negotiate a price that will provide both divisions with a profit, and hence an incentive to undertake the transfer. The Industrial Division has *excess capacity*, so any transfer price greater than the variable cost of R6900 will yield a contribution margin for the Industrial Division. (If the total fixed costs of production do not change if the manufacture of G-grade glycerol takes place, then there is no need to cover these fixed costs in the transfer price.)

Let's check this logic by using the general formula:

$$\text{Transfer price} = \begin{array}{c}\text{additional outlay costs per unit}\\ \text{incurred by supplying division}\end{array} + \begin{array}{c}\text{opportunity cost per unit}\\ \text{to the supplying division}\end{array}$$
$$= R6900 + R0$$
$$= R6900$$

Scenario 5: No external market and no excess capacity in the supplying division

Where a product has no reliable external market and the supplying division is operating at *full capacity*, setting transfer prices becomes difficult. The manager in the Industrial Division will not wish to forgo the manufacture and sale of its regular product in order to supply G-grade glycerol to the Soap Division. Any transfer price that is decided on must take account of the opportunity cost, or the contribution margin forgone, for the supplying division. Remember that the Industrial Division makes a contribution margin of R3000 per tonne on the sale of regular-grade glycerol to external customers. Therefore, the minimum transfer price for the G-grade glycerol from the Industrial Division's point of view must be R9900, being the total of the variable cost of product of G-grade glycerol (R6900) and the opportunity cost on lost sales of regular grade glycerol (R3000). This is clearly not an attractive price for the Soap Division, which needs to spend a further R2000 per tonne to sell the final product for R11 000. Thus the transfer will not go ahead. The general formula confirms this transfer price:

$$\text{Transfer price} = \begin{array}{c}\text{additional outlay costs per unit}\\ \text{incurred by supplying division}\end{array} + \begin{array}{c}\text{opportunity cost per unit}\\ \text{to the supplying division}\end{array}$$
$$= R6900 + R3000$$
$$= R9900 \text{ per tonne}$$

Is this the 'correct' decision from the whole company viewpoint? Yes. Overall, profits of the company will be lower if the internal transaction takes place, as the contribution of the G-grade glycerol is R2100 per tonne, compared with the contribution on the regular-grade glycerol of R3000 per tonne. The Industrial Division (and the company) is better off using the capacity to produce glycerol for the external market.[4]

Summary of transfer pricing scenarios

The transfer prices that were calculated under the above scenarios are listed in Exhibit 12.11. Note that in each situation, the transfer price calculated using the general rule leads to goal-congruent behaviour. That is, the price will either encourage both divisional managers to transfer the product or not to transfer the product. In each case, the managers will make the decision because it enhances their own divisional profit and, as we have already demonstrated, it also enhances the profits of the company as a whole. Note that in some of these scenarios, negotiation may still take place between divisions to determine the final transfer price.

An important issue in implementing the general rule relates to how it is applied. Should it be used by corporate management to determine appropriate transfer prices? In decentralised organisations, it is usually not appropriate for 'someone on high' to determine the transfer price. However, the general rule may influence corporate transfer pricing policies. Also, the general rule may provide guidance for managers of business units when they are negotiating their transfer prices.

The influence of taxation

One aspect that cannot be ignored when examining transfer pricing practices is the impact of income taxation. International transfer pricing arises when a multinational company transfers goods or services between business units that are located in different countries. This practice effectively 'moves' profits from one country to another. Countries have different tax rates and different tax regulations. Therefore, there are incentives for companies to 'think carefully' about the prices they set for international transfers of goods and services, to ensure they comply fully with the taxation regulations of the countries involved and to maximise any tax advantages, if available.

Scenario	Transfer price calculated by the general rule	Transfer price	Will the transfer proceed?
External market and excess capacity in the supplying division	R7000 + R0	Minimum of R7000 ("variable cost plus" basis). The ceiling will be the market price of R10 000.	Yes. Some negotiation will take place to determine the final transfer price.
External market and no excess capacity in the supplying division	R7000 + R3000	R10 000 (market price)	It's uncertain. Both divisions will be indifferent to whether the transfer takes place.
External market and limited capacity in the supplying division	(R7000 × 30 tonnes) + (R3000 × 20 tonnes)	Minimum of R9000 and maximum of R10 000 (the market price)	Yes. Some negotiation will take place to determine the final transfer price.
No external market, and excess capacity in the supplying division	R6900 + R0	Minimum of R6900 (variable cost plus)	Yes. The price will be acceptable to both divisions. Some negotiation will take place to determine the final transfer price.
No external market, and no excess capacity in the supplying division	R6900 + R3000	Minimum of R9900	No. The price is not acceptable to the buying division, as it will lead to a loss.

Exhibit 12.11 Using the general rule for each transfer pricing scenario

It is beyond the scope of this book to consider these issues in detail. However, in multinational companies, tax considerations may influence the transfer prices that are used for domestic purposes.

Transfer pricing in service firms

Service industry firms and non-profit organisations may also use transfer pricing when services are transferred between business units. In banks, for example, the interest rate at which funds are transferred from the bank's head office to bank branches is a form of transfer price.

Transfer pricing and service level agreements

In recent years, managers in many decentralised organisations have created *service level agreements* between various sub-units. A **service level agreement (SLA)** is a contract between two sub-units of an organisation that establishes the service that will be provided by one unit to the other, and the responsibilities of the supplying and buying parties. The agreement may describe the nature of the service that will be delivered, the price of the service, the quality and the timing of the service delivery, the way in which the performance of both parties will be tracked and measured, performance targets, procedures for solving problems, and how the agreement can be changed or terminated. SLAs typically govern the supply relationship for one or two years. L.O. 12

Thus, operating divisions of a manufacturing company may enter into SLAs with shared service units such as the head office computer department and the centralised marketing department. Universities may enter into SLAs with the library, the human resources department and the international student recruitment office.

The price that is specified within the SLA is, of course, a transfer price, and can be determined in exactly the same way as in the manufacturing scenarios that we described in this chapter. An important feature of SLAs is that the focus is on establishing the characteristics of the 'complete' service delivery, not just the price. These agreements focus on setting up a competitive customer-buyer relationship within a decentralised organisation, and they are intended to encourage the supplier unit to adopt a customer focus. SLAs are similar to supplier contracts that are entered into by an organisation and their suppliers, as described in Chapter 16. The establishment of an SLA supports the principles of decentralisation and responsibility accounting.

Can SLAs also be used to govern the supply of goods between units of an organisation? 'SLA' is a term that is typically used for the supply of services, not goods. However, in many organisations formal agreements are set up for the supply of goods between sub-units, and these may be similar to an SLA.

Summary

Most organisations are structured into sub-units, each with its own operations and responsibilities. A major issue that must be considered is the extent to which decision-making should be delegated to managers in decentralised sub-units.

- The benefits of decentralisation include access to better information and skills, opportunities for managerial training, better motivation, more timely decisions, and more time for corporate management to devote to strategic decisions. The costs of decentralisation include the potential for decentralised managers to focus too narrowly on their own business without considering fully the consequences of their decisions for other sub-units, or on the wider organisational goals.
- Responsibility accounting can be used to encourage goal-congruent behaviour by managers in decentralised organisations. Organisational sub-units, or responsibility centres, can be designated as cost centres, revenue centres, profit centres or investment centres.
- In recent years, shared services units have emerged in large decentralised organisations as a means of improving the effectiveness of support services. Also, as many organisations move towards flatter management structures, there is greater use of self-managed work teams to manage operations.
- Performance measurement is a key part of responsibility accounting. Segmented profit statements and a hierarchy of financial performance reports may be prepared, comparing actual and budgeted data for the various cost centres and profit centres.
- To be most effective, performance reports should distinguish between the performance of sub-units and the performance of sub-unit managers.
- Real-time reporting is becoming a possibility in some organisations to provide more timely and relevant information for decision-making. However, achieving a virtual close to provide real-time reports is difficult in some firms, due to inadequate computer systems.
- Another issue that arises in decentralised organisations is transfer pricing. When goods and services are transferred between profit centres or investment centres in the same organisation, the sub-units' profit performance is affected by the transfer price.
- The general transfer pricing rule states that the transfer price should be equal to the outlay cost incurred to supply the transferred goods plus the opportunity cost associated with the transfer. This provides a minimum transfer price, which should lead to divisional managers making goal-congruent decisions.
- Transfer pricing systems may be based on market prices, cost or negotiated prices. Important aspects to consider when setting transfer prices include whether the supplying division has excess capacity, and whether there is a competitive external market price for the product. In most situations, it is inconsistent with the philosophy of decentralisation for corporate management to determine transfer prices. However, they may set general transfer pricing policies and assist in transfer pricing disputes.
- Service level agreements (SLAs) provide ways of formalising arrangements for the ongoing supply of services between various sub-units of an organisation. SLAs establish the responsibilities of both the buying and supplying parties.

References

Accenture 2005, 'Driving High Performance in Government: Maximising the Value of Public Sector Shared Services', January 2005.

Arivia.kom 2006, Annual Report.

BHP Billiton Ltd 2001, Annual Report.

Caplan, J 2001a, 'Sidebar: five technology issues in adopting a virtual close', CFO.com, www.cfo.com, 8 March.

Caplan, J 2001b, 'A virtual close: as easy as one, two, three', CFO.com, www.cfo.com, 8 March.

Chenhall, RH & Langfield-Smith, K 1998, 'Factors influencing the role of management accounting in the development of performance measures within organizational change programs', *Management Accounting Research*, vol. 9, no. 4, pp. 361–86.

De Beer, L & Evans, F 2006, 'XBRL officially launched in South Africa', XBRL SA Press release, 27 July.

Edcon 2006, Annual Report.

Evans, F 2004, 'JSE becomes first exchange globally to adopt standardised reporting system', JSE Press release, 10 December.

Gold Fields 2004, 'Building Long-term Shareholder Value', Financial Strategy Presentation by Nick Holland, CFO, 8 September.

Greenmeier, L 2001, 'IT as a profit center', *Information Week*, www.informationweek.com/story, 2 July.

Hays, RD 1996, *Internal Service Excellence*, Summit Executive Press, Sarasota, FL.

Institute of Management Accountants 2000, 'Implementing Shared Services Centres', statement no. 5G, Institute of Management Accountants, Montvale, NJ, February.

Kersnar, J 2002, 'Virtual Close: Not so Fast', CFO.com, www.cfo.com, 15 October.

Leahy, T 2000, 'The reality of real-time reporting', *Business Finance*, March, p. 93.

Pawling, GP 2001, 'Virtual finance: moving towards the one-day close', *Cisco iQ*, May–June.

Schulman, DS, Dunleavy, JR, Harmer, MJ & Lusk, JS 1999, *Shared Services – Adding Value to the Business Units*, John Wiley & Sons, New York, pp. 36, 163.

Vision Systems Ltd 2001, CEO and chairman's address to shareholders at AGM, Australian Stock Exchange, 26 October.

Williams, L 2005, 'XBRL for SA companies in US', *Business Day*, 7 February.

Self study

Self-study problem: transfer pricing

Stellar Systems Company's Microprocessor Division sells a computer module to the company's Guidance Assembly Division, which assembles completed guidance systems. The Microprocessor Division has no excess capacity. The computer module has variable costs of R10 000, and it can be sold in the external market to companies in the computer industry for R13 500.

Required:
Calculate the transfer price for the computer module using the general transfer pricing rule.

Solution to Self-study problem

Transfer price = outlay cost + opportunity cost
= R10 000 + (R13 500 − R10 000)
= R13 500

The R3500 opportunity cost of a transfer is the contribution margin that will be forgone if a computer module is transferred instead of sold in the external market.

Cybersearch

1 Find the website of a company that has implemented a shared services unit.
  (a) What type of shared services are involved?
  (b) What was the motivation for the move towards shared services?
  (c) Can you determine whether the shared services unit is a cost centre or a profit centre?
2 Look for some websites of companies that use work teams.
  (a) What role do the teams play within the organisation?
  (b) Have there been any positive outcomes from using the teams?
  (c) Are there any other details of the teams provided that are of interest?

Questions

12.1 Why is goal congruence important to an organisation's success? How can a responsibility accounting system foster goal congruence?

12.2 Discuss the benefits and costs of decentralisation.

12.3 Define the following terms: *cost centre, revenue centre, profit centre* and *investment centre.*

12.4 Select an organisation with which you are familiar and use this to provide an example of each of the four responsibility centres listed in Question 12.3.

12.5 Explain the meaning of *shared services* and outline their advantages.

12.6 How might a move towards a shared services operation change managers' responsibilities? What are the implications for responsibility accounting?

12.7 Contrast *hierarchical structures* and *flatter organisational structures.*

12.8 Explain how self-managed work teams differ from a conventional process-based production environment.

12.9 Explain how the formation of self-managed work teams might impact on responsibility accounting.

12.10 Explain what is meant by a *segmented profit statement,* and how it may be used.

12.11 Explain why some management accountants may choose *not* to allocate common costs in segmented reports.

12.12 Provide four examples of common costs that might occur in a fast food chain.

12.13 Why do some companies distinguish the performance of managers from that of their department or division?

12.14 Why might some companies decide not to distinguish the performance of managers from that of their department or division?

12.15 How can budgeting and variances be used to report the financial performance of responsibility centres?

12.16 Can a common cost for one sub-unit be attributed to another sub-unit? Provide an example to explain your answer.

12.17 How might *real-time reporting* contribute to the competitive advantage of an organisation?

12.18 Explain what is meant by a *virtual close* and explain how this relates to *real-time reporting.*

12.19 Why do decentralised businesses use transfer prices?

12.20 Select an organisation with which you are familiar and explain where transfer pricing might be used.

12.21 Describe the two components of the general transfer pricing rule. Select an organisation and provide some specific examples of outlay costs.

12.22 Explain the issues that must be considered when corporate management intervenes in transfer pricing decisions.

12.23 When is it more appropriate to use market-based transfer prices rather than cost-based transfer prices?

12.24 Explain why some organisations may choose to use variable cost rather than absorption cost as the basis for their cost-based transfer prices.

12.25 Why might some organisations use *standard cost* as the basis for their transfer prices rather than *actual cost*? Provide an example to illustrate your answer.

12.26 Explain the significance of *excess capacity* in the supplying division, when transfer prices are set using the general transfer pricing rule.

12.27 Explain the types of provisions that may be found in a *service level agreement*.

12.28 Describe the linkages between the following terms: *transfer pricing, service level agreements, decentralisation* and *responsibility accounting*.

Exercises

E12.29 Responsibility centres

Indicate the type of responsibility centre that is most appropriate for each of the following:

1. A cinema in a company that operates a chain of theatres.
2. A television station owned by a large broadcasting network.
3. The sales department in an insurance company.
4. The ticket sales division of a major airline.
5. A packaging department of a soft drink company.
6. An orange juice factory operated by a large orange grower.
7. A self-managed production team.
8. The Kenyan Division of a multinational market research company, with a head office in Johannesburg.
9. The outpatient clinic in a private hospital.
10. The garden maintenance department of a local government council.

E12.30 Decentralisation

For each of the following organisations:

(a) list the advantages and disadvantages of a decentralised organisational structure

(b) would you choose a centralised or decentralised structure if you were the organisation's chief executive?

1. A hospital.
2. A university.
3. A national department store chain.
4. A multinational manufacturing company.
5. A fast food chain.

E12.31 Assigning responsibility for skilled employees' wages: manufacturer

Alston Electronics Company manufactures complex circuit boards for the aerospace industry. Demand for the company's products has fallen in recent months, and the firm has cut its production significantly. Many unskilled workers have been temporarily laid off. Top management made a decision, however, not to lay off any highly skilled employees such as inspectors and machinery operators. Management was concerned that if these highly skilled employees were laid off, they would easily find new jobs elsewhere and not return when Alston's production returned to normal levels.

During the production cutback the skilled employees have been reassigned temporarily to the Maintenance Department. Here they are performing general maintenance tasks, such as repainting the interior of the factory, repairing the loading dock and building wooden storage racks for the warehouse. The skilled employees continue to receive their normal wages, which average R110 per hour. However, the normal wages for Maintenance Department employees average R75 per hour.

The supervisor of the Maintenance Department recently received the March performance report, which indicated that his department's actual labour cost exceeded the budget by R96 800, or 90 per cent. The department supervisor complained to the accountant.

Required:

As the accountant, how would you respond? Would you make any modifications to Alston's responsibility accounting system or performance measurement system? If so, list the changes you would make. Explain your reasoning.

E12.32 Responsibility accounting; equipment breakdown: manufacturer

How should a responsibility accounting system handle each of the following scenarios?

1 The Moulding Department manufactures a component, which is then used by the Assembly Department. The Moulding Department recently experienced a machine breakdown, which held up production of the component. As a result, the Assembly Department was forced to cease its own production, thereby incurring large costs of idle time. An investigation revealed that the machinery in the Moulding Department had not been properly maintained.

2 Refer to the scenario above, but suppose that an investigation revealed that the machinery in the Moulding Department had been properly maintained, and that the breakdown occurred because the machinery was faulty.

E12.33 Responsibility accounting; shared services: travel agency

Happy Wanderer Travel Agency has three divisions. Each division is a profit centre and effectively operates as a stand-alone business. The Corporate Travel Division is located in Johannesburg, the Holidays Division is in Cape Town, and the Adventure Travel Division is in Durban. The general manager of each division reports to the managing director in Head Office, which is located in Johannesburg. Each division maintains its own separate support service departments for accounts payable, payroll and staff training. Other support services in Head Office are Human Resources, Finance and Information Technology. The managers of these Head Office support departments report to the financial controller in the Head Office. The costs of running these departments are allocated to each division in proportion to divisional sales revenue.

The managing director recently attended a conference where he learnt about shared services units, and he has asked you to answer a few questions.

Required:

1 What are the advantages to Happy Wanderer Travel Agency of moving the three support departments, located in each division, to head office as a shared services unit?

2 Do you think that the restructure would disadvantage the divisions? Explain your answer.

3 Would you recommend that the shared services unit be set up as a cost centre or as a profit centre? Why?

E12.34 Responsibility accounting; teams: manufacturing

Duplex Paints manufactures paint in its factory in Polakwane. Until recently, the manufacturing plant consisted of three processing departments: blending, mixing and packaging. The manufacturing manager has now restructured the plant into work-based teams. Each team is responsible for all aspects of the production process for a particular product line. The processes that each team is responsible for include ordering and receiving material from suppliers, receiving production orders from customers, blending, mixing and packaging the product, and delivering product to the loading dock for distribution to the customer. Each team consists of 10 workers. To reflect the product line for which each team is responsible, the teams are named Exterior Paint Team, Interior Paint Team, Industrial Paint Team and Whitegoods Paint Team.

These teams were only formed six months ago, and will not achieve full self-management for several years.

Required:

1 Would you regard the teams as cost centres, profit centres or investment centres? Explain your answer.
2 What are some of the additional responsibilities that the teams may take on as they move towards self-management?
3 What are some of the measures that could be used to monitor the teams' performance?
4 What additional information might the teams need to manage their own operations?

E12.35 Service level agreements

Consider an organisation with which you are familiar and think of two opportunities where service level agreements could be established between a buying unit and a selling unit.

For each opportunity, describe the service that forms the focus for the SLA and consider the specific types of provisions that could be established to govern the relationship. (*Hint:* Search the Internet to find examples of the types of provisions that are usually found in SLAs.)

E12.36 Segmented profit statement: television company

Bambanani Television Network is organised into three divisions: Metro, Suburban and Regional. Data for these divisions for last year were as follows:

	Metro	Suburban	Regional
Service revenue	R 95 000000	R 75 000 000	R 35 000 000
Variable expenses	15 000 000	10 000 000	5 000 000
Controllable fixed expenses	35 000 000	27 000 000	10 000 000
Fixed expenses controllable by others	18 000 000	15 000 000	4 000 000

In addition to the expenses listed above, the company had R4 500 000 of common fixed costs last year that were not attributable to the three divisions. Income tax expense for the year was R24 500 000.

Required:

Prepare a segmented profit statement for Bambanani Television Network. Use the contribution format.

E12.37 Real-time reporting; segment reporting

Indicate whether each of the following statements is true or false:

1 Real-time reporting takes place when managers report the number of decisions they have made that have resulted in negative outcomes.
2 Flash reports are the reports that are quickly prepared at the end of each month.
3 One impediment to companies achieving real-time reporting is the lack of sophistication of their computer systems.
4 Reports that are structured using the contribution margin format make it more difficult for managers to understand cost behaviour.
5 Common costs are allocated to sub-units only when managers in the sub-units cannot influence those costs.
6 Segment reports indicate the revenues and costs for each cost centre.

E12.38 General transfer pricing rule: manufacturer

Win Ltd has two divisions: Assembly and Electrical. The Assembly Division transfers partially completed components to the Electrical Division at a predetermined transfer price. The Assembly Division's standard variable production cost per unit is R450. This division has excess capacity, and it could sell all its components to outside buyers at R570 per unit in a perfectly competitive market.

Required:

1 Determine a transfer price using the general rule.
2 How would the transfer price change if the Assembly Division had no excess capacity?
3 What transfer price would you recommend if there was no outside market for the transferred component, and the Assembly Division had excess capacity?

E12.39 Cost-based transfer pricing: manufacturer

Refer to Exercise 12.38. The Assembly Division's absorption cost of a component is R510, which includes R60 of applied fixed overhead costs. The transfer price has been set at R561, which is the Assembly Division's absorption cost plus a 10 per cent mark-up.

The Electrical Division has a special offer of R700 for its product. The Electrical Division incurs variable costs of R150 in addition to the transfer price for the Assembly Division's components. Both divisions currently have excess production capacity.

Required:

1 Is the Electrical Division manager likely to want to accept or reject the special offer? Why?
2 Is this decision in the best interests of Win Ltd as a whole? Explain.
3 How could the situation be remedied using the transfer price?

Problems

P12.40 Designating responsibility centres: hotel

The Woolloomooloo Sands Hotel is a prestigious five-star hotel, popular with both business travellers and tourists. Each of the four main departments of the Woolloomooloo Sands Hotel is headed by a manager. The Hospitality Department has three sections. The Front Desk, which is supervised by the Front Desk manager, handles the hotel's reservations, room assignments, guest payments and key security. The Concierge Desk is managed by the concierge and is responsible for greeting guests, front door service, assisting guests with their luggage, and delivering room service orders. The Guest Services unit, supervised by the manager of Guest Services, is responsible for assisting guests with local transportation arrangements, for advising guests on tourist attractions, and for such conveniences as valet and floral services.

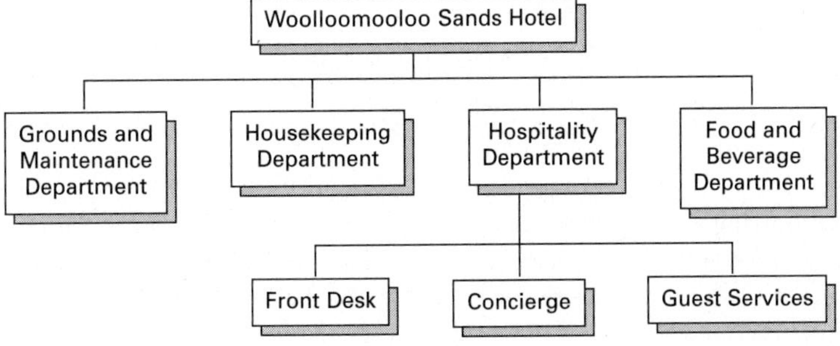

Required:

As an outside consultant, write a memo to the hotel's manager suggesting a responsibility centre designation for each of the sub-units shown in the organisation chart above. Explain your choices.

P12.41 Preparing a segmented profit statement; contribution margin format: retailer

Buy Best Department Stores Ltd operates a chain of department stores in South Africa. The company's organisation chart is shown below. Operating data for 20X7 are as follows:

Buy Best Department Stores
Operating Data for 20X7
(in R'000s)

	Western Division			Northern Division
	Wynberg store	**Tableview store**	**Parow store**	**(total for all stores)**
Sales revenue	R15 000	R7 200	R23 000	R63 000
Variable expenses:				
Cost of merchandise sold	9 000	6 000	18 000	36 000
Sales personnel: salaries	1 200	900	1 250	4 800
Sales commissions	200	120	270	600
Utilities	240	180	450	900
Other	180	105	360	750
Fixed expenses:				
Depreciation: buildings	R360	R270	R750	R1 410
Depreciation: furnishings	240	150	420	870
Computing and billing	120	90	225	480
Warehouse	210	180	600	1 350
Insurance	120	75	270	600
Property taxes	105	60	240	510
Supervisory salaries	450	300	1 200	2 700
Security	90	90	240	6 310

The following fixed expenses are controllable at the divisional level: depreciation (furnishings), computing and billing, warehouse, insurance and security. In addition to these expenses, each division annually incurs R150 000 in computing costs, which are not allocated to individual stores.

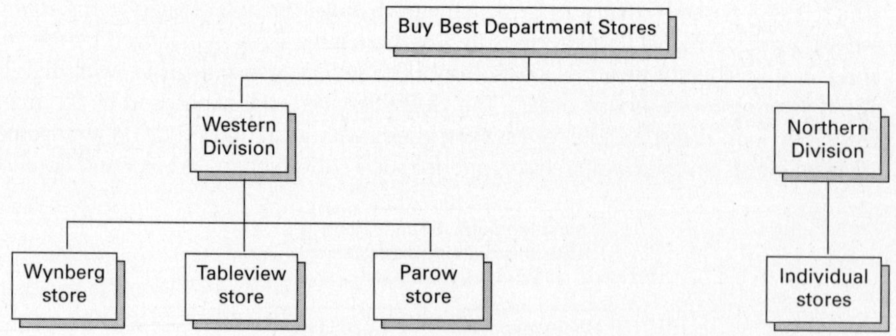

The following fixed expenses are controllable only at the company level: depreciation (building), property taxes and supervisory salaries. In addition to these expenses, each division incurs costs for supervisory salaries of R300 000, which are not allocated to individual stores.

Buy Best Department Stores incurs common fixed expenses of R360 000, which are not allocated to the two divisions. Income tax expense for 20X7 is R5 850 000.

Required:

1 Prepare a segmented profit statement, similar to that shown in Exhibit 12.5, for Buy Best Department Stores. The statement should have the following columns:

	Divisions of company		Western Division stores			
Buy Best Department Stores	**Northern Division**	**Western Division**	**Wynberg store**	**Tableview store**	**Parow store**	**Not allocated**

Prepare the statement in the contribution format, and indicate the controllability of expenses. Subtract all variable expenses, including cost of merchandise sold, from sales revenue to obtain the contribution margin.

2 How would the segmented profit statement help the managing director of Buy Best Department Stores to manage the company?

P12.42 Responsibility accounting; budgetary participation; behavioural issues: service firm

Reliable Cleaning Services was started a number of years ago by Rick Naidoo to provide cleaning services to both large and small businesses in his home city. Over the years, as local businesses reduced underutilised building maintenance staff, more and more cleaning services were subcontracted to Reliable. Reliable also expanded into other building services such as painting and local moving.

Reliable maintains a pool of skilled workers who are contracted to perform the non-cleaning services because these services do not recur on a day-to-day basis for the individual buildings. Many of Reliable's full-time employees have been with the firm for a number of years. Five zone managers are each responsible for providing ongoing nightly cleaning services to several businesses. In addition, the zone manager sells and schedules non-cleaning service jobs for the company's central pool of skilled employees. Informal meetings are held periodically to discuss Reliable's performance, personnel allocations, and scheduling problems. Reliable's budgeting and planning have been done by Naidoo, who also manages variations from budgets.

Naidoo recently decided to retire and sold the business to Commercial Maintenance Ltd (CML), which provides similar services in a number of metropolitan locations that surround Reliable's business area. After news of the sale, several of Reliable's long-term employees appeared resentful of the change in ownership and did not know what to expect.

CML's senior management met with Reliable's managers and announced that George Fowler would become president of Reliable and that Reliable would continue to operate as a separate subsidiary of CML. Furthermore, in accordance with CML's management philosophy, a responsibility accounting system would be implemented at Reliable. Also, in line with other CML subsidiaries, a participatory budgeting process is being considered. However, no decision will be made until an evaluation of Reliable's existing policies, operational culture and management is completed. In view of the significant change in management philosophy, CML has taken considerable time to explain how each system operates and to assure Reliable's managers that they are expected and encouraged to participate in both the planning and implementation of any of the systems that are to be adopted.

Required:

Two new initiatives are being considered at Reliable Cleaning Services:

(a) a responsibility accounting system

(b) a participatory budgeting system

For each of these new approaches:

1 Identify at least two behavioural advantages that could arise.
2 Identify at least two potential problems that could arise.
3 Discuss the likelihood that the new approach will contribute to the alignment of organisational and personal goals.

(You may wish to review budgetary participation in Chapter 9.)

(CMA adapted)

P12.43 Segmented profit statement; responsibility accounting: retailer

Hooray Party Supplies sells merchandise through three retail outlets – in Pretoria, Sandton and Randburg – and operates a general corporate headquarters in Sandton. A review of the company's profit statement indicates a record year in terms of sales and profits. Management, however, desires additional insights about the individual stores and has asked that Alison Ngoku, a newly hired accounting graduate, prepare a segmented statement of financial performance. The following information has been extracted from Hooray's accounting records:

- Sales volume, sales price, and purchase price data:

	Pretoria	Sandton	Randburg
Sales volume (units)	37 000	41 000	46 000
Unit selling price	R180.00	R165.00	R142.50
Unit purchase price	82.50	82.50	90.00

- The following expenses were incurred for sales commissions, local advertising, property taxes, management salaries, and other non-controllable (but traceable) costs:

	Pretoria	Sandton	Randburg
Sales commissions	6%	6%	6%
Local advertising	R165 000	R330 000	R720 000
Local property taxes	67 500	30 000	90 000
Sales manager salary	0	0	480 000
Store manager salaries	465 000	585 000	570 000
Other non-controllable costs	87 000	69 000	267 000

Local advertising decisions are made at the store manager level. The sales manager's salary in Randburg is determined by the Randburg store manager; in contrast, store manager salaries are set by Hooray's sales and marketing director.

- Non-traceable fixed corporate expenses total R2 884 500.
- The company uses a responsibility accounting system.

Required:

1 Assume the role of Alison Ngoku and prepare a segmented profit statement for Hooray Party Supplies.
2 Determine the weakest-performing store and present an analysis of the probable causes of poor performance.
3 Assume that an opening has arisen at the Sandton corporate headquarters and the company's chief executive officer (CEO) desires to promote one of the three existing store managers. In evaluating the store managers' performance, should the CEO use a store's segment contribution margin, the profit margin controllable by the store manager, or a store's segment profit margin? Justify your answer.

P12.44 Work teams; the management accountant's role: manufacturer

Inkco manufactures printing inks. The company employs 150 people, of whom 120 are production workers. The ink market is extremely competitive and, with a 20 per cent market share, Inkco has the third largest share of the South African market. The two market leaders manufacture high-volume black ink, while Inkco follows a niche market strategy: it produces high-quality coloured inks used in glossy magazines.

Four years ago the company made some changes in the manufacturing plant. Conventional production processing practices were reorganised and work teams were introduced. Each team consists of six production workers. They are self-managed work teams and, over the past few years, have been given increasing responsibilities. The team members have undergone training in quality concepts, as well as in communication and presentation skills. They are also multi-skilled – each member can operate all the machinery within the plant, inspect the quality of their product during processing, and has the skills to adjust the settings on machines when they detect any problems that need correction.

Walter Nklandla is a young management accountant who has been following these developments with interest. Recently, the general manager has asked him to act as an accounting adviser to some of the teams. Management considers that the teams are now mature enough to take on greater responsibilities. These responsibilities will include managing their own cost budgets and designing specific measures that they will use to monitor their own performance.

However, not all of the accountants are as interested in these developments as Walter Nklandla. Jackson Chambers, the budget officer, is critical of the new developments and of Nklandla's involvement. Chambers corners Walter in the company canteen:

Walter, how can you encourage this sort of caper? It is a waste of your time, and it distracts the production workers. They should be focusing on getting the product out, not doing our job. We are the experts in cost management and performance. We have used standard costs to control manufacturing performance for years, and I haven't heard any complaints. Our cost systems are well developed, and that is all we should be measuring. So the solution is clear. Why should these manufacturing teams develop their own measures? And how can management even think of letting them manage their own budgets!

Required:

1 List the reasons that may explain why a company like Inkco would introduce self-managed work teams.

2 Respond to each of the issues raised by Chambers.

3 What qualities could Walter Nklandla bring to the teams in his role as their accounting advisor?

P12.45 Transfer pricing problem: manufacturer

Blackwater Company manufactures windows for the home building industry sector and is focused on the low-cost housing segment of the sector. The window frames are produced in the Frame Division. The frames are then transferred to the Glass Division, where the glass and hardware are installed. The company's best-selling product is a 1 × 1.2 metre, double-paned window. The standard cost of the window is detailed as follows:

	Frame Division	Glass Division
Direct material	R30	R60*
Direct labour	40	30
Variable overhead	60	60
Total standard cost	R130	R150

*Not including the transfer price for the frame.

The Frame Division can also sell frames directly to custom home builders, who install the glass and hardware. The sales price for a frame is R160. The Glass Division sells its finished windows for R380. The markets for both frames and finished windows exhibit perfect competition.

Required:

1 Assume that there is no excess capacity in the Frame Division.
   (a) Use the general rule to calculate the transfer price for window frames.
   (b) Calculate the transfer price if it is based on standard variable cost with a 10 per cent mark-up.

2 Assume that there is excess capacity in the Frame Division.
   (a) Use the general rule to calculate the transfer price for window frames.
   (b) Explain why your answers to requirements 1(a) and 2(a) differ.
   (c) Suppose that the predetermined fixed overhead rate in the Frame Division is 125 per cent of direct labour cost. Calculate the transfer price if it is based on standard absorption cost plus a 10 per cent mark-up.
   (d) Assume the transfer price established in requirement 2(c) is used. The Glass Division has been approached by the management of a commercial construction company with a special order for 1000 windows at R310 each. From the perspective of the Blackwater Company as a whole, should the special order be accepted or rejected? Explain your answer.
   (e) Assume the same facts as in requirement 2(d). Would an autonomous Glass Division manager accept or reject the special order? Why?

3 Independent of requirements 1 and 2, assume that the Frame Division has limited capacity and can only supply half of the required 200 units of the double-paned window to the Glass Division. To supply all of the 200 units to the Glass Division, the Frame Division would have to forgo production and sales of 150 units of another product to external customers. These external sales typically yield a contribution of R80 per unit. Use the general rule to calculate the transfer price, and explain the likely decision that the two divisions will make about the transfer.

P12.46 Basic transfer pricing: manufacturer

Naledi Ltd has two manufacturing divisions: Costa Division and Margarita Division. The Costa Division produces electric motors, 20 per cent of which are sold to the Margarita Division of Naledi Ltd. The remainder are sold to outside customers. Naledi Ltd regards both divisions as investment centres and allows division managers to choose their sources of sale and supply. Corporate policy requires that all interdivisional sales and purchases be made at a transfer price based on standard variable cost. Costa Division's estimated sales and standard cost data for the year ending 31 December 20X8, based on capacity of 100 000 units, are as follows:

	To Margarita Division	To outside customers
Sales	R4 500 000	R40 000 000
Variable costs	−4 500 000	−18 000 000
Fixed costs	−1 500 000	−6 000 000
Gross margin	−1 500 000	16 000 000
Unit sales	20 000	80 000

Costa has an opportunity to sell the 20 000 units that it currently sells to Margarita to a new outside customer at a price of R375.00 per unit. Margarita can purchase its requirements from an outside supplier at a price of R425.00 per unit.

Required:

1 Assuming that Costa Division desires to maximise its profits, should Costa take on the new customer and drop its sales to Margarita in 20X8? Explain your answer.

2 Assume, instead, that Naledi Ltd permits division managers to negotiate the transfer price for 20X8. The managers agree on a tentative transfer price of R375.00 per unit, to be reduced based on an equal sharing of the additional gross margin to Costa resulting

from the sale to Margarita of 20 000 motors at R375.00 per unit. What would be the actual transfer price for 20X8?

3 Assume now that Costa Division has an opportunity to sell the 20 000 motors that Margarita Division would buy to the same customers that are buying the other 80 000 motors produced by Costa. Costa Division could sell all 100 000 motors to outside customers at a price of R500. What actions by each division manager are in the best interests of Naledi Ltd?
4 Under the scenario described in requirement 3, use the general transfer pricing rule to calculate the transfer price that Costa Division should charge Margarita Division for motors.
5 Will the transfer price calculated in requirement 4 result in the most desirable outcome from the standpoint of Naledi Ltd? Justify your answer.

(CPA, adapted)

P12.47 Multiple interdivisional transfers; accept or reject outside contract: manufacturer

Rabbid Industries Ltd consists of three decentralised divisions: Brentwood Division, Crater Division and Rand Division. The managing director of Rabbid Industries has given the managers of the three divisions the authority to decide whether to sell their products outside the company, or between themselves at a transfer price determined by the division managers. The external market for the company's products is very active and there are many competitors, so sales made internally or externally by the divisions will not affect market prices. Intermediate markets will always be available for Brentwood, Crater and Rand to purchase their manufacturing needs or sell their product. Each division manager attempts to maximise his contribution margin at the current level of operating assets for the division.

The manager of Crater Division is currently considering the following two orders:

- Rand Division needs 3000 units of a motor that can be supplied by Crater Division. To manufacture these motors, Crater would purchase components from Brentwood Division at a transfer price of R900 per unit. Brentwood's variable cost for these components is R450 per unit. Crater Division would further process these components at a variable cost of R750 per unit.
- Eros Company wants to order 3500 motors from the Crater Division. This is a custom-built product and the price will be R1875 per unit. Crater would purchase components for these motors from Brentwood Division at a transfer price of R750 per unit. Brentwood's variable cost for these components is R375 per unit. Crater Division will further process these components at a variable cost of R600 per unit.

Crater Division's plant capacity is limited, and the company can accept either the Eros order or the Rand order, but not both. The managing director of Rabbid Industries and the manager of Crater Division agree that it would not be beneficial to increase capacity.

If Rand Division cannot obtain the motors from Crater Division, it will purchase the motors from Frantic Company, which has offered to supply the same motors to Rand Division at a price of R2250 per unit. Frantic Company would also purchase 3000 components from Brentwood Division at a price of R600 for each of these motors. Brentwood's variable cost for these components is R300 per unit.

Required:

1 If the manager of Crater Division wants to maximise the division's short-run contribution margin, determine whether Crater Division should:
   (a) sell motors to Rand Division at the prevailing market price; or
   (b) accept the Eros Company order.
2 Independent of your answer to requirement 1, assume that Crater Division decides to accept the Eros Company contract. Determine if this decision is in the best interests of Rabbid Industries.

(CMA, adapted)

P12.48 Transfer pricing; negotiation; management incentives: manufacturer

Midas Technology Ltd (MTL) has two divisions: Ikapa and Tshwane. Tshwane currently sells a diode reducer to manufacturers of navigation systems for R15 500 per unit. Variable costs amount to R10 000, and demand for this product currently exceeds the division's ability to supply the marketplace.

Despite this situation, MTL's top management is considering another use for the diode reducer, namely, integration into a satellite positioning system that would be manufactured by Ikapa. The positioning system has an anticipated selling price of R28 000 and requires an additional R13 400 of variable manufacturing costs. A transfer price of R15 000 has been established for the diode reducer.

Top management is anxious to introduce the new positioning system. However, unless the transfer is made, an introduction will not be possible because of the difficulty of obtaining the needed diode reducers from the external market. Tshwane and Ikapa are in the process of recovering from financial problems, and neither division can afford any future losses. The company uses responsibility accounting and ROI to measure divisional performance, and awards bonuses to divisional management based on their division's performance.

Required:

1 How might Tshwane's divisional manager react to the decision to transfer diode reducers to Ikapa? Show calculations to support your answer.
2 How might Ikapa's divisional management react to the R15 000 transfer price? Show calculations to support your answer.
3 Assume that a lower transfer price is desired. Should top management lower the price or should the price be lowered by another means? Explain.
4 From a contribution margin perspective, does MTL benefit more if it sells the diode reducers externally or transfers the reducers to Ikapa? By how much?

P12.49 Transfer pricing; management: manufacturer

Rooiklip Industrial Resources Company (RIRC) has several divisions. However, only two divisions transfer products to other divisions. The Mining Division refines toldine, which is then transferred to the Metals Division. The toldine is processed into an alloy by the Metals Division, and the alloy is sold to customers at a price of R4500 per unit. The Mining Division is currently required by RIRC to transfer its total yearly output of 400 000 units of toldine to the Metals Division at total actual manufacturing cost plus 10 per cent. Unlimited quantities of toldine can be purchased and sold on the open market at R2700 per unit. While the Mining Division could sell all of the toldine it produces at R2700 per unit on the open market, it would incur a variable selling cost of R150 per unit.

Brian Jones, manager of the Mining Division, is unhappy with having to transfer the entire output of toldine to the Metals Division at 110 per cent of cost. In a meeting with the management of RIRC, he said:

Why should my division be required to sell toldine to the Metals Division at less than market price? For the financial year that has just ended, Metals' contribution margin was over R570 million on sales of 400 000 units, while Mining's contribution was just over R150 million on the transfer of the same number of units. My division is subsidising the profitability of the Metals Division. We should be allowed to charge the market price for toldine when transferring to the Metals Division.

The following table shows the detailed unit cost structure for both the Mining and Metals divisions during the most recent year:

	Mining Division	Metals Division
Transfer price from Mining Division	–	1 980
Direct material	360	180
Direct labour	480	600
Manufacturing overhead	960[1]	750[2]
Total cost per unit	R 1800	R 3 510

[1]Manufacturing overhead cost in the Mining Division is 25% fixed and 75% variable.
[2]Manufacturing overhead cost in the Metals Division is 60% fixed and 40% variable.

Required:

1 Explain why transfer prices based on total actual costs are not appropriate as the basis for divisional performance measurement.
2 Using the market price as the transfer price, determine the contribution margin for both the Mining Division and the Metals Division.
3 If Rooiklip Industrial Resources Company were to introduce the use of negotiated transfer prices and allow divisions to buy and sell on the open market, determine the price range for toldine that would be acceptable to both the Mining Division and the Metals Division. Explain your answer.
4 Use the general transfer-pricing rule to calculate the lowest transfer price that would be acceptable to the Mining Division. Is your answer consistent with your conclusion in requirement 3? Explain.
5 Identify which one of the three types of transfer prices (cost-based, market-based or negotiated) is most likely to elicit desirable management behaviour at RIRC. Explain your answer.

(*CMA adapted*)

P12.50 Interdivisional transfers; pricing the final product: manufacturer

Natural Industries is a diversified corporation with separate operating divisions. Each division's performance is evaluated on the basis of profit and return on investment.

The Soft-as-Air Division manufactures and sells air-conditioning units powered by small wind turbines. The coming year's budgeted profit statement, which follows, is based on a sales volume of 15 000 units.

Soft-as-Air Division
Budgeted Profit Statement

	Per unit	Total
Sales revenue	R 8 000	R 120 000 000
Manufacturing costs:		
Compressor	R1 400	21 000 000
Other direct material	740	11 100 000
Direct labour	600	9 000 000
Variable overhead	900	13 500 000
Fixed overhead	640	9 600 000
Total manufacturing costs	R 4 280	R 64 200 000
Gross margin	R 3 720	R 55 800 000
Operating expenses:		
Variable selling	R 360	R 5 400 000
Fixed selling	380	5 700 000
Fixed administrative	760	11 400 000
Total operating expenses	R 1 500	R 22 500 000
Net profit before taxes	R 2 220	R 33 300 000

The manager of the Soft-as-Air Division believes that sales can be increased if the price of the air-conditioners is reduced. A market research study by an independent firm indicates that a 5 per cent reduction in the selling price would increase sales volume by 16 per cent, or 2400 units. Soft-as-Air has sufficient production capacity to manage this increased volume with no increase in fixed costs.

Soft-as-Air uses a compressor in its units, which it purchases from an outside supplier at a cost of R1400 per compressor. The division manager of Soft-as-Air has asked the manager of the Compressor Division about selling compressor units to Soft-as-Air. The Compressor Division currently manufactures and sells to outside firms a unit that is similar to the unit used by Soft-as-Air. The specifications of the Soft-as-Air compressor are slightly different, which would reduce the Compressor Division's direct material cost by R30 per unit. In addition, the Compressor Division would not incur any variable selling costs in the units sold to Soft-as-Air. The manager of Soft-as-Air wants all the compressors it uses to come from one supplier, and has offered to pay R1000 for each compressor unit.

The Compressor Division has the capacity to produce 75 000 units. Its budgeted profit statement for the coming year, which follows, is based on a sales volume of 64 000 units, without considering Soft-as-Air's proposal.

Compressor Division
Budgeted Profit Statement

	Per unit	Total
Sales revenue	R2 000	R128 000 000
Manufacturing costs:		
Direct material	R240	15 360 000
Direct labour	160	10 240 000
Variable overhead	200	12 800 000
Fixed overhead	220	14 080 000
Total manufacturing costs	R820	R52 480 000
Gross margin	R1 180	R75 520 000
Operating expenses:		
Variable selling	120	7 680 000
Fixed selling	80	5 120 000
Fixed administrative	140	8 960 000
Total operating expenses	R340	R21 760 000
Net profit before taxes	R840	R53 760 000

Required:

1 Should the Soft-as-Air Division institute the 5 per cent price reduction on its air-conditioning units even if it cannot acquire the compressors internally for R1000 each? Support your conclusion with appropriate calculations.

2 Independent of your answer to requirement 1, assume that Soft-as-Air needs 17 400 units. Should the Compressor Division be willing to supply the compressor units for R1000 each? Support your conclusions with appropriate calculations.

3 Independent of your answer to requirement 1, assume that Soft-as-Air needs 17 400 units. Suppose that Natural Industries' top management has specified a transfer price of R1000. Would it be in the best interest of Natural Industries (as a whole) for the Compressor Division to supply the compressor units at R1000 each to the Soft-as-Air Division? Support your conclusions with appropriate calculations.

4 Is the transfer price of R1000 a goal-congruent transfer price? Refer to your answers to requirements 2 and 3.

Cases

C12.51 Segmented profit statement: manufacturer

Cost Brava Industries is a diversified company whose products are marketed both domestically and internationally. The company's major product lines are furniture, sports equipment and household appliances. At a recent meeting of the board of directors there was a lengthy discussion on ways to improve overall corporate profitability. The members of the board decided that they required additional financial information about individual corporate operations in order to target areas for improvement.

Danielle Marais, the financial controller, has been asked to provide additional data that would assist the board in its investigation. Marais believes that profit statements, prepared along both product lines and geographic areas, would provide the directors with the required insight into corporate operations. Marais had several discussions with the division managers for each product line and compiled the following information from these meetings:

	Product lines			
	Furniture	**Sports**	**Housewares**	**Total**
Production and sales in units	80 000	90 000	80 000	250 000
Average selling price per unit	R160	R400	R300	
Average variable manufacturing cost per unit	R80	R190	R165	
Average variable selling expense per unit	R40	R50	R45	
Fixed manufacturing overhead, excluding depreciation				R5 000 000
Depreciation of plant and equipment				R4 000 000
Administrative and selling expense				R11 600 000

- The division managers concluded that Marais should allocate fixed manufacturing overhead to both product lines and geographic areas on the basis of the ratio of the variable costs expended to total variable costs.
- Each of the division managers agreed that a reasonable basis for the allocation of depreciation on plant and equipment would be the ratio of units produced per product line (or per geographical area) to the total number of units produced.
- There was little agreement on the allocation of administrative and selling expenses, so Marais decided to allocate only those expenses that were traceable directly to a segment. For example, manufacturing staff salaries would be allocated to geographical areas. Marais used the following data for this allocation:

Manufacturing staff		**Sales staff**	
Furniture	R1 200 000	South Africa	R600 000
Sports	1 400 000	Portugal	1 000 000
Housewares	800 000	Singapore	2 500 000

- The division managers were able to provide reliable sales percentages for their product lines by geographical area.

	Percentage of unit sales		
	South Africa	**Portugal**	**Singapore**
Furniture	40%	10%	50%
Sports	40%	40%	20%
Housewares	20%	20%	60%

Marais prepared the following product-line profit statement based on the data presented above:

Cost Brava Industries
Segmented Profit Statement by product lines
for the year ended 30 June 20X7

	Product lines				
	Furniture	**Sports**	**Housewares**	**Un-allocated**	**Total**
Sales in units	80 000	90 000	80 000	–	
Sales	R12 800 000	R36 000 000	R24 000 000	–	R72 800 000
Variable manufacturing and selling costs	9 600 000	21 600 000	16 800 000	–	48 000 000
Contribution margin	3 200 000	14 400 000	7 200 000	–	24 800 000
Fixed costs:					
Fixed manufacturing overhead	1 000 000	2 250 000	1 750 000	–	5 000 000
Depreciation	1 280 000	1 440 000	1 280 000	–	4 000 000
Administrative & selling expenses	1 200 000	1 400 000	800 000	8 200 000	11 600 000
Total fixed costs	3 480 000	5 090 000	3 830 000	8 200 000	20 600 000
Operating profit (loss)	−280 000	9 310 000	3 370 000	−8 200 000	4 200 000

Required:

1 Prepare a segmented profit statement for Cost Brava Industries based on the company's geographical areas. The statement should show the operating profit for each segment.

2 As a result of the information disclosed by both segmented profit statements (by product line and by geographical area), recommend areas on which Cost Brava Industries should focus its attention in order to improve corporate profitability.

(CMA adapted)

C12.52 Segmented profit statement; responsibility accounting; bonuses; motivation; ethics: retailer

Elite Classic Clothes is a retailer that sells to professional business women. The firm leases space for large stores in upmarket shopping centres, and the organisational structure consists of regions, districts and stores. Each region consists of two or more districts; each district consists of three or more stores. Each store, district and region has been established as a profit centre. At all levels, the company uses a responsibility accounting system focusing on information and knowledge rather than on blame and control. Each year, managers, in consultation with their supervisors, establish financial and non-financial goals, and these goals are integrated into the budget. Actual performance is measured each month. The Gauteng Region consists of the Southern District and Northern District.

The Southern District includes the Johannesburg, Benoni and Boksburg stores. The Southern District's performance has not been up to expectations. For the month of May, the district manager has set performance goals with the managers of the Johannesburg and Benoni stores, who will receive bonuses if certain performance measures are exceeded. The manager of the Boksburg store decided not to participate in the bonus scheme. Since the district manager is unsure what type of bonus will encourage better performance, the Johannesburg manager will receive a bonus based on sales in excess of budgeted sales of R11 400 000, while the Benoni manager will receive a bonus based on net profit in excess of budgeted net profit. The company's net profit goal for each store is 12 per cent of sales. The budgeted sales revenue for the Benoni store is R10 600 000.

Other pertinent data for May are as follows:

- Southern District sales revenue was R30 000 000, and its cost of goods sold amounted to R12 675 000.
- The Southern District spent R1 500 000 on advertising.
- General and administrative expenses for the Southern District amounted to R3 600 000.

- At the Johannesburg store, sales were 40 per cent of Southern District sales, while sales at the Benoni store were 35 per cent of district sales. The cost of goods sold in both Johannesburg and the Benoni was 42 per cent of sales.
- Variable selling expenses (sales commissions) were 6 per cent of sales for all stores, districts and regions.
- Variable administrative expenses were 2.5 per cent of sales for all stores, districts and regions.
- Maintenance costs include cleaning and repair services and are a direct cost for each store. The store manager has complete control over this outlay. Maintenance costs were incurred as follows: Johannesburg, R150 000; Benoni, R12 000; and Boksburg, R90 000.
- Advertising is considered a direct cost for each store and is completely under the control of the store manager. The Johannesburg store spent two-thirds of the Southern District's total outlay for advertising, which was 10 times the amount spent by the Benoni store on advertising.
- Southern District rental expenses amounted to R3 000 000.
- The rental expenses at the Johannesburg store were 40 per cent of the Southern District's total, while the Benoni store incurred 30 per cent of the district total.
- District expenses were allocated to the stores based on sales.
- Gauteng Region general and administrative expenses of R3 300 000 were allocated to the Southern District. These expenses were, in turn, allocated equally to the district's three stores.

Required:

1. Prepare the May segmented profit statement for the Southern District and for the Johannesburg and Benoni stores.
2. Calculate the Boksburg store's net profit for May.
3. Discuss the impact of the responsibility accounting system and bonus structure on the managers' behaviour, and also the effect of their behaviour on the financial results for the Johannesburg store and the Benoni store.
4. The assistant financial controller for the Gauteng Region, Jack Fourie, has been a close friend of the Johannesburg store manager for over 20 years. When Fourie saw the segmented profit statement (as prepared in requirement 1), he realised that the Johannesburg store manager had really gone overboard on advertising expenditures. To make his friend look better to the regional management, he reclassified R500 000 of the advertising expenditures as miscellaneous expenses, and buried them in rent and other costs. Comment on the ethical issues in the assistant financial controller's actions. (Refer to specific ethical standards, which were given in Chapter 1).

C12.53 Divisional performance measurement and transfer pricing: manufacturer

Easy Living Industries manufactures carpets, furniture and cushions in three separate divisions. The company's operating statement for 20X7 is presented below:

Easy Living Industries
Operating Statement
for the year ended 31 December 20X7

	Carpet Division	Furniture Division	Cushion Division	Total
Sales revenue	R30 000 000	R30 000 000	R40 000 000	R100 000 000
Cost of goods sold	20 000 000	13 000 000	30 000 000	63 000 000
Gross profit	10 000 000	17 000 000	10 000 000	37 000 000
Operating expenses:				
Administration	3 000 000	5 000 000	4 000 000	12 000 000
Selling	6 000 000	6 000 000	5 000 000	17 000 000
Total operating expenses	9 000 000	11 000 000	9 000 000	29 000 000
Profit from operations before taxes	R1 000 000	R6 000 000	R1 000 000	R8 000 000

Additional information regarding Easy Living Industries' operations is as follows:

- Included in the Cushion Division's sales revenue is R5 000 000 that represents sales made to the Furniture Division. The transfer price for these sales was at variable cost.
- The three divisions' cost of goods sold comprise the following costs:

	Carpet Division	Furniture Division	Cushion Division
Direct material	R5 000 000	R10 000 000	R10 000 000
Direct labour	5 000 000	2 000 000	10 000 000
Variable overhead	7 500 000	500 000	10 000 000
Fixed overhead	2 500 000	500 000	0
Total cost of goods sold	20 000 000	13 000 000	30 000 000

- Administrative expenses include the following:

	Carpet Division	Furniture Division	Cushion Division
Divisional expenses:			
Variable	R850 000	R1 400 000	R400 000
Fixed	850 000	2 100 000	1 200 000
Head office expenses (all fixed):			
Directly attributable	1 000 000	1 200 000	2 000 000
General (allocated based on Sales Rands)	300 000	300 000	400 000
Total	R3 000 000	R5 000 000	R4 000 000

- All selling expenses are incurred at the divisional level. It is 80 per cent variable. Meg Johnson, manager of the Cushion Division, is not pleased with the company's report on operating performance. Johnson claims:

The Cushion Division makes a greater contribution to the company's profits than is shown. I sell cushions to the Furniture Division at cost and it gets our share of the profit. I can sell these cushions on the outside market at my regular mark-up, but I sell to Furniture for the wellbeing of the company. I think my division should get credit for those internal sales at market price. I think we should also revise our operating statements for internal purposes. Why don't we consider preparing these internal statements in a format that shows internal transfers at market price?

Required:

1 Meg Johnson believes that the transfers from the Cushion Division to the Furniture Division should be at market price rather than at cost, for divisional performance measurement.
   (a) Is Johnson correct? Explain your answer.
   (b) Describe another approach that the company could use to set transfer prices, other than manufacturing cost and market price.
2 Using transfer prices based on market prices, prepare a revised operating statement, by division, for Easy Living Industries for 20X7 that will facilitate the evaluation of divisional performance. Use the contribution margin format.

(CMA, adapted)

C12.54 Comprehensive transfer pricing case; use of general rule; cost analysis: manufacturer

St Kilda Products is a divisionalised furniture manufacturer. The divisions are autonomous segments, with each division responsible for its own sales, costs of operations, and equipment acquisition. Each division serves a different market in the furniture industry. Because the markets and products of the divisions are so different, there have never been any transfers between divisions.

The Commercial Division manufactures equipment and furniture that is purchased by the restaurant industry. The division plans to introduce a new line of counter and chair units featuring a cushioned seat for the counter chairs. Joan Nguni, the Commercial Division manager, has discussed the manufacture of the cushioned seat with Russ Daniels of the Office Division. They both believe that a cushioned seat currently made by the Office Division for use on its deluxe office stool could be modified for use on the new counter chair. Consequently, Nguni has asked Daniels for a price for 100-unit lots of the cushioned seat. The following conversation took place about the price to be charged for the cushioned seats:

Daniels: Joan, we can make the necessary modifications to the cushioned seat easily. The raw materials used in the new restaurant seat are slightly different and should cost about 10 per cent more than those used in our deluxe office stool. However, the labour time should be the same, because the seat fabrication operation is the same. I would price the seat at our regular rate: absorption cost plus a 30 per cent mark-up.

Nguni: That's higher than I expected, Russ. I was thinking that a good price would be your variable manufacturing cost. After all, your fixed costs will be incurred regardless of this job.

Daniels: Joan, I'm at capacity. By making the cushioned seats for you, I'll have to cut my production of deluxe office stools. Of course, I can increase my production of economy office stools. The labour time freed by not having to fabricate the frame or assemble the deluxe stool can be shifted to the frame fabrication and assembly of the economy office stool. Fortunately, I can switch my labour force between these two models of stools without any loss of efficiency. As you know, overtime is not a feasible alternative in our community. I'd like to sell the seats to you at variable cost, but I have excess demand for both the deluxe and economy office stools. I don't mind changing my product mix to the economy model if I get a good return on the seats I make for you. Here are my standard costs for the two stools and a schedule of my manufacturing overhead. (See the following schedules.)

Nguni: I guess I see your point, Russ, but I don't want to price myself out of the market. Maybe we should talk to corporate headquarters to see if they can give us any guidance.

Office Division
Standard Costs and Prices

	Deluxe office stool	**Economy office stool**
Direct materials:		
Framing	R81.50	R97.60
Cushioned seal:		
Padding	24.00	
Vinyl	40.00	
Moulded seat (purchased)		60.00
Direct labour:		
Frame fabrication (0.5 × R75 per hour)	37.50	37.50
Cushion fabrication (0.5 × R75 per hour)	37.50	0.00
Assembly	37.50[1]	22.50[2]
Manufacturing overhead	192.00[3]	102.40[4]
Total standard cost	R450.00	R320.00
Selling price (including 30% markup)	R585.00	R416.00

[1]0.5 × R75.00 per hour
[2]0.3 × R75.00 per hour
[3]1.5 × R128.00 per hour
[4]0.8 × R128.00 per hour

Office Division Manufacturing Overhead Budget		
Overhead item	**Description**	**Amount**
Supplies	Variable, at current market prices	R4 200 000
Indirect labour	Variable	3 750 000
Supervision	Fixed	2 500 000
Power	Use varies with activity; unit rates are fixed	1 800 000
Heat and light	Fixed; light is fixed regardless of production, while heat and air-conditioning vary with fuel charges	1 400 000
Property taxes and insurance	Fixed; any changes in amounts and rates are independent of production	2 000 000
Depreciation	Fixed	17 000 000
Employee benefits	20% of supervision, direct and indirect labour	5 750 000
Total overhead		R38 400 000
Capacity in direct labour hours		300 000
Overhead rate per direct labour hour		R128.00

Required:

1 Joan Nguni and Russ Daniels did ask St Kilda Products' corporate management for guidance on an appropriate transfer price. Corporate management suggested that they consider using a transfer price based on outlay cost plus opportunity cost. Calculate a transfer price for the cushioned seat based on this rule.

2 Which alternative transfer pricing system (absorption cost, variable cost, or outlay cost plus opportunity cost) would be better as the underlying concept for the company's transfer pricing policy? Explain your answer.

(CMA, adapted)

Endnotes

1 These amounts have been allocated to the hotels in Exhibit 12.6 for the purposes of reconciling the year-to-date figures.

2 The term 'transfer price' is often used in South African business to refer to prices charged for the international transfer of goods and services, and this is of interest to specialists in income tax. Businesses often use the term 'internal service charge' to refer to domestic transfer pricing.

3 This section has benefited from the assistance of Nihal Mudalige of Monash University.

4 There is some value from having spare capacity as it permits companies to react quickly to changes in demand. It may also act as a signal to potential competitors that the company will react aggressively to new competition.

CHAPTER

Financial Performance Measures for Investment Centres, and Reward Systems

❖ LEARNING OBJECTIVES

After completing this chapter, you should be able to:

1. calculate an investment centre's return on investment (ROI);
2. describe some advantages and limitations of ROI as a measure of performance of investment centres;
3. explain how the negative behavioural incentives associated with using return on investment to evaluate performance can be minimised;
4. calculate residual income (RI) for an investment centre, and describe some advantages and disadvantages of using RI to evaluate performance;
5. recognise the reasons for the various definitions of profit and invested capital that can be used in the calculation of return on investment and residual income;
6. explain the concept of shareholder value;
7. evaluate and calculate economic value added (EVA®) and shareholder value added (SVA) as measures of investment centre performance;
8. explain how reward systems can be designed and used to enhance goal congruence;
9. recognise the difference between intrinsic and extrinsic sources of motivation;
10. describe the differences between Herzberg's two-factor theory and the expectancy theory of motivation;
11. identify the different forms of performance-related reward systems used in organisations;
12. outline the advantages and disadvantages associated with group versus individual rewards; and
13. recognise the importance of the timing of the payment of rewards for enhancing motivation.

Introduction

In Chapter 12 we introduced decentralisation and responsibility accounting, and examined the nature of financial performance reports for responsibility accounting units. In this chapter, we will extend that discussion by looking at financial performance measures used in investment centres. That is, we will consider the advantages and disadvantages of measuring financial performance using return on investment (ROI), residual income (RI), profit, and economic value added (EVA®).[1] In South African organisations, linking remuneration to individual or group performance is becoming more widespread. In this chapter, we will also consider the various forms of reward systems that can be used to enhance motivation and goal congruence.

Financial measures in investment centres

As well as relying on detailed reports to communicate the financial performance of various responsibility centres, summary financial performance measures are commonly used to assess the performance of profit centres and investment centres. While some measure of profit is used to measure the performance of profit centres, for investment centres many firms employ measures that are based on profit and invested capital. We will illustrate these measures using the business and management structure of BHP Billiton, which is one of the world's major resources companies as well as being a leading integrated aluminium producer. The company divides its operations into segments which the company calls Customer Sector Groups (CSGs). In its aluminium customer sector group, the company is involved in the exploration and mining of bauxite, and processing and marketing of aluminium and alumina.

Responsibility accounting at BHP Billiton aluminium division

The aluminium division of BHP Billiton supplies bauxite, alumina and aluminium to domestic and international markets. BHP Billiton represents a merger of BHP, an Australian company and Billiton, a South African company which moved its listing to London.

The chief executive officer of each of these Customer Sector Groups is given wide decision-making authority by corporate management. This allows them to manage their business with little day-to-day interference, but in accordance with policies and authorities specified by and delegated from headquarters. The following business units of BHP Billiton's aluminium division form a vertically integrated operation:

- *Bauxite mining.* The main bauxite mine is at Worsley in Western Australia. Bauxite is supplied to the alumina refineries in which BHP Billiton has an interest, as well as to external customers.
- *Alumina refining.* Bauxite is processed into aluminium powder (alumina) and sold to smelting operations within BHP Billiton as well as to external customers.
- *Smelting.* Alumina is processed into aluminium for distribution to a variety of customers. The main smelters are in South Africa (Hillside and Bayside) and Mozambique (Mozal). In BHP Billiton, as in many large, decentralised businesses, corporate management uses a series of performance measures to evaluate the performance of each business unit. An important financial measure is return on investment.

In the following sections we will examine return on investment and other financial measures that can be used to evaluate the financial performance of investment centres.[2]

Return on investment

L.O. 1

Return on investment (ROI) is defined as follows:

$$\text{Return on investment (ROI)} = \frac{\text{profit}}{\text{invested capital}}$$

Invested capital is the assets that the investment centre has available to generate profit.[3] Let's assume that in the previous year, the Alumina Refining and Smelting businesses generated profits of R320 million and R480 million on investments of R2000 million and R4000 million respectively. The return on investment for the Refining and Smelting businesses can be calculated as follows:

$$\text{Refining} = 320/2000 = 0.16 \text{ or } 16\%$$
$$\text{Smelting} = 480/4000 = 0.12 \text{ or } 12\%$$

Notice how the ROI calculation for each investment centre takes into account *both investment centre profit and the capital invested* in that business unit. This is important. Suppose that each business was evaluated only on the basis of its profit. Smelting reported a higher profit than Refining; however, this does not necessarily mean that Smelting had the better financial performance, as it used a much larger amount of invested capital to earn that profit. The Smelting business had double the assets of the Refining business.

The focus of ROI is not on how much profit each investment centre earned, but rather on how effectively each investment centre used its invested capital to earn a profit.

Focusing on the components of ROI

The ROI formula can be expanded as follows:

$$\text{Return on investment} = \frac{\text{profit}}{\text{invested capital}}$$

$$= \frac{\text{profit}}{\text{sales revenue}} \times \frac{\text{sales revenue}}{\text{invested capital}}$$

Expanding the ROI formula highlights the components of return on investment. Profit divided by sales revenue is called the **return on sales**, and is expressed as a percentage. This term measures the percentage of each sales rand that remains as profit after all expenses are covered. Sales revenue divided by invested capital is called the **investment turnover**, and is expressed as a number of times or the number of sales rands generated for every rand of invested capital (assets). Sales revenue from Refining is R2200 million whilst sales revenue from Smelting is R4300 million. The return on sales, investment turnover and ROI for the two business units are calculated below:

$$\text{Return on sales} \times \text{Investment turnover} = \text{ROI}$$

$$\text{Refining: } 320/2200 \times 2200/2000 = 0.16 \text{ or } 16\%$$

$$\text{Smelting: } 480/4300 \times 4300/4000 = 0.12 \text{ or } 12\%$$

The Refining business' return on sales is 14.55 per cent (R320 million profit ÷ R2200 million sales revenue). Thus, each rand of sales resulted in about 14.55 cents profit. The business unit's investment turnover was 1.1 times (R2200 million sales revenue ÷ R2000 million invested capital). Thus, for Refining, R1.10 of sales revenue was generated by each rand of capital invested.

Improving ROI

How could the Refining business improve its return on investment? Since ROI is the product of return on sales and the investment turnover, ROI can be improved by increasing either, or both, of these two components. For example, if the return on sales increased to 18 per cent, while the investment turnover remained constant at 1.1 times, the ROI would climb from 16 per cent to 19.8 per cent:

New ROI = return on sales × investment turnover
= 18% × 1.1 times
= 19.8%

How might the Refining managers increase the return on sales to 18 per cent? They could increase profit to R396 million on sales of R2200 million (R396 million ÷ R2200 million = 18 per cent return on sales). This could be achieved in several ways, including increasing selling prices, increasing sales volume, and decreasing expenses. In the Refining business, prices might be set by reference to international pricing mechanisms and not influenced by business unit managers. However, there are several ways that sales volume could be increased. On the expense side, care should be taken in cost efficiency drives to ensure that there are no adverse effects on product quality or customer service. Otherwise, sales may be lost in the future.

An alternative way of increasing the Refining business' ROI would be to increase its investment turnover. If the investment turnover could be increased to 1.5 times, while the return on sales remained constant at 14.55 per cent, the business unit's ROI would climb from 16 per cent to 21.8 per cent:

New ROI = return on sales × investment turnover
= 14.55% × 1.5 times
= 21.8%

There are two ways to improve investment turnover: increase sales revenue or reduce the business unit's invested capital. There are several ways in which the level of invested capital can be reduced. The business unit manager can reduce inventories, or sell plant or other non-current assets. However, reducing inventories may have adverse effects on prompt deliveries to customers. Disposal of assets may have longer-term consequences of reduced capacity, which may reduce future returns.

While we can isolate ROI into the two components of return on sales and investment turnover, any actions taken with the sole purpose of making these ratios more favourable can have adverse effects on performance in future years.

The advantages of ROI

L.O. 2 ROI is used by many decentralised businesses in South Africa and overseas to evaluate the performance of investment centres. It has some positive features:

- It encourages managers to *focus on both profits and the assets required to generate those profits.* Thus, managers of investment centres must consider the relationships between revenues, costs and invested capital. It discourages excessive investment in assets, which may occur if performance is measured only on absolute profit.
- ROI can be used to *evaluate the relative performance of investment centres,* even when those business units have different scales of operations. Thus, we can compare the ROI of a small business with that of a large business.

The limitations of ROI

Against these advantages, a significant emphasis on achieving ROI can encourage dysfunctional decisions:

- It can encourage managers to focus on *short-term financial performance, at the expense of the long term.* Many ways of increasing ROI can result in reduced performance in the future. Excessive cost-cutting activities can improve short-term ROI, but weaken the business' future competitiveness. For example, research and development, or training expenditure, can be deferred. Reducing employee numbers can increase profit but may affect product quality or the level of customer service.
- ROI can encourage managers to *defer asset replacement.* Asset replacement may be deferred (particularly when those old assets are fully written off), as any new assets would boost the size of the invested capital. Deferring the placement of assets may improve ROI in the short term, but erode the competitiveness and profits of the business in later years. Disposing of productive assets can decrease the investment base, but also reduce the capacity of the business.
- ROI may *discourage managers from investing in projects* that are acceptable from the total organisation's point of view. This will occur where the project decreases the investment centre's ROI. An example of this problem is provided below.

The disincentive to invest in new projects

Let's suppose that the manager of the Smelting business is considering investing in modifications to one of the smelters. The modifications will cost R500 million, and will save the business R45 million in operating expenses in the first year. The accountant of the Smelting business has calculated that the investment will yield a return of more than 12 per cent over its life, which is greater than the minimum of, say, 8 per cent rate of return that headquarters might expect on investments of this nature. There may also be strong qualitative reasons for making this investment. It might reduce waste emissions and so would satisfy new, soon-to-be-enacted, environmental standards. If the Smelting business does not invest in the modifications, the continuing emission by the smelter may be viewed adversely by the local community. Viewed from the perspective of the company as a whole, the investment is desirable. However, how will the project affect the ROI of the business unit in the first year of operation?

Smelting return on investment (Year 1)

Without investment	With investment	
Rm	Rm	
480	525	[480 + 45]
4000 = 12.0%	4500 = 11.67%	[4000 + 500]

If the performance of the manager of the Smelting business is evaluated predominantly based on his business unit's ROI, he would have an economic incentive not to invest in the project. Without the modifications, the business unit ROI is 12 per cent, but if he proceeds with the project, the business unit ROI will fall to 11.67 per cent in the first year. While the modifications may provide a larger ROI in years to come, the manager may be rewarded on current ROI, rather than future ROI. Many managers are more concerned with the immediate financial performance rather than long-term performance.

Even though the investment may satisfy headquarters' economic criteria for new investments, and promote environmental standards, the Smelting manager may be reluctant to acquire the new equipment on economic grounds alone. Thus, when ROI is used as a primary measure of performance evaluation, goal congruence problems can arise.

Minimising the behavioural problems of ROI

L.O. 3

The problems associated with ROI can be minimised in the following ways:

- Using ROI as only one of a series of performance measures that focus on both short-term and long-term performance. This approach is taken by many companies. A more balanced set of measures (both financial and non-financial) can counter the dysfunctional incentives associated with ROI. These measures are examined in Chapter 14.

- Considering alternative ways of measuring invested capital, so that the replacement of an asset is less likely to result in a reduction of ROI. Many businesses measure invested capital at its written-down book value, which is often low at the time of asset replacement. If alternative measures of invested capital, such as market value or replacement cost, are used, the replacement decision will not cause a major change in the investment base. This is considered in a later section of this chapter.
- Using alternative financial measures, such as residual income or economic value added.

Residual income

L.O. 4

One suggested solution for overcoming the problems associated with ROI is to use a measure of residual income to evaluate performance. **Residual income** is defined as follows:

Residual income = profit − (invested capital × imputed interest rate)
where the imputed interest rate = the firm's required rate of return.

Unlike ROI, residual income is a rand amount, not a ratio. It is the amount of an investment centre's profit that remains (as a residual) after subtracting an **imputed interest charge**. The imputed interest charge is the rate of return that the firm expects from its investment in that division of the organisation. It may be based on the firm's minimum required rate of return on invested capital. In other companies it may be based on the organisation's **weighted average cost of capital (WACC)**. The weighted average cost of capital is the weighted average of the cost of funds from all sources of borrowings and equity. (The WACC is explained in greater detail in a later section of this chapter.) In some firms, investment centres that have different levels of risk may be assigned different imputed interest rates.

The advantage of residual income

To demonstrate the advantage of residual income over ROI, we will revisit the example of the modification project of the Smelting business. The residual income of the Smelting business is calculated below, both with and without the investment in the new project. We will assume that the imputed interest rate is 8 per cent.

Notice that the Smelting business' residual income will increase if the modifications are undertaken. If the managing director were evaluated on the basis of residual income instead of ROI, there would be an incentive to make the investment. Thus, *goal congruence* may be achieved when residual income is used to measure business unit performance.

Why did residual income facilitate goal congruence whereas ROI did not? The residual income formula incorporates an important piece of data that is excluded from the ROI formula: the organisation's required rate of return on invested capital. Any investment that, in any year, has a return that exceeds the minimum required rate of return will yield a positive residual income.

Smelting business' residual income

	Without investment		With investment	
		Rm		Rm
Business unit profit		480		525
Less: Imputed charge				
Invested capital	4 000		4 500	
× imputed interest rate	8%		8%	
Imputed interest charge		−320		−360
Residual income		160		165

Although there has been an increase in residual income, this depends on the level of the imputed interest charge. At an interest rate of 10 per cent, there would have been a reduction in residual income. Will this lead to the same problem with using ROI? No. Why? If residual income falls then it means that the *incremental* net income from the new investment is less than the cost of financing. The incremental net income of R45m (525−480) exceeds the cost of financing of R40m (R500m × 8 per cent). However, at an interest rate of 10 per cent, this would result in a negative residual income of R5m (R45m − R50m). What this all means is that a fall in residual income means that the profit for that year does not exceed the cost of financing. If the ROI falls, this does not necessarily mean that the investment should not go ahead. For example, assume the current ROI is 12 per cent and this is expected to fall to 11.67 per cent. The incremental ROI is 9 per cent (45/500), while the imputed interest cost is 8 per cent. The investment should go ahead even though there has been a fall in ROI. We should base decisions on whether the *incremental* ROI exceeds the cost of financing, not on whether the firm's ROI will rise with the investment.

Disadvantages of residual income

Residual income has a serious drawback: it should not be used to compare the performances of different-sized businesses, because as a Rand measure it incorporates a bias in favour of larger businesses. Thus, when evaluating the performance of investment centres of different sizes, ROI is preferred over residual income. However, because of its short-term focus and its ability to be manipulated, ROI should be used as part of a range of measures.

Like ROI, residual income can also encourage a short-term orientation, but it is often considered superior to ROI when evaluating capital expenditure projects. If we refer to our example, the incremental income from the investment in later years could be significantly higher than the net income of R45m for next year. Our decision should be based on the residual income levels in future years.

The term *residual income* is not widely used in South African companies. However, in recent years a series of *shareholder value* measures have emerged, one of which (EVA®) is similar to the residual income measure. This will be discussed in a later section of this chapter.

Measuring profit and invested capital

L.O. 5

How should profit and invested capital be measured for calculating ROI and residual income?

There are several approaches used in practice, and the choice may result in different behavioural incentives. While it can be argued that some definitions are superior to others, an important issue is that a particular measure is clearly defined and is used consistently throughout the one organisation.

How should we define 'invested capital'?

We will focus on the Smelting business to illustrate several alternative approaches to measuring invested capital. Exhibit 13.1 lists some illustrative assets and liabilities of the Smelting business at the end of the previous year. Notice that there are no non-current liabilities such as debentures. Although the company as a whole may have long-term debt, it would not be meaningful to assign portions of that corporate debt to the company's individual investment centres, such as the Smelting business; the managers in those businesses do not manage or control these liabilities.

Which assets should be included?

Exhibit 13.1 shows that Smelting had balances at the end of the financial year of R925 million in current assets; R3500 million in non-current assets such as plant and equipment; and R75 million tied up in plant under construction. In addition, the balance of current liabilities was R550 million.

		Rm
Assets		
Current assets (cash, receivables, inventories etc.)		925
Non-current assets (land, buildings, plant, equipment etc.)		
Acquisition cost	4900	
Less Accumulated depreciation	1400	
Net book value		3500
Plant under construction		75
Total assets		4500
Liabilities		
Current liabilities (accounts payable, provisions for employee entitlements)		550

Exhibit 13.1 Assets and liabilities of the Smelting business*

*These assets and liabilities are hypothetical.

There are several ways of defining *invested capital*:

- *Total assets.* This measure of invested capital is appropriate if the investment centre manager is responsible for decisions about all of the assets of the investment centre, including nonproductive assets.
- *Total productive assets.* In some companies, investment centre managers may be directed by corporate management to retain non-productive assets such as vacant land or construction in progress. In such cases it is appropriate to exclude these non-productive assets from the measure of invested capital. Under this alternative, R4425 million would have been used in the ROI and residual income calculations (total assets of R4500 million less R75 million for the plant under construction).
- *Total assets less current liabilities.* In some companies, managers in investment centres manage certain short-term liabilities, including short-term bank loans and employee entitlements such as the provision for long-service leave. In these cases, invested capital can be measured as total assets less current liabilities. This approach encourages the managers to minimise resources tied up in assets and to manage the use of short-term credit to finance operations. If this approach had been used by the Smelting business, the invested capital would have been R3950 million (total assets of R4500 million less current liabilities of R550 million).

Average or end-of-year balances

ROI and residual income are usually calculated for a period of time such as a year or a quarter and, during that period, asset balances will change. Therefore, it is more accurate to use average balances of assets to calculate ROI and residual income rather than to use end-of-year balances. For example, if the Smelting business' invested capital (based on total assets) was R4000 million at the start of the year and R4500 million at the end of the year, we would use the average invested capital of R4250 million [(R4000 million + R4500 million) ÷ 2] in the ROI and residual income calculations. This assumes that the investment was made halfway through the year. However, many financial analysts use either closing book values or opening book values to calculate ROI.

Allocating assets to business units

Some companies manage certain assets centrally, although these assets are needed to conduct operations in the investment centres. Common examples are cash and accounts receivable. Investment centres need cash in order to operate, but many companies control cash balances centrally in order to minimise their total cash holdings and maximise returns on invested funds.

When certain assets are controlled centrally, these asset balances may be allocated to investment centres so that they can be reported in their individual statements of financial position. For example, cash may be allocated based on the budgeted cash needs in each investment centre, or on the basis of business units' sales. Accounts receivable may be allocated on the basis of sales. If investment centre managers are able to manage or control these allocated assets, there is an argument for including them as part of invested capital.

Asset measurement: original cost, net book value or market value?

Another decision to make in choosing a measure of invested capital is whether to use original acquisition cost, net book value or market value when measuring non-current assets.

Using the data in Exhibit 13.1, if net book value is used, the invested capital would be R4500 million. However, if gross book value is used, invested capital would be R5900 million. There are advantages and disadvantages associated with using either gross book value or net book value as a measure of invested capital.

Advantages of net book value (disadvantages of gross book value)

- Using net book value maintains consistency with the statement of financial position prepared for external reporting purposes.
- Using net book value to measure invested capital is also consistent with the definition of profit, which is used in the ROI and residual income calculations. In calculating profit, the current period's depreciation on non-current assets is deducted as an expense.

Advantages of gross book value (disadvantages of net book value)

- The usual ways of calculating depreciation, such as straight-line or diminishing value methods, are arbitrary. Hence, they should not be allowed to affect ROI or residual income calculations.
- When non-current assets are depreciated, their net book value declines over time. Using net book value as a measure of invested capital may result in a misleading increase in ROI and residual income across time. It may provide a disincentive to invest in new equipment. This will be examined in more detail.

Incentives created by using net book value

Exhibit 13.2 provides an example of the ROI that rises steadily across a five-year horizon if invested capital is measured at net book value. However, using gross book value eliminates this problem. Note that if the diminishing value method is used instead of the straight line method, the increasing trend in ROI would be even more pronounced! We have calculated ROI on opening book value.

The increasing ROI that results when using the net book value of assets is misleading. Has performance actually improved? Probably not! The increase in ROI is solely the effect of the invested capital reducing due to the accounting method of depreciation. However, this phenomenon can provide incentives for investment centre managers to make dysfunctional decisions. Managers may defer investing in new equipment that, from a competitive perspective, may be a desirable investment. An investment centre's assets may become obsolete, making it uncompetitive.

Inflation even at low rates will make this problem even worse. Why? As profit increases with inflation, depreciation will remain constant as it is based on historical cost. In our example, assuming an inflation rate of 5 per cent per year, then the profit (before depreciation) would increase by 5 per cent per year, so that the ratio of profit to a historical cost which is being reduced by depreciation will rise over time due to depreciation and inflation and not due to an improved utilisation of the asset. This is depicted in Exhibit 13.3.

One way of preventing these problems is to use some measure of the *market value of assets*. As some South African companies periodically update the value of their non-current assets, current

	R000		
Acquisition cost of equipment	5600	Useful life	7
Profit (before deducting depreciation)	1500	Salvage value at end of 7 yrs	0
Depreciation (straight-line)	800		

Year	1	2	3	4	5	6	7
Figures in thousands							
Profit before depreciation	1500	1500	1500	1500	1500	1500	1500
Annual depreciation	−800	−800	−800	−800	−800	−800	−800
Profit after depreciation	700	700	700	700	700	700	700
Opening net book value	5600	4800	4000	3200	2400	1600	800
Annual depreciation	−800	−800	−800	−800	−800	−800	−800
Closing net book value	4800	4000	3200	2400	1600	800	0
ROI based on net op. book value	**12.5%**	**14.6%**	**17.5%**	**21.9%**	**29.2%**	**43.8%**	**87.5%**
Gross book value	5600	5600	5600	5600	5600	5600	5600
ROI based on gross book value	**12.5%**	**12.5%**	**12.5%**	**12.5%**	**12.5%**	**12.5%**	**12.5%**

Exhibit 13.2 Increase in ROI over time (using net and gross book value)

Year	1	2	3	4	5	6	7
Figures in thousands							
Inflation adjusted profit (infl. = 5%)	1500	1575	1654	1736	1823	1914	2010
Annual depreciation	−800	−800	−800	−800	−800	−800	−800
Profit after depreciation	700	775	854	936	1023	1114	1210
ROI based on net op. book value	**12.5%**	**16.1%**	**21.4%**	**29.3%**	**42.6%**	**69.7%**	**151.3%**
ROI based on gross book value	**12.5%**	**13.8%**	**15.2%**	**16.7%**	**18.3%**	**19.9%**	**21.6%**

Exhibit 13.3 Increase in ROI over time (using net and gross book value) with profit adjusted for inflation

data are sometimes available. There are South African companies such as Tiger Brands and PPC which have assets that are almost fully depreciated but are still generating revenue. This results in very high ROI but, as companies replace assets, the high ROI will fall.

Measuring profit

As described in Chapter 12, there are several different definitions that can be used to measure the profit of investment centres (or profit centres). Exhibit 13.4 illustrates these measures for an investment centre. The *profit margin controllable by the investment centre manager* (line 2) may be considered a suitable profit measure if the focus is to measure the *performance of the manager* of the investment centre. Remember that the overall objective of the performance measure is to provide incentives for goal-congruent behaviour. Some managers believe that no performance measure can motivate managers to make decisions about costs they cannot control.

Evaluating an investment centre as a viable economic investment is a different matter altogether. For this purpose, the *profit margin attributable to the investment centre* (line 3) should be used to calculate the investment centre ROI or residual income.

Remember, an important reason for considering business and managerial performance separately is to prevent penalising good managers who are asked to manage poorly performing divisions or departments.

Other profit definitions

The other measures of profit shown in Exhibit 13.4 (lines 4, 5 and 6) are also used by some companies. The rationale behind these profit measures is that all corporate costs have to be covered by the operations of the investment centres. Allocating corporate costs, interest and income taxes to the investment centres makes investment (or profit) centre managers aware of these costs.

	Sales revenue	9 000 000
	Variable expenses	−3 800 000
1	Divisional contribution margin	5 200 000
	Fixed expenses controllable by investment centre manager	−1 600 000
2	Profit margin controllable by investment centre manager	3 600 000
	Fixed expenses, attributable to investment centre, but controlled by others	−1 200 000
3	Profit margin attributable to investment centre	2 400 000
	Common fixed expenses, allocated from corporate headquarters	−400 000
4	Investment centre profit before interest and taxes	2 000 000
	Interest expense allocated from corporate headquarters	−250 000
5	Investment centre profit before taxes	1 750 000
	Income taxes allocated from corporate headquarters	−507 500
6	Investment centre net profit	1 242 500

Exhibit 13.4 Various definitions of profit

Measures of shareholder value

L.O. 6

In Chapter 1 *shareholder value* (sometimes called economic value) was defined as improving the worth of the business from the shareholders' perspective. Shareholders are interested in increased profitability, increased share price and increased dividends, and management is charged with the responsibility of delivering these outcomes. Similarly, other types of business owners are concerned with profits and a return on their investment. Throughout the various chapters in this book we have considered how management accounting can assist managers in creating shareholder value. However, we have not considered *how value may be measured and used to manage performance within firms*. The rationale behind measuring shareholder value is to determine whether a business is generating value for its shareholders or owners.

Value-based management

When organisations use shareholder value analysis to manage their business, they are said to be practising **value-based management** (**VBM**). VBM is a framework for making key business decisions that add economic value to the business. A particular strategy or decision creates shareholder value, where the return on capital is greater than the cost of capital. Thus, managers need to understand how to generate, evaluate and select business strategies, or undertake activities that will increase the value of the firm. This involves being able to measure the value created from decisions, such as whether to acquire a new business or move into new markets. Product lines or segments of a business that are not providing sufficient value may be deleted, and the outcomes of a proposed project or asset acquisition can be analysed in terms of value creation. There are four aspects of VBM: valuation, strategy, finance and corporate governance (Morin & Jarrell, 2001). We will examine each of these aspects.

Valuation

Value can be measured in several ways. Discounted cash flow (DCF) models are commonly used to measure value. (Chapters 21 and 22 contain details of how to calculate DCF.) The use of DCF to measure shareholder value makes sense, as investors and the capital markets often value a business based on the future cash flows of the business, discounted by the risk associated with those cash flows. In some cases, however, it is difficult to measure such cash flows, so surrogates may be used. (For example, the market capitalisation of the company – that is, the market price per share multiplied by the number of shares on issue – may be used.)

To increase the value of a firm, managers need to understand the drivers of value. **Value drivers** are the activities or actions that create value for a business. These drivers include:

- *spread*, which is the degree to which a firm can earn a return that is greater than its cost of capital;
- *growth* in funds available to invest in value-creation activities;
- the *sustainability* of those funds over many years; and
- the *cost of capital*.

The first three drivers maximise cash flow, which interacts with the cost of capital to increase shareholder value.

Strategy, finance and corporate governance

The other three aspects of VBM are strategy, finance and corporate governance. Strategic decisions have a substantial and continuing impact on the value of a business. Valuation techniques can assist managers to compare the value created by alternative differentiation or cost strategies. (The various types of business strategies are discussed in Chapter 1.) Financial policies, such as the adoption of particular financial and capital structures that reduce the cost of capital, will also influence value creation.

Corporate governance involves selecting and implementing systems that contribute to value creation. Performance measures can be developed to measure the value-creating performance of business units and managers. Managerial reward systems can be designed to link managers' compensation to their performance in creating value, as well as to guide managers' value creation activities. The formulation of performance measures under VBM will be discussed below, followed by a discussion of compensation systems.

There are several performance measures used by companies in South Africa and overseas within the VBM framework. These include economic value added (EVA®) and shareholder value added (SVA).

Economic value added (EVA®)

L.O. 7 **Economic value added (EVA®)** measures the value created over a single accounting period, measured by the spread between the return generated by business activities and the cost of capital. This can be stated as:

EVA® = net operating profit after tax − (capital employed × weighted average cost of capital)[4]

Thus, EVA® can be calculated as the company's net operating profit after tax (NOPAT), less a charge based on the book value of the assets of the business (described as capital employed or invested capital) multiplied by the firm's weighted average cost of capital (Stewart, 1991).

Let's assume that in 20X7, the profit after tax for the Siyanda Manufacturing Company is R81.6m, and the capital employed is R300m. The company obtains its funds from long-term debt and equity, and the weighted average cost of capital is estimated to be 12 per cent.

EVA® = net profit after tax (NOPAT) − (capital employed × weighted average cost of capital)
= R81.6m − (R300m × 0.12)
= R81.6m − R36m
= R45.6m

Thus, the Siyanda Manufacturing Company has generated R45.6m of value for shareholders during the year.

The weighted average cost of capital

We saw in an earlier section that the weighted average cost of capital is sometimes used in the calculation of residual income. It is also used to calculate economic value added. The WACC is usually calculated for the entire company, not for each business unit. How is this calculated?

Weighted average cost of capital (WACC) can be calculated as follows:

$$\text{WACC} = \frac{\begin{matrix}\text{after-tax cost} \\ \text{of debt capital}\end{matrix} \times \begin{matrix}\text{market value} \\ \text{of debt}\end{matrix} + \begin{matrix}\text{cost of equity} \\ \text{capital}\end{matrix} \times \text{market value of equity}}{\text{Market value of debt} + \text{market value of equity}}$$

Let's assume that Siyanda's Manufacturing Company has debt of R120m and the interest rate on that debt is 11 per cent before tax. The taxation rate is 29 per cent. As interest on debt is tax deductible, the company's after-tax cost of debt capital is 7.81 per cent [11 per cent × (1 − 0.29)]. The market value of the company's equity capital is R180m, and we will assume that the return that Siyanda's investors could earn from an investment similar to their investment in Siyanda is 14 per cent.

$$\text{WACC} = \frac{(0.0781) \times (\text{R120m}) + (0.14) \times (\text{R180m})}{\text{R120m} + \text{R180m}}$$

$$= 11.52\% \text{ or approximately } 11.5\%$$

Comparing RI and EVA®

You may notice that the formula for EVA® resembles that of residual income (R1). However, it differs in several ways. First, the definition of net profit after tax is not necessarily the same as the accounting measure of profit used in the residual income formula. Adjustments may need to be made to convert accrual accounting data to cash-based figures, and to eliminate the effects of gearing. (There are up to 164 possible adjustments that may be made!)[5]

Second, the weighted average cost of capital is used in the calculation of EVA®, whereas in RI this is not always the case. In the calculation of RI, an imputed interest is used, which is the required rate of return that the company expects of a division. Sometimes this is the WACC, but not in all cases.

Finally, in the EVA® formula, capital employed is often calculated as the company's total assets, less non-interest-bearing current liabilities. In the RI formula, as in ROI, invested capital can be defined in a variety of ways.

What strategies can management use to maximise EVA®? To improve EVA®, managers can:

- improve profitability without employing any additional capital;
- reduce capital without reducing profits;
- borrow additional funds if the firm can earn profits on those funds which are in excess of the cost of borrowing; and
- pay off debt by selling assets, as long as the savings in reduced interest are greater than profits lost through reducing the asset base (Barbara & Coyte, 1999);
- invest in projects that offer returns that are higher than the company's WACC;
- reduce the company's WACC.

These strategies are similar to those that can be used to improve residual income. However, the adjustments to NOPAT are thought to result in more accurate indications of economic value.

The use of EVA® does have its downside. EVA® suffers from the same limitations as ROI and RI, in that it is a single period measure of performance. Thus, the potential for manipulation and a short-term orientation can still arise. The value of a business is a function of several years of managerial decision making and firm performance. As with ROI, the use of the book value of assets may result in decisions not to invest in assets, owing to the unfavourable impact of depreciation in the early years of use. However, EVA provides solutions to the problems arising from short-term gains that negatively impact on long-term performance. The 'Real life' later in the chapter provides an example of how a South African company uses EVA®. In the next section, Professor Joel Stern, the founder of EVA, offers us his perspective on EVA.

REAL LIFE: ECONOMIC VALUE ADDED (EVA™) BY JOEL STERN

Professor Joel Stern is the founder of EVA. He has been instrumental in advancing the cause of shareholder value management and has had an immeasurable effect on the development of corporate finance. He is CEO of Stern Stewart. Joel has written or co-authored eight books, and writes for the Financial Times, Finance Week *and the* Wall Street Journal. *He is associated with a number of graduate schools and has taught at Columbia, the Australian Graduate School of Management (AGSM) and the University of Cape Town. He offers us a brief overview on why EVA is preferable to using free cash flow to evaluate performance.*

The theory of modern finance sees a firm's enterprise value (debt plus shareholders' funds) as the present value of the expected future Free Cash Flow (FCF). Although simple to use, its practical value is limited by the fact that projects can only be evaluated over their useful life. FCF can be measured contemporaneously, year by year, but it has no strategic meaning. FCF is NOPAT minus I, trading profit after taxes paid minus net new investment.[6] If the expected rate of return (R) exceeds the required rate of return (C), new investment adds to shareholder value. Thus, if R>C, maximizing I maximizes value, but hopefully current year's FCF is negative (i.e. NOPAT − I = −FCF) because I > NOPAT, and this is good.

In contrast, the EVA framework already is expressed in terms of present value. It says enterprise value is equal to Net Asset Value plus the present value of expected future EVA. Thus, in any year, any increase in EVA suggests a greater enterprise value. EVA is total capital multiplied by the difference [R − C]:

$$EVA = TC\,[R - C]$$

Thus, three motives of behaviour maximize EVA growth:

1 Grow the firm (TC[7]) as long as R>C.
2 Improve performance on existing capital (increase R).
3 Harvest losers where R < C and where there is little hope for improvement.

Finally, no model can hope to result in value maximization unless it is reinforced with incentive contracts that provide management (and potentially all employees) with an economic interest in improving EVA, one that pays out over time based on sustainability of performance.

Shareholder value added (SVA)

Another measure of economic value is **shareholder value added (SVA)**, which is defined as the corporate value of the company, less the market value of the debt (Rappaport, 1986).

$$\text{Shareholder value} = \text{corporate value} - \text{the market value of debt}$$

The **corporate value** of the company is calculated as the present value (PV) of the future cash flows and the **residual value** of the business. The PV of cash flows from operations is for a certain forecast period (such as 10 years). The residual value of the business is the value of the firm at the end of the forecast period. The weighted average cost of capital is used to discount these amounts to their present value.[8]

There are other forms of shareholder value measures, including Total Shareholder Returns (TSR) and Total Business Returns (TBR) (promoted by the Boston Consulting group). Further details can be found in Barbara & Coyte (1999), Ehrbar (1998) and Morin & Jarrell (2001).

REAL LIFE: EVA® AND PERFORMANCE

A number of prominent South African companies use EVA®, including the JD Group and SABMiller. We will now study SABMiller which reports on its EVA within its annual report.

The use of EVA to measure performance at SABMiller

SABMiller has become one of the world's major brewers. The group is now listed in London but it remains a South African company as it expanded globally from South Africa. SABMiller has over 53 000 employees and operates in over 60 countries. Sales for the year ended 31 March 2006 amounted to US$15.3 billion (US$14.53 billion in the year ending 31 March 2005).

The company's share price has performed strongly since listing in London in 1999. SABMiller believes in maximising shareholder value and the company has implemented the EVA™ system to measure performance. The company disclosed the rationale for using EVA in the company's annual report for the year ending 31 March 2005.

In focusing on shareholder value added, the group uses EVA™ as a key indicator of annual performance. As noted previously, SABMiller is continually investing in new brewing operations and most new investments impact negatively on EVA™ in the short term. Key factors to be borne in mind are: EVA™ is calculated using operating profit after tax, adjusted for exceptional and non-recurring items; the capital charge is calculated on opening economic capital – adjusted for acquisitions, any impairments of assets of continuing business units, and goodwill previously eliminated against reserves. The group's weighted average cost of capital (WACC) is applied against the resulting investment; and WACC, at 8.75% (as in 2004), takes account of relevant individual country risk profiles and the group's overall debt profile. SABMiller returned EVA™ of US$505 million in the year under review (2004: US$241 million). This increase is the result of the improved business performance outlined earlier, partially offset by a higher capital charge that reflects the acquisitions made during 2005.

SABMiller indicates how it calculated the company's EVA in its 2005 annual report. The company did not refer to this in the 2006 annual report.

Calculation of EVA™ SABMiller	**2005 US$m**	**2004 US$m**
Economic profit statements		
Profit on ordinary activities before interest and tax	2 361	1 579
Taxation on profit on ordinary activities	−850	−579
Tax deduction on financing costs	−58	−65
Adjustment for non-recurring items	140	308
Net operating profit after tax	1 593	1 243
Capital charge	−1 088	−1 002
Economic profit (EVA™)	505	241
Economic balance sheets		
Fixed assets	12 287	11 483
Working capital	−530	−203
Accumulated adjustment for non-recurring items	1 034	894
Economic Capital	12 791	12 174
Non-interest bearing funding	−462	−405
Provisions	−796	−866
Net operating assets	11 533	10 903

Exhibit 13.5 Calculation of EVA of SABMiller [Source: SABMiller annual report 2005]

In an interview with Malcolm Wyman, who is a South African chartered accountant and CFO of SABMiller, he indicated that although the WACC of SABMiller is 8.75 per cent, he will use a project-based cost of capital rather than use a single WACC to evaluate all investments. He also states as reported in the publication, the *Financial Director* (September 2005), that:

From year to year you do have variations in EVA depending on what capital you put down and acquisitions that you may make, but over the longer term, looking at Delta EVA is a way of making sure that you are consistently adding value and that you are not losing sight of the fact that you're not getting back what your cost of capital is.

Wyman explains that because of the additional investment that usually has to be made to upgrade a new acquisition, SABMiller will normally expect a new business to go EVA positive after about three to five years.

This is interesting as SABMiller does not focus on short-term EVA but evaluates changes to EVA (delta EVA) over a number of years. Due to high levels of investments made, EVA may be negative for a number of years after which the incremental investments will generate increased returns which will then ensure that EVA becomes positive.

How successful has SABMiller been? As the company reports in its 2006 financial statements, it measures its return to its shareholders in the form of Total Shareholder Return (TSR) which is the combination of share price appreciation and dividends returned. Since SABMiller moved its primary listing from Johannesburg to the London Stock Exchange in March 1999, the FTSE 100 has produced a total shareholder return of 20 per cent to 31 March 2006, whilst SABMiller has produced a TSR of 215 per cent over the same period.

Reward systems

To encourage goal congruence, part of an employee's remuneration may be tied to achieving certain levels of performance. A **reward system** consists of processes, practices and systems that are used to provide levels of pay and benefits to employees. At any level of the organisation, employee remuneration may consist of a base salary, performance-related pay, and non-financial rewards (such as a better computer or office, overseas travel, or even dinner at a restaurant for the family!).

Tying some part of employee rewards to achieving financial or non-financial performance targets can provide strong positive incentives for managers and employees to maximise their performance. However, if the performance measurement system is not designed correctly, there may be incentives to manipulate results. (For example, an excessive emphasis on achieving a high ROI can lead to dysfunctional decisions, as we saw earlier in this chapter.)

Designing a reward system that encourages goal-congruent behaviour is complex. It is difficult to reward managers and employees for *past actions and decisions* while at the same time encouraging them to *improve their future performance.* Issues to consider include the composition of the incentive payments (cash, shares or other means), whether rewards are to be tied to individual or group performance achievements, and the timing of payment of rewards (immediate and deferred).

Managers also need to understand what types of rewards motivate their employees.

Motivation

L.O. 9 Motivation is a complex topic. However, an understanding of some of the theories of motivation can help guide managers' thinking about designing and implementing reward systems. **Motivation** refers to the processes that account for an individual's intensity, direction and persistence of effort towards attaining goals (Robbins et al., 2004, p. 184). The level of employee motivation is situation specific. That is, it can vary between individuals in the one organisation, and within the same individual over time.

Intrinsic and extrinsic motivation

Rewards paid to employees often take the form of cash bonuses or shares in the company, and these are thought to motivate some employees. **Extrinsic rewards** are rewards that flow from an external source. They often take the form of financial rewards, but may also include non-financial outcomes such as congratulations from a senior manager.

Some employees are motivated by other less tangible aspects of their job. **Intrinsic rewards** are the rewards that an employee gets from the work itself (Robbins et al., 2004). Intrinsic motivation can arise when employees experience the following:

- *Choice*: the employee has the opportunity to select activities that make sense and to perform these in ways that seem appropriate.
- *Competence*: the accomplishment that follows when activities that have been chosen by the employee are skilfully performed.
- *Meaningfulness*: the opportunity to pursue a worthy task, which matters in the larger scheme of things.
- *Progress*: employees feel that they have made significant advancement in achieving the task's purpose (Robbins et al., 2004; Thomas, 2000).

Intrinsic motivation has been found to increase job satisfaction and employee performance. *How can an organisation encourage intrinsic motivation?* Clearly, the design of the job that is assigned to employees is relevant. However, some of the concepts that have been discussed in other chapters of this book, such as *employee participation* and *empowerment* are also important. Intrinsic motivation cannot be 'given' to employees. Managers can design jobs and systems to encourage intrinsic motivation. However, this may not be successful unless they can also encourage the development of an organisational culture where feelings of personal achievement and the intangible aspects of work are valued. This is no easy task!

How do managers choose which form of rewards to emphasise to encourage motivation and goal achievement? The effectiveness of reward systems will depend on many aspects of the organisation, including the design of jobs and systems, as well as the preferences of the people who work there. It will also depend on management's view about what motivates employees.

L.O. 10

Theories of motivation

Some of the best-known theories of motivation were developed in the 1950s, and you may have already studied some of these in other subjects. Early theories include Maslow's hierarchy of needs, McGregor's Theory X and Theory Y, and Herzberg's two-factor theory (see Maslow, 1954; McGregor, 1960; Hertzberg et al., 1959). Later theories include McClelland's theory of needs, goal setting theory, equity theory and expectancy theory (see Robbins et al., 2004, Chapter 6). In this section we will consider two widely used theories – Herzberg's two-factor theory and expectancy theory.

Herzberg's two-factor theory

Herzberg suggested that there are two factors that affect employee behaviour (Herzberg, 1968). **Hygiene factors** are those factors that provide the necessary setting for motivation but do not themselves motivate employees. Examples include working conditions, wage levels, rules and regulations, relationships with colleagues and job security. When these factors are adequate, employees will not be dissatisfied, but also they will not be satisfied. **Motivators** are factors that relate to job content or to outcomes of the job that will provide motivation. Examples include achievement, recognition, the nature of the work, responsibility and opportunities for personal growth. These factors are said to be *intrinsically rewarding*.

Thus, employees need a certain level of hygiene factors to prevent dissatisfaction. However, adding more of these factors will not result in motivation, or even satisfaction. Only the motivators will do this.

While this theory has been criticised, it does highlight the fact that many people are not motivated just by increased pay and conditions – attention needs to be paid to their 'higher-order needs'.

Expectancy theory

Another interesting theory of motivation is expectancy theory (Vroom, 1964). This theory is particularly relevant for the design of reward systems, as it focuses on the effect of incentives. **Expectancy theory** states that employee motivation is a function of the strength of expectancy, instrumentality and valence. These three terms will be explained in the context of performance measurement systems:

- *Expectancy (effort → performance)*: an individual's perceptions that the effort he or she puts into a task will lead to a certain performance (as measured by the performance measure);
- *Instrumentality (performance → rewards)*: the perception that achieving the performance will lead to the attainment of a desired outcome (a reward); and
- *Valence (rewards → personal goals)*: the degree to which the reward satisfies the individual's goals, and the attractiveness of the reward for that individual.

Motivational theories and rewards

How can these theories of motivation help managers to design and implement reward systems?

Expectancy theory suggests that individuals will be motivated to perform when they perceive a close linkage between their effort and achieving the performance measure (high level of expectancy); when they have confidence that the reward will be provided (high instrumentality); and when they value the particular reward that is offered (high valence). Thus, the effectiveness of a reward system in motivating employees may depend on whether employees perceive that the performance target is achievable and will lead to a reward that is valued. Some employees may value monetary rewards, while others may value the sense of achievement that comes with meeting a challenging goal.

Herzberg's theory suggests that it is not hygiene factors but factors such as achievement, recognition and responsibility that are strong motivators. However, expectancy theory suggests that employees may be motivated only if they value certain rewards. As noted above, the culture of the organisation must encourage the appreciation of intrinsic rewards for them to be valued and considered motivational by employees. Herzberg also suggests that extrinsic rewards are not motivators but provide only the setting for these intrinsic rewards. However, the proliferation of performance-related pay systems in South African companies suggests that many managers believe extrinsic rewards to be motivational!

We will now focus on the various ways in which rewards may be distributed as part of employee remuneration schemes.

Performance-related reward systems

L.O. 11 **Performance-related pay systems** (or **incentive compensation schemes**) base rewards on achieving or exceeding some performance target. Under these systems, employees are paid a base pay, and then additional pay will be awarded based on individual or group performance. Once performance-related pay was considered to only apply to middle and senior management. However, from the early 1990s a number of South African companies started to consider the various ways in which they could recognise and reward good performance and encourage future performance at all levels of the organisation. Organisations can choose to implement a variety of incentive compensation plans at the same time. The various types of incentive compensation schemes include individual incentive plans which are based on individual performance and compensation plans based on the performance of the group, team or the company as a whole (including profit-sharing plans, employee share plans, gainsharing and team-based incentives).[9]

Individual incentive plans

Individual incentive plans reward individuals for achieving individual performance targets. The major advantage of these schemes is that individual effort is clearly tied to outcomes and rewards (the essential elements of expectancy theory!). Rewards may be in the form of cash bonuses, or they may be non-cash rewards, including the award of certificates of achievement or gift vouchers. However, at the operational level it may be difficult to design measures that reflect an individual's performance. In these cases, subjective means may be used to evaluate performance and provide rewards.

Individual incentive plans are very common at the senior level of an organisation, and performance related bonuses can form a large percentage of a salary package, as indicated in the 'Real life' below.

Profit-sharing plans

Under **profit-sharing plans**, employees are paid cash bonuses based on a specified percentage of the company's profit. These schemes reward individuals but are based on the overall performance of the organisation. Bonuses may be distributed to employees in many ways, such as in equal shares or in proportion to their base pay. These bonuses do not become part of an employee's base salary. Profit-sharing schemes are designed to encourage employees to identify with the performance of the entire company – *to think like the owners.*

Employee share plans

Employee share plans (or **share option plans**) provide employees with the *right to purchase* shares in their company, at a specified price at some specified future time. Why is this regarded as a form of performance-related pay? Let's suppose that on 1 January 20X7 a company allows each of its senior managers the right to purchase 10 000 shares at the current market price of R10 per share by 31 December 20X8. If the managers intend to purchase the shares, they then have the opportunity to improve the firm's performance over the next two years in order to lift the market price of the shares. The managers can then choose to sell their shares at that higher share price and make a cash profit. Alternatively, they can hold on to their shares and work harder to increase the share price in the future! Some companies do not allow managers to exercise their option until some performance hurdle has been reached. For example, a company may set a hurdle of a 20 per cent increase in share price before senior managers can exercise their options.

Gainsharing

Gainsharing is a system where cash bonuses are distributed to employees when the performance of their segment of the company (the group or plant) exceeds some performance target. Performance targets are often based on achieving some productivity gains that can be directly influenced by employees – for example, labour cost, labour usage and material usage. A proportion of the performance gain will accrue to the company and to the employees, based on some formula. The employees' share may go into a pool each quarter and then be distributed to all employees at the end of the year, usually in equal amounts. Gainsharing schemes are based on the belief that employees should share in the gains from any contribution that they make to a firm's performance. Compared to profit-sharing plans, gainsharing programs are often considered to be more motivational as the group or plant performance is thought to be more controllable by employees.

Team-based incentive schemes

Team-based incentive schemes involve individuals being rewarded based on their work team exceeding certain performance targets. These schemes are designed to encourage teamwork and co-operation among employees. Like profit-sharing plans and gainsharing, these schemes do not tie individual effort to rewards. However, where the team is small, this may not be a serious problem.

REAL LIFE: IS SENIOR EXECUTIVE PAY LINKED TO PERFORMANCE?

In recent years, the high level of remuneration paid to senior managers, and particularly to chief executive officers, has been criticised by shareholders, the government and the media. A large part of the remuneration is due to short-term and long-term incentive payments, which often include share options. In the early 1990s, executives received up to 90 per cent of their pay package in base salary. More than ten years later, it is not uncommon for 55 per cent or less of salary to be base pay.

The level of executive pay is under scrutiny in South Africa. In 2005 Whitey Basson, the CEO of Shoprite, earned R58 million in remuneration. It was reported that over 20 per cent of the shareholders, including the Public Investment Corporation (PIC), voted against the resolution approving the directors' remuneration.[10] South African companies have performed well mainly due to a strong economy, lower interest rates, and an increasing affluence amongst black South Africans. Yet executive remuneration levels sometimes assume that it is only thanks to the management team that such performance was achieved.

How do companies justify such payment to their shareholders? A common argument put forth by Boards and the CEOs themselves is that the pay packages of senior managers in South Africa need to be globally competitive to attract the best management talent. Another argument is that the high levels of remuneration are a result of linking executive pay to corporate performance. Increasingly, executive pay packages in South Africa consist of a moderate base pay, a yearly bonus to provide short-term incentives, and share options to provide long-term incentives. Executives need to achieve certain performance hurdles to achieve the bonuses.

However, there are many reported examples where executive pay packages are not closely linked to performance.

Share options are a very common form of incentive scheme for senior managers, and some companies are also now offering them to more junior managers and employees. While senior managers may have some influence on improving the company's share price, for those at more junior levels the impact of their efforts on the share price may not be as direct. Despite this, some companies believe that offering these benefits to lower-level managers and employees is motivational, as it helps employees to identify with the fortunes of the company, encouraging goal congruence and motivating them to achieve high performance. According to Joel Stern, share options issued to management should have a rising exercise price equal to the company's cost of capital less the dividend yield, as option holders do not receive a dividend.[11]

According to Deloitte (South Africa), individual performance will be increasingly taken into account in the allocations and awards that are made and very few share schemes will be introduced in the future that do not have absolute or relative company performance as part of the vesting conditions.[12]

Unfortunately, these schemes may encourage 'freeloaders' – employees who gain rewards through the efforts of their fellow team members.

Team-based rewards may be in the form of cash bonuses, or they may be non-cash rewards. These may include a dinner for the team members and their families at a restaurant, or a plaque indicating that the team has attained a certain level of achievement.

L.O. 12

Group versus individual performance

Some of the reward schemes outlined above are based on group performance – company, division or team – while other rewards are based on individual performance. What are the advantages and disadvantages of these two approaches?

- *Identification with the group.* Incentive schemes based on group performance are designed to encourage employees to identify with the company, division or team. They can enhance goal congruence and encourage teamwork.
- *Equity among employees.* Group schemes provide the same rewards to each employee. In some organisations, employees consider this to be important, as differential rewards are seen as divisive.
- *Competitiveness between employees.* Individual rewards can encourage excessive competitiveness between employees, and may encourage employees to make dysfunctional decisions to maximise their own performance.
- *Relating individual effort to reward.* It is often difficult for employees, particularly at operational levels, to understand how their own performance can directly influence overall company performance. When rewards are based on individual performance, the relationship is clearer.
- *Rewarding only good performers.* Group schemes do not discriminate between employees who are good performers and those who are bad performers. Bad performers may still be rewarded. This is not the case when rewards are based on individual performance achievements.

REAL LIFE: REMUNERATION POLICIES AT SASOL

Sasol is a major South African energy company with global operations. The company produces petroleum products, chemicals and is involved in gas to liquid fuel projects. The following extract from the company's 2006 annual report indicates the company's remuneration policy and casts light on the company's policies in respect to fixed and variable pay.

In addition to salary and benefits, each executive director and member of group management participates in an annual executive performance bonus scheme to reward the achievement of agreed group financial, business unit financial (where applicable), business unit strategic and personal performance objectives.

The approved principles of the executive performance bonus scheme for the year 1 July 2005 to 30 June 2006 were based on group, individual, business and personal criteria and metrics. The group financial performance target relates to earnings per share growth compared against inflation. The weighting dedicated to improved group business results varies from 50% for group executive committee members, 60% for executive directors to 70% for the deputy and chief executive. The balance of weightings is aimed at incentivising the meeting of group strategic business and personal objectives.

Performance criteria and metrics in the group may vary depending on business-specific strategic value drivers and personal objectives as agreed by the boards. Divisional financial targets measure mainly operating profit improvements and fixed cash cost savings, while focused value drivers derived from group business objectives include targets agreed for safety (in all businesses) and employment equity (for businesses based in South Africa).

The compensation committee previously agreed that the chief executive may, with effect from 1 July 2005, earn an annual performance bonus of up to 100% of fixed remuneration (previously 80%) and the deputy chief executive up to 80% in line with market benchmarks.

Executive directors and members of group management participate in the Sasol Share Incentive Scheme, which is designed to recognise the contributions of senior staff to the growth in the value of the group's financial position and performance and to retain key employees. Within the limits imposed by the company's shareholders and the JSE Limited, options are allocated to executive directors and senior staff in proportion to their contribution to the business as reflected by their seniority and the group's performance.

The options, which are allocated at the closing market price ruling on the trading day immediately preceding the granting of the options, vest after stipulated periods and are exercisable up to a maximum of nine years from the date of allocation. Options granted vest as follows:

- *two years – first third*
- *four years – second third*
- *six years – final third*

On retirement the share options vest immediately and the nine year expiry period remains unchanged. On resignation, share options which have not yet vested will lapse and share options which have vested may be taken up before the last day of service. The trustees of the Sasol Share Trust grant share options as follows:

- *The number of shares offered in the form of share option grants is determined in accordance with the following formulae:*
  - *the number of shares offered for promotions is based on a multiple of total annual cash salary divided by the moving average share price over 24 months, prior to the grant; and*
  - *the number of supplementary shares offered is based on an individual rating factor and meeting the company's performance growth targets in profit compared with the South African consumer price index (CPI). The individual's performance is based on an assessment of the participants' annually agreed performance targets aiming to reward performance exceeding expectations, while not rewarding substandard performance. The company performance factor is determined when the company's profit growth exceeds the current level of inflation, thereby ensuring that executives are rewarded for achieving real growth in earnings when tested against CPI.*

Timing of incentive payments

L.O. 13 Some people argue that it is preferable to reward employees frequently to ensure continued motivation. Thus, in some organisations, bonuses may be paid quarterly. This practice also helps employees to see more clearly the relationship between their effort, performance outcomes and rewards (as described in expectancy theory). However, senior managers are often rewarded less frequently, often annually. Annual performance rewards can encourage a short-term focus, particularly when managers are rewarded on achieving a single performance measure, such as ROI or profit. Sometimes, to encourage a long-term focus, senior managers' incentive payments may be deferred for some years.

Under deferred schemes, managers' rewards may accumulate in a fund for some years, with only a percentage of the fund being available for withdrawal. This prevents managers from making

REAL LIFE: DO PAY-FOR-PERFORMANCE SCHEMES DELIVER?

While performance-related pay schemes are becoming increasingly common in South African companies, it is not clear that they are leading to improved performance. So what are the problems?

A study of performance-related pay schemes revealed that poor design and implementation ensured they were not a success. One system was intended to develop quantitative performance measures and targets, and an individual manager's performance was to be rated annually on a five-point scale to form the basis for cash rewards. This was not the experience:

- Appraisal of managers tended to be subjective because of the difficulties of assigning quantitative ratings to qualitative performance criteria.
- Many supervisors were reluctant to provide senior officers with negative feedback when their performance was deficient.
- It was difficult to determine who was responsible for successful policy outcomes, which often involved many managers from a number of departments.
- Performance-related pay was regarded by some managers as divisive and alien to the collective nature of the public service.

Source: O'Donnell (1997)

decisions that maximise short-term profits at the expense of medium- and long-term profits. Share option schemes are also designed to encourage a long-term performance orientation.

An important criterion that can influence whether or not a particular incentive scheme encourages a short-term or long-term perspective is whether the performance measures have a short-term or long-term orientation. In an earlier section we saw that measures could be designed to address both perspectives.

Summary

In this chapter we examined the types of summary financial measures that can be used to evaluate performance in investment centres, and the various types of reward systems used in organisations to enhance motivation, improve performance and enhance shareholder value. Key points include:

- Return on investment (ROI), which is the profit divided by invested capital, is a summary measure that can be used to evaluate the financial performance of investment centres.
- ROI has several advantages. It can:
  - encourage managers to focus on profit and the assets required to generate those profits; and
  - be used to evaluate the relative performance of investment centres.
- ROI has several limitations, including:
  - encouraging managers to focus on short-term financial performance;
  - encouraging managers to defer asset replacement; and
  - discouraging managers from investing in projects that may be acceptable from the organisation's viewpoint.
- The behavioural problems of ROI can be minimised by using a series of measures to evaluate performance that focus on both the short term and the long term, using alternative

measures of profit and invested capital in the ROI calculation, and using alternative summary financial measures, such as EVA®.

- Residual income (RI) is the amount of profit that remains after subtracting an imputed interest charge.
- RI will partially overcome the disincentives encouraged by ROI, but is not a good comparative measure.
- A question to be considered by corporate management is the appropriate way to define the measures of profit and invested capital, to be used in ROI or RI to minimise any dysfunctional consequences of using either measure.
- Some companies use shareholder value measures, including economic value added (EVA®) and shareholder value added (SVA) to assess overall financial performance, to analyse alternative strategies and to reward managers. Each of these measures has its own set of advantages and limitations as a performance measure.
- Various forms of reward systems may be used to encourage goal congruent behaviour and achieve organisational performance.
- Extrinsic motivation depends on rewards that flow from an external source, such as increases in pay or congratulations from a senior manager. Intrinsic motivation arises from rewards that an employee gets from the work itself.
- Knowledge of motivational theories, such as Herzberg's two-factor theory of motivation and expectancy theory, can help managers to understand how to design reward systems.
- Various types of performance-related reward systems, such as individual incentives, profit-sharing plans, employee share plans, gainsharing and team-based incentives, may be used to encourage motivation and hence improve employee and firm performance.
- The timing of incentive payments can have an impact on the effectiveness of rewards on individual performance.

We continue our focus on performance measures in the following chapters. In Chapter 14 we will consider contemporary approaches to measuring and managing performance throughout the organisation, including the use of non-financial performance measures, benchmarking, and the use of balanced scorecard approaches to performance measurement and management. In Chapters 15 and 16 we consider the use of performance measures to assist in the management of various critical aspects of the business, including cost, time, quality, suppliers and customers.

References

Barbara, M & Coyte, R 1999, *Shareholder Value Demystified*, University of New South Wales Press, Sydney.

De Cieri, H, Kramer, R, Noe, RA, Hollenbeck, JR, Gerhart, B & Wright, PM 2003, *Human Resource Management in Australia*, McGraw-Hill, Sydney.

Ehrbar, A 1998, *EVA – The Real Key to Creating Wealth*, John Wiley & Sons, New York.

Herzberg, F, Mausner, B & Snyderman, B 1959, *The Motivation to Work*, Wiley, New York.

Herzberg, F 1968, 'One more time: how do you motivate employees?', *Harvard Business Review*, January–February, pp. 53–62.

Maslow, A 1954, *Motivation and Personality*, Harper and Rowe, New York.

McGregor, D 1960, *The Human Side of Enterprise*, McGraw-Hill, New York.

Morin, RA & Jarrell, SL 2001, *Driving Shareholder Value*, McGraw-Hill, New York.

O'Donnell, M 1997, 'Creating a performance culture? Performance-Based Pay in the Australian Public

Service', working paper, School of Industrial Relations and Organisational Behaviour, University of NSW.

Rappaport, A 1986, *Creating Shareholder Value: The New Standard for Business Performance,* The Free Press, New York.

Robbins, SP, Millett, B & Waters-Marsh, T 2004, *Organisational Behaviour,* Pearson Education Australia, Frenchs Forest.

Stern Stewart & Co. 1999, 'EVA® in Action: Client Stories: James Hardie', viewed 1 November, www.eva.com/action/hardie.php.

Stern, Joel, 2006, 'Fair Pay: How to ensure executives are remunerated fairly', *FinWeek,* 2 November 2006, p.34

Stewart, GB 1991, *The Quest for Value,* Harperbusiness, New York.

Thomas, KW 2000, *Intrinsic Motivation at Work,* Berrett-Koehler, San Francisco.

Vroom, VH 1964, *Work and Motivation,* John Wiley, New York.

Annual reports: Sasol Ltd, SABMiller and Murray & Roberts.

Self study

Self-study problem: Financial performance measures for investment centres

Stellar Systems Company manufactures guidance systems for rockets that are used to launch commercial satellites. The company's Software Business Division reported the following results for 20X7:

Profit	R3 000 000
Sales revenue	20 000 000
Invested capital	30 000 000

The company's required rate of return is 9 per cent.

Required:

1 Calculate the Software Business Division's return on sales, investment turnover and return on investment for 20X7.

2 If profit and sales remain the same in 20X8, but the investment turnover increases to 0.8 times, calculate the following for 20X8:

(a) invested capital

(b) ROI

3 What is the residual income in 20X7?

Solution to Self-study problem

1 Return on sales $= \dfrac{\text{profit}}{\text{sales revenue}}$

$= \dfrac{\text{R3 000 000}}{\text{R20 000 000}}$

$= 15\%$

Investment turnover $= \dfrac{\text{sales revenue}}{\text{invested capital}}$

$= \dfrac{\text{R20 000 000}}{\text{R30 000 000}}$

$= 0.667$ times

Return on investment $= \dfrac{\text{profit}}{\text{invested capital}}$

$= \dfrac{\text{R3 000 000}}{\text{R30 000 000}}$

$= 10\%$

2 (a) Investment turnover $= \dfrac{\text{sales revenue}}{\text{invested capital}}$

$= \dfrac{\text{R20 000 000}}{\text{invested capital}}$

$= 0.80$ times

therefore, Invested capital = $\frac{R20\,000\,000}{0.80}$

= R25 000 000

(b) New ROI = 15% × 0.80 times = 12%

3 Residual income

Divisional profit	3 000 000
Less Imputed interest charge:	
invested capital × imputed interest rate	
R30 000 000 × 0.09	−2 700 000
Residual income	300 000

Cybersearch

1 There are several alternative names for return on investment (ROI), including *return on capital employed (ROCE)* and *return on assets*. Find the websites of two South African companies that use ROI or a similar measure.

(a) How do the two companies calculate the measure?

(b) How are *profit* and *invested capital* (or their equivalents) defined within the measures?

(c) How does each of the companies use the measures?

2 Log on to the Stern Stewart website at www.eva.com. From that page you can access a video online, which shows senior managers from a range of companies explaining their use of EVA®.

(a) Choose two companies from the video, and explain the advantages of EVA® for that company.

(b) Did any companies mention any problems that they experienced in adopting EVA®? Outline the problems.

3 Find a website that contains a report discussing the structure of remuneration packages for managers in a particular company.

(a) Describe the components of the remuneration package.

(b) What incentives are in place to provide certain motivational effects for the managers?

Questions

?

13.1 Define *return on investment* and describe its two components.

13.2 Explain why it is useful to focus on the two component ratios of the ROI calculation, rather than on the ROI ratio itself.

13.3 Explain how return on investment and residual income can be used as part of a responsibility accounting system.

13.4 Outline some positive outcomes that may occur if the manager of a manufacturing division is asked to improve the division's ROI.

13.5 Outline some negative consequences that may occur if the manager of a manufacturing division is asked to improve the division's ROI.

13.6 Outline some of the steps that can be taken to minimise the negative behavioural effects of ROI.

13.7 If there are so many difficulties associated with using ROI to evaluate the performance of investment centres, why do many businesses continue to use it?

13.8 Explain why ROI is not used to measure the performance of profit centre managers.

13.9 Prepare an example showing how residual income is calculated. What information used in this calculation is not used in calculating ROI?

13.10 Can the residual income measure eliminate all of the disadvantages associated with ROI? Explain your answer.

13.11 Why is there typically a rise in ROI or residual income over time? What dysfunctional decisions may be encouraged by this phenomenon?

13.12 Distinguish between the following measures of invested capital, and briefly explain when each should be used: (a) total assets (b) total productive assets (c) total assets less current liabilities

13.13 Why do some companies use gross book value instead of net book value to measure invested capital?

13.14 Does it matter how invested capital and profit are defined for the purposes of measuring ROI or residual income?

13.15 Explain the meaning of *value-based management* (VBM).

13.16 Describe each of the four aspects of VBM.

13.17 What is meant by *value* under VBM? Why is it important to measure it?

13.18 In your own words, outline negative strategies that managers might use to maximise economic value added.

13.19 Describe the measure of shareholder value added (SVA). How does it differ from EVA®?

13.20 Explain the difference between the imputed interest charge used in the calculation of residual income and the WACC used to calculate EVA.

13.21 Outline the differences between extrinsic and intrinsic motivation, and explain how intrinsic motivation can arise.

13.22 Distinguish between Herzberg's two-factor theory of motivation and expectancy theory.

13.23 What are the advantages and disadvantages of basing individual rewards on group performance?

13.24 What is a share option? Will the inclusion of share options in remuneration packages lead to extrinsic or intrinsic motivation?

13.25 Describe the difference between a gainsharing scheme and a profit-sharing plan.

13.26 Use principles of expectancy theory to compare the advantages and disadvantages of awarding individual bonuses based on group performance and on individual performance.

13.27 Which is better: rewards based on individual performance or rewards based on group performance? Explain your answer.

Exercises

E13.28 Return on investment; residual income

Classify each of the following statements as true or false. In each case, provide reasons for your answer.

1 Return on investment can be used to evaluate the return on new projects.
2 Return on investment provides a good measure of customer value.
3 As residual income increases, the balance of assets decreases.
4 Residual income can encourage managers to defer asset replacement.
5 Return on investment can be improved by deferring research and development expenditure and increasing marketing expenditure.

E13.29 Value-based management

Classify each of the following statements as true or false. In each case, provide reasons for your answer.

1 Value-based management is a method of increasing return on sales.
2 Economic value added is a multi-period measure.
3 Economic value added is equivalent to residual income.
4 The measure of economic value added has similar disadvantages to residual income.
5 Measures of shareholder value can be used to evaluate new business strategies, as well as mergers and acquisitions.

E13.30 Components of ROI; improving ROI; residual income: retailer

Office Go is a retailer that specialises in office supplies. It is a division of a large retail company. The following data relate to 20X7:

Profit	R8 000 000
Sales revenue	100 000 000
Average invested capital	40 000 000

Required:

1 Calculate Office Go's return on sales, investment turnover and return on investment for 20X7.
2 Demonstrate two ways in which the manager of Office Go could improve its ROI, increasing it to 25 per cent.

3 Assume that the retail company has a required rate of return of 10 per cent, and calculate the residual income for Office Go for 20X7.

E13.31 Improving ROI: manufacturer

The following data pertain to Merafong Mining Company, a producer of sand, gravel and cement, for 20X7:

Sales revenue	R6 000 000
Cost of goods sold	R3 300 000
Operating expenses	R2 400 000
Average invested capital	R3 000 000

Required:

1 Calculate the company's return on sales, investment turnover and ROI for 20X7.
2 If the sales and average invested capital remain the same in 20X8, to what level would total expenses have to be reduced in order to increase the firm's ROI to 15 per cent?
3 Assume that expenses are reduced, as calculated in requirement 2. Calculate the firm's return on sales. Show how the new return on sales and the old investment turnover together result in a ROI of 15 per cent in 20X8.

E13.32 ROI as a comparative performance measure

Assume that you have just been employed at Southern Coast Health Foods as an assistant accountant and you are concerned with the high level of reliance on ROI to evaluate and compare the performance of the three divisions of the company. You are aware that one division has assets that it purchased 10 years ago, and they now need replacement; the second division acquired its assets only three years ago; and the third division is the most profitable division and has relatively few assets.

Write a memo outlining any issues that you see with this situation. You might like to refer to Exhibit 13.2 to support your arguments.

E13.33 Comparing the performance of two divisions: retail company

Padstow Fabrics Ltd has two retail divisions, which reported the following results for 20X6:

	Furnishing Division	Dressmaking Division
Profit	R2 700 000	R600 000
Average invested capital	R18 000 000	R3 000 000
ROI	15%	20%

Required:

1 Which was the more successful division in 20X6? Think carefully about this, and explain your answer.
2 Calculate each division's residual income for 20X6 under each of the following assumptions about the firm's required rate of return:
(a) 15 per cent (b) 18 per cent (c) 22 per cent

E13.34 Weighted average cost of capital; ROI: service firm

The Williamstown Construction Company is a real estate developer and building contractor. The company has two sources of long-term capital: debt and equity. The cost of issuing debt is the after-tax cost of the interest that relates to the debt. (Interest paid on debt is tax deductible.) The cost of the company's equity capital is the investment opportunity rate of Williamstown's investors. This is the rate that investors could earn on investments that are of similar risk to Williamstown Construction. The interest rate on the company's R90 million of long-term debt is 10 per cent per annum, and the company's tax rate is 29 per cent. The cost of the company's equity capital is 15 per cent, and the market value (and the book value) of the company's equity is R135 million. The following data relate to the two divisions of the Williamstown Construction Company in 20X6:

	Total assets	Current liabilities	Operating profit before tax
Real Estate	R150 000 000	R9 000 000	R30 000 000
Construction	90 000 000	6 000 000	27 000 000

Required:

1 Calculate the weighted average cost of capital of Williamstown Construction Company.
2 Use the weighted average cost of capital to calculate the EVA® for each of the two divisions in 20X6.

E13.35 ROI and EVA®: service firm

Mbashe Rentals Ltd consists of two divisions. The Equipment Rental Division rents machinery, such as cement mixers and scissor lifts, to building contractors. The Truck Rental Division rents forklift trucks and removal trucks. The financial results for the two divisions in 20X6 are as follows:

	Equipment Rental Division R'000	Truck Rental Division R'000
Operating profit after tax	R22 500	R55 000
Total assets	375 000	1 500 000
Current liabilities	40 000	125 000

Mbashe Rentals obtains its financing from long-term debt and shares, and the weighted cost of capital is estimated to be 12 per cent. To calculate ROI, invested capital is defined as total assets less current liabilities.

Required:

1 Calculate the ROI for the two divisions for 20X6.
2 Calculate the EVA® for each division. Note that Mbashe Rentals does not make any adjustments to its NOPAT.
3 Which division has performed better in 20X6? Explain your answer.

E13.36 Performance measurement and reward systems

Classify each of the following statements as true or false. In each case give reasons for your answer.

1 According to Herzberg, employees need both hygiene factors and motivators to improve motivation.
2 Performance-related reward systems are most effective when rewards are provided for improved group performance.
3 An important reason for many performance-related pay systems not encouraging improved performance is that they are not linked to an effective performance measurement system.
4 Individual reward systems work better at the senior levels of an organisation rather than at the operational level.

E13.37 Reward systems: manufacturer

Grant Lawson has just been appointed as the new financial controller of Safety Chemicals Ltd, which has three separate divisions: Industrial Chemicals, Paints, and Household Chemicals. During his first week on the job, Lawson receives a visit from the managing director, who says:

I'm so glad you have arrived. We can now put into place our new profit-sharing plan. I want all employees across the divisions to share in the rewards of our good financial perform-

ance. Starting next quarter, 5 per cent of the company's quarterly profit will go into a pool, and at the end of the financial year, this will be distributed to employees in proportion to their base pay. This will really give our employees increased motivation to strive harder!

Required:

Write a memo to the managing director, outlining the advantages and disadvantages of the type of reward system that has been suggested.

Problems

P13.38 ROI; residual income: manufacturer

Lamington Industries has manufactured prefabricated houses for over 20 years. The houses are constructed in sections to be assembled on customers' lots. Lamington expanded into the pre-cut housing market in 20X1 when it acquired Ram Company, one of its suppliers. In this market, various types of timber are pre-cut into the appropriate lengths, banded into packages, and shipped to customers' lots for assembly. Lamington designated the Ram Division as an investment centre. Lamington uses return on investment (ROI) as a performance measure with investment defined as the average of the beginning and end of year assets. Management bonuses are based in part on ROI. All investments are expected to earn a minimum return of 15 per cent before income taxes. Ram's ROI has ranged from 19.3 to 22.1 per cent since it was acquired. Ram had an investment opportunity in 20X7 that had an estimated ROI of 18 per cent. Ram's management decided against the investment because it believed the investment would decrease the division's overall ROI. The 20X7 profit statement for Ram Division follows. The division's productive assets were R25 200 000 at the end of 20X7, a 5 per cent increase over the 20X6 year-end balance.

Ram Division
Profit Statement
for the year ended 31 December 20X7
(in R'000s)

Sales revenue		R48 000
Cost of goods sold		31 600
Gross margin		R16 400
Operating costs:		
Administrative	R4 280	
Selling	7 200	11 480
Profit from operations before income taxes		R4 920

Required:

1 Calculate the following performance measures for 20X7 for the Ram Division:
(a) return on investment (ROI) (b) residual income

2 Would the management of the Ram Division have been more likely to accept the investment opportunity if residual income had been used as a performance measure instead of ROI? Explain your answer.

(CMA, adapted)

P13.39 ROI and residual income; missing data: manufacturer

Papyrus Corporation has three divisions. The Plumbing Division manufactures copper pipes for tradespersons and home renovators. These areas of the economy are in decline.

The Plumbing Division is operating with spare capacity and is using machinery that was acquired many years ago. The Industrial Division produces pipes for heavy manufacturing industries involved in chemical refining and gas exploration. This division is machine-intensive, using advanced computerised equipment to manufacture pipes to precise tolerance levels. The Retail Division operates a hardware store. The following data relate to the three divisions. The company's required rate of return is 8 per cent.

	Plumbing Division	Industrial Division	Retail Division
Sales revenue	R40 000 000	?	?
Profit	R8 000 000	R1 600 000	?
Average investment	R10 000 000	?	?
Return on sales	?	20%	25%
Investment turnover	?	1.0 times	?
ROI	?	?	20%
Residual income	?	?	R480 000

Required:

1 Fill in the blanks in the data above.
2 Explain three ways in which the Industrial Division's manager could improve the division's ROI. Use numbers to illustrate these possibilities.
3 Suppose that the Retail Division's return on sales increased to 25 per cent, while its investment turnover remained constant. Calculate the division's new ROI.
4 Does ROI provide a suitable basis for comparing the performance of these three divisions? Explain your answer.

P13.40 ROI; EVA®: manufacturer

Raddington Industries produces tool and die machinery for car manufacturers. The company expanded in 20X2 by acquiring one of its suppliers of alloy steel plates, Reigis Steel Company. In order to manage the two separate businesses, the operations of Reigis are reported separately as an investment centre. Raddington monitors its divisions on the basis of both divisional contribution margin and return on investment (ROI). Investment is defined as average total assets. Management bonuses are based on ROI, but the company is considering using EVA® in the future. All investments in operating assets are expected to earn a minimum return of 11 per cent after income taxes.

Reigis' cost of goods sold is considered to be entirely variable, while the division's administrative costs are not dependent on volume. Selling costs are a semi-variable cost with 40 per cent attributed to sales volume. Reigis' ROI, after tax, has ranged from 11.8 to 14.7 per cent since 20X2. During 20X6 Reigis' management considered a project with an estimated ROI of 11.5 per cent. However, division management decided against the investment because it believed that it would decrease Reigis' overall ROI. The 20X6 profit statement for Reigis follows. The division's total assets were R15 750 000 on 31 December 20X6, a 5 per cent increase over the 20X5 year-end balance.

Reigis' funds are obtained from both debt and equity and the weighted average cost of capital is 10 per cent. The income tax rate is 28 per cent.

Reigis Steel Division
Profit Statement
for the year ended 31 December 20X6
(in R'000s)

Sales revenue		R25 000
Less costs:		
Cost of goods sold	R16 500	
Administrative costs	3 955	
Selling costs	2 700	23 155
Profit from operations before income taxes		R1 845

Required:

1 Calculate the divisional contribution margin for Reigis Steel Division, for the 1 484 000 units that were produced and sold during 20X6.
2 Calculate the following performance measures for 20X6 for the Reigis Steel Division: (a) after-tax return on investment (ROI) (b) economic value added (EVA®)
3 Would the management of the Reigis Steel Division be more likely to accept the project that was considered in 20X6 if EVA® rather than ROI was used as a performance measure?
4 The Reigis Steel Division is a separate investment centre within Raddington Industries. Identify several items that Reigis' management should have authorisation to control if it is to be evaluated fairly by either ROI or EVA®.
5 Calculate Reigis Steel Division's contribution margin per unit in 20X6. Briefly discuss the pros and cons of using divisional contribution margin versus the contribution margin per unit as a divisional performance measure.

(CMA, adapted)

P13.41 ROI and residual income; evaluation of new investment: retailer

Megamarket is a retailer of electrical products and has four divisions. At the end of each year the four divisional managers are evaluated and bonuses are awarded based on ROI. Last year, the company as a whole produced an ROI of 13 per cent.

During the past week, management of the company's Bloem Electrical Division was approached about the possibility of buying the operations of a competitor, SuperEl, which wished to cease its retail operations. The following data relate to recent performance of the Bloem Electrical Division and SuperEl.

	Bloem	SuperEl
Sales	R42 000 000	R26 000 000
Variable costs	70% of sales	65% of sales
Fixed costs	R10 750 000	R8 350 000
Invested capital	R9 250 000	R3 125 000

If the acquisition occurs, the operations of SuperEl will be absorbed into the Bloem Electrical Division. The operations of SuperEl will need to be upgraded to meet the high standards of Megamarket, which would require an additional R1 875000 of invested capital.

Required:

1 Calculate the current ROI and residual income of the Bloem Electrical Division and the ROI of the division if SuperEl is acquired.
2 What is the likely reaction of divisional management towards the acquisition? Why?
3 What is the likely reaction of Megamarket's corporate management to the acquisition? Explain why.
4 Would the division be better off if it did not upgrade the operation of SuperEl to Megamarket's standards? Show calculations to support your answer.
5 Assume that Megamarket uses residual income to evaluate performance and desires a 12 per cent minimum return on invested capital. Calculate the current residual income of the division and the division's residual income. Will divisional management be likely to change its attitude towards the acquisition? Explain why.

P13.42 ROI versus residual income; incentives; bonus schemes: manufacturer

Fun Time Company (FTC) is a subsidiary of New Age Industries. FTC manufactures go-carts, water skis and motorised scooters. With the increasing popularity of electronic arcade games, New Age has been encouraging FTC to diversify into some of these other recreational areas. Arcade Unlimited Ltd (AUL) is a large manufacturer of arcade games and it is looking for a friendly buyer. New Age's top management believes that AUL's assets could be acquired for an investment of only R16 million and has strongly urged Will Kelly, the divisional manager of FTC, to consider acquiring AUL.

Kelly has reviewed the financial statement of AUL and he believes that the acquisition may not be in the best interests of FTC. However, he knows that if he does not acquire AUL, New Age management is not going to be at all pleased! Kelly exclaims to his divisional management team: 'If only we could convince them to base our bonuses on something other than ROI.'

New Age has always evaluated the divisions on the basis of ROI, and the target ROI for each division is 20 per cent. The management team of any division that reports an annual increase in their ROI is given a bonus, but the managers of divisions where the ROI declines must provide a very convincing explanation as to why they should get a bonus. Where ROI has declined, the bonus is limited to only 50 per cent of the bonus that is paid to the divisions that report an increase in ROI.

The following data relate to the most recent financial year:

	FTC	AUL
Sales revenue	R15 500 000	R47 500 000
Less:		
Variable expenses	−6 500 000	−30 000 000
Fixed expenses	−6 000 000	−7 500 000
Operating profit	3 000 000	10 000 000
Current assets	9 500 000	11 500 000
Long-term assets	5 500 000	28 500 000
Total assets	15 000 000	40 000 000
Current liabilities	4 250 000	7 000 000
Long-term liability	6 000 000	19 000 000
Shareholders' equity	4 750 000	14 000 000
Total liabilities and equity	15 000 000	40 000 000

Required:

1 Explain why FTC may be reluctant to acquire AUL. Provide calculations.
2 If New Age were to use residual income to measure divisional performance and evaluate managers, would FTC be more likely to acquire AUL? Provide calculations.
3 Comment on the current bonus scheme and outline two other schemes that New Age could use to deliver bonuses to divisional managers.

(CMA adapted)

P13.43 Behavioural implications of ROI: computer-integrated manufacturer

Mkhondo Ltd made a capital investment of R100m in new equipment for its Sandman Division two years ago. The analysis at that time indicated that the equipment would save R35m in operating expenses per year over a five-year period. Discounted cash flow methods were used to evaluate the proposal. Before the purchase, the division's ROI was 20 per cent.

Tim Namusi, the division manager, believed that the equipment had lived up to its expectations. However, the divisional performance report showed that the overall return on investment for the first year in which the equipment was used was less than that in the previous year! Namusi asked the Accounting Department to break down the figures related to this investment to find out why it did not contribute to improving the division's ROI.

The Accounting Department was able to identify the equipment's contribution to the division's operations. The report presented to the division manager at the end of the first year is as follows:

Reduced operating costs due to new equipment	R35m
Less depreciation, 20% of cost	20m
Contribution	R15m
Investment, beginning of year	100m
Investment, end of year	80m
Average investment for the year	90m

ROI = 15/90 = 16.7%

Tim Namusi was surprised that the ROI was so low, because the new equipment performed as expected. The staff analyst in the Accounting Department replied that the ROI used for performance evaluation differed from the methods used to evaluate capital investment proposals.

Required:

1 Explain why the new equipment has not resulted in the expected improvement in financial performance.
2 Discuss the behavioural problems that can be associated with using ROI as a divisional performance measure. What might Tim Namusi do the next time a new equipment purchase is proposed?

(CMA, adapted)

P13.44 Weighted average cost of capital; EVA; ROI; performance report: agricultural company

Gum Leaf Ltd is a forestry company and has three divisions: Retail Plantations, Pine Forests and Large Growth Forests. The company obtains its capital from debt and equity. The interest rate on Gum Leaf's R400 million debt is 9 per cent per annum, and the company pays 30 per cent income tax. The cost of Gum Leaf's equity capital is 12 per cent, and the market value of the equity is R600 million. The book value of equity is only R430 million, but this does not reflect the current value of the company assets, which include some unrecorded intangibles. The following data (in millions) relate to the three divisions:

	Operating profit before tax	Current liabilities	Total assets
Retail Plantations	R14	R6	R70
Pine Forests	45	5	300
Large Growth Forest	48	9	480

Required:

1 Calculate Gum Leaf's weighted average cost of capital.
2 Calculate the EVA for each division, as well as the ROI.
3 Write a brief report evaluating the company's performance and the relative performance of each division.

P13.45 ROI and performance evaluation: manufacturer

Wash and Wear Industries manufactures a range of household products. Roger Wilkie is head of the Hardware Division and he has just experienced a terrible nine months. 'If it could go wrong it did. Sales are down, profits are down, inventories are out of control and I am starting to get worried about my job.'

Wilkie's performance is based on his division's ROI. The following data relate to the past nine months:

Sales	R7 200 000
Operating profit	540 000
Invested capital	9 000 000

In an effort to make something out of nothing and to salvage the current year's performance, Wilkie is considering some of the following strategies:

1 Write off and discard R90 000 of obsolete inventory.
2 Accelerate the collection of R120 000 of overdue customer accounts receivable.
3 Stop advertising for the next three months and reduce expenditure on repairs and maintenance. This will save the division R225 000.
4 Acquire two competitors that are expected to have the following financial characteristics:

	Projected sales	Projected operating expenses	Projected invested capital
Abacus	R4 500 000	R3 600 000	R7 500 000
Palamino	6 750 000	6 180 000	7 125 000

Required:

1 Calculate ROI and the two component ratios for the Hardware Division for the last nine months.
2 Evaluate the first two strategies, by considering their effect on the division's last nine months' performance. Should these strategies be adopted?
3 Evaluate the third strategy. Should it be adopted?
4 Calculate the ROI of the investment in Abacus and then in Palamino. Should Wash and Wear reject both acquisitions, acquire one or acquire both? Assume that there is sufficient capital available to fund both investments.

P13.46 Review of Chapters 12 and 13; ROI and EVA®; centralised versus decentralised service units: service company

Twelve Apostles Fisheries operates a chain of budget seafood restaurants, as well as its own fishing fleet, which operates off the south coast of South Africa. Twelve Apostles is structured into three divisions: the Northern Division and the Southern Division, which manage the restaurants, and the Fishing Fleet Division. Each division operates as a separate standalone business, and is designated as an investment centre.

The company uses return on investment to evaluate the performance of each division. For the purposes of calculating divisional ROI, investment capital is defined as total assets less current liabilities, and divisional operating profit after tax is used. Each division is required to achieve an ROI of at least 9 per cent after tax. To calculate divisional EVA® the weighted average cost of capital of 8 per cent is used. The company income tax rate is 29 per cent.

The following data relate to financial performance for 20X7:

	Southern Division	Northern Division	Fishing Fleet Division
Operating profit before tax	R18 000 000	R4 000 000	R3 000 000
Total assets	175 000 000	20 000 000	84 000 000
Current liabilities	40 000 000	10 000 000	8 000 000

In 20X5, the Fishing Fleet Division replaced most of its fleet. The Southern Division is the oldest division and owns all of its assets, while the Northern Division leases most of its restaurant sites. The lease payments are treated as an expense.

Required:

1 Calculate the return on investment for each division for 20X7.
2 Which division has the best performance in 20X7? Is there any other information in the case that needs to be taken into account when interpreting divisional performance using ROI?
3 Calculate the EVA® for each division for 20X7.
4 Compare the financial performance of each division using both ROI and EVA®.

5 Would you recommend any adjustments to the divisional accounting data, to provide figures for ROI and EVA® that can be more readily compared?

Cases

C13.47 Review of Chapters 12 and 13; divisional performance reporting and evaluation; ethics

Huis Corporation is a major producer of prefabricated low-cost houses. The corporation consists of two divisions: the Bell Division, which acquires the raw materials to manufacture the basic house components and assembles them into kits, and the Cornish Division, which takes the kits and constructs the homes for final home buyers. The corporation is decentralised, and the performance of the management of each division is measured by divisional profit and return on investment.

Bell Division assembles seven separate house kits using raw materials purchased at the prevailing market prices. The seven kits are sold to Cornish for prices ranging from R45 000 to R98 000. The prices are set by Huis's corporate management using prices paid by Cornish when it buys comparable units from outside sources.

The smaller kits with the lower prices have become the larger portion of the units sold, because the final house buyer is faced with prices that are increasing more rapidly than personal income. The kits are manufactured and assembled in a new plant just purchased by Bell this year. The division had been located in a leased plant for the past four years.

All kits are assembled upon receipt of an order from the Cornish Division. When the kit is completely assembled, it is loaded immediately onto a Cornish truck. Thus, Bell Division has no finished goods inventory.

Bell Division's accounts and reports are prepared on an actual cost basis. There is no budget, and standards have not been developed for any product. A manufacturing overhead rate is calculated at the beginning of each year. The rate is designed to charge all overhead to the production each year. Any underapplied or overapplied overhead is closed into the cost of goods sold account.

Bell Division's annual performance report follows below. This report forms the basis of the evaluation of the division and its management.

Bell Division
Performance report
for the year ending 31 December 20X6

			Increase (decrease from 20X5)	
Summary data	**20X6**	**20X5**	**Amount**	**Per cent change**
Net profit (in R000)	34 222	31 573	2 649	8.4%
Return on investment	37%	43%	−6%	−14.0%
Production data				
Kits started	2 400	1 600	800	50.0%
Kits shipped	2 000	2 100	−100	−4.8%
Kits in process at year-end	700	300	400	133.3%
Increase (decrease) in kits in process at year-end	400	−500		
Financial data (in R000s)				
Sales revenue	138 000	162 800	−24 800	−15.2%
Production cost of units sold:				
Direct material	32 000	40 000	−8 000	−20.0%
Direct labour	41 700	53 000	−11 300	−21.3%
Manufacturing overhead	29 000	37 000	−8 000	−21.6%
Cost of units sold	102 700	130 000	−27 300	−21.0%
Other costs:				
Corporate charges for:				
Personnel services	228	210	18	8.6%
Accounting services	425	440	−15	−3.4%
Financing costs	300	525	−225	−42.9%
Total other costs	953	1175	−222	−18.9%
Adjustment to profit:				
Unreimbursed fire loss	0	52	−52	−100.0%
Raw material losses due to improper storage	125	0	125	–
Total adjustments	125	52	73	140.4%
Total deductions	103 778	131 227	−27 449	−20.9%
Divisional profit	34 222	31 573	2 649	8.4%
Divisional investment	92 000	73 000	19 000	26.0%
Return on investment (ROI)	37%	43%	−6%	−14.0%

Additional information regarding corporate and divisional practices follows:

- The corporation head office does all the personnel and accounting work for each division.
- Corporate personnel costs are allocated to divisions on the basis of the number of employees in each division.
- Accounting costs are allocated to divisions on the basis of total costs, excluding corporate charges.
- Divisional administration costs are included in overhead.
- The financing charges include a corporate imputed interest charge on divisional assets.
- The divisional investment for the ROI calculation includes divisional inventory and plant and equipment at gross book value.

Required:

1 Discuss the value of the annual performance report presented for the Bell Division in evaluating the division and its management in terms of:
(a) the accounting techniques employed in the measurement of divisional activities;
(b) the manner of presentation;
(c) the effectiveness with which it discloses differences and similarities between years.
Use the information in the problem to illustrate your answer.

2 Present specific recommendations for the management of Huis Corporation that would improve its accounting and financial reporting system.

3 Suppose that Bell Division's chief accountant, Jake Thompson, was approached on 28 December by the divisional general manager with the following request:

Jake, we've got a firm order for 50 kits that won't be finished and shipped until 8 January. I want you to book the sale before the end of the year. The total sales figure on the order is R850 000. That will bump this year's net profit up over R35 000 000. The division will look better, and we'll all get a bonus.

What are Jake Thompson's ethical obligations in this situation?

(*CMA, adapted*)

C13.48 Financial performance measures and reward systems; behavioural issues: manufacturer
Motheo Ltd is a large and successful manufacturer of engines. The company consists of two divisions: the Automotive Engine Division and the Outboard Motor Division. Motheo has recently acquired a new company which will become a third division. The new Couch Division is a small manufacturer of lawnmower motors. It has been owned and managed by one person for 40 years. The prior owner treated all employees as part of his family. The company was noted for the lack of a 'them and us' attitude between employees and management, and there was free and open communication between all staff. Unfortunately, Couch is not a strong performer; the lawnmower market is in decline and profits have slipped.

Motheo is known for its modern management systems and would like all managers at Couch to participate in the performance-related pay system that is used in the other two divisions. The profit-sharing plan applies to senior divisional managers only. It is based on placing 10 per cent of Motheo's profits before interest and income tax into a pool, which is then shared by the senior divisional managers in direct proportion to their base salaries. The senior managers in the two original divisions received bonuses of 11 per cent and 12 per cent of their salaries in 20X5 and 20X6 respectively.

The profit results for 20X7, the first financial year following the acquisition of the Couch Division, are as follows:

	Outboard	Automotive	Couch
Sales revenue	80 000 000	100 000 000	20 000 000
Cost of goods sold	−40 000 000	−60 000 000	−15 000 000
Gross margin	40 000 000	40 000 000	5 000 000
Administrative costs	−12 000 000	−9 000 000	−3 000 000
Marketing and selling costs	−16 000 000	−9 000 000	−1 000 000
Total costs	−28 000 000	−18 000 000	−4 000 000
Profit before interest and taxes	12 000 000	22 000 000	1 000 000

Senior management salaries included in the above costs, and divisional assets at the end of 20X7, are as follows:

	Outboard	Automotive	Couch
Senior management salaries	20 000 000	14 000 000	7 000 000
Divisional assets	40 000 000	40 000 000	8 000 000

Prior to the acquisition by Motheo, all Couch employees, including the senior managers, participated in a gainsharing program. Under this program, the financial impact of improvements in labour productivity and delivery performance were quantified each quarter, and 50 per cent of this amount was accumulated in a pool. At the end of each year, each employee received an equal share of the pool. The scheme was discontinued when Motheo purchased Couch.

Required:

1 Which division has the best performance in 20X7?
2 Determine the bonus pool available for 20X7, and calculate the percentage bonus that each senior manager would receive.
3 Discuss the behavioural problems that could arise among the senior managers of the Outboard and Automotive divisions as a result of the 20X7 bonuses.
4 Discuss the behavioural problems that may arise within the Couch Division from the changes in the performance-related pay system.
5 Suggest some changes that could be made to improve Motheo's performance-related pay system and alleviate some of the problems identified in requirements 3 and 4.

C13.49 Analysing financial performance and evaluating alternative strategies, including outsourcing and closure

African Business School (Pty) Ltd ('ABS') is a registered training organisation that operates from three training sites in Irene (close to Pretoria), Magaliesburg and Randburg. ABS focuses on providing one- to three-day courses on managerial development topics to middle and senior management personnel. Courses are held during weekdays and facilities are closed over weekends. ABS leases the three training sites.

The Irene and Randburg training sites can accommodate a maximum of 30 people per day and the Magaliesburg site 40 people per day. Standard course rates are charged per person per day and there is no difference in the daily prices for one-, two- and three-day courses. The Magaliesburg training site is situated on the outskirts of the town of Magaliesburg within a small game reserve. The facility includes a lodge that can accommodate training course attendees overnight. Attendees on two- and three-day courses stay over at the lodge and all meals are included in the course rates. This site currently charges such attendees an extra R400 per night for meals and accommodation. The land on which the lodge and training site are situated is leased from the owners of the game reserve. The lease has recently been renewed for a further ten years.

The head office of ABS is responsible for scheduling of courses, marketing, finance and administration. The head office is situated on the Randburg site and the allocation of rent and related fixed overheads is based on the relative floor space occupied by the head office and the Randburg training facility. Salient information regarding the operational and financial performance of the three training sites and the lodge for the year ended 28 February 20X6 is summarised below:

African Business School (Pty) Ltd
Financial information for the year ended 28 February 20X6

	Notes	Irene training site	Randburg training site	Magaliesburg training site	Magaliesburg lodge
		R	R	R	R
Revenue		1 215 000	2 025 000	2 160 000	1 052 000
Course fees	1	1 215 000	2 025 000	2 160 000	0
Accommodation and meals		0	0	0	800 000
Bar revenue	2	0	0	0	252 000
Operating costs		−1 322 488	−1 760 980	−1 670 645	−1 225 887
Variable expenses	3	−172 125	−273 375	−360 000	−397 500
Fixed costs	4	−925 000	−1 112 000	−910 000	−680 000
Head office costs	5	−225 363	−375 605	−400 645	−148 387
Operating profit/(loss)		−107 488	264 020	489 355	−173 887

Notes:

1 The course fee per person per day during the 20X6 financial year was R600 at all ABS training venues. The number of people who attended courses during 20X6 and site capacities are set out below:

	Irene training site	Randburg training site	Magaliesburg training site
Maximum number of days available for training in the 20X6 financial year	225	225	225
Maximum number of people who could have attended courses in 20X6	6 750	6 750	9 000
Actual number of people attending training courses			
One-day courses	1 425	1 695	240
Two-day courses	150	420	720
Three-day courses	100	280	640

2 The lodge marks up alcohol and beverages sold in its bar by 60 per cent.

3 Variable costs at the training sites include costs of hiring external presenters, course materials and refreshments served during courses. ABS employs a limited number of presenters at each training site on a permanent basis and contracts with external presenters for specific courses as required. Variable costs at the lodge comprise the costs of alcohol and beverages, and catering costs.

4 Fixed costs in the 20X6 financial year were made up as follows:

	Irene training site	Randburg training site	Magaliesburg training site	Magaliesburg lodge	Head Office
Administration and finance costs	0	0	0	0	680 000
Cleaning costs	90 000	95 000	85 000	165 000	75 000
Kitchen staff salaries and overheads	0	0	0	275 000	0
Bar staff salaries	0	0	0	60 000	0
Marketing expenses	0	0	0	0	80 000
Rental of premises	215 000	235 000	115 000	105 000	85 000
Presenter salaries	450 000	510 000	590 000	0	0
Scheduling costs	0	0	0	0	230 000
Other fixed costs	170 000	272 000	120 000	75 000	0
	925 000	1 112 000	910 000	680 000	1 150 000

5 Head office costs were fully allocated to each training site and the lodge in 20X6 based on each site's revenue (excluding bar revenue) as a percentage of total ABS revenue.

ABS has been under pressure from the shareholders because of the performance of the company over the last three years. At the last shareholders' meeting, management was requested to identify and explore strategies to improve the financial performance of the company.

Management has subsequently identified the following three strategies for improving profitability:

- Closing the Irene training venue,
- Outsourcing the catering at the Magaliesburg training facility, and
- Using the Magaliesburg site as a wedding venue over weekends.

Option 1 Closing the Irene training venue

As the Irene site seems to be the least profitable, management is investigating the implications of closing this training facility, based on two possibilities: The first is to close the facility completely, and the second is that the University of Pretoria (UP) operate the facility on behalf of ABS.

Courses currently offered at Irene could be offered at the Randburg site, and initial feedback indicates that 75 per cent of ABS clients would attend courses at Randburg if the Irene site were closed. Other relevant information relating to the potential closure of the Irene training facility:

- The presenters currently employed in Irene could be offered positions at Randburg;
- The rental agreement for the Irene premises expires on 28 February 20X7;
- The estimated costs of retrenching employees at Irene, excluding presenters, would be R200 000; and
- Other site closure costs would amount to R75 000.

The UP has offered to operate the Irene training site on behalf of ABS. UP will assume full operational responsibility for the site including marketing, course scheduling, finance and administration. In addition, UP will pay all operational expenses associated with the site, except for head office charges, and will collect course fees directly from attendees. Apart from course presenters the current Irene employees will be employed by UP. ABS will retrench the presenters at Irene at a total cost of R350 000.

Essentially ABS will provide course material to UP and allow them to operate the training site as an ABS facility. In return, UP will pay ABS a fee amounting to 5 per cent of course revenue. UP has undertaken to charge the same course fee per person per day as is charged at other ABS sites.

Option 2 Outsourcing of the catering at Magaliesburg lodge

Management also investigated the possibility of outsourcing the catering at the lodge. Though the catering is of a very high standard and receives mostly positive comments on course evaluations, management is of the opinion that the costs of providing this service are too high. Brilliant Catering has made the following proposal for taking over the catering and bar functions on an exclusive basis at the lodge:

- Existing kitchen and bar staff will be offered employment by Brilliant Catering. Employees who refuse the offer will be retrenched by ABS. If no employee accepts the Brilliant Catering offer, the estimated retrenchment cost will amount to R230 000.
- Accommodation functions at the lodge will remain the responsibility of ABS.
- If Brilliant Catering takes over the catering and the bar, and kitchen and bar staff elect to join Brilliant Catering, the fixed costs at the lodge payable by ABS will decrease by an estimated R325 000 per annum.
- ABS will continue to pay rental for the premises as well as the fixed overheads associated with provision of accommodation facilities.
- Brilliant Catering will charge ABS a fixed fee of R125 per person per day for meals provided. Brilliant Catering will operate the bar for profit and amounts spent by attendees on alcohol and beverages will be recovered from ABS, who in turn will recover it from attendees.

Option 3 Using the Magaliesburg lodge as a wedding venue

As ABS does not use the Magaliesburg training site and lodge over weekends, management is keen to investigate the possibility of using the facilities as a wedding venue. However, the facilities will need to be upgraded and expanded to make them suitable for this purpose. An initial estimate from a reputable building contractor put the alteration cost at R1 250 000. These alterations would enable the lodge to cater for wedding parties of up to 200 guests. The management of ABS has consulted with various wedding planners and the consensus is that the upgraded Magaliesburg facility could be hired out for 30 weddings in a normal calendar year.

Required:

1 Critically analyse and discuss the financial performance of the training sites and the lodge during the 20X6 financial year.
2 Advise the management of ABS, with reasons, on the most appropriate strategy with regard to the Irene training site namely:

- to continue operating the Irene training site on the current basis,
- to close the site, or
- to outsource the operations to the University of Pretoria.

Your answer should include the financial considerations involved in each alternative as well as any other factors to be considered before making a final decision.

(South African Institute of Chartered Accountants QE)

Endnotes

1 EVA® is a registered trademark of the consulting company Stern Stewart & Co. (which developed the measure) in South Africa, the US and other countries.

2 We have structured the examples using products and processes from the aluminium industry. We have also used terms likely to be consistent with the investment centre activities of a company such as BHP Billiton; however, the issues and circumstances are illustrative only and bear no resemblance to any of the actual financial data of that company.

3 Within the ROI formula, invested capital can also be called total assets or investment.

4 This formula is derived from the following:
EVA® = (rate of return − cost of capital) × capital employed
= (rate of return × capital employed) − (cost of capital × capital employed)
Given that the rate of return on capital employed = net profit after tax/capital employed
rate of return × capital employed = net profit after tax
therefore EVA® = net operating profit after tax − (capital employed × weighted average cost of capital).

5 Stern Stewart & Co., the consulting firm that developed EVA® (Stewart, 1991), states that in practice only a few adjustments are typically undertaken. These include capitalising research and development expenditure and operating lease expenses, and adding back amortisation of goodwill. The accounting standards have now caught up with Stern Stewart and goodwill is no longer required to be amortised. We will see what will happen with operating leases in the future.

6 Alternatively, one may add back current year's depreciation to NOPAT resulting in COPAT, after-tax cash operating profit, but then to obtain FCF, one must subtract gross new investment from COPAT.

7 I is net new investment, the change in total capital, Δ TC.

8 The calculation of present value is described in Chapter 21.

9 See De Cieri et al. (2003) for more details of performance-related pay.

10 The share price of Shoprite increased from about R6 in 2002 to R25 in 2006. This represents an annual compound return of 43 per cent per year. Perhaps Mr Basson deserved his payment. Yet if you had bought Shoprite at its high point of R13 in 1997, the annual return over the nine years would have amounted to a much more modest 7.5 per cent per year (excluding dividends). Mr Whitey Basson was CEO of Shoprite then and now.

11 '*Fair Pay: How to ensure executives are remunerated fairly*', by Joel Stern, *FinWeek*, 2 November 2006, p.34.

12 Refer to Deloitte website, www.deloitte.co.za., under the newsroom section, and see the *press release* entitled *New Age Incentive Schemes,* issued on 18 September 2006.

Contemporary Approaches to Measuring and Managing Performance

❖ LEARNING OBJECTIVES

After completing this chapter, you should be able to:

1. recognise the various purposes of performance measurement systems and the role of these systems in enhancing customer value and shareholder value;
2. explain why conventional financial measures are not sufficient for managing an organisation;
3. describe the characteristics of contemporary approaches to performance measurement;
4. explain the advantages that non-financial performance measures offer over financial measures, as well as the problems;
5. describe the four perspectives of the Kaplan and Norton (1996) balanced scorecard;
6. demonstrate the causal linkages within the balanced scorecard;
7. explain the relationships between lead and lag indicators;
8. formulate a balanced scorecard for an organisation, selecting objectives, and lead and lag measures for each of the four perspectives;
9. complete a Du Pont chart, to link non-financial measures to financial measures and performance;
10. describe the basic steps of benchmarking and understand how benchmarking can improve competitiveness;
11. outline the major warning signs of an inadequate performance measurement system;
12. describe the criteria for designing effective performance measurement systems; and
13. outline the issues that are relevant to selecting performance measures in service organisations.

14 Introduction

Performance measurement systems measure performance of areas of the business (or individuals) by comparing performance with some target. These systems are an essential part of the planning and control process, and may help managers to assess the value added by the various operations and activities in which they engage. In this chapter, we explain that many organisations use performance measurement systems that go beyond the measurement of financial performance. These contemporary approaches to performance measurement may entail placing a greater emphasis on non-financial measures, implementing balanced scorecards, and using benchmarking techniques to manage resources better and hence improve performance.

The purposes of performance measurement

L.O. 1

In Chapter 12 we saw that responsibility accounting provides the foundation for planning and control, and that performance measurement is a key aspect of responsibility accounting. Let's consider the many ways in which performance measures can be used within a planning and control system:

- Performance measures can be used to *communicate the strategy and plans of the business and align employees' goals* with those of the organisation. Thus, a wisely designed performance measurement system can encourage goal congruence.
- Managers use performance measures to *track their performance against targets*. This feedback allows managers at all levels of the business to assess progress in achieving targets, and to take corrective actions if necessary. It may also indicate the need to amend plans and targets when there have been changes in the internal or external environment of the business.
- Reporting performance allows managers to *identify problem areas*. This can occur at all levels of the business. This is of greater value if actual performance is compared with some benchmark, which may be a budgeted target or an external benchmark.
- Senior managers may use performance measures to *evaluate subordinates' performance* and as the *basis for rewards*. Enterprises need a range of performance measures that reflect their competitive environment and strategies, to ensure that managers are motivated and rewarded for achieving the 'things that matter'.
- Performance measures may be used by senior managers to *guide them in developing future strategies and operations*. Performance measures should not just inform managers of the outcomes of past decisions and operations; they should give an indication of the capability of the firm to compete effectively in the future and point to areas for future growth.

Conventional performance measurement

L.O. 2

The financial performance measures used in typical conventional management accounting systems were described in Chapters 12 and 13 and are outlined in Exhibit 14.1. You will notice that the measures focus on profit and its components, revenues and costs. Performance measurement systems like these have been used for many decades. Profitability is the ultimate goal for most business owners. Profit performance is watched by owners, the financial markets and creditors, and therefore it must be important to managers too.

However, over the past decade we have seen many companies change their performance measurement systems, often broadening the focus away from financial measures. Why has this happened?

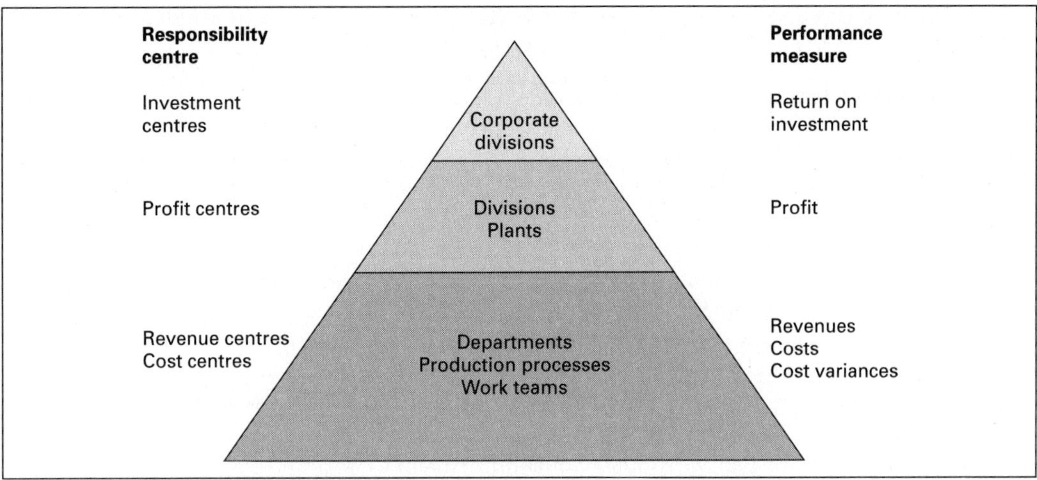

Exhibit 14.1 Conventional financial performance measures

Problems with conventional financial performance measures

1 *Conventional financial performance measures are not actionable.* Why are measures of profit, and its components, costs and revenues, not useful in controlling the business? It is because they describe consequences, not causes. They describe what has happened, not *why* it has happened. They are too aggregated and they do not tell operational managers what needs fixing.[1] Also, financial measures are often reported at the end of each month, so they are not timely. Businesses cannot afford to wait that long.

2 *Financial performance measures emphasise only one perspective of performance.* Businesses need to manage the determinants of future financial performance, and this is where strategy plays a role. Top management determines the strategies that will be implemented to enable the business to achieve long-term goals. Managers need a performance measurement system that assesses how well they perform across the full range of strategically important areas, such as quality and delivery performance, as well as cost.

3 *Financial performance measures provide limited guidance for future actions.* Financial measures do not allow managers to assess areas that need to be developed in the future for the organisation to be successful in the long term. For example, to ensure future growth, managers need to determine how effectively they have invested in areas such as new product development, development of staff, and actions to ensure customer loyalty. Financial measures report only on the immediate financial outcomes of actions and decisions.

4 *Financial performance measures may encourage actions that decrease both shareholder and customer value.* Financial performance measures may encourage managers to achieve short-term financial performance at the expense of long-term performance. This happens particularly when there is excessive pressure on managers to achieve short-term profit improvements, and where remuneration systems are closely tied to short-term profit achievement. For example, managers can improve short-term performance by reducing expenditure on new product development, quality initiatives, human resource development (including training), information systems, and customer and market developments. While these spending cuts cause an immediate increase in profits, they can seriously erode future profits and growth potential, and thus decrease shareholder value. Retaining outdated technology and systems can reduce competitiveness, and a lack of attention to

products, customers and the market can lead to a reduction in customer value and customer loyalty, leaving a company open to competitive threats.

These limitations arise largely from the particular orientation of financial performance measurement systems – they focus on the outcomes of past actions, not on the determinants of outcomes. However, to improve performance, managers at all levels need to manage the determinants of performance. Consider performance in sport. Let's say Arsenal are beaten by Chelsea in a Premiership match. The score is Chelsea 2, Arsenal 0. The score is the ultimate result and is of crucial interest to the clubs' supporters; it is the outcome of the teams' actions. However, it is not particularly useful to the Arsenal coach. He needs to know why Arsenal lost. Arsenal aimed to play short passes wherever possible to keep the game flowing freely. They aimed to minimise free kicks given away and maximise free kicks received. They planned to drive the ball through the centre of the ground rather than using the wings. These were the team's strategies. So the Arsenal coach needs to know the number of corners, how many free kicks were given and received, and how many passes and kicks went through the players in the centre of the ground compared with the number that went through the players on the wings. A strategy might have been to retain possession as much as possible. What percentage possession did the team retain during the game? These performance measures will help the coach to assess how well the team performed. Then he can determine which areas need improving. If the team performed well in each of the measures and still lost, then he needs to consider new tactics that will drive improved performance.

Performance measurement in not-for-profit organizations

The financial measures described in Exhibit 14.1 are used by businesses that have profitability as their primary goal, but may not always be appropriate for not-for-profit organisations. For example, the goals of many public sector organisations and private not-for-profit enterprises focus on social factors, such as client welfare, rather than on profit, and their performance measurement systems tend to monitor effectiveness in these areas. However, even in these organisations financial management is important, and some financial measures, such as costs, will be monitored. The criticisms of conventional financial performance measures may be just as relevant in not-for-profit organisations, as are some of the new approaches to performance measurement, described below.

Contemporary performance measurement systems

L.O. 3

We have discussed the limitations of conventional financial performance measurement systems in assisting managers to focus on both customer value and shareholder value, and noted that many organisations have broadened their performance measurement system. What are the characteristics of contemporary performance measurement systems? Contemporary performance measurement systems often have the following features:

- *Non-financial and financial measures.* Contemporary performance measurement systems include a range of financial and non-financial performance measures. Non-financial measures have been used for many decades, particularly at the operational levels, but they have not always been part of the formal performance measurement system. For example, manufacturing managers may have 'privately' measured the quality of their production processes, and sales managers may have monitored customer satisfaction. However, those managers may have been evaluated using financial measures such as cost and sales revenue.
- *A strategic orientation.* Performance measures may be selected to directly measure areas that provide competitive advantage and that increase customer and shareholder value. This entails monitoring performance in those areas that the organisation believes to be critical to the long-term success of the business, such as quality, innovation, customer satisfaction and delivery, as well as cost.

- *External benchmarks.* Contemporary performance measurement systems often use external benchmarks to provide an indication of whether performance is as good as that of competitors, or of best practice companies. In conventional performance measurement systems it is common to compare actual performance with last year's performance, or with budget targets that have been set within the organisation. However, this does not provide any assurance that the business' performance is good enough.
- *Continuous improvement.* Contemporary performance measurement systems often build continuous improvement into performance targets and into the way performance is measured. This may involve making performance targets more challenging over time, and measuring performance more precisely.

In the following sections we will elaborate on all of these features.

Non-financial measures for operational control

L.O. 4

If conventional performance measures are not actionable and have the wrong perspective, this must be obvious to the managers and other employees who use them. How have they responded? For a number of years, managers, particularly operational managers, have often supplemented conventional financial performance measures with their own non-financial performance measures.

What advantages do non-financial performance measures offer over financial measures?

- Non-financial measures can reflect the *drivers of future financial performance.* For example, managers may consider that improved quality and customer satisfaction will flow through to improved financial performance.
- They are *more actionable.* For example, it is easier for operational managers to investigate the sources of product defects and customer complaints than it is to investigate cost variances, as defects and customer complaints relate more directly to activities and operations.
- They are *more understandable and easier to relate to,* particularly at the operational level. Shopfloor employees may find it easier to understand the meaning of 'rejects per 100 units' or 'number of delivery days', compared with variable overhead cost variances.

We will now describe how managers at a major auto manufacturer used operational performance measures to help manage performance.

Performance measurement at an auto manufacturer

In the 1990s managers of a major auto manufacturer were surveyed to identify what measures they used to evaluate performance in their areas of responsibility. The results are shown in Exhibit 14.2. The company has a very sophisticated standard costing system that reports detailed cost variances right down to the shopfloor supervisor. However, you will see that managers at all levels collected additional information about performance.

The additional measures served two purposes. First, they helped managers to monitor performance in areas of strategic importance, such as quality and delivery. The company was opening up export markets in the US and Europe, and high-quality cars, delivered on time, were essential to its success. Second, they provided timely, actionable feedback to operational managers. On the shop floor, the measures focused on causes of problems, not consequences, and were available daily or sometimes hourly. Like the conventional financial performance measures, the additional measures were more detailed at the shop floor level and more aggregated at the upper levels of management.

The results of the investigation worried some managers. While they could see some value in all of the measures, they were concerned about their proliferation. Were all these measures essential

CORPORATE MANAGEMENT	
Quality	**Viability**
Customer satisfaction audits Warranty cost per unit Warranty defects per 100 vehicles Owner surveys: defects per vehicle	Profit Sales numbers Actual manufacturing costs Standard cost variances Actual output Variances between actual and planned output

PLANT MANAGER		
Delivery	**Quality**	**Cost/Productivity**
Number of good units completed in plant Daily shortages Stock status	Customer satisfaction audit Statistical process control Top 50 recurring defects in plant Percentage good units first time through plant Number of defects per unit per day in plant Number of defects from this plant found at final line Internal quality audit reports (e.g. paint thickness audits)	Overtime hours Cost of scrap Standard cost variances

SHOPFLOOR MANAGERS			
Delivery	**Quality**	**Cost/Productivity**	**Resource management**
Number of good units completed in work area Number of units achieved by each work area Schedule adherence Daily shortages Stock status	Percentage good units first time through shop Number of defects per unit per day in shop Top 50 recurring defects in shop Number of defects from this shop found at final line Number of vehicles scrapped in shop Number of units reworked in shop Internal quality audit reports (e.g. paint thickness audits)	Labour hours per car Overtime hours Cost of scrap Standard cost variances	Degree of multi-skilling Absence reports Accident reports Hours of machine breakdowns Number of machine breakdowns Equipment monitoring

SHOPFLOOR SUPERVISORS			
Delivery	**Quality**	**Cost/Productivity**	**Resource management**
Number of good units completed in work area Number of units achieved by each work area Schedule adherence	Percentage good units first time through work area Number of defects per unit per day Number of defects by source within work area Internal quality audit reports (e.g. paint thickness audits)	Labour hours per unit Overtime hours Cost of scrap Standard cost variances	Hours of machine breakdowns Equipment monitoring Accident reports

Exhibit 14.2 Performance measures at auto manufacturer

to achieving quality and delivery at a reasonable cost? What was the relationship between all these measures and the ultimate company goal – profit?

A closer look at some non-financial measures

Exhibit 14.2 contains some non-financial performance measures that may be new to you. Let's look more closely at some of these performance measures, and consider how they may be designed and calculated.

Customer satisfaction

This may be measured by a survey containing a series of questions designed to gauge aspects of the product or service that result in customer satisfaction or dissatisfaction. The survey may be administered to a sample of customers every three months. Degrees of customer satisfaction may be expressed as percentages – for example, 45 per cent of customers are highly satisfied with our service, and 30 per cent are mildly satisfied. This measure is important in assessing whether customer value is increasing. (Customer-related measures are discussed in more detail in Chapter 16.)

Number of defects from this plant found at final line

A defect is a fault in a product that occurs during the manufacturing process. It is better that defects are detected early in the production process rather than later (at the final production line), so that minimal resources are expended on a defective product. When defects are found early in the process, the partly completed product may be reprocessed, repaired or scrapped. A low-defect measure is critical in supporting a high-quality strategy.

Internal quality audits

The quality of a product may be determined by periodic inspections or testing of products during the production processing. High quality products support the competitive strategy of quality.

Productivity

Productivity is the ratio of outputs produced per unit of input. It is a measure of efficiency. Traditionally, manufacturing plants have measured labour productivity as follows:

$$\text{Labour productivity} = \frac{\text{number of units produced}}{\text{number of direct labour hours}}$$

Thus, labour productivity may be expressed, for example, as 3 units of product per DLH. Clearly direct labour is only one input to production and, with the growth in automation, it is decreasing in importance. Thus, **total factor productivity** measures the ratio of outputs produced to all production inputs, and may be calculated as follows:

$$\text{Total factor productivity} = \frac{\text{number of units produced}}{\text{cost of all inputs to production}}$$

Thus, total factor productivity may be expressed as, for example, 0.50 units of output per Rand of input costs. Productivity measures support a cost leadership strategy, as productivity is a driver of costs.

Stock status

This is the balance of inventory on hand. A company may have a target level of inventory that it wishes to keep available which is high enough to satisfy production demands, but not too high, as inventory entails storage costs for the company. Managing inventory is discussed in detail in Chapter 16.

Accident report

This measure is often called a 'safety report', and refers to the number of accidents that employees may experience per day or per week in the production plant.

Multi-skilling

This is a measure of the number of employees who have achieved a certain level of multi-skilling. In other words, it measures the number of employees who have completed training and acquired skills that allow them to undertake their own task as well as the tasks of other workers in the production area.

Machine downtime

This is measured as the number of hours, or percentage of total production hours in a week or month, that machines are unable to operate. This may be due to many factors, including the machine breaking down, employees refusing to work, electricity outages or set-up time. **Set-up time** is the time that it takes to get the machine and materials ready to start producing a product. Set-up time can take 10 minutes in some plants and two hours in others. By decreasing machine downtime in set-up, the timeliness of deliveries to customers can be improved.

Schedule adherence or delivery on time

This is a measure of whether the required products or services were provided to the customers by a certain targeted time. It may be calculated in several ways. For example, it might be the percentage of orders that were delivered to customers within three days of the customer order, or the percentage of orders delivered to customers at the promised time. Prompt delivery to customers is an important driver of customer value.

The problems with non-financial performance measures

Exhibit 14.2 highlights some of the problems that can occur when performance measurement systems are broadened to include non-financial performance measures:

- There is a *wide choice of non-financial measures* available. As you can see, quality is measured in many ways. Are all of these measures necessary? How do managers select appropriate quality measures?
- The development can be *ad hoc and undirected*. A proliferation of measures can occur over time, as new measures are adopted in response to a particular problem. However, old measures may not be discontinued.
- Managers must necessarily make *trade-offs*. Exhibit 14.2 indicates that there are many measures to focus on at each level of management. Which measures are the most important? What should a manager do if certain actions improve some measures but not others? For example, improving the quality measure 'number of defects' may result in an increase in the cost driver measure 'labour hours per unit'.
- Some non-financial measures may *lack integrity*. Data used to calculate non-financial performance measures may be gathered in a variety of ways – manually, computerised, by an external party – and because the accuracy of the data may be difficult to verify (compared with financial data recorded in the accounting system), there is potential for manipulation and error.
- Some non-financial measures *may not easily translate into financial outcomes*. Some managers 'take it on faith' that improving measures such as number of machine breakdowns, customer satisfaction or the number of on-time deliveries will lead to improved profits. We will consider this issue later in this chapter.

The auto manufacturer clearly needed a *systematic method* to redesign its performance measurement system and, over the following years, worked on developing a balanced scorecard.

Measuring performance with a balanced scorecard

L.O. 5

Like those at our auto manufacturing company, managers and other employees in businesses often supplement the *formal* performance measures with a wide range of non-financial performance measures, particularly at the operational level. As stated above, this can lead to several problems. How can these measures be integrated into a coherent performance measurement system? Some management accountants began to search for a system for reporting performance in all key strategic areas, in a form that was useful for the various levels of management. The aggregated financial and other strategic measures appropriate for upper-level managers needed to be translated into detailed operational measures for lower-level managers. One response has been the development of balanced scorecards. A **balanced scorecard** is a performance measurement system that identifies and reports on performance measures for each key strategic area of the business. Performance measures are developed for each level of the organisation. While there are a number of approaches to developing balanced scorecards, they all tend to be based on similar principles.[2]

A popular approach to developing a balanced scorecard is that of Kaplan and Norton (1996). This framework translates the organisation's mission and strategies into objectives and performance measures. The first step in the process is to consider the mission and the specific strategies of the organisation, and then translate these strategies into specific objectives that reflect four perspectives: financial, customer, internal business processes, and learning and growth. For each perspective, performance measures and targets are developed that relate to the specific objectives.

1 *Financial perspective.* This perspective includes financial objectives, which provide a view of performance from the perspective of the shareholders. To determine the specific financial objectives, the following question may be asked: *If we succeed, how should we look to our shareholders?* From this objective, a series of measures is developed. Financial measures summarise the financial outcomes of decisions and actions. Measures may include various cost and profit measures, return on investment, measures based on cash flow, and shareholder value measures (these were discussed in Chapter 13).

2 *Customer perspective.* The customer perspective includes measures of the company's success in achieving customer value. Specific customer objectives are formulated based on an understanding of customer value. The question can be asked: *If we achieve our vision, how should we look to our customers?* Specific measures that measure achievement of customer objectives may include customer satisfaction, customer profitability, market share and the number of new customers. These can be considered outcome, or lag, measures. More specific measures that may drive these outcome measures may include on-time delivery, the number of new products launched and the number of product defects.

3 *Internal business processes.* Objectives must be formulated for specific processes that contribute to achieving customer and financial objectives. These processes can be identified by asking the question: *To satisfy our shareholders and customers, at which business processes must we excel?* The internal business processes may be those in the areas of product design, operations, marketing, sales, distribution and customer service. Measures that are included under this perspective are designed to monitor the internal processes that are critical to delivering products or services to customers and achieving financial strategies. They can include measures of cost, product quality, and time-based measures of existing business processes. Long-term measures may be created to monitor new product development, or processes that determine the changing needs of customers.

4 *Learning and growth.* This perspective focuses on the capabilities of the organisation that must be developed in order to achieve superior internal processes that create both customer value and shareholder value. These capabilities can be identified by asking the

following question: *To achieve our vision, how will we sustain our ability to change and improve?* This perspective concentrates on the infrastructure that firms put in place to deliver long-term growth and improvement. Measures may focus on employee capabilities (measures of employee satisfaction, training, absenteeism and skills); on information system capabilities (measures such as the percentage of customer service employees having real-time access to customer information); and on the organisational climate for employee motivation and initiative (measures such as the number of employee suggestions made and implemented, and the number of employees whose goals are aligned with those of the organisation).

Cause and effect linkages

L.O. 6 Performance measures are cascaded down through the various levels of the organisation to communicate what aspects of the business are important at each level. You may have noted in the above discussion that there are linkages between objectives and measures under each of the four perspectives. That is, the scorecard is structured to reflect 'cause and effect' relationships between the objectives (and measures) in the various perspectives. This process is illustrated in Exhibit 14.3. An overall measure of shareholder value, economic value added, is chosen to capture achievement of the financial objectives. This measure may be influenced by the level of customer satisfaction, which in turn is caused by having a high number of product variations available and few customer complaints. These are the two customer measures.

The critical business processes on which management has chosen to focus are the product development cycle and production processes. Increasing the number of products under development will lead to an increase in the number of product variations to be offered. Increasing the number of good units completed will reduce the number of customer complaints. Finally, one of the key drivers of the two measures of internal business processes is employee satisfaction. Increasing the level of employee satisfaction, a measure of learning and growth, will lead to improving the two internal business process measures.

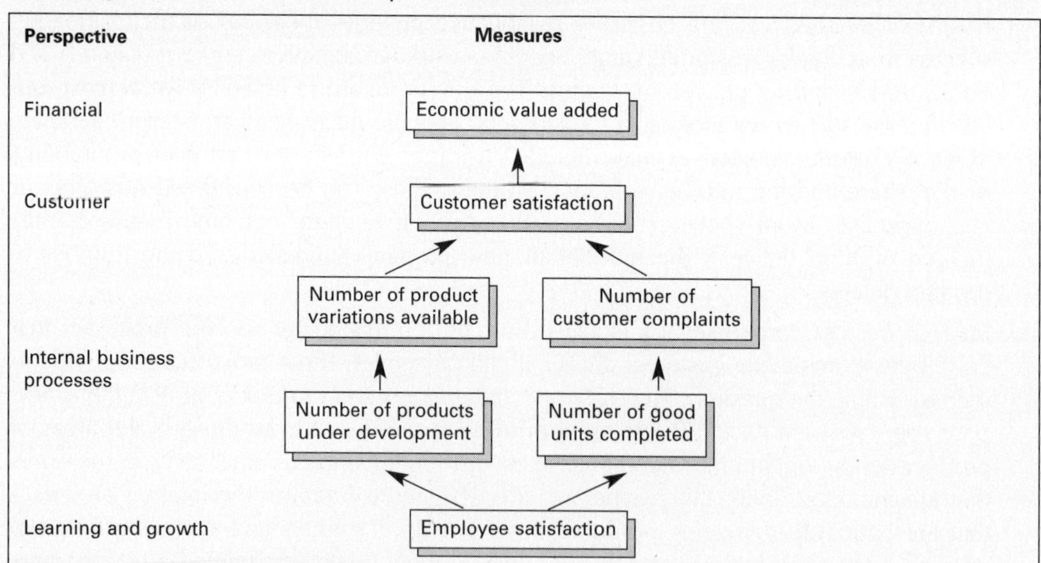

Exhibit 14.3 Causal linkages in the balanced scorecard

Lead and lag indicators

L.O. 7 Exhibit 14.4 contains an example of some objectives and performance measures for each of the four perspectives. Note that some measures are called *lag indicators* (*outcome measures*), and others are *lead indicators* (or *drivers* of those measures). **Lag indicators** monitor progress towards objectives. While these measures provide important information for managers about outcomes of decisions and operations, they may be difficult to manage directly. Examples of lag measures include many of the summary financial measures, market share information, and even customer satisfaction measures. These measures are often used as the basis for managers' performance contracts.

Objectives	Performance measures	
	Lag indicators	**Lead indicators**
1 Financial		
Improve returns to shareholders. Increase profits.	Return on equity Economic value added Product profitability	Sales mix Cost per product
2 Customer		
Increase customer satisfaction. Expand the customer base.	Customer satisfaction Market share Number of new customers Number of customers retained	Number of product returns On-time delivery Number of product variations available Number of customer complaints Number of good units completed
3 Internal business processes		
Improve the quality of products. Create new, innovative products. Improve production processes.	Number of good units completed Number of products under development	Product defects Number of product returns Product development time Production cycle time Number of machine breakdowns
4 Learning and growth		
Improve employee satisfaction. Develop employees' technical skills.	Employee satisfaction survey Number of employees participating in training programs	Improvements made to employee facilities Time spent developing employee programs

Exhibit 14.4 Objectives and performance measures for a balanced scorecard

Lead indicators are measures that drive the outcomes and provide information that is actionable and manageable. Lead indicators often relate to the processes and activities of the business, and improvements in these indicators should flow through to lag indicators over time. Lead indicators are often used as the focus for process improvement or cost management. This is because they are the drivers of activities and processes. When you study Chapter 15, you will see that various cost management approaches focus on identifying, managing and monitoring cost drivers.

In examining Exhibit 14.4 you will notice that measures that are lag indicators of one perspective may be lead indicators of another perspective. For example, market share is an outcome measure of the customer perspective, given the objective of expanding the customer base, but also a lead indicator of the financial perspective, as market share drives profitability.

In summary, the measures in the balanced scorecard provide balance between:

- short-term and long-term objectives;
- financial measures, customer measures, measures of business processes, and measures of learning and growth;
- outcome measures (lag indicators) and measures of the drivers of those outcomes (lead indicators); and
- objective and easily quantified measures and subjective performance measures.

Performance measures in practice

There are many variations in the way that organisations structure their performance measurement systems. Some organisations use lag and lead indicators but do not go as far as adopting a balanced scorecard. A range of alternative terms is used in companies to describe lead and lag indicators. For example, lag indicators may be called *outcome measures* or *key performance indicators (KPIs)*. Lead indicators may be called *drivers of measures* or *key performance drivers (KPDs)*. In addition, some organisations identify **critical success factors (CSFs)**. These are the factors that are critical to the survival of the business, such as quality, cost or innovativeness. The performance measurement system focuses on these factors because without any one of them, the company would fail.

The structure of the balanced scorecard that is used by some companies will vary. Some companies may use scorecards that have more than four perspectives, or perhaps the names of their perspectives are different. The two 'Real lifes' that follow show how some organisations have customised their balanced scorecard. The factors that should be common to all scorecard approaches are:

- the measures should support the objectives and strategy of the business;
- they should cascade down through the various levels of the organisation; and
- the measures chosen should include both short-term and long-term measures, as well as financial and non-financial measures, to reduce the likelihood of dysfunctional behaviour.

In practice it is very difficult to achieve these factors. The second 'Real life' below outlines how the National Research Foundation developed its measure for the difficult area of learning and growth.

REAL LIFE: CUSTOMISING THE BALANCED SCORECARD

How widely used is the balanced scorecard?

In 1999, an executive survey of management practices by Bain and Co found that 55 per cent of those surveyed in the US and 45 per cent in Europe used some form of balanced scorecard. Similarly, in 2000 a study by Renaissance Worldwide found that over 30 per cent of companies that were included in the BRW top 500 companies in Australia used balanced scorecards. In South Africa, the use of balanced scorecards is statutory in relation to meeting Black economic empowerment objectives as well as measuring public sector performance. Further, balanced scorecards are used by the majority of mining companies. However, the design of the balanced scorecards can vary across organisations.

Some organisations include more than four perspectives in their balanced scorecards. Other organisations and companies may customise the balanced scorecard that makes it more relevant to their industry. For example, Implats and other mining companies in South Africa will focus on safety and environmental targets. Further, in South Africa, the government is using a balanced scorecard approach to set Black Economic Empowerment targets in relation to industry charters, but more about this later.

At the University of Cape Town Library, the balanced scorecard is used to translate the library's vision and strategies into a set of performance measures. There are four perspectives: User, Finance, Internal Process, and Learning and Growth. Within these perspectives key measures include user satisfaction, the relevance of the library's services, and staff skill levels. So how does the library measure performance in these key areas?

1 *User perspective*: The library uses general user surveys to monitor user satisfaction with its services. The library uses other information such as the level of market penetration, monitoring the use of electronic resources as well as hits on the library web page.

2 *Finance perspective*: The library monitors the library budget as a percentage of the institution's budget as well as monitoring the books per student, loans per student, the number of students per seat and the information expenditure per student.
3 *Internal Processes perspective*: The library keeps track of turnaround time in regard to functions such as cataloguing, processing speeds and undertaking staff surveys.
4 *Learning and Growth perspective*: The library evaluates this area in terms of staff attendance at conferences and workshops, and staff participation in further education. The library also monitors the percentage of computers out of action and the replacement rate of library computers.

Impala Platinum Holdings Limited (Implats) is a major global company which mines, refines and markets platinum group metals. The CEO of the company states that:

Being primarily a mining operation, our key imperatives are cost-efficient production to ensure superior returns to our shareholders, without causing harm to our employees or the environment.

The company set out the following scorecard for the company in 2006 whereby the company monitored its performance in relation to the targets set in 2005. Again, we see the company customised the scorecard in terms of its priorities.

Table: Our Scorecard.

What we said in FY2005	**What we achieved in FY2006**
Achieving a 33% reduction in LTIFR year-on-year, with a long-term objective of zero injuries. [LTIFR= Lost time injury frequency rate]	χ Our safety goals are tough and while the target was not met, injuries were reduced, with an improvement in the overall Implats LTIFR by 4.48%, from 3.57 (FY2005) to 3.41 (FY2006). A special initiative, with full leadership support, was launched to ensure we move towards achieving our goal of 'Zero Harm'.
Converting our ISO 14001: 1996 certificates to incorporate the requirements of the 2004 standards.	√ This was achieved at all the operations that already had ISO 14001: 1996 certification, as well as at Ngezi operations (Zimplats).
Reducing fresh water consumption by 5% year-on-year.	χ Total consumption per production unit was reduced by 6% year-on-year, but the potable water consumption was reduced by only 1%.
Ensuring continued implementation of our Employment Equity Plans at all South African operations.	√ Transformation Committees were established to drive the process and meet quarterly. The aim of these committees is to: ■ Identify and address issues that create barriers to transformation; ■ Ensure the achievement of objectives, goals and targets; and ■ Assist line management to achieve targets through appropriate action plans.
Containing the HIV prevalence rate at our operations to lower than the levels reported for similar populations in surrounding areas.	√ The HIV prevalence rate at our Rustenburg operations remains stable at 16%. This is well below the reported level of 26% for the North West province. The prevalence rate at Refineries and Mimosa has not been quantified, whereas that at Zimplats is 20%.
Finalising sulphur dioxide abatement strategy for Rustenburg operations.	√ A new sulphur dioxide abatement strategy was completed and submitted to the regional Chief Air Pollution Control Officer, and a permit was negotiated accordingly.

In the mining sector due to the depth of mining operations, safety and avoiding injuries and fatalities is an important issue and this is often reflected in company reports. Harmony, the gold mining company, for example, reported in 2005 that;

The group's year-end LTIFR was 16.53 per million man-hours worked in FY2005, compared with 19.63 in FY2004.

Municipalities in South Africa are required to use key performance indicators to monitor performance in relation to the provision of services. For example, Tshwane and the City of Cape Town have introduced balanced scorecards to monitor performance. The City of Cape Town stated the following in a report in 2006:

The Balanced Scorecard (BSC) is a management system (not only a measurement system) that enables the City to clarify its vision and strategy and translates it into action. It integrates the City's strategy with four major perspectives, i.e. (Customer/Community, Financial, Internal Business Process, and Learning and Growth) and a limited number of Indicators within these perspectives. It provides feedback around the internal business processes and external outcomes in order to continuously improve strategic performance results.

There is also some variation among South African users of balanced scorecards in the extent to which companies link the measures within their balanced scorecard into cause-and-effect chains, across perspectives, and whether they identify measures of outcomes (lag indicators) and drivers (lead indicators).

Sources:
Karen de Jager, 2004,'Counting what matters – to measure what counts', University of Cape Town, presentation to the Conference on Quality Assurance Issues at Academic Libraries, University of Stellenbosch, October.

Impala Platinum Holdings, Social Responsibility Report, June 2006 (see www.implats.co.za)

City of Cape Town, Integrated Development Plan, 2006

REAL LIFE: USING A BALANCED SCORECARD APPROACH TO MEASURE BLACK ECONOMIC EMPOWERMENT IN SOUTH AFRICA

The economic empowerment of black South Africans has become a business imperative and government has introduced legislation to ensure that broad-based Black Economic Empowerment (B-BBEE) occurs in a meaningful way. There are agreements between government and industry sectors, known as *industry charters*, which set out empowerment targets for each industry. The government has introduced a balanced scorecard to give meaning and to measure compliance with economic empowerment. Prior to the industry charters, the focus was on the transfer of ownership, while the balanced scorecard approach includes targets in relation to ownership, management control, skills development, employment equity and procurement. There is a scoring system to measure BEE compliance.

The following generic scorecard was presented in the *Government Gazette* dated 7 February 2007:

Element	Weighting (points)	Code ref.
Ownership	20	100
Management control	10	200
Employment equity	15	300
Skills development	15	400
Preferential procurement	20	500
Enterprise development	15	600
Socio-Economic Development initiatives	5	700
	100	

B-BBEE Status	Qualification (points)	B-BBEE recognition level
Level One Contributor	100	135%
Level Two Contributor	≥85 but <100	125%
Level Three Contributor	≥75 but <85	110%
Level Four Contributor	≥65 but <75	100%
Level Five Contributor	≥55 but <65	80%
Level Six Contributor	≥45 but <55	60%
Level Seven Contributor	≥40 but <45	50%
Level Eight Contributor	≥30 but <40	10%
Non-compliant Contributor	<30	0%

Each element has a code which discloses in greater detail the composition of the points for that element. For example, in relation to ownership, there is a further balanced scorecard which allocates points under this element for the voting rights (5 points) and economic interest (7 points) held by black people, realisation points for net value (7 points) and ownership (1 point) as well as bonus points for involvement in the ownership of the enterprise of black new entrants (2 points) and employee ownership schemes (1 point). You can refer to these codes to analyse how points are scored for each element. Also, refer to the Department of Trade and Industry (DTI) website, www.dti.gov.za, which has a section on BEE.

General

In implementing the balanced scorecard many organisations have found the 'learning and growth' perspective the most challenging. There can be uncertainty over the focus of this perspective as well as how to identify meaningful measures of individual and organisational performance. In the literature, the perspective itself has been referred to sometimes as 'learning and growth', and at other times as 'innovation and learning'. In practice there are many additional variations on this theme because, as for any management accounting information, the learning and growth perspective of the balanced scorecard should be tailored to the specific information needs of the organisation.

The National Research Foundation, for example, will measure performance of staff in terms of the number of peer-reviewed journal articles produced for the year and the number of books and chapters in books as well as the published proceedings of conferences. This is also true for the university sector.

Developing a balanced scorecard for a bus company

To illustrate the development of a balanced scorecard, we will examine how this was achieved at a bus company.[3] It offers the public a series of regular bus routes within the city, seven days a week. The company also undertakes one-day tours to major tourist attractions outside the city. The company is structured into four units. The Commuter Travel Division consists of a manager and bus drivers who operate the daily bus routes within the city. The Long-haul Trips Division consists of managers, tour hosts and bus drivers who undertake the tours to popular tourist destinations. This **L.O. 8**

division has much larger and more luxurious buses than those used by the Commuter Travel Division. The Marketing and Sales Department manages advertising and promotions for the entire company. Managers in the Head Office unit oversee the operation of the three divisions, and undertake general administration.

The transport market is highly competitive, so the managers need to consider carefully how to manage their performance. There are many competing transport companies that would be very pleased to expand their businesses into the lucrative tourist travel market, as well as the commuter market. The managing director of the company has hired a consulting firm to provide a market analysis and to investigate the determinants of customer value. The consulting firm has found that all of the customers are highly sensitive to the price charged by the companies for bus tickets, and value a highly prompt service. In addition, the tourist market places great value on a comfortable bus service and innovative tourist routes.

1 The starting point in developing a balanced scorecard is to identify the vision and objectives of the company. The vision of the company is:

   To be the leading bus company in the province, through providing superior customer service to the community.

   The objectives of the bus company are to:

   - *Achieve a 98 per cent on-time reliability performance.*
   - *Provide an increase in the number of creative tours to exciting tourist destinations.*
   - *Achieve a return on investment of 10 per cent within 5 years.*

   Clearly, to achieve these objectives the strategies of the firm will centre on cost, reliability of service and product innovation.

2 For each of the four perspectives in the balanced scorecard, specific objectives were formulated. These objectives were derived from the overall objectives and business strategies of the company. Lag and lead indicators were then designed to support the objectives in each perspective. The balanced scorecard in Exhibit 14.5 shows all of the measures for the company.

3 To operationalise the balanced scorecard, measures and targets that are consistent with those in the balanced scorecard were selected for managers in each of the units of the company. For senior managers in each unit the measures were aggregate and broad, and for lower levels of the company, such as the bus drivers, the measures were specific and narrow. Specific targets for each measure were formulated for the first year of operation, as well as plans to achieve these targets. For example, the manager of the Commuter Travel Division was responsible for achieving targets for all of the lead and lag indicators under the customer and internal business process perspectives relating to commuter travel. Each bus driver in the division would have his or her own individual targets for the percentage of bus trips made within published schedules, the number of breakdowns per shift, and the average bus downtime per shift. Managers in the Marketing and Sales Department would have prime responsibility for achieving many of the customer measures. These include the average time to respond to customer complaints, and amount of advertising spending per month.

4 Regular performance reports, which compare actual results to the target for each measure, are prepared for managers at various levels in the company, and bus drivers.

Objectives	Performance measures: Lag indicators	Performance measures: Lead indicators
1 Financial		
Improve profitability. Increase profits.	Return on investment Profitability of each bus route	Number of new passengers per month Cost of diesel fuel Average ticket cost per kilometre
2 Customer		
Increase customer satisfaction. Improve quality of facilities on the bus. Offer innovative tours.	Customer satisfaction measure Market share Number of new passengers per month Number of regular customers retained Maintenance/repairs on buses	Number of customer demands for refunds Average time to respond to customer complaints Number of customer complaints Average advertising expenditure per month Number of monthly bus passes sold Number of bus accidents Number of new tourist routes offered Percentage of journeys made within published schedule
3 Internal business processes		
Improve the reliability of the bus services. Improve productivity.	Percentage of journeys made within published schedule Cost per journey	Number of bus breakdowns per shift Average bus downtime per shift Average capacity utilisation of each bus
4 Learning and growth		
Improve employee satisfaction. Develop employees' skills in managing the bus communication systems.	Employee satisfaction survey Number of employees participating in training programs	Improvements made to communication systems on the buses Improvements to lunchroom facilities Technical training provided to bus drivers

Exhibit 14.5 Balanced scorecard for a bus company

Linking non-financial measures to financial performance measures and financial performance

L.O. 9

Focusing on objectives, strategies and identifying performance measures at all levels of the business is the rationale underlying balanced scorecard approaches. However, ultimately, most organisations measure their performance as a whole in financial terms, as profitability is a critical measure of success from a shareholder's point of view.

In describing the cause and effect linkages in Exhibits 14.4 and 14.5, it is apparent that some measures within a scorecard have a clear link with profit. For example, improvements in the number of good units completed will feed through to reduced cost and hence increased profit. However, the relationship between improving performance in non-financial measures and improving profit is not always so direct. For example, it is not possible to identify the financial impact of an increase in the number of product variations or an increase in customer satisfaction.

Effective management of non-financial measures at the operational level should ensure improved profitability. However, this is not always so. An electronics company in the US, over a three-year period, achieved dramatic improvements in its operational performance measures. Defect rates dropped from 500 to 50 parts per million, on-time delivery improved from 70 per cent to 96 per cent, and yield increased from 26 per cent to 51 per cent. Nevertheless, these improvements were not mirrored in the company's financial results nor in its share price, which fell by two-thirds (Kaplan & Norton, 1996, p. 32). How can this happen?

Improvements in non-financial measures will not result in improved profits if management has selected the *wrong critical success factors*. If this happens, the performance measurement system may be directing employees to focus on areas that will not lead to success. For example, a firm may believe that high-quality innovative products are critical success factors, and will design performance measures to communicate this strategy to all employees. However, if customers do not value quality and are unwilling to pay extra for this, and if they are perfectly satisfied with the standard range of products, then the company may find that it is out of step with the market. It has not understood what it is about their products that customers value. The strategy will not lead to improved profitability. Hopefully, the performance measures of the company should provide warning signals before the company is in too much trouble!

Another reason for improvements in non-financial measures not flowing through to improved profit performance can relate to the *failure to utilise freed-up resources*. Many improvements in areas such as productivity and quality effectively expand the productive capacity of the business. When cycle time reduces, more units of product can be produced in a shorter time. When reject rates improve, fewer products are reworked and the need for inspections may be reduced. This means that employees and equipment may be underutilised. Improvements in these areas will not translate into cost savings and improved profits unless the idle resources (equipment and employees) are used by the company to undertake profitable activities elsewhere in the business and to increase the level of production, or are disposed of. However, many of the resources that are freed up may be committed costs; for example, it may be difficult to dispose of equipment or rationalise staff levels immediately. Also, it may be difficult, in the short term, to increase sales, and hence production, to use the idle resources. Thus, improvements in a range of non-financial areas will benefit a firm only if they can be translated into higher capacity utilisation and increased sales, or cost reductions.

A final reason for improvements in non-financial measures not flowing through to improved financial performance may relate to the *incorrect design of the performance measurement system*. Performance measures can provide incentives to engage in dysfunctional decisions, which maximise performance in some areas of the business, at the expense of other areas. In addition, the measures may be easy to manipulate and falsify, so that 'real' performance is not as high as the measures indicate. Some of these behavioural issues are described in the 'Real life' below.

While it can be difficult to establish direct links between the non-financial performance measures at operational levels and profitability, some companies design their performance measurement system explicitly to build in this link. We saw that this is the thinking underlying the design of balanced scorecards. An alternative approach to linking non-financial performance measures to profitability is to use a **Du Pont chart**, which identifies linkages between key performance drivers, key performance indicators and financial performance measures. Exhibit 14.6 shows a Du Pont chart for a mining company. The original Du Pont chart was developed by the Du Pont chemical company in the early 20th century, and included only financial measures.

Benchmarking

L.O. 10

Many organisations use benchmarking as part of their performance measurement systems. **Benchmarking** involves comparing the products, functions and activities of an organisation against external businesses in order to identify areas for improvement and to implement a program of continuous improvement (Reider, 2000). These external businesses are sometimes called **best practice companies**, which are businesses that are high performers in relation to a particular practice or process. In benchmarking, a business may not simply compare its own performance against a benchmark; it may follow a more formal procedure where the processes that the best practice companies have used to achieve their high levels of performance are examined. The business will then use this information as a basis for implementing continuous improvement.

REAL LIFE: INFLUENCING PERFORMANCE THROUGH ELECTRONIC MONITORING

Many managers believe that 'what you measure is what you get', and so attempt to design measures that will encourage employees to behave in certain ways. Electronic performance monitoring of employees is becoming common in a number of areas of business in South Africa and overseas, and may influence performance – although not always in a goal-congruent way – as shown in these examples:

- Some grocery distribution companies use a sophisticated computer program to determine the standard time for an employee to process a particular customer order. Employees log into the system and enter their employee number and customer order number, which then activates the time clock. Employees' actual performance is compared with the standard performance, and if they fail to meet the standard, they may be counselled and disciplined, or, over time, even dismissed!
- In a telecommunication company's customer service division, a computer is used to monitor employees' activities. At the end of each day, team leaders receive printouts of performance information on each of their team members. This details the precise time spent on incoming and outgoing calls, and the time taken for meal and toilet breaks. Weekly reports rank relative performance for each work team, which is benchmarked against best practice standards to encourage employees to speed up their responses to customer inquiries.
- A common measure of productivity in the call centres or customer service centres of banks and other companies is the time employees take to answer a telephone call, and the time spent on each call. Shorter times indicate improved efficiency. However, these measures may inadvertently encourage employees to provide poor customer service by cutting short calls, or even abandoning calls. This in turn can lead to reduced customer satisfaction, which can have a negative impact on profits.

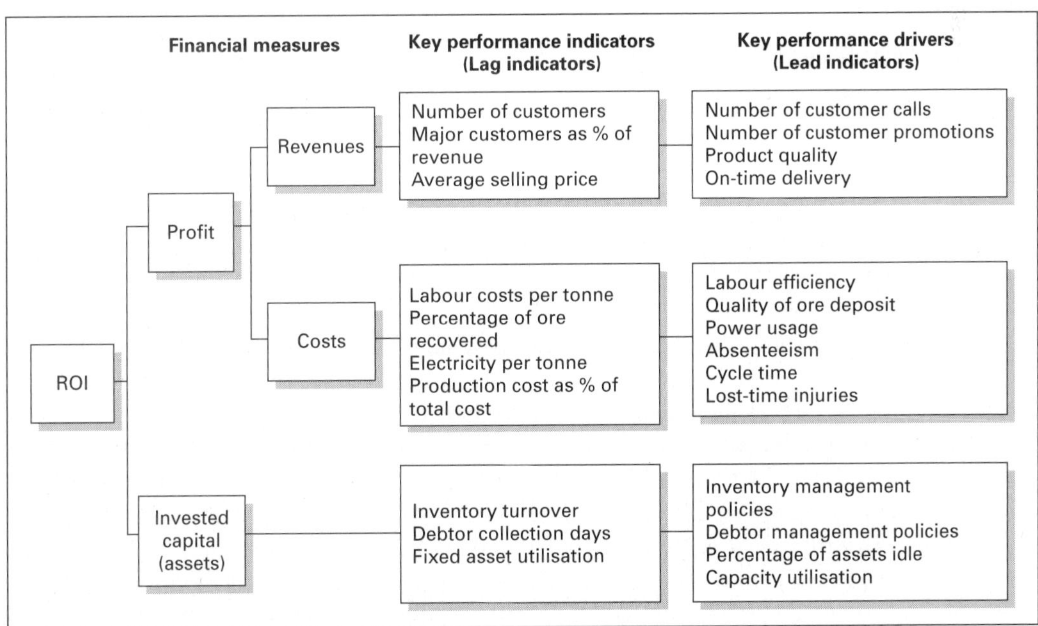

Exhibit 14.6 Du Pont chart, linking financial and non-financial measures

Steps in the benchmarking process

Formal benchmarking may involve the following steps (Shetty, 1993):

1 *Identifying the functions or activities to be benchmarked, and performance measures.* The functions and activities to be benchmarked will be those that are vital to the achievement of the business' objectives. They may include areas in which the company is experiencing performance problems. Performance measures are developed for these processes. The measures may be focused around cost or quality, customer service, delivery performance or other product-related characteristics. It is very important that the appropriate performance measures, which reflect the competitive strategy of the business, are selected.

2 *Selecting benchmark partners.* These are organisations that are regarded as the best performers in particular areas; they are not always in the same industry.

3 *Data collection and analysis.* Visits may be made to benchmark partners to examine their performance measures, and to study their processes and practices – the means to achieving their best performance. Many benchmarking visits are undertaken by teams that include employees at all levels, not just managers. This is consistent with ideas of employee empowerment, and often results in extensive improvements. Those closest to the operations are in the best position to learn and implement improvements. Indirect sources of benchmarking data may include information obtained from customers, trade journals, annual reports, company publications and public seminars. The objective of this phase is to identify **performance gaps**, which are the extent to which a business needs to improve in order to reach best practice.

4 *Establishing performance goals.* This involves planning new processes and practices to achieve performance goals and narrow the performance gap.

5 *Implementing plans.* Implementation of improved practices requires frequent measurement of performance to assess the extent of the performance gap, and taking corrective actions to improve performance where necessary.

These steps are outlined in Exhibit 14.7.

Forms of benchmarking

Formal benchmarking can be classified into four types (Reider, 2000; McNair & Leibfried, 1992):

1 *Internal benchmarking* involves benchmarking between business units within the same company. For example, BMW at Midrand in Gauteng benchmarks its key processes with other manufacturing plants that are part of the global BMW group. This is the simplest form of benchmarking, as access to benchmarking partners is easy to establish. However, it may not provide the world's best benchmarks, as companies outside the business group, including competitors, may be better performers.

2 *Competitive benchmarking* involves a company identifying the strengths and weaknesses of competitors in order to assist them to prioritise areas for improvement. The objective is to catch up or surpass the competitors' performance, using continuous improvement processes. However, formal benchmarking access may be difficult to arrange with direct competitors. Companies must rely on other external sources for data, including trade journals; newspaper reports; conference presentations; consultants; industry experts; patent records; public reports, such as annual reports; consumer reports; and material on the Internet. An example of competitive benchmarking occurs when a manufacturing company collects data relating to its main competitors to determine how those competitors are able to manufacture and deliver a product to customers within three days of the customer order.

Exhibit 14.7 The benchmarking process

3 *Industry benchmarking* is broader than competitive benchmarking as it involves comparing a company against companies that have similar interests and technologies, in order to identify performance and trends within an industry. The advantage of this form of benchmarking is that there may be technological processes and market characteristics that are common to both the business and the benchmarking partners. This means that performance measures and practices are directly comparable. For example, a retail bank may gather benchmarking data on the new forms of automation used in the financial services industry, and the various processes used to manage customers within the branches. Direct access to companies may be possible if those companies operate in the same type of business but compete in different markets. As industries become more globalised and directly compete in the same markets, opportunities of this nature diminish.

4 *Best-in-class or process benchmarking* involves benchmarking against the best practices that occur in any industry. For example, measures of the percentage of deliveries made to customers on time, or of the percentage of rejects, are of interest to managers in many different types of businesses, as are safety practices and measures of human resources practices. The difficulty with this approach is that many characteristics of best practice businesses may not be common to other companies. For example, a best practice company may achieve 98 per cent of its deliveries to customers on time because it has only a few major customers who place orders many weeks in advance. Also, the company

may have only a few products and state-of-the-art technology that assists it to achieve such high performance. Thus, these performance measures may not be directly comparable with those in another company that does not have the same advantages. Some businesses try to normalise the measures to make them directly comparable. **Normalisation** refers to the practice of removing the effects of factors outside the control of the organisation, so that narrowing the performance gap is achievable. However, some managers do not normalise data, despite differences in technology or processes, as the benchmark is still the level of performance that the company needs to strive for in order to achieve greater competitiveness.

It should be noted that, while many South African businesses claim to be engaged in benchmarking, they do not always follow the steps described in Exhibit 14.7. Benchmarking may be practised as a much more informal process, and may sometimes consist of no more than measuring performance against a difficult target, determined within or outside the organisation.

Benchmarking against competitors' cost structures

It is important for most businesses to reassess continually the cost competitiveness of their products and processes, particularly if their competitive strategy is focused on minimising cost. This requires an understanding of *competitors'* cost structures. Benchmarking provides a methodology for assessing performance gaps between a firm's costs and that of competitors (or other best practice companies), and examining the processes and practices used by those other firms to achieve their high levels of performance.

Can a firm directly determine competitors' costs? Competitors' costs can be deduced by using publicly available information, such as sales volume, market share, product mix, cost of goods sold, raw material costs, labour costs and overhead costs (Chalos, 1992). However, the resulting product costs are likely to be very imprecise.

In South Africa the opportunities for assessing competitors' cost structures are increasing with the emergence of some industry-sponsored databases and the development of benchmarking databases by consulting firms. Company research reports prepared by stockbroking firms also contain costs within an industry and for specific firms. However, these need to be used with caution, as sometimes the costs are only estimates. Some consulting firms offer benchmarking data, which include costs, to clients. Benchmarking groups or networks are sometimes formed by a group of organisations in order to compare processes and activities, and membership is by invitation only.

Warning signs of an inadequate performance measurement system

L.O. 11 How does an organisation know when its performance measurement system is inadequate? Managers need to be aware of several warning signs that may indicate that their system needs review (Vitale, 1995; Eccles, 1991; Meyer & Gupta, 1992).

1 *Performance is acceptable on all dimensions, except profit.* Non-financial performance measures, such as those related to quality, delivery time and cycle time, may be showing considerable improvements. At the same time, profits may not be increasing. How can this happen? There are several possible explanations. First, the non-financial measures may not relate to the organisation's strategies. If delivery responsiveness is not of strategic importance, because it is not what customers require, then improving this measure may not translate to increased sales and profits. Second, resources that may have been freed up by improvements in areas such as cycle time or reject rates may not have been utilised to improve profitability. This was explained in an earlier section. Third, there may be a lag between improving drivers and improving profits. How long does it take for improved

REAL LIFE: BENCHMARKING ACTIVITIES AT BENSA AND MARKINOR

Bensa is a South African organisation that generates benchmarking data on industry sectors. Consulting firms, accounting firms and other organisations may purchase data to enable them to assess performance in the area of costs, as well as in other areas such as market share and sales growth. Despite the difficulties in estimating competitors' costs, it is clear that some companies routinely estimate this type of information. For example, the managers at a manufacturing firm received an unsolicited approach from a Chinese manufacturer who had correctly estimated the current manufacturing cost of the company's main product and was offering to manufacture that product at 60 per cent of the cost.

Markinor, the market research firm, undertakes market surveys, which are often used for benchmarking purposes. The company undertakes loyalty surveys and the following reflect some of the results of a retail banking survey undertaken in 2006.

Call Centre	Score	Electronic Banking	Score
FNB	80%	FNB	72%
ABSA	69%	Standard Bank	59%
Nedbank	64%	ABSA	52%
Standard Bank	58%	Nedbank	47%
Ease of use of ATM	**Score**	**Teller Staff**	**Score**
FNB	87%	Nedbank	71%
Standard Bank	76%	FNB	68%
Nedbank	76%	Standard Bank	63%
ABSA	64%	ABSA	57%

Source: Bizcommunity.com, 19 July 2006

Companies within the sector can use the information produced by Markinor to improve service levels and increase the value of brands. Companies pay for these detailed reports. For example the cost of the full loyalty report was over R62 000, which is a small amount considering the impact of such information.

delivery performance to be turned into increased sales from existing customers and sales from new customers?

2 *Customers do not buy, even when prices are competitive.* If sales have not improved, even when performance measures indicate that quality, costs and delivery have improved, it may be that, relative to competitors, the organisation's performance is still not good enough. Wherever possible, performance in critical areas should be benchmarked against best practice. It is not enough to know that performance is improving; the test is whether performance is improving relative to that of competitors.

3 *No one notices when performance reports are not supplied.* This is a clear indicator that reports are considered to be of no use by managers – the reports are not giving managers any information that they can use! This can occur because managers consider that the performance measurement system focuses on the wrong things. The reports may be too detailed, or not detailed enough, or arrive too frequently, or not frequently enough. In particular, performance reports may provide no new information to managers.

4 *Significant time is spent debating the meanings of measures.* This can occur when measures are not clearly related to strategy, or when they are too aggregated, so that the

signals provided by the measures are subject to different interpretations. For example, an increase in customer satisfaction may be due to many factors. Unless these drivers are also measured, the causes and hence the means for improving customer satisfaction will not be apparent.

5 *The measures have not changed for some time.* This may mean that the system is out of date, and unable to assist in managing within the continually changing business environment.

6 *The business strategy has changed.* A change of strategy provides a signal, or a welcome excuse, to review the organisation's performance measurement system. Over time it is very common for organisations to add new measures to their systems as they encounter problems, and measures can proliferate throughout the business as a result. This can confuse those employees who are required to meet an ever-increasing range of performance targets.

Designing an effective performance measurement system

L.O. 12

Over the past decade we have seen major changes in the types of performance measurement systems that organisations use. There are many alternatives to financial performance measures, and strategic performance frameworks, such as the balanced scorecard, may help managers to focus on what is important for the business in both the short term and long term. However, many organisations get it wrong! Earlier in this chapter we recognised that improvements in *non-financial* measures may not translate into improved *financial* measures because of an inadequate performance measurement system.

Designing and implementing a good performance measurement system is very difficult. It is not sufficient merely to select a range of non-financial performance measures to support the four perspectives of a balanced scorecard, or to support critical success factors. Designing a performance measurement system requires careful analysis and frequent reviews, and an understanding of how people behave and react to particular performance measurement systems. It is not simply a case of replacing or supplementing financial performance measures with non-financial performance ones. In this section we identify the characteristics of good performance measurement systems, consider how to build continuous improvement into performance measures, and discuss the behavioural implications of new performance measurement systems.

Characteristics of good performance measurement systems

Good performance measurement systems should have the following characteristics:

- *Link to strategy and the goals of the organisation.* This helps to promote goal congruence and ensure that employees are encouraged to focus their efforts in the right direction. Contemporary frameworks, such as the balanced scorecard, use this principle.
- *Be simple.* Measures should be understandable and easy to communicate to employees. Employees who are using, or are being evaluated by, a measure must be able to understand how the measure was calculated and what they need to do to improve their performance in this area. In operational and administrative areas, performance measures are often displayed graphically, close to work areas, in order to help employees identify with the performance measures, to encourage them to discuss performance and to motivate them to achieve further improvements.
- *Recognise controllability.* When employees are responsible for achieving certain performance measures, these measures should relate to activities and processes that are under

their control. In Chapter 12 we saw that this was the principle used when separating divisional managers' performance from their business unit performance. Similarly, in Chapters 10 and 11, responsibility for standard cost variances was assigned to employees based on controllability.

- *Emphasise the positive.* To motivate improvements, performance measures should be expressed in positive rather than negative terms. It is considered more motivational to express delivery performance as 80 per cent on time rather than 20 per cent late, or to measure customer satisfaction at 78 per cent rather than customer dissatisfaction at 22 per cent.
- *Be timely.* Performance measures should be reported as close as possible to the period to which they relate. This gives immediate feedback to employees and managers, and allows timely corrective action to be taken.
- *Include benchmarking.* To lift performance to meet the demands of the customer and competition, it is important that performance measures are benchmarked to high external standards.
- *Embrace participation and empowerment.* To encourage managers and employees to accept performance measures as fair, it is important that they are involved in their formulation and operation. At the operational level, employees may be empowered to identify their own performance measures linked to the business' strategies and to take actions to improve performance.
- *Include only a few performance measures.* Too many performance measures can confuse and obscure real performance. A rule of thumb that is sometimes used is that no person should be held responsible for more than four or five measures.
- *Link to rewards.* Many companies believe that performance measures are more motivational if they are linked to reward systems. Reward systems were discussed in Chapter 13.

Designing measures for continuous improvement

To become and remain world-class, an enterprise must strive for **continuous improvement**, which refers to the ongoing search for improved methods to reduce or eliminate waste and improve performance in areas such as cost, quality and customer service. In many organisations employees play an active part in continuous improvement activities. In today's fast-paced environment customers continually upgrade their requirements and competitors continually improve their performance. This means that organisations have to continually improve their performance to remain competitive.

Continuous improvement can be built into performance measurement systems by:

1 *Selecting relevant performance measures.* The emphasis on continuous improvement means that, as changes are made throughout the business, some performance measures should be dropped and others added. Some companies focus their improvement efforts on problem areas, and then move on to other areas when performance has improved.

2 *Defining and redefining the measure.* In Exhibit 14.2 we saw that there are many measures that can be used to monitor quality, cost and delivery. Continuous improvement can be built into our selection of the appropriate measure. When a new performance measure is first introduced it may be defined loosely. For example, if prompt delivery to customers was very poor, then we could define *on-time delivery* as orders delivered to the customer within a specified period from the time the order was placed. Initially, performance may be only 45 per cent on time. Over time, as employees achieve high performance on this measure, of say 98 per cent, on-time delivery can be defined more

tightly, for example as complete orders delivered to customers within a specified time period. Note that in the initial measure we did not ascertain whether the *complete* order was delivered – if an item was missing, employees might have delivered it a few days later. When the new tighter measure is adopted, performance may immediately slip to, say, 70 per cent, but over time there is the opportunity to improve that performance. Why would a company design the loose measure initially? If the measure is perceived as not too difficult, employees may be motivated to achieve this measure. As their performance improves, there becomes little room for improvement, so the measure is made more challenging to provide a new improvement cycle.

3 *Making the performance target more challenging.* Employees may be set performance targets that increase in difficulty over time. Continuing our on-time delivery measure example, employees may have been given a series of monthly targets, which, once they were achieved, were increased in difficulty.

Behavioural implications of changing performance measures

Performance measurement is undertaken to encourage goal-congruent behaviour, and any selection of performance measures should include an assessment of their behavioural implications. The issues of resistance to change discussed with reference to implementing activity-based costing in Chapters 8 and 15, also apply to implementing performance measurement systems.

It is becoming increasingly common for reward systems to be linked to achieving certain performance targets in order to encourage goal-congruent behaviour. However, it is important to realise that performance-based reward systems can also decrease goal congruence. This can occur if inappropriate performance measures and targets are emphasised. For example, if employees are held responsible for achieving performance targets that are considered to be unfair or unachievable, this could decrease goal congruence. Moreover, changes to performance measures may be resisted if they are believed to adversely affect an individual's pay.

In general, new performance measures are most likely to succeed if they are supported across the entire organisation. Although many of the new performance measurement methodologies begin at the top of the organisation with the identification of business strategies and critical success factors, a bottom-up approach can be used to identify the drivers of these factors. The development of a balanced scorecard may have some appeal to people at various levels of the organisation. Many of the non-financial measures will not be new, but now they will be seen as a logical inclusion in a comprehensive performance measurement system rather than an 'add on' to an inadequate performance measurement system.

L.O. 13

Measuring performance in the service sector

So far, our discussion of performance measures has concentrated on manufacturing organisations. Although balanced scorecards can be used in service businesses, we need to remember that the outputs for service businesses are very different from manufactured products, and that service organisations therefore need different types of performance measures (Fitzgerald et al., 1991).

Exhibit 14.8 lists some of the performance measures identified in a survey of state-of-the-art performance measurement systems used by some service enterprises in the UK. Notice that this exhibit focuses on outcome measures and drivers. The emphasis placed on each dimension depends on the nature of the service business, its competitive environment and its strategic objectives. The main difference between service and manufacturing performance measurement systems is in the types of measures. For example, the quality of a service depends on factors such as responsiveness, friendliness and courtesy, while the quality of a manufactured product depends largely on physical attributes that can be monitored by measures such as the number of defects and warranty claims.

	Dimensions of performance	Types of measures
Outcome measures	Competitiveness	Relative market share and position Sales growth Measures of the customer base
	Financial performance	Profitability Liquidity Capital structure Market ratios
Drivers	Quality of service	Reliability Responsiveness Aesthetics/appearance Cleanliness/tidiness Comfort Friendliness Communication Courtesy Competence Accessibility Availability Security
	Flexibility	Volume flexibility Delivery speed flexibility Specification flexibility
	Resource utilisation	Productivity Efficiency
	Innovation	Performance of the innovation process Performance of individual innovations

Source: adapted from Fitzgerald et al. (1991)

Exhibit 14.8 Performance measures in service businesses

A difficulty in service firms is the qualitative or intangible nature of outputs. Consider how difficult it is to measure courtesy, accessibility and responsiveness. Of course, some manufacturing measures, such as customer satisfaction, relate to both the goods and services provided by the business.

Summary

In this chapter we considered contemporary approaches to designing and managing performance. Key points include:

- Performance measurement systems are systems that measure performance by comparing actual results with some form of benchmark.
- The five main purposes of performance measurement systems are to:
  - communicate the strategy and plans of the business and align employees' goals with those of the organisation;
  - track performance against targets;
  - identify problem areas;
  - evaluate subordinates' performance as the basis for rewards; and
  - guide senior managers in developing future strategies and operations.
- Conventional performance measurement systems are financially based, and many organisations broaden their performance measurement systems to include non-financial measures.

- The problems with conventional financial performance measures include the following:
  - measures are not actionable;
  - they emphasise only one perspective of performance;
  - they provide limited guidance for future actions; and
  - they encourage actions that may decrease both customer and shareholder value.
- Contemporary performance measurement systems consist of a mix of financial and non-financial measures, have a strategic orientation, utilise external benchmarks, and focus on continuous improvement.
- Non-financial measures offer several advantages over financial measures. These include:
  - non-financial measures are the drivers of financial performance;
  - they are more actionable; and
  - they are more understandable and easier to relate to.
- Non-financial measures also have their problems:
  - it is difficult to select measures from such a wide choice;
  - the development of such measures can be *ad hoc* and undirected;
  - using such measures involves trade-offs;
  - measures may lack integrity; and
  - it may not be easy to translate those measures into financial outcomes.
- The balanced scorecard (Kaplan & Norton, 1996) identifies and reports performance from four perspectives: financial, customer, internal business processes, and learning and growth. Within the four perspectives, there are causal linkages between objectives and measures, as well as between lag measures (outcome measures) and lead indicators (drivers of those outcomes measures).
- A Du Pont chart can be used to link non-financial measures with financial measures and financial performance.
- Benchmarking provides a process of comparing the products, functions and activities of a business against external businesses in order to identify areas for improvement and to implement a program of continuous improvement.
- There are five steps in a formal benchmarking process:
  - identify the functions or activities to be benchmarked, and performance measures;
  - select benchmark partners;
  - collect and analyse data;
  - establish performance goals; and
  - implement plans.
- Warnings of an inadequate performance measurement system include:
  - performance is acceptable on all dimensions, except profit;
  - customers do not buy the product, even when prices are competitive;
  - no one notices when performance reports are not supplied;
  - significant time is spent debating the meaning of measures;
  - measures have not changed for some time; and
  - the business strategy has changed.
- Good performance measurement systems:
  - have measures linked to strategy and goals;
  - are simple;

- recognise controllability;
- emphasise the positive;
- are timely;
- include benchmarking;
- embrace participation and empowerment;
- include only a few measures; and
- link to rewards.

■ Continuous improvement should be a part of all good performance measurement systems.

In the following two chapters we will consider the role that performance measures play in the management of cost and time, and in the management of suppliers, customers and quality.

References

Beischel, ME & Smith, KRT 1991, 'Linking the shop floor to the top floor', *Management Accounting* (US), October, pp. 25–9.

Chalos, P 1992, *Managing cost in today's manufacturing environment,* Prentice Hall, Englewood-Cliffs, NJ.

Eccles, RG 1991, 'The performance measurement manifesto', *Harvard Business Review,* January–February, pp. 131–7.

Fitzgerald, L, Johnston, R, Brignall, S, Silvestro, R & Voss C 1991, *Performance Measurement in Service Businesses,* The Chartered Institute of Management Accountants, London.

Kaplan, RS & Norton, DP 1996, *The Balanced Scorecard,* Harvard Business School Press, Boston, MA.

Lynch, RL & Cross, KF 1991, *Measure Up: Yardsticks for Continuous Improvement,* Basil Blackwell, Cambridge, MA.

McNair, CJ & Leibfried, KHJ 1992, *Benchmarking: A Tool for Continuous Improvement,* Omneo, Essex Junction, VT.

Meyer, MW & Gupta, V 1992, 'The performance paradox', in B Staw & LL Cummings (eds), *Research in Organizational Behavior,* JAI Press, Greenwich, CT, pp. 309–69.

Reider, R 2000, *Benchmarking Strategies: A Tool for Profit Improvement,* John Wiley & Sons, New York.

Shetty, YK 1993, 'Aiming high: competitive benchmarking for superior performance', *Long Range Planning,* vol. 26, no. 1, pp. 39–44.

Vitale, M 1995, 'How effective is your performance measurement system?', *Management Accounting* (US), August, pp. 43–7.

Self study

Self-study problem: Balanced scorecard

Super Chicken operates a chain of takeaway chicken shops. The company is operating in a very competitive market, and it is difficult to gain and maintain market share. Management believes that it is important to monitor competitors' actions closely, and to continually offer new products and special promotions to create high visibility among customers. The management team has recently reviewed its mission, which is: *To be a caring and environmentally responsible company, providing fresh and nutritious meals at an affordable price.*

Required:

Consider the four perspectives of Kaplan and Norton's balanced scorecard. For each perspective, develop objectives and a series of performance measures. Consider both lag and lead indicators. Make sure that your objectives and measures support the mission of Super Chicken.

Solution to Self-study problem

	Performance measures	
Objectives	**Lag indicators**	**Lead indicators**
1 Financial		
Improve returns to shareholders.	Return on equity Product profitability	Number of new outlets opened
2 Customer		
Increase customer satisfaction.	Customer satisfaction measure Market share Increase in sales revenue	Number of new products released each quarter Number of customer complaints Number of customers participating in special promotion Average time to serve a customer Average price per meal
3 Internal business processes		
Maintain the quality of products. Create new, innovative products. Improve efficiency of production processes. Improve environmental performance.	Number of products currently under development Average cost per meal	Time to develop new products Material wastage in kitchen Cycle time Electricity used per 10 kg output Labour productivity Kg packaging recycled
4 Learning and growth		
Improve employee satisfaction. Improve employees' knowledge of company systems.	Employee satisfaction survey Number of employees completing company training program	Improvements in working conditions Number of employee suggestions Number of employees achieving 'gold star' status

Cybersearch

1 Find websites with examples of organisations that use balanced scorecard approaches to manage their businesses.
   (a) Compare the features of their balanced scorecards with that of the Kaplan and Norton model.
   (b) Outline the advantages that the balanced scorecard has provided for the organisation.
2 Locate some websites of agencies that offer benchmarking services.
   (a) What type of benchmarking data is provided?
   (b) Does the agency provide benchmarking of processes and procedures?

Questions

14.1 Describe the various ways in which performance measurement systems can support customer value.

14.2 Outline the major limitations of conventional financial performance measures.

14.3 Why do many operational managers develop their own non-financial measures of performance? What are the problems with this approach to performance measurement?

14.4 Does adding non-financial measures always improve a performance measurement system?

14.5 Describe the problems associated with non-financial performance measures.

14.6 What advantages do non-financial performance measures offer for managing resources and creating value, compared with financial measures?

14.7 Describe the Kaplan and Norton balanced scorecard approach to performance measurement.

14.8 Select a business with which you are familiar, and, for each of the four perspectives of Kaplan and Norton's balanced scorecard, select two performance measures that could be used for this business.

14.9 Explain why the effective management of non-financial measures may not always flow through to improved financial performance.

14.10 Distinguish between *lead* and *lag indicators*. Provide an example to illustrate your answer.

14.11 What is a *Du Pont chart*? How can it help in managing performance?

14.12 Outline the characteristics of a good performance measurement system.

14.13 Describe the various ways in which continuous improvement can be built into a performance measurement system. Illustrate your answer with examples.

14.14 Outline the various warning signs that may indicate that an organisation has an inadequate performance measurement system.

14.15 Describe the meanings of *productivity, set-up time* and *machine downtime*. Which competitive strategies might these measures support?

14.16 How do performance measures for service firms differ from those for manufacturers?

14.17 Outline the features of contemporary performance measurement systems.

14.18 Outline the steps involved in benchmarking.

14.19 What are the advantages and limitations of the four types of benchmarking?

14.20 Explain the following terms, as they relate to benchmarking: *performance gap, normalisation, best practice company*.

14.21 What role can management accountants play in benchmarking activities?

Exercises

E14.22 Financial and non-financial measures

Classify each of the following statements as true or false. In each case give reasons for your answer.

1 Financial performance measures provide essential information in order to assist managers at the operational level to take actions to correct problems.
2 Non-financial measures assist managers to manage the drivers of future financial performance.
3 Both financial and non-financial measures can assist in communicating the strategy of the business and in encouraging goal congruence.
4 Financial measures provide an indication of how well the organisation has performed across a range of strategically important areas.

E14.23 Non-financial performance measures

For each of the following businesses, select three performance measures that could be used to support the competitive strategy of quality. Make sure that your measures are specific to each type of business.

1 An accounting firm.
2 A company that manufactures electric garden equipment.
3 A firm that designs advertising campaigns for sporting events.
4 A company that sells children's toys.
5 A pizza and pasta restaurant.
6 A taxi company.

E14.24 Non-financial performance measures: manufacturer

Elundini Fabrics (Pty) Ltd weaves fine wool, which it then manufactures into woollen clothing. The senior management team believes that critical success factors for the business are cost effectiveness, product innovation and time to market.

Required:

For each of the critical success factors, suggest three performance measures.

E14.25 Financial and non-financial performance measures: service firm

Canny Catering Ltd specialises in catering for office parties. Over the past six months, business has started to pick up, particularly as the number of 'employee farewell' parties has increased in the larger corporations. The prime control tool is the monthly performance report, which contains comparisons between actual and budgeted revenues and costs. Budgeted costs were developed last year; and now, with the increased business activity, monthly cost variances are always unfavourable. The budget was based on an average of two parties per week, whereas the company is currently catering for three parties per week.

The manager of Canny Catering says she has little use for the monthly cost and revenue reports – revenues always seem to be favourable and costs unfavourable. However, she has noticed that in the recent quarterly profit statement, the actual profit margin was 3 per cent, whereas the budgeted profit margin was 5 per cent. 'How can this be?' she asks.

Required:

1 How can monthly cost and revenue variances be favourable when the quarterly profit margin percentage is below budget?
2 Can you suggest how Canny Catering can improve its monthly performance reporting system?

3 Explain to the manager of Canny Catering the advantages of expanding the monthly performance reports to include non-financial measures.

E14.26 Benchmarking: manufacturer

Sleepy Time is a multinational manufacturer of herbal teas. The South African plant, located at Clanwilliam in the Western Cape, is currently attempting to lift its performance through benchmarking activities. The best performing plant in the Sleepy Time Group is located in Zurich, Switzerland. The general manager of the Clanwilliam plant has approved a benchmarking visit to the Zurich plant by a team of employees. The benchmarking team consists of the manufacturing manager, two manufacturing team leaders, a member of a third manufacturing team and the plant's human resources manager. The functions that the benchmarking team has identified for study include employment contracts, the operation of self-managed teams in manufacturing, and the processes that have resulted in high safety performance and short cycle times at the Zurich plant.

Required:

1 What type of benchmarking is the Clanwilliam plant planning to undertake?
2 Explain the advantages and limitations of this type of benchmarking.
3 What are the advantages of forming a multidisciplinary benchmarking team similar to the one used by the Clanwilliam plant?

E14.27 Performance measures: manufacturer

Juggernaut Industries manufactures mobile telephones, a product that has one of the fastest growing markets in South Africa. Juggernaut's accountant is considering designing a new performance measurement system for the company. As part of this process, the management team has established the following objectives for the company for the coming year:

- To achieve 10 per cent increase in sales revenue.
- To achieve a return on investment of 15 per cent.
- To provide mobile phones that meet customers' needs for leading-edge design and performance at a reasonable price.

Management has taken each objective and established the following critical success factors: customer satisfaction, cost effectiveness and new product introduction.

Required:

1 For each of the three objectives, suggest another critical success factor.
2 Suggest two performance measures that would support each of the company's critical success factors listed in the question.

E14.28 Performance measures in a service business

Identify specific lead and lag measures that may be used in each of the following three businesses to measure:

(a) quality (b) customer loyalty

1 An insurance company.
2 A school.
3 A market research company.

E14.29 Performance measures in a service environment

The head of the Accounting Department at the University of Utopia wants to develop a performance measurement system to improve the performance of her department in both teaching and research.

Required:

You are hired as a consultant to identify performance measures for the Accounting Department. Suggest three objectives for the Accounting Department. List the performance measures that should be included and give reasons for each measure chosen. (*Hint*: As a customer of an Accounting Department, you should have some great ideas about how performance in teaching can be measured and improved!) What problems do you envisage in the implementation of these performance measures?

E14.30 Key performance indicators and key performance drivers; Du Pont chart: service firm
Fetakgomo Bank is currently redesigning its performance measurement system. Up until now it has relied heavily on monthly cost variance reports to control the costs in each bank branch, and would now like to have a more comprehensive performance measurement system that can help the bank to detect problem areas before they become significant.

The bank is committed to achieving a high return on investment for shareholders and believes that careful management of customer service and costs will help to achieve that goal.

Required:

1 Identify some key performance indicators (KPIs) for the bank and some key performance drivers (KPDs) that could be used to manage operations at the bank branch level. Draw these in the form of a Du Pont chart.
2 Explain how continuous improvement could be built into the KPDs, to help encourage improved performance over time.

Problems

P14.31 Performance measures in manufacturing
Joe Tindane is a line supervisor in the Paint Shop of the East London Car Company (ELCC). The ELCC manufactures cars for the domestic and export markets. Jim Kent is the manager of the Finishing Department, which includes the Paint Shop. It is the end of the first week in May when Kent approaches Tindane for help.

Kent: Joe, here are the results for our department for the month of April. I need your help to explain these variances at the meeting with the plant manager tomorrow. Just look at them. I'm in for a really hard time.

(Tindane examines the performance report for the Finishing Department for April, which is shown below.)

Tindane: Jim, why do you bother with these measures? They're not worth the paper they're written on. Tell those blokes at the top that when they introduce some decent measures they'll start to get some decent results!

Finishing Department Performance Report for April		
Direct material:		
Standard cost	R301 225	
Material usage variance	1 950	F
Material price variance*	75	U
Actual material cost	299 350	
Direct labour:		
Standard cost	196 500	
Direct labour efficiency variance	7 000	F
Direct labour rate variance	2 400	U
Actual labour cost	191 900	
Manufacturing overhead:		
Applied to production	200 000	
Variable overhead efficiency variance	5 000	F
Variable overhead spending variance	4 000	U
Fixed overhead volume variance	10 000	F
Fixed overhead budget variance	15 000	U
Actual overhead	204 000	

*Material price variance is based on actual quantity used.

Required:

1 Outline the major criticisms of standard costing variances as measures of performance. (*Hint*: You may find it useful to review Chapters 10 and 11.)
2 Use the variance data to provide a brief report on the performance of the Finishing Department.
3 Suggest some alternative performance measures for the Finishing Department that might be useful.

P14.32 Designing a performance measurement system; Du Pont chart: service firm

Fleur Flowers is a chain of florists that has been operating successfully for the past two years. However, competition is becoming more intense, particularly in the trendier suburbs of the city. Mark Fleur, the managing director, no longer directly manages any of the florist shops and is interested in developing a performance measurement system that can help him to evaluate the relative performance of each shop and to anticipate any problems. It is important that he knows of any problems, particularly those concerning customers and profitability, as soon as they happen. He would like to know this information for each of his eight shops. In this type of business, customer loyalty can be short-lived and profits may be erratic.

Required:

1 Advise Mark Fleur on how he should set about designing a performance measurement system. In your answer, consider the various features of an effective performance measurement system.
2 Select some performance measures that may address the various concerns of Fleur.
3 Develop a Du Pont chart, similar to that in Exhibit 14.6, to show how the performance measures flow through to improving customer satisfaction and cost effectiveness, and ultimately to profit.

P14.33 Developing a balanced scorecard: bank

Search the website of a major bank and find information about the bank's business strategy, services and operations.

Required:

1 Outline the long-term goals of the bank and its business strategy.
2 Develop a balanced scorecard for the bank, including lead and lag indicators for each of the four perspectives.

3 Explain how the performance measures in your balanced scorecard may be used to motivate managers' performance.

P14.34 Balanced scorecard: service firm

Clean Living Ltd is a travel company that specialises in 'green tours' – package tours to environmentally sensitive destinations. These types of tours are growing in popularity, and while Clean Living has had little problem attracting customers, it has noticed that a number of competing businesses have just commenced operations. Even some of the regular travel companies are starting to offer green tours.

Saffron Jordaan, the managing director, has asked the financial controller, Clarence Kent, to design and implement a new performance measurement system that may help to protect the business against competitors. Jordaan has spent many years working for large multinationals and appreciates the value of strategic planning and a good performance measurement system. Recently she attended a seminar on balanced scorecards.

To provide the foundation for the new performance measurement system, all of the managers of the company participated in a strategic planning retreat. The managers used the Kaplan and Norton approach to outline a set of objectives to support the four perspectives of a balanced scorecard:

Perspectives	Objectives
Financial	Increase net profit
	Improve cash flow
Customer	Increase market share
	Improve customer satisfaction
Internal business processes	Improve office cost-effectiveness
	Develop innovative tours
Learning and growth	Improve environmental knowledge of employees

Required:

For each of the four perspectives, provide lead and lag indicators that would support the objectives. Make sure that your measures relate specifically to Clean Living Ltd.

P14.35 Performance measures for operational control: manufacturer

South African Plastics Ltd manufactures a range of moulded plastic products, such as kitchen utensils and desk accessories. The production process in the Tshwane plant is highly automated. The plant uses a just-in-time production management system. An automatic material-handling system is used to transport products between production operations.

Each month the accountant prepares a production efficiency report, which is sent to corporate headquarters. The data compiled in these reports, for the first six months of the current year, are as shown in the table below.

South African Plastics Ltd: Tshwane Plant Production Efficiency Report 1 January to 30 June							
	Jan.	Feb.	Mar.	Apr.	May	June	Average
Overtime hours	60	70	75	80	85	105	79.2
Total setup time (hours)	70	70	65	64	62	62	65.5
Cycle time (average in hours)	20	20	19	18	19	17	18.8
Percentage of orders filled	100%	100%	100%	100%	100%	100%	100%
Percentage of on-time deliveries	99%	98%	99%	100%	96%	94%	97.7%
Inventory value/sales revenue	5%	5%	5%	4%	5%	5%	4.8%
Number of defective units, finished goods	80	82	75	40	25	22	54
Number of defective units, in process	10	30	35	40	60	60	39.2
Number of raw material shipments with defective materials	3	3	2	0	0	0	1.3
Number of products returned	0	0	0	0	0	0	0
Power consumption (kWh, '000s)	800	795	802	801	800	800	799.7
Machine downtime (hours)	30	25	25	20	20	10	21.7
Bottleneck machine downtime* (hours)	0	0	2	0	15	2	3.2
Number of unscheduled machine maintenance calls	0	0	1	0	2	3	1

*The concept of bottlenecks is explained in Chapter 15.

Required:

1 Write a memo to the managing director of South African Plastics Ltd, evaluating the Tshwane plant's performance. Structure your report by dividing it into the following parts:
(a) production processing and productivity
(b) product quality and customer satisfaction
(c) delivery performance
(d) raw material, scrap and inventory
(e) machine maintenance
(Some measures may be relevant to more than one area of performance.)

2 Identify any areas of concern in your memo and suggest appropriate action for management.

P14.36 Performance measures for operational control: manufacturer

Medical Systems Corporation manufactures diagnostic testing equipment used in hospitals. The company practises JIT production management and has a state-of-the-art manufacturing system. The following non-financial data were collected every two weeks in the Port Elizabeth plant during the first quarter of the current year:

	Fortnightly measurement period					
	1	2	3	4	5	6
Cycle time (days)	1.5	1.3	1.3	1.2	1.2	1.1
Number of defective finished products	4	4	3	4	3	3
Customer complaints	6	7	6	5	7	8
Unresolved complaints	2	1	0	0	0	0
Products returned	3	3	2	2	1	1
Warranty claims	2	2	2	0	1	0
In-process products rejected	5	5	7	9	10	10
Average number of units produced per day per employee	410	405	412	415	415	420
Percentage of on-time deliveries	94%	95%	95%	97%	100%	100%
Percentage of orders filled	100%	100%	100%	98%	100%	100%
Inventory value/sales revenue	2%	2%	2%	1.5%	2%	1.5%
Machine downtime (minutes)	80	80	120	80	70	75
Bottleneck machine downtime* (minutes)	25	20	15	0	60	10
Overtime (minutes) per employee	20	0	0	10	20	10
Average setup time (minutes)	120	120	115	112	108	101

*The concept of bottlenecks is explained in Chapter 15.

Required:

1 For each non-financial performance measure, indicate which of the following areas of manufacturing performance is involved:
(a) production processing
(b) product quality
(c) customer satisfaction
(d) in-process quality control
(e) productivity
(f) delivery performance
(g) raw material and scrap
(h) inventory
(i) machine maintenance
(Some measures may relate to more than one area.)

2 Write a memo to management commenting on the performance data collected for the Port Elizabeth plant. Be sure to note any trends or other important results you see in the data. Evaluate the Port Elizabeth plant in each of the areas listed in requirement 1.

P14.37 Problems with conventional performance measures; strategy and performance measures: manufacturer

Grassy Park Mowers Ltd manufactures lawnmowers and grass-slashers. The manufacturing plant has three production departments: Metalwork, Mechanical Work and Assembly. The company uses monthly standard costing reports to evaluate performance and control costs in the manufacturing areas. Typically, these reports are distributed to managers within two weeks of the end of the month.

Required:

1 Identify the performance measures that are likely to be included in the monthly standard costing reports. (You may need to revisit Chapters 10 and 11.)

2 How useful do you think this information will be for:
(a) the managing director
(b) the manufacturing plant manager
(c) production department managers
(d) production line foremen and supervisors?
Explain your answer in each case.

3 Suggest strategic areas, apart from cost, where the company is likely to want to manage its performance.

4 Pick one strategic area that you have identified in requirement 3, and suggest an objective and two performance measures for each of the four management levels listed in (a) to (d) of requirement 2.

P14.38 Balanced scorecard: service firm

Rice Porterhouse and Company is a large chartered accounting firm. The company has four departments that work directly with clients: Auditing, Taxation, Management Consulting and Liquidation. In addition, the firm has an Administration Department. The managing partner uses the measures shown below to monitor the firm's performance.

	Performance measures
Overall business	Return on investment
	Market share
Client departments	Revenues
	Costs
	Percentage of available time charged to clients
Administration Department	Costs

At the end of each month the managing partner compares the actual results for these measures with budgeted results. Department managers are asked to explain any significant variances. Rice Porterhouse has always been successful, but recently its profitability has declined. The managing partner asks the Management Consulting Department to review the firm's performance measurement system.

Required:

Prepare a report for the managing partner that includes the following information:

1 Identification of the type of business strategies that might be followed in a service firm such as Rice Porterhouse,

2 A review of the existing performance measurement system, assessing:
   (a) how well it measures performance to support the firm's strategies
   (b) any potential adverse effects that the existing system may have on performance

3 A balanced scorecard system for the business that includes:
   (a) objectives for the business, and each perspective
   (b) lead and lag indicators for each perspective

4 An explanation of the advantages that the balanced scorecard offers over the existing performance measurement system.

P14.39 Financial and non-financial performance measures: fresh produce delivery firm

You have been offered employment over the summer break by your uncle, who operates a large fresh produce delivery service. The business sources and packs orders for fresh fruit and vegetables and makes about 400 deliveries per day, usually to hotels, restaurants and private residences. The company is currently evaluating the monthly performance of each of its divisions, using return on investment.

You are employed at the main depot, and over the past few weeks you have noticed that there appears to be a fair degree of wastage occurring. The business has been running at a loss, and customer complaints have been increasing. These complaints relate mainly to the quality of the product and the accuracy of the order delivered. You have suggested to your uncle that one way of managing this problem would be to design a new performance measurement system.

To assist you in your task, you have been told that the critical success factors of the business are delivery time, product quality and a wide product range. The managers believe that if these factors are focused on, sales revenue and profit will follow.

Required:

1 For each of the critical success factors, suggest two objectives and two performance measures for each objective. Make sure that your measures suit the particular operations of the business.

2 Explain how you could build continuous improvement into the performance measurement system. Use the performance measures developed in requirement 1 to illustrate your answer.

3 Non-financial performance measures, compared with financial measures, are better suited to monitoring the operations of a business and provide a more effective way of improving performance.
   (a) Explain why some people believe the above statement.
   (b) Outline the arguments against this claim.

P14.40 Benchmarking: manufacturer

Makhado Plastics Pty Ltd manufactures plastic kitchenware at its Castle Hill factory. Its manufacturing equipment consists of large plastic extrusion machines that were purchased 15 years ago. Makhado Plastics produces in small production runs, and although the machinery is old, it is reliable.

The company's products are much sought after by speciality gift stores and upmarket department stores such as Woolworths. It also sells its products to Saks of Fifth Avenue in

New York. While Makhado Plastics has many products, among the most popular is the Puchi salad bowl and servers. This product is made of clear plastic with gold flecks, and competes very favourably with the latest Italian salad bowls.

Makhado Plastics has just begun its first benchmarking activity. It has subscribed to an international benchmarking group that provides benchmarking data specifically tailored to different industries.

The benchmarking data supplied by the agency, relating to the plastics industry, include product cost per kilogram of finished product; cycle time; reject rate; and direct labour and raw material costs per kilogram of product. The manufacturing manager, Pascale Roux, suspects that the benchmark data must relate to the famous Speedy Plastics, renowned as the world's best plastics manufacturer. This company is a mass-producer of multicoloured school lunch boxes and picnic cutlery, and uses high-speed, computer-controlled plastic extrusion machines.

The management accountant of Makhado Plastics, Brian Khoza, has prepared a report comparing the performance of Makhado Plastics with the benchmark data:

Performance measure	Makhado Plastics	Benchmark data
Product cost per kg of product	R85	R66
Direct labour per kg of product	R20	R10
Raw material cost per kg of product	R45	R10
Cycle time per 100 units	60 minutes	15 minutes
Reject rate	2%	3%

Pascale is concerned about the size of some of the performance gaps between Makhado Plastics' measures and best practice, and has asked Brian to investigate.

Required:

1 Explain the concept of benchmarking and how it can be used to help a business improve its performance.

2 Should Pascale be concerned about the size of the performance gaps? In your answer, consider each performance measure separately.

3 Assuming that the benchmarking data relate to Speedy Plastics, will they provide suitable benchmarks for Makhado Plastics? If not, can you suggest what types of data may be more suitable?

Cases

C14.41 Review of Chapters 13 and 14; financial performance measures; reward systems; behavioural issues: manufacturing and service organisation

Young International has its head office in Gauteng, and operates throughout South Africa, Namibia and parts of Nigeria. There are three main divisions:

- Brewing Division – this is the oldest division, and it operates major breweries in Benoni, Nigeria and Cape Town.
- Newspaper Division – owns leading tabloid newspapers in several cities.
- Satellite Television Division – operates satellite television services in Namibia and South Africa. This is a high-risk, growing market.

Each division is headed by a managing director who has been given a high level of decision-making authority. Each managing director effectively runs his or her division as a stand-alone business within the general policy guidelines provided by the board of directors in the head office. Each managing director agrees to achieve a series of targets: return on investment (ROI), market share and sales growth. These targets are developed as part of the annual budget-setting process. Intense lobbying takes place between each managing director and the board of directors to determine the most suitable targets.

Each managing director receives an annual cash bonus based on achieving the target divisional ROI. The company defines ROI as operating profit, before interest and taxes, divided by divisional assets (measured at original cost less accumulated depreciation). Senior managers are each eligible for a cash bonus of R2 million if they reach their divisional ROI target. If performance is above target, share options are awarded at the rate of 10 000 shares for every additional point over target. Thus, if the ROI target is 13 per cent and the division achieves 15 per cent, the manager would be awarded 20 000 share options. These options are at the prevailing market price on the last day of the financial year, and must be taken up within two years of the award. The market price of the company's shares increased from R200 on 30 June 20X6 to R300 on 30 June 20X7. If the ROI target is not reached, there are no bonuses or share options, and the managing director has to give convincing reasons for the poor performance. As a consequence of the performance measurement and reward system, the managing directors are highly motivated to achieve – and exceed – their ROI targets.

Janice Mokoena has just been appointed as the new management accountant in the head office, charged with redesigning the performance measurement system. As her first task, she has obtained the financial data for the past two years for each division. A summary of the financial information for 20X6 and 20X7, in millions of Rands, is as follows:

	Operating profit		Sales revenue		Divisional assets		Target ROI	
	20X6	**20X7**	**20X6**	**20X7**	**20X6**	**20X7**	**20X6**	**20X7**
Newspaper	44.0	53.9	258.8	260.0	440.0	490.0	10%	10%
Brewing	95.0	110.0	475.0	450.0	500.0	647.1	18%	16%
Satellite Television	20.0	35.0	180.0	85.0	666.0	700.0	2%	3%

Leonard Smith, the managing director of the Brewing Division, is concerned that his market share, and hence his ROI, is likely to suffer in the current financial year, 20X8, as his main competitor has recently purchased new brewing technology. While his own brewing equipment is only 10 years old, it is unable to produce the new variety of beers that customers are demanding, and maintenance and operating costs are increasing.

Smith is considering a proposal to invest R1000 million in new equipment. This will probably increase operating profit for his division in 20X8 by R100 million. Smith has analysed the future cash flows of this proposal, and the new acquisition will easily satisfy the minimum required rate of return of 10 per cent for all new investments that is set for the Young Group. Without this acquisition, Smith expects his 20X8 ROI to drop to 14 per cent.

Required:

1 Calculate the ROI for each division for 20X6 and 20X7, as well as the two components of ROI: profit margin and return on assets. Comment on the relative performance of the three divisions.
2 Calculate the bonus that each managing director would earn in 20X6 and 20X7.
3 Explain why Leonard Smith is reluctant to invest in the new brewing equipment. Provide calculations to back up your answer.
4 Janice Mokoena is considering expanding the divisional targets to include a range of non-financial measures. She is interested in developing a balanced scorecard for each division. For each of the three divisions:

(a) formulate objectives for each of the four dimensions of the Kaplan and Norton balanced scorecard
(b) suggest lead and lag indicators for these objectives

C14.42 Performance measures and reward systems; behavioural issues; benchmarking; continuous improvement

Refer to Case 14.41.

Janice examined the performance-related pay system used to reward the managing directors, and has prepared a report that recommends three changes:

- Add a more long-run emphasis to the bonus system.
- Base rewards on achieving company-wide as well as division-based performance measures.
- Include targets that are designed specifically to consider the competitive challenges facing the managers of each division.

Required:

1 Suggest how the three proposed changes could be included in the bonus plan for each divisional managing director. Consider each division and be specific in your suggestions.
2 Outline any difficulties that could arise in implementing the changes to the bonus system.
3 Janice has also recommended that the performance measurement system should make greater use of benchmarking and incorporate continuous improvement to improve overall company performance. Why would she recommend benchmarking? Suggest the specific steps that would need to be undertaken to introduce benchmarking at the Newspaper Division.
4 Suggest how continuous improvement processes could be incorporated into the performance measurement system at the Newspaper Division. Provide some examples of performance measures to illustrate your answer.

C14.43 Review of chapters 12, 13 and 14; responsibility accounting, transfer pricing; reward systems: manufacturer

Monoclean Ltd is a multinational company that manufactures and markets household cleaners in a batch-process manufacturing environment, and ABC is used to allocate overhead to production. Recently, Monoclean has under gone a major structural reorganisation to assist it to compete more effectively in the Sub-Sahara African region.

Under the old structure, the Sub-Sahara African region was divided into 12 business units along geographical lines. Each business unit had a managing director (MD) responsible for manufacturing as well as marketing and selling operations of the business units' products. Each MD was evaluated and remunerated on the business unit profitability, which was as reported in a monthly business unit profit statement. Managers within each business unit were evaluated and remunerated according to their personal, department and business unit performance.

About a year ago the number of manufacturing plants in the region was reduced from 12 to 5. The 12 business units continued to exist, except that 7 of the business units were now only responsible for the marketing and selling of products. Only 5 business units continued to include manufacturing plants, which were now responsible for supplying all of the business units in the Sub-Sahara African region. Each business unit with a manufacturing plant has a manufacturing manager. While the MD of those business units have ultimate responsibility for the marketing and sales operations and all other aspects of the business unit, in practice the MD does not interfere with the manufacturing manager, who is given full responsibility for manufacturing in the business unit. The MD is principally evaluated and remunerated on the profit generated from marketing and sales activities. Marketing profit reflects actual sales revenues less standard manufacturing costs and actual sales and marketing costs. The manufacturing manager is evaluated on the profit from manufacturing. Manufacturing profit consists of sales revenue less actual manufacturing costs. There is also a manufacturing director for the region who has ultimate responsibility for all the manufacturing managers.

Under the new company structure, monthly profit statements are prepared for each business unit. In addition to these reports, a manufacturing profit statement is prepared for the region and a total company profit statement is prepared. The transfer price for goods transferred between manufacturing and marketing areas within the same business unit is at standard manufacturing cost. The transfer price for goods transferred between manufacturing and marketing, not within the same business unit, is at standard cost plus 5 per cent.

Some business unit managers have raised concerns about some of the decisions that have been made since the restructure, and wonder if the right incentives are in place. Some specific examples and issues follow:

- Marketing and sales managers are in the best position to influence the level of slow-moving and obsolete stock, through choosing whether to sell off these products or allow them to be written off. In recent months there have been high levels of obsolete stock that have had to be written off profit. However, the impact of these write-offs affects the manufacturing profit statement. There is little incentive for marketing staff to sell off or manage slow or old inventory as they simply purchase goods at standard cost from manufacturing as required.
- Inventory shipping and transportation is managed by manufacturing staff and the cost of this is charged to the manufacturing profit. However, the cost of these activities is heavily influenced by the deals that the sales force makes with their customers. Sales staff can negotiate three shipping and transportation options; the purchaser picks up the stock from Monoclean's warehouse, the stock is shipped by Monoclean to a central warehouse of the customer, or Monoclean transports the stock to the customer's supermarkets. Each of these options attracts different costs, which are charged to the manufacturing profit.
- When there is a change in product or raw material sourcing, the business units that include manufacturing areas absorb the manufacturing variances from standard cost (favourable or unfavourable). This results in an adjustment to standard cost in subsequent periods and affects the profit of the marketing units. For example, if a favourable purchasing variance results from the activities of the manufacturing company the transfer price will decrease.
- Another issue of concern is the role of the MD in the capital expenditure approval process. It is the manufacturing director, not the MD of each business unit, who initiates all capital expenditure requests. Capital expenditure decisions affect business unit profits through the timing of cash flows, depreciation on assets, maintenance cost and so on.

Some business unit managers believe that there may be a problem in the alignment between business unit responsibility, transfer pricing policy, performance evaluation systems and management remuneration. The profits of some business units are below budget and, in the current competitive environment, head office management is concerned.

Required:

You are part of a management consulting team and have been asked by the regional finance director of Monoclean Ltd to prepare a report outlining any issues that may be working against effective performance measurement and incentive systems in the business units. In your report, identify clearly any underlying problems and recommend a solution that considers appropriate responsibility centre type, transfer pricing policy, performance evaluation system and management remuneration package.

(Contributed by David Brown, UTS)

Endnotes

1 As explained in Chapter 1, the term operational (or operations) managers usually refers to manufacturing managers and manufacturing supervisors who have responsibility for manufacturing activities. They include production line supervisors, foremen, department managers and plant managers in manufacturing firms. In service businesses they include office managers, supervisors and front-line employees.

2 See, for example, Lynch & Cross (1991); Beischel & Smith (1991).

3 This example is based on the experience of a real company.

CHAPTER 15 Managing Costs and Time for Customer Value

❖ LEARNING OBJECTIVES

After completing this chapter, you should be able to:

1 define *cost management* and explain how it differs from conventional approaches to cost control;

2 use the four steps of activity-based management to reduce costs and increase customer value;

3 identify opportunities for cost reduction by undertaking value analysis;

4 select activity-based performance measures to manage cost, time and other sources of customer value;

5 recognise the impediments to implementing activity-based management;

6 describe the four major steps involved in business process re-engineering, to manage costs and other sources of value;

7 analyse life cycle costs and revenues and understand how to use life cycle management to reduce costs;

8 estimate target costs and describe the processes of target costing that lead to cost reduction and enhanced customer value;

9 explain how time-based management can be used to manage time drivers as well as costs and other sources of customer value; and

10 undertake analyses, using the theory of constraints and throughput accounting, to manage costs and time.

Introduction

In earlier chapters we described the changes that have swept through the business world over the past two to three decades. With the evolution of global markets, the rapid rate of technological innovation, the emerging 'e-environment' and the increasing importance of customer satisfaction, businesses need to offer a wider range of high-quality goods and services, at lower prices, developed in anticipation of customers' requirements and delivered on time. Some businesses have been able to meet this challenge and have prospered. Others have failed.

As well as developing new approaches to performance measurement, management accounting has responded to the changing business environment by paying increased attention to managing resources – in particular, costs, time and quality, which are not only key cost drivers but important sources of customer value. In this chapter, we consider various approaches to reducing costs and managing time. We revisit the Mason & Cox case, from Chapter 8, to illustrate activity-based management, a model that provides information to managers to help reduce costs and improve other sources of customer value. We describe other approaches to controlling and reducing costs, namely business process re-engineering and also life cycle management and the related concept of target costing. We also explore the role that management accounting can play in managing time, both time to develop new products (and services) and delivery time, paying particular attention to the concepts of throughput accounting and the theory of constraints. In Chapter 16 we consider the role that management accountants play in managing quality, as part of the broader processes of managing suppliers and customers.

Cost management

L.O. 1

Conventional management accounting systems include a range of financial performance reports and measures to provide managers with information for cost control. Contemporary management accounting systems also include various tools and techniques that provide information for cost management. What is 'cost management', and how does it differ from conventional approaches to cost control? **Cost management** is the improvement of an organisation's cost effectiveness through understanding and managing the real causes of costs. Although the predominant focus is on costs, most contemporary approaches to cost management also focus on improving other aspects of performance, such as quality and delivery.

The major differences between conventional approaches to cost control and contemporary cost management are:

- *Drivers of costs.* Under the conventional approach, managers control costs by bringing them into line with some predetermined goal, such as budgeted or standard costs. The focus is on cost results or outcomes. Cost management reduces costs by identifying wasted resources and eliminating this waste through identifying the factors that really drive costs.
- *Strategic perspective.* The primary focus of conventional approaches is on controlling costs within the organisation – an internal perspective. Contemporary cost management is also concerned with achieving value for the customer – a strategic perspective.
- *Process perspective.* Conventional systems tend to control costs by reporting results for responsibility centres based on functional areas of the business, such as production, marketing and administration. Contemporary cost management recognises that customers' needs are met by processes, which flow across the business and may cross functional areas.

A number of separate approaches have evolved to managing costs, including:

- activity-based management;
- business process re-engineering;
- life cycle management; and
- target costing.

As described below, each of these techniques can be used independently to reduce costs, although in some instances they may also be complementary. For example, activities, which are the foundation for activity-based management, can also provide a useful framework for business process re-engineering, life cycle management and target costing. Moreover, target costing reduces costs by applying life cycle management principles.

Activity-based management

In Chapter 8 we described how Mason & Cox implemented an activity-based product costing (ABC) system, and found that its conventional system had distorted product costs and undermined strategic decision making. The distorted product costs appeared to have eroded the ability of the company to compete successfully; activity-based product costing helped to solve the problem. However, this is only half of the story. We now return to Mason & Cox to examine the role that activity-based costing and activity-based management can play in managing costs and improving business performance.

Returning to Mason & Cox

You will recall that Mason & Cox is a large independent foundry, producing metal castings for a wide range of local industries and export customers. Production begins with drawing and issuing patterns, which are used to build up moulds. Molten metal is poured into the moulds, and when the metal is set, the castings are knocked out. The castings are 'finished' by smoothing, grinding, welding and heat treating. Mason & Cox had been in business for a long time, but by the 1990s its profits had declined. The cause of the problem was not clear from the company's existing conventional management accounting system. As accounting manager at Mason & Cox, Olivia Buthelezi knew that an improved product costing system would help with strategic decision-making. However, ultimately the company must reduce its costs and improve performance in other key areas in order to survive.

Mason & Cox had a conventional planning and control system based on standard costing and budgeting. Managers investigated variances between actual and budgeted results and instigated corrective action. This approach to planning and control is similar to that found in many businesses today, and these types of performance reports and measures have changed little since they were first developed in the 1920s. While Buthelezi provided managers at Mason & Cox with regular variance reports to help them control their costs, she was concerned about the usefulness of this information. She decided to explore the possibility of using activity-based management to improve Mason & Cox's performance.

Activity-based management at Mason & Cox

Exhibit 15.1 shows that activity-based costing can have two dimensions: costing and activity management.[1] Costing is used to calculate the cost of cost objects, such as products. The activity management dimension is a dynamic view that reports what is happening in the business.

When Buthelezi first encountered the term 'activity-based management' she was not sure how it differed from activity-based costing. Now she understood that **two-dimensional activity-based costing** provides information about activities, cost drivers and performance, as well as about the costs of cost objects such as products. **Activity-based management (ABM)** refers to the process of using information from activity-based costing to analyse activities, cost drivers and performance so

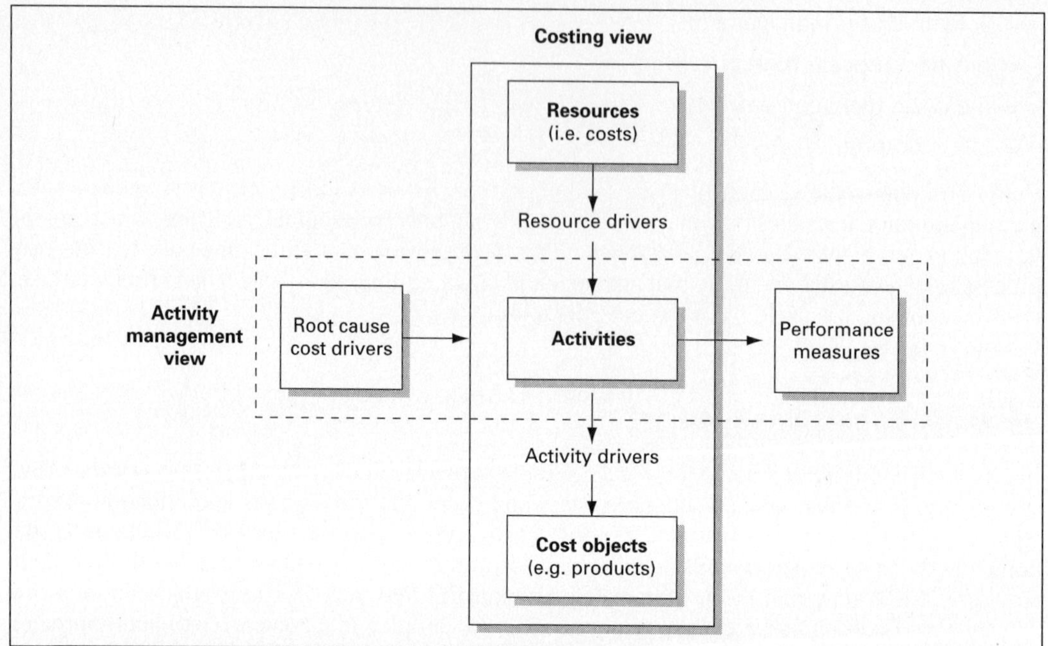

Source: adapted from p. 96 of *Common Cents: The ABC Performance Breakthrough* by Dr Peter B.B. Turney, President and CEO of Cost Technology Inc., a management consulting firm specialising in ABC/ABM implementations. Cost Technology Inc., 1991. Reprinted by permission of the publisher.

Exhibit 15.1 An activity-based costing model

that customer value and profitability are improved. You will remember from Chapter 1 that **customer value** is the value that a customer places on particular features of a product or service. ABM would enable Buthelezi to reduce costs and manage other important aspects of performance.

Let's now consider how this can be achieved.

Using ABM to reduce costs

L.O. 2 To reduce costs, Buthelezi worked through four steps:

1. Identify the major opportunities for cost reduction.
2. Determine the real causes of these costs.
3. Develop a program to eliminate the causes and, therefore, the costs.
4. Introduce some new performance measures to monitor the effectiveness of cost reduction efforts.

Identifying the major opportunities for cost reduction

L.O. 3 The pivotal point of the ABC model is the identification and costing of activities. **Activities** are the units of work performed within the organisation. Exhibit 15.2 reproduces Mason & Cox's activities and their costs, which were calculated in Chapter 8.

To identify opportunities to reduce costs, Buthelezi undertook a **value analysis** (or **activity analysis**), where she classified activities as value-added or non-value-added. **Value-added activities** provide essential value to the customer, or are essential to the functioning of the business. Exhibit 15.2 shows that the value-added activities included:

- basic production activities that contribute to the final product, such as making moulds and pouring metal; and

- essential administrative activities, such as managing the business and preparing annual reports.

Non-value-added activities do not add value to a product or service from the customers' perspective or for the business and, therefore, can be eliminated without detriment to either. In many businesses, major sources of non-value-added activity include waiting, inspection, rework, and the unnecessary movement and storage of inventories. Exhibit 15.2 shows the non-value-added activities at Mason & Cox, which accounted for 18 per cent of the total activity costs.

	Value-added	Non-value-added
Corporate management		
Manage business (CEO)	R500 000	
Manage business (Board)	1 000 000	
Prepare annual accounts	175 000	
Produce annual report	275 000	
Administration		
Process receivables	474 500	
Correct invoices		440 000
Process payables	1 290 500	
Operate IT system	1 500 000	
Prepare payroll	573 500	
Maintain grounds	256 500	
Sales and dispatch		
Process sales order	1 250 000	
Factory management		
Program production	1 305 500	
Manage plant	564 500	
Metal melting		
Pour metal	15 075 000	
Moulding		
Make CT moulds	4 075 000	
Make job moulds	3 900 000	
Make cores	875 000	
Move material		1 225 000
Inspect moulds		1 000 000
Finishing		
Oxy cut casting	721 250	
Grind castings		2 007 500
Weld defects		1 390 000
Operate shot blast machine	3 662 500	
Set up heat treat furnace	2 135 000	
Operate heat treat furnace	3 260 000	
Expedite castings		1 082 500
Inspect castings		591 250
Pattern design		
Design method	1 250 000	
Issue pattern	625 000	
Rework pattern		535 000
Maintenance		
Repair shot blast machine		875 000
Repair heat treat furnace		925 000
Preventative maintenance	835 000	
TOTAL COSTS	**R45 578 750**	**R10 071 250**

Exhibit 15.2 Activity costs and value status, Mason & Cox

The analysis and elimination of non-value-added activities can require considerable resources. Like many businesses, Mason & Cox decided to target their major non-value-added activities. The major non-value-added activities were 'Grind castings', 'Weld defects', 'Move material', 'Expedite castings' and 'Inspect moulds'. These five activities accounted for two-thirds of the cost of all non-value-added activity at Mason & Cox.

Determining the real causes of non-value-added costs

To eliminate non-value-added costs, Buthelezi began by building activities into processes. Then she analysed those processes to find the causes of the non-value-added activities.

Building activities into processes

Eliminating non-value-added activities requires a clear understanding of the way work is done in an organisation. One way of developing this understanding is to identify, for each activity, the preceding activities that supply its inputs (that is, its suppliers) and the subsequent activities that consume its outputs (its customers). This information can be used to link activities together into processes. A **process** (or **business process**) is a series of activities that are linked together to achieve a specific objective. Processes cut across conventional responsibility centres such as functional departments. Exhibit 15.3 illustrates the process of filling a customer order for a custom-made casting at Mason & Cox. Notice:

- the horizontal flow of activities across the business, which crosses functional areas such as product design, manufacturing, sales and administration; and
- the interdependence between activities, where a preceding activity is the supplier of a subsequent activity (or the subsequent activity is the customer for the preceding activity).

The process perspective helps to identify cost drivers and establish relevant performance measures. Also, using processes can simplify activity management as, in many cases, it may be possible to manage fewer aggregated processes rather than many detailed activities. Activities in a process may share common cost drivers and performance measures.

Cost driver analysis

Once the processes had been identified, Buthelezi attempted to identify the root cause cost drivers of the five major non-value-added activities at Mason & Cox. **Root cause cost drivers** are the basic factors that cause activities to be performed and their costs to be incurred. For example, the quality of the moulds built up in the Moulding Centre appeared to be a root cause cost driver for the non-value-added activities 'Grind castings' and 'Weld defects' in the Finishing Centre. The poorer the quality of the moulds, the higher was the number of defects in the castings, and the more grinding and welding was required to rectify them.

Buthelezi used **cost driver analysis** to identify root cause cost drivers for the major non-value-added activities. The number of defects from oxy cutting castings also *appeared* to drive the activities 'Grind castings' and 'Weld defects'. Each defect must be ground and welded, but is this a root cause cost driver? What causes these defects: is it impurities in the metal? or is it the poor quality of moulds used to make the casting? If metal impurities are a major problem, what causes these impurities? Does Mason & Cox need to seek new metal suppliers or negotiate more stringent quality requirements with its existing suppliers? The search for root cause cost drivers inevitably involves continually asking why. Exhibit 15.4 lists possible root cause cost drivers for the five major non-value-added activities at Mason & Cox.

Developing a program for reducing costs

The next step for Buthelezi was to develop a program to eliminate the root causes of the major non-value-added activities. This can be a complex task and will involve managers from across the organisation. For example, Buthelezi identified metal impurities as a primary cause of defects in castings and, therefore, as a major cause of the non-value-added activities 'Grind castings' and 'Weld defects'. She worked with the purchasing manager to improve the quality of metal used in

Exhibit 15.3 Process of filling a customer order at Mason & Cox

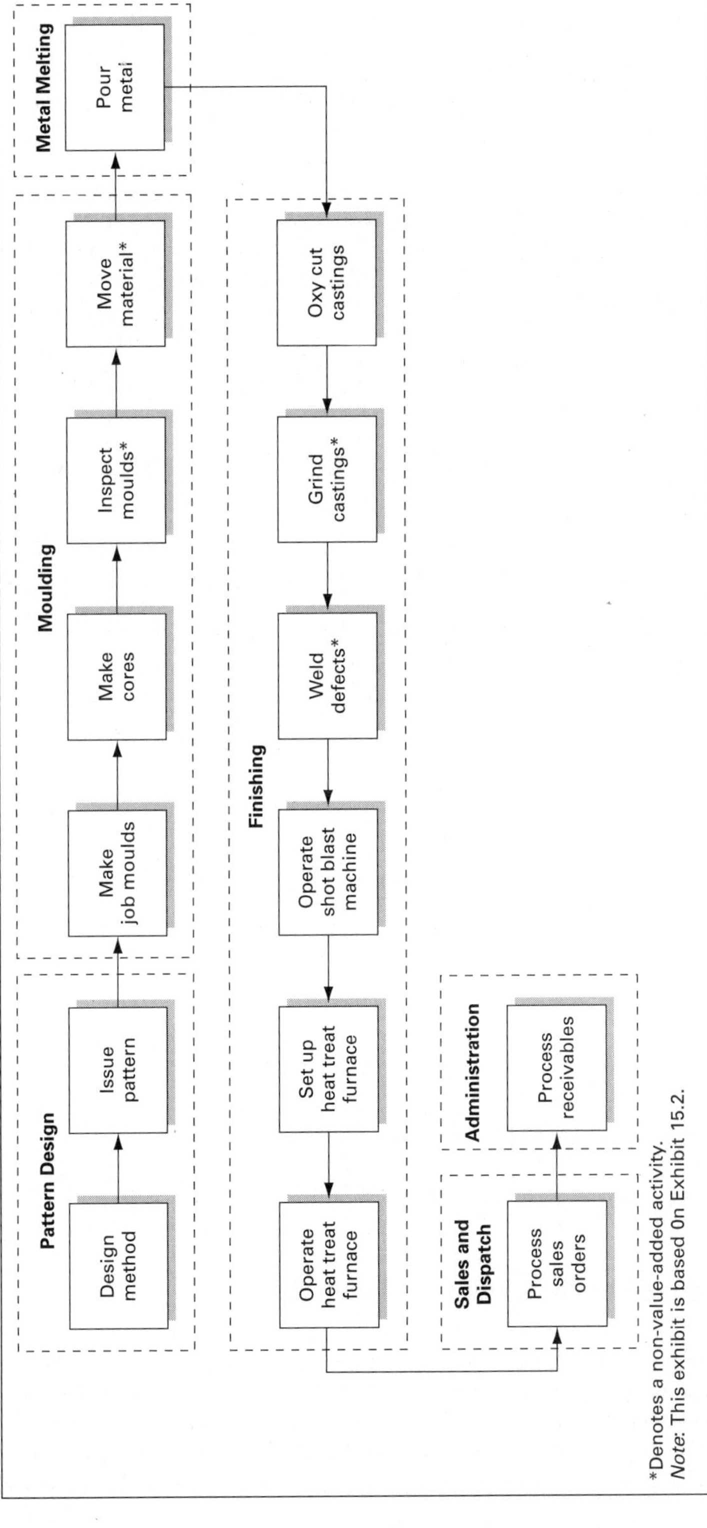

*Denotes a non-value-added activity.
Note: This exhibit is based 0n Exhibit 15.2.

Activity	Possible root cause cost drivers
Grind castings	Complexity of the casting Defects in moulds Defects during 'Oxy cut castings' Metal impurities
Weld defects	Complexity of the casting Defects in moulds Defects during 'Oxy cut castings' Metal impurities
Move material	Plant layout Supplier delivery arrangements
Expedite castings	Complexity of casting Poor scheduling, poor IT support Inadequate notice from customers Material unavailable Defects in moulding and casting
Inspect moulds	Complexity of the casting Complexity of pattern design Defects in moulding materials Inadequate employee training in moulding

Exhibit 15.4 Root cause cost drivers, Mason & Cox

castings. She found the activity 'Expedite castings' was caused by poor scheduling, and worked with the production scheduling staff to improve scheduling methods, the IT staff to improve the IT support for production scheduling, and the sales staff to improve the notice from customers.

Eliminating root cause cost drivers may involve tackling individual activities. Alternatively it may require a fundamental restructure of processes, called business process re-engineering, which is described later in this chapter.

Measuring performance

L.O. 4 Activity-based performance measures can be used to monitor the effectiveness of cost reduction efforts, as well as other key sources of customer value. Mason & Cox's management identified three aspects of performance that it believed were critical to the achievement of strategies and, therefore, to the success of the business: quality, delivery time and cost. (These are critical success factors for many businesses.)

Buthelezi identified performance measures that reflected both costs and cost drivers. She also introduced activity-based performance measures to monitor quality and delivery. In some cases these measures were interrelated. For example, a number of the quality and delivery measures, such as defects and cycle time, were also cost drivers. To illustrate this concept, Exhibit 15.5 lists some performance measures for cost, quality and delivery for each of the activities in the Finishing Centre.

By monitoring the measures over time, managers could obtain feedback on their performance. Targets could be set and corrective actions could be instigated where required. You will notice that by focusing on performance across key sources of customer value, ABM can be used in conjunction with the contemporary approaches to performance measurement described in Chapter 14.

The impact of activity-based management at Mason & Cox

The activity-based costing system had been expensive to implement at Mason & Cox. It was more complex than the conventional management accounting system and more expensive to maintain. Nevertheless, even though the new system had not been in place for long, ABC and ABM seemed to be improving profitability at Mason & Cox. Part of the improvement was due to the more accurate product costs, which provided a reliable basis for strategic decision making, as described in Chapter 8. For example, the cost of high volume, relatively simple products was no longer over-

Finishing Centre activities	Cost/cost drivers	Quality	Delivery
Oxy cut castings	R240.40 per hour No. of defects in moulds	No. of broken castings No. of defects during oxy cut	No. of castings Cycle time: 7.5 min. per casting
Grind castings	R125.45 per hour No. of defects in moulds No. of defects during oxy cut	No. of spots reground No. of defects during grinding	Cycle time: 5.3 per min.
Weld defects	R106.90 per hour No. of defects in moulds No. of defects during oxy cut	No. of cavities rewelded No. of defects during welding	Cycle time: 11.2 min. per casting
Operate shot blast machine	R1144.55 per load Cycle time	No. of defects during shot blasting	Cycle time: 180 min. per load
Set up heat treat furnace	R533.75 per setup Cycle time	No. of faulty setups	Cycle time: 214 min. per setup
Operate heat treat furnace	R0.60 per kilogram-hour Cycle time	No. of defects due to heat treatment	Cycle time: 110 min. per casting
Expedite castings	R1353.15 per order No. of defects in moulding and casting	No. of orders that fail to make due date	No set time, depends on reason for expediting
Inspect castings	R59.15 per casting No. of defects in welding	No. of customer returns	Cycle time: 2.8 min. per casting

Exhibit 15.5 Performance measures in the Finishing Centre, Mason & Cox

stated and the cost of low volume, speciality products was no longer understated. Cost-based prices now seemed to fit better with competitors' pricing and customers' expectations. However, part of the improvement was due to the company's better cost management. Cost savings had been achieved by targeting the most significant non-value-added activities. Their real cost drivers had been identified, and managers from across the business were working to eliminate them.

Moreover, part of the improvement was due to increased customer satisfaction. The drop in the price of the high-volume lines had met with customer approval. And, in addition to tracking cost drivers, activity-based performance measures enabled the company to monitor and improve quality and delivery, key sources of customer value. Instead of aggregated, outdated, financial measures of their performance, the new approach provided timely information about factors that were important to customers and factors that employees could control.

There was no doubt that ABM was helping Mason & Cox to improve both profitability and customer value! The two 'Real life' examples below describe South African businesses that have used activity-based management to improve their profitability and customer value.

Using the costing dimension of ABC to help manage costs

Most of the information for managing costs and improving customer value at Mason & Cox was obtained from the activity management dimension of the ABC model. However, some businesses use information from the costing dimension to reduce costs; for example, they may use ABC to obtain information about customer and supplier costs. Alternatively, they may use budgeted activity costs as a framework for control.[2]

Impediments to implementing ABM

Unlike activity-based product costing, the benefits from ABM are not limited to organisations with particular cost and product structures. ABM offers any organisation the opportunity to simultaneously manage costs better and improve customer value. There is limited evidence of the extent L.O. 5

of activity-based management in practice, although it is safe to say that the adoption rate has been relatively slow (Booth & Giacobbe, 1997). Why is this so?

Perhaps ABM suffers from some of the same impediments as activity-based product costing (described in Chapter 8). These included a lack of awareness, uncertainty over potential benefits, extensive resource requirements and resistance to change. The activity management dimension requires far more detailed analyses of activities and costs than the product costing dimension, and if ABM results in continuous improvement, activity and cost data may become outdated quickly. The costs of implementing and maintaining such a detailed system are likely to be substantial, although businesses may choose to implement ABM as a one-off exercise rather than as an ongoing system. Any new management approach is likely to encounter some resistance. However, the focus of activity-based management on highlighting non-value-added activities and identifying possible labour savings can result in substantial resistance among employees. (Resistance to change was dealt with in Chapter 8 and you may like to revisit that material at this stage.)

REAL LIFE: EXPERIENCES OF ABM AT SOUTH AFRICAN AND AUSTRALIAN COMPANIES

Barloworld, which is a major South African industrial group, has indicated that the roll-out of activity-based costing (ABC) across the business units of the group enabled the company to identify the true costs associated with each aspect of Barloworld's business. As indicated in Chapter 8, the company got out of business activities that were unprofitable and refocused management's attention on profitable operations. Activity-based costing also led the company to outsource certain non-strategic activities.

Anecdotal evidence suggests that the activity management perspective of ABC may offer as much, if not more, promise than the product costing perspective. Lamond (1992) cited three cases of Australian manufacturers that had adopted ABC and discovered the benefits of ABM:

- Parke Davis, a major pharmaceuticals manufacturer, attributed better investment decisions, as a result of more accurate product costs, to its ABC system. It also achieved better resource utilisation because of an activity management perspective. Parke Davis expected its ABC system to result in future cost savings and improved quality and service.
- Comalco Rolled Products (CRP), a manufacturer of rolled aluminium products, introduced ABC to improve its product costing system. As a result, it was able to drop a product group that had appeared profitable under its conventional system but was shown to be unprofitable under ABC. In addition, CRP found the activity management perspective of ABC invaluable because of its performance measures and its focus on the way work is done.
- ICI (now Orica) implemented ABC and ABM in its Film Products division, a major manufacturer of plastic-based film. The business experienced 'clear and measurable benefits' from the improved product costs resulting from the ABC system. The company decided to extend its ABC model to include activity management so that it could support total quality management (TQM) and similar programs.

In reviewing the role of activity-based costing in these three companies, Lamond concluded that ABM is becoming an important force in management accounting – even though most companies are using only some aspects of ABM.

In 1990 the Chemical and Plastics Division of ICI (C&P) also implemented ABM. C&P produced products such as polythene, polypropylene and vinyls, and employed about 3000 people in plants located throughout Australia. The division's ABM implementation focused on activities and processes, to identify costs and cost drivers, and to understand how customer value was created. In addition, ABM played a role in the identification of performance measures.

Sources: Lamond (1992); Chenhall & Langfield-Smith (1998a); www.barloworld.co.za

REAL LIFE: ACTIVITY-BASED MANAGEMENT IN SERVICE ORGANISATIONS

In Chapter 8 we described the real-life experiences of UNISA and Medscheme with activity-based product costing. Medscheme had implemented activity-based product costing to improve the allocation of overhead costs to products and to provide better information for strategic decisions about products. The company's ABC system also included an activity management dimension. With the increase in medical costs, Medscheme needed to accurately determine product costs, reduce costs and improve its competitiveness. The company wished to also determine customer profitability. Management at UNISA used ABM to identify and reduce non-value-added costs, monitor performance and determine the cost per course and cost per activity.

Some local councils have adopted activity-based product costing to increase the accuracy of estimated service costs. In Chapter 8, we referred to the case of the Buffalo City Municipality (which includes East London, King William's Town and Bisho), which was the first municipality to use ABC and ABM to set strategic priorities and tariffs for such services as refuse removal and electricity distribution. The City of Johannesburg is also committed to using ABM and ABC to set tariffs in the future.

The introduction of ABM and ABC at the local government level is expected to result in significant cost savings and improved services. The focus on ABM and ABC for local government follows the experience in Australia. Changes to legislation required local councils to open up a minimum of 50 per cent of their operating budget to competitive tendering. To compete in the tendering process, councils required accurate estimates of the complete costs of providing services. In addition, councils were expected to reduce costs by 15 to 20 per cent of gross expenditure. Annual savings to ratepayers were projected at nearly $400 million. Councils turned to ABM to achieve these savings. A study of the corporate services division of one large Melbourne council found that the top five activities consumed 45 per cent of the division's total expenditure and were largely non-value-added. For example, 92 per cent of the costs of the activity 'Mail management' were classified as non-value-added. Bayside City Council examined its accounts payable function, where the two major activities were 'processing invoices' and 'chasing invoices'. Chasing invoices, which involved following up documents that were not returned by other departments, accounted for 40 per cent of the accounts payable total activity time.

Sources: Newbold (1997); Hoban (1995); Lewis (1999)

In Chapter 8 we presented survey evidence to indicate that the adoption rate for ABC is likely to increase in the future, although it is not clear to what extent this applies to activity management, to activity-based product costing, or to both (Booth & Giacobbe, 1997; Chenhall & Langfield-Smith 1998b). However, it is clear that there are still many companies that have not adopted ABC/ABM.

Business process re-engineering

L.O. 6

Business process re-engineering is another approach to managing costs and improving customer value that has become popular since the early 1990s. **Business process re-engineering (BPR) or process re-engineering** is the fundamental rethinking and radical redesign of business processes in order to achieve dramatic improvement in critical areas of performance such as cost, quality and delivery (Hammer & Champy, 1993, p. 32; Manganelli & Klein, 1994).

BPR should focus on the processes that are essential to achieving the company's business objectives and strategies; that is, its **strategic processes**. Common processes include developing new products, manufacturing products, acquiring customer orders, fulfilling orders and developing human resources, although processes may differ from one organisation to the next. These processes cut across functional or departmental boundaries of the business. (For example, the process of filling a customer order at Mason & Cox, described in Exhibit 15.3, cuts across manufacturing departments, sales and administration.) The aim of BPR is to totally reorganise the way in which work is done by identifying and enhancing the value-added activities and eliminating all the non-value-added activities for a process. For example, re-engineering Mason & Cox's process of filling a customer order would aim to eliminate the non-value-added activities 'Inspect moulds', 'Move material', 'Grind castings' and 'Weld defects'. The value-added activities in the process would also be enhanced.

Once a process has been identified for re-engineering, BPR involves four major steps:

1. *Prepare a business process map.* A flowchart of the activities that make up the business process, called a **business process map**, is prepared. An example is shown in Exhibit 15.3.[3]
2. *Establish goals.* Management establishes clear goals for the re-engineered process, based on the business' sources of customer value. These are likely to include required quality and delivery performance, as well as cost. Depending on the business' strategies they may also include innovation, flexibility, and so on.
3. *Reorganise work flow.* Management works out how to reorganise the flow of work so that these goals can be achieved. For example, in re-engineering the process of filling a customer order at Mason & Cox, it may be possible to develop new, highly reliable moulding techniques to eliminate the need to inspect moulds. It may be possible to develop new oxy cutting techniques that eliminate the need for subsequent grinding and welding of defects. It may be possible to house custom-cast production and dispatch in one area where material movement is minimised, and staff are so highly trained that the need to inspect moulds, grind castings and weld defects is significantly reduced. (Reconfiguring the business around processes rather than functional departments is a common outcome for business process re-engineering.)
4. *Implementation.* The final step is implementation. Of course, you will have realised that business process re-engineering involves substantial change, and our earlier warnings about employees' resistance to change apply here. The behavioural aspects of BPR are best managed through the use of re-engineering project teams that involve employees from all functional areas affected by the process, and from all levels of the organisation.

REAL LIFE: BUSINESS PROCESS RE-ENGINEERING AT CONSOL

Consol is the leading manufacturer of food and beverage glass packaging in South Africa. The company was de-listed after Brait, a private equity group, acquired the company in 2006.

The company was very involved in re-engineering its business prior to its sale. In fact, Consol combined an expansion in capacity with a focus on innovation and business process re-engineering. The following is taken from a JSE SENS statement made by the company in May 2005:

Innovation in the Group is driven by an absolute commitment to delivering exceptional value to customers. Innovation takes many forms, from improving customer service, to exploiting IT, introducing new products and creating new uses for established products. Over the past year Consol has been successful in designing and developing lightweight glass containers in the wine, beer and carbonated soft drink (CSD) categories offering improved efficiencies and costs, and improved consumer branding and enjoyment. Within the information systems arena we have continued to invest to further improve operating performance and competitiveness. After two years of business process re-engineering and systems design, we have recently completed the overhaul of the SAP platform by implementing the mySAP business suite in the glass business.

REAL LIFE: RADICAL TRANSFORMATION AT TRANSNET

The appointment of Maria Ramos as CEO of Transnet signalled the beginning of a process of significant re-engineering at Transnet, a group that had been incurring sizeable operating losses, despite owning valuable assets. Ramos refocused the group on its core business units of rail freight, ports, fuel and gas pipelines, and the rolling stock maintenance division.

In the Transnet 2006 Annual Report, Maria Ramos states:

We have initiated a far-reaching business reengineering programme to build Transnet's core business units into efficient, profitable and customer-oriented entities as envisaged in the four point turnaround strategy. The key elements of this project focus on unlocking synergies and improving interfaces between rail and ports, and growing Transnet's market share and profitability.

The programme – Vulindlela – will continue over several years. Vulindlela consolidates all of our internal reengineering and efficiency improvement initiatives, and is expected to contribute significantly to the bottom-line over the next three years. It is designed to boost the sustainability of our strategic initiatives.

We have established a Vulindlela Programme Office in the Corporate Centre to coordinate the reengineering process. After a rigorous search, we appointed an international consultancy with a track record in the field of business transformation, to provide strategic support to this process, in partnership with a respected local black economic empowerment firm. A Vulindlela Steering Committee has been established to ensure accountability and high standards of governance, as well as grant a platform for peer review.

Vulindlela is initially focusing on:

- *The optimisation of Spoornet's iron ore line, the general freight business and the coal line;*
- *Improving maintenance practices and culture;*
- *Containing costs, simplifying processes and improving service delivery;*
- *Upgraded procurement processes;*
- *Improving safety; and*
- *Attention to Spoornet's National Operating Centre, which is focusing on the scheduling of trains.*

Whilst these projects will run for several years, significant benefits are already evident. For example, the reengineering team has been able to improve delivery times on the coal line by more than 10% since September 2005 with the introduction of a new scheduled operating system. The maintenance team working on this programme has decreased outage time on the main line from 64.4 to 21.6 hours.

Another example where our activities will pay dividends in the long-term, is in procurement, where reengineering efforts are focused on achieving economies of scale, setting policy and coordinating procurement practices throughout the business. Negotiating with top suppliers and leveraging economies of scale will achieve substantial savings for Transnet, and we are already beginning to see the benefits of this.

Vulindlela is integral to Transnet's focus on reducing the cost of doing business in South Africa through improved efficiency, capacity building and enabling appropriate freight to be railed instead of using road transport.

REAL LIFE: ADVISING ON BUSINESS PROCESS RE-ENGINEERING

PricewaterhouseCoopers (PwC), one of the 'Big Four' auditing and consultancy firms, provides clients with advice on business re-engineering. PwC uses advanced tools to achieve process improvements for clients and the firm goes beyond the measures of success – 'on time, to cost and to specification'. PwC follows a life cycle approach to obtaining benefits from business process re-engineering.

In executing process reengineering assignments PricewaterhouseCoopers makes use of a comprehensive set of tools. Our approach for business transformation, streamlining and simplification, together with our access to our Global Best Practices database and benchmarking tools enables us to fasttrack the identification of operational process issues and opportunities. PwC has selected Casewise Corporate Modeller as our advanced process modelling tool to complement other flowcharting tools already used in our practice. We acknowledge that some assignments may require only a simple process mapping tool to manage a small number of "flat" flowcharts. However, in other client engagements the processes subject to improvement may require the capturing of additional information or relationships between process components for further analysis (i.e. transaction volumes, processing times, people, locations, technologies). Thorough analysis may also require simulation to facilitate resource planning, cycle time improvement, queue management or bottleneck identification and resolution. Casewise Corporate Modeller is deployed where clients require a more advanced approach to process reengineering.

Source: www.pwc.com [Follow the links from Services, then performance improvement and then process improvement]

Is business process re-engineering the same as ABM?

Activity-based costing provides a good foundation for BPR, as it enables the identification of current processes and activities. ABC also provides information about the costs and value status of the activities within the business process. However, the focus of ABM is on **process improvement**, which is the incremental continuous improvement of processes, whereas BPR involves fundamental changes to the way processes are structured.

Life cycle costing

L.O. 7

Life cycle costing is an alternative approach to cost management which accumulates and manages costs over a product's life cycle (Adamany & Gonsalves, 1994; Artto, 1994; Susman, 1989). There are two important aspects to life cycle costing: the focus on the product cost and the inclusion of all upstream and downstream costs. A **product life cycle** is the time from the conception of a product through to its abandonment – that is, 'from cradle to grave'. From a production perspective, product life cycles usually cover four stages:

1 product planning and initial concept design;
2 product design and development;
3 production; and
4 distribution and customer (or logistical) support.

The length of a product's life cycle varies from one product to the next. For example, clothing and fashion goods tend to have a life cycle of one year or less. A Japanese auto manufacturer plans on a life cycle of four to five years from the time a new model is conceived to the time its production is discontinued. They allow another 10 years for the production of spare parts for discontinued models.

A **life cycle budget** can be developed to compare planned costs with predicted revenue over each year of the product's life. To complete the planning and control cycle, life cycle costing should be linked to the annual budgeting and performance reporting process to monitor the actual costs and revenues each year over the product's life cycle and compare them with the planned outcomes.

Life cycle budgeting enables a comprehensive assessment of the profitability of a product over its entire life, which can help managers to decide which products to produce.[4] Conventional costing systems enable product cost and profitability to be assessed each year, but this approach ignores upstream and downstream costs and the effects of life cycle stages.[5] In cost-plus pricing, cost should be based on the product's cost over its entire life cycle. This is especially important where products have short life cycles and high upstream and downstream costs. In this situation, prices must be set to recover all costs plus make a profit in a relatively short time.

We will illustrate these concepts with MPSA.

Life cycle budgeting: MPSA (Pty) Ltd

MPSA (Pty) Ltd manufactures MP3 players. Let's suppose that MPSA began the development of a revolutionary MP3 system, MP Super, in 20X4. The system was introduced into the market at the beginning of 20X5, with an expected life of four more years. Exhibit 15.6 shows the life cycle budget for MP Super. Over its life cycle, MP Super is expected to make a profit of R48.5 million, although it will be unprofitable in 20X5, the first year of production. If product profitability was assessed year-by-year, management may have decided to drop MP Super after 20X5! The company uses cost-plus pricing, and the life cycle budget helps management to set a price that covers all the costs that are expected to be associated with MP Super over its life.

	20X4	20X5	20X6	20X7	20X8	Total
Revenue	0	6 000 000	45 000 000	67 500 000	30 000 000	148 500 000
Costs:						
Product planning & concept design	3 000 000					3 000 000
Design and development	1 000 000	6 000 000				7 000 000
Production		3 000 000	20 000 000	27 000 000	12 000 000	62 000 000
Distribution & customer support		500 000	7 500 000	10 000 000	10 000 000	28 000 000
Total costs	4 000 000	9 500 000	27 500 000	37 000 000	22 000 000	100 000 000
Profit (Loss)*	−4 000 000	−3 500 000	17 500 000	30 500 000	8 000 000	48 500 000

*This analysis ignores the time value of money.

Exhibit 15.6 Life cycle budget, MPSA (Pty) Ltd

Managing costs through a life cycle perspective

The life cycle budget provides useful information for managing and reducing costs. For example, it can be used to carefully plan capacity requirements. More important, major cost savings can be achieved by recognising the trade-off between costs incurred prior to production and costs incurred once production begins. Exhibit 15.7 shows that nearly all of a product's costs are actually committed during the pre-production stages of its life cycle when the product and its production processes are designed. The design of the product, and of the processes that will be used to produce it, is a major determinant of subsequent production costs (and customer support costs). Spending more on the design phase can lead to significant savings during the production phase. Target costing, described below, is based on this principle and evaluates alternative product and process designs to identify the most cost-effective design.

Conventional systems, such as standard costing, focus on controlling production costs when they are incurred. However, far greater cost reductions can be achieved by designing efficient and effective production processes than by trying to control the costs of the processes once they are in place. Cost controls applied once production has begun can be expected to have only a relatively minor impact. Moreover, most conventional costing systems tend to treat pre-production (upstream) and post-production (downstream) costs as period costs, rather than recognising and managing them as product-related costs.

Impediments to life cycle costing

Although the concepts of life cycle costing make sound management sense, as yet they are not widely used in practice (Adamany & Gonsalves, 1994). This may reflect lack of awareness, or uncertainty about how to calculate life cycle costs (Booth, 1994). Life cycle budgeting is not easy, particularly for products with longer lives. It is very difficult to predict the effects of changing consumer tastes and the impact of competitors. The effects of inflation must also be considered. There is limited information in conventional budgeting systems for constructing life cycle budgets because conventional systems have a short-term (usually annual) cycle and focus on responsibility centres rather than on products, although the capital budgeting process may support the development of life cycle budgets. Activity-based costs can also play a useful role in estimating budgeted and actual life cycle costs, based on the activities performed in each year of the life cycle.

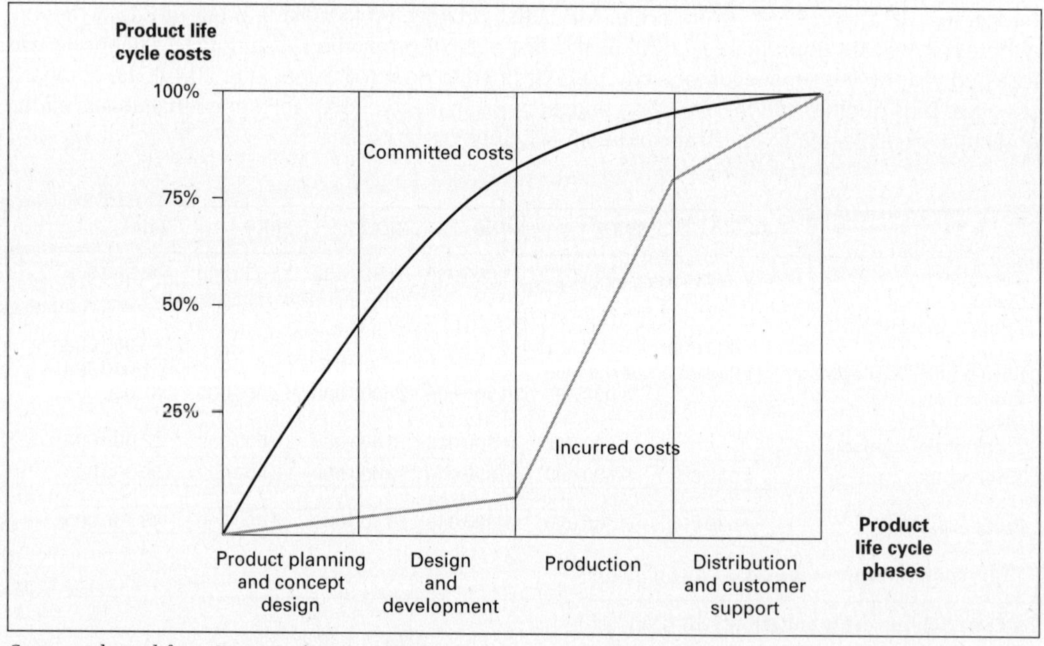

Source: adapted from Burstein (1988, p. 261)

Exhibit 15.7 Life cycle costs and cost commitment for a typical product

Target costing

L.O. 8

Target costing is a system of profit planning and cost management. The required features and performance of the proposed product are established. Then target costing determines the life cycle cost at which the product must be produced, to generate the firm's desired level of profit, given the product's anticipated selling price (Cooper and Slagmulder, 1999, p. 166). Note that target costing

REAL LIFE: THE LIFE CYCLE COSTS OF COMPACT DISCS

The costs of pressing a CD account for only a small part of its life cycle costs. There are high costs associated with marketing CDs, such as advertising and promotional videos, copyright costs for the music, and the recording artist's fees and royalties. Some of these costs do not vary with the level of production or sales, and have to be spread over the total number of units sold. The market in South Africa is much smaller than in the US, so the cost per CD is much higher. Based on a Canadian study in 2004, it is estimated that the retail price of CDs is 'divided up' as follows:

Compact discs	% of price
Manufacturing costs	8.8%
Artist & songwriting payments	11.8%
Recording costs and video production	18.8%
Promotion and marketing costs	12.9%
Label profit	7.1%
Record company distribution, sales & overhead	11.8%
Retailer	28.8%
	100.0%

Source: The Changing Face of Music Delivery: The Effects of Digital Technologies on the Music Industry, Department of Canadian Heritage, FAD Research, 2004.

However, some of these costs are fixed in nature. For example, the costs of recording, mixing and producing the music are upfront costs as well as some of the marketing and promotion costs. Recording labels may recover part of the recording costs from the artist in the future if the artist succeeds. Although the music industry is suffering from the effect of downloads and file sharing, it is also true to say that music artists feel that record companies do not pass over enough of the price of a music CD to artists in royalties whilst consumers consider that the prices of CDs are too high in relation to the underlying production cost. Artists are increasingly selling music over the Internet and are making money from live gigs rather than CD sales. The impact of myspace.com has also been instrumental in exposing bands and artists to the public. However, making money from making music is not easy.

is not a method for *product costing,* it is a technique for *cost management.* It was devised in Japan, where it is used widely, particularly in the automobile, electrical and equipment manufacturing industries (Lorino, 1995). With the effects of globalisation, it is gradually gaining acceptance in the Western world.

Remember the revolutionary MP3 system, MP Super, which MPSA (Pty) Ltd began developing in 20X4 and introduced into the market in 20X5? We can extend this example to illustrate target costing. In developing the life cycle budget, shown in Exhibit 15.6, MPSA's management accountant identified the planned selling price for MP Super and the planned number of units to be sold. Let's assume that the budgeted life profit of R48.5 million assumed sales of 50 000 units at a planned selling price of R2970 and a planned cost, including upstream and downstream costs, of R2000 per unit. The selling price was based on the planned cost per unit plus a planned profit markup of 48.5 per cent on cost (or 32.66 per cent of selling price). The planned costs were derived from the management accountant's understanding of the current production technology and facilities available to the company.

If the company had used target costing, the preparation of the life cycle budget and the planned level of profit might have been very different. Let's say that market research indicated to MPSA that to sell 50 000 units the MP Super would have to be priced at R1900. Given this information we can estimate the target cost for MP Super as:

Target cost = target selling price − target profit margin
= R1900 − (0.3266 × R1900)
= R1279.46

Notice that this cost is well below the planned cost of R2000 per unit. (Indeed, the target selling price is below the planned cost!) Substantial cost reduction would be required before the MP Super would earn a return of 32.66 per cent on selling price.

The target costing process

We have used the MP Super to illustrate the basic calculations involved in setting target costs, but it is important that you also understand the processes that would be used to drive the current cost down towards the target cost. Exhibit 15.8 describes the three steps to reducing costs through the target costing process (Cooper & Slagmulder, 1999):

1 market-driven costing;
2 product-level target costing; and
3 component-level target costing.

We will continue with the MP Super to illustrate these steps.

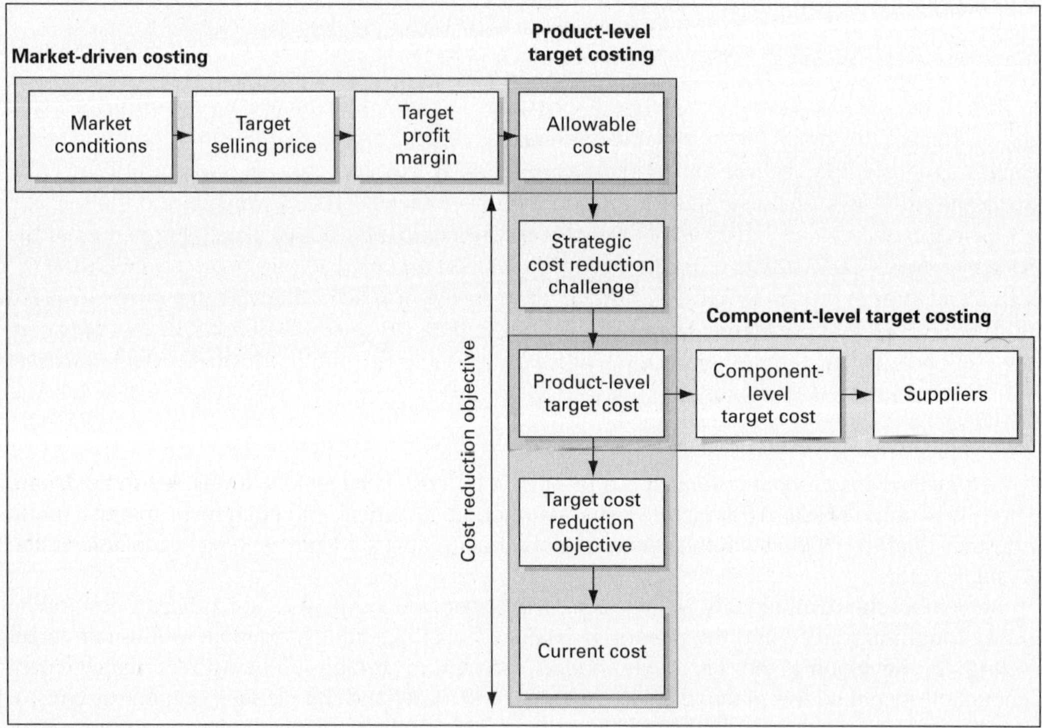

Source: Cooper & Slagmulder (1999, p. 166)

Exhibit 15.8 The target costing process

Market-driven costing, the target cost in an ideal world

Early in the product planning stage, MPSA would have developed a clear picture of the product features required to meet customers' expectations, and the level of performance required for each feature. This would have involved identifying the size of the MP Player, the quality of the sound, the length of play before recharging, and so on. The MP Super's **target selling price**, which is the anticipated market price for the product, would be based on market considerations, such as customers' needs and expectations and competitors' behaviour, as well as the business' strategic objectives for the product.

MPSA would then determine its **target profit margin**, based on an assessment of the return on sales required to make an acceptable profit on the MP Super. This would be influenced by the profit performance of similar products and the long-term profit objectives of the business. Based on this information, the MP Super's **allowable cost** can be estimated, which is the target cost at which the product must be produced if it is to be sold at the target selling price and generate the rate of return required by the business. Thus:

Allowable cost = target selling price − target profit margin

The target cost of R1279.46, identified for the MP Super in our simplified illustration above, is in fact the allowable cost.

Product-level target costing: connecting with reality

You will notice that the allowable cost is driven primarily by market considerations. It does not take into account whether or not MPSA has the capabilities to achieve this cost for the MP Super through its product designers, production capabilities, and material and component suppliers. The degree of cost reduction required to achieve the allowable cost is called the *cost reduction objective*. To calculate this objective, MPSA would need to estimate the cost, including upstream and downstream costs, for which the MP Super could be manufactured, given the current design and resources but prior to any cost reduction activities. This is called the **current cost**, which was estimated (in the life cycle budget) at R2000. Thus, as indicated in Exhibit 15.8, the **cost reduction objective** is the difference between the allowable cost and the current cost. At MPSA the cost reduction objective for the MP Super would be R720.54 (the current cost, R2000, minus the allowable cost, R1279.46).

To be effective, the MP Super's target cost would need to be challenging but achievable, otherwise the target costing process would lose credibility and targets would not be taken seriously at MPSA.[6] For this reason, some businesses distinguish between the *achievable* and *non-achievable* part of the cost reduction objective. The achievable part is called the **target cost reduction objective** and is determined by making a *realistic assessment* of the ability of the product designers, production engineers and suppliers to remove cost from the product. This task is often undertaken by a cross-functional team, which is set up to manage the target costing process. This team may consist of members representing key activities across the value chain, such as production engineering, product design, purchasing, marketing and accounting. In setting the target cost reduction objective there may be extensive negotiation between team members to locate where in the value chain the cost savings will be found. How much cost reduction can be achieved in product design? How much in the manufacturing process? How much in reduced material and component costs? The **product-level target cost** is then determined as the difference between the current cost and the target cost reduction objective:

Product-level target cost = current cost − target cost reduction objective

Let's say that, after an aggressive search for cost savings, MPSA's design engineers estimated that, given the company's current capabilities, cost savings of R500 per unit could be achieved. That is, the MP Super could be produced for R1500 per unit, including all upstream and downstream costs. The R500 cost saving becomes the target cost reduction objective, and the product-level target cost for the MP Super becomes R1500 (the current cost, R2000, minus the target cost reduction objective, R500).

The unachievable part of the cost reduction objective is the **strategic cost reduction challenge**, which for the MP Super amounted to R220.54 (the product-level target cost, R1500, minus the allowable cost, R1279.46). We would hope that this figure is not too high, as it indicates either that the business is less efficient than its competitors, or that its target profit margin is higher than that of competitors. The business will not earn its target profit margin until its product-level target cost is equal to (or less than) the allowable cost. This will only happen when the strategic cost reduction challenge has been eliminated. However, at the start of the target costing process the product-level target cost becomes the target for cost reduction activities, not the allowable cost, as it is an achievable target, although only with considerable effort and creativity.

Once the *target cost reduction objective* had been determined, MPSA would have to find ways of achieving the product-level target cost. Individual targets would be set for various functional departments, product components and materials, and value engineering would provide a way of reducing costs while enhancing the functionality of the new product (this is described in the next section). Under target costing, all functions of the business must make a firm commitment to designing, producing and distributing the product with total life cycle costs equal to the product level target cost.

Component-level target costing: focusing on the detail

The target costing team breaks down the product-level target cost into **component-level target costs**, which are target costs for major sub-assemblies and components of the new product. For example, at MPSA target costs would be set for the assembly process and the packaging process, as well as for distribution. In this way each major area in the business would have its own target cost and cost reduction objective to achieve. Techniques such as value engineering could be used to find creative ways of achieving some of these targets. **Value engineering (VE)** involves analysing the design of the product and the production process to eliminate any non-value-added elements, in order to achieve target cost while maintaining or increasing customer value. VE may involve design engineers modifying the design of some components to make them easier to manufacture and maintain, substituting more cost-effective material which does not reduce customer value, and improving the efficiency of the production processes. Thus, in undertaking VE, it is critical that engineers and product designers have a clear understanding of customer value. Value engineering will also involve working with suppliers to provide components or raw materials that meet target costs.

Most businesses rely on outsourced components, to some degree. In setting component-level target costs, the business' product designers may work with suppliers to reduce costs, which may then create a cycle of target costing within supplier organisations. At MPSA this would involve setting target costs for the plastic case, speakers and battery packs, which are sourced from external suppliers.

Given that suppliers will seek to maximise the price they receive and the business will seek to minimise the cost it pays, negotiations between the business and its suppliers are likely to be very intense. The relationship with suppliers needs to be managed carefully so that suppliers do not feel unreasonable pressure. Often the business' and the suppliers' design teams work together to achieve the component-level target cost. As with product-level target costs, component-level target costs need to be demanding but achievable in order to maintain the credibility of the target costing process.

Pursuing continuous improvement once production begins

If production of the MP Super began before the gap between the current cost and the product-level target cost had been eliminated completely, actual costs would be monitored against the target, and the various approaches to cost management described in this chapter, such as value analysis and cost driver analysis, would be used to drive the actual cost closer to the product-level target cost. During this stage, the emphasis would be on continuous, incremental improvements to production processes.

MPSA would not earn its target profit margin until the product-level target cost is reduced to the allowable cost. The business would continue to seek to meet the strategic cost reduction challenge to narrow this gap.

Target costing for cost management

The key features of target costing are that it:

- is price led (it begins with the expected market price and works backwards to set the target cost);
- focuses on the customer (the product features and quality required to meet customer expectations are established and taken as given, prior to setting the target cost);
- is based on the principles of life cycle management, placing primary emphasis on managing production and downstream costs by focusing on the design and development phase; and
- is cross-functional, involving managers from right across the value chain.

In its initial life cycle budget, MPSA used a cost-plus approach to pricing. The target costing study indicates that the planned level of sales of 50 000 units would not be achievable at this price. Target costing would enable MPSA to plan how to manage costs in order to achieve the desired level of sales.

Like life cycle costing, target costing has a major role to play in developing and managing new products, although it can also be used to manage the costs of existing products, especially product upgrades.

REAL LIFE: TARGET COSTING IN THE AUTOMOTIVE SECTOR

As in Japan, target costing plays a major role in the South African automotive industry sector. For example, the major car manufacturers use target costing to actively pursue cost reduction. Instead of being based on market price, target costs are set at the component level, based on the component cost in the previous model, adjusted for any changes in the engineering specifications for the new model. For example, a side protector moulding on a new model may be wider than on the existing model, and may include a new reflective strip. To establish the target cost for this component, the costs of the extra material and the extra processing time required to add the reflective strip would be added to the cost of the side protector moulding on the existing model. A target cost for the new model is obtained by adding the target costs for the individual components used to manufacture the vehicle.

At Toyota, target costing is one of a series of cost management tools used by the company. The target costing process is managed by the Cost Planning Team, which consists of people drawn from the purchasing, engineering, manufacturing and sales areas of the business. People from these areas are included because each of them can control some aspect of cost. The team is chaired by the National Manager of Management Accounting, and the target costing process is coordinated by the Accounting Division of Toyota, as the system interfaces with other major planning and control tools, including long-term business plans, budgeting and performance measurement.

Target costing is a suitable method of cost control for Toyota, as the selling price of new vehicles is determined by a fiercely competitive market, and cost effectiveness needs to be improved to continue viability and to increase market share.

Initially, detailed cost and profit analysis is undertaken for the new product by considering the variations required to produce the new model over the current model. Throughout the product development phase, progressive targets are set for all members of the Cost Planning Team, who are responsible for reducing costs in their particular area of responsibility. For example, the Purchasing Division will be responsible for meeting cost targets for the supply of component parts for the new vehicle. (There may be up to 3000 parts used in a motor vehicle.) The Cost Planning Team meets monthly to review progress on targets.

Toyota considers that the major opportunities for managing costs occur during the product development phase, before product design and tooling are locked in. The product development phase lasts about 30 months. Major sources of cost reduction are achieved through value engineering.

Once production commences, cost management still takes place. Cost reduction targets are set as part of the budgeting processes. Continuous improvement (or *Kaizen*) occurs over the production life of the vehicle, using value analysis. Any cost reductions achieved during the production phase will be used when the target costing process is undertaken for the next model.

Courtesy of Toyota

During the design phase, target costing teams may use value engineering to identify and eliminate any non-value-added aspects of the design. Target costs are also set for purchased parts and materials, and these need to be achieved by suppliers. Once production begins, the emphasis is on process improvements in order to continually narrow the gap between the actual cost and the target cost.

Sources: Langfield-Smith & Luckett (1999); Thorne (1997)

Managing time

L.O. 9

So far, our primary focus in this chapter has been on managing costs. However, most managers understand that time is an important driver of both costs and revenue. Time costs money because:

- time dictates the rate at which products and services are produced and revenue is generated;
- time determines how long resources are tied up during processing and therefore unavailable for other profit-generating activities;
- time delays often cause a build-up of inventories and associated holding costs; and
- for some businesses, innovation is a critical success factor. They compete on the basis of time to develop new products or to produce existing products, and delays will lead to a loss of current and potential customers.

Not only does effective cost management require effective time management, time itself can be a source of competitive advantage for many businesses.

Time-based management

Managing time focuses on compressing the time it takes to undertake all of the business' processes, from product development through to production and delivery. At the extreme, **time-based management (TBM)** considers time as the primary focus for managers' decisions.

Time is a universal characteristic of every activity and process, and, according to TBM, information about time is far easier to obtain and more timely than information about costs. Managers are encouraged to shift from the cost control focus of conventional management accounting to a time management mindset, making the organisation more customer-oriented and responsive. In managing time, as in managing costs, non-value-added activities must be identified and eliminated. Managing time will result in lower costs and better quality, but time remains the fundamental focus. The aim is to reduce new product development time, throughput time and delivery time (Mouritsen & Bekke, 1999).

Measures of time

Although most businesses do not adopt all of the principles of time-based management and focus on time to the exclusion of other considerations, many businesses do recognise the importance of time, by measuring and managing:

- time taken to develop new products and services; and
- time taken to fulfil customer orders for products and services.

Developing new products and services

Innovation can be a key source of competitive advantage for some businesses. For example, digital camera producers, such as Canon and Pentax, constantly compete on the basis of new and enhanced product features, such as picture resolution, zoom capability and image storage capacity. The sooner an innovative product can be released into the market the better, and many businesses measure **new product** (or **service**) **development time** (also known as **time-to-market**), which is the time from the identification of an initial concept through to the release of the product (or service) for sale. (Indeed, this is a common measure for firms that use a balanced scorecard performance measurement system, described in Chapter 14.)

Break-even time (BET), which measures the time from the identification of an initial concept through to when the product has been introduced and has generated enough profit to pay back the original investment, is another measure of the effectiveness of the new product development process (Kaplan & Norton, 1996).[7] This measure was developed by Hewlett-Packard and emphasises the importance of the speed, efficiency and profitability of the new product development process. However, BET can encourage incremental projects rather than major innovations, as incremental projects are likely to involve lower development costs, and returns that flow more quickly, easily and predictably. In contrast, major innovations are likely to involve longer life cycles, with later sales significantly exceeding sales early in the life cycle. Moreover, the BET measure is not timely, as it cannot be estimated until some time after the product development cycle has been completed.

Let's explore new product development at MPSA (Pty) Ltd, the business that manufactures portable MP3 players. The market for portable MP3 systems is very competitive, with global players such as Sony, Apple and Philips constantly developing products with enhanced features, in terms of sound quality, portability and battery life. To remain competitive MPSA must compete on the basis of innovation as well as cost. Indeed, you will remember that MPSA was in the process of developing a revolutionary MP3 system, MP Super. The sooner this product enters the market, the better, as its superior sound quality and lightweight, long-life battery will give MPSA a definite edge over its competitors. MPSA has a cross-functional team working on the design of MP Super, to develop product and process designs to meet its target cost.

It is likely that this team will also have a targeted *new product development time* to ensure that the MP Super is available in the market as soon as possible, and to provide a timeline for planning production and marketing resources. Product planning and concept design for the MP Super commenced at the beginning of 20X4 and the life cycle budget for the MP Super, in Exhibit 15.6, indicates that the 'Design and development' phase was completed sometime in 20X5. Thus, the MP Super was developed during a two-year period, but we would need to know the exact completion date to get a more precise measure of the new product development time.

	Cumulative initial investment (during 'Planning and concept design' and 'Design and development')	Profit (Sales revenue – production and distribution costs)	Investment yet to be recovered
20X4	R4 000 000	R0	R4 000 000
20X5	10 000 000	2 500 000	7 500 000
Jan 20X6	0	1 458 000	6 042 000
Feb 20X6	0	1 458 000	4 584 000
Mar 20X6	0	1 458 000	3 126 000
April 20X6	0	1 458 000	1 668 000
May 20X6	0	1 458 000	210 000
June 20X6	0	1 458 000	0

Exhibit 15.9 Break-even time, MP Super

Exhibit 15.9 shows that the *break-even time* for the MP Super will be 2 years and 6 months (assuming that the product performs according to its life cycle budget, shown in Exhibit 15.6). The original investment in the MP Super consists of the R10 million of costs incurred during the product 'Planning and concept design' and the 'Design and development' phases. Ignoring these design costs, profits of R2.5 million and R17.5 million were forecast for 20X5 and 20X6 respectively. Assuming that the profit from sales flows evenly during the year, the R17.5 million profit in 20X6 would be earned at approximately R1 458 333 per month (R17.5 million ÷ 12). (Note that R1 458 000 has been used in Exhibit 15.9 for simplicity.)

Time taken to fulfil a customer's order

Another important aspect of time management is the time taken to respond to a customer's order for a product or request for a service, which is measured by customer response time. Exhibit 15.10 shows that **customer response time** is made up of three major elements: order receipt time, production lead (or cycle) time (which can be divided into waiting time and production time), and delivery time.

Consider, for example, the customer response time at MPSA. When the MP Super enters the market it will be sold to electronic goods distributors as well as direct to major retail chains. To encourage minimal delays, MPSA will measure the time between receiving a customer order and delivering that order to the customer – that is, the *customer response time*. When MPSA's sales department receives an order for the MP Super, the time between receiving the order and placing it with the manufacturing department is the **order receipt time**. Once manufacturing receives the order, it may need to wait for various resources to become available, such as materials, components or machine capacity, before production can begin. This delay is the order **waiting time**. **Production time** refers to the duration of the manufacturing process for the MP Super. **Production lead** (or **cycle**) **time** (or **manufacturing cycle time**) measures the period from when the order for the MP Super enters the manufacturing department to when the manufacture of MP players is complete, and includes the *waiting time* and *production time*. The production lead (or cycle) time captures all the processes that MPSA must control to produce what the customer expects, which is a quality product in the shortest possible time. (Almost all customers prefer short lead (or cycle) times!) Indeed many businesses estimate **average cycle time**, which is the ratio of total processing time to total good units produced, as a measure of process efficiency. **Delivery time** refers to the time taken to deliver the MP Super order to the customer and reflects the efficiency of MPSA's distribution processes.

While customer response time is of interest to almost all customers, in some industries, such as fast food and banking, customer response time is a key source of competitive advantage. In the late 1990s McDonald's offered customers their meal free of charge if their order was not filled within two minutes. A bank providing home loans measures the time between the receipt and resolution of funding applications. An insurance company may measure the time between receiving a claim and payment. Minimising the time it takes to settle claims may offer the company a competitive advantage.

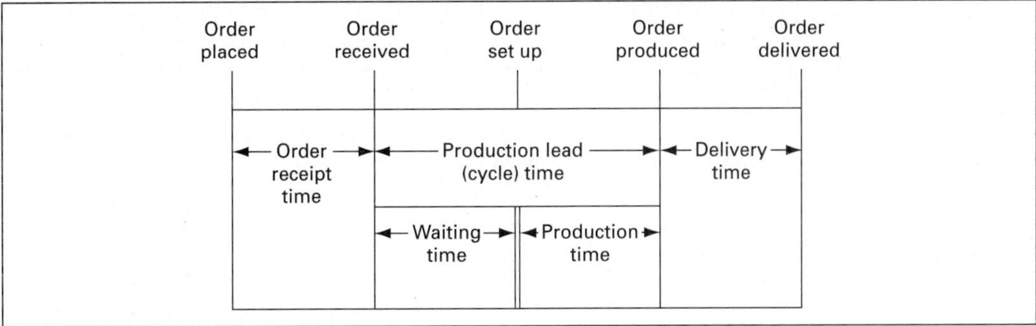

Exhibit 15.10 Customer response time

Reliability in meeting scheduled delivery dates

The effectiveness of meeting customer orders can also be measured through **delivery schedule reliability**, which assesses the extent to which a business meets predetermined delivery schedules. For example, SA Post offers a guaranteed overnight delivery service. One indicator of the effectiveness of SA Post's time management would be to measure the percentage of packages delivered by the next day. Telkom may measure the number of reported service faults remedied within 24 hours. Airlines, rail services and bus companies measure the percentage of services that arrive on time.

Note that a business can improve its delivery schedule reliability by building longer customer response times into the schedule, but customers may not perceive this as better time management!

Identifying and managing the drivers of time

Each of the measures described above monitors the effectiveness of time management. However, managers will only be able to improve time management by understanding and managing the drivers of time. A **time driver** is any factor that changes the duration of an activity. Exhibit 15.11 identifies common time drivers and suggests possible approaches to managing them.

Time drivers	Possible management approaches
Poorly structured order, production and delivery processes	Conduct value analysis to identify and remove non-value-added activities. Implement continuous improvement processes. Use business process re-engineering to completely redesign processes.
Bottlenecks in order, production and delivery processes	Manage throughput by identifying and resolving bottleneck resources. Attempt to minimise 'lumpiness' and unpredictability in customer demand.
Poor quality	Develop a total quality management (TQM) culture, supported by appropriate measures of quality costs and quality drivers.*
Inefficient inventory management	Improve supply chain management to minimise delays caused by inadequate and poor quality supplies.*
Poorly structured R & D processes in developing new products and services	Use target costing to manage the product design and development process. Ensure that value engineering minimises production time as well as cost.

*TQM and supply chain management are described in Chapter 16.

Exhibit 15.11 Customer response time

As you work your way through this chapter, you will notice that many of the approaches used to manage time are the same as those used to manage costs. For example, removing non-value-added activities or re-engineering business processes saves both time and money. Likewise, managing throughput focuses on speeding up the production processes, which results in more rapid revenue generation and lower costs. Managing quality can reduce delays and save costs. And target costing can be used to minimise production time as well as costs.

Some companies even use their cost accounting system to manage time. They allocate overhead costs to business units and products using production lead (or cycle) time as the overhead allocation base. Even though many overhead costs may not be driven by time, this allocation process makes managers aware of the importance of managing time, especially if managerial rewards systems are linked to measures of cost or profit. However, performance can be managed far more effectively using a more comprehensive range of performance measures that acknowledge the causal relationships between cost, time and quality, such as those used in a balanced scorecard performance measurement system described in Chapter 14. The 'Real life' below describes how both time and costs were managed at two healthcare centres.

REAL LIFE: MANAGING TIME AND COSTS FOR CUSTOMER VALUE

Many of the techniques described in this chapter to manage time and costs more efficiently and effectively have been developed in manufacturing settings. However, most of them can also be applied to the service environment. Public health care systems are increasingly under budgetary constraints in countries such as Australia, the UK and South Africa. This means that hospitals need to be innovative about reducing costs, managing time and creating value for patients.

Tygerberg Children's Hospital

Dealing with unequal access to medical services and healthcare has been a major challenge for South Africa's government. City and tertiary hospitals traditionally received the major part of public funding while patients in rural areas were subject to a poor level of healthcare service. The government has been directing funds away from the tertiary hospitals to the district hospitals and rural clinics. However, budget cuts at hospitals such as Groote Schuur and Tygerberg have also created problems such as queues for operations, a reduced level of specialised care, and cuts in the investment in medical equipment. The drop in the number of available beds has reduced the number of patients that are able to be examined by specialists. Yet demand remains high. One way of cutting costs and offering specialist medical services at rural and district hospitals is to adopt a telemedicine model. This is what Dr Nel and Dr Gie (with funding from the Rotary Club) set up at Tygerberg Children's Hospital, which is linked to a number of district hospitals. How does the system work? Doctors at district hospitals scan X-ray images and electrocardiographs and these are emailed to the Tygerberg Children's Hospital. Emails also include digital photographs and blood test results. The specialist doctors at Tygerberg then analyse the data and images and will email their results and diagnosis to the district doctors and will consult remotely with the doctors about treatment alternatives. The South African government is now implementing more sophisticated telemedicine systems in order to reduce costs and achieve a higher level of healthcare service to patients at district hospitals and rural clinics.

Telemedicine has other benefits such as savings relating to the travelling costs for patients as well as on accommodation costs for family members accompanying children. Further, interacting with specialists on cases raises the knowledge base and diagnostic skills of district doctors and radiographers.

Source: www.bridge.org [ICT-enabled development case studies: Series Africa]

The following refers to an actual case from an Australian hospital.

Flinders Medical Centre

Public hospitals within Australia rely on a mix of funding from federal and state governments and frequently face severe financial constraints, which in turn have an adverse impact on customer value. Over the past decade there has been considerable publicity around the issue of public hospital budget deficits and quality of service problems, which are often attributed to insufficient funding. Two of the most significant problems have been excessive waiting times for patients requiring medical care, and cancellations of planned medical procedures (that is, operations) due to insufficient resources. Certainly these problems have affected Flinders Medical Centre, a major public hospital in South Australia, which has one of Australia's busiest Accident and Emergency Departments, treating more than 50 000 patients each year.

In the winter of 2003, Flinders Medical Centre cancelled dozens of planned medical procedures as the hospital diverted its resources to cope with the seasonal inflow of emergency services patients. Queues in the Accident and Emergency Department grew, and patients admitted for operations were left on trolleys lined up in the hospital's corridors, sometimes for many hours. In one month, more than 1000 people waited in the Accident and Emergency department for more than eight hours, and in another month 230 operations were cancelled.

In response to this situation, in 2004 the hospital introduced a program entitled 'Redesigning Care', which focused on improving the flow of patients through the hospital, reducing duplication, error and rework and, in doing so, minimising risk. With this program Flinders Medical Centre was able to reduce waiting times and cancellations of procedures dramatically, using a production line approach to ensure the smooth flow of patients through hospital services. For example, in the Accident and Emergency Department, one approach was to process separately patients who could be treated and discharged quickly. This has been likened to 'the supermarket eight-items-or-less checkout concept'. Indeed, throughout the hospital patients were tracked from the moment they arrived until they departed.

The program was expected to take three to five years to complete, although some improvements were experienced within the first six months. For example, in the first half of 2003, 86 medical procedures were cancelled, whereas in the same period in 2004 only 13 were cancelled. Flinders Medical Centre set a goal of seeing 90 per cent of Accident and Emergency patients within four hours. In the first six months of 2004 only 50 per cent of patients had been seen within four hours; however, this was an improvement of 10 per cent over the previous year, and average waiting time during this period was reduced by approximately 90 minutes.

In addition, the Redesigning Care program sought to develop a culture which placed a much greater emphasis on customer value – in this case, patient care. The new culture urged staff to see things 'through the eyes of the patient'. To this end, hospital staff were subjected to simulated patient experiences, including leaving the doctors lying on hospital trolleys!

According to the acting CEO of Flinders Medical Centre, Mr Michael Szwarcbord, 'the problems are far from solved. However, this is a good start ... We want to smooth the patient's journey through the hospital, and, by being more efficient, we can become safer as well. Carmakers work on the notion of about 3 errors per million cars, while in a hospital it can be as high as 1 in 14.'

Source: Crouch (2004)

Managing throughput

L.O. 10 Earlier in this chapter we recognised that the effective management of bottlenecks is vital to managing time and costs. There is a school of thought that considers managing bottlenecks – or, more generally, managing throughput – to be the key to profitability. This approach is based on the theory of constraints.[8]

The theory of constraints

The **theory of constraints** is an approach to managing costs and improving quality and delivery performance, by focusing on identifying and removing bottlenecks. According to the theory of constraints, the rate of production is limited to the capacity of the constraints (or bottlenecks) that exist in the organisation. Production cannot flow through the plant faster than it can move through the bottlenecks. In the short term, therefore, the rate of production through all areas should be limited to the rate at which products can pass through the bottleneck. Any attempt to improve efficiency in non-bottleneck areas will not improve performance; it will only cause inventory to build up at the bottleneck. While this inventory build-up ensures that the bottleneck does not become idle, it also implies increased holding and handling costs. In the longer term, management efforts should focus on removing bottlenecks. Inadequate labour or machinery can cause bottlenecks. Labour resources can be improved with overtime, hiring and training, but constraints involving plant and equipment are more difficult to rectify. Applying the theory of constraints enables a business to increase revenue, reduce costs and improve customer response time. Removing bottlenecks may also improve quality, as defective units, hidden in the inventory stockpile at the bottleneck, will now be detected more quickly during further processing.

We will continue with our example of the company MPSA to illustrate this concept.

Managing throughput at MPSA

MPSA (Pty) Ltd manufactures portable MP3 players. Once again we will focus on MPSA's exciting new product, MP Super, which is now in production and has met with very high demand. Production facilities at MPSA are highly automated, with three separate departments:

- *Moulding*, which uses sophisticated injection moulding machines to produce 600 plastic cases per hour.
- *Assembly*, which uses robots to pick and place motors and other components into the plastic cases. The output from Assembly is 500 units per hour.
- *Testing and Packaging*, which X-rays the completed MP players to identify any defects before packing them ready for sale. This department can process 800 units per hour.

Products are then shipped to customers, who consist of electronic goods distributors and retail chains. Aware of the potential market, the manager of the Moulding Department has just begun a productivity drive to increase the output of his department from 600 to 900 units per hour. As shown in Exhibit 15.12, this proposal will have no effect on the rate at which MP players are shipped to customers, which is limited by the Assembly Department to 500 units per hour. The Assembly Department is the *bottleneck*. If the Moulding Department increases its output, the extra moulded cases will simply pile up in the Assembly Department, waiting to be assembled. Rather than improve profitability, work-in-process inventory and inventory-related costs will increase. Any attempts to improve the level of production should focus on the Assembly Department.

Throughput accounting

Many of the non-financial performance measures described in Chapter 14, such as machine downtime, set-up time and the various measures of cycle or process time can be used to identify and manage bottlenecks. However, the pioneer of throughput management, Goldratt, recommends

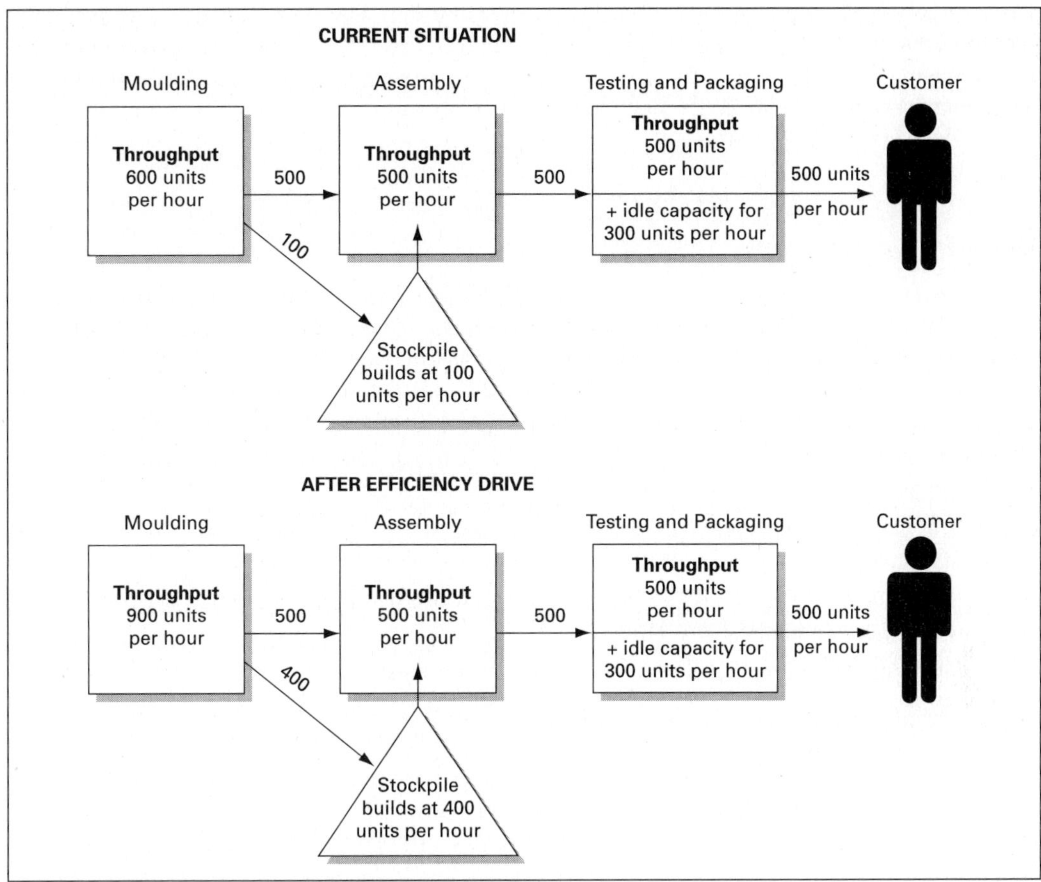

Exhibit 15.12 Managing throughput, MPSA (Pty) Ltd

managing performance with financial performance measures. This approach has been called *throughput accounting*. According to the throughput accounting approach, the ultimate business goal is to make money. The relevant performance measures are, therefore, net profit, return on investment (ROI) and cash flow as an indicator of survival. (Aspects such as customer satisfaction, quality and flexibility do not need to be measured as they are a means of achieving profitability, rather than goals in their own right.) The problem with these conventional financial measures is that they provide no indication of the impact of operational decisions on profitability. The solution, according to **throughput accounting**, is to measure the effects of bottlenecks and operational decisions using *financial* measures of throughput, inventory and operating expense. *Throughput* measures the rate at which a business generates money through sales. *Inventory* measures all the money that the business spends in buying things that it intends to sell. *Operating expense* measures all the money that the business spends in turning inventory into throughput.

The impact on profit of a change in any one of these three measures can be identified easily. When throughput is increased with no change in inventory or operating expense, then net profit, ROI and cash flow will increase. Likewise, when operating expense decreases with no change in throughput or inventory, then profit, ROI and cash flow will increase. Decreases in inventory will also increase profit, ROI and cash flow. Therefore, these measures can be used to guide decision-making and assess performance.

The problem of linking operational measures to business profitability does not exist because the operational measures are financial.

Throughput accounting concentrates on the short term. Constraints are often short-term problems and, once identified, can be overcome. Many critics of throughput management argue that performance should not be guided and assessed solely by short-term considerations. As explained in Chapter 14, to survive, a business must identify strategic objectives, which should form the basis for identifying critical success factors and related performance measures. While throughput accounting has a role to play in the identification and elimination of constraints, clearly it has some limitations over the longer term.

Summary

Management accounting has responded to the changing business environment by paying increased attention to managing resources – in particular, costs, time and quality, which are not only key cost drivers but also important sources of customer value. In this chapter we considered various approaches to reducing costs and managing time. Key points include:

- Many organisations have moved from controlling costs to managing them. Cost management improves an organisation's cost effectiveness through understanding and managing the real causes of costs.
- Activity-based management (ABM) can be used to manage costs, as well as other sources of customer value. Reducing costs through ABM involves four steps:
  - identifying the major opportunities for cost reduction;
  - determining the real causes of these costs;
  - developing a program to eliminate the causes and, therefore, the costs; and
  - introducing some new performance measures to monitor the effectiveness of cost reduction efforts.
- Value analysis can be used to identify opportunities for cost reduction. Costs can be reduced (and customer value increased) by identifying non-value-added activities, which are activities that do not add value to a product or service from a customer's perspective or for the business.
- The real causes of costs, called root cause cost drivers, can be identified through cost driver analysis, which involves an in-depth search for the underlying reasons that activities are performed. A good starting point for cost driver analysis is to link activities into business processes, to identify the supplier of and customer for each activity.
- Cost reduction programs should focus on reducing and eventually eliminating the root causes of major non-value added activities.
- Performance measures can be identified for each activity or business process to monitor improvements in cost, cost drivers, and other sources of customer value such as quality and delivery.
- Despite the benefits offered by activity-based management, it is not widespread in practice. Impediments to its implementation include a lack of awareness, uncertainty over potential benefits, extensive resource requirements, and resistance to change.
- Business process re-engineering (BPR) can also be used to reduce costs and improve other sources of customer value. Unlike ABM, BPR involves radical changes to the way an organisation works. The four steps involved in BPR are:
  - prepare a process map;
  - establish goals;
  - reorganise the work flow; and
  - implement the re-engineered process.
- A product's costs will vary with the stage in its life cycle. Life cycle costing and budgeting accumulates the revenues and costs associated with a product over its entire life cycle. The

life cycle perspective helps management to minimise total product cost by recognising the trade-off between costs incurred prior to production, in design and development, during production and in post-production.

- Another approach to cost management, target costing, is based on this trade-off. A product's target cost is based on the difference between its expected selling price and the firm's target profit margin. The design phase of a product's life cycle is driven towards meeting a target cost, as well as the usual specifications about product form and performance. In managing their costs, some firms differentiate between this target cost, called the 'allowable cost', and an achievable target cost given the firm's current capabilities, called the 'product-level target cost'.
- Time is a cost driver and it can also be a significant source of customer value. Some businesses compete on innovation and therefore need to manage the duration of the innovation process. Duration measures include new product development time and break-even time (BET). Most customers also value speedy delivery, and businesses can benefit by managing the duration of their order, production and delivery processes. Useful measures include customer response time and its components, order receipt time, order waiting time, production time and delivery time. Many businesses also measure delivery schedule reliability.
- Bottlenecks can have a major impact on the duration of processes. The theory of constraints provides a framework for identifying and managing bottlenecks. Throughput accounting focuses on measures of throughput, inventory and operating expenses, to speed up production and improve the management of revenue, costs and time.

In Chapter 14 we introduced broad frameworks for managing performance. In this chapter we have explored two key facets of performance in more detail: costs and time. In Chapter 16 we will consider other important aspects of managing performance – namely customers, suppliers and quality. In each case, you will notice that these approaches are designed to help an organisation develop strategies and achieve its objectives.

References

Adamany, HG & Gonsalves, FAJ 1994, 'Life cycle management: an integrated approach to managing investments', *Journal of Cost Management,* Summer, pp. 35–49.

Artto, KA 1994, 'Life cycle cost concepts and methodologies', *Journal of Cost Management,* Fall 1994, pp. 28–32.

Booth, P & Giacobbe, F 1997, 'Activity-based costing in Australian manufacturing firms: key survey findings', *Issues,* Report 5, Management Accounting Centre of Excellence, Australian Society of CPAs.

Booth, R 1994, 'Life cycle costing', *Management Accounting,* June, p. 10.

Burstein, MC 1988, 'Life cycle costing' in *Accounting in the 90s,* Institute of Management Accountants, Montvale, NJ, p. 260.

Chenhall, RH & Langfield-Smith, K 1998a, *Innovative Costing Systems: An Australian Perspective,* Management Accounting Centre of Excellence, Australian Society of CPAs.

Chenhall, RH & Langfield-Smith, K 1998b, 'Adoption and benefits of management accounting practices: an Australian study', *Management Accounting Research,* vol. 9, no. 1, pp. 1–20.

Cooper, R & Slagmulder, R 1999, *Supply Chain Development for the Lean Enterprise,* The IMA Foundation for Applied Research, Productivity Inc., Portland, OR.

Crouch, B 2004, 'Hospital wait time slashed', *Sunday Mail,* October 17, p. 21.

Goldratt, EM 1990, *Theory of Constraints,* North River Press, Croton-on-Hudson, NY.

Goldratt, EM & Cox, J 1992, *The Goal,* 2nd edn, North River Press, Croton-on-Hudson, NY.

Hammer, M & Champy, J 1993, *Reengineering the Corporation: A Manifesto for Business Revolution,* Harper Business, New York.

Hoban, B 1995, 'ABC in local government', *Australian Accountant,* August 1995, pp. 29–36.

Kaplan, RS & Norton, DP 1996, *The Balanced Scorecard,* Harvard Business School Press, Boston, MA.

Lamond, S 1992, 'Activity-based management: an Australian perspective', *Journal of Cost Management,* Summer, pp. 42–6.

Langfield-Smith, K & Luckett, P 1999, *Target Costing for Effective Cost Management,* study no. 10, Financial and Management Accounting Committee, IFAC, New York.

Lewis, M 1999, 'Defining the organisation: the process of ABC', *Australian CPA,* April.

Lorino, P 1995, 'Target costing – practice and implementation', Articles of Merit, 1995 Competition, FMAC Award Program for Distinguished Contribution to Management Accounting, IFAC, pp. 101–20.

Manganelli, RL & Klein, MK 1994, *The Reengineering Handbook: A Step by Step Guide to Business Transformation,* ANACOM, New York.

Mouritsen, J & Bekke, A 1999, 'A space for time: accounting and Time Based Management in a high technology company', *Management Accounting Research,* vol. 10, no. 2, June, pp. 159–80.

Newbold, K 1997, 'Process reengineering: the full story', presentation to the Australian Centre for Management Accounting Development, Victorian Division, 20 February.

Raffish, N & Turney, PBB (eds) 1991, 'Glossary of activity based management', *Journal of Cost Management,* Fall, pp. 53–63.

Ruhl, J 1996, 'An introduction to the theory of constraints', *Journal of Cost Management,* Summer, pp. 43–8.

Susman, G 1989, 'Product life cycle management', *Journal of Cost Management,* Summer 1989, pp. 8–22.

Thorne, H 1997, 'Target costing: achieving a competitive edge', *CPA Solutions,* Australian Society of CPAs, March.

Turney, PBB 1991, *Common Cents: The ABC Performance Breakthrough,* Cost Technology Inc., Hilsboro, OR.

www.barloworld.co.za

Self study

Self-study problem 1: Activity-based management

PJ Rogers Ltd manufactures timber bookcases in two production processes: cutting and assembly. The company has adopted an activity-based costing system and has identified the following activities:

- Inspect incoming timber.
- Dispose of substandard timber.
- Store timber.
- Move timber to production.
- Set up circular saw.
- Operate circular saw.
- Inspect sawn planks.
- Recut planks that are too long.
- Dispose of planks that are too short.
- Move sawn planks to assembly area.
- Sand planks.
- Assemble bookcase.
- Paint bookcase.
- Inspect bookcase.
- Move finished bookcase to shipping.

Required:

1 Explain why the activities 'Inspect sawn planks' and 'Recut planks that are too long' can be classified as non-value-added activities.

2 Suggest possible root cause cost drivers for these two activities.

3 Identify the other non-value-added activities at PJ Rogers Ltd.

Solution to Self-study problem 1

1 The activities 'Inspect sawn planks' and 'Recut planks that are too long' can be classified as non-value-added activities because they do not add value for the customer. If the planks had been cut properly in the first place, they would not require inspection or rework.

2 Possible root cause cost drivers for these two activities might include the following:

   - 'Inspect sawn planks': circular saw not set up properly; poor workmanship in the use of the circular saw.
   - 'Recut planks that are too long': poor training in setup procedures for the circular saw; poor training in the operating procedures for the circular saw; inadequate procedures for recruiting skilled trades employees.

3 Other non-value-added activities include the following:

   - Inspect incoming timber.
   - Dispose of substandard timber.
   - Store timber.

- Move timber to production.
- Dispose of planks that are too short.
- Move sawn planks to assembly area.
- Inspect bookcase.
- Move finished bookcase to shipping.

Self-study problem 2: Life cycle management and target costing

Hiliters Ltd manufactures fluorescent marking pens in Benoni. One of its top-selling lines is the Hilite pen, which is fluorescent yellow and has a special tip that does not dry out when the cap is left off. Earlier this year a Korean company entered the market offering a similar pen at a price 25 per cent below the Hilite price of R10.00 per unit. Company policy at Hiliters requires a profit margin equal to 30 per cent (on sales) on each of its products.

Required:

1 What allowable cost would have to be set for the Hilite pen to remain competitive and still meet the target profit margin of the company?

2 Explain how the company could apply the principles of life cycle management to achieve this cost.

3 Assume that Hiliters examines the current cost for the Hilite pen and its existing capabilities, and decides that the allowable cost is not achievable. Explain how the company could persist with target costing by adjusting the allowable cost, and assess the implications of this situation for the company's target profit margin.

Solution to Self-study problem 2

1 The allowable cost for the Hilite pen to remain competitive and meet the company's target profit margin would be R5.25.

Target price to remain competitive = R10.00 − 25% of R10.00 = R7.50

Allowable cost to achieve a 30% profit margin = R7.50 − (30% × R7.50) = R5.25

2 Hiliters could examine the distribution of expected costs over the remainder of Hilite pen's life cycle. The aim should be to examine each stage of the life cycle in order to identify ways in which non-value-added activities can be removed. It may be possible to spend more money in the design phase and reduce costs in subsequent stages, such as manufacturing and selling costs. It may also be feasible to spend more money during manufacturing, for example to improve quality, and to reduce subsequent costs such as customer complaints.

3 If Hiliters establishes that the cost reduction objective is not achievable, given the company's capabilities, it could identify the level of cost savings that is achievable (the target cost reduction objective), and set a product-level target cost which is based on the difference between the current cost and the target cost reduction objective. Hiliters would then work towards achieving this cost. If the pen includes externally purchased components, Hiliters could work with the component supplier to reduce component costs.

As long as the product-level target cost is greater than the allowable cost, Hiliters will not earn its target profit margin on the Hilite pen.

Cybersearch

1 Look for websites of consulting firms that offer activity-based costing and activity-based management services.
   (a) Do the concepts of ABC and ABM fit with those described in the chapter? If not, describe any differences.
   (b) What benefits do the consultants suggest may be expected from ABC and/or ABM?
   (c) Do the consultants acknowledge any impediments to the implementation of ABC/ABM?
2 Find the website of an organisation that uses target costing to manage costs and profitability.
   (a) Compare the organisation's approach to target costing with that described in the chapter.
   (b) Outline the advantages that target costing has provided for the organisation.
3 Locate websites that contain examples of businesses that measure and manage customer response time.
   (a) Compare their approach to managing customer response time with that described in the chapter.
   (b) From your search, what industries seem particularly interested in this aspect of time management?

Questions

?

15.1 Describe the conventional approaches to controlling costs, used by many South African businesses. How does cost management differ from these approaches?

15.2 Outline the key features of the two-dimensional activity-based costing model described in the chapter.

15.3 What is *activity-based management*? What is its relationship to *activity-based costing*?

15.4 How can an organisation use activity-based management to identify opportunities to reduce costs?

15.5 What role can cost driver analysis play in the management of a business?

15.6 What role can value analysis play in the management of a business?

15.7 What are *value-added activities* and *non-value-added activities*? Give three examples of each for a university department that teaches management accounting.

15.8 Explain the role of activity-based performance measures in reducing costs.

15.9 'Measuring performance in ABM involves more than managing costs.' Explain.

15.10 Activity-based management is not widespread in practice. Why?

15.11 What is business *process re-engineering*? How does it differ from *process improvement*?

15.12 What is a product life cycle? Describe the four stages of a product's production life cycle.

15.13 Select three products, state whether each would be expected to have a long life cycle or a short life cycle, and explain your answers.

15.14 Why is it important to assess product profitability using a life cycle approach?

15.15 Explain the trade-off between pre-production and production costs over the product life cycle. How can understanding this trade-off help a business manage its costs?

15.16 What is target *costing*? How can a business use target costing to reduce costs and plan profits?

15.17 Explain the difference between an allowable cost and a product-level target cost. Why do some businesses use the product-level target cost instead of allowable cost as their target cost?

15.18 Explain the meaning of the *strategic cost reduction challenge* in target costing, and outline its implications for the target profit margin.

15.19 Why is it important for a business to manage time?

15.20 What is *time-based management (TBM)*? Do you agree that it makes more sense to manage time than costs?

15.21 Describe two measures of new product development performance. Are these measures relevant to all firms?

15.22 Explain the meaning of customer response time and its four components. Are these measures relevant to a service firm? Illustrate your answer by using an example.

15.23 Explain the theory of constraints. What implications does this theory have for managing costs?

15.24 According to throughput accounting, how should performance be measured at the operational level? What advantages and disadvantages do these measures offer?

Exercises

E15.25 Conventional costing systems; activity-based costing; activity-based management

Classify each of the following statements as true or false. In each case, give reasons for your answer.

1 Conventional standard costing systems are useful for controlling manufacturing costs.
2 Conventional costing systems do not provide any useful information for controlling other critical sources of value, such as quality or delivery performance.
3 ABC estimates activity costs, while ABM involves identifying the root cause cost drivers of activities.
4 ABC and ABM identify cost drivers, but so do conventional costing systems.
5 ABM focuses on processes, but so do conventional management accounting systems.

E15.26 Non-value-added activity: service firms

Non-value-added activities also occur in service firms. Identify four potential non-value-added activities in:

1 An airline.
2 A supermarket.
3 A bank.

Give your reasons.

E15.27 Non-value-added activity: restaurant

Visit a local restaurant for a meal or think carefully about your most recent restaurant experience.

Required:

1 List as many activities as you can think of that would have been performed by the restaurant's employees for you as a customer.
2 For each activity indicate whether it is value-added or non-value-added.
3 Indicate the possible root cause for each activity.

E15.28 Activity-based management; non-value-added activity; cost drivers; performance measures: manufacturer

Favio Pty Ltd manufactures high-impact plastic bike helmets. The A-1 helmet is produced in two processes: plastic extruding and assembly. The company has adopted an activity-based costing system. For 20X6, the following activities have been defined:

- Design A-1 helmet.
- Store materials.
- Move raw materials to production.
- Set up extruding machine.
- Operate extruding machine.
- Move product to assembly area.
- Assemble helmet.
- Label helmet.

- Inspect and test helmet.
- Package helmet.
- Move finished helmet to shipping.
- Advertise A-1 helmet.

Required:

1 Identify the non-value-added activities at Favio Pty Ltd.

2 Select three non-value-added activities and identify two possible root cause cost drivers for each one.

3 Use a process (supplier or customer) perspective to suggest a possible performance measure for the activity 'Inspect and test helmet'.

E15.29 Activity-based management; cost driver analysis; performance measures: manufacturer

Teskor Pty Ltd manufactures paintbrushes in Hermanus. The management accountant, Mary Malone, has developed an activity-based costing system for the company. The activities in the wooden handle area are as follows:

Activity	Description
Set up saw	Saw set up to cut timber into designated lengths
Operate saw	Timber cut into lengths
Set up lathe	Lathe set up to produce a designated handle shape
Operate lathe	Timber lengths shaped into handles
Inspect handles	Handles inspected to identify faults
Rework handles	Faulty handles reworked
Move handles	Handles moved to assembly area

From the cost assignment module in her ABC system, Malone knows that the activities 'Inspect handles' and 'Rework handles' are costly. She considers both to be non-value-added and therefore candidates for elimination.

Required:

1 Explain why the activities 'Inspect handles' and 'Rework handles' can be classified as non-value-added activities.

2 Suggest possible root cause cost drivers for these two activities.

3 Suggest possible performance measures for the activity 'Operate lathe' which might help eliminate the activities 'Inspect handles' and 'Rework handles'.

E15.30 Business process re-engineering

Consider the various activities that were undertaken when you enrolled in your course this semester.

Required:

1 List those activities in the sequence in which they occurred.

2 Prepare an activity analysis: discuss the activity linkages and cost drivers.

3 Re-engineer the various steps in the enrolment process to:

(a) improve the effectiveness of the process from the students' perspective

(b) improve the effectiveness of the process from the institution's perspective

E15.31 Life cycle costing

Classify each of the following statements as true or false. In each case give reasons for your answer.

1 Life cycle budgeting is impossible because of the problems in predicting the sales and costs for a product many years into the future.

2 Per unit product costs are likely to be stable across all stages of a product's life cycle.

3 Life cycle costing is relevant only to products with short product life cycles.

4 The biggest impact on reducing costs can be achieved by using tight cost controls during production. That is why standard costing is so important.
5 Product mix decisions should be based on a life cycle assessment of product profit.

E15.32 Target costing

Classify each of the following statements as true or false. In each case give reasons for your answer.

1 Target costing is relevant only to new products.
2 Target costing is not relevant to service entities.
3 Target costing has an internal focus rather than a customer focus.
4 Target costing is consistent with Japanese culture but will not work in Western economies.
5 It is the product designer's job to achieve the target cost for a product.

E15.33 Life cycle costing: manufacturer

Integral Data Dynamics Ltd manufactures components for personal computers. It is planning to develop a new CD ROM drive, CDII, to improve the quality of data retrieval. On the basis of its current product range, the company expects CDII to have prime costs (that is, direct material and direct labour costs) of R150 and applied manufacturing overhead costs of R100. The marketing manager estimates that CDII will sell for around R400, with sales of around 10 000 units per year for three years, but will then become technically obsolete.

Required:

1 Should Integral Data Dynamics Ltd introduce CDII?
2 What costs, other than the manufacturing costs, should be considered in assessing the profitability of CDII? How high would these costs need to go to deter the company from introducing CDII?

E15.34 Life cycle management and target costing: manufacturer

Solarcare Ltd manufactures plastic lenses for sunglasses in Midrand, Gauteng. One of its top-selling lines is the XRP Lens, which has a scratch-resistant polarised surface. Earlier this year, a Chinese company entered the market offering a similar lens at a price 20 per cent below the XRP price of R15.00 per unit. Solarcare's parent company has a target profit margin equal to 40 per cent (on sales) on each of its products.

Required:

1 What allowable cost would have to be set for the XRP to remain competitive and meet the requirements of Solarcare's parent company?
2 Explain how Solarcare could apply the principles of life cycle management to achieve this cost.
3 Under what circumstances would Solarcare identify a product-level target cost, and how would this impact on the target profit margin?

E15.35 Customer response time

The Magic Mushroom Company (MMC) manufactures a range of designer T-shirts, which it produces to order for major department stores. On 5 March the sales department at MMC received an order from retail company, Edgars, for 5000 glitter Ts. The sales department at MMC forwarded the order to its manufacturing department on 12 March. On receiving the order, the manufacturing department placed an order with its supplier of glitter fabric. This fabric was received by the manufacturing department on 28 March, but there was no spare capacity on the T-shirt pattern and cutting machines until 5 April, when MMC commenced the order. The order was completed on 14 April and delivered to the warehouse. The warehouse accumulated this order with others from Edgars. The MMC delivery, including the glitter Ts, was received by Edgars on 1 May.

Required:

1 What is the customer response time for the glitter Ts order, in days?
2 Estimate order receipt time, waiting time, production time, production lead (or cycle) time and delivery time for the glitter Ts order.
3 Suggest steps that MMC might take to improve its customer response time.

E15.36 The theory of constraints: manufacturer

Life is simple at the ABC Company. The business produces a single product in a straightforward production process involving machines A, B and C, each run by a separate department. The process begins at machine A, where raw material is converted into a single component. The component passes through machine B where it is converted into the finished product. The completed product passes to machine C where it is tested and packaged. It is then shipped to the customer. The demand for this product is unlimited. Aware of the potential market, the manager of Department B has just begun an efficiency drive to increase the rate of output of his department by 50 per cent.

Required:

Assess the effectiveness of the Department B manager's proposal for each of the following situations. In each case, identify the current rate of output for the company, and the effect of the proposed efficiency drive on this rate; where appropriate, suggest an alternative approach to increase ABC's rate of output.

1 Machine A completes 60 units per hour, machine B completes 35 units per hour, machine C completes 55 units per hour.
2 Machine A completes 60 units per hour, machine B completes 70 units per hour, machine C completes 65 units per hour.
3 Machine A completes 60 units per hour, machine B completes 70 units per hour, machine C completes 50 units per hour.

E15.37 The theory of constraints: fast (?) food outlet

Mick and Donald run a fast food outlet on the N1 national road between Bloemfontein and Johannesburg. The N1 road is the main transport corridor all the way from Cape Town to Gauteng. For most of the day, Mick and Donald are able to keep up with demand and serve customers quickly. However, from 4 p.m. to 8 p.m. the shop is inundated with truck drivers, most of whom want one of Mick's famous 'hamburgers with the lot'. Queues build, tummies rumble and truck drivers grumble.

Mick decided to solve this problem by setting up a hamburger production line from 4 p.m. to 8 p.m. each day. His wife, Minnie, would take over the sales counter. He would cut, toast and butter the bread rolls (he can complete 20 per hour). Donald would cook the meat patties, eggs, bacon and onions (he can complete 40 serves per hour). Donald's wife, Daisy, would chop the lettuce and tomato and place it in a toasted bread roll along with the meat patty, egg, bacon, onion, and, of course sauce (she can complete 25 hamburgers per hour).

The new system was put in place, and the next day, an average of 30 customers per hour ordered 'a hamburger with the lot' between 4 p.m. and 8 p.m.

Required:

1 Draw a diagram similar to that shown in Exhibit 15.12 to identify the number of customers per hour who received their orders.
2 How many customers were unfed by 8 p.m?
3 Identify the bottlenecks in Mick's production process and suggest how they might be overcome to meet the customers' requirements.

Problems

P15.38 Key features of activity-based costing and activity-based management: manufacturer

You are the management accountant for Runmoe Springs Ltd, a company that manufactures suspension components for the automotive industry. Currently, costing in the manufacturing area is based on a standard costing system using overhead applied on direct labour hours. Departmental budgets are used to monitor costs in the non-manufacturing areas. The company is contemplating switching to activity-based costing (ABC). The senior managers have just attended a one-day course on ABC, run by a large management consulting firm, but Runmoe's managing director is feeling frustrated.

It's always the same. We pay a fortune to attend these courses. The consultants peddle their wares, and no matter what the new gimmick is, they tell us that our business is likely to fail without it. They used to talk about using ABC to improve our product costing. Now they talk about using ABM to improve our control. They see activity-based management as a cure for all ills. I don't understand why we need a new costing system or how activity-based costing works.

Even the terminology has got me beaten. What's the difference between activity-based costing and activity-based management? What are these things called activity attributes, root cause cost drivers, non-value-added activities, activity performance measures and processes? How could I use them to improve control at Runmoe?

Required:

Write a clear and concise report to Runmoe's managing director, explaining:

1 the potential problems with Runmoe's existing system for control;
2 the key features of the two-dimensional activity-based costing model;
3 the difference between activity-based costing and activity-based management; and
4 how ABM could be used to improve Runmoe's control.

P15.39 Activity analysis; non-value-added costs; cost drivers: manufacturer

Contemporary Kitchen Furnishings, Inc. (CKF) manufactures a variety of homewares for the consumer market. The company's three major product lines are cooking utensils, tableware, and flatware. CKF implemented activity-based costing four years ago and now has a well-developed ABC system in place for determining product costs. Only recently, however, has the ABC system been systematically used for the purposes of activity-based management. As a pilot project, CKF's controller asked the ABC project team to complete a detailed activity analysis of the purchasing activity. The following specific activities were identified:

1 Receipt of parts specifications from the Design Engineering Department.
2 Follow-up with design engineers to answer any questions.
3 Vendor (supplier) identification.
4 Vendor consultations (by phone or in person).
5 Price negotiation.
6 Vendor selection.
7 Ordering (by phone or mail).
8 Order follow-up.
9 Expediting (attempting to speed up delivery).
10 Receipt of orders.
11 Inspection of parts.
12 Return of parts not meeting specifications.

13 Consultation with design engineers and production personnel if parts do not satisfy intended purpose.
14 Further consultation and/or negotiation with vendor if necessary.
15 Shipping parts back to vendor if necessary.
16 If satisfactory, moving parts to storage.

Required:

1 Identify the root cause cost drivers for each of the following activities in CKF's purchasing activity analysis:
  (a) Follow-up with design engineers (activity 2)
  (b) Expediting (activity 9)
  (c) Inspection of parts (activity 11)
  (d) Return of parts (activity 12)
  (e) Consultation with design engineers and production personnel (activity 13)
2 Identify four activities in CKF's list of activities that may be non-value-added. Explain why.
3 Choose four activities in CKF's purchasing function, and suggest a performance measure for each of these activities.

P15.40 Cost drivers; non-value-added costs: manufacturer

Northern Lights Company manufactures a variety of small parts for the automotive industry. The company's manufacturing overhead cost budget for the current year is as follows:

Electric power	R225 000	Purchasing	R400 000
Supervision	880 000	Waste collection	20 000
Machine maintenance: labour	455 000	Custodial labour	200 000
Machine maintenance: materials	115 000	Telephone service	35 000
Natural gas (for heating)	175 000	Engineering design	340 000
Factory supplies	200 000	Inspection of raw materials	100 000
Set-up labour	150 000	Receiving	100 000
Lubricants	50 000	Inspection of finished goods	150 000
Property taxes	125 000	Packaging	310 000
Insurance	175 000	Shipping	150 000
Depreciation on manufacturing equipment	525 000	Wages of parts clerks (find parts for production depts)	300 000
Depreciation on trucks and forklifts	350 000		
Depreciation on material conveyors	75 000	Wages of material handlers	350 000
Building depreciation	800 000	Fuel for trucks and forklifts	350 000
Grinding wheels	25 000	Depreciation on raw-material warehouse	250 000
Drill bits	10 000	Depreciation on finished-goods warehouse	290 000

These budgeted overhead costs total R7 680 000, and the budgeted amount of direct labour for the year is 40 000 hours.

Required:

1 Calculate the predetermined overhead rate based on direct labour hours.
2 Management has decided to implement an activity-based costing system. The cost drivers under consideration are the following:
  - Production (in units).
  - Raw material cost.
  - Factory space.
  - Machine hours.
  - Number of production runs.
  - Number of shipments of finished goods.
  - Number of shipments of raw materials.
  - Number of different raw materials and parts used in a product.

- Engineering specifications and change orders.

Divide Northern Lights' manufacturing overhead costs into separate cost pools, and identify a cost driver for each cost pool.

3 Which of the overhead costs are candidates for elimination as non-value-added costs?

4 Suppose that inspection of raw materials and receiving were combined to form an activity cost pool, with the number of shipments of raw materials identified as the cost driver. Calculate a rate for this cost pool, assuming that 400 shipments are anticipated.

P15.41 Basic elements of a production process; non-value-added activities; business process re-engineering: bakery

Bagels Ltd manufactures a variety of bagels, which are frozen and sold in supermarkets. The production process consists of the following steps:

1 Ingredients, such as flour and raisins, are received and inspected. They are then stored until needed.

2 Ingredients are carried on handcarts to the mixing room.

3 Dough is mixed in 40 kilogram batches in four heavy-duty mixers.

4 Dough is stored on large boards in the mixing room until a bagel machine is free.

5 A board of dough is carried into the bagel room. The board is tipped and the dough slides into the hopper of a bagel machine. This machine pulls off a small piece of dough, rolls it into a cylindrical shape, and then squeezes it into a doughnut shape. The bagel machines can be adjusted in a setup procedure to accommodate different sizes and styles of bagels. Workers remove the uncooked bagels and place them on a tray, where they are kept until a boiling vat is free.

6 Next, the trays of uncooked bagels are carried into an adjoining room, which houses three 50-litre vats of boiling water. The bagels are boiled for approximately one minute.

7 Bagels are removed from the vats with a long-handled strainer and are placed on a wooden board. The boards full of bagels are carried to the oven room, where they are kept until an oven rack is free. The two ovens each contain eight racks that rotate but remain upright, much like the seats on a Ferris wheel. A rack full of bagels has finished the baking process after one complete revolution in the oven. When a rack full of bagels is removed from the oven, a fresh rack replaces it. The oven door is opened and closed as each rack completes a revolution in the oven.

8 After the bagels are removed from the oven, they are placed in baskets for cooling.

9 While the bagels are cooling, they are inspected. Misshapen bagels are removed and set aside. (Most are eaten by the staff!)

10 After the bagels are cool, the wire baskets are carried to the packaging department. Here the bagels are dumped into the hopper on a bagging machine. This machine packages six bagels in each bag and seals the bag with a twist-tie.

11 Then the packaged bagels are placed in cardboard boxes, each box holding 24 bags. The boxes are placed on a forklift and driven to the freezer, where the bagels are frozen and stored for shipment.

Required:

1 Draw a diagram of the production process for bagels.

2 Identify the non-value-added activities that might be present in the process. Explain each choice.

3 Suggest ways in which the process could be re-engineered.

P15.42 Activity-based management; cost cutting: manufacturer

Readers.Com is a small company that sells books and software over the Internet. A recent article in a trade journal has caught the attention of management, given that the company has experienced soaring inventory handling costs. The article noted that similar firms have purchasing, warehousing, and distribution costs that average 13 per cent of sales, which is attractive when compared with Readers.Com's results for the past year.

The following information is available:

Activity (Cost)	Cost driver	Cost driver quantity	Percentage of cost driver activity for books	Percentage of cost driver activity for software
Incoming receipts (R600 000)	Number of purchase orders	2 000	70%	30%
Warehousing (R720 000)	Number of inventory moves	9 000	80	20
Outgoing shipments (R450 000)	Number of shipments	15 000	25	75

Book sales totalled R7 800 000 and software sales totalled R5 200 000. A review of the company's activities found various inefficiencies with respect to the warehousing of books and outgoing shipments of software. These inefficiencies resulted in an extra 550 inventory moves and 250 shipments, respectively.

Required:

1 What is activity-based management? What is a non-value-added activity?

2 How much did non-value activities cost Readers.Com this past year?

3 Cite several examples of situations that may have given rise to non-value-added activities for Readers.Com.

4 Will the elimination of non-value-added activities allow Readers.Com to achieve purchasing, warehousing and distribution costs that average 13 per cent of sales for each of the product lines? Show calculations.

5 Does either of the two product lines require additional cost cutting to achieve the target percentage? If so, how much additional cost cutting is needed, and what tools (methods) might the company use to achieve the cuts? Briefly describe.

P15.43 Non-value-added activities; throughput management: manufacturer

Pickwick Paper Company's Mount Gambier plant manufactures paperboard. Its production process involves the following operations:

(a) Harvested trees arrive by rail in the wood-yard and are stored outside.

(b) Logs are moved by a forklift truck into the plant, where they are passed through a debarker and cut up into chips.

(c) The chips are stored in large bins near the chipping machines.

(d) The chips are then transported by small trucks to another building and placed in a digester – a large pressure cooker where heat, steam and chemicals convert the chips into moist fibres.

(e) The fibres are stored near the digester.

(f) In the next step, the fibres are loaded by workers onto a conveyor belt, which carries the fibres to a depressurised blow-tank. This operation separates the fibres.

(g) The separated fibres are placed on wooden pallets and are stored next to the blow-tank.

(h) Forklifts are used to carry the separated fibres to the refining area, where the fibres are washed, refined and treated with chemicals and caustic substances until they become pulp.

(i) The wood pulp then enters the paper machines through a headbox, which distributes pulp evenly across a porous belt of forming fabric.

(j) Water is removed from the pulp by passing it over a wire screen.

(k) Additional water is removed from the pulp in a series of presses.

(l) Dryers then remove any remaining water from the pulp.

(m) The thin, dry sheets of pulp are then smoothed and polished by large rollers called 'calenders'.

(n) The paperboard is wound into large rolls, and workers place the rolls on wooden pallets.
(o) Forklifts are used to move the rolls of paperboard to the labelling building.
(p) There, the rolls are labelled and stored for shipment.
(q) The rolls of paperboard are shipped to customers from the loading dock in the labelling building.

The partially processed product is sometimes stored between production operations for two to three days. This delay can be caused either by a faster production rate in the earlier processes than in the later processes, or by breakdowns in the production machinery.

Required:

1 Identify the non-value-added activities that might be present in Pickwick Paper's plant layout and production process. Explain each choice.
2 What criteria did you use to assess whether an activity was valued-added or non-value-added?
3 Explain why the theory of constraints appears to be relevant to managing costs at Pickwick Paper. Besides costs, what other aspects of performance could be improved with better throughput management?

P15.44 Business process re-engineering; throughput management; time-based management: manufacturer

Refer to the data for Pickwick Paper Company in Problem 15.43.

Required:

1 Draw a diagram of the current production process.
2 Suggest ways in which the process could be re-engineered.
3 Select some specific time-based performance measures that could be used by Pickwick Paper. How might these benefit the company?
4 Throughput management has been criticised for its short-term perspective. Does your re-engineered process reflect a short-term perspective or a strategic perspective? Explain your answer.

P15.45 Break-even time: manufacturer

Zelda Ltd manufactures toys and games. The table below shows the costs and revenues of a toy called Dragon Mouth over the first five years of its life. Dragon Mouth is a plastic monster that swallows and regurgitates miniature animals.

	20X4	20X5	20X6	20X7	20X8
Revenue	0	4 000 000	7 000 000	9 000 000	6 000 000
Costs:					
Product planning and concept design	400 000				
Design and development	1 600 000	1 600 000			
Production		2 200 000	4 000 000	5 200 000	3 600 000
Distribution and customer service		1 000 000	1 400 000	1 800 000	1 200 000
Profit (Loss)	**−2 000 000**	**−800 000**	**1 600 000**	**2 000 000**	**1 200 000**

Required:

1 What is the break-even time (BET) for Dragon Mouth?
2 How can Zelda's management use the BET to better manage the business?
3 What problems may be encountered when BET is used to monitor new product development?
4 Why is the time taken to develop new products an important consideration in Zelda Ltd? Is it an important consideration in all companies? Explain your answer.

P15.46 Non-value-added costs; root cause cost drivers; activity-based performance measures: manufacturer

Welkom Autoworks Company manufactures a variety of small parts for the automotive industry. The company's manufacturing overhead cost budget for 20X6 is as follows:

Supervision	R1 920 000
Machine maintenance labour	780 000
Machine maintenance materials	200 000
Electrical power	500 000
Natural gas (for heating)	300 000
Factory supplies	400 000
Set-up labour	300 000
Lubricants	100 000
Property taxes	250 000
Insurance	350 000
Depreciation on manufacturing equipment	1 050 000
Depreciation on trucks and forklifts	700 000
Depreciation on material conveyors	150 000
Building depreciation	1 600 000
Grinding wheels	50 000
Drill bits	20 000
Purchasing	800 000
Waste collection	40 000
Security staff wages	400 000
Telephone service	50 000
Engineering design	700 000
Inspection of raw materials	200 000
Receiving	200 000
Inspection of finished goods	300 000
Packaging	600 000
Shipping	300 000
Wages of parts clerks (find parts for production departments)	600 000
Wages of material handlers	700 000
Fuel for trucks and forklifts	300 000
Depreciation on raw materials warehouse	500 000
Depreciation on finished goods warehouse	600 000
Total budgeted manufacturing overhead	R14 960 000

The budgeted amount of direct labour in 20X6 is 20 000 hours.

Required:

1 Which of the overhead costs are candidates for elimination as non-value-added costs?
2 Suggest four non-value-added activities that are likely to occur in this company, and identify two possible root cause cost drivers for each one.
3 Suggest four value-added activities and recommend two possible performance measures for each one.
4 How could Welkom Autoworks' management use activity-based management to help reduce or eliminate some of the overhead costs? Be specific.

P15.47 Delivery schedule reliability and customer response time: fast food firms

Hungry Jills (HJs) makes and delivers burgers for the takeaway market. Its home delivery service (in its local suburb) is a source of competitive advantage for the company, as most other fast food burger restaurants cater to the takeaway market but do not offer home delivery. Because speedy, reliable delivery is a critical success factor for HJs, the company measures its customer response time on all deliveries. At the beginning of the year, HJs advertised that 50 per cent of orders would be delivered in 15 minutes, and 95 per cent within 30 minutes. The following data relate to the first quarter of the year:

Time from receipt of order to delivery	January	February	March	Total
Orders delivered within 15 minutes	1 200	1 300	1 350	3 850
Orders delivered between 16 and 30 minutes	800	900	1 200	2 900
Orders delivered between 31 and 45 minutes	400	300	50	750
Total orders	**2 400**	**2 500**	**2 600**	**7 500**

Required:

1 Analyse the above data to determine if HJs achieved its advertised delivery reliability over each month.

2 Did the company's delivery performance improve over the quarter?

3 Suggest ways in which HJs could improve its delivery performance.

P15.48 The theory of constraints; business process re-engineering: service organisation

In a recent municipality budget, the Motor Registration and Licensing Office suffered substantial cutbacks. As a result, each department has been asked to submit a cost budget for the coming year that is 10 per cent lower than the costs for the current year.

The Licensing Department, which employed 50 people, issues driver's licences to qualified applicants. On average the department processes 250 licences per hour. To achieve the required cost saving, the branch manager has decided to re-engineer the process. The proposed process will consist of 5 consecutive activities and require a staff of 45 people:

- Area A would have a staff of 5 people and be responsible for receiving each application and checking that it is complete. They could process 250 applicants per hour.
- Area B would have a staff of 8 people, who confirm that the applicant is qualified to drive. They could process 350 applicants per hour.
- Area C would have a staff of 10 people, who take the applicant's photo. They could process 150 applicants per hour.
- Area D would have a staff of 17 people, who complete the licence card by adding the photo and a driver's licence number to the card. They could process 140 applicants per hour.
- Area E would have a staff of 5 people, who issue the licence to the applicant and process his or her payment. They could process 280 applicants per hour.

Required:

1 How many driver licence applicants would be processed per hour using the re-engineered process?

2 Identify the bottlenecks that would have to be removed to reach the current level of output.

3 Make recommendations on the number of staff that is required for each area in order to achieve the current level of output. Remember that to achieve the required cost savings, the maximum staff size is 45.

P15.49 Life cycle budgeting; product profitability: manufacturer

Frenzied Fashions Pty Ltd produces clothes for the teenage market. The design department is currently working on two potential product lines: elegant evening wear and casual country wear. The marketing department is keen to introduce both, but currently the company has only enough surplus production capacity to introduce one new product line. Both product lines are estimated to have a life cycle of three years – one year for design and development and two years on the retail market. The company accountant reviewed the budget estimates for both of the product lines and estimated their profitability for each year in the retail market as follows:

	Evening Wear	Country Wear
Sales revenue	R3 500 000	R6 500 000
Cost of goods sold	2 500 000	4 500 000
Gross margin	R1 000 000	R2 000 000

The marketing manager, whose performance is evaluated on sales, is keen to introduce the Country Wear and uses the profitability analysis to support this view. However, the company accountant is concerned about some of the other costs he has uncovered. The Evening Wear will be sold in a limited, exclusive market and involve relatively little promotion and distribution cost. In contrast, the Country Wear, a higher-volume line, will be distributed to a large number of retailers and require substantial support costs.

	Evening Wear	Country Wear
Design costs*	R200 000	R1 000 000
Promotion costs†	40 000	400 000
Distribution costs†	60 000	1 200 000
	R300 000	R2 600 000

*These costs are to be incurred in the year prior to the products' release on the market.
†These costs will be spread equally over the two years in which the products are sold.

Required:

1 Which product line appears the more profitable, using the conventional profitability analysis?
2 Prepare a profit statement for each product line for each of the three years of the life cycle. Which product appears to be the more profitable now? Why?
3 If Frenzied Fashions uses a cost-plus pricing system, which approach to costing – life cycle costing or conventional costing – would be more useful in setting product prices? Explain your answer.
4 Outline some more information that you might need to undertake a complete profitability analysis for the two product lines.

P15.50 Life cycle costing; time-based management: manufacturer

Ellipsis Electronics Ltd produces speakers for high-fidelity sound systems. Because of the rapid rate of technological innovation in the hi-fi market, most of the company's products have short life cycles. The marketing manager, Jean Plaatjies, believes that new product introductions are the key to Ellipsis's success. However, the managing director, Joseph Lacopetta, is concerned that the frequent changes in product lines are eroding the company's profitability. He believes that many of the new products have such short life cycles that they never fully recover their costs. He asks the management accountant, Stan Willox, to help him.

Willox decides to review the profitability of the Easy Ear Speaker System (EESS), which has just been phased out after only three years on the market. First, Willox prepares a conventional analysis of the profitability of the EESS:

	Year 1	Year 2	Year 3
Sales revenue	R750 000	R1 425 000	R525 000
Less Cost of goods sold:*			
Direct materials	150 000	285 000	105 000
Direct labour	75 000	142 500	52 500
Applied manufacturing overhead	112 500	213 750	78 750

*The company uses a JIT system, which means that inventories are minimal and all manufacturing costs flow directly to cost of goods sold.

In addition to these manufacturing costs, Willox is able to isolate the following costs associated with the EESS:

	Year 0	Year 1	Year 2	Year 3
Research and development	170 000			
Product design	100 000			
Process design	150 000	50 000	30 000	
Tooling costs	200 000			
Marketing costs	80 000	120 000	60 000	80 000
Warranty claims		100 000	40 000	10 000
After-sales service		30 000	55 000	20 000

Required:

1 Assess the profitability of the EESS in years 1, 2 and 3 using the conventional approach, which includes manufacturing costs only.
2 Assess the profitability of the EESS based on its life cycle costs.
3 Given this information, what action should Lacopetta take when considering future products?
4 Discuss the advantages and disadvantages of developing life cycle budgets for proposed new products.
5 Estimate the break-even time for the EESS.
6 What other performance measures might the company introduce to manage its new product development more effectively?

P15.51 Life cycle budgeting; life cycle management; target costing: manufacturer

The marketing department of Bream Hot Water Ltd has recommended that the company introduce a new solar hot water system, to be called the Sunstruck. To compete effectively with existing models offered by other companies, the Sunstruck would need to be priced at R8000. The company requires a target profit margin on sales for all new products of at least 30 per cent of sales. The technology in solar energy is developing rapidly, and therefore the Sunstruck is expected to be obsolete within three years of entering the market. Initial estimates of the Sunstruck's cost of manufacture per unit are:

Direct material	R2 500
Direct labour	1 250
Manufacturing overhead*	1 250
	R5 000

*Manufacturing overhead is applied at 100 per cent of direct labour cost

The Marketing Department is keen to introduce the Sunstruck as soon as possible. However, the management accountant is concerned about the non-manufacturing costs likely to be associated with the new product. He asks the departments that are upstream and downstream of manufacturing to estimate the costs in their departments associated with the development, production and sale of the Sunstruck. He receives the following information:

Estimated costs associated with the proposed Sunstruck (in R'000s)					
Department	20X4	20X5	20X6	20X7	20X8
Research and Development	15 000				
Product and Process Design	30 000	7 000			
Marketing	10 000	8 000	5 000	4 000	
Customer Support		2 500	8 000	7 500	2 000

The forecast sales of the Sunstruck are as follows:

20X5	17 000 units
20X6	9 000 units
20X7	4 000 units

Required:

1 Calculate the allowable cost for the Sunstruck that will meet the target selling price of R8000 and the target profit margin of 30 per cent on sales. Compare this with the estimated manufacturing cost. On this basis, would you recommend the development and introduction of the Sunstruck model?

2 Sunstruck considers the allowable cost is unachievable given its capabilities. Describe how the company could establish a product-level target cost that it considers achievable.

3 Prepare a life cycle budget for the Sunstruck that covers each year from 20X4 to 20X8.

4 What is the estimated average unit cost of the Sunstruck over its entire life cycle? On this basis, would you recommend the development and introduction of the Sunstruck model?

5 Explain how Bream could use life cycle management to reduce the manufacturing cost of the Sunstruck solar hot water system. Which part of the value chain may warrant additional expenditure? Explain.

Cases

C15.52 Using an activity-based costing system to modify behaviour: manufacturer[9]

The Hospital Instruments Division of MedLife Technology Corporation manufactures a variety of electronic medical equipment. The principal product of the Hospital Instruments Division is a sophisticated instrument for measuring and graphically displaying a variety of medical phenomena, such as heart and respiration rates. The culture throughout the division was primarily engineering-oriented. One result of this culture was that the company's design engineers generally designed new products from scratch, rather than relying on modification of a current design. While this approach usually resulted in an 'elegant' design from an engineering standpoint, it often resulted in the use of new or unique parts that were not already being used in the company's other products.

The strategy of the Hospital Instruments Division's management was to position the division as a product differentiator and price leader, not as the industry's low-cost producer.

This meant that the division generally led the medical instruments market with new products that exhibited greater functionality than competing products, and that the products were priced at a premium. The company's competitors then would emulate a new product, produce it at a lower cost, and undercut the MedLife Technology price. However, by then MedLife Technology had moved on to a new product with even greater functionality.

This strategy had been quite successful until the Japanese entered the medical instruments market in a major way. MedLife Technology's new competitors were able to set product prices some 25 per cent below those of MedLife Technology, while maintaining close to the same level of functionality. In order to compete, the Hospital Instruments Division had to lower its prices below its reported product costs. This resulted in significant losses for the division.

To remedy the situation, the Hospital Instruments Division's management began an extensive continuous improvement program. The division changed its production and inventory management system to a JIT system; ideas of total quality control were aggressively pursued; and management attempted to develop an empowered workforce. All of these efforts paid off dramatically. However, production costs were still relatively high for the industry, and cycle times were considered too long by management. The general feeling was that in order to remain competitive in the long run, the division would have to further lower its production costs and shorten its production cycle times. As management contemplated the high production costs, one problem that kept coming up was the division's part number proliferation. As the engineering-dominated company continued to introduce new products, the number of different parts and components that had to be stocked in inventory continued to increase. Some members of management felt that the division's cost-reduction goals could be achieved (at least partially) by solving the problem of part number proliferation.

As management was pondering the division's cost-reduction goal, the financial controller was contemplating the introduction of activity-based costing and activity-based management in the Hospital Instruments Division.

Required:

1 Explain how the problem of part number proliferation could increase the division's production costs.
2 Explain how long production cycle times may increase the division's production costs.
3 How could an ABC/ABM system be used to help reduce costs by attacking the problem of part number proliferation? The following specific questions may help in completing this requirement.
   (a) What was the division's strategy in the marketplace?
   (b) How were prices being determined at that time?
   (c) Did management really need more accurate product costs, given its strategy and the reality of market-driven prices?
   (d) What was the goal of management?
   (e) What was (at least partially) to blame for high production costs?
   (f) Who was (at least partially) to blame for high production costs?
   (g) How could an ABC system help to solve the problem and reduce production costs?
4 Following up your answer to requirement 3, what cost drivers could be employed to help to solve the problem of part number proliferation? Which cost driver would work best? Explain.
5 How could an ABC system help to highlight and solve the problem of production cycle times that are too long?

C15.53 Activity-based costing; activity-based management; non-value-added costs; target costing: manufacturer

Schmidtke's Meat Pty Ltd manufactures smoked meat products in the Worcester Valley, using processes that have been handed down from one generation of Schmidtkes to the next. Recently, one of the company's major high-volume-selling products, mettwurst, has come under intense pressure from a Durban manufacturer that uses modern manufacturing processes. Schmidtke's mettwurst sells for R34.93 per 500-gram stick, based on a cost-plus pricing system. (The company applies manufacturing overhead using a plantwide overhead rate based on the number of direct labour hours worked. Prices are based on absorption cost plus a 40 per cent mark-up.) The Durban competitor sells its mettwurst for R27.50 per 500-gram stick. The owner and manager of Schmidtke's, Hans Schmidtke, is not particularly worried about the problem, but his wife Frieda, the marketing manager, is concerned.

Frieda: Hans, you are putting your head in the sand. The Durban mettwurst has the potential to destroy our business. All our years of work will be lost. By the time our children, Wolfgang and Heidi, finish university there will be no more Schmidtke's Meat! Where will they work?

Hans: Frieda, stop worrying. The Durban mettwurst will disappear from the market after a while. There is no way they can be making a profit at that price. Just think about it. They're located in a city where rent and rates are high. They've got all that fancy new machinery to pay for. They're playing games, trying to get a share of our market. To survive in the longer term, they'll have to increase their price. Anyway, they don't have a recipe like ours that has been in the family for years. And they don't have our reputation for quality.

Heidi: Dad, I'm not sure you're right. You should taste this Durban mettwurst. There's no problem with their recipe or their quality. The customers know this already and that's why our mettwurst sales are down. At the university, we've been learning about a new costing system called 'activity-based costing'. I'd like to use it to work out what our problem is.

Hans: I've told you, I've told your mother: we don't have a problem, or we won't in the longer term. In the meantime, if you want to waste your vacation playing around with a new costing system that we don't need, go right ahead!

Heidi developed an activity-based costing system and identified the following bill of activities for the production of mettwurst:

Mettwurst: Bill of Activities
Annual volume: 5000 sticks
Batch size: 250 sticks

Activity	Quantity of activity driver used	Cost per unit activity driver	Annual cost
Inspect meat	20 inspections	R 150.00 per inspection	R 3 000.00
Dispose of substandard meat	500 kilograms	R 5.00 per kilogram	R 2 500.00
Move to mincing room	60 barrow-loads	R 40.00 per barrow	R 2 400.00
Load mincer*	40 loads	R 135.00 per load	R 5 400.00
Operate mincer	3000 kilograms	R 2.50 per kilogram	R 7 500.00
Unload mincer*	40 loads	R 105.00 per load	R 4 200.00
Move to mixing room	40 barrow-loads	R 45.00 per barrow	R 1 800.00
Load mixer*	60 loads	R 100.00 per load	R 6 000.00
Operate mixer	60 loads	R 200.00 per load	R 12 000.00
Unload mixer*	60 loads	R 80.00 per load	R 4 800.00
Move to packing room	60 barrow-loads	R 25.00 per barrow	R 1 500.00
Pack meat into skins	5000 skins	R 2.50 per skin	R 12 500.00
Move to smokehouse	100 trolley-loads	R 20.00 per trolley	R 2 000.00
Move to truck	100 trolley-loads	R 50.00 per trolley	R 5 000.00
Annual cost of all direct labour and manufacturing overhead activities			R 70 600.00
Activity cost per unit			R 14.12
Direct material cost per unit			10.83
Cost per unit			R 24.95

*These activities have to be performed more than once per batch because of the limited capacity per machine.

Required:

1 Suggest some reasons why the Durban company may be able to sell its mettwurst at R27.50 over the longer term.
2 Calculate the cost per stick of mettwurst under the existing absorption costing system.
3 Hans is convinced that Heidi's activity-based cost for the mettwurst is wrong. Identify the likely causes of the difference between the absorption cost and the activity-based cost per unit and explain to Hans why the absorption cost is likely to be wrong. (*Hint*: If you have problems with this you should revisit Chapter 8.)
4 What target cost would Schmidtke's have to set for its mettwurst if it wished to match the Durban price and maintain its existing mark-up?
5 Review the activities included in the bill of activities and identify any candidates for elimination as non-value-added activities. For each activity, explain why you consider it to be non-value-added.
6 Suggest possible root cause cost drivers for each of the non-value-added activities.
7 Does Schmidtke's need business process re-engineering or process improvement to eliminate its non-value-added activities? Explain.
8 Assume that by the next year of operations, the company has been able to reduce the cost of the following non-value-added activities by 30 per cent:
   - Inspect meat.
   - Dispose of substandard meat.
   - Move to mincing room.
   - Load mincer.
   - Unload mincer.
   - Move to mixing room.
   - Load mixer.
   - Unload mixer.
   - Move to packing room.
   - Move to smokehouse.
   - Move to truck.

   What will be the activity-based cost per unit (including direct material)?
9 Assuming the activity-based cost calculated in requirement 8, will the company be able to add its 40 per cent mark-up and compete effectively with the Durban mettwurst? If not, what would you recommend?

C15.54 Conventional approaches to control; activity-based management; performance measures: manufacturer

Refer to the data for Schmidtke's Meat Pty Ltd in Case 15.53.

Schmidtke's Meat Pty Ltd has a conventional approach to planning and control.

The company is divided into three departments: Manufacturing, Marketing and Administration. Each month, Hans Schmidtke checks a report which compares actual costs for the departments with budgeted costs. The budgeted costs are based on the costs for the previous year, adjusted for any major changes planned for the coming year. He also looks at actual versus budgeted revenue for the Marketing Department. When his father was running the business, he was able to 'keep his finger on the pulse' without any formal performance reports. Even in those days, the business had a reputation for fine quality and reliable delivery performance. However, the company has grown since then, and the existing approach to planning and control simply evolved.

In her first year at university, Hans' daughter, Heidi, learned about standard costing. She extolled the virtues of the standard costing variances and the principles of management by exception, and advised Hans to update his planning and control system. If he did not, she warned that he would never have effective control of his costs and Schmidtke's Meat would eventually fall to its competitors. Hans discussed Heidi's ideas with his long-time accountant, Otto Werner, but they decided it would involve a lot of effort setting standards for each of the company's products. The business seemed to be reasonably profitable and costs appeared to be under control.

In her second year at university, Heidi learned about activity-based costing and activity-based management. At about this time, the company experienced problems with sales of its mettwurst, described in the preceding case, and Heidi spent her summer vacation implementing an activity-based costing system. Initially, she used the system to cost products, but she also used the activity management dimension to identify and reduce the non-value-added activities associated with the production of mettwurst. But she was still not completely happy with the company's information for planning and control. She had identified non-value-added activities but she wanted to be sure that these were being eliminated as planned. Also, she wanted information to manage other critical aspects of performance for each activity, on an ongoing basis.

Hans was not convinced. Only a year ago Heidi was insisting that he throw out the existing system and implement standard costing. Now she was brutal in her condemnation of standard costing and was insisting on masses of activity-based information. 'Ah!' he said to himself, 'The impetuosity of youth knows no bounds, but nor does it understand that conservatism is the essence of good business.'

Required:

1 Identify the major weaknesses of the existing approach to planning and control at Schmidtke's Meat Pty Ltd.
2 If Hans had implemented a standard costing system, would it have given him a sound basis for planning and control? Explain your answer. (You may find it useful to revisit Chapters 10 and 11 to help answer this question.)
3 What aspects of performance do you think that Heidi would like to monitor at Schmidtke's Meat? Explain.
4 How could these requirements be met through activity-based management?
5 Identify a root cause cost driver for the activity 'Dispose of substandard meat' and use the process (supplier/customer) perspective to suggest a suitable performance measure for the preceding activity 'Inspect meat'.
6 When Hans hears that Heidi wants to measure several aspects of performance for each activity, he is horrified. 'We will spend all our time measuring rather than making mettwurst!' How could Heidi's approach be simplified?
7 (Only attempt this question if you have completed Chapter 14.) How does Heidi's proposal differ from the balanced scorecard approach to performance measurement described in Chapter 14?

Endnotes

1 The terminology used in this section is based on a glossary of terms about activity-based management prepared for CAM-I and published in Raffish & Turney (1991).

2 Customer and supplier cost analysis is described in Chapter 16 and activity-based budgeting is discussed in Chapter 11.

3 A more complete process map would include inputs, outputs and key aspects of performance.

4 The introduction of new products should be treated like any other capital investment decision. As described in Chapters 21 and 22, in evaluating these decisions, the expected cash inflows and outflows are identified year by year over the life of the planned project and discounted for the time value of money. For a new product introduction, the cash flows can be used to develop a life cycle budget for the product.

5 As discussed in Chapter 4, some businesses include upstream and downstream costs in their product costing system, but many confine product costs to manufacturing costs to comply with external reporting requirements.

6 The behavioural issues associated with setting target costs are similar to those involved in setting budget targets, as described in Chapter 9.

7 You will notice that BET is very similar to the payback period described in Chapter 21.

8 E.M. Goldratt pioneered this approach. See, for example, Goldratt (1990) and Goldratt & Cox (1992). For a good summary of the theory of constraints see also Ruhl (1996).

9 This case draws on a scenario described in the following sources: Peter B.B. Turney, *Common Cents: The ABC Performance Breakthrough* (Hillsboro, OR: Cost Technology, 1991), pp. 34, 106, 139, 150, 156, 164, 182, 213, 214, 217, and 220; and Peter B.B. Turney and Bruce Anderson, 'Accounting for Continuous Improvement', *Sloan Management Review* 30, no. 2 (1991), pp. 37–48.

Managing Suppliers, Customers and Quality

❖ Learning Objectives

After completing this chapter, you should be able to:

1. describe how e-commerce technologies and enterprise resource planning (ERP) systems can be used to enhance supply chain management;
2. recognise the value of creating close relationships with suppliers, and use activity-based techniques to analyse supplier costs;
3. explain how supplier relationships can be evaluated from both the supplier's and the firm's perspective;
4. use the EOQ formula to calculate the ordering cost and carrying cost, and determine the optimum order quantity and reorder point for inventory items;
5. discuss the philosophy underlying JIT systems, as well as their key features;
6. explain how customer relationship management (CRM) can be used to create long-term relationships with customers;
7. use activity-based methods to undertake customer profitability analysis;
8. measure customer performance and understand the relationships between various customer performance measures;
9. define quality and explain how it can be measured;
10. describe the four types of quality costs, and prepare and interpret cost of quality reports;
11. describe the key features of a total quality management system;
12. explain the concept of quality accreditation; and
13. (after studying the appendix) recognise the difference between backflush costing and conventional costing, and account for cost flows using backflush costing.

Introduction

Many organisations in the 21st century are focused on managing activities and costs across the value chain of the business, as well as creating and managing close relationships with suppliers and customers. In Chapter 14 contemporary frameworks for measuring performance were examined, and in Chapter 15 we focused on contemporary measures and approaches for managing costs and time. In this chapter we continue the theme of contemporary cost management and performance measurement by considering the management of suppliers, customers and quality. We describe methods that can be used to better manage supplier costs, supplier performance, and relationships with suppliers. Just-in-time inventory management systems, which allow firms to manage inventory and production more effectively, are outlined. We also consider customer relationship management, which involves understanding more about customers' needs and behaviours in order to develop stronger and lasting relationships with customers. Customer profitability and focused performance measures are also examined. The chapter finishes with an examination of the role of quality and total quality management.

All of the topics in this chapter are important for management accountants, as they provide tools and approaches for the efficient management of resources across the value chain of the organisation. The effective management of suppliers, inventory and quality also has an impact on enhancing customer value, and improving profitability and shareholder value.

Supply chain management

Supply chains are the interlinked customers and suppliers that work together to convert, distribute and sell goods and services among themselves, leading to a specific end product (NRC, 2000). **Supply chain management (SCM)** is the management of key business processes that extend across that supply chain, from the original suppliers to the final customers. SCM can involve managing costs, accelerating the time-to-market of new products, and creating close relationships with suppliers and customers. It may include the adoption of e-commerce technologies and cost management and process analysis techniques to improve efficiency, customer value and competitiveness. Many of the cost management techniques described in Chapter 14 can be used to achieve these objectives.

In practice, many organisations that use SCM consider only linkages and activities that involve their immediate suppliers and customers, and focus on optimising the value chain across those linkages. Exhibit 16.1 illustrates the supply chain of a business, which includes linkages with suppliers and customers.

E-commerce applications

L.O. 1 Electronic commerce (e-commerce) is a major change impacting on business and accounting systems. **E-commerce** involves the use of electronic transmission media to engage in the buying and selling of products and services, which are delivered electronically or physically (Greenstein & Vasarhelyi, 2002; Rayport & Jaworski, 2001).

E-commerce technologies may be used to create electronic linkages with suppliers and customers who are at either end of a firm's value chain. The term **B2B** (or **business-to-business**) refers to the e-commerce activities that take place between a business and its suppliers or customers (Rayport & Jaworski, 2001). In the case of suppliers, these activities include purchasing and procurement, supplier management and inventory management. For customers, they include Internet-based facilities for customer inquiries, ordering, payments and support. Such technologies may lead to enhanced communications and co-ordination across the supply chain – between the company and its suppliers and customers, and within the company itself.

B2B activities may utilise **electronic data interchange (EDI)**, which links a firm's computer system with that of its customers (and suppliers). For example, a computer link between a whole-

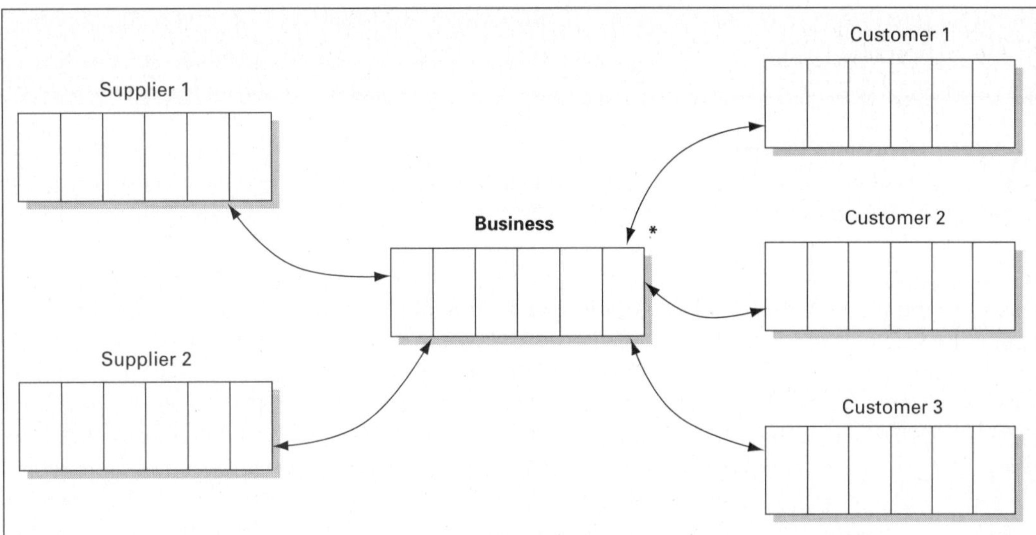

*These boxes represent activities within the value chain of each business.

Exhibit 16.1 The supply chain of a business

saler and its retail customers may allow the wholesaler to analyse the customers' daily sales activity and to determine when customers require additional stock. Customers also gain from these systems, as they receive products from their suppliers as soon as they are required without having to incur the expense associated with raising and processing purchase orders.

B2C (or **business-to-consumer**) refers to e-commerce exchanges between a business and its non-business customers. These systems are typically less extensive than B2B. Customers may purchase and pay for products and services online, make sales inquiries, and search for and receive customer support and assistance.

Within a firm, **enterprise resource planning (ERP) systems** may assist in achieving the objectives of supply chain management. Despite the name, ERP systems do not focus specifically on planning. Rather, they are complex software packages that support information systems that span many different functional areas of a business. Thus, areas as diverse as accounts payable, accounts receivable, human resource management, purchasing, inventory management and the general ledger may be integrated within an ERP system, and operate off common databases. Examples of popular ERP systems that are used by South African and overseas companies include SAP, Peoplesoft and Oracle. ERP systems may be difficult and expensive to implement successfully and are, therefore, more suited to larger organisations. They provide the advantages of consistency and standardisation of data definitions and business processes across a firm, more efficient retrieval of information for managers' decisions, and electronic access and data sharing across an organisation. ERP systems may also include e-commerce capabilities, to allow suppliers and customers to engage in online transactions and to gain access to relevant data.

The 'Real life' below provides three examples of technology-enhanced supply chain management. Focusing on Harley-Davidson, Komatsu and PPC, it illustrates the importance of the supply end of the value chain as a driver for improving performance throughout an organisation, and flowing through to positive customer outcomes. Clearly, effective supply chain management may enhance customer value as well as shareholder value.

Managing suppliers

As purchased material and components can make up a large proportion of the cost of producing a product, many organisations have come to realise the importance of carefully selecting suppliers and creating and managing ongoing relationships with them.

REAL LIFE: USING TECHNOLOGY TO MANAGE SUPPLY CHAINS IN THE USA, AUSTRALIA AND SOUTH AFRICA

Many businesses have implemented IT-based supply chain initiatives to improve their competitiveness. As the following case studies show, this approach enables organisations to dramatically improve their efficiency and effectiveness, benefiting their suppliers and customers.

In 1995 the US motorbike manufacturer Harley-Davidson re-engineered its supply chain to overcome production constraints and problems in meeting customer demand. At that time customers had to wait up to 18 months for their order! Using web-based technologies, the company reduced the number of its suppliers from 4000 to 800, improved defect rates from an average of 10 000 parts per million to 48 parts per million for most of its suppliers, reduced material costs by approximately US$40 million, and cut product development time by 30 per cent. Harley now uses the web to ensure suppliers have access to electronic ordering and vital information about design, quality and scheduling. And its customers can go online for ordering, processing product warranties, investigating service histories, and searching for spare parts and technical information.

Komatsu Australia (KA) is Australia's second largest distributor of earthmoving equipment. Supplies are sourced from KA's parent company in Japan and approximately 50 other businesses in Australia. Customers range from large government departments and mining companies to very small businesses such as plumbers. A major part of KA's activity focuses on the sales of spare parts and services and the testing of oil samples. KA's supply chain had been managed around an in-house system developed more than 16 years ago. From 2000 the company implemented a comprehensive supply chain management program, costing $4 million, based on a software system that supports customer relationship management (discussed later in this chapter) and provides data warehousing capabilities and a sophisticated electronic procurement hub. Different levels of customer service are available for customers, depending on their own e-business capabilities. Although it is early days for its supply chain management program, Komatsu Australia has identified major benefits, both in terms of cost savings and creating customer value.

PPC is the largest supplier of cement in South Africa and the company transports 3 million tons of cement each year to 14 000 customer destinations from 12 dispatch points. PPC produces 48 products which require a combination of standard and specialised equipment. About 500 deliveries are made each day in Southern Africa. PPC spends over R200 million each year on road transportation and its distribution requirements are complex. Payment of 120 000 freight invoices was managed on a decentralised basis and there was limited information about turnaround times and vehicle utilisation or on-time deliveries.

Barloworld Logistics provided an integrated logistics solution to PPC which included the following aspects:

- Design and optimisation of a new transportation process
- New software
- Daily demand planning and scheduling of vehicles
- Electronic integration of PPC, the transport suppliers and the customers, and
- Management information.

The new supply chain solution provided PPC with cost savings and improvements in customer service levels. An Internet portal was created and all communication regarding scheduling of transportation was over the Internet. Intensive training of transport operators took place to ensure that they achieved benchmarked key performance indicators (KPIs).

These cases demonstrate the power of technology-based supply chain management to enhance shareholder and customer value. You may also like to think about how intertwined supply chains can become, as the outputs of Harley-Davidson, Komatsu and PPC become inputs for the supply chains of their customers!

Sources: Sullivan (2001); Department of Communications, Information Technology and the Arts (2003a and 2003b), www.barloworld-logistics.com

REAL LIFE: SUPPLY CHAIN MANAGEMENT IN SOUTH AFRICA

Barloworld Logistics produce an annual survey of supply chain management in South Africa. The following represent some of the findings of the 2007 survey:

- Globalisation is expected to create extended supply chains as well as increase the complexity of such supply chains.
- About 74 per cent of CEOs regard currency fluctuations to be very challenging for sourcing globally.
- There is a realisation that a new approach to supply chain management is required due to weaknesses in current practices and poor infrastructure.
- The main supply chain objectives for the next year include improving the service offered to customers, lower sourcing and procurement costs, improving collaboration in the supply chain, achieving lower transportation costs and lower warehousing and distribution costs as well as decreasing lead times.
- The challenges to meet these objectives included planning and forecasting capabilities, the diverse needs of customers, increased volumes and complexity and the state of the distribution network.
- Procurement is seen as key to achieving cost reductions.
- About 40 per cent of supply chain strategy is either only partly aligned or not aligned with a firm's business strategy
- Logistics service providers are used mainly for forwarding and clearing, outbound distribution and warehousing.
- Marketing, finance and IT executives are unresponsive to supply chain issues and there is a lack of integration and collaboration.
- About 19 per cent of respondents do not know what their supply chain costs are in relation to sales.
- For most firms, the cost of a company's supply chain will vary from 5 to 17.5 per cent as a percentage of sales with 7.6 to 10 per cent being the most common range.
- Over 55 per cent of companies tend mostly not to share demand forecasts with their logistics service providers (from their point of view).

In the USA logistics costs rose to close to 10 per cent of GDP and there has been a 20 per cent increase in domestic freight transportation in the past 10 years, Yet, international shipments are expected to increase by 85 per cent over the next decade.

Source: www.barloworld-logistics.com

Relationships with suppliers

Improved supplier relationships can help to minimise supplier and inventory-related costs, which is particularly relevant if the strategic focus of the firm is cost leadership. Manufacturers' product quality may also be enhanced, and production lead time improved, which is consistent with a product differentiation strategy. (Remember from Chapter 15 that production lead time is the period from when an order enters the manufacturing department to when the finished products are ready for delivery.) In recent years, many companies in South Africa have put considerable effort into developing and strengthening supplier relationships. For example, South African motor vehicle manufacturers, such as Toyota, BMW, General Motors and VW, have worked at developing such relationships, and in some cases, they have created strategic alliances with certain suppliers. **Strategic alliances** are formal co-operative arrangements between two or more parties, involving the sharing of resources and activities to enhance the strategies of all participants. This includes undertaking joint product development, outsourcing information technology or distribution services, alliances to introduce quality manufacturing practices in suppliers, and joint construction projects. Some examples of strategic alliances with suppliers are described in the 'Real life' below.

REAL LIFE: DEVELOPING CO-OPERATIVE SUPPLIER RELATIONSHIPS

Increasingly South African companies are finding that there are many benefits to be gained from developing co-operative relationships and strategic alliances with their suppliers. These relationships may be mutually beneficial as they can give greater security to suppliers through long-term contracts and increased business, and allow firms to extend their quality improvement and cost management activities into their suppliers' operations.

Toyota South Africa introduced its supplier development strategy in the early 1990s. This involved assessing each supplier on a range of criteria, including delivery, quality and price, and directly assisting suppliers to improve the efficiency and quality of their own manufacturing processes. Toyota gained many advantages from helping suppliers to improve their production systems: reduced material costs, improved product quality, reduced inventory-related costs under a just-in-time delivery system, and cost savings from a reduction in variability of production schedules. Many of Toyota's suppliers have also reaped the benefits of more productive and cost-effective manufacturing operations, as well as achieving long-term supply contracts with Toyota. A number of suppliers have passed these same principles on to their own suppliers.

Toyota is manufacturing the Hilux model in South Africa for the local market and for export to Europe. Toyota is investing R2.4 billion in the manufacturing facility including R400 million for the tooling of its suppliers.

Courtesy of Toyota

Analysing supplier costs

L.O. 2 Selecting the best suppliers is a vital part of managing a business and achieving business strategies, and cost information should enter into this decision. However, conventional costing systems provide only limited information for helping managers to select suppliers, apart from details of the price paid for purchases. Many businesses recognise that the costs of dealing with suppliers include not only the purchase price of materials, but also a range of costs that are triggered by the purchase activity or by the supplier. These supplier costs, known as the **total cost of ownership**, are the costs associated with dealing with a particular supplier. They include the following (Carr & Ittner, 1992):

- *Costs of purchasing.* These include the costs of ordering inventory, delivery, receiving and inspection.

- *Costs of holding inventory.* These are carrying costs, including storage, insurance, obsolescence, and opportunity costs associated with holding inventory.
- *Costs of poor quality.* These include the costs of rework, scrap, returning defective material to suppliers, and downtime caused by using low-quality material.
- *Costs of delivery failure.* These are the costs triggered by late (or early) delivery by a supplier, and include expediting costs, additional labour costs to receive late or early deliveries, downtime due to late deliveries, and lost contribution margin from lost sales due to failed deliveries.

Many of the above costs tend to be hidden within overhead in a conventional costing system, even though they may be significant and may vary between suppliers. Focusing solely on the purchase price offered by suppliers may encourage managers to select the lowest priced suppliers, without regard to the other costs of managing suppliers. This may particularly be the case if managers' own performance is evaluated using material price variances from a standard costing system. Activity-based costing techniques can be used to solve this problem. (Activity-based costing for products was covered in Chapter 8.)

Calculating the total cost of ownership

Activity-based costing can be used to estimate the total costs of dealing with suppliers by regarding suppliers as the cost object and assigning to each supplier the costs of purchases and all supplier-related activities. This analysis may also involve the search for cost drivers, and so provide opportunities for cost management.

To illustrate the principles of analysing the total cost of ownership, we will focus on Hardy Saucepans (Pty) Ltd. Hardy Saucepans manufactures and sells saucepans and other kitchen equipment directly to customers, as well as to retail stores. To produce its saucepan sets, the company purchases raw materials and components from a range of suppliers. We will focus on the two suppliers of the plastic handles for the standard saucepan sets: Plastex Industries, and Handles Ltd. Hardy Saucepans has been dealing with these suppliers for several years and uses two suppliers for the one component because the purchasing manager believes this practice is less risky than being tied to a single supplier. Plastex Industries is used for most orders, as it charges only R20 per handle, whereas Handles Ltd charges R22 per handle.

In the past year, Hardy Saucepans purchased a total of 10 000 units from Plastex Industries and 6000 units from Handles Ltd. The accountant and the purchasing manager have just completed an analysis of the costs of dealing with both suppliers during that year. The first step was to analyse the major activities that were driven by suppliers, determine their activity drivers and calculate the cost per unit of activity driver. This information is contained in Exhibit 16.2, along with the number of activities consumed by each supplier.

		Number of activities	
Activity	**Cost per unit of activity driver**	**Plastex**	**Handles Ltd**
Place purchase order	R1 200 per order	12	10
Receive a delivery	R800 per delivery	60	45
Inspect material	R400 per delivery	60	45
Store inventory	R280 per unit stored per year	200	100
Rework product due to poor-quality material	R500 per unit reworked	45	5
Downtime due to poor-quality material	R450 per hour of downtime	30	4
Receive and inspect late deliveries	R2 500 per late delivery	10	1

Exhibit 16.2 Activities and activity cost for suppliers, Hardy Saucepans

The next step was to determine the total cost of ownership, by calculating the total costs of supplier-related activities for the year. In Exhibit 16.3, the supplier costs have been calculated in total, and as a cost per unit. This allows us to estimate the total cost per unit for each supplier. Note that the purchase price must be included in the analysis.

	Plastex Industries		Handles Ltd	
Purchase price per unit		R 20.00		R 22.00
Supplier activity costs:*				
Place purchase order	14 400		12 000	
Receive a delivery	48 000		36 000	
Inspect material	24 000		18 000	
Store inventory	56 000		28 000	
Rework product due to poor-quality material	22 500		2 500	
Downtime due to poor-quality material	13 500		1 800	
Receive and inspect late deliveries	25 000		2 500	
Total supplier activity costs	203 400		100 800	
No. of units	10 000		6 000	
Total supplier activity cost per unit		20.34		16.80
Total cost of ownership per unit		R 40.34		R 38.80

*The supplier costs for each activity are based on the number of times the activity was performed, multiplied by the cost per unit of activity driver (from Exhibit 16.2).

Exhibit 16.3 The total cost of ownership, Hardy Saucepans

What can management conclude from the data in Exhibit 16.3? In the past year, it was cheaper to deal with Handles Ltd than with Plastex Industries. This was due mainly to the higher costs of receiving late deliveries from Plastex, as well as the costs of rework. Like many companies, Hardy Saucepans had made the initial decision – to engage Plastex Industries rather than Handles Ltd as the main supplier – based on purchase price. Both suppliers were considered equally capable of supplying high-quality products as required. However, the data in Exhibit 16.3 clearly show that delivery and quality performance were much better for Handles Ltd. The management of Hardy Saucepans now has some useful data to consider in its future supply decisions. It may decide to place a greater reliance on Handles Ltd in the future, or it may inform Plastex Industries that it will have to improve its performance if it wishes to be retained as a major supplier to the company.

Note that total cost of ownership may be understated when a supplier's delivery performance is poor, or where there is downtime and rework resulting from poor supplier performance, as the cost of the contribution margin on lost sales cannot be estimated with any accuracy.

Evaluating supplier performance

L.O. 3 The above analysis of supplier costs can form the basis for evaluating suppliers' performance. For example, one technique that we can use to compare the performance of a range of suppliers is to calculate a **supplier performance index (SPI)**. This is simply the ratio of supplier costs to the total purchase price (Carr & Ittner, 1992). For the two suppliers to Hardy Saucepans, the SPI can be calculated as follows:

Plastex Industries	Handles Ltd
$\text{SPI} = \dfrac{\text{Total supplier activity costs*}}{\text{Total purchase price}}$	$\text{SPI} = \dfrac{\text{Total supplier activity costs}}{\text{Total purchase price}}$
$= \dfrac{\text{R}203\,400}{10\,000 \times \text{R}20.00}$	$= \dfrac{\text{R}100\,800}{6000 \times \text{R}22.00}$
= R1.017	= R0.7636

*The total supplier activity costs are taken from Exhibit 16.3.

Thus, Plastex Industries costs more per rand of purchase than does Handles Ltd. This confirms our original conclusion that Handles Ltd is more cost-effective to deal with than Plastex.

However, firms may evaluate suppliers' performance using a variety of criteria, including the ability to supply at the contracted purchase price, material quality, supplier delivery performance, and the quality of relationships between employees, unions and management. As part of establishing long-term contracts with suppliers, specific performance measures and targets for these criteria are often developed. Examples of supplier performance measures are outlined in Exhibit 16.4.

Criteria	Examples of measures	Explanation
Delivery	% of orders delivered on time. Average lead time* for deliveries.	Suppliers may be required to deliver an order within a short timeframe (e.g. 2 hours, 1 day, 2 days).
Quality	% of orders rejected.	Quality inspections may not be undertaken on all deliveries, and financial penalties may be levied on suppliers that deliver defective or inadequate material.
	Achievement of quality certification.	A firm may set targets for suppliers achieving certain quality accreditations. These may be international quality standards (e.g. ISO 9000), or quality standards developed by the firm itself.
Cost	Success at meeting cost-down targets.	Firms may set suppliers targets for 'cost downs' – that is, suppliers may be expected to reduce the price that they charge to the firm for materials/components by a certain percentage each year.
	Achievement of manufacturing cost reduction targets.	A firm may assist suppliers to reduce their manufacturing cost, and set targets to measure suppliers' cost reduction performance.
Organisational change	Implementation of team structures. Adoption of EDI system.	Firms may require suppliers to make changes in their production methods and administrative systems and may assist the supplier to achieve this over time.
Relationship	Supplier satisfaction surveys. Number of disputes between suppliers and firm resolved within 7 days. Number of days of downtime due to industrial actions.	Measures may be developed to assess the quality of the relationships between the supplier and the firm. This includes surveying purchasing and manufacturing employees within the firm to gauge their level of satisfaction with the supplier. Industrial actions at the suppliers' plants can lead to late or no supply to the firm.

*Lead time for deliveries is the time between placing an order for inventory with a supplier and receiving that inventory.

Exhibit 16.4 Supplier performance measures

Of course, relationships involve two parties, and some firms will also *assess their own performance* in relation to the management of suppliers and the development of supplier relationships. The ability of suppliers to meet performance measures imposed by a firm (the buyer) may be directly impacted by the performance of the buyer. Performance criteria may focus on the purchasing, production planning, accounts payable and information systems areas of a firm. Measures may include the following (Hines et al., 2000):

- number of approved suppliers;
- number of new suppliers contacted;
- number of supplier/joint innovations generated;
- response time to supplier queries;
- provision of future order information to suppliers on time;
- percentage of orders processed through electronic means;
- percentage of payments processed electronically;
- reduction in number of suppliers;
- number of expedited orders.

Managing inventory

The effective management of inventory can help to reduce supplier costs, as well as manufacturing and production costs. Manufacturing, wholesale and retail businesses often hold significant amounts of inventory that could alternatively be invested in areas such as new equipment or staff training, or just invested to earn interest. So why do some organisations hold high levels of inventory?

Why hold inventories?

The reasons for carrying inventories vary from one business to the next. Common reasons include the following:

1 to cope with uncertainties in customer demand and in production processes, such as machine breakdowns – the inventory acts as a buffer against the possibility of running out of a needed item;
2 to qualify for discounts available on large orders – called **quantity discounts**;
3 to avoid future price increases in raw materials;
4 to avoid the costs associated with placing numerous relatively small orders with suppliers.

Inventory decisions have broad implications. They can influence customer service and quality, as well as costs, and thus have a significant impact on the competitiveness of the firm. The conventional approach to managing inventory focuses on minimising inventory costs by assessing how much inventory to purchase or manufacture in-house, and how often.

Conventional approaches to inventory management

Conventional approaches to inventory management consider the balance between three classes of costs: ordering costs, carrying costs and shortage costs. **Ordering costs** refer to the incremental costs of placing an order for inventory. Where inventory is purchased, the ordering costs include any costs associated with placing the purchase order and receiving the stock. Where inventory is *manufactured in-house*, the ordering costs include the costs of placing the work order and, more importantly, the costs of setting up the plant to produce the required inventory item. **Carrying costs** are the costs of carrying inventory in stock. **Shortage** (or **stock-out**) **costs** refer to the costs of running out of inventory. Examples of costs in each of these categories are given in Exhibit 16.5. (**Expediting costs** refer to the extra costs of processing purchase or production orders more quickly than normal.)

REAL LIFE: SUPPLY CHAIN MANAGEMENT AT ANGLOGOLD ASHANTI PLC

AngloGold Ashanti is a major global gold-mining company that has significant mining operations in South Africa. The company has placed a critical focus on Procurement and Supply Chain management. The following is an extract from the company's website in relation to careers in the company and offers us a clear perspective of what supply chain management encompasses at AngloGold Ashanti.

Mission

The Procurement and Supply Chain discipline (PSC) mission is to ensure that the mining operations and other clients get the appropriate quality goods and services at the right place and time in order to enable them to mine gold safely and profitably.

Business role

Besides being a critical link in the physical supply chain, the role of the PSC is increasingly being recognised as a key contributor to shareholder returns through cost containment and reductions of the overall input costs and maximisation of returns on assets. To be able to fulfil this role the PSC maintains an intimate knowledge of the internal business strategies, objectives and processes, as well as an expert knowledge-base of the external supply chain environment and factors affecting the supply and demand of goods and services.

Specific activities

Specific areas of PSC activity include:

- *Purchasing & procurement function*: general sourcing of goods and services from suppliers and service providers;
- *Materials management function*: definition of the business requirements, management of materials and services quality standards, vendor selection and performance, especially technical service providers, and the disposal of redundant and obsolete assets;
- *Logistics management function*: management of the inbound logistics supply chain, inventory and warehouse management, internal distribution of goods;
- *Contract management*: administration of supply contracts, negotiation of pricing applications and management of supplier relationships;
- *Strategic sourcing*: the specialised procurement of certain key and strategic commodities and services, with a specific focus on reducing the overall total cost of ownership (TCO) and ensuring a stable source of supply. Strategic sourcing includes identification and maximising the leverage opportunities created through Group commodity consolidation and collaboration with various external parties, such as other AA plc companies;
- *Information systems*: the design and maintenance of systems and processes to enable, facilitate and support all PSC activities. Extensive use is made of mainframe-, mid-range- and PC-based systems and including extensive use of web-based and e-business technologies.

Source: www.anglogold.com/Careers/Career+Choices

Economic order quantity (EOQ)

The **economic order quantity (EOQ) model** has been used since the early 1900s. The EOQ model determines the optimum order size for individual inventory items. An **optimum order size** is one that minimises the total of the ordering costs and carrying costs. If the inventory is purchased, the EOQ model estimates the ideal size of the purchase order. If inventory is manufactured, the model estimates the ideal size of the work order (that is, the production run). L.O. 4

Ordering costs: inventory that is purchased	**Carrying costs**
Costs of finding suitable suppliers	Storage costs (e.g. warehouse cost)
Clerical costs of preparing purchase order	Handling costs
Transportation costs	Insurance
Costs of receiving the order (e.g. unloading and inspecting)	Spoilage and obsolescence
Costs of processing the invoice	Theft
Costs of expediting orders	Forgone return on funds tied up in inventory
Ordering costs: inventory that is manufactured in-house	**Shortage costs**
Clerical costs of preparing the work order	Lost sales (current and future)
Costs of setting up for production	Costs of interrupted production when raw materials are not available
Preparing equipment and facilities for production of the item	Wages of idle workers
Wages of idle workers during setup	Extra machinery setup costs (see 'ordering costs' in the text)
Cost of idle machines during setup	Costs of expediting
Cost of test runs	

Exhibit 16.5 Inventory ordering, carrying and shortage costs

Let's return to Hardy Saucepans and consider how the EOQ model can be used to manage the ordering of one of their key raw material components, plastic pellets, which is used by Hardy Saucepans to make parmesan cheese graters. This product consists of a cylindrical plastic casing and handle, with a stainless steel grater. The EOQ model can be used to determine the size and frequency of orders of plastic pellets.

Plastic pellets are purchased in 25 kilogram bags, and 4800 bags are used each year. Each bag costs R100. The incremental cost of placing and receiving a typical order for plastic pellets is estimated at R600, and the annual cost of carrying plastic pellets in inventory is R25.00 per bag per year.[1]

The total annual cost of ordering and carrying inventory is given by the following equation:

$$\text{Total annual cost} = \left(\frac{\text{annual requirement}}{\text{order quantity}} \times \text{cost per order}\right) + \left(\frac{\text{order quantity}}{2} \times \text{annual carrying cost per unit}\right)$$

The economic order quantity is the order size at which the total annual cost is minimised. By using calculus we can arrive at the following formula for the economic order quantity (or EOQ):

$$\text{Economic order quantity} = \sqrt{\frac{2 \times \text{annual requirement} \times \text{cost per order}}{\text{annual carrying cost per unit}}}$$

Applying this formula to the order problem yields the following EOQ:

$$EOQ = \sqrt{\frac{2 \times 4800 \times 600}{25.00}}$$

$$= 480 \text{ bags}$$

Another way of solving the EOQ problem is the graphical method, which is presented in Exhibit 16.6. Notice that the ordering cost line slants downwards to the right. This indicates a decline in total order costs as the order size increases and the order frequency decreases. However, as the order size increases, the average inventory on hand increases. This results in an increase in total carrying costs, as indicated by the positive slope of the carrying cost line. The EOQ is at 480 bags, where the best balance is struck between these two costs. In this situation total inventory-related costs are R12 000 (10 × R600 + 240 × R25).

Timing of orders under EOQ

The EOQ model is used to determine how much to order at a time. Another important decision is when to order – that is, the inventory reorder point. The **inventory reorder point (ROP)** is the quantity of inventory on hand that serves as a trigger for the placement of an order from the suppliers. This decision depends on the lead time and the rate at which inventory is used. The **lead time** associated with inventory is the length of time between placing an order and receiving an order. In the case of purchased inventory, the lead time is the period between placing and receiving the purchase order. For manufactured inventory, it is the time between placing the work order and the completion of the goods. We can use the following formula to calculate the reorder point:

$$\text{ROP} = \text{inventory used per period of time} \times \text{order lead time}$$

Suppose the lead time for plastic pellets is two weeks. Since Hardy Saucepans uses 4800 bags of plastic pellets per year, then (assuming the production rate is constant throughout the year) this implies that 96 bags are used each week.[2] The reorder point is:

$$\begin{aligned}\text{ROP} &= 96 \text{ bags} \times 2 \text{ weeks} \\ &= 192 \text{ bags}\end{aligned}$$

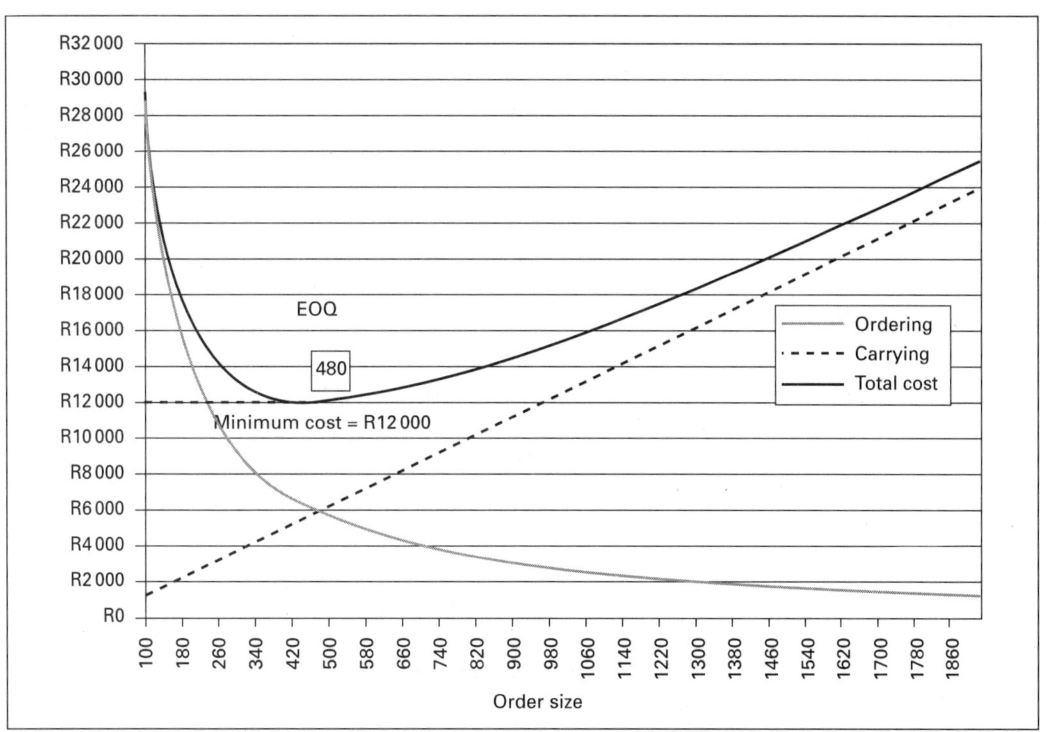

Exhibit 16.6 Graphical solution to economic order quantity for plastic pellets

Therefore, plastic pellets should be ordered in the economic order quantity of 480 bags, when the inventory level falls to 192 bags. By the time the new order arrives, two weeks later, the 192 bags in inventory will have been used in production. Exhibit 16.7 illustrates this pattern of ordering and using inventory. By placing an order early enough to avoid a stock-out, management reduces the potential costs of shortages.

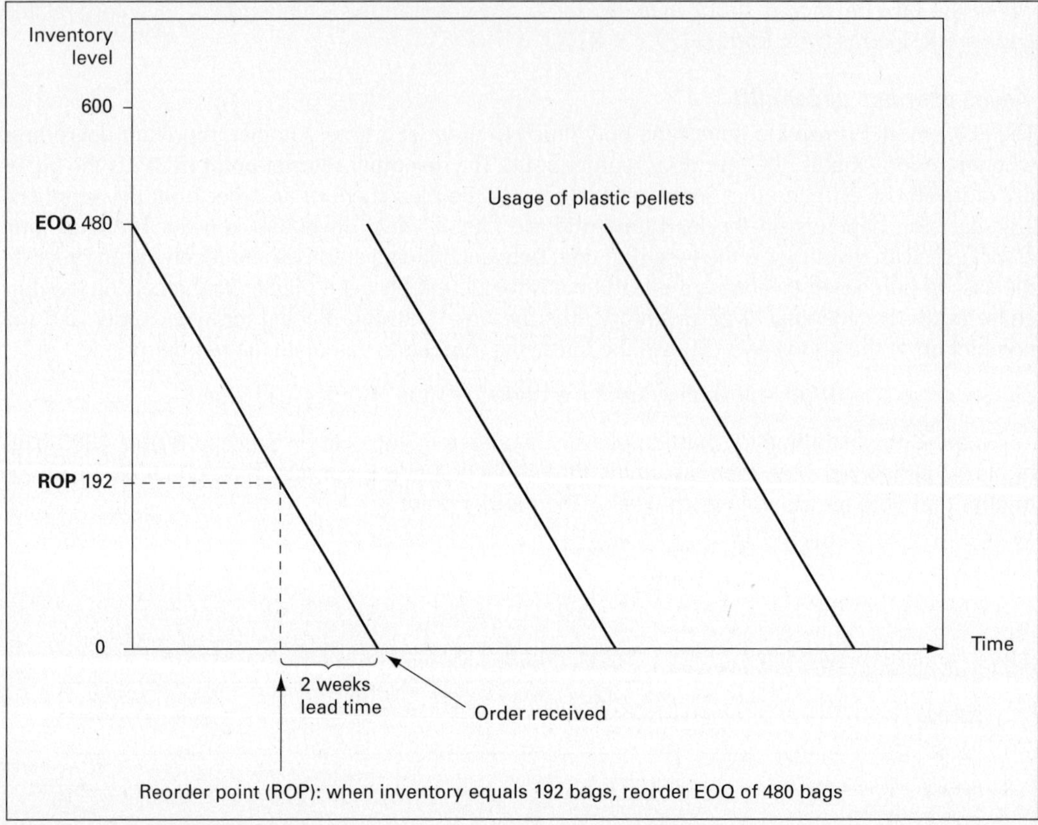

Exhibit 16.7 Ordering, lead time and usage of plastic pellets inventory

Safety stock

Our example assumed that 96 bags of plastic pellets were used every week. Suppose instead that weekly usage fluctuates between 86 and 106 bags. Although the average weekly usage is still 96 bags, there is the potential for stock shortages of up to 10 bags in any week. In light of this uncertainty, management may wish to keep a **safety stock** – extra inventory to cover above-average usage. The safety stock needed to cover stock shortages during the two-week lead time is 20 bags. We could calculate this reorder point using the following formula:

$$\begin{aligned} \text{ROP} &= (\text{inventory used per period of time} \times \text{order lead time}) + \text{safety stock} \\ &= (96 \text{ bags} \times 2 \text{ weeks}) + 20 \text{ bags} \\ &= 212 \text{ bags} \end{aligned}$$

Allowing for 20 extra bags to be kept as safety stock results in a reorder point of 212 bags. Thus, an order for 480 bags should be placed whenever the plastic pellets inventory falls to 212 bags. During the two weeks' lead time, another 172 to 212 bags of plastic pellets will be consumed in production. Although a safety stock will increase inventory-carrying costs, it will minimise the potential costs caused by shortages. Some businesses use more sophisticated reorder point models, which find the balance between the extra carrying costs for safety stock and the extra shortage costs from potential stock-outs.

Assumptions underlying EOQ

Like most decision-making models, the EOQ model is based on a number of simplifying assumptions, including the following:

1 Demand is known and constant.

2 Incremental ordering costs are known and are constant per order.

3 Acquisition cost per unit is constant.
4 The entire order is delivered at one time.
5 Carrying cost is known and is constant per unit.
6 On average, one-half of inventory is in stock at any one time.

Organisations using the EOQ model need to assess how reasonable these assumptions are for the business. Will the EOQ model provide useful information, or will it need to be adapted? The EOQ model can be altered to allow for the quantity discounts that many suppliers offer for large orders. It can also be adapted to allow for different delivery patterns. For example, when inventory is manufactured instead of purchased, it is likely to be delivered bit by bit, rather than the entire order delivered at the one time. However, in many organisations EOQ models are not used to manage inventory, as there are more effective systems available, including just-in-time approaches.

Just-in-time (JIT) systems

L.O. 5

Since the late 1970s just-in-time (or JIT) inventory and production management has become increasingly popular. The JIT philosophy, made famous by Toyota, has been credited as the key to success of many of the world's leading manufacturers. Tremendous cost savings have been realised by many companies that have adopted the JIT philosophy.

A **just-in-time** (or **JIT**) **inventory and production system** is a comprehensive system for controlling the flow of manufacturing in a multistage production environment. The underlying philosophy is the *simplification of the production process* by removing non-value-added activities. A full-scale JIT system covers all aspects of the production process, not just inventories. However, as inventory can be a major cause of *non-value-added activity*, inventory management is a critical focus. One goal of JIT is to reduce or eliminate inventories at every stage of production, from raw materials to finished goods. Clearly, this is a very different approach to inventory management, compared with EOQ.

To visualise the JIT approach, examine Exhibit 16.8, which illustrates the production of the Parmesan cheese grater at Hardy Saucepans. The flow of manufacturing activity is depicted by the solid arrows running from one production stage to the next. However, the signal that triggers more production activity in each stage comes from the *next* stage of production. These signals, depicted by the dashed-line arrows, run upwards. We begin with sales at the bottom of the exhibit. Ideally, a sales order for the cheese grater triggers their production and they are *pulled* from Packaging by sending a signal that more product is needed. Similarly, when production employees in Packaging need more inputs (more cheese graters) to pack and seal into boxes, they send a signal back to the Assembly stage. This triggers the purchase of the stainless steel component and the assembly of the three components of the cheese grater. Working our way back to the beginning of the process, the purchase of the plastic pellets is triggered by a signal that they are needed in the Plastic Moulding process. Thus, under JIT, production and inventory purchases are *pulled* through the system, driven by the *actual demands of the final customer.*

The **pull system** of production management is an important characteristic of the JIT approach, and results in significantly reduced inventory levels. This can be compared with a push system, which is found in conventional inventory management and production systems. Under a **push system** goods are purchased or produced to meet inventory requirements rather than to meet actual customer demand. We saw this under an EOQ approach, where budgeted annual customer demand for a product determines annual inventory requirements, which in turn drive the EOQ. Inventory, rather than actual customer demand, *pushes* production. Under JIT the focus is on meeting immediate customer needs for product and inventory, and customer demand pulls production.

Key features of JIT production

The key features of JIT production include the following:

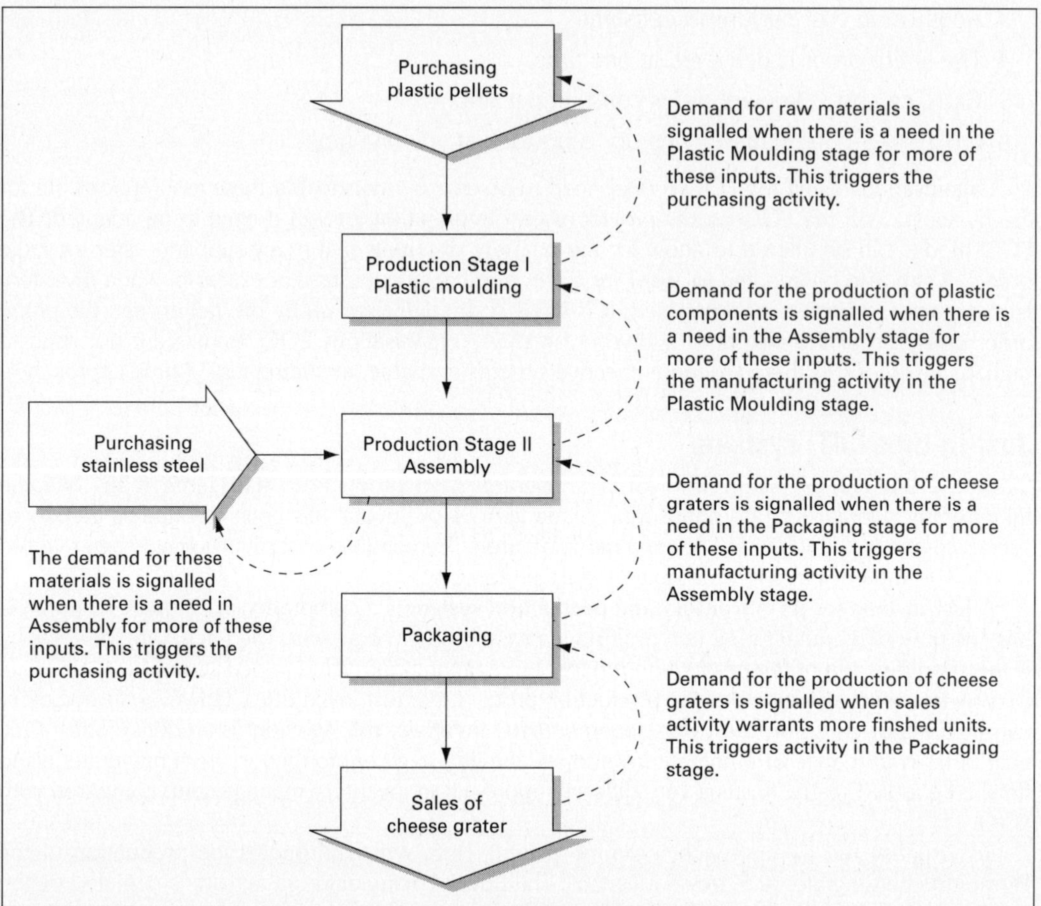

Exhibit 16.8 Just-in-time (JIT) system for the Parmesan cheese grater

1 *A pull method of coordinating production.* Goods are produced in each manufacturing stage, and materials are purchased only when they are needed at the next stage. The signal that triggers production in each stage is sent in the form of a '*kanban*'. ***Kanban*** is the Japanese term for card or visible record. Nothing is manufactured at any stage until its need is signalled from the subsequent stage, via a *kanban*. As a result, no components or finished goods are produced until they are needed, and therefore no inventories build up.

2 *Simplified production processes.* An important goal of JIT is to simplify the production flow, beginning with the arrival of materials from suppliers and ending with the delivery of goods to customers. Non-value-added activities are identified and removed throughout the production process. Techniques for managing activities were outlined in Chapter 15.

3 *Purchase of materials, and manufacture of sub-assemblies and products in small lots.* As materials are purchased and goods produced only as required, batch sizes tend to be small and inventory levels are low.

4 *Quick and inexpensive set-ups of production machinery.* To produce in small batches, set-up times must be reduced, or the production line will be too slow to meet customer delivery requirements. In some companies set-ups can take more than an hour, while in other companies only 10 minutes may be required. Value analysis and the use of advanced technologies may help to reduce this time.

5 *High quality levels for raw materials, components and finished products.* If raw materials, components and sub-assemblies are to arrive 'just in time' for production, they must be 'just right' for their intended purpose. Otherwise, the production line will be shut down and significant non-value-added costs of waiting will result. Managing inventory and managing quality go hand in hand, and most businesses with JIT systems also have total quality management (TQM) programs. Quality is not only a requirement of JIT; it is a result. Under JIT, any quality problems become apparent immediately because defective outputs are input into the next stage of the production process. Under a conventional approach, the defective units may be hidden in work in process inventory and not discovered for days or even weeks.

6 *Effective preventive maintenance of equipment.* If goods are to be manufactured just in time to meet customer orders, production delays must be avoided, so frequent maintenance of equipment is essential.

7 *Flexible work teams.* To facilitate JIT, many businesses restructure their production processes from rigid assembly lines into work-based teams. Employees in these teams are multi-skilled, being trained to complete all aspects of the production process. This assists in eliminating bottlenecks in the production process and non-value-added idle time.

JIT purchasing

A JIT system involves JIT purchasing as well as JIT production. Indeed, some organisations take a JIT approach only to purchasing, and not to production. The aim of JIT purchasing is to purchase raw materials from outside suppliers only as they are needed, to avoid costly inventory build-ups. JIT purchasing includes the following key features:

1 *Only a few suppliers.* Under JIT, many companies dramatically reduce the number of suppliers that they deal with, and work on developing close relationships with individual suppliers, who must be able to deliver high-quality goods on time.

2 *Long-term contracts with suppliers.* Long-term contracts that include supply price, quality, design specifications and delivery terms may be negotiated with suppliers.

3 *Materials and parts delivered in small lots as needed.* The aim of JIT is to avoid holding costly inventories by having supplies arrive 'just in time' to be placed into production. This results in many small orders delivered more often. Orders may be received daily, or weekly, or hourly, depending on the company.

4 *Minimal inspection of delivered materials and parts.* Under JIT, suppliers are selected according to their ability to meet stringent quality standards and deliver the correct amount of materials on time. Once the quality of suppliers is proven, the level of quality testing is reduced.

5 *Electronic ordering and payments.* JIT systems may utilise e-commerce applications, including EDI, often as part of a wider ERP system. This may allow firms to place orders electronically with suppliers, or will provide suppliers with online access to a firm's inventory files to determine purchase requirements and to provide orders. Invoices from suppliers and payments to suppliers will also be managed electronically. These systems reduce costly paperwork for both supplier and purchaser.

We have described the key features that are common to many JIT production and purchasing systems in manufacturing businesses. JIT purchasing is also used in retail, wholesale and service firms to reduce warehouse inventories and to streamline the purchasing function.

Clearly, JIT purchasing is a critical aspect of managing suppliers, and JIT production and JIT purchasing have implications for enhancing customer satisfaction.

REAL LIFE: 'OH WHAT A FEELING, LOW INVENTORY'

Auto component manufacturers form an important part of the South African manufacturing sector. In fact, the auto industry accounts for one third of South Africa's manufacturing base. Up to recently, many auto component manufacturers carried large inventories in order to ensure that production at the OEMs (original equipment manufacturers) such as Toyota, BMW, Audi and VW were not held up due to a lack of components. However, this was costly. Auto component manufacturers have begun to adopt JIT inventory systems, have redesigned plant layouts and have eliminated warehouse rentals and other costs. Companies have moved to *kanban* systems and in some cases inventory has fallen from over 17 days' supply to only a few days' supply. A motor manufacturer such as Toyota demands frequent small deliveries of components so that it can minimise inventories of purchased parts. It also insists that production is never held up due to a lack of parts.

Physical location is important in order to facilitate JIT. For example, Foxtec-Ikwezi is an auto component firm in East London that manufactures ready-to-fit forged aluminium suspension struts. It is envisaged that 1.5 million parts will be manufactured in 2007 and production will increase to 4.5 million in 2008 with some 80 per cent of the parts destined for the export market. Foxtec-Ikhwezi is 4kms away from the harbour and under a kilometre away from DaimlerChrysler which will take up 20 per cent of production for the new C-Class Mercedes Benz model, allowing for just-in-time (JIT) supply to markets.

Source: *Daily Despatch*, 3 July 2006.

Toyota's production system

Courtesy of Toyota

Costs and benefits of JIT

A JIT system often entails a substantial investment in setting up the production facilities to minimise non-value-added activities, such as material handling and other work associated with poor quality and excessive inventories. A JIT system can also increase the risk of incurring inventory shortage costs. This may lead to disrupted production, the costly expediting of materials, and lost sales. The 'Real life' below illustrates this point. Another issue is that it may be difficult for JIT to deliver benefits to small suppliers. While small firms may need to comply with the JIT requests of large and powerful customers, they may not have the muscle to push those same systems onto their own suppliers. Thus, small suppliers may keep excessive raw materials inventory and finished goods inventory on hand, to meet the JIT requirements of their customers.

On the other hand, the benefits of JIT extend beyond the obvious savings in inventory carrying costs: reduced storage and handling costs; lower insurance costs; fewer losses due to spoilage, obsolescence and theft; and decreased opportunity costs associated with having money tied up in inventory. The aim of JIT is to eliminate all non-value-added activity, not just excessive inventories.

JIT can improve productivity, manufacturing lead times and quality. Under a successful JIT system, customers' needs are satisfied more quickly and more effectively.

In theory, the JIT ideal is zero inventories. In practice, businesses must weigh up the substantial costs that may result from inventory shortages and compare them with the benefits of holding minimal inventories. In many companies, the JIT approach involves streamlining the production of products and reductions in inventory balances – not necessarily the elimination of inventory. As in so many of the management decisions we describe, it is not possible to quantify all these costs and benefits, and management judgement therefore plays a vital role.

What can be done to reduce the risks of JIT in South Africa? If possible, a company should not rely only on one supplier for a particular component. Toyota, the originator of JIT, had to learn this the hard way. The sole supplier of brakes to Toyota experienced a major fire at its manufacturing facility and this resulted in Toyota having to shut down its own assembling plants, resulting in major financial losses. If it is not possible to have more than one supplier for a component, then a company should consider carrying inventory of that component, just in case.[3]

The role of the management accountant in managing inventory

With its emphasis on the elimination of non-value-added activity and the improvement of quality, the JIT approach requires a range of non-financial performance measures linked to business strategies to supplement the conventional, largely financial, performance measures. JIT management

REAL LIFE: IS JIT TOO RISKY?

Since the early 1980s better inventory management practices have resulted in falling average inventory levels in South African companies. Much of this improvement has been driven by JIT. Many adopters of JIT practices claim high levels of cost savings.

However, there are risks associated with adopting JIT. One of the biggest potential risks relates to disruption in supply of inventory. South African motor vehicle manufacturers are known for their widespread use of JIT systems. The possibility of labour strikes and industrial action by employees can have a dramatic impact on the whole manufacturing process so that a strike at a single auto component manufacturer may mean that the VW plant, for example, cannot continue with production of motor vehicles. The strikes at Hulamin and Daimler SA are indicative of the risks that the South African motor industry can face from just-in-time inventory systems. In 2006 Mittal Steel SA began to ration the sale of steel to local customers including the South African auto industry, because it had run out of inventory of iron ore which is a key component for the manufacture of steel.

The use of JIT is also widespread in the Australian auto industry. In 2001 a strike by 350 employees at Tristar, a supplier of steering parts to the four Australian car manufacturers, led to a shutdown of production lines at the manufacturers and at a range of car component suppliers. Under JIT, production ceased as there was no supply of steering parts, and thus there was no need for parts from other suppliers, who then also needed to cease their production. Over 12 000 vehicle builders were stood down across the industry. The strike lasted for more than 14 days and the cost to the automotive industry was high. At Holden alone, it was estimated that the strike resulted in losses of about $20 million a day. These were losses due to lost production and hence lost sales, and losses arising from damage to Holden's international reputation.

The diagram illustrates the timing of deliveries from suppliers for the manufacture of Holden vehicles at the Elizabeth plant in Adelaide. Clearly, any delay in the delivery of components such as exhaust systems or axles (delivered every 40 minutes, and installed immediately), or problems in the quantity or quality of the delivered components, would result in production stoppages, lost sales, lost profits and lost market share.

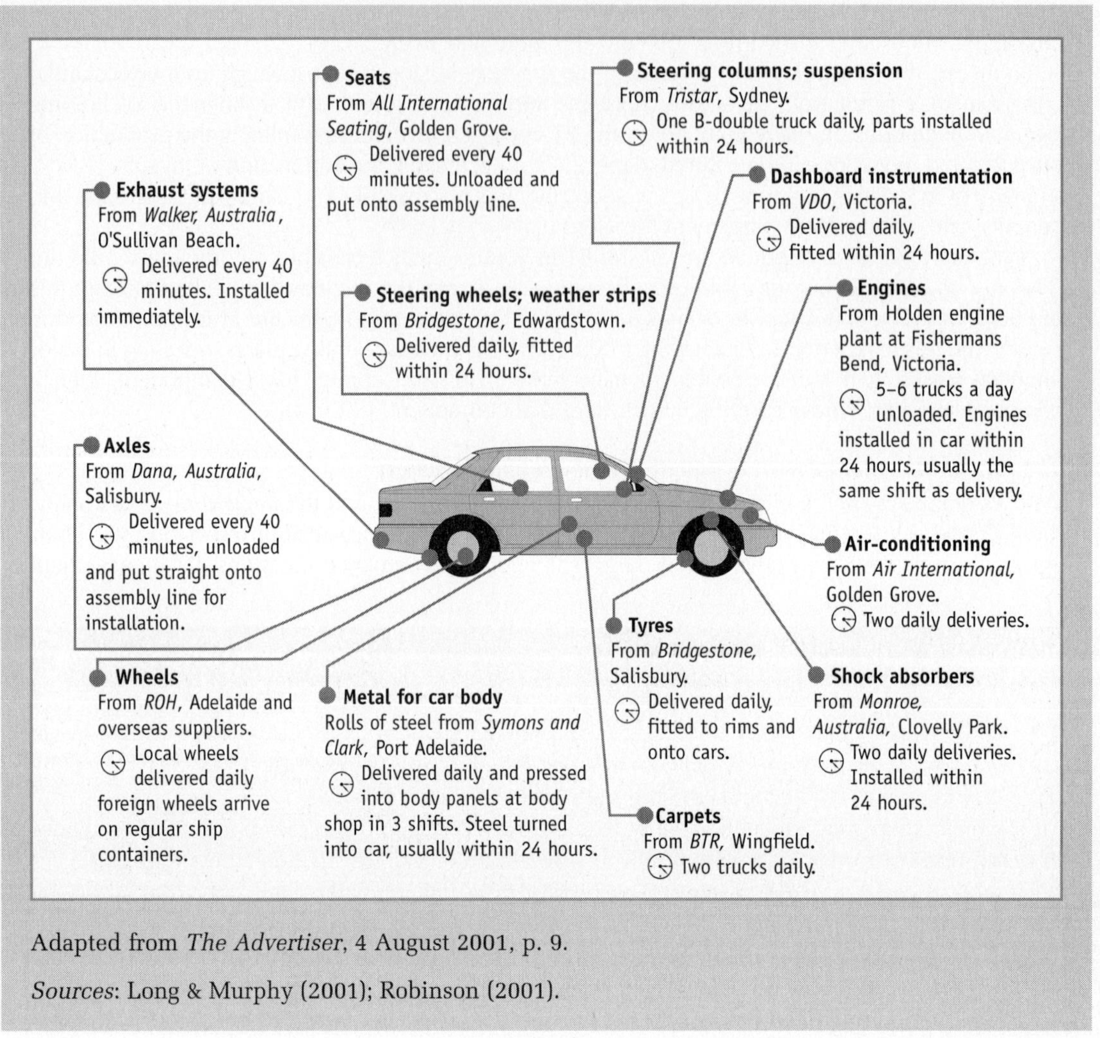

Adapted from *The Advertiser*, 4 August 2001, p. 9.

Sources: Long & Murphy (2001); Robinson (2001).

requires just-in-time information. Useful measures include manufacturing lead time, throughput, days of inventory on hand, set-up time and rework. Many of these measures may be captured by employees within the work teams, but management accountants may coordinate the collection of this information, analyse, and report it to various levels of management. This issue was covered in greater depth in Chapter 14. Some businesses using JIT have switched to backflush costing, which reduces the complexity of the costing system. Backflush costing is described in the appendix to this chapter.

Managing customers

A key aspect of supply chain management is the effective management of customers. Many organisations are placing increasing importance on improving customer relationships and enhancing customer value. This requires the organisation to work towards better understanding and satisfying customers' specific needs.

Customer relationship management

L.O. 6

Customer relationship management (CRM) is an important activity in many organisations. CRM refers to collecting and analysing data to understand customers' behaviour patterns and needs, and to develop strong relationships with customers. This involves a shift away from mass marketing based on products, to marketing that is tailored to individual customers, or customer types. It is often associated with technologies and software that are used to bring together information from across the organisation concerning customers, sales, marketing effectiveness, market trends and the firm's responsiveness to customers. An effective CRM system can lead to improved customer service, retention of existing customers, the acquisition of new customers, more effective and efficient marketing and sales activities, and increased sales revenue and customer profitability.

CRM involves considering the type of data that should be collected, and how such data can be made available for real-time use across the organisation (Greenstein & Vasarhelyi, 2002). For example, customer inquiries arise from many sources, including the Internet, call centres and postal inquiries. These data should be collected and made available to sales and marketing staff to help them better understand customers' needs and preferences. Easily accessible and detailed profiles of specific customers stored in a centralised database may be used for targeted marketing campaigns. Much of the data that is collected as part of a CRM system may already have existed within the organisation, but may not have been centralised on a single database, or utilised to manage customers better. CRM software is often a component of an ERP system.

E-commerce: a customer perspective

Increasingly, firms are establishing electronic relationships with their customers, which allow existing customers and potential customers access to interactive websites and enable transactions between a firm and its customers to be initiated and processed over the Internet. EDI connections allow sales orders, invoicing, payments and analyses to be undertaken electronically. Customers also gain from these systems, as they receive products as soon as they are required, without having to incur the expense associated with raising and processing purchase orders. Strategic alliances may be formed with customers. This may entail joint advertising and joint product planning, and the expenses of warehousing and distribution channels may be shared.

As in the case of suppliers, strategic alliances with customers can provide significant cost advantages for an organisation, as well as cost savings for its customers. For example, as part of the *product life cycle approach*, a manufacturing company may design its products to reduce their whole-of-life costs. (Life cycle approaches were described in Chapter 15.) The improved design of a piece of equipment may mean less after-sales service and fewer warranty claims for a manufacturer, and so result in savings in these customer service costs. Also, better product design can provide *advantages for the customer*. The equipment may require less ongoing maintenance and have a longer useful life. Providing these benefits for customers can be a source of *competitive advantage for the manufacturer*.

Customer profitability analysis

L.O. 7

Activity-based costing techniques can be used to determine the profitability of customers. Customers can be identified as cost objects, and ABC can be used to estimate the costs of doing business with particular customers or with groups of customers that require similar service levels. Customers may be grouped by size, industry, market or distribution channel. For example, in the food-processing industry it may be useful to group customers by distribution channel, distinguishing between supermarket chains, independent grocers and smaller outlets such as 24-hour convenience stores.

How do we define customer groups? Marketing managers often identify the customers of their business as belonging to certain segments. These segments may be determined by considering similarities and differences in customers' buying behaviours and customer preferences. Companies often develop certain products and particular marketing campaigns to target specific market segments. While many marketing managers have analysed the sales and estimated the approximate profitability of different customer segments, it is only in recent years that activity-based techniques have started to be used to undertake customer cost analysis and customer profitability analysis.

With **customer cost analysis**, the costs of products purchased by the customer are assigned to customers, along with the costs of any other customer-driven activities.[4] Customer-driven activities may relate to marketing and selling, packaging, order entry, loading and shipping goods, invoicing and collecting sales revenue, technical and administrative support, and after-sales service. Exhibit 16.9 outlines the components of customer cost analysis. In **customer profitability analysis** the costs of all the activities used to support a customer or a customer group are accumulated and compared with the revenue generated by that customer or customer group. The relative profitability of particular customers or groups of customers can be determined and used for a range of strategic decisions.

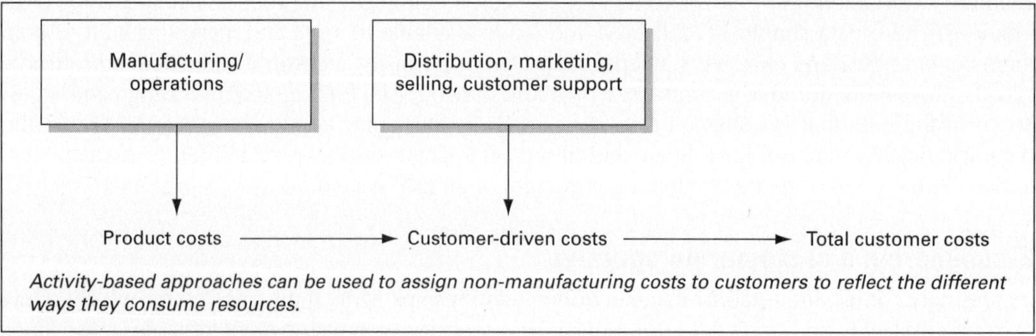

Exhibit 16.9 Customer cost analysis

How do customers differ?

Differences in customer profitability may be due to *differences in revenues charged* to customers and to *differences in resources used* (costs) to service customers. Differences in revenue can arise because customers are charged different prices (when they operate in different markets) or are given different discounts, sales volumes differ or customers purchase a range of different products.

Differences in the cost of servicing customers usually relate to manufacturing costs and the costs of downstream activities. They may include the following:

- *Customisation of products.* Some customers may require additional features to be added to products. For example, a large hotel group may require a manufacturer to add monograms to the towels and sheets that it purchases.
- *Marketing and selling activities.* Advertisements may be developed to attract specific customer groups, or industries. Some customers may purchase products online, while other customers may depend on direct calls from sales representatives. Customers who place frequent sales orders will use more resources than will those who place only occasional orders.
- *Distribution channels.* Products may be offered to customers through various distribution channels. For example, some customers may purchase products directly from the firm, while other sales are made through warehouses, agents or the Internet.
- *Customer support activities.* Various levels of support are offered to customers, including technical support, training, on-site visits and help lines. These activities may not be dependent on the products sold but on the particular type of customer.

In the past, it was often assumed that many of the above activities were consumed uniformly across all customers. However, different customers or customer groups may differ in their requirements. Exhibit 16.10 contains examples of activities that may be consumed by high-cost customers and low-cost customers.

Activity	High-cost customer	Low-cost customer
Manufacturing	Customer requires customized features for products.	Customer requires standard products.
Order entry	Salesperson takes orders directly from the customer.	Customer submits orders electronically.
Distribution	Customer requires overnight delivery.	Customer is satisfied with 3-day delivery.
Credit collection	Customer pays in 90 days by cheque, and requires receipt.	Customer pays in 7 days by electronic direct deposit.
Technical support	Customer requires specialized training for their staff.	Customer provides own in-house training.

Exhibit 16.10 Comparison of activities used by high-cost and low-cost customers

In determining customer profitability, it is usually not practical to identify the profitability of individual customers, unless there are only a few of them. Therefore, customers may be grouped by size, industry, market or distribution channel.

Why calculate customer profitability?

In many businesses, *customer-driven costs* are a growing proportion of overall costs, and the resources expended on particular customers or groups of customers may vary widely. For example, in the computer software industry, a large proportion of costs are incurred after the point of sale, and include providing technical support to customers and solving their problems. These costs may be associated with particular customers or customer groups, not with the products that they purchase.

How can information about the relative profitability of customers be used in strategic decisions? Customer profitability analysis can be used to address questions such as:

- Which customers generate the greatest profits? And how can we retain those customers?
- Which customers generate the lowest profits? And what can we do to make those customers more profitable?
- On what types of customers should we focus our business efforts in order to maximise profitability?

Customer profitability analysis can lead to interesting findings. A manufacturing company may find that it is more expensive (per unit of product) to deal with small individual customers than with large distributors, so management may decide to encourage the smaller customers to purchase from the distributors rather than buy direct from the manufacturer. This may help the company to improve its cost performance relative to that of its competitors. Alternatively, the manufacturer may look for ways of reducing the costs of servicing the smaller customers without reducing the level of service.

Customer profitability analysis provides a different perspective on the profitability of the business, and allows managers to make a series of strategic decisions about which customers, markets or distribution channels to focus on. It also helps to identify areas for cost control and cost reduction.

Calculating customer costs

Activity-based costing techniques can be used to determine customer costs. Recognition of a hierarchy of customer-driven activities can help us assign costs to customer groups more accurately. (We saw in Chapter 8 that similar principles are used in product costing under activity-based costing.) There are four levels of customer-driven costs:

1 *Order level activities* are triggered each time an order is placed by a customer, and are driven directly by the selling and delivery of individual customer orders. Examples include

processing a customer's order, raising an invoice, packing the products ordered, delivering the goods and collecting amounts owed.

2 *Customer level activities* are related to acquiring new customers or maintaining each customer or customer group. Negotiating with a new customer may trigger activities, such as credit evaluation and making the initial sales call. Maintaining an existing customer can involve ongoing sales calls, technical support, complaint handling, provision of samples and catalogues, and cash collections.

3 *Market level activities* are related to a particular market, or class of customers. These activities are performed to define and analyse customer needs, develop new technologies to satisfy customer needs, maintain a presence in a particular market and attract new customers. Examples include advertising, market research and trade shows.

4 *Facility level activities* are not driven by customers, and are necessary to run the business. As with product costing using activity-based costing, these costs should not be allocated to customers or customer groups for decision-making purposes.

Customer profitability example

To illustrate the principles of customer profitability analysis, we will focus on the profitability of customer groups at Hardy Saucepans (Pty) Ltd during the past year. Hardy Saucepans sells two products to three groups of customers: direct customers, small retail and large retail. Activity-based costing has been used to analyse manufacturing activities and determine product costs for the two products: the standard saucepan set and the premium saucepan set. The selling prices and the manufacturing costs were as follows:

	Selling prices	Manufacturing cost
Standard saucepan set	R1600 per set	R300 per set
Premium saucepan set	R2400 per set	R600 per set

Exhibit 16.11 contains a summary of customer-driven activities for the three customer groups. Direct customers make up the largest customer group, and involve the highest number of orders, deliveries and complaints. The large retailers consist of only four customers, but they have the greatest sales volume. Thus, different amounts of activities and resources are spent on the three customer groups.

As a first step in customer profitability analysis, the company has identified seven customer related activities and determined the total cost of these activities. Activity drivers have also been identified for each activity and used to allocate activity costs to the three customer groups. Exhibit 16.12 shows the activity costs by customer group.

	Direct customers	Small retailers	Large retailers
No. of customers	50	25	4
Sales units – standard saucepan sets	1 800	600	3 600
Sales units – premium saucepan sets	1 200	3 000	5 800
No. of sales orders	2 100	72	120
No. of deliveries	2 200	110	140
No. of sales calls	–	100	70
No. of complaints	95	80	25

Exhibit 16.11 Customer activity, Hardy Saucepans

The next step is to determine the profitability of each customer group, by comparing sales revenues with the manufacturing costs of the products purchased and customer-related costs. Exhibit 16.13 indicates that in the past year, direct customers generated a loss of R3 429 000. The data in Exhibits 16.11 and 16.12 indicate that this is largely due to the high number of orders and deliv-

Exhibit 16.12 Activity costs by customer group, Hardy Saucepans

Activity	Activity cost	Cost per unit of activity driver†	Activity costs*		
			Direct customers	**Small retailers**	**Large retailers**
Order level					
Processing an order	5 615 400	R 2 450 per order	5 145 000	176 400	294 000
Delivering the product	2 695 000	R 1 100 per delivery	2 420 000	121 000	154 000
Customer level					
Sales calls	1 360 000	R 8 000 per call	–	800 000	560 000
Handling customer complaints	240 000	R 1 200 per complaint	114 000	96 000	30 000
Market level					
Market research – retail market	800 000	Equal proportion to retail customer groups	–	400 000	400 000
Advertising in retail trade magazines	700 000	Assignment to retail customers in proportion to sales revenue	–	205 000	495 000
Advertising in consumer magazines	250 000	Direct assignment	250 000		
Total activity costs	11 660 400		7 929 000	1 798 400	1 933 000

*The costs per customer group for order level and customer level activities are based on the number of times the activity was performed (from Exhibit 16.11), multiplied by the cost per unit of activity driver.

†Costs per unit of activity driver for order level and customer level activities are based on activity cost divided by the total number of times the activity was performed (from Exhibit 16.11).

eries for this class of customers. Large retailers were the most profitable, contributing 93 per cent of the total profits, while small retailers contributed only 31 per cent of the profits. This data is summarised in a customer profitability graph in Exhibit 16.14.

	Direct customers	Small retailers	Large retailers	Total
Sales revenue	5 760 000	8 160 000	19 680 000	33 600 000
Costs of goods sold	1 260 000	1 980 000	4 560 000	7 800 000
Gross margin	4 500 000	6 180 000	15 120 000	25 800 000
Customer costs (from Exhibit 16.12)	7 929 000	1 798 400	1 933 000	11 660 400
Contribution to company profits	−3 429 000	4 381 600	13 187 000	14 139 600
% contribution	−24%	31%	93%	100%

Exhibit 16.13 Customer profitability analysis, Hardy Saucepans

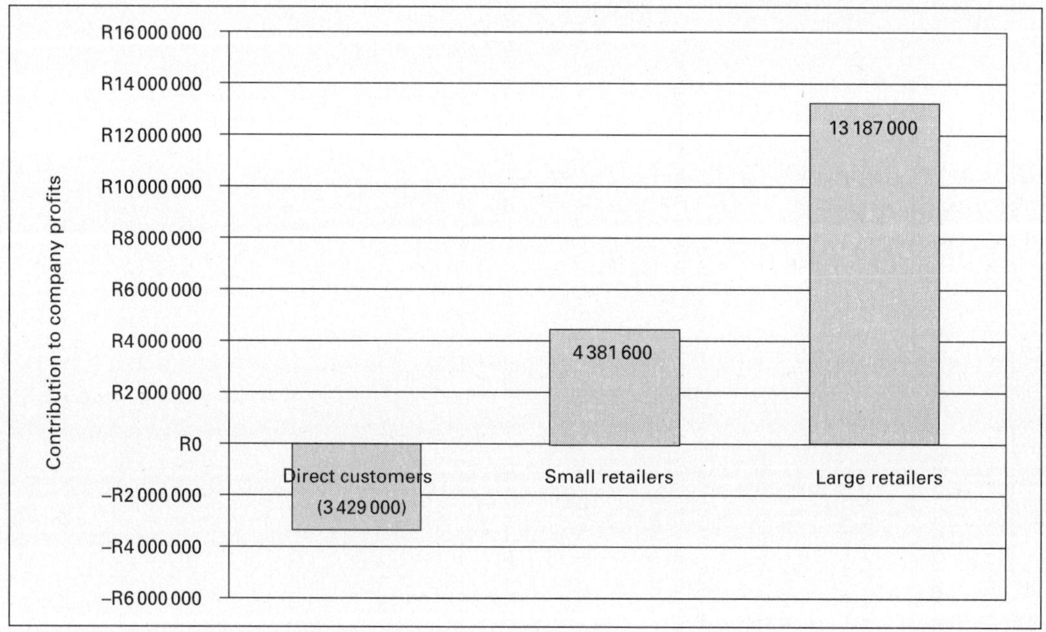

Exhibit 16.14 Customer profitability graph, Hardy Saucepans

This information can raise a variety of questions that are of strategic importance to the management of Hardy Saucepans. Should the company continue to sell directly to customers? Can those customers be encouraged to purchase from small and large retailers? Can the cost of servicing direct customers be reduced? Can small retailers be encouraged to purchase in larger order sizes? Does the company need to make as many sales calls to small retailers? Can the company direct more effort towards attracting more large retailers? What steps can the company take to ensure that the current large retailers stay with the company?

Customer performance measures

L.O. 8 In Chapter 14 we learned that the customer perspective was one of the four perspectives of the balanced scorecard, and that achieving customer objectives is critical to the achievement of financial objectives. Key to this process is defining and monitoring customer performance measures. Five core customer measures that apply to all forms of organisations are market share, customer retention, customer acquisition, customer satisfaction and customer profitability. These core measures are defined in Exhibit 16.15, and the various ways in which these can be measured are described. Exhibit 16.16 highlights how the five measures relate to each other as part of a causal chain. Thus,

REAL LIFE: CUSTOMER PROFITABILITY ANALYSIS BY BANKS

In the 1990s banks started increasingly to measure the profitability of each customer. In order to measure customer profitability, a bank will include the fees and interest earned on a customer's accounts. The bank will deduct the costs of servicing accounts such as transaction costs, the cost of a customer's use of banking services, interest and deposit insurance. What banks have found is that about 20 per cent of the bank's customers may generate 110 per cent of the bank's total profit, while the bottom 20 per cent of the bank's customers represent losses for the bank. Why acquire customers that are going to destroy value for the bank? Banks have started to divide customers into different segments and have started offering high-value customers special services such as relationship managers, and classifying them as 'gold' or 'premium' customers, which may result in special benefits. The information on customer profitability provides customer ratings which are sent to the frontline staff such as tellers so that, by looking on the screen, a staff member can tell how valuable a customer is to the bank. For example, customers can be rated from 5 stars to 1 star reflecting a customer's profitability to the bank. This will affect the relationship between customers and the staff members at the bank. It will affect what the frontline staff can offer to each customer and what each staff member will promote. For example, a bank may suggest to valuable customers that they make use of the bank's investment adviser and wealth management services. Alternatively, if you find that a teller at the bank is not being friendly, it may just be that based on the bank's analysis of customer profitability; you are just not worth it. When you threaten to take your business elsewhere, this may be exactly what the bank wants you to do! Generally, however, the bank will try and charge higher interest rates and reduce services to customers who are currently identified as loss makers, in order to lead them back to profitability.

Of course, it is important for a bank to measure the value of each customer rather than just their current profitability. A student doing a B.Com (Hons) degree, and who is going to be a chartered accountant in a few years' time, may currently be costing the bank money, but will generate a high level of profitability for the bank over his/her lifespan. At the same time an elderly customer with lots of cash may currently be very profitable but may not have long to go in terms of being of value to the bank.

Branches cost banks money (rent, salaries, security and other costs) and customers who use ATMs and Internet banking services will cost significantly less to service than customers that visit the branches. However, it has been found that often a bank's most valuable customers as well as the bank's biggest loss makers visit branches. So a bank has to be careful with the visitors to the branches and ensure that it looks after its valuable customers (perhaps directing them upstairs to sit in a comfortable lounge while the loss makers stand in long queues downstairs).

Banks have come a long way from measuring the financial performance of each bank, to measuring the profitability of each product and now to measuring the profitability of each customer.

customer satisfaction contributes to increased customer acquisition and customer retention, as well as improved customer profitability. Increased market share is influenced by the rate of customer acquisition and customer retention. These five measures can be regarded as lag (or outcome) measures. Some of the lead measures that drive these customer measures can be found in Chapter 14.

Managing quality

In this final part of the chapter, we will look at how businesses manage quality. Achieving high quality is an important aspect of supply chain management. A failure to manage quality at the sup-

Customer measure	Definition	Measurement
Market share	The proportion of sales in a given market	The proportion of customers, sales revenue or sales volume of the business, as a proportion of the market size.
Customer acquisition	The rate at which an organisation attracts and wins new customers	The number of new customers. Total sales to new customers. Sales to new customers as a proportion of total sales.
Customer retention	The rate at which a business retains, or maintains, ongoing relationships with customers	Proportion of total sales to sales from existing customers. Customer loyalty: percentage of growth of business from existing customers.
Customer satisfaction	The satisfaction of customers, in terms of specific aspects of value	Customer satisfaction surveys that address the degree of satisfaction with specific aspects of the service or product: telephone, mail surveys, interviews.
Customer profitability	The net profit attributable to a customer or customer group	Change in customer profitability per quarter. Proportion of loss customers compared to profitable customers.

Source: adapted from Kaplan & Norton (1996, p. 68)

Exhibit 16.15 Measurement of core customer measures

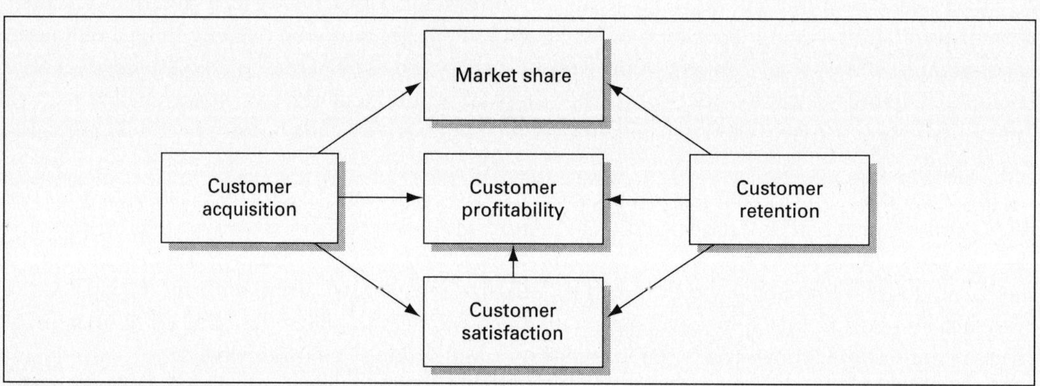

Source: adapted from Kaplan & Norton (1996, p. 68)

Exhibit 16.16 Core customer measures

plier stage, or within manufacturing, can impact on the ability of a firm to meet customer orders in a timely manner, or to supply quality products. This can reduce customer satisfaction and profitability. Organisations manage quality in many different ways. Some firms include quality measures as part of their performance measurement systems. Others implement total quality management systems to gain quality accreditation, and some firms regard total quality management as an end in itself.

The meaning of quality

L.O. 9 What do we mean by 'quality'? **Quality** may mean different things to different people. However, in many organisations quality is defined in terms of products or services meeting customers' needs and expectations. There are two concepts that need to be considered in meeting those needs:

- **Quality of design**: the degree to which the product's design specifications meet customers' expectations. For example, a coffee mug designed with a handle that is too small for the user's fingers would have poor quality of design.
- **Quality of conformance**: the degree to which the product meets its design specifications. A coffee mug with an appropriately sized handle may be well designed, but if the handle breaks off due to shoddy manufacturing the mug will be useless. Such a mug has poor quality of conformance as it fails to conform to its design specifications.

How does quality relate to customer value? Companies need to design products or services to satisfy customer expectations – *quality of design* – and then put in place processes to ensure that the design specification are met – *quality of conformance*. Thus, a clear understanding of customer value is essential in order to provide customers with a high-quality product or service. Remember that customer value is the value that a customer places on particular aspects of a product or service.

Measuring quality

Once customers' needs and expectations are known, managers need to be able to *measure* quality in order to improve and maintain it. Measures such as defect rates, yield, warranty claims and customer complaints are examples of performance measures that focus on quality.

How do these quality measures fit into the balanced scorecard? There is no specific quality perspective in Kaplan and Norton's balanced scorecard. However, quality measures, such as customer complaints and delivery-on-time, may drive customer satisfaction, and thus are lead measures under the Customer Perspective. In addition, quality measures such as defect rates, yield, waste, scrap and rework rates would be lag indicators under the Internal Business Process Perspective of the balanced scorecard.

The costs of quality

Quality costs focus on the costs of the quality of conformance. There are four types of quality costs: **L.O. 10**

1. **Internal failure costs**: the costs incurred when defective products or services are detected before leaving the business.
2. **External failure costs**: the costs incurred because defective products or services are provided to customers.
3. **Appraisal costs**: the costs of determining whether defects exist.
4. **Prevention costs**: the costs incurred in preventing defects and in minimising appraisal activities.

Exhibit 16.17 shows the types of costs included in each category. Notice that quality costs include costs not measured by the accounting system, such as the lost profit contribution due to internal and external failures.

Exhibit 16.18 shows a sample **cost of quality report** for Hardy Saucepans. Note that the internal and external failure costs do not include the opportunity costs associated with scrapped products and lost sales. These costs are excluded because they are difficult to estimate, but they can be considered qualitatively when making decisions. It has been estimated that these 'hidden' costs of quality amount to 'at least three times and up to ten times the visible cost of quality' (Petty, 1996).

Using cost of quality information

How do the managers at Hardy Saucepans use the monthly cost of quality report? These reports can help managers to reduce costs and improve quality. For example, managers can analyse the quality costs as a percentage of total sales and look at the trend over time. They can also classify the quality costs as fixed or variable with respect to the level of sales so that they can compare them with a flexible budget.

Internal failure costs	External failure costs
Scrap Rework Downtime Material disposals Lost contribution margin from scrapped products	Sales returns Warranty claims Processing customer complaints Legal fees Service call-outs Lost contribution margin from current and future sales
Appraisal costs	**Prevention costs**
Monitoring Inspecting materials Inspecting work in process Inspecting finished goods Testing equipment	Quality engineering Quality planning Employee training Quality improvement plans Quality reporting

Exhibit 16.17 Quality costs

	Current month's cost	Percentage of total
Internal failure costs		
Scrap in production	R 20 000	4.54%
Scrapped finished goods	30 000	6.82%
Rework	20 000	4.55%
Downtime	10 000	2.27%
Total internal failure costs	R 80 000	18.18%
External failure costs		
Warranty costs	R 70 000	15.91%
Out-of-warranty repairs and replacement	30 000	6.82%
Servicing customer complaints	10 000	2.27%
Transportation losses	20 000	4.55%
Total external failure costs	R 130 000	29.55%
Appraisal costs		
Materials inspection	R 30 000	6.82%
In-process inspection	20 000	4.54%
Finished goods inspection	20 000	4.55%
Laboratory testing	40 000	9.09%
Total appraisal costs	R 110 000	25.00%
Prevention costs		
Quality training	R 40 000	9.09%
Quality planning	10 000	2.27%
Quality reporting	20 000	4.55%
Quality systems development	50 000	11.36%
Total prevention costs	R 120 000	27.27%
Total quality costs	**R 440 000**	**100.00%**

Exhibit 16.18 Costs of quality, Hardy Saucepans

Other aspects that can be considered include the possible *interactions* between the costs in the four categories (Carr & Ponemon, 1994). High levels of prevention costs should result in low internal and external failure costs, and may allow a low level of appraisal activity. High appraisal costs may cause high internal failure costs but should also result in low external failure costs.

There are two views among quality experts about how these costs interact. The traditional view is that there is some *optimal level of quality* (as measured by the percentage of defects) beyond which any further improvement will cause the total costs of quality to increase. This view is illustrated in Exhibit 16.19. This is based on the assumed interaction of prevention and appraisal costs, on the one hand, with failure costs on the other hand. Initially, as more money is spent on prevention and appraisal, the level of defects decreases and the failure costs decline. The savings in failure costs more than offset the increases in prevention and appraisal costs. But, after a certain point, any further attempts to drive the defect rate down cause increases in prevention and appraisal costs that are greater than the savings in failure costs. Total quality costs are minimised by driving the defect rate down to this point, called the **acceptable quality level (AQL)**, and no further. This viewpoint is not driven by customer value; rather, it is concerned with optimising resources.

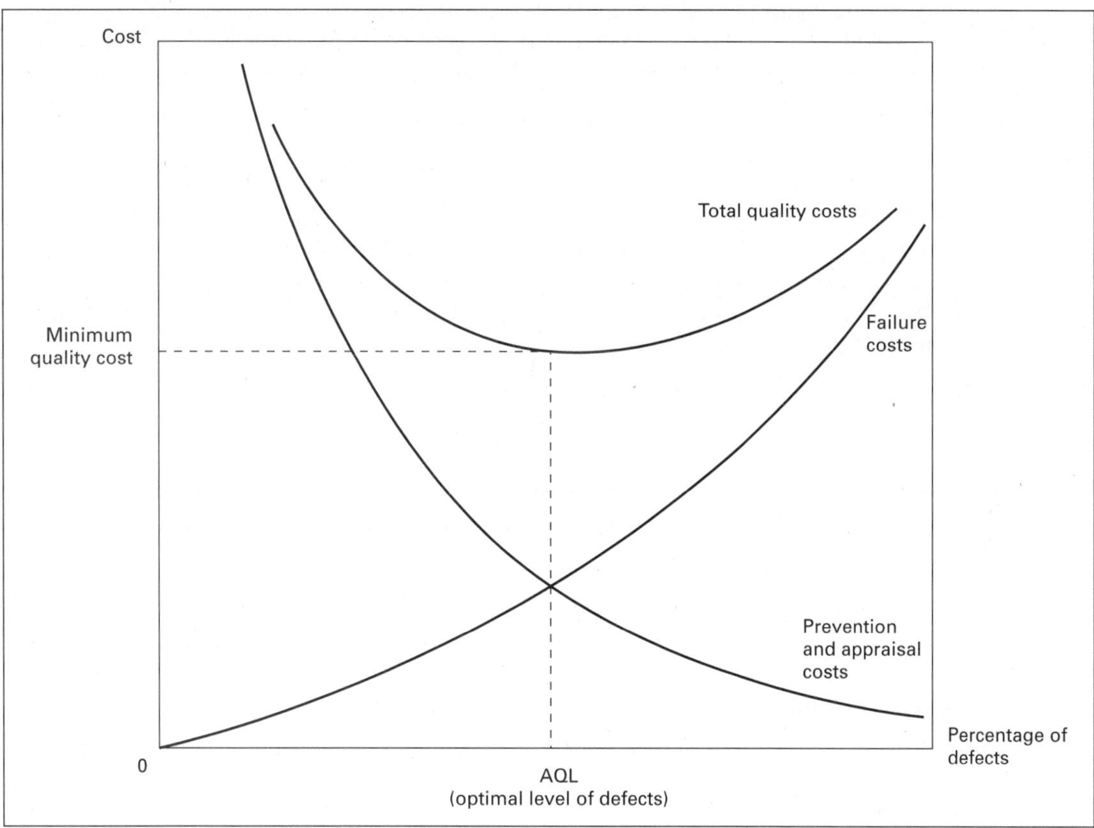

Exhibit 16.19 Optimal level of quality performance

The alternative view is that a business should aim to push its level of quality (or defect rate) towards zero rather than accepting some *apparently* optimal level. Three arguments support this view:

1 Quality is recognised as *a source of customer value* in its own right. Thus, the level of defects should be pushed below that level that minimises costs. (This argument assumes that customers value zero defects, which may not be correct.)

2 Many businesses underestimate the costs of failure, particularly the more nebulous costs of external failure such as lost future sales, which means that the optimal level of defects will be much lower than that estimated.

3 Experience has shown that, as businesses increase prevention and appraisal costs, failure costs reduce. As failure costs reduce, businesses discover that they can reduce prevention and appraisal costs. In fact, the traditional view of a trade-off between prevention and appraisal costs on the one hand, and failure costs on the other hand, does not hold. The costs in all four categories go down. Quality costs move towards zero as the level of defects is driven towards zero.

Finally, it should be pointed out that cost of quality reports are *not used by some companies,* as some managers believe that the emphasis on tracking costs is not an appropriate way to manage quality.

Total quality management (TQM) and a quality culture

L.O. 11 With the realisation that quality underlies the competitive strengths of many businesses, total quality management became increasingly popular during the late 1980s and 1990s. **Total quality management (TQM)** is a management approach that centres on meeting customer requirements by achieving continuous improvement in products or services. Although the TQM concept has not received as much attention in the new millennium, the quality culture associated with TQM has permeated many businesses and has provided the framework for managing costs and all other sources of customer value.

The key features of TQM are as follows:

1 *TQM is organisation-wide.* TQM needs to infiltrate all aspects of a business, and involve all employees – it is not the exclusive concern of manufacturing. A quality management program should encompass the *entire value chain,* from research and development through production to customer services. In addition, TQM can focus on relationships with external suppliers. Only suppliers with a commitment to quality, and accredited suppliers, are engaged.

2 *TQM is customer-driven.* Quality is defined by the needs and expectations of customers. Employees need to understand the requirements of their **internal customer**, who is the next person or group in the process.

3 *TQM involves empowerment.* In order for shop-floor employees to manage their own quality inspection and to correct problems, extensive training is required.

4 *TQM has a process perspective.* A **process perspective** focuses on the smooth flow of activity across the organisation rather than within functional departments.

5 *TQM is supported by a quality management system.* Although TQM is more a philosophy than a set of techniques, it should be supported by documented quality procedures and practices to keep the entire TQM process under control.

6 *TQM involves continuous improvement.* Given the goal of meeting customers' requirements, and because customers' requirements are constantly changing, continuous improvement is an essential part of TQM.

The development of total quality management has largely been attributed to 'quality pioneers' such as Deming, Juran, Crosby and Ishikawa. Although their models differ, the six features listed above are recognised as key elements of TQM by each of these quality experts (Dotchin & Oakland, 1992; Shank & Govindarajan, 1994).

Quality in service organisations

TQM has evolved from concepts such as inspection, quality control and quality assurance that have been developed and used largely in manufacturing organisations. However, as the 'Real life' below shows, a quality culture is just as important in a service environment.

Quality accreditation

L.O. 12 One of the driving forces behind the growth in quality management in South Africa has been the quality accreditation process. **Quality accreditation** is obtained by meeting a series of quality standards set out in the international ISO 9000 series. The standards cover the systems, documentation, process controls and delivery methods that an organisation must have in place to deliver quality products and services. The certifications are issued by approved quality auditors.

The take-up of the ISO 9000 series was strong in the 1980s and 1990s. During this period of staggering growth in quality accreditation, certification was seen as necessary or useful in gaining access to local and overseas customers. For example, ISO 9000 was not mandatory but was often used as a guide to awarding tenders.

REAL LIFE: QUALITY ASSURANCE IN THE SERVICES SECTOR

Generally, service organisations have been less enthusiastic about TQM than have manufacturers. However, as the following cases show, the development of a quality culture has had a substantial impact in some service businesses.

Independent Regulatory Board for Auditors

The Independent Regulatory Board for Auditors (IRBA) is tasked with regulating the auditing profession in South Africa. The IRBA sets auditing and ethical standards which are internationally comparable and sets out a framework for the education and training of auditors. The IRBA will inspect and review the work of registered auditors to ensure that it is in line with professional standards. Corporate collapses such as Enron, Leisurenet, and Fidentia have made such regulation more urgent.

Professional bodies such as the South African Institute of Chartered Accountants (SAICA) are required to be accredited by IRBA. Accreditation criteria include;

- Continuing professional development;
- Discipline code and procedures;
- Register of members;
- Technical support to registered auditors;
- Recognised academic programs;
- Core assessment programs;
- Recognised education and training programs.

Auditors in South Africa will be chartered accountants and will be members of SAICA which is currently the only accredited professional body whose members can undertake the audit of companies. However, in the future, it is expected that other professional bodies may be accredited in relation to enabling their members to undertake the audit function.

Council for Health Service Accreditation of Southern Africa (Cohsasa)

Cohsasa provides accreditation to hospitals in South Africa that adhere to internationally recognised standards set by the International Society for Quality in Healthcare (ISQua). Hospitals are required to meet specified performance indicators. The *South African Medical Journal* (February 2006, Vol. 96, No.2) reported that only 27 of the 502 hospitals (public and private) working with Cohsasa met the accreditation criteria. However, there were many hospitals that had previously been accredited and had not maintained their accreditation. There are many hospitals that are working with Cohsasa to achieve accreditation and there are a number of private hospitals that adhere to other quality assurance programs. When accrediting a healthcare facility, Cohsasa will measure up to 3000 criteria, and will examine 37 areas of operation including clinical and non-clinical performance indicators.

Discovery Health, a medical insurance company, has implemented a rating index system for hospitals that will provide doctors and patients with information about the quality and cost of care at South African hospitals. Hospitals are scored on the basis of clinical outcomes as measured by mortality rates, readmissions and healthy discharges as well as the cost of facilities such as intensive care and cost of drugs and other services.

By the late 1990s, quality accreditation seems to have slipped from favour in South Africa, as ISO systems are expensive to implement and maintain, and they appear to have little relevance to many small businesses and service organisations. Many government purchasing agencies have softened their quality accreditation requirements.

Quality accreditation versus total quality management

Does a quality-accredited organisation practise *total quality management*? Probably, but not necessarily. Total quality management is a philosophy or body of ideas. It is much broader than quality accreditation, which is a documentation process – it may encourage employees to think about ways to improve quality but it has no broad, underlying philosophy to guide management or employees. One consultant referred to the 'hill that represents improvement in the business' and used the following analogy to distinguish between TQM and quality accreditation: 'TQM is pushing the ball up that hill ... Certification is a way of ensuring the ball does not roll back down the hill' (James, 1993).

REAL LIFE: SIYAKHULA – 'WE ARE GROWING'

How SABS is helping small businesses achieve quality accreditation

The South African Bureau of Standards (SABS) is accredited to provide certification that South African companies comply with international quality standards such as ISO 9001. SABS will audit a company's systems, processes and products to ensure that they comply with the requisite standard.

The audit process to acquire certification is a demanding process, particularly for small, medium and micro enterprises (SMMEs). Tenders and contractors may require that firms have formal certification in order to qualify for the awarding of contracts. SABS has introduced Siyakhula Certification to assist small businesses in obtaining certification such as ISO 9001:2000 Quality Management Systems, as this may be required in contracts that small and medium enterprises are entering into particularly with larger companies and export customers. Siyakhula means 'we are growing' in Xhosa and small firms follow a three-phase process to acquire certification. SABS states that the Siyakhula Certificate is based on eight quality management principles, being;

- Customer focus;
- Leadership;
- Involvement of people;
- System approach;
- Process approach;
- Continual improvement;
- Factual approach to decision-making;
- Supplier relationships.

In the SABS 2006 annual report, the company reports as follows:

SABS provided tailor-made training to 135 SMMEs in various fields such as clothing & textiles (42), industrial chemicals (34), civil, building, fishing and electrical engineering. ISO 9001/14001, Eurogap and HACCP training has been provided to 28 SMMEs. 3 SMMEs made history when they obtained ISO 9001:2000 certification which was achieved with the previous quality certification via the Siyakhula Certificate. SABS has assisted 45 SMMEs in obtaining capability reports for submission of proper tenders. Through the subsidy scheme 99 SMMEs were supported to test their products at SABS laboratories.

The increasing focus on procurement in determining a company's BEE status means that SABS can assist smaller BEE companies to achieve certification and comply with tender and contract requirements.

Summary

In this chapter we explored several aspects that need to be managed to achieve effective supply chain management. These were suppliers, inventory, customers and quality.

- Supply chain management involves streamlining supply chains by managing costs, accelerating the time-to-market of new products, and creating close relationships with suppliers and customers. E-commerce technologies and ERP systems provide increased potential for firms to achieve these objectives.
- Selecting the best suppliers and managing supplier relationships is an important aspect of supply chain management. Activity-based costing techniques can be used to analyse supplier costs, to compare suppliers' cost performance. In addition, as part of the contract with long-term suppliers, a variety of performance measures and targets may be set for suppliers.
- An important aspect of managing the supply chain is the management of inventory. Conventional approaches to inventory management, such as the economic order quantity (EOQ) model, accept that inventories are necessary and focus on ways to minimise inventory ordering, holding costs and shortage costs.
- More contemporary inventory management systems, such as just-in-time (JIT) systems, have focused on reducing the size and associated costs of inventory holdings. JIT inventory management systems focus on minimising inventories by purchasing or producing final products just in time to meet actual customer demands.
- Customer relationship management is an approach that allows organisations to target the preferences of specific customer groups more effectively. E-commerce technologies can provide not only the facility for building and analysing databases of customer information, they can provide increased customer service through online transactions.
- Organisations can evaluate customer profitability using activity-based techniques. Through a series of customer-related performance measures, an organisation can monitor its progress in achieving improved customer satisfaction.
- The management of quality remains an important aspect that contributes to improved customer value. Quality can be defined in terms of quality of design and quality of conformance.
- An organisation can assess its performance in achieving quality using quality-based performance measures, as well as cost of quality reports. Cost of quality reports recognise four quality costs:
  - internal failure costs;
  - external quality costs;
  - appraisal costs; and
  - prevention costs.

- Total quality management (TQM) is a broad system that focuses on meeting customer requirements by achieving continuous improvement in products or services. It is a culture that focuses on quality, from 'top floor to shop floor', across the entire value chain.
- The requirements for quality accreditation are much narrower than the broad concept of TQM. In recent times there has been some dissatisfaction with quality-accreditation processes among small businesses and service entities in South Africa, particularly with costs and the lack of flexibility.

References

Andon, P, Baxter, J & Bradley, G 2001, 'Calculating the economic value of customer to an organisation', *The Australian Accounting Review*, vol. 11, no. 1, pp. 62–72.

Carr, LP & Ittner, CD 1992, 'Managing the cost of ownership', *Journal of Cost Management,* Fall, pp. 42–51.

Carr LP & Ponemon, LA 1994, 'The behaviour of quality costs: clarifying the confusion', *Journal of Cost Management,* Summer, pp. 26–34.

Correia, C 2003, 'From just-in-case to just-in-time (and back again)?', *Accountancy SA,* May.

Department of Communications, Information Technology and the Arts 2003a, *Advancing with e-Business – Berri Limited,* www.dcita.gov.au/ie/publications/2003/08/e-bus_supp_chain/berri_limited

— 2003b, *Advancing with e-Business – Komatsu Australia,* www.dcita.gov.au/ie/publications/2003/08/e-bus_supp_chain/komatsu

DeLuzio, MC 1993, 'Management accounting in a JIT environment', *Journal of Cost Management,* Winter, pp. 6–15.

Dotchin, JA & Oakland, JS 1992, 'Theories and concepts in total quality management', *Total Quality Management,* vol. 3, no. 2, pp. 133–5.

Greenstein, M & Vasarhelyi, M 2002, *Electronic Commerce: Security, Risk Management and Control,* McGraw-Hill, New York.

Hines, P, Lamming, R, Jones, D, Cousins, P & Rich, N 2000, *Value Stream Management: Strategy and Excellence in the Supply Chain,* Prentice Hall, Harlow, England.

James, D 1993, 'No escaping new quality standard', *Business Review Weekly,* 7 May, pp. 67–8.

Kaplan, RS & Norton, DP 1996, *The Balanced Scorecard,* Harvard Business School Press, Boston, MA.

Levin, RI, Rubin, DS & Stinson, JP 1986, *Quantitative Approaches to Management,* McGraw-Hill, New York.

Long, S & Murphy, K 2001, 'Car workers defy return-to-work order', *The Australian Financial Review,* 8 August, p. 3.

NRC, 2000, *Surviving Supply Chain Integration: Strategies For Small Manufacturers,* Committee on Supply Chain Integration, Board on Manufacturing and Engineering Design, Commission on Engineering and Technical Systems, National Research Council, National Academy Press, Washington DC.

O'Guin, MC & Rebischke, SA 1993, 'Customer-driven costs using activity-based costing', in Brinker, B (ed.) *Handbook of Cost Management,* Warren, Gotham & Lamont, New York.

Petty, J 1996, 'QA and the new MA', Australian Society of CPAs, National Management Accounting Conference, Management Accounting: The Business Driver, Sydney.

Petty, J & Goodman, K 1996, 'Customer profitability analysis', *Management Accounting Issues,* Report no. 3, May, Management Accounting Centre of Excellence, Australian Society of CPAs, Melbourne.

Rayport, JF & Jaworski, BJ 2001, *e-Commerce,* McGraw-Hill, New York.

Robinson, P 2001, 'Jobs in danger as campaign spreads', *The Age,* 3 August, p. 1.

Shank, JK & Govindarajan, V 1994, 'Measuring the cost of quality: a strategic cost management perspective', *Journal of Cost Management,* Summer, pp. 5–17.

Sullivan, M 2001, 'High-octane hog', *Forbes,* vol. 168, item 6, pp. 8–10.

www.barloworld-logistics.com

Self study

Self-study problem 1: Customer profitability analysis

Softtowel Ltd manufactures towels for department stores and residential hotels. The financial controller is concerned that the profits in 20X5 were 15 per cent below the previous year, and plans to calculate the profitability of the three main customer groups: department stores, small hotels and large hotels.

In 20X5 the selling price and manufacturing costs from the three major products – bath sheets, bath towels and hand towels – and sales to customer groups, were as follows:

	Bath sheets	Bath towels	Hand towels
Selling price	R 200	R 175	R 100
Manufacturing cost	R 100	R 75	R 35
Sales units:			
Department stores	500	1 000	300
Small hotels	400	300	300
Large hotels	800	1 200	850
Total sales units	1 700	2 500	1 450

In 20X5 the customer-driven activities, cost per unit of activity driver, and activities for each customer group were as follows:

		Number of activities		
Activities	**Cost per unit of activity driver**	**Department stores**	**Small hotels**	**Large hotels**
Process sales order	R 400 per order	40	60	25
Deliver order	R 750 per delivery	60	60	28
Invoice customer	R 150 per invoice	38	60	30
Process payment	R 100 per payment	45	58	25
Handle complaint	R 200 per complaint	10	7	8
Investigate bad debt	R 250 per investigation	6	4	10
Visit customers	R 600 per visit	30	26	20
Advertise in hotel magazines	R 250 000 (to be shared equally between small and large hotels)			

Required:

1. Calculate the customer-driven costs for each customer group.
2. Prepare a profitability statement in order to determine the contribution of the three customer groups to company profits. Within your profit statement, include percentage contributed by each customer group to sales revenue, gross margin and contribution to company profits.
3. Contrast the relative profitability of the three customer groups, and provide suggestions for improving performance.

Solution to Self-study problem 1

1

Activities	Cost per unit of activity driver	Activity costs		
		Department stores	Small hotels	Large hotels
Order level				
Process sales order	R400 per order	R16 000	R24 000	R10 000
Deliver the order	R750 per delivery	45 000	45 000	21 000
Invoice customer	R150 per invoice	5 700	9 000	4 500
Process payment	R100 per payment	4 500	5 800	2 500
Customer level				
Handle complaint	R200 per complaint	2 000	1 400	1 600
Investigate bad debt	R250 per investigation	1 500	1 000	2 500
Visit customers	R600 per visit	18 000	15 600	12 000
Market level				
Advertising in hotel magazines	Equal share to hotel customer groups	0	125 000	125 000
Total activity costs		**R 92 700**	**R 226 800**	**R 179 100**

2

	Profitability of customer groups			
	Department stores	Small hotels	Large hotels	Total
Sales revenue:				
Bath sheets	R100 000	R80 000	R160 000	
Bath towels	175 000	52 500	210 000	
Hand towels	30 000	30 000	85 000	
Total sales revenue	R305 000	R162 500	R455 000	R922 500
	33.06%	17.62%	49.32%	100%
Manufacturing cost:				
Bath sheets	50 000	40 000	80 000	
Bath towels	75 000	22 500	90 000	
Hand towels	10 500	10 500	29 750	
Total manufacturing cost	R135 500	R73 000	R199 750	R408 250
Gross margin	169 500	89 500	255 250	514 250
	32.96%	17.40%	49.64%	100%
Customer-related costs	92 700	226 800	179 100	498 600
	18.59%	45.49%	35.92%	100%
Contribution to profits	R76 800	−R137 300	R76 150	R15 650
	490.73%	−877.32%	486.58%	100%

3 The above analysis indicates that the company is making modest profits from the department stores and large hotels, whereas small hotels are generating a loss. Each customer group generates about the same gross margin percentage on sales (55 to 56 per cent), so the reason for the difference in bottom-line profitability lies in the differential consumption of customer activities.

	Department stores	Small hotels	Large hotels
Total sales	R305 000	R162 500	R455 000
Gross margin	R169 500	R89 500	R255 250
Gross profit percentage	56%	55%	56%

- Small hotels contributed a loss of R137 300. While small hotels generated 17.62 per cent of the sales revenue and 17.4 per cent of the gross margin, they consumed 45.49 per cent of the customer costs. The customer-related activity costs were higher than were those for the other groups, mainly due to the high number of sale orders, deliveries, invoices and payments. Clearly, if the company wants to continue selling to this group, then the company must look for ways of encouraging small hotels to order in larger order sizes. If this is not viable, the small hotels could be encouraged to purchase the products from department stores, with the department stores providing some form of discount.
- Large hotels and department stores made a profit of R76 150 and R76 800 respectively. While large hotels earned significantly more gross margin than did department stores, they consumed more customer costs. This was largely due to advertising costs in hotel magazines. To increase the profitability of these two groups, the company could consider various ways of managing customer costs. Techniques such as activity-based management or business process re-engineering could be considered in an attempt to reduce the cost of order level activities.

Self-study problem 2: Cost of quality report

The following costs were incurred by Ansell Company to maintain the quality of its products during May 20X7:

- Inspecting incoming materials, R8000.
- In-process inspections, R30 000.
- Repairs of faulty products identified in finished goods inspection, R30 000.
- Reworking faulty products discovered during processing, R19 000.
- Quality training program for machine operators, R29 000.
- Processing customers' complaints, R40 000.
- Legal fees related to product recall, R9000.
- Inspection of goods as they arrive at the finished goods warehouse, R17 000.
- Lost contribution on goods that were scrapped as result of finished goods inspection, R50 000.
- Quality improvement seminar for production supervisors, R5000.

Required:
Prepare a cost of quality report similar to the report shown in Exhibit 16.18.

Solution to Self-study problem 2

Ansell Company
Cost of Quality Report
April 20X7

	Current month's cost	Percentage of total
Internal failure costs		
Repairs: Finished goods	R30 000	
Repairs: Work in process	19 000	
Lost contribution on scrapped products	50 000	
	R99 000	41.8%
External failure costs		
Customer complaints	40 000	
Product recall	9 000	
	R49 000	20.7%
Prevention costs		
Quality training	R34 000	14.3%
Appraisal costs		
Inspecting incoming materials	8 000	
Inspecting work in process	30 000	
Inspecting finished goods	17 000	
	R55 000	23.2%
Total quality costs	R237 000	100%

Cybersearch

1 Find the websites of two companies that have implemented customer relationship management systems.
   (a) What were the difficulties encountered in implementing these systems?
   (b) What advantages did the two companies obtain from CRM?
   (c) Does either company use customer performance measures or customer profitability analysis?

2 Go to the South African Bureau of Standards (SABS) website, www.sabs.co.za, a body that assists South African organisations to achieve quality accreditation. Access the sections that detail 'Accreditations' and 'Certification', and provide answers to the following questions:
   (a) Explain briefly what organisations need to do to achieve certification under the ISO 9000/1 series of standards for quality management. Also, go to Centurion Quality Management at www.cqm.co.za and indicate how they define and explain ISO 9001.
   (b) After considering your answer to part (a), explain whether or not achieving certification under ISO 9000/1 provides assurance that an organisation is meeting customers' expectations for quality.

3 Look for a website on supply chain management that will help you answer the following questions:
   (a) Briefly detail the advantages of supply chain management described on this website.
   (b) How important are e-commerce applications to the operation of supply chain management?
   (c) How do cost management tools fit into supply chain management?

Appendix to Chapter 16

JIT and backflush costing

L.O. 13 The key to JIT is simplification, and this can also flow through to costing. Some firms with JIT production systems have adopted a simplified costing system called **backflush costing**.[5]

Exhibit 16.20 shows the journal entries that Hardy Saucepans could use in backflush costing, as well as the corresponding entries under a conventional costing system. Note that backflush costing makes no distinction between raw material inventory and work in process inventory. After all, in a JIT environment these inventories are kept very low and, ideally, any purchases are placed directly into production. Each journal entry under backflush costing is described below:

1 Raw material purchases are recorded directly in an account called **raw and in process inventory** (the **RIP account**) (entry (a)).

2 Direct labour cost is combined with manufacturing overhead in a single account. *Actual* conversion costs are accumulated by debiting a temporary account with a title such as 'Conversion costs' (entry (b)). Additional details may be recorded by first entering these amounts in various departmental labour and overhead accounts, and then closing these temporary accounts to the conversion costs account.

3 When goods are finished, this triggers the release of direct material costs from the RIP account to the finished goods inventory (see entry (c)). Conversion costs are *applied* to finished goods inventory by crediting the conversion costs account (entry (c)). Any difference between actual and applied conversion costs (overapplied or underapplied conversion costs) is closed to cost of goods sold at the end of the period.

4 Finally, costs are transferred from finished goods to cost of goods sold (entry (d)).

Several variants of backflush costing are observed in practice. One common variant is to replace entries (c) and (d) with the following single entry:

Cost of goods sold	R3 500 000
Raw and in process inventory	R2 000 000
Conversion costs	R1 500 000

Under JIT, finished goods inventories are minimal, as goods are sold virtually as they are produced. Therefore, costs can be transferred directly to cost of goods sold as soon as the goods are finished.

Backflush costing compared with conventional costing

You will notice two major differences between the backflush costing and conventional costing systems in Exhibit 16.20. Each difference is a logical response to the JIT production environment.

1 In conventional costing systems, raw material purchases are added to the raw materials inventory account when they are purchased, and are then moved into the work in process inventory account as materials are drawn into production. Under backflush costing, raw material purchases are added directly to the RIP account. After all, under JIT, materials are ordered only as they are needed for production.

2 In conventional costing systems, direct labour and manufacturing overhead costs are charged to work in process inventory. These costs are moved to the finished goods inventory only when the goods are completed. Under backflush costing, these conversion costs

Exhibit 16.20 Product costing in a JIT setting

Event	Journal entries: backflush system			Journal entries: conventional system		
1 Purchase of raw material	(a) Raw and in process inventory	R2 000 000		Raw material inventory	R2 000 000	
	Accounts payable		R2 000 000	Accounts payable		R2 000 000
2 Raw material requisitioned for production	No entry			Work in process inventory	R2 000 000	
				Raw material inventory		R2 000 000
3 Direct labour cost incurred				Work in process inventory	R500 000	
3 and 4	(b) Conversion costs	R1 450 000		Wages payable		R500 000
	Wages payable		R500 000			
4 Actual manufacturing overhead costs incurred	Accounts payable		R950 000	Manufacturing overhead	R950 000	
				Accounts payable		R950 000
5 Application of manufacturing overhead to work in process inventory (predetermined overhead rate is 200% of direct labour cost)	No entry			Work in process inventory	R1 000 000	
				Manufacturing overhead		R1 000 000
6 Products are completed	(c) Finished goods inventory	R3 500 000		Finished goods inventory	R3 500 000	
	Raw and in process inventory		R2 000 000	Work in process inventory		R3 500 000
	Conversion costs*		R1 500 000			
7 Goods are sold	(d) Cost of goods sold	R3 500 000		Cost of goods sold	R3 500 000	
	Finished goods inventory		R3 500 000	Finished goods inventory		R3 500 000

*Applied conversion costs include direct labour of R500 000 and applied manufacturing overhead of R1 000 000. Notice that overhead is overapplied by R50 000 under both systems. Under the conventional system, we have actual overhead of R950 000 and applied overhead of R1 000 000. Under the JIT system, we have actual conversion costs of R1 450 000 and applied conversion costs of R1 500 000. Under both approaches, the R50 000 of overapplied costs will be closed into cost of goods sold at the end of the period.

are moved directly to the finished goods inventory. Under JIT, work in process inventories should be minimal so the costs move rapidly into finished goods inventory.

While conventional costing tracks costs sequentially through the physical flow of manufacturing, backflush costing waits until the manufacturing sequence is complete and then works backwards to flush the product costs out of the system.

Costs and benefits of backflush costing

Backflush costing is simpler and less expensive than conventional product costing, but it provides much less detailed information. There is a cost–benefit decision to be made as to whether the cost savings justify the loss in detailed information. Although the use of backflush costing is becoming more common, it is still used by only a small minority of manufacturers.

Questions

16.1 Describe the major components of supply chain management.

16.2 In your own words, explain the difference between a *strategic alliance* and a *supplier relationship.*

16.3 Why is it inappropriate to select suppliers by comparing only the purchase prices?

16.4 Explain how activity-based costing can be used to determine *the total cost of ownership.*

16.5 Describe some measures that can be used to evaluate supplier delivery performance and the quality of the supplier relationship.

16.6 How can a firm assess its own performance in managing and developing supplier relationships?

16.7 What types of businesses are likely to hold significant amounts of inventory? Describe the major forms of inventory held by three different types of businesses.

16.8 What is the *economic order quantity model*? What can it be used for?

16.9 What is the *inventory reorder point*? What variables affect it?

16.10 What are the likely implications for a business that uses EOQ data, if some of the underlying assumptions do not match reality? Provide an example to illustrate your answer.

16.11 Briefly describe the JIT philosophy.

16.12 Why do some organisations continue to use EOQ models, when JIT methods are available?

16.13 List seven key features of a just-in-time inventory and production management system.

16.14 List five key features of a just-in-time purchasing system.

16.15 Explain why quick and inexpensive setups and effective preventive maintenance are important features of a JIT production management system.

16.16 Comment on this statement: 'JIT just doesn't make sense and companies that implement JIT are putting themselves in danger of costly down time and stock shortages.'

16.17 Under EOQ approaches, order costs can be minimised by placing large infrequent orders of inventory. However, under JIT, inventory-related costs are reduced by ordering frequently and in small quantities. Can you explain why both of these statements are correct?

16.18 Explain the advantages and disadvantages for suppliers if they agree to delivery to their customers under a JIT system.

16.19 What are the advantages, for an organisation and its customers, of creating close customer relationships?

16.20 Outline some advantages that may arise for a company that engages in a strategic alliance with their customers.

16.21 Explain how customer groups may be determined. In your answer, select a company with which you are familiar and identify the type of customer groups that might be relevant to its needs.

16.22 Provide examples to illustrate how customer profitability analysis can be used in strategic decisions.

16.23 Consider a company that you are familiar with and provide two examples of differences that might occur in downstream activities for some specific customer groups.

16.24 Explain why some organisations consider it important to measure customer retention and customer satisfaction.

16.25 Define *quality* and explain the difference between *quality of design* and *quality of conformance.*

16.26 Explain the relationship between the four categories of quality costs.

16.27 What is *quality accreditation,* and how does it differ from *total quality management*?

16.28 (appendix) Describe the major differences between backflush costing and conventional costing.

Exercises

E16.29 Supplier relationships: manufacturers

Motor vehicle manufacturers are renowned for creating close relationships with their suppliers, and several South African motor vehicle manufacturers have committed significant resources to developing their supplier programs. These supplier programs have resulted in advantages, not only for the motor vehicle manufacturers but also to the component suppliers and to the automotive industry at large.

Required:

1 Explain the nature of the advantages that are referred to in the above statement.

2 How can a successful supplier program support a business' competitive strategy that is focused on:
(a) product quality (b) cost leadership?

E16.30 Supply chain management, supplier relationships and supplier costs

Classify each of the following statements as true or false. In each case give reasons for your answer.

1 Supply chain management focuses primarily on supplier performance measures.

2 Enterprise resource planning (ERP) systems assist managers to plan the resources used to manage suppliers and customers.

3 Strategic alliances with suppliers may provide a way of enhancing the competitiveness of suppliers.

4 An analysis of the total cost of ownership can assist managers to select suppliers and evaluate supplier performance.

5 The main aspect of difference between supplier costs is the purchase price.

E16.31 Supplier performance: delivery firm

Cascade of Roses (COR) is a business that specialises in the delivery of arrangements of roses. COR uses six main suppliers of roses, and has worked hard over the past two years to establish close cooperative relationships with them. COR is now keen to put in place comprehensive systems to evaluate the ongoing performance of suppliers. These measures will be incorporated into new long-term contracts that are currently being formulated between COR and its suppliers.

Taking into account the nature of this business, can you suggest specific measures that could be developed to:

(a) assess supplier performance
(b) assess COR's performance in managing and developing supplier relationships?

E16.32 Economic order quantity
For each of the following independent cases, use the EOQ equation to calculate the economic order quantity:

	Case A	Case B	Case C
Annual requirement (in units)	7290	4563	150
Incremental cost per order	R500	R10	R100
Annual carrying cost per unit	R9	R15	R12

E16.33 Lead time and safety stock
Alligator Ltd uses 840 tonnes of a chemical each year in its manufacturing processes. Monthly demand for the chemical fluctuates between 55 and 85 tonnes. The lead time for each order is one month, and the economic order quantity is 130 tonnes.

Required:
1 Determine the safety stock required for the chemical.
2 Calculate the reorder point in tonnes for the chemical.

E16.34 Customer-related costs
Classify the following customer-related activities as order level, customer level, market level or facility level activities:
1 Processing a customer invoice.
2 Holding a cocktail function to attract new customers.
3 Renting a Bloemfontein sales office.
4 Following up customers' complaints.
5 Printing catalogues of new products.
6 Carrying out market research to determine customer preferences.
7 Solving customer problems using a phone-in helpline.

E16.35 Customer relationship management: manufacturer
Moni Sausages (Pty) Ltd is a medium-sized company that produces gourmet beef and chicken sausages for a highly competitive market. Moni's sausages are sold to major supermarket chains, as well as to retail butchers and speciality delicatessens. The company holds only about 15 per cent of the gourmet sausage market and struggles to maintain that market share. Joe Moni, the sales manager, has put a lot of energy into visiting new and potential customers to try to understand their needs. However, he is aware that customers do complain about some aspects of the products and services that are provided by the company. Joe is finding it difficult to retain customers and find new customers, as the market leaders are very aggressive and seem to have some form of superior market intelligence that allows them to anticipate changing customer preferences. Joe feels that his company is a follower rather than a leader when it comes to dealing with customers.

Joe has recently heard of customer relationship management and is wondering whether this could provide any advantages for his company.

Required:
1 Describe what is meant by customer relationship management (CRM).
2 How might CRM assist Moni Sausages to retain customers and attract new ones?
3 How might e-commerce solutions help?

E16.36 Customer performance measures: manufacturing
Refer to the information provided in Exercise 16.35.

Joe Moni is interested in monitoring the performance of the various customer groups over time, and in tracking the company's overall sales and marketing performance using customer performance measures.

Required:
Select some specific customer performance measures that may be suitable for this type of business, and explain to Joe Moni how they might be used to improve the company's performance.

E16.37 Customer profitability graph: service firm
Swish Designs specialises in designing commercial office space in Sandton. The CEO, Ralph Radebe, has reviewed the financial results for 20X6 and has noticed that operating profits were below budget. He also has access to a customer profitability graph that shows the operating profit for each of the six main customers for October 20X6.

Swish Designs
Profit Statement for the month ended 31 October 20X6

Sales revenue	R3 000 000
Cost of service provided	2 550 000
Gross margin	450 000
Marketing and administrative costs	300 000
Operating profit	R150 000

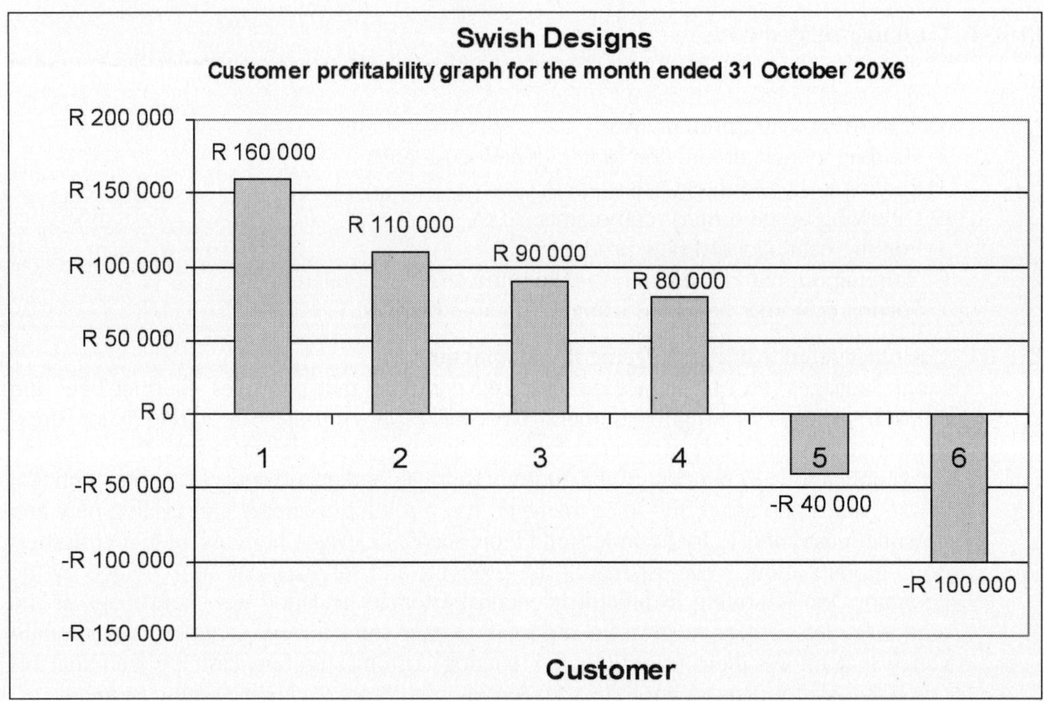

In his usual way, the CEO has just run into your office on his way to an executive meeting. He has asked you to prepare a few notes that he can use in that meeting to comment on the financial results. You have only 10 minutes.

Required:
Write some brief notes for the CEO that address the company's financial results and the customer profitability graph. Make sure that you include the following: implications of the customer profitability analysis; issues that need to be considered by the management team; further information that you need to undertake a more thorough analysis.

E16.38 Classifying quality costs

Classify each of the following as internal failure costs, external failure costs, prevention costs or appraisal costs. Why is it useful to classify quality costs in this way?

1 Sales commissions on faulty products.
2 Defective units that are scrapped.
3 Contribution margin forgone on units scrapped.
4 Supplier evaluation program.
5 Rework on defective units.
6 Quality inspection in the goods receiving area.
7 Legal fees for product liability cases.
8 Quality inspection during processing.
9 Product recall.
10 Finished goods product testing.
11 Quality training programs.
12 Contribution margin forgone on lost future sales.
13 Engineering costs to solve problems detected during process inspection.
14 Lost time to correct production line quality problem.
15 Design engineering to ensure quality.
16 Laboratory testing of products.

E16.39 Cost of quality report: manufacturer

The following costs were incurred by Hamble Metals Company to maintain the quality of its products during April:

- Operating an X-ray machine to detect faulty welds, R5700.
- Repairs to faulty products returned by customers, R5000.
- Cost of rewelding faulty joints discovered during processing, R900.
- Cost of sending machine operators to a three-week quality training program, R4900.
- Cost of recalling faulty products, R8000.
- Legal fees related to product recall, R2900.
- Product inspection into finished goods warehouse, R3700.
- Cost to confirm a supplier's quality accreditation, R300.
- Cost of faulty goods that were scrapped, R6200.

Required:

1 Prepare a cost of quality report similar to the report shown in Exhibit 16.18.
2 Comment on the relative proportions of each of the four categories of quality costs.

E16.40 Cost of quality report: manufacturer

Universal Circuitry manufactures electrical instruments for a variety of purposes. The following costs, related to maintaining product quality, were incurred in May:

Inspection of electrical components purchased from outside suppliers	R24 000
Costs of rework on faulty instruments	38 000
Replacement of instruments already sold that were still covered by warranty	85 000
Costs of defective parts that cannot be salvaged	12 200
Training of quality control inspectors	10 000
Tests of instruments before sales	20 000

Required:

1 Prepare a cost of quality report similar to the report shown in Exhibit 16.18.
2 How do you think management should react to the relative size of the four categories of quality costs?
3 Do you think that Universal Circuitry has identified all of its external failure costs? Explain.

E16.41 Managing quality; cost of quality: service firm

In 20X1 Tindane and Partners, a legal firm, embarked on a TQM program that was supported by a cost of quality reporting system. At that time, cost of quality accounted for 20 per cent of revenue. Between 20X4 and 20X7, annual revenue remained stable at R8 000 000, quality costs decreased by 40 per cent, and the distribution of quality costs changed in the following way:

	20X4	20X7
Internal failure	20%	15%
External failure	50%	21%
Prevention	12%	35%
Appraisal	18%	29%

Required:

1 What was the cost of quality?
(a) in 20X1 (b) in 20X4

2 Calculate the amount of each cost of quality category in 20X4 and in 20X7. Analyse these costs and suggest what the firm's approach to improving quality has been.

E16.42 Backflush costing in a JIT setting: manufacturer (appendix)

Albany Lighting Corporation manufactures a wide range of lighting fixtures for the housing industry. The company recently adopted backflush costing. The following events occurred in April:

(a) Raw material costing R500 000 was purchased on credit.
(b) Direct labour costs of R220 000 and actual manufacturing overhead costs of R370 000 were incurred. These amounts have not yet been paid in cash.
(c) Conversion costs of R540 000 were applied to finished products. These goods included raw material costing R410 000.
(d) Goods costing R840 000 were sold for R1 000 000 on credit.
(e) Overapplied or underapplied conversion costs were closed to cost of goods sold.

Required:

Prepare journal entries to record these events under the company's new backflush costing system.

Problems

P16.43 Analysis of supplier costs; strategic decisions: service firm

Giyani Builders is undertaking an analysis of supplier costs in order to evaluate the relative costs and performance of each supplier. For 20X6 they have isolated a range of activities that are consumed by suppliers, identified activity drivers, and estimated the cost per unit of activity driver:

Activity	Cost per unit of activity driver	
Order material	R1250	per order
Receive order	R900	per delivery
Inspect order	R1500	per delivery
Return material to supplier	R1100	per return
Pay supplier	R950	per invoice
Dispute invoiced amount	R2800	per dispute

In 20X6, the three major suppliers to the company consumed the following number of activities:

Activity	Wallace Lumber	Gromit Supplies	Sean Insulation
Order material	40	48	30
Receive order	40	60	38
Inspect order	40	60	38
Return material to supplier	5	4	15
Pay supplier	12	48	12
Dispute invoiced amount	2	0	13

The cost of material purchased from each supplier during 20X6 was as follows:

Wallace Lumber	R400 000
Gromit Supplies	R500 000
Sean Insulation	R250 000

Required:

1 Calculate the total cost of ownership for each of the three suppliers.
2 Determine the supplier performance index for each supplier.
3 Discuss the relative performance of each supplier.
4 Do you have any recommendations on supplier selection for the management of Giyani Builders?

P16.44 Supplier relationships

Jack Nkosi recently ran into an old colleague, Bob Barnard, at a cocktail party. They had both worked together at a major accounting firm until five years ago. Jack started telling Bob about the just-in-time inventory management system that his company was planning to implement:

Jack: It really is a different approach. We hold seminars for our suppliers and we send some of our purchasing people out to inspect their plants. Most of our suppliers now deliver raw material a couple of times a week, rather than once a month. And our receiving staff save a lot of time because there is no inspection. We are also saving money in the administrative area, as we do not raise separate purchase orders or receive separate invoices from suppliers for each delivery. Our inventories are almost non-existent, so we have no storage costs!

Bob: But how can your company even think of doing this? We both remember the problems we used to find on our audits. How are you going to keep effective control over payments to suppliers? And how can your company save money when they are reducing the size of orders and increasing the number of orders delivered? And what about the risk of running down the levels of inventory?

Required:

Respond to each of the criticisms made by Bob. In your answer, explain the rationale behind improving supplier relationships and the impact on competitive strategy of introducing a just-in-time system.

P16.45 Economic order quantity: equation approach; effects of JIT purchasing: manufacturer

Rally Communications Company manufactures glass fibres used in the communications industry. The company's materials and parts manager is currently revising the inventory ordering policy for XL-20, one of the chemicals used in the production process. The chemical is purchased in 10-kilogram canisters for R950 each. The firm uses 4800 canisters per year. The accountant estimates that the incremental costs of ordering and receiving XL-20 are R1500 per order. The annual cost of storing XL-20 is R40 per canister.

Required:

1 Use the EOQ formula to determine the optimal order quantity for XL-20.
2 What is the total annual cost of ordering and storing XL-20 at the economic order quantity?
3 How many orders will be placed per year?
4 Rally's accountant, Frank Mallard, recently attended a seminar on JIT purchasing. Afterwards, he analysed the cost of storing XL-20, including the cost of wasted space and inefficiency. He was shocked to find that the real annual carrying cost was R200 per canister. Mallard then met with Doug Kaplan, Rally's purchasing manager. Together they contacted Chemical Industries, the supplier of XL-20, about a JIT purchasing arrangement. After some discussion and negotiation, Kaplan concluded that the cost of placing an order for XL-20 could be reduced to just R300.
   (a) Calculate the new EOQ for XL-20.
   (b) How many orders will be placed per year?

P16.46 Economic order quantity; graphs; reorder point and safety stock: manufacturer

Refer to the data given in Problem 16.45 for Rally Communications Company prior to the JIT purchasing agreement. The lead time required to receive an order of XL-20 is one month.

Required:

1 Assuming stable usage of XL-20 each month; determine the reorder point for XL-20.
2 Draw a graph showing the usage, lead time and reorder point for XL-20.
3 Suppose that monthly usage of XL-20 fluctuates between 300 and 500 canisters, although annual demand remains constant at 4800 canisters. What level of safety stock should the materials and parts manager keep on hand for XL-20? What is the new reorder point for the chemical?
4 Explain the types of changes that Kaplan may have negotiated with the supplier to reduce the cost of placing an order from R1500 to just R300.

P16.47 Economic order quantity; effects of JIT purchasing: wholesaler

Egoli Glass Company is a distributor of car windscreens. The windscreens are manufactured in Japan and shipped to Egoli. Management is expecting an annual demand of 10 800 windscreens. The purchase price of each windscreen is R2000. Other costs associated with ordering and maintaining an inventory of these windscreens are shown below.

- The ordering costs incurred in the purchase order department for placing and processing orders for the years 20X3 to 20X5 are:

Year	Orders placed and processes	Total processing costs
20X3	20	R61 500
20X4	55	R62 375
20X5	100	R63 500

- Management expects these ordering costs to increase by 16 per cent over the amounts and rates experienced in the last three years.
- Each order is inspected by South African customs officers. A fee of R375 is charged.
- A clerk in the receiving department receives, inspects and secures the windscreens as they arrive from the manufacturer. This activity requires 8 hours per order received. This clerk has no other responsibilities and is paid at the rate of R45 per hour. Related variable overhead costs in this department are applied at the rate of R12.50 per hour.
- Additional warehouse space will have to be rented to store the new windscreens. Space can be rented as needed in a warehouse at an estimated cost of R12 500 per year plus R26.75 per windscreen.
- Breakage cost is estimated to average R15 per windscreen.

- Insurance on the inventory costs R5.75 per windscreen.
- Other carrying costs amount to R52.50 per windscreen.

Egoli Glass Company works a 6-day week for 50 weeks each year. The firm is closed for two weeks each year. Six working days are required from the time the order is placed with the supplier until it is received.

Required:

1 Assuming that all costs other than order costs remain the same in 20X6, calculate the following amounts for the Egoli Glass Company for 20X6:
   (a) the value of the ordering cost that should be used in the EOQ formula (*Hint*: Use the high–low method to estimate the incremental processing cost per order)
   (b) the value of the carrying cost that should be used in the EOQ formula
   (c) the economic order quantity
   (d) the minimum annual relevant cost of ordering and carrying at the economic order quantity
   (e) the reorder point in units

2 Management has been able to negotiate a JIT purchasing agreement with the Japanese manufacturer, and the inspection fee has been renegotiated with the customs officials. The purchasing manager has determined that JIT purchasing would enable the company to reduce the cost per order to R162.00. Moreover, she has analysed the cost of storing windscreens, taking care to include the cost of wasted space and inefficiency. She estimates that the real annual cost of carrying inventory is R300 per windscreen.
   (a) Calculate the new EOQ, given the purchasing manager's new cost estimates.
   (b) How many orders would now be placed per year?
   (c) Calculate the new minimum annual relevant cost of ordering and carrying inventory.

(*CMA, adapted*)

P16.48 Economic order quantity; reorder point and safety stock; cost behaviour: manufacturer

Alfred Wood operates a factory that manufactures bread and cakes. One of the major raw materials used is organic maize, which he buys for R5 per kilogram. The factory operates for 350 days each year. The following information has been provided:

Annual usage of maize	80 000 kg
Average time between placing and receiving order	4 days
Estimated cost of ordering and receiving inventory (per order)	R8
Estimated annual cost of carrying a kilogram of maize in stock	R0.50

Required:

1 Use the above data to calculate:
   (a) the economic order quantity (EOQ)
   (b) the number of orders per year

2 Wood has recently heard of just-in-time (JIT) purchasing, and wonders if he should use it in his business. However, he is very concerned that the cost of placing many frequent orders will be too high. Explain the advantages of JIT purchasing and address specifically his concerns about cost.

3 After a brief analysis of the cost of storing maize, including the cost of wasted space and inefficiency, you have discovered that the annual carrying cost can be reduced to R0.20 per kilogram. Wood has asked you to help him to negotiate a JIT purchasing arrangement with a major supplier. After some discussion you have discovered that the cost of placing an order for maize can now be reduced to just R2 per order. Calculate:
   (a) the new EOQ
   (b) the new number of orders per year

4 Marco Martin, who manages a competing factory, also wishes to use the EOQ model. However, because he has no formal accounting training, he is struggling with the com-

plexity of the model. Specifically, he is having trouble determining a cost per order to be used in the EOQ formula. Ordering-cost data for the previous four years are shown below:

Year	Number of orders placed	Total ordering cost
20X2	40	R6 000
20X3	25	R2 000
20X4	120	R10 500
20X5	125	R10 000

Using the high–low method described in Chapter 3, calculate the cost per order to be used in the EOQ formula.

P16.49 Just-in-time production: manufacturer

Electro Mobiles Ltd (EML) manufactures electric golf carts, electric sand buggies and electric senior citizen scooters. Each of the three products has two or three models. Because of the erratic product demand and the lead-time needed for the setup for a model changeover, EML has been increasing its raw material and finished good inventories. Work-in-process inventories are relatively low and the cost of WIP inventory is consistent from one month to the next.

During the last five years, EML has experienced increased inventory costs, decreasing profit margins and increasing customer complaints concerning the long lead time to fill sales orders. EML's managing director, Leonard Williams, is concerned about these problems and has been discussing ways to change this situation with his senior production, marketing and accounting staff.

For the past few months this top management group has been looking at how a just-in-time manufacturing system utilising a *kanban* concept could be used in their company. The team has assembled data which indicates that EML could change its production process from a push system to a pull system, by rearranging their production floor into manufacturing cells that would be dedicated to one of the three products produced. Slight modification to the equipment in the cell would be needed for a changeover from one model to the next. Cell production teams would be responsible for cell performance, maintenance on machines and equipment, solving their own production problems and training.

The management team has reached a point where it now needs an outside consultant, and has hired Greg Fransman. EML wants Fransman to explain the procedures and issues involved in changing from a push to a pull production process.

Required:

1 Discuss the effect on EML's planning and operating processes if the company implements a pull production system.
2 Identify and describe at least five benefits to EML that should result from the new approach.
3 Discuss how the changes might impact production employees, and consider how these employees might react to the changes that are proposed.

P16.50 Just-in-time purchasing; cost savings: manufacturer

Yebo Player Ltd has recently decided to adopt a just-in-time inventory policy to curb its steadily rising costs and to free up cash for investment. The company anticipates that inventory will decrease from R72 000 000 to R12 000 000, and the freed-up funds can be invested at 12 per cent per annum. The following data apply:

- Reduced inventory should produce savings in insurance and property taxes of R540 000 per annum.
- The company will lease 75 per cent of its existing warehouse to another firm for R40 per square metres per year. The warehouse has 30 000 square metres.

- Because there is now the need to handle an increased number of small deliveries from suppliers, Yebo player will need to remodel its production and receiving dock at a cost of R12 000 000. These construction costs will be depreciated over a 10-year life.
- A change in suppliers is expected to result in more expensive raw materials. However, these materials should give rise to fewer warranty and repair problems after Yebo Player's finished products are sold, resulting in a net savings of R500 000 per year.
- Two employees who currently earn R600 000 each will be transferred to other positions in the company, due to the introduction of JIT. A further employee who also earns R600 000 per annum will be terminated.
- Reduced raw material inventory levels and accompanying stock-outs will cost the company about R1 400 000 per year.

Required:

1 Calculate the annual financial impact of the decision to adopt the JIT system.
2 If the JIT decision is implemented in a proper fashion, what is the likelihood of excessive raw material stock-outs?
3 Adoption of a JIT purchasing system will often result in less need for the inspection of incoming parts and materials. Explain why.
4 Compared to a traditional purchasing system, why does a JIT system give rise to an increased number of small deliveries to the buying firm?

P16.51 JIT implementation; cost savings: manufacturer

Farm First Ltd is a manufacturer of farm equipment that is sold by a network of distributors across South Africa. The Service Division manufactures spare parts for the various models of farm equipment and sells these through the distribution centres. In January last year, a JIT system was implemented in the Service Division to reduce inventory costs. This has now been in place for a year, and the results are as follows:

- The average inventory of spare parts has now reduced from R11 000 000 to R3 000 000.
- Projected annual insurance costs of R1 600 000 have declined by 60 per cent due to the lower average cost of inventory.
- A leased 8000 square metre warehouse, previously used for inventory storage, was not used all year. The division paid R224 000 annual rent for the warehouse and was able to sub-let three-quarters of the building to several tenants at R50 per square metre. The remainder of the space was not used.
- Two warehouse employees whose services were no longer needed were transferred to the purchasing department of the Service Division in January last year at the start of the JIT implementation, to assist in the coordination of the JIT program. Their total annual cost was R760 000, which continued to be charged to the indirect labour portion of the fixed overhead.
- Even though employees needed to work overtime to manufacture 7500 spare parts, lost sales due to stock-outs totalled 3800 spare parts. The overtime premium amounted to R112.00 per part manufactured. The use of overtime to manufacture spare parts was virtually non-existent prior to the introduction of JIT.

Prior to the decision to implement JIT, the Service Division of Farm First had completed its budget. The budgeted profit statement, without any adjustments for the JIT system, is as follows. Farm First's incremental cost of borrowing is 15 per cent per annum.

Farm First Ltd **Service Division** **Budgeted Profit Statement (in R'000s)**		
Sales revenue (280 000 spare parts)		R123 200
Cost of goods sold:		
Variable	53 200	
Fixed	22 400	
		75 600
Gross margin		R47 600
Selling and administrative expenses:		
Variable	14 000	
Fixed	11 100	
		25 100
Operating profit		R22 500
Other revenue		1 500
Profit before interest and income taxes		R24 000
Interest expense		3 000
Profit before income taxes		R21 000

Required:

1 Calculate the cash savings (or loss) for the Service Division of Farm First Ltd for the first year of operation of JIT. (*Hint*: you will need to include the forgone contribution margin on lost sales that has resulted from the introduction of JIT.)

2 Discuss any factors that should be considered before a company implements JIT.

P16.52 Customer profitability analysis: manufacturer

Feather Light manufactures optic cables for the telecommunications industry. The cost management staff have just completed a customer profitability analysis, at the request of the marketing manager. The following information forms the basis for the analysis:

Customer-related activities	Cost driver	Cost driver rate
Sales activity	Sales visits	R20 000
Order taking	Purchase orders	4 000
Special handling	Units handled	1 000
Special shipping	Shipments	10 000

Cost driver data for two of Feather Light's major customers for the most recent year:

Customer-related activities	CaesarStream	NeroCom
Sales activity	8 sales visits	6 sales visits
Order taking	15 purchase orders	20 purchase orders
Special handling	800 units handled	600 units handled
Special shipping	18 shipments	20 shipments

The following data relate to those same two customers:

	CaesarStream	NeroCom
Sales revenue	R3 800 000	R2 476 000
Cost of goods sold	1 600 000	1 240 000
General selling costs	480 000	360 000
General administrative costs	380 000	320 000

Required:

1 Prepare a customer profitability analysis for CaesarStream and NeroCom.
2 Prepare a customer profitability graph, similar to the one in Exhibit 16.14, for the two customers.
3 Comment on the relative profitability of the two customers.

P16.53 Customer profitability; product profitability; competitive strategy: service firm

Gravitt and Runn is a medium-sized parcel-delivery firm. Lately the firm has been finding it difficult to retain existing customers and to gain new ones. The mergers between some of the major delivery firms have given those firms tremendous competitive advantages. The big firms are now far more cost-competitive than Gravitt and Runn, and they are able to offer expert services in all areas of delivery.

The senior managers of Gravitt and Runn have called a crisis meeting to consider what they can do to survive in this newly structured market. Currently the firm offers three types of services: same-day delivery, overnight delivery and international delivery. A number of strategic options are proposed at this meeting.

Carmen Jansen, the overnight delivery manager, argues that the firm should offer only overnight delivery, as this is the potential growth area of the future and it currently generates the most revenue for the firm. Jack Gravitt, the managing director, has suggested that the firm should continue to offer the full range of services, but only to corporate customers. He suggests that small customers should be dropped. Leslie Nkatlo, the finance manager, proposes that the decision be deferred until the profitability of the three main areas of the business, and of corporate and small customers, is investigated.

In preparation for the next meeting, Nkatlo prepared some information for last year:

- The sales revenues and direct costs of the three services offered by Gravitt and Runn during that year were as follows:

	Same-day delivery	Overnight delivery	International delivery
Sales revenue	R9 000 000	R27 000 000	R23 000 000
Direct costs	5 000 000	19 000 000	16 000 000

- The percentage of sales revenue of the three services to the two customer groups was calculated:

	Percentage of sales revenue	
	Small customers	**Corporate customers**
Same-day delivery	30	70
Overnight delivery	20	80
International delivery	30	70

- Customer-driven activities were identified, the total cost of each activity during the year was determined, and the activity cost per unit of activity driver was calculated:

Activity	Activity cost per unit of activity driver	
Process invoice	R1 000	per monthly invoice
Receive cheque	R250	per cheque
Handle disputed invoice	R1 500	per dispute
Follow up an overdue account	R2 000	per overdue account
Handle customer complaints	R800	per complaint
Investigate delivery	R2 000	per investigation
Make initial sales call to corporate customers	R4 500	per initial call
Make credit check on corporate customers	R3 500	per check

- The number of customer-driven activities consumed by the two customer groups was determined:

Activity	Small customers	Corporate customers
No. of invoices processed	8000	500
No. of cheques received	8000	600
No. of invoices disputed	200	50
No. of customer complaints	60	35
No. of delivery investigations	70	20
No. of overdue accounts followed up	200	30
No. of initial sales calls to corporate customers	–	70
No. of credit checks on corporate customers	–	40
Promotions to attract new small customers	R500 000	–
Advertisements to attract new corporate customers	–	R2 500 000

Required:

1 Calculate the contribution to profits of the three types of services offered by Gravitt and Runn during the past year.
2 Prepare a profit statement and calculate the profitability of the two customer groups.
3 Discuss the relative profitability of the three products and the two customer groups.
4 Based on your financial analysis, do you agree with the recommendations of the overnight delivery manager, or of the managing director?

P16.54 Quality costs analysis: manufacturing company

Lightning Technologies Ltd (LTI) produces two extrusion machines that are very popular with plastics manufacturers: model ABC and model XYZ. Model ABC has an average selling price of R30 000, and model XYZ sells for about R27 500. The company is concerned about the differing performance of the two machines is relation to quality, and has collected the following information:

	Model ABC	Model XYZ
No. of machines (units) produced and sold	160	200
Warranty costs:		
Average repair cost per unit	R900	R350
Percentage of units needing repairs	70%	10%
Reliability engineering at R150 per hour	1600 hours	2000 hours
Rework at LTI's manufacturing plant:		
Average rework cost per unit	R1900	R1600
Percentage of machines needing rework	35%	25%
Manufacturing inspection at R50 per hour	300 hours	500 hours
Transportation costs to customer sites to fix problems	R29 500	R15 000
Quality training for employees	R35 000	R50 000

Required:

1 Classify the above quality costs as prevention, appraisal, internal failure or external failure.
2 Prepare a cost of quality report for model ABC in Rands, using a similar format to Exhibit 16.18. In addition, add a further column showing all quality costs as a percentage of sales revenue.
3 Prepare a similar cost of quality report for model XYZ.
4 Comment on the two reports, noting whether the company is 'investing' its quality expenditure differently for the two machines.

Cases

C16.55 Supplier costs; just-in-time systems; cost management; performance measurement: manufacturer

Fast Lane Ltd manufactures 125cc motorbikes and is located in Durban. More than 70 per cent of the cost of the company's motorbikes consists of material and components, which are purchased from South African suppliers. About three years ago Fast Lane introduced a comprehensive supplier evaluation system to monitor the performance of its suppliers. Each supplier was given a three-year contract that guaranteed large orders as long as it performed according to Fast Lane's strict requirements. Each supplier's performance was measured by considering its adherence to delivery schedules (Fast Lane works on a just-in-time system), accuracy of orders delivered, number of components rejected on delivery, and its achievements in reducing its production costs (and, therefore, its material and component prices) over the contract period. Performance in all of these areas will determine whether Fast Lane renews the supplier's contract or offers the contract to another supplier. The suppliers are aware that there are many alternative component suppliers who would be eager to enter into a long-term contract with Fast Lane.

After holding discussions with the purchasing manager, as part of the review process, the financial controller has conducted a study to determine the full cost of dealing with suppliers. While the company uses a series of non-financial performance measures to measure most aspects of supplier performance, the financial controller believes that the calculation of the total cost of ownership will provide an additional perspective to viewing supplier performance. For 20X7, the following supplier-related activities and costs have been identified:

Activity	Total cost	Number of activities
Order components from supplier	R1 200 000	6000 orders
Receive order	9 000 000	10 000 deliveries
Return reject components to supplier	38 500	55 returns
Receive late deliveries	260 000	130 late deliveries
Production downtime due to late delivery	1 200 000	800 hours
Production downtime due to defective material	3 600 000	3000 hours
Process invoice and pay supplier	1 050 000	3000 invoices
Dispute invoiced amount	20 000	50 disputes

Fast Lane obtains its exhaust systems from two suppliers: Hot Exhausts and Chrome Manufacturers. In 20X7, Fast Lane purchased 3000 units from Hot Exhausts at R100 per unit, and 4000 units from Chrome Manufacturers at R90 per unit. Both suppliers provide an identical component.

The analysis revealed that in 20X7, the following activities related to the two suppliers:

Activity	Hot Exhausts	Chrome Manufacturers
Order components from supplier	90 orders	130 orders
Receive order	90 deliveries	150 deliveries
Return reject components to supplier	15 returns	16 returns
Receive late deliveries	6 late deliveries	28 late deliveries
Production downtime due to late delivery	45 hours	59 hours
Production downtime due to defective material	20 hours	29 hours
Process invoice and pay supplier	12 invoices	130 invoices
Dispute invoiced amount	3 disputes	8 disputes

Required:

1 Determine the cost per unit of activity driver for each supplier-related activity.
2 Calculate the total cost of ownership and the total cost per unit for the two suppliers.
3 Calculate the supplier performance index for the two suppliers.
4 Compare the performance of the two suppliers.
5 Describe the changes that the purchasing manager and financial controller could implement to minimise supplier-related costs.
6 Consider the various criteria used by Fast Lane to determine whether or not supplier contracts should be renewed. For each criterion, suggest two performance measures that Fast Lane might use to evaluate suppliers' performance.
7 Fast Lane is considering implementing electronic systems for transacting with suppliers. Outline some advantages that might accrue to both Fast Lane and its suppliers from such systems.

C16.56 JIT production management and TQM: manufacturer

Toyan Ltd is a major motor vehicle producer, located in Durban. The company has experienced declining sales and increasing costs over the last few years. At the beginning of this year, Toyan was taken over by a Japanese multinational company that has car manufacturing interests in most Western economies. An audit team from the Japanese parent company has just completed its evaluation of Toyan and recommended sweeping changes to the company's inventory, production and quality management. The major recommendations include the following:

- Inventories of raw materials, work in process and finished goods are to be halved during the next year and then reduced by a further 10 per cent per year over the following three years.
- Defect rates in work in process and finished vehicles are to be reduced by 20 per cent per annum. The company's goal is zero defects in five years' time.
- The number of raw material suppliers is to be reduced to just one or two suppliers for each major raw material.
- Shop floor employees are to be trained to stop the production line the moment they identify a quality problem and to start it again once they have corrected the problem.
- Shifts in each area are to start 15 minutes early to allow for a quality meeting, which is to be attended by all managers and line employees.
- Vehicle manufacturing times are to be reduced by 25 per cent over the next two years.
- Employees are to focus on processes and on the needs of customers, both internal and external.

Johan Smit has been the managing director of Toyan for the past 20 years. He is stunned by the report from Japan and discusses it with his plant manager, Jay Reddy, who also has years of experience at Toyan.

Smit: This is a recipe for disaster! If we cut our inventories, the unions will have a field day. Every time they call a stop-work meeting, we'll run out of cars for our customers. There'll be no stockpile to tide us over. Our suppliers will also be able to hold us to ransom. A stoppage in their plant will shut us down, especially if we confine ourselves to only one or two suppliers for each of our major materials.

Reddy: You're right. And imagine if the shop floor people can stop the line whenever they feel like it. With virtually no inventories, every delay will mean a delay in meeting customer orders. Even if we could cut defects by 20 per cent per year, we'd have a lot of stoppages, especially in the first year or two.

Smit: That's another point. How are we supposed to cut defects by that amount each year? The Japanese don't understand the South African way of doing things whereby 'near enough is good enough'. We spend big money on quality inspections so that we can find defects. The easiest way to cut the defect rate in the factory is to cut inspections!

Reddy: It's not just their lack of local knowledge; these Japanese blokes aren't logical. How could we cut vehicle manufacture time by 25 per cent and shut down the production line every time we have a quality problem? We would just be encouraging our people to work more slowly. Don't they see, we're going to get slower, not faster! Anyway, they don't understand our problems with factory layout. As we've grown, our layout has become chaotic. We have material and work in process that has to be moved all over the plant. Shorter manufacturing times will require a huge capital investment.

Smit: And what about these meetings every morning? What a joke. Most of the shop-floor people won't make the meeting, although I bet they'll collect the extra pay. Even if they did come, they're not going to open up to you and me about the problems on the shop floor. They're into hiding problems, not talking about them. As if they're going to confess to all their mistakes! Anyhow, why talk to shopfloor people when we can talk to their managers? What a waste of time and managerial talent!

Reddy: The Japanese don't seem to understand the basic principles of management. We know that the best way to run this place is to hold the managers responsible for the performance of their department. Look at Fred's Paint Department. He is evaluated on the number of cars that are painted each day and he pushes them through to reach his targets. Paint fair flies. Sometimes there's a bit of overspray but Fred gets his numbers. Not like poor Jack in the Trim Department, who never keeps up with the cars transferred from the Paint Department. Cars are lined up everywhere and he's always making excuses, like complaining about paint overspray that has to be cleaned off, but basically, Jack is just a lousy manager.

Smit: If we start using a customer focus, Jack will make Fred's life miserable, always carrying on about overspray. In this place, managers know that they have to make their own department work, not the department next door. It's obvious that if every department does its best, then the company will be doing its best too.

Reddy: Johan, I think the Japanese just don't understand the South African manufacturing culture. You'll have to go to Japan and sort this out. If we implemented these recommendations, Toyan would go broke within two years. Then where would you and I be?

Required:

Before going to Japan, Smit consults you, Toyan's management accountant. Prepare a report for Smit that explains the rationale behind each of the Japanese recommendations. Suggest any accompanying changes that will be needed to achieve the goals set by the parent company.

C16.57 Customer profitability analysis; product profitability; cost management: manufacturer

Jacaranda (Pty) Ltd assembles personal computers for home and business use. Three years ago, it implemented an activity-based costing system. Both the management accountants and the manufacturing managers are very pleased with the results, as they now have accurate product costing information that they can use for a variety of decisions. However, the ABC system focuses only on product design and manufacturing costs. The activity-based costs of Jacaranda's major products are as follows:

	Average product		
Activity	**PIII**	**PIV**	**PIV+**
Designing	R100	R110	R125
Purchasing	150	95	130
Assembling	890	1 200	1 400
Finishing	260	250	250
Total activity cost	R1 400	R1 655	R1 905

In July Hannah Allen, the assistant accountant, noticed that over the last six months the spending in both the Customer Support Department and the Sales Department had been steadily increasing. The previous month's costs had been 20 per cent above budget! The customer support supervisor, Bill Dominico, is able to explain exactly why this is happening. He has had to employ new staff, there is more overtime being worked, and some of the service calls have been outsourced to a third-party maintenance company. But all this was necessary, as he explains:

If a customer has a problem, we have to fix it! And if we have spent more than our budget, then that is just too bad. It is important to keep customers happy. Why, only the other day the managing director was telling us how important our customers are and how customer satisfaction is critical to the company's success.

Hannah asks Bill if she can have access to the records of his department for the past three months (June quarter). She intends to analyse the service calls to see exactly where the extra money is being spent. She also plans to analyse the selling expenses that have occurred during June quarter. The analysis reveals the following data:

- The cost of selling and customer support activities, and average selling price for each product, are as follows:

	PIII	PIV	PIV+
Activities:			
Selling	R39 000	R33 750	R9 000
Customer support	78 300	123 750	20 200
Average selling price per unit	R2 000	R2 600	R2 800

- The company's customers can be analysed into three main groups: home entertainment, educational and professional. The sales (in units) to these groups during the June quarter are detailed below:

Customer groups	PIII	PIV	PIV+
Educational institutions	150	40	5
Professional	20	30	30
Home entertainment	130	80	5
Total sales	300	150	40

- The costs of customer support and selling activities for each customer group are as follows:

	Educational	Professional	Home entertainment
Selling expenses	R28 000	R25 750	R28 000
Customer support	86 000	49 750	86 500

Required:

1 Calculate the profitability of each customer group and each product line, and present this in a customer profitability graph.
2 What can you conclude from your analysis in requirement 1?
3 Would you recommend dropping the loss-making products or customers? Explain your answer.
4 Can you think of some specific steps that could be taken to reduce expenditure in the problem areas?
5 How could the introduction of product life cycle management help to reduce customer support expenditure in the future?

C16.58 Measuring and managing quality costs: manufacturer

Loots Ltd is a major South African bicycle manufacturer. Over the last decade, bicycle manufacturers from Taiwan and Korea have been able to price their bikes below those of the Loots products, but the company has retained its market share due to the poor quality of the imported bikes. Recently, however, the quality of the imported bikes has improved, and Loots has had to cut prices to maintain market share. The managing director, John Loots, is concerned about the viability of the business at these lower prices and asks the accountant, Nabila Moolla, to investigate the problem.

Moolla's initial investigation indicates that the lower prices cannot be sustained in the longer term, as they do not cover the costs of manufacture, let alone contribute to the company's selling and administrative costs. She looks for possible cost reductions. The company has always had a reputation for high quality, but Moolla feels that there are substantial costs incurred in attaining this level of quality. She knows that there are extensive quality inspection checks throughout the production process and that many employees spend part of their time reworking defective parts. She has also noticed the buckets full of scrapped parts and components spread throughout the factory. These costs are not recorded separately in the existing accounting system. Moolla asks Loots to support the development of a cost of quality system.

Loots: What do you mean, a system that records the costs of poor quality! Our bikes are among the best in terms of quality!

Moolla: I know that, John, and we know what it costs us to make our bikes, but we've got no idea how much of that cost is related to ensuring quality. I think the cost of quality here is very high. What if it's a third of our manufacturing costs? And what if we could reduce it without compromising our quality? We could keep our prices down and still make a good profit.

Loots: Okay, Nabila. Give your cost of quality system a try, though I don't see how it will help. Everybody knows that good quality costs money. Even if we do find out our cost of quality, I don't see how it will help us reduce it.

Moolla: John, good quality doesn't seem to cost money in Taiwan and Korea. Their prices haven't gone up, even though their quality has. You'll soon see that understanding quality costs can help you to reduce them and to improve quality at the same time.

Over the next six months Moolla identifies the following costs of quality:

- Cost of replacement bikes provided under warranty, R50 000.
- Cost of bikes returned by customers and scrapped, R50 000.
- Sales commissions on faulty bikes returned by customers, R5000.
- Contribution margin forgone on bikes returned by customers, R10 000.
- Rework on defective wheels, R80 000.
- Quality inspection in the goods receiving area, R150 000.
- Quality inspections during processing, R230 000.
- Laboratory testing of bikes and components, R130 000.
- Contribution margin forgone on lost future bike sales, R50 000.
- Engineering costs to correct production line quality problems, R150 000.
- Lost contribution on machine downtime during correction of production line quality problems, R250 000.
- Operating an X-ray machine to detect faulty welds, R150 000.
- Cost of repairs under warranty, R10 000.
- Cost of rewelding faulty joints discovered during processing, R190 000.
- Cost of quality training programs, R30 000.
- Inspection of bikes put into finished goods warehouse, R160 000.
- Cost of faulty components that are scrapped, R40 000.
- Cost of faulty bikes that are scrapped after finished goods inspection, R100 000.

During this period, total manufacturing costs were R6 000 000.

Required:

1 Prepare a cost of quality report similar to the report shown in Exhibit 16.18.

2 Use the information in this report to suggest ways in which the company could reduce its cost of quality.

3 When John Loots receives the cost of quality report, he is amazed and says, 'Nabila, you're the accountant. Why didn't you tell me before that our quality costs were this high?' Explain to Loots why Moolla was unable, because of the existing accounting system, to tell him much about the cost of quality.

Endnotes

1 We can calculate the incremental cost per order by identifying how total order costs change for different numbers of orders processed. The cost per order equals the change in total order costs divided by the change in the number of orders processed. Thus, the cost per order used in the EOQ model does not include a portion of the fixed order costs. See Levin, Rubin & Stinson (1986) for a further discussion of this issue.

2 The weekly usage is based on the annual requirement of 4800 bags divided by the number of weeks in the production year, 50 (assuming the equivalent of a two-week shutdown over the year for public holidays).

3 This section is drawn from an article in *Accountancy SA* (May 2003) by C Correia entitled 'From Just-in-Case to Just-in-Time (and back again)?'

4 Good references include O'Guin & Rebischke (1993), Petty & Goodman (1996), Andon, Baxter & Bradley (2001).

5 Backflush costing can be used in any production setting, although it is most appropriate where inventories are low or stable. The discussion in this chapter is confined to its role in a JIT environment. For a further discussion of product costing under JIT, see DeLuzio (1993).

CHAPTER

Environmental and Social Management Accounting

❖ Learning Objectives

After completing this chapter, you should be able to:

1 explain the meaning of corporate social responsibility and why it is considered important by many organisations;

2 describe how triple bottom line reporting provides a broader perspective than conventional approaches to reporting performance;

3 explain the meaning of environmental management accounting (EMA);

4 describe the range of techniques that are used in environmental management accounting;

5 outline the benefits of recognising and measuring environmental and social impacts;

6 explain the difficulties in recognising and measuring environmental and social impacts;

7 define environmental costs and describe the five tiers of environmental costs;

8 analyse environmental costs as prevention, appraisal and internal and external failure costs;

9 integrate environmental costs in information for decision making;

10 assess the effects of environmental and social factors when managing suppliers and customers;

11 describe the types of measures that can be used to assess environmental and social performance;

12 define the term social audit and outline the benefits of social audits; and

13 include environmental and social factors in capital investment analyses.

Introduction

In Chapter 1 we explained that management accounting focuses on supporting managers within the organisation in their quest to enhance both shareholder and customer value. However, organisations are increasingly recognising the broader information needs of a wider range of stakeholders. For example, a number of South African businesses now use triple bottom line reporting to communicate the economic, environmental and social dimensions of their activities to stakeholders, and many organisations require a range of information to practise environmental management.

In this chapter, we briefly examine the triple bottom line approach to reporting to external stakeholders, and then move on to explore how management accounting can help an organisation to manage its environmental and social performance, which can benefit both the organisation and society. An important aspect of contemporary management accounting is the inclusion of both financial and non-financial information, and this can extend to include social and environmental information. Management accountants have the skills to monitor performance along a variety of social and environmental dimensions, and to gather and analyse the financial and non-financial data provided in reports. Accounting for environmental and social factors can benefit the organisation and enhance shareholder value, as well as contribute to a more sustainable environment and society.

Corporate social responsibility and external reporting

L.O. 1

Corporate social responsibility involves organisations taking into account the social and environmental impact of corporate activity when making decisions (Adams and Zutshi, 2004). This approach is regarded by many senior managers as leading to increased profitability, and as a determinant of long-term survival (Simms, 2002).

It is becoming more common for organisations to communicate their performance on environmental and social issues within external reports to stakeholders. This information may be reported as part of the annual report, or as separate stand alone reports. These separate reports have a variety of titles, including *triple bottom line reports, environmental reports, stakeholder impact reports, social impact reports* and *social audits.*

Triple bottom line reports

L.O. 2 **Triple bottom line (TBL) reports** focus on three aspects of performance: financial (or economic), social and environmental. Traditionally, financial information has been the focus of the reports presented to shareholders, with information about social and environmental issues being provided on an *ad hoc* basis. Triple bottom line reporting is a more comprehensive reporting process aimed at a broader range of stakeholders, including various environmental and social interest groups. **Social performance** refers to the impact of an organisation's behaviour on society including the broader community, employees, customers, and suppliers. **Environmental performance** refers to the impact of an organisation's performance on the environment, including the natural systems such as land, air and water as well as on people and living organisms. Social and environmental performance are both concerned with people. Environmental performance includes the impact on people outside of the organisation that results from an organisation's good or poor environmental performance. Occupational health and safety problems usually appear in the social performance report, but they may be the result of poor environmental practices within the organisation and be included in environmental performance.[1]

Triple bottom line reporting is used by many different types of organisations. Mining companies, such as Goldfields, and energy producers, such as Engen, produce triple bottom line reports because of the obvious community concern about their environmental performance. Manufacturing organisations may cause a range of environmental and social impacts and produce social and environmental reports to account for these activities. Service organisations can improve their environmental performance by reducing the energy they consume as well as recycling consumables such as paper and toner cartridges. In addition, service industries can encourage their suppliers to act in an ethical and environmentally and socially responsible way. Government entities and not-for-profit organisations may produce triple bottom line reports to focus attention on their environmental and social activities and performance as well as their financial performance.

One of the drivers for organisations adopting TBL is the Global Reporting Initiative (GRI), an international collaboration to develop guidelines for triple bottom line reporting. The GRI was launched in 1997 by the Coalition for Environmentally Responsible Economies and the United Nations Environment Program. Its work is continuing, as it develops global reporting guidelines for TBL reporting.

Some people believe that triple bottom line reporting is used by some organisations to produce 'a good public face', without there being any genuine intention of improving environmental and social performance. However, it can be argued that if social and environmental performance is reported publicly, this may encourage the organisation to actively manage these issues. Organisations that produce these reports may be more likely to 'walk the talk' and adopt responsible social and environmental practices.

However, triple bottom line reporting will not by itself improve environmental and social performance. We can expect performance to improve when managers and individuals in organisations integrate social and environmental goals and information into their daily practice. Management accounting is an important information source, which can help improve both environmental and social performance. The 'Real life' on page 852 outlines how BHP Billiton integrates corporate social responsibility into their management approach and practices, and provides details of its TBL reporting.

The relevance of sustainability to South African companies

Sustainability is important to future economic progress. Financial performance should be matched with progress in a company's environmental, health and social equity record. South African companies are increasingly turning their attention to triple bottom line reporting, rather than focusing only on financial performance. Further, investors are demanding to invest in companies that place sustainability and social responsibility at the heart of their business strategy and operations. The importance for companies to be included in such indices as the JSE SRI Index, the FTSE4Good or the Dow Jones Sustainability Index is relevant as asset managers and investors are demanding that companies are included in these indices. Companies are producing lengthy sustainability reports which depict a company's performance in employee relations, environmental impact, community involvement and corporate governance.

In South Africa, a significant dimension to sustainability involves transformation and Broad-Based Black Economic Empowerment initiatives. In fact, some companies such as Standard Bank combine black economic empowerment with other measures of sustainability. It is relevant to remember the reasons why there has been a move towards corporate social responsibility and sustainability. Firstly, the introduction of new legislation and laws has dramatically increased the liability of companies to adhere to safe labour practices, address environmental issues such as pollution and the rehabilitation of mines, achieve Broad-Based Black Economic Empowerment targets and undertake social investments. Socially responsible investing has become an integral part of the investment landscape, and investors demand to know what a company's economic, social and environmental performance is prior to investing in a company's shares. This has led to the creation of a number of social responsibility indices, and companies have to comply with social, economic and environmental criteria to form part of these indices. Globalisation means for example that a mining company's impact on a local community in a far-flung place cannot be hidden, as the company may be listed in London or New York and any disclosure of harmful effects will carry real consequences. Litigation is also now a real possibility as stakeholders are ready to take on companies in the courts. Codes and certification in terms of ISO 14001, which relates to environmental management standards, also play an important role in impacting on corporate practices. Further, we would like to think that the corporate sector is increasingly conscious of its commitments to society and its stakeholders and will do the right thing.

Environmental management accounting

L.O. 3

Environmental management accounting (EMA) consists of environmentally related management accounting systems and practices. These systems and practices can include life cycle costing, environmental cost accounting, environmental performance measures, assessment of environmental benefits and strategic planning for environmental management (IFAC, 1998). EMA focuses on material and energy flow information, environmental costs, and other related cost and physical information.

These data are identified, collected, estimated, analysed and reported for use by internal decision makers within an organisation (Savage, 2003). EMA *does not usually include* external costs to society or the environment for which an organisation is not legally accountable. In our description of triple bottom line reporting earlier in this chapter we defined *environmental performance* as the impact of an organisation's performance on the environment, including the natural systems such as land, air and water as well as on people and living organisms. This definition may include external costs, in contrast to the EMA approach to assessing environmental performance.

The interest in EMA is growing globally. In the early 1990s the US Environmental Protection Agency set up a formal program to promote the adoption of EMA, and in 2004 the International Federation of Accountants (IFAC) issued an exposure draft *International Guidelines on Environmental Management Accounting (EMA)* (IFAC, 2004).[2]

EMA techniques

L.O. 4

EMA consists of a range of environmental management accounting techniques, some of which produce *financial information* and some that produce *physical information.* In this chapter we will consider primarily techniques that produce financial information.[3]

Financially oriented EMA

Financially oriented EMA focuses on supplying financial information to management about the environmental impact of the organisation's activities. Techniques are similar to many of those described in other chapters of this book, although they will have a broader scope to include the environmental costs and benefits resulting from the organisation's activities. In many management accounting systems this information may be hidden in more aggregated classifications, such as overhead cost and sales revenue. Under EMA, these financial impacts become more visible.

Environmental costs are the costs that an organisation incurs to prevent, monitor and report environmental impacts. Examples include the costs of waste management systems (acquisition costs and ongoing running costs), environmental training, legal activities and fines, record keeping and reporting, as well as costs of preventing, mitigating and remediating environmental impacts. Environmental costs are described in more detail in a later section of this chapter.

Environmental product costing involves tracing direct and indirect environmental costs to products, and covers the costs of waste management, permits and fees, and recycling. Under EMA there is an emphasis on tracking environmental costs and benefits directly to the specific processes and products that cause those costs or benefits, rather than spreading them across all products. Costing techniques covered in Chapters 4, 5, 7 and 8 are relevant.

Environmental performance indicators can also be used to set targets and to monitor environmental performance, using both financial and physical measures. In Chapter 14 we studied a range of approaches to developing and using financial and non-financial performance measures, including the balanced scorecard. As we will see later in this chapter, some companies have adapted the balanced scorecard to include both environmental and social performance indicators.

Environmentally induced capital expenditure describes capital investment that is driven by the desire to improve the organisation's environmental impacts or by the need to comply with environmental regulations. Techniques for evaluating capital investment decisions are covered in Chapters 21 and 22.

Environmentally induced revenues (or **benefits**) are revenues that arise from positive environmental actions of an organisation. These may include increased revenue resulting from the sale of recyclable materials and higher profit contributions from producing greener products, or charging higher prices for enhanced environmentally friendly products. More intangible benefits from adopting environmentally responsible practices may also be considered, including increased customer satisfaction, improved employee morale and increased future profits. These future benefits are difficult to quantify, but may be relevant in decision making.

Life cycle costing is an approach to managing costs over the life of a product, as described in Chapter 15. In identifying a product's life cycle costs, organisations that practise EMA will identify and often assign a cost to the environmental consequences of the product, including the costs of recycling waste and the disposal of products and equipment.

Under EMA, information produced for tactical management decisions, such as decisions to make or buy a product, or to produce a special order, or to delete or add a new product, will include environmental costs and benefits that are relevant to the decision. These techniques are described in Chapter 19.

Physically oriented EMA

Physically oriented EMA includes techniques that focus on supplying information to management that accounts for the organisation's impact on the natural environment, measured in physical terms. Physical measures include kilograms, tonnes, kilowatt hours and decibels. Thus, information provided to management for tactical decisions and capital investment decisions will include information about the physical environmental impacts of a decision alternative, such as the quantities of noxious emissions, energy used or solid waste produced.

Environmental management systems and EMA

The growth of interest in EMA is closely linked to increased interest in environmental management systems. **Environmental management systems (EMS)** are the systems that organisations put in place to manage their environmental performance. An EMS may include recycling systems and systems to monitor and control levels of liquid, material and atmospheric discharge and waste. In 1996, ISO 14001 was released, which is an international standard for environmental management systems and their audit. By 2001 over 10 000 companies around the world were certified ISO 14001 compliant (Gray and Bebbington, 2001).

The growth of EMS and the adoption of ISO 14001 by many organisations is of interest to management accounting, as it requires that environmental performance be measured against policies, objectives and targets. Many conventional and contemporary management accounting techniques can be adapted to meet these needs. Further environmental standards have been released, including ISO 14010 Environmental Audits and ISO 14031 Environmental Performance Indicators, which are discussed later in this chapter.

The benefits of recognising environmental and social impacts

L.O. 5

Management accountants have often been too busy identifying financial impacts of decisions to take on the additional difficult task of measuring environmental and social performance and preparing decision-making information that addresses environmental and social issues. In addition, many accountants may believe that their role is to create value for major stakeholders, and not for the broader community. However, many organisations and their accountants are increasingly now acknowledging the broad consequences of their behaviour, including their impacts on the wider

REAL LIFE: INTERNATIONAL ENVIRONMENTAL MANAGEMENT STANDARDS—ISO 14001

Gold Fields and Harmony, two of the largest South African gold mining groups, have adopted the ISO 14001 environmental management system. Gold Fields was the first gold mining company in South Africa to achieve ISO 14001 certification. The company states:

The system caters for macro issues, such as rehabilitation of disturbed land and the mitigation of potential impacts on a regional scale, through to micro issues that may arise from daily activities, such as the correct handling and disposal of all waste products that may ultimately present a cumulative impact. Furthermore, the ISO 14001 system requires environmental concerns to be fully integrated into everyday practices and responsibilities.

Environmental management systems at the operations focus on prevention strategies, which are inherently more cost-effective, for example the construction of a spillage containment facility will ultimately be more cost efficient than the remediation costs associated with constantly having to rehabilitate spillages. Other environmental cost savings are effected by setting specific targets for reductions in the consumption of water, compressed air and electricity. Other benefits flowing from ISO 14001 certification are the recycling of waste which results in revenue generation, lower environmental liabilities, and increased investor, public and regulatory confidence.

Source: Gold Fields 2006 Annual Report

community. And many managers now accept that social and environmental responsibility is important to the long-term sustainability of their organisation. The 'Real life' on James Hardie and Cape plc/Gencor below provides a sobering tale of the consequences of not acknowledging the social dimensions of performance.

There are great benefits in recognising, managing and reporting environmental and social impacts. These include attracting and retaining highly skilled employees who wish to work for a responsible employer; enhancement of the organisation's reputation as a responsible and caring organisation; identification of potential cost savings; and reduction in the risk of current and future activities (Group of 100, 2003).

Environmental management accounting will allow an organisation to assess a broader range of the costs and benefits of its operations, and help managers manage their resources more effectively. For example, by identifying the cost of disposing of waste material from production, management can consider ways to reduce these costs by reprocessing the waste or by changing production processes.

Environmental and social accounting can also lead to improvements in competitiveness. Some customers may prefer to buy from companies that follow good environmental practices, or which produce products and services responsibly. The reputation of the organisation can thereby be greatly enhanced.

Remember that in Chapter 1 we explained that it is important to consider both financial and non-financial information within the management accounting system. This helps to ensure that all aspects of relevant activities and performance information are available to assist managers to enhance shareholder and customer value. Environmental and social impacts can have both financial and non-financial perspectives.

REAL LIFE: ASBESTOS—A TRAGIC LEGACY

South Africa and Australia have been affected by the long-term and tragic consequences of mining and processing asbestos.

AUSTRALIA

James Hardie is one of Australia's largest building material groups. In the 1920s the company started to mine and process asbestos. However, in 1968 the company started to phase out the mining of blue asbestos, the most lethal form of asbestos, and by 1986 it claimed that all of its products were asbestos-free. Blue asbestos is a fibrous mineral that has been linked to lung cancer and mesothelioma, a rare form of cancer affecting the chest or abdomen.

At the time that James Hardie started to process asbestos, there was relatively limited knowledge of the serious health effects that this activity could have on its workforce and the public into the future. Nor was there any realisation of the high value that society in the future would place on a company's obligation to manage a safe workplace.

In 2001 James Hardie started a fund, with a payment of $293 million, to pay damages to people exposed to the asbestos used in its products. It then shifted its head office from Australia to the Netherlands. The New South Wales government set up an inquiry chaired by David Jackson, a former Federal Court judge. Jackson found that the fund needed at least $1.5 billion to meet all claims. However, the liability may exist for decades, as new cases emerge every week around Australia. In December 2004, after extensive media coverage of the dispute and very public negotiations, James Hardie, the ACTU (representing the trade unions) and various asbestos victim groups arrived at an agreement to ensure that the company continues to fund current and future asbestos victims and their families. There is no limit on how much can be paid to victims, and the commitment will extend for at least 40 years. However, there is a maximum amount that James Hardie can pay in any year, which is set at 35 per cent of the company's free cash flow.

If environmental information had been understood and included in James Hardie's decision-making, the company would have been aware of the social impact of its manufacturing operations. (In fact, it might have decided not to mine and process asbestos products at all!) This lack of recognition has had serious financial consequences for James Hardie and for its reputation as a responsible company.

SOUTH AFRICA

In South Africa, communities in the Northern Cape were deeply affected by the mining and processing of asbestos by Cape plc and Gencor. Minimal protection was offered to workers from the asbestos dust and fibres that caused illness or death for many workers later on. Litigation in the English courts for compensation was contested by Cape plc but finally a settlement was reached and £21 million was to be made available to 7500 claimants. During the period of litigation, the share price of Cape plc collapsed, and fell from £1.50 to £0.11. If Cape plc had lost the case, then it would have probably gone into liquidation and so the claimants decided to reach a settlement with the company. Liquidation would have also drawn out the case and over 300 claimants died whilst the case was in progress. However, the settlement was not realised due to financial problems at Cape plc. At the same time an action was brought against Gencor in South Africa by asbestos victims at its mines. As most of the 7500 claimants had also worked at Gencor mines or

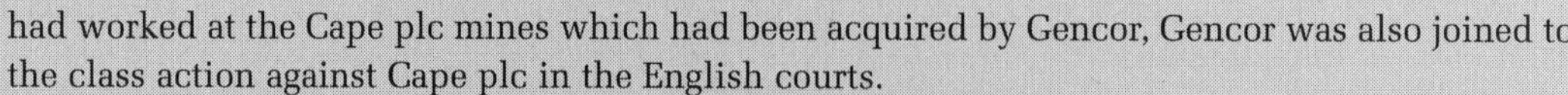

had worked at the Cape plc mines which had been acquired by Gencor, Gencor was also joined to the class action against Cape plc in the English courts.

On the unbundling of Impala Platinum from Gencor, a settlement of £37.5 million (about R460 million at the time) was reached with the asbestos victims of Gencor and an additional £3.21 million was paid to the Cape plc claimants who had also worked at Gencor mines. Cape plc ended up making a settlement of £7.5 million. Gencor also made about R40 million available for the rehabilitation of the asbestos mining areas in the Northern Cape. In July 2007 the market capitalisation of Cape plc was close to £250 million and the share price has increased from £0.17 to about £3.00, an increase of over 1600 per cent from 2003 to 2007. The settlement with the claimants permitted Cape plc to survive and prosper, whilst its asbestos workers in the Northern Cape slowly died. After the unbundling, Gencor ceased to exist. We wonder if Gencor would have acquired the mines of Cape plc if it had known about the potential future liability arising from the asbestos claims. Even today, the communities in towns such as Prieska, in the Northern Cape, live with the tragic legacy of asbestos.

Sources: http://quote.bloomberg.com/apps/news; www.mirg.org/mesothelioma; www.actu.asn.au/public/news/1103593342_21819.html
Legal Resources Centre and Legal Resources Trust, Annual Report for the year ending 31 March 2004.
'Asbestos fight comes home', see http://news.bbc.co.uk/1/hi/world/africa/506167.stm
Cape plc, 2006 Annual Report
McCulloch, J 'Asbestos Mining in Southern Africa, 1893–2002', *Int J Occup Environ Health*, Vol.9, No. 3, Jul/Sep 2003
Meeran, R 'Cape plc: South African Mineworkers Quest for Justice', *Int J Occup Environ Health*, Vol.9, No. 3, Jul/Sep 2003
McCulloch, J 'Beating the Odds: The Quest for Justice by South African Asbestos Mining Communities', *Review of African Political Economy*, No. 103:63–77

L.O. 6

Difficulties in recognising and measuring environmental and social impacts

Conventional management accounting excludes the measurement of many environmental and social impacts. In some companies, the costs of these impacts remain hidden, even though they may be substantial. Exhibit 17.1 provides some examples.

Some organisations now measure some of these 'forgotten' costs. For example, a drop in the value of brands and in corporate image as a result of adverse environmental or social impacts of an organisation's activities may be recognised, and the impact sometimes estimated in Rands.

However, environmental and social impacts can be difficult to recognise and report because:

- future ecological and social issues are not yet known;
- many costs and benefits are external—that is, they occur outside of the organisation; and
- many costs and benefits are difficult to measure in financial terms (Gluch and Baumann, 2004).

Future ecological and social issues are not yet known

It may be difficult to determine the future environmental and social impact of current decisions and operations, particularly as we do not know what aspects of the environment and of society may be valued by future generations. Even now, there are probably many work practices and operations that will have future environmental and social impacts that we are not able to currently assess.

One example is the growing interest in developing and growing genetically modified (GM) crops. This provides great business opportunities for many organisations. However, while many scientists believe that these crops will have no future adverse impact on the environment or on the population who consume these products, we do not really know what the long-term consequences will be.

Measuring impacts external to the organisation

Traditionally, management accountants have recorded only the costs and benefits that occur inside the organisation. In Chapter 16 we explained that value chain approaches encourage us to think about and measure the impacts of decisions on suppliers and customers. While it can be difficult to determine the impact of our actions on suppliers and customers, it can be even more difficult to assess the environmental and social impacts outside the organisation.

The 'Real life' on CFCs below demonstrates the problem that occurred when GE developed a chemical that increased efficiency and eliminated work hazards in refrigeration manufacturing plants, but provided later generations with global environmental problems. Limiting the assessment of environmental and social effects within our organisation may cause us to overlook many long-term problems that our firm may create!

Costs we measure	Costs we forget
The cost of collecting and disposing of waste	The long-term cost to society of dumping waste.
Cost of control systems to minimise emissions into rivers or air	Damage to water sources and air as a result of legal emissions. Impact on the health of neighbours.
Packaging costs	Costs to customers and society of disposing of unwanted packaging.
Compensation paid to the estate of an employee killed at the plant	Devastating loss to employee's family and friends. Damage to morale of employees.
Cost of a new waste water treatment plant	Poor corporate image because we dump waste water.

Exhibit 17.1 Environmental and social costs: measured or forgotten

REAL LIFE: GENERAL ELECTRIC AND CHLOROFLUOROCARBONS (CFCs)

In the United States, General Electric (GE) developed chlorofluorocarbons (CFCs) in the 1930s. These were used by GE in its domestic refrigeration products. CFCs were believed to be a major advance over the ammonia and sulphur methods of refrigeration, as they were non-flammable and non-toxic, and they increased production efficiency. Over time, CFCs came to be used in a variety of products, including air-conditioning and as the propellant in aerosols.

It was not until the 1970s that scientists began to realise that this commonly used gas was dangerous to the environment, and was one of the pollutants causing a hole in the ozone layer. Today CFCs are rarely used and South Africa's use of CFCs is limited to medical sprays. Under the Montreal Protocol the production and consumption of CFCs was banned in developed countries from 1 January 1996, except for essential uses that must meet a very limited range of essential use criteria. Developing countries have until 2010 to phase out CFCs completely.

In the 1970s no company would have predicted that the products it manufactured could cause significant environmental damage. Scientists believe that it will take until 2050 for the atmosphere to recover from the environmental damage caused by CFCs. In the future, scientists and companies will be much more careful before widespread adoption of a new chemical.

Sources: www.abc.net.au/rn/talks/natint/stories/s682544.htm; EPA (2000)

The difficulty of measuring costs

While some environmental and social impacts can be measured in physical terms, it is sometimes difficult to measure these in financial terms. In this chapter we look at new techniques that will help in this process, and focus on physical units as well as financial terms. In the CFC case it would have been almost impossible for engineers in the 1930s to measure the financial costs of the potential damage of the new chemical, even if they had recognised the possible future environmental problems.

Defining environmental costs

L.O. 7 As explained in an earlier section, environmental costs are the costs that an organisation incurs to prevent, monitor and report environmental impacts. They can also include the costs an organisation incurs when it does not comply with environmental regulations, some of which may extend well into the future. Some organisations may define environmental costs very narrowly, including only costs that have a direct effect on profits. Other organisations may include costs that result from the organisation's activities and operations but are external to it. As part of a management accounting system, an organisation may report any or all of these types of environmental costs, depending on how managers intend to use the information.

The United States Environment Protection Authority has defined five tiers of environmental costs, from Tier 1 to 5, as shown in Exhibit 17.2 (EPA, 1995):

- Tier 1 costs, conventional costs, can be found in the accounting systems of most organisations. However, they may not be reported in a form that can be readily used by managers to assess environmental expenditure. These include the costs of purchasing equipment and plant that will prevent environmental impacts.
- Tier 2 costs, hidden costs, include the costs of monitoring and reporting activities to comply with regulations. These costs also can be found in the accounting system, but may not be easy to find and report, as they are often hidden in various overhead accounts and in the cost of wages and salaries.
- Tier 3 costs, contingent costs, include costs that may be incurred in the future, depending on future events. These costs may be recognised within internal company reports. They are also disclosed in the notes to the accounts of external financial reports, but only if there is a high probability that the company will be obliged to pay these costs in the future and if they are material in value. In external reports, these contingent liabilities are often limited to costs that may arise from existing legal actions.
- Tier 4 costs, relationship and image costs, reflect perceptions of various stakeholders, which are rarely measured in standard information systems and are difficult to measure objectively.
- Recognition of Tier 5 costs, societal costs, would be very difficult to achieve because of the cost of estimating the impacts, and the specialised environmental knowledge that might be needed to do so. In some cases, it may be easier to use physical measures to understand external impacts.

The first four tiers can be described as **private costs**, as these are environmental costs that directly affect the profit of the organisation or are costs for which the organisation can be held legally accountable.

Analysing environmental costs

L.O. 8 Many of the management accounting techniques described in other chapters of this book can help to measure and analyse environmental costs. These include activity-based costing, conventional overhead analysis and life cycle costing. The framework for analysing quality costs, described in Chapter 16, is particularly useful.

You may remember that quality costs can be categorised as prevention costs, appraisal costs, internal failure costs and external failure costs. When applying this framework to environmental

1 **Conventional costs**
Direct costs associated with capital expenditures, raw materials, and other operating and maintenance costs.

2 **Hidden costs**
Hidden regulatory costs from activities such as monitoring and reporting of environmental activities and emissions, cost of searching for environmentally responsible suppliers, and the ongoing cost of cleaning up contaminated land.

3 **Contingent costs**
Contingent liabilities arising from failure to clean up contaminated sites, and fines and penalties for non-compliance with regulations.

4 **Relationship and image costs**
Less tangible costs and benefits that relate to consumer perceptions, and employee and community relations.

5 **Societal costs**
These are the costs that organisations impose on others—the environment and society—for which they may not be held legally responsible and which cannot be compensated for in the legal system.

Source: adapted from EPA (1995)

Exhibit 17.2 Five tiers of environmental costs

costs, the goal is to control and reduce environmental costs overall. As with quality management, an initial focus on prevention and appraisal activities may, in time, significantly lower failure costs. However, the definition of each cost category differs from those used under quality management (Hughes and Willis, 1995).

- *Prevention activities* are designed to solve environmental problems before they occur, or even to turn problems into opportunities. Costs incurred under this category can be viewed as investment, as they can reduce later outlays and provide long-term benefits. For example, efforts to reduce and eliminate pollutants can provide a long-term cost advantage over competitors, as well as possible marketing and reputation advantages. The cost of prevention activities includes the cost of employee training and the cost of installing environmentally responsible equipment, processes and activities.
- *Appraisal activities* monitor the level of environmental impacts and include measuring damage, inspecting processes and products, and auditing supplier performance. Appraisal costs include depreciation of testing equipment, costs of supplies used in testing and monitoring, and costs of obtaining external certifications and tests.
- *Internal failure activities* correct environmental breakdowns that have been discovered in appraisal activities.[4] For example, internal failure costs may include the costs of cleaning up the plant following a chemical explosion or leakage, and costs of occupational health and safety claims.
- *External failure activities* occur when the resolution or remediation efforts fall outside of the company's management. These costs may include the cost of cleaning up polluted sites, fines for environmental damage, and losses associated with a loss of reputation (and future sales) due to public awareness of the organisation's failure to engage in environmentally responsible actions. As with the analysis of quality costs, it is often difficult to recognise and measure the cost of external failure.

Let's look at an example of a company that reports and analyses environmental costs. Lithgow Cleaners manufactures chemicals for the cleaning industry and is very aware that some of its processes and practices may impact on the external environment. The warehousing manager has undertaken an assessment of the cost for its materials handling operations of all activities performed to reduce the company's impact on the environment. These costs are listed in Exhibit 17.3.

Environmental costs			Percentage of total environ-mental cost
Prevention costs:			
Auditing environmental risks	R22 500		
Training for staff on how to reduce waste	14 800		
Recycling of packaging from suppliers' materials	56 500		
Depreciation—air cleaning system attached to exhaust	83 550		
		R177 350	9.36%
Appraisal costs:			
Monitoring the level of air pollution	R26 500		
		R26 500	1.40%
Internal failure:			
Cost of cleaning plant following chemical spillage	R282 000		
Employee medical costs arising from spillage of toxic chemicals	152 900		
		R434 900	22.94%
External failure:			
Fines for environmental damage	R1 256 750		
		R1 256 750	66.30%
Total environmental costs		**R1 895 500**	**100.00%**

Exhibit 17.3 Analysis of environmental costs

How could the managers at Lithgow Chemicals use this information? Some activities are related to prevention, such as training, auditing, and recycling of packaging materials (which helps to prevent environmental damage). Managers could also reduce the recycling cost by asking their suppliers to reduce their level of packaging. The monitoring of air pollution levels is an appraisal cost. This is an important activity to safeguard employees and to prevent unnecessary pollutants from entering the environment.

The internal failure costs relate to a chemical spillage and make up about 23 per cent of the total environmental costs. Management may decide to investigate the underlying causes of this spillage to prevent any future accidents from occurring. The investigation may lead to increased prevention and appraisal activities. The external failure cost relates to a fine for environmental damage, and this is the highest component of all of the environmental costs. The managers may undertake an assessment to consider how this could have been prevented. Managers at Lithgow may look at ways of undertaking more prevention activities (increase prevention costs) to prevent these types of problems from occurring in the future. In the short run, increasing the costs of prevention and appraisal may reduce the risk of failure costs. Introducing more sophisticated monitoring equipment and engaging in more employee environmental awareness training may help to minimise future internal and external failures.

L.O. 9

Improved decision making at Cormack Manufacturing

Cormack is a plastic injection moulding business employing 90 people. There are two production processes. Plastic granules are injection moulded to form container caps and tops for the food, cosmetics and pharmaceutical industries. The components of the food packaging are then assembled. Most waste is recycled; there are no toxic chemicals used in the process, and no hazardous waste outputs; and there are limited requirements for environmental compliance.

Relevant costs	Current accounting treatment	Revised treatment: stage 1
Tier 1		
Materials packaging	Packaging and materials costs are hidden within cost of goods sold in the company accounts.	New account codes for Materials and Packaging to be created within cost of goods sold in the company accounts.
Light and power	One account for each product cost centre is maintained in the manufacturing business unit for all energy costs (lighting, machinery, office equipment etc.). The allocation of costs between the product cost centres is fairly arbitrary, based on assumed management estimations of energy usage.	To be separated out into new account codes, 'Lighting' and 'Moulding Energy', for each product cost centre within the manufacturing business unit. This will improve understanding of how the costs are generated. The remainder will remain in the Energy Overhead account. The allocation basis between product cost centres will be updated and based on actual readings taken during the trial, replacing the previous management estimation basis.
Stock variance	All stock losses are accumulated in the manufacturing business unit at a consolidated level. These include obsolete stock, spills, wastage on the production lines and misappropriation. There is no allocation between the product cost centres and no identification of particular comments of the cost—for example, how much relates to waste.	Obsolete stock costs to be separated into a new manufacturing business unit account code, with costs allocated across the product cost centres. The remainder will stay within the Stock Variance account for the time being.
Tier 2		
Direct labour Depreciation External repairs and maintenance	There are already separate account codes in the manufacturing business unit. Costs are allocated directly to the product cost centres to which they relate.	No change requested. Current accounts and the bases of allocation appear reasonable.
Waste	No cost data recorded. The materials cost of waste is hidden within the Stock Variance account in the manufacturing business unit, as noted above. Energy and labour costs of waste are hidden in the Energy and Salaries accounts, respectively, in the manufacturing business unit.	The weight of plastic waste produced (by product category) by the moulding and assembly operations is to be set up as a KPI in summary management accounts. Although not separating the costs of waste at this stage, this KPI at least provides management with a measure for monitoring and controlling waste, and identifying where and why it is generated. Waste costs (including raw materials, labour, energy etc.) will be separated out in the future.
Compliance	Minimal environmental compliance costs.	No change requested.
Tiers 3, 4 and 5	Not being captured by the accounting system.	Quantitative and qualitative data to be included in the summary management accounts and brought into decision making.

Source: ICAA (2003b, pp. 44–5)

Exhibit 17.4 Environmental costing information, Cormack Manufacturing

The need for environmental management accounting does not look strong. However, the company did implement an environmental management accounting project, which provided improved costing and environmental outcomes. The company analysed its costs using a modified tier structure similar to that outlined in Exhibit 17.3. This is detailed in Exhibit 17.4. As discussed earlier, it is unlikely that we will find management accounting systems that report environmental costs at the higher tiers.

Part of the motivation for the project undertaken at Cormack was to develop environmental information that could direct employee behaviour towards more environmentally responsible actions. The existing costing system provided very little financial information relating to key areas of environmental performance. In the new system, a decision was made to collect financial data to direct attention to various critical areas where environmental performance could be improved, such as the cost of material waste, energy use by various machines, packaging and lighting.

The new systems at Cormack included many changes. We will discuss two of the major initiatives to show how improved management accounting can encourage managers and employees to adopt more environmentally supportive behaviours.

Integrating production and environmental costs

At Cormack, plastic products are manufactured using either a cold runner process or a hot runner process to inject molten plastic into moulds. The cold runner process generates waste that needs to be hand sorted for recycling, whereas the hot runner process generates waste that cannot be recycled and is sent to landfill. The two processes generate different amounts of waste and use different amounts of energy and labour. Exhibit 17.5 compares the total annual production cost and the environmental cost of waste for the same product, using the hot runner or the cold runner processes.

	Hot runner		Cold runner	
	Estimated cost	Environmental waste cost element	Estimated cost	Environmental waste cost element
Materials (FG)*	R958 680		R959 680	
Energy (FG)*	28 990		30 490	
Materials (waste)†	132 210	R132 210	115 080	R115 080
Labour (waste)†	22 160	22 160	62 160	62 160
Energy (waste)†	1 500	1 500	1 320	1 320
Total	R1 143 540	R155 870	R1 168 730	R178 560
Cost of waste as % of production cost		13.6%		15.3%

* FG indicates the monetary value of the material that is included in the finished goods.
† Waste indicates the monetary value of material that is diverted into a waste stream.
Source: ICAA (2003b, p. 47)

Exhibit 17.5 Comparison of the cost of hot runner and cold runner processes, Cormack Manufacturing

Overall, management was surprised at the cost of environmental waste. For the hot runner process, the cost of environmental waste was 13.6 per cent of production costs, and for the cold runner process was 15.3 per cent of production costs. The cold runner process resulted in higher waste costs. The material cost of this waste was cheaper than for the hot runner process, as it could be recycled, but the labour cost was higher because of the hand sorting. However, this is not the whole story. Although it was cheaper to produce the product using the hot runner process and there were lower internal environmental waste costs, the hot runner process produced 1844 kg of waste that needed to be disposed of in landfill, compared to 1605 kg for the cold runner process. In addition, the hot runner process produced environmentally damaging CO_2 emissions of 47 tonnes compared to 49 tonnes for the cold runner.

Management can use either the hot runner or cold runner processes, and may use the cost and environmental information to help make this decision. How will they integrate the cost information with the environmental information? How will they weigh up the relative damage to the environment from the production of CO_2 gas compared to waste in landfill? On balance, they may argue that the CO_2 emissions are similar and given the lower measured environmental waste cost then the hot runner process may look superior. But perhaps not!

The cost of recycling waste

In the plastic injection industry, much of the waste produced can be re-used in future production. This appears sensible on environmental grounds—plastics use up scarce hydrocarbons and their waste causes environmental damage. Cormack used its new costing system to assess whether recycling the waste and re-using it in production was better for the company than the current system of selling waste plastic to an external recycler. The major saving associated with recycling and re-using the plastic waste relates to raw material savings, with some minor increases in costs for energy and labour to run the waste regrinding machine. In this case, what is clearly a good decision for the environment is also a good decision for the company from a financial viewpoint, as is shown in Exhibit 17.6. A detailed financial analysis like this may help Cormack to think about ways to make the recycling process even more efficient.

The 'Real life' below, on improving the costing systems at G H Michell & Sons, provides a further demonstration of how environmental costs can be taken into account.

Costs/benefits	
Depreciation of the waste regrinding machine	R19 500
Energy needed to run the regrinding machine	1 310
Labour cost of running the regrinding machine	30 870
Recycling sales revenue foregone	31 750
Total costs	83 430
Raw material saved	476 280
Net benefits from recycling waste for re-use in production	R392 850

Source: adapted from ICAA (2003b, p. 49)

Exhibit 17.6 The costs and benefits of recycling waste at Cormack Manufacturing

Improving supply chain management through environmental and social accounting

L.O. 10

Environmental and social management accounting may provide useful information to assist managers to achieve competitive advantage. This approach may result in cost savings and product and process improvements at each stage in the supply chain. Although some advantages may go to both suppliers and customers, there may be financial advantages for an organisation and advantages for the environment and society. (You may remember that supply chain management was explained in Chapter 16.)

Suppliers

An organisation may be willing to pay more for supplies that are known to have reduced adverse impacts on society and the environment. However, there may be other incentives for an organisation to work with suppliers to adopt responsible environmental and social practices, as sometimes these changes can lead to reductions in cost.

For example, in the 'Real life' at G H Michell, bales of wool transported to the processing plant included a high percentage of waste material, which needed to be disposed of prior to and during processing. Thus, part of the cost of transport related to transporting waste material. Additional

REAL LIFE: ENVIRONMENTAL COSTING AT G H MICHELL & SONS

G H Michell & Sons is Australia's largest wool and leather processor, processing between 30 and 35 million kilograms of wool every year. Michell's traders purchase several grades of wool for the company at wool auctions. They are provided with the estimated processing cost for each grade of wool, which influences the prices that they are willing to pay.

Michell redesigned its costing system to reflect more closely the resources used to process the various grades of wool. These changes also helped the company to reduce the environmental impacts of its wool processing.

G H Michell uses a carbonising process to process low grade or 'dirty' wool. The process is more complex than that used for the top grade wools, as there are large amounts of dirt, vegetable matter and salts that must be removed from the wool. The dirty wool goes through the following stages:

1 *Opening*. This separates the fibres that have been firmly packed by a wool press at the shearing shed. Pressing reduces transportation costs but creates costs for the processor.
2 *Scouring*. Four scourers work in a row, using detergent to clean the wool.
3 *Acidification*. The burrs and vegetable matter are acidified and turned to ash that can be removed from the wool.
4 *Centrifuge*. Water is removed from the wool.
5 *Dry baking*. The wool undergoes dry baking.
6 *Crushing/dusting*. The crushing/dusting process removes vegetable matter, carbon and dust from the wool fibre.
7 *Neutralising*. Water, sodium carbonate and hydrogen peroxide are used to neutralise any acid.
8 *Blending*. The wool fibres are blended ready for manufacture.
9 *Packing*. The wool is packed ready for transport.

At each stage in the process there are inputs, some of which deplete resources, and outputs, some of which are potentially harmful to the environment.

Under the existing costing system the costs of processing were allocated evenly across all wool products on a per bale basis. As we learned in Chapter 8, averaging costs in this way does not cause any distortions in product costs if all products use a similar amount of resources. However, at Michell this was not the case. Dirty wool used more energy, water, detergent, acid and transportation costs per unit of output than top grade wools. It was more difficult to process dirty wool; it had a much lower yield than top grade wool and the production processes caused more environmental costs. In addition, the dirty wool was more expensive to transport from the suppliers because a significant part of the weight of each bale was lost during the carbonising process due to the removal of contaminants. If only 50 per cent of the bale is usable wool, then half of the transport cost has been wasted.

The redesigned costing system took account of the expected yields of various wool grades—for dirty wool the yield was as low as 50 per cent. The changes in product costs resulting from the new system were lower than 10 per cent across all products, but this was significant as profit margins were very low. Also, the new product costs sent a signal to the traders to pay less for dirty wool, which costs the company and the environment in terms of usage of energy and chemicals.

The new costing system reduces the number and cost of preventive activities—the wool now no longer needs the heavy processing it once did. And Michell has other procedures that support sound environmental management. Wool grease, which is obtained more efficiently from better wools, can be sold for $2 a kilogram. The sludge from the carbonising process is reprocessed for compost for vineyards, although this costs Michell $15 per tonne.

Source: ICAA (2003a), based on a study by Craig Deegan

greenhouse emissions were also created by these wasteful transport and processing activities. If the supplier could remove the waste material from the wool bales prior to transport, this might result in lower transport costs for the supplier and lower processing costs for G H Michell, as well as resulting in reduced environmental impacts. Thus, both costs and environment impacts would be reduced by this change. Sometimes an organisation may be committed to following environmentally responsible practices, only to find that its supplier is using non-biodegradable and hazardous materials or avoiding using recycled materials. This may not be detected easily in a management accounting system, although an environmentally responsible supplier cost analysis (see Chapter 16) could include measuring the level of non-environmentally friendly materials used or produced by a supplier.

Exhibit 17.7 shows how an organisation might evaluate its suppliers by taking into account a range of environmental and social factors. This idea was developed at Commonwealth Edison, a United States electricity supply organisation (EPA, 2000). For each supplier, a rating from 1 to 7 can be given for each criteria, and a total score can then be calculated for the supplier. The difficulty for any organisation in calculating this score is how to weigh up the importance of each criteria in its evaluation and comparison of suppliers.

Evaluation area	Criteria	worst → 1	2	3	4	5	6	best 7
Purchasing and supply management	Cost Vendor performance Shelf life Packaging safety Storage requirements							
Environment	Material regulated by EPA Disposal required off-site							
Safety and hygiene	Adequate labelling on containers Inhalation risk Hazardous decomposition Carcinogenic potential							
Analytical	Specification analysis Frequency of testing							
Source: adapted from EPA (2000), p. 14								

Exhibit 17.7 Financial and environmental criteria for evaluating suppliers

Customers

Manufacturers and service organisations can work with customers to reduce adverse social and environmental impacts. These impacts include harm to customers, other people and the environment when the service is being delivered or the product is being used, as well as damage to the environment when the product is disposed of. This approach may lead manufacturers to help their customers recycle a used product. It may also encourage the customer to use the product or service in a way that will cause the least damage to the environment.

There are many examples of organisations that encourage their customers to recycle using methods that include 'take back' and 'disposal' programs. The European auto industry is required by law to design cars in a way that they can be recycled once the customer has finished with the car. The directive of the European Union is that the car must be designed so that 85 per cent of the weight of its materials can be recycled. This provides a significant challenge to car designers, especially in reducing the use of plastics and in using recyclable plastics. The goal is that by 2015, 95 per cent of a car will be recyclable (www.azom.com; www.planetark.com).

Management accounting can help an organisation identify the cost savings from recycling or better environmental use of a product in the hands of a customer. For Cormack there was an advantage in working with its customer. The company's new costing system showed that packaging costs accounted for 48 per cent of manufacturing profit, and therefore were a prime area for improvement. As a result of this information, a trial was conducted using containers that could be recycled four times. Even though it was expensive to redesign processes and purchase the new containers, the analysis in Exhibit 17.8 shows that over the four-year life of the containers there were net cost savings for Cormack. Of course, this particular initiative relied on the customer being willing to accept an alternative packaging form. This example shows the advantages in working with the customer, and the cost savings could have been used to negotiate a lower selling price for the customer.

Costs and benefits		
One-off setup costs for using returnable cartons:		
■ purchase of new cutting equipment		
■ design and print costs		
■ additional cost of purchasing returnable cartons (compared to non-returnable cartons)		
Initial net outlay		−R75 000
Cost reductions to the business from using returnable cartons as compared to using disposable cartons (based on existing order quantities and lead times):		
■ fewer cartons required (reduced purchase costs)		
■ increased cartage (higher collection charges)		
■ increased liner cost (more liners required for smaller cartons)		
■ labour differences are negligible		
Net benefit per annum		47 900
Net benefit over expected life (4 years) of returnable cartons	[47 900 × 4 −75 000]	R116 600
Intangible benefits		
■ industry reputation		
■ customer relationship		
■ meeting obligations under Packaging Covenant and avoiding future regulation		
■ reduced packaging waste in the supply chain		
Net intangible benefit		Unquantifiable
Source: ICAA (2003b, p. 50)		

Exhibit 17.8 Cost and benefits to Cormack Manufacturing of introducing recyclable containers[5]

Management accounting information can help managers to make decisions that not only result in lower costs but also lead to favourable environmental impacts. In some cases, the analysis may show that it is more expensive to provide a more environmentally friendly product or service, and the organisation may still decide to adopt these practices but to charge more to customers.

Some customers may be happy to pay more for a product that they believe to be more environmentally responsible. However, this depends on the nature of the product or service being offered, and the characteristics and preferences of the customers. Clearly, marketing and strategic considerations come into these pricing decisions, and information such as that used in the Cormack case above is essential for making these decisions.

Measuring environmental and social performance

L.O. 11

We saw in Chapter 14 that performance measurement systems that combine financial and non-financial measures may provide a balanced perspective of the overall performance of an organisation. Performance measurement systems provide important information to assist managers in monitoring and controlling activities, and to motivate and reward managers. They are also used to direct attention to aspects that are considered important by the organisation. As with many important aspects of business activity, it is difficult to quantify environmental and social impacts. It is even more difficult to express these in Rand terms. However, a well-designed environmental management system should include measures of performance.

ISO 14031 environmental performance indicators

ISO 14031 is an international standard that assists organisations to develop environmental performance measures. This standard suggests that three types of indicators (or measures) should be used: operational performance indicators, management performance indicators and environmental condition indicators.

1 **Operational performance indicators** provide information, such as waste levels and energy consumption, relative to volume of production, sales or some other activity. Thus, an organisation may measure the number of kilograms of waste material disposed of in landfill, or waste material as a percentage of material used or as a percentage of production output. In this case, we could measure the quantity in kilograms as well as in Rands. Another example is the kilowatts of electricity and the cost of electricity used per production output or production hour. Again, both a physical and a financial measure can be provided.

2 **Management performance indicators** measure the efforts of management to improve the environmental performance of their organisation. These include the cost of supplier audits, the number of cases of non-compliance with regulations and any cost of correcting non-compliance, and the cost and time devoted to staff environmental training. These are not outcome measures as they do not capture the impact of an organisation's activities. They can be described as input measures, and compliance may or may not lead to improved environmental outcomes.

3 **Environmental condition indicators** measure the actual condition of the environment at a local, national or global level. This is a difficult area to quantify, as many organisations and other factors may contribute to the condition of the local environment. Thus, it may be difficult to single out the impact of a single organisation. Nevertheless, there are examples where distinct changes in environmental conditions can be closely linked to the activities of a specific organisation. For example, the level of noise pollution experienced close to an airport may be linked to the activities of that airport, and so the airport owner could monitor the noise level. Alternatively, a sewage processing plant that is allowed to pump recycled output into the ocean could monitor the quality of the water. In both of these cases, it is possible to measure the impact in quantitative terms—average and maximum decibels of noise and percentage of bacteria per litre of discharge.

As with all performance measures, these indicators may be presented as *absolute measures* relative to another activity (for example, to sales), or as a percentage *relative to a baseline*. Some organisations might benchmark them against other organisations. To be useful to managers, these indicators need to be reported and monitored over time using a consistent measurement approach.

When indicators are initially developed, there may not be an appropriate benchmark against which to measure the relative performance. For example, for the disposal of wastewater, either the total discharge or the total discharge per Rand of production may be reported. However, over time, a measure such as wastewater discharge per kilogram of production may provide more useful information. In addition, the financial cost of a social or environmental problem may galvanise management attention more than a physical or relative measure.

Eco-intensity measures are measures of the *input* (such as kilohertz of power) *to output* (such as kilograms of aluminium). You may recognise this as a form of productivity measure (see Chapter 14). In this case, it indicates the level of environmental inputs used to produce a level of output. This approach could be used to indicate which organisations use the scarce water from the Vaal river in the most responsible way.

An **eco-efficiency measure** relates *output to input.* For example it could relate the product value measured in Rands against the resources used. For the Vaal river water, a farm producing cotton could assess the production or financial value of cotton produced relative to how much water was used. The farm might see that its long-term viability might be in doubt if another form of agriculture, such as vineyards, produced greater income for each kilolitre of water used.

The release of environmental reports to external stakeholders is becoming more common. These reports often contain a range of performance indicators.

The socially balanced scorecard

In Chapter 14 the balanced scorecard was described. You may remember that the Kaplan and Norton scorecard consists of four dimensions: financial, customer, internal business processes, and growth and learning. For each dimension, there is an objective as well as lead and lag indicators. We also learned that in some organisations different dimensions are included.

Some organisations have added a social and environmental dimension to the balanced scorecard. Two examples are Novo Nordisk and Shell (Zingales and Hockerts, 2003). Novo Nordisk is a Danish pharmaceutical manufacturer. As the company has a major investment in people and in research and development (R&D), the CEO wanted to understand the company's performance in these two areas. He realised that relying on conventional performance indicators was not enough, as it takes some time before people and R&D performance impact on these data. In the late 1990s the company adopted a balanced scorecard and integrated social and environmental measures. Novo Nordisk's scorecard has four perspectives: Finance, Business Processes, Customers and Society, and People and Organisation. The Customers and Society, People and Organisation and Business Processes dimensions incorporate a range of environmental and social targets and indicators. Performance across the balanced scorecard is reported as part of the company's triple bottom line external reports, and managers' bonuses are based on performance against criteria in the balanced scorecard. Exhibit 17.9 outlines some of the performance indicators for the People and Organisation perspective. Targets are set for each performance indicator, and the performance of the manager responsible is monitored against these targets.

Royal Dutch Shell is a very large multinational petrol company, based in the Netherlands. The balanced scorecard used at Shell contains a dimension called Sustainable Development, as a replacement for the usual learning and growth perspective. At Shell, managers' bonuses are linked to this dimension to encourage them to focus their attention on achieving these outcomes. Shell uses 'strategy maps' to articulate the cause and effect linkages between the different perspectives.

These maps allow the managers to understand how a focus on sustainable development can influence performance across the whole organisation, and create value for stakeholders. An example of the type of linkages found in the strategy map at Shell is shown in Exhibit 17.10.

Measuring and reporting social values

So far in this chapter we have focused primarily on management accounting responses to environmental rather than social issues, although Novo Nordisk and Shell provide examples of measures of social impacts. There are other examples of organisations that have well-developed measures of social performance, particularly in the human services sector of the economy, such as welfare agencies and hospitals. Given their community service roles, organisations like these will want to track the impact they have on the community.

Performance measures that focus on social and environmental issues may be developed in all types of organisations. Some organisations publish these in their external financial reports or in triple bottom line and other special reports, as management may believe they enhance the reputation and profile of their organisation. From a management accounting perspective, we are interested in understanding how these measurement and reporting systems can be used to manage and monitor operations and whether they are effective in directing the behaviour of decision makers within the organisations, from the CEO to employees at operational level.

Critical success factors (CSFs)	CSF—rationale	Key performance indicators (KPIs)
Attraction and retention of staff	High retention of employees will secure our knowledge and competitive advantage	Reduction of unwanted turnover in selected business units
Development of people	Development of people is a key objective for managers	No. of managers with development of people as a personal target
Customer relations	Improving customer retention is essential for improving sustainable business processes	No. of dialogues between patients and employees
Winning culture	Developing a winning culture will help us strive for stretch targets	No. of team targets
Social responsibility	Increasing equal opportunities and diversity throughout the entire company is one of our objectives	No. of plans for increasing equal opportunity

Source: adapted from Zingales & Hockerts (2003, p. 9)

Exhibit 17.9 CSFs and KPIs for the People and Organisation perspective at Novo Nordisk

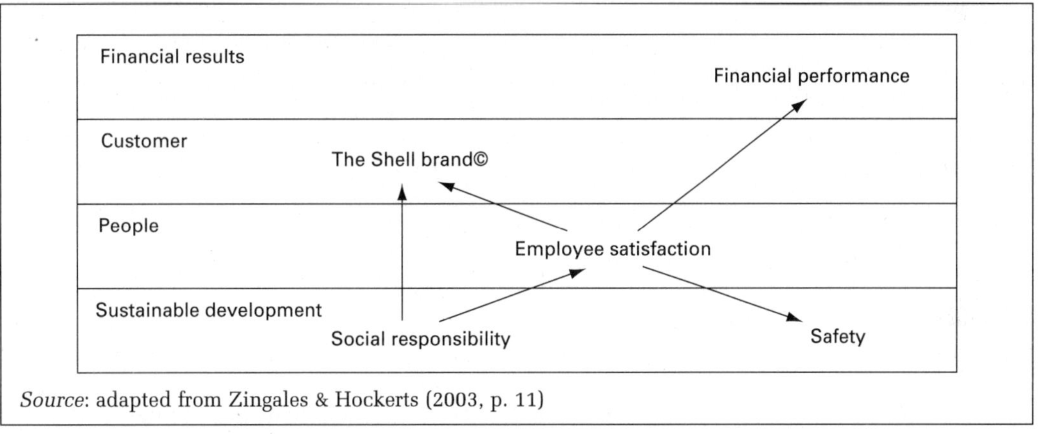

Source: adapted from Zingales & Hockerts (2003, p. 11)

Exhibit 17.10 A strategy map at Shell[6]

Social audits

L.O. 12

Social auditing is a formal process where organisations measure and report the extent to which they have operated in accordance with their stated shared values and objectives. Social auditing requires the involvement of stakeholders, such as employees, customers, suppliers and the local community, who will provide some of the feedback on the organisation's performance. The outcomes of a social audit are usually verified by an external party or panel to give credibility to the findings. Thus, the social audit provides a form of accountability to a broad range of stakeholders. An organisation may adopt this practice to enhance its reputation in the eyes of its stakeholders. Just as lapses in behaviour, real or perceived, can destroy or reduce the reputation of an organisation, a 'good' reputation can give an organisation a competitive advantage. As part of a social audit, an organisation may identify potential or existing problems and then invite stakeholders to assist in possible solutions. Another goal of social audits is to help management not only to understand stakeholder concerns, but also to anticipate them.

Environmental outcomes: capital expenditure analysis

L.O. 13

Techniques used to evaluate capital expenditure proposals are described in Chapters 21 and 22. When social and environmental factors are included the evaluation processes remain the same, except that we need to exercise care when identifying all the costs and benefits. The challenge for many organisations is that a project may not be economically viable for the organisation, but once the external costs and benefits are included it may be considered more attractive. The alternative is that a project may be viable on financial grounds, but if all the environmental costs and benefits are included it may appear less attractive for the organisation. In some situations, these analyses indicate whether the organisation is willing to put the broader interests of society above its own interests. Of course, some capital expenditures are driven by the organisation's need or desire to be environmentally responsible. These are the environmentally induced capital expenditures described in an earlier section of this chapter. In this section we will look at two examples that demonstrate how environmental factors may be accounted for in capital investment decisions.

At Cormack the energy that was consumed by air compressors was considered to be a major part of the total energy cost of the moulding process. Cormack needed to purchase a new compressor, but in the past had assumed that a more energy-efficient compressor may be too expensive.

A cost analysis revealed that, while an energy-efficient compressor would cost R175 000 more than the conventional model, it would save R45 000 per year in energy cost. Clearly, the extra cost of purchasing the energy-efficient compressor would be recovered in the first four years of its operations. Even a discounted cash flow approach (see Chapter 21) to analysing the energy savings over the 15-year life of the compressor indicated that an energy-efficient compressor would result in significant savings. In addition, the environment would benefit from the reduction in 773 tonnes of CO_2 over the 15-year life of the compressor.

In this type of decision, the identifiable benefits to an organisation could include:

- savings in energy;
- reductions in the cost of disposing of waste and emissions;
- reduced insurance and costs of cleaning up environmental damage;
- reduced materials and packaging; and
- new by-products that can be sold.

Exhibit 17.11 shows a range of less tangible factors that may be considered in making such a decision.

Our second example relates to the purchase of a piece of equipment by a furniture manufacturer. Dubbo Whitewoods, a large manufacturer of pine furniture, is considering the purchase of a paint mixer to mix paint continuously instead of in batches (adapted from the Anderson case, EPA 2000). The new mixer would also have several environmental advantages compared to the old mixer. An evaluation has shown that the new mixer would have a high initial purchase price, but would result in reductions in many costs.

The first step in the analysis is to estimate the financial costs and benefits of the purchase. Some of these are relatively easy to estimate. Exhibit 17.12 indicates that the replacement of the paint mixer would yield savings of R1 950 100 per annum. However, there are other cost savings or quantitative factors that can be identified but may be difficult to quantify.

Two examples are as follows:

- *Material handling charges.* The reduction in the use of paint and solvents results in a substantial reduction in the costs of handling and storing the materials.
- *Waste handling and storage.* Less waste will mean fewer costs in handling toxic waste products.

Management may wish to include estimates of these costs in the financial analysis. A full cash flow analysis can then be prepared for the life of the asset, using evaluation tools such as net present

Productivity	**Future regulation**
■ Product quality	■ Stricter enforcement of current regulations
■ Production throughput	■ Modification of current regulations
■ Production flexibility	■ New regulations
■ Production reliability	
■ Worker absenteeism	**Insurance**
■ Worker morale	■ Workers' health insurance
	■ Workers' compensation
Potential liability	■ General property core fire insurance
■ Business shutdown costs	■ General liability/hazard
■ Non-compliance fines	■ Environmental liability
■ Site clean-up costs	■ Unemployment
■ Legal costs	
	Company image
■ Personal injury claims	■ Access to customers and markets
■ Property damage claims	■ Access to financing
■ Natural resource damage claims	■ Public relations

Source: Tellus Institute (2000), cited by the United Nations (2001)

Exhibit 17.11 Important factors in capital investment analysis

Reductions in:	**Material reductions**	**Annual savings**
Workers' compensation:*		
Reduced insurance premiums due to reduced employee exposure to hazardous materials		R 100 000
Paint use and waste:		
Paint—purchase and freight inwards	14 100 litres	1 003 740
Waste treatment, transport and disposal		143 870
Emission investigations	600 kg	1 620
Solvents and waste:		
Solvents—purchase and freight	35 000 litres	587 100
EPA charges	1500 kg	5 600
Flush solvents:		
Purchases	10 000	106 870
Emissions	2000 kg	1 300
Total annual savings		**R1 950 100**

* Workers' compensation premiums are insurance premiums paid by the company to compensate employees if they suffer injuries during employment.

Exhibit 17.12 Financial benefits from the paint mixer replacement project at Dubbo Whitewoods

value, internal rate of return or the payback period. This analysis would take into account the initial cost of the mixer, as well as the annual cost savings.

However, there are other intangible factors that need to be considered in this decision, which cannot enter into the formal financial analysis:

- *Benefits to the environment.* The reduction in toxic emissions and the dumping of waste paint may result in significant benefits to the environment. It may also lead to local residents developing a more positive attitude towards the plant.
- *Improved labour attitudes.* The elimination of dangerous jobs of cleaning up toxic wastes not only reduces workers' compensation insurance premiums, but may result in a positive impact for employees who no longer engage in risky and unpleasant tasks.

The final decision will involve considering these additional intangible factors alongside the results of the financial analysis. The final outcome may well rest on how much management values the benefits to the environment and to the community.

REAL LIFE: TRANSFORMATION AND BROAD-BASED BLACK ECONOMIC EMPOWERMENT IN THE FINANCIAL SECTOR

The Financial Sector Charter was enacted in February 2007, in terms of the Broad-Based Black Economic Empowerment Act, 2003 (Act No. 53 of 2003). This was in terms of a commitment made by the financial sector in 2002 to achieve transformation in the sector. The charter sets out targets that should be achieved by banks and other financial institutions in relation to black ownership, human resource development, such employment equity and skills development, procurement from BEE suppliers, enterprise development and increasing the access to financial services by providing affordable banking services and providing credit to small and micro enterprises. The targets are to be achieved by 2008 and there is a Charter Council to oversee the implementation of the Charter. There is a scoring system and the charter indicates the maximum points (%) that a company can achieve in terms of each component. Companies are rated from A to E in terms of a company's level of transformation as measured by its score. Government will take cognizance of this score when awarding tenders.

Tendering to Govt.		
Score %	**Rating**	**Weighting to be given by Govt.**
<40%	E	0%
40%–55%	D	25%
55%–70%	C	50%
70%–80%	B	75%
>80%	A	100%

Standard Bank states that for the group, 'sustainable business requires the balancing of short-term results with long-term objectives and impacts—on the economy, society and environment.'

Standard Bank sets out its transformation scorecard in its 2006 *Sustainability and Black Economic Empowerment Report*, and this is set out as Exhibit 17.13. Standard Bank has increased its score from 52.94 points in 2004 to 92.31 points in 2006. Standard Bank would be classified as A-rated in terms of Broad-Based Black Economic Empowerment legislation as set out in the financial charter.

Empowerment ratings

In South Africa, Broad-Based Black Economic Empowerment (BEE) is seen as a business imperative and BEE ratings by independent rating agencies play an important role in the verification of a company's BEE status. This is particularly important for government and companies wishing to determine the BEE status of their suppliers which impacts on their own BEE score in terms of the points allocated to procurement from BEE companies. Empowerdex is a company which provides BEE ratings to the South African corporate sector and to the public sector. Empowerdex also compiles the annual *Financial Mail Top Empowerment Companies* survey which indicates the top 200 most empowered listed companies. The top 10 empowerment companies in the *Financial Mail* 2007 survey were as follows:

1 Enaleni Pharmaceuticals
2 Adcorp Holdings
3 The Don Group
4 Oceana Group
5 Hosken Consolidated
6 Sekunjalo
7 Cadiz
8 Bytes Technology
9 Metropolitan
10 Bidvest Group

	Maximum possible points	Audited results 2006	Audited results 2005	Audited results 2004
Charter category				
Human resources development	20.00	19.27	15.80	14.45
Management employment equity	15.00	15.00	12.50	11.20
Skills development spend	3.00	3.00	3.00	2.94
Black learnerships	2.00	1.27	0.30	0.31
Access to financial services	18.00	14.76	11.41	3.38
Access to financial services	8.00	6.64	5.94	0.00
Origination	8.00	6.12	3.47	1.38
Consumer education	2.00	2.00	2.00	2.00
Empowerment financing	22.00	22.00	20.11	14.09
Targeted investment	17.00	17.00	15.11	10.73
BEE transaction financing	5.00	5.00	5.00	3.36
Procurement and enterprise development	15.00	13.80	11.40	6.00
Ownership and control	22.00	19.48	18.45	12.02
Ownership	14.00	12.00	12.00	12.00
Board of directors	3.00	3.00	3.00	0.02
Control: Top 50 executive management	5.00	4.48	3.45	0.00
Corporate Social Investment	3.00	3.00	3.00	3.00
Total score	100.00	92.31	80.17	52.94

Exhibit 17.13 Standard Bank Transformation Score in terms of the Financial Charter

Socially Responsible Investing (SRI) Indices

Socially responsible investing focuses on the triple bottom line and evaluates a company's performance on three criteria: economics, society and the environment. In 2004 the JSE Securities Exchange launched its Social Responsibility Investments (SRI) Index in order to identify JSE listed companies that incorporate the principles of the triple bottom line into their business operations. The SRI Index also includes criteria in relation to corporate governance. Investors can use the SRI Index to identify companies to invest in that comply with the following three pillars:

- *Pillar 1—Environmental sustainability.* Companies are required to measure and minimise their impact on the environment. Companies should ensure the sustainable use of resources as well as seeking ways of improving operations to save on the consumption of resources. Mining companies have a large environmental impact but even companies such as banks and hotels can implement policies to achieve energy savings.
- *Pillar 2—Economic sustainability.* Although financial performance is an important component of measuring economic sustainability, this pillar goes beyond the company's current level of financial performance. The fundamental question is whether a company is taking actions to maximise its longer-term growth and its longer-term profitability even if this may imply sacrificing short-term performance. Is the company's business model sustainable in the long term? Is the company ready to change its mode of operations to take into account new economic realities?
- *Pillar 3—Social sustainability.* Companies are corporate citizens and should reflect society and its values. Companies are required to promote diversity, employment equity, transformation, and health and safety in the work place. Companies are expected to adhere to fair labour practices and are required to undertake social investments that result in poverty reduction and

social upliftment. For example, the investment in mobile clinics by a mining company in South Africa is an important contribution as mining companies have a direct relationship with communities, often in far-flung places.

In relation to *Corporate Governance*, companies should adhere to the principles and practices espoused by the King Report on Corporate Governance ('King II'). Companies are assessed on each criterion and are scored relative to their performance in each category. However, in terms of environmental sustainability, companies are evaluated on the basis of their environmental impact. There are over 50 companies that are included in the SRI Index. In April 2006 the JSE indicated that the top performers in each of the impact categories were:

- *High environmental impact category*—jointly, Anglo-American plc and AngloAmerican Platinum Ltd;
- *Medium environmental impact category*—Woolworths Holdings Ltd;
- *Low environmental impact category*—Nedbank Group Ltd.

Dow Jones Sustainability World Index (DJSI)

The Dow Jones Sustainability World Index is determined by assessing 2500 companies in the Dow Jones Global Index. Companies are ranked on the basis of sustainability criteria and the index consists of the top 10 per cent of the companies in each industry group. This is a relative ranking and only companies in the top 10 per cent of their industry sector are included so that companies may be part of the index in one year and may fall out in the following year, due to the improved sustainability performance by other companies in the same sector. For example, Standard Bank was part of the index in 2005 but its score in 2006 was not enough to enable Standard Bank to make it into the top 10 per cent of companies in the financial sector. This is something that Standard Bank is addressing and the same applies to Sasol, which won the Ernst and Young Excellence in Sustainability Reporting Award in 2006 but just missed making it onto the Dow Jones Sustainability World Index in 2006. This reflects increasing competition by companies to form part of this index. The index outperformed the MCSI (Morgan Stanley) global index in the five years to August 2006 and increasingly investors and asset managers are using this information to decide where to invest their funds.

The Dow Jones Sustainability World Index includes over 300 companies from about 58 industry sectors. The criteria used to rank companies on the basis of sustainability include the factors indicated in Exhibit 17.14.

Economic	Environmental	Social
Corporate Governance Risk & Crisis Management Anti-Corruption & Bribery Industry-Specific Criteria	Environmental Performance (Eco-Efficiency) Environmental Reporting Industry-Specific Criteria	Human Capital Development Talent Attraction & Retention Labour Practice Indicators Corporate Citizenship/ Philanthropy Social Reporting Industry-Specific Criteria

Exhibit 17.14 Dow Jones Sustainability World Index criteria

The industry leaders in terms of sustainability in 2006/07 are set out in Exhibit 17.15.

Name	Market Sector	Country
BMW	Automobiles & Parts	Germany
Westpac Banking Corp.	Banks	Australia
Norsk Hydro	Basic Resources	Norway
DSM NV	Chemicals	Netherlands
Holcim	Construction & Materials	Switzerland
Sodexho Alliance SA	Travel & Leisure	France
Statoil	Oil & Gas	Norway
Investa Property Group	Financial Services	Australia
Unilever	Food & Beverage	Netherlands
Novartis	Healthcare	Switzerland
3M Company	Industrial Goods & Services	USA
Allianz	Insurance	Germany
ITV Plc	Media	UK
Procter & Gamble Co.	Personal & Household Goods	USA
Kesko	Retail	Finland
Intel Corp.	Technology	USA
BT Group Plc	Telecommunications	UK
Veolia Environment	Utilities	France

Exhibit 17.15 Dow Jones Sustainability World Index industry leaders

There are no South African companies that are industry leaders. In fact, out of over 300 companies that make up the index, there are only four South African companies. The South African companies in the Dow Jones Sustainability World Index in 2006 were Bidvest, Investec, African Bank and Nedbank. Australia had 18 companies in the Index. Companies such as BHP Billiton, Anglo-American and SABMiller which have South African roots and a relatively high proportion of South African shareholders, form part of the Index but are classified as UK companies as their primary listing is in London.

FTSE4Good Index

The UK-based FTSE4Good Index is an index that includes companies that comply with stated corporate responsibility criteria. There are four tradable and four benchmark index series, UK, Europe, US and Global. Companies that are part of FTSE indices are eligible to be considered for inclusion. Companies that are excluded are: tobacco producers, manufacturers of whole weapon systems, companies providing parts or services for manufacturing whole nuclear weapon systems as well as owners of nuclear power stations and those mining or producing uranium. Then, the remaining companies have to comply with the selection criteria:

- Working towards environmental sustainability;
- Upholding and supporting human rights;
- Positive relations with stakeholders.

FTSE is currently introducing climate change as a criterion and will evaluate the policies and disclosure of greenhouse gas emissions and will in the next few years also evaluate the measures that companies take to achieve greenhouse gas reductions.

Conclusion

In the USA it has been estimated that the amount of SRI investments under management is over $2 trillion. SRI Indices enable investors to identify and invest in companies that practise sustainable and socially responsible business practices. For companies, inclusion in an SRI index may result in cost savings as companies focus on reducing energy bills, water use, and waste-removal costs. Further, companies are able to attract and retain talented employees, thereby impacting positively on recruitment costs and on productivity levels. Companies are also able to enhance

their reputation and create a relationship of trust with their customers and other stakeholders. Further, companies are required to consider their environmental and social impacts. Changes in policies to adhere to SRI requirements may also reduce legal, reputational and operational risks as well as future financial consequences. In any case, it is the right thing to do.

REAL LIFE: BHP BILLITON—SUSTAINABLE DEVELOPMENT POLICY

'Healthy People + Safe Workplaces + Environmental Commitment + Social Responsibility + Economic Contribution + Sound Governance = LICENCE TO OPERATE'

Although BHP Billiton's primary listing is in London, the company has deep roots in Southern Africa and Australia. The company is a mining company in South Africa and operates a number of aluminium smelters. The company's Sustainable Development Report is lengthy at over 500 pages.

We have reproduced the company's sustainable development policy below from the company's 2006 Sustainable Development Report. We have also included one of BHP Billiton's case studies regarding actions taken to protect the environment in South Africa. The company was the leading mining company in the Dow Jones Sustainability World Index in 2006.

BHP Billiton's Sustainable Development Policy

At BHP Billiton our objective is to be the company of choice—creating sustainable value for our shareholders, employees, contractors, suppliers, customers, business partners and host communities. We aspire to Zero Harm to people, our host communities and the environment and strive to achieve leading industry practice. Sound principles to govern safety, business conduct, social, environmental and economic activities are integral to the way we do business.

Wherever we operate we will develop, implement and maintain management systems for sustainable development that drive continual improvement and ensure we:

- *do not compromise our safety values, and seek ways to promote and improve the health of our workforce and the community*
- *identify, assess and manage risks to employees, contractors, the environment and our host communities*
- *uphold ethical business practices and meet or, where less stringent than our standards, exceed applicable legal and other requirements*
- *understand, promote and uphold fundamental human rights within our sphere of influence, respecting the traditional rights of Indigenous peoples and valuing cultural heritage*
- *encourage a diverse workforce and provide a work environment in which everyone is treated fairly, with respect and can realise their full potential*
- *set and achieve targets that promote efficient use of resources and include reducing and preventing pollution*
- *enhance biodiversity protection by assessing and considering ecological values and land-use aspects in investment, operational and closure activities*
- *engage regularly, openly and honestly with people affected by our operations, and take their views and concerns into account in our decision-making*
- *develop partnerships that foster the sustainable development of our host communities, enhance economic benefits from our operations and contribute to poverty alleviation*

- *work with those involved through the lifecycles of our products and by-products to promote their responsible use and management*
- *regularly review our performance and publicly report our progress.*

In implementing this Policy, we will engage with and support our employees, contractors, suppliers, customers, business partners and host communities in sharing responsibility for meeting our requirements. We will be successful when we achieve our targets towards Zero Harm, are valued by our host communities, and provide lasting social, environmental and economic benefits to society.

REAL LIFE: THE EMALAHLENI WATER RECLAMATION PROJECT

Ingwe Collieries (a subsidiary of BHP Billiton) is taking action at a closed colliery to tackle a major environmental issue. The closed mines in the area have been found to have significant amounts of contaminated water which poses a risk to the Olifants River catchment area. Environmental legislation has also placed the responsibility on mining companies to minimise the harmful effects of mining operations. In a joint venture with Anglo Coal, the company will convert the contaminated water into high-quality potable (i.e. drinking) water at a water treatment facility at a rate of 20 megalitres per day. The treated high quality drinking water will be transported to the Witbank Town reservoir where it will be blended with the town's normal water supply. The town has been facing a water shortage and this will mean that the town will not need to draw water from the Vaal River catchment area. Further, some water will be discharged into local streams to maintain flows and revive local river eco-systems. Therefore, a negative impact from mining has turned into a positive impact by providing water to the local community.

REAL LIFE: GOLD FIELDS—DEALING WITH THE HIV/AIDS CHALLENGE IN SOUTH AFRICA

Gold Fields Ltd is one of South Africa's leading gold mining companies. HIV/AIDS is a major challenge for South African society and for South African business. Most South African companies have HIV/AIDS policies in place. Gold Fields' HIV/AIDS and TB strategy consists of prevention, treatment, care and support. Yet, the company faces immense challenges and it is estimated that about 30 per cent of its employees are HIV positive. The company provides education and free condoms to workers. The company provides free testing for HIV and promotes those who test negative to protect themselves and the company's motto is 'Protect your HIV-free status with your LIFE'. For workers that test positive, the company encourages them to adopt life-prolonging lifestyle changes. Gold Fields offers treatment for all employees infected with HIV. The following case study is an extract from Gold Fields' 2006 Sustainable Development report.

CASE STUDY:

The Gold Fields ART programme

Dr Wendy Neethling, the Programme Manager, explains: 'The programme has grown exponentially, now employing eight staff members and starting between 30 and 40 employees per month on treatment. The first employee ever enrolled, on 1 January 2004, still remains on the programme. He initially had disseminated TB and a CD4 count of 21. Today, his CD4 is 486 and he still has an undetectable viral load. Amazingly, he is still taking the initial treatment regimen and has shown no evidence so far of developing drug resistance.' He is not the only one. An evaluation of the programme's efficacy conducted in 2005 by Kimera Consulting, the company's disease management advisors, found that after 12 months of treatment 83 per cent of patients had suppressed their circulating viral load to undetectable levels. They praised the results, stating 'the virological responses to ART are excellent indicating high levels of adherence, and are superior to many published results of 'first world' programmes'. Dr Neethling finds it rewarding to see employees gain weight, recover and return to work, and is very proud of their adherence to the treatment regimen. She attributes this to rigorous health education given by the registered nurse that heads up the clinic, Sr Lydia Mkefa, who is passionate about HIV and ART. A former member of the TAC, her niece died of Aids before ART became available through the government rollout programme. Sr Lydia has made it her life's mission to ensure employees accessing the programme understand their disease and treatment, and that they implement lifestyle changes. She runs a two-hour education session each morning at the clinic and, with an interactive style, facilitates debates on a range of Aids-related topics. As a consequence, patients are extremely well informed about their disease and are active participants in their disease management.

Source: Sustainable Development, Gold Fields 2006

REAL LIFE: THE BEST COMPANY TO WORK FOR

How do companies measure how they are doing in terms of attracting and retaining talented staff? Deloitte undertakes an annual survey of South African firms which requires participating firms to send their employee lists to Deloitte. Employees are randomly selected on the basis of race, gender and level in the firm. The survey addresses the following issues:

- Job satisfaction
- Leadership
- Management style
- Communication
- Relationships & trust
- Training and development
- Policies & Procedures
- Rewards, Recognition & Performance Management
- Diversity
- Change & Transformation
- Values & Culture

The top company to work for in 2005 was Pretoria Portland Cement (PPC) whilst in 2006 it was the DAV Professional Placement Group. In 2007, it was The LR Group (Pty) Ltd. Other companies in the top 20 companies to work for in 2007 included Microsoft SA, PPC, Cadiz, WesBank, and Flight Centre SA. The top three large companies to work for in 2007 were Wesbank, ABSA and Santam. We would expect companies to increasingly make use the Deloitte survey results to benchmark their management of human resources against other firms in the industry.

Source: www.bestcompany.co.za

REAL LIFE: THE FIRSTRAND GROUP—SUSTAINABILITY IN ACTION

The FirstRand Group includes companies such as First National Bank, Rand Merchant Bank, OUTsurance, WesBank, Momentum and Discovery Health. In its 2006 Sustainability Report, the company refers to cases whereby the company is applying sustainability criteria in its operations and investments.

WesBank's new head office will include lighting control which senses when a room is empty and will automatically switch off the lighting. Water from the air-conditioning system will be used for irrigating the landscape and solar energy will be used for water heating in some areas. The building will be insulated to reduce energy required for heating and cooling the building. Systems will be implemented to enable the recycling of waste products.

First National Bank has focused on reducing electricity and energy consumption at its Bank City complex. FNB installed new control equipment for lighting and air-conditioning which has resulted in the company reducing electricity consumption from 11640KvA in 2004 to 7487KvA in 2006. FNB is also extending banking services to low-income areas so that 1 in 4 branches are now in previously disadvantaged areas.

Discovery Health has over 800 000 principal members and offers members benefits of joining its Vitality scheme. There are 250 000 Vitality members that belong to gyms, with generous cost advantages and thereby promoting fitness and a healthy lifestyle amongst its members.

OUTsurance has sponsored Gauteng anti-hijacking Task Teams which has helped in reducing the hijacking of vehicles in the region by 33 per cent.

Summary

In this chapter we have explained how environmental and social management accounting can be used by organisations. Key points include:

- Corporate social responsibility involves managers taking social and environmental factors into account when making decisions, and is regarded by some managers as a key to increasing profitability and long-term sustainability.
- Triple bottom line (TBL) reporting is a form of external reporting aimed at a range of stakeholders. TBL reports on financial, environmental and social performance.
- Environmental management accounting (EMA) focuses on material and energy flow information, environmental costs, and other related cost and physical information, which are identified, collected, estimated, analysed and reported for use by decision makers within an organisation.
- Recognising environmental and social impacts can provide a range of benefits for organisations, including:
  - the attraction and retention of highly skilled employees;
  - enhancement of the organisation's reputation as a responsible and caring organisation;
  - identification of cost savings; and
  - reduction in the risk of current and future activities.
- However, environmental and social impacts can be difficult to recognise because:
  - future ecological and social issues are not yet known;

- many costs and benefits occur outside of the organisation; and
- many costs and benefits are difficult to measure in financial terms.

- Environmental costs are the costs that an organisation incurs to prevent, monitor and report environmental impacts. They can also include the costs an organisation incurs when it does not comply with environmental regulations. These costs may extend well into the future.
- The five tiers of environmental costs include:
  - conventional costs;
  - hidden costs;
  - contingent costs;
  - relationship and image costs; and
  - societal costs.
- Environmental costs can be used in a variety of management decisions. One form of analysis to is to classify costs as prevention, appraisal, internal failure and external failure costs.
- EMA techniques can improve a range of management decisions, where both cost performance is enhanced and environmental benefits are achieved.
- Environmental and social costs can be used in managing the supply chain. Suppliers' performance can be assessed in terms of their ability to deliver responsible environmental and social performance.
- Organisations can work with customers to enhance environmental outcomes for both parties.
- Performance measurement systems can include social and environmental indicators, sometimes as part of a balanced scorecard.
- Social audits are used by some organisations to measure and report the extent to which they have operated in accordance with their stated shared values and objectives.
- Environmental and social factors can be taken into account in capital investment decisions to assess a broader set of inputs into the proposal, as well as outcomes.

References

Adams, C & Zutshi, A 2004, 'Corporate social responsibility: Why business should act responsibly and be accountable', *Australian Accounting Review*, vol. 14, no. 3, pp. 31–9.

Burritt, R, Hahn, T & Schaltegger, S 2002, 'Towards a comprehensive framework for environmental management accounting', *Australian Accounting Review*, vol. 12, no. 2, pp. 39–50.

CPA 2004, *Triple Bottom Line: A Study of Assurance Statements Worldwide*, CPA Australia, Melbourne.

EPA 1995, *An Introduction to Environmental Accounting as a Business Management Tool: Key Concepts and Terms*, United States Environmental Protection Agency, Office of Pollution Prevention and Toxics, Washington, DC.

EPA 2000, *Enhancing Supply Chain Performance with Environmental Cost Information: Examples from Commonwealth Edison*, Andersen Corporation and Ashland Chemical, United States Environmental Protection Agency, Office of Pollution Prevention and Toxics, Washington, DC.

Gluch, P & Baumann, H 2004, 'The life cycle costing (LCC) approach: a conceptual discussion of its usefulness for environmental decision-making', *Building and the Environment*, vol. 39, pp. 571–80.

Gray, R & Bebbington, J 2001 *Accounting for the Environment*, 2nd edn, Sage Publications, London.

Group of 100, 2003, *Sustainability: A Guide to Triple Bottom Line Reporting*, Group of 100 Incorporated, Sydney.

Hughes, SB & Willis, DM 1995, 'How quality control concepts can reduce environmental expenditures', *Journal of Cost Management*, Summer, pp. 15–19.

ICAA 2003a, 'G H Michell and Sons Pty Ltd', in *Environmental Management Accounting: An Introduction and Case Studies for Australia*, Institute of Chartered Accountants in Australia, Sydney, pp. 55–63.

ICAA 2003b, 'Cormack Manufacturing Pty Ltd', in *Environmental Management Accounting: An Introduction and Case Studies for Australia*, Institute of Chartered Accountants in Australia, Sydney, pp. 42–53.

IFAC 1998, *Environmental Management in Organizations: The Role of Management Accounting*, Financial and Management Accounting Committee, International Federation of Accountants, Study no. 6, New York.

IFAC 2004, *Exposure Draft: International Guidelines on Environmental Management Accounting (EMA)*, International Federation of Accountants, New York.

Savage, D 2003, 'A primer on environmental management accounting', *Business and the Environment*, March 2003, pp. 2–3.

Schaltegger, S & Burritt, R 2000, *Contemporary Environmental Accounting—Issues, Concepts and Practice*, Greenleaf Publishing, Sheffield, UK.

Simms, J 2002, 'Business: corporate social responsibility—you know it makes sense', *Accountancy*, vol. 130, no. 1311, pp. 48–50.

UN, 2001, *Environmental Management Accounting Procedures and Principles*, United Nations Division for Sustainable Development, New York.

Zingales, F & Hockerts, K 2003, 'Balanced scorecard and sustainability: Examples from literature and practice', INSEAD working paper 30, Fontainebleau, France.

Self study

Self-study problem 1: Social and environmental costs

Mafube Casual Coffee has made an evaluation of the social and environmental costs of its coffee roasting facility. The total cost of running the roasting facility is R9 876 540, including R6 890 010 for the cost of unroasted beans and environmental costs of R911 730, as shown below.

Depreciation of oven fume extractor system	R43 250
Employee training costs to reduce environmental accidents	56 000
Monitoring system to detect fumes	48 910
Fine from municipality for dumping coffee grounds into the sewer	56 910
Inspection of drainage systems to detect problems with discharge	12 410
Reduction in value of nearby houses due to odour	536 510
Routine cleaning of extractor system to remove coffee residues	25 610
Disposal of waste coffee grounds	56 520
Medical costs relating to employees' inhalation of fumes	75 610
Total	R911 730

Required:

1 Identify the social costs that relate to the operation. Is there a link here between social costs and environmental costs?

2 Prepare an environmental cost analysis of the existing cost of R911 730, highlighting appraisal, prevention and failure costs.

Solution to Self-study problem 1

1 The reduction in value of nearby houses is a social cost, as is the medical cost of employees who have inhaled fumes. In the first case, the real cost is the reduction in the quality of the residents' lifestyle, but the reduction in value of the houses emphasises the potential financial loss that could be realised if the houses were sold. There is a link between social and environmental costs. The medical cost of treating employees who have inhaled fumes will be classified as an environmental cost (internal failure cost). However, it also has a social impact, as it affects the health of employees.

2 Environmental cost analysis

Prevention:		
Depreciation of oven fume extractor system	R43 250	
Employee training costs to reduce environmental accidents	56 000	
Routine cleaning of extractor system to remove coffee residues	25 610	
		R124 860
Appraisal:		
Monitoring system to detect fumes	R48 910	
Inspection of drainage systems to detect problems with discharge	12 410	
		R61 320
Internal failure:		
Disposal of waste coffee grounds	R56 520	
Medical costs relating to employees' inhalation of fumes	75 610	
		R132 130
External failure:		
Fine from municipality for dumping coffee grounds into sewer	56 910	
		R56 910
Total		R375 220

In this example, the reduction in the value of nearby houses has not been included as an environmental cost, as it does not reflect a cost incurred by the company. However, some companies may choose to include this. At this stage most of the cost relates to prevention activities. This is not necessarily a problem as these activities may help to reduce failure costs. Internal failure costs are also high, accounting for 35 per cent of the total environmental costs. Management may need to consider if there are any preventive activities that could be undertaken to minimise the need to dispose of waste coffee grounds. There may also be ways of preventing future problems with fume inhalation. Appraisal activities may need to be improved to prevent future failure costs.

Self-study problem 2: Environmental cost analysis

Jozini Foundry operates two plants, one in Saldanha Bay, on the West Coast and the other at Newcastle, in KwaZulu-Natal. There has been a reduction in demand for their products and it is not viable to operate both plants. Management need to decide which of the two plants it will continue to operate in the coming year.

A preliminary investigation shows that the Saldanha plant is able to process material at a faster rate than the Newcastle plant. However, this is because of an inefficient heating process. Transport costs are cheaper at Saldanha as it is located closer to the major suppliers. The following information relates to the two plants for the past year:

	Saldanha Bay	Newcastle
Material cost per kg of cast metal	R35.00	R31.50
Other variable operating costs per kg of cast metal	R125.00	R75.00
Fixed cost of the plant per annum	R3 750 000	R1 950 000
Net cost of closing the plant	R11 000 000	R8 000 000
Transport costs inward per kg (included in operating variable costs)	R1.50	R3.80
Lost days due to injury per annum	56	21
Number of employees	56	39
Emissions per annum	60 tonnes	45 tonnes
Waste disposal sent to landfill (per kg of cast metal)	15 kg	10 kg

Currently, both plants process 150 tonnes of castings per annum, and both plants have operating equipment that can be used for another five years with no residual value.

Required:

1 Calculate the annual running cost of the two plants and evaluate which of the two plants seems more efficient.

2 What social and environmental factors might you also consider in assessing which plant should be retained?

3 What would you recommend?

Solution to Self study problem 2

1 Financial comparison of the two plants.

		Saldanha Bay	Newcastle
Material cost:			
	R 35.00 per kg × 150 tonnes × 1000	R5 250 000	
	R 31.50 per kg × 150 tonnes × 1000		R4 725 000
Other variable costs:			
	R 125.00 per kg × 150 tonnes × 1000	R18 750 000	
	R 75.00 per kg × 150 tonnes × 1000		R11 250 000
Fixed overhead		13 750 000	11 950 000
Total production costs		R37 750 000	R27 925 000
Production cost per kg	[Total production costs / (150 × 1000)]	R251.67	R186.17
Transport costs inward per kg (included in operating variable costs)		R1.50	R3.80
Net cost of closing the plant		R11 000 000	R8 000 000

The Newcastle plant appears to be the more efficient plant, with an average production cost per kg of R186.17 compared to the Saldanha Bay cost of R251.67. This is despite the cost of transport being higher at Newcastle. It would cost more to close the plant and terminate employees if the Saldanha Bay plant were closed, but this is a one-off cost. Overall, on financial grounds the Newcastle plant seems the more attractive option.

2 While the Newcastle plant is the more attractive on financial grounds, there are other issues that the company may need to take into account:

- Lost days due to injuries at the Saldanha Bay plant average 1 (56/56) per employee, compared to 0.538 (21/39) per employee at the Newcastle plant.
- Suppliers need to travel further if the Saldanha Bay plant is closed and this entails more greenhouse emissions, which are harmful for the environment.
- The Saldanha Bay plant is more inefficient in its energy use, which is more harmful for the environment compared to the Newcastle plant.
- The Saldanha Bay plant disposes of more waste in landfill compared to the Newcastle plant.
- The company may also consider the social and economic impact on employees and their families of closing the Saldanha Bay plant, and any financial hardships that this may cause.

3 Overall, the Newcastle plant is still the more attractive option. It is not only more cost effective, it is more efficient in the waste that it produces, in its emissions and in employee injuries. The transport cost is higher at Newcastle, and this also has undesirable environmental impacts. The company may consider using more locally based suppliers.

Cybersearch

1 Find the triple bottom line report of at least one South African organisation. How might this report contribute to improving the environmental and social management practices of the organisation?

2 Find the website for BHP Billiton and find the page on sustainability. Here you will find case studies of environmental management. Select one of these case studies and outline how management accounting might assist in achieving the environmental goals of the organisation.

3 Locate the Sanlam website, and find the company's latest Sustainability Report. Review the results and consider how management might use these reports to improve Sanlam's performance in these areas of social responsibility.

Questions

17.1 Explain the meaning of corporate social responsibility and why some managers may wish to adopt this approach.

17.2 Define the term triple bottom line reporting. Explain some of the benefits that may arise to companies that provide these reports to stakeholders.

17.3 Explain the meaning of environmental management accounting and describe some of the techniques that are used.

17.4 What is an environmental management system? How does it relate to environmental management accounting?

17.5 Outline the major benefits that may arise from recognising, managing and reporting environmental and social impacts.

17.6 Explain why it is difficult to recognise and measure environmental and social impacts.

17.7 Explain why managers might wish to recognise Tier 4 and Tier 5 environmental costs, which are external to the organisation.

17.8 Provide an example of a cost for each tier of the five tiers of environment costs.

17.9 List five social and environmental costs that may not be easy to find in the management accounting system.

17.10 Explain how social and environmental cost information may change management decision making. Provide two examples.

17.11 Provide an example of how a firm might reduce environmental cost by increasing the cost and time involved in product design.

17.12 Review the criteria listed in Exhibit 17.7 that may be used to evaluate supplier performance. Which criteria could you: (a) quantify in financial terms (b) quantify in non-financial terms (c) treat only as a qualitative factor?

17.13 Outline the major types of performance indicators that may be used under ISO 14031. Provide two examples of each type.

17.14 How can the balanced scorecard be adapted to take into account social and environmental issues?

17.15 Discuss how the capital expenditure evaluation process can take account of social and environmental costs.

17.16 What measurement issues may arise for a hospital that is interested in measuring and reporting social performance?

17.17 List five different social costs that may exist in an after-school childcare centre.

17.18 An organisation is looking at a new location for its warehouse. What environmental costs might it consider and how could they be measured?

17.19 Provide three examples of approaches to addressing social and environmental factors that may: (a) increase financial costs, and (b) decrease financial costs.

17.20 Provide an example of a social and environmental impact that, if reduced, could also reduce costs for: (a) a local government council (b) a motor vehicle repairer (c) a university

17.21 Give two examples of how an organisation might reduce the cost of its services or products by increasing social and/or environmental costs.

17.22 Give two examples of how an organisation might increase the cost of its services or products by increasing social and/or environmental costs.

Exercises

E17.23 Decision making; considering social and environmental factors: manufacturer

Livingstone Bikes is looking at two alternatives for disposing of an annual production of 287 kilolitres of waste paint, both of which are acceptable to the local municipality:

- Livingstone can pay paint recyclers to remove the waste paint at a cost of R52.70 per kilolitre. The recycler would then process the waste into 5 kg of solid waste compound per kilolitre and dispose of this in landfill.
- Rent a recycling machine which strips the residues and produces 10 kg per kilolitre of waste compound, which then needs to be disposed of in landfill. The annual rent of the machine is R12 500 and the operating cost is R0.21 per kilolitre.

Required:

1 Which alternative is superior on financial grounds?

2 List five social and environmental factors that Livingstone may need to consider before selecting an alternative.

E17.24 Cost analysis: winery

Rooi River Winery has developed the following analysis of its environmental costs and revenues for the last financial year:

Employee training costs to improve the management of effluent disposal	R56 000
Scrap value of broken bottles	−125 610
Cleaning of exhaust fans	48 910
Fine for minor leakage of untreated waste into the Rooi River	125 690
Inspection of drainage systems	154 210
Restoring land where wastes were dumped in the 1980s	169 860
Study tour to California to select new equipment to reduce wastes	47 690
Developing air pollution monitoring systems	148 970
Lost sales due to poor environmental reputation	37 870
Workers' compensation claim due to poor environmental practices	56 520
Obtaining ISO 14001 certification	679 080
Total	R1 399 190

Total costs for the plant were R13 096 700 per annum.

Required:

1 Prepare an environmental cost report showing appraisal, prevention, and internal and external failure costs.

2 Use this cost report to recommend what the winery might do to improve its environmental performance.

E17.25 Life cycle costing: orchard

Vermaak Orchards and Cannery is considering buying high pressure cleaning equipment that vacuums waste liquids into a storage tank and then purifies the waste. The waste water can then be pumped back onto orchards. The system will avoid any leakage of liquid waste into the local river, which has happened once every two years, and will avoid the related workers' compensation claims that have arisen every five years. The operating characteristics are as follows:

Initial outlay for new equipment, 10-year life, no residual value	R4 893 450
Annual operating cost over 10-year life	R159 040 p.a.
Depreciation	10% p.a.
Savings in water cost due to reclaimed water	R159 870 p.a.
Total cost of cleaning and maintaining system every 4 years	R149 000
Workers' compensation claim	R55 000

Required:

1 Prepare a summary of the total costs for the waste cleaning system for the next 10 years.
2 Should Vermaak Orchards invest in this equipment even if it is uneconomic?

E17.26 Costing for decisions: refinery

An aluminium refinery in Newcastle is planning to implement an environmental management project. The project is to purchase new equipment that will lower operating costs and reduce emissions from the factory, which is currently spread over nearby residential districts.

	Additional costs	Cost savings	Reduction in emissions (tonnes of airborne particles)
Initial outlay	R2 890 000		
Year 1	1 455 000	R205 000	50
Year 2	1 300 000	205 000	50
Year 3	1 250 000	205 000	50
Year 4	1 250 000	205 000	50
Year 5	1 250 000	205 000	50

It is estimated that each tonne of emissions currently causes health costs that average R10 per annum for each of Newcastle's 50 000 residents.

Required:

1 Calculate the net financial cost to the refinery of investing in the new equipment.
2 Calculate the financial cost or benefit to the community over the five years.
3 What other information might you need to gather in order to undertake a more comprehensive analysis of the project?

E17.27 Selecting a supplier: milk producer

Cunning Custards is looking for a new supplier of milk. It needs approximately 2 000 000 litres per annum. The following data have been collected for each supplier:

	Dalby Dairies	Longreach Lite	Hughenden Herefords	Charleville Cows
Transport distance (km)	427	379	705	199
Transport costs per litre	R0.15	R0.125	R0.25	R0.05
Pesticide (litres) used per kilolitre of milk produced	15	0	5	0
Milk quality rating	AA	B	A	B
Milk purchase cost per litre	R2.05	R1.95	R2.05	R1.90
Percentage of product rejected on delivery	1.0%	5.0%	0.5%	2.0%
Antibiotic used per cow (ml per month)	50	0	10	15

Required:

1 Analyse the above financial information to decide which supplier Cunning Custards might use.

2 Consider the other information supplied, and make your overall recommendation.

E17.28 Classifying costs for environmental reporting

Classify each of the following environmental costs as relating to prevention, appraisal, internal failure, and external failure costs:

1 Medical costs of employees injured by chemical leakage.
2 Increased workers' compensation insurance following chemical leakage.
3 Decreased sales due to loss of reputation as an environmentally responsible company.
4 Cost of new waste monitoring system.
5 Cost of new environmental reporting systems.
6 Depreciation of waste emission system.
7 Fines for violation of waste disposal laws.
8 Cost of attaining ISO 14001 certification.
9 Cost of audit of EMS systems.
10 Cost of testing waste disposal systems.
11 Cost of environmental training programs for staff.
12 Salary of the environmental quality manager.
13 Engineering costs to solve environmental problems detected during process inspection.
14 Lost time to correct environmental emission problem.
15 Legal costs associated with land contamination.
16 Cost of restoring contaminated land and water.

E17.29 Environmental cost report: manufacturer

The following costs were incurred by Grouse Plating Company during June:

- Operating cost of waste reprocessing, R157 000.
- Repairs to faulty waste management equipment, R150 000.
- Cost of retraining employees in new waste management processes, R9 000.
- Cost of disposing of chemicals in landfill, R349 000.
- Cost of processing chemicals ready for landfill recalling, R280 000.
- Legal fees related to chemical spill during transport to landfill, R229 000.
- Cost of independent environmental audit, R237 000.
- Cost to achieve ISO 14001 certification, R343 000.
- Cost of protective clothing for employees, R162 000.

Required:

1 Prepare an environmental cost report highlighting prevention, appraisal internal failure and external failure costs.

2 Comment on the implications of the relative proportions of each of the four categories of environmental costs.

E17.30 Performance measurement: community organisation

Meals-on-Wheels provides daytime meals for senior citizens and disadvantaged people in their homes. It is developing a performance measurement system to monitor the performance of each branch across South Africa.

Required:

1 Identify five performance indicators that Meals-on-Wheels might use to reflect its social and financial goals.

2 Discuss any difficulties that Meals-on-Wheels might experience in gathering data to measure these indicators.

E17.31 Performance measurement: hotel

Return to the Woolloomooloo Sands Hotel problem in P12.40. For each department, provide two different examples of performance measures that could be used to monitor social or environmental factors.

E17.32 ISO 14031: manufacturer

Penrith Parts manufactures components for the European auto industry and needs to be compliant with ISO 14031. Oriana Daries has been hired by the CEO to develop a system of performance measures. So far, she has found that the company uses the following measures:

Staff occupational health and safety training	487 hours
Air pollution in Penrith district	25 ppm
Energy consumption	1278.5 kwh
Waste dumped in landfill	4.8 tonnes
Management audits of the casting plant	3 per annum
Supplier audits of environmental practices	2% per annum
Production volume	2800 tonnes of castings
Staff environmental training	57 hours

Required:

1 Assist Oriana by separating the measures into the following three categories and presenting them in an appropriate report format: (a) operational performance indicators (b) management performance indicators (c) environmental condition indicators

2 Suggest some further measures that could be added to improve the performance measurement system.

E17.33 Balanced scorecard: airline industry

The Environmental Guidelines of Lufthansa Airlines state:

Environmental protection is a high priority goal—protecting the environment is an expression of corporate responsibility. We aim for constant improvement—we adhere to environmental regulation. However, we want to do more: we employ the best available technology within the limits of our economic possibilities to continuously reduce the negative impact of our activities on the environment.

The Lufthansa balanced scorecard has the following perspectives and performance measures:

Shareholders:	*Customers:*	*Employees:*
■ Profitability	■ Customer loyalty	■ Employee engagement
■ DCF yield	■ Quality image	■ Management qualities
■ Sales growth	■ Global presence	■ Service culture

Required:

1 Explain why Lufthansa might not have included measures that address its environmental goals in the scorecard.

2 Suggest some measures that Lufthansa might include if it were to have a fourth perspective for social and environmental performance.

Problems

P17.34 Analysis of environment costs: local government

Buffalo City Council is looking at buying two new minibuses for transporting senior citizens. A bus is expected to travel 250 000 kilometres per annum, and will last 3 years, with zero disposal value. There are three types of buses that look attractive: a conventional petrol engine that can be converted to LPG, a petrol electric (battery) model, and a diesel bus. The operating information for each bus is below:

	Petrol/LPG	Petrol Electric Model	Diesel
CO_2 emissions	290 gms per km	15 gms per km	250 gms per km
Purchase price	R1 050 000	R1 770 000	R1 170 000
Maintenance costs per km	R2.76	R3.36	R5.34
Fuel consumption	35 litres per 100 km of petrol 15 litres per 100 km on LPG	10 litres per 100 km	15 litres per 100 km
Fuel price	R6.30/R 2.70	R6.30*	R6.60
Life of the engine	400 000 km	450 000 km	1 000 000 km
Cost of replacement engine	R84 000	R114 000	R210 000

*Cost of petrol. Assume that fuel costs for electric power are insignificant.

Required:

1 Consider which of the three buses is the more attractive option on financial grounds. State clearly any assumptions that you need to make.
2 Repeat the analysis again, but only taking into account the environmental criteria.
3 Write a recommendation to council outlining which bus it should purchase.

P17.35 Analysis of social and environmental costs: manufacturer

Durban Sofa Company is thinking of setting up a plant in Chengdu, China. Operating data for Durban and Chengdu are as follows:

	Durban	Chengdu
Material per sofa	R309	R237
Labour time per sofa	30 mins	90 mins
Labour cost per hour	R45.00	R9.00
Waste per sofa	15 kg	35 kg
Effective working weeks per annum per employee	40	49
Fixed manufacturing cost	R300 000 p.a.	R150 000 p.a.
Delivery time	7 days	27 days

If the Chengdu plant is opened, then the Durban plant will be closed. If the Durban plant is closed the workers will almost certainly be unemployed. There is consternation in the local community about the closure, especially among older workers. The plant appears to have few airborne pollutants and does not contaminate waterways and sewers.

Required:

1 Rank the alternatives using financial data only.
2 Rank the alternatives using only social and environmental data.
3 Write a recommendation to the board outlining the issues it should consider when making this decision.

P17.36 Life cycle costs: manufacturer

Visser Chemicals in King Williamstown wants to purchase cooling systems for its new materials handling equipment in the warehouse. The warehouse is located near a residential district so management wants to ensure that there is minimal disruption to local residents. There are three different systems currently on the market.

	System 1—water cooled	System 2—aircooled	System 3—refrigerant
Initial outlay	R275 000.00	R465 000.00	R685 150.00
Cost of coolant p.a.	R115 000.00	R0.00	R4 000.00
Maintenance costs p.a.	R45 000.00	R35 000.00	R17 500.00
Energy costs p.a.	R47 500.00	R37 500.00	R26 000.00
Waste p.a.	230 000 kilolitres of water	–	50 litres of refrigerant
Major refurbishment	R35 000.00 every 5 years	R20 000.00 every 10 years	R40 000.00 every 5 years
Sound tiers	95 db*	75 db*	55 db*
* db = decibels			

Required:

1 Prepare a life cycle analysis over the next 10 years for the three systems, taking into account all of the above costs. (If you have studied Chapter 21, calculate the NPV using a 10 per cent discount rate.)

2 Prepare a recommendation to the board as to which system it should adopt.

P17.37 Environmental cost analysis: manufacturer

Amajuba Paint Ltd produces industrial paint. Senior management has recently expressed concern at the waste management systems that are currently used at its Mossel Bay plant. During the last year, the plant was prosecuted for excessive chemical emissions as well as for leakage of wastewater into the local bay.

The financial controller, the plant manager and other members of the management team have met to discuss these issues. While there are already some environmental systems in place, the management team knows that there must be areas where performance can be improved. At the end of last year, the plant took its first step in improving environmental practices: new environmental monitoring systems were implemented, upgrades were made to production equipment, and employees were trained in responsible environmental practices. The next stage is to implement an ongoing reporting system to help monitor environmental costs. The financial controller has isolated the environmental costs for the last financial year. These are as follows:

Depreciation of plant fume extractor system	R543 000
Employee training costs to reduce environmental accidents	158 000
Depreciation on new monitoring systems to detect fumes	248 000
Cost of upgrading of production systems to reduce waste	380 000
Fine for dumping waste into the waterways	456 910
Inspection of drainage systems to detect problems with discharge	325 000
Fine for excessive emissions	600 000
Cost of legally dumping chemical waste in landfill	250 000
Routine cleaning of extractor system	25 610
Inspection of waste water monitoring systems	120 000
Medical costs relating to employees' inhalation of chemical fumes	90 000
Investigation of waste water leakage problem	250 000

Required:

1 Prepare an environmental cost report highlighting appraisal, prevention, internal failure and external failure costs for the past year.

2 Explain the benefits that may arise for the Mossel Bay plant if it analyses environmental costs in this manner.

3 Use the environmental cost report to recommend areas for improvement.
4 Explain how the company might take account of social costs in this analysis.

P17.38 Environmental cost analysis: manufacturer

Western Dairies has four plants in the Western Cape. The environmental cost reports show the following information:

Plant	Prevention	Appraisal	Internal failure	External failure	Total
Knysna	R210 000	R290 000	R1 500 000	R400 000	R2 400 000
Mossel Bay	120 000	380 000	170 000	170 000	840 000
George	1 320 000	620 000	440 000	80 000	2 460 000
Paarl	10 000	30 000	60 000	400 000	500 000
Total costs	R1 660 000	R1 320 000	R2 170 000	R1 050 000	R6 200 000

Managers in all four plants have been instructed by the head office in Stellenbosch to try to cut the wastage of milk. Wastage occurs when refrigeration fails, and where there are delays in milk collection and transport. In the past, spoilt milk was poured into open pits, but head office managers no longer believe that this is an acceptable arrangement.

The Paarl and Knysna plants are the oldest plants, and they both drain waste milk into a septic system. There is no control over airborne pollutants that result from this practice. The George plant has purchased a system where all wastes are reprocessed, and the final waste can be used as fertiliser on vineyards. The system relies on careful monitoring of waste levels. The manager of Mossel Bay monitors the waste levels in a closed vat, and waits until complete biological breakdown occurs before piping the waste onto local apple orchards.

Required:

1 Which plant appears to be an environmental leader? Be specific in any assumptions that you need to make.
2 Which plant appears to be the worst performing from an environmental viewpoint? What could be done to improve this performance?
3 A Cape Town share analyst wishes to invest in companies that are environmentally friendly. Would you recommend Western Dairies?

P17.39 Balanced scorecard; triple bottom line reporting: travel company

In Chapter 14 you may have studied Problem 14.34. This problem referred to Clean Living Ltd, a travel company that specialises in 'green tours' (package tours to environmentally sensitive destinations). Review this problem now.

Clean Living's objectives, based on the structure of its balanced scorecard, were as follows:

Perspectives	Objectives
Financial	Increase net profit
	Improve cash flow
Customer	Increase market share
	Improve customer satisfaction
Internal business processes	Improve office cost effectiveness
	Develop innovative tours
Learning and growth	Improve environmental knowledge of employees

Clean Living has now been taken over by Greenlink, which is a market leader in the provision of environmentally focused tours. The CEO of Greenlink, Barry Forest, is intrigued by the balanced scorecard that has been used by Clean Living—he has never come across this idea before. However, he is concerned that the focus of the scorecard promotes economic performance, and pays only token attention to the environmental dimension. Investors in Greenlink focus on the social responsibility aspects of the company's performance, which are an important part of its mission. Forest believes that his company should 'walk the talk' in all aspects of its operations, not just in the products that it provides.

Required:

1 Consider the structure of the balanced scorecard that has been used by Clean Living, and explain to Forest how it may be modified to take into account his concerns.
2 Be creative—use your imagination to add an environmental and social flavour to the balanced scorecard. Identify the dimensions, objectives and some possible lead and lag indicators. State clearly any assumptions that you need to make.

Cases

C17.40 Social auditing; environmental issues; ethics: manufacturer[7]

Erica Hopkins has recently joined the staff of a chemicals factory located in Welkom, Free State. She is employed as an internal auditor.

Erica is a well-respected and experienced accountant who also has a strong interest in 'green' issues. She is an active member of Friends of the Earth. For the last six years she has been living with Geoffrey Benn, a mining engineer. Geoffrey shares her concerns about the environment and is very engaged in promoting a more responsible attitude towards mining and mining communities. This has brought him into many conflicts with mine managers and colleagues over values.

Until now, Erica has been able to keep her professional work and her personal interests separate, but she is no longer able to do so. From her internal audit she has discovered that the factory is very wasteful of energy resources and is inefficient in its use of equipment and investment funds. Particularly serious is the plant's practice of depositing untreated toxic waste into a river, for which Erica believes it could incur a R50 million fine.

Senior management informs her that, as an internal auditor, she has no right to criticise how they operate the business. They stress that running the business is difficult enough, given the competition from overseas companies. They remind her that they are employing 2000 staff, and they do not wish to put their own positions or the jobs of their employees in jeopardy. There is already a high level of unemployment in the region.

Erica counters that if they ran their plant more efficiently they could save money, which could then be invested in treating the toxic waste. She also warns them that they might have to face a substantial fine for dumping the toxic waste. The managers disagree. They consider that she does not have the scientific or technological background to qualify her to judge the matter. Moreover, as managers, it is they who have to assess the risks involved, not the internal auditor.

George Holt, the financial director of the chemical factory, supports Erica privately but has made it clear that he will not do so openly. 'It is more than my job is worth,' he states emphatically.

Erica tries to appeal to George's sense of social responsibility: 'What about the health of the people in this area and the irreversible damage to the environment? What about the legacy we shall be leaving to future generations if activities like this are allowed to continue?', Erica argues.

George remains unimpressed. 'What have future generations done for me?' he snaps. 'I owe a duty of loyalty to this firm, my colleagues and the shareholders. If I blow the whistle now this plant will be seriously harmed and will either go out of business or be closed down.'

Erica is very unhappy about what she has found out. She decides to discuss her problem with Brian Hanekom, a professional accountant friend. Brian advises her to keep strictly to the accustomed role of auditing the books and not to be concerned with the other issues, such as harm to public health and the environment and the efficient use of energy resources and investment.

His advice is:

Erica, I really do not believe your role as an internal auditor is to engage in a social audit of firms. Your training and expertise is in financial auditing, and you should leave to others the question of social auditing. You will invite criticism of accountants if you go off half-cocked on this one and stir up trouble on matters that are not concerned with the traditional role of internal auditors. My advice is to keep your professional and your private concerns separate. I realise that you have a deep-felt concern for the environment and you wish to try to prevent harm being done to our beautiful country. I respect this in you, and I support you personally and privately in what you are doing as an active member of the Friends of the Earth.

Erica is in a dilemma and does not know where to turn for further professional and personal help.

Required:

1 What are the ethical issues expressed in this case? (You may need to revisit Chapter 1.)
2 Do you agree with Brian's advice?
3 Are there any ethical justifications for Erica, and other accountants who are similarly placed, to adopt a stand on 'green' issues in particular, and social auditing in general?
4 What are the likely implications for all concerned if Erica leaks information to the media on the chemical plant?
5 How should the management of the chemical factory handle Erica's complaints?
6 To whom could Erica turn for professional and personal help?

C17.41 Analysis of information for decisions: manufacturer

Parks Spice Company is considering making dramatic changes to the company. It currently has production facilities in Durban, as well as in South East Asia. The CEO, Jayne Parker, is concerned about several issues currently facing the company and she would like to solve these in a socially and environmentally sound way.

First, the major supplies of spices are imported from the small countries of Vendor and Celadon. In both countries toxic chemical sprays are used on plantations, and these sprays have a long life. The spice processors in both countries pay their employees only R9 per hour. The employees work long hours and breathe in chemical fumes, which over time may burn the lungs. Jayne is considering setting up a factory for preliminary processing of spices in Vendor. Finance manager, Cedric Blanche, believes that setting up this factory is a good idea, as the setup costs will be only R3.6 million. The current cost of processing spices at Durban is R0.99 per kg but will fall to R0.33 per kilogram if pre-processing is undertaken in Vendor. The current Durban figure is based on the following costs:

			Cost per kg
Direct labour	R57 per hour to process	126 kg	R0.452
Variable overhead	R15 per hour to process	126 kg	R0.119
Fixed overhead	R435 000 per year to produce	1 039 427 kg	R0.419
Total cost per kg			R0.990

Geoff Tureen, the production manager, believes that the quality of the final spice products will not reduce if the pre-processing is undertaken offshore.

Second, although the Durban plant currently meets the required environmental emissions standards, it has been prosecuted in the past for several violations of air pollution standards, and neighbours still complain about the smell. An improved filtering system would cost R870 000 to purchase and R52 500 per annum to run. Cedric believes there would be no financial benefits in improving the air quality since the facility meets government standards. He does not think that the new system should be purchased. The quality manager, Ravi Nath, disagrees and believes that the improvements would enhance the company's reputation and reduce discolouration of the buildings. The local newspaper has twice run stories that were critical of Parks Spice. A recent story suggested that they were also water polluters, an assertion that the company claims is untrue. No contaminated water is released into the waterways; it is all evaporated using recycling ponds and a septic system.

The third problem is continuing low employee morale at the Durban plant. The previous production manager came to the plant from the army, and ran the factory very smoothly and efficiently, but using a military style. This led to serious clashes with some of the production staff and 12 of these staff continue to be unhappy. Jayne has thought about offering these staff redundancies at a total cost of R855 000. Another alternative is to engage an external consultant to act as a mediator between management and staff, to see if problems can be resolved and to help improve the morale. The approximate cost of the consultant would be R129 000. Cedric is opposed to this as the performance indicator for staff in the company's social and environmental report is already satisfactory and is getting better every year. The money would therefore be wasted in trying to calm only 12 staff.

Required:

For each of the three problems outlined above:

1 Outline the financial, environmental and social issues that the company needs to take into account.

2 Highlight any further information that the company may need to gather before it can resolve these issues.

C17.42 Environmental performance indicators; triple bottom line reporting: insurance company

WealthWise Insurance has recently set up an internal information system to improve social and environmental practices within the company. The company has its head office in Johannesburg and offices in all capital cities and every regional city with a population of more than 50 000 people. One of the underlying principles of the company is to be socially and environmentally responsible. This principle has been in place for many years, dating back to the firm's founder, Jeannette De Villiers, who felt that she would like to contribute to society rather than simply maximising profits.

The company is a major contributor to charities, particularly those that focus on the homeless and the poor. It actively promotes environmental management in all of the company operations. It sponsors a program that provides scholarships to disadvantaged students to allow them to attend university, and it is proud to offer employment in the company to long-term unemployed and the poor. Each year it publishes a triple bottom line report that summarises its achievements across each area of performance.

Over time these activities have become a marketing strength of WealthWise. The social and environmental stance taken by the company has attracted many customers to the company. Listed on the JSE Securities Exchange in 20X4, the company has also become a preferred stock of ethical and green investment funds.

The mission statement of WealthWise states that it will aim to:

- support employees in achieving their personal and career goals;
- act in a socially responsible way when dealing with insurance clients and the general community; and
- promote a better social and physical environment for the world.

However, the current CEO, Sylvia Dludlu, thinks that the firm has become complacent and is resting on its past achievements. She is concerned that the firm has built up a reputation for good social and environmental practices but is not 'walking the talk'. There is some level of discontent among employees about the way that management treats staff, and this is impacting on employee satisfaction. There have also been negative reports in the media of its treatment of businesses in Mozambique that were damaged in the floods of 20X7. The reports claim that the company has tried to minimise the amounts paid to these businesses by strictly applying clauses in the insurance contracts that cover storm damage but not flood damage.

In 20X7 the company's net profit rose by 15 per cent to R173 million on an asset base of R1 235 million. This is the third consecutive year of increased profits. Earnings per share were 62 cents on a R2 par value share, and the market value was R5.40 per share. The board is concerned that WealthWise makes a loss on its insurance business, while its investments yield a strong return and are the main reason for the increase in profitability. Its investment portfolio includes shares in BHP Billiton, Anglo-American, Tiger Brands and Kumba Resources.

The board adopts a triple bottom line approach to viewing its performance and uses the following key performance indicators to assess company performance:

Financial:

- Net profit
- Gross insurance premiums
- Return on investment

Social indicators:

- Employee satisfaction ratings
- Percentage of women in the top three tiers of management
- Number of previously disadvantaged employees
- Customers' ethical ranking of sales staff
- Number of staff hired who were previously unemployed teenagers

Environmental indicators:

- Tonnes of paper recycled per annum
- Percentage reduction in electricity usage
- Litres of fuel per Rand of sales

Required:

1 Explain what is meant by triple bottom line reporting and why a publicly listed insurance company like WealthWise may adopt this approach.
2 Consider the list of key performance indicators used by WealthWise. Explain how these measures could be used to help achieve the mission.
3 Suggest alternative performance measures that could be included in the performance measurement system to assist WealthWise to achieve its mission.
4 Write a report address to the CEO explaining what steps she can take to encourage staff to behave in a socially and environmentally responsible way. Specifically, explain to her how the performance measurement system could be used in a balanced way to support the achievement of the company's goals.

Endnotes

1 In South Africa, the National Business Initiative (NBI) is an organisation that promotes social, economic and environmental stability. Members include many of South Africa's leading companies. See www.nbi.org.za.

2 There are also websites devoted to EMA, including the environmental accounting site of the US EPA (www.epa.gov/oppt/acctg/), the Centre for Social and Environmental Accounting Research (CSEAR) (www.gla.ac.uk/departments/accounting/csear/index.html) and the Environmental Management Research and Information Centre (www.emawebsite.org).

3 These descriptions are based on material in Schaltegger and Burritt (2000) Chapter 6, and Burritt, Hahn and Schaltegger (2002).

4 Under cost of quality approaches, internal failure costs are linked to the company's inability to meet customer specifications, resulting in product-specific rework and scrap. Under the environmental approach, internal failure is linked to production processes (Hughes and Willis, 1995).

5 If the savings over the four years were discounted to recognise the time value of money, then the net benefit would be lower. Net present value and discounting techniques are described in Chapter 21.

6 In the strategy map reported in Zingales and Hockerts (2002) there was no arrow between the brand image and financial performance. However, this would be a logical causal linkage.

7 Copyright CPA Australia. Reproduced with the permission of CPA Australia and acknowledgment of the authors.

PART 4
Information for Creating value

Part Contents

In Chapter 1 we learned that the objective of management accounting is to provide information to assist managers in managing resources and creating value. The use of information for managing resources was considered in Part 3. In this section we consider how management accounting information can be used to create both shareholder and customer value.

Cost volume profit (CVP) analysis is a simple tool that provides an overview of the effects on revenue and costs of all types of short-run changes. It helps management to understand the profit effects of changes in selling prices, costs, income tax rates and the organisation's mix of products or services. In particular, CVP analysis can be used to determine the break-even point. CVP analysis is studied in Chapter 18, in the context of a theatre company.

In Chapter 19 we consider how management accounting information can be used for a variety of tactical decisions. These decisions include accepting or rejecting special orders; make or buy (outsourcing) decisions; adding or deleting a product, service or department; and selling or processing further a joint product. Both quantitative and qualitative information may be relevant information for decisions. Decisions faced by Wings Airlines and the International Chocolate Company form the focus of this chapter.

The use of accounting information in pricing and product mix decisions is the topic of Chapter 20. The factors that influence the setting of prices are outlined, and the importance of understanding customer value is emphasised. Various pricing strategies are studied, including value-based pricing, economic-value pricing and cost plus pricing. The strategic pricing of new products is considered, as is pricing for competitive bidding. Particular restrictions relevant to setting prices in South Africa are discussed. In this chapter, consideration is also given to both short-term and long-term product mix decisions.

Capital expenditure decisions are covered in Chapters 21 and 22. These are long-term decisions and they usually take into account the time value of money. Discounted cash flow techniques, the payback period and accounting rate of return methods are techniques that are studied. A capital expenditure decision of a medical centre is the focus of Chapter 21. In Chapter 22, the impact of income taxes on capital expenditure decisions is considered, as well as the difficulty of ranking alternative investment projects. The processes used to justify investments in advanced technologies in both manufacturing and service firms are also evaluated.

CHAPTER

Cost Volume Profit Analysis

❖ Learning Objectives

After completing this chapter, you should be able to:

1. calculate the break-even point in sales units using the CVP equation;
2. calculate the contribution margin ratio, and use it to find the break-even point in sales Rands;
3. prepare a cost volume profit graph and explain how it is used;
4. use the break-even formula to determine the sales units or sales revenue required to achieve a target net profit;
5. apply CVP analysis to determine the effect on profits of changes in fixed costs, variable costs, sales prices and sales volume;
6. calculate the break-even point and prepare a profit volume graph for a multi-product enterprise;
7. include income taxes in CVP analysis;
8. describe the limitations and potential uses of CVP analysis in practice;
9. use activity-based approaches within CVP analysis and understand the limiting assumptions implicit in this analysis;
10. explain how financial planning models can be used for sensitivity analysis and to develop more sophisticated profit models; and
11. after studying the appendix, explain the concepts of cost structure and operating leverage, and measure operating leverage.

Introduction

How will KLM's profit change if it adds an additional flight on the Cape Town to Amsterdam route? How will the South African Ballet's profit change if there is a 10 per cent increase in the number of tickets sold for performances of *Swan Lake*? How many people need to attend a Johnny Clegg concert before the promoters start making a profit? Will your answer change if the location of the concert is moved from the Artscape Theatre to the Bellville Velodrome?

All these questions can be addressed by using an analytical technique called **cost volume profit analysis**, or **CVP analysis** for short. This technique can be used to determine the effects of changes in an organisation's sales volume on its costs, revenue and profit. Cost volume profit analysis can also be used to analyse the effects on profit of changes in selling prices, costs, income tax rates and the organisation's mix of products or services. What will happen to profit, for example, if SARFU increases the ticket prices for seats? In short, CVP analysis provides managers with an overview of the effects on revenue and costs of a range of short-run changes. This enables them to make decisions that will improve profitability and enhance owners' wealth. CVP analysis can also help managers to understand the implications of cost behaviour for profitability and, in this way, manage resources more effectively.

Although the word 'profit' appears in the term, cost volume profit analysis is not confined to profit-seeking enterprises. Managers in not-for-profit organisations, such as hospitals and charities, may also use CVP analysis to examine the effects of changes in sales volume and other short-run changes on revenue and costs. CVP analysis can be used as a tool by managers at such diverse not-for-profit institutions as hospitals, libraries, universities, art galleries and local government bodies. For example, CVP analysis could be used to help managers decide whether to introduce a physiotherapy clinic to their hospital's outpatient services and, if so, how many sessions to offer each week.

CVP analysis at the Cape Town Theatre Company

To illustrate the various analytical techniques used in cost volume profit analysis, we will focus on a performing arts organisation. We will call this arts company, the Cape Town Theatre Company (CTC).[1] It is a not-for-profit company and is a part of the University of Cape Town. It is run by a board of management and has full-time and part-time employees. The senior managers of the company are as follows:

- *Artistic director.* The artistic director directs a number of the plays. Responsibilities include production (wardrobe, scenery, stage management) and the management of artistic staff (actors, set designers, wardrobe).
- *General manager.* The general manager is responsible for administrative functions, such as accounting and marketing activities, and provides support for the artistic side of the company.
- *Finance and administration director.* Reporting to the general manager, the finance and administration director's responsibilities include managing the support infrastructure of the company, preparing contracts and other legal documents, designing and producing financial accounting reports, and undertaking the management accounting functions.
- *Marketing director.* Reporting to the general manager, the marketing director is responsible for promoting new plays.

The CTC is a professional theatre company with resident directors, production staff, stage management, stage designers, wardrobe staff and lighting designers. Actors are contracted when needed for individual plays.

Most of the company's performances are held at either the Baxter Theatre or Artscape. The company has two main seasons of plays each year, amounting to about 15 different plays. Each play is rehearsed for about four weeks, and 18 to 40 performances of the play are spread over a three- to six-week period.

Revenues and costs at the CTC

The CTC is not a profit-seeking company. Its primary focus is on providing a high-quality artistic programme of plays. Consistent with this objective, the artistic director acts as the chief executive of the company. However, the managers are very conscious of the company's financial constraints. Ticket sales are the largest source of revenue for the CTC but are extremely difficult to forecast or control. Box office sales for individual plays are monitored closely each day by the accounting and marketing staff. Other main sources of revenue are sponsorships of plays, special touring programs, and other organisations such as the National Lottery and the National Arts Council.

In common with many profit-seeking enterprises, the CTC has administrative functions that are needed to support the main activities. About 60 per cent of the costs of the business are administrative overheads, consisting mainly of fixed labour costs. These include the salaries of the accounting and marketing staff, and the cost of maintaining the CTC premises. The remaining costs of the business relate to the staging of individual plays. The direct costs of each play are determined as accurately as possible for budgeting and control purposes. The revenues and costs are estimated to determine a budgeted profit for each play. Some of the costs of staging a play are variable with respect to sales volume, but most are fixed. While each play usually generates a profit, the profits in total from all plays need to be large enough to support the high administrative overheads of the company. Throughout the year, the finance and administration director closely monitors the actual revenues and costs of each play in order to detect, and hopefully correct, any potential out-of-control situations.

Projected revenues and costs

During the coming summer season, seven plays are to be staged. As part of the preparation for the season, the finance and administration director has estimated revenues and costs for all productions. For example, she has estimated that the following costs will be incurred for the production of *Calypso*:

Revenue	
Price per ticket	R100.00
Variable costs per ticket	
Royalties	R18.75
Theatre rental	16.25
	R35.00
Fixed costs of the play	
Creative:	
Director	R30 000
Stage designer	25 000
Lighting designer	12 500
Extra artistic staff	5 000
Actors	350 000
Pre-production:	
Sets and props	R60 000
Wardrobe	25 000
Freight	7 500
Stage management	89 000
Set up and demolish stage	20 000
	R624 000

Importance of recognising different cost behaviours

Notice that the costs of the play have been categorised according to their cost behaviour: fixed or variable. Analysing an organisation's cost behaviour (the topic of Chapter 3) is a necessary first step in any cost volume profit analysis. For the CTC play, only two costs are considered to be variable with respect to sales volume: royalties that are paid to the author of the play, and theatre rental. Both these costs are paid on the basis of the number of tickets sold. Included in the fixed costs are the salary costs of the creative staff, including the actors and director. You may remember from examples in Chapter 3 that in many companies the rental of offices or buildings is considered fixed, while labour costs are often treated as variable with respect to the level of activity. Thus it is important to realise that the classification of costs as variable or fixed depends on how those particular costs behave in the organisation in question.

In Chapter 3 we also recognised that in many organisations costs may be driven by a range of cost drivers, rather than simply by production volume as is assumed in the conventional variable and fixed cost classification. Later in this chapter we consider how to accommodate a range of cost drivers in CVP analysis.

The break-even point

As the first step in the CVP analysis for the Cape Town Theatre Company, we will find the break-even point for the play *Calypso*. The **break-even point** is the volume of sales at which the total revenues and costs are equal. At this level of sales, there is no profit or loss; the operation *breaks even*. The break-even point can be calculated for an entire organisation or, as in the CTC example, for individual projects or activities that an organisation undertakes.

The break-even formula

L.O. 1

Calypso will break even when the revenue from ticket sales is equal to the total cost of staging the play. We know that profit can be calculated as sales revenue minus costs, and that these expenses consist of variable and fixed costs:

$$\text{Sales revenue} - \text{variable costs} - \text{fixed costs} = \text{profit}$$

This equation can be restated as follows:

$$\begin{pmatrix}\text{unit} & & \text{sales}\\ \text{sales} & \times & \text{volume}\\ \text{price} & & \text{in units}\end{pmatrix} - \begin{pmatrix}\text{unit} & & \text{sales}\\ \text{variable} & \times & \text{volume}\\ \text{cost} & & \text{in units}\end{pmatrix} - \text{fixed costs} = \text{profit} \qquad (1)$$

To find the play's break-even volume of tickets, the profit in equation (1) will equal zero:

$$(\text{R}100 \times X) - (\text{R}35 \times X) - \text{R}624\,000 = 0$$

where X denotes the number of units of sales (tickets) required to break even. This equation can be solved for X:

$$\text{R}100X - \text{R}35X - \text{R}624\,000 = 0$$

$$\text{R}65X = \text{R}624\,000$$

$$X = 9600 \text{ tickets}$$

Therefore, the CTC must sell 9600 tickets for the play to break even.

We can check this answer by constructing a profit statement for the play, for sales of 9600 tickets:

Sales revenue	9600 × R100.00	R960 000
Variable costs	9600 × R35.00	336 000
Total contribution margin		R624 000
Fixed costs of the play		624 000
Profit from the play		R0

Thus the play will make zero profits, or break even, when it sells 9600 tickets. Note that this profit statement segregates the variable and fixed costs, and can be termed a **contribution margin** (or **variable costing**) statement.[2] The **total contribution margin** is the difference between the sales revenue and the variable costs. It is the amount available to cover fixed costs and then contribute to profits.

An alternative way of calculating the break-even point is to emphasise the **unit contribution margin**, which is the difference between sales price per unit and variable cost per unit. In the CTC example, each ticket sells for R100, but R35 of this is used to cover the variable cost per ticket. This leaves R65 per ticket as the *unit contribution margin.* Equation (1) can be reconsidered:

$$\left(\begin{matrix}\text{unit}\\\text{sales}\\\text{price}\end{matrix} \times \begin{matrix}\text{sales}\\\text{volume}\\\text{in units}\end{matrix}\right) - \left(\begin{matrix}\text{unit}\\\text{variable}\\\text{cost}\end{matrix} \times \begin{matrix}\text{sales}\\\text{volume}\\\text{in units}\end{matrix}\right) - \text{fixed costs} = \text{profit}$$

Sales volume in units can be isolated on the left-hand side of the equation, and, as we are determining the break-even point, profits will equal zero:

$$\begin{matrix}\text{sales}\\\text{volume}\\\text{in units}\end{matrix} \times \left(\begin{matrix}\text{unit}\\\text{sales}\\\text{price}\end{matrix} - \begin{matrix}\text{unit}\\\text{variable}\\\text{cost}\end{matrix}\right) - \text{fixed costs} = 0$$

The unit contribution margin is now recognised, and fixed costs are moved to the right-hand side of the equation:

$$\text{Sales volume in units} \times \text{unit contribution margin} = \text{fixed costs}$$

Thus, after dividing both sides of the equation by the unit contribution margin, the general formula for calculating the break-even point in sales units can be determined:

$$\text{Break-even point (in units)} = \frac{\text{fixed costs}}{\text{unit contribution margin}} \qquad (2)$$

Applying the data for the play, the break-even point can be calculated:

$$\text{Break-even point (in units)} = \frac{\text{fixed costs}}{\text{unit contribution margin}}$$

$$= \frac{\text{R624 000}}{\text{R65}}$$

$$= 9600$$

Contribution margin ratio

L.O. 2 Sometimes management prefers to calculate the break-even point in sales *Rands* rather than *units.* The break-even point for the play in sales Rands is calculated as follows:

Break-even point in units (tickets)		9 600
Sales price per unit	×	R100
Break-even point in sales Rands		R960 000

There is also a formula for determining the break-even point in sales Rands:

$$\text{Break-even point (in sales Rands)} = \frac{\text{fixed costs}}{\text{unit contribution margin/unit sales price}}$$

$$= \frac{\text{R624 000}}{0.65}$$

$$= \text{R960 000}$$

The unit contribution margin divided by the unit sales price (R65/R100) is called the **contribution margin ratio** (0.65 in this example). This ratio can also be expressed as a **contribution margin percentage** (65 per cent here). Thus, the break-even point in sales Rands may be calculated by dividing the fixed costs by the contribution margin ratio. The logic behind this approach is that 65 per cent of each sales Rand is available to make a contribution towards covering fixed costs, and generating profit. The general formula is as follows:

$$\text{Break-even point (in sales Rands)} = \frac{\text{fixed costs}}{\text{unit contribution margin ratio}} \qquad (3)$$

Equations (2) and (3) are two equivalent formulas for finding the break-even point. Both methods reach the same conclusion, so personal preference dictates whether the break-even point is calculated in terms of sales units or sales Rands.

Graphing cost volume profit relationships

L.O. 3 While the break-even point may convey useful information to management, it does not show how costs, revenue or profits change as sales volume changes. To illustrate these relationships, a **cost volume profit (CVP) graph** may be used. The steps below are used to prepare a CVP graph for the play *Calypso*. The graph is displayed in Exhibit 18.1. Notice that the graph shows the relevant range, which is the range of sales volume for which the cost behaviour is assumed to be valid. The marketing director expects the number of seats sold for the play to be between 7000 and 12 000, so estimates for the variable and fixed costs for the play were developed for that range of sales volume.

Step one: Draw the axes of the graph.
Label the vertical axis in Rands and the horizontal axis in units of sales volume (tickets sold). (Note that in CVP analysis, costs are assumed to be fixed or variable with respect to production volume, and production volume is assumed to be equal to sales volume.)

Step two: Draw the fixed cost line.
This is parallel to the horizontal axis, since fixed costs are assumed not to change despite changes in sales volume.

Step three: Draw the total cost line.
First, calculate total costs at any volume. For example, select a volume of 8000 tickets:

Variable costs	8000 × R 35.00 per ticket	280 000
Fixed costs of the play		624 000
Total costs (at 8000 tickets)		R904 000

Plot this point (R904 000 at 8000 tickets) on the graph—see point A on the graph in Exhibit 18.1. Second, draw the total cost line passing through point A and the intercept of the fixed cost line on the vertical axis (R624 000). The difference between this line and the fixed cost line is equal to variable costs.

Step four: Draw the total revenue line.
First, calculate total sales revenue at any convenient volume. We will choose 8000 tickets again. Total revenue is R800 000 (8000 × R100 per ticket). Plot this point (R800 000 at 8000 tickets) on the graph—see point B on the graph in Exhibit 18.1. Second, draw the total revenue line passing through point B and the origin.

Step five: Find the break-even point.
This occurs at the intersection of the total revenue line and the total cost line.

Interpreting the CVP graph

Several conclusions can be drawn from the CVP graph in Exhibit 18.1.

Break-even point

The break-even point in units, and in sales Rands, can be determined by the coordinates of the point at the intersection of the total revenue line and the total cost line. The play breaks even at

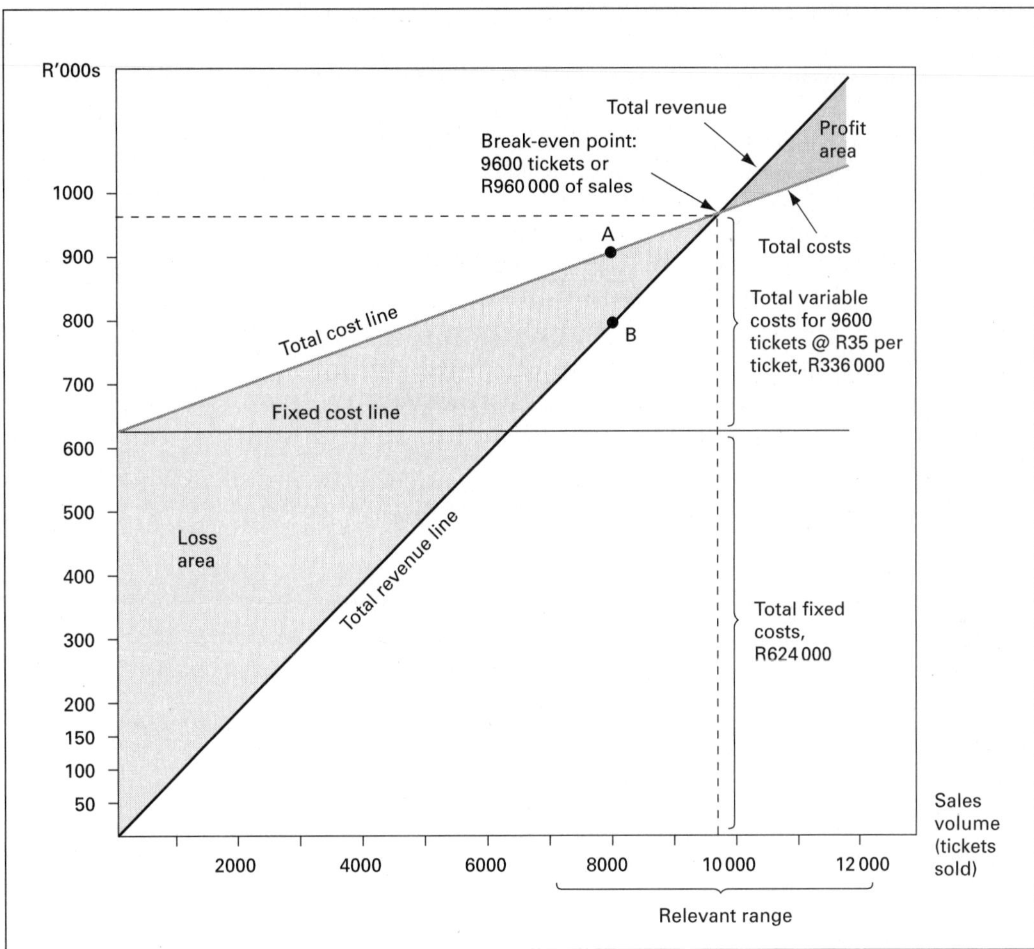

Exhibit 18.1 Cost volume profit graph, Cape Town Theatre Company production of *Calypso*

9600 tickets or R960 000 of ticket sales. This corresponds with our calculations in the preceding section.

Profit and loss areas

The CVP graph discloses more information than does the break-even calculation. From the graph, we can see the effects on profit of changes in volume. The vertical distance between the total revenue and total cost lines in the graph represents the profit or loss at a particular sales volume. If the CTC sells fewer than 9600 tickets for the play, the organisation will suffer a loss. The magnitude of the loss increases as ticket sales decline. The CTC will make a profit on the play only if sales exceed 9600 tickets.

Implications of the break-even point

The level of the break-even point provides important information to management. Let's assume that the play will be staged at the Baxter Theatre, which seats 660 people. The CTC has planned 19 performances of the play, and on average about 80 per cent of seats will be filled for each performance. Thus, while the maximum number of tickets that can be sold for the run of the play is 12 540 (660 seats × 19 performances), based on past experience only about 10 032 seats (12 540 × 80 per cent) will be sold. Notice how, in this example, the play's break-even point (9600 tickets) is close to the probable sales volume. This would be a cause for concern in a company like the CTC, which has limited financial resources.

What could management do to improve this situation? One possibility is to schedule additional performances.[3] However, this might not be feasible due to the non-availability of the theatre or actors. Also, these performances may entail additional fixed costs such as increased payments for the actors and production crew, and there is no guarantee that enough tickets for the additional performances would be sold to cover extra fixed costs. Other possible solutions are to raise ticket prices or to reduce costs. These issues will be explored later in the chapter.

The CVP graph will not resolve this potential problem for the management of the CTC but it will direct management's attention to the situation.

Profit volume graph

Another approach to graphing cost volume profit relationships is displayed in Exhibit 18.2. This **profit volume (PV) graph** highlights the total amount of profit or loss at different sales volumes. Notice that the graph intercepts the vertical axis at the amount equal to fixed costs. The graph crosses the horizontal axis at the break-even point. The vertical distance between the horizontal axis and the profit line, at a particular level of sales volume, is the profit or loss at that volume.

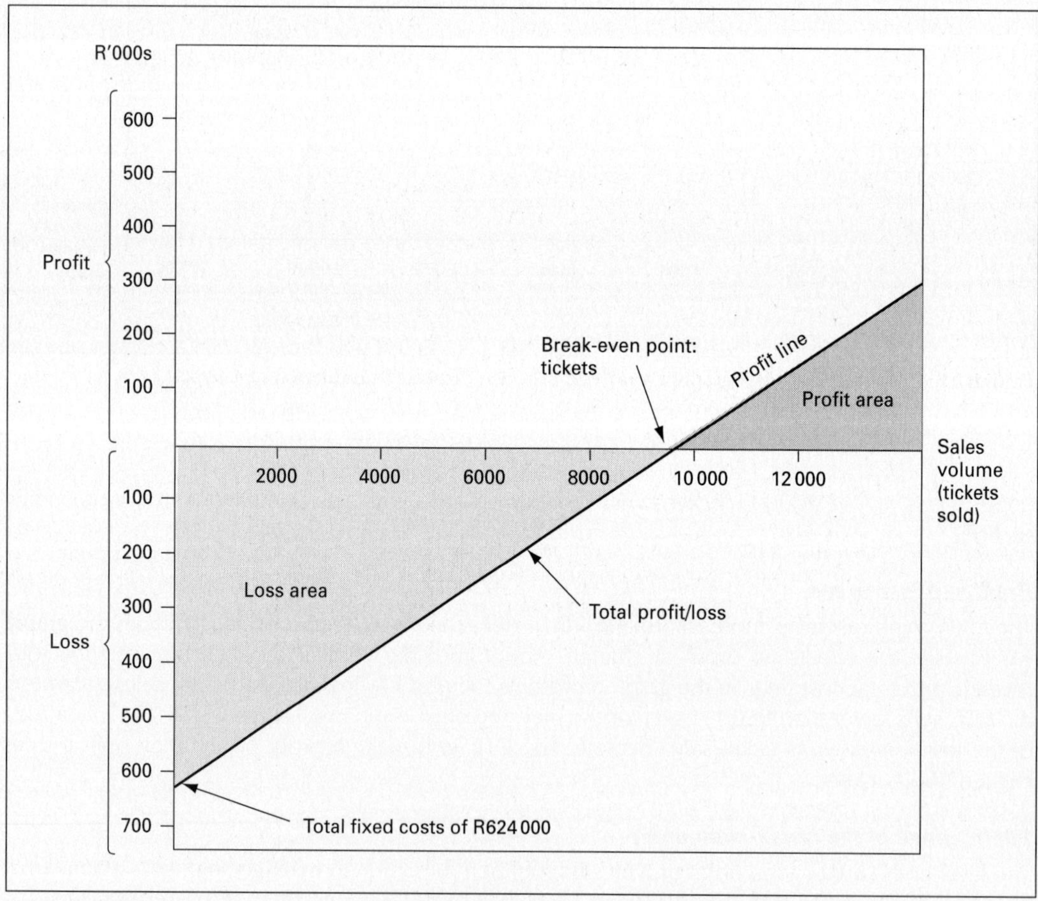

Exhibit 18.2 Profit volume graph, Cape Town Theatre Company production of *Calypso*

The hospitality industry makes extensive use of cost volume profit analysis, especially in managing hotels, as discussed in the 'Real life' that follows.

REAL LIFE: CVP ANALYSIS IN THE HOSPITALITY INDUSTRY

Major hotel management companies in South Africa depend on a variety of management accounting information to manage their internal operations. Management decision-making depends on a good understanding of the drivers of revenue and cost. CVP analysis and contribution margin analysis are used to manage the yield of a hotel. The concept of yield used in the hotel management industry is similar to that used in the airline industry. Yield management in the hotel industry is the maximisation of revenue through balancing room rates and occupancy rates. In the accommodation business, the variable cost per room is low, so the contribution margin per room is high. This leads to considerable flexibility in setting room rates. Thus, CVP analysis can be used to determine the number of room nights to sell in order to break even at a minimum staff structure. Through recognising cost structures, the effect on profit of changes in room prices and occupancy rates can be determined easily.

The hotel sector in South Africa is experiencing high occupancy rates. Globally, the hotel sector is also performing well. In the USA the profit per room was estimated to be $6005 in 2007, while this was only $3803 in 2004. The increase in profitability has been due to the industry being able to reduce fixed costs such as taking advantage of lower interest charges, the elimination of middle-management positions, and the reduction in the number of employees needed per 100 occupied rooms. Internet bookings and other uses of technology have also resulted in lower costs. The net effect of reducing fixed costs has been to reduce the occupancy rate required to break even. PWC reported that, in 1990, the required occupancy level was 65 per cent, whilst in 2007 the required occupancy level to break even was only 52 per cent. The estimated occupancy level in the USA was 63 per cent in 2007. In South Africa the City Lodge group of hotels achieved an occupancy level of 82 per cent in 2007. When you consider that the City Lodge caters mainly to the business travellers, thereby resulting in slower demand over weekends, this is really a major achievement. This has been reflected in the change in City Lodge's share price in the five years to 2007.

Of course, hotels may change room rates throughout the day depending on the probability of having empty rooms for the night. So later on in the day, room rates may fall.

Airlines use information systems to determine the probability of filling planes on certain days of the week and prices may reflect the weaker demand for flights on certain days. For example, Mondays and Fridays tend to be more expensive due to higher demand on these days. Why not go to www.flymango.com and check out a destination's prices—make a note and come back to the site the next day and see if prices have changed.

Source: Glenn Haussman, 'Profits up, but not like they could be', 15 December 2006, see www.hotelinteractive.com. Also, see presentation by Bjorn Hanson at the 2007 Americas lodging investment summit—presentation under Hospitality & Leisure, publications at www.pwc.com.

Target net profit

L.O. 4 The break-even point formula can be used to determine the sales units or sales revenue required to achieve a target profit. A **target profit** is a desired profit level determined by management.

The board of management of the CTC would like to run a series of free workshops for young actors and aspiring playwrights, but it is only willing to do this if it can generate sufficient profits from the play to cover the costs of the workshops: teachers' salaries and rental of space at a local college. If the CTC makes a surplus of R70 000 from the play, then the workshops can be held. The board has asked the finance and administration director to determine how many theatre tickets must be sold during the play's run to make a target net profit of R70 000.[4] We will use R70 005 to avoid rounding effects.

Modifying the break-even formula

The problem of calculating the volume of sales required to earn a particular target net profit is very similar to the problem of finding the break-even point. After all, the break-even point is merely the sales volume (in units or Rands) required to earn a target net profit of zero. The formula in equation (2) can be modified to include the target profit:

$$\text{Target sales volume (in units)} = \frac{\text{fixed costs} + \text{target profit}}{\text{unit contribution margin}} \tag{4}$$

$$= \frac{\text{R624 000} + \text{R70 005}}{\text{R65}}$$

$$= 10\,677 \text{ units}$$

Thus, if the CTC sells 10 677 tickets for the play, it will make a profit of R70 005, which can be used to fund the drama workshops. The total Rand sales required to earn a target net profit can be found by multiplying the required sales of 10 677 tickets by the ticket price of R100. Alternatively, the formula in equation (3) can be modified:

$$\text{Target sales volume (in Rands)} = \frac{\text{fixed costs} + \text{target profit}}{\text{contribution margin ratio}} \tag{5}$$

$$= \frac{\text{R624 000} + \text{R70 005}}{0.65}$$

$$= \text{R1 067 700}$$

The graphical approach

The profit volume graph in Exhibit 18.2 can be used to find the sales volume required to earn a target net profit. First, locate the target net profit of R70 005 on the vertical axis. Then move horizontally until the profit line is reached. Finally, move down from the profit line to the horizontal axis to determine the required sales volume (10 677 tickets).

Using CVP analysis for management decision-making

L.O. 5 The cost volume profit relationships that underlie break-even calculations and CVP graphs have wide-ranging applications for management decisions. We will look at several common applications.

Safety margin

The safety margin of an enterprise is the difference between the budgeted sales revenue and the break-even sales revenue. The marketing director of the CTC expects 80 per cent of all seats to be sold for the play *Calypso*. Therefore, the budgeted sales revenue is R1 003 200 (660 seats × 19 performances of each play × 0.80 × R100 per ticket). Since break-even sales revenue is R960 000, the organisation's safety margin is R43 200 (R1 003 200 − R960 000). The safety margin gives management a feel for how close projected operations are to the break-even point. The safety margin concept is discussed in greater detail in the appendix to this chapter.

Changes in fixed costs

When undertaking CVP analysis it should be remembered that fixed costs are only fixed in the short term. When estimates of fixed costs are revised, this will change the break-even point. In other situations we may recognise different estimates of fixed costs for different levels of sales volume. This will result in more than one break-even point. These two cases will be considered separately.

Revised estimates of fixed costs

What would happen to the break-even point if estimates of fixed costs changed? In the case of the play *Calypso*, suppose that the initial estimate for setting up and demolishing the stage, R20 000, is now considered too low. The stage manager has just found out that the sets have to be struck and transported from the theatre immediately after the last performance of the play instead of the next morning. This will attract higher wages (overtime rates) and, with the higher cost of transporting the scenery and equipment, will increase the cost by R40 000. The break-even calculations based on both the original and the new estimate of fixed costs are as follows:

		Original estimate	New estimate
Set up and demolish stage		R20 000	R60 000
Total fixed costs		R624 000	R664 000
Break-even calculation		R624 000 / R65.00	R664 000 / R65.00
Break-even point (units ie. No. of tickets)	=	9 600	10 215
Price	×	R100.00	R100.00
Break-even point (Rands)		R960 000	R1 021 500 *

* If we use a contribution margin of 0.65, then B/E (Rands) = R664 000/0.65 = R1 021 538 (slight difference due to rounding)

The estimate of fixed costs has increased by 6.4 per cent, since the increase in costs of R40 000 is 6.4 per cent of R624 000. Notice that the break-even point also increased by 6.4 per cent—the additional 615 (10215–9600) tickets that must be sold are equal to 6.4 per cent of 9600 tickets. This relationship will always exist.

$$\text{Break-even point (in units)} = \frac{\text{fixed costs}}{\text{unit contribution margin}}$$

$$\text{Break-even point (in units)} \times 1.064 = \frac{\text{fixed costs} \times 1.064}{\text{unit contribution margin}}$$

Recognising step-fixed costs

It can be seen from Exhibit 18.1 that the estimate of fixed costs for *Calypso* is constant for sales volumes between 7000 and 12 000 tickets—that is, for the relevant range. However, management may also be interested in knowing the break-even point for sales volumes outside this range. If the number of planned performances of the play were to decrease from 19 to 10, the number of tickets sold would fall below 7000. Management may decide to negotiate lower rates for the actors in order to reduce the fixed costs of the play. Let's assume that the estimated fixed costs are R390 000 for sales volumes of less than 7000 tickets.

Where two levels of fixed costs are recognised, two break-even points may be calculated. We saw earlier that for sales between 7000 and 12 000 tickets, the break-even point is 9600 tickets.

For the lower volume of sales, the break-even point is calculated as follows:

$$\text{Break-even point} = \text{R390 000/R65}$$
$$= \text{6000 tickets}$$

The graph illustrating the two break-even points is shown in Exhibit 18.3. Note that as the fixed costs are stepped, the total cost line is also stepped. In this example, the point of discontinuity is 7000 tickets. The graph indicates that if the sales volume is likely to be less than 7000 tickets, then the CTC needs to ensure that it sells more than 6000 tickets for the play in order to recover its costs. However, if the volume of tickets sold is 7000 or greater, then the level of fixed costs will be higher, and the play will not yield a profit unless it sells more than 9600 tickets.

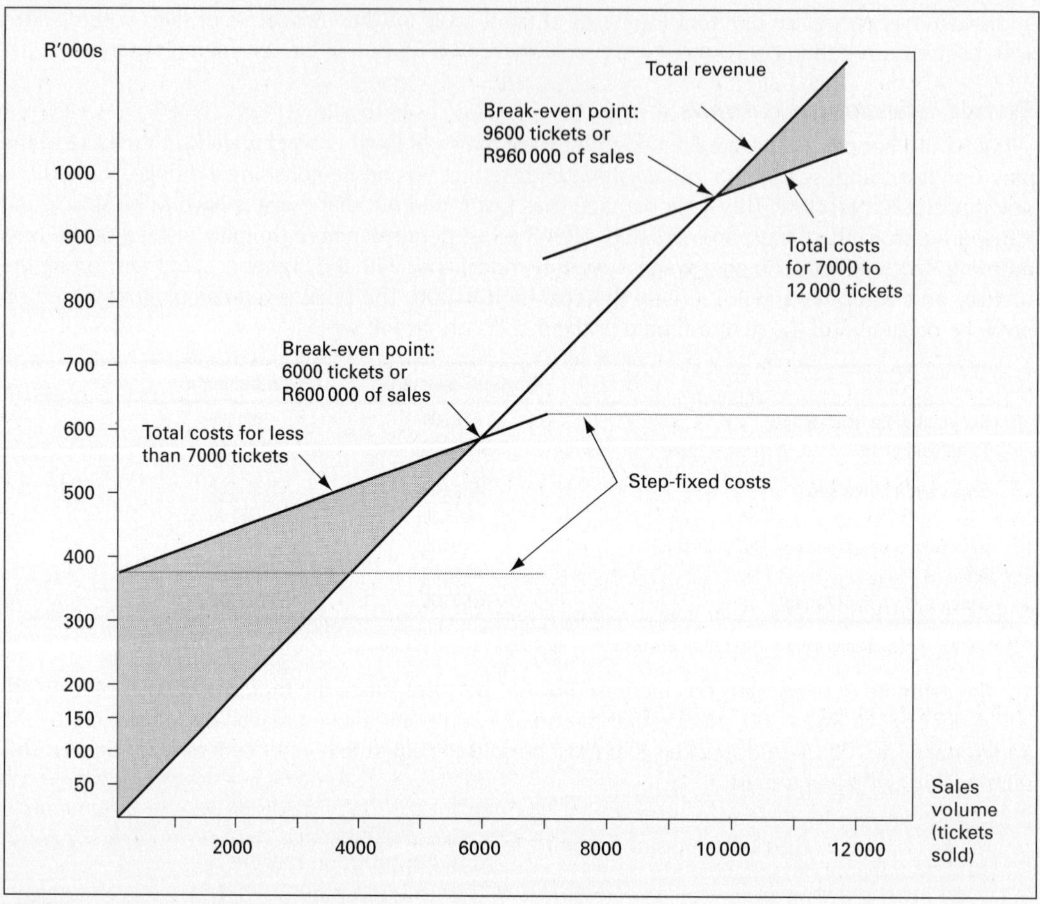

Exhibit 18.3 Cost volume profit graph with step-fixed costs, Cape Town Theatre Company production of *Calypso*

Changes in the unit contribution margin

What would happen to the play's break-even point if the cost of the theatre rental increased by R6.25 per seat (that is, per ticket sold)? What would be the effect if the ticket price increased from R100 to R110? These two situations will be considered separately.

Change in unit variable costs

If the variable costs per ticket for the play increase from R35 to R41.25 because of the increased cost of renting the theatre, the unit contribution margin will fall from R65 to R58.75.

The original and new break-even points are calculated as follows:

		Original estimate	New estimate
Variable costs per ticket		R35.00	R41.25
Unit contribution margin per ticket		R65.00	R58.75
Break-even calculation		R624 000	R624 000
		R65.00	R58.75
Break-even point (units ie. No. of tickets)	=	9 600	10 622 [rounded-up]
Price	×	R100.00	R100.00
Break-even points (Rands)		R960 000	R1 062 200 *

* If we use a contribution margin of 0.5875, then B/E (Rands) = R624 000/0.5875 = R1 062 128 (slight difference due to rounding)

If this increase in unit variable costs occurs, the play would not break even unless the CTC was able to sell more than the expected 80 per cent of seats for each performance. While a total of 12 540 seats are available (660 seats × 19 performances), only 10 032 (80 per cent) are likely to be sold. Once again, CVP analysis will not solve this problem for management, but it will direct management's attention to potentially serious difficulties.

Change in sales price

Changing the unit sales price will also alter the unit contribution margin. Suppose the management of the CTC raises the ticket price from R100 to R110 per seat. This change will increase the unit contribution margin from R65 to R75. A R10 increase in the ticket price will lower the break-even point from 9600 tickets to 8320 tickets (R624 000 ÷ R75). Is the increase in prices desirable? A lower break-even point decreases the risk of loss if sales volume decreases. However, higher ticket prices may discourage some people from buying tickets. It could be that the company may make higher profits by not increasing the ticket price. Ultimately, the decision to increase the ticket price depends on management's assessment of the likely effect on ticket sales.

Management's decision about the ticket price increase will also be influenced by the values and mission of the CTC. The CTC was formed to bring drama to the people of Cape Town. The lower the ticket price, the more accessible are the theatre's productions to people of all income levels. An increase in ticket price may conflict with the overall mission of the company. While CVP analysis provides valuable information, it is only one of several elements that will influence management's decisions.

Multiple changes in key variables

To stimulate demand for its play, suppose that management is considering decreasing ticket prices from R100 to R90 per seat, and engaging in an advertising campaign to promote the play. The campaign will cost R26 000 and increase the fixed costs to R650 000. These actions are expected to increase ticket sales from 10 032 to 12 500 for the play. What effect will these changes have on profit? The calculations are as follows:

Ticket price	Unit contribution margin	Forecast demand	Fixed costs of the play
R100.00	R65.00	10 032	R624 000
R90.00	R55.00	12 500	R650 000

The expected profit under the two scenarios is calculated below:

		Ticket price	
		R100.00	**R90.00**
Sales revenue:			
Currrently	10 032 × R100.00	R1 003 200	
New	12 500 × R90.00		R1 125 000
Less Variable costs:			
Currently	10 032 × R35.00	R351 120	
New	12 500 × R35.00		R437 500
Total contribution margin		R652 080	R687 500
Less Fixed costs of the play		R624 000	R650 000
Profit		R28 080	R37 500

The difference in expected profit at the two ticket prices, R9420 (37 500 − 28 080), is due to three factors:

1 The unit contribution margin decreased from R65 to R55 per unit.

2 Sales volume increased by 2468 (12 500 − 10 032) tickets.

3 The fixed costs of the play increased by R26 000 (650 000 − 624 000).

Incremental approach

Rather than presenting the entire profit calculation under each alternative ticket price, we can use an incremental approach. This analysis focuses on the *difference* in the total contribution margin, fixed costs and profits under the two alternatives. If the price is decreased to R90 per ticket:

Expected contribution margin @ R90 ticket price: 12 500 × (R90 − R35)	R687 500
Expected contribution margin @ R100 ticket price: 10 032 × (R100 − R35)	R652 080
Increase in total contribution margin	R35 420
Increase in fixed costs	R26 000
Total increase in profits	R9 420

The expected total contribution margin is R35 420 higher with the R90 ticket price following increased ticket sales, but this is offset by increases in fixed costs of R26 000 due to an advertising campaign. As discussed later in this chapter, businesses tend to use spreadsheet modelling to assess the possible effects of changes in the variables underlying the profit equation, especially where multiple changes are involved.

Even though the CTC is not a profit-making organisation, it may still have strong reasons for wanting to increase profit on its plays. For example, the board needs to consider the administrative overheads that must be covered; it may need to accumulate cash reserves to be used in difficult times; or perhaps it would like to use profits to provide free outdoor plays for the people of Cape Town.

L.O. 6

CVP analysis with multiple products

CVP examples often assume that an organisation or a project has only one product. Most firms have more than one product, but to include multiple products increases the complexity of the analysis. Let's suppose that the management of the CTC have decided to adopt a different pricing strategy. They will offer two different seat prices for performances of *Calypso*. Tickets in A reserve seats will cost R125 and in B reserve seats will cost R85. B reserve seats have reduced visibility of the stage compared with A reserve seats, and are located at the back of the theatre or the ends of the seating rows. The following data are estimated for the two seat types:

Seat type	Unit ticket price	Unit variable cost	Unit contribution margin	Number of seats in theatre
A	R125	R35	R90	495
B	R85	R35	R50	165

Notice that 75 per cent of the available theatre seats are A reserve, and 25 per cent are B reserve. This is called the **sales mix**, which, for any organisation selling multiple products, is the relative proportion of each type of product sold. The sales mix is an important assumption in multi-product CVP analysis, as it is used to calculate a **weighted average unit contribution margin**. This is the average of the products' unit contribution margins, weighted by the relative sales proportion of each product. The weighted average unit contribution margin for the play is calculated as follows:

$$\text{Weighted average unit contribution margin} = (\text{R}90 \times 75\%) + (\text{R}50 \times 25\%)$$
$$= \text{R}80$$

The break-even point in units for the play is calculated using the following equation:

$$\text{Break-even point} = \frac{\text{fixed costs}}{\text{weighted average unit contribution margin}} \qquad (6)$$

$$= \frac{\text{R624 000}}{\text{R80.00}}$$

$$= 7800 \text{ tickets}$$

The break-even point of 7800 tickets must be interpreted in light of the sales mix. The play will break even if 7800 tickets are sold as follows:

A reserve: 7 800 × 75%	5 850 tickets
B reserve: 7 800 × 25%	1 950 tickets
	7 800 tickets

We can check the break-even point:

Sales revenue:		
A reserve seats:	5 850 × R125	R731 250
B reserve seats:	1 950 × R85	165 750
Total revenue: 7800 seats in total		R897 000
Less Variable costs:	7 800 × R35	273 000
Total contribution margin		R624 000
Less Fixed costs of the play		624 000
Profit		0

The break-even point of 7800 tickets is *valid only for the sales mix* that was used in calculating the weighted average unit contribution margin. If 7800 tickets are sold in any other mix of A and B reserve, the organisation will not break even.

Notice that the break-even formula in equation (6) is a modification of the formula in equation (2) given earlier in the chapter. The only difference is that equation (6) uses the weighted average unit contribution margin.

The CTC's finance and administration director has constructed the profit volume (PV) graph shown in Exhibit 18.4. The PV graph shows the play's profit at any level of total sales, assuming the sales mix of 75 per cent A reserve seats and 25 per cent B reserve seats. For example, if 9000 tickets in total are sold at the assumed sales mix, the PV graph indicates that the profit will be R96 000.

With multi-product CVP analysis, we can investigate the impact on profit of changes in sales volume, prices, variable costs, fixed costs, or the sales mix itself. For example, what would be the effect on the play's break-even point if the sales mix were 80 per cent A reserve seats and 20 per cent B reserve seats? With this sales mix, the weighted average unit contribution margin is calculated as follows:

$$\text{Weighted average unit contribution margin} = (\text{R90} \times 80\%) + (\text{R50} \times 20\%)$$

$$= \text{R82}$$

At this new sales mix, the break-even point will decline from 7800 tickets to approximately 7610 tickets as a result of the higher proportion of A reserve seats (with a higher contribution margin) in the sales mix.

$$\text{Break-even point} = \frac{\text{fixed costs}}{\text{weighted average unit contribution margin}}$$

$$= \frac{\text{R624 000}}{\text{R82.00}}$$

$$= 7610 \text{ tickets}$$

The 'Real life' that follows describes the problems in sorting out the sales mix in veterinary practices!

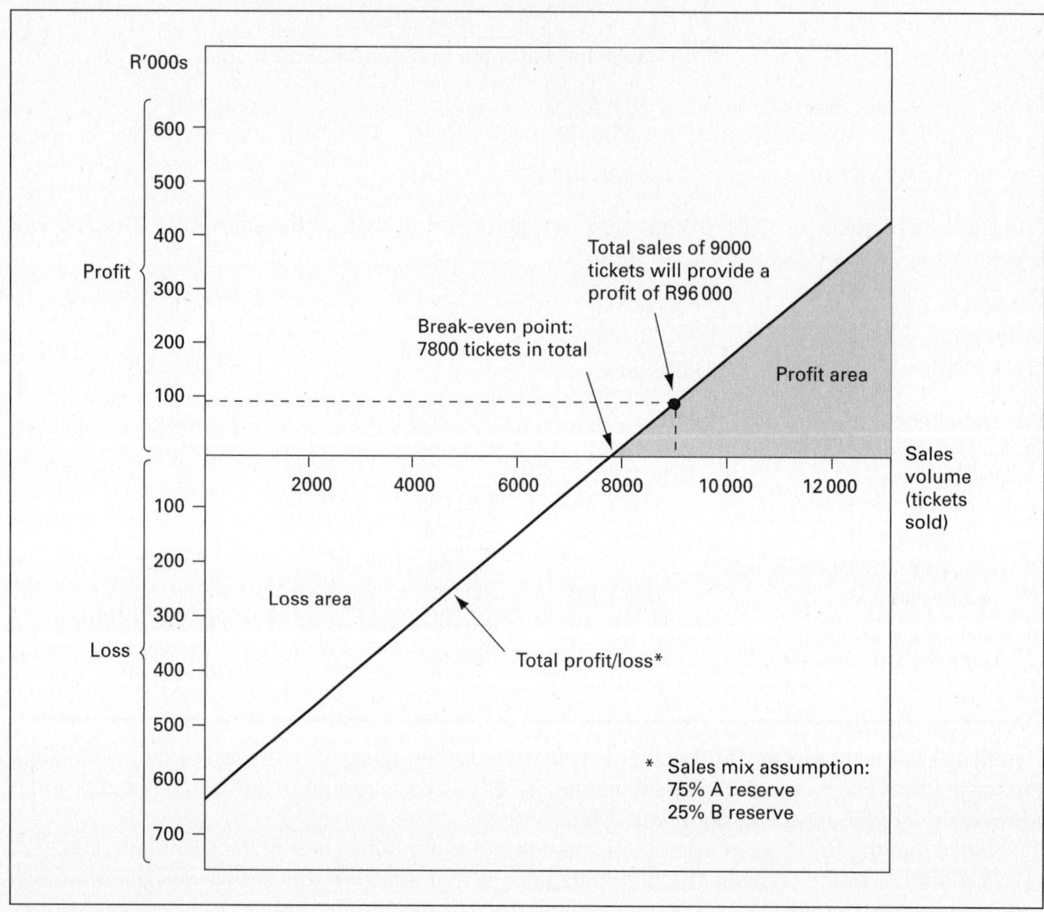

Exhibit 18.4 Profit volume graph with multiple products, Cape Town Theatre Company production of *Calypso*

Including income taxes in CVP analysis

L.O. 7 The Cape Town Theatre Company does not pay income taxes. However, for many other organisations that do pay taxes, income tax is a further factor to be included in CVP analysis.

To explain this issue we will use the example of KubiliTime (Pty) Ltd, a company that manufactures electronic time clocks (with smart cards) that are used to measure employee attendance. Suppose that KubiliTime (Pty) Ltd must pay income taxes of 28 per cent of its profit before tax. The following shows the company's profit statement for the year just ended:

Sales	20 000 × R375.00	R7 500 000
Variable costs*	20 000 × R250.00	5 000 000
Contribution margin		R2 500 000
Fixed costs		1 750 000
Profit before taxes		R750 000
Income tax expense	28%	210 000
Net profit after tax		R540 000

* Variable cost per unit is R250: variable manufacturing cost of R225 plus variable selling and administrative costs of R25.

The requirement that a firm pay income taxes affects its cost volume profit relationships. To earn a particular after-tax profit requires greater before-tax profit. How much profit before tax must be

REAL LIFE: COST VOLUME PROFIT ANALYSIS IN THE ANIMAL WORLD

In an article on practice management, *Vet Advisor* recommends that veterinary practice managers use cost volume profit analysis to establish the break-even point for their practices. However, the author acknowledges the difficulties of establishing which costs are fixed and which are variable. Fixed costs will include rent, depreciation, insurance, staff salaries and legal costs. Variable costs will include food, drugs, medical supplies and payments to relief staff. To estimate the break-even point for the practice it is necessary to calculate the weighted average contribution margin. This requires an understanding of the sales mix for the range of veterinary services provided by the practice and the contribution margin of each service. The sales mix for most veterinary practices will include surgical procedures, laboratory tests, animal hospital services, examinations and vaccinations, and animal care (treatment, dentistry and other care).

The article also recommends using CVP analysis for a range of short-term decisions, especially in setting prices for services. For example, prices set for 'shot clinics' and for advertised program specials, such as 'national pet week', should be developed using the cost volume profit model to ensure that these specials add to profits rather than create losses.

Dr Stephan Gray
Courtesy of Valerie Reed

Source: McFerson (1998)

earned in order to achieve a particular target profit after tax? This relationship between target profit and income tax expense is expressed in the following formula:

$$\text{Target net profit after tax} = (\text{target profit before tax}) - t \times (\text{target profit before tax})$$

where t denotes the income tax rate.

Rearranging this equation yields the following formula:

$$\text{Target net profit after tax} = (\text{target profit before tax})(1 - t)$$

or

$$\text{Target net profit before tax} = \frac{\text{target net profit after tax}}{(1 - t)}$$

Now we are in a position to calculate the number of clocks that KubiliTime must sell in order to achieve a particular net profit after tax. Let's assume that the company's target net profit after tax is R540 000 and its fixed costs are R1 750 000. We can modify the formula in equation (4), presented earlier in the chapter, to calculate the sales units required to earn a target net profit after tax:

$$\text{Number of units of sales required to earn target net profit after tax} = \frac{\text{fixed costs} + \dfrac{\text{target net profit after tax}}{(1 - t)}}{\text{unit contribution margin}} \quad (7)$$

$$= \frac{\text{R}1\,750\,000 + \dfrac{\text{R}540\,000}{0.72}}{(375.00 - 250.00)}$$

$$= 20\,000 \text{ units}$$

In terms of sales revenue, KubiliTime must achieve sales of R7 500 000 (20 000 units × R375 sales price). These calculations can be verified by reviewing KubiliTime's profit statement on page 892.

REAL LIFE: THE 'HARMONY WAY' AT GOLD FIELDS

In late 2004 Harmony made a hostile takeover bid for Gold Fields. Both these companies are major gold producers in South Africa and also own foreign mining operations. One of the reasons given for the takeover bid was that Harmony would be able to reduce the break-even cost of mining gold at Gold Fields' extension projects at the Driefontein and Kloof mines. In a Harmony presentation in March 2005, entitled 'The Value Proposition in Merging Harmony and Gold Fields', it was indicated that the proposed merger and mining 'the Harmony way' would have the following impacts on the break-even point of producing gold at the Driefontein and Kloof mines, stated in terms of Rands per Kg of gold produced. If we convert to ounces and assume a $/Rand exchange rate of R7 = $1, then this would equate to the following US$ prices per ounce which may be compared to the price of gold of about $700 at the time of writing.

Mines	Break-even price per kg under GF management	Break-even price per kg under HAR management	Break-even price in $ per oz. under GF management	Break-even price in $ per oz. under HAR management
Driefontein				
9#	R97 382	R82 775	$432	$368
5#	R85 057	R72 298	$378	$321
Kloof				
Kea	R89 056	R75 698	$395	$336
EBA	R86 198	R73 268	$383	$325

The proposed takeover did not succeed and today, Harmony and Gold Fields remain independent gold producers. Yet reducing the break-even price of mining was indicated as a major reason for the proposed merger. Further, Gold Fields' management have given greater attention to achieving cost savings at their mines. In the above analysis we focused on the minimum price of gold to ensure continued production. However, an important break-even indicator in the mining sector is called the 'cut-off grade'. Harmony defines this as the 'lowest grade at which an orebody can be mined'. In the gold mining sector, grades refer to how much gold you can extract from every ton of ore. The cut-off grade firstly depends on the gold price. As the gold price increases, the cut-off grade will fall as it becomes profitable to mine ore that previously was uneconomical to mine.

The cut-off grade is also dependent on the cash operating costs per ton, planned production rates and the mine recovery factor. Ore reserves reflect indicated resources above the cut-off grade.

It has been argued by mining companies that any royalty imposed by government on mining production will have the effect of increasing the cut-off grade and reducing the life span of South Africa's mines.

The grades have been falling at South African gold mines, so that most mines produce at grades of 4–8 grams of gold for every ton milled. Milling refers to the process of extracting gold from mined ore. This involves a process of crushing, grinding, acidulation and leaching. Remember this fact—that for every ton of ore mined and milled, only a few grams of gold will be extracted.

REAL LIFE: BREAK-EVEN AT ATMS

The decision by a bank to install an Automated Teller Machine (ATM) would be expected to be influenced by the ATM's break-even point. In terms of revenue, this will depend on the expected types of transaction such as cash withdrawals, balance enquiries, bank transfers and so on. Each type of transaction will have an attached fee and we need to estimate the expected mix of transactions and thereby determine the revenue mix. The fixed costs include installation, rent, and depreciation and planned maintenance. Variable costs will be determined by the number of transactions and this will include such costs as paper, replacing deposit envelopes and cash, and the variable components of the cost of information services as well as the cost of communications.

Of course, the placing of ATMs inside a store may result in additional sales for the store as customers have immediate access to cash. It may also reduce the rental costs as well as reduce security costs for the bank. In the USA a study found that an ATM needed to achieve an average of 4444 transactions per month to break even if no surcharges were imposed on the ATM by other bank card holders.

REAL LIFE: BREAK-EVEN OF A MAJOR RADIATION MEDICINE CENTRE

iThemba LABS is proposing to invest in advanced radiation and diagnostic equipment at an expected cost of US$96 million (about R700 million). iThemba is a group of research laboratories that are administered by the National Research Foundation. The new Major Radiation Medicine Centre (MRMC) project will have other benefits such as the training of oncologists in South Africa and will enable South African oncologists to undertake advanced cancer research. The new facility will provide a wide range of radiation treatments for cancer patients such as protons, neutrons and photons. In terms of the MRMC business plan, it is estimated that the expected revenue would be $40.7 million per year, while the break-even revenue was determined to be $27.4 million. Projections assume that 2850 patients will be treated annually in a mix of 1000 for photons, 1500 for protons and 350 for neutrons. It is estimated that 36 per cent will be international patients paying $30 000 for proton therapy and $4300 for photon treatment. South African patients are expected to pay R40 000 for protons and R15 000 for photons. The new facility requires the recruitment of an additional 158 personnel, of whom 75 are medical staff. While financing the R700m MRMC project has been a challenge for iThemba, break-even analysis is critical to ensuring that this project gets the final go-ahead.

Source: Refer to 'Major projects' at www.nac.co.za

REAL LIFE: BREAK-EVEN IN THE AIRLINE INDUSTRY

Delays in production can have a significant impact on break-even points. Airbus initially needed to sell 270 A380s to break even. However, delays to production have now resulted in the break-even point being significantly increased so that Airbus will now need to sell 420 A380s to break even. Break-even is only expected to be achieved by 2017. Airbus currently has 159 orders for the A380. Boeing's Dreamliner, the 787, has already achieved about 700 orders, easily passing its required break-even point. The Dreamliner uses less fuel, resulting in a lower break-even load factor for the airlines that purchase the planes. The selling price of the 787 plane is expected to be between $150 million and $200 million per plane.

Most aircraft have a break-even load factor of about 70 per cent. However, SAA some years ago invested in the Airbus A340 rather than buying more Boeing 747s, as it estimated that this would reduce its break-even load factor from 70 per cent to about 55 per cent. This was due to the greater fuel efficiency of the A340 as compared to the 747.

Practical issues in CVP analysis

L.O. 8 CVP analysis can provide a useful tool to assist in management decisions. However, it should be used with caution. In this section we consider the assumptions underlying conventional approaches to CVP analysis, and the ways in which CVP analysis may be used in practice.

Assumptions underlying CVP analysis

So far in this chapter we have considered conventional approaches to CVP analysis. For CVP analysis to be valid, the following assumptions must be reasonably satisfied:

1 *The behaviour of total revenue is linear (a straight line).* This implies that the selling price per unit of the product will not change as sales volume varies within the relevant range.

2 *The behaviour of total costs is linear over the relevant range.* This implies the following more specific assumptions:

   (a) Costs can be categorised as fixed, variable or semivariable. Total fixed costs remain constant as the sales volume changes, and the unit variable cost remains unchanged as the sales volume changes.

   (b) Labour productivity, production technology and market conditions do not change. If these were to change, then we could no longer assume that costs were linear with respect to sales volume.

   (c) There are no capacity additions during the period under consideration. This ensures that there are no increases in fixed costs, or changes in variable cost per unit.

3 For both variable and fixed costs, sales volume is the only cost driver.

4 In multi-product organisations, the *sales mix remains constant* over the relevant range.

5 In manufacturing firms, *the levels of all inventory at the beginning and end of the period are the same.* This implies that the number of units produced during the period equals the number of units sold.

Can CVP analysis be used for longer-term decisions?

The CVP model is usually described as a short-term (or tactical) decision tool. For example, we can use it to consider what would happen if we put up our price, or sales volume drops, or the price of our inputs increases. The classification of costs as fixed or variable, which underlies the CVP model, is essentially short term, as in the longer term 'fixed' costs are likely to change in response to changes in production capacity and other infrastructure requirements. But does this mean that CVP analysis cannot be used in considering long-term decisions, such as the introduction of a new product, the acquisition of new technology to produce a specific product, or the establishment of a new sales outlet? While it is possible to isolate the costs and revenues associated with these projects from the organisation's broader activities and to analyse their financial impact using CVP analysis, we need to be able to classify their costs as fixed and variable, and these cost behaviours must hold over time. Strictly speaking, where the life of the project extends over the longer term, it is more appropriate to analyse the financial impact using the capital budgeting techniques described in Chapters 21 and 22.

Treating CVP analysis with caution

You will realise from discussions in other chapters of this book that very few of the assumptions outlined above are satisfied in practice! How many companies have a constant sales mix, or consider production volume as the sole cost driver? When using CVP analysis we must remember that it is merely a *simplified model* that must be used with caution.

At the CTC, CVP analysis was regarded as an important management tool. The tool was sufficiently accurate to provide useful information about the impact of changes in costs, revenues and other important factors. The 'Real life' examples in this chapter demonstrate that CVP analysis is used across a range of businesses, including hotels, airlines, veterinary practices and, as below, in farming. However, it is clear that these businesses are less complex than many larger companies. CVP analysis can also be useful in larger, more complex companies, particularly in analysing individual projects and proposals. To be relevant, these projects must have fixed and variable cost behaviours that are constant; and the direct revenues and costs associated with each project must be distinguishable from existing operations. In the CTC case, each play was viewed as a distinct project, and only the direct costs relating to each project were considered.

REAL LIFE: BREAK-EVEN FOR WINE PRODUCERS IN SOUTH AFRICA

In an article in *Wynboer*, Johan Truter and Paiter Botha describe how to determine break-even bulk wine prices at varying yield levels per hectare. What is the break-even cost of producing 1 litre of wine? The article uses the average production cost for the industry, but this cost excludes interest and depreciation, which would increase the break-even price. The production cost (in 2001) amounted to R9933 per hectare and the average recovery was 773 litres of wine per ton. If a wine farm produces 10 tons per hectare, then the cost of production would amount to R1.28 per litre (R993 per ton). If the farm is able to produce at 20 tons per hectare, then the break-even cost would be R0.64 per litre (R497 per ton). Yields can have a significant impact on the break-even price at the farm level. At 15 tons per hectare, the break-even cost is R0.86 per litre.

Then there are the cellar costs, which amount to an additional cost of R0.93 per litre. Cellar costs exclude interest and depreciation. The combined cost of production at 15 tons per hectare amounts to R1.79 (R0.86 + R.93) per litre, while even at 20 tons yield per hectare the cost is R1.57 (R0.64 + R0.93) per litre. Truter and Botha state that, in 2001, the average bulk selling price for white wine was R1.39 per litre and that 40 per cent of all bulk wine was sold for less than R1.25 per litre. This means that most farmers were not achieving break-even prices on the sale of bulk wine. Further, these costs did not include depreciation or interest which means that the true break-even price would be higher.

It was reported that in 1998, only 1 per cent of bulk wine was sold at below R1.25 per litre but this had increased to 40 per cent in 2001. The result was that producers were selling at below the cost of producing bulk wine.

The break-even price for selling branded bottled wine would require that we take into account bottling and marketing costs. Also, we may need to store wines for a few years prior to selling and this may mean that we need to include the carrying costs which will include storage costs and financing costs.

In 2007 the situation of wine growers had not improved due to the worldwide over-supply of wine and the relatively strong Rand. Although bulk wine prices had increased since 2001, costs had also increased. The *Cape Times* in March 2007 reported that there were many wine farms for sale due to low wine prices. In some places vines were unpicked. It was reported that some wine farmers were selling their farms as they could not keep producing grapes at a loss. The producers of bottled premium wines were still making money but this no longer applied to the bulk wine suppliers. Of course, consumers of wine are now able to buy wine at low prices—at least for a while.

The situation in the wine sector indicates the importance of determining the break-even price of producing wine. If farmers know that they are producing below break-even, then at least they can plan ahead or stop producing wine—at least until the market recovers or the Rand depreciates to make exporting more viable.

Source: Truter, J. and Botha, 'Ensure that you make a profit on your wine', *Wynboer*, February 2002

REAL LIFE: COUNTING THE COSTS OF CROPS

An agricultural newsletter advises farmers to assess the break-even point for their crops. According to the author, the fixed costs of cropping will include lease and interest payments on land, and lease payments on the harvester and other cropping equipment. The variable costs will include the costs of preparing the land (spraying, seeding, watering, fertilising); harvesting costs such as fuel and casual labour; maintenance of equipment; and motor vehicle expenses. Revenue depends on the selling price per tonne and the crop yield.

New crops should not be introduced unless they are expected to break even. Rather than taking a short-term approach, the article recommends a longer-term view, arguing that some fixed costs should be spread over two to three years of cropping, although all variable costs should be recovered for each crop.

Source: Blessing (1998)

A wheat crop

Courtesy of Grain Corp

Where the assumptions of CVP analysis are not met—for example, where price is influenced by sales volume or where costs are driven by a number of factors in addition to sales volume—businesses may need to modify the profit equation underlying CVP analysis. More sophisticated approaches to modelling a business' financial characteristics are considered later in this chapter.

An activity-based approach to CVP analysis

L.O. 9 Under conventional CVP analysis it is assumed that all costs can be divided into two categories: costs that vary in proportion to sales volume (variable costs) and those that do not vary with sales volume (fixed costs). (Remember, under CVP analysis we assume that production volume equals sales volume.) However, our study of activity-based costing has taught us that in many businesses costs that are fixed with respect to production volume may in fact be driven by other cost drivers. We can improve the accuracy of CVP analysis by taking an activity-based approach and recognising a range of cost drivers.

Including unit, batch, product and facility level costs in CVP analysis

You may remember from Chapter 8 that, under activity-based costing, instead of classifying costs as variable and fixed with respect to production volume we can classify them as:

- *unit level*, which are related to the number of units produced (that is, production volume);
- *batch level*, which are related to the number of batches produced;
- *product level*, which are related to particular product lines; and
- *facility level*, which are incurred to run the business but are not specifically related to products.

To illustrate the impact of activity-based costing on CVP analysis, let's return to KubiliTime (Pty) Ltd, a company that manufactures a single product—an electronic clock. The clock is assembled from components purchased from outside suppliers, and is then packaged. Following a change in processing technology and the launch of a new model of the clock, the company has implemented an activity-based costing system. This involved undertaking a detailed analysis of planned activity costs and cost drivers (as described in Chapter 8). The planned activities and costs are shown in Exhibit 18.5.

Activity	Level of activity	Planned costs	
Administration	Facility	R1 144 000	
Production and process design	Product	R150 000	
Moving components to assembly	Batch	R700	per batch
Setting up assembly line	Batch	R1 200	per batch
Assembly per clock	Unit	R55	per unit
Inspection per clock	Unit	R5	per unit
Packaging per clock	Unit	R20	per unit

Exhibit 18.5 Planned activities and costs, KubiliTime Pty Ltd

The *facility level costs*, R1 144 000, consist of the factory manager's salary and certain selling and administrative costs, and could be regarded as 'fixed' because, in the short term, they do not appear to vary with any activity driver. The *product level costs* usually include the costs incurred to support each product line, such as product and process design costs, and, as such, can be considered to vary with the number of product lines. As KubiliTime has only one product, the R150 000 cost relates directly to that product.

Batch level costs consist of the activities of setup and material handling. The total cost per batch has been estimated at R1900. The costs of the assembly, inspection and packaging activities are *unit level costs*, as they vary with the number of units produced. The total unit level costs have been estimated at R80 per unit. In addition, the accountant has estimated that direct materials, consisting of components, will cost R170 per unit.

Under an activity-based approach, profit is no longer determined by a simple relationship between revenue, costs and sales volume. Why? Because it is recognised that some costs are driven by non-volume-related cost drivers, such as the number of setups and number of product lines. To estimate the break-even point under an activity-based approach, we need to modify the basic CVP equation:

Profit = sales revenue
− (unit level costs
+ batch level costs
+ product level costs
+ facility level costs)
= (sales price × number of units sold)
− [(activity costs per unit × number of units produced*)
+ (activity costs per batch × number of batches produced)
+ (activity costs per product × number of product lines produced)
+ facility level costs]

* assuming that the number of units produced is equal to the number of units sold.

To break even, the business must generate sufficient sales revenue to cover the total costs of the business. To obtain the break-even point, the total batch, product and facility level costs can be added together and divided by the difference in the selling price per unit and the unit level costs per unit. The selling price for the clocks is R375 per unit. The unit level costs consist of the activity costs of assembly, inspection and packaging, as well as the direct material cost per unit. Let's assume that the average batch size for clocks that will be produced during the coming year is 60 units. This means that the total batch level costs will vary, depending on the number of batches that need to be undertaken to produce the break-even number of production units.

Given these plans, the break-even point can be estimated as follows:[5]

$$\text{Break-even point (in units)} = \frac{\text{Total batch, product and facility level costs}}{\text{selling price} - \text{unit level costs per unit}}$$

$$= \frac{[(\text{break-even units/batch size}) \times \text{R1900}] + \text{R150 000} + \text{R1 144 000}}{\text{R375} - (\text{R170} + \text{R80})}$$

$$= \frac{[(\text{break-even units / 60}) \times \text{R1900}] + \text{R1 294 000}}{\text{R125}}$$

$$= \text{13 864 units}$$

We could also determine the number of units that the company would need to sell to make a target profit of R1 million:[6]

$$\text{Sales volume required to earn target net profit} = \frac{[(\text{break-even units / 60}) \times \text{R1900}] + \text{R1 294 000} + \text{R1 000 000}}{\text{R125}}$$

$$= \text{24 579 units}$$

Limiting assumptions of CVP analysis using activity-based costs

In the above example, to undertake CVP analysis we needed an estimate of the likely batch size to calculate the total batch level costs, and the total batch costs were partially dependent on the likely production levels. The formula then gave us a break-even volume, or target sales volume, which was valid for that number of batches. Of course, if management vary the size of the production batches then this will change both the break-even volume and the production volume required to achieve a target profit.

In the above example, we assumed that there was only one product, the electronic clock, and therefore all product level costs related to this product. If KubiliTime produced more than one product line, we would need to identify specific product level costs with those product lines to implement this model.

Thus, the results of CVP analysis using activity-based costs must be interpreted with caution. It may be necessary to use more complex financial models, described below, to allow for the effects of non-volume-related costs and possible interactions between production volume and batch and product level cost drivers.

Despite these difficulties, activity-based CVP analysis may offer an improvement on conventional approaches as it allows a broader recognition of a business' cost behaviour. The activity analysis may also facilitate a better understanding of cost behaviour and CVP relationships. Once again, the issue of costs versus benefits needs to be considered in deciding whether to build more complex models for CVP analysis.

Including customer-related costs in CVP analysis

As discussed in Chapter 16, some activity-based costing systems also identify customer-related costs. Costs are classified as:

- *order level,* if they are related to the number of customer orders received;
- *customer level,* if they are related to the number of customers serviced;
- *market level,* if they are related to the number of markets served; and
- *facility level,* if they are incurred to run the business but not specifically related to customers.

The inclusion of customer-related costs requires further modification to the basic CVP equation, giving the following:

$$\begin{aligned}\text{Profit} = \text{sales revenue} - (&\text{unit level costs} + \text{batch level costs}\\ &+ \text{product level costs} + \text{order level costs} + \text{customer level costs}\\ &+ \text{market level costs} + \text{facility level costs})\end{aligned}$$

The variables in the profit equation would now include sales price, activity costs per unit, number of units sold, activity costs per batch, number of batches, activity costs per product, number of product lines, activity costs per customer order, number of orders, activity costs per customer, number of customers, activity costs per market, number of markets and facility level costs! Any organisation using this approach will need to develop a comprehensive financial model, as discussed below.

Financial planning models

In Chapter 9 we recognised that many organisations construct computer models to assist with their budgeting processes. These models can also assist with CVP analysis, in order to test the sensitivity of decisions to changes in the variables underlying the profit equation and to develop more comprehensive profit equations.

Sensitivity analysis and CVP analysis

Conventional CVP analysis is based on specific estimates of a set of variables. Since these variables are rarely known with certainty, it may be helpful to run a CVP analysis several times with different combinations of estimates. This approach is called **sensitivity analysis**. Sensitivity analysis is an approach that examines how a result or outcome may change if there are variations in the predicted data or underlying assumptions. By developing a simple spreadsheet model using software such as Microsoft Excel®, a sensitivity analysis can be run using a variety of estimates for one or more of the critical variables. For example, KubiliTime's finance manager might run the CVP analysis using a range of different estimates for the electronic clock prices and associated sales volumes, as shown in Exhibit 18.6.

In the initial CVP analysis for KubiliTime, shown on page 892, it was assumed that the electronic clock would sell for R375, and if 20 000 clocks were sold at that price the company would make an after-tax profit of R540 000. The sensitivity analysis in Exhibit 18.6 assesses how 'sensitive' this profit estimate is to the assumed selling price of R375 and the assumed sales volume of 20 000 units. For example, if the price drops to R325 a loss will result, despite the expected increase in sales volume associated with the lower price. Alternatively, if the price is increased to R425 the profit will increase dramatically, despite the expected fall in sales volume. Using this model, the finance manager can test 'what if ' prices rise or fall, sales volumes increase or decrease, or any other variable changes, and in doing so help management to make the best decision in the light of uncertainty.

In addition, the results of sensitivity analysis often indicate that profit is very sensitive to changes in some variables (that is, minor changes in the variable will cause major changes in profit) but not so sensitive to changes in other variables. More care can then be taken in estimating the variables that have the most effect on profit.

Some companies use more sophisticated financial planning software or spreadsheet software packages to build profit models and conduct sensitivity analysis. Common approaches include

Microsoft Excel - Sensitivity%20analysis(2).xls

A19 Net profit after tax

	A	B	C	D	E	F	G
1							
2	**BASE ASSUMPTIONS**						
3	Sales price	R 375					
4	Units sold	20,000					
5	Variable cost per unit	R 250					
6	Fixed expenses	R 1,750,000					
7	Income tax rate	28%					
8							
9	**CHANGES TO ASSUMPTIONS**						
10	Number of clocks sold		24,000	22,000	20,000	18,000	16,000
11	Selling price		R 275	R 325	R 375	R 425	R 475
12							
13	Sales		6,600,000	7,150,000	7,500,000	7,650,000	7,600,000
14	Variable expenss		-6,000,000	-5,500,000	-5,000,000	-4,500,000	-4,000,000
15	Contribution margin		600,000	1,650,000	2,500,000	3,150,000	3,600,000
16	Fixed expenses		-1,750,000	-1,750,000	-1,750,000	-1,750,000	-1,750,000
17	Profit before taxes		-1,150,000	-100,000	750,000	1,400,000	1,850,000
18	Income tax		0	0	-210,000	-392,000	-518,000
19	Net profit after tax		**-R 1,150,000**	**-R 100,000**	**R 540,000**	**R 1,008,000**	**R 1,332,000**

Exhibit 18.6 | Exhibit 18.6 image | Exhibit 18.8 | 18.8 image

Exhibit 18.6 Sensitivity analysis at KubiliTime Pty Ltd[7]

'goal seek' and 'what-if' analyses. These functions are available on many spreadsheet packages and allow the analyst to test a range of scenarios. **Goal seek** allows you to specify the outcome of an analysis (for example the target profit), and then it requires the software to determine the necessary inputs to allow that goal to be achieved. **What-if analysis** allows the analyst to input changes in assumptions and data in a financial model, and to examine the effect of those changes on the output.

Developing more sophisticated profit models

As we recognise above, many business situations do not satisfy the assumptions underlying CVP analysis. For example, costs may be driven by a range of product-related and customer-related drivers rather than simply by production volume. Often these organisations construct more sophisticated profit models than those used in conventional CVP analysis, in order to reflect more accurately a range of cost drivers and real business conditions. These models may be run using computerised spreadsheets or financial planning software.

We can extend the KubiliTime example to consider how the company could develop a profit model to reflect a wider range of cost drivers. Let's assume that the R1144 000 facility level costs identified in Exhibit 18.5 actually included customer-related costs of R400 000, with the remaining R744 000 being true facility level costs, as shown in Exhibit 18.7.

Activity level	Cost per activity (cost) driver	Volume of activity (cost) drivers	Estimated cost
Order	R7.50	15 000	112 500
Customer	R30.00	8 000	240 000
Market	R47 500	1	47 500
Facility			744 000
Total cost			1 144 000

Exhibit 18.7 Customer-related costs at KubiliTime Pty Ltd

It is now possible to develop a model of KubiliTime's profit, as shown in Exhibit 18.8, by separately identifying sales price, activity costs per unit, number of units sold, activity costs per batch, number of batches, activity costs per product, number of product lines, activity costs per customer order, number of orders, activity costs per customer, number of customers, activity costs per market, number of markets and facility level costs in the profit equation. When this model is set up in a spreadsheet it is a relatively simple task for KubiliTime's director of finance and administration to identify the number of units required to break even, or the implications of changing any other key variable, such as the cost per batch, the number of batches, the cost per customer, the number of customers and so on.

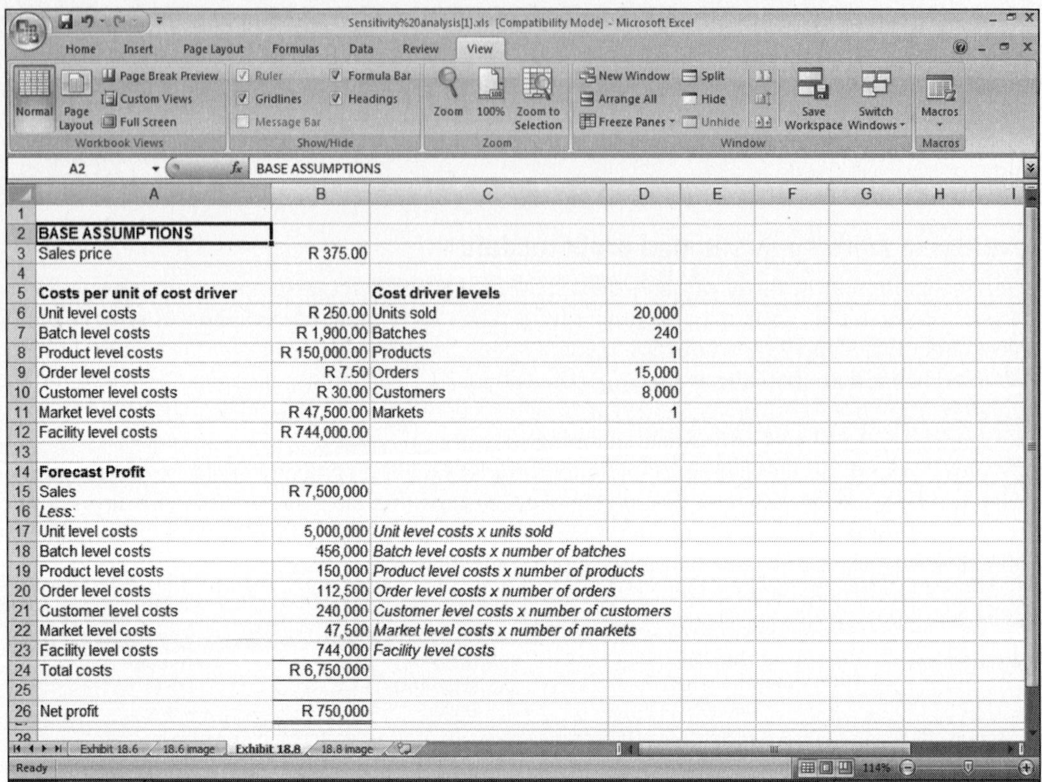

	A	B	C	D
1				
2	**BASE ASSUMPTIONS**			
3	Sales price	R 375.00		
4				
5	**Costs per unit of cost driver**		**Cost driver levels**	
6	Unit level costs	R 250.00	Units sold	20,000
7	Batch level costs	R 1,900.00	Batches	240
8	Product level costs	R 150,000.00	Products	1
9	Order level costs	R 7.50	Orders	15,000
10	Customer level costs	R 30.00	Customers	8,000
11	Market level costs	R 47,500.00	Markets	1
12	Facility level costs	R 744,000.00		
13				
14	**Forecast Profit**			
15	Sales	R 7,500,000		
16	*Less:*			
17	Unit level costs	5,000,000	*Unit level costs x units sold*	
18	Batch level costs	456,000	*Batch level costs x number of batches*	
19	Product level costs	150,000	*Product level costs x number of products*	
20	Order level costs	112,500	*Order level costs x number of orders*	
21	Customer level costs	240,000	*Customer level costs x number of customers*	
22	Market level costs	47,500	*Market level costs x number of markets*	
23	Facility level costs	744,000	*Facility level costs*	
24	Total costs	R 6,750,000		
25				
26	Net profit	R 750,000		

Exhibit 18.8 Profit model for KubiliTime Pty Ltd under activity-based costing

Summary

In this chapter we described cost volume profit (CVP) analysis, a technique that can be used to assess the effects on profit of all types of changes in sales volume, sales prices, sales mix and costs. CVP analysis provides a useful planning and decision tool for managers to manage resources effectively and make decisions that enhance profitability. Key points include:

- The break-even point estimates the level of sales needed to just cover costs—that is, to make neither a profit nor a loss. It can be estimated as the number of units sold required to break even, by dividing the fixed costs by the unit contribution margin. The unit contribution margin is the selling price per unit minus the variable cost per unit.
- The break-even point can also be estimated as the Rands of sales revenue required to break even, by dividing fixed costs by the contribution margin ratio. The contribution margin ratio is the contribution margin per unit divided by the selling price per unit, or total contribution margin divided by total sales revenue.
- We can use a cost volume profit graph to show how revenues, costs and profits change as sales volume changes. The firm will break even at the sales volume where total revenue equals total costs. Above this point the firm will make a profit, and below it will make a loss. An alternative approach is the profit volume graph, which shows the changes in profit as sales volume changes.
- We can modify the break-even formula to estimate the level of sales required to earn a target net profit, by dividing the sum of the fixed costs and the target net profit by either the

contribution margin per unit (for sales units) or the contribution margin ratio (for sales revenue).

- The CVP model can be used to identify the effect on profit of changes in fixed costs, variable costs, sales prices and sales volume, although we need to be aware of possible interdependencies between these variables, which are not recognised in the model. For example, sales price can influence sales volume.
- Most businesses produce more than one product. The CVP model can be used in multi-product situations by estimating a weighted average contribution margin (or weighted average contribution margin ratio), based on the sales mix.
- Income taxes do not affect the break-even point, as income tax expenses are incurred only when a profit is made. However, when income tax is included in the CVP analysis, it is necessary to calculate the net profit before tax needed to earn the target profit after tax. This involves dividing the target net profit after tax by (1 − the tax rate).
- Although CVP analysis has the potential to help managers make decisions, particularly in the short term, the CVP model is based on a number of assumptions, including revenue and cost functions being linear, volume being the only cost driver, a constant sales mix and stable inventories. The usefulness of CVP analysis may be undermined where these assumptions are not met.
- CVP analysis can be expanded to include the effects of activity-based costing, recognising the hierarchies of product-related costs (unit, batch, product and facility) and customer-related costs (customer, order, market and facility). However, more sophisticated profit models are required to obtain meaningful estimates of the sales needed to break even or earn a target profit.
- Financial planning models can be used to develop more sophisticated profit models, as well as to check how sensitive profit is to changes in a range of key variables.
- As discussed in the appendix, a firm's cost structure refers to the relative proportion of fixed and variable costs, and operating leverage describes the extent to which the firm uses fixed costs in its cost structure. The higher the operating leverage, the higher the proportion of fixed costs, and the greater will be the change in profit from a given change in sales. But the higher the proportion of fixed costs, the higher the break-even point and, therefore, the greater the risk of not making any profit at all! In managing the firm's cost structure, managers must decide what level of risk they are willing to accept.

Despite its limitations, CVP analysis can be a useful technique to support managers' planning and decision making, particularly in the short term. In Chapter 19 we give further consideration to information to support short-term, or tactical, decisions.

References

Blessing, P 1998, 'Break-even analysis', *The Australian New Crops Newsletter*, Issue no. 10, www.newcrops.uq.edu.au/newslettncnl1010.html, July.

McFerson, G 1998, 'Practice management', *Vet Advisor*, www.vetadvisor.com/financial1.html

Self study

Self-study problem: Cost volume profit analysis

Mountain View is a small, romantic bed and breakfast hotel located near Grahamstown. The charge of R500 per double room is for one night's accommodation excluding breakfast. (Patrons can walk across the road to an independent coffee shop for a delicious breakfast.) The retired couple who own and manage the hotel estimate that the variable cost per room is R200 per day. This includes such costs as electricity, laundry, cleaning and utilities. The hotel's fixed costs, which include council rates, water rates and land taxes, total R420 000 per year. The hotel has 10 double rooms. The hotel charges per room and a couple sharing a room will pay the same rate as a single person per room. Any difference in costs is immaterial and in fact almost all of the hotel's clientele will check in as couples sharing a room.

Required:

Calculate the following:

1. contribution margin per unit of service (a unit of service is one night's accommodation per room);
2. contribution margin ratio;
3. annual break-even point in units of service and in Rands of service revenue;
4. the number of units of service required to earn a target net profit of R600 000 for the year (ignore income taxes).

Solution to Self-study problem

1

Contribution margin per unit of service = nightly charge/room − variable cost/room
= R500 − R200
= R300

2

$$\text{Contribution margin ratio} = \frac{\text{contribution margin per unit}}{\text{nightly room charge}}$$

= R300/R500
= 0.60

3

$$\text{Annual break-even point in units of service} = \frac{\text{fixed costs}}{\text{contribution margin per unit}}$$

= R420 000/R300
= 1400 nights of accommodation

$$\text{Annual break-even point in Rands of service} = \frac{\text{fixed costs}}{\text{contribution margin per unit}}$$

= R420 000/0.60
= R 700 000

4

$$\text{Number of units of service required to earn a target net profit} = \frac{\text{fixed costs + target net profit}}{\text{contribution margin per unit of service}}$$

= R1 020 000/R300
= 3400 nights of accommodation

Cybersearch

1 Find websites containing the key term *break-even analysis.*
   (a) Find examples of businesses or industries where CVP analysis is used.
   (b) Do you notice any common features among the businesses or industries that use CVP analysis? What are these?
2 Locate websites containing the term *cost volume profit analysis.*
   (a) Does your search indicate that the term 'CVP analysis' is used more widely by practitioners or by educational institutions?
   (b) What is the difference between break-even analysis and CVP analysis?
   (c) What uses for, or examples of, CVP analysis have you discovered in your search?
3 After studying the appendix, find the websites of businesses that offer financial planning software.
   (a) Do any of the packages include CVP analysis? If so, describe the CVP features that they offer.
   (b) Do any of these packages provide information about the firm's cost structure and/or operating leverage? Give examples of this information.

Appendix to Chapter 18

Cost structure and operating leverage

The cost structure of an organisation is the relative proportion of its fixed and variable costs.[8] Cost structures differ widely between industries and between firms within an industry. A company using a computer-integrated manufacturing system has a large investment in plant and equipment, which results in a cost structure dominated by fixed costs. In contrast, the cost structure of a retail store has a much higher proportion of variable costs (particularly salaries). The highly automated manufacturing firm is capital-intensive, whereas the retail store is labour-intensive.

An organisation's cost structure has a significant effect on the sensitivity of its profit to changes in volume. A convenient way to portray a firm's cost structure is shown in Exhibit 18.9, which describes the cost structures of three firms: A, B and C. Although these three firms have the same sales revenue (R500 million) and net profit (R50 million), they have very different cost structures. Company B's production process is largely manual, and its cost structure is dominated by variable costs. It has a low contribution margin ratio of only 0.20. (In the chapter we calculated the contribution margin ratio using unit contribution margin ÷ sales price. It can also be based on total contribution margin ÷ total sales revenue, as shown here.) In contrast, Company C has a highly

Figures in millions	Company A		Company B (manual system)		Company C (automated system)	
	Amount	%	Amount	%	Amount	%
Sales	R500	100%	R500	100%	R500	100%
Variable costs	300	60%	400	80%	50	10%
Contribution margin	R200	40%	R100	20%	R450	90%
Fixed costs	150	30%	50	10%	400	80%
Net profit	R50	10%	R50	10%	R50	10%

Exhibit 18.9 Comparison of cost structures

automated production process, and its cost structure is dominated by fixed costs. The firm's contribution margin ratio is 0.90. Company A falls between these two extremes with a contribution margin ratio of 0.40.

Suppose that sales revenue increases by 8 per cent, or R40 million, in each company. The resulting increase in each company's profit is calculated in Exhibit 18.10.

	Increase in sales revenue (Rm)	×	Contribution margin ratio	=	Increase in net profit (Rm)	Percentage increase in net profit
Company A	R40	×	0.40	=	R16	32% [16/50]
Company B (high variable costs)	R40	×	0.20	=	R8	16% [08/50]
Company C (high fixed costs)	R40	×	0.90	=	R36	72% [36/50]

Exhibit 18.10 Effect on profit of increase in sales revenue

Notice that Company B, with its high variable costs and low contribution margin ratio, shows a relatively low percentage increase in profit. In contrast, the high fixed costs and large contribution margin ratio of Company C result in a relatively high percentage increase in profit. Company A falls between these two extremes. *The greater the proportion of fixed costs in a firm's cost structure, the greater the impact on profit from a given percentage change in sales revenue.*

Operating leverage

The extent to which an organisation uses fixed costs in its cost structure is called **operating leverage**. The operating leverage is greatest in firms with a large proportion of fixed costs, a low proportion of variable costs, and the resulting high contribution margin ratio. Exhibit 18.10 shows that Company B has low operating leverage, Company C has high operating leverage, and Company A falls in between. To a physical scientist, *leverage* refers to the ability of a small force to move a heavy weight. To the manager, *operating leverage* refers to the ability of the firm to generate an increase in net profit when sales revenue increases.

Measuring operating leverage

We can measure a firm's operating leverage, *at a particular sales volume,* using the **operating leverage factor**:

$$\text{Operating leverage factor} = \frac{\text{contribution margin}}{\text{net profit}}$$

Using the data in Exhibit 18.9, the operating leverage factors of companies A, B and C are calculated as follows:

	Contribution margin (Rm)	÷	Net profit (Rm)	=	Operating leverage factor
Company A	R200	÷	R50	=	4
Company B	R100	÷	R50	=	2
Company C	R450	÷	R50	=	9

The operating leverage factor is a measure, at a particular level of sales, of the percentage impact on net profit of a given *percentage* change in sales revenue. Multiplying the percentage change in sales revenue by the operating leverage factor yields the percentage change in net profit:

	Percentage increase in sales revenue	×	Operating leverage factor	=	Percentage change in net profit
Company A	8%	×	4	=	32%
Company B	8%	×	2	=	16%
Company C	8%	×	9	=	72%

The percentage change in net profit shown above for each company may be verified by re-examining Exhibit 18.10.

Break-even point and the safety margin

A firm's operating leverage also affects its break-even point. Since a firm with relatively high operating leverage has proportionally high fixed costs, the firm's break-even point will be relatively high. This fact is illustrated using the data from Exhibit 18.9:

	Fixed costs (Rm)	÷	Contribution margin ratio	=	Break-even sales revenue (Rm)
Company A	R150	÷	0.4	=	R375.0
Company B	R50	÷	0.2	=	R250.0
Company C	R400	÷	0.9	=	R444.4

The safety margin is also affected by a firm's operating leverage. Suppose the budgeted sales revenue for each of the three companies is R500 million. Then the safety margin, defined as the budgeted sales revenue minus the break-even point, is calculated as follows:

	Budgeted sales revenue (Rm)	–	Break-even sales revenue (Rm)	=	Safety margin (Rm)
Company A	R500	–	R375.0	=	R125.0
Company B	R500	–	R250.0	=	R250.0
Company C	R500	–	R444.4	=	R55.6

To summarise, Company C's high fixed costs result in a high break-even point and a low safety margin. Company B displays the opposite characteristics, and Company A falls between the two extremes.

Labour-intensive versus automated production processes

The effects of labour-intensive (manual) production processes and highly automated manufacturing systems, illustrated by companies B and C respectively, are typical. As Exhibit 18.11 shows, a movement towards a more highly automated manufacturing environment often results in a higher operating leverage, higher break-even point, and a lower safety margin. High-technology manufacturing systems are generally designed to have greater throughput, thus allowing greater potential for profitability. However, what must be considered is the increased risk if the expected high demand for a product is not realised.

Cost structure and operating leverage: a cost–benefit issue

An organisation's cost structure plays an important role in determining its cost volume profit relationships. A firm with proportionately high fixed costs has relatively high operating leverage. The result of high operating leverage is that the firm can generate a large percentage increase in net profit from a relatively small percentage increase in sales revenue. On the other hand, a firm

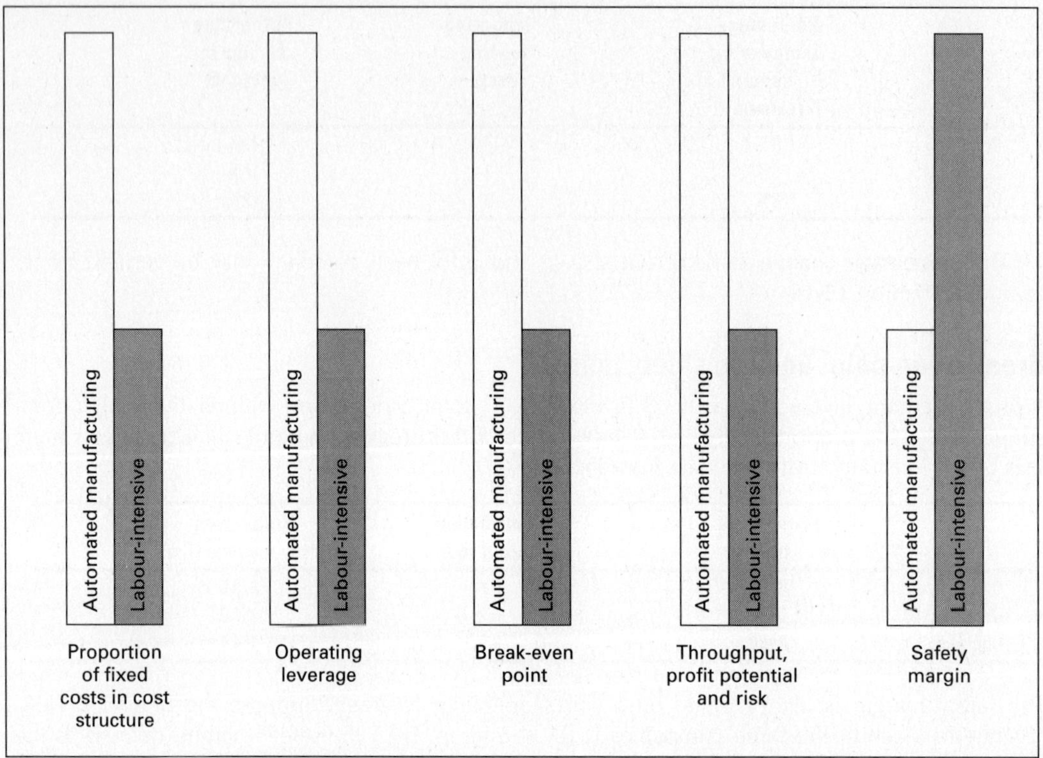

Exhibit 18.11 Labour-intensive production processes versus automated manufacturing system

with high operating leverage has a relatively high break-even point. This entails some risk to the firm.

The optimal cost structure for an organisation involves a trade-off. Management must weigh the benefits of high operating leverage against the risks of large, committed fixed costs and the associated high break-even point.

Questions

18.1 What is the meaning of the term unit contribution margin? Contribution to what?

18.2 Briefly explain how the break-even point is calculated:
(a) in sales units (b) in sales Rands (c) using a graph.

18.3 What information is conveyed by a cost volume profit graph in addition to a company's break-even point?

18.4 How can a profit volume graph be used to predict a company's profit for a particular sales volume?

18.5 'To estimate the contribution margin ratio we need to know the price per unit and variable cost per unit. Fixed costs are irrelevant.' True or false? Explain why.

18.6 What does the term safety margin mean? How can managers use this information to create shareholder value?

18.7 Suppose that a medical practice's variable costs per patient increase. What sort of costs might these be? What will happen to the practice's break-even point?

18.8 In a strategy meeting, the manufacturing director said, 'If we raise the price of our product, the company's break-even point will be lower.' The financial director responded by saying, 'Then we should raise our price. The company will be less likely to incur a loss.' Do you agree with the manufacturing director? Give reasons. Do you agree with the financial director? Explain your answer.

18.9 What will happen to a company's break-even point if the sales price and the unit variable cost of its only product increase by the same Rand amount?

18.10 A not-for-profit art gallery covers its operating expenses by charging a small admission fee. A local arts enthusiast has just pledged to make an annual donation of R5000 to the gallery. How will the donation affect the gallery's break-even attendance level?

18.11 What is the difference between a company's gross margin and its total contribution margin?

18.12 Explain the meaning of the sales mix. How is a weighted average contribution margin calculated and used in CVP analysis?

18.13 Explain the limitations associated with using CVP analysis in multi-product companies. Does this mean that CVP analysis is of little value in these situations?

18.14 Explain how income taxes affect the calculation of the break-even point.

18.15 'I've studied economics, so I know that the price of a product can influence the quantity sold. CVP ignores this.' Discuss.

18.16 A car-rental agency rents small, medium and family-sized cars. What assumptions would be made about the agency's sales mix for the purpose of a cost volume profit analysis? How and why would the weighted average unit contribution margin be calculated for this business?

18.17 'We all know that the greater the quantity of goods a retailer buys, the lower the price per unit it pays, because of quantity discounts. CVP ignores this.' Discuss.

18.18 How could cost volume profit analysis be used in budgeting and making a decision about advertising?

18.19 Why do many operating managers use a contribution profit statement instead of a traditional income statement?

18.20 Explain how sensitivity analysis can be used to help deal with uncertainty in cost volume profit analysis.

18.21 Two companies have identical products, total fixed costs and variable costs per unit, yet one company is able to set a much lower price for its product and still be as profitable as the other company. Explain how this can happen.

18.22 Explain briefly how an activity-based approach to analysing production costs and customer-related costs would affect cost volume profit analysis.

18.23 List the variables that are likely to be included in the profit equation for a business that uses an activity-based approach to analyse its production and customer-related costs. Explain how a computer-based financial planning model could be used to analyse the relationship between costs, volume and profit in this business.

18.24 Describe the assumptions underlying CVP analysis. Given the nature of these assumptions, can it be relied upon as a useful management tool?

18.25 (appendix) East Ltd manufactures electronic equipment using a completely automated production process. West Ltd also manufactures electronic equipment, but its products are assembled manually. How will these two firms' cost structures differ? Which company will have a higher operating leverage factor?

18.26 (appendix) When sales volume increases, which company will experience a larger percentage increase in profit: company X, which has mostly fixed costs, or company Y, which has mostly variable costs? Explain.

18.27 (appendix) 'The obvious strategy to increase profitability is to focus on cost structure and ensure high operating leverage. I just don't understand why more firms don't go this way.' Discuss.

Exercises

E18.28 Basic CVP analysis: retailer

University Pizza delivers pizzas to the residential colleges and flats near a major university. The company's annual fixed costs are R216 000. The sales price of a pizza is R40, and it costs the company R24 to make and deliver each pizza. (In the following requirements, ignore income taxes.)

Required:

1 Using the contribution margin approach, calculate the company's break-even point in units (pizzas).
2 What is the contribution margin ratio?
3 Calculate the break-even point in sales Rands. Use the contribution margin ratio in your calculation.
4 How many pizzas must the company sell to earn a target net profit of R240 000? Use the CVP equation.

E18.29 CVP analysis and decisions: manufacturer

Alloy Metals Ltd manufactures wheel rims systems for high performance motor vehicles. The firm's fixed costs are R2 000 000 per year. The variable cost of each wheel rim is R1000, and the wheel rims are sold for R1500 each. The company sold 7000 wheel rims during the previous year. (In the following requirements, ignore income taxes.)

Required:

Treat requirements 1 to 4 as independent situations:

1 Calculate the break-even point in units.
2 What will the new break-even point be if fixed costs increase by 5 per cent?
3 What was the company's net profit for the previous year?
4 The sales manager believes that a reduction in the sales price to R1400 will result in orders for 1000 more wheel rims each year. What will the break-even point be if the price is changed?
5 Should the price change discussed in requirement (4) be made? Explain.

E18.30 Missing data; basic CVP relationships

Fill in the missing data for each of the following independent cases. (Ignore income taxes.) Figures are in thousands.

	Sales revenue	Variable costs	Total contribution margin	Fixed costs	Net profit	Break-even sales revenue
1	R55 000	R11 000	?	?	R19 000	?
2	?	60 000	?	R60 000	?	R80 000
3	160 000	?	R30 000	?	?	160 000
4	?	120 000	240 000	?	150 000	?

E18.31 CVP graph: sports team

The Soweto All Stars, a soccer team, play their weekly games at a stadium in Soweto. The stadium holds 6000 people and tickets sell for R20 each. The team's management estimate that the team's annual fixed costs are R360 000 and that the variable cost per ticket sold is R2. (In the following requirements, ignore income taxes.)

Required:

1 Draw a cost volume profit graph for the sports team. Label the axes, the break-even point, profit and loss areas, fixed costs, variable costs, total cost line and total revenue line.
2 If the stadium is two-thirds full for each game, how many games must the team play to break even?

E18.32 Profit volume graph; safety margin: sports team

Refer to the data given in Exercise 18.31. (Ignore income taxes.)

Required:

1 Prepare a fully labelled profit volume graph for the Soweto All Stars.
2 What is the safety margin if the team plays a 10 game season and the team management expects the stadium to be 45 per cent full for each game?
3 If the team plays a 10 game season and the stadium is 40 per cent full for each game, what ticket price would the team have to charge in order to break even?

E18.33 CVP analysis with multiple products: retailer

TourForce Bicycle Shop sells 21-speed racing bicycles. For the purposes of a cost volume profit analysis, the shop owner has divided sales into two categories, as follows:

Product type	Sales price	Invoice cost	Sales commission
Road bikes	R5 000	R2 750	R250
Track bikes	R3 000	R1 350	R150

Seventy per cent of the shop's sales are track bikes. The shop's annual fixed costs are R742 500. (In the following requirements, ignore income taxes.)

Required:

1 Calculate the unit contribution margin for each product type.
2 What is the shop's sales mix?
3 Calculate the weighted average unit contribution margin, assuming a constant sales mix.
4 What is the shop's break-even sales volume in Rands? Assume a constant sales mix.
5 How many bicycles of each type must be sold to earn a target net profit of R495 000? Assume a constant sales mix.

E18.34 CVP analysis with income taxes: service firm

Maseko Scaffolding provides services to building contractors. The firm's contribution margin ratio is 0.25, and its annual fixed costs are R2 000 000. The firm's income tax rate is 40 per cent.

Required:

1 Calculate the firm's break-even revenue.
2 How much before-tax profit must the firm earn to make an after-tax net profit of R1 200 000?
3 What level of revenue must the firm generate to earn an after-tax net profit of R1 200 000?
4 Suppose the firm's income tax rate falls to 28 per cent. What will happen to the break-even level of revenue?

E18.35 Contribution margin statement; operating leverage (appendix): manufacturer

Pacific Rim Publications specialises in reference books that keep abreast of the rapidly changing economic issues in the Asia-Pacific region. The company also sells economic data. The results of the company's operations during the past year are given below. All units produced during the year were sold. (Ignore income taxes.)

Sales revenue	R5 000 000
Manufacturing costs:	
Fixed	1 250 000
Variable	2 500 000
Selling costs:	
Fixed	125 000
Variable	250 000
Administrative costs:	
Fixed	300 000
Variable	75 000

Required:

1 Prepare a traditional profit statement and a contribution margin statement for the company.
2 What is the firm's operating leverage factor for the sales volume generated during the past year?
3 Suppose that sales revenue increases by 12 per cent. What will be the percentage increase in net profit?

4 Which profit statement would an operating manager use to answer requirement 3? Why?

E18.36 Cost structure and operating leverage (appendix): service firm

A contribution margin statement for Impala Lodge, a small game farm, is shown below. (Ignore income taxes.)

Revenue	R3 000 000
Variable costs	1 800 000
Contribution margin	R1 200 000
Fixed costs	900 000
Net profit	R300 000

Required:

1 Show the hotel's cost structure by indicating the percentage of the hotel's revenue represented by each item on the contribution margin statement.

2 Suppose the hotel's revenue declines by 20 per cent. Use the contribution margin ratio to calculate the resulting decrease in net profit.

3 What is the hotel's operating leverage factor when revenue is R3 000 000?

4 Use the operating leverage factor to calculate the increase in net profit resulting from a 25 per cent increase in sales revenue.

E18.37 Cost structure and operating leverage (appendix): service firm

Refer to the data given in Exercise 18.36.

Prepare a new contribution margin statement for Impala Lodge in each of the following independent situations (ignore income taxes):

1 The hotel's volume of sales increases by 25 per cent, and fixed costs increase by 50 per cent.

2 The ratio of variable costs to revenue doubles. There is no change in the hotel's volume of sales. Fixed costs decline by R200 000.

Problems

P18.38 CVP calculations; multiple break-even points; CVP graph: manufacturer

Sabiye Backpacks Pty Ltd has estimated that budgeted production and sales of its backpacks during the coming year will be 70 000 units at an average price of R300 per unit. Variable manufacturing costs are estimated to be R120 per unit, and variable marketing costs R60 per unit sold. Fixed costs are expected to amount to R5 400 000 for manufacturing and R2 160 000 for marketing. There will be no beginning or ending work in process inventory, or finished goods inventory. (Ignore income taxes.)

Required:

1 Calculate the company's budgeted break-even point in sales Rands for the coming year.

2 Calculate the number of sales units required to earn a net profit of R5 400 000 during the coming year.

3 If the company's variable manufacturing costs are 10 per cent higher than budgeted, calculate the break-even point in sales Rands.

4 If the variable manufacturing costs are 10 per cent higher than budgeted, calculate the selling price that would yield the same contribution margin ratio in the coming year.

5 The company has estimated that if sales are less than 50 000 units, then budgeted manufacturing fixed costs will drop to R3 000 000. Other budgeted costs remain unchanged. Calculate the break-even point at the new level of sales volume.
6 Prepare a graph similar to that in Exhibit 18.3, highlighting the two break-even points.

(CMA, adapted)

P18.39 Basic CVP relationships: manufacturer

Surreal Images manufactures and sells DVDs. Price and cost data are as follows:

Selling price per unit		R100.00
Variable costs per unit:		
Direct material		R32.80
Direct labour		R16.00
Manufacturing overhead		R24.00
Selling costs		R6.40
Total variable costs per unit		R79.20
Annual fixed costs:		
Manufacturing overhead		R1 152 000
Selling and administrative		1 656 000
Total fixed costs		R2 808 000
Forecast annual sales	140 000 units	R14 000 000

(In the following requirements, ignore income taxes.)

Required:

1 What is Surreal Images' break-even point in units?
2 What is the company's break-even point in sales Rands?
3 How many units would Surreal Images have to sell in order to earn a profit of R1 560 000?
4 What is the firm's safety margin?
5 Management estimate that direct labour costs will increase by 10 per cent next year. How many units will the company have to sell next year to reach its break-even point?
6 If Surreal Images' direct labour costs do increase by 10 per cent, what selling price per unit of product must it charge to maintain the same contribution margin ratio?

(CMA, adapted)

P18.40 Basic CVP relationships; income taxes: manufacturer

Refer to the data given in Exercise 18.39. Now assume that Surreal Images pays income taxes of 28 per cent.

Required:

1 What is Surreal Images' break-even point in units?
2 What is the company's break-even point in sales Rands?
3 How many units would Surreal Images have to sell in order to earn a profit of R1 600 000 after tax?
4 What is the firm's safety margin?
5 If Surreal Images' direct labour costs increase by 10 per cent, what selling price per unit of product must it charge to maintain the same contribution margin ratio?

(CMA, adapted)

P18.41 Cost volume profit equation; sensitivity analysis: manufacturer

Refer to the data given in Problem 18.39 for Surreal Images Pty Ltd.

Required:

1 Using a contribution margin format, prepare an electronic spreadsheet (using a software package such as Microsoft Excel®) in order to estimate Surreal Images' profit at the forecast sales level of 140 000 units.

2 Surreal Images' marketing department has predicted that changing the selling price of DVDs will impact on sales volume. Develop your spreadsheet to show the effect on profit of the various forecast combinations of selling prices and sales volumes, as detailed in the following table:

Selling price	Sales volumes (in units)
R132	110 000
R124	120 000
R112	130 000
R100	140 000
R88	150 000
R76	160 000
R64	170 000

3 How could this information help Surreal Images' management?

P18.42 Basic CVP relationships; impact of operating changes: manufacturer

Polakwane-based Comp Tronics manufactures audio speakers for desktop computers. The following data relate to the period just ended, when the company produced and sold 42 000 speaker sets:

Sales	R16 128 000
Variable costs	4 032 000
Fixed costs	10 944 000

Management are considering relocating its manufacturing facilities to China to reduce costs. Variable costs are expected to average R86.40 per set; and fixed costs are anticipated to be R9 523 200. (Ignore income taxes.)

Required:

1 Calculate the company's current profit and determine the level of Rand sales needed to double that figure, assuming that manufacturing operations remain in Polakwane.
2 Determine the break-even point in speaker sets if operations are shifted to China.
3 Assume that management desire to achieve the China break-even point; however, operations will remain in Polakwane.
   (a) If unit variable costs remain constant, what must management do to fixed costs? By how much must fixed costs change?
   (b) If fixed costs remained constant, what must management do to the variable cost per unit? By how much must unit variable costs change?
4 Determine the impact (increase, decrease, or no effect) of the following operating changes:
   (a) effect of an increase in direct material costs on the break-even point
   (b) effect of an increase in fixed administrative costs on the unit contribution margin
   (c) effect of an increase in the unit contribution margin on net profit
   (d) effect of a decrease in the number of units sold on the break-even point

P18.43 CVP relationships; evaluating alternatives: manufacturer

Cele's Canopy Company (CCC) manufactures and sells adjustable canopies attached to bakkies. The market covers both new units as well as replacement canopies. The company developed its business plan for the coming year, based on the assumption that canopies would sell at a price of R3200 each. The unit variable cost of the canopy is projected at R1600, and fixed costs are budgeted at R800 000. The company's after-tax target net profit is R1 920 000; the company's tax rate is 28 per cent.

While CCC's sales usually rise during the April to June quarter, the May financial statements reported that sales were not meeting expectations. For the first five months of the year, only 350 units had been sold at the established price, with variable costs as planned. It was clear that the planned after-tax profit objective would not be reached unless action was taken. The company's CEO, Melanie Grand, assigned a management committee to analyse the situation and develop several alternative courses of action. The following mutually exclusive alternatives were presented to the CEO:

- Reduce the sales price by R320. The sales organisation forecasts that with a significantly reduced sales price, 2700 units can be sold during the remainder of the year. Total fixed and unit variable costs will stay as budgeted.
- Lower variable costs per unit by R200 through the use of less expensive raw materials and slightly modified manufacturing techniques. The sales price would also be reduced by R240 and sales of 2200 units for the remainder of the year are forecast.
- Cut fixed costs by R80 000 and lower the sales price by 5 per cent. The variable cost per unit will be unchanged. Sales of 2000 units are expected for the remainder of the year.

Required:

1 If no changes are made to the selling price or cost structure, determine the number of units that Cele's Canopy Company must sell to break even.

2 Determine which of the alternatives management should select to achieve its annual after-tax profit objective.

(CMA adapted)

P18.44 CVP relationships; indifference point: manufacturer

Naidoo Electronics Pty Ltd is studying the acquisition of two electrical component insertion systems for producing its sole product, the universal gismo. Data relevant to the two systems follow:

- Model A: variable costs, R8.00 per unit; annual fixed costs, R1 971 200.
- Model B: variable costs, R6.40 per unit; annual fixed costs R2 227 200.

Naidoo Electronics' selling price for the universal gismo is R32 per unit, which is subject to a 5 per cent sales commission. (Ignore income taxes.)

Required:

1 How many gismos must the company sell to break even, if model A is selected?

2 Which of the two systems would be more profitable if sales and production were expected to average 184 000 units per year?

3 Assume Model B requires the purchase of additional equipment that is not reflected in the preceding figures. The equipment will cost R900 000 and will be depreciated over a five-year life by the straight line method. How many units must the company sell to earn a profit of R1 912 800 if Model B is selected?

4 Ignoring the information presented in requirement 3, at what volume will management be indifferent to whether Model A or Model B is acquired? (In other words, at what volume level will the annual total cost of each system be equal?)

P18.45 Break-even analysis; PV graph: service firm

Town Roadshow Ltd owns and operates a nationwide chain of cinemas. The 450 properties in the Town Roadshow chain vary from low-volume, small-town, single-screen theatres to high-volume, big-city, multi-screen theatres. The firm's management is considering installing popcorn machines, which would allow the cinemas to sell freshly popped corn rather than pre-popped corn. This new feature would be advertised to increase patronage at the company's cinemas. The fresh popcorn will be sold for R7.00 per box. The annual rental costs and the operating costs vary with the size of the popcorn machines. The machines' capacities and costs are shown below (ignore income taxes):

	Popper model		
	Economy	Regular	Super
Annual capacity	40 000 boxes	80 000 boxes	120 000 boxes
Costs:			
Annual machine rental	R32 000	R44 000	R80 000
Popcorn cost per box	R0.52	R0.52	R0.52
Other costs per box	R4.88	R4.56	R4.20
Cost of each cardboard box	R0.32	R0.32	R0.32

Required:

1 Calculate the break-even sales in units (measured in boxes of popcorn) for each model of popcorn popper.
2 Prepare a profit volume graph for the Super Popper.
3 Calculate the sales volume at which the Economy Popper and the Regular Popper earn the same profit or loss in cinema.

(*CMA, adapted*)

P18.46 CVP and activity-based analysis; manufacturer

Commercial Crates (Pty) Ltd manufactures polystyrene crates for transporting fresh fruit and vegetables. The budgeted data for next year are as follows:

Selling price	R100	
Direct material	R52	
Activities:		
Assembling crates	R36	per unit
Packaging crates	R4	per unit
Setting up production line	R90	per batch
Inspection	R50	per batch
Moving material to production	R50	per batch
Advertising and promotion	R50 000	
Production units	50 000	
Average batch size	100	

Facility costs for the plant are estimated to be R180 000.

Required:

1 Calculate the total budgeted production costs for next year.
2 Calculate the break-even point for next year.
3 The financial controller is surprised by the high level of the break-even volume, and after discussion with the manufacturing manager has decided that the source of the problem must be the small batch size. Recalculate the break-even point, assuming that the batch size has been changed to 2000 units.
4 Management has decided to produce all crates in 2000-unit batches next year to save costs. Do you consider this to be a good idea? Explain why or why not.

P18.47 CVP analysis and special projects; sales mix: professional service organization

Dr Mentoor is a radiologist at Mitchell's Plain Hospital, and he has estimated the following costs for his Radiology Department for next year:

Materials	R50 per film
Radiologists' salaries	R1 900 000
Technicians' salaries	900 000
Office staff salaries	100 000
Supplies	400 000
Depreciation on equipment	300 000
Rental	150 000

This budget is based on an estimate of 25 000 films being processed next year using the current X-ray machines, which will be operating at their maximum capacity. These machines originally cost R1 000 000 each when they were purchased 10 years ago. The average fee charged to clients for processing a film is R250.

Dr Mentoor is considering the purchase of an additional X-ray machine, which will cost R3 750 000 and is expected to last for 3 years. This purchase would increase the capacity of the department by 50 000 films per year. As this machine can process more intricate films, the average fee for each film is expected to be R300. An additional technician would need to be hired to operate the machine at a cost of R400 000 and the cost of supplies would increase by R450 000 per year. Materials for this machine will be R80 per film.

Required:

1 Use the budgeted data to calculate the break-even point in number of films, and the budgeted profit of the department, assuming the new machine is not purchased.
2 What is the break-even point if the new machine is purchased? (Assume a sales mix based on the maximum capacity.)
3 What will be the new budgeted profit, assuming the department operates at full capacity?
4 Dr Mentoor is amazed at the new budgeted profit, and has asked you to explain why the addition of the new machine has caused the budgeted profits to increase so much.
5 Dr Mentoor now explains that in the first year of operation, demand for the new machine may be as low as 20–30 per cent of capacity. Prepare a report for Dr Mentoor advising whether or not the acquisition of the machine is advisable. In your report consider issues such as the margin of safety and the break-even point associated with the new machine. Is there any additional financial analysis that you would recommend?

(CMA, adapted)

P18.48 CVP analysis; sales mix and employee reward systems: manufacturer

Premier Corporation sells two models of home ice-cream makers, Mr Ice Cream and Cold King. Current sales total 60 000 units, consisting of 21 000 Mr Ice Cream units and 39 000 Cold King units. Selling price and variable cost information follows:

	Mr Ice Cream	Cold King
Selling price	R370.00	R430.00
Variable cost	205.00	325.00

Salespeople currently receive flat salaries that total R2 million per year. Management are contemplating a change to the commissions paid to salespeople in an effort to boost the company's presence in the marketplace. Two plans are under consideration:

- Plan A: 10 per cent commission calculated on gross Rand sales. Mr Ice Cream sales are anticipated to be 19 500 units. Cold King sales are expected to be 45 500 units.
- Plan B: 30 per cent commission calculated on the basis of production contribution margins. Mr Ice Cream sales are expected to total 39 000 units. Cold King sales are anticipated to be 26 000 units.

Before considering the questions below, you may wish to revisit the material on reward systems in Chapter 13.

Required:

1 Define the term 'sales mix'.
2 Compare Plan A to the current compensation arrangement:
   (a) Will Plan A achieve management's objective of an increased presence in the marketplace? Briefly explain.
   (b) Given the proposed change in compensation, are salespeople likely to promote Mr Ice Cream or Cold King? Briefly discuss.

(c) Explain whether the sales force is likely be satisfied with the result of Plan A.
(d) Explain whether Premier is likely be satisfied with the resulting impact of Plan A on company profitability. Why?

3 Assume that Plan B is more likely to be adopted.
(a) Compare Plan A and Plan B with respect to total units sold and the sales mix. Comment on the results.
(b) In comparison with flat salaries, is Plan B more attractive to the sales force? To the company? Show calculations to support your answers.

P18.49 CVP analysis; changes in sales prices and costs: manufacturer

Saturn Games Ltd manufactures computer games. Last year Saturn sold 25 000 games at R500 each. Total costs amounted to R10 500 000, of which R3 000 000 was considered fixed.

In an attempt to improve its product, the company is considering replacing a component part that has a cost of R50 with a new and improved part costing R90 per unit in the coming year. A new machine would also be needed to increase plant capacity. The machine would cost R360 000, have a useful life of 6 years and no salvage value. It is estimated that all other variable costs will be at the same cost per unit in the coming year. The only increase in fixed costs, over the preceding year, would be caused by the installation of a new machine to increase plant capacity. The company uses straight line depreciation on all plant assets. (Ignore income taxes.)

Required:

1 What was Saturn's break-even point in number of units last year?
2 How many units of product would the company have had to sell last year to earn R2.8 million profit?
3 If Saturn holds the sales price constant and makes the suggested changes, how many units of product must be sold in the coming year to break even?
4 If the firm holds the sales price constant and makes the suggested changes, how many units of product will the company have to sell in the coming year, to make the same net profit as last year?
5 If Saturn wishes to maintain last year's contribution margin ratio in the coming year, what selling price per unit of product must it charge to cover the increased direct material cost?

(CMA, adapted)

P18.50 CVP; multiple products; changes in costs and sales mix: manufacturer

Groendrome Gardening Tools Ltd (GGT) manufactures a line of electric garden tools that are sold in general hardware stores. The company's accountant, Tim Basson, has just received the sales forecast for the coming year for GGT's three products: hedge clippers, weeders and leaf blowers. GGT has experienced considerable variation in sales volumes and variable costs over the past two years, and Basson believes that the forecast should be carefully evaluated from a cost volume profit viewpoint. The preliminary budget information for the coming year is as shown below.

	Weeders	Hedge clippers	Leaf blowers
Unit sales	50 000	50 000	100 000
Unit selling price	R840	R1 080	R1 440
Variable manufacturing cost per unit	R390	R360	R750
Variable selling cost per unit	R150	R120	R180

For the coming year, GGT's fixed manufacturing overhead is budgeted at R60 million, and the company's fixed selling and administrative costs are forecast to be R18 million. GGT has a tax rate of 28 per cent.

Required:

1 Determine GGT's budgeted net profit for the coming year.

2 Assuming the sales mix remains as budgeted, determine how many units of each product GGT must sell in order to break even in the coming year.

3 After preparing the original estimates, management determined that the variable manufacturing cost of leaf blowers would increase by 20 per cent, and the variable selling cost of hedge clippers could be expected to increase by R30 per unit. However, management have decided not to change the selling price of either product. In addition, management have learned that the leaf blower has been perceived as the best value on the market, and they can expect to sell three times as many leaf blowers as each of their other products. Under these circumstances, determine how many units of each product GGT would have to sell in order to break even in the coming year.

P18.51 CVP relationships: retailer

Boundaries (Pty) Ltd has two retail stores, one in the city and a store in a shopping mall. The stores sell books, DVDs and music CDs. Condensed monthly profit data are presented below for November 20X5 (ignore income taxes):

	City store	Mall store	Total
Sales	R240 000	R360 000	R600 000
Less Variable costs	96 000	252 000	348 000
Contribution margin	144 000	108 000	252 000
Less Fixed costs	60 000	120 000	180 000
Operating profit	R84 000	−R12 000	R72 000

Additional information:

- Management estimate that closing the mall store would result in a 10 per cent decrease in the city store's sales, while closing the city store would not affect mall store sales.
- One-quarter of each store's fixed costs would continue until 31 December 20X6 if either store were closed.
- The operating results for November 20X5 are typical of all months.

Required:

1 Calculate the increase or decrease in Boundaries' monthly operating profit during 20X6 if the mall store is closed.

2 The management of Boundaries are considering a promotional campaign at the mall store that would not affect the city store. Annual promotional costs at the mall store would be increased by R180 000, spread equally over 12 months, in order to increase mall store sales by 10 per cent. What would be the effect of this promotional campaign on the company's monthly operating profit during 20X6?

3 One-half of the mall store's Rand sales are from items sold at their variable cost to attract customers to the store. Boundaries' management are considering the deletion of these items, a move that would reduce the mall store's direct fixed costs by 15 per cent and result in the loss of 20 per cent of the mall store's remaining sales volume. This change would not affect the city store. What would be the effect on Boundaries' monthly operating profit if the items sold at their variable cost were discontinued?

(CMA, adapted)

P18.52 CVP analysis; income taxes; marketing decisions: manufacturer

Modack Telco Equipment Ltd (MTE) manufactures telecommunications equipment. The company has always been production-oriented, and sells its products through agents. Agents are paid a commission of 15 per cent of the selling price. MTE's budgeted profit statement for next year follows:

Modack Telco Equipment Ltd Budgeted Profit Statement for the year ending 31 December (in R'000s)		
Sales		R72 000
Manufacturing costs:		
Variable	R32 400	
Fixed overhead	10 530	42 930
Gross margin		29 070
Selling and administrative costs:		
Commissions	R10 800	
Fixed marketing costs	630	
Fixed administrative costs	8 010	R19 440
Net operating profit		9 630
Less Fixed interest expense		2 430
Profit before income taxes		7 200
Less income taxes	28%	2 016
Net profit		R5 184

After the profit plan was completed for the coming year, MTE's sales agents demanded that the commissions be increased to 22.5 per cent of the selling price. This demand was the latest in a series of actions that Jannie Mulder, the company's managing director, believed had gone too far. He asked Maureen Petersen, the most sales-oriented officer in his production-oriented company, to estimate the cost to MTE of employing its own sales force. Petersen's estimate of the additional annual cost of employing its own sales force, exclusive of commissions, follows. Sales personnel would receive a commission of 10 per cent of the selling price in addition to their salary.

Estimated annual cost of employing a company sales force (in R'000s)	
Salaries:	
Sales manager	R450
Sales personnel	4 500
Travel and entertainment	1 800
Fixed marketing costs	4 050
Total	R10 800

Required:

1 Calculate MTE Ltd's estimated break-even point in sales Rands for next year:
   (a) if the events represented in the budgeted profit statement take place
   (b) if MTE employs its own sales force
2 If MTE continues to sell through agents and pays the increased commission of 22.5 per cent of selling price, determine the estimated volume in sales Rands for next year that would be required to generate the same net profit as projected in the budgeted profit statement.
3 Determine the estimated volume in sales Rands that would result in equal net profit for next year, regardless of whether MTE Ltd continues to sell through agents and pays a commission of 22.5 per cent of selling price, or employs its own sales force.

(CMA, adapted)

P18.53 Basic CVP relationships; reward systems; cost structure; operating leverage (appendix): wholesaler

Pneumo Tech Ltd is studying the addition of a new valve to its product line. The valve would be used by manufacturers of pneumatic equipment. The company anticipates starting with a relatively low sales volume and then boosting demand over the next several years. A new salesperson must be hired because Pneumo Tech's current sales force is working at full capacity. Two salary packages are under consideration:

- Plan A: An annual salary of R99 000 plus a 10 per cent commission based on gross Rand sales.
- Plan B: An annual salary of R297 000 and no commission.

Pneumo Tech will purchase the valve for R225 and sell it for R360. Anticipated demand during the first year is 6000 units. (Ignore income taxes.)

Before considering the questions below, you may wish to revisit the material on reward systems in Chapter 13.

Required:

1 Calculate Pneumo Tech's break-even point for Plan A and Plan B.
2 What is meant by the term operating leverage?
3 Analyse the cost structures of both plans at the anticipated demand of 6000 units. Which of the two plans is more highly leveraged? Why?
4 Assume that a general economic downturn occurred during Year 2, with product demand falling from 6000 to 5000 units. Determine the percentage decrease in company net profit if Pneumo Tech had adopted Plan A.
5 Repeat requirement 4 for Plan B. Compare Plan A and Plan B, and explain a major factor that underlies any resulting differences.
6 Briefly discuss the likely profitability impact of an economic recession for more highly automated manufacturers. What can you say about the risk associated with these firms?

P18.54 Basic CVP relationships; cost structure; operating leverage (appendix): manufacturer

Zaduma Ltd has decided to introduce a new product, which can be manufactured by either a computer-assisted manufacturing system or a labour-intensive production system. The manufacturing method will not affect the quality of the product. The estimated manufacturing costs relating to the two methods are as follows:

	Labour-intensive production system		Computer-assisted manufacturing system	
Direct material		R42.00		R37.50
Direct labour	0.08 DLH @ 67.50	54.00	0.50 DLH @ 90.00	45.00
Variable overhead	0.80 DLH @ 45.00	36.00	0.50 DLH @ 45.00	22.50
Fixed overhead*		R9 900 000		R18 300 000

* These costs are directly traceable to the new product line. They would not be incurred if the new product line were not produced.

The company's marketing research department has recommended an introductory unit sales price of R225. Selling expenses are estimated to be R3 750 000 annually, plus R15 for each unit sold. (Ignore income taxes.)

Required:

1 Calculate Zaduma's estimated break-even point in annual unit sales of the new product if the company uses:
   (a) the labour-intensive production system
   (b) the computer-assisted manufacturing system
2 Determine the annual unit sales volume at which the company would be indifferent to which of the two manufacturing methods is chosen.
3 Management must decide which manufacturing method to employ. One factor it should consider is operating leverage. Explain the concept of operating leverage. How is this concept related to Zaduma's decision?
4 Describe the circumstances under which the company should employ each of the manufacturing methods.
5 Identify some business factors other than operating leverage that management should consider before selecting the manufacturing method.

Cases

C18.55 Activity-based costing; ethical issues: manufacturer

This case should be completed in conjunction with Problem 18.49.

Refer to the original data given for Saturn Games Ltd in Problem 18.49. An activity-based costing study has revealed that Saturn's fixed costs include the following components:

Set up (40 set-ups @ R8000 per set-up)	R320 000
Engineering (500 hours @ R500 per hour)	250 000
Inspection (1000 inspections @ R600 per inspection	600 000
General factory overhead	1 230 000
Total	R2 400 000
Fixed selling and administrative costs	600 000
Total 'fixed' costs	R3 000 000

Management are considering the installation of new highly automated manufacturing equipment that would significantly alter the production process. In addition, management are planning a move towards just-in-time inventory and production management. If the new equipment is installed, set-ups will be quicker and less expensive. Under the proposed JIT approach, there would be 300 set-ups per year at R1000 per setup. Since a total quality management program would accompany the move towards JIT, only 100 inspections would be anticipated annually at a cost of R900. After the installation of the new production system, 800 hours of engineering would be required during the year at a cost of R560 per hour. General factory overhead would increase to R3 322 000. However, the automated equipment would allow Saturn to cut its unit variable cost by 20 per cent. Moreover, the more consistent product quality anticipated would allow management to raise the price per computer game to R520 per unit. (Ignore income taxes.)

Required:

1 Upon seeing the activity-based analysis given in the problem, Saturn's manufacturing manager exclaimed to the financial controller: 'I thought you told me this R3 000 000 was fixed. These don't look like fixed costs at all. What you're telling me now is that setup costs us R8000 every time we set up a production run. What gives?'
As Saturn's financial controller, write a short memo explaining to the manufacturing manager what is going on.

2 Calculate Saturn's new break-even point if the proposed automated equipment is installed.

3 Determine how many units Saturn will have to sell to show a profit of R2 800 000, assuming that the new technology is adopted.

4 If Saturn adopts the new manufacturing technology, will its break-even point be higher or lower? Will the number of sales units required to earn a profit of R2 800 000 be higher or lower? (Refer to your answers to the first two requirements of the preceding problem.) Are the results in this case consistent with what you would typically expect to find? Explain why.

5 The decision as to whether to purchase the automated manufacturing equipment will be made by Saturn's board of directors. In order to support the proposed acquisition, the manufacturing manager asked the financial controller to prepare a report on the financial implications of the decision. As part of the report, the manufacturing manager

asked the financial controller to calculate the break-even point assuming the installation of the equipment. The controller complied, as in requirement 2 of this problem.

When the manufacturing manager saw that the break-even point would increase, he asked the financial controller to delete the break-even analysis from the report. What should the financial controller do? Which ethical standards for accountants are involved here? (*Hint*: Refer to the appendix of Chapter 1 for a description of these ethical standards.)

6 Describe the difficulties that can arise using activity-based costing in cost volume profit analysis. Have these difficulties affected the CVP analysis in this case? Explain your answer.

C18.56 CVP and comprehensive activity-based analysis; financial planning model: manufacturer

Indaba Camping Company is a major manufacturer of tents, which are sold directly to discount department stores and camping equipment suppliers. The company has recently introduced activity-based costing and the following activities and costs have been identified:

Activity	Level of activity	Planned costs
Production costs:		
Production and process design	Product	R250 000 per product
Moving materials to cutting area	Batch	R500 per batch
Setting up pattern cutting machines	Batch	R1 250 per batch
Moving materials to sewing area	Batch	R600 per batch
Setting up sewing machines	Batch	R900 per batch
Cutting pattern	Unit	R75 per tent
Stitching	Unit	R225 per tent
Waterproofing seams	Unit	R50 per tent
Inspection	Unit	R55 per tent
Packaging	Unit	R20 per tent
Customer-related costs:		
Processing customer order	Order	R350 per order
Delivering the product	Order	R700 per order
Sales calls	Customer	R750 per customer
Handling customer complaints	Customer	R375 per customer
Advertising in retail trade magazines	Market	R120 000
Other costs:		
Administration	Facility	R1 100 000

The company expects to manufacture and sell 75 000 tents next year, at a selling price of R1025 each. It is estimated that this will involve producing 1875 batches of tents, for 185 customers, who will place a total of 3750 orders during the year. The direct material cost per tent is estimated to be R350.

Required:

1 Use a spreadsheet to develop a profit model for Indaba Camping Company and estimate the planned level of profit. (*Hint*: Refer to Exhibit 18.8.)

2 Use your profit model to estimate how many tents the company would need to break even.

3 Use your profit model to estimate how many tents the company would need to sell to make a pre-tax profit of R4.75 million.

4 Estimate the company's safety margin and explain the significance of this information to the company's management.

5 The company's marketing department has forecast that sales could be increased by 10 000 units if the selling price were decreased by R75 per unit, and by 20 000 units if the selling price were decreased by R100 per unit. Use your profit model to assess the

effects of these changes. The number of batches produced and customers' orders placed will increase proportionately, but the number of customers will remain unchanged at 185.

6 The marketing manager has recommended that the company cease trading with camping equipment suppliers and concentrate on the discount department store market. It is estimated that this will decrease sales by 15 000 tents, reduce the number of customers by 110 and the number of orders by 2700. Production will be based on the same batch size as currently used. Use your profit model to assess the effects of these changes.

7 Write a report to the company's management explaining the profit implications of the initial forecast level of activity and recommending whether the company should:
   (a) decrease its selling price and, if so, by how much
   (b) cease trading with camping equipment suppliers

C18.57 Break-even analysis; safety margin: service firm[9]

Steven Mashonga and two of his colleagues are considering opening a law office in Johannesburg that would make inexpensive legal advice available to those who could not otherwise afford legal services. The intent is to provide easy access for their clients by having the office open 360 days per year, 16 hours each day from 7 a.m. to 11 p.m. The office would be staffed by two recently qualified lawyers, a paralegal, a legal secretary and a clerk-receptionist for each of the two eight-hour shifts.

To determine the feasibility of the project, Mashonga hired a marketing consultant to assist with market projections. The results of this study show that if the firm spends R240 000 on advertising in the first year, 50 new clients are expected each day. Mashonga and his associates believe that this number is realistic and are prepared to spend the R240 000 on advertising. Other pertinent information about the operation of the proposed business follows:

- The only charge to each new client would be R100 for the initial consultation. All cases that warrant further legal work will be accepted on a contingency basis with the firm earning 25 per cent of any favourable settlements or judgments. Mashonga estimates that 20 per cent of new client consultations will result in favourable settlements or judgments averaging R8000 each. It is not expected that there will be repeat clients during the first year of operations.
- The hourly wages of the staff are projected to be R100 for each lawyer, R70 for the paralegal, R50 for the legal secretary and R30 for the clerk-receptionist. Labour on-costs will be 20 per cent of wages paid. A total of 400 hours of overtime is expected for the year; this will be divided equally between the legal secretary and the clerk-receptionist positions. Overtime will be paid at one and a half times the regular wage, and the labour on-costs will apply to the total wages paid.
- Mashonga has located 300 square metres of suitable office space that can be rented for R560 per square metre annually. Associated expenses will be R54 000 for council services and R74 000 for utilities.
- It will be necessary for the group to purchase professional indemnity insurance, which is expected to cost R180 000 annually.
- The initial investment in office equipment will be R120 000. This equipment has an estimated useful life of four years.
- The cost of office supplies has been estimated to be R8 per new client consultation.

Required:

1 Determine how many new clients must visit the law office being considered by Steven Mashonga and his colleagues in order for the venture to break even during its first year of operations.

2 Calculate the law firm's safety margin.

3 Describe the assumptions that underlie your analysis and the limitations that they imply.

(*CMA adapted*)

C18.58 Contribution margin statement; CVP analysis: manufacturer

Dollie Products Ltd is a regional firm with three major product lines: cereals, breakfast bars and dog food. The following income statement was prepared by product line. (Ignore income taxes.)

Dollie Products Ltd
Income Statement
for the year ended 30 June
(in R'000s)

	Dog food	Cereal	Breakfast bars	Total
Sales (in kg)	2 000	500	500	3 000
Sales revenue	R5 000	R2 000	R1 000	R8 000
Costs of goods sold:				
Direct material	R1 650	R800	R500	R2 950
Direct labour	450	200	100	R750
Manufacturing overhead	540	240	120	R900
Total cost of goods sold	R2 640	R1 240	R720	R4 600
Gross margin	R2 360	R760	R280	R3 400
Operating expenses:				
Selling expenses:				
Advertising	R250	R150	R100	R500
Commissions	250	200	100	550
Salaries and on-costs	150	100	50	300
Total selling expenses	R650	R450	R250	R1 350
General and administrative expenses:				
Licenses	250	100	75	R425
Salaries and on-costs	300	125	75	500
Total general & administrative expenses	R550	R225	R150	R925
Operating profit before taxes	R1 160	R85	−R120	R1 125

Other data:

- Cost of goods sold. The company's inventories of raw materials, work in process and finished products do not vary significantly from year to year. (The inventories on 30 June were essentially identical to those on 30 June in the previous year.)

  Manufacturing overhead was applied to products at 120 per cent of direct labour Rands. The manufacturing overhead costs for the year ended 30 June were as follows:

Indirect labour and supplies (variable)	R75 000
Employee on-costs on indirect labour (variable)	150 000
Supervisory salaries and on-costs	175 000
Plant occupancy costs	500 000
Total	R900 000

  There was no overapplied or underapplied overhead at year-end.
- Advertising. The company has been unable to determine any direct causal relationship between the level of sales volume and the level of advertising expenditures. However, because management believe that advertising is necessary, an annual advertising program is implemented for each product line. Each product line is advertised independently of the others.
- Commissions. Sales commissions are paid to the sales force at the rate of 5 per cent on sales of dog food and 10 per cent on sales of breakfast bars and cereal.
- Licences. Various licences are required for each product line. These are renewed annually for each product line.

- Salaries and on-costs. Sales and administrative personnel devote time and effort to all product lines. Their salaries and wages are allocated on the basis of management's estimates of time spent on each product line.

Required:

1 The accountant of Dollie Products Ltd has recommended that the company do a cost volume profit analysis of its operations. As a first step, the accountant has requested that you prepare a revised profit statement that employs a contribution margin format, which will be useful in CVP analysis. The statement should show the contribution margin for each product line and the operating profit before taxes for the company as a whole.

2 The accountant of Dollie Products is going to prepare a report to present to the other members of top management, explaining cost volume profit analysis. Identify and explain the following points, which the accountant should include in the report:
   (a) the advantages that CVP analysis can provide to the company
   (b) the difficulties the company could experience in the calculations involved in CVP analysis
   (c) the dangers that management should be aware of in using the information derived from the CVP analysis

(CMA, adapted)

C18.59 Break-even analysis; CVP relationships: hospital

Kloof Medical Centre operates a general hospital. The medical centre also rents space and beds to separately owned entities rendering specialised services, such as Paediatrics and Psychiatric Care. Kloof charges each separate entity for shared services, such as patients' meals and laundry, and for administrative services such as billings and collections. Space and bed rentals are fixed charges for the year, based on bed capacity rented to each entity. Other charges are variable, based on the number of annual patient-days in each entity. Kloof Medical Centre charged the following costs to Paediatrics for the year ended 30 June 20X5:

	Variable	Fixed
Dietary	R3 600 000	
Janitorial		R420 000
Laundry	1 800 000	
Laboratory	2 700 000	
Pharmacy	2 100 000	
Repairs and maintenance		180 000
General and administrative		7 800 000
Rent		9 000 000
Billings and collections	1 800 000	
Total	R12 000 000	R17 400 000

During the year ended 30 June 20X5, Paediatrics charged each patient an average of R1800 per day, had a capacity of 60 beds, and had revenue of R36 million for 365 days. In addition, Paediatrics directly employed personnel with the following annual salary costs per employee: supervising nurses, R150 000; nurses, R120 000; and aides, R54 000. Kloof Medical Centre has the following minimum departmental personnel requirements, based on total annual patient-days:

Annual patient-days	Aides	Nurses	Supervising nurses
Up to 21 900	20	10	4
21 901 to 26 000	25	14	5
26 001 to 29 200	31	16	5

Paediatrics always employs only the minimum number of required personnel. Salaries of supervising nurses, nurses and aides are therefore fixed within ranges of annual patient-days.

Paediatrics operated at 100 per cent capacity on 90 days during the year ended 30 June 20X5. Administrators estimate that on these 90 days, Paediatrics could have filled another 20 beds above capacity. Kloof Medical Centre has an additional 20 beds available for rent for the year ending 30 June 20X6. Such additional rental would increase Paediatrics' fixed charges based on bed capacity, and would need to be rented for the full year. (Ignore income taxes.)

Required:

1 Calculate the minimum number of patient-days required for Paediatrics to break even, for the year ending 30 June 20X6, if the additional 20 beds are not rented. Patient demand is unknown, but assume that revenue per patient-day, cost per patient-day, cost per bed, and salary rates will remain the same as for the year ended 30 June 20X5.

2 Assume that patient demand, revenue per patient-day, cost per patient-day, cost per bed, and salary rates for the year ending 30 June 20X6 remain the same as for the year ended 30 June 20X5. Prepare a schedule of Paediatrics' increase in revenue and increase in costs for the year ending 30 June 20X6. Determine the net increase or decrease in Paediatrics' earnings from the additional 20 beds if Paediatrics rents this extra capacity from Kloof Medical Centre.

(CPA, adapted)

Endnotes

1 This case is a simplified version of the processes used by a theatre company to estimate and control the costs of plays. The financial data for the fictional play, *Calypso*, may not represent the actual revenues and costs of staging a play.

2 Contribution margin statements are discussed in more detail in Chapters 7 and 12.

3 We will assume that the length of time the play is on will not affect the percentage of seats filled for each performance. If a play is successful, and it is not be possible to add additional performances right away, it should be possible to re-stage the play at a later time in the year.

4 We will set the target at R70 005 rather than R70 000 in order to avoid rounding effects as we do not wish our answer to reflect fractional units.

5 In order to make this easier to follow, let break-even = B, so that B = [(B/60)R1 900 + R1 294 000]/R125]
B125 = (B/60)1 900 + R1 294 000
B125 − (B1 900/60) = R1 294 000
B125 − (B31.6667) = R1 294 000
B(125 − 31.6667) = R1 294 000
B = R1 294 000/R93.3333
B = 13 864.286 (rounded to 13 864)

6 Simply divide (R1 294 000 + R1 000 000) by R93.333 (R125 − 31.6667) to get to the sales volume required to earn the target profit. This results in a break-even of 24578.58 units, which we have rounded up to 24579 units.

7 The tax is zero at selling prices of R275 and R325 as the company is not required to pay tax on losses. However, in the real world, the company may be able to set off losses on one product against profits on other products so that tax losses may result in tax savings elsewhere in the firm. This will reduce potential losses and will therefore reduce the risk of a new product. Further, even if this does not apply, then the firm will be able to carry forward losses to set off against profits in later years.

8 Note that is a conventional management accounting concept. Costs are classified as fixed or variable with respect to production or sales volume.

9 Lawyers are permitted to charge contingency fees ('no success, no pay') in South Africa to enable all people to have access to legal resources. Contingency fees have been described as 'the poor man's key to the courthouse'. Contingency fees are subject to strict guidelines in South Africa.

CHAPTER

Information for Tactical Decisions

❖ LEARNING OBJECTIVES

After completing this chapter, you should be able to:

1 explain the differences between tactical decisions and long-term decisions;

2 describe the steps in the decision-making process, and the management accountant's role in that process;

3 describe the characteristics of relevant information;

4 select and analyse relevant information for special order decisions;

5 select and analyse relevant information for make or buy decisions;

6 select and analyse relevant information for decisions to add or delete a product or department;

7 explain how to treat joint product costs in decisions about whether to sell a product or process it further;

8 complete relevant cost analysis using activity-based costs;

9 discuss the linkage between decision making and incentives;

10 identify the pitfalls to avoid in using accounting data in decisions; and

11 after studying the appendix, use various approaches to allocating joint costs to products, and evaluate the usefulness of these approaches for managerial decision-making.

Introduction

Decision-making is a fundamental part of management. The effectiveness of an organisation in creating customer value and shareholder wealth depends on managers being able to identify opportunities or recognise problems, and make the most appropriate decision. Decisions that have to be made about the acquisition of equipment, mix of products, methods of production, and pricing of goods and services confront managers in all types of organisations. This chapter covers the role of management accounting information in a variety of decisions. The primary focus is on tactical decisions related to implementing an organisation's strategies, although many of the underlying concepts are also applicable to long-term decisions.

The management accountant's role in decision-making

The management accountant's role in the decision-making process is to provide relevant information to the managers and teams who make the decisions. Production managers make decisions about alternative production processes and schedules; marketing managers make pricing decisions; and specialists in finance are usually involved in decisions about major acquisitions of equipment. In a manufacturing company, production teams make decisions about day-to-day operations. In a service business, such as a consulting company, managers make decisions about which clients to service and which staff to assign to particular jobs. All these people require specific information to assist in those decisions.

Tactical versus long-term decisions

L.O. 1 Many of the decisions examined in this chapter can be classified as **tactical decisions**. Tactical decisions do not usually require significant increases or decreases in capacity-related resources, such as factory space and equipment, and the impact may be short term. Thus, in these decisions many overhead costs are considered fixed. It is also assumed that tactical decisions can be changed quickly or reversed to take advantage of better opportunities that may arise. Examples of tactical decisions include whether to accept or reject a special order, and whether to sell or process further a joint product. In considering tactical decisions, we often focus on the incremental revenues and costs arising from each alternative.

In contrast, **long-term decisions** tend to be more strategic in nature, and may involve large outlays of (or decreases in) capacity-related resources. The effects of these decisions tend to be more difficult to reverse and may extend for longer time periods. Examples of long-term decisions include the closing of a business unit, the acquisition of automated computer equipment, and the introduction of a new product line.

In reality, many of the so-called tactical decisions do have longer-term implications. For example, if, during one month, management decide to reduce the production of a particular product due to limited production capacity, a long-term loss of customers and lower profits may result. The process of identifying relevant costs and benefits is largely the same whether the decision is viewed from a tactical or long-term perspective.

One additional factor that is relevant in a long-term analysis, however, is the time value of money. When the impact of a decision spans several years, the analyst should account for the fact that a R1 cash flow today is worth more than a R1 cash flow in future years. A Rand received today can be invested to earn interest, while the Rand received in five years' time cannot be invested over the intervening time period. The analysis of long-term decisions requires recognition of the time value of money. We explain this concept further in Chapter 21.

Types of decisions

In this chapter, we examine the following types of decisions:

- whether to accept or reject a special order;
- whether to make or buy (or outsource) a product or service;
- whether to add or delete a product, service or department;
- joint products: sell or process further?

Pricing and product mix decisions are covered in Chapter 20, while capital expenditure decisions are the focus of Chapters 21 and 22.

A model of the decision-making process

L.O. 2

The processes that managers undertake when making decisions are often described as a series of logical, sequential steps. To illustrate this process we will use a decision for Wings Airlines.

Wings Airlines is based in Johannesburg and flies routes from South Africa to the US, Europe and several Asian cities. Wings Airlines is facing increasing competition in its overseas operations. In particular, it is having difficulty maintaining its cost competitiveness. Senior management is considering closing its hub operation in London. Airlines establish hubs at airports where many of their routes intersect. Hub operations include facilities for in-flight food preparation, aircraft maintenance and storage, and administrative offices. The steps involved in making the decision about whether to close the hub operation in London are as follows:

1 *Clarify the problem.* Sometimes the decision to be made, or the problem, is clear. For example, if a company is asked to supply a special order of its most popular product at a price below the usual market price, the decision is whether to accept or reject the order. In the case of Wings Airlines, the problem is whether to close the London hub or keep it open.

   However the decision is seldom so clear and unambiguous. Perhaps a company has unused capacity in its manufacturing plant because demand for its product is declining. What exactly is causing this decreased demand: Increasing competition? Declining quality control? Has a competitor just introduced a similar product into the market? Before a decision can be made, the problem needs to be clarified and defined in more specific terms. Considerable management skill is required to define a problem in terms that can be addressed effectively.

2 *Identify alternative courses of action.* A decision involves selecting from two or more possible courses of action. If a machine breaks down, what are the possible courses of action? The machine can be repaired, or replaced, or a replacement can be leased. In the case of Wings Airlines, two possible alternatives are to close the London hub or to keep it open.

3 *Collect relevant costs and benefits.* Although management accountants are often involved in steps 1 and 2, they are chiefly responsible for steps 3 and 4. Selecting data pertinent to decisions is one of the management accountant's value-adding roles in an organisation. This often involves predictions about the outcomes (costs and benefits) of various possible courses of action. This requires a good understanding of what it is that drives costs, and factors that influence revenues. (Cost drivers have been considered in earlier chapters. See Chapter 20 for a discussion of factors that influence sales revenue.) For Wings Airlines, the management accountant will need to predict the future costs and benefits of continuing to operate the London hub, and to determine the costs that would be saved by closing the hub. The accountant needs to distinguish between relevant and irrelevant data.

4 *Compare the costs and benefits of each possible course of action.* In this stage the accountant will prepare an analysis of the relevant costs and benefits of each possible course of action. Both quantitative and qualitative information should be included. It is important that the impact of each option on the organisation's strategic direction is

considered. For example, if Wings Airline's strategies include improving customer service and cost competitiveness, then it is important to determine how each alternative—closing the hub and continuing to operate the hub—will impact on these strategies.

5 *Select a course of action.* Once the relevant information is collected, managers will select the course of action that will provide the greatest net benefit to the organisation.

These steps are illustrated in Exhibit 19.1.

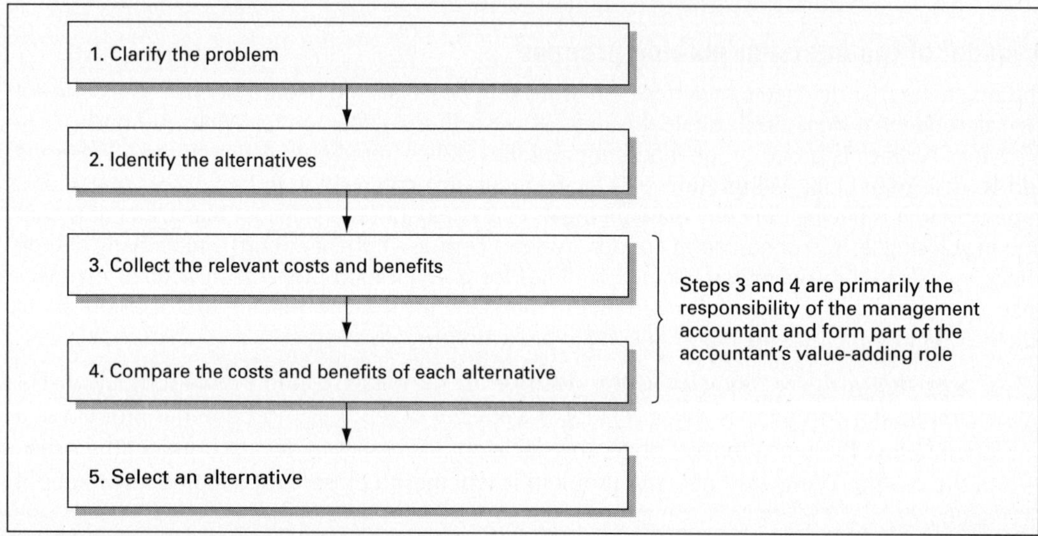

Exhibit 19.1 Steps in the decision-making process

While the decision-making process is described as a series of steps, it must be recognised that this is merely a model. It assumes that managers follow rational processes and systematic methods when making decisions. However, decisions are often made by managers without necessarily following each step. The full range of possible courses of action may not be considered, or data may not be collected and used to assess each option. Several of the steps may be completed concurrently, rather than sequentially. We may even find examples where data are produced by the management accountant to confirm a decision that management has already made!

These practices may be dictated by the need to make quick decisions in some situations, or they may merely reflect the preferred style of decision making of certain managers.

Determining relevant information

L.O. 3

A primary theme of this chapter is learning how to decide what information is relevant to various common decisions. In general, relevant information is information—such as costs or revenues—that differs between alternative courses of action. However, there are other characteristics of relevant information. These characteristics are now examined.

Characteristics of relevant information

Relevant information is different under competing courses of action

Relevant information involves costs or benefits that are different for each course of action. Therefore, costs or benefits that are the same across all the available courses of action need not be considered within a decision.

Let us consider Wings Airlines and its decision about whether or not to close the London hub. If Wings Airlines intends to maintain its reservations office in London, then the costs of operating the reservations office are irrelevant to the decision about whether or not to eliminate the London hub. The cost of running the reservations office is the same for both alternatives: keeping the hub, or closing it.

Opportunity costs are also relevant to many decisions. An **opportunity cost** is the potential benefit that is given up when one course of action is chosen over another. Opportunity costs can arise in a variety of different decision contexts, and they are just as relevant as out-of-pocket costs. Out-of-pocket costs are those incremental costs that will be incurred if a particular course of action is selected. These may include additional wages, materials and equipment.

Relevant information relates to the future

The outcomes of decisions affect the future, not the past. Therefore, for information to be relevant it must also relate to the future. Costs that have already been incurred are termed **sunk costs**. They are irrelevant as they do not affect any future costs and cannot be changed by any current or future action. The acquisition cost of equipment currently used in the London hub is an example of a sunk cost.

The cost information relevant to Wings Airlines' decision concerning its London operations involves only those costs that will be incurred in the future under either of the two alternatives. Costs that were incurred in the past in the airline's London operations cannot be changed and are irrelevant to the decision at hand.

Note that in predicting relevant costs and benefits, the accountant will often use historical data to estimate future cost behaviour. These data may include cost drivers. There is an important and subtle issue here. Relevant costs and benefits are those that may be realised in the future. However, the accountant's predictions of those costs and benefits are often based on data from the past.

Timeliness versus accuracy

Relevant information is only of value if it is timely. **Timely information** is information that is available in time for a decision. However, relevant information should also be accurate. In some situations a trade-off needs to be made between the accuracy and the timeliness of information. More accurate information may take longer to produce. Therefore, as accuracy improves, timeliness suffers, and vice versa. For example, in deciding whether or not to close the London hub, it could take considerable time to determine accurately the compensation to be paid to retrenched employees. If the decision has to be made as soon as possible, then an estimate of the likely payout may be used in the analysis. A long wait to obtain more precise information may unduly delay management's decision.

Information may be quantitative or qualitative

Relevant information may be quantitative or qualitative. **Quantitative information** is expressed in numerical terms, such as Rand estimates of the effects on profit or costs. When a manager makes a final decision, however, qualitative information can be as important as the quantitative information. **Qualitative information** consists of factors relevant to a decision that cannot be expressed effectively in numerical terms. In Wings' decision concerning whether or not to eliminate the London hub, the analysis of the quantitative data may indicate that closing the operation yields the highest profits. In making their decision, however, the company's managers will consider qualitative issues such as the effect of the closure on the morale of their remaining employees in the airline's Johannesburg, Frankfurt, Atlanta and Singapore hubs.

Review of relevant information

Relevant information must satisfy the following criteria:

- It differs between courses of action—out-of-pocket and opportunity costs are relevant.
- It affects the future—sunk costs are irrelevant to a decision.
- It provides a balance between timeliness and accuracy.
- It may consist of both quantitative and qualitative information.

The importance of providing only relevant information

Why is it important for the management accountant to provide only the relevant costs and benefits in a decision analysis? There are several reasons. First, generating information is a costly process. The relevant data must be sought and analysed, and this requires time and effort. By focusing only on the relevant information, the management accountant can simplify and shorten the data gathering and analysis process.

Second, it is costly to have managers' limited time spent on reading and processing information that is not relevant to a decision. Thus, supplying irrelevant information can result in a waste of managerial resources.

Finally, as we recognised in Chapter 1, people can effectively use only a limited amount of information. Beyond this, they experience information overload and their decision-making effectiveness declines. By providing only relevant costs and benefits, the likelihood of information overload may be reduced.

Information for unique versus repetitive decisions

Many of the decisions that are outlined in this chapter can be classified as unique decisions that arise infrequently or only once. Wings Airlines' decision regarding its London hub is an example. Compiling information for unique decisions usually requires a special analysis by the management accountant. The relevant information will often be found in diverse places, both inside and outside the organisation.

In contrast, repetitive decisions are made over and over again, at either regular or irregular intervals. For example, an airline may make scheduling decisions every six months. Such a decision makes it worthwhile for the management accountant to ensure that information relevant to the scheduling decision is produced on a regular basis.

Cost predictions relevant to repetitive decisions may draw on a large amount of historical data. Since the decisions have been made repeatedly in the past, the data to support those decisions should be readily available. Information relevant to unique decisions is harder to generate. The management accountant will have to give more thought to deciding which data are relevant, and will have less historical data available upon which to base predictions.

Information for decisions

What costs and benefits are relevant when a manager must decide whether to add or drop a product or service? What data are relevant when deciding whether to produce or buy a particular service or component? For many of the decisions that are examined in this section, the relevant information focuses on the incremental costs and incremental revenues associated with choosing a particular course of action. **Incremental revenue** is the additional revenue that will be gained as a result of choosing one course of action over another. Similarly, **incremental costs** are the additional costs that arise from choosing that alternative.

In other decisions, the focus of the relevant information is on determining the avoidable and unavoidable costs. Avoidable costs are those costs that will not be incurred in the future if a particular decision is made. Unavoidable costs are costs that will continue to be incurred, no matter which course of action is chosen. Unavoidable costs are irrelevant to the decision.

Let's now consider the information that is needed for decisions that managers often make.

Accept or reject a special order

L.O. 4 In a special order decision, managers are faced with deciding whether or not to supply a customer with a single, one-off order for goods or services, at a special price. The incremental costs associated with the decision will often be the direct costs of producing the product for the special order. However, sometimes costs of special equipment or other activities related to the special order are also included. For example, producing the special order may entail product design costs and special distribution arrangements.

Jim Wright, Wings Airlines' operations manager, has been approached by a Perth tourist agency that has requested a one-off special flight. The tourist agency has offered Wings Airlines R750 000 for a round-trip flight between Perth and Mauritius. The airline does not usually fly this route, so the decision requires a special analysis by Jim Wright.

Special orders and excess capacity

In some situations, a special order will utilise **spare (excess) production capacity**, which exists when there is equipment, labour or other inputs that are not being utilised and are therefore available for other purposes. In other cases, accepting the special order may mean using capacity that would normally be used for producing regular products. In general, if a business has excess or spare capacity in its operational facilities, then any special order that has incremental revenue greater than the incremental costs is acceptable as it will contribute some additional profits for the company.

Jim Wright knows that Wings Airlines will have a jumbo jet idle at the time the agency requires the special flight. To help make his decision, Wright asks the accountant to provide cost estimates. These are based on a typical round-trip jumbo jet flight of the same distance as the special flight.

Variable cost of the flight	R450 000
Fixed costs allocated to the flight	R500 000

The variable costs cover reservations and ticketing costs, aircraft fuel and maintenance, flight crew costs, in-flight meals and services, and landing fees. The fixed costs allocated to each flight are facility level costs that relate to the entire operations of Wings Airlines and include aircraft depreciation, maintenance and depreciation of facilities, and administrative costs.

If Jim Wright had not understood management accounting, he might have done the following incorrect analysis:

Price of special flight	R750 000
Total cost of flight	R950 000
Loss on special flight	−R200 000

This calculation suggests that the special charter offer should be declined. What is the error in this analysis? The mistake is the inclusion of allocated fixed costs in the total cost of the special flight. This is an error because the total fixed costs of the company will not increase if the charter flight is undertaken. Since the fixed costs will not change under either alternative, they are irrelevant.

Fortunately, Jim Wright does not make this mistake. He knows that only the incremental costs of the proposed charter are relevant. Moreover, Wright determines that the variable costs of the charter would be lower than those of a typical flight because Wings Airlines would not incur the costs of reservations and ticketing. These costs amount to about R25 000 for a scheduled flight. Wright's correct analysis of the charter offer is shown in Exhibit 19.2.

Incremental revenue:		
Price of the special flight		R 750 000
Incremental costs:		
Variable cost of a routine flight	R 450 000	
Less Savings on reservations and ticketing	25 000	
Direct cost of special flight		R 425 000
Contribution from special flight		R 325 000

Exhibit 19.2 Incremental revenues and costs of special flight with excess capacity, Wings Airlines

Wright's analysis shows that the special charter flight will contribute R325 000 towards covering the airline's fixed costs and profit. This is because the incremental revenue from the special flight is greater than the incremental costs. Since the airline has excess flight capacity due to an idle aircraft, the optimal decision is to accept the special charter offer. Note that this solution assumes that the airline has no other uses for the idle aircraft.

Special orders and no excess capacity

Now we shall consider how the analysis appears if the airline has no idle aircraft (that is, if there is no excess capacity). Suppose that in order to fly the charter between Perth and Mauritius, the airline would make an aircraft available by cancelling a flight on its least profitable route, which is between Perth and Durban. This flight normally contributes R400 000 towards covering the airline's fixed costs and profit. Therefore, if the charter offer is accepted, the airline will lose R400 000, which is the forgone contribution margin on the Perth–Durban flight. We will assume that there are no long-term effects of cancelling this flight. This amount is an opportunity cost, and must be included in the decision analysis. Wright's analysis appears in Exhibit 19.3.

Incremental revenue:		
Price of the special flight		R750 000
Incremental costs:		
Variable cost of a routine flight	R450 000	
Less Savings on reservations and tickets	−25 000	
Direct cost of special flight		R425 000
Contribution from special flight		R325 000
Less Opportunity cost—forgone contribution from cancelling flight		400 000
Loss if special flight accepted		−R75 000

Exhibit 19.3 Incremental revenues and costs of special flight with no excess capacity, Wings Airlines

Thus, if Wings Airlines has no excess flight capacity (that is, no idle aircraft), then Jim Wright should reject the special charter offer as the company would be worse off by R75 000. Another way of interpreting this solution is to realise that the contribution to profits from accepting the special flight (R325 000) is R75 000 less than the contribution from the cancelled flight which is R400 000.

Qualitative factors

As with all decisions, the management of Wings Airlines must consider any other relevant factors that may impact on the decision. In this case, Wright needs to consider whether or not providing the special flight will have any adverse effects on regular business. For example, will profits on other flights be reduced because some existing customers choose to fly on the Perth charter to Mauritius rather than on other regular flights of the company?[1]

The significance of a one-off decision

A key assumption in analysing a special order decision is that it is a once-only decision. If the tourist agency is likely to approach Wings Airlines in the future with the same request, there may be two further issues to consider.[2]

First, if the company has excess capacity that it is continually using for the 'special' flight between Perth and Mauritius, it can be argued that this flight should be regarded as part of the regular business of the airline. As such, it may be considered that the order should not be accepted unless the price of the flight is set to cover both direct and facility level costs.[3] Thus, while the relevant costs associated with the decision may not change, management may consider reviewing the agreed price. If existing customers were to learn about this 'special pricing', customer dissatisfaction might result. Setting prices for one class of customer that cover only the incremental costs of the flight leads to other customers being charged a price high enough to cover all of the other costs of the business.

Second, if there is no spare capacity, the airline may choose to increase capacity rather than sacrifice current profitable flights. This may entail leasing or purchasing an additional aircraft and incurring more overheads to service this capacity. In this situation, the relevant costs of the decision may increase. This will also cause the company to review the most suitable price for the flight. (Pricing issues are explored further in Chapter 20.)

Note that in both of these situations, the one-off special order has become a long-term decision.

Review of relevant costs for special order decisions

The decision to accept or reject a special order is a tactical decision that is common to firms in both service and manufacturing industries. The correct analysis of such decisions focuses on the incremental costs and benefits. Several costs, such as fixed, facility level costs, are usually irrelevant to the decision as it is assumed that these costs will not change in total, whether the order is accepted or rejected.

When excess capacity exists, the relevant costs will usually be only the incremental costs associated with the special order. In general, when the incremental revenues from a special order are in excess of the incremental costs of producing that order, then, on financial grounds, the order should be accepted. This is because the special order generates a contribution to the company profits. When there is no excess capacity, the same rule applies except that the opportunity cost of using the firm's facilities for the special order is also relevant to the decision. Qualitative issues, such as the impact on existing customers of accepting the special order, should always be considered.

Make or buy a product

L.O. 5

In a make-or-buy decision, an organisation is faced with the choice of whether to produce particular goods or services itself, or purchase them from an external supplier. Sometimes this entails the outside supplier producing a custom-made product especially for the business.

James Swart is Wings Airlines' manager of in-flight services. He supervises the airline's flight attendants and all of the firm's food and beverage operations. Swart currently faces a decision regarding the preparation of in-flight dinners at the airline's Johannesburg hub. In the Johannesburg flight kitchen, dinners are prepared and packaged for long-haul flights that start at Johannesburg (O. R. Tambo). Swart has received a call from a Johannesburg bakery, which has offered to produce the airline's desserts. Currently, all the desserts are baked and packaged in the flight kitchen. Swart's decision, therefore, is whether to make or buy the dessert portion of the in-flight dinners. To help guide his decision, Swart has assembled product costing information, shown in Exhibit 19.4, which shows a total cost per dessert of R1.25.

The Johannesburg bakery has offered to supply the desserts for R1.05 each. Swart's initial inclination is to accept the bakery's offer, since it appears that the airline would save 20 cents per dessert. However, the management accountant reminds Swart that not all the costs listed in Exhibit 19.4 are relevant to the make-or-buy decision. Swart asks the management accountant to prepare an analysis of the relevant costs of the decision for a one-month period. The accountant's report, displayed in Exhibit 19.5, compares the total costs of producing, or purchasing, the 1 000 000 desserts, which is the flight kitchen's average monthly volume.

	Cost per dessert
Variable costs:	
Direct material (food and packaging)	R0.30
Direct labour	0.20
Electricity	0.20
Fixed costs (allocated to products):	
Supervisory salaries	0.20
Depreciation of kitchen equipment	0.35
Total cost per dessert	R1.25

Exhibit 19.4 Cost of in-flight dessert, Wings Airlines

	Alternatives	
	Make desserts	Buy desserts
Cost of purchasing desserts		R1 050 000
Variable costs:		
Direct material (avoidable)	R300 000	
Direct labour (avoidable)	200 000	
Electricity (avoidable)	200 000	
Fixed costs:		
Supervisory salaries (avoidable)	50 000	
Supervisory salaries (unavoidable)	150 000	150 000
Depreciation (unavoidable)	350 000	350 000
Total costs	R1 250 000	R1 550 000
Additional cost per month of purchasing desserts	R300 000	

Exhibit 19.5 Total costs of the make-or-buy decision, Wings Airlines

A key to determining the financial impact of the alternatives in a make-or-buy decision is to consider which costs are avoidable and which are not. In a make-or-buy decision, the avoidable costs are those costs that will not be incurred in the future if the decision is taken to buy the product or service rather than make it in-house. The unavoidable costs are those costs that will still be incurred whether the product or service is manufactured in-house or by an external party.

It can be seen in Exhibit 19.5 that if Wings Airlines buys the desserts, it will not incur the variable costs of producing the desserts—these are avoidable costs. Also, some of the 'fixed' costs are avoidable. If the desserts are purchased, R150 000 of the cost of supervisory salaries would still be incurred. However, R50 000 would be avoided as the airline kitchen could operate with fewer kitchen supervisors. The remaining fixed cost of depreciation would still be incurred even if the desserts were purchased. The analysis indicates that the incremental costs of buying the desserts is R300 000 per month. In light of the analysis, it seems that the airline should continue to make its own desserts.

Note that the solution in Exhibit 19.5 compares the total costs of the two alternatives. Another solution, based on incremental costs, can be presented:

Cost of purchasing desserts		R1 050 000
Less Cost savings due to purchasing the desserts:		
Direct material	R300 000	
Direct labour	200 000	
Electricity	200 000	
Supervisory salaries	50 000	750 000
Additional costs of purchasing desserts		R300 000

This presentation considers only those costs that differ between the two alternatives. The costs that are unavoidable are common to both alternatives and have been left out of the decision analysis, without changing the outcome. In Exhibit 19.5 we have included these irrelevant costs in the analysis to make the example easier to understand. In real life, this redundant information would not be estimated, as this would lengthen the time and cost of the data-gathering process. Nor would it be included in the analysis, as this would add unnecessary detail to the presentation.

Opportunity costs

In a make-or-buy decision, opportunity costs may also be relevant. Suppose that by choosing to buy desserts from the bakery, the kitchen could use the freed-up capacity to produce additional main courses. These could be sold to another airline for R450 000 per month. It is estimated that the additional costs of producing these extra meals would amount to R125 000. Thus, there is an opportunity cost associated with using the freed-up capacity, amounting to R325 000 (R450 000 – R125 000). Once again, the incremental costs associated with the decision can be focused on:

Cost of purchasing desserts		R1 050 000
Less Cost savings due to purchasing desserts:		
Direct material	R300 000	
Direct labour	200 000	
Electricity	200 000	
Supervisory salaries	50 000	750 000
Additional costs of purchasing desserts		R300 000
Additional profit from using freed capacity to produce main courses (opportunity cost)		325 000
Cost savings of purchasing desserts		R25 000

Notice that in this case, the 'opportunity cost' is not a cost at all. Instead of giving up a potential benefit when the desserts are purchased, Wings will gain a potential benefit from using the freed-up space to make and sell extra main courses. Another way of looking at this is that the potential profit from using the freed-up space is an opportunity cost of continuing to produce desserts in-house, as shown in Exhibit 19.6. This exhibit analyses the costs of each alternative. In this decision, buying the desserts and using the excess capacity of the kitchen to produce additional main courses would result in a cost saving of R25 000 per month.

	Alternatives	
	Make desserts	Buy desserts
Cost of purchasing desserts		R1 050 000
Variable costs:		
Direct material (avoidable)	R300 000	
Direct labour (avoidable)	200 000	
Electricity (avoidable)	200 000	
Fixed costs:		
Supervisory salaries (avoidable)	50 000	
Supervisory salaries (unavoidable)	150 000	150 000
Depreciation (unavoidable)	350 000	350 000
Opportunity costs of using spare capacity to produce additional meals	325 000	
Total costs	R1 575 000	R1 550 000
Net cost savings per month by purchasing desserts and using facilities to produce extra meals	R25 000	

Exhibit 19.6 Total costs of the make-or-buy decision with opportunity costs, Wings Airlines

Qualitative and strategic issues

The above cost analysis, which includes the opportunity cost, indicates that it is cheaper to purchase the desserts from the outside bakery than to manufacture them in-house. However, a range of qualitative issues should also be considered: Would the quality of those purchased desserts be consistent? Would the delivery schedule be suitable? For how long would the price per dessert remain unchanged? Also, could production in the flight kitchen be easily resumed if the decision were reversed?

Qualitative issues are particularly important in a make-or-buy decision. When goods or services cease to be produced and are purchased from a supplier, the organisation effectively loses some control over a range of important factors, which may then impact on customer value. Factors to be considered include:

- the quality of the outsourced product;
- the delivery responsiveness of the supplier;
- the technical capabilities of the supplier;
- labour relations at the supplier;
- the financial stability of the supplier; and

- the ability of the supplier to respect confidential information gained in the course of the relationship.

When companies are seeking to enhance customer value, they must avoid making decisions that may impact negatively on those aspects of the product or service that are important to customers.

Beware of unit cost data

In many organisations, fixed costs are often allocated to individual units of product for product costing purposes, or for determining the full profitability of a product. For decision-making purposes, however, allocating fixed costs to units of production can be misleading, as it can imply that these costs vary with the rate of production. However, the manner in which 'fixed' costs change under different decision alternatives can be specific to the particular decision. As the cost analysis in Exhibit 19.5 shows, only R50 000 in 'fixed' monthly costs will be avoided if the desserts are purchased. The remaining R500 000 of monthly fixed costs will continue whether the desserts are made or purchased. Swart's initial cost analysis implied that each dessert cost the airline R1.25 to produce. However, as shown in Exhibit 19.4, that R1.25 cost includes 55 cents of allocated fixed costs. Most of these fixed costs will remain unchanged regardless of the outcome of the make-or-buy decision. They will not all be avoided if the decision is made to buy the desserts. By allocating fixed costs to individual products, they may appear to act as variable costs, even though they are not.

Review of relevant costs for make-or-buy decisions

In a make-or-buy decision, it is important to distinguish between avoidable and unavoidable costs. Unavoidable costs are irrelevant to the decision and so can be omitted from the decision analysis without affecting the outcome.[4] In the analysis of any fixed costs it is wise to focus on total fixed costs rather than on per unit costs, and consider how or if those fixed costs will change as a result of the decision. Opportunity costs may also be relevant to the decision if unused facilities can be used for another purpose. Qualitative factors are particularly important in make-or-buy decisions as the operations of the outside supplier are largely beyond the control of the purchasing organisation.

Outsourcing decisions

Outsourcing describes situations in which part of a manufacturing process, or another function normally undertaken within an organisation, is contracted to an outside business (Langfield-Smith, Smith & Stringer, 2000; Domberger, 1998). The term 'outsourcing' is sometimes used interchangeably with make-or-buy, as it involves choosing to source goods or services either inside or outside the firm. However, outsourcing tends to imply more long-term arrangements. It is becoming common for organisations to outsource part or all of their information-processing function, payroll, training, inventory management, distribution and manufacturing processes, or even the accounting function!

Many organisations choose to outsource in order to manage escalating costs or to take advantage of the high level of skills and expertise of an outside specialist firm. This was the case for Edcon, as described in the 'Real life' below. While the criteria used to recognise relevant costs and benefits for an outsourcing decision are similar to those for make-or-buy decisions, the longer time frame may require a greater range of qualitative factors to be considered. Once a function is outsourced it can be difficult to reverse that decision, as both the infrastructure necessary to carry out the function and the expertise of in-house personnel may need to be re-established. For example, if the manufacture of a component is outsourced, specialised equipment may be disposed of and employees may lose their expertise. Also, the external provider may develop unique specialised skills and knowledge that, over time, exceed those of the original manufacturer. This may make it very difficult for the manufacturer to take production back in-house if there is dissatisfaction with price increases, delivery responsiveness or quality. The qualitative considerations that are relevant in make-or-buy decisions become even more important in an outsourcing decision. Many organisations have found that the benefits of outsourcing do exceed the costs even when qualitative factors are taken into account, as is shown in the Edcon example below.

REAL LIFE: OUTSOURCING AT EDCON

Edgars Consolidated Stores (Edcon) is the leading clothing, textiles and footwear retailing group in Southern Africa. The group operates over 900 stores and the group includes such store formats as Edgars, CAN, Jet, Red Square and Boardmans. The group has over 20 000 employees. The group is a leading credit retailer and has over 4 million cardholders. As you read this, you may have an Edgars' card close to you. The company's sales revenue is over R17 billion.

The group was one of the first major companies in South Africa to outsource its Information Technology (IT) capabilities and systems. Although many companies have started to outsource IT, Human Resources and other back office functions that are considered to be non-core, Edcon was different as it considered its IT capabilities as a source of competitive advantage. In fact, IT was considered to be core to its business operations. Edcon appointed Accenture to transform its IT systems in the late 1990s. Accenture would manage Edcon's application systems, maintenance, achieve system integration, undertake training, standardise systems and introduce new IT capabilities. These included introducing a new supply chain management system, retail demand forecasting and price management modules, a new sales monitoring system and a new credit management system. Edcon is the largest credit retailer in Southern Africa. Accenture is a global management consulting, technology services and outsourcing company which employs about 146 000 people in 49 countries and generated close to US$17 billion in revenue in 2006.

So what happened to Edcon since outsourcing its IT capabilities to Accenture? For example, what is the impact of the new sales monitoring system? Henri Slabbert, the chief information officer at Edcon, states: 'With this system, we know every day what's happening with about one million active items in our stores, giving us the ability to act quickly on mistakes.' We are sure that it also enables Edcon to react quickly to successes so that the group will order more of items selling well to ensure that orders are placed well in advance of running out of inventory.

In financial terms, Edcon has increased its sales revenue from about R6 billion to over R16 billion in about 8 years and the company's share price increased from about R2 to about R45. While there were significant external forces such as lower interest rates and a strong economy that have bolstered Edcon's revenues, the fact is that its investment in new IT systems and its outsourcing arrangements with Accenture gave the group the capability to achieve and manage the significant pressures that strong growth places on systems and the distribution networks. Outsourcing and upgrading its IT capabilities has enabled the group to increase its stock turnover from 3.4 to 6.1 in five years and it has enabled the group to increase its distribution to 275 million units in 2006. Yet, the cost of IT as a percentage of sales has fallen from about 5 to 3.8 per cent.

The focus by Edcon to undertake outsourcing is not simply to achieve cost savings, it is about creating value. As Slabbert states: 'Some people think you can only outsource the things that are non-core. That's a misconception. Working with Accenture, we benefit from their worldwide experience in the retail business and in systems development. We leverage off that capability, knowing that we are getting international best practice and solutions that we are confident will work.' It is an interesting perspective. In 2007 Bain Capital undertook South Africa's largest private equity buyout to date by purchasing Edcon for over R25 billion. This means that Edcon is no longer listed on the JSE Securities Exchange and is now owned by Bain Capital.

Source: www.accenture.com and www.edcon.co.za

REAL LIFE: OUTSOURCING, YOU CAN BANK ON IT!

Banks have been at the forefront of the outsourcing revolution. Banks are outsourcing Information Technology (IT), electronic payments, cheque processing, human resources, custodial services, security, and account administration. Banks can even outsource the internal audit function, and may also outsource asset management by using independent fund managers. The South African Reserve Bank is concerned about banks outsourcing the compliance function. Although there have been some problems with the initial outsourcing process undertaken by some of the major banks in the 1990s, the process is irreversible.

BusinessWeek (30 January 2006) reported a Deutsche Bank executive saying about outsourcing: 'The issue is if you don't do it, you won't survive.' Banks are moving skilled work to other countries such as India and China. This is called offshore outsourcing. Businesses talk about 'labour arbitrage', which means that the cost of labour is much lower in India and China. However, this may be temporary. What is also important is to acquire talented people and that is where one-third of the world's population resides. Outsourcing makes costs more variable although firms will enter into contracts that last a few years.

What about investment banks? The reality is that firms such as J.P. Morgan and Morgan Stanley are using Indian firms or setting up subsidiaries in India to undertake financial modelling, to determine ratios and undertake comparative analyses. The high-level financial and qualitative analysis is done in the USA. The cost of an analyst in India is about 25 per cent of the cost of an analyst in New York. It is only a matter of time before this trend reaches South Africa.

In relation to business process outsourcing, South Africa is a destination for multinational firms. We have seen call centres being set up in South Africa to handle customer queries on behalf of a number of companies from the Netherlands, Germany, the UK and the USA.

All this outsourcing raises questions about what makes a firm. Let's look at the firm, **ATM Solutions** to whom banks outsource a key function of their business. ATMs are either owned by banks or are owned and operated by independent firms. There may be revenue sharing arrangements with the banks. ATM Solutions is a company that focuses on placing and operating ATMs in locations not traditionally serviced by the banks and in convenient locations for their clients, for example, petrol service stations and retail outlets. ATM Solutions is now the market leader and controls close to 50 percent of the off-premise ATM market in South Africa. The company controls and manages the operations of each ATM which includes cash management, ATM monitoring and maintenance, security, transaction processing, and daily balancing and reconciliations all of which is supported by a customer support centre.

The company however outsources most of these functions to its strategic partners. The ATMs are from **Triton**, who is the leading provider of off-premise ATMs in the USA. The company uses software from **Postilion**, which is a leading provider of electronic funds transfer (EFT) software, to drive the network of machines. The firm uses **Symetrix** to manage and maintain the ATM IT systems in South Africa. G4S (formerly known as Fidelity) ensures that the machines are always loaded with cash. G4S is the leading provider of cash-in-transit services in South Africa and transports about R400 billion annually for all its clients. **Absa** is the major transaction acquiring bank however the company has relationships with all the major banks. **Connectnet** provides bi-directional wireless data communications to the ATM Solutions' network. The outsourcing of the firm's critical functions is core to the company's business model, yet the company retains control of the business and this has been proven very successful.

REAL LIFE: DOES OUTSOURCING WORK?

Many organisations view outsourcing as an effective way of managing and reducing the complexities in their business. Outsourcing can provide firms with opportunities to meet the challenges of globalisation, can lead to overcoming resource constraints and may provide access to specialised skills and expertise. A well-managed outsourcing arrangement can lead to cost savings as well as improvements in customer service, product quality and competitiveness.

When the outsourced functions are simple, benefits can be more easily achieved. Hotels for example can outsource the housekeeping function to an independent firm, whose staff may wear the hotel uniforms and may be supervised by the hotel managers. A hotel no longer has to become involved in complex labour and time-consuming human resource management issues. It can achieve cost savings and high levels of customer service thanks to negotiating a well-thought-out and detailed service agreement with the independent firm. The detailed arrangements are reviewed each year and updated.

Outsourcing can be used as a competitive tool. Airlines can make significant progress against other airline competitors by outsourcing, or threatening to outsource, in-house functions in order to reduce labour costs. Employees may be asked to bid against outsourcers to retain their jobs. These moves have allowed some airlines to reduce ticket prices, to increase their market share, and to survive in a climate of discount pricing in the airline industry. Lufthansa outsourced the maintenance of its Boeing fleet to SAA in order to achieve cost savings.

In addition, as indicated in the case of Edcon, outsourcing can provide firms with access to high levels of skills and expertise that they could not hope to achieve within their own firm. Using Accenture provided Edcon with access to a global pool of IT experts who could be called on to provide assistance with specific problems and could be relied upon to always be at the cutting edge of technology.

Sources: Langfield-Smith, Smith & Stringer (2000); Long (2001); Tolhurst (2001); Bennett (2001)

Add or delete a product, service or department

L.O. 6

The decision to eliminate a product, service or department involves considering which costs and benefits will disappear if the decision is taken. The decision to add a product, service or department involves estimating the additional costs and revenues that will arise from that decision. These decisions clearly have long-term implications. Here we will simply focus on identifying the relevant costs and benefits.

Deleting a department

Wings Airlines offers its passengers the opportunity to join its World Hoppers Club. Club membership entitles a traveller to use the club facilities at Johannesburg Airport, which include a private lounge, meals and beverages, and the use of a small health spa. John Masiza, the managing director of Wings Airlines, is worried about the World Hoppers Club not being profitable. The monthly profit statement for the club is shown in Exhibit 19.7.

At his weekly staff meeting Masiza states that he is concerned about the World Hoppers Club running at a loss and is considering whether it should be dropped. However, the management accountant points out that not all of the costs on the club's profit statement would be eliminated if the club were discontinued. The sales manager adds that the club is vital to the business as it helps Wings Airlines to attract and maintain passengers that it might otherwise lose to a competitor. As the meeting adjourns, Masiza asks the management accountant to prepare an analysis of the costs and benefits associated with dropping the World Hoppers Club. This analysis is displayed in Exhibit 19.8.

Sales revenue		R1 000 000
Less Variable costs:		
Food and beverages	R350 000	
Personnel wages	200 000	
Electricity and telephone	125 000	675 000
Contribution margin		325 000
Less Fixed costs:		
Depreciation of furnishing and equipment	R150 000	
Supervisiory salaries	100 000	
Insurance	25 000	
Rent	50 000	
General administrative costs (allocated)	50 000	375 000
Net loss		−R50 000

Exhibit 19.7 World Hoppers Club Monthly Profit Statement, Wings Airlines

	Alternatives	
	Retain club	Eliminate club
Sales revenue	R1 000 000	0
Less Costs:	R1 050 000	R200 000
Food and beverages (avoidable)	350 000	
Personnel wages (avoidable)	100 000	
Personnel wages (unavoidable)	100 000	100 000
Electricity and telephone (avoidable)	125 000	
Depreciation (avoidable)	150 000	
Supervisory salaries (avoidable)	100 000	
Insurance (avoidable)	25 000	
Rent (unavoidable)	50 000	50 000
General administrative costs (allocated)	50 000	50 000
Net loss	−R50 000	−R200 000
Additional loss per month by eliminating the club	R150 000	

Exhibit 19.8 Total revenues and costs of decision to drop the World Hoppers Club, Wings Airlines

In the first column of this report the management accountant has listed the revenues and costs that are incurred each month if the club is retained. The second column shows the costs that would not be avoided if the club were eliminated. The depreciation, supervisory salaries and insurance will be avoided if the club is eliminated. However, the R50 000 rental fee paid to the airport for the privilege of operating the club must continue to be paid because there is a long-term contract in place. The club's allocated portion of general administrative expenses, R50 000, is unavoidable. Wings Airlines will incur these expenses regardless of which alternative it chooses. Also, R100 000 of the personnel wages will remain because the airline has recently placed some personnel on a one-year contract.

It can be seen that if the club is closed, the airline will be worse off by R150 000 per month. However, this is not the final answer. As the sales director pointed out, the World Hoppers Club is attractive to many travellers. The management accountant estimates that if the club were discontinued, the airline would also lose R300 000 each month in forgone contribution margin from decreased airline ticket sales. This loss would result from losing passengers (who would otherwise have been attracted to Wings Airlines by its World Hoppers Club) to a competing airline. This R300 000 in forgone contribution margin is an opportunity cost of the option to close down the club. An incremental analysis of the full decision is presented in Exhibit 19.9.

As Exhibit 19.9 shows, when the opportunity cost is considered, the loss to the airline by discontinuing the club amounts to R450 000 per month. That is, Wings Airlines' monthly profit will decrease by R450 000 if the club is closed. The financial analysis indicates that the club should be retained.

Sales revenue forgone		−R1 000 000
Less Cost saved by eliminating the club:		
Food and beverages	R350 000	
Personnel wages	100 000	
Electricity and telephone	125 000	
Depreciation	150 000	
Supervisory salaries	100 000	
Insurance	25 000	R850 000
Net loss by eliminating the club		−R150 000
Lost contribution from decreased sales		−300 000
Overall loss by eliminating the club		−R450 000

Exhibit 19.9 Overall loss from the decision to drop the World Hoppers Club, Wings Airlines

Adding a product

The sales manager of Wings Airlines, Jayne Le Roux, has suggested to senior management that they should introduce a new flight route—a round trip from Cape Town to the Antarctic Circle. Another South African airline has introduced similar flights, and demand has been growing. Le Roux believes that a competitive price is R3000 for the round trip. Like its competitor, Wings Airlines would provide champagne, drinks, meals by a leading chef and entertainment as part of the service.

The management accountant has estimated the direct costs per trip:

Meals & drinks	R250	per seat
Fuel	R100 000	
Salaries of pilots	R25 000	
Salaries of flight attendants	R12 500	
Entertainment	R6 000	

The aircraft that would be used seats 200 passengers, and would be filled with passengers to 70 per cent capacity. An average of two flights would be scheduled each month. From this information, Le Roux calculates the contribution to profits for the first year of operation:

Sales revenue (R3000 × 200 × 0.70 × 24 flights)		R10 080 000
Less Direct costs:		
Meals & drinks (R250 × 200 × 0.70 × 24)	R840 000	
Fuel (R100 000 × 24)	2 400 000	
Salaries of pilots (R25 000 × 24)	600 000	
Salaries of flight attendants (R12 500 × 24)	300 000	
Entertainment (R6000 × 24)	144 000	R4 284 000
Contribution to profits		R5 796 000

The management accountant points out that Le Roux has not considered the impact of introducing the new product on the overheads of the airline. However, he has difficulty determining, from the accounting system, the likely increases in aircraft maintenance expenses and administrative expenses. To cost existing products, the management accountant allocates overheads to products at a predetermined rate, based on the number of air-kilometres travelled. However, this does not reveal by how much overheads will change with the introduction of the new flight. Air-kilometres are not an accurate cost driver for the range of overheads that the airline incurs. If the company had an activity-based costing system, then the impact of the new product on costs would be clearer.

The management accountant, in consultation with Jayne Le Roux, determines that the new flight will cause increased selling and advertising costs, airline maintenance, and landing and airport gate fees. The cost of reservations and ticketing, and administrative costs, are not expected to increase, as the new business created by the addition of this flight is relatively small. There will be no additional aircraft depreciation, as this would have been incurred whether or not the flight was introduced. The full analysis of the decision is presented in Exhibit 19.10. The financial analysis indicates that the introduction of the new flight to Antarctica will generate additional profits of R3 946 000 in its first year.

Incremental sales revenue		R10 080 000
Less Incremental costs:		
Meals	R840 000	
Fuel	2 400 000	
Salaries of pilots (now including on-costs)	800 000	
Salaries of flight attendants (now including on-costs)	370 000	
Entertainment	144 000	
Aircraft maintenance	250 000	
Selling and advertising	1 000 000	
Landing fees	250 000	
Airport gate fees	80 000	R6 134 000
Incremental profits for first year of operation		R3 946 000

Exhibit 19.10 Incremental revenues and costs from the new flight, Wings Airlines

Misleading accounting data

Both the 'deleting a department' and 'adding a product' examples indicate that care should be taken in relying on conventional accounting profit statements and conventional product costs. These often contain allocations of costs which may not be avoided if the product or department is deleted. Also, these allocated costs do not help in determining the increases in indirect costs that may result if a new product, service or department is introduced. In considering the addition of a product, service or department, it is the incremental costs and revenues that are relevant to the decision.

Qualitative and strategic issues

As with all decisions, an alternative cannot be chosen by relying solely on financial data. In decisions to delete a product, service or department, a range of other factors must be considered. For example, will there be an impact on any other part of the business if a department is deleted? Will we lose customers if a product or service is discontinued? Is it preferable to continue to sell some loss-making products in order to ensure higher sales of other products? Another issue that may be relevant in the decision to drop a department is the impact on the morale of employees working in other departments.

In the decision to add a new flight, the focus was on determining the relevant costs and revenues of the decision. These are the additional costs and revenues that will be incurred if the new flight is introduced. However, any decision to introduce or delete a product or service is a strategic decision. Such a decision may entail changes in capacity to accommodate the increased or decreased activities resulting from the decision. The pricing structure needs careful attention, and any decision to change product mix should involve considering any impact on the organisation's competitive position. These issues are reviewed in Chapter 20.

The addition or deletion of a product or department affects operations and profits over the long term. In most situations it is wiser to analyse cost and revenue flows that extend over some years, taking into account the time value of money. (This approach is described in Chapter 21.) The cash flows associated with the introduction of a new product should be estimated over the life cycle of the product in order to determine the financial impact on the business. Examples of life cycle analysis are included in Chapter 15.

Review of add or delete decisions

In deciding whether to delete a product or department, the analysis focuses on which costs and revenues will cease if the decision goes ahead. Care should be taken when costs have been allocated to the product or department. These costs will not be avoided if the decision is taken to eliminate the product or department. In deciding whether to add a product or department, the incremental revenues and costs are the focus of the analysis.

Joint products: sell or process further

L.O. 7

So far in this chapter we have examined three types of decisions that may arise in either service or manufacturing situations. Decisions about whether to sell a joint product or to process it further tend to be associated with manufacturing companies, so we will examine this type of decision in a manufacturing context.

What are joint products? **Joint products** are two or more products that are produced simultaneously from the one production process. A common example of joint products occurs in the oil-refining industry, where petroleum, LPG, kerosene and other products are produced from the one process. Another example occurs in the chicken-processing industry, where joint products would include the various cuts of a chicken—drumsticks, wings and breasts—as well as chicken feet, feathers and the carcass. The dilemma, from a financial accounting point of view, is that because we are unable to identify individual products during processing, we cannot determine precisely the cost of each individual product. To value inventory and cost of goods sold, accountants have to use some arbitrary method for allocating the joint production costs to products. For management decisions, however, we must interpret joint production costs carefully. We will illustrate this using an example based on the International Chocolate Company.

Manufacturers with joint production processes must sometimes decide whether a joint product should be sold at the split-off point or processed further before being sold. The **split-off point** is that stage in the production process where the joint products are identifiable as separate products. Such a decision recently confronted Bill Pandey, the managing director of the International Chocolate Company. Pandey's firm imports cocoa beans and processes them into cocoa powder and cocoa butter.

Only a portion of the total cocoa powder is used by the International Chocolate Company in the production of chocolate bars. The remainder is sold to an ice-cream producer. Pandey is considering the possibility of processing this cocoa powder into an instant cocoa mix to be marketed under the brand name 'ChocoTime'. Data relating to the production process are displayed in Exhibit 19.11.

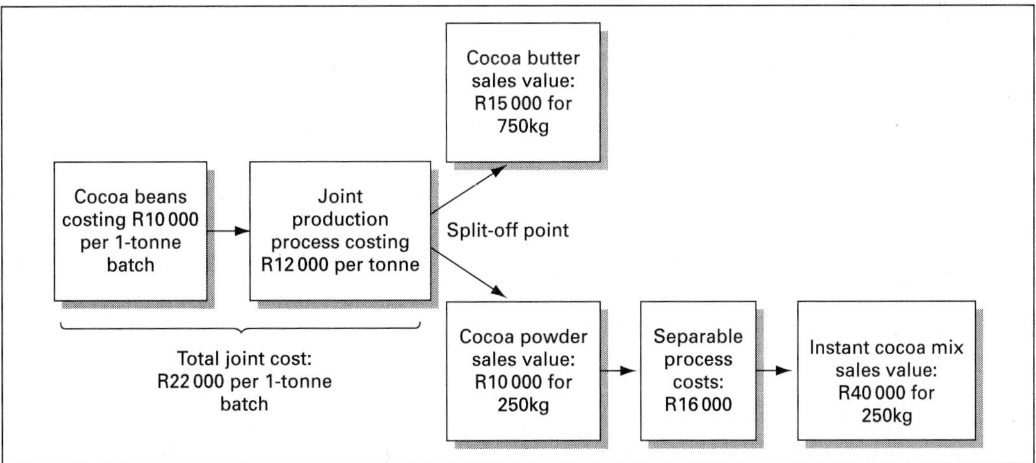

Exhibit 19.11 Joint processing of cocoa beans, International Chocolate Company

Notice from the diagram that cocoa beans are processed in 1-tonne batches. The total cost of the cocoa beans and the joint processing is R22 000. This is called the **joint cost**, which is the manufacturing cost incurred in the production of joint products. The output of the joint process is 750 kilograms of cocoa butter and 250 kilograms of cocoa powder.

How should Bill Pandey approach the decision about processing the cocoa powder into instant cocoa mix? What are the relevant costs and benefits? First, let's consider the joint cost of R22 000. Is this cost relevant to the decision at hand? The joint cost is not a relevant cost, because it will not change regardless of the decision Pandey makes.

However, suppose that the R22 000 joint cost had been allocated to the two joint products for product costing purposes. A common method for allocating a joint cost is the **relative sales value method**, in which the joint cost is allocated to the joint products in proportion to their sales value at the split-off point. (Other methods for allocating joint costs are covered in the appendix to this chapter.) The International Chocolate Company would make the joint cost allocation shown below.

Joint products	Sales value at split-off point	Relative proportion*	Joint cost	Allocation of joint cost
Cocoa butter	R15 000	0.6	R22 000	R13 200
Cocoa powder	R10 000	0.4	R22 000	R8 800
Total joint cost allocated				R22 000

* (15 000/(15 000 + 10 000)) = 0.6
* (10 000/(15 000 + 10 000)) = 0.4

Does this allocation of the R22 000 joint cost make it relevant to the decision about processing cocoa powder into an instant cocoa mix? The answer is still no! The R22 000 joint cost does not change in total, whether or not the cocoa powder is processed further. The joint cost is irrelevant to the decision at hand. This can be demonstrated by considering the total costs of the two alternatives, as presented in Exhibit 19.12.

	Alternatives	
	Sell cocoa powder at split-off point	Process cocoa powder into instant cocoa mix
Sales revenue:		
Cocoa butter	R15 000	R15 000
Cocoa powder	10 000	
Instant cocoa mix		40 000
Less Costs:		
Joint costs	22 000	22 000
Separable cost of processing cocoa powder into instant cocoa mix		16 000
Profit	R3 000	R17 000
Incremental profit from processing further	→ R14 000 ←	

Exhibit 19.12 Total revenues and costs of the decision to sell or process further, International Chocolate Company

The analysis in Exhibit 19.12 indicates that if cocoa powder is processed further, profits will increase by R14 000 a batch. However, this analysis contains many irrelevant costs. The only costs and benefits relevant to Pandey's decision are those that differ between the two alternatives. We can simplify the analysis by considering only the incremental costs and revenues of the decision as follows:

Incremental profits to be gained from processing further:		
Sales value of cocoa mix	R40 000	
Less Sales value of cocoa powder	10 000	R30 000
Less Incremental costs of processing further		16 000
Incremental profits to be gained from processing further		R14 000

This analysis provides the same answer as derived in Exhibit 19.12, and indicates that the joint production cost is not relevant to the decision. Many manufacturing companies allocate joint production costs to joint products using arbitrary methods. For decision purposes, we must remember that these costs are not relevant to the decision to either sell a product or process it further. This issue is explored further in the appendix to this chapter.

Implications of activity-based cost analysis for decisions

L.O. 8

You will have noticed that in the decisions discussed in this chapter it was often assumed that costs could be divided easily into variable and fixed components, and variable costs were often expressed in terms of production volume (such as variable cost per unit). When an activity-based approach to cost analysis is used, costs are analysed in more detail—identifying both volume-based and non-volume-based cost drivers—and costs are assigned to cost objects (such as products or departments) more accurately.

Issues such as identifying relevant costs, incremental costs, opportunity costs, sunk costs and avoidable costs do not change under an activity-based approach. However, more accurate cost information is available, based on a better understanding of the cost drivers, which increases the ability of management accountants to identify the precise cost implications of various decision alternatives. This will be illustrated with another example from the International Chocolate Company.

The company makes fine chocolates in its Msunduzi-Pietermaritzburg plant. The chocolates are packaged in 1-kilogram and 2-kilogram gift boxes which are manufactured at the same plant. The plant manager, Alice Bell, was recently approached by a packaging company with an offer to supply the 1-kilogram gift boxes at a price of R9.00 each. The annual requirement for the gift boxes is 1 million. Bell is aware that the manufacturing accountant, David Naidoo, has just completed a pilot project using activity-based costing. Naidoo offered to analyse the make-or-buy decision using the new activity data.

Naidoo identified the activities performed at the Msunduzi-Pietermaritzburg plant and assigned labour and overhead costs to them. He then estimated the cost per unit of activity driver for each activity. (The procedures used in activity-based costing are described in detail in Chapter 8.) He used this information to prepare the bill of activities, shown in Exhibit 19.13 below, for the 1 kilogram gift boxes. Note that in this analysis, different levels of activity are recognised and some non-manufacturing costs are included, such as the costs of product development. The cost of direct material has been added to the total activity cost to provide the total product cost per unit.

Using the ABC (activity-based costing) data, Naidoo completed a relevant cost analysis of the make-or-buy decision, as shown in Exhibit 19.14. This analysis indicates that all the activity costs assigned to the gift box operation could be avoided if the gift boxes were purchased. The purchase of the gift boxes would result in a net saving of R1 016 000.[5]

Naidoo showed the ABC relevant costing analysis to Bell. After some discussion they agreed that various qualitative issues needed to be explored before a final decision was made. For example, would the new supplier be reliable, and would the gift boxes be of good quality?

To summarise: under activity-based costing the concepts underlying relevant cost analysis do not change. However, the better recognition of cost drivers under activity analysis may result in more accurate information and better decisions.

Incentives for decision makers

L.O. 9

In this chapter we have studied how managers make decisions by focusing on the relevant costs and benefits. However, in an earlier part of this chapter it was also stated that managers do not always follow rational processes or systematic methods when making decisions. Various incentives may be created within organisations—intentionally or unintentionally—that may influence the ways in which managers make decisions. For example, there is an important link between decision

Bill of Activities: gift boxes					
Activities	Cost per unit of activity driver		Annual quantity of activity driver consumed	Annual activity cost of gift boxes	
Product level costs:					
Product development	R2 000	per product specification	2	4 000	
Supervision of product line	R800	per supervisory hour	15	12 000	
				R16 000	
Batch level costs:					
Material handling	R360	per move	1 000	360 000	
Inspection	R640	per inspection	1 000	640 000	
Setting up box machine	R4 000	per setup	1 000	4 000 000	
				R5 000 000	
Unit level costs:					
Material cutting	R2.00	per unit	1 000 000	2 000 000	
Box assembly	R1.00	per unit	1 000 000	1 000 000	
				R3 000 000	
Total activity cost (annual and per unit)				R8 016 000	R8.016
Direct material cost per unit					R2.000
Total product cost per unit					R10.016

Exhibit 19.13 Make-or-buy decision using activity-based costing data, International Chocolate Company

Cost of purchasing gift boxes		R9 000 000
Less Costs avoided:		
Product level costs	R16 000	
Batch level costs	R5 000 000	
Unit level costs	R3 000 000	
Direct material	R2 000 000	10 016 000
Cost savings through purchasing gift boxes		R1 016 000

Exhibit 19.14 Cost analysis of the make-or-buy decision, International Chocolate Company

making and managerial performance evaluation. Managers typically make decisions that maximise their reported performance and rewards. This is human nature. If we want managers to make decisions that are consistent with the organisation's goals and strategies, then the performance measurement system and reward structure should be consistent with that perspective. This issue is investigated further in Chapter 13.

The correct treatment of sunk costs in decision making illustrates this issue. Earlier in this chapter it was stated that sunk costs should be ignored, as they are irrelevant. For example, the original cost of a machine used to produce a particular product is irrelevant when making a decision about whether to make or buy a product. Suppose that a manager correctly ignores that original cost and, as part of the 'buy' alternative, a recently purchased machine is disposed of. If the buy alternative is taken, the unfortunate manager may be criticised by his superior for 'taking a loss' on this machine and for disposing of a machine for which he had to fight so hard to get permission to purchase. What is our manager likely to do the next time he faces a similar decision? He may favour the 'make' alternative to retain the machine in order to justify his prior decision to purchase it (and avoid criticism). This may not be in the best interests of the firm!

Cost systems may be designed explicitly to encourage biases in certain decisions. It has even been argued that less accurate cost systems can be designed to direct employees' attention towards certain issues in order to help them learn and to motivate them (Merchant & Shields, 1993). An example of such a system occurred at the Portable Instrument Company in the US (Cooper & Turney, 1988). The company implemented a just-in-time/total quality management system. Material support costs, such as for purchasing, receiving, inspection, storage and handling, constituted about

50 per cent of overheads. To cost products, the company chose a single overhead cost driver: the number of parts. This system was designed to encourage engineers to reduce the number of parts in newly developed products. Thus, the more parts involved in a new product, the more costly that product appeared. While employees knew that not all overhead costs were driven by the number of parts, the system focused attention on factors that were considered by management to be critical to the company's cost strategy. The new system encouraged designers to use fewer parts in new products, which, in turn, resulted in lower costs for receiving, storage, handling and manufacturing. Once the system had achieved its purpose, more cost drivers were identified and a more accurate product costing system was developed.

The message here is that if we want managers and employees to make certain decisions, we must design systems with incentives that encourage that behaviour. These issues are considered further in other chapters of the book, including Chapter 13.

Pitfalls to avoid in using accounting data for decisions

L.O. 10

Identification of the relevant costs and benefits is an important step in making any decision. Nonetheless, both managers and management accountants often overlook relevant costs or incorrectly include irrelevant data. In this section, we review four common mistakes that should be avoided in decision making:

1. *Sunk costs.* Sunk costs cannot be changed by any current or future course of action, so they are irrelevant in decision making. Nevertheless, a common behavioural tendency is to give importance to past costs. People may seek to justify their past decisions by refusing to delete a product or department, even when this is contrary to the formal analysis. *The moral:* Ignore sunk costs.
2. *Unitised costs.* For product costing purposes, fixed costs are often divided by a measure of production volume and assigned to individual units of product. Similarly, under activity-based costing, facility level costs, product level costs and batch level costs may also be expressed at a rate per unit of product. While there may be legitimate reasons for this practice from a product costing perspective, it can lead to inaccuracies when used in decision making. Therefore, in a decision analysis it is usually wise to consider total costs and how they will be affected by a decision, rather than to base an analysis on costs per unit. *The moral:* Beware of using unitised fixed costs in decision making.
3. *Allocated costs.* It is common in many companies to allocate fixed costs to divisions, departments or product lines. A possible result is that a product or department may appear unprofitable when in reality it does make a contribution towards covering fixed costs and profit. Before deciding to eliminate a product or department, be sure to ask which costs will be avoided if a particular alternative is selected. A fixed cost that has been allocated to a product or department may continue, in total or in part, even after the product or department has been eliminated. *The moral:* Beware of allocated costs; identify the avoidable costs.
4. *Opportunity costs.* People tend to overlook opportunity costs or to treat such costs as less important than out-of-pocket costs. Yet opportunity costs are just as real and important in making a correct decision as are out-of-pocket costs. *The moral:* Pay special attention to identifying and including opportunity costs in a decision analysis.

Summary

In this chapter we examined the use of information for tactical decisions. The types of decisions considered were about whether to accept or reject a special order; to make or buy a product; to add or delete a product, service or department; and to sell or process further joint products. Key points include:

- Tactical decisions do not require significant or permanent resource commitments and can be changed or reversed if better opportunities arise. The impact of such decisions is short term and the financial impact of alternatives is usually analysed by considering the incremental revenue and costs of each alternative. This can be compared to long-term decisions, which tend to be more strategic in nature and involve large increases or decreases in capacity-related resources.
- The steps involved in decision making are as follows: clarify the problem, identify the alternative courses of action, collect relevant cost and benefits, compare the cost and benefits of each possible course of action, and select a course of action.
- Relevant information differs under the various alternative courses of action, relates to the future, must observe the trade-off between timeliness and accuracy, and may be quantitative or qualitative. It is important to supply only relevant information for decisions, as too much information can result in information overload, which may reduce decision-making effectiveness.
- In selecting relevant information for decisions, the focus is usually on incremental revenues and incremental costs. Assessing the relevant incremental costs for some decisions requires an understanding of avoidable and unavoidable costs.
- In the decision to accept or reject a special order, where there is excess capacity, the analysis will focus on incremental revenue and incremental costs of the alternatives. Fixed facility level costs are usually irrelevant, as they will not change. Where there is no excess capacity, the opportunity costs of using the facilities are also included in the analysis. Qualitative issues must also be considered in the special order analysis.
- In the decision to make or buy a product, avoidable costs that may result from each alternative course of action will be relevant. Opportunity costs may also be relevant where there are alternative uses for freed-up capacity. Strategic issues and other qualitative concerns will also be included in the analysis.
- Outsourcing decisions imply more long-term arrangements, compared to make or buy decisions. An organisation may choose to contract part of a manufacturing process, or another function normally undertaken within the business, to an outside party. In these situations the decision to outsource may be difficult to reverse, as capacity may have been reduced.
- In the decision to delete a product, service or department, the analysis will focus on revenues and costs that will be avoided if a decision goes ahead. When considering whether to add a product, service or department, the focus will be on incremental revenue and costs of the decision. The decision to add or delete a product, service or department tends to have strategic implications, and may involve the analysis of cash flows over some years.
- Decisions about whether to sell a joint product or to process it further involve focusing on the incremental revenues and costs associated with processing further. Allocated joint product costs are not relevant to the decision.
- The use of activity-based costs may result in more accurate cost information for decisions, as we are able to more accurately predict the changes in costs that may result from alternative courses of action. This is because activity-based costs are based on a better understanding of the drivers of cost.

- While the decision-making process and the specification of relevant information appear to be rational and systematic, various incentives may influence the way in which managers select information, analyse that information and select alternatives. For example, managers may make decisions that maximise their reported short-term performance and rewards, which may not maximise the long-term performance of the firm.
- Mistakes to avoid in using accounting data for decisions include:
  - including sunk costs in an analysis, as these are irrelevant and cannot be changed;
  - analysing fixed costs at a unit level as if they behaved in a per-unit manner. It is safer to consider how total costs will change under the various alternative courses of action;
  - including allocated costs in an analysis, when these costs may not be avoided under any alternative course of action; and
  - overlooking opportunity costs associated with a course of action. These are just as relevant as out-of pocket costs.

We will continue to focus on information for decisions in the following chapters. In Chapter 20, pricing decisions and product-mix decisions are discussed. In Chapters 21 and 22, we consider the analysis of information for capital expenditure decisions.

References

Bennett, B 2001, 'Pitfalls on contracts in inexperienced hands', *The Australian Financial Review*, 26 September, p. 10.

Cooper, R & Turney, P 1988, *Tektronix: The Portable Instruments Division*, Harvard Business School, Case 9–188–142/4.

Domberger, S 1998, *The Contracting Organization*, Oxford University Press, New York.

Langfield-Smith, K, Smith, D & Stringer, C 2000, *Managing the Outsourcing Relationship*, University of New South Wales Press, Sydney.

Long, S 2001, 'Outsourcing gave Qantas the edge', *The Australian Financial Review*, 1 October, p. 7.

Merchant, K & Shields, MD 1993, 'When and why to measure costs less accurately and improve decision making', *Accounting Horizons*, vol. 7, no. 2, pp. 76–81.

Tolhurst, C 2001, 'New challenges for firms cutting in-house activities', *The Australian Financial Review*, 26 September, p. 15.

Self study

Self-study problem 1: Relevant costs

Lansing Camera Company has received a special order for photographic equipment that it does not normally produce. The company has excess capacity, and the order could be manufactured without reducing production of the firm's regular products.

Required:
Discuss the relevance of each of the following items in calculating the cost of the special order:

1 Equipment to be used in producing the order has a book value of R20 000. The equipment has no other use for Lansing Camera Company. If the order is not accepted, the equipment will be sold for R15 000. If the equipment is used in producing the order, it can be sold in three months for R8 000.

2 If the special order is accepted, the operation will require some of the storage space in the company's plant. If the space is used for this purpose, the company will rent storage space temporarily in a nearby warehouse at a cost of R180 000. The building depreciation allocated to the storage space to be used in producing the special order is R120 000.

3 If the special order is accepted, it will require a sub-assembly. Lansing Camera can purchase the sub-assembly for R240 per unit from an outside supplier, or the company can make it for R300 per unit. The R300 cost per unit was determined as follows:

Direct material	R100.00
Direct labour	R60.00
Variable overhead	R60.00
Allocated fixed overhead	R80.00
Total unit cost of sub-assembly	R300.00

Solution to Self-study problem

1 The book value of the equipment is a sunk cost, irrelevant to the decision. In calculating the cost of the special order, the relevant cost of the equipment is R7000. This is determined as follows:

Sales value of equipment now	R15 000
Sales value after producing special order	8 000
Decrease in cost due to accepting the special order	R7 000

2 The R120 000 portion of building depreciation allocated to the storage space to be used for the special order is irrelevant. First, it is a sunk cost. Second, any costs relating to the company's factory building will continue whether or not the special order is accepted. The relevant cost is the R180 000 rent that will be incurred only if the special order is accepted.

3 Lansing Camera should make the sub-assembly. The sub-assembly's relevant cost is R220 per unit.

Relevant cost of making sub-assembly (per unit)		Relevant cost of purchasing sub-assembly (per unit)	
Direct material	R100.00	Purchase price	R240.00
Direct labour	R60.00		
Variable overhead	R60.00		
Total	R220.00		

Notice that the unitised fixed overhead, R80, is not a relevant cost of the sub-assembly. Unless we are told otherwise, we can assume that in the short term Lansing Camera Company's total fixed cost will not change, whether or not the special order is accepted.

Cybersearch

1 Find websites of companies that have outsourced part of their business.
   (a) Have the organisations been able to determine the amount of cost savings resulting from the outsourcing?
   (b) What are some of the other positive or negative outcomes that have been identified by the organisations?
2 Locate the website of an organisation that has considered the issue of excess capacity in its decision-making processes.
   (a) What type of decision is mentioned?
   (b) Is it clear as to why the issue of excess capacity was relevant to this decision?
3 Look for a company website that contains a description of the types of relevant information that were considered when making a certain decision. Such decisions may include the purchase of new plant, the manufacture of new products or adopting new production processes.
   (a) What was the decision?
   (b) What information (financial and non-financial) did the company use when making the decision?
   (c) Were there any trade-offs that had to be considered in making the decision?

Appendix to Chapter 19

L.O. 11

Allocating joint production costs

In this chapter we saw that for product costing purposes and profit determination, joint production costs are usually allocated to joint products. The relative sales value method of joint cost allocation was presented within the chapter. In this appendix, three other methods commonly used to allocate joint costs are explained. Remember, joint cost allocation is not useful in deciding whether to process a joint product further. It is simply a method that allows us to determine product costs and cost of goods sold, for financial accounting purposes.

Allocation methods

To illustrate allocation methods, the International Chocolate Company example will be used. A description of the production process is presented in Exhibit 19.15. Note that in contrast to the chapter, we now recognise that cocoa butter may be further processed into tanning cream. Exhibit 19.16 shows the data relating to the relative sales value method, which was included in the chapter. It also shows three other commonly used methods: the physical units method, the constant gross margin method, and the net realisable value method.

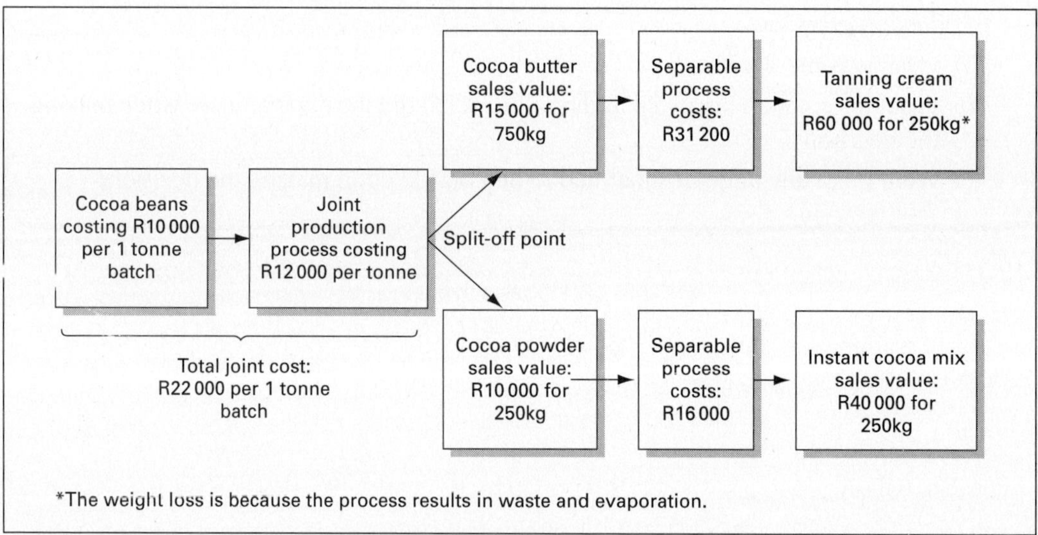

Exhibit 19.15 Joint processing of cocoa beans, International Chocolate Company

Physical units method

Under the physical units method, joint costs are allocated based on some physical characteristic of the joint products at the split-off point. Exhibit 19.16 shows this allocation method for the International Chocolate Company using the weight of the joint products as the allocation basis: three-quarters of the joint cost is allocated to cocoa butter, which represents three-quarters of the weight of the total production at the split-off point.

Constant gross margin method

Under the constant gross margin method, joint costs are allocated to joint products so that the gross margin for each joint product is identical. The first step is to calculate the gross margin for the entire production process:

Total sales value (R60 000 + R40 000)	R100 000
Less Production costs (R22 000 + R31 200 + R16 000)	69 200
Gross margin	30 800
Gross margin as a percentage of sales value	30.80%

Note that we have used the sales value of the final products (tanning cream and instant cocoa mix), and both the joint and separable production costs. The amount of joint cost allocated to the two joint products is based on the amount of joint cost needed to ensure that each of the joint products ends up with the same gross margin of 30.8 per cent. The various steps are illustrated in Exhibit 19.16. Using the constant gross margin method, the required profit for each joint product is calcu-

Physical units method

Joint cost	Joint products	Weight at split-off point	Relative proportion	Allocation of joint cost
R22 000	Cocoa butter	750 kg	750/1000	R16 500
	Cocoa powder	250 kg	250/1000	R5 500
	Total joint cost allocated			R22 000

Relative sales value method

Joint cost	Joint products	Sales value at split-off point	Relative proportion	Allocation of joint cost
R22 000	Cocoa butter	R15 000	15/25	R13 200
	Cocoa powder	R10 000	10/25	R8 800
	Total joint cost allocated			R22 000

Constant gross margin method

Joint cost	Joint products	Gross margin %	Sales revenue	Required gross margin	Separable cost of processing	Allocation of joint cost
R22 000	Cocoa butter	30.8	R60 000	R18 480	R31 200	R10 320
	Cocoa powder	30.8	R40 000	R12 320	R16 000	R11 680
	Total joint cost allocated					R22 000

[60 000 − 18 480 − 31 200 = 10 320] & [40 000 − 12 320 − 16 000 = 11 680]

Net realisable value method

Joint cost	Joint products	Sales value of final product	Separable cost of processing	Net realisable value	Relative proportion	Allocation of joint cost
R22 000	Tanning cream	R60 000	R31 200	R28 800*	28.8/52.8	R12 000
	Instant cocoa mix	R40 000	R16 000	R24 000*	24/52.8	R10 000
	Total joint cost allocated					R22 000

* Sales value of final product − separable cost of processing = net realisable value
Tanning cream: R60 000 − R31 200 = R28 800
Instant cocoa mix: R40 000 − R16 000 = R24 000

Exhibit 19.16 Methods for allocating joint product costs, International Chocolate Company

lated based on the gross margin of 30.8 per cent multiplied by the sales revenue of each final product. The amount of joint cost allocated to each product is the amount of costs required to achieve that profit, which is equal to the sales revenue minus the separable processing costs and the required gross margin for each product. The **separable processing costs** are incurred after the split-off point, and can be traced directly to the two products.

Net realisable value method

Under the **net realisable value method**, we calculate the net realisable value of the final products, which is the total sales value of the final products less any separable processing costs incurred after the split-off point. The joint cost is allocated to the joint products according to the relative magnitude of the final products' net realisable values. This allocation method is illustrated in Exhibit 19.16.

Costing by-products

A joint product that has very little value when compared with the value of other joint products and is not the main motivation for undertaking the joint process is termed a **by-product**. For example, whey is a by-product in the production of cheese. In the South African gold mining sector, uranium is a by-product of gold mining operations. A common practice in accounting is to subtract a by-product's net realisable value from the cost of the joint process. Then the remaining joint cost is allocated to the major joint products.

An alternative procedure is to value the by-product at its sales value at split-off. The by-product's sales value is then deducted from the total production cost of the main products.

Profitability under each method

Once the joint costs have been allocated to each product, we can calculate the total costs of producing each product, and determine profitability. Exhibit 19.17 contains a comparison of the product cost and profitability using each of the four methods. The profits of the two joint products (cocoa butter and cocoa powder) are calculated, assuming that the whole 1-tonne batch is sold at split-off. This implies that further processing does not take place. You can see that under each

	Product costs				Profits†			
	Physical units	Relative sales value	Constant gross margin	Net realisable value	Physical units	Relative sales value	Constant gross margin	Net realisable value
Joint products:								
Cocoa butter	R16 500	R13 200	R10 320	R12 000	−R1 500	R1 800	R4 680	R3 000
Cocoa powder	5 500	8 800	11 680	10 000	4 500	1 200	−1 680	0
					3 000	3 000	3 000	3 000
Final products:*								
Tanning cream	R47 700	R44 400	R41 520	R43 200	R12 300	R15 600	R18 480	R16 800
Cocoa mix	21 500	24 800	27 680	26 000	18 500	15 200	12 320	14 000
					30 800	30 800	30 800	30 800

* Costs for final products are based on joint cost plus the separable cost of R31 200 for the tanning cream or R16 000 for the cocoa mix.

† Profits based on the sales values shown in Exhibit 19.15 minus the product costs shown above.
Examples of workings: [15 000 − 16 500 = −1 500] & [10 000 − 5 500 = 4 500]
[60 000 − 47 700 = 12 300] & [40 000 − 21 500 = 18 500]

Exhibit 19.17 Product costs and profits using each joint cost allocation method, International Chocolate Company

method the total profits are constant at R3000 per batch, but the break-up of the profits between the two products is different. Note that under the physical units method, cocoa butter makes a 'loss', while under the constant gross margin method, cocoa powder is a loss product. The profitability of the final products (tanning cream and instant cocoa mix) is also calculated. The total profit that would result from further processing of the joint products is R30 800 per 1-tonne batch. Once again, the profits of the individual products differ under each method. Which method results in more 'accurate' product costs and profits?

Evaluation of the joint cost allocation methods

Notice how different the cost allocations are under the four methods, particularly under the physical units method. Each method results in different product costs and different profits. However, it is difficult to argue that any one of these methods is preferable to the others, because of the nature of a joint process. By definition, a joint process produces two or more products simultaneously—it is not possible to identify separate individual products until the split-off point. Thus, all the resources used within the joint production process benefit all the joint products, and these costs cannot be separated. All four methods for allocating joint costs are arbitrary allocation methods.

Despite this, some researchers argue that the physical units approach is the least preferred as it is not based on the economic characteristics of the joint products. That is, the physical weights have no relationship to the revenue-producing power of the individual joint products. However, an important issue to consider is that if an objective of determining product costs is to set selling prices, then the net realisable value, relative sales value and constant gross margin methods should not be used. This is because of the circular reasoning of using current selling prices to determine the allocation of joint costs that are then used to determine future selling prices.

There is no correct way of allocating joint production costs to products because of the very nature of the joint production process—we cannot identify joint products until after the joint production process is complete. There are few reasons for allocating joint production costs to joint products, apart from the need to estimate cost of goods sold and value inventory for external reporting requirements. From a management accounting perspective, allocated joint costs are unreliable due to their arbitrary nature and should not be used in pricing or in any other management decisions.

Let's consider the profit information in Exhibit 19.17. Under the physical units method cocoa butter appears to be a loss product. Can we use this information to make a decision about discontinuing the product? We have already stated that it is difficult to argue that one joint cost method is superior to the other, because they are all arbitrary cost allocations. Therefore, we must be cautious in using any allocated cost data in decisions. However, there is a more fundamental issue here. Because of the very nature of a joint process, we cannot 'discontinue' the production of a joint product. Cocoa butter will be produced from this joint process whether we want to produce it or not! A joint process is so called because individual products cannot be separately identified until the end of processing.

Questions

19.1 Explain the difference between tactical and long-term decisions. How does the information required to support each of these types of decisions differ?

19.2 List the steps in the decision-making process. Do all managers apply this process? Explain.

19.3 Explain the role of the management accountant in the decision-making process.

19.4 Distinguish between qualitative and quantitative information. Select a decision and provide three examples of each type of data.

19.5 'All decisions come down to an assessment of the relevant costs and benefits, and a good management accountant should be able to quantify these.' Discuss.

19.6 What is meant by each of the following characteristics of information: relevant, accurate and timely? Is objective information always relevant? Is objective information always accurate? In each case give examples to support your answer.

19.7 Provide two examples of information for decisions that illustrate the trade-off between timeliness and accuracy.

19.8 Is the book value of inventory on hand a relevant cost? Explain your answer.

19.9 Why might a manager want to consider sunk costs in making a decision? Provide two examples of sunk costs and explain why they are irrelevant in decision making.

19.10 Select a specific decision and give an example of an irrelevant future cost. Why is it irrelevant?

19.11 Define the term opportunity cost. Select two decisions and provide specific examples of relevant opportunity costs. What behavioural tendency do people often exhibit with regard to opportunity costs?

19.12 Briefly describe the appropriate approach for making a decision about adding or dropping a product line. Is this a tactical or long-term decision? Explain your answer.

19.13 Explain how avoidable and unavoidable costs enter into the decision to either make or buy a product.

19.14 Distinguish between the following terms: incremental costs, avoidable costs and relevant costs.

19.15 Explain how the existence of excess production capacity can affect the choice of whether to accept or reject a special order.

19.16 Explain what is meant by outsourcing. Is this the same as a make-or-buy decision? Explain your answer.

19.17 Describe some qualitative factors that may be relevant to an outsourcing decision.

19.18 What is a joint production process? Provide two examples of joint production situations (apart from those mentioned in this chapter).

19.19 Are allocated joint processing costs relevant when making a decision about whether to either sell a joint product at the split-off point or to process it further? Explain your answer and describe the correct approach to making this decision.

19.20 'There is an important link between the topics of decision making and managerial performance evaluation.' Explain.

19.21 Explain four potential pitfalls in using accounting data in decision making.

19.22 'Accounting systems should produce only relevant data and forget about the irrelevant data. Then I'd know what was relevant and what wasn't!' Comment on this remark by a company's managing director.

19.23 Are the concepts underlying relevant cost analysis still valid in an advanced manufacturing environment? Are these concepts valid when activity-based costing is used? Explain.

19.24 What are unitised fixed costs, and how can they cause errors in decision making?

19.25 (appendix) Explain briefly how to use the physical units, relative sales value, net realisable value and constant gross margin methods of joint cost allocation. Which method is the best?

Exercises

E19.26 Steps in the decision-making process

Choose an organisation with which you are familiar and a particular decision situation. For that decision, describe each step in the decision-making process, as illustrated in Exhibit 19.1.

E19.27 Irrelevant information

Redo Exhibit 19.5 without the irrelevant information. Which is the better approach? Explain.

E19.28 Obsolete inventory: manufacturer

Cape York Ltd manufactures auto parts. The company currently has a R21 000 inventory of parts that have become obsolete due to changes in design specifications. The parts could be sold for R9000, or modified for R12 000 and sold for R22 300.

Required:

1 Which of the data above are relevant to the decision about the obsolete parts?
2 Specify the two alternatives and analyse the relevant costs.

E19.29 Joint products: manufacturer

Castille Industries produces chemicals for the swimming pool industry. In one joint process, 10 000 litres of GSX are processed into 7000 litres of xenolite and 3000 litres of banolide. The cost of the joint process, including the GSX, is R20 000. Castille allocates R14 000 of the joint cost to the xenolite and R6 000 of the cost to the banolide. The 3000 litres of banolide can be sold at the split-off point for R2 500, or they can be processed further into a product called kitrocide. The sales value of 3000 litres of kitrocide is R10 000, and the additional processing cost is R8 100.

Required:

Castille's managing director has asked your consulting firm to make a recommendation as to whether the banolide should be sold at the split-off point or processed further. Write a letter providing an analysis and a recommendation.

E19.30 Drop product line: retailer

Day Street Deli's owner is disturbed by the poor profit performance of his ice-cream counter. He has prepared the following profit analysis for 20X5:

Sales		R202 500
Less Cost of food		90 000
Gross margin		112 500
Less Operating expenses:		
Wages of counter personnel	R54 000	
Paper products (e.g. cups, serviettes)	18 000	
Utilities (allocated)	13 050	
Depreciation of counter equipment and furnishings	11 250	
Depreciation of building (allocated)	18 000	
Deli manager's salary (allocated)	13 500	R127 800
Loss on ice-cream counter		−R15 300

Required:

1 Evaluate the above analysis that has been prepared by the manager.

2 Provide a correct analysis and assess whether or not the ice-cream counter should be continued.

E19.31 Special order: manufacturer

Global Chemical Company (GCC) recently received an order for a product that it does not normally produce. Since the company has excess production capacity, management are considering accepting the order. In analysing the decision, the assistant accountant is compiling the relevant costs of producing the order. Production of the special order would require 8000 kilograms of theolite. GCC does not use theolite for its regular product, but the firm has 8000 kilograms of the chemical on hand from the days when it used theolite regularly. The theolite could be sold to a chemical wholesaler for R217 500. The book value of the theolite is R30 per kilogram. GCC could buy theolite for R36.00 per kilogram.

Required:

1 What is the relevant cost of theolite for the purpose of analysing the special order decision?

2 Discuss each item of numerical data given in the exercise with regard to its relevance in making the decision.

E19.32 Special order: manufacturer

Refer to the data given in Exercise 19.31.

GCC's special order also requires 1000 kilograms of genatope, a solid chemical regularly used in the company's products. The current stock of genatope is 8000 kilograms at a book value of R121.50 per kilogram. If the special order is accepted, the firm will be forced to restock genatope earlier than expected, at a predicted cost of R130.50 per kilogram. Without the special order, the purchasing manager predicts that the price will be R124.50 when normal restocking takes place. The order size for genatope is 5000 kilograms.

Required:

1 What is the relevant cost of genatope?

2 Discuss each item of numerical data detailed in this exercise in terms of its relevance to the decision.

E19.33 Further processing; relevant costs; cost volume profit analysis: manufacturer

Hercules Cleaning Company produces cleaning compounds and solutions for industrial and household use. While most of its products are processed independently, a few are related. Grit 337, a coarse cleaning powder with many industrial uses, costs R32 per kilogram to make and sells for R40 per kilogram. A small portion of the annual production of this product is retained for further processing in the Mixing Department; there, it is combined with several other ingredients to form a paste, which is marketed as a silver polish selling for R80 per jar. This further processing requires 0.25 kilogram of Grit 337 per jar.

Costs of other ingredients, labour, and variable overhead associated with this further processing amount to R50 per jar. Variable selling costs are R6 per jar. If the decision were made to cease production of the silver polish, R112 000 of the Mixing Department's fixed costs could be avoided. Hercules has limited production capacity for Grit 337, but unlimited demand for the cleaning powder.

Required:
Calculate the minimum number of jars of silver polish that would have to be sold to justify the further processing of Grit 337.

(*CMA, adapted*)

E19.34 Closing a department: insurance company

Trusty Insurance Company is considering the elimination of its Payroll Department. Management has received an offer from an outside firm to process all of Trusty's payroll. To help her make the decision, Trusty's managing director has asked the chief accountant for an analysis of the cost of running the Payroll Department. Included in that analysis is R111 000 of rent per annum, which is the Payroll Department's allocation of rent of Trusty's head office. If the Payroll Department is eliminated, the freed-up space will be used to store insurance files. Currently, Trusty rents storage space in a nearby warehouse for R130 000 per year. The warehouse rental would no longer be necessary if the Payroll Department were eliminated.

Required:

1 Discuss each item of numerical data given in the exercise with regard to its relevance to the decision to close the Payroll Department.
2 What type of cost is the R130 000 warehouse rental, from the viewpoint of the Payroll Department?

E19.35 Closing a department: insurance company

Refer to the data given in Exercise 19.34.

If Trusty Insurance closes its Payroll Department, the department manager will be appointed manager of the Accounts Payable Department. The Payroll Department manager is paid a salary of R510 000 per year. Hiring a new accounts payable manager would cost Trusty R660 000 per year.

Required:
Discuss the relevance of each of these salary figures to the decision to close the Payroll Department.

E19.36 Machine replacement: pizza parlour

The owner of Riviera Pizza Parlour bought his current pizza oven two years ago for R10 500, and it has one more year of life remaining. He is using straight line depreciation for the oven. He could purchase a new oven for R2200, but it would only last one year. The owner figures the new oven would save him R3000 in annual operating expenses compared to the existing one. Consequently he has decided against buying the new oven since doing so would result in a loss of R500 over the next year.

Required:

1 Explain how the owner arrived at a R500 loss for the next year if the new pizza oven were purchased.
2 Evaluate the owner's analysis and decision.
3 Prepare a correct analysis of the decision.

E19.37 Pros and cons of outsourcing

Visit the website of any major company.

Required:

1 Briefly describe the company's operations and activities.

2 Choose an activity that is necessary for the company's operations and discuss the arguments for and against outsourcing that activity.

E19.38 Joint cost allocation (appendix): manufacturer

Crunch-Time Cereal Company manufactures two breakfast cereals in a joint process. Cost and quantity information follows:

Joint Cost	Cereal	Quantity at split-off point	Sales price per kg
R400 000	Yummies	12 000 kilograms	R20.00
	Crummies	8 000 kilograms	R25.00

Required:

Use the following methods to allocate the company's joint production cost between Yummies and Crummies:

1 The physical units method.

2 The relative sales value method.

3 The constant gross margin method.

E19.39 Joint cost allocation; net realisable value method (appendix): manufacturer

Refer to the data given in Exercise 19.38. Crunch-Time Cereal Company has an opportunity to further process its Crummies into a mulch for ornamental shrubs. The additional processing operation costs R7.50 per kilogram, and the mulch will sell for R40.00 per kilogram.

Required:

1 Should Crunch-Time process Crummies into the mulch? Explain your answer.

2 Suppose the company does process Crummies into the mulch. Use the net realisable value method to allocate the joint production cost to the mulch and to the Yummies.

Problems

P19.40 Closing an unprofitable department: retailer

Contemporary Trends sells paint and paint supplies, carpet and wallpaper at a single-store location in suburban Durban. Although the company has been very profitable over the years, management has seen a significant decline in wallpaper sales and earnings. Much of this decline is attributable to the customers increasingly purchasing products on the Internet and to companies that advertise deeply discounted prices in magazines and offer customers free shipping and toll-free telephone numbers. Recent figures follow:

	Paint and supplies	Carpeting	Wallpaper
Sales	R1 900 000	R2 300 000	R700 000
Variable costs	1 140 000	1 610 000	560 000
Fixed costs	280 000	375 000	225 000
Total costs	R1 420 000	R1 985 000	R785 000
Operating profit/loss	R480 000	R315 000	−R85 000

Management are studying whether to drop wallpaper because of the changing market and accompanying loss. If the line is dropped, the following changes are expected to occur:

- The vacated space will be remodelled at a cost of R62 000 and will be devoted to an expanded line of high-end carpet. Sales of carpet are expected to increase by R600 000, and the line's overall contribution margin ratio will rise by 5 percentage points.
- Contemporary Trends can cut wallpaper fixed costs by 40 per cent. Remaining fixed costs will continue to be incurred.
- Customers who purchased wallpaper often bought paint and paint supplies. Sales of paint and paint supplies are expected to fall by 20 per cent.
- The firm will increase advertising expenditures by R125 000 to promote the expanded carpet line.

Required:

1 Should Contemporary Trends close its wallpaper operation? Show your calculations.

2 Assume that Contemporary Trends' wallpaper inventory at the time of the closure decision amounted to R118 500. How would you have treated this additional information in making the decision?

3 What advantages might the Internet- and magazine-based firms have over Contemporary Trends that would allow these organisations to offer deeply discounted prices—prices far below those that Contemporary Trends can offer?

P19.41 Make or buy: manufacturer

For several years, Reddy Flow Technology (RFT) has purchased 10 000 pumps annually from Prime Ltd. Because the price keeps increasing, reaching R1020 per unit last year, RFT's management has asked for an estimate of the cost of manufacturing the pump in RFT's facilities. RFT makes stampings and castings and has little experience with products requiring assembly.

The Engineering, Manufacturing and Accounting Departments have prepared a report for management that includes the estimate shown below for an assembly run of 10 000 pumps. Additional production employees would be hired to manufacture the pumps, but no additional equipment, space or supervision would be needed.

The report states that total costs for 10 000 units are estimated at R14 355 000, or R1435.50 a unit. The current purchase price is R1020 a unit, so the report recommends continued purchase of the product.

Components (outside purchases)	R1 800 000
Assembly labour*	4 500 000
Manufacturing overhead†	6 750 000
General and administrative overhead‡	1 305 000
Total costs	R14 355 000

* Assembly labour consists of hourly production workers.

† Manufacturing overhead is applied to products on a direct labour Rand basis. Variable overhead costs vary closely with direct labour Rands.

Fixed overhead	50% of direct labour Rands
Variable overhead	100% of direct labour Rands
Manufacturing overhead rate	150% of direct labour Rands

‡ General and administrative overhead, which is a fixed cost, is applied at 10 per cent of the total cost of material (or components), assembly labour and manufacturing overhead.

Required:

Consider the analysis prepared by RFT Engineering, Manufacturing and Accounting Departments, and their recommendation to continue purchasing the pumps. Explain whether you think this analysis was correct. In your answer, include any supporting calculations you consider necessary.

(CMA, adapted)

P19.42 Introducing a new product: manufacturer

Martinair is a small firm involved in the production and sale of electronic business products. The company is well-known for its attention to quality and innovation.

During the past 15 months a new product has been under development that allows users mobile access to online radio stations from around the world. The device can be used in a car. Martinair named the product 'Wireless Wizard' and has been quietly designing two models: Standard and Enhanced. Development costs have amounted to R1 815 000 and R2 625 000, respectively. The total market demand for each model is expected to be 40 000 units, and management anticipate being able to obtain the following market shares: Standard, 25 per cent; Enhanced, 20 per cent. Forecast data follow:

	Standard	Enhanced
Projected selling price	R3 750.00	R4 950.00
Production cost per unit:		
Direct material	420.00	675.00
Direct labour	225.00	300.00
Variable overhead	360.00	480.00
Fixed overhead	540.00	720.00
Marketing and advertising per product line	R1 950 000	R3 000 000
Sales salaries per product line	R855 000	R855 000
Sales commissions*	10%	10%

* Calculated on the basis of sales Rands

Since the start of development work on the Wireless Wizard, advances in technology have altered the market somewhat, and management now believe that the company can introduce only one of the two models. Consultants confirmed this fact not too long ago, with Martinair paying R345 000 for an in-depth market study.

Required:

1 Calculate the per unit contribution margin for both models.
2 Which of the data above should be ignored in making the product introduction decision? For what reason?
3 Prepare a financial analysis and determine which of the two models should be introduced.
4 What other factors should Martinair consider before a final decision is made?

P19.43 JIT cost savings: manufacturer

Margro Ltd is an automotive supplier that uses automatic screw machines to manufacture precision parts from steel bars. Margro's inventory of raw steel averages R6 000 000, with a turnover rate of four times per year.

John Oates, managing director of Margro, is concerned about the cost of carrying inventory. He is considering the adoption of just-in-time (JIT) inventory procedures in order to eliminate the need to carry any steel inventory. Oates has asked Karin Gorman, Margro's accountant, to evaluate the feasibility of JIT for the company. Gorman identified the following effects of adopting JIT:

- Without scheduling any overtime, lost sales due to stock-outs would increase by 35 000 units per year. However, by incurring overtime premiums of R400 000 per year, the increase in lost sales could be reduced to 20 000 units. This would be the maximum amount of overtime that would be feasible for Margro.
- Two warehouses presently used for steel bar storage would no longer be needed. Margro rents one warehouse from another company at an annual cost of R600 000. The other warehouse is owned by Margro and has 12 000 square metres of storage space. Three quarters of the space in the owned warehouse could be rented out for R15.00 per square metre per year.
- Insurance totalling R140 000 per year would be eliminated.

Margro's projected operating results for 20X6 are shown below. Long-term capital investments by Margro are expected to produce a rate of return of 20 per cent before taxes.

Margro Ltd
Budgeted Income Statement
for the year ending 31 December 20X6

		(in R'000s)
Sales (900 000 units)		R108 000
Cost of goods sold:		
Variable	R40 500	
Fixed	R14 500	55 000
Gross margin		R53 000
Selling and administrative expenses:		
Variable	R9 000	
Fixed	R15 000	R24 000
Profit before interest and income taxes		R29 000
Interest expense		9 000
Profit before taxes		R20 000

Required:

1 If Margro adopts JIT, is it more cost effective to schedule overtime or not?
2 Calculate the estimated savings or loss for Margro Ltd that would result in 20X6 from the adoption of just-in-time inventory methods. (Ignore income taxes.)
3 Identify and explain the conditions that should exist in order for a company to install JIT successfully.

(CMA, adapted)

P19.44 Special order; financial and production considerations: manufacturer

Mercury Stapler (Pty) Ltd manufactures staplers. Several weeks ago, the firm received a special-order inquiry from Siyanda Ltd. Siyanda desires to market a stapler similar to one of Mercury's, and has offered to purchase 11 000 units if the order can be completed in three months. The cost data for Mercury's Champion model stapler are as follows:

Direct material				R16.40
Direct labour	0.25 hours	@	R18 per hour	R4.50
Total manufacturing overhead	0.50 machine hours	@	R40 per hour	R20.00
Total				R40.90

The following additional information is available:

- The normal selling price of the Champion model is R53.00; however, Siyanda has offered Mercury only R31.50 because of the large quantity it is willing to purchase.
- Siyanda requires a modification of the design that will allow a R4.20 reduction in direct material cost.
- Mercury's production supervisor notes that the company will incur R7400 in additional setup costs and will have to purchase a R4800 special device to manufacture these units. The device will be discarded once the special order is completed.
- Total manufacturing overhead costs are applied to production at the rate of R40 per machine hour. This figure is based, in part, on budgeted yearly fixed overhead of R1 500 000 and planned production activity of 60 000 machine hours (5 000 per month).
- Mercury will allocate R3600 of existing fixed administrative costs to the order as 'part of the cost of doing business'.

Required:

1 Assume that present sales will not be affected. Should the order be accepted from a financial point of view, that is, is it profitable? Why? Show calculations.

2 Assume that Mercury's current production activity consumes 70 per cent of planned machine-hour activity. Can the company accept the order and meet Siyanda's deadline?

3 What options might Mercury consider if management truly wanted to do business with Siyanda in hopes of building a long-term relationship with the firm?

P19.45 Outsourcing decision; relevant costs; ethics: manufacturer

The Gauteng Division of Hord Motor Corporation (HMC) manufactures sub-assemblies that are used in their final products. Lynn Van der Westhuizen of the Gauteng Division's Profit Planning Department has been assigned the task of determining whether a component, JY-65, should continue to be manufactured by the Gauteng Division or purchased from Marley Company, an outside supplier. JY-65 is part of a sub-assembly manufactured by the Gauteng Division.

Marley has submitted a bid to manufacture and supply the 32 000 units of JY-65 that the Gauteng Division will need for 20X7 at a unit price of R86.50. Marley has assured HMC that the units will be delivered according to HMC's production specifications and needs. While the contract price of R86.50 is only applicable in 20X7, Marley is interested in entering into a long-term arrangement beyond 20X7.

Van der Westhuizen has gathered the following information regarding the Gauteng Division's cost to manufacture JY-65 in 20X6. These annual costs will be incurred to manufacture 30 000 units.

Direct material	R975 000
Direct labour	600 000
Factory space rental	420 000
Equipment leasing costs	180 000
Other manufacturing costs	1 125 000
Total manufacturing costs	R3 300 000

Van der Westhuizen has also collected the following information related to manufacturing JY-65.

- Direct materials used in the production of JY-65 are expected to increase by 8 per cent in 20X7.
- The Gauteng Division's direct-labour contract calls for a 5 per cent increase in 20X7.
- The facilities used to manufacture JY-65 are rented under a month-to-month rental agreement. Thus, the Gauteng Division can withdraw from the rental agreement without any penalty. The Division will have no need for this space if JY-65 is not manufactured.
- Equipment leasing costs represent special equipment that is used in the manufacture of JY-65. This lease can be terminated by paying the equivalent of one month's lease payment for each year left on the lease agreement. Gauteng has two years left on the lease agreement, through to the end of the year 20X8.
- Forty per cent of the other manufacturing overhead is considered variable. Variable overhead changes with the number of units produced, and this rate per unit is not expected to change in 20X7. The fixed manufacturing overhead costs are not expected to change regardless of whether JY-65 is manufactured or not. Equipment other than the leased equipment can be used in the Gauteng Division's other manufacturing operations.

John Porter, the manager of the Gauteng Division, stopped by Van der Westhuizen's office to voice his concern regarding the outsourcing of JY-65. Porter commented:

I am really concerned about outsourcing JY-65. I have a son-in-law and a nephew, not to mention a member of our bowling team, who work on JY-65. They could lose their jobs if we buy that component from Marley. I really would appreciate anything you can do to make sure the cost analysis comes out right to show we should continue making JY-65. Corporate is not aware of the material increases and maybe you could leave out some of those fixed costs. I just think we should continue making JY-65!

Required:

1 (a) Prepare an analysis of relevant costs that shows whether or not the Gauteng Division of HMC should make JY-65 or purchase it from Marley Company for 20X7.

(b) Based solely on financial results, recommend whether the 32 000 units of JY-65 for 20X7 should be made by the Gauteng Division or purchased from Marley.

2 Identify and briefly discuss three qualitative factors that the Gauteng Division and HMC should consider before agreeing to purchase JY-65 from Marley Company.

3 By referring to the standards of ethical conduct for managerial accountants described in Chapter 1, explain why Lynn Van der Westhuizen might consider the request of John Porter to be unethical.

(*CMA adapted*)

P19.46 Joint products; sell or process further: manufacturer

Talor Chemical Company is a diversified chemical-processing company. The firm manufactures swimming pool chemicals, chemicals for metal processing, specialised chemical compounds and pesticides.

Currently, the Norwood plant is producing two derivatives, RNA-1 and RNA-2, from the chemical compound VDB developed by Talor's research laboratories. Each week, 1 200 000 kilograms of VDB is processed, at a cost of R246 000, into 800 000 kilograms of RNA-1 and 400 000 kilograms of RNA-2. The proportion of these two outputs cannot be altered, because this is a joint process.

RNA-1 has no market value until it is converted into a pesticide with the trade name Fastkil. Processing RNA-1 into Fastkil costs R240 000. Fastkil wholesales at R50 per 100 kilograms.

RNA-2 is sold as is for R80 per 100 kilograms. However, management has discovered that RNA-2 can be converted into two new products by adding 400 000 kilograms of compound LST to the 400 000 kilograms of RNA-2. This joint process would yield 400 000 kilograms each of DMZ-3 and Pestrol, the two new products. The additional direct material and related processing costs of this joint process would be R120 000. DMZ-3 and Pestrol would each be sold for R57.50 per 100 kilograms. The company's management have decided not to process RNA-2 further, based on the analysis presented in the schedule below.

		Process further		
	RNA-2	**DMZ-3**	**Pestrol**	**Total**
Production (kg)	400 000	400 000	400 000	
Revenue	R320 000	R230 000	R230 000	R460 000
Costs:				
VDB costs	R82 000*	R61 500	R61 500	R123 000†
Additional direct materials and processing of RNA-2		60 000	60 000	120 000
Total costs	R82 000	R121 500	R121 500	R243 000
Weekly gross profit	R238 000	R108 500	R108 500	R217 000

* R82 000 is one-third of the R246 000 cost of processing VDB. When RNA-2 is not processed further, one-third of the final output is RNA-2 (400 000 out of a total of 1 200 000 kilograms).

† R123 000 is one-half of the R246 000 cost of processing VDB. When RNA-2 is processed further, one-half of the final output consists of DMZ-3 and Pestrol. The final products then are: 800 000 kilograms of RNA-1; 400 000 kilograms of DMZ-3; and 400 000 kilograms of Pestrol.

Required:

Evaluate Talor Company's analysis, and make any revisions that are necessary. Your critique and analysis should indicate:

1 whether management made the correct decision; and

2 the gross savings or loss per week resulting from the decision not to process RNA-2 further, if different from management's analysis.

(CMA, adapted)

P19.47 Add a product line: manufacturer

Camilla's, a high-fashion dress manufacturer, is planning to market a new evening dress for the coming year. The company operates in a niche market as it is not possible to compete against imports in other lines such as casual wear. This strategy has started to work for the company.

Four metres of material are required to lay out the dress pattern. Some material remains after cutting, which can be sold as remnants. The leftover material could also be used to manufacture a matching wrap and handbag. However, if the leftover material is used for the wrap and handbag, more care will be required in the cutting operation, which will increase the cutting costs.

The company expects to sell 1250 dresses. Market research reveals that dress sales will be 20 per cent higher if a matching wrap and handbag are available. The market research indicates that the wrap and handbag will be saleable only as accessories with the dress. The combination of dresses, wraps and handbags expected to be sold by retailers is as follows:

	Percentage of total
Complete sets of dress, wrap and handbag	70%
Dress and wrap	6%
Dress and handbag	15%
Dress only	9%
Total	100%

The material used in the dresses costs R200 a metre or R800 for each dress. The cost of cutting the dress if the wrap and handbag are not manufactured is estimated at R320 a dress, and the resulting remnants can be sold for R80 per dress. If the wrap and handbag are manufactured, the cutting costs will increase by R144 per dress and there will be no saleable remnants. The selling prices and the costs to complete the three items once they are cut are as shown below.

	Selling price per unit	Unit cost to complete*
Dress	R3 200.00	R1 280.00
Wrap	440.00	312.00
Handbag	152.00	104.00

*excludes cost of material and cutting operation

Required:

1 Calculate Camilla's incremental profit or loss from manufacturing the wraps and handbags in conjunction with the dresses. Assume that Camilla's produces only sufficient product to meet sales demand.

2 Identify any qualitative factors that could influence Camilla's management in their decision to manufacture wraps and handbags to match the dresses.

(CMA, adapted)

P19.48 Relevant costs and benefits: not-for-profit organisation

Janice Watson was recently appointed executive director of the National Foundation for the Education of Children. The Foundation supports schools in impoverished communities by supplying books, computers and other learning materials. The foundation raises most of the money for its activities through an annual mail campaign. Although the mail campaign raises large amounts of money, the year-to-year growth in donations has been lower than expected by the Foundation's board. In addition, the board wants the mail campaign to project the image of a well-run and financially responsible organisation in order to build a base for greater future contributions. Consequently, Watson's efforts in her first year will be devoted to improving the mail campaign.

The campaign takes place each spring. The Foundation staff work hard to secure media coverage of the Foundation's activities for weeks before the mail campaign. In previous years, the Foundation mailed brochures to millions of people, describing its activities and requesting contributions. The addresses for the mailing are generated from the Foundation's own database of past contributors and from mailing lists purchased from brokers.

The Foundation staff are considering three different brochures for the upcoming campaign. All three will measure 90 × 280 millimetres. The simplest, and the one sure to be ready in time for bulk mailing, is a sheet of white paper with a printed explanation of the Foundation's program and a request for funds. A more expensive brochure, on coloured stock with pictures as well as printed copy, may not be ready in time to take advantage of bulk postal rates. It will be ready in time for mailing at regular postal rates. The third option is a brochure printed on glossy paper. The printer has promised that it will be ready to meet the regular mailing schedule, but has asked for a delivery date one week later just in case there are production problems.

The Foundation staff have assembled the following cost and revenue information for mailing the three different brochures to 2 000 000 potential contributors:

	Brochure costs				Potential revenue (R'000s)		
Type of brochure	Design	Type-setting	Unit paper cost	Unit printing cost	Bulk mail	Regular mail	Late regular mail
Plain paper	R3 000	R1 000	R0.05	R0.03	R12 000		
Coloured paper	10 000	8 000	R0.08	R0.10	20 000	R22 000	
Glossy paper	30 000	20 000	R0.18	R0.40		25 000	R22 000

The postal rates are R0.20 per item for bulk mail and R1.30 per item for pre-sorted regular mail. Regular mail is more likely to be delivered on a timely basis than is bulk mail. The charge by outside companies to handle the mailing is R0.10 per unit for the plain and coloured paper brochures, and R0.20 per unit for the glossy paper brochure.

Required:

1 Calculate the net revenue contribution (that is, excess of donations over solicitation costs) for each brochure with each viable mailing option.

2 The foundation must choose one of the three brochures for this year's campaign. The criteria established by the board are:

(a) net revenue raised;

(b) image as a well-run organisation; and

(c) image as a financially responsible organisation.

Evaluate the three different brochures in terms of these three criteria.

(CMA, adapted)

P19.49 Make or buy a component: relevant costs, opportunity costs and quality control: manufacturer

Ukuza Manufacturing uses 10 units of part KJ37 each month in the production of paper making equipment. The cost of manufacturing one unit of KJ37 is as follows:

Direct material	R3 000
Material handling (20% of direct material cost)	600
Direct labour	24 000
Manufacturing overhead (150% of direct labour)	36 000
Total manufacturing cost	R63 600

Material handling represents the direct variable costs of the Receiving Department, which are applied to direct material and purchased components at 20 per cent of the cost of the direct material or components delivered. This is a separate charge in addition to manufacturing overhead. Ukuza's annual manufacturing overhead budget is one-third variable and two-thirds fixed. Scott Supply, one of Ukuza's reliable vendors, has offered to supply part KJ37 at a unit price of R45 000.

Required:

1. If Ukuza purchases the KJ37 from Scott, the capacity that Ukuza used to manufacture these parts would be idle. If Ukuza decides to purchase the part from Scott, by what amount would the unit cost of KJ37 increase or decrease?
2. Assume Ukuza is able to rent out all of its idle capacity for R75 000 per month. If Ukuza decides to purchase the 10 units from Scott Supply, by how much would Ukuza's monthly cost for KJ37 increase or decrease?
3. Assume that Ukuza does not wish to commit to a rental agreement but could use its idle capacity to manufacture another product that would contribute R156 000 per month. If Ukuza elects to manufacture KJ37 in order to maintain quality control, what is Ukuza's opportunity cost from using the space to manufacture part KJ37?

(CMA, adapted)

P19.50 Analysis of special order: manufacturer

Krotoa Industries Ltd received an order for a piece of special machinery from Rex Company. Just as Krotoa completed the machine, Rex Company declared bankruptcy, defaulted on the order, and forfeited the 10 per cent deposit paid on the selling price of R217 500.

Krotoa's manufacturing manager identified the costs already incurred in the production of the special machinery for Rex Company as follows:

Direct material		R49 800
Direct labour		64 200
Manufacturing overhead applied:		
Variable	R32 100	
Fixed	16 050	48 150
Fixed selling and administrative costs		16 215
Total		R178 365

Another company, Kaytell Corporation, will buy the special machinery if it is reworked to Kaytell's specifications. Krotoa offered to sell the reworked machinery to Kaytell as a special order for R205 200. Kaytell agreed to pay the price when it takes delivery in two months' time. The additional identifiable costs to rework the machinery to Kaytell's specifications are as follows:

Direct materials	R18 600
Direct labour	12 600
Total	R31 200

Another option available to Krotoa is to convert the special machinery to the standard model, which sells for R187 500. The additional identifiable costs for this conversion are as follows:

Direct materials	R8 550
Direct labour	9 900
Total	R18 450

A third option for Krotoa is to sell the machine as is for a price of R156 000. However, the potential buyer of the unmodified machine does not want it for 60 days. This buyer has offered to pay R21 000 immediately, with the remainder due upon delivery.

The following additional information is available regarding Krotoa's operations:

- The sales commission rate on sales of standard models is 2 per cent, while the rate on special orders is 3 per cent.
- Normal credit terms for sales of standard models are 2/10, net/30. This means that a customer receives a 2 per cent discount if payment is made within 10 days, and payment is due no later than 30 days after billing. Most customers take the 2 per cent discount. Credit terms for a special order are negotiated with the customer.
- The allocation rates for manufacturing overhead and fixed selling and administrative costs are as follows:

Manufacturing:	
Variable	50% of direct labour cost
Fixed	25% of direct labour cost
Fixed selling and administrative	10% of the total of direct material, direct labour and manufacturing overhead costs

- The amount allocated as variable overhead is considered to be a reasonable approximation for actual variable overhead resources used in producing the particular products.
- Normal time required for rework is one month.

Required:

1 Determine the Rand contribution that each of the three options will add to Krotoa's before-tax profit. Identify the best option.

2 Kaytell is willing to negotiate a new price. What is the lowest price that Krotoa can accept for the reworked machinery? Explain your answer.

3 Discuss the influence that fixed manufacturing overhead cost should have on the sales price quoted by Krotoa for special orders.

(CMA, adapted)

P19.51 Conventional versus activity-based costing analyses; relevant costs: manufacturer

South African Can Company Ltd (SACC) produces metal cans and canisters for a range of food manufacturers. The plant manager, Ricardo Jacobs, was recently approached by the Chinese manufacturer, Xian Canister Company, with an offer to supply the canisters at a price of R0.75 each. The company produces 760 000 canisters. SACC's conventional product costing system assigns the following costs to canister production:

Direct material		R244 000
Direct labour	9000 hours @ R15 per hour	135 000
Variable overhead	R10 per direct labour hour	90 000
Fixed overhead	R45 per direct labour hour	405 000
Total cost		874 000

Unit costs: R874 000 ÷ 760 000 canisters = R1.15 per canister

Jacobs's conventional make-or-buy analysis indicated that Xian's offer should be rejected, since only R550 000 of costs would be avoided (including R60 000 of supervisory salaries and R21 000 of machinery depreciation). In contrast, the firm would spend R570 000 buying the canisters. The factory accountant, Susan Philander, came to the rescue with an activity-based costing analysis of the decision. Philander concluded that the activity costs and cost driver information associated with the production of 760 000 canisters are as shown in the following table:

Activities	Activity cost per unit of activity driver	Quantity of activity driver consumed
Product level:		
Product development	R75.00 per product specification	1
Engineering analysis	R30.00 per engineering hour	10
Batch level:		
Material handling	R15.00 per move	2 000
Inspection	R24.00 per inspection	2 000
Setting up metal press	R75.00 per setup	2 000
Unit level:		
Metal pressing	R0.10 per unit	760 000
Canister printing	R0.05 per unit	760 000

Required:

1 Show how Jacobs arrived at the R550 000 of cost savings in his conventional make-or-buy analysis.

2 Using Philander's activity cost data, determine the costs that will be saved by purchasing the canisters.

3 Complete the relevant costing analysis of the make-or-buy decision using the activity data. Should the firm buy from Xian Canister Company?

4 If the conventional and activity-based analyses yield different conclusions, briefly explain why.

P19.52 Special order: manufacturer

Klep Ltd, located in the Free State, manufactures a variety of industrial valves and pipe fittings that are sold to customers in the mining sector. Currently, the company is operating at about 70 per cent of capacity and is earning a satisfactory return on investment. Management have been approached by Glasgow Industries Ltd of Scotland with an offer to buy 120 000 units of a pressure valve. Glasgow Industries manufactures a valve that is almost identical to the pressure valve produced by Klep; however, a fire in Glasgow Industries' valve plant has shut down its manufacturing operations. Glasgow needs the 120 000 valves over the next four months to meet commitments to its regular customers. Glasgow is prepared to pay R190 each for the valves. The cost of the pressure valve produced by Klep, which is based on current attainable standards, is R200, calculated as follows:

Direct material	R50.00
Direct labour	60.00
Manufacturing overhead	90.00
Product cost	R200.00

Manufacturing overhead is applied to production at the rate of R180 per standard direct labour hour. This overhead rate is made up of the following components:

Variable manufacturing overhead	R60.00
Fixed manufacturing overhead (traceable)	80.00
Fixed manufacturing overhead (allocated)	40.00
Applied manufacturing overhead rate	R180.00

Additional costs incurred in connection with sales of the pressure valve include sales commissions of 5 per cent of sales, and freight expense of R10 per unit. However, the company does not pay sales commissions on special orders that come directly to management. In determining selling prices, Klep adds a 40 per cent markup to total product cost. This provides a R280 suggested selling price for the pressure valve. The Marketing Department, however, has set the current selling price at R270 in order to maintain market share. Production management believe that they can handle the Glasgow Industries order without disrupting the department's scheduled production. The order would, however, require additional fixed factory overhead of R120 000 per month in the form of supervision and clerical costs. If management accept the order, 30 000 pressure valves will be manufactured and shipped to Glasgow Industries each month for the next four months. Glasgow's management have agreed to pay the shipping charges for the valve.

Required:

1 Determine how many direct labour hours would be required each month to fill the Glasgow Industries order.
2 Prepare an analysis showing the impact of accepting the Glasgow Industries order.
3 Calculate the minimum unit price that management at Klep could accept for the Glasgow Industries order without reducing net profit.
4 Identify the factors, other than price, that Klep Ltd should consider before accepting the Glasgow Industries order.

(CMA, adapted)

P19.53 Joint costs: manufacturer

Mpumalanga Sawmill Ltd manufactures two timber products from a joint milling process. The two products are mine support braces (MSB) and lengths of unseasoned commercial building timber (CBT). A standard production run incurs joint costs of R7 500 000 and results in 60 000 units of MSB and 90 000 lengths of CBT. Each MSB sells for R50, and each length of CBT sells for R100.

Required:

1 Calculate the amount of joint cost allocated to the commercial building timber (CBT) on a physical units basis.
2 Calculate the amount of joint cost allocated to the mine support braces (MSB) on a relative sales value basis.
3 Assume the commercial building timber is not marketable at split-off but must be further planed and sized at a cost of R10 000 000 per production run. During this process, 10 000 lengths are unavoidably lost; these spoiled units have no value. The remaining lengths of commercial building timber are saleable at R250 per unit. The mine support braces, although saleable immediately at the split-off point, are coated with a sticky preservative that costs R2 500 000 per production run. The braces are then sold for R125.00 each. Using the net realisable value method, calculate the cost assigned to each length of commercial building timber.
4 If Mpumalanga Sawmill chooses not to process the mine support braces beyond the split-off point, by how much would the contribution from the joint milling process increase or decrease?
5 Did you use the joint cost allocation results in answering requirement 3? If so, how did you use it? Why did you use or not use the allocation results?

(CMA, adapted)

P19.54 Joint costs; allocation and production decisions (appendix): manufacturer

Ster Industries is a manufacturer of chemicals. One of the processes used by Ster produces SPL-3, a chemical used in swimming pools; PST-4, a chemical used in pesticides; and RJ-5, a product that is sold to fertiliser manufacturers. Ster uses the net realisable value method to allocate joint production costs. The ratio of output quantities to input quantities of direct material used in the joint process remains consistent from month to month. In valuing its finished goods inventories, Ster Industries assumes that the units produced first are sold first.

Data for Ster's operations for the month of November are as shown below. During this month, Ster incurred joint production costs of R1 700 000 in the manufacture of SPL-3, PST-4 and RJ-5.

	SPL-3	PST-4	RJ-5
Finished goods inventory, litres (1 Nov.)	18 000	52 000	3 000
November sales in litres	650 000	325 000	150 000
November production in litres	700 000	350 000	170 000
Additional processing costs	R874 000	R816 000	R60 000
Final sales value per litre	R4.00	R6.00	R5.00

Required:

1 Determine Ster Industries' allocation of joint production costs for the month of November. (Carry the calculation of relative proportions to four decimal places.)

2 Determine the Rand values of the finished goods inventories for SPL-3, PST-4 and RJ-5 as at 30 November. (Round the cost per litre to the nearest cent.)

3 Suppose that Ster Industries has a new opportunity to sell PST-4 at the split-off point for R3.80 per litre. Prepare an analysis showing whether Ster should sell PST-4 at the split-off point or continue to process this product further.

(CMA, adapted)

P19.55 Joint costs; allocation and production decisions; ethics (appendix): manufacturer

Chemco Ltd manufactures two products, Compod and Ultrasene, out of a joint process. The joint costs incurred are R750 000 for a standard production run that generates 120 000 litres of Compod and 80 000 litres of Ultrasene. Compod sells for R6.00 per litre while Ultrasene sells for R9.75 per litre.

Required:

1 If there are no additional processing costs incurred after the split-off point, calculate, for each production run, the amount of joint cost allocated to Compod on a physical units basis.

2 If there are no additional processing costs incurred after the split-off point, calculate, for each production run, the amount of joint cost allocated to Ultrasene on a relative sales value basis.

3 Suppose the following additional processing costs are required beyond the split-off point in order to obtain Compod and Ultrasene: R0.30 per litre for Compod and R3.30 per litre for Ultrasene.

(a) Calculate, for each production run, the amount of joint cost allocated to Ultrasene on a physical units basis.

(b) Calculate the amount of the joint cost of each production run allocated to Compod on a net realisable value basis.

4 Assume the same data as in requirement 3. What costs would be allocated to the two products using the constant gross margin method?

5 Assume the same data as in requirement 3. Suppose that Compod can be processed further into a product called Compodalene at an additional cost of R1.20 per litre. Compodalene will be sold for R7.80 per litre by independent distributors. The distributor's commission will be 10 per cent of the sales price. Should Chemco sell Compod or Compodalene?

6 Independent of your answer to requirement 5, suppose that Christine Dalton, the assistant accountant, has completed an analysis showing that Compod should not be processed further into Compodalene. Before presenting her analysis to top management, however, she got a visit from Jack Turner, Chemco's director of research. Turner was upset upon learning that Compodalene, a product he had personally developed, would not be manufactured. The following conversation takes place:

Turner: The company's making a big mistake if it passes up this opportunity. Compodalene will be a big seller and get us into new markets.

Dalton: But the analysis shows that we'd be losing money by every litre of Compod that we process further.

Turner: I know, Christine, but it's a temporary problem. Eventually, we will bring down the cost of making Compodalene.

Dalton: Can you find me some estimates of the cost reduction you expect?

Turner: I don't have a crystal ball, Christine. Look if you could just fudge the numbers a little bit to help me get approval to produce Compodalene, I can get this product off the ground. I know the cost reduction will come.

Comment on the ethical issues in this scenario. What should Christine Dalton do?

7 Assume the same data as given in requirements 3 and 5. The industrial chemical industry has experienced a downturn, which has left Chemco with idle capacity. Suppose that Chemco can sell only half of the Compod made in each production run, but the remainder could be sold as Compodalene. Should Chemco process the remaining Compod into Compodalene?

(*CMA, adapted*)

Cases

C19.56 Analysis of production choices: manufacturer

Real Africa Toy Ltd manufactures and distributes doll's houses. The toy industry is a seasonal business; most sales occur in late winter and spring.

The projected sales in units for next year are shown in the following schedule. With a sales price of R75 per unit, the total sales revenue for next year is projected at R9 million. Management schedule production so that finished goods inventory at the end of each month, exclusive of a safety stock of 4 000 doll's houses, should equal the next month's sales. Thirty minutes of direct labour time is normally required to produce each doll's house. Using the production schedule followed in the past, the total direct labour hours (by month) required to meet the next year's sales estimate are also shown in the schedule.

Real Africa Toy Ltd
Projected sales and planned production
for the year ending 31 December

	Projected sales (in units)	Direct labour hours
January	8 000	4 000
February	8 000	4 000
March	8 000	4 000
April	8 000	4 000
May	8 000	5 000
June	10 000	6 000
July	12 000	6 000
August	12 000	6 500
September	13 000	6 500
October	13 000	6 000
November	12 000	4 000
December	8 000	4 000*
Total	120 000 units	60 000 hours

* Sales for January in the following year are projected to be 8000 units

The production schedule followed in the past requires scheduling overtime hours for any production over 8000 units (4000 direct labour hours) in one month. While the use of overtime is feasible, management have decided to consider two other possible options: hiring temporary help from an agency during peak months, or expanding the labour force and adopting a level production schedule.

The employees, who are highly skilled, are paid R90 per hour for regular time; the labour on-costs average 20 per cent of regular pay. For hours worked in excess of 4000 hours per month, employees receive time and a half, but labour on-costs average only 10 per cent on these additional wages. Past experience has shown that labour inefficiencies occur during overtime. This increases the direct labour hours required during overtime by an additional 5 per cent. This 5 per cent inefficiency was not included in the direct labour hour estimates presented in the schedule.

Instead of paying overtime to its regular labour force, the company could hire temporary employees when production exceeds 8000 units per month. The temporary workers can be hired at the same labour rate of R90 per hour, but there would be no labour on-costs. Management estimates that the temporary workers would require 25 per cent more time than that taken by the regular employees (on regular daytime hours) to produce the doll's houses.

If Real Africa Toy Company adopts a level production schedule, the labour force would be expanded but no overtime would be required. The same labour rate of R90 per hour, and the labour on-costs rate of 20 per cent, would apply.

The manufacturing facilities have the capacity to produce 18 000 doll's houses per month. On-site storage facilities for completed units are adequate. The estimated annual cost of carrying inventory is R10 per unit. The company is subject to a 29 per cent income tax rate.

Required:

1 Prepare an analysis comparing the costs associated with each of Real Africa Toy Company's three options:
 (a) schedule overtime hours
 (b) hire temporary workers
 (c) expand the labour force and schedule level production
2 Identify and discuss briefly the qualitative factors that are difficult to estimate, which management should consider in conjunction with the cost analysis prepared in requirement 1.

(CMA, adapted)

C19.57 Cost analysis of alternative vendors; ethics: manufacturer

'It's nice to have supply options, but I'm going bananas trying to sort out these slit steel bids,' exclaimed Christopher Lane, purchasing manager for Sarbec Ltd.

'I see what you mean,' responded Jack Nell, Lane's assistant. 'Let me call my friend over in the accounting office. He'll have some suggestions for us.'

Sarbec Ltd needs a total of 125 tonnes of sheet steel—50 tonnes of 4 centimetre width and 75 tonnes of 8 centimetre width—for a customer's job. Sarbec can purchase the sheet steel in these widths directly from Jensteel Ltd, a steel manufacturer, or it can purchase sheet steel from Jensteel that is 48 centimetres wide and then have it slit into the desired widths by Precut Pty Ltd. Both vendors are local and have previously supplied materials to Sarbec.

Precut specialises in slitting sheet steel, provided by a customer, into any desired width. When negotiating a contract, Precut tells its customers that there is a scrap loss in the slitting operation, but that this loss has never exceeded 2.5 per cent of input tonnes. Precut recommends that if a customer has a specific tonnage requirement, it should supply an adequate amount of steel to yield the desired quantity. Precut's charges for steel slitting are based on good output, not input handled.

The 48 centimetre-wide sheet steel is a regular stock item of Jensteel and can be shipped to Precut within five days of receipt of Sarbec's purchase order. If Jensteel is to do the slitting, shipment to Sarbec would be scheduled for 15 days from receipt of the order. Precut has quoted delivery at 10 days after receipt of the sheet steel. In dealings in the past Sarbec has found both Jensteel and Precut to be reliable vendors with high-quality products:

Jensteel Ltd rates

Size	Gauge	Quantity	Cost per tonne
4 cm	14	50 tonnes	R2 100
8 cm	14	75 tonnes	R2 000
48 cm	14	25 tonnes	R1 800

Precut Pty Ltd steel slitting rates

Size	Gauge	Quantity	Price per tonne of output
4 cm	14	50 tonnes	R180
8 cm	14	75 tonnes	R150

Freight and handling charges

Destination	Cost per tonne
Jensteel to Sarbec	R100
Jensteel to Precut	R50
Precut to Sarbec	R75

In addition to the above information, Precut has informed Sarbec that if Sarbec purchases 100 output tonnes of each width, the per-tonne slitting rates would be reduced by 12 per cent.

Sarbec knows that the same customer will be placing a new order in the near future for the same material and estimates it would have to store the additional tonnage for an average of two months at a carrying cost of R15 per month for each tonne. There would be no change in Jensteel's prices for additional tonnes delivered to Precut.

As Nell's friend in the accounting office, you have just received a phone call for help.

Required:

1 Prepare an analysis to determine whether Sarbec Ltd should:
   (a) purchase the required slit steel directly from Jensteel Ltd; or
   (b) purchase the 48 centimetre-wide sheet steel from Jensteel and have it slit by Precut Pty Ltd into 50 output tonnes, 4 centimetres wide and 75 output tonnes, 8 centimetres wide; or
   (c) take advantage of Precut's reduced slitting rates by purchasing 100 output tonnes of each width.

Round all cost figures to the nearest cent.

2 Independent of your answer to requirement 1, present three qualitative arguments as to why Sarbec Ltd may favour the purchase of the slit steel directly from Jensteel Ltd.

3 Independent of your answers to requirements 1 and 2, suppose that Christopher Lane's final analysis shows that purchasing slit steel directly from Jensteel is Sarbec's least costly option. Before making his decision, Lane receives a call from a good friend who is the production manager at Precut. His friend has called to urge Lane to use Precut's services. 'We're really hurting here at Precut, Chris,' his friend insists. 'If we don't get this job, it's going to be a long cold winter for some of us.'

   Discuss Christopher Lane's ethical obligations in this matter.

(CMA, adapted)

C19.58 Drop a product line: manufacturer

Levitt Corporation, a small manufacturing company in Welkom, produces three types of pumps: R-pumps, F-pumps and S-pumps. For many years the company has been profitable and has operated at full capacity. However, for the last two years, prices on all pumps have been reduced and selling expenses increased to meet competition and to keep the plant operating at capacity. The results for the second quarter, which follow, typify recent experience:

Levitt Corporation
Profit Report
Second quarter
(in R'000s)

	R-pump	F-pump	S-pump	Total
Sales	4 800	2 700	2 700	10 200
Cost of goods sold	3 144	2 310	2 850	8 304
Gross margin	1 656	390	−150	1 896
Selling and administrative expenses	1 110	555	405	2 070
Profit before taxes	546	−165	−555	−174

Maria Levitt, Levitt's managing director, is concerned about the results of the pricing, selling and production policies. After reviewing the third-quarter results, she asked her management staff to consider her proposed course of action, comprising the following three changes to operations:

- Discontinue the S-pump line immediately. S-pumps would not be returned to the product line unless the problems with the pump could be identified and resolved.
- Increase quarterly sales promotion by R300 000 on the R-pump product line in order to increase sales volume by 15 per cent.
- Cut production on the F-pump line by 50 per cent, and cut the traceable advertising and promotion for this line to R60 000 each quarter.

Joe Sojola, the management accountant, suggested a more careful study of the financial relationships to determine the possible effects on the company's operating results of the managing director's proposed course of action. The managing director agreed and assigned Joanne Rhoda, the assistant accountant, to prepare an analysis. Rhoda has gathered the following information:

- The unit sales prices for the three pumps are as follows:
  R-pump R600
  F-pump R270
  S-pump R540
- The company is manufacturing at capacity and is selling all pumps it produces. All three pumps are manufactured with common equipment and facilities.
- The quarterly general selling and administrative expense is allocated to the three pump lines in proportion to their Rand sales volume.
- Special selling expenses (primarily advertising, promotion and shipping) are incurred for each pump as follows:

	Quarterly advertising and promotion	Shipping expense
R-pump	R 630 000	R30 per unit
F-pump	300 000	12 per unit
S-pump	12 000	30 per unit

The unit manufacturing costs for the three products are as follows:

	R-pump	F-pump	S-pump
Raw material	R93	R51	R150
Direct labour	120	60	180
Variable manufacturing overhead	135	90	180
Fixed manufacturing overhead	45	30	60
Total	R393	R231	R570

Required:

1 Joanne Rhoda says that Levitt Corporation's product line profit report for the second quarter is not suitable for analysing proposals and making decisions such as the ones suggested by Maria Levitt.
   (a) Explain why the product line profit report, as presented, is not suitable for analysis and decision making.
   (b) Describe an alternative profit reporting format that would be more suitable for analysis and decision making, and explain why it is better than the original.

2 Use the operating data presented for Levitt Corporation and assume that the managing director's proposed course of action was implemented at the beginning of the second quarter. Then evaluate the managing director's proposal by specifically responding to the following points:
   (a) Is each of the three proposed changes cost effective? Support your discussion with an analysis that shows the net impact on profit before taxes for each of the three proposed changes.
   (b) Was the managing director correct in proposing that the S-pump line be eliminated? Explain your answer.
   (c) Was the managing director correct in promoting the R-pump line rather than the F-pump line? Explain your answer.
   (d) Does the proposed course of action make effective use of Levitt's capacity? Explain your answer.

3 Are there any qualitative factors that Levitt Corporation's management should consider before it drops the S-pump line? Explain your answer.

(CMA, adapted)

Endnotes

1 Australians normally like to fly Wings Airlines to South Africa to visit the wild nature game reserves. Some visitors may now decide to visit Mauritius rather than South Africa, so that the charter may result in a loss of passengers for Wings Airlines' normal routes.

2 We will assume that Wings Airlines will be able to obtain landing rights from the local aviation authorities.

3 If the company had a permanently idle 747 jet, then we may need to also consider any opportunity cost as the company may be able to lease the plane to another airline. An airline may have some spare aircraft to ensure continued operations at all times. For example, if one plane experiences technical problems on a scheduled flight, then the airline can immediately send out a replacement aircraft to ensure that there are no serious delays to scheduled flights that may impact on future passenger and freight demand.

4 We can further argue that depreciation is really a sunk cost as it refers to the orginal cost of plant and equipment and so only incremental costs are relevant. However, in the long term, if we continue to make any product, we would in most cases need to replace equipment in the future and we need to consider this future cost in making our decision but we will also need to discount any future cash flows. We will come back to this issue in Chapters 21 and 22. In the public sector, government has been in some cases 'outsourcing' activities such as airports and roads mainly due to the huge costs required to finance the expansion in airports, the road network and other major infrastructural assets such as the rail network.

5 This is equal to the difference between the price per unit of R9.00 and the activity-based cost per unit of R10.016, multiplied by the number of boxes required, 1 000 000.

CHAPTER

Chapter 20 Pricing and Product Mix Decisions

❖ Learning Objectives

After completing this chapter, you should be able to:

1. list and describe the major influences on pricing decisions;
2. explain and use the economic profit-maximising pricing model;
3. explain value-based, economic-value and cost-price pricing strategies, and use these methods to calculate prices;
4. determine prices using the time and material pricing approach;
5. explain how product cost distortions can undermine a firm's pricing policy;
6. discuss the issues involved in the strategic pricing of new products;
7. set prices in special order or competitive bidding situations by analysing the relevant costs;
8. describe the restrictions imposed on pricing, administered by the South African Competition Commission;
9. identify which information is relevant for tactical and long-term product mix decisions; and
10. after studying the appendix, use linear programming in short-term (tactical) product mix decisions.

Introduction

Setting the price for an organisation's goods or services is one of the most important decisions a manager faces, as prices have a major influence on both customer and shareholder value. The pricing decision arises in virtually all types of business. Manufacturers set prices for the goods they manufacture; retailers set prices for the goods they sell; service organisations set prices for insurance policies, train tickets, rock concerts and bank loans. Not-for-profit organisations often set prices too—for example, government enterprises price vehicle registrations and national park entrance fees. The optimal approach to pricing often depends on a variety of factors. Pricing a mature product that a firm has sold for many years may be quite different from pricing a new product. However, in setting a price it is critical that managers understand the product's value to the customer. In some areas, prices are regulated or monitored by outside bodies, such as the South African Competition Commission.

Another important decision for managers is selecting the appropriate mix of goods or services to produce and sell. In the short term this may involve producing products or offering services to maximise the benefits that can be generated from available resources. When considering long-term product mix, a range of strategic issues comes into play.

In this chapter, we will study pricing decisions and product mix decisions, with an emphasis on the role of management accounting information. The setting for our discussion is Cape Sailing Supplies, a manufacturer of sailing supplies and equipment.

Major influences on pricing decisions

L.O. 1

The major factors that affect a company's pricing decisions may be both internal and external to the firm. They include:

1 market positioning;

2 product cost;

3 customer value;

4 competitor behaviour; and

5 legal, political and ethical issues.[1]

The influence of these factors on price is shown in Exhibit 20.1. Note that in setting the price, in most situations the cost of the product or service is the lower limit of the price, whereas customer value sets the upper level of the price. If a price is set lower than cost, then the product will make a loss. If the price is set higher than customer value, then customers will regard this as too expensive and will not purchase the product.

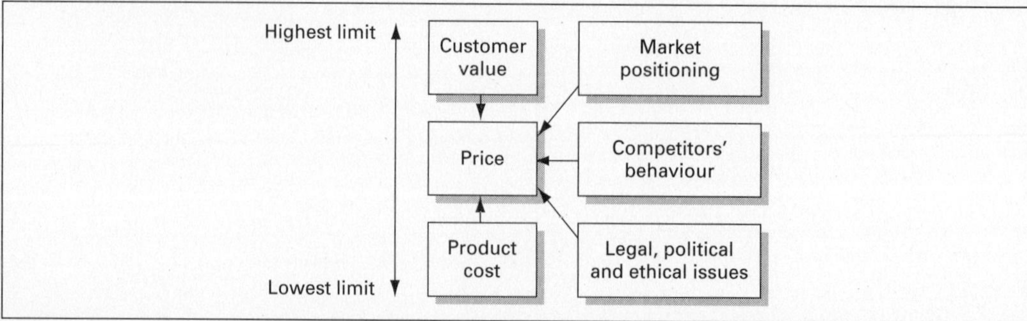

Exhibit 20.1 Factors that influence price

Market positioning

Companies choose to position themselves in certain markets, and this may influence product prices. For example, McDonald's operates in the takeaway food industry, so it will price products at a level that is affordable for families and teenagers. On the other hand, a firm with a reputation for very high quality and prestigious products may set a high price that is consistent with its image. The price that it charges will be high in order to appeal to the appropriate market and to represent a certain quality. (For example, a French champagne company positions its product to appeal to high-income consumers.) However, with many high-priced prestige brands, as we have all discovered, similar products may be available in a discount store at much lower prices.

Where a company positions its product to cater for a high-price market, an overemphasis on price cutting can damage a product's image and reduce profitability. This is because regular price discounting can weaken the positioning of the product. Customers become used to the price being discounted and will delay purchasing the product until the price is discounted. As a reaction, companies may cut prices to encourage sales. The market declines in profitability as a result, and the loyalty of customers to brands is reduced.

Product costs

In most situations, the cost of a product or service sets the lower limit for the price. Clearly, to make a profit, businesses must produce at a cost below the market selling price. However, the importance of costs in price setting varies widely across industries. For example, costs influence prices in the construction industry, in a wide range of consulting firms and in the electrical contracting trade. Even when market forces may cause an organisation to price a product below cost—a loss leader—it is still important for managers to be aware of the product cost.

For some agricultural products (such as dairy products and sugar), there were statutory marketing boards that set prices. Their decisions were usually based on a consideration of both production costs and customer demand. For utilities, such as electricity and water, prices are often influenced by a regulatory agency of the government. Production costs and the firm's cost of capital may be important in justifying increases in utility prices.[2]

Customer value

A critical aspect of price setting is understanding customer value. Customers base their buying decision on two criteria: price, and the perceived benefits of a particular product or service. In Chapter 1 we defined customer value as the value that a customer places on particular features of a product or service. Another way of looking at customer value, which is useful for setting prices, is to define customer value as the difference between the value that a customer gains by owning and using the product, and the price paid for the product.

The delivery of superior value is a key to achieving business success. However, companies must understand the specific aspects of their products or services that provide value to the customers. Let's consider a particular yacht that is produced by Cape Sailing Supplies. What are the features of the yacht that customers value? Is it the colour? Is it the streamlined shape? Is it the state of the art navigation technology? Is it the safety features? Is it the low price?

Managers should not simply guess customer preferences—to do so may result in developing a product that no customers will want. Understanding customer preferences requires a great deal of research: surveying or talking to customers about preferences, analysing customer behaviour in the marketplace, and test-marketing new aspects of the product. It is important to understand that a particular product at a particular price will satisfy only some segments of the market. For example, you might create an ultra-low-cost house that no one wants to purchase; or a cappuccino machine that makes coffee instantly, but the coffee is undrinkable; or an electric toaster with all the features desired by customers, but at such a high price that no one is willing to purchase it!

An understanding of customer value should flow through to all aspects of the product/service creation—each area within the value chain needs to contribute to enhancing customer value. The importance of understanding customer value in modern cost management techniques was discussed in Chapter 15.

Competitor behaviour

Competitors' behaviour can affect a company's pricing decisions. In the 1990s and into the 2000s the dominance of South Africa's major airline, South African Airways (SAA), was challenged by new competitors, such as Comair (operating as British Airways) and Nationwide. In 2001, Comair introduced the low-cost airline kulula.com. In 2004, 1Time Airlines entered the market by also offering low fares. In order for these new entrants to gain market share, they offered lower prices than the market leader. SAA responded in 2006 by launching its own budget airline, Mango. As described in the 'Real life' below, these changes resulted in a competitive environment characterised initially by price wars.

REAL LIFE: BATTLING FOR SOUTH AFRICA'S SKIES

South Africa's airline industry has become increasingly competitive with the development of the low cost or budget segment of the market, and the arrival of each new competitor has led to price wars. kulula.com began operations as a low-cost airline in 2001. kulula.com offered a no-frills, low-cost flying experience with some funny advertisements and 'fun' in-flight announcements. The main airline carriers prior to the entry of the low-cost airlines were South African Airways, Comair (BA) and Nationwide. kulula.com is a subsidiary of Comair. In 2004 a new low-cost airline, 1Time, took to the skies. SAA resisted but finally launched its own low-cost provider, called Mango, in late 2006. Internet booking is a feature of the low-cost segment of the airline sector. Mango began operations by offering flights on the Johannesburg–Cape Town route for under R200! The website crashed due to the excessive number of people trying to obtain flights at these fares. kulula.com, who were significantly affected by the lower fares offered by Mango, indicated that this represented unfair competition. Why? Mango's parent company, SAA, is government-owned and could therefore subsidise fares and incur losses in order to obtain market share.

Mango is leasing 737-800s from SAA and has increased the number of seats in the planes as well as flying the planes more often. Mango is also using retired SAA pilots. The 737-800s are also more fuel-efficient than the older planes operated by kulula.com and 1Time. However, the R200 fare was an opening price which attracted substantial interest from customers. *The Pretoria News* (31 October 2006) reported the CEO of kulula.com as saying that 'Mango will go vrot' and would be a drain on South African taxpayers.

The CEO of kulula.com was further quoted as saying: 'We introduced low-fare air travel more than five years ago and in that time have doubled the size of the market, have treated more than 5 million clients to low fares, and we have become South Africa's biggest online retailer.'

How has the pricing changed for Mango? Well, in August 2007, you could still obtain a special fare of R239 (excluding airport charges) from Cape Town to Johannesburg. However, most fares were in the range of R450–R599 for a one-way ticket. In the same week in August 2007 kulula.com was quoting most one-way fares from Cape Town to Johannesburg in the range R499 to R659. So, it seems that the dust has mostly settled on ticket pricing.

In 2007 kulula.com was warning that increasing and excessive airport charges were going to negatively affect future air travel. The Airports Company of South Africa (ACSA) operates the major airports in South

Africa and, as the company has no competition and is in effect a monopoly, it has a high degree of pricing power. ACSA is extremely profitable and is currently engaged in spending billions of Rands to expand the airports which will only result in higher airport charges. The airlines such as Mango and kulula.com quote prices excluding airport charges so that customers can see what the airport is charging and how this cost is escalating over time.

Australia has also seen the growth in low-cost airlines which include Virgin Blue and Jetstar, a subsidiary of Qantas. Jetstar entered the market with a bang, with an amazing introductory offer of 100 000 seats at $29 each (about R180) to destinations around the nation. It's a big country. In its first day of operation, Jetstar's Internet booking site attracted more than 2.5 million hits. With the website processing 5000 bookings every 30 minutes, 20 000 tickets were snapped up within a couple of hours of opening.

It is interesting to ponder whether there are any real winners in price wars. Mango is reported to be losing money. The airline industry in South Africa has endured dramatic increases in fuel prices and airport charges, and the introduction of Mango and 1Time have led to a very competitive environment in which it is difficult to pass on cost increases to customers. While the price wars between Mango, 1Time and Kulula.com resulted in some real bargains for customers, ultimately customers will be served best by airlines setting competitive but sustainable prices.

Sources: *Pretoria News* 31 October 2006; www.kulula.com; www.flymango.com; Oakes (2004); Bawden (2004)

Cape Sailing Supplies' managers would like their company to have the sailing market to itself, but they are not so fortunate. Domestic and foreign competitors are striving to sell their products to the same customers. Thus, as Cape Sailing Supplies' management design products and set prices, they must keep a watchful eye on the firm's competitors. If a competitor reduces its price of sails, Cape Sailing Supplies may have to follow suit to avoid losing its market share. Yet the company cannot follow its competitors blindly. Predicting competitors' reactions to its product design and pricing strategy is a difficult but important task for management.

When considering the reactions of competitors or customers, management must take care to define the company's product and market correctly, and hence identify its competitors. Should Cape Sailing Supplies' managers define its product narrowly as 'sailing supplies and equipment', or more broadly as 'recreational supplies'? For example, if the company raises the price of its two-person sailing dinghy, will this encourage potential customers to switch to canoes, rowboats, jet skis and mountain bikes? Or will most potential dinghy customers react to a price increase only by price shopping at competing manufacturers? The way in which Cape Sailing Supplies' management answer these questions can profoundly affect the company's marketing and pricing strategies.

Legal, political and ethical issues

Many organisations need to take account of legal issues when setting prices. Managers must adhere to certain laws. The law generally prohibits companies from discriminating between their customers in setting prices. Also prohibited is collusion in price setting, which is where firms within an industry agree to set their prices at certain levels.[3] These legal restrictions imposed by the South African Competition Commission are discussed in a later section of this chapter.

Political considerations can also be relevant to setting prices. If a firm operates in an industry that is perceived by the public as reaping excessive profits, then there may be political pressure on legislators to tax those profits differentially or to intervene in some way to regulate prices. For example, when the major South African banks announce record profits, this often results in outcries from customers about the high levels of account-keeping charges and the high price (interest rates) of housing loans. High prices for resources have caused the South African government to consider introducing a windfall tax on the mining and petroleum sectors.

Ethical considerations may also be taken into account when setting prices. For example, some dishonest firms may develop quite complex pricing schemes, so that the price that a customer pays for a product may be only the first of many expenditures that will need to be incurred before the product is suitable for use. Such deceptive practices may be prosecutable under the Trade Practices Act of 1976.

Economic profit-maximising models

L.O. 2

In this section we consider economic profit-maximising models to determine price. Generally speaking, economic models assume that as the price of a product is increased the quantity demanded declines, and vice versa. As we will see in the following section, there are more realistic models that can be adopted to determine price.

Profit-maximising price and quantity

Cape Sailing Supplies is interested in finding out the optimal price and sales quantity that will maximise profit for its two-person sailing dinghy, the Wave Darter. The first step is to consider the trade-offs between charging a higher price and gaining a higher sales quantity. This can be shown in the shape of the firm's **total revenue curve**, which graphs the relationship between total sales revenue and quantity sold. Panel A of Exhibit 20.2 shows that total revenue increases as the quantity sold each month increases, but the rate of increase declines as the monthly sales quantity increases. Panel B shows that the profit-maximising sales quantity, q^*, for the Wave Darter is determined by the intersection of the marginal cost curve and the marginal revenue curve. The optimal price, p^*, is determined from the demand curve for that same quantity. These curves will now be explained.

The **marginal revenue** curve shows the change in total revenue that accompanies a change in the quantity sold. The marginal revenue curve in panel B of Exhibit 20.2 shows that total revenue increases at a declining rate as the quantity sold each month increases. The **demand curve** shows the relationship between the sales price and the quantity of units demanded. The demand curve shows that any decrease in the sales price brings about an increase in the monthly sales quantity. The demand curve is also called the average revenue curve, since it shows the average price at which any particular quantity can be sold.

Profit is determined by both revenue and cost. How does total cost behave as the number of Wave Darters produced and sold by Cape Sailing Supplies changes? The firm's **total cost curve** (panel A) graphs the relationship between total cost and the quantity produced and sold each month.[4] Total cost increases throughout its range, although the rate of increase is not constant.

Closely related to the total cost curve is the marginal cost curve, which is graphed in panel B of Exhibit 20.2. The marginal cost curve shows the change in total cost that accompanies a change in quantity produced and sold. It can be seen (panel A) that at the profit-maximising quantity (and price), the distance between the total revenue curve and the total cost curve, which is equal to total profit, is maximised. A tabular presentation of the revenue, cost and profit data is shown in panel C of Exhibit 20.2. Notice that monthly profit is maximised when the price is set at R9250 and 40 Wave Darters are produced and sold each month.

Price elasticity

The impact of price changes on sales volume is called the **price elasticity**. Demand is elastic if a price increase has a large negative impact on sales volume, and vice versa. Demand is inelastic if price changes have little or no impact on sales quantity. **Cross-elasticity** refers to the extent to which a change in a product's price affects the demand for other substitute products. For example,

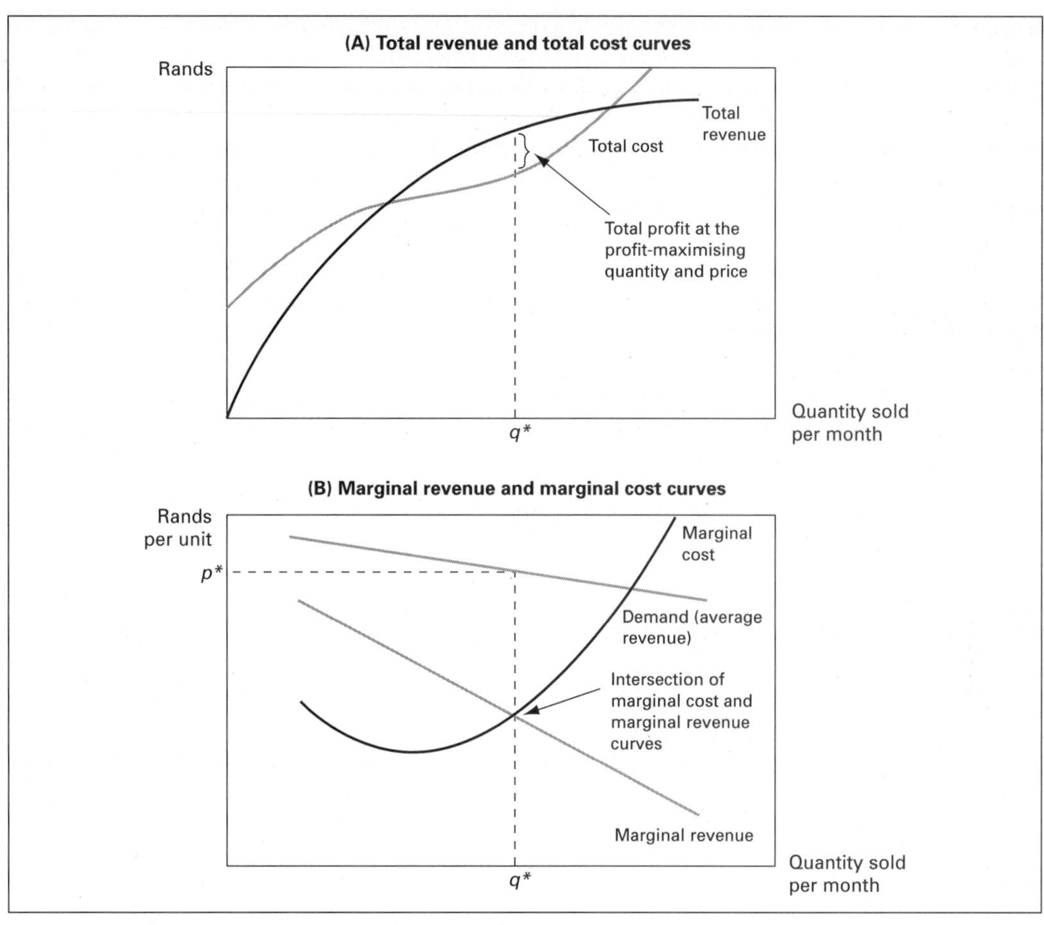

(C) Tabular revenue, cost and profit data

	Quantity produced and sold per month	Unit sales price	Total revenue per month	Total cost per month*	Profit (loss) per month
	10	R12 250	R122 500	R185 000	−R62 500
	20	R11 000	220 000	230 000	−10 000
profit-	30	R10 000	300 000	275 000	25 000
maximising →	40	R9 250	370 000	320 000	50 000
price	50	R8 000	400 000	365 000	35 000
	60	R7 000	420 000	410 000	10 000

*We will come back to the determination of total cost later in the chapter.

Exhibit 20.2 Determining the profit-maximising price and quantity, Cape Sailing Supplies

if Cape Sailing Supplies raises the price of its two-person sailing dinghy, there may be an increase in demand for substitute recreational craft, such as jet skis, canoes or windsurfers.

Measuring price elasticity and cross-elasticity is an important objective of market research. Having a good understanding of these economic concepts helps managers to determine the profit-maximising price.

Limitations of the economic model

The economic model of the pricing decision serves as a useful framework for approaching a pricing problem. However, it does have several limitations. First, the firm's demand curve and marginal revenue curve are difficult to determine with precision. Although market research is designed to gather data about product demand, it rarely enables management to predict accurately the effects of price changes on the quantity demanded. Also, many other factors in addition to price affect product demand. Product design and quality, advertising and promotion, and company reputation can significantly influence customer demand for a product.

Second, the marginal revenue–marginal cost paradigm is not valid for all forms of markets. In an **oligopolistic market**, where a small number of sellers compete among themselves, the simple economic pricing model is no longer appropriate. In an oligopoly, such as the car industry, the reactions of competitors to a firm's pricing policies must be taken into account. While economists have studied oligopolistic pricing, the state of the theory is not sufficient to provide a thorough understanding of the impact of prices on demand.

The third limitation of the economic pricing model involves the difficulty of measuring marginal cost. Costing systems are not usually designed to measure the marginal changes in cost incurred as production and sales increase unit by unit. This would entail the design of a very costly information system.

As discussed below, pricing strategies are often based on models that contain more realistic assumptions than that of the above economic model.

Pricing strategies

L.O. 3

How can an understanding of customer value, product cost or competitor's costs help an organisation to set prices for its products or services? There are various pricing strategies that can be used. We will examine value-based pricing, economic-value pricing and cost-based pricing. With all pricing strategies, we need to focus on a particular customer segment of the market. As different customers in different segments have different preferences, they will attach different levels of economic value to a product, and hence the price will be different.

Value-based pricing

Value-based pricing is where customers' perceptions of the value of the product or service guide the pricing. Thus, prices cannot be set until the organisation has a firm understanding of customers' needs and their perceptions of the value of the product or service. In Exhibit 20.1, this is depicted as the upper limit of the price.

But how do we determine customer value? How much extra is a consumer willing to pay for an airline seat that has 20 per cent extra leg room? Or for a pizza served in the comfort of the restaurant, as opposed to pizza purchased as takeaway? One approach is to ask consumers how much extra they would pay for the additional benefit of extra leg-room, or how much extra they are willing to pay to be served in the restaurant. This will represent the value of those features to the customer.

Economic-value pricing

Economic-value pricing specifically estimates the costs and benefits experienced by the customer that extend beyond the initial purchase price (Forbis & Mehta, 2000). For example, switching from one brand of computer to another may require the customer to engage in staff training costs, installation costs, rewriting of software, and construction costs to house the new computer. Economic-value pricing is often used in industrial markets, where the goods or services that are purchased enter into the production of other goods or services that are then sold, leased or supplied to others (Kotler, Adam, Brown & Armstrong, 2003, p. 352). Economic-value pricing allows companies to differentiate their products from those of competitors, on the basis of economic value to customers.

The first step in economic-value pricing is to select a reference product. This is a product that customers currently use that satisfies the same underlying needs as the firm's product. The choice of product is critical and may be a specific product of a competitor, or the last generation of the firm's own product.

This strategy assumes that there are two reasons for a customer to switch from their current product to the firm's product. First, the firm's product may have better functionality. (For example, it may complete a task faster, have greater accuracy or be more visually appealing.) Second, the firm's product may entail lower operating costs than the reference product.

We can now see that the **economic value to the customer (EVC)** is the price that customers are willing to pay for the product, given the price that they pay for the reference product and the added functionality and any operating cost reduction provided by the product.

Exhibit 20.3 illustrates the EVC process. Cape Sailing Supplies is considering introducing a new model of the 10-metre yacht, to be called the SuperSwift. Market research has indicated that the new yacht will appeal to a particular market sector, identified as 'weekend cruise operators'. The most popular 'equivalent' yacht currently used by this segment is that of a competitor—the Dolphin. This will be used as the reference product. The Dolphin currently sells for R125 000. The new features, or improved functionality, that the SuperSwift has over the Dolphin are its increased speed, more attractive sails, more appealing shape and larger capacity. Let's assume in this case that market research indicates that the improved functionality is valued at R15 000 by customers. The start-up costs for the SuperSwift, which include insurance, training, and customisation of fittings and seats, are expected to be R15 000, compared to R10 000 associated with the Dolphin. In addition, the operating costs of the SuperSwift are expected to be R20 000 over the life of the product, compared to R25 000 for the Dolphin. As indicated in Exhibit 20.3, the economic value to the customer is R140 000. Thus, Cape Sailing Supplies could charge R140 000 for the SuperSwift. In reality, this figure represents the maximum price that the company could charge, and it would probably charge less than R140 000. Note that a more accurate analysis of the economic value to the customer would make allowance for the time value of money.

	Dolphin	SuperSwift	EV to the customer
Purchase price	R125 000		R125 000
Additional functionality		R15 000	15 000
Startup cost	10 000	15 000	−5 000
Post-purchase costs	25 000	20 000	5 000
Total EVC			R140 000

Exhibit 20.3 Economic value pricing, the SuperSwift

Cost-plus pricing

Most managers consider product costs to some degree when setting prices. There are several reasons for this. First, most companies sell a range of different goods or services. There simply is not enough time to do a thorough market analysis for every product. Managers must rely on quick and straightforward methods for setting prices, and cost-based pricing formulas provide a fairly simple base for setting prices. Second, even though market considerations may ultimately determine the final product price, a cost-based pricing formula gives the manager a place to start. Finally, and most importantly, the cost of a product or service provides a floor, and the price cannot be set below this floor in the long run. Although a product may be 'given away' at a price below cost when it is first launched, ultimately a product's price should usually cover its costs in the long term. In some situations, an organisation may choose to offer a product at a price below cost even over the long run, where sales of that product lead to customers purchasing a range of more profitable products.

Many businesses, particularly some professional service firms, service shops and smaller manufacturers, use cost-plus pricing. Cost-plus pricing formulas have the following general form:

$$\text{Price} = \text{cost} + (\text{mark-up percentage} \times \text{cost})$$

This approach is called **cost-plus pricing**, because the price is equal to cost plus a mark-up. As we have learnt in previous chapters, there are a variety of different definitions of 'product cost'.

These include variable cost and absorption cost, and broader definitions of product cost that may include product-related costs that occur outside of manufacturing.

Suppose Cape Sailing Supplies' production plan calls for 480 (40 × 12) Wave Darters to be manufactured during the year. The cost data relating to this decision are shown in Exhibit 20.4.

Variable costs:		
Manufacturing	R1 920 000	
Sales commission	240 000	
Total variable costs		R2 160 000
Fixed costs (allocated):		
Manufacturing	R1 200 000	
Selling and administrative	480 000	
Total fixed costs		R1 680 000
Total costs		R3 840 000
Variable manufacturing cost per unit	R1 920 000	/ 480 = R4000
Absorption cost per unit		
Variable Manufacturing Costs	R1 920 000	
Fixed Manufacturing Costs	1 200 000	
	R3 120 000	/ 480 = R6500
Total variable cost per unit		
Manufacturing	R1 920 000	
Sales commission	240 000	
	R2 160 000	/ 480 = R4500
Note: Total monthly cost at 40 units = 40 × R4500 + (R1680 000/12) = R320 000		

Exhibit 20.4 Product cost for the Wave Darter, Cape Sailing Supplies

Exhibit 20.4 indicates that the absorption cost of the Wave Darter is R6500 per unit. (Remember from Chapter 7 that absorption cost includes both variable and fixed manufacturing costs.) If management decide that the required mark-up is 30 per cent on absorption cost, then the price will be determined as follows:

Price = R6500 + (0.30 × R6500)
= R8450

If a narrower cost definition is used—variable costing—then management may use a greater mark-up percentage, as there are more costs that need to be covered by the mark-up for the firm to remain in profit.

Cost-plus pricing requires us to consider two issues:

1 What is the best definition of cost?

2 How will the mark-up be determined?

There is no one best definition of product cost for pricing purposes. The decision often depends on whether we want to determine a short-term price, or a long-term price.

Absorption cost pricing formulas

Most companies that use cost-plus pricing use either absorption manufacturing cost, or a broader definition of product cost that includes product-related upstream and downstream costs, as the basis for pricing products or services.[5] Some reasons for this are as follows:

1 Absorption cost (or broader cost) pricing formulas provide a justifiable price that tends to be perceived as equitable by all parties. Consumers generally understand that a company must make a profit on its product to remain in business. Basing a price on the total cost of production and other product-related costs that occur outside production, plus a reasonable profit margin, seems fair to many customers.

2 Absorption cost information is usually provided by a firm's costing system because it is required for external financial reporting under IAS 2 *Inventories,* the International

Accounting Standard. Since absorption cost information already exists, it is cost-effective to use it for pricing. The alternative would involve preparing special product cost data specifically for the pricing decision. In a firm with hundreds of products, such data could be expensive to produce.

The primary disadvantage of absorption cost or broader product cost definitions is that they obscure the cost behaviour pattern of the firm. Since allocated fixed costs are included, it is not clear from these data how the firm's total costs will change as production and sales volumes change. Another way of stating this criticism is that absorption cost data are not consistent with cost volume profit (CVP) analysis. (CVP analysis was discussed in Chapter 18.) CVP analysis emphasises the distinction between fixed and variable costs. This approach enables managers to predict the effects of changes in prices and sales volume on profit. Absorption and broader product cost information obscures the distinction between variable and fixed costs.

Variable cost pricing formulas

Some managers prefer to use cost-plus pricing formulas based on either variable manufacturing costs or total variable costs. In Exhibit 20.4, the variable manufacturing cost is R4000 per unit, while the total variable cost per unit is R4500.

Three advantages are attributed to this pricing approach:

1 Variable cost data do not obscure the cost behaviour pattern by unitising fixed costs and making them appear variable. Thus, variable cost information is consistent with cost volume profit analysis, which may be used by managers to assess the profit implications of changes in price and volume.

2 Variable cost data do not require allocation of fixed costs to individual product lines. For example, the annual salary of Cape Sailing Supplies' sales director is a cost that must be borne by all of the company's product lines. Arbitrarily allocating a portion of his salary to the Wave Darter product line is not meaningful.

3 Variable cost data are exactly the type of information managers need when facing certain tactical short-term pricing decisions, such as whether to accept a special order. This decision, examined in Chapter 19, often requires an analysis that separates fixed and variable costs in order to determine the incremental costs of the special order. Where there is excess capacity, the price of the special order may be set just above the variable costs of producing the order.

The primary disadvantage of variable cost pricing formulas is that, in the long term, prices must be set to cover all costs and a normal profit margin. If managers perceive the variable cost of a product to be the floor for the price, they may tend to set the price too low for the firm to cover its fixed costs. Ultimately, such a practice could result in the failure of the business. If variable cost data are used as the basis for cost-plus pricing, managers must understand the need for higher mark-ups in order to ensure that all costs are covered.

Determining the mark-up

Regardless of which definition of cost is used, Cape Sailing Supplies must determine its mark-up on the Wave Darter. If management use a variable cost pricing formula, the mark-up must cover all fixed costs and a reasonable profit. If management uses an absorption costing formula, the mark-up must still be sufficient to cover the firm's selling and administrative costs and required profit on the Wave Darter product line. Even with broader definitions of product cost, the mark-up must be sufficient to generate profit on the Wave Darter. What constitutes a reasonable or normal profit margin? While managers will often rely on their judgement and experience in determining the most suitable mark-up, a more formal method is based on the target return on investment.

Return on investment pricing

One common approach to determining the profit margin in cost-plus pricing is to use **return on investment (ROI) pricing**, which bases the profit margin on the firm's target return on investment. Let's consider the decision to price the Wave Darter.

Suppose that the year's average investment in the Wave Darter product line is R3 000 000. If Cape Sailing Supplies' target return on investment for the Wave Darter line is 20 per cent, the required annual profit is calculated as follows:

$$\text{Average invested capital} \times \text{target ROI} = \text{target profit}$$
$$\text{R3 000 000} \times 20\% = \text{R600 000}$$

The mark-up percentage required to earn Cape Sailing Supplies a R600 000 profit on the Wave Darter line depends on which definition of product cost is used. We will calculate the mark-up percentage using two definitions of product cost:

1 Cost-plus pricing based on absorption cost. Exhibit 20.4 indicates that the absorption cost of a Wave Darter is R6500 per unit. The mark-up percentage applied to absorption cost must be sufficient to cover the target profit of R600 000 and the selling and administrative costs. We will assume that sales are not affected by the mark-up percentage. The mark-up can be calculated using the following formula:

$$\text{Mark-up percentage} = \frac{\text{target profit} + \text{total selling and administrative costs}}{\text{annual volume} \times \text{cost per unit}}$$

$$= \frac{\text{R600 000} + \text{R720 000}}{480 \times \text{R6500}}$$

$$= 42.3\% \text{ (rounded from 42.3077\%)}$$

2 Cost-plus pricing based on total variable costs. The total variable cost of a Wave Darter is R4500 per unit (Exhibit 20.4). The mark-up percentage applied to variable cost must be sufficient to cover both the target profit of R600 000 and total annual fixed costs of R1680 000. The required mark-up percentage is calculated as follows:

$$\text{Mark-up percentage on total variable cost} = \frac{\text{target profit} + \text{total annual fixed cost}}{\text{annual volume} \times \text{total variable cost per unit}}$$

$$= \frac{\text{R600 000} + \text{R1 680 000}}{480 \times \text{R4 500}}$$

$$= 105.6\% \text{ (rounded from 105.5556\%)}$$

The general formula for calculating the mark-up percentage in cost-plus pricing to achieve a target ROI is as follows:

$$\text{Mark-up percentage} = \frac{\text{profit required to achieve target ROI} + \text{total annual costs not included in cost base}}{\text{annual volume} \times \text{cost base per unit used in cost-plus pricing formula}}$$

L.O. 4 Time and material pricing

Another cost-based approach to pricing is called **time and material pricing**. Under this approach, the company determines one charge for the labour used on a job and another charge for the materials. The labour charge typically includes the direct cost of the employees' time, and a charge to cover various overhead costs and generate a profit. The material charge generally includes the direct cost of the materials used in a job plus a charge for material handling and storage. As mentioned in Chapter 6, time and material pricing is widely used by a range of service businesses including construction companies, printers and repair shops. It is also used by some professional firms, especially in engineering, law and public accounting businesses.

To illustrate, we will examine a special job undertaken by Cape Sailing Supplies. The company's sales director, Richard Hendricks, was approached by a successful local physician about refurbishing her yacht. She wanted an engine overhaul, complete refurbishment and redecoration of the cabin facilities, and stripping and repainting of the hull and deck. The work would be done in the Repair Department of the company's Yacht Division, located in Hout Bay.

Budgeted data regarding the operations of the Repair Department are as follows:

Labour rate, including on-costs	R54 per hour
Required profit per labour hour	R21 per hour
Annual labour hours	10 000 hours
Annual overhead costs:	
Material handling and storage	R120 000
Other overhead costs (supervision, utilities, insurance and depreciation)	R600 000
Annual cost of materials used in Repair Department	R3 000 000

Based on these data, the Repair Department calculated its time and material prices as follows.

Time charges

The hourly profit charge is set at a level to ensure that a particular profit margin is achieved.

$$\text{Time charge (hourly rate)} = \text{hourly labour cost} + \left[\frac{\text{annual overhead (excluding material handling and storage)}}{\text{annual labour hours}}\right] + \text{hourly charge to cover profit margin}$$

$$= \text{R}54 + \frac{\text{R}600\,000}{10\,000} + \text{R}21$$

$$= \text{R}135 \text{ per labour hour}$$

Material charges

$$\text{Material charge} = \text{material cost incurred on job} + \left[\text{material cost incurred on job} \times \frac{\text{annual material handling and storage costs}}{\text{annual cost of materials used in Repair Department}}\right]$$

$$= \text{material cost incurred on job} + \left[\text{material cost incurred on job} \times \frac{\text{R}120\,000}{\text{R}3\,000\,000}\right]$$

R0.04 per Rand of material cost

The material charges formula includes a charge for the costs incurred in the handling and storage of materials.

Richard Hendricks estimates that the yacht refurbishment job will require 200 hours of labour and R24 000 in materials. Hendricks' price quotation for the job is shown in Exhibit 20.5. Included in the R51 960 price quotation for the yacht refurbishment are charges for labour costs, overhead, material costs, material handling and storage costs, and a normal profit margin. Some companies also charge an additional mark-up on the materials used in a job in order to earn a profit on that component of their services. Cape Sailing Supplies' practice is to include a high enough profit charge on its labour to earn an appropriate profit for the Repair Department.

Price Quotation Yacht Division: Repair Department Job: Refurbishment of 10-metre yacht, *Pride of the Sea*		
Time charges:	Labour time	200 hours
	× rate	× R135 per hour
	Total	27 000
Material charges:	Cost of materials for job	24 000
	+ charge for material handling and storage	960*
	Total	24 960
Total price for job:	Time	27 000
	Material	24 960
	Total	R51 960

*Charge for material handling and storage = (R24 000 material cost) × (R0.04 per Rand of material cost)

Exhibit 20.5 Time and material pricing, Cape Sailing Supplies

Target costing and pricing

In Chapter 15 we introduced the concept of target costing for cost management. Target costing is often described as an approach to pricing. However, this is not correct. As explained in Chapter 15, the first step in using target costing for cost management does involve setting a target price for the product. This is usually based on an estimate of the price required to achieve a particular market share, informed by market research about sources of customer value and competitors' actions, as well as by the firm's strategic objectives for the product. Once the target price has been established, the firm's target profit margin is deducted to obtain an estimate of target (or allowable) cost, which is the cost at which the product must be produced in order to achieve the desired profit margin. All attention is then focused on finding ways to produce the product at this cost. As you can see, target costing is primarily concerned with reducing and managing a product's cost. The product price is not derived from its target cost—on the contrary, the allowable product cost is derived from the target price.

Cost-plus pricing: summary and evaluation

In setting prices, managers cannot ignore market forces, nor can they ignore costs. In practice, cost-plus pricing is used widely to establish a starting point in the process of determining a price. Cost-plus formulas are simple; they can be applied mechanically without taking up the time of top management. They make it possible for a company with hundreds of products or services to cope with the tasks of updating prices for existing products and setting initial prices for new products.

Cost-plus pricing formulas can be used effectively with a variety of cost definitions, but the mark-up percentage must be appropriate for the type of cost used. It is imperative that managers understand that, in the long term, the price must cover all costs and a normal profit margin. Absorption cost-plus, or broader cost-plus pricing, has the advantage of focusing the manager's attention on covering total manufacturing costs or the full range of costs across the business respectively. The variable cost-plus formulas have the advantage of highlighting important information about cost behaviour.

Cost-plus pricing formulas establish a starting point in setting prices. The price setter must then consider market conditions, likely actions of competitors, and general business conditions. Thus, effective price setting requires a constant interplay of market considerations and cost awareness.

Product cost distortion and pricing: the role of activity-based costing

L.O. 5 It is clear from discussions in earlier chapters that the use of a conventional volume-based product costing system may result in significant cost distortions between product lines. In many cases, high-volume and relatively simple products are overcosted, while low-volume and complex products are undercosted. This results from the fact that high-volume and relatively simple products require proportionately less overhead support activities per unit than do low-volume and complex products. Yet a conventional product costing system, in which all overhead is allocated on the basis of a single unit level activity, such as direct labour hours, fails to capture the cost implications of product diversity. In contrast, an activity-based costing system can measure the extent to which each product line consumes costs of the key support activities.

Since pricing decisions often utilise product costs (which are developed for external financial reporting purposes), decision makers should be aware that cost distortions can result in overpricing high-volume and relatively simple products while low-volume and complex products are underpriced. The competitive implications of such pricing errors can be disastrous.[6]

Strategic pricing of new products

L.O. 6

Pricing a new product is an especially challenging decision problem. The newer the concept of the product, the more difficult it is to determine an appropriate price. For example, if Cape Sailing Supplies develops a new two-person sailing dinghy, its pricing problem is far easier than the pricing problem of a company that, for the first time, markets products that use a radically new technology. Genetic engineering, superconductivity, artificial hearts and space-grown crystals are all examples of such frontier technologies.

Pricing a new product is more difficult than pricing a mature product because of the magnitude of the uncertainties involved. For example, what obstacles will be encountered in manufacturing the product, and what will be the costs of production? When the product is available, will anyone want to buy it and, if so, at what price? If Cape Sailing Supplies decides to market a new two-person sailing dinghy, management can make a reasonable estimate of both the production costs and the potential market for the product. The uncertainties here are far smaller than the uncertainties facing a company developing many new products.

In addition to the production and demand uncertainties, new products pose another challenge. There are two widely differing pricing strategies that a producer of a new product can adopt. One strategy is called **skimming pricing**, in which the initial product price is set high, and short-term profits are reaped on the new product. The initial market will be small, due in part to the high initial price. It is important that the quality and image of the product are consistent with the high price. This pricing approach is often used for unique products, where there are people who 'must have it' whatever the price. Many products entailing new technology fall into this category. Consider mobile phones, software packages, digital cameras, computers and DVDs. All of these products entered the market at high prices, and could be afforded by only a few buyers. As the products gained acceptance, the price was gradually lowered. Eventually, these products were priced in a range that appealed to a wide range of consumers.

REAL LIFE: PRICING IN THE TELECOMMUNICATIONS INDUSTRY

The pricing of telecommunications services has become a central issue in South Africa, with the entry of a competitor for Telkom in the fixed line sector. In a 2005 study by the South African Foundation of telecommunications prices in South Africa as compared to other countries, it was stated that 'the pricing evidence clearly states that Telkom's pricing structure is excessive'. Further, the cost of cellular calls is high and MTN and Vodacom dominate the market. The entrance of Cell C has offered some competitive pricing, but switching costs were initially high due to difficulties of migrating telephone numbers when customers switched from one provider to another. This has now changed and Cell C has been advertising this fact extensively to promote the migration of Vodacom and MTN customers to Cell C. There have also been allegations about MTN overcharging Cell C for interconnection fees and MTN was reported to owe Cell C about R200m in 2007.

A fixed line operator such as Telkom makes substantial profits from international calls and although the company is dominant, there is growing competition from call back services and VoIP (Voice over Internet Protocol). The impact of technology has resulted in some competition (eg Skype) and Telkom has been reducing international rates and raising domestic call rates. In the period 1997 to 2003, the cost of a peak-rate, 3-minute local call increased by 316 per cent and the cost of peak-rate international calls fell by 32 per cent between 1998 and 2002. There is also an increased focus on line rentals rather than calls and this has become a useful pricing strategy for Telkom. This results in a more stable cash flow for Telkom, and customers will always wish to have access to a telephone line.

Telkom was criticised for overcharging Internet Service Providers for access to ADSL lines. This was based on a comparative analysis of fees charged in other countries. The Independent Communications Authority of South Africa (ICASA) examined the issue of Telkom increasing the cost of bandwidth services it provides to resellers who then were forced to pass on the increased costs to their customers. MTN in 2007 were considering building their own fixed-line network to save on the levies payable to Telkom for Internet access. Companies such as Vodacom (50 per cent owned by Telkom), Cell C and MTN lease lines from Telkom in order to connect the base stations to the national telecommunications grid. It was argued by some presenters to ICASA that customers should not pay a rental for an ADSL subscription, as the same copper line is used for telephone and ADSL access and so Telkom was not incurring additional costs on cabling.

It is difficult to focus on the incremental or marginal cost of providing a service. As we have discussed in this chapter, when a narrow definition of cost is used, then clearly the mark-up must be very high to cover the remaining costs of the business and make a profit.

It is difficult to recommend the appropriate prices that Telkom and the cellular operators should charge competitors for access to their networks. If the prices are set too high, this would constrain the development of a competitive market and limit any flow-on of benefits to customers. New entrants to the market would be 'held to ransom' by monopoly prices and might attempt to set up their own rival networks. If the prices are set too low, this would discourage the major existing operators from continuing to invest in modernising their networks. Clearly, the pricing issue is an important determinant of the success or failure of the newly deregulated telecommunications industry. In the 2005 study, it was reported that South Africa had the most expensive broadband service of the 15 countries surveyed and was about 9 times more expensive than Singapore.

In relation to ADSL services, the ICASA inquiry and increasing competition from MWeb and the cellular services (3G) has resulted in a fall in the price of ADSL services at the time of writing in 2007.

Courtesy of Nokia

Source: South Africa Foundation, 'Telecommunications prices in South Africa: An international peer group comparison', Occasional Paper, No.1/2005.

An alternative initial pricing strategy is called **penetration pricing**, in which the initial price is set relatively low. By setting a low price for a new product, management hope to gain wide acceptance of the product and quickly attract a large market share. This pricing approach is often used for products that are of good quality but do not stand out as vastly better than competing products. In 2007 Telkom and other ISPs were following very aggressive pricing strategies to create customer demand for broadband. The price of broadband access has been reduced significantly to move customers from the dial-up mode of Internet access to the much faster ADSL facility. Increased competition from cellular services, MWeb and other service providers has also added impetus to Telkom's pricing strategy.[7] The choice between skimming pricing and penetration pricing depends on the type of product and involves trade-offs of price versus volume. Skimming pricing results in much slower acceptance of a new product but higher unit profits. Penetration pricing results in greater initial sales volume but lower unit profits. To determine the profit implications of both approaches, a good understanding of product costs is required.

Competitive bidding

L.O. 7

In Chapter 19 we examined whether a special order should be accepted or rejected. The analysis focused on identifying the relevant costs of the special order. The existence of excess capacity was an important factor. Accepting a special order when there is excess capacity entails no opportunity cost. But when there is no excess capacity, one relevant cost of accepting a special order is the opportunity cost incurred by using the firm's limited capacity for the special order instead of for some other order. After all of the relevant costs of the order have been identified, the decision maker compares those costs with the price offered. If the price exceeds the relevant costs, then, on financial grounds, the order should be accepted.

This approach is similar to that used when setting a price for a competitive bid. Whether the decision makers are setting a price or have been offered a price, they must identify the relevant costs of producing the product.

In a **competitive bidding** situation, two or more companies submit sealed bids (or prices) to a potential buyer for a product, service or project. The buyer selects one of the companies on the basis of the bid price and the design specifications for the job. Competitive bidding complicates a manager's pricing problem because now the manager is in direct competition with one or more competitors. If all the companies submitting bids offer a roughly equivalent product or service, the bid price becomes the sole criterion for selecting the contractor. The higher the price that is bid, the greater will be the profit on the job if the firm gets the contract. However, a higher price also lowers the probability of winning the contract. Thus, there is a trade-off between bidding high to make a good profit, and bidding low to land the contract. Some say there is a 'winner's curse' in competitive bidding, meaning that the company bidding low enough to beat its competitors may be bidding too low to make an acceptable profit on the job. Despite these problems, competitive bidding is a common form of selecting contractors in many types of business.

Bidding where there is excess capacity

Richard Hendricks, the sales director at Cape Sailing Supplies, was approached recently by the Nelson Mandela Bay Yacht Club to bid for the building of an extension to the marina for moderate-sized sailing vessels. Hendricks decided that his company's Marine Construction Division should submit a bid for the job. The Yacht Club announced that three other firms would also be submitting bids. Since all four companies were equally capable of building the extension to the marina to the Yacht Club's specifications, Hendricks assumed that the bid price would be the deciding factor in selecting the contractor.

Hendricks consulted the divisional accountant and chief engineer of the Marine Construction Division, and the following data were compiled:

Direct labour requirements	1500 hours @ R36 per hour	R54 000
Direct material requirements		90 000
Petrol, lubricants and supplies		22 500
Total incremental costs of the marina job		R166 500
Fixed overhead (allocated on the basis of direct labour)	1500 hours @ R24 per hour	R36 000

Fixed overhead costs are allocated to jobs on the basis of direct labour hours, and include depreciation on vehicles and construction equipment, depreciation of the division's buildings, and supervisory salaries. The total fixed costs of the company are not expected to increase if the marina job is taken on.

It was up to Richard Hendricks to decide on the bid price for the extension to the marina. In his meeting with the divisional accountant and the chief engineer, Hendricks argued that the marina job was important to the company for two reasons. First, the Marine Construction Division had been operating well below capacity for several months. The marina job would not stop the firm from taking on any other construction work, so it would not entail an opportunity cost. Second, the marina job would provide a highly visible profile for Cape Sailing Supplies. City residents would see the firm's name on the project, and this would promote sales of the company's boats and sailing supplies.

Relying on these arguments, Hendricks pressed for a bid price that just covered the incremental costs of completing the order and allowed for a modest contribution margin. After some discussion among the senior managers, a bid price of R180 000 was finally agreed upon.

In competitive bid contracts, when a firm has excess capacity, a price that exceeds the incremental costs of producing the product will contribute towards covering the company's costs and profit. In the example, it was assumed that none of the Marine Construction Division's fixed costs would increase as a result of taking on the marina job. Thus, a bid price of R180 000 would cover the R166 500 of variable costs on the job and contribute R13 500 towards profits. Naturally, Cape Sailing Supplies' management would like to make a larger profit on the marina job, but bidding a higher price means running a substantial risk of losing the job to a competitor.

Bidding where there is no excess capacity

What if the Marine Construction Division has no excess capacity? If management expects to have enough work to occupy the division fully, a different approach may be used to set the bid price.

If the Marine Construction Division has no excess capacity, the incremental costs of producing the marina job would still be relevant. However, there is now an opportunity cost of not producing regular jobs that must be taken into account. As we saw in Chapter 19, the opportunity cost would be the contribution margin forgone on regular products if the marina job is taken on. Thus, the bid price may be higher than the price that was set when there was excess capacity. However, consideration of the relevant costs, including opportunity costs, is only one factor in setting the 'correct' bid price.

Marketing and strategic issues in competitive bids

Managers will need to consider a range of issues that are difficult to quantify. These may include marketing and strategic issues. Richard Hendricks pointed out that there would be valuable promotional benefits to Cape Sailing Supplies if its Marine Construction Division builds the marina. He believes that once his company has completed building the extension to the marina, the company will have demonstrated its reliability and expertise, and may have a strong chance of attracting future tenders. Hendricks will have to make a judgement regarding just how important the marina job is to the company. It may be that the price is pitched below the incremental costs, just to obtain the tender. The greater the perceived strategic benefits, the lower the bid price may be set to maximise the likelihood that the company will be awarded the contract.

Legal restrictions on pricing

L.O. 8

Businesses are not always free to set any price they wish for their products or services. The Competition Commission, which was formed in 1998, is a statutory body which has wide-reaching responsibilities for surveillance and enforcement of anti-competitive restrictive trade practices law, and of consumer law. In regulating prices and restrictive trade practices, the aim of the Competition Commission is to promote competition.

The South African Competition Act 89 of 1998 contains provisions placing restrictions on a wide range of commercial activities, including pricing. In particular, the Competition Act prohibits:

- companies taking advantage of their market power to eliminate or substantially damage a competitor;
- preventing entry of companies into a market; and
- deterring or preventing a company from competing in a market.

The aims here are not just to preserve competition, but also to protect the interests of consumers.

Some of the ways that companies may take advantage of their market power are through various pricing practices, including:

- **Predatory pricing**, which occurs when a company attempts to eliminate a competitor by reducing the price of its products or services to such a low level that the competitor is forced out of the market.
- **Price discrimination**, which occurs when companies offer different prices, discounts, services or payment terms to different customers for the same goods or services. If the discrimination is based on differences in costs incurred to produce, sell or deliver the product or service, or if it is undertaken to meet a competitor's price, then it is allowable. The purpose of this prohibition is to protect small purchasers from the price discrimination that could be practised by a dominant supplier. It also gives protection to small suppliers, who might otherwise be eliminated by the pricing behaviour of a large supplier.
- **Resale price maintenance**, which occurs when a supplier dictates the minimum price at which a product or service is to be resold by a buyer to the retail or wholesale market. This practice is restricted, as it may limit price competition between companies which deal with those products or services, and thus may impact consumers in the form of higher prices.
- **Price-fixing contracts**, which are also forbidden by the Act. These are arrangements that result in the fixing, control or maintenance of prices of goods or services. For example, a clothing wholesaler may enter into a contract with a series of retailers to fix the retail prices of its goods. Further examples are discussed in the 'Real life' below.

Product mix decisions

L.O. 9

Product mix decisions involve determining the most appropriate range of products (or services) to offer to customers. Tactical product mix decisions frequently involve changing the product mix temporarily, often because of some constraint on resources available, or because of unusual customer demands. Long-term product mix decisions are concerned with whether new products should be adopted or existing products discontinued.

Decisions about product mix are linked to pricing decisions. Prices influence product profitability, which may influence decisions about whether to change the product mix. Both require us to pay close attention to customer behaviour and competitor reactions. Product cost information can provide some useful parameters for these decisions.

REAL LIFE: PRICE FIXING – IT'S A BUSY TIME FOR THE COMPETITION COMMISSION

British Airways was fined \$546 million (about £270m) in 2007 for colluding with Virgin Atlantic on the setting of fuel surcharges on transatlantic flights. In a similar situation, the Competition Commission of South Africa referred the major domestic airlines such as South African Airways (SAA), SA Airlink, SA Express and Nationwide to the Competition Tribunal for a ruling on the collusion by the airlines to simultaneously introduce a fuel levy of equal amount in 2004. Comair (BA and kulula.com) applied for corporate leniency in terms of which it admitted that it had contravened the Act and would assist the Commission in setting its case before the Competition Tribunal. SAA came to an agreement with the Competition Commission to pay a fine of R40 million for collusion on setting fuel levies, as well as price-fixing by SAA and Lufthansa in relation to bilateral agreements between the two airlines.

In July 2007 the Competition Commission undertook a search and seizure operation on the Reclamation Group (Reclam), which is involved in the recycling of scrap metals, glass, rubber and other materials. It was suspected that Reclam was involved in fixing prices with other companies in the sector.

In early 2007 Clover applied for corporate leniency and would provide information to the Competition Commission regarding price fixing in the milk industry. Other companies implicated were Parmalat, Ladismith, Woodlands, Lancewood, Nestlé and CSA. This relates to the exchange of information on milk procurement prices so that the competitors could fix the purchase price of raw milk. There were also exchange agreements to sell surplus milk to companies in the cartel rather than to customers, in order to maintain high prices. The companies could be fined 10 per cent of their turnover if they are found to have engaged in price-fixing.

The major bread producers in South Africa, including Sasko, Duens (Pioneer Foods) and Albany Bakeries (Tiger Brands), were investigated for price-fixing. Blue Ribbon Bakery (Premier Foods) has asked for corporate leniency for co-operating with the Competition Commission. The Competition Commission stated that the companies held meetings and discussions on pricing. The companies simultaneously raised prices and fixed the discounts offered to distributors. Tiger Brands was fined R99 million and the CEO resigned over this issue.

Tactical product mix decisions involving limited resources

Managers will aim to produce combinations of products that will maximise profits. However, if there are limited production resources, then the optimum product mix may be based on the products with the greatest contribution margin per unit of the limited resources. This will now be explained.

Limited resources

In the short term, organisations often have limited resources that restrict the range or quantity of products that they can produce. There may be limitations on floor space, machine time, labour hours or raw materials. Thus, a firm must often choose between sales orders, deciding which orders to fill and which ones to decline. In making such decisions, managers need to know which product is the most profitable. This is not as simple as just comparing relative profits per unit; it involves considering how individual products utilise the limited resources.

To illustrate: suppose that Cape Sailing Supplies' Accessories Plant manufactures and sells two components for yachts: cleats and shackles. The contribution margin for each of these products is calculated in Exhibit 20.6.

A glance at the contribution margin data suggests that shackles are more profitable than are cleats. Shackles contribute more towards covering the company's fixed cost and profit than do

REAL LIFE: MITTAL STEEL CHARGING 'EXCESSIVE PRICES'

The Competition Tribunal found that Mittal Steel SA (now Arcelor Mittal Steel) had contravened the Competition Act by charging excessive prices for its flat steel products. In terms of the Competition Act, it is unlawful for a dominant firm to charge excessive prices. The tests relate to the degree of dominance and evidence that excessive pricing has occurred. A company will be defined as superdominant if the following applies to the sector:

- There are very high barriers to entry.
- The market share of such a firm must be close to 100 per cent.
- There is no realistic prospect of new entrants.
- The market must be unregulated.

The market for flat steel products was found to have all these characteristics and the Competition Tribunal found Mittal to be a superdominant company in the sector. The definition of 'excessive price' is stated in the Competitions Act as 'a price for a good or service which bears no reasonable relation to the economic value of that good or service'. Mittal Steel applied an import parity pricing system which means that Mittal set the price to its South African customers on the basis of what it would cost South African customers to import the products, including freight, clearing charges and import duties, and the company was even reported to include a 'hassle' factor of 5 per cent. Lack of competition resulted in the company being able to set prices on an import parity pricing basis. The Competition Tribunal held that Mittal Steel had charged excessive prices for its flat steel products.

Source: Mark Garden and Amy Lob, 'Of giants and tyranny, flat-steel products and excessive pricing', in *Business Day*, 14 May 2007. See also the Competitions Act, 1998.

	Cleats	**Shackles**
Sales price	R30.00	R42.00
Less Variable costs:		
Direct material	R9.00	R11.25
Direct labour	6.00	7.50
Variable overhead	9.00	11.25
Variable selling and administrative costs	3.00	6.00
Total variable costs	27.00	36.00
Contribution margin per unit	R3.00	R6.00

Exhibit 20.6 Contribution margin per unit, Cape Sailing Supplies

cleats. However, an important consideration has been ignored in the analysis so far. The plant's capacity is limited by its available machine time. Only 700 machine hours are available in the plant each month. Cape Sailing Supplies can sell as many cleats and shackles as it can produce, so production is limited only by the constraint of machine time.

To maximise the plant's total profits, management should strive to use each machine hour as profitably as possible. This realisation alters the analysis of product profitability. The relevant question is not which component has the highest contribution margin per unit, but which component has the highest contribution margin per machine hour. This question is answered with the calculation in Exhibit 20.7.

A machine hour spent in the production of cleats will contribute R150 towards covering fixed cost and profit, while a machine hour devoted to shackles contributes only R120. Hence, the company's most profitable product is cleats, when the plant's scarce resource is taken into account.

		Cleats	Shackles
(a)	Contribution margin per unit	R3.00	R6.00
(b)	Machine hours required per unit	0.02	0.05
(a) ÷ (b)	Contribution margin per machine hour	R150.00	R120.00

Exhibit 20.7 Contribution margin per machine hour, Cape Sailing Supplies

Suppose that the plant manager, Roger Engelbrecht, is faced with a choice between two sales orders, one for cleats and one for shackles, of which only one can be accepted. Only 80 hours of unscheduled machine time remains in the month, and it can be used to produce either cleats or shackles. The relative profits obtained from producing either cleats or shackles can be calculated:

	Cleats	Shackles
Contribution margin per machine hour	R150	R120
Total contribution from 80 machine hours	R12 000	R9 600

This calculation indicates that Engelbrecht should devote the 80 hours of machine time to filling the order for cleats. Note that although this decision can be regarded as short term or tactical, consideration must also be given to any long-term implications. For example, delaying the order for shackles could damage the company's long-term relationship with that customer; however, if the cleats customer is willing to wait for the order, then Engelbrecht might consider manufacturing shackles first, despite this not being the optimum solution in the short term.

Thus, a decision about the best use of a limited resource should be made on the basis of the contribution margin per unit of the scarce resource, not contribution margin per unit.

Multiple scarce resources

Suppose that the Accessories plant had a limited amount of both machine hours and labour hours. Now the analysis of product profitability is more complicated. The choice as to which product is most profitable will typically involve a trade-off between the two scarce resources. Solving such a problem requires a mathematical tool called linear programming. This technique is described in the appendix to this chapter.

Long-term product mix decisions

In Chapter 19 we learned how to determine relevant costs and revenues in decisions about whether to add or delete a product or service in the short term. This information is also important in long-term product mix decisions. However, decisions to delete or add products are strategic decisions that have long-term implications for market share, cost levels and profits. Many of the costs that we assume are unchanged in short-term product mix decisions may change when products are added or deleted. Adding or deleting products can lead to changes in the resources that are used across the business. In the short term, fixed costs are not usually relevant to product mix decisions; but in the long term, the firm has the opportunity to adjust its capacity and resources (and therefore its fixed costs) to match the new production requirements.

When the product mix is changed, facility level costs may increase or decrease. For example, new equipment may be added, and staffing levels may be increased. Product level costs, such as product design and advertising, will be incurred when new product lines are added, and will disappear when product lines are deleted. Batch level costs will change if a product that is normally manufactured in a large batch size is replaced by products that require smaller batches. In the old language: 'fixed' costs will change when the product mix is changed.

Caution should be taken when considering eliminating a product. When product profitability studies reveal loss-making products, firms can choose a range of alternative responses:

- The firm may choose to increase product prices. Of course, this may not be acceptable if competitors are offering similar products at lower prices, although there may be other ways of offering improved services to differentiate products from those of competitors, to justify the higher prices.

- Managers may implement various cost management techniques (described in Chapter 15) to try to reduce the cost of producing that product.
- The firm may offer customers incentives (such as quantity discounts) to encourage them to purchase greater quantities of the product. This may have the effect of reducing some product costs per unit and hence improving product profitability.
- The firm can choose to retain a loss-making product. This may happen where the product forms part of a range of products that the firm would like to continue to offer to customers.
- The firm may choose to discontinue the product if the firm is certain that there will be no ill effects on the sales of other products. Discontinuing a product may lead to a decrease in sales of related products.

Product elimination decisions can have far-reaching effects on profits and market share. Therefore, it is critical that all relevant costs are considered.

Summary

In this chapter we considered how goods and services may be priced, which is one of the most challenging decisions faced by management. We also considered how managers may make decisions about the appropriate mix of goods or services to produce and sell. Key points include:

- Many factors influence pricing decisions: market positioning, product cost, customer value, competitor behaviour, and legal, political and ethical issues.
- Economic theory shows that, under certain assumptions, the profit-maximising price and quantity are determined by the intersection of the marginal revenue and marginal cost curves. While the economic model serves as a useful conceptual framework for the pricing decision, it is limited by its assumptions and the informational demands it implies.
- Pricing strategies that may be used by organisations include value-based pricing, economic-value pricing and cost-based pricing.
  - Value-based pricing involves setting the price to reflect the value of the product or service to the customer.
  - Economic-value pricing entails setting a price that recognises that the purchase price of a product or service is only one of the possible costs for the customer. This pricing method involves setting a price so that it takes into account the full costs of ownership to the customer, as well as customer value.
  - Cost-plus pricing formulas add a mark-up to product cost, which may be defined as variable cost, absorption cost or a broader product cost that includes product-related costs that occur outside of manufacturing. Mark-ups are often set to earn the company a target profit on its products, based on a target rate of return on investment. When companies set prices, they need some awareness of the costs of producing those goods or services.
- In industries such as construction, repairs and maintenance, and printing, and in professional service firms, time and material pricing is often used. Under this approach the price is calculated as the sum of a labour cost component and a material cost component. Either or both of these components may include a mark-up to ensure that the company earns a profit on its services.
- The distortions inherent in conventional product costing systems can undermine cost-plus pricing, and managers should consider the advantages of using activity-based costing for cost-plus pricing decisions.

- Strategic pricing of new products is an especially challenging problem for management.
- Various pricing approaches, such as skimming pricing or penetration pricing, may be appropriate, depending on the nature of the product and its positioning in the market.
- Pricing special orders and determining competitive bid prices entail an analysis of the relevant costs to be incurred to complete the job. The relevant cost analysis should take account of the existence of excess capacity or full capacity.
- The South African Competition Commission imposes legal restrictions to prevent pricing practices by companies that may lessen competition, or harm consumers. These practices include predatory pricing, price discrimination, resale price maintenance and price fixing.
- Product costs may also be useful in both tactical (short-term) and long-term product mix decisions. In tactical product mix decisions, we can focus on maximising profitability, subject to any limited resource. As with pricing decisions, customer behaviour and reactions of competitors are important factors in determining long-term product mix.

In this chapter, a marketing orientation was taken to explain the factors that influence the prices of goods and services. While it is important to have an understanding of the costs of providing goods and services, costing information is certainly not the major driver of prices in most organisations.

References

Bawden, T 2004, 'Virgin flying into the facts of life', *The Advertiser*, 20 November, pp. 75–6.

Competitions Act, No. 89 of 1998.

Forbis, JL & Mehta, NT 2000, 'Economic value to the customer', *McKinsey Quarterly*, no. 3.

Garden, M and Lob, A 2007, 'Of giants and tyranny, flat-steel products and excessive pricing', in *Business Day*, 14 May 2007.

Gordon, L, Cooper, R, Falk, H & Miller, D 1981, *The Pricing Decision*, National Association of Accountants, New York.

Govindarajan, V & Anthony, RN 1983, 'How firms use cost data in pricing decisions', *Management Accounting*, vol. 65, no. 1, July, pp. 30–6.

Kotler, P, Adam, S, Brown, L & Armstrong, G 2003, *Principles of Marketing*, Prentice Hall, Sydney.

Lovelock, CH, Patterson, PG & Walker, RH 2001, *Services Marketing: An Asia-Pacific Approach*, 2nd edn, Prentice Hall, Sydney.

Oakes, D 2004, 'Fare war erupts on the internet', *The Age*, www.theage.com.au/articles/2004/02/26/1077676864517.html, 26 February.

South Africa Foundation, 'Telecommunications prices in South Africa: An international peer group comparison', Occasional Paper, No.1/2005.

www.comp.com.co.za

www.comptrib.co.za

Self study

Self-study problem: cost-plus pricing

Kitchenware Corporation manufactures high-quality copper pots and pans. Janet Cooke, one of the company's price analysts, is involved in setting a price for the company's new Starter Set. This set consists of seven of the most commonly used pots and pans. During the next year the company plans to produce 10 000 Starter Sets, and the accountant has provided Cooke with the following cost data:

Predicted costs of 10 000 starter sets	
Direct material per set	R120
Direct labour per set, 2 hours @ R40	80
Variable selling costs per set	10
	R210
Variable overhead rate	R16 per direct labour hour
Fixed manufacturing overhead rate	R24 per direct labour hour
Total fixed manufacturing overhead	R480 000
Total fixed selling and adminstrative cost	R40 000

Required:

1 Calculate the cost of a Starter Set, using variable manufacturing cost and absorption cost.

2 Determine the mark-up percentage required for the Starter Set product line in order to earn a target profit of R635 000 before taxes during the next year. Use the absorption cost definition in the cost-plus formula.

Solution to Self-study problem

1

Variable manufacturing cost per unit:	
Direct material	R120
Direct labour	80
Variable overhead (2 labour hours @ R16 per hour)	32
Total variable manufacturing cost	R232
Absorption cost per unit:	
Total variable manufacturing cost	R232
Applied fixed overhead cost (2 labour hours @ R24 per hour)	48
Total absorption cost	R280

2

$$\text{Mark-up percentage} = \frac{\text{target profit} + \text{total selling and administrative costs}}{\text{annual volume} \times \text{cost per unit}}$$

$$\text{Mark-up percentage on absorption cost} = \frac{635\,000 + 140\,000^*}{10\,000 \times 280} = 27.68\%$$

*Total annual costs not included in the cost base = fixed selling and administrative costs + variable selling costs

Variable selling & administrative costs 10 000 × R10 =	R100 000
Fixed selling & administrative costs	40 000
	R140 000

Proof:

Price = absorption cost + 27.68% × absorption cost

= R280 + [27.68% × R 280]

= R357.50

Profit statement			
Sales revenue	10 000 × R357.50		R3 575 000
Less variable costs:			
Direct material	10 000 × R120.00	R1 200 000	
Direct labour	10 000 × R80.00	800 000	
Variable overhead	10 000 × R32.00	320 000	
Variable selling and administrative costs	10 000 × R10.00	100 000	
Total variable costs			R2 420 000
Contribution margin			R1 155 000
Less Fixed costs:			
Manufacturing overhead		R480 000	
Selling and administrative cost		40 000	
Total fixed costs			520 000
Profit			R635 000

Cybersearch

1 Find websites with newspaper reports about organisations that have adopted pricing practices that are contrary to the Competition Act.

(a) What form of illegal pricing activity were the organisations engaged in?

(b) Describe the details of the illegal activity.

2 Many public sector and not-for-profit organisations place details of their 'pricing policies' on the Internet. Find websites with examples of this.

(a) What factors does the organisation take into account when setting its prices?

(b) Are these factors similar to those discussed in the chapter?

Appendix to Chapter 20

Linear programming

In this chapter we considered a simple example of determining product mix where there was a single resource limitation. Where there is more than one constraint, linear programming techniques can be used. L.O. 10

We will again focus on Cape Sailing Supplies and the production of cleats and shackles. Exhibit 20.8 provides data relevant to the problem.

Linear programming involves identifying linear relationships between decision variables to determine the optimal solution, given a number of constraints. It includes the following steps:

1 Identify the **decision variables**. These are the variables about which a decision must be made. Cape Sailing Supplies' decision variables are as follows:

$$X = \text{number of cleats to produce each month}$$
$$Y = \text{number of shackles to produce each month}$$

2 Determine the **objective function**, which is an algebraic expression of the firm's goal. Cape Sailing Supplies' goal is to maximise its total contribution margin. Since cleats have a contribution margin of R3 per unit, and shackles a contribution margin of R6 per unit (which is twice that of cleats), the firm's objective function is the following:

$$\text{Objective function: Maximise } Z = X + 2Y$$

where Z = total contribution margin

3 Determine the **constraints**. These are algebraic expressions of the limitations faced by the firm, such as those limiting its productive resources. The company has constraints for machine time and direct labour.

There is a maximum of 700 machine hours and a maximum of 5000 labour hours available each month. As shown in Exhibit 20.8, cleats require 0.02 machine hours per unit, and shackles use 0.05 machine hours per unit. Also, cleats require 0.20 direct labour hours per unit and shackles require 0.25 direct labour hours per unit. Thus, the constraints can be explained algebraically:

$$\text{Machine time constraint: } 0.02X + 0.05Y \leq 700$$
$$\text{Labour time constraint: } 0.20X + 0.25Y \leq 5000$$

	Cleats	Shackles
Contribution margin per unit	R3.00	R6.00
Machine hours per unit	0.02	0.05
Direct labour hours per unit	0.20	0.25
	Machine hours	**Direct labour hours**
Limited resources: hours available per month	700	5000

Exhibit 20.8 Data for determining product mix, Cape Sailing Supplies

Suppose, for example, that management decided to produce 10 000 units of cleats and 6000 units of shackles. The machine time used would appear as follows:

$$(0.02 \times 10\,000) + (0.05 \times 6000) = 500$$

Thus, at these production levels, the machine time constraint would be satisfied, with 200 machine hours to spare.

Graphical solution

To understand how linear programming can help Cape Sailing Supplies' management to solve their product mix problem, examine the graphs in Exhibit 20.9. The two broken lines in panel A represent the constraints. They indicate that the production quantities of cleats and shackles must lie on or below these lines. The space between the axes and constraints form an area called the **feasible region**, in which the solution to the linear program must lie.

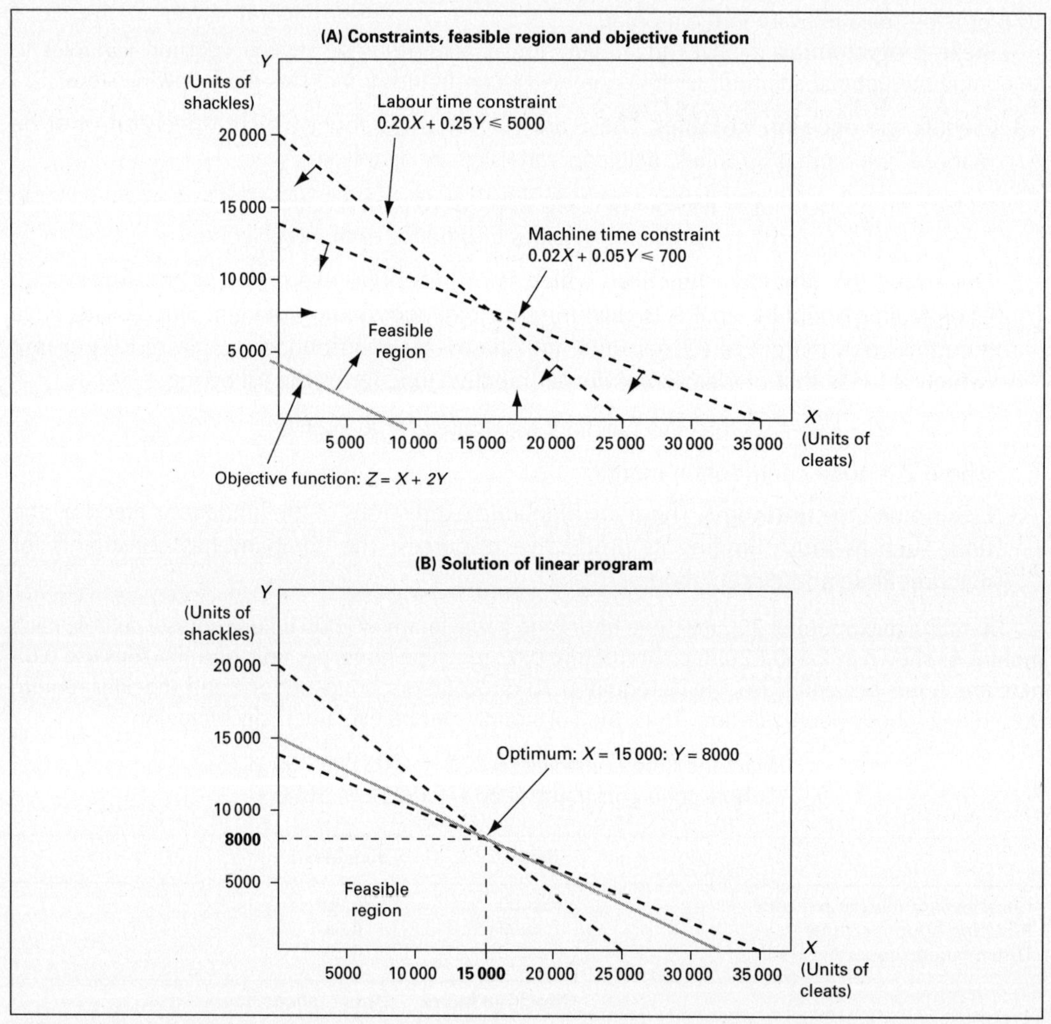

Exhibit 20.9 Product mix problem expressed as linear program, Cape Sailing Supplies

The solid grey line in graph A represents the objective function. The objective function equation can be rearranged as follows:–

$$Z = X + 2Y \rightarrow Y = \frac{Z}{2} - \frac{1}{2}X$$

This form of the objective function shows that the slope of the equation is $-\frac{1}{2}$, which is the slope of the objective function line in the exhibit. Management's goal is to maximise total contribution margin, denoted by Z. To achieve the maximum, the objective function line must be moved as far outward and upward in the feasible region as possible, while maintaining the same slope. This goal is represented in panel A by the arrow that extends from the objective function line.

The result of moving the objective function line as far as possible in the indicated direction is shown in panel B of the exhibit. The objective function line intersects the feasible region at exactly one point, where X equals 15 000 and Y equals 8000. Thus, the optimal product mix is 15 000 cleats and 8000 shackles per month. The total contribution margin is calculated as follows:

$$\begin{aligned}\text{Total contribution margin} &= (15\,000 \times \text{R}3) + (8000 \times \text{R}6)\\ &= \text{R}93\,000\end{aligned}$$

Simplex method and sensitivity analysis

Although the graphical method is instructive, it is a cumbersome technique for solving a linear program. Fortunately, mathematicians have developed a more efficient solution method called the simplex algorithm. A computer can apply the algorithm to a complex linear program and determine the solution in seconds. In addition, most linear programming computer packages provide a sensitivity analysis of the problem. This analysis shows the decision maker the extent to which the estimates used in the objective function and constraints can change without changing the solution.

Whilst the simplex method may result in highly complex equations for firms with multiple products and multiple constraints, we will solve the objective function, maximise $Z = X + 2Y$, for Cape Sailing Supplies, by using the simplex method. The equations are restated as follows:

$$\begin{aligned}0.02\,X + 0.05\,Y &\le 700\\ 0.20\,X + 0.25\,Y &\le 5\,000\end{aligned}$$

We will firstly eliminate X to determine Y, but we could also firstly eliminate Y to determine X. Once we have determined either X or Y we can solve for the remaining variable. To eliminate X, we can multiply the first equation by 10 and then subtract equation 1 from equation 2 so that $X = 0$ and $0.25Y = 2000$.

$$\begin{aligned}0.20\,X + 0.50\,Y &\le 7\,000\\ \underline{0.20\,X + 0.25\,Y} &\le \underline{5\,000}\\ 0.25\,Y &\le 2\,000\\ Y &\le 8\,000\end{aligned}$$

We divide 2000 by 0.25 so that $Y = 8000$. We can now use either equation 1 or equation 2 to determine X. We know that Y is 8000 and we can calculate the remaining variable, X as follows:

$$\begin{aligned}0.02\,X + 0.05\,Y &\le 700\\ 0.02\,X + 400 &\le 700\\ 0.02\,X &\le 300\\ X &\le 15\,000\end{aligned}$$

If we multiply Y, which is 8000, by 0.05 we obtain 400 and so we have $0.02X = 300$ so that $X = 300/.02 = 15\,000$. As you can see, we have reached the same solution as the graphical method that to maximise the total contribution of the firm we need to produce 15 000 cleats (X) and 8000 shackles (Y).

Linear programming can be used in a variety of business decisions. These include blending, in the petroleum and chemical industries; scheduling of personnel, trains and aircraft; and the mixing of ingredients in the food industry.

Questions

?

20.1 List and briefly describe the major influences on pricing decisions.

20.2 Comment on the following remark made by a consulting company: 'The prices of our consulting services are determined by whatever our competitors charge for similar services. Costs are irrelevant.'

20.3 'All this marginal revenue and marginal cost stuff is just theory. Prices are determined by production costs.' Evaluate this assertion.

20.4 Explain what is meant by the following statement: 'In considering the reactions of competitors, it is crucial to define your product.'

20.5 Explain the following statement: 'Price setting generally requires a balance between market forces and cost considerations.'

20.6 Explain why an understanding of customer value is important in setting prices.

20.7 Think of an industry in which political considerations are important in the setting of prices. Explain what the product is and why political issues are important.

20.8 Briefly explain the concept of *economic profit-maximising pricing*. It may be helpful to use graphs in your explanation.

20.9 Describe the limitations of the economic profit-maximising model of pricing.

20.10 Contrast *value-based pricing* and *economic-value pricing*. Describe situations in which value-based pricing and economic-value pricing might be used.

20.11 Explain the meaning of *economic value to the customer* and where this fits into pricing models.

20.12 'Determining the best approach to pricing requires a cost–benefit trade-off.' Explain.

20.13 Write the general formula for cost-plus pricing, and briefly explain its use.

20.14 List the various cost bases commonly used in cost-plus pricing. How can they all result in the same price?

20.15 List the reasons often cited for the use of variable costing as the cost base in cost-plus pricing formulas. What is the primary disadvantage of basing the cost-plus pricing formula on variable cost?

20.16 Explain the disadvantages that can result when cost-plus prices are based on absorption costs.

20.17 Briefly explain the concept of *return on investment pricing*.

20.18 'Time and material pricing is a rip-off for our customers. We mark up everything: our labour, our materials and our overhead costs.' Discuss.

20.19 Explain the importance of the excess capacity issue in setting a competitive bid price.

20.20 The identification of relevant costs and benefits in decisions to accept or reject a special order, and the selection of a price for a competitive bid, may be based on similar principles. Explain.

20.21 Describe the *skimming pricing* and *penetration pricing* approaches to pricing new products. Provide two examples of each (other than those provided in the chapter).

20.22 Explain what is meant by *predatory pricing* and *resale price maintenance.*

20.23 Explain the role of the South African Competition Commission in regulating pricing.

20.24 Briefly explain the potential negative consequences that can arise when using conventional volume-based product costs to set prices.

20.25 Briefly describe the correct approach to making a production decision when limited resources are involved.

20.26 What is meant by the term *contribution margin per unit of scarce resource*? How is this concept used in making product mix decisions?

20.27 Outline the issues that are important in a long-term product mix decision.

20.28 (appendix) Explain the meaning of the following terms: *constraints, decision variables, feasible region* and *objective function.* Explain their relevance to product mix decisions.

Exercises

E20.29 Marginal revenue and marginal cost curves: retailer

The marginal cost, marginal revenue and demand curves for the retailer Home and Garden's deluxe wheelbarrow are shown in the graph below:

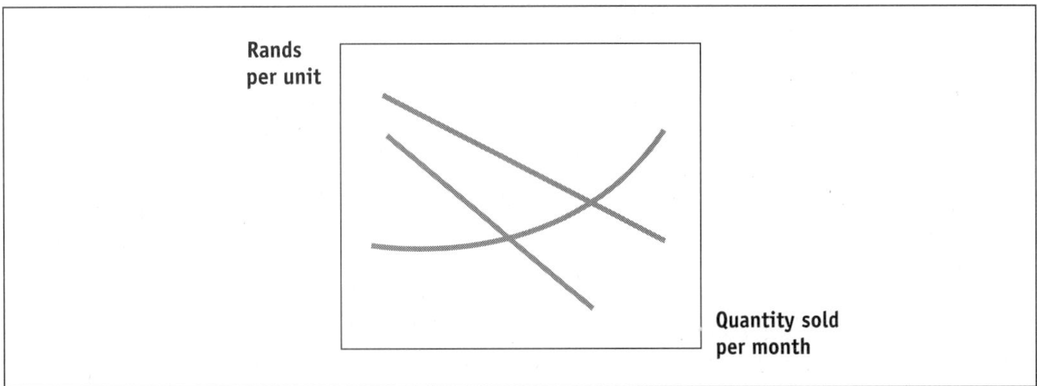

Required:

Before completing any of the following requirements, read the entire list (1–3).

1 Trace the graph shown above onto a blank piece of paper, and label all parts of the graph.
2 Draw a companion graph directly above the traced graph. Use this graph to draw the firm's total revenue and total cost curves.
3 Show the retailer's profit-maximising price on the lower graph and its profit-maximising quantity on both graphs.

E20.30 Demand and revenue data: manufacturer

The Buffalo City Division of Spectrum Sound manufactures MP3 players with unusual features. The divisional sales manager has estimated the following demand curve data:

Quantity sold per month	Unit sales price
20	R500
40	R475
60	R450
80	R425
100	R400

Required:

1 Prepare a table containing columns of the following charter: quantity sold per month, unit sales price, total revenue per month, changes in total revenue.

2 Draw a graph that shows the total revenue curve.

E20.31 Continuation of Exercise 20.30; cost data: manufacturer

Refer to the data given in Exercise 20.30. The divisional accountant at Spectrum Sound's Buffalo City Division has estimated the following cost data for the division's MP3 players. (There are no fixed costs.)

Quantity produced and sold per month	Average cost per unit
20	R450
40	R425
60	R410
80	R430
100	R445

Required:

1 Prepare a table of data, using the following column headings: quantity produced and sold per month, average cost per unit, total cost per month, changes in total cost.

2 Draw a graph that shows the total cost curve.

E20.32 Profit-maximising price: manufacturer

Refer to the data given in Exercises 20.30 and 20.31.

Required:

1 Prepare a table of revenue, cost and profit relationships. For guidance, refer to panel C of Exhibit 20.2.

2 Draw a graph similar to that in panel A of Exhibit 20.2, reflecting the data tabulated in requirement 1.

3 To narrow down the pricing decision, the Buffalo City Division's sales manager has decided to price the MP3 player at one of the following prices: R400, R425, R450, R475 or R500. Which price do you recommend? Why?

E20.33 Determining mark-up percentage; target ROI: manufacturer

Refer to the cost and production data for the Wave Darter in Exhibit 20.4. The target profit is R900 000.

Required:

Use the general formula to calculate the required mark-up percentages for each of the following cost-plus formulas:

1 Variable manufacturing cost.

2 Absorption cost.

E20.34 Cost-plus pricing formulas; missing data: manufacturer

The following data pertain to LawnMate Ltd's bottom-of-the-line lawnmower.

Variable manufacturing cost	R275
Applied fixed manufacturing cost	R55
Variable selling and administrative cost	R66
Allocated fixed selling and administrative cost	?

To achieve a target price of R495 per lawnmower, the mark-up percentage is 12.5 per cent on total unit cost.

Required:

1 What is the fixed selling and administrative cost allocated to each unit of LawnMate's bottom-of-the-line mower?

2 For each of the following cost bases, develop a cost-plus pricing formula that will result in a target price of R495 per mower:
(a) variable manufacturing cost (b) absorption manufacturing cost (c) total variable cost.

E20.35 Pricing; advertising; and special order decisions: manufacturer

Umklomelo Ltd produces a single product in its Gauteng plant, which currently sells for R75.00 per unit. Fixed costs are expected to amount to R900 000 for the year, and all variable manufacturing and administrative costs are expected to be incurred at a rate of R45.00 per unit. Umklomelo has two salespeople who are paid strictly on a commission basis. Their commission is 10 per cent of the sales Rands they generate. (Ignore income taxes.)

Required:

1 Suppose that management alter their current plans by spending an additional amount of R75 000 on advertising, and increase the selling price to R90.00 per unit. Calculate the profit on 60 000 units.

2 The Salente Company has just approached Umklomelo to make a special one-time purchase of 10 000 units. These units would not be sold by the sales personnel and, therefore, no commission would have to be paid. What is the price Umklomelo would have to charge per unit on this special order to make an additional profit of R300 000?

(*CMA, adapted*)

E20.36 Cost-plus pricing formulas: manufacturer

The following data pertain to Legion Lighting Company's oak-clad, contemporary chandelier:

Variable manufacturing cost	R300
Applied fixed manufacturing cost	105
Variable selling and administrative cost	45
Allocated fixed selling and administrative cost	75

Required:

For each of the following cost bases, develop a cost-plus pricing formula that will result in a price of R600 for the oak chandelier:

1 Variable manufacturing cost.

2 Absorption manufacturing cost.

3 Total cost.

4 Total variable cost.

E20.37 Time and material pricing: manufacturer

Refer to Exhibit 20.5. Suppose that the Repair Department of Cape Sailing Supplies adds a mark-up of 10 per cent on the material charges of a job (including the cost of material handling and storage).

Required:

1 Rewrite the material component of the time and material pricing formula to reflect the mark-up on material cost.

2 Calculate the new price to be quoted on the yacht refurbishment described in Exhibit 20.5.

20.38 Product mix; limited resources: manufacturer

Duo Company manufactures two products, Uno and Dos. Contribution margin data follow:

	Uno	Dos
Unit sales price	R13.00	R31.00
Less:		
Direct material	R7.00	R5.00
Direct labour	1.00	6.00
Variable overhead	1.25	7.50
Variable selling and administrative costs	0.75	0.50
Total variable cost	R10.00	R19.00
Unit contribution margin	R3.00	R12.00

Duo Company's production process uses highly skilled labour, which is in short supply. The same employees work on both products and earn the same wage rate.

Required:

Which of Duo Company's products is the more profitable? Explain.

E20.39 Linear programming; formulate and solve graphically (appendix): manufacturer

Welkom Chemical Company manufactures two industrial chemical products, called Zanide and Kreolite. Two machines are used in the process, and each machine has 24 hours of capacity per day. The following data are available:

	Zanide	Kreolite
Selling price per drum	R108	R126
Variable cost per drum	R84	R84
Hours required per drum on machine I	2 hours	2 hours
Hours required per drum on machine II	1 hour	3 hours

The company can produce and sell partially full drums of each chemical. For example, a half-drum of Zanide sells for R54.

Required:

1 Formulate the product mix problem as a linear program.
2 Solve the problem graphically.
3 What is the value of the objective function at the optimal solution?

Problems

P20.40 Cost-plus pricing; bidding: wholesaler

Hall Pharmaceuticals is a wholesaler that specialises in packaging bulk drugs, in standard dosages, for local hospitals. The company has been in business for seven years and has been profitable since its second year of operation. Don Magadla, the assistant accountant, installed a standard costing system after joining the company three years ago.

Ikhwezi Memorial Hospital has asked Hall to bid on the packaging of 1 million doses of medication at total product cost plus a mark-up on total cost of no more than 15 per cent. Ikhwezi defines 'total product cost' as including all variable costs of performing the service, a reasonable amount of fixed overhead, and reasonable administrative costs. The hospital will supply all packaging materials and ingredients. Ikhwezi has indicated that any bid over R0.09 per dose will be rejected.

Magadla has accumulated the following information prior to the preparation of the bid:

Direct labour	R48 per direct labour hour (DLH)
Variable overhead	R36 per DLH
Fixed overhead	R60 per DLH
Incremental administrative costs	R6 000 for the order
Production rate	2 000 doses per DLH

Required:

1 Calculate the minimum price per dose that Hall Pharmaceuticals could bid for the Ikhwezi Memorial Hospital job without reducing Hall's profit.

2 Calculate the bid price per dose using total product cost and the maximum mark-up specified by Ikhwezi Memorial Hospital.

3 Independent of your answer to requirement 2, suppose that the price per dose that Hall calculated, using the cost-plus criterion specified by Ikhwezi Memorial Hospital, is greater than the maximum bid of R0.09 per dose allowed by Ikhwezi. Discuss the factors that Hall Pharmaceuticals should consider before deciding whether or not to submit a bid at the maximum price of R0.09 per dose that Ikhwezi allows.

(CMA, adapted)

P20.41 Time and material pricing: service firm

Suburban Heating Ltd installs heating systems in new homes. Jobs are priced using the time and materials method. The managing director of Suburban Heating, B.T. Jantjies, is pricing a job involving the heating systems for six houses to be built by a local developer. His estimates are:

Labour hours	400
Material cost	R225 000

The following predictions relate to the company's operations:

Labour rate, including on-costs	R60 per hour
Annual labour hours	12 000 hours
Annual overhead costs:	
Material handling and storage	R93 750
Other overhead costs	R405 000
Annual cost of materials used	R937 500

Required:

Suburban Heating adds a mark-up of R15 per hour on its time charges, but there is no mark-up on material costs.

1 Develop formulas for:

(a) the company's time charges (b) the company's material charges

2 Calculate the price for the job described above.

3 What would be the price of the job if Suburban Heating also added a mark-up of 10 per cent on all material charges (including material handling and storage costs)?

P20.42 Pricing of special order: manufacturer

Swartland Industries Ltd manufactures flour milling machinery according to customer specifications. The company operated at 75 per cent of practical capacity during the year just ended, with the following results (in thousands):

Sales revenues	R12 500
Less Sales commissions (10%)	1 250
Net sales	R11 250
Costs:	
Direct material	R3 000
Direct labour	3 750
Manufacturing overhead—variable	1 125
Manufacturing overhead—fixed	750
Corporate administration—fixed	375
Total costs	R9 000
Profit before taxes	R2 250
Income taxes (28%)	630
Net profit	R1 620

Swartland, which expects continued operations at 75 per cent of capacity, recently submitted a bid of R82 500 on custom-designed machinery for Premier Foods Ltd. Swartland used a pricing formula in deriving the bid amount; the formula being based on last year's operating results. The formula follows:

Estimated direct material	R14 600
Estimated direct labour	28 000
Estimated manufacturing overhead @ 50% of direct labour	14 000
Estimated corporate overhead @ 10% of direct labour	2 800
Estimated total costs excluding sales commissions	59 400
Add 25% for profit and taxes	14 850
Suggested price (with profit) before sales commissions	R74 250
Suggested total price: R74 250 ÷ 0.9 to adjust for 10% commission	R82 500

Required:

1 Calculate the impact the order would have on Swartland's net profit if the R82 500 bid were accepted by Premier Foods Ltd.

2 Assume that Premier has rejected Swartland's bid but has stated it is willing to pay R63 500 for the machinery. Should Swartland manufacture the machinery for the counter-offer of R63 500? Explain your answer and show calculations.

3 At what bid price will Swartland break even on the order?

4 Explain how the profit performance in the coming year would be affected if Swartland accepted all of its work at prices similar to Premier's R63 500 counter-offer described in requirement 2.

P20.43 Economic-value pricing; strategic pricing of new products

Razzle Ltd is developing a new clothes dryer, Dry Master, that it plans to sell to coin-operated laundries. Currently, the market leader is a product called DryWell, which is sold by a competitor. The managing director of Razzle Ltd, Fred Jansen, has engaged a marketing research agency to help assess the appropriate selling price for the new clothes dryer.

The agency has surveyed a range of laundries and determined the following data for the DryWell:

Selling price	R12 000
Installation costs	R200
Yearly maintenance cost	R800
Expected useful life	8 years
Disposal value	zero

Engineering estimates have determined that the Dry Master will entail maintenance costs of R600 per annum, and will have a useful life of 9 years with a disposal value of zero. In addition, the new product will dry clothes more quickly than the DryWell and will result in softer and fluffier clothes. The value of this improved functionality to the customer is estimated at R400. Customers will need to incur average installation costs for the Dry Master of R300 per machine.

Required:

1 Determine the economic value to the customer of the Dry Master. (Do not consider the time value of money.)
2 What price should Razzle charge for the new product? Explain your answer.
3 What additional factors and information should Fred Jansen consider before he sets the price for the new product?

P20.44 Product cost distortion and product pricing; departmental overhead rates: manufacturer

Super Sounds Ltd manufactures two models of stereo speaker sets for computers and MP3 players. The company uses an absorption product-costing system, which means that both variable and fixed overhead are included in the product cost. Cost estimates for the two models for the coming year are as follows:

	Standard model	Deluxe model
Direct material	R720	R1 170
Direct labour (10 hours @ R63 per hour)	630	630
Manufacturing overhead*	450	450
Total cost per set	R1 800	R2 250

*The predetermined overhead rate is R45 per direct labour hour.

Each stereo speaker set requires 10 hours of direct labour. Each Standard model set requires 2 hours in Department I and 8 hours in Department II. Each set of the Deluxe model requires 8 hours in Department I and 2 hours in Department II. The manufacturing overhead costs expected during the coming year in Departments I and II are as shown below:

	Department I	Department II
Variable overhead per direct labour hour (DLH)	R36.00	R18.00
Fixed overhead	675 000	675 000

The expected operating activity for the coming year is 37 500 direct labour hours in each department.

Required:

1 Show how Super Sounds derived its predetermined overhead rate.
2 What will be the price of each model stereo speaker set if the company prices its products at absorption manufacturing cost plus 15 per cent?
3 Suppose that Super Sounds were to use departmental overhead rates. Calculate these rates for Departments I and II for the coming year.
4 Calculate the absorption cost of each model stereo speaker set using the departmental overhead rates calculated in requirement 3.

5 Suppose that management sticks with its policy of setting prices equal to absorption cost plus 15 per cent. Calculate the new price for each speaker model using the product costs developed in requirement 4.

6 Should Super Sounds use plant wide or departmental overhead rates? Explain your answer.

P20.45 Bidding on a special order: manufacturer

Ibhotile Industries Ltd is a manufacturer of standard and custom-designed bottling equipment. Early in December 20X6, Lyan Company asked Ibhotile to quote a price for a custom-designed bottling machine to be delivered in April. Lyan intends to make a decision on the purchase of such a machine by 1 January, so Ibhotile would have the entire first quarter of 20X7 to build the equipment.

Ibhotile's pricing policy for custom-designed equipment is 50 per cent mark-up on absorption cost. Lyan's specifications for the equipment have been reviewed by Ibhotile's Engineering and Cost Accounting departments, which made the following estimates for direct material and direct labour:

Direct material	R768 000
Direct labour (11 000 hours @ R45 per hour)	R495 000

Manufacturing overhead is applied on the basis of direct labour hours. Ibhotile normally plans to run its plant at a level of 15 000 direct labour hours per month, and assigns overhead on the basis of 180 000 direct labour hours per year. The overhead application rate for 20X7 of R27 per hour is based on the following budgeted manufacturing overhead costs for 20X7:

Variable manufacturing overhead	R2 916 000
Fixed manufacturing overhead	1 944 000
Total manufacturing overhead	R4 860 000

Ibhotile's production schedule calls for 12 000 direct labour hours per month during the first quarter. If Ibhotile is awarded the contract for the Lyan equipment, production of one of its standard products would have to be reduced. This is necessary because production levels cannot be increased beyond 15 000 direct labour hours each month without considerable notice. Furthermore, Ibhotile's employees are unwilling to work overtime. If the special order is taken on, no increase or decrease in fixed overhead costs is expected.

Sales of the standard product equal to the reduced production would be lost, but there would be no permanent loss of future sales or customers. The standard product for which the production schedule would be reduced has a unit sales price of R36 000 and a cost structure as follows.

Direct material	R7 500
Direct labour (250 hours @ R45 per hour)	11 250
Manufacturing overhead (250 hours @ R27 per hour)	6 750
Total cost	R25 500

Required:

Ibhotile Industries plans to submit a bid to Lyan Company for the manufacture of the custom-designed bottling equipment.

1 Calculate the bid that Ibhotile would submit if it follows its standard pricing policy for custom-designed equipment.

2 Calculate the minimum bid that Ibhotile could submit on the Lyan equipment that would result in the same total contribution margin as planned for the first quarter of 20X7.

(CMA, adapted)

P20.46 Make or buy; use of limited resources: manufacturer

Stewart Industries has been producing two bearings, components B12 and B18, for use in production. Data regarding these two components are as follows:

	B12	B18
Machine hours required per unit	2.5	3.0
Standard cost per unit:		
Direct material	R22.50	R37.50
Direct labour	40.00	45.00
Manufacturing overhead:		
Variable*	20.00	22.50
Fixed†	37.50	45.00
	R120.00	R150.00

* Variable manufacturing overhead is applied on the basis of direct labour hours.
† Fixed manufacturing overhead is applied on the basis of machine hours.

Stewart's annual requirement for these components is 8000 units of B12 and 11 000 units of B18. Recently, Stewart's management decided to devote additional machine time to other product lines, leaving only 41 000 machine hours per year for producing the bearings. An outside company has offered to sell Stewart its annual supply of the bearings at prices of R112.50 for B12 and R135.00 for B18. Stewart wants to schedule the otherwise idle 41 000 machine hours to produce bearings so that the firm can minimise costs (maximise net benefits).

Required:

1 Calculate the net benefit (loss) per machine hour that would result if Stewart Industries accepts the supplier's offer of R135.00 per unit for component B18.
2 Choose the correct answer.
Stewart Industries will maximise its net benefits by:
(a) purchasing 4800 units of B12 and manufacturing the remaining bearings
(b) purchasing 8000 units of B12 and manufacturing 11 000 units of B18
(c) purchasing 11 000 units of B18 and manufacturing 8 000 units of B12
(d) purchasing 4 000 units of B18 and manufacturing the remaining bearings
(e) purchasing and manufacturing some amounts other than those given above
3 Suppose that management have decided to drop product B12. Independently of requirements 1 and 2, assume that Stewart Industries' idle capacity of 41 000 machine hours has a traceable, avoidable annual fixed cost of R440 000, which will be incurred only if some of the idle capacity is used. Calculate the maximum price Stewart Industries should pay a supplier for component B18.

(CMA, adapted)

P20.47 Production decisions; limited capacity: manufacturer

Chef Gourmet Company has assembled the following data relating to its two most popular products:

	Blender	Food processor
Direct material	R180	R330
Direct labour	120	270
Manufacturing overhead @ R480 per machine hour	480	960
Cost if purchased from an outside supplier	600	1 140
Annual demand (units)	20 000	28 000

Past experience has shown that the fixed manufacturing overhead component included in the cost per machine hour averages R300. Management have a policy of filling all sales orders, even if it means purchasing units from outside suppliers.

Required:

1 If 50 000 machine hours are available, and management desire to follow an optimal strategy, how many units of each product should the firm manufacture? How many units of each product should be purchased?

2 With all other things constant, if management are able to reduce the direct material for a food processor to R180 per unit, how many units of each product should be:
(a) manufactured (b) purchased?

(CMA, adapted)

P20.48 Excess production capacity: manufacturer

Handy Dandy Tools Company manufactures electric carpentry tools. The Production Department has met all production requirements for the current month and has an opportunity to produce additional units of product with its excess capacity. Unit selling prices and unit costs for three different saw models are as follows:

	Basic model	Deluxe model	Pro model
Selling price	R348	R390	R480
Direct material	96	120	114
Direct labour (@ R60 per hour)	60	90	120
Variable overhead	48	72	96
Fixed overhead	96	30	90

Variable overhead is applied on the basis of direct labour Rands, while fixed overhead is applied on the basis of machine hours. There is sufficient demand for the additional production of any model in the product line.

Required:

1 If the company has excess machine capacity and can add more labour as needed (that is, neither machine capacity nor labour is a constraint), the excess production capacity should be devoted to the production of which product? (Assume that the excess capacity will be used for a single product line.)

2 If the company has excess machine capacity and a limited amount of labour time, the excess production capacity should be devoted to producing which product or products?

(CMA, adapted)

P20.49 Short-term product mix; limited capacity: manufacturer

Umoya Industries Ltd produces and sells three products, which are manufactured in a factory with four departments. Both labour and machine time are applied to the products as they pass through each department. The machines and labour skills required in each department are so specialised that neither machines nor labour can be switched from one department to another.

Umoya Industries' management are planning their production schedule for the next few months. The planning is complicated because there are labour shortages in the community and some machines will be down several months for repairs.

Management have assembled the following information regarding available machine and labour time by department, and the machine hours and direct labour hours required per unit of product. These data should be valid for the next six months.

	Department			
	1	2	3	4
Monthly capacity available				
Normal machine capacity, in machine hours	3 500	3 500	3 000	3 500
Capacity of machine being repaired, in machine hours	−500	−400	−300	−200
Available machine capacity in machine hours	3 000	3 100	2 700	3 300
Available labour in direct labour hours	3 700	4 500	2 750	2 600
Labour and machine specifications per unit of product				
Product **Labour and machine time**				
401 Direct labour hours	2	3	3	1
Machine hours	1	1	2	2
403 Direct labour hours	1	2	–	2
Machine hours	1	1	–	2
405 Direct labour hours	2	2	2	1
Machine hours	2	2	1	1

The Sales Department believes that the monthly demand for the next six months will be as follows:

Product	Monthly sales volume in units
401	500
403	400
405	1 000

Inventory levels are satisfactory and need not be increased or decreased during the next six months. Unit price and cost data that will be valid for the next six months are shown:

	Product		
	401	403	405
Unit costs			
Direct material	R21	R39	R51
Direct labour:			
Department 1	36	18	36
Department 2	63	42	42
Department 3	72	–	48
Department 4	27	54	27
Variable overhead	81	60	75
Fixed overhead	45	30	96
Variable selling costs	9	6	12
Unit selling price	R588	R369	R501

Required:

1 Calculate the monthly requirement for machine hours and direct labour hours for the production of products 401, 403 and 405, and determine whether the monthly sales demand for the three products can be met by the factory.

2 What monthly production schedule should Umoya Industries select in order to maximise its profits? Explain how you selected this production schedule, and present a schedule of the contribution to profit that would be generated by your production schedule.

3 Identify the various courses of action that Umoya Industries might consider so that it can supply its customers with all of the product they demand.

(CMA, adapted)

P20.50 Linear programming; formulate and solve graphically (appendix)

Galaxy Chocolate Company manufactures two popular chocolate bars, the Eclipse bar and the Nova bar. Both chocolate bars go through a mixing operation, in which the various ingredients are combined, and then enter the Coating Department, where the bars from the Mixing Department are coated with chocolate. The Eclipse bar is coated with both white and dark chocolate to produce a swirled effect. A material shortage of an ingredient in the Nova bar limits production to 300 batches per day. Production and sales data are presented in the following table. Both chocolate bars are produced in batches of 200 bars.

	Use of capacity in hours per batch of product		
	Available daily capacity in hours	**Eclipse**	**Nova**
Mixing	525	1.5	1.5
Coating	500	2.0	1.0

Management believe that Galaxy can sell all of its daily production of both the Eclipse and Nova bars. Other data follow:

	Eclipse	**Nova**
Selling price per batch	R600	R700
Cost per batch	200	450
Monthly fixed costs (allocated evenly between both products)	750 000	750 000

Required:

1 Formulate the objective function and all of the constraints in order to maximise contribution margin. Be sure to define the variables.

2 How many batches of each type of chocolate bar (Eclipse and Nova) should be produced to maximise the total contribution margin?

3 Calculate the contribution margin at the optimal solution.

P20.51 Linear programming (appendix): service firm

Great Cooking Company offers monthly service plans for providing prepared meals that are delivered to customers' homes. The target market for these meal plans includes double-income families with no children, and retired couples in upper income brackets.

Great Cooking offers two monthly plans: Premier Cuisine and Haute Cuisine. The Premier Cuisine plan provides frozen meals that are delivered twice each month; this plan generates a contribution margin of R600 for each monthly plan sold. The Haute Cuisine plan provides freshly prepared meals delivered on a daily basis; this plan generates a contribution margin of R450 for each monthly plan sold.

Great Cooking's reputation provides the company with a market that will purchase all the meals that can be prepared. All meals go through food preparation and cooking steps in the company's kitchens. After these steps, the Premier Cuisine meals are flash-frozen. The time requirements per monthly meal plan and the hours available per month are as follows:

	Preparation	**Cooking**	**Freezing**
Hours required:			
Premier Cuisine	2	2	1
Haute Cuisine	1	3	0
Hours available	60	120	45

For planning purposes, Great Cooking uses linear programming to determine the most profitable number of Premier Cuisine and Haute Cuisine monthly meal plans to produce.

Required:

1 Using the notation *P* for Premier Cuisine and *H* for Haute Cuisine, state the objective function and the constraints that Great Cooking should use to maximise the total contribution margin generated by the monthly meal plans.

2 Graph the constraints on Great Cooking's meal preparation process. Be sure to label the graph clearly, including the optimal solution.

3 Using the graph prepared in requirement 2, determine the optimal solution to Great Cooking's production planning problem in terms of the numbers of each type of meal plan to produce.

4 Calculate the value of Great Cooking's objective function at the optimal solution.

5 If the constraint on preparation time could be eliminated, determine the revised optimal solution.

(CMA, adapted)

P20.52 Linear programming; formulate and discuss (appendix): manufacturer

CoffeeTime Ltd manufactures two types of electric coffeemakers, Regular and Deluxe. The major difference between the two appliances is capacity. Both are considered top-quality units and sell for premium prices. Both coffeemakers pass through two manufacturing departments: Plating and Assembly. The company has two assembly operations, one automated and one manual. The Automated Assembly Department has been in operation for one year and was intended to replace the Labour Assembly Department. However, business has expanded rapidly in recent months, and both assembly operations are still being used. Workers have been trained for both operations and can be used in either department. The only difference between the two departments is the proportion of machine time versus direct labour used. Data regarding the two coffeemakers are presented in the following schedules:

	Machine-hour data		
	Plating	**Labour Assembly**	**Automated Assembly**
Machine hours required per unit	0.15	0.02	0.05
Machine hours available per month	25 000	1 500	5 000
Annual machine hours available	300 000	18 000	60 000

	Unit variable manufacturing costs			
	Plating Department		**Labour Assembly**	**Automated Assembly**
	Regular	**Deluxe**		
Raw material:				
Casing	R31.00	R59.80	–	–
Heating element	24.00	24.00	–	–
Other	33.00	33.00	–	–
Direct labour:				
@ R40 per hour	R8.00	R8.00	–	–
@ R48 per hour	–	–	R12.00	R2.40
Manufacturing overhead:				
Supplies	R5.00	R5.00	R6.00	R6.00
Power	4.80	4.80	3.00	3.00

	Sales data	
	Regular mode	**Deluxe mode**
Selling price per unit	R180.00	R240.00
Variable selling expense per unit	12.00	12.00
Annual allocated fixed overhead	3 600 000	3 600 000

CoffeeTime produced and sold 600 000 Deluxe coffeemakers and 900 000 Regular coffeemakers last year. Management estimate that total unit sales could increase by 20 per cent or more if the units can be produced. CoffeeTime already has contracts to produce and sell 35 000 units of each model each month. CoffeeTime has a monthly maximum labour capacity of 30 000 direct labour hours in the Plating Department and 40 000 direct labour hours for the assembly operation (Automated Assembly and Labour Assembly combined). Sales, production and costs occur uniformly throughout the year.

Required:

1 CoffeeTime's management believe that linear programming could be used to determine the optimum mix of Regular and Deluxe coffeemakers to produce and sell. Explain why linear programming is appropriate to use in this situation.

2 Management have decided to use linear programming to determine the optimal product mix. Formulate and label:
(a) the objective function (b) the constraints
Be sure to define your variables.

(CMA adapted)

Cases

C20.53 Pricing a special order; ethics: manufacturer

Bloem Ltd manufactures one product, a combination fertiliser-weedkiller called Fertikil. The product is sold nationwide to retail nurseries and gardening stores. Taylor Nursery plans to sell a similar fertiliser-weedkiller through its regional nursery chain under its private label. Taylor has asked Bloem to submit a bid for a 25 000 kilogram order of the private brand compound. While the chemical composition of the Taylor compound differs from that of Fertikil, the manufacturing process is very similar. The Taylor compound would be produced in 1000 kilogram batches. Each batch would require 60 direct labour hours and the following chemicals:

Chemicals	Quantity (kg)
CW-3	400
JX-6	300
MZ-8	200
BE-7	100

The first three chemicals (CW-3, JX-6, MZ-8) are all used in the production of Fertikil. BE-7 was used in a compound that Bloem has discontinued. This chemical was not sold or discarded because it does not deteriorate and Bloem has adequate storage facilities. Bloem could sell BE-7 at the prevailing market price, less 20 cents per kilogram for selling and handling expenses.

Bloem also has on hand a chemical called CN-5, manufactured for use in another product that is no longer produced. CN-5, which cannot be used in Fertikil, can be substituted for CW-3 on a one-for-one basis without affecting the quality of the Taylor compound. The quantity of CN-5 in inventory has a salvage value of R5000. Inventory and cost data for the chemicals that can be used to produce the Taylor compound are as follows:

Raw material	No. of kg in inventory	Actual price per kg when purchased	Current market price per kg
CW-3	22 000	R8.00	R4.50
JX-6	5 000	5.50	3.00
MZ-8	8 000	14.00	8.00
BE-7	4 000	6.00	3.25
CN-5	5 500	7.50	*

* Salvage value of R5000 for entire inventory on hand.

The current direct labour rate is R70 per hour. The manufacturing overhead rate is established at the beginning of the year using direct labour hours as the base. The predetermined overhead rate for the current year, based on a two-shift capacity of 400 000 total direct labour hours with no overtime, is as follows:

Variable manufacturing overhead	R22.50	per direct labour hour
Fixed manufacturing overhead	37.50	per direct labour hour
Combined rate	R60.00	per direct labour hour

Bloem's production manager reports that the present equipment and facilities are adequate for manufacturing the Taylor compound. However, Bloem is within 800 hours of its two-shift capacity this month before it must schedule overtime. If need be, the Taylor compound could be produced on regular time by shifting a portion of Fertikil production to overtime. Bloem's pay rate for overtime hours is one-and-a-half the regular pay rate, or R105.00 per hour. There is no allowance for any overtime premium in the manufacturing overhead rate. Bloem's standard markup policy for new products is 25 per cent of absorption manufacturing cost.

Required:

1 Assume Bloem Ltd has decided to submit a bid for a 25 000 kilogram order of Taylor's new compound, to be delivered by the end of the current month. Taylor has indicated that this one-time order will not be repeated. Calculate the lowest price Bloem can bid for the order and not reduce its net profit.

2 Independently of your answer to requirement 1, assume that Taylor Nursery plans to place regular orders for 25 000 kilogram lots of the new compound during the coming year. Bloem expects demand for Fertikil to remain strong, so recurring orders from Taylor will put Bloem over its two-shift capacity. However, production can be scheduled so 60 per cent of each Taylor order can be completed during regular hours, or Fertikil production could be shifted temporarily to overtime so that Taylor orders could be produced on regular time. Bloem's production manager has estimated that prices of all chemicals will stabilise at current market rates for the coming year. All other manufacturing costs are expected to be maintained at the same rates or amounts. Calculate the price Bloem Ltd should quote Taylor Nursery for each 25 000 kilogram order of the new compound, assuming there will be recurring orders during the coming year. Assume that Bloem's management believe new products sold on a recurring basis should be priced to cover their total production costs plus the standard markup.

3 Suppose Bloem Ltd has submitted a bid to Taylor Nursery. However, Dalton Industries, a competitor to Bloem, has submitted a lower bid. Before accepting Dalton's bid, the owner of Taylor Nursery telephones his golfing friend, who is Bloem's production manager:

I've got some bad news for you. Bloem's been outbid on the private label order by Dalton Industries. I've been thinking, though. It looks to me like Bloem included some cost in its bid that could be eliminated. If you'd like to revise the Bloem bid, we might be able to steer this deal your way. If it would help, I can show you Dalton's figures.

Discuss the ethical issues in this scenario.

(CMA, adapted)

C20.54 Adding a product line; limited capacity: manufacturer

Sami Chetty, Sportway Corporation's production manager, had requested a lunch meeting with the company's managing director. Chetty wanted to put forward his suggestion to add a new product line. As they finished lunch, Meg Truter, the managing director, said: 'I'll give your proposal some serious thought, Sami. I think you're right about the increasing demand for skateboards. What I'm not so sure about is whether the skateboard line will be better for us than will our tackle boxes. Those have been our bread and butter the past few years.'

Chetty responded: 'Let me get together with one of the accountants. We'll run a few numbers on this skateboard idea that I think will demonstrate the line's potential.'

Sportway is a wholesale distributor supplying a wide range of moderately priced sports equipment to large chain stores. About 60 per cent of Sportway's products are purchased from other companies, while the remainder of the products are manufactured by Sportway. The company has a Plastics Department that is currently manufacturing moulded fishing tackle boxes. Sportway is able to manufacture and sell 8000 tackle boxes annually, making full use of its direct labour capacity at available work stations. The selling price and costs associated with Sportway's tackle boxes are as follows:

Selling price per box		R258.00
Costs per box:		
Moulded plastic	R24.00	
Hinges, latches, handle	27.00	
Direct labour (@ R45 per hour)	56.25	
Manufacturing overhead	37.50	
Selling and administrative cost	51.00	R195.75
Profit per box		R62.25

Because Sportway's sales manager believes the company could sell 12 000 tackle boxes if it had sufficient manufacturing capacity, the company has looked into the possibility of purchasing the tackle boxes for distribution. Maple Products, a steady supplier of quality products, would be able to provide up to 9 000 tackle boxes per year at a price of R204 per box delivered to Sportway's facility.

Sami Chetty has come to the conclusion that the company could make better use of its Plastics Department by manufacturing skateboards. Chetty has a market study that indicates an expanding market for skateboards and a need for additional suppliers. Chetty believes that Sportway could expect to sell 17 500 skateboards annually at a price of R135 per skateboard.

After his lunch with the company managing director, Chetty worked out the following estimates with the assistant accountant:

Selling price per skateboard		R135.00
Costs per skateboard:		
Moulded plastic	R16.50	
Wheels, hardware	21.00	
Direct labour (@ R45 per hour)	22.50	
Manufacturing overhead	15.00	
Selling and administrative cost	27.00	R102.00
Profit per skateboard		R33.00

In the Plastics Department, Sportway uses direct labour hours as the application base for manufacturing overhead. Included in the manufacturing overhead for the current year is R150 000 of factory-wide, fixed manufacturing overhead that has been allocated to the Plastics Department. For each unit of product that Sportway sells, regardless of whether the product has been purchased or is manufactured by Sportway, there is an allocated R18 fixed overhead cost per unit for distribution that is included in the selling and administrative cost for all products. Total selling and administrative costs for the purchased tackle boxes would be R30 per unit.

Required:

1 In order to maximise the company's profitability, prepare an analysis that will show which product or products Sportway Corporation should manufacture or purchase.
2 First determine which of Sportway's options makes the best use of its scarce resources. How many skateboards and tackle boxes should be manufactured? How many tackle boxes should be purchased?
3 Calculate the improvement in Sportway's total contribution margin if it adopts the optimal strategy rather than continuing with the status quo.

(CMA, adapted)

C20.55 Pricing for a professional conference

Systems Planners Institute (SPI), a professional association for systems analysts and computer programmers, has 50 000 members. SPI holds a conference each October, and planning for the 20X8 conference is progressing smoothly. The conference budget for promotional brochures, fees and expenses for 20 speakers, equipment rental for presentations, the travel and expenses of 25 staff, consultant fees, and volunteer expenses is R1.65 million. This amount does not include the hotel charges for meeting rooms, luncheons, banquets or receptions.

SPI has always priced each function at the conference separately. Members select and pay for only those functions they attend. Members who attend the conference pay a registration fee that allows them to attend the annual reception and meeting. The Annual Conference Committee has recommended that SPI set a single flat fee for the entire conference; registered members would be entitled to attend all functions.

The following table presents the conference functions, the percentage of attendees that can be expected to attend each function, the price SPI would charge for each function if it were priced separately, and the hotel charges for food, service and meeting rooms. The percentage of attendees expected to attend each function is based on past experience and is expected to hold regardless of the pricing scheme used.

	Percentage of attendees who will participate	Separate price of function	Hotel charge
Function:			
Registration fee	100%	R250	none
Reception	100%	free	R125 per attendee
Annual meeting	100%	free	R10 000 for meeting hall
Keynote luncheon	90%	R200	R125 per attendee
Six concurrent sessions*	70%	R300	R1 000 per room or R6 000 in total
Plenary session	70%	R250	R10 000 for meeting hall
Six workshops*	50%	R500	R1 000 per room or R6 000 in total
Banquet	90%	R250	R150 per attendee

* Attendee selects one session or workshop for the fee

The hotel's package of services to SPI and the conference attendees is as follows:

- Three free rooms for conference headquarters and storage.
- Twenty per cent discount for all conference attendees who stay in the hotel during the three-day conference. The types of rooms, the regular posted rate, and the proportion of each type of room taken by attendees are as shown below. Attendees are to make room reservations directly with the hotel, and all hotel room charges are the responsibility of the attendees.

Type	Regular rate per night	Proportion rented
Single	R500	10%
Studio	525	10%
Double	625	75%
Suite	1 000	5%

- SPI is given credit for one free double room for three days for every 50 conference registrants who stay at the hotel. The credit will be applied to the room charges of staff and speakers.
- Meeting rooms and halls are free if food is served at the function.
- Meeting rooms and halls for professional sessions are free if 1000 members are registered at the hotel.
- The hotel receives all revenue from bar sales at the reception and before the luncheons and banquet. The hotel estimates that the average consumption at each of these functions will be one cocktail per attendee at a cost to the hotel of R7.50 per cocktail.

If SPI continues to price each conference function separately, the prices given in the first table will apply. Expected attendance under this type of pricing scheme is 2000 members.

The Annual Conference Committee has estimated the conference attendance for three different single flat-fee pricing structures as follows:

Proposed single flat fee	Estimated number of attendees
R1 625	1 600
1 500	1 750
1 375	1 900

SPI estimates that 60 per cent of the people who attend the conference will stay in the conference hotel, and each attendee will need a separate room for an average stay of three nights.

Required:

SPI wants to maximise its contribution margin from its annual conference. Recommend whether SPI should price each function at the conference separately or charge one of the three single flat fees for the conference. Support your recommendation with an appropriate analysis.

(CMA, adapted)

C20.56 Pricing; possible plant closure: manufacturer

Handy Household Products Ltd is a multiproduct company with several manufacturing plants. The Epping plant manufactures and distributes two household cleaning and polishing compounds, standard and commercial, under the Clean & Bright label. The forecast operating results for the first six months of the current year, when 100 000 cases of each compound are expected to be manufactured and sold, are presented in the following statement:

Clean & Bright Compounds, Epping plant
Forecast results of operations
for the six-month period ending June 30
(in R000s)

	Standard	Commercial	Total
Sales	40 000	60 000	100 000
Cost of goods sold	32 000	38 000	70 000
Gross profit	8 000	22 000	30 000
Selling and administrative expenses:			
Variable	8 000	14 000	22 000
Fixed*	4 800	7 200	12 000
Total selling & administrative expenses	12 800	21 200	34 000
Profit (loss) before taxes	−4 800	800	−4 000

* The fixed selling & administrative expenses are allocated between the two products on the basis of Rand sales volume.

The standard compound sold for R400 a case and the commercial compound sold for R600 a case during the first six months of the year. The manufacturing costs, by case of product, are presented in the schedule below. Each product is manufactured on a separate production line.

Annual normal manufacturing capacity is 200 000 cases of each product. However, the plant is capable of producing 250 000 cases of standard compound and 350 000 cases of commercial compound annually.

	Cost per case	
	Standard	Commercial
Direct material	R140.00	R160.00
Direct labour	80.00	80.00
Variable manufacturing overhead	20.00	40.00
Fixed manufacturing overhead	80.00	100.00
Total manufacturing cost	R320.00	R380.00
Variable selling and administrative costs	R80.00	R140.00

The following schedule reflects the consensus of top management regarding the price-volume alternatives for the Clean & Bright products for the last six months of the current year. These are essentially the same alternatives management had during the first six months of the year.

Standard compound		Commercial compound	
Alternative prices (per case)	Sales volume (in cases)	Alternative prices (per case)	Sales volume (in cases)
R380	120 000	R520	175 000
R400	100 000	R540	140 000
R420	90 000	R600	100 000
R440	80 000	R640	55 000
R460	50 000	R700	35 000

Handy Household Products' top management believe that the loss for the first six months reflects a tight profit margin caused by intense competition. Management also believe that many companies will leave this market by next year and profit should improve.

Required:

1 What unit selling price should management select for each of the Clean & Bright compounds for the remaining six months of the year? Support your selection with appropriate calculations.

2 Independently of your answer to requirement 1, assume that the optimum alternatives for the last six months were as follows: a selling price of R460 and volume of 50 000 cases for the standard compound, and a selling price of R700 and volume of 35 000 cases for the commercial compound.

(a) Should management consider closing down the plant's operations until January 1 of the next year in order to minimise its losses? Support your answer with appropriate calculations.

(b) Identify and discuss the qualitative factors that should be considered in deciding whether the Epping plant should be closed down during the last six months of the current year.

(CMA, adapted)

Endnotes

1 Further information on pricing can be found in Kotler, Adam, Brown & Armstrong (2003) and Lovelock, Patterson & Walker (2001).

2 Statutory marketing boards came to an end in the late 1990s. However, producer associations and duties on imports (ex. sugar) will enable companies to charge higher prices. In 2007, Eskom was permitted to raise the price of electricity by over 14% to enable Eskom to finance the cost of expanding the number of power stations required to increase electricity generation and reduce the rolling blackouts experienced across South Africa. Petroleum prices are regulated by government and taxation also affects the pricing of petroleum products. Tobacco and alcohol are affected by the duties ('sin taxes') imposed by government and which form part of the pricing of such products. In sectors such as cement, high transportation costs due to the nature and weight of cement allow regional producers to charge higher prices.

3 At the time of writing in 2007, British Airways was fined £270m by the British and USA regulatory authorities for colluding with Virgin Atlantic in setting surcharges on transatlantic fares. Virgin Atlantic escaped penalties by 'whistle blowing' and disclosing the cartel to the authorities. However, a class action by passengers is pending and the amount claimed was expected to be a further £300m, payable by both BA and Virgin. Collusion can be costly.

4 The demand and revenue curves are based on the quantity sold, while the cost curves are based on the quantity produced. For simplicity, it is assumed that Cape Sailing Supplies' monthly sales and production quantities are the same.

5 For further discussion of cost-plus pricing, see Govindarajan & Anthony (1983) and Gordon, Cooper, Falk & Miller (1981).

6 The Mason & Cox illustration in Chapter 8 provides a good example of how prices can be inappropriate when based on inaccurate conventional product costs.

7 Telkom would also need to consider the opportunity cost of dial-up. Most customers on dial-up would not be able to make or receive telephone calls whilst connected to the Internet. This costs Telkom money. ADSL enables customers of fixed lines to make and receive normal telephone calls while connected to the Internet.

Capital Expenditure Decisions: An Introduction

❖ Learning Objectives

After completing this chapter, you should be able to:

1. explain the nature and purpose of capital expenditure decisions;
2. describe a typical capital budgeting approval process;
3. explain the importance of, and account for, the time value of money in capital budgeting decisions;
4. use the net present value method to evaluate a capital expenditure proposal;
5. use the internal rate of return method to evaluate a capital expenditure proposal;
6. compare the net present value and internal rate of return methods;
7. describe the assumptions underlying the net present value and internal rate of return methods;
8. apply the appropriate techniques to select the least-cost decision in capital expenditure analysis;
9. account for depreciation in capital expenditure analysis;
10. use the net present value and the internal rate of return to compare alternative capital expenditure proposals;
11. use the payback method to evaluate capital expenditure proposals, and evaluate its usefulness;
12. use the accounting rate of return method to evaluate capital expenditure proposals, and evaluate its usefulness;
13. explain the value of post-audits of capital expenditure projects;
14. explain the potential conflict between using discounted cash flow analysis for evaluating capital expenditure projects and using accrual accounting data for evaluating managers' performance; and
15. after studying the appendix, calculate future values and present values over several time periods.

Introduction

In managing the resources of an organisation to create shareholder and customer value, managers face major decisions that involve cash flows over several years. Decisions involving the acquisition of machinery, vehicles, buildings or land are examples. Other decisions may involve significant changes to a production process or the addition of a major new line of products or services to the organisation's activities. These capital investments can have a significant effect on the competitive position of a business.

Capital expenditure decisions

L.O. 1

Decisions that require the evaluation of cash inflows and outflows over several years to determine the acceptability of the project are called **capital expenditure** (or **capital budgeting** or **capital investment**) **decisions**. These are usually described as long-term decisions.[1]

The focus on projects

Capital expenditure decisions focus on specific projects or programs. Should the City of Cape Town purchase a new street-cleaner? Which new project should BHP Billiton undertake? Should a university buy a new electron microscope? Should a manufacturing firm acquire a computer-integrated manufacturing system?

The City of Cape Town would need to consider whether the cost savings that would be generated by purchasing the new street cleaner justified the expenditure. Non-financial issues must also be considered in this decision. For example, the City of Cape Town must consider the poor performance of the current street-cleaning machine, and the dissatisfaction this is causing among residents. This is very difficult to quantify as it has no immediate cost implications, but it is important in the capital expenditure decision.

Over time, as managers make decisions about a variety of specific programs and projects, the organisation as a whole becomes the total of its individual investments, activities, programs and projects. We can view the organisation's performance over a year as the combined result of all the projects under way during that year. Exhibit 21.1 depicts this project viewpoint of an organisation's activities.

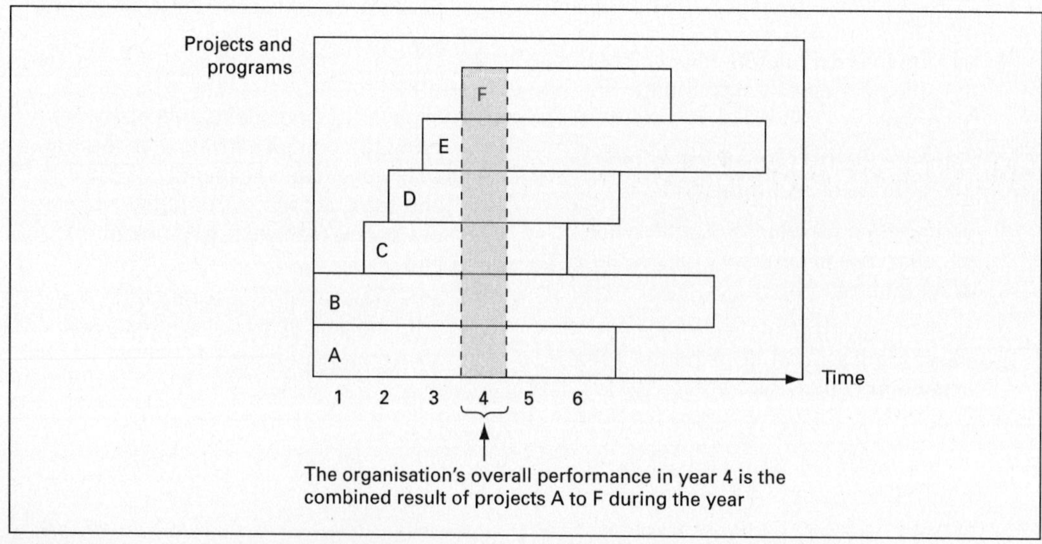

Exhibit 21.1 An organisation as a collection of projects and programs

Decisions to invest in long-term projects often form part of the strategic planning process. Large investments in manufacturing technology and major asset purchases may be undertaken to change, or enhance, the competitiveness of the business. This is shown in the 'Real life' below.

REAL LIFE: CAPITAL EXPENDITURE CAN BOOST COMPETITIVENESS AND GROWTH

Many South African companies undertake significant capital expenditure to improve their competitiveness in domestic and international markets and ensure growth in sales revenue and profits. Here are some examples.

In August 2007 Gold Fields, a leading gold producer, announced that it would spend R13 billion over the following two financial years on capital projects to expand production and access more ore reserves. The company's largest project was South Deep, which is one of the deepest gold deposits in the world (about 4 km down) but was also a mine with the largest reserves of gold. Other projects include mining projects outside South Africa.

In February 2007 Pretoria Portland Cement (PPC), the leading supplier of cement in South Africa, announced a R604 million inland cement milling upgrade and expansion project. This new project is in addition to the Dwaalboom Batsweledi R1.4 billion expansion project (see pictures) which will result in an increase of 1.25 million tons of cement capacity. Further, investment in state of the art technology would result in an increased capacity of 300 000 tons per annum. The demand for cement and aggregates in South Africa increased by 50 per cent between 2002 and 2006 and PPC was forced to import cement in order to supply the South African market. The growth in cement demand was unprecedented, yet PPC had a legacy of excess capacity for two decades prior to the boom in construction that occurred in South Africa after 2003.

Sources:

Business Day, Nicola Mawson, 'Gold Fields embarks on R13bn growth drive', 15 August 2007.
www.goldfields.co.za
www.ppc.co.za, press release 'PPC announces R604 million Capital Expansion Project', 27 February 2007.

The capital expenditure approval process

L.O. 2

An organisation's long-term health can be affected significantly by its capital budgeting decisions, so many large organisations have elaborate capital expenditure approval processes that are often highly formalised. Specific forms are used, and requests are reviewed at several levels of management. Some businesses have capital budgeting staff whose function is to analyse all capital budgeting proposals.

Six stages of the capital expenditure decision process can be identified (Emmanuel, Otley & Merchant, 1990):

1 *Project generation.* In many large companies, projects are initiated by managers of business units (such as cost or profit centres). The choice of projects may need to be consistent with the strategic plan developed by corporate management and with corporate guidelines concerning what projects are likely to be acceptable to the organisation. Also,

managers may use their discretion not to submit projects which may have been acceptable to the business, but which they feel may entail some personal risk for them or their business unit.

2 *Estimation and analysis of projected cash flows.* The cash flows of a project must be estimated for the life of the project. A range of alternative techniques can be used to analyse the cash flows, some of which are described in the next section of this chapter. There is some evidence that project initiators may bias the cash flows for their proposals in order to make them more attractive. This is difficult to detect in situations where particular managers have the best knowledge of their business and their market.

3 *Progress to approval.* The level of authority for approval of capital budgeting proposals differs between organisations. The larger the cost of a proposal, the higher in the organisation is the authority for final approval. Most substantial capital expenditure proposals require senior management approval, and project initiators often have to 'sell' their proposals to corporate management. A political process often takes place, since in many businesses there is strong competition for limited resources. Managers may need to rally support for their particular project and prepare convincing justifications to show why their project is superior to others. The analysis of financial data is only one aspect of the capital expenditure proposal. There must also be powerful arguments presented to justify the adoption of a project; these are often made on strategic, marketing or environmental grounds.

4 *Analysis and selection of projects.* Following the 'promotional' activity by project initiators, projects will be examined and selected by corporate management.

5 *Implementation of projects.* Successful projects will be implemented. This may involve the construction or purchase of a new asset, the employment of new staff, and the training of existing staff.

6 *Post-completion audit of projects.* This may occur a year or even longer after the project is implemented and may entail an evaluation of the accuracy of the initial plans and cash flow estimates, and progress reports on the outcomes of the project in operational and financial terms.

Of course, not all projects are approved in this way. In many small businesses the process is far more informal. In large organisations, managers in business units are typically authorised to make certain capital expenditures without seeking corporate approval; for example, a manufacturing manager may only need to gain approval from his or her divisional manager to undertake projects that exceed R100 000.

In the remainder of this chapter, and in Chapter 22, we will consider in greater detail the various steps that are undertaken in managing the capital expenditure process.

Techniques for analysing capital expenditure proposals

How do businesses decide whether or not to undertake a particular project? Clearly, the financial impact of the project must be considered. That is, the costs of each project must be compared with the benefits that it will generate. In capital expenditure decisions, these costs and benefits extend over several years; they are known as cash outflows and cash inflows respectively. **Cash outflows** include the initial cost of the project and any increases in costs that will be incurred as a result of the project over its life. **Cash inflows** include cost savings and additional revenues and any proceeds of the sale of assets that result from the project. For example, if the City of Cape Town is considering purchasing the new street-cleaning machine, the outflows would include the initial purchase of the machine and any increase in operating costs of the new machine over its useful life. The relevant cash inflows would include proceeds from the sale of the old machine, ongoing cost savings that result from using the new machine, and the disposal value at the end of the new machine's life.

Several different techniques can be used to analyse these cash flows: the payback method, the accounting rate of return, and discounted cash flow (DCF) techniques. The first two methods do not consider the time value of money—that is, they assume that a Rand received in a future period is as valuable as a Rand received in the current period. Discounted cash flow techniques explicitly consider the effect of the time value of money.

We will examine how each of these techniques can be used by focusing on a capital expenditure decision that took place at a medical centre.

Capital expenditure decisions at a medical centre

Since the 1990s, South Africa's private and public hospitals have been subject to many pressures and changes and, in the face of tighter health budgets, many have adopted commercial business practices. The Government changed the way it funded public hospitals and this has forced both private and public hospitals to place greater emphasis on performance improvement, in both patient care and costs. Hospitals have also adopted more formalised accounting techniques and information systems, including systems for evaluating capital expenditure.

Organisational structure

Let's analyse a medical centre which we will call Metro Medical Centre (MMC) and which has structured its operations into business units. Exhibit 21.2 shows that there were five production divisions and three service divisions. In the hospital environment the production divisions were known as clinical divisions. These divisions were regarded as profit centres. (Responsibility accounting and structures were studied in Chapter 12.) Each division was headed by a chairman or director who was responsible for the profits generated by their division.

A capital expenditure decision in the CT Scanning Department

We will focus on a decision relating to the purchase of a CT scanner. A CT scanner is a computerised axial tomography system. It is used to take a range of images of thin slices of any part of the human body. These slices show muscle, blood vessels and bone, and can be used to diagnose a range of medical problems including back pain, brain tumours and various other forms of cancer.

MMC had one CT scanner that was acquired in 1986. It was located in the CT Scanning Department of the Imaging Division. Since the mid-1990s the demand for CT services at MMC had almost doubled. The extra demand was covered by the introduction of late evening and Saturday services. Demand for CT scans was expected to increase further as the neurosciences, and accident and emergency areas, expanded.

It became clear to the chairman of the Imaging Division that the old CT machine was too unreliable. Several machine breakdowns led to delays in patient treatment. Doctors in the clinical divisions were very concerned about the deterioration of service provided by the CT Scanning Department. Inpatients often had to wait three days for a scan.[2] For outpatients, the waiting time had grown to three weeks. Patients were often referred to MMC because of the high level of skills and interventional procedures that MMC offered. The chairman could see that if these delays continued, they might affect not only the quality of healthcare, but also MMC's good reputation. Another problem to be considered was the decreasing level of staff efficiency in the CT Scanning Department. When the existing CT scanner broke down or was being repaired, the staff were unoccupied, and then they often needed to work overtime to complete work when the scanner was back in operation.

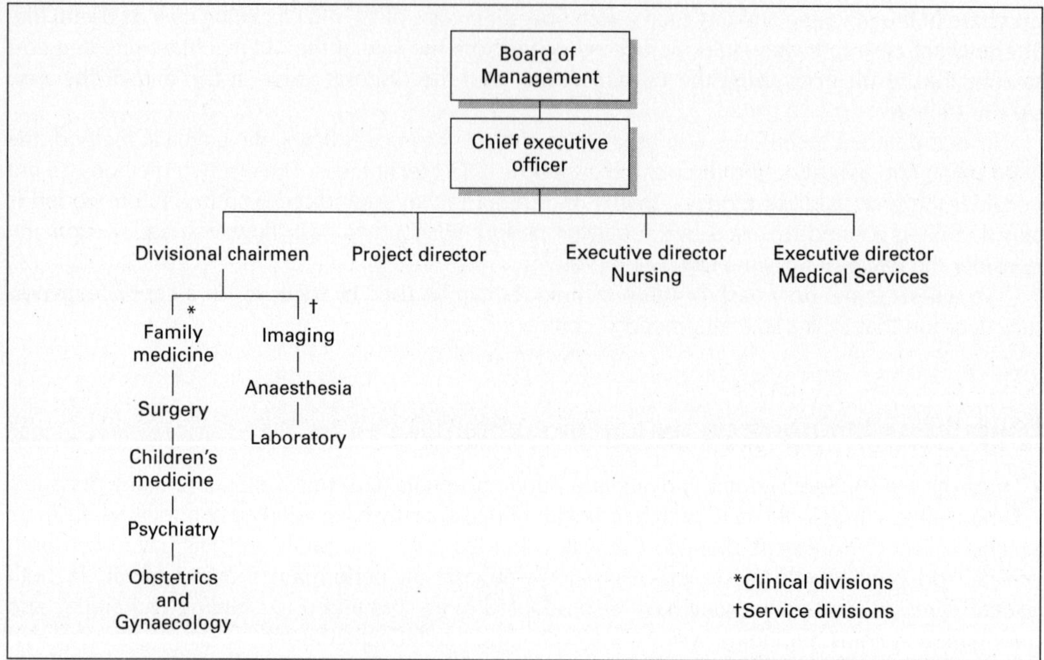

Exhibit 21.2 Organisation chart of the Medical Centre

The chairman of the Imaging Division had no doubt that changes needed to be made in the CT Scanning Department. There were several options available. The newly appointed project director stepped in to analyse two alternative solutions: should MMC purchase an additional CT scanner and retain the old machine, or simply replace the old CT scanner with a new one?

The project director needed to prepare a detailed report for the board of management outlining the nature of the problem, presenting arguments in support of each alternative and the cost implications. She would conclude the report with her recommendation.

Alternative One: purchase an additional CT scanner

A second CT scanner would provide additional capacity to enable the CT Scanning Department to meet current requirements and the expected future increase in demand for its services. It would reduce the current waiting time and thus provide better service to both inpatients and outpatients. The increased capacity would allow the Department to see more patients and earn additional revenue. Also, the shorter waiting times would reduce the length of stay for inpatients in the clinical divisions. This reduced length of stay would result in significant savings for the hospital.

The old and new CT machines would be positioned so that they could be operated by the existing staff, and only an additional part-time operator would be needed. The extra salary cost would be offset by savings in overtime payments. The costs of extra chemicals, supplies and service for the second machine were also important to the decision.

The cash flows relating to the project were estimated and are summarised in column 1 of Exhibit 21.3. These are the incremental cash inflows and outflows that would result if Alternative One were chosen. The existing cash inflows and outflows of the CT Scanning Department, and of the hospital at large, are not included in the analysis as they are not relevant to the decision.[3] This is because they will not change under either alternative. You can see that the cost savings extend to five years; to estimate beyond that time involved too many uncertainties.

The purchase price of the machine was estimated at R5 850 000 and it would cost R747 150 to install it. Therefore, the initial outlay was estimated as R6 597 150. Additional expenditure for replacement parts, service cost and chemicals would amount to R1 070 000 per year. Opportunities for additional revenue, due to the increased capacity of the CT Scanning Department, were estimated at R900 000 per year. Savings due to reduced lengths of stay of inpatients were expected to amount to R2 000 000 per year.

Alternative Two: replace the current CT scanner

There were strong arguments in favour of simply replacing the old CT scanner. The new CT scanner would alleviate many problems currently occurring in the CT Scanning Department; it would be larger and more sophisticated than the new machine envisaged under Alternative One. The breakdowns that were causing delays in servicing patients would cease, and staff would no longer have to work overtime and on Saturdays. The larger machine would increase throughput in the clinical divisions of the hospital and help to reduce the waiting list for a CT scan. However, there would not be sufficient increased capacity to allow the Department to take on extra revenue-earning activities. There was also the possibility that the increase in capacity created by this new machine would not be sufficient to accommodate the expected increase in demand for CT scans in the future.

The cash flows relating to this alternative are listed in column 2 of Exhibit 21.3. The cost of the replacement scanner was estimated at R6 760 000. This was more expensive than the cost of the additional CT scanner to be purchased under Alternative One, as it was a larger and more sophisticated machine. Unlike Alternative One, however, there would be no installation cost, as the structural work needed to accommodate two scanners would not be required. The proceeds from the sale of the old scanner, R1 500 000, would reduce the cost of the investment. The new machine could be operated more efficiently than the old scanner, and provide annual operating cost savings of R630 000. The savings resulting from reductions in the average length of stay of inpatients were estimated at R800 000 per year. There would be a one-off cost in year 1 of R150 000 to train staff to operate the more sophisticated machine.

How can these cash flows be analysed? At this point we will concentrate on the first alternative.

	Alternative One: Purchase an additional CT scanner	Alternative Two: Replace the current CT scanner
Initial investment (time 0)		
Acquisition cost	−R5 850 000	−R6 760 000
Installation	−747 150	0
Proceeds of sale	0	1 500 000
Net investiment (time 0)	**−R6 597 150**	**−R5 260 000**
Cash flow (years 1–5)		
Increase/savings in operating costs	−R1 070 000	R630 000
Additional revenue due to increased capacity	900 000	0
Savings due to reduced stay of inpatients	2 000 000	800 000
Training for new machine (year 1)	0	−150 000
Annual cost savings	**R1 830 000**	**R1 280 000**
	(Years 1–5)	(Year 1 only) R1 430 000 (Years 2–5)

Exhibit 21.3 CT scanner: cash flows for the two alternatives

Discounted cash flow analysis

The cash flows for the alternatives involve different sums over the five years. One way we can analyse these cash flows is to 'discount' them back to their present value.

The time value of money

L.O. 3 To use discounted cash flow methods in order to analyse capital expenditure decisions such as those faced by the medical centre, we first need to understand the basic concept of the time value of money. Would you rather receive R100 today or a letter promising the R100 in a year's time? Most of us would rather have the cash now. There are two reasons for this choice. First, if we received the money today, we could spend it now instead of waiting a year. Second, as an alternative strategy, we could invest the R100 received today at, say, 7 per cent interest; then, at the end of one year, we would have R107. Thus, there is a time value associated with money. A R100 cash flow today is not equivalent to a R100 cash flow in one year, two years or ten years.

When analysing cash flows that extend over several years, it is incorrect simply to add them all together. The proper approach is to use **discounted cash flow analysis**, which takes account of the time value of money. We need to discount the cash flows of future years to make them equivalent to those in the current year. In Part 1 of the appendix to this chapter, the concepts of present and future values of cash flows are explained in detail. If you are unfamiliar with these ideas, you should read this appendix carefully before proceeding with the following analysis.

There are two widely used methods of discounted cash flow analysis: the net present value method and the internal rate of return method. Each of these will be used to analyse the cash flows relating to the CT scanner decision at MMC.

Net present value method

L.O. 4 The net present value method calculates the present value of the future cash flows of a project. Four steps are needed to complete a net present value analysis of an investment proposal:

1 Prepare a table showing the cash flows during each year of the proposed investment.
2 Calculate the present value of each cash flow, using the required rate of return. The **required rate of return** (or **hurdle rate** or **discount rate**) is the minimum acceptable rate of return on investments. It usually reflects the firm's cost of capital. (This is discussed in greater detail on page 1045.)
3 Calculate the **net present value (NPV)**, which is the sum of the present values of the cash flows in each period.
4 If the NPV is positive, the project is acceptable on financial grounds. The higher the net present value, the more acceptable is the project. You will remember from the discussion in Chapter 19 that financial information is only one input to a decision. Strategic or other qualitative issues may carry equal or even greater weight in management decisions.

NPV of the cash flows for the additional CT scanner

The cash flows relating to the purchase of the additional CT scanner (Alternative One) were presented in Exhibit 21.3. In Exhibit 21.4, the same cash flows are presented in a way that emphasises their timing. The initial investment in the CT scanner takes place, by convention, at time 0. Each cash flow for years 1 to 5 can be discounted back to time 0, using individual net present value factors.[4] The discount rate used is 10 per cent per annum. One way to discount the cash flows is to use the present value factors that can be found in Table C at the back of the book. These factors are shown in Exhibit 21.4 for each of the five years. Other methods are to use a software package, such as Microsoft Excel®, or a financial calculator.

The decision under NPV

The net present value analysis indicates that the purchase of the additional scanner (R6 597 150) would yield cost savings or additional revenue (with a present value of R6 936 981), which exceeds the new machine's acquisition cost. The net present value of the cash inflows exceeds the cash outflows by R339 831. Thus, the NPV analysis favours the purchase of the additional machine.

	Yearly cash flows					
	0	1	2	3	4	5
Initial investment	−6 597 150					
Yearly cost savings – additional revenue		1 830 000	1 830 000	1 830 000	1 830 000	1 830 000
	−6 597 150	1 830 000	1 830 000	1 830 000	1 830 000	1 830 000
Present value of R1* at 10%	× 1.0000	0.9091	0.8264	0.7513	0.6830	0.6209
	−6 597 150	1 663 653	1 512 312	1 374 879	1 249 890	1 136 247

Present value of cost savings	R6 936 981
Initial investment	−6 597 150
Net present value at time 0	R339 831

* Discount factors taken from Table C at the back of the book

Exhibit 21.4 The net present value method: Alternative One—additional CT scanner

Internal rate of return method

L.O. 5

An alternative discounted cash flow method for analysing investment proposals is the internal rate of return method. A project's **internal rate of return** (or **time-adjusted rate of return**) is the actual economic return earned by the project over its life. Another way of stating this is that a project's internal rate of return (IRR) is the discount rate at which the present value of expected cash inflows is equal to the present value of cash outflows; thus the IRR is the discount rate that makes the NPV of the cash flows equal to zero.

What is the internal rate of return on the medical centre's proposal to purchase the additional CT scanner? Recall that the project has a positive net present value, given a discount rate of 10 per cent.

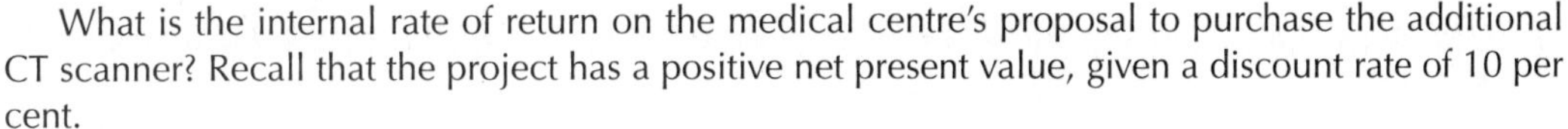

Would you expect the project's IRR to be higher than or lower than 10 per cent? The higher the discount rate used in a net present value analysis, the lower the present value of all future cash flows. This is because a higher discount rate means that it is even more important to have the money earlier rather than later. Thus, in this example, a discount rate higher than 10 per cent would be required to drive the net present value of future cash flows down to zero.

Finding the internal rate of return

The internal rate of return can be calculated by solving for r in the following formula:

$$p = \sum_{t=1}^{n} \frac{C_1}{(1 + r)^n}$$

where p = initial outlay
C_t = net cash flow generated by the project in period t
n = life of the project
r = the internal rate of return

Of course, the easy way to find the exact internal rate of return is to use a financial calculator, or a software program such as Microsoft Excel®. We can also use trial and error methods. By testing a range of discount rates in the above formula, it is possible to determine the exact internal rate of return for a project. This is the rate for which the net present value is zero. This method, however, is particularly difficult where cash flows in each period are different. Exhibit 21.5 shows that when the discount rate is 12 per cent, the NPV for the proposed investment is very close to zero. Thus, the internal rate of return for Alternative One, the purchase of the additional CT scanner, is 12 per cent.[5]

	Yearly cash flows					
	0	1	2	3	4	5
Initial investment	−6 597 150					
Yearly cost savings – additional revenue		1 830 000	1 830 000	1 830 000	1 830 000	1 830 000
	−6 597 150	1 830 000	1 830 000	1 830 000	1 830 000	1 830 000
Present value of R1 at 12% ×	1.0000	0.8929	0.7972	0.7118	0.6355	0.5674
	−6 597 150	1 634 007	1 458 876	1 302 594	1 162 965	1 038 342

Present value of cost savings	R6 596 784
Initial investment	−6 597 150
Net present value at time 0	−R366

Exhibit 21.5 Internal rate of return method: Alternative One—additional scanner

The decision under IRR

Now that we know that the investment proposal's internal rate of return is 12 per cent, how can the Metro Medical Centre use this information in its decision?

An investment proposal is acceptable on financial grounds if its internal rate of return is greater than the required rate of return. The internal rate of return of the proposal, 12 per cent, exceeds the hospital's required rate of return, 10 per cent. Thus, the discounted cash flow analysis supports the purchase of the additional CT scanner. However, we would need to do the same analysis for Alternative Two.

To summarise: with the internal rate of return method of discounted cash flow analysis, the following steps are undertaken:

1 Prepare a table showing the cash flows during each year of the proposed investment. These cash flows are the same as those prepared under the net present value method. (See column 1 of Exhibit 21.3.)

2 Calculate the internal rate of return for the proposed investment. This is accomplished using a financial calculator or a software program. Alternatively, trial and error is used to find the discount rate that yields a zero net present value for the proposed investment.

3 If the internal rate of return is greater than the required rate of return, then the project is acceptable on financial grounds.

Comparing the NPV and IRR methods

L.O. 6

In this case, the NPV and IRR methods both support the purchase of the additional CT scanner. When considering whether to accept or reject a single project, the methods usually will either both support or both not support the proposal.

Advantages of net present value method

The net present value method has many advantages over the internal rate of return method. First, if the investment analysis is calculated manually, it is easier to calculate a project's NPV than its IRR. This advantage is not important, however, when a computer or financial calculator is available.

A second advantage of the NPV method is that the analyst can adjust for risk. For some investment proposals, the further into the future a cash flow occurs, the less certain the analyst may be about the size of the cash flow. Thus, the later a projected cash flow occurs, the riskier it may be. It is possible to adjust a net present value analysis for such risk factors by using a higher discount rate for later cash flows than for earlier cash flows. It is not possible to include such a risk adjustment in the internal rate of return method, because the analysis solves for only a single average discount rate, the project's IRR.

The third advantage is that the NPV always yields one answer. When cash flows change from positive to negative over the life of the project, more than one IRR can be calculated for the one project. This may happen, for example, if there is a negative cash flow in year 3, followed by positive cash flows in years 4 and 5 and a negative cash flow in year 6.

The reinvestment assumption

A final advantage of NPV over IRR concerns the reinvestment assumption implicit in IRR. In the IRR analysis, cash flows available during the life of the project are assumed to be reinvested at the same rate as the project's internal rate of return. This assumption may be unrealistic if the internal rate of return of the project is much higher than the firm's required rate of return. NPV makes the more realistic assumption that cash flows are reinvested at the firm's required rate of return.

A further disadvantage of IRR compared with NPV relates to the ranking of projects. The use of IRR can lead to sub-optimal decisions compared with decisions made using the NPV method. This issue is discussed in a later section of this chapter.

In general, the NPV technique is usually regarded as superior to the IRR technique when evaluating capital investment proposals.[6]

Assumptions underlying discounted cash flow analysis

L.O. 7

Like any decision model, discounted cash flow methods are based on assumptions. In addition to the reinvestment assumption discussed above, discounted cash flow methods are based on two important assumptions:

1. *The year-end timing of cash flows.* In the present value calculations used in the NPV and IRR methods, all cash flows are treated as though they will occur at year-end. However, if the Medical Centre were to purchase the additional CT scanner, the R1 830 000 in annual cost savings and additional revenue would occur at different points throughout each year. The additional computational complexity that would be required to reflect the exact timing of all cash flows would complicate an investment analysis considerably. The error introduced by the year-end cash flow assumption is generally considered not large enough to cause concern.
2. *The certainty of cash flows.* Discounted cash flow analyses treat the cash flows associated with an investment project as though they are known with certainty. Although methods of capital budgeting under uncertainty have been developed using probability distributions for cash flows, they are not widely used in practice. Many managers do not believe that the additional benefits of more accurate financial information are worth the additional complexity. As mentioned above, however, risk adjustments can be made to the discount rate in an NPV analysis to account partially for the uncertainty of the cash flows.

In practice, these assumptions are rarely satisfied. Nevertheless, discounted cash flow models provide an effective and widely used method of investment analysis. The improved decision making that could result from using more complex models may not be worth the additional cost of information and analysis.

Determining the required rate of return

The required rate of return used to discount the cash flows in an NPV analysis, or as the hurdle rate with the IRR method, is usually based on the organisation's weighted average cost of capital. The **cost of capital** is the minimum return needed to compensate suppliers of capital for committing resources to a project.[7] A new project should increase the wealth of shareholders by generating cash flows that exceed the costs of acquiring the funds that are going to be used in the project.

The cost of capital is based on the costs of all sources of a firm's funds. How do organisations generate funds? Governments and government business enterprises often acquire funds through special bond issues, or by borrowing from financial institutions. Profit-oriented enterprises generate funds by issuing shares, or through borrowings. Therefore, as described in Chapter 13, the cost of capital will be a weighted average of the cost of funds from each of these sources.

To evaluate projects, the required rate of return is based on the firm's weighted average cost of capital, which may be adjusted for the risk associated with the particular project.

A rate of 10 per cent was used to discount the yearly cash flows for the CT scanner project. This rate was chosen because it was the average cost that the Medical Centre pays to acquire its funds.

Least-cost decisions

L.O. 8 In some situations a capital expenditure decision may be approved by management even though the proposal has a negative NPV, or a lower than acceptable IRR. For example, a new computer system may be a necessity for the Medical Centre in order to provide the level of service required by customers and to serve management information needs. However, it may be very difficult to quantify the additional cash inflows that will result from this acquisition, and the main arguments for the acquisition will be qualitative in nature. Here we may still complete a discounted cash flow analysis, but the objective will be to select the course of action that has the lowest cost. This is called the **least-cost decision**: rather than maximising the NPV of cash inflows minus cash outflows, the objective is to minimise the NPV of the costs to be incurred.

Other examples where a least-cost decision may be taken include the purchase of safety equipment, or expenditure on equipment that is needed to satisfy environmental standards, such as emission control or waste disposal.

Depreciable assets

L.O. 9 When a long-term asset is purchased, its acquisition cost is charged against profit over several time periods through depreciation. However, we did not include any depreciation charges in our discounted cash flow analysis. Both the NPV and IRR methods focus on cash flows and periodic depreciation charges are not cash flows. Suppose that the Medical Centre depreciates assets using the straight-line method, and the useful life of a CT scanner is five years. If the Medical Centre purchased the additional CT scanner for R6 597 150, then the depreciation charges would be recorded as shown in Exhibit 21.6.

However, the only cash flow in Exhibit 21.6 is the R6 597 150 cash outflow incurred to acquire the new machine. The R1 319 430 annual depreciation charges are not cash flows. Thus, we record the acquisition cost as a cash flow in our investment analysis, but we do not record the annual depreciation charges—they are not relevant to our discounted cash flow analysis.

Depreciation charges in a taxable business

Suppose that our capital expenditure decision had focused on a business that was liable for income taxes, instead of the Medical Centre.[8] For example, the retailer Woolworths might consider the purchase of a new computer system. This would not change our treatment of the annual depreciation charges in cash flow analysis—depreciation charges are still not cash flows. However, depreciation is a tax deduction. Tax payments themselves are cash flows, and the reduction in tax due to depreciation should be included in the cash flow analysis. The next chapter will consider the tax implications of depreciable assets in capital expenditure analyses.

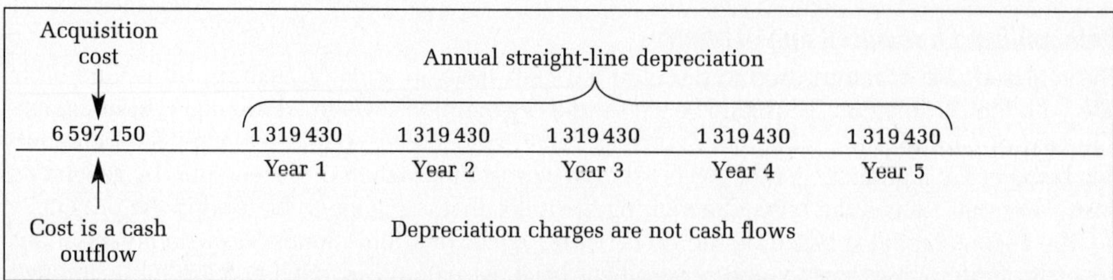

Exhibit 21.6 Additional CT scanner: cash flows versus depreciation charges

Comparing two alternative investment projects

L.O. 10

We saw that there were two possible solutions to the problems in the CT Scanning Department of the Medical Centre. The first alternative was to purchase an additional CT scanner. There were strong arguments in favour of this alternative, and it was also supported by the discounted cash flow analyses, which yielded a positive NPV and an IRR of 12 per cent (greater than the Medical Centre's required rate of return). The second alternative was to replace the old CT scanner.

The cash flows relating to both alternatives were presented in Exhibit 21.3. We will now consider a comparison of both alternatives using discounted cash flow techniques. Exhibit 21.7 displays a net present value analysis of the two alternatives. The net present value of purchasing an additional CT scanner is compared with that of replacing the old machine. While the NPV of both alternatives is positive, Alternative One yields an NPV that is R315 495 greater than Alternative Two.

		Yearly cash flows					
		0	1	2	3	4	5
Alternative One: Additional CT scanner							
Acquisition cost		−5 850 000					
Installation cost		−747 150					
Incremental operating costs			−1 070 000	−1 070 000	−1 070 000	−1 070 000	−1 070 000
Incremental revenue			900 000	900 000	900 000	900 000	900 000
Savings due to reduced stay by inpatients			2 000 000	2 000 000	2 000 000	2 000 000	2 000 000
Total cash flows		−6 597 150	1 830 000	1 830 000	1 830 000	1 830 000	1 830 000
Discount factor (see Table C)	10%	1.0000	0.9091	0.8264	0.7513	0.6830	0.6209
Present value of cash flows		−6 597 150	1 663 653	1 512 312	1 374 879	1 249 890	1 136 247
Net present value of cash flows					R339 831		
Alternative Two: Replace CT scanner							
Acquisition cost		−6 760 000					
Proceeds from sale		1 500 000					
Incremental operating savings			630 000	630 000	630 000	630 000	630 000
Savings due to reduced stay by inpatients			800 000	800 000	800 000	800 000	800 000
Training costs			−150 000				
Total cash flows		−5 260 000	1 280 000	1 430 000	1 430 000	1 430 000	1 430 000
Discount factor (see Table C)	10%	1.0000	0.9091	0.8264	0.7513	0.6830	0.6209
Present value of cash flows		−5 260 000	1 163 648	1 181 752	1 074 359	976 690	887 887
Net present value of cash flows					R24 336		
Difference in net present value					R315 495		

Exhibit 21.7 CT scanner—net present value analysis

IRR for the two alternatives

We have already calculated the IRR of Alternative One as 12 per cent. Given the low positive NPV of Alternative Two (R24 336 in Exhibit 21.7), we can predict that its IRR will be close to 10 per cent. The exact IRR can be calculated by trial and error, or by using a financial calculator. The IRR for Alternative Two is 10.18 per cent. This can be checked by estimating the net present value of the cash flows with this discount rate and finding that it is equal to zero (or almost zero due to rounding).

Completing the analysis for the CT scanner

We now have the financial information that the project director needs for her report. The discounted cash flow analyses support the purchase of the additional scanner, while the replacement alternative was very close to the required rate of return:

	Alternative One	Alternative Two
NPV (at 10%)	339 831	24 336
IRR	12.00%	10.18%

In this case both the NPV and the IRR analyses lead to the same conclusion: that Alternative One is superior to Alternative Two.

For any two projects, the NPV and IRR analyses will usually give the same ranking, though this is not always the case. If the NPV analysis and the IRR analysis provide different rankings, and if only one of the projects can be undertaken, then the project with the highest NPV should be undertaken. Due to the assumption that cash flows can be reinvested at the IRR, the IRR technique can sometimes rank projects incorrectly. However, the NPV technique will always result in projects being correctly ranked.

We saw earlier that the project director at the Medical Centre presented strong qualitative arguments in favour of acquiring the additional CT scanner, while the arguments for the replacement decision were not as strong. The financial analysis also supports the first alternative.

What would happen if the second alternative had a higher NPV than the first alternative? What if the first alternative had a negative NPV? Given the strong advantages of having an additional machine, the qualitative arguments may carry greater weight than do the financial considerations.

The project director concluded that the best alternative was to purchase an additional machine. Her completed report was sent to the board of the Medical Centre to allow it to consider her recommendations and how the machine would be funded. In her report the project director considered both financial and qualitative information when making her recommendation. This is often the way capital expenditure decisions take place in businesses. While an accurate analysis of the financial implications of proposals is vital for the decision, the proposals must be strongly supported on a variety of other grounds, including strategic or competitive concerns. The importance of considering these other concerns, as well as the timing of capital expenditure, is illustrated in the 'Real life' below.

REAL LIFE: MAKING THE RIGHT INVESTMENTS AT THE RIGHT TIME

Capital investment is essential for providing the basis for maintaining long-term competitiveness and profitability. However, the timing and the quality of the investment must be considered. Capital investment can be misdirected.

The airline industry is highly competitive and operates with tight margins. Airline companies compete by offering the latest planes and technologies, excellent safety records, and high-quality, innovative in-flight service. The capital investment required to achieve these outcomes must be an integral part of the strategic planning process. Many former airline companies have learnt the lesson that cutting back on fleet investment and airline maintenance can lead to disastrous outcomes. The increase in fuel costs has resulted in the airlines with older planes incurring higher operating costs due to lower levels of fuel efficiency. The investment in newer planes with lower operating costs and higher levels of fuel efficiency has become a primary concern for airlines operating in a highly competitive sector. In other sectors, the timeline required to increase capacity may be years and a current shortage due to a strong economy may result in additional capacity coming on stream at the time when the economy is slowing down. This has happened in the steel sector and in the cement sector although having all that additional capacity helps when the next boom comes around.

Other techniques for analysing capital expenditure proposals

The strength of the discounted cash flow methods that we have used so far lies in the fact that they take account of the time value of money. However, in spite of the conceptual superiority of discounted cash flow decision models, managers sometimes use other techniques for analysing the cash flows of an investment decision. Such techniques include the payback method and the accounting rate of return method. Sometimes, these alternative techniques are used alongside a discounted cash flow analysis, and sometimes they are used alone. There are many reasons for a business to choose these other techniques. Let's reconsider the cash flows relating to the two proposals for the CT Scanning Department at a Medical Centre.

L.O. 11

Payback method

The **payback period** of a capital investment proposal is the amount of time it will take for the cash inflows from the project to accumulate to an amount that covers the original investment.[9] The following formula defines an investment project's payback period.

$$\text{Payback period} = \frac{\text{initial investment}}{\text{annual cash flow}}$$

There is no adjustment in the payback method for the time value of money. A cash inflow in year 5 is treated in the same way as a cash inflow in year 1.

The calculation of the payback period for the purchase of the additional CT scanner is now shown:

$$\begin{aligned}\text{Payback period} &= \frac{\text{initial investment}}{\text{annual cash flow}}\\ &= \frac{6\,597\,150}{1\,830\,000}\\ &= 3.61 \text{ years}\end{aligned}$$

Thus, the first alternative—to purchase an additional CT scanner—will 'pay back' its initial investment in its fourth year.

Payback period with uneven cash flows

The simple payback formula will not work if a project has an uneven pattern of cash flows. Instead, the cash flows must be accumulated on a year-to-year basis until the accumulation equals the initial investment. The payback period for Alternative Two, which has uneven cash flows in this way, is calculated in Exhibit 21.8.

According to the payback method, Alternative Two is as desirable as Alternative One. Both alternatives pay back their initial investments during year 4. However, this method ignores cash flows that occur after year 4 and fails to consider the time value of money. These two limitations are discussed next.

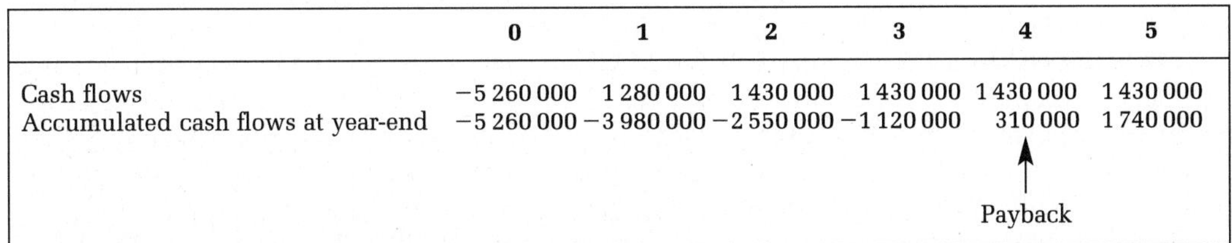

	0	1	2	3	4	5
Cash flows	−5 260 000	1 280 000	1 430 000	1 430 000	1 430 000	1 430 000
Accumulated cash flows at year-end	−5 260 000	−3 980 000	−2 550 000	−1 120 000	310 000	1 740 000
					↑ Payback	

Exhibit 21.8 Payback period with uneven cash flows: Alternative Two—replace the CT scanner

Payback: the pros and cons

The payback method of evaluating capital investment proposals has two serious drawbacks:

1. It ignores the time value of money. The payback method assumes that cash flows received in the future are as valuable as cash flows received in the current period. This ignores the fact that we need to discount future cash flows to make them equivalent to current cash flows, because current cash flows can be invested to earn a return in the future. However, while the payback method fails to consider the time value of money, there is no reason why discounted cash flows could not be incorporated into the analysis.
2. It ignores cash flows beyond the payback period. Only the cash flows up to the end of the payback period are considered relevant in this analysis, and so the payback method provides an incomplete picture of the financial impact of a capital investment proposal. All cash flows occurring after the payback period are ignored.

Despite these shortcomings, the payback method is widely used in practice, for several reasons:

- *Simplicity.* The payback period is easy to calculate and understand compared with discounted cash flow methods.
- *Screening investment projects.* The payback method provides a tool for roughly screening investment proposals. If a project does not meet some minimum criterion for the payback period, management may wish to reject the proposal, despite potential large cash flows predicted well into the future.
- *Cash shortages.* When a firm is experiencing a shortage of cash, it may be crucial to select investment projects that recoup their initial investment quickly. A cash-poor firm may not be able to wait for the big payoff of a project that has a long payback period but a favourable NPV. Even in these cases, it is wise not to rely on the payback method alone; it should be used in conjunction with a discounted cash flow analysis.
- *Risk of a project.* The payback technique provides some insight into the risks of a project. The earlier cash flows are considered more certain than those received in later years. The further into the future the cash flows are expected to occur, the greater is the level of uncertainty.

Accounting rate of return method

L.O. 12

The **accounting rate of return** method focuses on the incremental accounting profit which results from a project. Accounting profit is based on accrual accounting procedures. Thus, revenue is recognised during the period of sale, not necessarily when the cash is received; expenses are recognised during the period in which they are incurred, not necessarily when they are paid in cash. The following formula is used to calculate the accounting rate of return on an investment project:

$$\text{Accounting rate of return} = \frac{\text{average annual profit from the project}}{\text{initial investment}}$$

Note that the formula for accounting rate of return is similar to that for return on investment (ROI), which was introduced as a performance measure in Chapter 13. The accounting rate of return is effectively an average annual ROI for an individual project.

Let's consider Alternative One in the Metro Medical Centre example—purchasing an additional CT scanner. To apply the accounting rate of return method, the cash flows shown in Exhibit 21.3 need to be re-analysed in terms of revenues and costs. (In this example, we will assume that the cash inflows shown in Exhibit 21.3 are recognised as revenues or cost savings in that year. In addition, the yearly cash outflows are recognised as expenses in the same year.)

The incremental revenues from the project are estimated at R900 000 per annum. The incremental costs are negative, as they consist of net cost savings of R930 000. This is made up of cost savings of R2 000 000 plus additional operating costs of R1 070 000. Like most businesses, MMC depreciates its non-current assets. Assuming the CT scanner has a useful life of five years, and the straight-line depreciation method is used, the yearly depreciation charge will be calculated as follows:

$$\text{Yearly depreciation} = \frac{\text{investment}}{\text{useful life}}$$

$$= \frac{\text{R6 597 150}}{5}$$

$$= \text{R1 319 430 per year}$$

The accounting rate of return on the purchase of the additional CT scanner is as follows:

Total cash flows	R1 830 000
Depreciation	− R1 319 430
Net income	R510 570

Accounting rate of return = R510 570 / R6 597 150 = 7.74% (rounded)

Note that the project's accounting rate of return, at 7.74 per cent, is much lower than its IRR of 12 per cent.

Use of the average investment

Some managers prefer to calculate the accounting rate of return using the average amount invested in a project for the denominator, rather than the project's full cost. The formula is modified as follows:

$$\text{Accounting rate of return} = \frac{\text{average annual profit from the project}}{\text{average investment}}$$

A project's average investment is the average accounting book value over the project's life. The average book value of the CT scanner is calculated as follows:

$$\text{Average investment} = \frac{(\text{initial investment} + \text{salvage value})}{2}$$

$$= \frac{(\text{R6 597 150} + 0)}{2}$$

$$= \text{R3 298 575}$$

Thus, the accounting rate of return using average investment is 15.48 per cent, that is:

R510 570 / R3 298 575 = 15.48%

Note that this version of the accounting rate of return yields a significantly higher return than the project's internal rate of return, which was calculated as 12 per cent. Generally, the following relationships will be observed:

Accounting rate of return < internal rate of return < accounting rate of return
(using initial investment) (using average investment)

Accounting rate of return: pros and cons

The advantages of the accounting rate of return method, compared with other techniques, are as follows:

1 *Screening investment projects.* Like the payback method, the accounting rate of return method is a simple way of screening investment proposals.

2 *Consistency with financial accounting methods.* Some managers use this method because it parallels financial accounting statements, which are also based on accrual accounting.

3 *Consistency with profit-based performance evaluation systems.* Unlike discounted cash flow methods, there is consistency between the accounting rate of return method and accounting-based performance measures, such as return on investment. This issue is discussed later in the chapter.

4 *Consideration of the entire life of the project.* Unlike the payback method, the accounting rate of return method considers the entire life of the project.

The disadvantage of the accounting rate of return method is that, like the payback method, it does not consider the time value of money.

Many different terms for the accounting rate of return are used in practice, including simple rate of return, rate of return on assets, unadjusted rate of return or return on investment (ROI).

The accountant's role In capital expenditure analysis

To use discounted cash flow analysis in decisions about investment projects, managers need accurate cash flow projections. This is where the management accountant can play a role. The accountant is often asked to predict cash flows related to operating cost savings, additional working capital requirements, or incremental costs and revenues. Such predictions are difficult to make in a world of uncertainty. We often draw upon historical accounting data to help in making cost predictions. Knowledge of market conditions, economic trends and the likely reactions of competitors can also be important in projecting cash flows.

Two techniques are used in practice to analyse investment proposals where the cash flow projections are very uncertain:

1 The required rate of return may be increased. The greater the uncertainty about a project's cash flows, the higher the required rate of return. Using the IRR method, businesses may increase the required rate of return above the firm's cost of capital for projects with uncertain cash flows. With the NPV method, the discount rate applied to uncertain cash flows can be increased.

2 The analyst may use sensitivity analysis.

Sensitivity analysis

In Chapter 18 we described how sensitivity analysis can be used to assess the sensitivity of cost volume profit analysis to uncertain variables. Sensitivity analysis can also be used in capital expenditure analysis to determine how much cash flow estimates would have to change in order for a decision not to be supported. To illustrate, let's return to the Medical Centre's decision about the CT scanner. The relevant data for Alternative One were as follows:

Type of cash flow	Cash flow	Discount factor	Present value
Acquisition cost	−6 597 150	1.0000	−6 597 150
Projected annual cost savings			
(5 year annuity @ 10%)	1 830 000	3.7908	6 937 164
Net present value[4]			340 014

Suppose the project director is uncertain about the amount of the annual cost savings. How low could the annual cost savings be before the decision would result in a negative NPV? An equivalent question is: What is the amount of annual cost savings that would result in a zero NPV in this decision? When there is a zero NPV, then the present value of annual cost savings is equal to the acquisition cost:

$$\text{Acquisition cost} = \text{PV of annual cost savings}$$
$$= \text{annual cost savings} \times \text{annuity discount factor}$$

Therefore:

$$\text{Annual cost savings} = \text{acquisition cost / annuity discount factor}$$
$$= \text{R6 597 150/3.7908*}$$
$$= \text{R1 740 305}$$

* Annuity discount factor for n = 5 and r = 10%, from Table D

If the annual cost savings were R1 740 305, the NPV of Alternative One would be zero [R6 597 150 − (R1 740 305 × 3.7908) = 0]. Thus, the originally projected annual cost savings of R1 830 000 could fall as low as R1 740 305 for the project to remain acceptable on financial grounds.

Post-completion audits of capital expenditure decisions

L.O. 13

The desirability of a capital expenditure project depends heavily on the accuracy of cash flow projections. If they are highly inaccurate, they may lead to acceptance of undesirable projects or rejection of projects that would have had positive returns. Because of the importance of the capital budgeting process, some organisations systematically follow up on projects to see how they turn out. This procedure, where the actual cash flows associated with a project are compared with the cash flows projected in the capital budget proposal, is called a **post-completion audit (PCA)** or a **post-audit**.

If the project has not lived up to expectations, an investigation may be warranted to learn what went astray. The PCA is used to provide feedback on the accuracy of initial estimates for the project and thus improve managerial learning. Sometimes a PCA will reveal shortcomings in the cash flow projection process. In such cases, action may be taken to improve future cash flow predictions. While two types of errors can occur in capital expenditure decisions—undesirable projects may be accepted and desirable projects rejected—the PCA can examine only those projects that were accepted. It cannot evaluate the quality of projections for projects that were rejected.

As in any performance evaluation process, a PCA should not be used punitively. The focus of a post-audit should be to provide information to the capital budgeting staff, the project manager and the management team. A PCA is intended to facilitate learning and to improve the practice of cash flow predictions and capital budgeting decisions.

Controlling capital investment projects

Many investment projects require a long time to complete, such as building a new power plant or developing an oilfield. The benefits from the completed project are realised over an even longer timeframe. To help control capital expenditure projects, managers can rely on the many concepts and tools that are studied in the other chapters in this book. Budgets can be compared with actual results, variances can be calculated, and periodic performance reports can be prepared.[10] The control process is more difficult for capital expenditure projects. Accounting systems are often not designed to keep track of individual capital projects. Also, because each project is unique, there may be no past performance to guide the accountant, and it may be difficult to determine whether the actual results are out of line or whether the projections were faulty. Nevertheless, periodic project performance reports can direct management's attention to where it is needed most.

Performance evaluation: a behavioural issue

L.O. 14

Take another look at Exhibit 21.1, which depicts an organisation as a collection of investment projects. As the diagram indicates, the organisation's performance in a particular time period comprises the combined results of the performance of the projects operating during that period. In practice, there is a potential conflict between the criteria for evaluating individual projects and those used to evaluate the overall performance of managers and business segments. This conflict is best understood through an example. Suppose the chairman of the Medicine Division at the Medical Centre is considering the purchase of a new cardiology machine. Over its five-year life it is expected to generate considerable increases in revenue for the Medical Centre. The new system's acquisition cost, projected revenues and costs, and net present value (using a discount rate of 10 per cent), are shown in Exhibit 21.9.

Cost	Cost savings				
0	1	2	3	4	5
−8 000 000	1 400 000	1 500 000	2 600 000	2 800 000	3 000 000
1.0000	0.9091	0.8264	0.7513	0.6830	0.6209
−8 000 000	1 272 740	1 239 600	1 953 380	1 912 400	1 862 700
Net present value	R240 820				

Exhibit 21.9 Net present value of new cardiology machine

Although the new system has a positive NPV, the revenues for the earlier years are quite low. This is because there will be considerable excess capacity in the first two years, which will not be filled until the later years. Why might this create a problem? Like many businesses, the Medical Centre uses divisional profits to evaluate the performance of the chairman of the Medicine Division. Suppose the new machine is depreciated using the straight-line method over its five-year life. The new project's incremental revenue and cost, net of the annual depreciation charge, are as follows:

Cost savings	R1 400 000	R1 500 000	R2 600 000	R2 800 000	R3 000 000
Less Depreciation	1 600 000	1 600 000	1 600 000	1 600 000	1 600 000
Incremental profits	−R200 000	−R100 000	R1 000 000	R1 200 000	R1 400 000

The depreciation charges are not cash flows, and so these costs were not included in the net present value analysis. Nevertheless, annual depreciation charges are subtracted under accrual accounting procedures to determine periodic profit. Thus, a conflict can exist between discounted cash flow methods and accrual accounting performance evaluation methods. This problem is less likely to occur when the accounting rate of return method (return on investment) is used to evaluate capital expenditure proposals. However, it should be noted that when divisions and managers are evaluated using return on investment, this is usually undertaken on a year-to-year basis, whereas if the accounting rate of return is used as a method to evaluate a project, it is calculated as an average annual return over the life of the project. So, while the accounting rate of return method may be acceptable for a project, a predicted low ROI in initial years may provide a disincentive for managers to invest in a project.

Similarly, a manager may reject a project that has a positive NPV and is acceptable to the organisation as a whole. This is because it will reduce divisional profits in its early years and imply that the manager is not performing well. Of course, in the longer term, the project will result in higher profits for the division, but this is some years into the future. The current manager may not even be the head of the division by that time. (This issue was also explored in Chapters 13 and 14 of this book.)

A potential solution to the behavioural problem described above is to de-emphasise the use of profit-based performance measures. When decision makers are asked to use a discounted cash flow approach in choosing investment projects, their performance evaluation can be based on post-audits of those projects. However, performance measures based on accrual accounting are well entrenched in practice. Perhaps the most practical solution to the problem is to enlighten managers about the conflict between accrual accounting and discounted cash flow analysis. If performance is evaluated using both accrual accounting methods and post-audits of particular investment projects, the conflict may be overcome. Or perhaps there are other solutions? The 'Real life' below examines this issue in greater detail.

REAL LIFE: CAPITAL INVESTMENT AND CEO INCENTIVES

Large capital expenditure in new plant, equipment or systems can yield significant competitive advantages, but often the outcomes will not be achieved for some years. For example, capital projects in the mining industry may cost in excess of R500 million, but may take many years to complete. Therefore, it is a courageous chief executive who invests millions to improve the value of the business in the long term, in an environment dominated by shareholder pressures for short-term returns. Performance-linked remuneration packages are often linked to achieving today's profits or share price growth, which may also be a disincentive to engage in long-term investments that may only yield returns after the term of the CEO has expired.

So how can a CEO 'sell' this long-term view to shareholders, fund managers and other stakeholders?

- Organisations must integrate capital expenditure plans within their corporate and business strategies. In this way, the magnitude of capital expenditure investments and the timing and size of expected returns are 'approved' by investors in advance.
- Senior managers must communicate their strategies to investors. Senior executives should continually talk to fund managers, who are major investors, about how capital expenditure plans fit into their overall strategies. Many companies include extensive information on their websites detailing capital expenditure projects and the expected long-term gains.
- Businesses should tie bonuses to the achievement of shareholder value measures, as part of executive remuneration. Companies may use shareholder value creation as a performance criterion. This provides an incentive for managers to focus on both the short and long term when making decisions.

Sources: McCallum (2001); Stern Stewart (2001)

REAL LIFE: CAPITAL INVESTMENT METHODS IN USE

Which capital budgeting methods are firms using in practice? Du Toit and Pienaar (2005) found that 71.9 per cent of firms used the IRR method and 71.9 per cent of firms also used the NPV method to evaluate capital projects. Only 40.6 per cent of the firms in this survey used the payback method. However, another 23.4 per cent of firms used present value payback, which represents how long it takes for discounted cash flows to cover cost. Accounting rate of return was used by 35.9 per cent of the firms and 10.9 per cent of firms used a profitability index, which is the present value of future cash flows divided by cost. The IRR method was the most important primary method used in practice. It was found that 37.1 per cent of the firms used IRR as the primary method to evaluate projects whilst 27.4 per cent of the firms used the NPV method as the primary method to evaluate projects. Only a few firms used payback or the accounting rate of return as the primary method to evaluate projects. The primary capital budgeting methods used in South Africa as indicated by Du Toit and Pienaar are set out in the following table:

Primary capital budgeting method used to evaluate projects	%
Internal rate of return	37.10%
Net present value	27.40%
Profitability index	0.00%
Accounting payback	8.10%
Present value payback	8.10%
Accounting return on investment	11.30%
Adjusted internal rate of return	0.00%
Other methods	8.00%
Total	100.00%

Gilbert (2003) found in a survey of manufacturing firms that the following methods were used in practice:

Payback	85%	Net Present Value (NPV)	74%
ROI	77%	Internal rate of return (IRR)	67%
Accounting rate of return	23%		

Cramer and Correia (2007) found that 82.1% of Chief Financial Officers (CFOs) always or almost always use the NPV method whilst 78.6% of CFOs always or almost always use IRR. Only 53.6% of CFOs always or almost always use the payback period method to evaluate projects.

It is interesting to compare the methods used in South Africa to those used in the USA. A survey by Ryan (2002) found that USA companies used the following methods to evaluate investment projects.

	Always or often used (> = 75%)
Net Present Value (NPV)	85%
Internal rate of return (IRR)	77%
Payback	53%
Discounted Payback	38%
Profitability Index	21%
Accounting rate of return	15%
Modified internal rate of return (MIRR)	9%
Economic Value Added (EVA)	31%

A higher proportion of US firms use NPV and a high proportion of US firms use Economic Value Added (EVA) to evaluate projects.

Increasingly, firms are using discounted cash flow (DCF) methods such as NPV and IRR to evaluate projects, rather than the accounting rate of return method. Although firms use payback, generally this is used for small projects and firms will often use this measure as a supplementary indicator of measuring the risk of projects.

Summary

This chapter presented the basic techniques for analysing future cash flows for capital expenditure decisions. Key points include:

- Capital expenditure decisions involve analysing cash flows over several future periods of time. Such decisions focus on specific projects or programs, and are often undertaken to change or enhance the competitiveness of the business.
- The capital expenditure approval process typically consists of the following steps:
  - *Project generation.* Projects are generated by managers of business units and should be consistent with corporate guidelines and strategic plans.
  - *Estimation and analysis of projected cash flows.* Cash flows are estimated over the life of the project and analysed using a variety of techniques.
  - *Progress to approval.* In the light of scarce resources, managers need to make a strong case to support the approval of their project to senior management.
  - *Analysis and selection of projects.* Senior management approve some projects and reject others.
  - *Implementation of projects.* This may include the construction or purchase of a new asset, employment of new staff and staff training.
  - *Post-completion audit of projects.* This may occur at least a year after the project commences, to assess actual cash flows and outcomes against plan.
- Since capital budgeting decisions involve cash flows over several time periods, the cash flows should be discounted to recognise the time value of money. There are two discounted cash flow (DCF) methods: the net present value method and the internal rate of return method.
  - Under the net present value (NPV) method, an investment proposal may be accepted if its net present value is zero or positive. A project's NPV is the present value of the project's future cash flows less its initial acquisition cost. In calculating the NPV of the cash flows, the discount rate is based on the organisation's cost of capital.
  - Under the internal rate of return (IRR) method, an investment proposal is acceptable if its IRR equals or exceeds the organisation's required rate of return. A project's IRR is the discount rate required to make the project's net present value equal to zero.
  - Both the NPV and the IRR methods are based on assumptions: the year-end timing of cash flows, the certainty of cash flows, and assumptions about the reinvestment of cash flows. The NPV method is somewhat easier to apply. It also has the advantage of allowing the decision maker to increase the discount rate for highly uncertain cash flows. Sensitivity analysis is another technique for dealing with uncertainty in capital budgeting decisions.
- Besides DCF analysis, some organisations use the payback method and the accounting rate of return method to analyse capital budgeting decisions. Since these methods do not account for the time value of money, they are conceptually inferior to DCF methods.
- Because of the importance of capital expenditure decisions, in many large businesses there are routine systems for requesting capital expenditure and for monitoring and controlling that expenditure. These include the use of budgets to monitor spending on individual projects, and the use of post-completion audits.
- A potential conflict can arise when DCF techniques are used for evaluating capital expenditure proposals and yearly accrual accounting data is used to evaluate managers' performance. This may lead to managers making decisions that enhance their yearly performance measures, but do not maximise the long-term performance of the firm.

In the following chapter we will extend the discussion of capital expenditure techniques to encompass more complex situations, and to include the impact of income taxation. We will also consider the appropriateness of capital expenditure techniques to justify investments in advanced technology.

References

Correia, C, Flynn, D, Uliana, E & Wormald, M 2007, *Financial Management*, Juta & Co., 6th edn, Chapters 8 and 9. Also see Chapter 2 for time value of money.

Cramer, P & Correia, C 2007, 'Cost of capital, capital structure and capital budgeting: A survey of South African listed companies', presented at the South African Accounting Association Regional Conference, in Cape Town, 8 November 2007, at the Cape Peninsula University of Technology.

Du Toit, MJ and Pienaar, A 2005, 'A review of the capital budgeting behaviour of large South African firms', *Meditari Accounting Research*, Vol.13, No.1.

Emmanuel, C, Otley, DT & Merchant, KJ 1990, *Accounting for Management Control*, 2nd edn, Chapman and Hall, London.

Gilbert, E 2003, 'Do managers of South African manufacturing firms make optimal capital investment decisions?', *South African Journal of Business Management*, 34(2).

McCallum, J 2001, 'Tough at the Top', *Business Review Weekly*, 22 June, pp. 54–9.

Ryan, PA 2002, 'Capital budgeting practices of the Fortune 1000: how have things changed?', *Journal of Business and Management*, Vol. 8, No. 4, Winter.

Stern Stewart, 2001, 'James Hardie Industries Limited', Stern Stewart & Co., www.sternstewart.com/action/hardie.shtml, 10 October.

Self study

Self-study problem: capital expenditure analysis

Moroka Mines is considering replacing its excavation equipment. The new equipment will cost R5.2 million to purchase and a further R1.3 million to install. It is estimated that the new machine will generate annual cost savings of R1.9 million over the next six years, and annual maintenance costs of R400 000 will be incurred.

At the end of four years, the machine will be overhauled at a cost of R900 000, and at the end of six years it will be sold for R2 million.

If the new equipment is purchased, the old equipment would be sold immediately for R324 000. The company has a required rate of return of 12 per cent.

Required:

1 Calculate the net present value of the new machine.

2 Determine the internal rate of return.

3 Calculate the payback of the new equipment.

Solution to Self-study problem

1 Calculation of net present value:

	Yearly cash flows						
	0	1	2	3	4	5	6
Cost of equipment	−5 200 000						
Installation	−1 300 000						
Sale of old equipment	324 000						
Overhaul					−900 000		
Annual cost savings		1 900 000	1 900 000	1 900 000	1 900 000	1 900 000	1 900 000
Maintenance		−400 000	−400 000	−400 000	−400 000	−400 000	−400 000
Sale of equipment							2 000 000
	−6 176 000	1 500 000	1 500 000	1 500 000	600 000	1 500 000	3 500 000
Present value of R1 at 12%	× 1.0000	0.8929	0.7972	0.7118	0.6355	0.5674	0.5066
	−6 176 000	1 339 350	1 195 800	1 067 700	381 300	851 100	1 773 100
	Net present value at time 0			R432 350			

2 Internal rate of return:

Using a financial calculator, you can determine that the IRR = 14.19 per cent. This is the internal rate of return that would make the net present value of cash flows equal to zero.

Proof:

	Yearly cash flows						
	0	1	2	3	4	5	6
Cost of equipment	−5 200 000						
Installation	−1 300 000						
Sale of old equipment	324 000						
Overhaul					−900 000		
Annual cost savings		1 900 000	1 900 000	1 900 000	1 900 000	1 900 000	1 900 000
Maintenance		−400 000	−400 000	−400 000	−400 000	−400 000	−400 000
Sale of equipment							2 000 000
	−6 176 000	1 500 000	1 500 000	1 500 000	600 000	1 500 000	3 500 000
Present value of R1# at 14.19%	× 1.0000	0.8757	0.7669	0.6716	0.5881	0.5151	0.4511
	−6 176 000	1 313 550	1 150 350	1 007 400	352 860	772 650	1 578 850
	Net present value at time 0			−R 340*			

* Note that the NPV is not exactly zero as we have rounded our IRR to 14.19%. The actual IRR is 14.18764194%

We do not have Tables with 14.19%, and so we have used the formula, $1/(1 + r)^n$ to determine each year's PV factor. For example, the PV factor for year 2 is $1/(1 + 0.1419)^2 = 0.7669$.

3 The payback period:

The payback period formula cannot be used here, as the yearly cash flows are unequal. Using the table in part 1, the yearly cash flows (without taking into account the time value of money) can be added to determine that payback occurs within year 5.

	Yearly cash flows						
	0	1	2	3	4	5	6
Total cash flows	−6 176 000	1 500 000	1 500 000	1 500 000	600 000	1 500 000	3 500 000
Cumulative cash flows	−6 176 000	−4 676 000	−3 176 000	−1 676 000	−1 076 000	424 000	3 924 000
						↑ Payback	

The cumulative cash flows at the end of year 4 = (R1 076 000)

The cumulative cash flows at the end of year 5 = R424 000

Cybersearch

1 In a 'Real life' in this chapter, the potential conflict between capital expenditure and executive remuneration was discussed. Find websites of organisations that have introduced longer-term performance measures to encourage managers to take a longer-term view of expenditures. Explain whether you think this will help to minimise or eliminate the conflict.

2 Find websites of public sector entities that describe the techniques they use to evaluate capital expenditure. Are these methods consistent with those discussed in this chapter?

Appendix to Chapter 21

Part 1: Calculating future values and present values

L.O. 15 Part 1 of this appendix presents in greater detail the concepts of compound interest, present value and future value. An understanding of these concepts is necessary to use discounted cash flow techniques in the analysis of cash flows of capital expenditure decisions.

Compound interest and future values

Suppose you invest R100 today (time 0) at 10 per cent interest for one year. How much will you have after one year? The answer is R110, as Exhibit 21.10 shows.

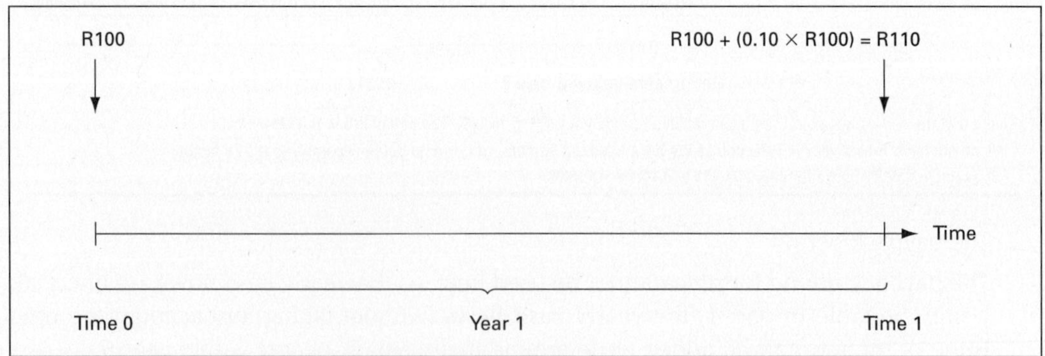

Exhibit 21.10 Estimating the future value of R100 in one year

The R110 at time 1 (end of one year) is composed of two parts:

Principal, time 0 amount	R100
Interest earned during year 1 (0.10 × R100)	10
Amount at time 1	R110

Thus, the R110 at time 1 consists of the R100 at time 0, called the principal, plus the R10 of interest earned during the year.

Now suppose that you leave your R110 invested during the second year. How much will you have at the end of two years? As Exhibit 21.11 shows, the answer is R121.

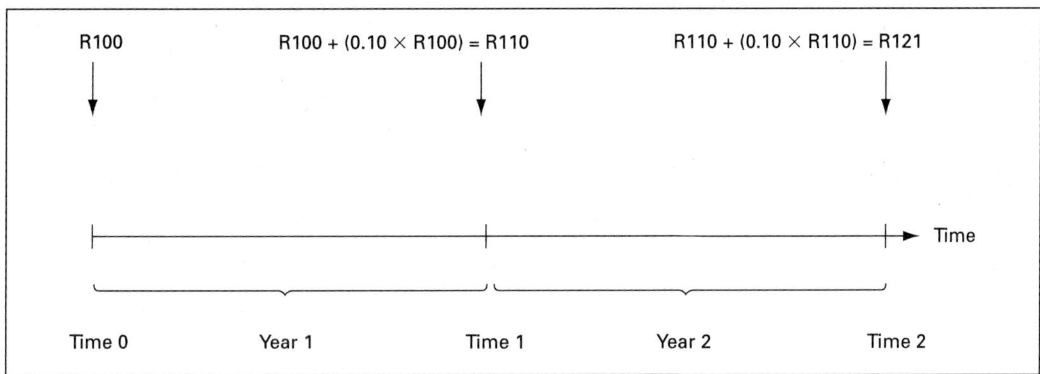

Exhibit 21.11 Estimating the future value of R100 in two years

We can break down the R121 at time 2 into two parts as follows:

Amount at time 1	R110
Interest earned during year 2 (0.10 × R110)	11
Amount at time 2	R121

Note that you earned more interest in year 2 (R11) than in year 1 (R10). During year 2, you earned 10 per cent interest on the original principal of R100 and also 10 per cent interest on the year 1 interest of R10. When interest is earned on the interest of prior periods, it is called **compound interest**. Exhibit 21.12 shows how the invested funds would grow over a five-year period of investment: the **future value** of the initial R100 investment is R161.05 after five years.

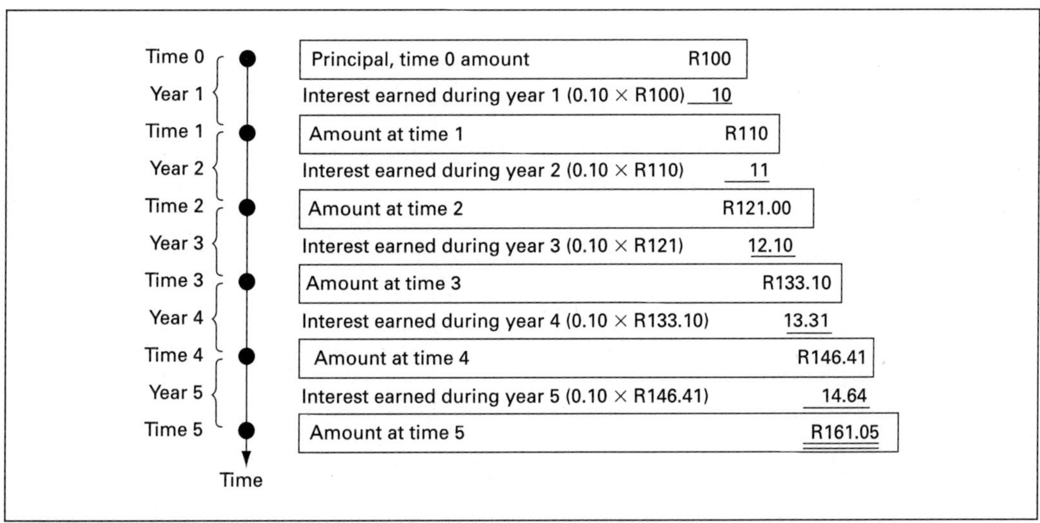

Exhibit 21.12 Compound interest and future value

As the number of years in an investment increases, it becomes more cumbersome to calculate the future value of the investment using the method shown in Exhibit 21.12. Fortunately, the simple formula shown below can be used to calculate the future value of any investment:

$$F_n = P(1 + r)^n \tag{1}$$

where F_n = future value after n years
P = principal
r = interest rate per year
n = number of years

Using formula (1) to calculate the future value of your R100 investment after five years, we have the following calculation:

$$\begin{aligned} F_n &= P(1 + r)^n \\ &= \text{R}100(1 + 0.10)^5 \\ &= \text{R}100 \times 1.61 \\ &= \text{R}161 \end{aligned}$$

The value of $(1 + r)^n$ is called the **accumulation factor**. The values of $(1 + r)^n$ for various combinations of r and n are listed in Table A at the back of the book.

Exercise

Use formula (1) and the values in Table A to calculate the future value, after 10 years, of an R800 investment that earns interest at the rate of 12 per cent per year.[11]

Present value

In the discussion above, we calculated the future value of an investment when the original principal is known. Now consider a slightly different problem. Suppose that you know how much money you want to accumulate at the end of a five-year investment. The problem is to determine how much your initial investment needs to be in order to accumulate the desired amount in five years. To solve this problem, start with formula (1):

$$F_n = P(1 + r)^n \tag{1}$$

Now divide each side of the equation by $(1 + r)^n$

$$P = Fn\left(\frac{1}{(1 + r)^n}\right) \tag{2}$$

In formula (2), P denotes what is commonly called the **present value** of the cash flow F_n, which occurs after n years when the interest rate is r.

Let's use formula (2) in the investment problem that we analysed in Exhibit 21.12. Suppose you do not know the value of the initial investment required if you want to accumulate R161.05 at the end of five years in an investment that earns 10 per cent per year. We can determine the present value of the investment as follows:

$$P = F_n\left(\frac{1}{(1 + r)^n}\right) \tag{3}$$

$$\begin{aligned} P &= \text{R}161.05\left(\frac{1}{(1 + 0.10)^5}\right) \\ &= \text{R}161.05 \times 0.6209 \\ &= \text{R}100 \end{aligned}$$

Thus, as we knew already, you must invest R100 now in order to accumulate R161.05 after five years in an investment earning 10 per cent per year. The present value of R100 and the future value of R161.05 at time 5 are economically equivalent, given that the annual interest rate is 10 per cent. If you had the choice of receiving R100 now and investing it at 10 per cent per annum, or R161.05 at the end of five years, you should be indifferent between the two, as they both result in the same outcome at the end of five years.

When we used formula (2) to calculate the present value of the R161.05 cash flow at time 5, we used a process called discounting. The interest rate used when discounting a future cash flow to calculate its present value is called the **discount rate**. The value of $1/(1 + r)^n$, which appears in formula (2), is called the **discount factor**. Discount factors for various combinations of r and n are given in Table C at the back of the book.

Exercise

Suppose you want to accumulate R18 000 to go on holiday in four years' time, and you can earn interest at the rate of 8 per cent per year on an investment you make now. How much do you need to invest now? Use formula (2) and the discount factors in Table C to calculate the present value of the required R18 000 amount needed at the end of four years.[12]

Present value of a cash flow series

The present value problem solved above involved only a single future cash flow. Now consider a slightly different problem. Suppose that you have just won R50 000 in a lottery. You want to spend some of the cash now, but you have decided to save enough to rent a beach house during summer for each of the next three years. You would like to deposit enough in a bank account now so that you can withdraw R10 000 from the account at the end of each of the next three years. The money in the bank account will earn 8 per cent per year. The question, then, is: How much do you need to deposit? Another way of asking the same question is: What is the present value of a series of R10 000 cash flows at the end of each of the next three years, given that the discount rate is 8 per cent? (See Exhibit 21.13.)

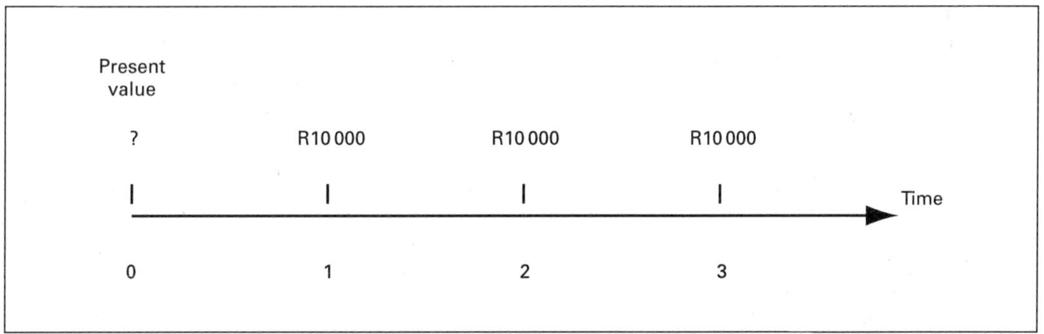

Exhibit 21.13 Present value of R10 000 received each year for the next three years

One way of solving this problem is to calculate the present value of each of the three R10 000 cash flows and add the amounts together. We can use formula (2) for these calculations, as shown in panel A of Exhibit 21.14. Notice that the present value of each of the R10 000 cash flows is different, because the timing of the cash flows is different. The earlier the cash flow occurs, the higher its present value.

Now look more closely at Exhibit 21.14. We obtained the R25 770 total present value by adding three present value amounts. Each of these amounts is the result of multiplying R10 000 by a discount factor. Notice that we can obtain the same result by adding the three discount factors first, and then multiplying by R10 000.

This approach is taken in panel B of Exhibit 21.14. The sum of the three discount factors is called an **annuity discount factor**, because a series of equivalent cash flows is called an **annuity**. Annuity discount factors for various combinations of r and n are given in Table D at the back of the book.

(A) Present Value of cash flows using 3 present value calculations		Cash flow		$\frac{1}{(1+r)^n}$		Cash flow		PV Factor 8%		PV
Present value of time 1 Cash Flow	1	10 000	×	$1/(1+0.08)^1$	=	10 000	×	0.9259	=	9 259
Present value of time 2 Cash Flow	2	10 000	×	$1/(1+0.08)^2$	=	10 000	×	0.8573	=	8 573
Present value of time 3 Cash Flow	3	10 000	×	$1/(1+0.08)^3$	=	10 000	×	0.7938	=	7 938
										25 770
(B) Present Value of cash flows using the annuity discount factor		Cash flow		$\frac{1-1/(1+r)^n}{r}$		Cash flow		Annuity 8%		PV
Present value of annuity	3	10 000	×	$\frac{(1-1/(1+0.08)^3)}{0.08}$	=	10 000	×	2.5771	=	25 771

There is a very slight difference between the two approaches, due to rounding. If we add the individual year PV factors we will get 2.5770, due to rounding to 4 decimal places. It should add up to 2.5771. See Table D.

Exhibit 21.14 Present value of a series of cash flows

Now let's verify that R25 771 is the required amount for financing your three summer holidays. Exhibit 21.15 shows how your bank account will change over the three-year period as you earn interest and then withdraw R10 000 each year.

		0		1		2	3
Deposit / opening balance		25 771		25 771		17 833	9 259
Interest for the period	8%			2 062		1 426	741
Accumulated amount		25 771		27 833		19 259	10 000
Withdrawals to cover cost of each year's holiday		–		(10 000)		(10 000)	(10 000)
Balance at end of year		25 771		17 833		9 259	–
	Yr						
Interest	1	25 771	×	8%	=	2 062	
Interest	2	17 833	×	8%	=	1 426	
Interest	3	9 259	×	8%	=	741	

Exhibit 21.15 Verification of present value calculation for cash flow series

Future value of a cash flow series

To complete the discussion of present value and future value concepts, let's consider the series of R10 000 rental payments for the beach house from the landlord's perspective. Suppose that the owner of the beach house invests each R10 000 rental payment in a bank account that pays 8 per cent interest per year. How much will the owner have accumulated at the end of the three-year period? An equivalent question is: What is the future value of the three-year series of R10 000 cash flows, given an annual interest rate of 8 per cent? Exhibit 21.16 answers the question in two ways. In panel A, three separate future value calculations are made using formula (1). Notice that the R10 000 cash flow at time 1 is multiplied by $(1.08)^2$, since it has two years to earn interest. The R10 000 cash flow at time 2 has only one year to earn interest, and the time 3 cash flow has no time to earn interest.

(A) Future Value of cash flows using 3 Future Value calculations		Cash flow		$(1 + r)^n$		Cash flow		FV Factor 8%		FV
Future value of time 1 Cash Flow	1	10 000	×	$(1 + 0.08)^2$	=	10 000	×	1.1664	=	11 664
Future value of time 2 Cash Flow	2	10 000	×	$(1 + 0.08)^1$	=	10 000	×	1.0800	=	10 800
Future value of time 3 Cash Flow	3	10 000	×	$(1 + 0.08)^0$	=	10 000	×	1.0000	=	10 000
								3.2464		32 464
(B) Future Value of cash flows using the annuity accumulation factor		Cash flow		$\frac{(1 + r)^n - 1}{r}$		Cash flow		Annuity 8%		FV
Future value of annuity	3	10 000	×	$\frac{(1 + 0.08)^3 - 1}{0.08}$	=	10 000	×	3.2464	=	32 464

Exhibit 21.16 Future value of a series of cash flows

In panel B, the three-year **annuity accumulation factor** is used. This factor is the sum of the three accumulation factors used in panel A. The annuity accumulation factors for various combinations of *r* and *n* are given in Table B at the back of the book.

Part 2: Future value and present value tables

Using the tables correctly

When using the tables to solve future value and present value problems, be sure to select the correct table: Table A is used to find the future value of a single cash flow, and Table C is used to find the present value of a single cash flow; Table B is used to find the future value of a series of identical cash flows, and Table D is used to find the present value of a series of identical cash flows. Take care not to confuse future value with present value, or a single cash flow with a series of identical cash flows. If you have a calculator that will exponentiate (raise a number to a power), you do not need the tables. Just use the correct formula and calculate the appropriate factor yourself. Otherwise, use a financial calculator to determine present values, future values and a project's IRR. Excel can also be used to determine a project's NPV and IRR. Tables A, B, C and D are presented at the back of the book.

Part 3: The use of Excel® and financial calculators

Using Excel® and financial calculators to determine net present value, internal rate of return, present values and future values

In the real world, managers tend to use Excel to determine a project's net present value (NPV) and internal rate of return (IRR). Further, Excel has many built-in functions to solve time value of money problems and we can use these functions to determine future values and present values. Excel is useful for financial modelling and it enables us to undertake sensitivity analysis as well as permitting us to place cash flows within a time dimension. Cells are used to indicate time periods. This is very useful when projects have uneven cash flows. It is best to place values within cells so that we can change these values easily to measure the effect on a project's NPV and IRR.

We can use the =NPV function to discount a range of cell values at a specified discount rate. The =IRR function is used to determine a project's IRR. The NPV function assumes that the first cash flow occurs in a year's (period's) time. The NPV function requires that we indicate the discount rate and range of cells to be discounted. We place in a cell, =NPV(rate, range). In the following example, we have placed the discount rate in Cell B2. Assume the cash flows occur at the end of each period. The NPV is R256 456.65. The formula within Cell B6 is set out below B6 in Exhibit 21.17. If there is a cost outflow in time 0 of R175 000, then the NPV is R81 456.65. You will notice that as the NPV function assumes that the first value in a range occurs in a year's time, we are determining the present value of the cash flows for the period years 1 to 5 and we add to this the cost outflow in time zero, so that the formula becomes, = NPV(B2, C10:G10) + B10.

	A	B	C	D	E	F	G
2	Interest rate	10.00%					
3		0	1	2	3	4	5
4	Cash flows		60 000	80 000	70 000	40 000	90 000
5							
6	**NPV**	**256 456.65** [1]					
7		1 =*NPV(B2,C4:G4)*					
8							
9		0	1	2	3	4	5
10	Cash flows	−175 000	60 000	80 000	70 000	40 000	90 000
11							
12	**NPV**	**81 456.65** [2]					
13		2 =*NPV(B2,C10:G10) + B10*					
14							
15	**IRR**	**26.6%** [3]					
16		3 =*IRR(B10:G10,0.14)*					

Note: IRR requires you to insert an estimated IRR. We indicated 0.14 but you can select any rate.

Exhibit 21.17 Using Excel to determine the NPV and IRR of a series of cash flows

We can use Excel to determine the NPV of the cash flows set out in Exhibit 21.4 in the chapter. The difference in NPV is due to rounding PV factors to four decimal places in Exhibit 21.4.

	A	B	C	D	E	F	G	H	I
1									
2						**Yearly cash flows**			
3	Discount rate	10%		**0**	**1**	**2**	**3**	**4**	**5**
4	Initial investment			−6 597 150					
5	Yearly cost savings – additional revenue				1 830 000	1 830 000	1 830 000	1 830 000	1 830 000
6				−6 597 150	1 830 000	1 830 000	1 830 000	1 830 000	1 830 000
7									
8		NPV		339 990					
9				=*NPV(B3,E6:I6) + D6*					
10		IRR		12.0%					
11				=*IRR(D6:I6, 0.13)*					

Exhibit 21.18 Using Excel to determine the NPV and IRR of the cash flows set out in Exhibit 21.4

We can also use Excel to solve numerous *time value of money* problems. This is similar to using Excel as a financial calculator.

The main functions in Excel to solve time value of money problems are:

Future Value: = FV (rate, nper, pmt, PV, type)
Present Value: = PV (rate, nper, pmt, FV, type)
Interest rate: = RATE (nper, pmt, PV, FV, type)
Number of periods: = NPER (rate, pmt, PV, FV, type)
Payment: = PMT (rate, nper, PV, FV, type)

Most of the terms are self-explanatory, and nper refers to the number of periods whilst type refers to whether the first cash flow occurs at the beginning or end of each period. If the cash flow occurs at the beginning of each period, then indicate the type as 1. If the cash flow occurs at the end of each period, then indicate the type as 0 (or omit).

Let's apply Excel to solve a few time value problems indicated in this appendix.

	A	B	C	D	E	F
1	***Future Value***			***Present Value***		
2						
3	Present Value	100.00		Future Value	161.05	
4	Payment	0.00		Payment	0.00	
5	Periods	5		Periods	5	
6	Rate	10%		Rate	10%	
7	Type	0		Type	0	
8	**Future Value**	161.05		**Present Value**	100.00	
9						
10	What is in Cell B8?	= FV(B6,B5,B4,−B3,B7)		What is in Cell E8?	= PV(E6,E5,E4,−E3,E7)	
11		= fv(rate, nper, pmt, pv, type)			= PV(rate, nper, pmt, fv, type)	

Exhibit 21.19 Using Excel to determine FV and PV

We have set the payment as zero as there are no payments but only a single future value or present value. In the appendix, we also calculated the future value of a series of equal cash flows of R10 000 per year for 3 years at an interest rate of 8 per cent, and we determined the future value at the end of 3 years to be equal to R32 464. The present value of a series of equal cash flows of R10 000 required per year to undertake a holiday was R25 771.97.

	A	B	C	D	E	F
1	***Future Value***			***Present Value***		
2						
3	Present Value	0.00		Future Value	0.00	
4	Payment	−10 000.00		Payment	−10 000.00	
5	Periods	3		Periods	3	
6	Rate	8%		Rate	8%	
7	Type	0		Type	0	
8	**Future Value**	32 464.00		**Present Value**	25 770.97	
9						
10	What is in Cell B8?	= FV(B6,B5,B4,−B3,B7)		What is in Cell E8?	= PV(E6,E5,E4,−E3,E7)	
11		= fv(rate, nper, pmt, pv, type)			= PV(rate, nper, pmt, fv, type)	

Exhibit 21.20 Using Excel to determine FV and PV of a series of equal cash flows

Using financial calculators

We can use financial calculators to compute future values and present values and to solve other time value of money problems. You need to enter the data using the relevant Input keys which for the HP-10B*II* are as follows:

N	I/YR	PV	PMT	FV

Where:
N = number of periods
I/YR = interest rate as a percentage. Enter a number, so if the rate is 10 per cent, enter 10, not 0.10. Other calculators may reflect the interest rate per period as [i] and the number of periods as [n].
PV = present value
PMT = annuity payment. Specify this as a zero when working with single sums only
FV = future value

In most cases, three or four inputs will be specified, and the financial calculator will solve for the remaining variable. On some calculators you will need to first press the COMPUTE key prior to pressing the missing input key.

What to watch out for when using a financial calculator?

Outflows are recorded as negative cash flows. An investment will be recorded in present value terms as a negative amount. If you borrow, you will receive the loan amount today which will be recorded as a positive cash flow and the repayments will be reflected as negative amounts. Ensure that you clear the memory. Enter a zero for any variable that is not relevant in a particular case. For example, when determining the future value of a single sum investment, enter a zero for the PMT key.

Ensure that the financial calculator is programmed for annual compounding by doing the following steps:

Enter *1,* then press *SHIFT* key and then the PMT *(P/YR)* key. We will make adjustments later for non-annual compounding.

Let's do some of the previous examples by using an HP-10B*II* financial calculator.

An investment of R100 invested for 10 years earning 12 per cent per year compound interest will result in a future value of R310.6. Key in the following input values and press the FV key for the solution.

Seq.	*2*	*3*	*1*	*4*	
	N	I/YR	PV	PMT	FV
	10	12	−100	0	**310.6**

First enter the present value as a negative number, −100 or press 100 followed by (−), depending on the calculator being used, and then press the PV key. Then enter 10 and press N, enter 12 and press I/Y, enter 0 and press PMT and then press FV (or Comp FV) to find the answer.

If given a FV of 310.6 with the number of periods being 10 and an interest rate of 12 per cent, press in the following sequence and then press the PV key to find the answer of −100.

Seq.	*2*	*3*		*4*	*1*
	N	I/YR	PV	PMT	FV
	10	12	**−100**	0	310.6

What is the interest rate that will achieve a present value of R100 growing to R310.60 within 10 years? Enter the inputs in the following sequence, then press the [I/YR] key to determine the interest rate of 12 per cent.

Seq.	2		1	3	4
	N	I/YR	PV	PMT	FV
	10	**12**	−100	0	310.6

We have assumed so far that the company has annual compounding. If the compounding period is less than a year, then we will need to input the number of compounding periods per year. This requires us to press the number of periods per year, then press the *SHIFT* key and (*P/YR*).

Let's go back to the first example and assume monthly compounding. We need to program the financial calculator for monthly compounding by undertaking the following steps:

Enter *12,* and then press the *SHIFT* (yellow) key and then the PMT (*P/YR*) key. [*P/YR* / PMT]

This means that the financial calculator is now programmed for monthly compounding. The present value is R100, the interest rate is 12 per cent per year and N is 120 months.

Seq.	2	3	1	4	
	N	I/YR	PV	PMT	FV
	120	12	−100	0	**330**

Remember to input the *annual* interest rate. The financial calculator will divide it by the number of compounding periods per year. The effect of compounding interest each month rather than each year is to increase the future value from R310.6 to R330. Remember to input the number of *months.*

Present values

What is the present value of an annuity of R100 per year for three years at an interest rate of 12 per cent?

Seq.	2	3		1	4
	N	I/YR	PV	PMT	FV
	3	12	**240.18**	−100	0

The present value is R240.18. This assumes that the annuity occurs at the end of each year. What is the present value of an annuity that starts at the beginning of each year? Firstly, set the calculator to the beginning of year by pressing the *SHIFT* key and press the *BEG/END* key. Then enter PMT of −100, N of 3, I/YR of 12, FV of 0 and then press PV to find the answer of R269.

Seq.	2	3		1	4
	N	I/YR	PV	PMT	FV
	3	12	**269**	−100	0

Remember to reset your financial calculator back to end of period mode by pressing the *SHIFT* key and the *BEG/END* key. Usually we will assume that cash flows occur at the end of each period. Remember always to ensure that you clear the memory and all previous inputs by pressing the *SHIFT* key and then the *C ALL* key.

How do we use a financial calculator to determine the present value of an uneven stream of cash flows? We will use the CF_j and the *I/YR* keys to input data and press the *NPV* key for the answer. Let's assume an interest rate of 10% per year and that Project A has the following cash flows:

	Year	**1**	**2**	**3**
CF	Rm	16	5	5

Assume there is no cash flow now today, i.e. time zero. You will still need to input a value, so enter zero. Firstly, input 0 then press the CF_j key, then input 16 and press the CF_j key, input 5 and press the CF_j key, input 5 and press the CF_j key, input 10 and press the *I/YR* key and then press the SHIFT key followed by pressing the *NPV* key to find the answer of R22.4343m.

0 [CFj] 16 [CFj] 5 [CFj] 5 [CFj] 10 [I/YR] *SHIFT* [NPV]

22.4343

[Source for section on Financial Calculators: Correia, C, Flynn, D, Uliana, E & Wormald, M, *Financial Management*, Juta & Co., 6th Edn, 2007, Chapter 2. Copyright ©: Juta & Co. and Carlos Correia. Used by kind permission.]

Questions

?

21.1 Explain how capital expenditures can impact on a firm's competitiveness.

21.2 How do capital expenditure decisions differ from tactical decisions? Give two examples of each type of decision.

21.3 Describe the various stages involved in the capital investment decision process.

21.4 'We can view the organisation's performance over a year as the combined result of all the projects under way during that year.' True or false? Explain your answer.

21.5 Briefly explain the concept of discounted cash flow analysis. Explain the essential difference between the two common methods of discounted cash flow analysis.

21.6 List the steps to be taken when using the net present value method.

21.7 'The greater the discount rate, the greater the present value of a future cash flow.' True or false? Explain your answer.

21.8 'The lower the interest rate, the greater the future value of a current cash flow.' True or false? Explain your answer.

21.9 Define the term internal rate of return and explain how to calculate the internal rate of return for a project.

21.10 State the decision rule used to accept or reject an investment proposal under each of these methods of analysis:
(a) net present value method
(b) internal rate of return method.

21.11 List and explain briefly the advantages that the net present value method has over the internal rate of return method.

21.12 Compare and contrast the assumptions underlying the net present value and IRR methods of discounted cash flow analysis.

21.13 In a least-cost decision, what is the objective of the discounted cash flow analysis?

21.14 Under what circumstances can the IRR method of discounted cash flow analysis lead to inappropriate capital expenditure decisions?

21.15 'In using discounted cash flow analysis, one of the most difficult things is to identify cash outflows associated with depreciation.' True or false? Explain your answer.

21.16 What is meant by the term payback period? What are the main drawbacks of this method for evaluating capital expenditure decisions?

21.17 Given the limitations of the payback method, why do many businesses continue to use it?

21.18 Explain how to calculate a project's accounting rate of return. Would you expect a project's accounting rate of return or the internal rate of return to be higher? Explain your answer.

21.19 Discuss the pros and cons of the accounting rate of return as an investment criterion.

21.20 Briefly describe two techniques commonly used when the cash flows of an investment proposal are highly uncertain.

21.21 What is meant by a post-audit of an investment project? Why do so few businesses complete post-audits of their capital expenditure decisions?

21.22 'My annual salary bonus is based on my business unit's return on investment. There is no way that I will approve capital expenditure projects which do not generate an accounting profit each year.' Discuss the implications of this statement.

21.23 Discuss the relative importance of quantitative and qualitative information in capital expenditure decisions.

21.24 (appendix) What is meant by the terms compound interest, present value and annuity?

21.25 (appendix) Explain in words the following future value formula: $F_n = P(1 + r)^n$.

21.26 (appendix) 'If the interest rate is 10 per cent, then a present value of R100 and a future value of R161.05 at the end of five years are economically equivalent.' Explain this statement.

Exercises

E21.27 Net present value: local council

The Nelson Mandela Bay Municipality Council is considering the purchase of a site for a new sanitary landfill. The purchase price for the site is R2 340 000 and preparatory work will cost R880 800. The landfill would be useable for 10 years. The Council hired a consultant, who estimated that the new landfill would cost R480 000 per year less to operate than the current landfill. The current landfill will also last 10 more years. For a landfill project, the Municipality can borrow money from the government at a subsidised rate. The Municipality's required rate of return is only 6 per cent for this project.

Required:

Calculate the net present value of the new landfill. Should the council approve the project?

E21.28 Internal rate of return: local municipality

Refer to the data given in Exercise 21.27.

Required:

Calculate the internal rate of return for the landfill project. Should the council approve the project?

E21.29 Net present value: not-for-profit organisation

Jack and Jill's Place is a not-for-profit preschool run by the parents of the enrolled children. Since the preschool is out of town, it has a water storage tank rather than city water supply. After chemicals accidentally were poured into the tank, the tank water became contaminated. The preschool has had to bring in bottled drinking water. The school's management committee is considering building a larger, more modern water storage system. The committee estimates that this would cost R28 250 and save the preschool R5 000 annually for 10 years. The preschool's required rate of return is 8 per cent.

Required:

Calculate the new water tank's net present value. Should the management committee approve the new project?

E21.30 Internal rate of return: not-for-profit organisation

Refer to the data given in Exercise 21.29.

Required:
Calculate the internal rate of return on the new water tank using a financial calculator or Excel (or any other spreadsheet programme). Should the management committee approve the new tank?

E21.31 Internal rate of return: school

The Head of Mendelsson Secretarial College is considering the replacement of the college's computer system. The proposed new computer system would cost R655 000 and have a life of five years. The college's current computer system would also last five more years, but it does not have sufficient capacity to meet the college's expanding needs. If Mendelsson College continues to use the old computer system, it will have to purchase additional computer time, on a time-share basis, from the local university. The cost of the additional computer time is projected at R140 000 annually. The old computer system can be sold now for R115 000.

Required:
Use a financial calculator or Excel (or any other spreadsheet programme) to calculate the internal rate of return on the proposed purchase of a new computer system.

E21.32 Internal rate of return; uneven cash flows: school

The trustees of the Umcolo School of Art and Music, located in Manguang, are considering a major overhaul of the school's audio system. With or without the overhaul, the system will be replaced in two years. If an overhaul is done now, the trustees expect to save the following repair costs during the next two years: year 1, R30 000; year 2, R50 000. The overhaul will cost R66 640.

Required:
Use trial and error to calculate the internal rate of return on the proposed overhaul. (*Hint*: The NPV of the overhaul is positive if an 8 per cent discount rate is used, but the NPV is negative if a 16 per cent rate is used.)

E21.33 Net present value with different discount rates: theatre company

The board of management of the Pretoria Shakespearian Theatre is considering the replacement of the theatre's lighting system. The old system requires two people to operate it, but the new system would need only a single operator. The new lighting system will cost R865 000 and save the theatre R180 000 annually over the next eight years.

Required:
Prepare a table showing the proposed lighting system's net present value for each of the following discount rates: 8 per cent, 10 per cent, 12 per cent, 14 per cent and 16 per cent. Use the following headings in your table. Comment on the pattern in the right-hand column.

Discount rate	Annuity discount factor	Annual savings	Acquisition cost	Net present value

E21.34 Sensitivity analysis: theatre company

Refer to the data given in Exercise 21.33. Suppose that the Pretoria Shakespearian Theatre's board is uncertain about the cost savings with the new lighting system.

Required:
How low could the new lighting system's annual savings be such that the proposal is still acceptable to the board of directors? Assume that the theatre's discount rate is 12 per cent.

E21.35 Payback period; net present value; even cash flows: bank

The management of North West National Bank is considering an investment in automatic teller machines. The machines would cost R2 565 000 and have a useful life of seven years. The bank's finance manager has estimated that the automatic teller machines will save the bank R550 000 during each year of their life. The machines will have no salvage value.

Required:

1 Calculate the payback period for the proposed investment.
2 Calculate the net present value of the proposed investment, assuming a discount rate of:
   (a) 10 per cent
   (b) 12 per cent
   (c) 14 per cent
3 What can you conclude from your answers to requirements 1 and 2 about the limitations of the payback method?

E21.36 Payback period; net present value; uneven cash flows: publishing company

Parkes Book Company's management is considering an advertising program that would require an initial expenditure of R1 655 000 and bring in additional sales over the next five years. The projected additional sales revenue in year 1 is R750 000, with associated expenses of R250 000. The additional sales revenue and expenses from the advertising program are projected to increase by 10 per cent each year.

Required:

1 Calculate the payback period for the advertising program.
2 Calculate the advertising program's net present value, assuming a required rate of return of 12 per cent.

E21.37 Accounting rate of return: manufacturer

Iliwa Spring Water Company recently purchased a new delivery truck for R500 000. Management expects the truck to generate the following additional revenue and expenses during its useful life.

Average incremental revenue	R250 000
Average incremental expenses, not including depreciation	100 000

The truck has an expected life of six years and is depreciated using the straight line method.

Required:

1 Prepare a schedule showing the incremental revenue, incremental operating expenses and incremental depreciation during each of the next six years.
2 Calculate the accounting rate of return on the delivery truck, using the initial investment as the denominator.

E21.38 Performance evaluation; behavioural problems: government department

The supervisor of the eThikweni Water Authority is considering the replacement of a utility truck. A new truck costs R605 000 and has a useful life of five years. The Authority depreciates all assets on a straight line basis. The supervisor estimates that the new truck would result in substantial savings over the next five years. He has projected the following pattern of operating cost savings (cash flows):

Year	Cost savings
1	R110 000
2	115 000
3	130 000
4	180 000
5	200 000

After giving the proposal some thought, the supervisor decided against purchasing the new utility truck. He said to his deputy supervisor: 'If we go for that truck, the managing director will fry us. With R121 000 in depreciation each year, the truck won't even pay its own way until three years out. By then, you and I will be unemployed!'

Required:
The Water Authority's required rate of return is 6 per cent. Did the supervisor make a wise decision? Explain your answer. Comment on the behavioural problem evident in this situation.

E21.39 Future value and present value (appendix)
Answer each of the following independent questions. Ignore personal income taxes.

1 Suppose that you invest R5000 in an account bearing interest at the rate of 14 per cent per year.
   (a) What will be the future value of your investment in six years?
   (b) Prepare a diagram similar to that in Exhibit 21.12 to show how your accumulation grows each year to the estimated future value after six years.
2 Your best friend won the lottery and has offered to give you R10 000 in five years' time when he has made his first million Rands. You reason that if you had the money today, you could invest it at 12 per cent interest per annum. What is the present value of your friend's future gift?
3 In four years, you would like to buy a small cabin in Mpumalanga. You estimate that the property will cost you R525 000 by the time you are ready to buy. How much money will you need to invest each year in an account bearing interest at the rate of 6 per cent per year in order to accumulate the R525 000 purchase price?
4 You have estimated that your educational expenses over the next three years will be R55 000 per year.
   (a) How much money do you need in your account now in order to withdraw the required amount each year? Your account bears interest at 10 per cent per year.
   (b) Prepare a diagram similar to that in Exhibit 21.15 to verify the amount you need in order to fund your educational expenses.

E21.40 Future value and present value (appendix)
You plan to retire at age 40 after a successful but short career. You would like to accumulate enough money by age 40 to withdraw R225 000 per year for 40 years. You plan to pay into your account 15 equal instalments, beginning when you are 25 and ending when you are 39. Your account bears interest of 12 per cent per year. Ignore personal income taxes.

Required:
1 How much do you need to accumulate in your account by the time you retire?
2 How much do you need to pay into your account in each of the 15 equal instalments?
3 Is this a future value problem or a present value problem? Explain.

Problems

P21.41 Net present value; qualitative issues: not-for-profit organisation
Special People Industries is a not-for-profit organisation that employs only people with physical or intellectual disabilities. One of the organisation's activities is to make biscuits for its snack food store. On 31 December 20X7, Special People Industries purchased a special biscuit-cutting machine. This machine has now been used for three years.

Management is considering the purchase of a newer, more efficient machine. If purchased, the new machine would be acquired on 31 December 20X3.

Management expects to sell 300 000 dozen biscuits in each of the next six years. The selling price is expected to average R11.50 per dozen.

Special People Industries has two options: continue to operate the old machine, or sell the old machine and purchase the new machine. No trade-in was offered by the seller of the new machine. The following information has been assembled to help management decide which option is more desirable:

	Old machine	New machine
Original cost of machine at acquisition	R800 000	R1 200 000
Remaining useful life (number of years)	6	6
Expected annual cash operating expenses:		
Variable cost per dozen	R4	R3
Total fixed costs	R210 000	R110 000
Estimated cash value of machines:		
31 December 20X3	R400 000	R1 200 000
31 December 20X9	R70 000	R200 000

Assume that all operating revenues and expenses occur at the end of the year.

Required:

1 Use the net present value method to determine whether Special People Industries should retain the old machine or acquire the new machine. The organisation's required rate of return is 16 per cent.

2 Independent of your answer to requirement 1, suppose the quantitative differences between the two alternatives are so slight that management is indifferent between the two proposals. Identify and discuss any qualitative factors that management should consider.

(CMA, adapted)

P21.42 Net present value; outsourcing: manufacturer

Sure Fire Company manufactures a variety of products in four plants located in Cape Town. The company is currently purchasing an electronic igniter from an outside supplier for R620 per unit. Because of supplier reliability problems, the company is considering producing the igniters internally in a manufacturing plant that is currently unused. Annual volume over the next five years is expected to total 400 000 units at a variable manufacturing cost of R600 per unit. Management must hire a factory supervisor and two assistants for a total annual salary and fringe benefit package of R950 000.

In addition, the company must acquire R600 000 of new equipment. The equipment has a five-year service life and R120 000 salvage value, and will be depreciated on the straight-line method. Repairs and maintenance are expected to average R45 000 per year in years 3–5, and the equipment will be sold at the end of its life. Ignore income taxes.

Required:

1 Should discounted cash flows be used in this outsourcing decision? Why?

2 Ignoring your answer to requirement 1, use the net present value method (total cost approach) and a 14 per cent hurdle rate to determine whether management should manufacture or outsource the igniters.

3 Suppose management is able to negotiate a lower purchase price from its supplier. At what purchase price would management be financially indifferent between manufacturing and outsourcing the igniters?

P21.43 Net present value: hospital

The board of trustees of St Mary's Hospital is considering the addition of a comprehensive medical testing laboratory. In the past, the hospital has sent all blood and tissue specimens to Diagnostic Testing Services, an independent testing service. The hospital's current contract with the testing service is due to expire, and the testing service has offered a new 4-year contract. Under the terms of the new contract, St Mary's Hospital would pay Diagnostic Testing Services a flat fee of R400 000 per year plus R120 per specimen tested.

Since St Mary's Hospital does not have its own comprehensive testing laboratory, the hospital staff are forced to refer some types of cases to a nearby hospital. If St Mary's Hospital had its own laboratory, these cases could be handled in-house. St Mary's Hospital's administrator estimates that the hospital loses R540 000 per year in contribution margin on the cases that currently must be referred elsewhere. This amounts to 1000 tests and the contribution loss of R540 000 refers to both the test fee contribution as well as the contribution from other hospital services provided to the patients.

The proposed new laboratory would not require construction of a new building, since it would occupy space currently used by the hospital for storage. However, the hospital would then be forced to rent storage space in a nearby warehouse at a cost of R90 000 per year. The equipment for the laboratory would cost R3.4 million.

Due to the rapid technological improvement of medical testing equipment, the equipment would have negligible salvage value after 4 years. Staffing the laboratory would require 1 supervisor and 4 technicians. Annual salary costs would run to R240 000 for the supervisor and R120 000 each for the laboratory technicians.

Fixed operating costs in the laboratory would be R150 000 per year, and variable costs would amount to R40 per medical test.

St Mary's Hospital requires 20 000 tests per year. The capacity of the laboratory would be 26 000 tests per year. St Mary's Hospital's administrator believes that physicians in private practice would utilise the laboratory's excess capacity by sending their own tests to St Mary's Hospital. The administrator has projected a charge of R120 per test for physicians in private practice. The hospital does not pay corporate tax. St Mary's Hospital's required rate of return is 12 per cent.

Required:

Prepare a net present value analysis of the proposed testing laboratory.

P21.44 Net present value: hospital

Gardenia Community Hospital is a non-profit hospital. The hospital's administrator is considering a proposal to open a new outpatient clinic in the nearby town of Njalo-njalo. The administrator has made the following estimates pertinent to the proposal:

Construction of the clinic building will cost R7.8 million in two equal instalments of R3.9 million, to be paid at the end of 20X0 and 20X1. The clinic will open on 2 January 20X2. All staffing and operating costs begin in 20X2.

- Equipment for the clinic will cost R1.5 million, to be paid in December 20X1.
- Staffing of the clinic will cost R8 million per year.
- Other operating costs at the clinic will be R2 million per year.
- Opening the clinic is expected to increase charitable contributions to the hospital by R2.5 million per year.
- The clinic is expected to reduce costs at Gardenia Community Hospital. Annual cost savings at the hospital are projected to be R10 million.
- A major refurbishment of the clinic is expected to be necessary towards the end of 20X5. This work will cost R1.8 million.
- Due to shifting population and medical needs, the administrator doubts the clinic will be needed after 20X9.
- The clinic building and equipment could be sold for R2.9 million at the end of 20X9.
- The hospital's required rate of return is 12 per cent.

Required:

1 Calculate the net present value of the proposed outpatient clinic.

2 Should the administrator recommend to the hospital's trustees that the clinic be built? Explain your answer.

P21.45 Net present value: government department

The chief ranger of the Department of Forestry is considering a new plan for fighting bushfires. The current plan uses 8 fire-control stations, which are scattered throughout the wilderness areas. Each station has a 4-person staff, whose annual salaries total R400 000 per station. Other costs of operating each base amount to R200 000 per year. The equipment at each base has a current salvage value of R240 000. The buildings at these stations have no other use. To demolish them would cost R20 000 each.

The chief ranger's new plan involves 4 fire-control stations, one on the perimeter of each wilderness area. Each station would require a 6-person staff, with annual salary costs of R600 000 per station. Other operating costs would be R220 000 per base. Building each perimeter station would cost R400 000. The perimeter bases would need helicopters and other equipment costing R1 million per station. Half the equipment from the current stations could be used at the perimeter stations. Therefore, only half the equipment at the current stations would be sold if the perimeter stations were built.

A required rate of return of 10 per cent is used for all capital investment projects.

Required:

1 Prepare a net present value analysis of the chief ranger's two fire-control plans—the current plan and the proposed new plan. Assume that the current fire-control stations will be demolished if the perimeter plan is selected. The chief ranger has decided to use a 10 year time period for the analysis.
2 What qualitative factors would the chief ranger be likely to consider in making this decision?

P21.46 Internal rate of return; even cash flows: airport

The chief executive of Hermanus Airport is considering approaching the Central Airport Authority to request permission to construct a longer runway at Hermanus Airport. Currently, the airport can handle only private aircraft and small jet commuters. A new, long runway would enable the airport to handle the midsized jets used on many budget domestic flights. Data pertinent to the decision are as follows:

Cost of acquiring additional land for runway	R700 000
Cost of runway construction	2 000 000
Cost of extending perimeter fence	298 400
Cost of runway lights	396 000
Annual cost of maintaining new runway	280 000
Annual incremental revenue from landing fees	400 000

In addition to the data given above, two other facts are relevant to the decision. First, a longer runway will require a new rolling machine, which will cost R1 million. The old roller can be sold now for R100 000. The new, larger roller will cost an additional R120 000 in annual operating costs. Second, the chief executive believes that the proposed long runway will ease the pressure on facilities at Cape Town Airport, and increase the total level of aircraft activity, particularly leisure aircraft.

In analysing the runway proposal, the chief executive has decided to use a 10 year time horizon. The hurdle rate for capital expenditure projects is 12 per cent. Ignore income tax.

Required:

1 Calculate the initial cost of the investment in the long runway.
2 Calculate the annual net cost or benefit from the runway.
3 Determine the IRR on the proposed long runway. (*Hint*: The answer is a whole number.) Should it be built?

P21.47 Net present value: airport

Refer to the data given in Problem 21.46.

Required:

1 Prepare a net present value analysis of the proposed long runway.
2 Should the runway be approved?
3 Which of the data used in the analysis are likely to be:
(a) the most uncertain (b) least uncertain? Why?

P21.48 Internal rate of return; sensitivity analysis: airport

Refer to the data given in Problem 21.46. The chief executive of Hermanus Airport believes that if the airport conducts a promotional effort costing R200 000 per year the proposed long runway will result in substantially greater economic development than was projected originally. However, he is uncertain about the actual increase in airport revenue that will result.

Required:

Suppose that the airport builds the long runway and conducts the promotional campaign. What would be the increase in the airport's annual revenue needed for the proposed runway's internal rate of return to equal the hurdle rate of 12 per cent?

P21.49 Net present value; behavioural issues; ethics: not-for-profit organisation

The Institute for Environmental Studies (IES) is a privately funded, not-for-profit scientific organisation based in eThikweni. The organisation's director of field research is scheduled to retire in two years, and the financial controller, Maria Daries, is hoping to be appointed to the post at that time. In her current position, Daries has significant administrative responsibilities, including the approval of research proposals and equipment acquisitions. Daries has developed a reputation for carefully scrutinising every proposed project, and keeping the Institute's field research branch within its budget. Daries has been so successful in her job that she has been quietly assured by several members of the IES board of directors that she is in line for her boss' job. She knows, however, that her prospects depend on her continued success in keeping the field research branch in sound financial shape.

IES recently signed a contract with the central government to undertake a five-year study of the effects of global warming on the migration of waterfowl. The contract fee is R5 000 000, payable in equal annual instalments over the contract term. Daries is now considering two alternative proposals for carrying out the study. Each proposal entails the purchase of equipment and the incurrence of various operating costs throughout the term of the contract. The projected costs are as follows:

Year	Type of cost	Research proposal I	Research proposal II
Time 0	Equipment acquisition*	R400 000	R700 000
Year 1	Operating costs	1 500 000	750 000
Year 2	Operating costs	1 200 000	750 000
Year 3	Operating costs	750 000	950 000
Year 4	Operating costs	400 000	950 000
Year 5	Operating costs	400 000	950 000

*The equipment will be obsolete at the end of the contract term.

Daries' normal procedure for project evaluation is to calculate each proposal's NPV, using an 8 per cent discount rate.

Required:

1 Calculate the NPV for each research proposal.
2 Which proposal should Maria Daries approve? Why?
3 After completing her NPV analysis, Daries was tempted to ignore it. These thoughts ran through her mind as she drove to work:

If I approve Proposal I, the financial picture for the field research branch will fall to pieces over the next two years. After a R400 000 initial investment in equipment, I'm going to show losses of R500 000 and R200 000 in the first two years. That's not going to look very good when the board considers my promotion.

When she arrived at the office, Daries wrote a memo approving Proposal II. Comment on the ethical issues in this situation.

P21.50 Internal rate of return; uneven cash flows: library

The board of management of the Ottery Public Library is considering the installation of an electronic security system to reduce the theft of books. Currently, the library spends R150 000 annually to replace lost books. The board estimates that 90 per cent of this cost is due to book theft. The remaining 10 per cent of the cost is unrelated to book theft and will be incurred regardless of whether a new security system is installed. The library currently employs people on a part-time basis to monitor the library's exit. However, this system is ineffective. The library incurs an annual cost of R120 000 on this monitoring activity.

The board could install an electronic security system, which would render the exit monitoring unnecessary. In order to install the new security system, the library's exits would have to be modified at a cost of R450 000. The equipment for the security system would cost R553 485 and have a useful life of 10 years. In addition, the new security system would require the placement of a sensor panel inside every book in the library, at a total cost of R90 000. This process, which would take place over a three-year period, would cost R30 000 during each of those years. Since the security system would not be completely in place for three years, the library would continue to incur some cost from stolen books over the three-year installation period. The projected cost of replacing stolen books during the proposed security system's life is as follows:

Year	Cost of replacing stolen books
1	R112 500
2	67 500
3	22 500
4 to 10	0

The board requires at least a 14 per cent internal rate of return on all capital projects.

Required:

1 Calculate the library's net savings during each of the next 10 years if the new security system is installed.
2 Calculate the system's internal rate of return using a financial calculator or a computer software package, or by trial and error.
3 Should the library's board purchase the new security system? Explain your answer.
4 Which of the cash flows mentioned in the problem would be:
(a) the most difficult to estimate (b) the least difficult? Why?

P21.51 Internal rate of return; net present value; uneven cash flows: library

Refer to the data for Problem 21.50. As stated, the total cost of installing the sensor plates in the books is R90 000. Suppose that the R90 000 expenditure could be spread out evenly over the next six years, instead of the next three years, without changing the projected cost of replacing stolen books each year. All other data remain the same.

Required:

1 Would you expect the new security system's internal rate of return to be higher or lower than it was, given the data in the preceding problem? Why? (Do not provide calculations.)

2 Calculate the proposed security system's net present value, given the change in the schedule of expenditures for the placement of sensor panels. Begin by revising the schedule of net savings developed in the preceding problem.

P21.52 Payback; accounting rate of return; NPV: manufacturer

Terry's Tiles Ltd is reviewing a capital investment proposal. The initial cost of the project and the net cash flows for each year are presented in the schedule below. It is estimated that there would be no salvage value at the end of the investment's life.

Year	Initial cost and book value	Annual net cash flows	Annual net profit
0	R1 050 000		
1	700 000	R500 000	R150 000
2	420 000	450 000	170 000
3	210 000	400 000	190 000
4	70 000	350 000	210 000
5	0	300 000	230 000

Terry's uses a required rate of return of 16 per cent to evaluate new capital investment proposals.

Required:

1 Calculate the project's payback period.
2 Calculate the accounting rate of return on the investment proposal. Base your calculation on the initial cost of the investment.
3 Calculate the proposal's net present value.

(CMA, adapted)

P21.53 Net present value; payback period; accounting rate of return: pancake parlour

The owner of Peter's Pancake House is considering an expansion of the business. He has identified two alternatives, as follows:

- Build a new restaurant near the mall.
- Buy and renovate an old building in the centre of the city for the new restaurant.

The projected cash flows from these two alternatives are shown below. The owner of the restaurant uses a 10 per cent discount rate.

	Cash outflow	Cash inflows	
Investment proposal	**Time 0**	**Years 1 to 10**	**Years 11 to 20**
Mall restaurant	R4 000 000	R500 000	R500 000
City restaurant	2 000 000	358 000	–

Required:

1 Calculate the net present value of each alternative restaurant site.
2 The owner of Peter's Pancake House will consider capital projects only if they have a payback period of six years or less. The owner also favours projects that exhibit an accounting rate of return of at least 15 per cent. The owner bases a project's accounting rate of return on the initial investment in the project.
   (a) Calculate the payback period for each of the proposed restaurant sites.
   (b) Calculate the accounting rate of return for each proposed site. (Assume that the average annual incremental profit is R500 000 for the mall restaurant and R358 000 for the city restaurant.)
   (c) If the owner of the restaurant sticks to his criteria, which site will he choose?
   (d) Comment on the pros and cons of the restaurant owner's investment criteria.

Cases

C21.54 Decision problem with alternatives; NPV; IRR; ethics: school

The board of management for the Charters Towers School is considering the acquisition of several minibuses to transport students to school. Five of the school bus routes are underpopulated, so the full-size buses on those routes are not fully utilised. After a careful study, the board has decided that it is not feasible to consolidate these routes into fewer routes served by full-size buses. The area in which the students live is too large for that approach, and the bus ride to school for some students would exceed 45 minutes.

The plan under consideration by the board is to replace five full-size buses with eight minibuses, each of which would cover a much shorter route than that covered by a full-size bus. The bus drivers in this school are part-time employees whose salaries cost the school district R54 000 per year for each driver. In addition to the driver's salary, the annual costs of operating and maintaining a full-size bus amount to R150 000. In contrast, the board projects that a minibus will cost only R60 000 annually to operate and maintain. A minibus driver earns the same wages as those earned by a driver of a full-size bus. The school accountant has estimated that it will cost the school a further R45 750, initially, to redesign its bus routes, pay for the installation of caution signs in certain hazardous locations, and retrain its drivers.

A minibus costs R189 000, whereas a full-size bus costs R360 000. The school uses straight-line depreciation for all its non-current assets. The board has two options regarding the five full-size buses. First, the buses could be sold now for R120 000 each. Second, the buses could be kept in reserve to use for field trips and sports events and to use as back-up vehicles when buses break down. Currently, the board charters buses from a private company for these purposes. The annual cost of chartering buses amounts to R90 000. The accountant has estimated that this cost could be cut to R15 000 per year if the five buses were kept in reserve. The five full-size buses have five years of useful life remaining, either as regularly scheduled buses or as reserve buses. The useful life of a new minibus is also projected to be five years.

Charters Towers School uses a required rate of return of 12 per cent to evaluate all capital expenditure projects.

Required:

1 Think about the decision faced by the board of management. What are the board's two main alternatives?
2 One of these main alternatives contains two options. What are those two options?
3 Suppose that the board of management chooses to buy the minibuses. Prepare a net present value analysis of the two options for the five full-size buses. Should the buses be sold now or kept in reserve?
4 From your answer to requirement 3, you know the best option for the board to choose regarding the full-size buses if the minibuses are purchased. Now you can ignore the other option. Prepare a net present value analysis of the board's two main alternatives:
   (a) continue to use the full-size buses on regular routes; or
   (b) purchase the minibuses.
   Should the minibuses be purchased?
5 Calculate the internal rate of return on the proposed minibus acquisition.
6 What information given in this case was irrelevant to the school board's decision? Explain why the information was irrelevant.

7 Independent of requirements 1 to 6, suppose the NPV analysis favours keeping the full-size buses. Michael Jeffries, accountant for the Charters Towers School, was prepared to recommend that the board not purchase the minibuses. Before doing so, however, Jeffries ran into a long-time friend at his tennis club. Peter Reynolds was the sales manager at the local Ford dealership where the minibuses would have been purchased. Jeffries broke the bad news of his impending recommendation about the minibuses to his friend. The two talked for some time about the pros and cons of the minibus alternative.

Reynolds: Michael, you and I go back a long time. I know you're not paid all that well at the school. Our top financial person is retiring next year. How would you like to come and work for the dealership?
Jeffries: That's pretty tempting, Peter. Let me think it over.
Reynolds: Sure, Michael, take all the time you want. In the meantime, how about rethinking that minibus decision? It's no big deal to you, and I could certainly use the business.
Jeffries: But Peter, I told you what the figures say about that.
Reynolds: Come on, Michael. What are friends for?

Discuss the ethical issues in this situation. What should Michael Jeffries do?

C21.55 Post-completion audit; net present value; internal rate of return: municipal council

The city of Keurboom is located on the southern coast. The city has enjoyed a booming tourist trade, primarily from fishing and boating enthusiasts. In the past, the small river on which Keurboom is located was navigable for most private vessels. In recent years, however, the river has become increasingly clogged with sand. This has reduced the draught of the boating channel in the river. As a result, Keurboom's tourist industry has fallen off dramatically.

In December 20X2, the Keurboom City Council approved a channel-dredging project. The river channel was dredged at a cost of R4 326 000. The Council charged half of this cost to local businesses, which would benefit from restored tourist trade. The City Council estimated that its revenue from parking and boating fees would increase by R630 000 annually over a five-year period as a result of the increased economic activity.

It is now early in 20X8, and the river channel is clogged again. The City Council is considering another channel-dredging operation. Before proceeding, however, the Council has directed its accountant, Bill Visser, to conduct a post-completion audit of the 20X2 channel-dredging project.

After a study of the Council's accounting records, Visser has determined that the actual increase in the Council's revenues amounted to R600 000 per year from 20X3 to 20X7.

The Council's required rate of return for capital expenditure projects is 10 per cent.

Required:

1 Calculate the net present value projected for the channel-dredging operation in 20X2.
2 Calculate the internal rate of return projected on the river project in 20X2.
3 Using the actual revenue discovered by Bill Visser, calculate the actual net present value of the channel-dredging operation to the end of 20X2.
4 Using the actual revenue data, calculate the actual internal rate of return earned on the 20X2 river project.
5 Prepare a post-completion audit report that compares the projection with the actual results of the channel-dredging project. Use the following format for your report:

Cost of 20X2 channel-dredging operation: ______________________
Cost to Council (50 per cent of total cost): ______________________

Annual increase in council revenue		
Projected	**Actual**	**Variance**

Net present value in 20X2		Internal rate of return	
Projected	**Actual**	**Projected**	**Actual**

Endnotes

1 Short-term decisions assume that the effects of the decision are confined to the current year. These decisions, often described as 'tactical decisions', were covered in Chapter 19.

2 Inpatients stay in the hospital for treatment. Outpatients do not stay overnight, but attend the hospital for specific services such as a CT scan or X-ray, or for a consultation with a particular specialist.

3 The concept of relevant costs and revenues is important in both tactical and long-term decisions. This was discussed in detail in Chapter 19.

4 An alternative method is to view the annual cash flows as comprising a five-year, R1 830 000 annuity, and to use the annuity discount factor to calculate the present value of the five years of cost savings. Thus, the present value of the annuity = R1 830 000 × 3.7908 (from Table D at the back of the book) = R6 937 164. The NPV of the project = R6 937 164 − R6 597 150 = R340 014. This is a slightly different answer from that obtained in Exhibit 21.4 of R339 831 using the PV of each year's cash flows, as each yearly present value factor was rounded to four decimal places.

5 The IRR is 11.998 per cent but we have used 12 per cent. It is close enough. If you use a discount rate of 11.998 per cent, the NPV will be exactly zero.

6 Further explanations can be found in Correia et al. (2007).

7 The calculation of the weighted average cost of capital was introduced in Chapter 13.

8 Public hospitals are not subject to income tax. However, private hospitals will be subject to income tax on profits earned. We have assumed up to now that the medical centre is not subject to income tax. Please note that depreciation rates for tax and accounting may differ. However, we will ignore this for now.

9 Many finance writers refer to after-tax cash flows. At this stage we are dealing only with before-tax cash flows. Tax considerations are introduced in Chapter 22.

10 The life cycle approach, presented in Chapter 15, is a useful framework for controlling capital investment projects. The initial data used for the capital investment proposal can be regarded as a life cycle budget, and actual results can be compared with the budget over the life of the project.

11 Using formula (1): $F = R800 \times (1 + 0.12)^{10}$. From Table A, $(1 + 0.12)^{10} = 3.1058$. Thus, the future value of the investment is (R800 × 3.1058) = R2 484.64. Compound interest will more than triple the original R800 investment in 10 years.

12 Using formula (2): $P = R18\,000 \times [1/(1 + 0.08)^4]$. From Table C, $[1/(1 + 0.08)^4] = 0.7350$. Thus, the present value of the required R18 000 amount is (R18 000 × 0.7350) = R13 230. An investment of R13 230 made now, earning annual interest of 8 per cent, will accumulate to R18 000 at the end of four years.

Further Aspects of Capital Expenditure Decisions

Learning Objectives

After completing this chapter, you should be able to:

1. explain the impact of income taxes on capital expenditure decisions in profit-seeking enterprises;
2. determine the after-tax cash flows in a capital expenditure analysis;
3. recognise and account for the effects of accounting versus taxation depreciation on after-tax cash flows;
4. assess the effects on after-tax cash flows of profits or losses on the disposal of non-current assets;
5. assess the effects of changes in working capital on after-tax cash flows;
6. evaluate a capital expenditure proposal using a discounted cash flow analysis, considering income tax effects;
7. incorporate the effects of income taxes in the calculation of the pay-back method and the accounting rate of return;
8. discuss the difficulty of ranking investment proposals using discounted cash flow techniques;
9. describe the process of justifying investments in advanced technologies in manufacturing and service firms;
10. explain the limitations of conventional capital expenditure analysis for evaluating investments in large-scale technologies; and
11. after studying the appendix, explain the impact of inflation on a capital budgeting analysis.

Introduction

In Chapter 21 we introduced approaches to evaluating capital expenditure decisions and explained the importance of these decisions for creating shareholder and customer value. Income taxes influence many decisions made in profit-seeking enterprises. Sometimes, tax considerations are so crucial in a capital expenditure decision that they dominate all other aspects of the analysis. In this chapter, we continue the discussion of capital expenditure decisions and discounted cash flow analysis, by focusing on income tax considerations.

We also consider the additional problems that arise when attempting to justify investments in advanced technologies. Often, conventional methods of determining and analysing cash flows cannot easily capture important strategic or competitive factors.

Income taxes and capital expenditure analysis

L.O. 1

When a business makes a profit, it usually pays income taxes. Since many cash flows associated with a capital expenditure proposal affect the business' profit, they also affect the firm's income tax liability. These income tax payments are cash flows, and they must be considered in any analysis of cash flows arising from a capital expenditure proposal.

After-tax cash flows

L.O. 2

The first step in an analysis of cash flows for a profit-seeking enterprise is to determine the after-tax cash flows associated with the investment projects under consideration. An **after-tax cash flow** is the cash flow expected after all tax implications have been taken into account. The financial aspects of a project must be examined carefully to determine its potential tax impact.

To illustrate the tax implications of a capital expenditure project, we will focus on a retail business. High Country Department Stores operates two department stores in Kwazulu-Natal. The firm has a large store in Durban (eThikweni) and a smaller store in Pietermaritzburg (Msunduzi). The company is quite profitable, and management is considering several capital expenditure projects that will enhance the firm's future profit potential. Before analysing these projects, let's pause to consider the tax issues that the company is likely to face. For the purposes of our discussion, we will assume that the current company tax rate is 29 per cent.[1] Thus, if the company's taxable profit is R10 000 000, its income tax expense will be R2 900 000 (R10 000 000 × 29 per cent).

The tax effect of an increase in sales

Suppose that High Country's management is considering the purchase of an additional delivery truck. As with the tactical decisions described in Chapter 19, we will consider the incremental revenues and incremental costs that may arise from this decision. The sales manager estimates that a new truck will allow the company to increase annual sales revenue by R1 100 000. These additional sales will involve an increase in cost of goods sold of R600 000. Thus, the additional gross profit resulting from the additional sales before tax is R500 000. What is High Country's after-tax cash flow from the incremental sales?

Incremental sales revenue		R1 100 000
Incremental expenses (cost of goods sold)		−600 000
Incremental gross profit		500 000
Incremental income tax	500 000 × 29%	−145 000
After-tax cash flow (net inflow after taxes)		R355 000

Although the incremental sales resulted in an additional cash inflow of R500 000, the cash outflow from income taxes increases by R145 000. Thus, the after-tax cash inflow from the increased sales is R355 000.

A quick method for calculating the after-tax cash inflow from increased sales is the following:

After-tax cash flow = (incremental sales revenue net of cost of goods sold) × (1 − tax rate)
= R500 000 × (1 − 0.29)
= R355 000

The tax effect of additional expenses

What are the tax implications of additional cash expenses associated with a project? Suppose that the addition of the delivery truck under consideration by High Country's management will involve hiring an additional three employees, whose combined annual salary plus on-costs will amount to R300 000.

Incremental expense		300 000
Reduction in income tax	300 000 × 29%	−87 000
After-tax cash flow (net outflow after taxes)		213 000

Although the additional employees' total salaries amount to R300 000, this expense is tax-deductible. Thus, the firm's income tax payment will be reduced by R87 000. As a result, the after-tax cash outflow from the additional expenditure is R213 000.

A quick method for calculating the after-tax cash outflow from an incremental cash expense is as follows:

After-tax cash flow = (incremental expense) × (1 − tax rate)
= R300 000 × (1 − 0.29)
= R213 000

Non-cash expenses

Not all expenses represent cash outflows in the current period. The most common example of a non-cash expense is depreciation expense. Suppose that High Country Department Stores' management are considering the purchase of a delivery truck that costs R400 000 and has no salvage value. Let's assume the truck will be depreciated for tax purposes, as shown in Exhibit 22.1.

As discussed in Chapter 21, the only cash flow shown in Exhibit 22.1 is the truck's acquisition cost of R400 000 at time 0. We assume that the truck has an estimated useful life of five years. The depreciation expense in each of the next five years is not a cash flow. However, depreciation reduces the firm's taxable profit. For example, the R80 000 depreciation expense in year 1 will reduce High Country's taxable profit by R80 000. As a result, the company's year 1 income tax payment will decrease as follows:

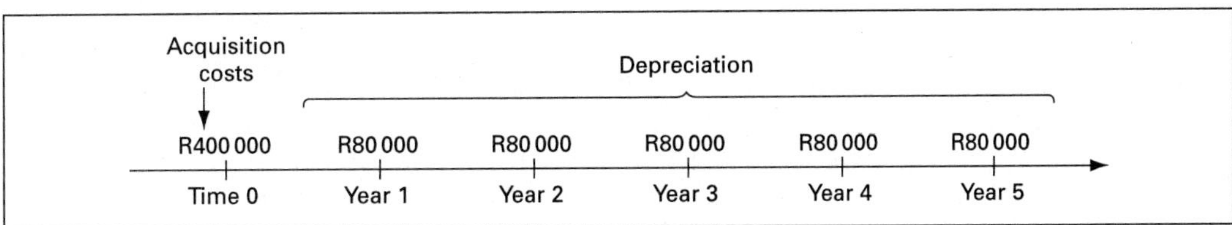

Exhibit 22.1 Depreciation charges on delivery truck, High Country Department Stores

Decrease in income tax = non-cash expense × tax rate
= R80 000 × 0.29
= R23 200

The annual depreciation expense associated with the truck provides a reduction in income tax expense equal to the firm's tax rate multiplied by the depreciation. Although depreciation is not a cash flow, it does cause a reduced cash outflow because it reduces the tax payable.

Cash flows not on the profit statement

Some cash flows do not appear on the profit statement in the same period in which they occur. They are not revenues or expenses. A common example of such a cash outflow is the purchase of an asset. If High Country Department Stores purchases the delivery truck, the R400 000 acquisition cost is a cash outflow but not an expense of the current period. A purchase is merely the exchange of one asset (cash) for another (a delivery truck). The expense associated with the truck's purchase is recognised through the depreciation expense, throughout the asset's depreciable life. Thus, the cash outflow resulting from the purchase of an asset does not affect profit and has no direct tax consequences. However, it is a cash flow for the purposes of capital expenditure analysis.

Net present value analysis, after tax cash flows

Now let's complete our example by preparing a net present value analysis of the proposed delivery truck acquisition. Exhibit 22.2 shows that there will be a positive NPV of R195 513, which supports the decision to purchase the delivery truck. (Note that an after-tax required rate of return of 12 per cent has been assumed.)

High Country Department Stores							
Purchase of delivery truck							
		0	1	2	3	4	5
Cost		−400 000					
Cash flow from additional sales	500 000 × 0.71		355 000	355 000	355 000	355 000	355 000
Cash flow form additional wages	−300 000 × 0.71		−213 000	−213 000	−213 000	−213 000	−213 000
Cash flow effect of depreciation	80 000 × 0.29		23 200	23 200	23 200	23 200	23 200
		−400 000	165 200	165 200	165 200	165 200	165 200
Discount factor @ 12%		1.0000	0.8929	0.7972	0.7118	0.6355	0.5674
		−400 000	147 507	131 697	117 589	104 985	93 734
		Net present value		**R 195 512**			

Exhibit 22.2 Net present value analysis with after-tax cash flows for purchase of delivery truck, High Country Department Stores

Assumptions about timing of tax payments

We have assumed in our analysis that the cash flows resulting from income taxes occur during the same year as that in which the before-tax cash flows occur. For example, High Country's management predict that sales revenue will increase by R1 100 000 per year if the truck is purchased. This will increase profit by R500 000, and will therefore increase the cash outflow from income taxes by R145 000. We have assumed that the R145 000 cash outflow from incremental taxes occurs in the same year as the R500 000 cash inflow from the incremental sales. In South Africa, while taxation regulations change yearly, many businesses make most of their tax payments after the close of their taxation year.

It is too difficult to illustrate these effects in this chapter, but they should certainly be included in any comprehensive capital expenditure analysis.

Timing of cash flows

Another assumption we have made in our analysis is that the cash flows of a proposal occur in the same year in which they are recognised as revenues and expenses. If you have studied financial accounting you will understand that this is not always the case. Under accrual accounting, recognition of revenues or expenses is not determined by the payment or receipt of cash. While we could recognise these slight timing differences in our analysis, the additional complexity would be hard to justify. Working capital adjustments can be made to move from the accrual to the cash basis.

As in the examples discussed in Chapter 21, we have assumed that all cash flows occur at yearend, for discounting purposes.

L.O. 3

Depreciation methods

The main concept underlying discounted cash flow analysis is the time value of money. We discount each cash flow to find its present value. Since money has a time value, it is advantageous for a business to take tax deductions as early as allowable under the tax law. South African tax law allows companies to depreciate their assets using the reducing balance method or the straight line method. The reducing balance method may allow higher depreciation rates to be used, based on the written-down value of the asset. The Income Tax Act provides a schedule of depreciation rates that can be used for various classes of assets.

Tax depreciation rates are expressed as a percentage per annum, such as 20 per cent straight line or 30 per cent reducing balance. These depreciation rates are applied to the original cost of the asset, without adjustments for salvage value or explicit consideration of life of the asset.[2]

Taxation depreciation versus accounting depreciation

It should be noted that in many businesses, the depreciation rates used for taxation purposes differ from those used for external reporting purposes. The South African Revenue Service will permit firms to use depreciation deductions that are specified in the Income Tax Act or in associated schedules and practice notes. Depreciation used for external reporting purposes is governed by the requirements of the International Accounting Standard on Depreciation, IAS 16. Under the standard, depreciation is a systematic method for allocating the cost of an asset over its useful life. In estimating this expense, the accountant must consider the estimated useful life of the asset and the pattern of usage over that life.

Thus, the amount of depreciation deducted for taxation purposes may differ from the depreciation expense used to calculate accounting profit.[3] In fact, the use of the reducing balance method for depreciation ensures that assets may be written off more quickly for tax purposes than for accounting purposes. In some smaller businesses, we may find taxation depreciation is used in the calculation of accounting profits.

When considering the impact on cash flows of a capital expenditure project, the accountant must be careful to consider the cash flow effect resulting from taxation depreciation, not accounting depreciation.

Depreciation deductions and cash flow

It is important to realise that a depreciation deduction is not a cash flow. However, a depreciation deduction will lower a firm's taxable income and this will result in a tax saving, which is a cash flow. The effect on the firm's cash flow is:

$$\text{Depreciation deduction} \times \text{tax rate}$$

An operating cash inflow is a cash flow subject to income tax and we consider the after-tax effect of this cash flow by recording the inflow and reducing the cash flow by any tax due. For example, the operating cash flow may be R10 million per year and we assume that this is subject to tax. The cash inflow is R10 million and the tax is R2.9 million (R10m × 29 per cent). The company thereby retains 71 per cent (1 − tax rate) of the cash flow. Depreciation is not a cash flow but it results in a tax saving of 29 per cent of such a deduction.

Depreciation deductions in terms of the Income Tax Act

The South African Revenue Service will often use depreciation deductions to encourage firms to invest in plant and equipment. In terms of section 12C of the Income Tax Act, a firm may qualify for a depreciation deduction of 40 per cent of cost in the first year and 20 per cent of cost in each of the subsequent three years. This only applies to manufacturing plant and machinery that is brought into use in the tax year. There is no apportionment of this deduction, so that acquiring plant and machinery at the end of a company's tax year will result in a full deduction for that year. If a company invests in plant and machinery that is used, then in terms of section 12C the firm will qualify for a straight-line depreciation deduction of 20 per cent of cost per year.

Buildings that are used in a process of manufacturing may qualify for a straight-line depreciation deduction of 5 per cent of cost per year. This deduction also applies to hotel buildings. There are special depreciation deductions for buildings constructed in designated urban redevelopment zones. Ships may be depreciated at a rate of 20 per cent of cost per year and this deduction may also apply to aircraft. If there are no specific deductions, then assets will qualify for a wear-and-tear allowance in terms of section 11(e) of the Income Tax Act. For example, the investment in motor vehicles will qualify for a straight-line wear and tear allowance (depreciation deduction) of 25 per cent per year, whilst furniture and fittings are subject to a wear-and-tear deduction of 20 per cent per year. Please refer to www.sars.gov.za for a full schedule of write-off periods for various assets. Search for 'depreciation' and Practice Notes 19 and 39.

Profit and loss on disposal – recoupments and scrapping allowances

L.O. 4 Capital expenditure decisions frequently involve the disposal of assets, and sometimes profits or losses result. We are not concerned with the accounting profit on the sale of an asset, as this is not a cash flow. However, if a company sells an asset at a price above the asset's tax value, then a recoupment will occur which is subject to tax. Thus, the tax effects of profits and losses on disposal of assets can be an important feature of a capital expenditure decision.

The **tax value** (or **written-down value**) of an asset is the asset's acquisition cost minus the accumulated tax depreciation to date. When an asset is sold for more than its current tax value, a **recoupment** is recorded. The recoupment is the difference between the proceeds from sale and the asset's tax value. A **scrapping allowance** is recorded when an asset is sold for less than its current tax value. When analysing the cash flows of a capital expenditure project, it is the tax value resulting from taxation depreciation that is relevant. The book value of a non-current asset recorded in the financial accounting records may differ from the asset's tax value because of the different depreciation rates used. (This was explained in the previous section.)

To illustrate, suppose High Country Department Stores owns a forklift that cost R100 000 and has currently accumulated tax depreciation of R60 000. The forklift's book value is calculated as follows:

$$\begin{aligned}\text{Tax value} &= \text{acquisition cost} - \text{accumulated tax depreciation to date}\\ &= \text{R}100\,000 - \text{R}60\,000\\ &= \text{R}40\,000\end{aligned}$$

Scenario 1: Recoupment (profit) on disposal

Suppose that High Country sells the forklift for R50 000. The recoupment on disposal is R10 000 (R50 000 proceeds minus R40 000 tax value) and this will be added to the firm's taxable income. If High Country's income tax rate is 29 per cent, the following cash flows will occur at the time of the sale:

Cash inflow: proceeds from sale		R50 000
Cash outflow: incremental income tax due to the profit on disposal	10 000 × 0.29	−2 900
Net cash flow		R47 100

Although High Country sold the forklift for R50 000, the company's net cash benefit is only R47 100. The firm must pay the other R2900 in increased income taxes on the R10 000 profit. In terms of the Income Tax Act, this is called a tax recoupment. Recoupments are limited to cost so that if an asset is sold above cost, then the recoupment will be limited to:

Recoupment = cost − tax value

Any amount above cost will be subject to capital gains tax, which we explain later in the chapter.

Scenario 2: Scrapping allowance (loss on disposal)

Now assume instead that High Country Department Stores sells the forklift for R32 000. The scrapping allowance (loss on the sale) is R8000 (R32 000 proceeds − R40 000 tax value). If High Country's income tax rate is 29 per cent, the following cash flows will occur at the time of the sale:

Cash inflow: proceeds from sale		R32 000
Cash inflow: incremental tax saving due to the loss on disposal	8000 × 0.29	2 320
Net cash flow		R34 320

Although High Country sold the forklift for only R32 000, the company's total benefit from the sale is R34 320. The extra R2320 comes from a reduction in income taxes due to the loss on the sale.

Implications for capital expenditure decisions

Why is the analysis above likely to be relevant in a capital expenditure decision? Suppose that High Country Department Stores has the opportunity to sell its old forklift for R32 000 and buy a new one for R120 000. The company will save R50 000 in annual operating expenses over the next 5 years if the new forklift is used instead of the old forklift. The market value of the new forklift in 5 years' time is R42 000. The new forklift qualifies for a straight-line section 12C depreciation deduction of 20 per cent per year. The old forklift is currently being depreciated for tax purposes on a straight-line basis and the current tax depreciation charge is R8000 per year. The market value of the old forklift in 5 years' time will be zero.

A net present value analysis of this replacement decision is presented in Exhibit 22.3. The tax impact of the loss on disposal of the old forklift is part of the machine replacement analysis. Without the tax savings associated with the loss on disposal, the net present value of the new forklift would have been cut by R34 320.[4] The tax payable due to the recoupment on the sale of the new forklift in 5 years' time is recorded as a cash outflow.

Capital Gains Tax

Since 1 October 2001 all gains above cost are subject to capital gains tax (CGT). Capital gains tax occurs only when an asset is sold and the base cost includes the acquisition cost and the cost of any improvements. Only 50 per cent (the current inclusion rate) of any capital gain is subject to capital gains tax. An example will illustrate the combined impact of CGT and normal tax on the sale of plant and machinery.

Example

Assume that Molo Ltd acquired used plant and machinery on 31 June 2002 at a cost of R2 million. The company qualified for a section 12C straight-line depreciation deduction of 20 per cent of cost per year. After three years, the company sells the plant and machinery for R3 million. The company will be subject to a recoupment of depreciation deductions and a capital gain of R1 million (R3m − R2m). The tax effects of the recoupment and the capital gain are shown in Exhibit 22.4

Investment in working capital

L.O. 5

Some capital investment proposals require additional outlays for working capital. **Working capital**, defined as the excess of current assets over current liabilities, often increases as the result of higher balances in accounts receivable or inventory necessary to support a project. Such increases are cash outflows and should be included in an analysis of cash flows.

To illustrate, suppose that the City of Kimberley has offered High Country Department Stores a contract to sell special T-shirts and mementos commemorating the city's 'Back to Diamonds'

Exhibit 22.3 Net present value analysis, forklift replacement decision, High Country Department Stores

High Country Department Stores
Forklift replacement decision

		0	1	2	3	4	5
Acquisition cost of new forklift		−120 000					
Proceeds of sale from old forklift		32 000					
Tax saving due to loss on sale*		2 320					
Proceeds on the sale of the new forklift							42 000
Tax due on recoupment							−12 180
Annual cost savings × (1 − tax rate)	50 000 × 71%		35 500	35 500	35 500	35 500	35 500
Depreciation deduction on new forklift	24 000 × 29%		6 960	6 960	6 960	6 960	6 960
Loss of depreciation deduction on old forklift†	8000 × 29%		−2 320	−2 320	−2 320	−2 320	−2 320
		−85 680	40 140	40 140	40 140	40 140	69 960
PV Factor	10%	1.0000	0.9091	0.8264	0.7513	0.6830	0.6209
Present values		−85 680	36 491	33 172	30 157	27 416	43 438
Net present value of new forklift [sum of present values]		R **84 994**					

		Old forklift	New forklift
Proceeds on sale of forklift		32 000	42 000
Tax value at time of disposal		40 000	0
Scrapping allowance/recoupment		−8 000	42 000
Tax saving/tax payable	29%	2 320	−12 180

* The assumption that the reduction in tax cash flows due to the loss on sale occurs at time 0 may be unrealistic. It may occur during year 1.

† By selling now we will not be able to claim future depreciation deductions on the old forklift.

Tax effects	Amount	Inclusion rate	Taxable	Tax rate	Tax
Recoupment	1 200 000	100%	1 200 000	29%	348 000
Capital Gain	1 000 000	50%	500 000	29%	145 000
	2 200 000				493 000
Cost		2 000 000			
Depreciation to date		1 200 000[R2m × 20% × 3 years]			
Tax value		800 000			
Proceeds (limited to cost)		2 000 000			
Tax value		(800 000)			
Recoupment		1 200 000			

Exhibit 22.4 Tax effects of a recoupment and capital gain on sale of plant and machinery

festival. The contract covers the three-year period leading up to the celebration. The sales proposal will require a R200 000 outlay for additional working capital throughout the three-year period. The increased working capital is largely due to a higher balance in inventory. In evaluating the contract, we would include the investment in working capital as an outflow at time zero. Since the increase in working capital is not released until the end of year 3, that R200 000 inflow is discounted. Even though the company will recover the working capital investment, the cash outflow occurs today and the inflow occurs only at the end of year 3.

Comprehensive illustration of income tax effects

L.O. 6

We have now covered most of the important aspects needed for analysing a capital expenditure proposal in a profit-seeking enterprise. A comprehensive illustration will help to consolidate your understanding of these concepts. High Country Department Stores' management are considering the installation of a new checkout system for the company's Durban store. The computerised system would include new cash registers at each checkout station. In addition, the new checkout system would include barcode readers so that most goods could be checked out automatically instead of manually. The advantages of the new system are increased accuracy in the checkout process, auto-

High Country Department Stores Computerised checkout system decision	
Old checkout equipment	
Remaining useful life, assuming overhaul in year 2	6 years
Cost of overhaul in year 2	R35 000
Current tax value (fully depreciated)	0
Current salvage value	12 000
Salvage value in six years' time	0
New checkout equipment	
Depreciation—25% straight-line	
Acquisition cost of new equipment	R500 000
Update of software required in year 3	40 000
Salvage value of new equipment in six years	10 000
Cost to retrain checkout staff	50 000
Cost to retag inventory	30 000
Annual data	
Annual operating cost savings	150 000
Annual cost of computer system operator	300 000
Annual cost of marketing data analysis	45 000
Annual incremental profits resulting from additional sales*	400 000
After-tax required rate of return	12%
Tax rate	29%

* Profits on increased sales generated from the marketing data analysis

Exhibit 22.5 Data for extended illustration

matic updating of computerised inventory records, and the ability to gather data about customers' buying patterns and trends. Exhibit 22.5 presents the data for the decision.

Notice that the old equipment has been fully depreciated already. However, its useful life can be extended to six more years if an overhaul is done in year 2. The new equipment also has an expected useful life of six years, and the equipment qualifies for a straight-line depreciation deduction of 25 per cent per year. Most of the data in Exhibit 22.5 are self-explanatory. The last two items under 'Annual data' relate to the new checkout system's capability for gathering data about customer demand patterns. The extra data analysis will cost R45 000 annually, but it is expected to generate increased sales which would result in additional profits of R400 000 per annum.

A net present value analysis of the new checkout system proposal is given in Exhibit 22.6. The present value of each financial item and the net present value are calculated for replacing the old equipment with new equipment. An explanation of each line in the exhibit follows. All discount factors are drawn from Table C.

	0	1	2	3	4	5	6
(1) Cost of retraining checkout staff	−35 500						
(2) Cost to retag retail inventory	−21 300						
(3) Update of software				−28 400			
(4) Overhaul avoided			24 850				
(5) Annual operating cost savings		106 500	106 500	106 500	106 500	106 500	106 500
(6) Annual cost of computer operator		−213 000	−213 000	−213 000	−213 000	−213 000	−213 000
(7) Annual cost of marketing analysis		−31 950	−31 950	−31 950	−31 950	−31 950	−31 950
(8) Annual profits from increased sales		284 000	284 000	284 000	284 000	284 000	284 000
	−56 800	145 550	170 400	117 150	145 550	145 550	145 550
(9) Cost of new equipment	−500 000						
(10) Proceeds on sale of old equipment	8 520						
(11) Proceeds on sale of new equipment							7 100
(12) Tax saving from depreciation deduction		36 250	36 250	36 250	36 250		
Cash flows	−548 280	181 800	206 650	153 400	181 800	145 550	152 650
PV Factor (12%)	1.0000	0.8929	0.7972	0.7118	0.6355	0.5674	0.5066
Present Values	−548 280	162 329	164 741	109 190	115 534	82 585	77 332
(13) NPV (sum of present values)	**163 431**						

Exhibit 22.6 Comprehensive example of net present value analysis with tax effects

(1) and (2) These one-time cash flows are required to retrain checkout personnel (R50 000) and retag inventory (R30 000) to accommodate the new bar code readers. Since these costs are tax deductions, we multiply by (1 − tax rate).

(3) The cost of updating the software in year 3 is a tax deduction, so we multiply R40 000 by (1 − tax rate) [R40 000 × 0.71 = R28 400]

(4) Investing in the new equipment means that the firm is not required to undertake the overhaul at a cost of R35 000 which is R24 850 after tax [R35 000 × (1−tax rate)]. This is a saving attributable to investing in the new equipment.

(5), (6), (7) and (8) These items are annual cash flows. We could have summed the cash flows, and then multiply the R205 000 annuity by (1 − tax rate) because each of the net cash flows is taxable.

(9) Line (9) records the acquisition cost of the new checkout equipment. This cash flow has no tax impact and does not need to be discounted, since it occurs at time 0.

(10) The old equipment can be sold in year 0 for R12 000. Since it has a tax value of zero, there will be a recoupment. We assume that the recoupment will occur at the same time as the sale of the equipment. The R12 000 proceeds are not taxed (line 10), but the recoupment of R12 000, being the difference between the proceeds and the tax value of zero, is taxable.

(11) The new equipment can be sold in year 6 for R10 000. Since it will be written down to zero at that time, there will be a recoupment. (The tax saving from the depreciation deduction is shown at line 12.) The R10 000 proceeds are not taxed (line 8), but the recoupment of R10 000, being the difference between the proceeds and the tax value of zero, is taxable.

(12) The annual depreciation deductions are not cash flows, but they do cause a reduction in income taxes. We multiply the depreciation deduction of R125 000 (R500 000 × 25 per cent) by the tax rate [R125 000 × 0.29 = R36 250].

(13) The net present value of the purchase of new equipment is R163 431.

The financial analysis supports the decision to purchase the new checkout equipment. The NPV of the new equipment is positive.

We could determine the before tax cash flows separately from the tax calculation as this is often done in practice. A single tax amount is included per period. The answer is always the same. We have done this in Exhibit 22.7.

Using after-tax profit for other capital expenditure analysis techniques

L.O. 7

Just as the effects of taxation can be incorporated into discounted cash flow analysis, the formulas for payback and accounting rate of return can also be amended to take account of taxation. In any taxable business, it is important to consider after-tax cash flows rather than before-tax cash flows when analysing cash flows for capital expenditure decisions. Thus, we can amend the formulas presented in Chapter 21:

$$\text{Payback period} = \frac{\text{initial investment}}{\text{annual after-tax cash inflow}}$$

$$\text{Accounting rate of return} = \frac{\text{average annual profit after tax from the project}}{\text{initial investment}}$$

Ranking investment projects

L.O. 8

Suppose that a company has several potential capital expenditure projects, all of which have positive net present values. If a discount rate is used based on the firm's weighted average cost of capital, then any project with a positive NPV will earn a return greater than the cost of funds required to support the project. It may be that, in practice, only a few higher ranking proposals are accepted—a form of capital rationing takes place. This may not always be because of a limited supply of investment capital, but because of other constraints. For example, managers may feel that they cannot devote sufficient attention to all the desirable projects. The solution, then, is to select only some of the positive NPV proposals. This requires a ranking of all the proposed projects.

However, there are difficulties in ranking independent investment projects with positive net present values and different lives. To illustrate, suppose that the management of High Country Department Stores is considering two investment opportunities:

	0	1	2	3	4	5	6
Cost of retraining checkout staff	−50 000						
Cost to retag retail inventory	−30 000						
Update of software				−40 000			
Overhaul avoided			35 000				
Annual operating cost savings		150 000	150 000	150 000	150 000	150 000	150 000
Annual cost of computer operator		−300 000	−300 000	−300 000	−300 000	−300 000	−300 000
Annual cost of marketing analysis		−45 000	−45 000	−45 000	−45 000	−45 000	−45 000
Annual profits from increased sales		400 000	400 000	400 000	400 000	400 000	400 000
	−80 000	205 000	240 000	165 000	205 000	205 000	205 000
Cost of new equipment	−500 000						
Proceeds on sale of old equipment	12 000						
Proceeds on sale of new equipment							10 000
Taxation	19 720	−23 200	−33 350	−11 600	−23 200	−59 450	−62 350
Cash flows	−548 280	181 800	206 650	153 400	181 800	145 550	152 650
PV Factor	1.0000	0.8929	0.7972	0.7118	0.6355	0.5674	0.5066
Present Values	−548 280	162 329	164 741	109 190	115 534	82 585	77 332
NPV (sum of present values)	**163 431**						
Taxation							
Taxable income/loss from operations	−80 000	205 000	240 000	165 000	205 000	205 000	205 000
Depreciation deduction: cost × 25%		−125 000	−125 000	−125 000	−125 000		
Recoupment on sale of new equipment							10 000
Recoupment on sale of old equipment	12 000						
Taxable income/loss	−68 000	80 000	115 000	40 000	80 000	205 000	215 000
Tax	−19 720	23 200	33 350	11 600	23 200	59 450	62 350

Exhibit 22.7 Comprehensive example of net present value analysis with separate tax calculation

- *Proposal A*: Open a small gift shop at Cape Point. High Country's management believe the benefits of this proposal would last only six years; after that, their competitors would move into Cape Point and eliminate High Country's advantageous position.
- *Proposal B*: Open a small gift shop at O R Tambo Airport. High Country Department Stores would sign a 10-year lease for this shop.

The predicted cash flows for these investment proposals are as follows:

Investment proposal	Cash outflow time 0	After tax cash inflows Years 1–6	Years 7–10	Present value of inflows 12%	Net present value	Internal rate of return
A (Cape Point)	−544 500	140 000	0	575 596	31 096	14.0%
B (Airport)	−1 017 000	190 000	190 000	1 073 538	56 538	13.3%

Both investment proposals have positive net present values. Suppose, however, that due to limited managerial time, High Country's management has decided to pursue only one project. Which proposal should be ranked higher? This is a difficult question to answer. Proposal B has a higher net present value but a lower internal rate of return. While Proposal A has a higher internal rate of return, this return of 14 per cent applies only to its six-year time horizon. If management accept Proposal A, what will happen in years 7 to 10? Will the facilities and equipment remain idle? Or could they be used profitably for another purpose? These questions are left unanswered by the analysis.

The main reason that the NPV and IRR methods of analysis yield different rankings for these two proposals is that the projects have different lives. Without making an assumption about what will happen in years 7 to 10 if Proposal A is accepted, the NPV and IRR methods do not help us to rank the proposals in any sound manner. One approach to the problem posed in this illustration is to accept that both projects are desirable, and that either could be selected. Each proposal exhibits a positive NPV and an IRR greater than the hurdle rate of 12 per cent.

Profitability index

One criterion that managers sometimes apply in ranking investment proposals is called the **profitability index** (or **excess present value index**), which is defined as follows:

$$\text{Profitability index} = \frac{\text{present value of cash flows, exclusive of initial investment}}{\text{initial investment}}$$

The profitability indices for High Country's two investment proposals are calculated as follows:

Investment proposal	PV/Cost	Profitability Index	NPV	IRR
A (Cape Point)	$\frac{575\,596}{544\,500}$ =	1.06	31 096	14.0%
B (Airport)	$\frac{1\,073\,538}{1\,017\,000}$ =	1.06	56 538	13.3%

Although Proposal A has a lower NPV than Proposal B, and Proposal A exhibits a higher IRR than Proposal B, they both have the same profitability index! If one proposal had a higher profitability index than the other, could we rely on this? Unfortunately, this method suffers from the same drawbacks as those associated with the NPV or IRR methods. Both proposals exhibit a profitability index greater than 1.00, which merely reflects their positive NPVs. Thus, both projects are desirable. The unequal lives of the two proposals prevent the profitability index from indicating a theoretically correct ranking of the proposals. The relative desirability of proposals A and B depends on what will happen in years 7 to 10 if Proposal A is selected.

In summary: If a manager chooses not to accept all projects with positive NPVs, because of capital rationing, then the required ranking may ultimately need to be made on subjective criteria.

Justification of investments in advanced technologies

L.O. 9

The manufacturing environment has changed dramatically as many firms have adopted management philosophies such as total quality management (TQM) and just-in-time (JIT). In many industries there has been a move towards the adoption of computer-integrated manufacturing (CIM) systems. In non-manufacturing areas there may also be large investments in new technologies. Banks are continually evaluating and investing in computerised processing systems, including electronic funds transfer systems. In the tourism industry, large investments in information technology are also very common.

While many firms may consider making investments in technologically advanced systems, managers are often frustrated when the analysis indicates a negative net present value for a proposed investment. While they may believe intuitively that an investment will provide a competitive edge, managers are hindered when the NPV analysis points to rejection of the proposal.

What is the problem here? Are managers too optimistic about the advantages of new technologies? Or are discounted cash flow approaches inappropriate for such investment decisions? One problem with discounted cash flow exercises is the difficulty of quantifying the relevant benefits and costs that might arise from investments in advanced technologies, especially those with strategic implications.

REAL LIFE: JUSTIFYING 'SOFT' INVESTMENTS

Capital expenditure does not just involve the purchase of buildings, equipment and other 'hard' assets. It can also apply to investments in software systems, information technology, new product development and organisational restructuring projects. Many organisations are investing in enterprise resource planning (ERP) software, such as SAP and PeopleSoft®. These are integrated systems that have the potential to revolutionise the way in which an organisation manages its accounting, inventory, purchasing, manufacturing, human resources and other areas of the business. Such investments run into millions of Rands, and take several years to implement, so capital investment proposals may be needed to provide a strong business case. But can the benefits of such systems be justified? Can the outcomes of these investments be assessed?

In a survey of 30 directors of information technology in the US, many organisations were found not to justify their initial investment in ERP systems in quantitative terms, due to the difficulty of valuing the intangible benefits. The investment in ERP was simply looked on as providing a means for remaining competitive in the marketplace—it was the cost of doing business.

Nor did many of these same organisations use measures to assess the benefits once the initial investment had been made. Managers saw quantitative measures as inadequate, providing only a partial picture of the value provided by the investment. However, 42 per cent of respondents revealed that they did measure the value achieved from their ERP system. Common measures used in this post-audit, for the financial modules of such systems, included increased inventory turnover, reduced obsolete inventory, favourable material price variances and reductions in IT department costs. For human resource modules, measures included reduction in HR costs and reduction in time to execute payroll. Many of the managers believed that in the initial capital investment proposal it was essential to identify targeted benefits for the project, and then to assess achievement of those targets through performance measures. If the project is not a success, then a review of performance using these measures will indicate where the problems lie.

Source: Bradford & Roberts (2001)

Quantifying the strategic impact of a capital investment

Sometimes managers adopt capital investment proposals, even though they do not meet the required rate of return. This is due to the realisation that the analyses did not formally consider strategic issues.

Let's consider the example of a major South African chemical company that considered investing in new manufacturing technology. Many of its competitors in Japan, Korea and Taiwan were already using this technology. However, when the formal investment analysis was undertaken, the proposal was rejected because it did not pass the company's hurdle rate. The result of not investing in the technology meant that the company lost considerable market share over the next few years. Competitors who had installed the advanced equipment were able to exploit their low-cost advantage and achieve high-quality levels for their products. In the formal analysis of cash flows, the changes that would come about if the company did not invest in the new technology were overlooked. The types of issues that were ignored were the likely actions of competitors that could lead to a loss of market share.

Often the estimates of cash flows related to a capital investment project are compared with the wrong baseline. There is an implicit assumption in many capital expenditure analyses that, if a particular project is not approved, things will stay the same. This is rarely the case, as many large capital investment projects are of strategic importance; not investing can have a serious effect on the firm's competitive position. Exhibit 22.8 illustrates this point. In considering whether to invest in new leading-edge production technology, a reduction in cash flows or profits (line 3) may occur if the investment does not take place and competitors adopt the new technology. If the conventional approach is taken (line 2), the benefits of investment in new technologies may be understated. Conventional analysis would measure the cash flow implications of investing in a project as vertical line A, which assumes that things stay the same if the investment does not take place. However, this assumed status quo may be unrealistic. Rather, the cash flow implications of the proposed expenditure should be measured as the vertical line B—the difference between the cash flows of the new investment and the reduction in cash flows if the project does not proceed.

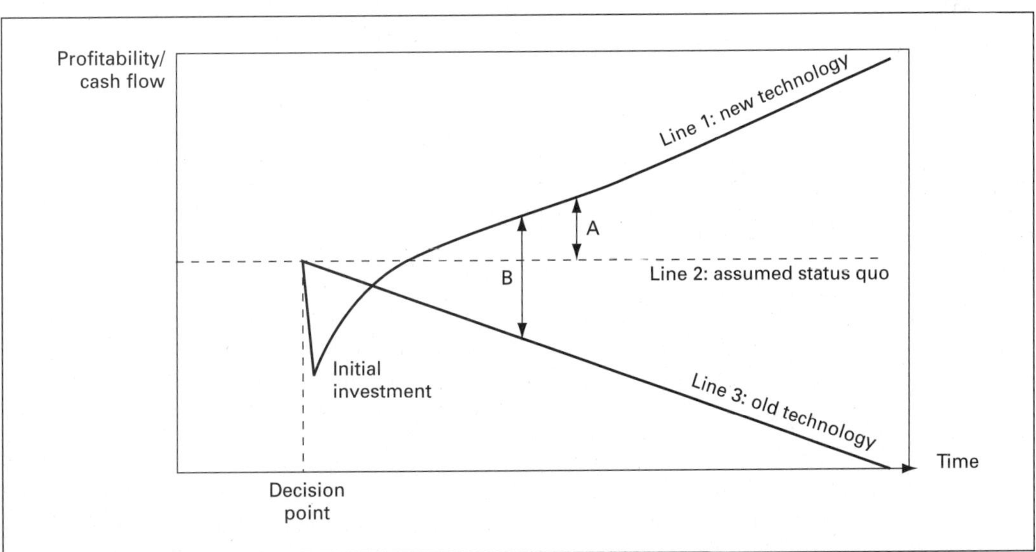

Source: Samson, Langfield-Smith & McBride (1991). Copyright CPA Australia. Reproduced with the permission of CPA Australia and acknowledgment of the authors.

Exhibit 22.8 The impact of not investing in new technology

Investing in new information and communications technologies

We are all aware of the very rapid changes that occur continually in information and communications technologies. Every day we are confronted by catalogues that remind us that our mobile phone is now outdated within six months of purchase, and our most up-to-date personal computer has faded into technological obscurity within a year! While this situation may be frustrating for us, it presents a major problem for businesses that rely on these technologies as a source of competitive advantage. Failure to invest in the latest technology may result in the demise of their business rather than the maintenance of the status quo.

The limitations of conventional capital expenditure analysis

L.O. 10 There are several issues that can limit the usefulness of conventional capital expenditure analyses and often cause blockages to the investment in large-scale technologies (Kaplan, 1986; Berliner & Brimson, 1988; Noble, 1990).

- *An unrealistic status quo.* As explained above, it should not be assumed that the current cash flow situation will be maintained if a project does not go ahead. Not investing may result in a loss of competitive advantage for the business. Sometimes there will be little choice but to invest in a project because of the need to maintain a certain competitive position. These considerations can be introduced into formal analyses as qualitative issues, or by comparing the cash flows of the new proposal to the reduction in cash flows that will occur if the project does not proceed.
- *Hurdle rates that are too high.* Sometimes businesses set hurdle rates that are too high. This can occur in large businesses where a high hurdle rate provides a form of capital rationing, or an insurance against the uncertainty of future cash flow estimates. The high rate may also be used by senior managers to provide an incentive for divisional managers to submit only those projects with very high returns. However, we must remember that the purpose of discounting cash flows is to account for the time value of money. The appropriate hurdle rate for any investment decision should be based on the cost of capital for other investment projects of equivalent risk.
- *Time horizons that are too short.* Another common limitation is to underestimate the time horizon of a capital investment project. The acquisition cost of new technologies can be enormous, and the benefits may be realised over a lengthy period of time. If the NPV analysis stops short of including the benefits in later years, it is biased against a favourable recommendation.
- *The difficulty of gaining approval for large projects.* Most firms require large investments to be authorised by senior managers. This creates an incentive for lower-level managers to request relatively small, incremental improvements in the manufacturing processes rather than large, comprehensive improvements, such as a move to computer-integrated manufacturing (CIM). For example, if the investment authorisation limit for a plant manager is R500 000, the manager may introduce a series of R400 000 improvements instead of requesting approval for one investment in a million-Rand flexible manufacturing system. A series of such incremental improvements may not result in the benefits that could be attained with a full commitment to advanced manufacturing technology.
- *Greater uncertainty about operating cash flows.* Managers often have greater uncertainty than usual about the cash flows that will result when an advanced manufacturing system or any new technology is implemented. This increased uncertainty is often due to the complexity of the hardware and software and to the firm's inexperience with such advanced systems.

- *Exclusion of benefits that are difficult to quantify.* The benefits to the firm of advanced technologies may be extensive. Some benefits are easy to estimate, such as lower inventory levels, less floor space, and improved product quality. Others that can be even more significant are often difficult to quantify. Some of these benefits are:
  - *The synergistic effects of adopting multiple capital expenditure proposals.* The sum of the benefits of individual capital investment projects may be less than that of a group of projects. For example, the benefits of some advanced manufacturing technologies may be greatest when several manufacturing activities are linked.
  - *Greater flexibility in the production process.* For example, a flexible manufacturing system (FMS) cell can often produce runs of several distinct products in the same day. Moreover, the machines in an FMS can serve as backups for each other, which reduces machine downtime. Flexible manufacturing systems also allow engineering changes to be made more easily as products are adapted to changing customer preferences.
  - *Shorter cycle times and reduced lead times.* For example, an FMS enables the firm to fill customer orders more quickly and to be responsive to customer requests.
  - *Reduction of non-value-added costs.* Some of the more recent technologies, such as ABC, JIT and FMS systems, encourage employees to seek out activities that can be made more efficient or can be eliminated.

Although it is difficult to quantify these benefits, few managers doubt their existence. Excluding them from a discounted cash flow analysis means they are being valued at zero. It may be preferable to make some estimate of these benefits, however crude, rather than to ignore them. If a manager believes it is impossible to make such an estimate, then the investment criteria should be expanded to place greater weight on these intangible benefits along with a proposal's NPV.

In service firms there are similar difficulties. The future cash flow implications of benefits associated with the investment in a new computerised booking system in an airline, or in an improved service costing system in a consulting firm, are difficult to quantify. These benefits include improved customer service, reduced customer complaints, greater employee satisfaction, increased efficiency of operations and greater access to more accurate management information.

To summarise: justification of investments in advanced technologies, including new manufacturing systems, is a difficult exercise. Discounted cash flow analysis is the appropriate tool for analysing such a decision, but estimating the cash flows presents a challenge. Managers should strive to make the best possible estimates of costs and benefits, and ultimately make a judgement that recognises the intangible benefits as well.

Summary

In this chapter we extended the basic material on capital expenditure analysis that was presented in Chapter 21, to incorporate the effect of income taxes, and to consider the limitations of using formal capital expenditure analysis to justify investing in large-scale advanced technologies. Key points include:

- Income taxes play an important role in the capital expenditure decisions of a profit-seeking enterprise. For any organisation subject to income taxes, in any capital expenditure analysis we must determine the after-tax cash flows of the investment proposal under consideration.
- When accounting for the impact of income taxation on cash flows, we must take account of cash flows that are not on the profit statement, and of the timing of tax payments; and we must recognise that the timing of cash flows may differ from when those same revenues and expenses are brought to account in the firm's profit statement.

- The difference between accounting depreciation and taxation depreciation must be recognised and accounted for in calculating cash flows. Taxation depreciation will reduce the organisation's income taxes paid, which is a cash outflow.
- A profit or loss on disposal of an asset will reduce or increase taxation payments, and hence after-tax cash flows. The South African Government has introduced an accelerated depreciation allowance that will reduce taxes payable in the first year of acquisition of an asset and in subsequent years.
- Some capital proposals entail additional outlays for working capital, and these cash outflows should be included in the capital expenditure analysis.
- The effects of taxation should also be incorporated into the calculation of payback and accounting rate of return.
- When ranking alternative projects using discounted cash flow techniques, it is difficult to choose between projects that have unequal lives.
- Discounted cash flow techniques can be used to help evaluate investments in advanced technologies, such as computer integrated manufacturing systems or new information systems. However, it must be kept in mind that there are many benefits associated with these new systems that are difficult to quantify and build into the analysis. The level of uncertainty that is often present when considering these decisions, and the importance of competitiveness, must be considered along with the financial analysis.
- Conventional capital expenditure analysis may disadvantage investments in large-scale technologies due to the following issues: an unrealistic status quo (it is assumed that the current cash flows will continue if the project does not proceed, which is unlikely); hurdle rates may be too high; time horizons may be too short; there may be difficulties in gaining approval of large projects; there is greater uncertainty in the operating cash flows; and benefits that are difficult to quantify are excluded.

References

Berliner, C & Brimson, JA (eds) 1988, *Cost Management in Today's Advanced Manufacturing*, Harvard Business Review Press, Boston MA.

Bradford, M & Roberts, D 2001, 'Does your ERP system measure up?', *Strategic Finance*, September, pp. 30–4.

Kaplan, RS 1986, 'Must CIM be justified by faith alone?', *Harvard Business Review*, March–April, pp. 87–95.

Noble, JL 1990, 'A New Approach for Justifying Computerintegrated Manufacturing', *Journal of Cost Management for the Manufacturing Industry*, Winter, pp. 14–16.

Samson, DA, Langfield-Smith, K & McBride, P 1991, 'The Alignment of Management Accounting with Manufacturing Priorities—A Strategic Perspective', *Australian Accounting Review*, vol. 1, no. 1, pp. 29–40.

Self study

Self-study problem: Capital expenditure analysis, including taxation

The Western Credit Bank (WCB) is considering expanding and updating its network of automatic teller machines (ATMs), which currently are installed in each of its branches. WCB will install machines in local shopping centres, where it has no branches. It will also replace the machines that it has in each branch. The following costs have been estimated:

Cost of new equipment and software	R60 000 000
Installation costs	1 250 000
Tax (book) value of machines that will be replaced	20 000 000
Salvage value of the machines that will be replaced	5 000 000
Annual increase in operating costs	3 000 000
Annual increase in revenue from additional ATM points	18 000 000
Software update in year 3	4 000 000

For taxation purposes, the new machines will be depreciated over four years, using a reducing balance depreciation method of 40 per cent per year. The salvage or residual value of the machines is estimated to be R11 168 000 at the end of year 4. The taxation rate is 29 per cent, and the company has a required rate of return of 11 per cent after tax.

The managing director of WCC is very keen to go ahead with the new investment. In fact, he believes that if the ATM network is not expanded and updated, then WCC will lose many customers to competitors.

Required:

1 Calculate the annual after-tax cash flows for the above proposal.

2 Calculate the net present value of the proposal.

3 On the basis of your cash flow analysis, would you recommend that the managing director of WCC proceed with the new investment?

4 How would the net present value change if the depreciation was straight-line over 4 years (25 per cent per year)?

Solution to Self-study problem

1 and 2

	0	1	2	3	4
Cost and installation	−60 000 000				
Installation cost	−1 250 000				
Proceeds from sale of old machines	5 000 000				
Increase in revenue		18 000 000	18 000 000	18 000 000	18 000 000
Increased costs		−3 000 000	−3 000 000	−3 000 000	−3 000 000
Software update				−4 000 000	
Residual value					11 168 000
Tax (see workings below)	4 350 000	2 755 000	−87 000	−632 200	−3 752 020
	−51 900 000	17 755 000	14 913 000	10 367 800	22 415 980
PV Factor (11%)	1.0000	0.9009	0.8116	0.7312	0.6587
	−51 900 000	15 995 480	12 103 391	7 580 935	14 765 406
	Net present value		−1 454 788		

We have calculated the tax effects as well as the depreciation deduction in a separate worksheet. We could have also taken into account the tax effects per each cash flow so that we multiply cash flows by (1 − tax rate) but we would multiply the depreciation deduction by the tax rate. Depreciation is not a cash flow—it only results in a tax saving which means that only the tax rate is relevant.

Tax		0	1	2	3	4
Increase in revenue			18 000 000	18 000 000	18 000 000	18 000 000
Increased costs			−3 000 000	−3 000 000	−3 000 000	−3 000 000
Software costs					−4 000 000	
Scrapping allowance (tax value − sales price of old machines)		−15 000 000				
Depreciation (see below for workings)			−24 500 000	−14 700 000	−8 820 000	−5 292 000
Recoupment (sales price of new equipment − tax value, which is zero in yr4)						3 230 000
		−15 000 000	−9 500 000	300 000	2 180 000	12 938 000
	× 29%	−4 350 000	−2 755 000	87 000	632 200	3 752 020
Determination of Depreciation						
Opening tax value		61 250 000	61 250 000	36 750 000	22 050 000	13 230 000
Depreciation − opening balance × depreciation rate	40%		−24 500 000	−14 700 000	−8 820 000	−5 292 000
Closing tax value		61 250 000	36 750 000	22 050 000	13 230 000	7 938 000

As there are losses in time 0 and 1, we are assuming that the firm can set off the losses from this project against the income from other projects in the same time period. This will result in a tax saving equal to the loss multiplied by the tax rate. Although the tax saving is from other products, the tax saving arises from this investment decision and we therefore have credited the project with the tax savings in years 0 and 1. If a firm has no other taxable income, then we need to carry forward any tax losses to later years.

3

The NPV of the proposal is −R1 454 788, which suggests that the proposal should not proceed. However, the managing director has said that if the proposal does not take place, WCC will lose business to its competitors. This factor has not been included in the cash flow analysis—the cash flow analysis assumes that if the proposal does not take place, then 'things will stay the same'. This is clearly an unrealistic assumption. The cash flows of the proposal should be compared with the decrease in cash flows from not investing. Exhibit 22.8 elaborates on this point.

4

	0	1	2	3	4
Cost and installation	−60 000 000				
Installation cost	−1 250 000				
Proceeds from sale of old machines	5 000 000				
Increase in revenue		18 000 000	18 000 000	18 000 000	18 000 000
Increased costs		−3 000 000	−3 000 000	−3 000 000	−3 000 000
Software update				−4 000 000	
Residual value					11 168 000
Tax (see workings below)	4 350 000	90 625	90 625	1 250 625	−3 148 095
After-tax cash flows	−51 900 000	15 090 625	15 090 625	12 250 625	23 019 905
PV Factor (11%)	1.0000	0.9009	0.8116	0.7312	0.6587
	−51 900 000	13 595 144	12 247 551	8 957 657	15 163 211
	Net present value		**−1 936 436**		

Tax		0	1	2	3	4
Increase in revenue			18 000 000	18 000 000	18 000 000	18 000 000
Increased costs			−3 000 000	−3 000 000	−3 000 000	−3 000 000
Software costs					−4 000 000	
Scrapping allowance (tax value − sales price of old machines)		−15 000 000				
Depreciation	61 250 000 × 25%		−15 312 500	−15 312 500	−15 312 500	−15 312 500
Recoupment (sales price of new equipment − tax value)						11 168 000
		−15 000 000	−312 500	−312 500	−4 312 500	10 855 500
	× 29%	−4 350 000	−90 625	−90 625	−1 250 625	3 148 095
Determination of Depreciation						
Opening tax value		61 250 000	61 250 000	45 937 500	30 625 000	15 312 500
Depreciation —cost × depreciation rate	× 25%		−15 312 500	−15 312 500	−15 312 500	−15 312 500
Closing tax value		61 250 000	45 937 500	30 625 000	15 312 500	0

The NPV is more negative now as the depreciation deduction is reduced in the early years.

Cybersearch

1 Find a website that describes a company's approach to evaluating capital expenditure proposals. How does the approach differ from those discussed in this chapter and in Chapter 21?

2 Locate websites of private or public sector organisations that undertake post-audits of capital expenditure projects. Outline the methods or techniques that the organisation uses to conduct this review.

Appendix to Chapter 22

Impact of inflation

L.O. 11 Since the 1990s inflation in South Africa has been relatively low. However, most countries have experienced inflation to some degree over the past 20 years. **Inflation** is defined as a decline in the general purchasing power of a monetary unit, such as a Rand, across time. At the time of writing in 2007 we are starting to see a rise in the inflation rate. Since capital expenditure decisions involve cash flows over several time periods, it is worthwhile examining the impact of inflation in capital expenditure analyses.

Inflation can be incorporated in a discounted cash flow analysis in either of two ways. Both approaches yield correct results, but the analyst must take care to be consistent in applying one approach or the other. The two methods are distinguished by the use of either nominal or real rates of return. These terms are defined below.

Real or nominal required rates of return

The real **required rate of return** is the rate of return that covers investment risk (but no allowance for inflation). This rate compensates investors for the time value of money and the risk of an investment. The **nominal required rate of return** includes the real rate of return, plus an additional premium to compensate for inflation.

Suppose the real required rate of return is 12 per cent, and inflation of 5 per cent per annum is projected. Then the nominal interest rate is determined as follows:

$$(1 + \text{real return})\ (1 + \text{inflation rate}) - 1$$
$$(1.12 \times 1.05) - 1.00 = 0.176$$

Rands: real or nominal

A cash flow measured in nominal Rands is the actual cash flow we observe. For example, a particular model of a notebook computer costs R10 000 in 20X2 but costs R12 155 in 20X6. Both the R10 000 cash flow in 20X2 and the R12 155 cash flow in 20X6 are measured in nominal Rands. A cash flow measured in real Rands reflects an adjustment for the Rand's purchasing power.

The following table shows the relationship between nominal and real Rands, assuming an inflation rate of 5 per cent:

Year	(a) Cash flow in nominal Rands	(b) Price index	(c) = (a) ÷ (b) Cash flow in real Rands
20X2	R10 000		R10 000
20X3	10 500	$(1.05)^1 = 1.0500$	10 000
20X4	11 025	$(1.05)^2 = 1.1025$	10 000
20X5	11 576	$(1.05)^3 = 1.1576$	10 000
20X6	12 155	$(1.05)^4 = 1.2155$	10 000

As the table shows, cash flows in nominal Rands must be deflated, which means dividing them by the price index to convert them to cash flows in real Rands. The real Rand cash flows are expressed in year 20X2 Rands.

Two approaches to capital expenditure analysis under inflation

A correct capital expenditure analysis may be done using either of the following approaches:

1 Use cash flows measured in nominal Rands, and a nominal required rate of return to determine the nominal discount rate.

2 Use cash flows measured in real Rands, and a real required rate of return to determine the real discount rate.

To illustrate these two approaches, we will focus on an equipment replacement decision faced by the management of High Country Department Stores. The company operates a repair service for the household appliances it sells. Management is considering the replacement of a sophisticated piece of testing equipment used in repairing TVs and DVDs. The new equipment costs R5000 and will have no salvage value. Over its four-year life, the new equipment is expected to generate the cost savings and depreciation deductions shown below. The real required rate of return is 12 per cent. The cash flows in column (f) of the table are the total after-tax cash inflows, measured in nominal Rands. Assume the tax rate is 33%.

	Measured in nominal Rands					
	(a)	(b)	(c)	(d)	(e)	(f)
Year	Acquisition cost	Cost savings	After-tax cost savings [(b) × (1 − tax rate)]	Depreciation deduction	Depreciation effect [(d) × tax rate]	Total after-tax cash flow [(c) + (e)]
20X2	R(5 000)					
20X3		R1 900	R1 273	R1 250	R413	R1686
20X4		2 000	1 340	1 250	413	1753
20X5		2 100	1 407	1 250	413	1820
20X6		2 500	1 675	1 250	413	2088

Approach 1: Nominal Rands and nominal discount rate

Under this capital budgeting approach, we discount the nominal Rand cash flows in the preceding table using the nominal discount rate. For High Country Department Stores, the real required rate of return is 12 per cent. With an inflation rate of 5 per cent, the nominal required rate of return is 17.6 per cent, as shown on page 1106. The net present value analysis is as follows:

Year	(a) Cash flow in nominal Rands	(b) Discount factor for nominal discount rate of 17.6%	(c) = (a) × (b) Present Value
20X2	R(5 000)	1.0000	R(5 000)
20X3	1 686	0.8503 [$1 \div (1.176)^1$]*	1 434
20X4	1 753	0.7231 [$1 \div (1.176)^2$]	1 268
20X5	1 820	0.6149 [$1 \div (1.176)^3$]	1 119
20X6	2 088	0.5228 [$1 \div (1.176)^4$]	1 092
Net present value			R(87)

* The 17.6% discount factor is calculated using formula (2) in Part 1 of the appendix to Chapter 21.

The financial analysis does not favour the purchase of the new testing equipment, since its NPV is negative.

Approach 2: Real Rands and real discount rate

Under this approach, we first convert the cash flows measured in nominal Rands to cash flows in real Rands, as follows:

Year	(a) After-tax cash flow in nominal Rands	(b) Price index	(c) = (a) ÷ (b) After-tax cash flow in real Rands*
20X2	R(5 000)	1.0000	R(5 000)
20X3	1 686	$(1.05)^1 = 1.0500$	1 606
20X4	1 753	$(1.05)^2 = 1.1025$	1 590
20X5	1 820	$(1.05)^3 = 1.1576$	1 572
20X6	2 088	$(1.05)^4 = 1.2155$	1 718

* Real Rand cash flows expressed in terms of year 20X2 Rands.

Now we discount the after-tax cash flows, measured in real Rands, using the real discount rate of 12 per cent. The net present value analysis is as follows:

Year	(a) Cash flow in real Rands	(b) Discount factor for real discount rate of 12%	(c) = (a) × (b) Present value
20X2	R(5 000)	1.0000	R(5 000)
20X3	1 606	0.8929	1 434
20X4	1 590	0.7972	1 268
20X5	1 572	0.7118	1 119
20X6	1 718	0.6355	1 092
Net present value			R(87)

Notice that the new testing equipment's negative NPV of –R87 is the same under both approaches. Both methods lead to the conclusion that High Country Department Stores should not purchase the new equipment.

Consistency is the key

Either approach will provide the correct analysis, as long as it is applied consistently. Use either nominal Rands and a nominal discount rate, or real Rands and a real discount rate. A common error in capital expenditure analysis is to convert the after-tax cash flows to real Rands, but then use the nominal discount rate. This faulty analysis creates a bias against acceptance of worthwhile projects.

To illustrate, suppose that High Country's management had made this error in its testing equipment analysis. The following incorrect analysis would result:

Incorrect analysis of testing equipment decision

Inconsistency (between (a) and (b))

Year	(a) Cash flow in real Rands	(b) Discount factor for nominal discount rate of 17.6%	(c) = (a) × (b) Present value
20X2	R(5 000)	1.0000	R(5 000)
20X3	1 606	0.8503	1 366
20X4	1 590	0.7231	1 150
20X5	1 572	0.6149	967
20X6	1 718	0.5228	898
Net present value			R(619)

This inconsistent and incorrect analysis will lead High Country's management to the wrong conclusion.

Questions

22.1 Explain how to calculate the after-tax amount of an increase in sales and an increase in expenses.

22.2 Give an example of a non-cash expense. What impact does such an expense have on a capital expenditure analysis? Explain how to calculate the after-tax impact of a non-cash expense.

22.3 Give an example of a cash flow that you would not find on the income statement. How do you determine the after-tax amount of such a cash flow?

22.4 Give two examples of cash flows relevant to capital expenditure decisions that are not included in a firm's income statement. Explain why these cash flows are omitted from the income statement.

22.5 What assumptions about the timing of tax payments and cash flows are made in the capital expenditure analysis illustrated in this chapter? Are these assumptions realistic and, if not, what adjustments should be made to the analysis?

22.6 'Depreciation is an accounting entry, not a cash flow and therefore is not relevant to capital expenditure analysis.' True or false? Explain your answer.

22.7 What is the reducing balance method of depreciation, and how does it differ from the straight line method? Why do some businesses prefer to use the reducing balance method of depreciation for tax purposes? Explain why the depreciation deduction for unused manufacturing plant and equipment is so favourable.

22.8 Explain why many companies use different depreciation methods for taxation purposes and for external reporting.

22.9 How should changes in working capital be included in capital expenditure analyses?

22.10 Explain how a profit or loss on disposal is handled in a capital expenditure analysis.

22.11 'The profit or loss on disposal of a non-current asset is an accounting entry and not a cash flow. For this reason it should not be considered in analysing capital expenditure decisions.' True or false? Explain your answer.

22.12 What is a depreciation deduction, and how should it be taken into account in an analysis of cash flows for a capital expenditure project?

22.13 What adjustments would be required to the formula for:
(a) the payback period (b) the accounting rate of return to include the impact of taxation?

22.14 Why is it difficult to rank capital expenditure projects with positive net present values and different lives?

22.15 What assumptions do we make when ranking capital expenditure projects with different lives, using:
(a) the net present value method (b) the internal rate of return method?

22.16 Why may the net present value and internal rate of return methods yield different rankings for investments with different lives?

22.17 Define the term profitability index. How can it be used in the ranking of investment proposals? Does it work under all circumstances?

22.18 Explain the difficulties often encountered in justifying an investment in advanced technology.

22.19 What limitations of conventional capital expenditure analysis undermine its usefulness for evaluating projects investing in new technologies?

22.20 In an investment proposal involving new technology, the cash flows related to the proposed project are often compared with the wrong baseline. Explain this statement.

22.21 'NPV should not be used for analysing projects that have strategic significance for the business, as this method cannot take strategic factors into account.' Explain this statement. Do you agree?

22.22 (appendix) Define the term inflation. How is inflation measured?

22.23 (appendix) Explain the differences between:
(a) real and nominal required rates of return (b) real and nominal Rands

22.24 (appendix) Briefly describe two methods for analysing net present values in an inflationary period. What would be the impact on a capital expenditure analysis of ignoring inflation?

Exercises

E22.25 After-tax cash flows: publishing company

Heeren Publishing Company recently purchased a truck for R600 000. Under the current tax rules, the first year's depreciation was R120 000. The truck driver's salary in the first year of operation was R140 000.

Required:

Show how each amount mentioned above should be converted to an after-tax amount. The company's tax rate is 28 per cent.

E22.26 Profit or loss on disposal: manufacturer

In December 20X6, Atlas Chemicals Ltd sold a forklift for R92 550. The machine was purchased on the last day of the 20X3 financial year for R500 000. In terms of section 12C of the Income Tax Act, the company qualified for a depreciation deduction of 40 per cent of cost in the first year and 20 per cent deduction in each of the subsequent three years.

Required:

1 What was the forklift's tax value at the time of sale?
2 Calculate the recoupment or scrapping allowance on the sale of the forklift.
3 Determine the after-tax cash flow from the sale of the forklift. The firm's tax rate is 28 per cent.

E22.27 The effects of depreciation: manufacturer

All Steel Fabrication Ltd purchased industrial tools costing R1 100 000. These tools are expected to last for four years and have a salvage value of R100 000 at that time.

Required:

1 Prepare a schedule setting out the depreciation deductions, and their implications for cash flow, for each of the four years using the straight line method and a depreciation rate of 25 per cent per year.

2 Repeat requirement 1 using the reducing balance method. Apply the same depreciation rate of 25 per cent per year.

E22.28 Payback period; even cash flows: retirement village

The management of Harmony Retirement Village, a small complex in Pinelands, are considering an investment in an electrified perimeter fencing system to protect residents. The fence would cost R186 300 and have a useful life of seven years. The village's finance manager has estimated that the new fencing system will save the village R40 500 per year after taxes in security costs. The fencing system will have no salvage value. The tax rate is 28 per cent.

Required:

1 Calculate the payback period for the proposed capital expenditure.

2 Calculate the net present value of the proposed investment, assuming a required rate of return after tax of:

(a) 10 per cent (b) 12 per cent (c) 14 per cent

E22.29 Payback period; uneven cash flows: service firm

Taste Sensation is a new speciality restaurant specialising in chocolate. The restaurant's management are considering an advertising program to explain to the public the health benefits of eating more chocolate, particularly at their restaurant. This will require an initial expenditure of R731 000 and would bring in additional sales over the next five years. The projected additional sales revenue in year 1 is R350 000, with associated expenses of R50 000. The additional sales revenue and expenses from the advertising program are projected to increase by 10 per cent each year. The tax rate is 28 per cent.

Required:

1 Calculate the payback period for the advertising program.

2 Calculate the advertising program's net present value, assuming that the required rate of return is 10 per cent.

3 What is the program's internal rate of return?

E22.30 Profitability index: retail

The owner of Black Hills Confectionery is considering the purchase of a new semi-automatic chocolate-vending machine. The machine will cost R125 000 and last 10 years. The machine is expected to have no salvage value at the end of its useful life. The owner projects that the new machine will generate R20 000 in after-tax savings each year during its life (including the tax effect of depreciation).

Required:

Calculate the profitability index for the proposed vending machine, assuming the after-tax required rate of return of:

(a) 8 per cent (b) 10 per cent (c) 12 per cent

E22.31 Inflation and capital budgeting (appendix): municipality

The Municipality of eThikweni is considering the purchase of a new mainframe computer for R1 000 000. A cost study indicates that the new computer should save the department R400 000, measured in real Rands, during each of the next five years.

The real required rate of return is 6 per cent and the inflation rate is 6.6 per cent. The Municipality of eThikweni pays no taxes.

Required:

1 Prepare a schedule of cash flows measured in real Rands. Include the initial acquisition and the cost savings for each of the next eight years.

2 Using cash flows measured in real Rands, calculate the net present value of the proposed computer. Use a real discount rate.

E22.32 Inflation and capital budgeting (appendix)
Refer to the data in Exercise 22.31.

Required:
1 Calculate the nominal required rate of return (round off to nearest percentage).
2 Prepare a schedule of cash flows measured in nominal Rands.
3 Using cash flows measured in nominal Rands, calculate the net present value of the proposed computer. Use a nominal discount rate.

Problems

P22.33 Net present value: manufacturer
VacuTech is a high-technology company that manufactures sophisticated testing instruments for evaluating microcircuits. These instruments sell for R35 000 each and cost R24 500 each to manufacture. An essential component of the company's manufacturing process is a sealed vacuum chamber in which the interior approaches a pure vacuum.

The technology of the vacuum pumps that the firm uses to prepare its chamber for sealing has been changing rapidly. On 2 January 20X3, VacuTech bought the latest in electronic high-speed vacuum pumps, a machine that allowed the company to evacuate a chamber for sealing in only six hours. The company paid R4 000 000 for the pump.

Recently, the manufacturer of the pump approached VacuTech with a new pump that would reduce the evacuation time to two hours. VacuTech's management are considering the acquisition of this new pump and have asked Melanie Prins, the management accountant, to evaluate the financial impact of replacing the existing pump with the new model. Prins has gathered the following information prior to preparing her analysis:

- The new pump would be installed on 1 January 20X6, and placed in service on the same date. The cost of the pump is R6 080 000, and the costs for installing, testing and debugging the new pump would be R120 000. For depreciation purposes, these costs would be considered part of the cost of the equipment. The pump is expected to have a salvage value of R800 000 when sold at the end of four years (20X9).
- The company would be able to claim the Section 12C depreciation deduction of 40 per cent of cost in the first year that the new pump is brought into use and 20 per cent in each of the subsequent three years.
- The old pump would be fully depreciated at the time the new pump is placed in service and would have a book and tax value of zero. If the new pump is purchased, arrangements would be made to sell the old pump for R500 000 on 31 December 20X5.
- At the current rate of production, the new pump's greater efficiency would result in annual cash savings of R1 250 000.
- VacuTech is able to sell all the testing instruments it can produce. Because of the increased speed of the new pump, output would be expected to be 30 units greater in 20X6 than in 20X5. In 20X7 and 20X8, production would be 50 units greater than in 20X5. The production in 20X9 would exceed the 20X5 production by 70 units. For all additional units produced, the manufacturing costs would be reduced by R1 500 per unit.
- VacuTech is subject to a 28 per cent tax rate. For evaluating capital investment proposals, VacuTech's management uses a 14 per cent after-tax discount rate.

Required:
1 Determine whether VacuTech should purchase the new pump by calculating the net present value of the proposal.

2 Determine the project's internal rate of return.
3 Describe some of the factors, other than the net present value and internal rate of return, that VacuTech should consider before making the pump replacement decision.

(CMA, adapted)

P22.34 Sensitivity analysis; NPV with taxes: retail

Refer to the data for High Country Department Stores' checkout equipment decision given in Exhibit 22.5. Also refer to the net present value analysis presented in Exhibit 22.6.

Required:

The annual incremental contribution from increased sales is estimated at R400 000. How low could this amount be and still result in a positive net present value for the new equipment?

P22.35 After-tax cash flows; NPV; automated material-handling systems: manufacturer

Ikapa Barley Ltd's management are considering a proposal to acquire new material handling equipment. The new equipment has the same capacity as the current equipment but will provide operating efficiencies in labour and power usage. The savings in operating costs are estimated at R2 250 000 annually.

The new equipment would cost R4 500 000 and would be purchased at the beginning of the year. The equipment dealer is certain that the equipment would be operational during the second quarter of the year in which it is installed. Therefore, 60 per cent of the estimated yearly savings can be obtained in the first year. The company would incur a one-off expense of R450 000 to install the new equipment. No loss of sales will occur because the processing facility is large enough to install the new equipment without interfering with the operations of the current equipment. The depreciation deduction on the equipment would be 20 per cent straight line.

The current equipment has been fully depreciated. Management have reviewed its condition and concluded that it can be used for an additional 5 years. The company would receive R75 000, net of removal costs, if it elected to buy the new equipment and dispose of its current equipment at this time. The new equipment would have no salvage value at the end of its useful life of 5 years.

The company is subject to a 28 per cent income tax rate and requires an after-tax return of at least 12 per cent on any investment.

Required:

1 Calculate the annual incremental after-tax cash flows for Ikapa Barley Ltd's proposal to acquire the new equipment.
2 Calculate the net present value of the company's proposal to acquire the new equipment using the cash flows calculated in requirement 1, and indicate what action management should take. For ease of calculation, assume that all annual cash flows take place at the end of the year.

(CMA, adapted)

P22.36 Automation; intangible benefits; NPV; ethics: manufacturer

Gauteng Automotives Ltd manufactures motorised utility equipment and trucks. The Assembly Department employs about 200 workers, and negotiations are currently under way between management and production workers to form an enterprise wage agreement that would take effect from 1 January 20X5. During negotiations, the plant's consultative committee has presented a proposal to management that covers the next four years. This proposal calls for an annualised salary for production workers of R100 000 for the first year of the agreement, increasing by 5 per cent per annum over the life of the contract. Under the enterprise agreement, production workers are paid the salary no matter how many hours they work each week—there are no extra wages paid for overtime. Production workers are currently paid an hourly rate of R40. The hourly rate would also increase at 5 per cent per annum after the first year. The company also pays labour on-costs of 20 per cent. Management are concerned that the increase in labour costs that will result from this enterprise agreement will eliminate most or all of its profits.

Gauteng Automotives' long-term plans call for expansion of the product line in the near future. Management are working with outside consultants on the design of a new automated plant that will double present capacity. The new plant is to be operational in December 20X8, at which time the existing facility will be sold.

The assembly activity in the new plant will be highly automated. Now, in response to the proposal of the consultative committee, management want to examine the possibility of automating the existing Assembly Department. Because the system has already been designed and developed, the production manager is confident that the equipment could be acquired and installed in late 20X4 to be operational in January 20X5.

The management accountant has been asked to provide an analysis of the proposal to automate the existing Assembly Department, based on the labour costs included in the consultative committee's proposal. The accountant has collected the following data:

- The sales revenues for the next four years are expected to be relatively stable.
- Production volume is uniform throughout the year. Currently, a total of 40 000 labour hours are worked annually in the Assembly Department, of which 3000 labour hours are subject to an overtime premium of 50 per cent of the wage rate.
- If the new automated facility is undertaken, only 10 production workers will be required at the annualised salary, compared with 21 workers under the existing production system.
- The new equipment will be purchased and installed in the Assembly Department in December 20X4 at a cost of R5 million. For tax purposes, the equipment will qualify for the section 12C depreciation deduction of 40 per cent of cost in the first year and 20 per cent of cost in each of the subsequent three years.
- Annual maintenance costs will increase by R24 000 with the new equipment.
- The existing facility can be sold for R3.2 million on 31 December 20X8. However, if the Assembly Department is automated, the plant can then be sold on 31 December 20X8 for R4 million. On 31 December 20X8, the tax value of the existing facility, exclusive of the new equipment, will be R2.8 million, whether or not the Assembly Department is automated.
- Gauteng Automotives is subject to a 28 per cent income tax rate.
- Management assume annual cash flows occur at the end of the year for evaluating capital investment proposals. The company uses a 14 per cent after-tax discount rate.

Required:

1 Assuming that the consultative committee's proposal for annualised salaries becomes part of the enterprise agreement, calculate the net present value on 31 December 20X4 of the company's proposal to automate the Assembly Department. Should the company invest in the automated equipment?

2 Discuss the potential difficulties of Gauteng Automotives using discounted cash flow analysis to make a decision about high-tech manufacturing equipment.

3 When the accountant presented his findings to the production manager, the production manager responded as follows:

I think it's a real mistake not to automate now. I can see what your figures say, but I know there will be other benefits to the firm if we move on this now. I'm talking about intangible benefits that you can't put your finger on. Look, Dave, here's what I want you to do. Revise your analysis and increase the projected labour savings by enough to make the overall NPV positive. Then we can get the board to approve it. What I'm asking may be a bit sneaky, but I've got a gut feeling the automation decision will prove to be a good one.

Discuss the ethical issues in this scenario. How should the accountant respond?

4 Suppose that the production manager can list some of the intangible benefits of automating. What would the annual before-tax total cash flow from these benefits have to be to bring the project's NPV to zero?

(CMA, adapted)

P22.37 After-tax cash flows; NPV; robotic equipment: manufacturer

Auto Frontiers Ltd manufactures equipment for use in the automotive sector. In December 20X4, the company's management were considering the acquisition of robotic equipment that would radically change its manufacturing process. The management accountant collected the following data pertinent to the decision:

- The robotic equipment would cost R10 million, to be paid at the end of December 20X4. The equipment would be placed into use at the beginning of 20X5. The equipment's useful life is projected to be 5 years. The equipment qualifies for the section 12C depreciation deduction of 40 per cent of cost in the first year and 20 per cent of cost in each of the subsequent three years.
- The robotic equipment requires software that will be developed over a two-year period—20X5 and 20X6. However, the equipment would be fully functional from the beginning of 20X5. Each software expenditure, which would amount to R250 000 per year, will be expensed during the year it is incurred.
- A computer systems operator would be hired immediately to oversee the operation of the new robotic equipment. The operator's annual salary would be R400 000.
- Maintenance technicians would be needed. The total cost of their wages and on-costs would be R1 200 000 per year.
- The changeover of the manufacturing line would cost R900 000, to be fully expensed in 20X5.
- Several of the company's employees would need retraining to operate the new robotic equipment. The training costs are projected as follows:

20X5	R350 000
20X6	250 000
20X7	100 000

- An inventory of spare parts for the robotic equipment would be purchased immediately at a cost of R600 000. This investment in working capital would be maintained throughout the five-year life of the equipment. At the end of 20X9, the parts would be sold for R600 000.
- The robotic equipment's salvage value at the end of 20X9 is projected to be R500 000. It would be fully depreciated at that time.
- Apart from the costs specifically mentioned above, management expect that the robotic equipment would save R7 800 000 per year in manufacturing costs.
- Switching to the robotic equipment would enable Auto Frontiers to sell some of its manufacturing machinery over the next two years. The following sales schedule is projected:

	Acquisition cost of equipment sold	Tax depreciation to date	Sales proceeds
20X5	R1 500 000	R1 000 000	R200 000
20X6	3 050 000	2 150 000	1 400 000

- The company tax rate is 28 per cent.
- The company's after-tax required rate of return is 11 per cent.

Required:

1 Prepare a year-by-year schedule including all the after-tax cash flows associated with the robotic equipment decision. Assume that each cash flow will occur at year-end.

2 Calculate the net present value of Auto Frontiers' proposed acquisition of robotic equipment. What is the internal rate of return?

P22.38 Various methods of investment analysis: manufacturer

Enviro Tech plans to replace an old piece of research equipment which is obsolete and becoming more unreliable under the stress of daily operations. The equipment is fully depreciated, its tax value is zero and no salvage value can be realised upon its disposal.

One piece of replacement equipment under consideration which has been used but is only one year old, would provide annual cash savings of R210 000 before income taxes. The equipment would cost R540 000 and have an estimated useful life of five years. The equipment is expected to have no salvage value at the end of five years.

Enviro Tech uses the straight line depreciation method on all equipment for both book and tax purposes. In terms of section 12C, the equipment qualifies for a 20 per cent straight-line depreciation deduction. The company is subject to a 28 per cent tax rate. The company has an after-tax required rate of return of 14 per cent.

Required:

1 Calculate, for Enviro Tech's proposed investment in new equipment, the after-tax:
(a) payback period (b) accounting rate of return (c) net present value (d) profitability index (e) internal rate of return (use a financial calculator or Excel)
Assume that all operating revenues and expenses occur at the end of the year.

2 Identify and discuss the issues that Enviro Tech's management should consider when deciding which of the five decision models identified in requirement 1 should be employed to evaluate alternative capital investment projects.

(CMA, adapted)

P22.39 After-tax cash flows; NPV: manufacturer

First Line Safety Pty Ltd manufactures fire extinguishers. One part used in all types of fire extinguishers is a unique pressure fitting, requiring specialised machine tools that now need to be replaced. First Line's production manager has concluded that the only alternative to replacing these machine tools is to buy the pressure fitting from Lonsdale Pipe and Fitting Company. First Line could buy the fittings for R200 if a minimum order of 70 000 fittings were placed annually. First Line has used an annual average of 80 000 fittings over the past three years. The production manager believes that this volume will remain constant for five more years.

Cost records indicate that unit manufacturing costs for the last several years have been as follows:

Direct material	R41.00
Direct labour	37.00
Variable overhead	17.00
Fixed overhead*	45.00
Total unit cost	140.00

* Depreciation accounts for two-thirds of the fixed overhead. The balance is for other fixed overhead costs of the factory that require cash expenditure.

If the specialised tools are purchased, they will cost R25 million and will have a disposal value of R1 million after their expected life of five years. Straight line depreciation is used for external reporting purposes, but in terms of section 12C of the Income Tax Act, the tools qualify for a depreciation deduction of 40 per cent of cost in the first year and 20 per cent of cost in each of the subsequent three years. The taxation rate is 28 per cent. Management require a 12 per cent after-tax return on investment.

The sales representative for the manufacturer of the new tools stated: 'The new tools will allow direct labour and variable overhead to be reduced by R16.00 per unit.' Data from another manufacturer, where identical tools were used and similar operating conditions were experienced, but with an annual average production of 110 000 units, confirm the direct labour and variable overhead savings. However, this manufacturer indicates that it experienced an increase in direct material cost to R45.00 per unit because of the higher quality material that had to be used with the new tools.

Required:

1 Prepare a net present value analysis covering the life of the new specialised tools to determine whether management should replace the old tools or purchase the pressure fittings. Include all tax implications.

2 Identify any additional factors which management should consider before a decision is made to replace the tools or purchase the pressure fittings.

(CMA, adapted)

P22.40 After-tax cash flows; net present value: manufacturer

Sonspeel Ltd is a niche toy manufacturer that will have excess capacity at its single plant after 20X6. The company has survived by focusing on quality toys for the upper end of the market. Sonspeel's management are currently studying two alternative proposals that would utilise this excess capacity:

Proposal 1

Sonspeel has been approached by GloriToys, one of its competitors, to manufacture a partially completed doll. GloriToys, owner of the distribution rights for the doll, would finish the dolls in its plant and then market them. The GloriToy doll would not compete directly with any of Sonspeel's products.

GloriToys would contract to purchase 5000 unfinished dolls each month at a price of R75.00 each for the period 20X4 to 20X9. Sonspeel's estimated incremental cash outlays to manufacture the doll would be R2.5 million per year during the six-year contract period. In addition, this alternative would require a R4 million investment in manufacturing equipment. The equipment would have no salvage value at the end of 20X9. Straight-line depreciation of 20 per cent per annum would be used for taxation purposes.

Proposal 2

Sonspeel is considering the production of a new stuffed soft toy lion to be added to its own product line. The stuffed lion would be sold at R150 per unit. The continuing success of *The Lion King* is expected to support sales of the lion. Expected annual sales over the estimated six-year product life (20X4–20X9) for the lion are as follows:

Year	Annual unit sales
20X4	65 000
20X5	90 000
20X6	90 000
20X7	65 000
20X8	50 000
20X9	50 000

The per-unit variable manufacturing and selling costs are estimated to be R60 and R10 respectively over this six-year period. The estimated annual incremental cash outlay for fixed costs would be R3 million. The manufacture and sale of the new stuffed toy would require a R7 million investment in new manufacturing equipment. The equipment would have no salvage value at the end of the six-year period.

Additional information relevant to the two proposals follows:

- Manufacturing equipment for either proposal would be acquired at the end of 20X3 and placed in service at the beginning of 20X4. Depreciation on the equipment would be recognised, starting in 20X4. Straight line depreciation of 20 per cent per annum would be used for tax purposes.

- Sonspeel Ltd is subject to a 28 per cent income tax rate.
- Sonspeel's management assume that annual cash flows occur at the end of the year for evaluating capital investment proposals. Sonspeel uses a 14 per cent after-tax discount rate.

Required:

1 Calculate the net present value, at 31 December 20X3, of the estimated after-tax cash flows for each of Sonspeel Industries' two proposals.

2 Independent of the net present value calculations in requirement 1, identify any other factors that would increase the attractiveness of the two proposals.

(CMA, adapted)

P22.41 Investment in advanced technologies: manufacturer

Sophia Milan, the production manager of Italiano Footwear, is concerned about the company's ability to maintain its competitive position in the footwear market in South Africa. There has been a recent surge of imported shoes priced well below Italiano's full product cost. One of Italiano's major competitors, Ster Shoes, has responded to this recent flood of cheap imports by introducing computer-integrated manufacturing (CIM).

Milan has identified that it would cost Italiano R160 million to purchase the relevant CIM equipment, which would have an expected life of 6 years and an estimated salvage value of R20 million at the end of this time. For tax purposes, the equipment will qualify for a depreciation deduction of 40% of cost in the first year and 20% of cost per year for the following three years.

Once the equipment is commissioned the following annual benefits/costs will occur:

- Fewer faulty products and less reworking, annual savings of R52 million.
- Lower rental payments due to reduced space required for warehousing, annual savings of R8 million.
- Increased revenue from improved quality resulting in higher price for shoes, annual revenue of R16 million.
- Cost of maintaining the CIM equipment, R16 million per year.

Other financial impacts will include:

- Reduced working capital associated with lower inventory and accounts receivable, R8 million. (Assume that these costs are incurred at the same time as the CIM investment is made.)
- One-off costs of implementing CIM, associated with staff development and production losses during the implementation phase, R40 million. (Assume that these costs are incurred at the same time as CIM investment is made and are capitalised with the initial purchase costs of R160 million.)

Italiano uses a required rate of return of 14 per cent to evaluate capital investment proposals. The company's tax rate is 28 per cent.

Required:

1 Prepare a schedule of Italiano Footwear's after-tax cash flows that will result from the proposed CIM investment.

2 Calculate the net present value of the CIM proposal. Should Italiano go ahead with this proposal, given its current investment criteria? Explain why.

3 Calculate the payback period (after-tax) for the CIM proposal.

4 Discuss the potential difficulties of Italiano Footwear using discounted cash flow analysis to make a decision about high-tech manufacturing equipment.

P22.42 Investment in robotic manufacturing equipment; net present value; payback: manufacturer

Ukusika Ltd manufactures three different models of paper shredders, including the waste container that serves as the base. While the shredder heads are different for the three models, the waste container is the same. The number of waste containers that Ukusika will need during the next five years is estimated as follows:

	20X5	20X6	20X7	20X8	20X9
Number of containers	80 000	100 000	120 000	60 000	50 000

The equipment used to manufacture the waste container must be replaced because it has broken and cannot be repaired. Management is considering the purchase of new equipment to replace the old machinery. The new equipment would have a purchase price of R9 450 000. There will be a 2 per cent discount if payment is made within 10 days. Company policy is to take all purchase discounts. The freight on the equipment would be R110 000, and installation costs would total R229 000. Freight and installation costs will be included in the equipment's asset cost for taxation depreciation purposes. The equipment would be purchased in December 20X4 and placed into service on 1 January 20X5. It would have a five-year useful life and would be depreciated for tax purposes at 20 per cent per annum using the straight-line method. This equipment is expected to have a salvage value of R120 000 at the end of its useful life in 20X9. The new equipment would result in a 25 per cent reduction in both direct labour and variable overhead. There will be an additional one-off permanent decrease in working capital requirements of R25 000, resulting from a reduction in direct material inventories. This working capital reduction would be recognised in the analysis at the time of equipment acquisition. The old equipment is fully depreciated, and it can be sold for R15000.

Rather than replace the equipment, one of Ukusika's production managers has suggested that the waste containers be purchased. Ukusika has no alternative use for the manufacturing space at this time, so, if the waste containers were purchased, the old equipment would be left in place. One supplier has quoted a price of R270 per container. This price is R80 less than Ukusika's current manufacturing cost, which is as follows:

Direct material		R80.00
Direct labour		100.00
Variable overhead		60.00
Fixed overhead:		
Supervision	R20.00	
Facilities	50.00	
General	40.00	R110 00
Total manufacturing cost per unit		R350.00

Ukusika employs a plantwide fixed overhead rate in its operations. If the waste containers are purchased outside, the salary and on-costs of one supervisor, included in the fixed overhead budget at R420 000, would be eliminated. There would be no further changes in the other cash and non-cash items included in fixed overhead, except depreciation on the new equipment. Ukusika is subject to a 28 per cent income tax rate. Management assumes that all annual cash flows and tax payments occur at the end of the year, and uses a 12 per cent after-tax discount rate.

Required:

1 Ukusika Ltd must decide whether to purchase the waste containers from an outside supplier or to purchase the equipment to manufacture the waste containers. Calculate the net present value of the estimated after-tax cash flows, and recommend which of these two options to pursue.
2 Explain why some companies calculate the payback period of an investment in addition to determining the net present value.
3 What is the payback period for the new equipment?

(CMA, adapted)

P22.43 Ranking investment proposals; NPV versus profitability index: service firm

The owner of the Red Bull Burger chain is considering an expansion of the business. He has identified two alternatives:

- Build a new restaurant in a neighbouring town.
- Set up a number of small Red Bull Burger canteens to capture the lunch trade by catering at selected factory sites. These canteens would have a useful life of 10 years.

The projected cash flows from these two alternatives are shown below. Red Bull uses a 10 per cent after-tax discount rate.

Investment proposal	Cash outflow time 0	Net after-tax cash inflows Years 1–10	Years 11–20
New restaurant	R3 600 000	R450 000	R450 000
Canteens	1 800 000	322 200	–

Required:

1 Calculate the net present value of each alternative restaurant site.
2 Calculate the profitability index for each alternative.
3 How do the two sites rank in terms of:
(a) NPV (b) the profitability index?
4 Comment on the difficulty of ranking the owner's two options for the new restaurant.

P22.44 Net present value; internal rate of return; payback; sensitivity analysis; taxes: manufacturer

Wes Corporation's management are considering the replacement of an old machine. It is fully depreciated but it can be used by the company through to the end of 20X9. The old machine would have no salvage value in 20X9. If management decide to replace the old machine, iLanga Ltd has offered to purchase it for R600 000 on the replacement date. If the replacement occurs, a new machine would then be acquired from Hillcrest Industries on 31 December 20X5. The purchase price of R10 million for the new machine would be paid in cash at the time of replacement. Due to the increased efficiency of the new machine, estimated annual cash savings of R3 million would be generated through to the end of 20X9, the end of its expected useful life. The new machine is not expected to have any salvage value at the end of 20X9. Wes' management require all investments to earn a 12 per cent after-tax return. The company's tax rate is 28 per cent.

Required:

1 Calculate the net present value of the machine replacement investment.
2 Calculate the internal rate of return on the machine replacement, using a trial and error, financial calculator or spreadsheet approach.
3 Calculate the machine replacement's payback period.
4 How much would the salvage value of the new machine have to be on 31 December 20X9, in order to turn the machine replacement into an acceptable investment?

(CMA, adapted)

P22.45 Inflation; NPV; nominal Rands (appendix): service firm

New Wave Cablevision Ltd provides a community television cable service to Gauteng. The firm's management are considering the construction of a new satellite dish. The new antenna would improve reception and the service provided to customers. The dish antenna and associated equipment would cost R2 million to purchase and install. The company's old equipment, which is fully depreciated, can be sold now for R200 000. The company's general manager expects the firm's improved capabilities to result in additional revenue of R900 000 per year during the dish's useful life of six years. There would be no salvage value at the end of year 6. The incremental operating expenses associated with the new equipment are projected to be R80 000 per year. These incremental revenues and expenses are expressed in terms of real Rands.

The new satellite dish would be depreciated for tax purposes at 20 per cent straight line. The company's tax rate is 28 per cent. New Wave Cablevision's general manager expects the real required rate of return to be 6 per cent. She expects the inflation rate, currently running at 6.6 per cent, to remain unchanged.

Required:

1. Prepare a schedule of cash flows projected over the project's life, measured in nominal Rands. The schedule should include the initial costs of purchase and installation, the after-tax incremental revenue and expenses, and the tax effect of depreciation. Remember to express the incremental revenues and expenses in nominal Rands.
2. Calculate the nominal required rate of return.
3. Prepare a net present value analysis of the proposed new satellite dish. Use cash flows measured in nominal Rands, and a nominal discount rate equal to the nominal required rate of return.

Cases

C22.46 Capital budgeting analysis of automated material-handling system; ethical issues: manufacturer

Leland Rhoda is a member of the planning and analysis staff for Instant Dinners Ltd (IDL), an established manufacturer of microwaveable frozen foods. He has been asked by Bill Rolland, chief accountant of IDL, to prepare a net present value analysis for a proposed capital equipment expenditure that should improve the profitability of their Western Plant. This analysis will be given to the board of directors for approval. Several years ago, as director of planning and analysis at IDL, Rolland was instrumental in convincing the board to open the Western Plant. However, recent competitive pressures have forced all IDL's manufacturing divisions to consider alternatives to improve their market position. To Rolland's dismay, the Western Plant may be sold in the near future unless significant improvements in cost control and production efficiency are achieved.

Western's production manager, an old friend of Rolland, has submitted a proposal for the acquisition of an automated material handling system. Rolland is anxious to have this proposal approved as it will ensure the continuation of the Western Plant and preserve his friend's position. The plan calls for a number of forklift trucks and operators to be replaced with a computer-controlled conveyor belt system that feeds directly into the refrigeration units. This automation would eliminate the need for a number of material handlers and increase the output capacity of the plant. Rolland has given this proposal to Rhoda and instructed him to use the following information to prepare his analysis:

Automated material-handling system projections	
Projected useful life (number of years)	6
Purchase and installation of equipment	22 500 000
Increased working capital needed*	5 000 000
Increased annual operating costs (exclusive of depreciation)	1 000 000
Equipment repairs to maintain production efficiency (end of year 3)	4 000 000
Increase in annual sales revenue	6 000 000
Reduction in annual manufacturing costs	2 500 000
Reduction in annual maintenance costs	1 500 000
Estimated salvage value of conveyor belt system	4 250 000

* The working capital will be released at the end of the useful life of the conveyor belt system.

The forklift trucks have a net book value (and tax value) of R5 million, with a remaining useful life of five years and no salvage value for depreciation purposes. If the conveyor belt system is purchased now, these trucks will be sold for R2 million. IDL is subject to a 28 per cent tax rate. The equipment qualifies for the section 12C depreciation allowance of 40 per cent of cost in the first year and 20 per cent of cost in each of the subsequent three years. The company uses a 12 per cent discount rate. For the purpose of analysis, all tax effects and cash flows from the equipment acquisition and disposal are considered to occur at the time of the transaction, while those from operations are considered to occur at the end of each year.

When Rhoda completed his initial analysis, the proposed project appeared quite healthy. However, after investigating equipment similar to that proposed, Rhoda discovered that the estimated salvage value of R4.25 million was very optimistic. Information previously provided by several vendors estimated this value to be only R2.5 million. Rhoda also discovered that industry trade publications considered 4 years to be the maximum life of similar conveyor belt systems. The estimated salvage value at the end of 4 years is expected to be R2.5 million. As a result, Rhoda prepared a second analysis based on this new information. When Rolland saw the second analysis, he told Rhoda to discard this revised material, warned him not to discuss the new estimates with anyone at IDL, and ordered him not to present any of this information to the board of directors.

Required:

1 Prepare a net present value analysis of the purchase and installation of the material handling system using the revised estimates obtained by Leland Rhoda.
2 Explain how Leland Rhoda should evaluate Bill Rolland's directives to repress the revised analysis. Take into consideration the ethical code of conduct presented in Chapter 1.
3 What could Leland Rhoda do to resolve this situation?

(CMA, adapted)

Endnotes

1 The corporate tax rate in South Africa in 2007 was 29 per cent. The corporate tax rate has fallen from 48 per cent about 15 years ago to a tax rate of 29 per cent in 2007. In early 2008, the tax rate was reduced to 28%. We will use 29% in the text and 28% in the questions.

2 The depreciation and wear and tear rates set by the South African Revenue Service include implicit assumptions about asset life. For example, a 20 per cent straight line rate assumes a life of five years.

3 The liability of provision for deferred income tax and the asset of future income tax benefit, which are often found in balance sheets, arises from recognition of timing differences: expenses are not always taxation deductions in the same accounting period. Other differences between accounting profit and taxable profit arise from permanent differences: there are tax deductions that will never be regarded as expenses, and expenses that will never be recognised as tax deductions. Similar issues exist for revenues and taxable income.

4 However, this will be reduced as we need to take into account the fact that if the old forklift is not sold, then we would continue to have the tax savings relating to the continuing depreciation of the old forklift in the future.

Further Questions from Professional Examinations

by Carlos Correia and Colin Smith

Whilst each chapter includes professional questions adapted from the Certified Management Accountant (CMA) examinations that are specific to the chapter topics, the objective of this chapter is to include further questions set by the South African Institute of Chartered Accountants (SAICA), the Association of Chartered Certified Accountants (ACCA) and the Chartered Institute of Management Accountants (CIMA). A number of these questions particularly at the higher levels (SAICA QE Parts 1 and II) and ACCA Paper 3.3 often represent integrated questions which are difficult to allocate to a single chapter topic. The questions at these levels are appropriate for students undertaking their final year of study (CTA, PGDA, BCom (Hons) or BCompt (Hons)) prior to writing Part 1 of SAICA's Qualifying Examination or Paper 3.3 of the ACCA examination. Questions from Paper 2.4 of ACCA or SAICA's AGA examinations may be set for students undertaking either a first course or second course in Management Accounting.

South African Institute of Chartered Accountants (SAICA)

The South African Institute of Chartered Accountants is a leading accountancy body in South Africa. SAICA has over 20 000 members and the institute plays a pivotal role in business, in education and in providing support services to its members in public practice and in commerce. Members are able to use the highly respected designation, CA(SA) after their names. Many of the leading CEOs and CFOs in South Africa are Chartered Accountants.

Chartered Accountants are required to have undertaken a Certificate in the Theory of Accountancy (CTA) or equivalent qualification at an accredited educational institution and then to have passed the Qualifying Examination (QE) which consists of two parts, as well as having completed a three-year training contract.

The Associate General Accountant (AGA) qualification from SAICA requires that members have a three-year degree, have undertaken a three-year training contract and have passed the AGA examination. Members use the AGA (SA) designation. Go to www.saica.co.za for more information.

In relation to the Qualifying Examination for the CA(SA) qualification, we have included questions from Part 1 but there are also a few questions from Part II. We have included a number of questions from the AGA examination.

Association of Chartered Certified Accountants (ACCA)

The Association of Chartered Certified Accountants (ACCA) is a global accountancy body with over 115 000 members in over 170 countries. ACCA is based in the United Kingdom but has over 80 offices around the world. Members are employed mainly in industry, financial services, the public sector and in public practice and members are licenced to be registered as auditors in the UK and in Europe.

The ACCA qualification consists of three levels (Professional Scheme Parts 1 to 3) and we have included questions from Paper 2.4 (Financial Management and Control) and Paper 3.3 (Performance Management). The new ACCA qualification with increased focus on ethics and corporate governance is effective from December 2007 and the most relevant papers are F5 (Performance Management) and P5 (Advanced Performance Management). However, we consider that the topics covered in the past Papers 2.4 and 3.3 will remain relevant for future examinations. Go to www.acca.co.uk for more information.

Chartered Institute of Management Accountants (CIMA)

The Chartered Institute of Management Accountants (CIMA) is internationally recognised as a leading Management Accounting professional body. CIMA has over 40 000 members worldwide and the CIMA qualification is one of the most highly rated financial qualifications in the United Kingdom.

We have included questions from the papers Management Accounting—Decision Management P2 and Management Accounting—Performance Evaluation P1. Go to www.cimaglobal.com for more information about the CIMA qualification.

Topics

The topics covered in each professional question set by SAICA, ACCA and CIMA are indicated in the following table:

SAICA

S	23.1	Just-in-time inventory, standard costing
S	23.2	Special order, break-even analysis
S	23.3	Break-even (CVP) analysis
S	23.4	Process costing, by and joint products, absorption and variable costing
S	23.5	Financial performance, relevant costing, outsourcing, decision analysis
S	23.6	Cost allocation, overhead costing, analysis of special order
S	23.7	Budgeting, absorption costing, standard costing, outsourcing
S	23.8	Budgeting, contribution analysis, special order, pricing
S	23.9	Break-even (CVP) analysis, budgeting, special order
S	23.10	Capital budgeting, break-even (CVP) analysis
S	23.11	Standard costing, contribution, overhead costing, outsourcing, special order
S	23.12	Costing systems, pricing, make or buy, special order
S	23.13	Cost allocation, break-even (CVP) analysis, ABC costing, alternatives

ACCA

A	23.14	Capital budgeting, financial performance, sources of finance, marginal costing
A	23.15	Budgeting, financial performance, not-for-profit organisations
A	23.16	Standard costing
A	23.17	Standard costing
A	23.18	Budgeting
A	23.19	Capital budgeting
A	23.20	Activity based costing

A 23.21 Not-for-profit organisations, zero-based budgeting, activity based budgeting
A 23.22 Standard Costing
A 23.23 Inventory, Economic Order Quantity (EOQ), just-in-time inventory system
A 23.24 Activity-based costing, performance measurement
A 23.25 Budgeting, break-even (CVP) analysis, decision analysis
A 23.26 Transfer pricing
A 23.27 Learning curve, performance management, target costing
A 23.28 Performance management
A 23.29 Just-in-time management, back-flush accounting, ledger accounts
A 23.30 Budgeting, benchmarking, balanced scorecard, activity based costing

CIMA

C 23.31 Budgeting, flexible budgets
C 23.32 Transfer pricing
C 23.33 Relevant costs, pricing decisions
C 23.34 Marginal costing, absorption costing and activity based costing
C 23.35 Production budgeting, marginal and absorption costing, cash flow
C 23.36 Joint products – sell or process further
C 23.37 Activity based costing
C 23.38 Process costing, by-products, further processing, variances
C 23.39 Outsourcing
C 23.40 Benchmarking
C 23.41 Performance management system

Notes:

The SAICA questions relating to Part 1 or Part II of the Qualifying Examination as well as the AGA examination have not been amended. The ACCA and CIMA questions have been slightly adapted but only in relation to changing the currency from Sterling or US Dollars into Rands, as well as sometimes making the numbers more realistic by multiplying the original sterling or US dollar numbers by a factor.

The marks allocated to each section have been included in order to indicate to students the relative importance of each section. In order to convert marks to time allocations, the following is relevant:

♦ SAICA AGA (1 mark = 1.2 minutes) ♦ SAICA QE Part I & II (1 mark = 1.5 minutes) ♦ ACCA (1 mark = 1.8 minutes) ♦ CIMA (1 mark = 1.8 minutes)

Questions

S23.1 Just-in-time inventory system, standard costing

Black Ink Ltd is a South African company whose core competencies centre round the production of commercial ink cartridges. Due to poor management the quality of its main product, Blink 1, was not up to standard in 2003 and 2004. The result was a loss of customer satisfaction leading to a significant drop in market share. In a last bid to restore the company's profitability, a new production manager, Mr Justin Good, was employed at the beginning of 2005. With lucrative incentives, Mr Good was tasked with turning the company around before the end of 2005. After a thorough analysis of the company, he recommended the introduction of a Just-In-Time system (JIT system) to improve the quality of the Blink 1 product so as to restore customer trust and loyalty. Management implemented a JIT system early in 2005. The company operates a standard costing system. The following standards were set in 2004 with regard to Blink 1.

Components	Per unit
Raw materials	
■ Ink	0.5 litres at R10 per litre
■ Plastic	2 kg at R5 per kg
Labour	1 hour at R25 per hour
Fixed overheads	R10 million
Other information	
Mark-up	50% on variable cost
Budgeted production / sales	1 million units

The company operates a variable costing system.

During 2005, Mr Good changed to a more reliable raw material supplier who provided the company with higher quality ink and plastic, reducing production down time. This, together with dynamic training of all staff, has improved the quality of Blink 1 which in turn increased market share and the profitability of the company. The company produces sufficient quantities to meet sales demand and because of the improved quality, demand in 2005 increased to 1.5 million units, creating sales revenue of R150 million. The actual costs and quantities for 2005 are summarised below:

Component	Cost information
Ink	675 000 litres at a cost of R8 100 000 (purchased and used)
Plastic	2 400 000 kg at R6.50 per kg (purchased and used)
Labour	Total labour cost for the year R38 250 000
	Time to produce one unit of Blink 1 was 0.85 hours
Fixed overheads	Actual fixed overheads for the year R8 million

Because of the dramatic improvement in the company's performance in 2005, Mr Good was expecting to receive a bonus at the end of the year. However management has informed him that because his performance evaluation is based on production variances, potential adverse material and labour variances may prevent him from receiving a bonus. Management is also evaluating whether the introduction of the JIT system was as successful as they had anticipated.

Required:

(a) Using the information provided above, prepare a statement reconciling the budgeted profit to the actual profit, providing as much detail of the variances as possible. (24)

(b) Based on the reconciliation statement you prepared in (a) above and on other information provided in the question, discuss whether the implementation of the Just-In-Time system was of value to the company. (4)

(c) Discuss whether Mr Justin Good should in your opinion receive a bonus. Motivate your answer. (3)

(d) Discuss the aims of a Just-In-Time system and describe the goals that this system is trying to achieve.(7)

(SAICA AGA 2006)

S23.2 Special order, break-even analysis

Loud Ltd is a company that manufactures hi-fi loudspeakers. The company has been operating in the South African market for ten years with little local or international competition. However, during the past few years a number of international brands have entered the market. Because of the increased competition, the company has forecast a 100 unit reduction in volume for the current year as well as future years. The company is currently working at 100 per cent capacity, and manufactured 2000 units last year. The company has the following cost structure:

	R
Direct materials (per unit)	250
Direct labour (per unit)	200
Variable factory overheads (per unit)	75
Selling expenses (per unit)	50
Fixed factory overheads (per unit charge)	475
Administration expenses (fixed)	200

An order for 250 units at R600 per unit has been received from a prominent hi-fi retail company. They plan to market the units under the brand name of their retail store at prices lower than the R800 currently charged by Loud Ltd. Loud Ltd can increase the capacity of their factory by 200 units at a fixed cost increase of R120 000 per annum. At the new level of production the company's variable manufacturing overheads would drop by R60 per unit for all production. No additional administration or selling expenses will be incurred on the special order. The Financial Director of Loud Ltd has asked you to evaluate the special order from a relevant costing perspective.

Required:

(a) Prepare a statement showing the additional budgeted profit or loss that will result from the acceptance of the special order. (You should address all cost items, and record reasons for any omissions.) (12)

(b) Calculate the minimum volume that Loud Ltd would have to manufacture for the special order to be viable. (10)

(c) State what other factors should be considered before the order is accepted or rejected. (10)

(d) The Financial Director is concerned that the calculations above do not agree with the accounting treatment required by IAS 2 (AC108) *Inventories.* Explain to the Financial Director how the costs would be treated in terms of generally accepted accounting practice, and why the treatment differs from the above. (7)

(SAICA AGA 2005)

S23.3 Break-even (CVP) analysis

This question consists of three unrelated parts.

PART A

ABC Ltd manufactures product A which is sold directly to retailers. The company is experiencing strong competition and the accounting report for the last trading year indicated that the company produced the lowest profit in five years. The forecast for 2004 indicates that the present deterioration in profits is likely to continue. The company considers that a profit of R90 000 should be achieved to provide an adequate return on capital. The financial director is of the opinion that a change in the present pricing and marketing policies will have the necessary effect. He has two proposals for improving the profit situation.

Proposal 1
Market research indicates that a 10 per cent reduction in selling price would increase demand by 40 per cent.

Proposal 2
Sell 55 000 units of product A annually to XYZ Ltd for resale in Namibia. XYZ Ltd will transport these products from ABC Ltd to their own warehouse. While ABC Ltd would not pay any sales commission, the company will provide special packaging at a cost of 40c per unit. ABC Ltd would also contribute R66 000 per annum towards the marketing campaign of the product in Namibia. The marketing director is of the opinion that in 2004 the sales from existing business would remain unchanged at 120 000 units, based on a selling price of R10 if this special order is undertaken. ABC Ltd has a maximum production capacity of 180 000 units.

ABC LTD
Profit and Loss Account for the year ending 31 December 2003

	R	R
Sales revenue [120 000 units at R10]		1 200 000
Factory cost of goods sold		−878 000
Direct materials	144 000	
Direct labour	420 000	
Variable factory overheads	64 000	
Fixed factory overheads	250 000	
Administration overheads		−168 000
Selling and distribution overheads		−132 000
Sales commission (2% of sales)	24 000	
Delivery cost (variable per unit sold)	60 000	
Fixed costs	48 000	
		22 000

Required:

(a) Calculate the break-even sales value based on the profit and loss account for 2003. (4)

(b) Do a financial evaluation of proposal 1 to calculate the number of units that ABC Ltd has to sell at the new price to achieve the target profit of R90 000. (10)

(c) Assuming that proposal 2 is implemented, calculate the minimum price that XYZ Ltd has to pay for the product—
  i to ensure that ABC Ltd would break even on the special contract; and (4)
  ii if the target profit for ABC Ltd must be achieved. (4)

PART B
Bubbles Ltd sells two products, namely product X and product Y. The budgeted sales are divided equally between these two products and the budgeted contribution is R10 per unit of product X and R6 per unit of product Y. The actual sales for the period consisted of 75 per cent for product Y and 25 per cent for product X. The annual fixed costs are R560 000. Actual costs and selling prices are identical to the budget.

Required:

(a) Calculate the break-even points for budgeted and actual sales. (4)

(b) Analyse your results. (4)

PART C

Required:

(a) Explain why contribution margin per unit becomes profit per unit above the break-even point. (3)

(b) Define the term margin of safety and explain how it can be used to measure operating risk. (4)

(c) Explain what is meant by the term operating leverage. What impact does increased leverage have on risk? (3)

(SAICA AGA 2004)

S23.4 Process costing, by and joint products, absorption and variable costing

This question consists of two parts, which are not related.

PART 1

Edible Oils Ltd manufactures sunflower cake, a product used as livestock feed. The sunflower cake is manufactured in two different, consecutive processes. The output of process 1 is used in process 2 and the output from process 2, which is the final product, is sent to the packing department. The following information relates to the week ended 5 October 2002 with regard to process 1:

Input	
Sunflower seed	60 000 kg at R8 per kg
Ingredient X	20 000 kg at R3 per kg
Labour	1 840 hours at R25 per hour
Normal loss	5% of input
Sale price of scrap	R2.80 per kg
Output	77 500 kg

During this week there was neither opening nor closing work in progress in process 1. Total overheads charged to process 1 and 2 amount to R280 000 for the week and were absorbed on the basis of labour hours. The labour hours worked in process 2 were 1660 hours. All scrap was sold for cash on the last day of the week.

Required:

(a) Prepare, using only the information provided above, the following accounts for the week ended 5 October 2002:

i Process 1 account;

ii Abnormal loss/gain account; and

iii Scrap account. (14)

(b) Briefly explain how to distinguish a by-product from a joint product. (4)

PART 2

You were involved in the preparation of the budget at the beginning of this year. Estimates of sales revenue and cost behaviour for a one-year period, on which your plans were based, are set out below. The company manufactures only one product.

Activity level	80%	100%
Sales and production	720 000 units	900 000 units
Sales	R5 760 000	R7 200 000
Production costs	R2 970 000	R3 420 000
Sales, distribution and administration costs	R1 864 000	R2 080 000

The production costs and the sales, distribution and administration costs include both variable and fixed costs. Fixed costs are incurred evenly throughout the year. The normal level of activity used for budgeting purposes is 900 000 units per annum.

The following information pertains to inventory for the quarter just ended:

- Opening inventory of finished goods 5000 units
- Units manufactured 240 000 units
- Units sold 228 000 units

The actual fixed costs incurred equal budgeted amounts.

Required:

(a) Calculate the following if absorption costing is used:
  i The total amount of fixed production overheads absorbed during the quarter that has just ended; (5½)
  ii The over-/under-absorption of fixed production costs for the quarter; and (2½)
  iii The profit for the quarter, as shown in the profit statement (a profit statement should be prepared). (8)

(b) Prepare the journal entry to record the over-/under-absorption calculated above. The narration may be omitted. (1)

(c) Calculate the net profit or loss for the quarter if variable costing (marginal or direct costing) is used. (You are advised to simply adjust the absorption costing profit figure already calculated, rather than drawing up a profit statement on a contribution basis.) (3)

(d) What should the value of inventories be in terms of South African Statements of Generally Accepted Accounting Practice, given that the high level of production is considered to be materially different from the budget? (2)

You may assume that sales revenue and variable costs per unit equal budgeted amounts. Ignore all forms of taxation.

(SAICA AGA 2003)

S23.5 Financial performance, relevant costing, outsourcing, decision analysis

African Business School (Pty) Ltd ('ABS') is a registered training organisation that operates from three training sites in Irene (close to Pretoria), Magaliesburg and Randburg. ABS focuses on providing one to three day courses on managerial development topics to middle and senior management personnel. Courses are held during weekdays and facilities are closed over weekends. ABS leases the three training sites.

The Irene and Randburg training sites can accommodate a maximum of 30 people per day and the Magaliesburg site 40 people per day. Standard course rates are charged per person per day and there is no difference in the daily prices for one, two and three day courses.

The Magaliesburg training site is situated on the outskirts of the town of Magaliesburg within a small game reserve. The facility includes a lodge that can accommodate training course attendees overnight. Attendees on two and three day courses stay over at the lodge and all meals are included in the course rates. This site currently charges such attendees an extra R400 per night for meals and accommodation. The land on which the lodge and training site are situated is leased from the owners of the game reserve. The lease has recently been renewed for a further ten years.

The head office of ABS is responsible for scheduling of courses, marketing, finance and administration. The head office is situated on the Randburg site and the allocation of rent and related fixed overheads is based on the relative floor space occupied by the head office and the Randburg training facility.

Salient information regarding the operational and financial performance of the three training sites and the lodge for the year ended 28 February 2006 is summarised below:

African Business School (Pty) Ltd
Financial information for the year ending 28 February 2006

	Notes	Irene training site	Randburg training site	Magaliesburg training site	Magaliesburg lodge
		R	R	R	R
Revenue		1 215 000	2 025 000	2 160 000	1 052 000
Course fees	1	1 215 000	2 025 000	2 160 000	0
Accommodation and meals		0	0	0	800 000
Bar revenue	2	0	0	0	252 000
Operating costs		−1 322 488	−1 760 980	−1 670 645	−1 225 887
Variable expenses	3	−172 125	−273 375	−360 000	−397 500
Fixed costs	4	−925 000	−1 112 000	−910 000	−680 000
Head office costs	5	−225 363	−375 605	−400 645	−148 387
Operating profit/(loss)		−107 488	264 020	489 355	−173 887

Notes

1 The course fee per person per day during the 2006 financial year was R600 at all ABS training venues. The number of people who attended courses during 2006 and site capacities are set out below:

	Irene training site	Randburg training site	Magaliesburg training site
Maximum number of days available for training in the 2006 financial year	225	225	225
Maximum number of people who could have attended courses in 2006	6750	6750	9000
Actual number of people attending training courses			
One day courses	1425	1695	240
Two day courses	150	420	720
Three day courses	100	280	640

2 The lodge marks up alcohol and beverages sold in its bar by 60 per cent.

3 Variable costs at the training sites include costs of hiring external presenters, course materials and refreshments served during courses. ABS employs a limited number of presenters at each training site on a permanent basis and contracts with external presenters for specific courses as required. Variable costs at the lodge comprise the costs of alcohol and beverages, and catering costs.

4 Fixed costs in the 2006 financial year were made up as follows:

Fixed costs for the year ended 28 Febrary 2006

	Irene training site	Randburg training site	Magaliesburg training site	Magaliesburg lodge	Head Office
	R	R	R	R	R
Administration and finance costs	0	0	0	0	680 000
Cleaning costs	90 000	95 000	85 000	165 000	75 000
Kitchen staff salaries and overheads	0	0	0	275 000	0
Bar staff salaries	0	0	0	60 000	0
Marketing expenses	0	0	0	0	80 000
Rental of premises	215 000	235 000	115 000	105 000	85 000
Presenter salaries	450 000	510 000	590 000	0	0
Scheduling costs	0	0	0	0	230 000
Other fixed costs	170 000	272 000	120 000	75 000	0
	925 000	1 112 000	910 000	680 000	1 150 000

5 Head office costs were fully allocated to each training site and the lodge in 2006 based on each site's revenue (excluding bar revenue) as a percentage of total ABS revenue.

ABS has been under pressure from the shareholders because of the performance of the company over the last three years. At the last shareholders' meeting, management was requested to identify and explore strategies to improve the financial performance of the company.

Management has subsequently identified the following three strategies for improving profitability:

- Closing the Irene training venue,
- Outsourcing the catering at the Magaliesburg training facility, and
- Using the Magaliesburg site as a wedding venue over weekends.

Option 1—Closing the Irene training venue

As the Irene site seems to be the least profitable, management is investigating the implications of closing this training facility, based on two possibilities: The first is to close the facility completely, and the second is that the University of Pretoria (UP) operate the facility on behalf of ABS. Courses currently offered at Irene could be offered at the Randburg site, and initial feedback indicates that 75 per cent of ABS clients would attend courses at Randburg if the Irene site were closed. Other relevant information relating to the potential closure of the Irene training facility:

- The presenters currently employed in Irene could be offered positions at Randburg;
- The rental agreement for the Irene premises expires on 28 February 2007;
- The estimated costs of retrenching employees at Irene, excluding presenters, would be R200 000; and
- Other site closure costs would amount to R75 000.

The UP has offered to operate the Irene training site on behalf of ABS. UP will assume full operational responsibility for the site including marketing, course scheduling, finance and administration. In addition, UP will pay all operational expenses associated with the site, except for head office charges, and will collect course fees directly from attendees. Apart from course presenters the current Irene employees will be employed by UP. ABS will retrench the presenters at Irene at a total cost of R350 000.

Essentially ABS will provide course material to UP and allow them to operate the training site as an ABS facility. In return, UP will pay ABS a fee amounting to 5 per cent of course revenue. UP has undertaken to charge the same course fee per person per day as is charged at other ABS sites.

Option 2—Outsourcing of the catering at Magaliesburg lodge

Management also investigated the possibility of outsourcing the catering at the lodge. Though the catering is of a very high standard and receives mostly positive comments on course evaluations, management is of the opinion that the costs of providing this service are too high. Brilliant Catering has made the following proposal for taking over the catering and bar functions on an exclusive basis at the lodge:

- Existing kitchen and bar staff will be offered employment by Brilliant Catering. Employees who refuse the offer will be retrenched by ABS. If no employee accepts the Brilliant Catering offer, the estimated retrenchment cost will amount to R230 000.
- Accommodation functions at the lodge will remain the responsibility of ABS.
- If Brilliant Catering takes over the catering and the bar, and kitchen and bar staff elect to join Brilliant Catering, the fixed costs at the lodge payable by ABS will decrease by an estimated R325 000 per annum.
- ABS will continue to pay rental for the premises as well as the fixed overheads associated with provision of accommodation facilities.
- Brilliant Catering will charge ABS a fixed fee of R125 per person per day for meals provided. Brilliant Catering will operate the bar for profit and amounts spent by attendees on alcohol and beverages will be recovered from ABS, who in turn will recover it from attendees.

Option 3—Using the Magaliesburg lodge as a wedding venue

As ABS does not use the Magaliesburg training site and lodge over weekends, management is keen to investigate the possibility of using the facilities as a wedding venue. However, the facilities will need to be upgraded and expanded to make them suitable for this purpose. An initial estimate from a reputable building contractor put the alteration cost at R1 250 000. These alterations would enable the lodge to cater for wedding parties of up to 200 guests. The management of ABS has consulted with various wedding planners and the consensus is that the upgraded Magaliesburg facility could be hired out for 30 weddings in a normal calendar year.

Required:

(a) Critically analyse and discuss the financial performance of the training sites and the lodge during the 2006 financial year. (15)

(b) Advise the management of ABS, with reasons, on the most appropriate strategy with regard to the Irene training site namely –
- to continue operating the Irene training site on the current basis,
- to close the site, or
- to outsource the operations to the University of Pretoria.

Your answer should include the financial considerations involved in each alternative as well as any other factors to be considered before making a final decision. (15)

(c) Evaluate and provide an initial recommendation as to whether outsourcing the catering at the lodge to Brilliant Catering will improve the profitability of ABS. List any additional aspects that should be considered before a final decision is taken. (8)

(d) Outline how the management of ABS should approach the evaluation of the financial feasibility of upgrading the Magaliesburg facility to make it suitable as a venue for weddings, and list the additional financial information they would require in order to make an informed decision. (7)

(SAICA QE Part 1 2006)

S23.6 Cost allocation, overhead costing, analysis of special order

Perfect Paints Ltd ('Perfect Paints') manufactures decorative paint at its factory in Wadeville, Johannesburg. Two basic product ranges are manufactured, namely the ProTouch and BestGuard ranges. ProTouch is available in 15 different colours and is for interior use. BestGuard, which is for outdoor use, has a textured, matt finish and is also available in 15 different colours. Paint is sold in 20 litre containers to hardware stores and paint shops. Perfect Paints also distributes 20 litre containers of paint directly to building contractors and property developers.

Perfect Paints has one production line and as a result paint is manufactured in batches. Standard production batches are 200 containers (20 litres each) of paint for ProTouch and 50 containers (20 litres each) of paint for BestGuard. The difference in batch size arises because more additives are required during the production of the BestGuard range to achieve the textured, matt finish. BestGuard also requires more labour time. Machines in the production line need to be reset and cleaned after each batch of paint has been produced and set-up costs are incurred for each new batch.

Perfect Paints estimates the demand for different colours in the two product ranges and manufactures accordingly. Pigments and colourants are added during the production process to produce the different colours. These pigments and colourants are purchased from one particular supplier, who supplies them in pre-measured quantities. Within each product range, there is no difference in the cost of manufacturing various colours. (In other words, the cost of producing a 20 litre container of light blue ProTouch is the same as for a 20 litre container of burnt orange ProTouch, and the same applies to BestGuard colours.)

The following is an extract from the budget of Perfect Paints for the year ending 29 February 2008:

PERFECT PAINTS LTD BUDGET FOR THE YEAR ENDING 29 FEBRUARY 2008			
	Notes	**ProTouch**	**BestGuard**
Number of 20 litre containers of paint to be produced and sold	1	100 000	50 000
		R	R
Selling price per 20 litre container	2	595.00	765.00
Manufacturing cost per 20 litre container		412.00	514.00
Materials		205.00	230.00
Direct labour		100.00	125.00
Manufacturing overheads	3	107.00	159.00
Gross profit per 20 litre container		183.00	251.00

Notes

1 Machine hours are limited to 6000 for the year ending 29 February 2008. Each machine hour yields 50 containers of ProTouch paint or 25 containers of BestGuard paint. Planned production of ProTouch is 8500 containers of paint per month for every month during the financial year except during December 2007, when production will decrease to 6500 containers of paint. Containers of BestGuard paint will not be manufactured during December 2007 and January 2008 because of builders' holidays. Planned production for the rest of the year is 5000 containers of BestGuard paint per month. Perfect Paints has budgeted to produce and sell 150 000 containers of finished product in the 2008 financial year based on feedback from customers regarding potential demand and published reports on industry growth.

2 Perfect Paints sells 20 litre containers of paint at the same price to retailers as it does to building contractors and property developers. However, any individual customer who purchases more than 5000 containers of ProTouch paint or 4500 containers of BestGuard paint during any financial year from Perfect Paints receives a volume rebate. Volume rebates are determined at the end of the financial year. In the case of customers who qualify for the volume rebate, 5 per cent of the total selling price of paint sold to them during the financial year is credited to their accounts and set off against purchases during the next year. Volume rebates are not transferable from one customer to another.

3 Budgeted manufacturing overheads for the year ending 29 February 2008:

Overhead costs	R'000	Nature of cost
Batch set-up costs	3 600	Fixed and variable
Electricity and water	4 500	Variable
Rental of factory premises	1 800	Fixed
Depreciation of machinery	2 750	Fixed
Salaries	4 800	Fixed
Other manufacturing overheads	1 200	Fixed and variable
Total manufacturing overheads	18 650	

Manufacturing overheads include both fixed and variable costs. Variable manufacturing overheads have been allocated to ProTouch and BestGuard products following a detailed analysis of production activities and related costs. However, fixed manufacturing overheads have been allocated to finished products based on the total planned production (150 000 containers of paint) of Perfect Paints for the year ending 29 February 2008. No distinction has been made between product ranges and the fixed overhead recovery rate is the same for the production of both ProTouch and BestGuard containers of paint. If Perfect Paints were to produce 150 000 containers of ProTouch paint and 50 000 containers of BestGuard paint during the financial year ending 29 February 2008, the budgeted total manufacturing overheads would be R88.75 per container of ProTouch and R140.75 per container of BestGuard paint produced, using the allocation bases described above.

Special order: Penumbra Civils

Perfect Paints has been approached by Penumbra Civils, a major building contractor in the Western Cape, to supply them with 7500 containers (20 litres each) of paint of a variation of the BestGuard paint. Penumbra Civils has requested a colour that Perfect Paints does not currently produce and which has a higher sheen finish than is currently being manufactured. While Perfect Paints can produce the required paint, it will have to purchase additional machinery, at a cost of R720 000 (excluding VAT), to add to the production line to enable it to manufacture the paint to the required specifications. Perfect Paints has no intention of including this variation of BestGuard in its standard product range in the foreseeable future.

The direct labour cost and variable manufacturing overhead cost per container of paint will remain the same for the special order, but the material cost will increase by R10 per container of paint produced. Manufacturing output is estimated to remain the same, namely at 25 containers of paint per machine hour.

Penumbra Civils has suggested a price of R5 million (excluding VAT) for the special order of 7500 containers of paint. They require delivery of 2500 containers of the ordered paint per month during the period June to August 2007. Penumbra Civils has offered to pay for any increased costs of delivering the paint to their head office in Cape Town.

Ignore any VAT implications.

Required:

(a) Calculate the total fixed manufacturing overhead costs and the variable manufacturing overhead costs per container of ProTouch and BestGuard paint in the budget of Perfect Paints Ltd for the year ending 29 February 2008. (7)

(b) For each individual item of fixed manufacturing overhead, identify and describe with reasons a more appropriate basis (if any) of allocating the expense item to finished products in the budget of Perfect Paints Ltd for the year ending 29 February 2008. (10)

(c) Analyse and calculate what impact the acceptance and fulfilment of the Penumbra Civils order may have on the profitability of Perfect Paints Ltd for the year ending 29 February 2008. (10)

(d) List the key factors to be considered by Perfect Paints Ltd in determining whether to accept the special order from Penumbra Civils. (9)

(e) Discuss the accounting treatment (including presentation) in the annual financial statements of Perfect Paints for the volume rebates granted to customers. (9)

(SAICA QE Part 1 2007)

S23.7 Budgeting, absorption costing, standard costing, outsourcing

Chem (Pty) Ltd is a manufacturer of liquid fertiliser. The company was established 12 years ago and has expanded over the years to become a niche player in the South African fertiliser market. Chem (Pty) Ltd is highly specialised and manufactures only one finished product.

The financial manager of Chem (Pty) Ltd has recently completed the draft budget for the financial year ending 31 March 2005 with significant input from production and sales personnel. The abridged income statement of this draft budget, which will shortly be presented to the board of directors of Chem (Pty) Ltd for approval, is set out below:

DRAFT BUDGET FOR THE YEAR ENDING 31 MARCH 2005
ABRIDGED INCOME STATEMENT

	Notes	R'000	
Revenue	1		27 060
Raw material costs	2		−8 140
Labour	4		−3 060
Variable manufacturing overheads			−5 526
Delivery costs	5	1 386	
Water and electricity	4	1 080	
Waste disposal costs	6	1 800	
Other overheads	4	1 260	
Fixed manufacturing overheads			−5 440
Depreciation on plant and machinery		1 450	
Depreciation on transport fleet		750	
Repairs and maintenance of plant		1 820	
Repairs and maintenance of transport fleet	5	550	
Other overheads		870	
Closing inventory			880
Finished product	2	440	
Work in progress	3	440	
Gross profit			5 774
Non-manufacturing overheads	7		−3 200
Profit before interest and tax			2 574

Notes

1 Chem (Pty) Ltd is budgeting to sell 33 000 litres of finished product at an average price of R820 per litre.

2 Planned production for the 2005 financial year is 35 000 litres of finished product. There will be no inventories at the end of March 2004 as the company will shut down the plant for two weeks before year end. Chem (Pty) Ltd shuts down the plant every three years to enable external contractors to perform major preventative maintenance on the plant. Raw materials are added at the start of the production process. The company produces 1 litre of finished product for every 1.1 litre of raw material input. The financial manager is uncertain how closing inventories should be recorded in the budget. Chem (Pty) Ltd has historically adopted variable costing to determine product costs and to value inventory for budgeting and planning as well as management accounting purposes. The company is considering a change to an absorption costing basis in the 2005 financial year. This will result in management accounts being prepared on a basis that is consistent with information contained in the annual financial statements. No adjustments have yet been made in the budgeted income statement with regard to the change in costing basis. Closing finished product and work in progress inventories in the budgeted income statement reflect only the estimated raw material costs associated with producing inventories. Raw material costs recorded in the above income statement are based on an average cost of R200 per litre of raw material introduced into the production process. Production involves one process by means of which raw materials are converted into finished product.

3 Work in progress at 31 March 2005 is budgeted to consist of 2000 litres of 50 per cent completed finished product. The budgeted income statement incorporates the variable costs associated with producing the budgeted work in progress at 31 March 2005.

4 Labour and other conversion costs are incurred evenly throughout the production process.

5 Chem (Pty) Ltd owns a fleet of tankers that delivers finished products to customers. Delivery costs in the draft budget represent forecast variable costs of operating the

tanker fleet. The budgeted repairs and maintenance costs of R550 000 are consistent with prior years. The company does not have workshop facilities and outsources the repair and maintenance of tankers.

6 The production process generates effluent water, which has to be removed from the premises, treated and recycled. An independent waste disposal company is contracted to perform these tasks.

7 Non-manufacturing overheads include all other overheads budgeted for the 2005 financial year.

8 Chem (Pty) Ltd is also considering introducing a standard costing system within the next year.

Outsourcing of transport of finished products

Chem (Pty) Ltd is considering the option of outsourcing the transportation of its finished products to a specialist third party transport company, namely TRB Tankers (Pty) Ltd. The parties are in advanced discussions regarding the outsourcing initiative. TRB Tankers (Pty) Ltd has proposed the following arrangements:

- TRB Tankers (Pty) Ltd will purchase Chem (Pty) Ltd's tanker fleet with effect from 1 April 2004 for a consideration equivalent to the carrying value of the assets as reflected in the annual financial statements of Chem (Pty) Ltd at 31 March 2004.
- A condition for purchasing the tanker fleet would be a five-year transportation services contract between TRB Tankers (Pty) Ltd and Chem (Pty) Ltd.
- TRB Tankers (Pty) Ltd proposes charging R11.50 per km for deliveries of Chem (Pty) Ltd's finished products to customers. This rate per km is based on the estimate by Chem (Pty) Ltd that the tanker fleet would travel 200 000 km in total to deliver finished products during the year ending 31 March 2005.
- Service level requirements, including pre-determined collection and delivery lead times, must be included in the outsourcing contract.
- Chem (Pty) Ltd will pay TRB Tankers (Pty) Ltd a minimum monthly transportation fee of R100 000 irrespective of whether Chem (Pty) Ltd uses its services.

Required:

(a) Recalculate the budgeted profit before interest and tax of Chem (Pty) Ltd for the financial year ending 31 March 2005, incorporating the necessary changes to value closing inventories on an absorption costing basis. (16)

(b) Discuss the potential benefits to Chem (Pty) Ltd of using a standard costing system to manage its business. (6)

(c) Discuss how Chem (Pty) Ltd should evaluate the financial feasibility of outsourcing the transportation of its finished products to TRB Tankers (Pty) Ltd. (8)

(d) List the factors, other than those outlined in (c) above, as well as the potential issues to be considered by Chem (Pty) Ltd in evaluating whether to outsource transportation to TRB Tankers (Pty) Ltd. (10)

(SAICA QE Part 1 2004)

S23.8 Budgeting, contribution analysis, special order, pricing

Aqua-systems Ltd has two divisions. The Pumpworks division manufactures standardised electric water pumps for industrial use and the Agri-water division manufactures irrigation systems for agricultural purposes. The normal production capacity of Pumpworks is 1000 units per month, while an average of 970 units are sold. Pricing is based on a set mark-up as prescribed by Aqua-systems Ltd.

During a recent management meeting, the management of Aqua-systems Ltd reviewed the budgeted income statement of Pumpworks for April 2005. The manager of the Pumpworks division explained that the division is slowly but surely turning the corner. The division had improved its performance over the past three months and profitability should improve soon. In fact, the manager of Pumpworks indicated that the loss of the division has decreased and that it should reach a break-even position in five months' time.

However, the management of Aqua-systems Ltd is not convinced of this and they approached you, the management accountant of the company, to advise them on the likelihood that the Pumpworks division will return to profitability soon.

PUMPWORKS DIVISION
BUDGETED INCOME STATEMENT FOR THE MONTH ENDING 30 APRIL 2005

	Notes	R
Sales (970 units)		1 703 320
Less: Cost of sales		1 578 260
Opening stock (24 casings @ R205 each)		4 920
Production cost (1000 finished units)		1 622 000
Closing stock (30 finished units)		−48 660
Gross profit		125 060
Insurance claim	1	54 300
Sales and administration cost	2	−148 400
Head Office allocation	3	−173 580
Loss for the month		−142 620

Notes

1 During June 2004 the Pumpworks production facilities were damaged in a fire caused by an electrical fault. After initial problems with the insurance company, Aqua-systems Ltd received a letter from it shortly before the completion of the April budget to the effect that the amount of R54 300 was awarded to the company for the damage.

2 25 per cent of sales and administration costs are variable.

3 Head Office overheads include a fee of R14 per water pump sold. The fee relates to a patent used on one of the components of the water pump.

Pumpworks has received two offers for contracts

1 The SA Mining Ltd offer

Pumpworks has been approached by SA Mining Ltd to supply 200 pumps for a project in the Limpopo Province in April 2005. They need a scaled down version of the water pumps that will be brought into use by the end of April 2005. 200 units will be required for the project, at R1600 per unit. SA Mining Ltd has indicated that they will approach a competitor of Pumpworks if the latter were not interested in the order.

The following information relates to the normal production costs of Pumpworks and the order from SA Mining Ltd:

The cost of the water pump components and related labour costs are set out below:

(a) Pipe connectors

These units are bought from an external supplier. One connector is used per pump system. Pumpworks recently bought 250 pipe connectors at R20 each for use on the standard system. Unfortunately the units were the wrong size and Pumpworks planned to return them to the supplier. However, the supplier offered Pumpworks a 50 per cent discount on the unit price for keeping the units. In anticipation of the possible contract to supply smaller water pumps to SA Mining Ltd, Pumpworks has now decided to accept the supplier's offer.

(b) Casings

Current casings could be modified to fit the specifications of the order. The modification will cost R54 and entail 30 labour minutes per casing. Information on the 24 standard casings that are in stock are as follows:

Cost	R205 each
Replacement cost	R230 each
Net replacement value	R225 each

(c) Impellers
One set of impellers is used per pump. Pumpworks is able to manufacture 1150 sets of impellers per month, at a total variable cost of R250 per set. It can sell any spare sets of impellers at R370 per set. No impellers are currently in stock. The total fixed cost for the production of impellers amounts to R132 000 per month, and represents depreciation on recently acquired machinery.

(d) Shafts
Shafts are cut from standard steel bars. Each bar is cut into one shaft. According to the stock sheets, the total cost (excluding labour) amounts to R175 per shaft. Pumpworks has the capacity to cut 1100 standard shafts per month. Depreciation and other fixed costs (excluding labour) related to this activity amount to R160 000 per month.

(e) Electric motors
Electric motors are bought at R450 per unit. One motor is used per pump system.

(f) Labour

- *Shaft cutting:* Shaft cutting labourers are highly skilled. They are paid R60 per hour and work 160 hours per month. Because of the high cost of training, all five shaft cutting labourers are full-time employees of the company.
- *Casings:* A total of 13 labourers are employed in this section. Each labourer receives a salary of R5000 per month and works 160 hours per month. Each standard casing takes two hours to manufacture. New casing casters can be trained at a cost of R5000 per employee. The minimum employment period for these workers is three months.
- *Impellers:* Labour consists of full-time machine operators. Existing operators will be able to handle any expansion.
- *Assembly:* Labourers are paid R50 per hour to do the assembly. One pump system takes two hours to assemble. Assembly hours are not limited and can be adjusted as necessary.

2 The Agri-water offer

As an alternative to the SA Mining Ltd order, Agri-water has offered to buy the 200 smaller pumps from Pumpworks at a price of R1400 per unit. The 200 pumps will be used for an irrigation project in the Makatini area in northern KwaZulu-Natal. Agri-water was approached by the government when the previous contractor became unable to complete the contract. The project is an initiative of the KwaZulu-Natal government and the contract price for the 200 irrigation systems on the Makatini project is R500 000. Agri-water has however been unable to source the correct water pumps for the project from any other supplier. Though the water pumps manufactured by Pumpworks are normally for industrial use and as such are very powerful and generally too expensive for agricultural purposes, they could be used for the Makatini project. Agri-water has sufficient capacity to complete the contract.

The cost for one irrigation system is as follows:

	Notes	R
Material (excluding piping)	1	1 800
Labour		342
Piping	2	174
Manufacturing fixed cost		210
Total cost		2 526

Notes

1 Material cost includes the cost of R1400 per unit that will have to be paid to Pumpworks.

2 Piping costs consist of both the piping used per unit and the maintenance of equipment. Previous records show that the cost per unit changes with changes in output. At an

output of 1000 units the cost per unit is R185 while the cost per unit at an output of 710 units is R197.68. Further, for every 100 unit increase (or part thereof) in output, maintenance costs increase by R10 000.

Required:

(a) Analyse and discuss the budgeted income statement for April 2005 and the detailed costs of Pumpworks, and
  i specifically comment on the statement by the manager of Pumpworks that the division is capable of returning to profitability within the next five months, and
  ii suggest possible actions that could lead to profitability for the division (25)

(b) Calculate the contribution per unit that Pumpworks would make if it accepted the order from SA Mining Ltd. (10)

(c) Advise the management of Aqua-systems Ltd on whether Pumpworks should supply Agri-water with 200 pumps as opposed to accepting the SA Mining Ltd order. Show all your workings and provide detailed reasons to support your answer (10)

(d) Comment on the pricing strategy used by Aqua-systems Ltd (5)

(SAICA QE Part 1 2005)

S23.9 Break-even (CVP) analysis, budgeting, special order

You have recently joined Slam (Pty) Ltd, a company that manufactures and distributes brake pads to the automotive industry, as a financial accountant. The managing director and majority shareholder has asked you to assist him in interpreting the draft financial results for the year ended 28 February 2003 and to review the budget for the new financial year.

As part of his preparations for the budget for the financial year ended 28 February 2003, the previous accountant completed a break-even analysis and concluded that the break-even production and sales volumes amounted to 20 500 units. The fact that the company only sold 20 000 units but is reporting a preliminary profit of R130 000 for the year ended 28 February 2003, has raised a concern about the integrity of the information generated by your department. You have been able to establish the following:

1 The draft income statement for the year ended 28 February 2003 is as follows:

	R
Sales	2 000 000
Cost of sales	1 700 000
Inventory at beginning of year	0
Raw materials	500 000
Direct labour costs	600 000
Production overheads absorbed	1 025 000
Inventory at end of year: Finished products	−425 000
Gross profit	300 000
Production overheads: over-recovery	90 000
Administration costs	−80 000
Selling costs	−180 000
Net income before tax	130 000

2 Sales and production had been budgeted for the 2003 year at 22 000 units. The budgeted selling price for the 2003 financial year was R100 per unit.

3 The company has access to a reliable supply of raw materials and therefore does not carry any raw materials inventory. There were no work-in-progress inventories at the beginning or end of the year.

4 Actual production volumes amounted to 25 000 units.

5 The actual unit costs and selling prices as well as fixed costs were all equal to budgeted amounts.

6 Production overheads and selling costs comprise both fixed and variable costs. Selling costs would have amounted to R190 000 at budgeted sales volumes of 22 000 units.
7 Administration costs are fixed.
8 For financial accounting purposes fixed production overhead absorption rates were set at R30 per unit at the beginning of the 2003 financial year. This was based on planned production volumes of 22 000 units.
9 Total actual and budgeted fixed production overhead costs incurred amounted to R660 000.
10 Production volumes of between 20 000 and 25 000 units per annum are regarded as being within the range of normal capacity.

Budget for 2004

As a result of the unexpected profit, a review of the 2004 budget was deemed necessary. Based on a discussion with the managing director and the sales and production managers, the following key assumptions were agreed upon:

1 Unit sales prices are expected to increase by 8 per cent.
2 Sales volumes are expected to be 22 000 units.
3 Raw materials costs are expected to increase by 20 per cent. All other unit variable costs are expected to increase by 10 per cent.
4 A key objective in the forthcoming financial year is to achieve a net income before tax of 5 per cent of turnover.
5 All fixed costs are expected to increase by 5 per cent.
6 Production volumes of 21 000 units are forecast.

Special order

As a result of the supply disruptions caused by the recent liquidation of one of its competitors, Slam (Pty) Ltd has been invited to quote for a special order of 4000 units, which is to be supplied during the course of the 2004 financial year. Product specifications vary from the existing brake pads that are produced and will accordingly require different machine settings. Therefore labour and variable production overhead costs are expected to be 50 per cent higher for the first batch of 1000 units than for the existing product. Thereafter an 80 per cent learning curve is expected to reduce unit costs. Material costs are not expected to differ from the existing product. No variable selling costs will be incurred.

This special order was not taken into account in the 2004 budget.

Because of current industry conditions, bidding for this order is likely to be highly aggressive. Slam (Pty) Ltd regards this order as an opportunity to gain a foothold in that market, which offers great expansion opportunities. As a consequence the managing director wants to quote the minimum price that can be charged while still producing profits that conform to the overall financial objectives of the company.

Required:

(a) Reperform the calculation of the break-even production and sales volumes based on the 2003 budget assumptions. (10)
(b) Discuss, with reasons, the apparent contradiction between the budgeted break-even sales and production volumes and the preliminary profit achieved in the 2003 financial year. (5)
(c) Calculate the budgeted profit before tax for the 2004 financial year. Ignore the effect of the special order. (10)
(d) Advise the managing director on possible steps that could be taken to enable the company to achieve its targeted profit before tax of 5 per cent of turnover. Support your advice with calculations on how the target profit could be achieved. Ignore the effect of the special order. (10)
(e) Discuss the factors to be considered in determining a selling price that should be quoted for the special order. (10)

(f) Discuss whether closing inventories at 28 February 2003 have been appropriately valued at R425 000 in terms of the South African Statements of Generally Accepted Accounting Practice. (5)

(SAICA QE Part 1 2003)

S23.10 Capital budgeting, break-even (CVP) analysis

VPharm (Pty) Ltd ('VPharm') is a manufacturer and supplier of a range of pharmaceutical products. The head office is based in Johannesburg and manufacturing plants are situated in Cape Town, Durban and Port Elizabeth. VPharm has expanded rapidly over the past five years through the acquisition of smaller pharmaceutical companies, which is why manufacturing plants are located in different cities.

The company manufactures tablets and capsules covering various therapeutic fields. Products are used as prescription treatments for respiratory, gastro-intestinal and cardiovascular ailments. VPharm also manufactures over-the-counter medicines that can be purchased without a prescription.

VPharm is currently negotiating a licence agreement with BSK plc, a major international pharmaceutical group, regarding the manufacture and distribution of their world leading anti-malaria tablets. It is envisaged that VPharm will acquire the exclusive rights to manufacture and distribute the anti-malaria tablets of BSK plc in sub-Saharan Africa for a period of ten years. The licence period will commence when the production facility has been commissioned and is operational.

The company will have to build a new manufacturing facility to produce the anti-malaria tablets. The existing manufacturing plants are operating at more than 80 per cent capacity and growth is expected in the existing product ranges. VPharm has decided that the new plant will be erected in Johannesburg and has prepared the following initial capital budget:

VPharm (Pty) Ltd
Anti-malaria tablet plant—Capital Budget

	Notes	Year 0 R000	Year 1 R000	Year 2 R000	Year 3 R000	Year 4 R000
Acquisition cost of licence	1	(8 000)				
Plant and equipment	2	(10 000)	(28 000)			
Revenue	3			45 000	80 000	120 000
Raw material costs				(17 100)	(28 000)	(42 000)
Factory overheads	4			(5 400)	(7800)	(10 600)
Quality control overheads	5			(1 800)	(1 890)	(1 985)
Gross profit margin				20 700	42 310	65 415
Warehouse expenses	5			(2 100)	(2 205)	(2 315)
Royalties	1			(3 375)	(6 000)	(9 000)
Rental of premises	6		(1200)	(1 296)	(1 400)	(1 512)
Sales and marketing expenses	7			(2 250)	(4 000)	(6 000)
Logistical expenses	8			(2 700)	(2 800)	(4 200)
Other indirect overheads	5			(6 200)	(6 510)	(6 835)
Allocated head office costs	9			(2 500)	(2 750)	(3 025)
Earnings before interest, tax, depreciation and amortisation				279	16 645	32 528
Working capital	10			(5 900)	(4 700)	(5 460)
Net cash flows		(18 000)	(29 200)	(5 621)	11 945	27068

Notes

1 The initial payment on signing the licence agreement with BSK plc is estimated to be R8 million. VPharm has approached the South African Revenue Service (SARS) for guidance regarding the tax allowance applicable to the licence agreement. The SARS

have agreed to an allowance of 10 per cent per annum (not to be pro rated) in terms of section 11(gC) of the Income Tax Act. The first allowance will be claimed in the first year of production (year 2). VPharm will pay a royalty of 7.5 per cent of revenue in respect of anti-malaria tablets produced and sold and SARS has indicated that it will permit a deduction of these royalties paid for income tax purposes.

2 VPharm is to engage an independent engineering company to build the manufacturing plant. It will take a year for the engineering firm to complete the order, assembly and installation of the manufacturing plant. VPharm will have to pay an upfront deposit of R10 million for the plant and equipment and the balance (R28 million) will be due once the plant has been installed and commissioned. The plant will have an expected useful life of ten years. After ten years, the plant could be decommissioned and sold piecemeal for an estimated 10 per cent of initial cost. Alternatively, the plant could be upgraded and used for the manufacture of other VPharm products. VPharm has approached the SARS for guidance regarding the tax allowances applicable to the plant and equipment. The SARS has indicated that a section 12C allowance for manufacturing activities may be claimed on the following basis:
   - 40 per cent in the year that the plant is brought into use, and
   - 20 per cent will be deductible in each of the three subsequent years.

   The current statutory normal tax rate for companies is 29 per cent.

3 Revenue is expected to increase over time as VPharm increases its share of the market for anti-malaria tablets. After year 4 revenue growth is expected to be 10 per cent per annum which is the current average growth in the anti-malaria tablet market.

4 50 per cent of factory overheads are variable in nature. Depreciation has not yet been calculated and as a result has not been included in factory overheads.

5 VPharm intends to have world-class quality control procedures in place to ensure that tablets are manufactured in accordance with BSK plc standards. Quality control costs, warehouse expenses and other indirect overheads will be fixed in nature and will not vary with production volumes.

6 The property on which the new manufacturing facility is to be erected is to be leased for a period of 11 years and rentals will escalate by 8 per cent per annum. Negotiations with the landlord are nearing completion and VPharm expects to enter into a lease agreement as soon as the licence agreement with BSK plc has been finalised.

7 VPharm employs 150 sales representatives to market and sell the company's basket of products. These sales representatives are remunerated mainly through sales commission, at a rate of 5 per cent of invoiced and banked revenue. These representatives will market anti-malaria tablets to VPharm's existing customer base of private health care providers and pharmacists.

8 Distribution of finished products to customers is to be outsourced to an independent third party. VPharm has negotiated a variable fee arrangement with the third party of 3.5 per cent of invoiced revenue subject to a minimum aggregate charge of R2.7 million per annum for services rendered.

9 Head office cost allocations relate to accounting and human resource functions performed on behalf of the anti-malaria division. It is estimated that it would cost the anti-malaria division R1.8 million in year 2 to provide these services in-house, and that the expense would increase by 5 per cent per annum thereafter.

10 The annual incremental investment in working capital is expected to increase by 10 per cent per annum from year 5 onwards.

11 VPharm forecasts that, for year 5 and thereafter –
   - gross profit margins will be 55 per cent; and
   - warehouse expenses, other indirect overheads and allocated head office expenses will increase by 5 per cent per annum.

12 For the purposes of the draft capital budget, it has been assumed that all cash flows occur at the end of the year. This is consistent with the normal policy of the company when evaluating potential new projects.

13 All cash flows are exclusive of VAT.
14 VPharm does not derive taxable income from any other source.

Cost of capital

VPharm has determined its cost of capital to be 15 per cent. The company has no external borrowings at present and has sufficient cash resources to fund the acquisition of the anti-malaria tablet plant.

MBX Ltd

MBX Ltd is a distributor of pharmaceutical products in Southern Africa. The company has recently been awarded various tenders to supply anti-malaria tablets to government departments in South Africa, Botswana and Mozambique. MBX Ltd has approached VPharm to purchase its entire planned production for year 2 and 3 to fulfill its supply obligations. MBX Ltd has also offered to collect finished products from VPharm's warehouse at their own cost, and be responsible for distribution of products to their customers. VPharm planned to supply products to the private sector (pharmacists and private health care providers) and had not intended to target the public sector. The board of directors of VPharm is considering the MBX Ltd proposal but is uncertain as to how to price the proposed order.

Required:

(a) Calculate the net present value at year 0 of the expected cash flows associated with the acquisition of the anti-malaria plant and equipment and with the operation of the division, using a discount rate of 15 per cent. (20)
(b) Calculate the revenue required in year 3 to enable the anti-malaria division to break even in that year. Include non-cash flow items but exclude tax. (9)
(c) Evaluate the minimum revenue that VPharm should derive from supplying MBX Ltd in years 2 and 3 in order to match the forecast profit contribution by the anti-malaria division. In addition, identify and list other key issues that should be considered in pricing the MBX Ltd order. (12)
(d) Identify and list the key risks facing VPharm in pursuing the anti-malaria project. (9)

(SAICA QE Part 1 2006)

S23.11 Standard costing, contribution per unit, overhead costing, outsourcing, special order

Fashion (Pty) Ltd, a manufacturer of denim jeans and T-shirts, is based in Cape Town. The company manufactures only its own brand of clothing, namely 'Bundai' jeans and T-shirts, which is sold to independent clothing stores. The Bundai brand is positioned as a unisex premium brand targeting young adults between the ages of 15 and 30. Garments are priced just below the levels commanded by international brands of jeans and T-shirts, and independent clothing stores have supported this pricing strategy. The company supplies approximately 200 independent clothing stores throughout South Africa, none of which account for more than 5 per cent of the turnover of Fashion (Pty) Ltd. Fashion (Pty) Ltd has not historically sold products through major national clothing chains.

The standard manufacturing cost per garment for the current financial year of Fashion (Pty) Ltd ending on 30 September 2002 is summarised below:

	Notes	Pair of Jeans R	T-shirt R
Material cost	1	32.00	7.50
Labour cost	2	24.00	15.00
Variable manufacturing overheads		9.60	6.00
Fixed manufacturing overheads	3	6.40	4.00
		72.00	32.50

Notes

1 Standard material cost is estimated on the basis of the expected usage of fabric and budgeted purchase prices of fabric. Standards have closely approximated actual costs in the past. Costs are averaged over the range of sizes and styles.

2 Standard labour costs are based on the expected time the machinists will spend on making a garment, multiplied by hourly labour rates. Machinists on average take 48 minutes to make a pair of jeans and 30 minutes to make a T-shirt. To improve production yields machinists specialise in making either jeans or T-shirts, and they work a standard 40 hours per week. Standard costs are based on normal production hours and it is assumed that machinists work 1900 hours per annum after taking into account public holidays and sick leave. Budgeted labour costs per machinist are an average of R30 per hour.

3 Budgeted fixed manufacturing overheads are estimated with care and allocated to product lines, based on expected annual production hours. The budget of Fashion (Pty) Ltd for the current financial year is based on the manufacture and sale of 118 750 pairs of jeans and 266 000 T-shirts.

The management accounts for the five-month period ended February 2002 indicate that the jeans production line is operating at full capacity and the T-shirt production line is operating at less than planned capacity. The company has experienced lower than expected T-shirt orders and production volumes are expected to remain below budgeted levels for the remainder of the current financial year. Machinists on the T-shirt production line are working normal hours, and could be assigned to the jeans production line. However, the machinists who usually make T-shirts are only able to manufacture on average one pair of jeans per hour.

The average selling price for a pair of jeans was R120 for the first five months of the financial year, and this is expected to remain stable. T-shirts have been sold at an average of R50 per item in this financial year, but prices are expected to decline to R45 per T-shirt over the next couple of months. Budgeted selling prices for the current financial year were R120 per pair of jeans and R52 per T-shirt.

Fashion (Pty) Ltd manufactured and sold 47 500 pairs of jeans and 79 800 T-shirts in the five months ended February 2002. The company is planning to produce and sell 71 250 pairs of jeans over the remainder of the financial year, as was initially budgeted. In view of the lower demand for T-shirts, it is estimated that only 119 700 T-shirts will be produced and sold in the remaining seven months of the 2002 financial year.

The normal production hours for the remainder of the financial year are as follows:

March	19 920 hours	July	19 680 hours
April	19 200 hours	August	19 680 hours
May	19 920 hours	September	18 720 hours
June	19 680 hours		

Machinists are paid 1.5 times the normal rate for overtime worked. However, overtime per employee is restricted to 80 hours per month.

Fashion (Pty) Ltd has been approached by a major clothing retail chain, GDF Stores, to fill an order totalling 30 000 pairs of jeans to be delivered in equal parcels of 6000 pairs per month. Production for this order is required to commence on 1 April 2002. GDF Stores has indicated that it will place further orders of around 7500 pairs of jeans per month commencing in October 2002 if the current order of 30 000 pairs successfully sells in its stores. Management of Fashion (Pty) Ltd are excited about the prospect of doing regular business with GDF Stores, given the potential impact on profitability, but they are uncertain about how to meet the continuing increased product demand. Two possible options have been put forward:

1 The company should re-assign certain machinists from the T-shirt line to the jean line, and offer employees on the jean line the opportunity to work overtime; or

2 The company should outsource some production to 'cut, make and trim' (CMT) manufacturers. A CMT manufacturer, Style Ltd, has offered to manufacture jeans on behalf of Fashion (Pty) Ltd subject to the latter supplying the fabric required for the production of jeans as and when required. Style Ltd has quoted a 'service' charge of R50 per pair of jeans manufactured, payable in cash on delivery of jeans to the premises of Fashion (Pty) Ltd. In terms of this arrangement Fashion (Pty) Ltd will be responsible for the raw material costs, while all other costs will be for the account of Style Ltd.

You may ignore VAT in your calculations.

Required:

(a) Calculate the price per pair of jeans that Fashion (Pty) Ltd should charge GDF stores for the order of 30 000 pairs, assuming that Fashion (Pty) Ltd wishes to achieve a R55 contribution per pair of jeans in respect of this order and decided to adopt option 1. (25)

(b) Discuss the basis adopted by Fashion (Pty) Ltd for the allocation of fixed manufacturing overheads in the calculation of standard product costs and suggest improvements. (5)

(c) Assuming that Fashion (Pty) Ltd obtains regular orders for 7500 pairs of jeans per month from GDF Stores, discuss and evaluate the cost effectiveness of outsourcing the manufacturing of jeans to Style Ltd. (7)

(d) List the factors to be considered prior to making the decision to outsource manufacturing to Style Ltd. (8)

(e) Discuss the issues Fashion (Pty) Ltd should consider in evaluating whether it should supply GDF Stores on a regular basis. (5)

(SAICA QE Part 1 2002)

S23.12 Costing systems, pricing, make or buy, special order

Azania Engineering (Pty) Ltd ('Azania') manufactures and supplies generator sets to customers in the hospitality, retail, telecommunications and health care industries. Over the past 18 months the demand for generator sets ('gensets') has increased significantly because of the frequent power outages experienced in major cities in South Africa and the perception that electricity demand will outstrip supply in the country over the next five to ten years. Gensets are primarily used as back-up power sources when the electricity supply is disrupted.

Azania produces diesel powered gensets at its factory situated in Wadeville, Johannesburg. The sales and marketing, procurement, finance and administrative functions are located in the same building. The business was founded in 1985 by Mr Diggory Lewis and has grown into one of the leading suppliers of diesel gensets. Mr Lewis retired in 2005 and his family trust still retains a 100 per cent shareholding in Azania. The business is run by the executive directors, who have all been employed by Azania for more than ten years.

The major components, by value, of a genset are the diesel engine, alternator, sheetwork (metal frames or canopies in which gensets are housed) and the electrical control panel. Azania has always imported diesel engines from various European suppliers renowned for the reliability and quality of engines supplied. Alternators, electrical control panel components and sheetwork are sourced from local suppliers. Azania designs gensets using computer assisted design software which it then uses for the assembly of the components. All assembly operations, including electrical wiring and instrumentation work, are performed at the Wadeville factory.

Azania produces custom-built gensets according to specific requirements of customers. This strategy, as opposed to building standard gensets, has differentiated Azania from other suppliers in South Africa. The company has found that most customers have unique requirements regarding power output, genset design, control systems, sound shields, etc., which are generally not met by standard genset product ranges. While some suppliers do sell standard gensets, this invariably means that their customers either acquire gensets which produce too much power for their needs (and incur unnecessary expense) or that there is some aspect of the standard genset design that does not suit their requirements. In the industries in which most of the company's customers operate, back-up power is a critical requirement. Customers accordingly place a high value on reliable and high quality gensets and tend to be less price sensitive in procurement decisions. Azania has many long standing customers.

Because of the tremendous increase in market demand for gensets, factory staff have worked extensive overtime at the Azania factory during the months of July, August and September. The company is considering expanding its premises and employing more factory staff to increase capacity.

Extracts from the detailed management accounts of Azania for the financial year ended 31 December 2005 and the nine months ended 30 September 2006, together with the revised budget for the year ending 31 December 2006, are summarised below:

AZANIA ENGINEERING (PTY) LTD
ABRIDGED INCOME STATEMENTS

	Notes	Actual results Dec-05 R'000	Year to date results Sep-06 R'000	Revised budget Dec-06 R'000
Revenue		42 360	55 060	75 616
Cost of sales				
Raw materials	1	−23 383	−32 045	−44 687
Direct labour		−4 092	−6 569	−9 140
Manufacturing overheads	2	−3 274	−3 277	−4 420
Gross profit		11 611	13 169	17 369
Non-manufacturing overheads		−4 550	−3 822	−5 605
EBITDA		7 061	9 347	11 764
Depreciation		−660	−480	−640
EBIT		6 401	8 867	11 124
Interest income		560	460	590
Profit before tax		6 961	9 327	11 714
Tax		−2 026	−2 706	−3 395
Profit after tax		4 935	6 621	8 319

Notes

1 Forward exchange contracts (FECs) are taken out specifically for all diesel engines imported from Europe. Azania does not bear any risk relating to fluctuating exchange rates and passes on FEC costs to customers. The contracts are entered into with the bank in the name of Azania and a separate agreement is entered into with each customer to transfer the costs of the relevant FEC to that customer. The Euro exchange rate has been particularly volatile during 2006. In early January 2006 the €:ZAR exchange rate was €1:R7.25 but by 30 September 2006 the rate had moved to €1:R9.40. The cost of diesel engines represented 55 per cent of the total cost of sales in the 2005 financial year.

2 Manufacturing overheads comprise water and electricity, assessment rates on property, insurance, allocated salaries, depreciation of plant and equipment and premises rental paid. Management is confident that overhead expenditure is accurately allocated to cost of sales and non-manufacturing overheads on the appropriate bases.

Manufacturing overheads are classified into fixed and variable costs:

	Actual results Dec-05 R'000	Year to date results Sep-06 R'000
Fixed costs	2 454	2 006
Variable costs	820	1 271
Total manufacturing overheads	3 274	3 277

Costing system

The procurement division prepares Excel spreadsheets for each customer order. The cost of the specific engine that will be imported for each particular genset is determined after obtaining supplier quotes and FEC rates from the company's commercial bank. Supplier quotes for other raw materials are also recorded and accumulated. Labour costs are estimated to a specific percentage of the total cost of raw materials, which was 15 per cent for the 2006 financial year. Manufacturing overheads are also estimated for the purposes of determining the cost of specific gensets. The policy for the past three years has been to include manufacturing overheads at 15 per cent of total raw material costs for the purposes of the costing spreadsheets.

Having estimated the total cost of sales for each order, Azania adopts a cost-plus pricing policy. For the past five years the mark-up has been 32.5 per cent. The depreciation of the rand has resulted in increased diesel engine costs – and therefore increased genset costs – during the current financial year.

Management analyses and reviews individual cost of sales expense items on a monthly basis to identify any production issues and monitor gross profit margins.

Special order: Axw Healthcare Ltd

Axw Healthcare Ltd ('Axw') has approached Azania to supply gensets to 15 of its hospitals throughout South Africa. The group has decided to replace some gensets because of the increasing cost of maintaining them and because the gensets are no longer reliable.

Azania is currently operating at peak production capacity during normal operating hours. Factory staff are already working overtime during the week and on weekends in order to fulfill customer orders. Axw wants the gensets to be delivered to their hospitals during the three-month period ending 31 March 2007. The procurement division has prepared a detailed costing spreadsheet, the salient information of which is summarised below:

COSTING ESTIMATE FOR Axw HEALTHCARE LTD SPECIAL ORDER
Order number: AZ10092

	€	FEC rate	R
Diesel engines	605 000	9.55	5 777 750
Alternators			1 425 000
Electrical control panels			940 000
Sheetwork			427 500
Other raw materials			880 000
Total raw material			9 450 250
Estimated direct labour costs			1 417 537
Estimated manufacturing overheads			1 417 538
Total cost of sales			12 285 325

The executive directors of Azania are uncertain as to how to price this special order. They are keen to secure the order, as it may lead to genset orders for the other 85 hospitals in the Axw group over the next three years. They would also prefer to minimise the potential risk of losing other customers because of an inability to supply them. However, the production manager of Azania, Mr Adam Zebra, has estimated that in order to manufacture and deliver the gensets for Axw during the period January to March 2007, factory staff will have to continue to work overtime. Furthermore, there is a risk that Azania may not have the capacity to accept orders from existing customers that may potentially be placed for delivery during this period.

Chinese imports

The executive directors are considering importing fully assembled gensets from Chinese suppliers. This possibility is being considered because of the production capacity problems currently being experienced at the Wadeville factory of Azania – a position which will be exacerbated if Azania accepts the Axw order.

Azania has examined and tested a number of different Chinese sourced gensets during the past two months. While the initial results indicate that these gensets should operate to acceptable standards, they are unlikely to meet the exact requirements of Azania customers. From those reviewed, the gensets produced by Zhexin Co Ltd ('Zhexin') were found to have the lowest cost, and they were the second best from a design and operational perspective. Fully assembled gensets can be imported from Zhexin at a price (including import duties) which would on average be 10 per cent lower than Azania's current total manufacturing cost for similar gensets.

The executive directors are uncertain about how much they should mark up the imported gensets from Zhexin.

Zebra (the production manager of Azania) recently spent two weeks inspecting the manufacturing facilities of Zhexin in China. The executive directors subsequently discovered that Mr Zebra spent an additional week at a holiday resort in Thailand, which was fully paid for by Zhexin. This discovery was made when Mr Zebra sent an e-mail message to friends in which he told them about the resort, and about various deep sea fishing trips and lavish dinners paid for by Zhexin, to which he inadvertently added the e-mail address of the managing director of Azania.

Maintenance contracts

Azania gensets carry a 12-month warranty for replacement or repair of any defective parts, subject to the gensets being operated in accordance with their design specifications. Azania has not in the past offered customers the additional option of maintenance contracts, but this option is now being explored by Azania. There are currently 750 gensets in use by customers, which Azania has supplied over the years.

Maintenance contracts will essentially entail routine three-monthly inspections of customer gensets by Azania personnel, as well as replacement of any worn parts (at the customer's expense) and general repair work required. Contracts would also provide customers with peace of mind, as Azania will guarantee that service personnel will repair gensets within eight hours of the breakdown being reported. It is expected that proactive and regular maintenance of gensets would be of great benefit to customers, by improving operating performance of equipment and prolonging the useful lives of gensets.

The following preliminary abridged budget has been prepared to evaluate the feasibility of establishing a maintenance division and to determine the pricing of the maintenance services:

AZANIA ENGINEERING (PTY) LTD
MAINTENANCE DIVISION FIRST DRAFT BUDGET

	2007 year R'000
Maintenance revenue (750 installed gensets @ R1500 per month	R13 500
Gross profit on expected sale of parts	4 500
Direct labour costs (15 technicians + 15 assistants + supervisor)	−6 600
Depreciation of motor vehicles	−560
Travelling expenses	−920
Contribution	9 920

Required:

(a) Analyse and compare the gross profit margin for the nine months ended 30 September 2006 with the gross profit margin for the year ended 31 December 2005. Identify possible reasons for the change and list issues that need to be investigated further. (15)

(b) Critically review the costing system currently used by Azania Engineering (Pty) Ltd to estimate genset costs and identify any potential weaknesses in the system. You should also outline possible improvements to the system. (15)

(c) Discuss the factors, other than the pricing of the order, that Azania Engineering (Pty) Ltd should consider in evaluating whether to accept the special order from Axw Healthcare Ltd. (10)

(d) Review the costing for the Axw Healthcare Ltd order and identify issues that should be investigated further or clarified. (6)

(e) List the key factors that should be considered in determining a selling price for the Axw Healthcare Ltd special order. Suggest a pricing range to the executive directors of Azania Engineering (Pty) Ltd and show all workings. (8)

(f) List the issues that should be considered in deciding whether to import gensets from Zhexin Co Ltd for supply to Azania Engineering (Pty) Ltd customers. (12)

(g) Discuss the ethical issues arising from the fact that the stay of Mr Zebra, the production manager, at a holiday resort in Thailand was paid for by Zhexin Co Ltd, from the perspective of Azania Engineering (Pty) Ltd. List any further information you would require in order to evaluate whether his actions were ethical or not. (10)

(h) Critically review and comment on the draft budget prepared for the proposed maintenance division of Azania Engineering (Pty) Ltd. What further information would you require to evaluate the feasibility of establishing the new division? (12)

(i) Identify and explain the key business risks facing Azania Engineering (Pty) Ltd. (12)

(j) Discuss the accounting implications of the FECs taken out for the imported diesel engines in the annual financial statements of Azania Engineering (Pty) Ltd. In your discussion consider recognition, measurement and presentation. Ignore deferred tax. (10)

(SAICA QE Part II 2006)

S23.13 Cost allocation, break-even (CVP) analysis, ABC costing, evaluation of alternatives

You are a management accountant in the Automatic Teller Machine (ATM) division of Brown Bank Ltd. As part of the bank's review of its customer service strategy, which aims to grow the market penetration in the medium to lower income segment of the personal market aggressively, you have been requested to assist in a review of the ATM strategy. While Brown Bank Ltd has an extensive branch infrastructure, ATMs have proved to be a cost effective way of servicing a large proportion of the basic banking requirements of its target market. It is therefore a strategic objective to move as many deposit and withdrawal transactions as possible out of the branch network to ATMs.

The bank makes use of two types of ATM devices:

- The XpressCash machine that currently costs R150 000 to purchase and allows customers to withdraw cash, make electronic transfers between accounts and obtain information such as account balances and abridged statements.
- The XpressTeller machine that currently costs R250 000 and allows customers to deposit cash (notes and cheques) in addition to all the functions performed by the XpressCash machine.

Brown Bank Ltd has 1200 of each of these machines in operation. Machine placements are a function of expected customer utilisation. A model developed some years ago to evaluate the viability of ATM sites has resulted in a generally accepted rule that an XpressCash machine needs a minimum of 4000 'value transactions' per month while an XpressTeller machine needs a minimum of 6000 'value transactions' per month to be economically viable.

For the purposes of the model, 'value transactions' comprise deposit and cash withdrawal transactions only. The costs associated with processing electronic transfers and information request transactions are negligible and therefore customers are not charged for these services.

Other actual relevant information relating to ATMs:

	XpressCash machines	XpressTeller machines
Average number of monthly transactions per ATM		
Cash withdrawals	7 500	12 000
Deposits	n/a	500
Average number of monthly servicing visits per ATM	20	50
Average number of 'value transactions' between ATM servicing visits	375	250

The bank uses an activity-based costing system. Activity-based costs (ABC) are reviewed annually and are designed to include all relevant direct and indirect costs on a fully absorbed basis. Where appropriate, detailed time and motion studies are performed to assist in deriving the ABC rates. The current relevant ABC information is as follows:

A Transaction costs

The relevant costs of processing a 'value transaction', regardless of whether the transaction has been initiated on an XpressTeller or XpressCash machine, are as follows:

Cost per transaction	Deposit R	Withdrawal R
Verify content of deposit envelope	0.75	
Compare amounts to transaction log	0.50	
Clear transaction	0.25	
Allocated network costs	0.75	0.75
Claims and queries	0.10	
General machine operating and maintenance costs	0.15	0.15
	2.50	0.90
ATM servicing costs—still to be determined	?	?
Total cost per transaction	?	?

Additional information

1 While the costs of the ATM servicing visits have been analysed (see note B below), the allocation of such costs to deposit and withdrawal transactions has yet to be performed.

2 The above ABC rates exclude depreciation expenses. Both types of ATM machines have a five-year economic life with negligible residual value.

B ATM Servicing costs

	XpressCash machines R	XpressTeller machines R
Unlock safe doors	7.50	7.50
Disable machine (off-line)	3.50	3.50
Clear machine counters and print transaction log	3.50	3.50
Clear deposits and confirm to log		37.00
Replenish and service cash dispenser	40.00	30.00
Service printers	28.00	28.00
Check and replace printer ribbons	21.50	20.00
Enable machine (on-line)	2.50	2.50
Secure safe doors	6.00	6.00
Servicing cost per ATM per visit	112.50	138.00

Additional information

1 ATMs are serviced frequently in order to replenish cash, service printers and collect deposit envelopes.

1.1 In the case of XpressCash machines, the servicing frequency is a function of cash withdrawal transaction volumes. A centralised ATM monitoring system warns service personnel when a machine reaches a minimum level of cash holding, triggering a service visit.

1.2 XpressTeller machines require servicing at least once a day, as deposits have to be cleared on a daily basis. On average every XpressTeller machine has at least one deposit transaction per day.

2 In order to service the ATMs, machines can be accessed in one of the following two alternative ways:

2.1 *From inside a branch:* These are serviced by a designated official (the ATM custodian), who is permanently stationed at the branch. The custodian also has other duties apart from servicing the ATMs. For security reasons, a branch-based custodian only services ATMs that can be accessed from inside the branch. About 60 per cent of all devices are serviced in this manner

2.2 *From central departments located in all major cities:* For these machines, a number of custodians are centrally employed, each with a set allocation of ATMs. Each custodian visits the allocated ATMs, accompanied by armed security guards. The routes used to travel to the ATMs are continually varied.

The servicing costs in the table above make no distinction between the differences in the forms of machine access. Travelling costs are not allocated to the servicing activities as they are too varied to be apportioned with any degree of reliability.

Revenue generation

Brown Bank Ltd does not charge its customers for deposit transactions. The question of charging customers for deposit transactions has been raised on numerous occasions in the past. The decision historically has been not to charge fees for deposit transactions as none of Brown Bank Ltd's competitors do.

Cash withdrawal transactions are charged a minimum fee of R1.50 per transaction plus an additional cost which is determined on a sliding scale depending on the amount of cash withdrawn. The average revenue (before deducting transaction costs) per cash withdrawal transaction is currently R2.10.

Consultants' review of ABC system

An outside firm of consultants was asked to assist in the review of the customer service strategy. Their report contained the following comment with regard to ATMs:

> The placement of XpressTeller and XpressCash machines is not optimised. The break-even calculations that have been used to establish the existing minimum transaction volumes of 4000 and 6000 transactions per month for XpressCash and XpressTeller machines, respectively, are outdated.

The general manager responsible for the ATM network is of the opinion that the viability of the ATM delivery channel can be improved considerably and has proposed two alternatives:

- Eliminate the functionality for taking deposits at ATMs entirely as this will significantly reduce the costs associated with servicing ATMs. This will furthermore enable the bank to concentrate on the cheaper XpressCash machines and make a much wider ATM presence in the market affordable; or
- As the cost associated with providing the deposit functionality results in a very small volume of transactions being responsible for a large incremental cost, it would be appropriate to recover the cost of providing this service from customers who make use of it. Even a nominal fee of R2.50 per deposit transaction would significantly enhance the ability to place additional machines.

In reply to the above suggestions the marketing general manager pointed out that research has indicated that customer behaviour in response to price increases in the past has shown a lack of sensitivity to the level of withdrawal fees. He expressed the view that an increase of 5 per cent in the withdrawal transaction fees would be a significantly better alternative than to charge for deposit transactions.

Required:

(a) Analyse the ATM servicing costs for withdrawals and deposits and recommend an allocation of these servicing costs to transaction costs for XpressCash and XpressTeller ATMs for each transaction type. (12)

(b) Recalculate the break-even monthly 'value transaction' volumes for XpressCash and XpressTeller machines given the revised transaction cost structures you have calculated in (a) above. You should assume for the purposes of this calculation that all ABC costs are variable in nature. (10)

(c) Highlight the issues, including those apparent from the results of your break-even analysis in (b), that Brown Bank Ltd should consider in the placement and rollout of further ATMs in pursuing its strategy of increasing market share. (12)

(d) Outline the key benefits and pitfalls of using ABC costing in a service organisation such as Brown Bank Ltd. (8)

(e) Evaluate the impact on profitability of increasing withdrawal transaction fees by 5 per cent and charging a fee of R2.50 per deposit transaction. (10)

(f) Critically evaluate and discuss the two alternative proposals by the general manager responsible for the ATM network to improve the viability of the ATM delivery channel. (8)

(SAICA QE Part II Financial Management 2005)

A23.14 Capital budgeting, financial performance, sources of finance, marginal costing

The finance director of GTK Ltd is preparing its capital budget for the forthcoming period and is examining a number of capital investment proposals that have been received from its subsidiaries. Details of these proposals are as follows:

Proposal 1

Division A has requested that it be allowed to invest R500 000 in solar panels, which would be fitted to the roof of its production facility, in order to reduce its dependency on oil as an energy source. The solar panels would save energy costs of R700 per day but only on sunny days. The Division has estimated the following probabilities of sunny days in each year.

	Number of sunny days	Probability
Scenario 1	100	0.30
Scenario 2	125	0.60
Scenario 3	150	0.10

Each scenario is expected to persist indefinitely, i.e. if there are 100 sunny days in the first year, there will be 100 sunny days in every subsequent year. Maintenance costs for the solar panels are expected to be R2000 per month for labour and replacement parts, irrespective of the number of sunny days per year. The solar panels are expected to be used indefinitely.

Proposal 2

Division B has asked for permission to buy a computer-controlled machine with a production capacity of 60 000 units per year. The machine would cost R221 000 and have a useful life of four years, after which it would be sold for R50 000 and replaced with a more up-to-date model. Demand in the first year for the machine's output would be 30 000 units and this demand is expected to grow by 30 per cent per year in each subsequent year of production. Standard cost and selling price information for these units, in current price terms, is as follows:

	R/unit	Annual inflation
Selling price	12	4%
Variable production cost	4	5%
Fixed production overhead cost	6	3%

Fixed production overhead cost is based on expected first-year demand.

Proposal 3

Division C has requested approval and funding for a new product which it has been secretly developing, Product RPG. Product development and market research costs of R350 000 have already been incurred and are now due for payment. R300 000 is needed for new machinery, which will be a full scale version of the current pilot plant. Advertising takes place in the first year only and would cost R100 000. Annual cash inflow of R100 000, net of all production costs but before taking account of advertising costs, is expected to be generated for a five-year period. After five years Product RPG would be retired and replaced with a more technologically advanced model. The machinery used for producing Product RPG would be sold for R30 000 at that time.

Other information

GTK Ltd is a profitable, listed company with several million Rands of shareholders' funds, a small overdraft and no long-term debt. For profit calculation purposes, GTK Ltd depreciates assets on a straight-line basis over their useful economic life. The company can claim writing down allowances on machinery on a 25 per cent reducing balance basis and pays tax on profit at an annual rate of 30 per cent in the year in which the liability arises. GTK Ltd has a before-tax cost of capital of 10 per cent, an after-tax cost of capital of 8 per cent and a target return on capital employed of 15 per cent.

Required:

(a) For the proposed investment in solar panels (Proposal 1), calculate:
  i the net present value for each expected number of sunny days;
  ii the overall expected net present value of the proposal;
  and comment on your findings. Ignore taxation in this part of the question. (9)

(b) Calculate the net present value of the proposed investment in the computer-controlled machine (Proposal 2) and advise whether the proposal is financially acceptable. Assume in this part of the question that tax is payable and that writing down allowances can be claimed. (15)

(c) Calculate the before-tax return on capital employed (accounting rate of return) of the proposed investment in Product RPG (Proposal 3), using the average investment method, and advise on its acceptability. (6)

(d) Discuss how equity finance or traded debt (bonds) might be raised in order to meet the capital investment needs of GTK Ltd, clearly indicating which source of finance you recommend and the reasons for your recommendation. (12)

(e) At the end of the first year of production after implementation of Proposal 2, the finance director noted that a mistake had been made in forecasting selling price inflation, which should have been 1.5 per cent instead of 4 per cent. He has gathered the following information regarding selling price and sales volume.
  Forecast standard selling price (4 per cent inflation) R12.48
  Actual selling price R12.36
  Forecast and actual standard variable cost R4.20
  Forecast sales volume 30 000 units
  Actual sales volume 32 000 units

Required:

i Using a marginal costing approach and ignoring the mistake in forecasting selling price inflation, calculate the selling price variance and the sales volume contribution variance, and reconcile budgeted contribution to actual contribution. (4)

ii Using a marginal costing approach, evaluate the selling price variance from an operational and planning perspective and discuss briefly whether your evaluation provides the finance director with useful information. (4)

[Note: part (d) is included here for completeness, but would not normally form part of a management accounting course and you may wish to ignore this part of the question]

(ACCA 2.4 June 2007)

A23.15 Budgeting, financial performance, not-for-profit organisations

Woodside is a local charity dedicated to helping homeless people in a large city. The charity owns and manages a shelter that provides free overnight accommodation for up to 30 people, offers free meals each and every night of the year to homeless people who are unable to buy food, and runs a free advice centre to help homeless people find suitable housing and gain financial aid. Woodside depends entirely on public donations to finance its activities and had a fundraising target for the last year of R700 000. The budget for the last year was based on the following forecast activity levels and expected costs:

Free meals provision:	18 250 meals at R5 per meal
Overnight shelter:	10 000 bed-nights at R30 per night
Advice centre:	3000 sessions at R20 per session
Campaigning and advertising:	R150 000

The budgeted surplus (budgeted fundraising target less budgeted costs) was expected to be used to meet any unexpected costs. Included in the above figures are fixed costs of R5 per night for providing shelter and R5 per advice session representing fixed costs expected to be incurred by administration and maintaining the shelter. The number of free meals provided and the number of beds occupied each night depends on both the weather and the season of the year. The Woodside charity has three full-time staff and a large number of voluntary helpers.

The actual costs for the last year were as follows:

Free meals provision:	20 000 meals at a variable cost of R104 000
Overnight shelter:	8760 bed-nights at a variable cost of R223 380
Advice centre:	3500 sessions at a variable cost of R61 600
Campaigning and advertising:	R165 000

The actual costs of the overnight shelter and the advice centre exclude the fixed costs of administration and maintenance, which were R83 000. The actual amount of funds raised in the last year was R620 000.

Required:

(a) Prepare an operating statement, reconciling budgeted surplus and actual shortfall and discuss the charity's performance over the last year. (13)

(b) Discuss problems that may arise in the financial management and control of a not-for-profit organisation such as the Woodside charity. (12)

(ACCA 2.4 June 2007)

A23.16 Standard costing

The following information relates to budget period 1 for Leysel Co:

	Budget 60 000 units	Budget 90 000 units	Actual for period
Sales	R9 000 000	R13 500 000	R12 400 000
Raw materials	4 500 000	6 750 000	6 324 000
Labour	1 550 000	2 075 000	1 652 000
Production overheads	1 900 000	2 350 000	2 380 000

Actual production and sales in budget period 1 were 80 000 units. Actual labour costs for the period included R500 000 of fixed labour costs. Actual production overheads for the period included R1 100 000 of fixed production overheads.

Required:

(a) Using a marginal costing approach, prepare a flexed budget for the period and calculate appropriate variances in as much detail as allowed by the information provided above. (10)

(b) In budget period 2, Leysel Co planned to absorb fixed production overheads of R1 125 000 on a standard labour hour basis. A total of 22 500 standard labour hours were budgeted but only 16 000 labour hours were actually worked in the period. Standard labour hours for actual production were 22 000 hours. Calculate the fixed production overhead efficiency variance for period 2 and explain its meaning. (4)

(c) Explain how budgeting can help organisations to achieve their objectives. (11)

(ACCA 2.4 December 2006)

A23.17 Standard costing

Ash Ltd recorded the following actual results for Product RS8 for the last month:

Product RS8	2 100 units produced and sold for R145.00 per unit
Direct material M3	1 050 kg costing R16 800
Direct material M7	1 470 kg costing R27 930
Direct labour	525 hours costing R36 750
Variable production overhead	R12 600
Fixed production overhead	R47 250

Standard selling price and cost data for one unit of Product RS8 is as follows.

Selling price	R150.00
Direct material M3	0.6 kg at R15.50 per kg
Direct material M7	0.68 kg at R17.50 per kg
Direct labour	14 minutes at R72.00 per direct labour hour
Variable production overhead	R21.00 per direct labour hour
Fixed production overhead	R90.00 per direct labour hour

At the start of the last month, 497 standard labour hours were budgeted for production of Product RS8. No stocks of raw materials are held. All production of Product RS8 is sold immediately to a single customer under a just-in-time agreement.

Required:

(a) Prepare an operating statement that reconciles budgeted profit with actual profit for Product RS8 for the last month. You should calculate variances in as much detail as allowed by the information provided. (17)

(b) Discuss how the operating statement you have produced can assist managers in:
 i controlling variable costs;
 ii controlling fixed production overhead costs. (8)

(ACCA 2.4 June 2006)

A23.18 Budgeting

Sine Ltd produces a single product, Product DG, and is preparing budgets for the next three-month period, July to September. The current cost data for Product DG is as follows.

Direct Material X	1.5 kg at	R35.00 per kg	R52.50
Direct Material P	2.0 kg at	R45.00 per kg	90.00
Direct labour	12 min at	R80.00 per hour	16.00
Variable production overhead		R10.00 per unit	10.00
Fixed production overhead		R30.00 per direct labour hour	6.00
			R174.50

Sine Ltd experiences seasonal changes in sales volumes and forecast sales for the next four months are expected to be as follows.

Month	July	August	September	October
Sales (units)	30 000	35 000	60 000	20 000

It has been decided that opening stocks of finished goods in August and September must be 20 per cent of the expected sales for the coming month. Closing stocks of finished goods in September must be 10 per cent of the expected sales in October. Stocks of finished goods at the start of July are expected to be 4000 units. Opening stocks of finished goods in July are valued at R698 000.

There will be 30 000 kg of Material X and 40 400 kg of Material P in stock at the start of July. These stocks will be bought in June at the current prices per kilogram for each material. Further supplies of Material X and Material P will need to be purchased for the higher prices of R38 per kg for Material X and R48 per kg for Material P due to supplier price increases. Opening stocks of each material will remain at the same level as the start of July.

In any given month, any hours worked in excess of 8000 hours are paid at an overtime rate of R120 per hour. Sine Ltd operates a FIFO (first in, first out) stock valuation system.

Required:

(a) Prepare the following budgets for July, August and September and in total for the three-month period:
  i Production budget, in units;
  ii Material usage budget, in kilograms;
  iii Production budget, in money terms. (10)

(b) Calculate the value of the closing stocks of finished goods at the end of the three-month period, and the value of cost of sales for the period. (3)

(c) Discuss the ways in which budgets and the budgeting process can be used to motivate managers to endeavour to meet the objectives of the company. Your answer should refer to:
  i setting targets for financial performance;
  ii participation in the budget-setting process. (12)

(ACCA 2.4 June 2006)

A23.19 Capital budgeting

Charm Ltd, a software company, has developed a new game, 'Fingo', which it plans to launch in the near future. Sales of the new game are expected to be very strong, following a favourable review by a popular PC magazine. Charm Ltd has been informed that the review will give the game a 'Best Buy' recommendation. Sales volumes, production volumes and selling prices for 'Fingo' over its four-year life are expected to be as follows.

Year	1	2	3	4
Sales and production (units)	150 000	70 000	60 000	60 000
Selling price (R per game)	R250	R240	R230	R220

Financial information on 'Fingo' for the first year of production is as follows:

Direct material cost	R54 per game
Other variable production cost	R60 per game
Fixed costs	R40 per game

Advertising costs to stimulate demand are expected to be R6 500 000 in the first year of production and R1 000 000 in the second year of production. No advertising costs are expected in the third and fourth years of production. Fixed costs represent incremental cash fixed production overheads. 'Fingo' will be produced on a new production machine costing R8 000 000. Although this production machine is expected to have a useful life of up to ten years, government legislation allows Charm Ltd to claim the capital cost of the machine against the manufacture of a single product. Capital allowances will therefore be claimed on a straight-line basis over four years. Charm Ltd pays tax on profit at a rate of 30 per cent per year and tax liabilities are settled in the year in which they arise. Charm Ltd uses an after-tax discount rate of 10 per cent when appraising new capital investments. Ignore inflation.

Required:

(a) Calculate the net present value of the proposed investment and comment on your findings. (11)

(b) Calculate the internal rate of return of the proposed investment and comment on your findings. (5)

(c) Discuss the reasons why the net present value investment appraisal method is preferred to other investment appraisal methods such as payback, return on capital employed and internal rate of return. (9)

(ACCA 2.4 June 2006)

A23.20 Activity based costing

Linacre Co operates an activity-based costing system and has forecast the following information for next year.

Cost Pool	Cost	Cost Driver	Number of Drivers
Production set-ups	R1 050 000	Set-ups	300
Product testing	R3 000 000	Tests	1 500
Component supply and storage	R250 000	Component orders	500
Customer orders and delivery	R1 125 000	Customer orders	1 000

General fixed overheads such as lighting and heating, which cannot be linked to any specific activity, are expected to be R9 000 000 and these overheads are absorbed on a direct labour hour basis. Total direct labour hours for next year are expected to be 300 000 hours.

Linacre Co expects orders for Product ZT3 next year to be 100 orders of 60 units per order and 60 orders of 50 units per order. The company holds no stocks of Product ZT3 and will need to produce the order requirement in production runs of 900 units. One order for components is placed prior to each production run. Four tests are made during each production run to ensure that quality standards are maintained. The following additional cost and profit information relates to product ZT3:

Component cost:	R10.00 per unit
Direct labour:	10 minutes per unit at R78.00 per hour
Profit mark up:	40 per cent of total unit cost

Required:

(a) Calculate the activity-based recovery rates for each cost pool. (4)

(b) Calculate the total unit cost and selling price of Product ZT3. (9)

(c) Discuss the reasons why activity-based costing may be preferred to traditional absorption costing in the modern manufacturing environment. (12)

(ACCA 2.4 December 2005)

A23.21 Not-for-profit organisations, zero-based budgeting, activity-based budgeting

Required:

(a) Discuss how costing information and principles may be applied in a not-for-profit organisation in the following areas:

i the selection of cost units;

ii the use of performance measures to measure output and quality;

iii the comparison of planned and actual performance. (10)

(b) Discuss the key features of zero-based budgeting and explain how it may be applied in a not-for-profit organisation. (8)

(c) Briefly discuss how activity-based budgeting might be introduced into a manufacturing organisation and the advantages that might arise from the use of activity-based budgeting in such an organisation. (7)

(ACCA 2.4 June 2005)

A23.22 Standard costing, variances

BRK Co operates an absorption costing system and sells three products, B, R and K, which are substitutes for each other. The following standard selling price and cost data relate to these three products:

Product	Selling price per unit	Direct material per unit		Direct labour per unit	
B	R140.00	3.00 kg at	R18.00 per kg	0.5 hrs at	R65.00 per hour
R	R150.00	1.25 kg at	R32.80 per kg	0.8 hrs at	R65.00 per hour
K	R180.00	1.94 kg at	R25.00 per kg	0.7 hrs at	R65.00 per hour

Budgeted fixed production overhead for the last period was R810 000. This was absorbed on a machine hour basis. The standard machine hours for each product and the budgeted levels of production and sales for each product for the last period are as follows:

Product	B	R	K
Standard machine hours per unit	0.3 hrs	0.6 hrs	0.8 hrs
Budgeted production and sales (units)	10 000	13 000	9 000

Actual volumes and selling prices for the three products in the last period were as follows:

Product	B	R	K
Actual selling price per unit	R145	R155	R190
Actual production and sales (units)	9 500	13 500	8 500

Required:

(a) Calculate the following variances for overall sales for the last period:

i sales price variance;

ii sales volume profit variance;

iii sales mix profit variance;

iv sales quantity profit variance, and reconcile budgeted profit for the period to actual sales less standard cost. (13)

(b) Discuss the significance of the sales mix profit variance and comment on whether useful information would be obtained by calculating mix variances for each of these three products. (4)

(c) Describe the essential elements of a standard costing system and explain how quantitative analysis can assist in the preparation of standard costs. (8)

(ACCA 2.4 June 2005)

A23.23 Inventory, Economic Order Quantity (EOQ), just-in-time inventory system

TNG Co expects annual demand for product X to be 255 380 units. Product X has a selling price of R19 per unit and is purchased for R11 per unit from a supplier; MKR Co. TNG places an order for 50 000 units of product X at regular intervals throughout the year. Because the demand for product X is to some degree uncertain, TNG maintains a safety (buffer) stock of product X which is sufficient to meet demand for 28 working days. The cost of placing an order is R25 and the storage cost for Product X is 10 cents per unit per year. TNG normally pays trade suppliers after 60 days but MKR has offered a discount of 1 per cent for cash settlement within 20 days. TNG Co has a short-term cost of debt of 8 per cent and uses a working year consisting of 365 days.

Required:

(a) Calculate the annual cost of the current ordering policy. Ignore financing costs in this part of the question. (4)

(b) Calculate the annual saving if the economic order quantity model is used to determine an optimal ordering policy. Ignore financing costs in this part of the question. (5)

(c) Determine whether the discount offered by the supplier is financially acceptable to TNG Co. (4)

(d) Critically discuss the limitations of the economic order quantity model as a way of managing stock. (4)

(e) Discuss the advantages and disadvantages of using just-in-time stock management methods. (8)

(ACCA 2.4 June 2005)

A23.24 Activity-based costing, performance measurement

At a recent board meeting of Spring Ltd, there was a heated discussion on the need to improve financial performance. The Production Director argued that financial performance could be improved if the company replaced its existing absorption costing approach with an activity-based costing system. He argued that this would lead to better cost control and increased profit margins. The Managing Director agreed that better cost control could lead to increased profitability, but informed the meeting that he believed that performance needed to be monitored in both financial and non-financial terms. He pointed out that sales could be lost due to poor product quality or a lack of after-sales service just as easily as by asking too high a price for Spring Ltd's products. He suggested that while the board should consider introducing activity-based costing, it should also consider ways in which the company could monitor and assess performance on a wide basis.

Required:

(a) Describe the key features of activity-based costing and discuss the advantages and disadvantages of adopting an activity-based approach to cost accumulation. (14)

(b) Explain the need for the measurement of organisational and managerial performance, giving examples of the range of financial and non-financial performance measures that might be used. (11)

(ACCA 2.4 December 2004)

A23.25 Budgeting, break-even (CVP) analysis, decision analysis

Wonderland Ltd, which is based in Robynland, owns Cinola Island, which is located off the coast of Robynland. On Cinola Island, Wonderland Ltd operates a circus and zoological gardens (zoo) both of which are open for 365 days per annum. The circus, which is widely regarded as the best in the world, can accommodate a maximum of 14 000 visitors per day. The zoological gardens, which opened on 1 December 1999, can accommodate a maximum of 20 000 visitors per day. Visitors travel to and from Cinola Island using petrol-driven ferries owned by Wonderland Ltd.

There is no other mode of transport to and from Cinola Island.

The following information is available in respect of the year ended 30 November 2006 and the year ending 30 November 2007.

1 The zoo and circus were open on each day of the year. The circus performed once per day and was always operated at maximum capacity.

2 Three types of ticket were sold as follows:

Ticket type	Admission to:
Z	Zoo
C	Circus
ZC	Zoo and Circus

The total of admissions to the zoo was 6 570 000. The total of admissions to the circus was 5 110 000. These totals include 4 380 000 type 'ZC' tickets.

3 Admission fees per visitor were as follows:

Category	Zoo only	Circus only
Adults	R40.00	R40.00
Children and senior citizens	R20.00	R20.00

Visitors who purchased ticket type 'ZC' received a discount of 25 per cent on the cost of separately purchasing a type 'Z' and a type 'C' ticket. Each ticket type was valid for one day only.

4 The visitor 'mix' for all ticket types was as follows:

Adults	40%
Children and senior citizens	60%

5 In addition to any admission fees payable, visitors paid a transport fee for the return journey to and from Cinola Island. The total transport fees received amounted to R25 550 000 of which R15 330 000 was attributable to the zoo, the remainder being attributable to the circus.

6 The management of Wonderland Ltd categorizes all operating costs, including those relating to the operation of its petrol-driven ferries, as fixed costs. These were as follows:

Zoo	Circus
R130m	R100m

Note: The petrol-driven ferries were fully depreciated as at 1 December 2006.

7 Wonderland Ltd received an annual fee of R10 million from an International media group under a fixed-term contract of three years' duration. The contract commenced on 1 December 2005 and relates to the rights to televise programmes which were filmed in the zoo and therefore the fee should be regarded as relating to the zoo.

8 Admission fees to the zoo and circus will be increased by 5 per cent with effect from 1 December 2006. Transport fees will remain unchanged.

9 It is anticipated that all operating costs will increase by 4 per cent per annum due to the impact of inflation during the year ending 30 November 2007.
10 The management of Wonderland Ltd expects that the number of visitors, visitor mix and ticket mix will remain unchanged during the year ending 30 November 2007.
11 Ignore taxation.

Required:

(a) Prepare the budgeted profit and loss account for Wonderland Ltd for the year ending 30 November 2007. (9)

(b) Calculate the percentage of maximum capacity at which the zoo will break even during the year ending 30 November 2007. You should assume that 50 per cent of the revenue from sales of ticket type ZC is attributable to the zoo. (7)

(c) The management of Wonderland Ltd are concerned regarding the extent to which fluctuations in zoo revenues will impact upon the total profitability of Wonderland Ltd during the year ending 30 November 2007. They are not concerned about fluctuations in circus revenues and are confident that it will remain at maximum capacity throughout the year. However, because Robynland has experienced considerable fluctuations in the rate of inflation during recent years, the management of Wonderland Ltd are also concerned regarding the impact upon profitability of any variation in the rate of inflation from the 4 per cent allowed for, as per Note (9).

The management of Wonderland Ltd have obtained the following forecasts regarding zoo revenues and the possible rates of inflation in respect of the year ending 30 November 2007.

Zoo revenues	Probability	Inflation	Probability
Increase by 10%	0.25	2%	0.30
No change	0.50	4%	0.40
Decrease by 10%	0.25	8%	0.30

Note: Transport revenues relating to the zoo would increase or decrease by the same percentage as zoo revenues.

Required:

i Using the above information, prepare a summary in an appropriate format which shows:

(1) the range of possible company net profit or loss outcomes
(2) the combined probability of each potential outcome
(3) the expected value of net profit for the year. (10)

ii Calculate the probability of the net profit being less than R75 million. (2)

(d) The management of Wonderland Ltd have become concerned about the increased level of operating costs associated with its petrol-driven ferries and have made a strategic decision to dispose of these. They are now considering entering into a contract with the Newman Steamship Company (NSC), a shipping organisation based in Robynland. The contract would entail NSC providing transport to and from Cinola Island for all visitors to the zoo and circus.

As a result of negotiations with NSC, the directors of Wonderland Ltd are considering two options whereby NSC will become responsible for the transportation of visitors to and from Cinola Island with effect from 1 December 2007 or 1 December 2008.

Additional information is available as follows:

(1) NSC would require Wonderland Ltd to pay for the necessary modifications to their steamships in order that they would satisfy marine regulations with regard to passenger transportation. The only firm which could undertake this work is currently working to full capacity and would require a payment of R2 450 000 in order to undertake the work necessary so that the ferries could be in operation by 1 December 2007. The same firm would require a payment of R1 725 000 in order to make the necessary modifications so that the ferries could be

in operation by 1 December 2008. The government of Robynland would be willing to pay a grant of 8 per cent towards the cost of getting the ferries into operation by 1 December 2007, but would not be willing to pay a grant in respect of any later date.

(2) On 1 December 2002 Wonderland Ltd paid R500 000 to the Port Licencing Authority of Robynland. This payment was for a licence which entitles Wonderland Ltd to use all harbour facilities in Robynland during the five-year period ending 30 November 2007. The licence could be renewed on 1 December 2007 at a cost of R150 000 per annum.

(3) Redundancy payments would need to be paid in respect of loss of employment. These would amount to R1 200 000 if the contract with NSC commenced on 1 December 2007. This amount would reduce to R750 000 if the contract commenced on 1 December 2008.

(4) Wonderland Ltd has a contract for the provision of petrol for its ferries which is due to expire on 30 November 2008. Early termination of the contract would incur a penalty charge of R76 000. An emergency reserve stock of petrol held by Wonderland Ltd, which cannot be used after 30 November 2007 due to marine regulations regarding the age of fuel, could be sold for R55 000 on 1 December 2007 but not on any date thereafter.

(5) The ferries could be sold for R3 300 000 on 1 December 2007. If retained after 1 December 2007 the ferries would require servicing during the year ending 30 November 2008 which would incur costs amounting to R150 000. The resale value of the ferries on 1 December 2008 would be R2 900 000.

(6) Stock of consumable items which originally cost R150 000 could be sold on 1 December 2007 for R110 000 and on 1 December 2008 for R50 000.

Required:

i On purely financial grounds, advise whether the management of Wonderland Ltd should enter into a contract with NSC with effect from 1 December 2007 or 1 December 2008. You may ignore the time value of money. (9)

ii Briefly discuss FOUR non-financial factors which might influence the above decision. (4)

(e) Briefly discuss FOUR initiatives that management might consider in order to further enhance profitability. (4)

(ACCA 3.3 December 2006)

A23.26 Transfer pricing

The Information Technology division (IT) of the RJ Business Consulting Group provides consulting services to its clients as well as to other divisions within the group. Consultants always work in teams of two on every consulting day. Each consulting day is charged to external clients at R7500 which represents cost plus 150 per cent profit mark up. The total cost per consulting day has been estimated as being 80 per cent variable and 20 per cent fixed.

The director of the Human Resources (HR) division of RJ Business Consulting Group has requested the services of two teams of consultants from the IT division on five days per week for a period of 48 weeks, and has suggested that she meets with the director of the IT division in order to negotiate a transfer price. The director of the IT division has responded by stating that he is aware of the limitations of using negotiated transfer prices and intends to charge the HR division R7500 per consulting day. The IT division always uses 'state of the art' video-conferencing equipment on all internal consultations which would reduce the variable costs by R500 per consulting day. Note: this equipment can only be used when providing internal consultations.

Required:

(a) Calculate and discuss the transfer prices per consulting day at which the IT division should provide consulting services to the HR division in order to ensure that the profit of the RJ Business Consulting Group is maximised in each of the following situations:

i Every pair of consultants in the IT division is 100 per cent utilised during the required 48-week period in providing consulting services to external clients, i.e. there is no spare capacity.

ii There is one team of consultants who, being free from other commitments, would be available to undertake the provision of services to the HR division during the required 48-week period. All other teams of consultants would be 100 per cent utilised in providing consulting services to external clients.

iii A major client has offered to pay the IT division R2 640 000 for the services of two teams of consultants during the required 48-week period. (12)

(b) Briefly explain THREE limitations of negotiated transfer prices. (3)

(ACCA 3.3 December 2006)

A23.27 Learning curve, performance management, target costing

The Great Western Cake Company (GWCC) is a well-established manufacturer of specialist flour confectionery products, including cakes. GWCC sells its products to national supermarket chains. The company's success during recent years is largely attributable to its ability to develop innovative products which appeal to the food selectors within national supermarket chains.

The marketing department of Superstores Ltd, a national supermarket chain, has asked GWCC to manufacture a cake known as the 'Mighty Ben'. Mighty Ben is a character who has recently appeared in a film which was broadcast around the world. The cake is expected to have a minimum market life of one year although the marketing department considers that this might extend to eighteen months.

The management accountant of GWCC has collated the following estimated information in respect of the Mighty Ben cake:

1 Superstores Ltd has decided on a launch price of R81.00 for the Mighty Ben cake and it is expected that this price will be maintained for the duration of the product's life. Superstores Ltd will apply a 35 per cent mark-up on the purchase price of each cake from GWCC.

2 Sales of the Mighty Ben cake are expected to be 100 000 units per month during the first twelve months. Thereafter sales of the Mighty Ben cake are expected to decrease by 10 000 units in each subsequent month.

3 Due to the relatively short shelf-life of the Mighty Ben cake, management has decided to manufacture the cakes on a 'just-in-time' basis for delivery in accordance with agreed schedules. The cakes will be manufactured in batches of 1 000. Direct materials input into the baking process will cost R28 000 per batch for each of the first three months' production. The material cost of the next three months' production is expected to be 95 per cent of the cost of the first three months' production. All batches manufactured thereafter will cost 90 per cent of the cost of the second three months' production.

4 Packaging costs will amount to R3.00 per cake. The original costs of the artwork and design of the packaging will amount to R96 000. Superstores Ltd will reimburse GWCC R32 000 in the event that the product is withdrawn from sale after twelve months.

5 The design of the Mighty Ben cake is such that it is required to be hand-finished. A 75 per cent learning curve will apply to the total labour time requirement until the end of month five. Thereafter a steady state will apply with labour time required per batch stabilising at that of the final batch in month five. The labour requirement for the first batch of Mighty Ben cakes to be manufactured is expected to be 6000 hours at R100 per hour.

6 A royalty of 5 per cent of sales revenue (subject to a maximum royalty of R4.4 million) will be payable by GWCC to the owners of the Mighty Ben copyright.

7 Variable overheads are estimated at R14.00 per direct labour hour.

8 The manufacture of the Mighty Ben cake will increase fixed overheads by R300 000 per month.

9 In order to provide a production facility dedicated to the Mighty Ben cake, an investment of R7 600 000 will be required and this will be fully depreciated over twelve months.
10 The directors of GWCC require an average annual return of 35 per cent on their investment over 12 months and 18 months.
11 Ignore taxation and the present value of cash flows.

Note: Learning curve formula: $y = ax^b$
where: y = average cost per batch
a = the cost of the initial batch
x = the total number of batches
b = learning index (= −0.415 for 75% learning rate)

Required:

(a) Prepare detailed calculations to show whether the manufacture of Mighty Ben cakes will provide the required rate of return for GWCC over periods of twelve months and eighteen months. (20)

(b) i Advise the directors of GWCC on specific actions which may be considered in order to improve the estimated return on their investment of R7 600 000. (8)
ii Briefly discuss TWO factors which could reduce the rate of return earned by the investment as per the results in part (a). (4)

(c) Explain the term 'target costing' and how it may be applied by GWCC. Briefly discuss any potential limitations in its application. (8)

(ACCA 3.3 June 2006)

A23.28 Performance management

You are the Senior Management Accountant of Better Gardens Ltd (BGL), a well-established manufacturer of a range of conservatories, summerhouses and large garden ornaments. The company's turnover and after-tax profits for the year ending 31 May 2007 are forecast to be R300 million and R60 million respectively. The company has 350 employees in total who are comprised as follows:

Function/level:	Number of employees
Directors/Senior managers	20
Sales staff	40
Assembly staff	250
Administrative & support staff	40

BGL's products are sold to specialist 'Garden Centres' by its sales staff, each of whom is home-based. The forty sales staff work from home and are supported by administrative and support staff who also undertake telephone-based selling activities.

The manufacture of conservatories and summer-houses is undertaken by 210 assembly staff, some of whom work in teams and others who work on an individual basis. The large garden ornaments, each of which is hand-finished, are produced by 40 assembly staff who are responsible for their individual output. The directors of BGL are considering whether to implement a reward scheme for all employees within the organisation. They have approached you for advice with regard to this matter. The production director recently stated 'if we implement a reward scheme then it is bound to be beneficial for BGL'.

Required:

(a) As Senior Management Accountant, prepare a memorandum to the directors of BGL which explains:
i the potential benefits to be gained from the implementation of a reward scheme; (6)
ii the factors that should be considered in the design of a reward scheme for BGL; (7)

iii whether you agree or not with the statement of the production director. (3)

(b) Briefly discuss how stakeholder groups (other than management and employees) may be rewarded for 'good' performance. (4)

(ACCA 3.3 June 2006)

A23.29 Just-in-time management, back-flush accounting, ledger accounts

(a) Explain the term 'backflush accounting' and the circumstances in which its use would be appropriate. (6)

(b) CSIX Ltd manufactures fuel pumps using a just-in-time manufacturing system which is supported by a backflush accounting system. The backflush accounting system has two trigger points for the creation of journal entries.

These trigger points are:

- the purchase of raw materials
- the manufacture of finished goods.

The transactions during the month of November 2005 were as follows:

Purchase of raw materials	R5 575 000
Conversion costs incurred:	
Labour	R1 735 000
Overheads	R3 148 000
Finished goods completed (units)	210 000
Sales for the month (units)	206 000

There were no opening inventories of raw materials, work-in-progress or finished goods at 1 November. The standard cost per unit of output is R48. This is made up of R26 for materials and R22 for conversion costs (of which labour comprises R8.20).

Required:

i Prepare ledger accounts to record the above transactions for November 2005. (6)

ii Briefly explain whether the just-in-time system operated by CSIX Ltd can be regarded as 'perfect'. (3)

(ACCA 3.3 December 2005)

A23.30 Budgeting, benchmarking, balanced scorecard, activity based costing

Better budgeting in recent years may have been seen as a movement from 'incremental budgeting' to alternative budgeting approaches. However, academic studies (e.g. *Beyond Budgeting* – Hope & Fraser) argue that the annual budget model may be seen as (i) having a number of inherent weaknesses and (ii) acting as a barrier to the effective implementation of alternative models for use in the accomplishment of strategic change.

Required:

(a) Identify and comment on FIVE inherent weaknesses of the annual budget model irrespective of the budgeting approach that is applied. (8)

(b) Discuss ways in which the traditional budgeting process may be seen as a barrier to the achievement of the aims of EACH of the following models for the implementation of strategic change:

i benchmarking;

ii balanced scorecard; and

iii activity-based models. (12)

(ACCA 3.3 June 2005)

C23.31 Budgeting, flexible budgets

AHW Ltd is a food processing company that produces high-quality, part-cooked meals for the retail market. The five different types of meat that the company produces (Products A to E) are made by subjecting ingredients to a series of processing activities. The meals are different, and therefore need differing amounts of processing activities.

Budget and actual information for October 2002 is shown below:

Budgeted data

	Product A	Product B	Product C	Product D	Product E
Number of batches	20	30	15	40	25
Processing activities per batch					
Processing activity W	4	5	2	3	1
Processing activity X	3	2	5	1	4
Processing activity Y	3	3	2	4	2
Processing activity Z	4	6	8	2	3

Budgeted costs of processing activities:	R000
Processing activity W	1 600
Processing activity X	1 300
Processing activity Y	800
Processing activity Z	2 000

All costs are expected to be variable in relation to the number of processing activities.

Actual data

Actual output during October 2002	Product A	Product B	Product C	Product D	Product E
Number of batches	18	33	16	35	28

Actual processing costs during October 2002:	R000
Processing activity W	1 580
Processing activity X	1 390
Processing activity Y	730
Processing activity Z	2 060

Required:

(a) Prepare a budgetary control statement (to the nearest R000) that shows the original budget costs, flexible budget costs, the actual costs, and the total variances of each processing activity for October 2002. (15)

Your control statement has been issued to the Managers responsible for each processing activity and the Finance Director has asked each of them to explain the reasons for the variances shown in your statement. The Managers are not happy about this as they were not involved in setting the budgets and think that they should not be held responsible for achieving targets that were imposed upon them.

Required:

(b) Explain briefly the reasons why it might be preferable for Managers not to be involved in setting their own budgets. (5)

(c) i Explain the difference between fixed and flexible budgets and how each may be used to control production costs and non-production costs (such as marketing costs) within AHW Ltd. (4)

ii Give two examples of costs that are more appropriately controlled using a fixed budget, and explain why a flexible budget is less appropriate for the control of these costs. (3)

Many organisations use linear regression analysis to predict costs at different activity levels. By analysing past data, a formula such as:

$$y = ax + b,$$

is derived and used to predict future cost levels.

Required:

(d) Explain the meaning of the terms y, a, x and b in the above equation. (3)

(CIMA Intermediate level Management Accounting – Performance Management, Nov 2002)

C23.32 Transfer pricing

MCP Ltd specialises in providing marketing, data collection, data processing and consulting services. The company is divided into divisions that provide services to each other and also to external clients. The performance of the Divisional Managers is measured against profit targets that are set by central management.

During October, the Consulting division undertook a project for AX Ltd. The agreed fee was R155 000 and the costs excluding data processing were R26 000. The data processing, which needed 200 hours of processing time, was carried out by the Data Processing (DP) division. An external agency could have been used to do the data processing, but the DP division had 200 chargeable skilled hours available in October.

The DP division provides data processing services to the other divisions and also to external customers. The budgeted costs of the DP division for the year ending 31 December 2002, which is divided into 12 equal monthly periods, are as follows:

	R
Variable costs	
Skilled labour (6000 hours worked)	1 200 000
Semi-skilled labour	960 000
Other processing costs	600 000
Fixed costs	2 400 000

These costs are recovered on the basis of chargeable skilled labour hours (data processing hours) which are budgeted to be 90 per cent of skilled labour hours worked. The DP division's external pricing policy is to add a 40 per cent mark-up to its total budgeted cost per chargeable hour.

During October 2002, actual labour costs incurred by the DP division were 10 per cent higher than expected, but other costs were 5 per cent lower than expected.

Required:

(a) Calculate the total transfer value that would have been charged by the DP division to the Consulting division for the 200 hours on its AX Ltd project, using the following bases:

i actual variable cost

ii standard variable cost + 40% mark-up

iii market price. (6)

(b) Prepare statements to show how the alternative values calculated in answer to requirement (a) above would be reflected in the performance measurement of the DP division and the Consulting division (12)

(c) Recommend, with supporting calculations, explanations and assumptions, the transfer value that should be used for the 200 hours of processing time in October. Your answer need not be one of those calculated in your answer to requirement (a) above. (7)

(CIMA Intermediate level Management Accounting – Performance Management, Nov 2002)

C23.33 Relevant costs, pricing decisions

H, a printing company, uses traditional absorption costing to report its monthly profits. It is seeking to increase its business by winning work from new customers. It now has the opportunity to prepare a quotation for a large organisation that currently requires a new catalogue of its services. A technical report on the resource requirements for the catalogues has been completed at a cost of R10 000 and its details are summarised below:

Production period

It is expected that the total time required to print and dispatch the catalogue will be one week.

Material A

10 000 sheets of special printing paper will be required. This is a paper that is in regular use by H and the company has 3400 sheets in inventory. These originally cost R14.00 per

sheet but the current market price is R15.00 per sheet. The resale price of the sheets held in inventory is R12.00 per sheet.

Material B

This is a special ink that H will need to purchase at a cost of R80 per litre. 200 litres will be required for this catalogue but the supplier has a minimum order size of 250 litres. H does not foresee any other use for this ink, but will hold the surplus in inventory. H's inventory policy is to review slow moving items regularly. The cost of any inventory item that has not been used for more than 6 months is accounted for as an expense of the period in which that review occurs.

Direct labour

Sufficient people are already employed by H to print the catalogue, but some of the printing will require overtime working due to the availability of a particular machine that is used on other work. The employees are normally paid R80 per hour, the order will require 150 hours of work and 50 of these hours will be in excess of the employees' normal working week. A rate of R100 per hour is paid for these overtime hours. Employees are paid using an hourly rate with a guaranteed minimum wage for their normal working week.

Supervision

An existing supervisor will take responsibility for the catalogue in addition to her existing duties. She is not currently fully employed and receives a salary of R5000 per week.

Machinery

Two different types of machine will be required:

Machine A will print the catalogues. This is expected to take 20 hours of machine time. The running cost of machine A is R50 per hour. There is currently 30 hours of unused time on machine A per week that is being sold to other printers for R120 per hour.

Machine B will be used to cut and bind the catalogues. This machine is being used to full capacity in the normal working week and this is why there is a need to work overtime. The catalogue will require 25 machine hours and these have a running cost of R40 per hour.

Dispatch

There will be a delivery cost of R4000 to transport the catalogues to the customer.

Fixed overhead costs

H uses a traditional absorption costing system to attribute fixed overhead costs to its work. The absorption rate that it uses is R200 per direct labour hour.

Profit mark-up

H applies a 30 per cent mark-up to its costs to determine its selling prices.

Required:

(a) In order to assist the management of H in preparing its quotation, prepare a schedule showing the relevant costs for the production of the catalogues. State clearly your reason for including or excluding each value that has been provided in the above scenario. (15)

(b) Explain how the use of relevant costs as the basis of setting a selling price may be appropriate for short-term pricing decisions but may be inappropriate for long-term pricing decisions. Your answer should also discuss the conflict between reporting profitability within a traditional absorption costing system and the use of relevant cost based pricing. (10)

(CIMA Management Accounting – Decision Management, May 2007)

C23.34 Marginal costing, absorption costing and activity based costing

KL manufactures three products, W, X and Y. Each product uses the same materials and the same type of direct labour but in different quantities. The company currently uses a cost plus basis to determine the selling price of its products. This is based on full cost using an overhead absorption rate per direct labour hour. However, the Managing Director is concerned that the company may be losing sales because of its approach to setting prices. He thinks that a marginal costing approach may be more appropriate, particularly since the workforce is guaranteed a minimum weekly wage and has a three month notice period.

Required:

(a) Given the Managing Director's concern about KL's approach to setting selling prices, discuss the advantages and disadvantages of marginal cost plus pricing **AND** total cost plus pricing. (6)

The direct costs of the three products are shown below:

Product	W	X	Y
Budgeted annual production (units)	15 000	24 000	20 000
	R per unit	R per unit	R per unit
Direct materials	350	450	300
Direct labour (R100 per hour)	400	300	500

In addition to the above direct costs, KL incurs annual indirect production costs of R10 440 000.

Required:

(b) Calculate the full cost per unit of each product using KL's current method of absorption costing. (4)

An analysis of the company's indirect production costs shows the following:

	R	Cost driver
Material ordering costs	2 200 000	Number of suppliers orders
Machine setup costs	1 000 000	Number of batches
Machine running costs	4 000 000	Number of machine hours
General facility costs	3 240 000	Number of machine hours

The following additional data relate to each product:

Product	W	X	Y
Machine hours per unit	5	8	7
Batch size (units)	500	400	1000
Supplier orders per batch	4	3	5

Required:

(c) Calculate the full cost per unit of each product using activity based costing. (8)

(d) Explain how activity based costing could provide information that would be relevant to the management team when it is making decisions about how to improve KL's profitability. (7)

(CIMA Management Accounting – Decision Management, Nov 2006)

C23.35 Production budgeting, marginal and absorption costing, cash flow

The management team at MN Ltd is considering the budgets it prepared for the year ending 31 December 2003. It has now been revealed that in June 2003 the company will be able to purchase on 10 000 litres of material Q (all other resources will be fully available). In the light of this new information, the management team wants to revise its plans for June to ensure that profits are maximised for that month.

MN Ltd can produce three products from the same labour and main raw material Q, though different amounts are required for each product. The standard resource requirements, costs and selling prices, and the customer demand for delivery in June (including those orders already accepted) for each of its finished products are as follows:

Resources per unit	Product V	Product S	Product T
Material Q	10 litres	8 litres	5 litres
Direct labour	8 hours	9 hours	6 hours
Selling prices and costs	R per unit	R per unit	R per unit
Selling price	145.00	134.00	99.00
Material Q	25.00	20.00	12.50
Other materials	10.00	4.00	8.50
Direct labour	40.00	45.00	30.00
Overheads:			
Variable	10.00	11.25	7.50
Fixed*	24.00	30.00	12.00
	109.00	110.25	70.50
Customer demand	1100 units	950 units	1450 units

*based on R95 000 per month

MN Ltd has already accepted customer orders for delivery in June 2003 as follows:

Product V	34 units
Product S	75 units
Product T	97 units

The management team has decided that these customer orders must be satisfied as the financial and non-financial penalties that would otherwise arise are very significant.

Given the shortage of material Q, the management team has now set the following stock levels for June:

	Opening stock	Closing stock
Material Q**	621 litres	225 litres
Product V	20 units	10 units
Product S	33 units	25 units
Product T	46 units	20 units

**This would mean that 10 396 litres of material Q would be available during the period.

Required:

(a) Prepare a production budget for June 2003 that clearly shows the number of units of each product that should be produced to maximise the profits of MN Ltd for June 2003. (12)

(b) Using your answer to requirement (a) above, calculate the number of units of each product that will be sold in June 2003. (3)

(c) Using your answer to requirement (b) above, calculate the profit for June 2003 using:
  i Marginal costing
  ii Absorption costing. (5)

The Managing Director of MN Ltd is concerned about the effect on cash flow caused by the scarcity of Material Q during June 2003. She is aware that monthly profit and cash flow are often unequal and has heard that marginal costing profits more closely resemble cash flow than do absorption costing profits.

Required:

(d) i Explain briefly why there is a difference between cash flow and profit.
 ii Briefly discuss the assertion that marginal costing profits are a better indicator of cash flow than absorption costing profits. (5)

(CIMA Management Accounting – Performance Management, May 2003)

C23.36 Joint products – sell or process further

Z is one of a number of companies that produce three products for an external market. The three products, R, S and T may be bought or sold in this market.

The common process account of Z for March 2007 is shown below:

Inputs	Kg	R		Kg	R
Material A	1 000	35 000	Normal loss	500	0
Material B	2 000	20 000	Outputs:		
Material C	1 500	30 000	Product R	800	35 000
Direct labour		60 000	Product S	2 000	87 500
Variable overhead		20 000	Product T	1 200	52 500
Fixed cost		10 000			
Totals	4 500	175 000		4500	175 000

Z can sell products R, S or T after this common process or they can be individually further processed and sold as RZ, SZ and TZ respectively. The market prices for the products at the intermediate stage and after further processing are:

Market price per kg:

	R
R	30.00
S	50.00
T	35.00
RZ	60.00
SZ	57.50
TZ	67.50

The specific costs of the three individual further processes are:

Process R to RZ variable cost of R14.00 per kg, no fixed costs
Process S to SZ variable cost of R9.00 per kg, no fixed costs
Process T to TZ variable cost of R10.00 per kg, fixed cost of R6000 per month

Required:

(a) Produce calculations to determine whether any of the intermediate products should be further processed before being sold. Clearly state your recommendations together with any relevant assumptions that you have made. (3)

(b) Produce calculations to assess the viability of the common process:
 (i) assuming that there is an external market for products R,S and T; and
 (ii) assuming that there is not an external market for products R,S and T.
 State clearly your recommendations. (7)

(CIMA Management Accounting – Decision Management, May 2007)

C23.37 Activity based costing

ZP Ltd is a marketing consultancy that provides marketing advice and support to small and medium sized enterprises. ZP Ltd employs 4 full time marketing consultants who each expect to deliver 1 500 chargeable hours per year and each receive a salary of R600 000 per year. In addition the company employs 6 marketing support/administration staff whose combined total salary cost is R1 200 000 per year.

ZP Ltd has estimated its other costs for the coming year as follows:

	R000
Office premises: rent, rates, heating	500
Advertising	50
Travel to clients	150
Accommodation whilst visiting clients	110
Telephone, fax, communications	100

ZP Ltd has been attributing costs to each client (and to the projects undertaken for them) by recording the chargeable hours spent on each client and using a single cost rate of R750 per chargeable hour. The same basis has been used to estimate the costs of a project when preparing a quotation for new work.

ZP Ltd has reviewed its existing client database and determined the following three average profiles of typical clients:

Client profile	D	E	F
Chargeable hours per client	100	700	300
Distance (km) to clients	100	140	200
Number of visits per client	3	8	3
Number of clients in each profile	10	5	5

The senior consultant has been reviewing the company's costing and pricing procedures. He suggests that the use of a single cost rate should be abandoned and, where possible, activities should be costed individually. With this in mind he has obtained the following further information:

- It is ZP Ltd's policy that where a visit is made to a client and the distance to the client is more than 100 km, the consultant will travel the day before the visit and stay in local accommodation so that the maximum time is available for meeting the client the following day.
- The cost of travel to the client is dependent on the number of km travelled to visit the client.
- Other costs are facility costs – at present the senior consultant cannot identify an alternative basis to that currently being used to attribute costs to each client.

Required:

(a) Prepare calculations to show the cost attributed to each client group using an activity based system of attributing costs. (7)

(b) Discuss the differences between the costs attributed using activity based costing and those attributed by the current system and advise whether the senior consultant's suggestion should be adopted. (9)

(c) In a manufacturing environment activity based costing often classifies activities into those that are: unit; batch; product sustaining; and facility sustaining. Discuss, giving examples, how similar classifications may be applied to the use of the technique in consultancy organisations such as ZP Ltd. (9)

(CIMA Management Accounting – Decision Management, Nov 2005)

C23.38 Process costing, by-products, further processing, variances

PQR Ltd is a chemical processing company. The company produces a range of solvents by passing materials through a series of processes. The company uses the First In First Out (FIFO) valuation method. In Process 2, the output from Process 1 (XP1) is blended with two other materials (P2A and P2B) to form XP2. It is expected that 10 per cent of any new input to Process 2 (that is, transfers from Process 1 plus Process 2 materials added) will be immediately lost and that this loss will have no resale value. It is also expected that in addition to the loss, 5 per cent of any new input will form a by-product, Z, which can be sold without additional processing for R20.00 per litre.

Data from Process 2 for April 2003 was as follows:

Opening work in process

Process 2 had 1200 litres of opening work in process. The value and degree of completion of this was as follows:

	R	% degree of completion
XP1	15 600	100%
P2A	15 400	100%
P2B	7500	100%
Conversion costs	37 900	40%
	76 400	

Input

During April, the inputs to Process 2 were:

		R
XP1	5 000 litres	156 790
P2A	1 200 litres	60 000
P2B	3 000 litres	45 000
Conversion costs		228 000

Closing work in process

At the end of April, the work in process was 1450 litres. This was fully complete in respect of all materials but only 30 per cent complete for conversion costs.

Output

The output from Process 2 during April was:

Z	460 litres
XP2	7 850 litres

Required:

(a) Prepare the Process 2 account for April 2003. (16)

The output from Process 2 (XP2) is readily identifiable as three different grades of solvent (P, Q and R). For reporting purposes, the costs of Process 2 are apportioned to the three products in the ratio of their output volumes. The output volumes for April were:

Product P	2700 litres
Product Q	3300 litres
Product R	1850 litres

The managers of PQR Ltd are currently deciding, for each individual product, whether they should sell it at the end of Process 2 or refine it further. The respective selling prices and further processing costs per litre are as follows:

Product	Selling price per litre at the end of Process 2 R	Selling price per litre after further processing R	Further processing costs per litre R
P	112.00	149.00	16.00
Q	92.00	126.00	24.00
R	65.00	86.00	12.00

The further processing costs are purely variable and they vary directly with the input volume. They are stated before any adjustment for revenue from further processing losses.

Further processing losses

- When product P is processed further, there is an expected loss of 15 per cent of input. This loss can be sold for R80.00 per litre.
- When product Q is processed further, there is an expected loss of 20 per cent of input. This loss has no scrap value.
- There is no loss expected when product R is processed further.

Required:

(b) Prepare a numerical statement that shows whether each of the products should be further processed. State clearly your conclusion in respect of each product. (10)

The standard input mix of materials XP1, P2A and P2B and their standard costs per litre are as follows:

	% mix	Cost per litre
XP1	50%	R 27.50
P2A	20%	R 60.00
P2B	30%	R 14.00

Required:

(c) Calculate the total material mix variance for April. (4)

(CIMA Management Accounting – Performance Management, May 2003)

C23.39 Outsourcing

The insurance industry is characterised by large organisations producing, packaging and cross-selling a number of different 'products' to their client base. Typical products include life insurance, health insurance, house insurance and house contents insurance. Therefore, cost efficiency, repeat business and database manipulation are of significant importance. BXA is a medium sized insurance company that has grown over the past fifty years by a number of relatively small mergers and acquisitions. Its business is focused on life, automobile and private property insurance. Over the last few years the insurance industry has undergone significant change with increasing consolidation and the squeezing of margins.

The Board of BXA recognises that it is quite old-fashioned in its approach to business, particularly in its attitude to information technology. Much of the computing is done on personal computers, many of which are not networked, using a variety of 'user written' programs. There are a number of different computer systems in the organisation that have been inherited from the companies that have been acquired in the past. However, these computer systems have not been fully consolidated. It is recognised that this lack of compatibility is causing efficiency problems.

BXA has recently been approached by CXA, an insurance company of a similar size, with a view to a merger. Although BXA has never combined with an organisation of this size before, the Board recognises that this merger could present an opportunity to develop into a company of significant size but that this may also present further problems of system incompatibility.

BXA has decided to proceed with the merger, but the Board recognises that this might only make the situation worse with regards to information management strategy of the resulting combined company. The Finance Director has asked you, as project accountant, to investigate the potential of outsourcing the information technology function as part of the post-merger consolidation process.

Required:

(a) Discuss the advantages and disadvantages of outsourcing the IT function for the merged organisation at each of the strategic, managerial and tactical levels of the organisation. (15)

(b) Briefly describe the characteristics of the supplier that BXA will be looking for in the selection of the contractor to take on the outsourcing. (5)

(c) Identify the factors which should be included in the service level agreement with which the contractor will be expected to comply in achieving the levels of performance that BXA will require. (5)

(CIMA Management Accounting – Business Strategy, May 2005)

C23.40 Benchmarking

PAL is a banking group specialising in loans for home purchase. It has a network of shops, cash machines and other outlets in and around the capital city (where it has headquarters) with all outlets within 140 kilometres. It monitors interest rates offered by competitors and strives to match or better the lowest rates. This strategy has been successful, but in order to compete more fully, it has introduced a range of additional customer services, including home insurance. A dedicated unit was established to extend existing benchmarking of price to other aspects of customer requirements. Following a survey, the following factors in addition to price have emerged as being relevant to customers:

- delivery
- technical content of literature
- customer service and correspondence

Required:

(a) Discuss the use of appropriate performance measures which home insurance could use as part of the proposed competitor benchmarking exercise. For each measure, advise on ways in which subjectivity might be dealt with. (12)

(b) Analyse the strategies followed by PAL so far and evaluate the possible effects of actions arising from benchmarking in supporting these strategies. (13)

(CIMA Management Accounting – Business Strategy May 2003)

C23.41 Performance measurement system

D is a management consultancy partnership providing complex computer modelling services to utility companies. Three partners started the business ten years ago but rapid growth in the past four years has seen it increase to fifteen partners. Each partner has a team working exclusively for, and reporting directly to, that partner. Competition between the teams is fierce and, sometimes, heated. The loyalty of each team to its respective partner is very strong. Members of each team are rewarded with an annual team bonus based on the amount of new business they bring in each year. However, recently it has been discovered that teams have been competing with each other for the same potential new client.

Partners recruit all consultants as trainees, usually after they have obtained a doctorate in pure mathematics or economics. After a six months' probationary period they are either confirmed in post or asked to leave. The rewards for those that stay are high with at least 60 per cent of income derived from the team bonus. Typically a basic salary of R400 000 would be boosted to R1 000 000 if the team has worked aggressively and found new clients.

The service that the partnership provides is highly specialised and at the forefront of available technology. Each team will write computer simulations to address its clients' problems. These models are not made available outside the company and, on some occasions, have not even been shared with other teams in the consultancy.

At a recent partners' meeting, it was agreed that the inter-team rivalry was not working in the partnership's best interest, since teams were competing in such a way as to damage the firm's reputation, profitability and its prospects for growth. Recognising that the current performance measurement system encouraged this behaviour, the partners agreed that an appropriate performance measurement system should be introduced which was less one-dimensional. The partners believed this would encourage better practice in terms of knowledge sharing and a coordinated approach to their existing clients and potential clients. They have recognised that the introduction of a multi-dimensional performance measurement system will involve a significant training programme for their teams to redirect their current focus away from only finding new business.

Required:

As a first stage in this process, you have been appointed as management accountant and practice manager.

(a) Advise the partners of the functions that an effective performance measurement system will perform for D. Note: You are not required to describe, in detail, any particular system. (10)

(b) Recommend the process that should be used in developing the performance measurement system to be used within D. (15)

(CIMA Management Accounting – Business Strategy, May 2007)

Glossary

A

abnormal spoilage spoilage that should not occur under efficient operating conditions
absorption costing all manufacturing costs are assigned to products: direct material, direct labour, variable and fixed manufacturing overhead
acceptable quality level (**AQL**) the defect rate at which total quality costs are minimised
account classification method (or **account analysis**) the process in which managers use their judgement to classify costs as fixed, variable or semivariable costs
accounting rate of return (or **simple rate of return, rate of return on assets, unadjusted rate of return** or **return on investment (ROI)**) the average annual profit from a project, divided by the initial investment
accumulation factor the value of $(1 + r)^n$ used in present value and future value calculations
activity a unit of work performed in the organisation
activity-based budgeting (**ABB**) a process of building up budgets from the major activities of the business
activity-based costing (**ABC**) (**system**) a methodology that can be used to measure the cost of cost objects and the performance of activities
activity-based management (**ABM**) the process of using information from activity-based costing to analyse activities, cost drivers and performance so that customer value and profitability are improved
activity centre a work area in which the activities have a common purpose
activity driver a cost driver used to estimate the cost of an activity consumed by the cost object
actual costing the process of assigning the actual amounts of direct material, direct labour and overhead to products
actual manufacturing overhead the manufacturing overhead costs incurred in production
actual overhead rate the actual amount of overhead divided by the actual volume of production
adjusted R^2 the coefficient of determination after adjusting for the effects of a relatively small number of observations
administrative expenses the costs of running a business as a whole, including the costs of senior management and administrative support departments
after-tax cash flow the cash flow expected after all tax implications have been taken into account
allowable cost the target cost at which the product must be produced if it is to be sold at the target selling price and generate the target profit margin
annual budget (or **master budget**) a comprehensive set of budgets that covers all aspects of a firm's activities
annuity a series of equal cash flows
annuity accumulation factor the sum of the accumulation factors used to determine the future value of an annuity
annuity discount factor the sum of the discount factors used to determine the PV of an annuity
applied manufacturing overhead an estimate of the overhead resources used to manufacture a product
appraisal costs the costs of determining whether defects exist
asset a measure of costs where the benefits extend into the future
average cycle time the ratio of total processing time to total good units produced
avoidable costs costs that will not be incurred in the future if a particular decision is made

B

B2B (or **business-to-business**) e-commerce activities that take place between a business and its customers, including purchasing and procurement, supplier management, inventory management, sales activities, payment management and customer service and support
B2C (or **business-to-consumer**) e-commerce exchanges between a business and its non-business customers, that may allow customers to purchase and pay for products and services, make sales inquiries, and search for and receive customer support and assistance, all online
back office the part of the service production process where the service is produced without the customer being present
backflush costing a simplified method of product costing where costing occurs after product is complete, by working backwards to flush costs from the system

balanced scorecard a performance measurement system that identifies and reports on performance measures for each key strategic area of the business
batch level activities activities performed for each batch of product
batch level costs costs relating to activities that are performed for a group of product units, such as a production batch or a delivery load
batch manufacturing processes processes in which individual products are produced in large batches and require a specific combination of direct materials and a specific sequence of production processes
benchmarking a process of comparing the products, functions and activities of an organisation against external businesses in order to identify areas for improvement and to implement a program of continuous improvement
best practice companies businesses that are high performers in relation to a particular practice or process
bill of activities a report identifying the activities, the cost per unit of activity driver, the quantity of activity drivers consumed and, therefore, the cost of the activities consumed by a product
bill of materials a list of all the materials required for a job
billable hours the number hours per year that an employee has available to service customers
billing system a system that estimates the fees to be charged to the client for the service, based on chargeout rates per billable hour for the various categories of labour consumed in producing the service
book value (or **written-down value**) an asset's acquisition cost minus the accumulated depreciation
bottom-up budgeting a participative process in which people at the lower managerial and operational levels play an active role in setting their own budget
break-even point the volume of sales at which the total revenues and costs are equal, and the operation breaks even
break-even time (**BET**) measures the time from the identification of an initial concept through to when the product has been introduced and has generated enough profit to pay back the original investment
budget a detailed plan summarising the financial consequences of an organisation's operating activities for a specified future time period
budget administration the procedures used to gather information and construct a budget
budget committee a committee consisting of senior managers that has responsibility for determining budget policy, and reviewing and approving budgets
budget manual a set of instructions that communicates budget procedures and deadlines throughout the company
budget (or **master budget**) **volume** the budgeted volume of cost driver for the year
budgetary slack the difference between the revenue or cost projection that a person provides and a realistic estimate of that revenue or cost
budgeted balance sheet a statement outlining the expected financial position of the firm at the end of the budget period
budgeted income statement a statement showing the expected revenues and planned expenses of the firm during the budget period
budgeting process the procedures and activities undertaken to develop the budget
budgeting system a system used to prepare a detailed plan, summarising the financial consequences of an organisation's operating activities for a future time period
business process map a flowchart of the activities that make up the business process
business process re-engineering (**BPR**, or **process re-engineering**) the radical redesign of business processes to achieve dramatic improvement in critical areas of performance such as cost, quality and delivery
business (or **competitive**) **strategy** the way a business competes within its chosen market
by-product a joint product with very little value compared with other joint products

C

capital expenditure budget a plan for the acquisition of long-term assets, such as buildings, plant and equipment
capital expenditure (or **capital budgeting** or **capital investment**) **decision** a long-term decision that requires the evaluation of cash inflows and outflows over several years to determine the acceptability of the project
carrying costs the costs of carrying inventory in stock
cash budget a budget that details expected cash receipts and planned cash payments for the budget period
cash inflows cost savings and additional revenues and any proceeds of sale of assets that result from a project
cash outflows the initial cost of the project and any increases in costs that will be incurred as a result of the project over its life

chargeout rates per billable hour the hourly charges to clients for the various categories of labour that have produced the service

coefficient of determination (*R^2*) a measure of a regression line goodness of fit, showing the proportion of the change in the dependent variable that is explained by the change in the independent variables

committed cost a cost resulting from an organisation's basic structure and facilities, and which is very difficult to change in the short term

committed resources resources, such as plant, equipment and supervision, supplied in advance of being used in production

common costs the costs of activities that are incurred for the benefit of more than one responsibility centre

competitive advantage the advantages that a business may have over another, which are difficult to imitate

competitive bidding where two or more companies submit sealed bids (or prices) to a potential buyer for a product, service or project

component-level target costs target costs for product subassemblies and components

compound interest the earnings of interest on the interest of prior periods

constant gross margin method a method of allocating joint costs to joint products so that the gross margin for each product is identical

constraints the limitations faced by the firm, including limited productive resources

continuous improvement the ongoing search for improved methods to reduce or eliminate waste and improve performance in areas such as cost, quality and customer service

contribution margin the difference between the sales revenue and variable costs

contribution margin format a reporting format in which costs are reported by cost behaviour, and a contribution margin is calculated

contribution margin percentage the unit contribution margin divided by the unit sales price, multiplied by 100

contribution margin ratio the unit contribution margin divided by the unit sales price

contribution margin (or **contribution** or **variable costing**) **statement** a profit report that separates fixed and variable costs and calculates a contribution margin

control putting mechanisms in place to ensure that operations proceed according to plan and that objectives are achieved

control systems the systems and procedures that provide regular information to assist in control

controllable cost a cost that a specific manager can control or significantly influence

conventional product costing system a product costing system that traces direct material and direct labour to products, and allocates manufacturing overheads to products using a predetermined overhead rate, which is usually based on a volume-based cost drive

conversion costs the costs of direct labour and manufacturing overhead incurred to convert raw material to a finished product

corporate social responsibility involves organisations taking into account the social and environmental impact of corporate activity when making decisions

corporate strategy decisions about the types of businesses in which to operate, which businesses to acquire and divest, and how best to structure and finance the organisation

corporate value the present value (PV) of both the future cash flows plus the residual value of the business

cost allocation the process of allocating costs in a cost pool to cost objects

cost allocation base some factor or variable that is used to allocate costs in a cost pool to cost objects

cost behaviour the relationship between a cost and the level of activity or cost driver

cost budgets a series of budgets that detail the cost of operations needed to support forecast sales

cost centre a sub-unit in which the manager is held accountable for costs incurred in that sub-unit

cost distribution the process of tracing and allocating all manufacturing overhead costs to production and support departments

cost driver any activity or factor that causes costs to be incurred

cost driver analysis a method that identifies root cause cost drivers of activities

cost estimation the process of determining the cost behaviour of a particular cost item

cost function an equation used to describe a cost behaviour

cost leadership a business strategy where a firm is a low-cost producer that allows the business to sell its goods or services at a lower price than competitors

cost management the improvement of cost effectiveness through understanding and managing the real causes of costs

cost management system a system that focuses on improving cost effectiveness through understanding and managing the real causes of costs

cost object an item which is assigned a separate measure of cost

cost of capital the minimum return needed to compensate suppliers of capital for committing resources to a project

cost of goods manufactured the cost of all direct materials, direct labour and manufacturing overhead incurred to produce finished products

cost of goods sold the cost of the products that are sold, matched against revenue received to determine gross margin

cost of goods sold expense the cost of the products that are sold, which is matched against revenue to determine gross margin

cost of quality report a report of the costs incurred in ensuring that the firm maintains a high level of quality, and the costs arising from having poor-quality products

cost per unit of activity driver the total cost of an activity divided by the quantity of its activity driver

cost pool a collection of costs that are to be allocated to cost objects

cost pool rate an alternative term for cost per unit of activity driver

cost prediction using knowledge of cost behaviour to forecast the level of cost at a particular level of activity

cost reduction objective the difference between the allowable cost and the current cost

cost structure the relative proportions of an organisation's fixed and variable costs

cost volume profit (CVP) analysis a technique used to determine the effects of changes in an organisation's sales volume on its costs, revenue and profit

cost volume profit (CVP) graph a graph that shows how costs, revenue and profits change as sales volume changes

costing system (or **cost accounting system**) a system that estimates the cost of goods and services, as well as the cost of organisational units, such as departments

cost-plus pricing the price calculated by adding a markup to cost

costs the resources given up to achieve a particular objective

critical success factors (CSFs) factors that derive from the competitive strategy, and are critical to the survival of the business

critical value the point at which a variance should be investigated

cross-elasticity the extent to which a change in a product's price affects the demand for other substitute products

current cost the cost that the new product could be manufactured for, including upstream and downstream costs, given the current design and resources but prior to any cost reduction activities

current replacement cost the cost that an entity would incur to replace an asset on the reporting date

curvilinear cost a cost that exhibits a cost behaviour that can be described by a curved line

customer cost analysis an analysis of the costs of products purchased by the customer as well as the costs of any other customer driven activities from any part of the value chain

customer profitability analysis a comparison of the costs of all the activities used to support a customer or a customer group with the revenue generated by that customer or customer group

customer relationship management (CRM) the collecting and analysing of data to understand customers' behaviour patterns and needs, and to develop strong relationships with customers

customer response time the time between a customer placing an order for a product or service and receiving that order

customer service costs the costs incurred in servicing customers, including after-sales support and warranty claims

customer support activities activities that support customers after the service production/delivery processes

customer value (1) the value that a customer places on particular features of a product or service **(2)** the difference between the value that a customer gains by owning and using the product, and the price paid for the product

D

decentralisation structuring of the organisation into subunits, and assigning particular operations and decision-making responsibilities to each unit

decision variables those variables about which a decision must be made

delivery schedule reliability the extent to which a business meets predetermined delivery schedules

delivery time the time taken to deliver the finished order to the customer

demand (or **average revenue**) **curve** a graph of the relationship between the sales price and the quantity of units demanded

denominator volume an estimate of the quantity of cost driver used to determine overhead rates
departmental overhead rates separate departmental overhead rates that allow us to recognise that overheads in each department are driven by different cost drivers
departmental production report a report that summarises the flow of production quantities and costs through the department, and the cost of product
dependent variable (***Y***) the variable that can be estimated by one or more independent variables (*X*)
design activities activities to design new services and service production processes
design costs all costs associated with the design of a product and of the processes that will produce the new product
direct cost a cost that can be identified with, or traced to, a particular cost object in an economic manner
direct labour the cost of salary, wages and labour on-costs for personnel who work directly on the manufactured product
direct labour efficiency variance a measure of the effect of using a different number of direct labour hours compared with the number of standard hours that should be used for the actual production output
direct labour rate variance a measure of the effect on cost of paying a different labour rate, compared with standard
direct material the cost of materials consumed in the manufacturing process to produce a product, where the cost can be traced to each product in an economic manner
direct material price variance (or **purchase price variance**) a measure of the effect on cost of purchasing inventory at a price different from standard
direct material quantity variance (or **direct material usage variance**) a measure of the effect on cost of using a different quantity of material in production, compared with the standard quantity that should have been used for the actual production output
direct method a method of allocating support department costs where each support department's costs are allocated directly to production departments that consume part of the support department's output
direct product costs manufacturing costs that can be traced to products in an economic manner
discount factor the value of $1 \div (1 + r)^n$ used in present value calculations
discount rate the interest rate used when discounting a future cash flow to its present value
discounted cash flow analysis a technique used in investment decisions to take account of the time value of money
discretionary cost a cost resulting from a management decision to spend a particular amount of money for some purpose, and where the decision can be changed easily
distribution costs the costs of storing, handling and shipping finished products
Du Pont chart a framework that identifies linkages between key performance drivers, key performance indicators and financial performance measures

E

e-commerce the use of electronic transmission media to engage in the buying and selling of products and services, delivered electronically or physically
eco-efficiency measures measures that compare output to input
eco-intensity measures measures that compare input to output
economic order quantity (**EOQ**) **model** a model for determining the optimum order size for individual inventory items in order to minimise total order costs and carrying costs
economic value added (**EVA®**) a measure of the value created over a single accounting period, measured by the spread between the return generated by business activities and the cost of capital
economic value to the customer (**EVC**) the price that customers are willing to pay for the product, given the price that they pay for the reference product and the added functionality and any operating cost reduction provided by the product
economic-value pricing a pricing strategy that takes into account the costs and benefits experienced by the customer that extend beyond the initial purchase price
electronic data interchange (**EDI**) electronic connections that link a firm's computer system with that of its customers and suppliers, to allow sales orders, invoicing, payments and analyses to be undertaken electronically
employee empowerment the practice of giving greater responsibility to employees at the operational levels of a business
employee share plans (or **share option plans**) plans that provide employees with the right to purchase shares in their company, at a specified price at some specified future time

engineered cost a cost that bears a defined physical relationship to the level of output
engineering method the study of the processes that result in the incurrence of a cost
engineering studies studies that identify the relationships that should exist between inputs and outputs
enterprise resource planning (ERP) systems software packages that support information systems that span different functional areas of a business
environmental condition indicators measure the actual condition of the environment at a local, national or global level
environmental costs the costs that an organisation incurs to prevent, monitor and report environmental impacts
environmental management accounting (EMA) environmentally related management accounting systems and practices
environmental management systems (EMS) systems that organisations put in place to manage their environmental performance
environmental performance the impact of an organisation's performance on the environment, including the natural systems (such as land, air and water) as well as on people and living organisms
environmental product costing tracing direct and indirect environmental costs to products, including the costs of waste management, permits and fees, and recycling
environmentally induced capital expenditure capital investment that is driven by the desire to improve the organisation's environmental impacts or by the need to comply with environmental regulations
environmentally induced revenues (or **benefits**) revenues (benefits) that arise from positive environmental actions of an organisation
equivalent units the production inputs that have been applied to physical units during production
expectancy theory a theory that assumes that employee motivation is a result of the relationships between three elements: expectancy, instrumentality and valence
expediting costs the extra costs of processing purchase or production orders faster than is normal
expense a cost used up in the generation of revenue
experience curve a graph illustrating how product costs, including costs from across the value chain, decrease as units of output increase
external failure costs the costs incurred because defective products or services are provided to customers
extrinsic rewards rewards that are given to employees from an external source

F

***F*-statistic** a statistic that tests the likelihood that the relationships in the regression equation have occurred by chance
facility level (or **facility-sustaining**) **activities** activities required to support the business as a whole, not caused by any particular product
facility level (or **facility-sustaining**) **costs** the costs incurred to support the business as a whole, not caused by any particular product
feasible region the space between the axes and constraints, within which lies the solution to a linear program
FIFO (first in, first out) method a method that assumes that the oldest inventory is completed before new production commences
financial accounting the practice of preparing and reporting accounting information for parties outside the organisation
financial budgets the budgeted income statement, budgeted balance sheet, cash budget and capital expenditure budget
financial performance report a report that shows the key financial results appropriate for the type of responsibility centre
financially oriented EMA financial information supplied to management about the environmental impact of the organisation's activities
finished goods inventory the manufactured goods that are complete and ready for sale
fixed cost a cost which remains unchanged in total despite changes in the level of activity
fixed manufacturing overhead costs indirect manufacturing costs that do not vary with the level of production
fixed overhead budget variance a measure of the difference between actual fixed overhead and budgeted fixed overhead
fixed overhead volume variance a measure of the difference between budgeted fixed overhead and fixed overhead applied to production

flash reports the daily online reporting of critical information
flat organisational structures organisational structures that have few layers of management
flexible budget a detailed budget that is prepared for a range of levels of activity
flexible budget report a report that shows flexible overhead budgets at various levels of activity
formula flexible budget a report that indicates total overhead costs at various levels of activity using the formula: budgeted variable overhead cost per unit of activity multiplied by the level of activity, plus fixed overhead
front office the part of the service production process in which the service is produced by staff interacting directly with customers
future value the accumulated value of a sum of money at a future point in time

G

gainsharing a system where cash bonuses are distributed to employees when the performance of the company, or of their segment of the company, exceeds some performance target
goal congruence a situation in which managers are committed to achieving the goals of the organisation while still satisfying their personal goals
goal seek approach an approach that allows the analyst to specify the outcome of the analysis so that the software can determine the necessary inputs

H

high–low method a method for estimating a cost function by considering data at the highest and lowest levels of activity
hybrid costing system a costing system that has the features of two or more costing systems, for example job costing and process costing
hygiene factors factors that provide the necessary setting for motivation but do not themselves motivate employees

I

idle time the cost of employees' non-productive time, arising from events such as equipment breakdowns or new setups of production runs
imputed interest charge the required rate of return that the firm expects of its investments, which is based on the organisation's cost of capital
incremental costs the additional costs that arise from choosing one course of action over another
incremental revenue the additional revenue that will be gained as a result of choosing one course of action over another
independent variable (***X***) a variable that can be used to estimate the dependent variable (*Y*)
indirect cost a cost that cannot be identified with, or traced to, a cost object in an economic manner
indirect labour any labour used in production that cannot be directly traced to individual products in an economic manner
indirect materials materials used in production that cannot be directly assigned to individual products in an economic manner
indirect product costs manufacturing costs that cannot be traced to products in an economic manner
inflation the decline over time in the general purchasing power of a monetary unit
intermediate products products that have no market outside the company and are processed further to become final products
internal customer the next person or group in a process
internal failure costs the costs incurred when defective products or services are detected before leaving the business
internal rate of return (or **time-adjusted rate of return**) the actual economic return earned by the project over its life
intrinsic rewards intangible rewards that arise from the positive experiences of being satisfied with performing well
inventoriable cost (or **inventoried cost**) another term for product cost, derived from the process of 'storing' the cost of inventory until the goods are sold
inventory reorder point (**ROP**) the level of inventory on hand that triggers the placement of a new order from a supplier

invested capital the assets that the investment centre has available to generate profit
investment allowance a one-off taxation deduction that businesses receive in the year of purchase of an asset
investment centre a sub-unit in which the manager is held accountable for profit generated and invested capital used to generate profit in that sub-unit
investment turnover the number of sales dollars generated by every dollar of invested capital (assets), calculated as sales revenue divided by invested capital

J

job (or **job order**) a distinct batch of production, or production undertaken to fill a particular customer order
job cost sheet a record of all costs that relate to a particular job
job costing a costing system that traces manufacturing costs to individual jobs
joint cost all manufacturing costs incurred in the production of joint products
joint products two or more products that are produced simultaneously from the one production process
joint rate efficiency variance the outcome of paying more for labour than the standard and using a greater number of labour hours than the standard number allowed
just-in-time (JIT) inventory and production system a comprehensive system for controlling the flow of manufacturing in a multistage production environment

K

kanban the Japanese term for card or visible record, which is used to signal a request for new production (or inventory)

L

labour on-costs the additional costs that are incurred to employ personnel, including payroll tax, workers' compensation and the employer's superannuation contributions
lag indicators measures of the outcomes of decisions that monitor progress towards objectives
lead indicators measures that drive the outcomes and provide information that is actionable and manageable
lead time the length of time between placing an order and receiving an order
learning curve a graphical expression of how production efficiency increases with experience
learning curve effect the reduction in labour time per unit that occurs as the labour force gains experience in manufacturing a new product
least-cost decision a capital expenditure decision where the objective is to minimise the NPV of the costs to be incurred
level of activity the level of work performed in the organisation
life cycle budget a budget that compares planned costs with predicted revenue over the product's entire life
life cycle costing a cost management approach where costs are accumulated and managed over a product's life cycle
line item budgeting a form of budgeting where resources are allocated to line items such as salaries, office supplies or telephone expenses
line management managers who are directly involved in the core activities of the business
linear programming a method for identifying linear relationships between decision variables to determine the optimal solution, given a number of constraints
long-term decisions decisions that tend to be more strategic in nature, and involve large increases (or decreases) in capacity related resources
loss on disposal the loss made when an asset is sold for less than its current book value

M

management accounting the processes and techniques that focus on the effective use of organisational resources, to support managers in their tasks of enhancing both customer value and shareholder value
management accounting system an information system that produces the information required by managers to manage resources and to create value
management by exception the practice of reporting only significant cost variances
management performance indicators indicators that measure the efforts of management to improve the environmental performance of their organisation
manufacturing costs (**1**) the production costs in a manufacturing business, which include all costs incurred within the factory (**2**) the cost of direct material, direct labour and manufacturing overhead

manufacturing overhead costs (or **indirect manufacturing costs** or **factory burden costs**) all manufacturing costs other than direct material and direct labour costs
marginal cost the cost of producing one additional unit of production
marginal cost curve a graph of the change in total cost that accompanies a change in the quantity of product produced and sold
marginal revenue curve a graph of the change in total revenue that accompanies a change in the quantity of product sold
marketing activities activities that focus on selling the services, as well as advertising and promotion
marketing costs the overall costs of selling goods and services
mass services entities organisations that serve many customers, with each one requiring limited staff time and little customisation; staff are mainly non-professional
material requisition form authorises the movement of raw materials from the warehouse to the production department
merchandising businesses businesses that purchase goods to sell to customers, without any further conversion processes
mission statement a statement that defines the purpose and boundaries of the organisation
motivation the processes that account for an individual's intensity, direction and persistence of effort towards attaining goal
motivators factors that relate to job content and provide motivation
multiple regression a statistical technique that estimates a linear relationship between one dependent variable and two or more independent variables

N

net present value (**NPV**) the sum of the present values of the cash flows in each period
net realisable value the estimated selling price in the ordinary course of business less the estimated costs of completion and the estimated cost necessary to make the sales
net realisable value method a method of allocating joint costs to the joint products according to the relative size of the final products' net realisable values
new product (or **service**) **development time** (or **time-to-market**) the time from the identification of an initial concept through to the release of the product (or service) for sale
nominal dollars a measure of the actual cash flow
nominal required rate of return the real rate of return plus a premium to compensate for inflation
non-manufacturing costs all costs incurred outside of manufacturing—that is, the cost of upstream and downstream activities
non-value-added activity an activity that does not add value to a product or service from the customers' perspective or for the business and, therefore, can be eliminated
non-volume-based cost driver a cost driver not directly related to production volume
normal costing a product costing system which assigns direct material and direct labour costs at actual amounts, but applies overhead using a predetermined overhead rate
normal spoilage spoilage that is inherent in the production process and occurs even under efficient operating conditions
normal volume the level of capacity that will satisfy average customer demand over the normal business cycle, taking account of seasonal, cyclical and trend factors
normalisation the practice of removing the effects of factors outside the control of the organisation, so that narrowing the performance gap is achievable
normalised overhead rate an overhead rate calculated over a relatively long period to smooth out fluctuations in overheads, and therefore product cost

O

objective function an algebraic expression of the firm's goal that is used in linear programming
objectives (or **goals**) specific statements of what the organisation aims to achieve, often quantified and relating to a specific period of time
oligopolistic market a market where a small number of sellers compete among themselves
operating budgets the sales budgets and various cost budgets that are directly associated with the operating activities of the organisation
operating leverage the extent to which an organisation uses fixed costs in its cost structure
operating leverage factor the percentage impact on net profit of a percentage change in sales revenue

operation costing a hybrid costing system used in a batch manufacturing environment to assign direct material costs to batches and conversion costs to departments or processes
operational managers managers who have responsibility for manufacturing activities in manufacturing firms, or for service delivery areas in service firms
operational performance indicators indicators that provide information such as waste levels and energy consumption, relative to volume of production, sales or some other activity
opportunity cost the potential benefit that is given up when one course of action is chosen over another
optimum order size an order size that minimises the total ordering and carrying costs
order receipt time the time between the sales department receiving a customer order and placing that order with the manufacturing department
ordering costs the incremental costs of placing an order for inventory
outlier a data point that falls far away from the other points in the scatter diagram
out-of-pocket costs the incremental costs that will be incurred if a particular course of action is selected
outsourcing situations in which part of a manufacturing process, or another function normally undertaken within an organisation, is contracted to an outside business
overapplied overhead the amount by which the total manufacturing overhead applied to production is greater than the total of the actual overhead costs incurred
overhead cost performance report a summary of the actual and budgeted costs for each overhead item, and the overhead variances
overhead costs in a service environment, these are the costs of supporting service production that cannot be traced directly to individual services in an economic manner
overtime premium the extra wages paid to an employee who works beyond normal working hours

P

***p*-value** a statistic used to test the significance of a result
padding the budget the practice of underestimating revenues or overestimating costs so that budget targets are easier to achieve
participative budgeting a process where managers who are held accountable for budget performance help to develop their own budget estimates
payback period the amount of time it will take for the cash inflows from the project to accumulate to cover the original investment
penetration pricing a strategy of setting the initial price of a new product relatively low to attract market share
perfection (or **ideal** or **theoretical**) **standards** the minimum attainable costs under near-perfect operating conditions
performance gap the extent to which a business needs to improve to reach best practice
performance measurement system a system that measures performance by comparing actual results with some target
performance-related pay systems (or **incentive compensation schemes**) systems that base rewards on achieving or exceeding some performance target
period costs costs that are expensed in the accounting period in which they are incurred
physical units all units currently in production, whether complete or partially complete
physical units method a method of allocating joint costs to joint products based on some physical characteristic of the joint products at the split-off point
physically oriented EMA techniques that focus on supplying information to management that accounts for the organisation's impact on the natural environment, measured in physical terms
planning a broad concept that is concerned with formulating the direction for future operations
plantwide overhead rate a single overhead rate that is calculated for the entire production plant
post-completion audit (**PCA**, or **post-audit**) a comparison of a project's actual cash flows with the projected cash flows
practical capacity the maximum level of production that a plant will produce under normal, efficient operating conditions (including downtime)
practical (or **attainable**) **standards** the minimum attainable costs under normal operating conditions, with allowances made for downtime and wastage
predatory pricing when a company reduces the price of its products or services to such a low level that a competitor is forced out of the market
predetermined (or **budgeted**) **overhead rate** an estimate of the overhead resources consumed per unit of cost driver

present value (of a cash flow) the future cash flows discounted to the present date
prevention costs the costs incurred in preventing defects and in minimising appraisal activities
price discrimination setting different prices, discounts, services or payment terms for different customers for the same goods or services
price elasticity the impact of price changes on sales volume
price-fixing contracts arrangements that result in the fixing, control or maintenance of prices for the supply of goods or services
prime costs the costs of direct material and direct labour
principal the initial sum of money lent or borrowed
private costs environmental costs that directly affect the profit of the organisation or are costs for which the organisation can be held legally accountable
process (or **business process**) a series of activities that are linked together to achieve a specific objective
process costing (system) a costing system that traces all production costs to processes or departments, and averages them across all units produced
process improvement the incremental continuous improvement of processes
process perspective the flow of activity across the organisation rather than within functional departments
product cost the cost assigned to goods that were either manufactured or purchased for resale
product costing system a system that accumulates product-related costs and uses a series of procedures to assign them to the organisation's final products
product differentiation a business strategy whereby a firm derives competitive advantage from offering goods or services that have characteristics superior to those offered by a competitor
product diversity the number of different products produced
product level (or **product-sustaining**) **activities** activities performed for specific products or product families
product level (or **product-sustaining**) **costs** costs relating to activities that are performed for specific products or product families
product-level target cost the difference between the current cost and the target cost reduction objective
product life cycle the time from the conception of a product through to its abandonment
product mix decision determining the most appropriate range of products to offer to customers
production and delivery activities activities undertaken to produce and deliver the services
production budget a budget that outlines the number of production units to be manufactured during the budget period to satisfy sales and to meet inventory requirements
production costs the costs incurred to collect and assemble the resources used to produce a product
production department a department that works directly on the product being produced
production lead (or **cycle**) **time** (or **manufacturing cycle time**) the period from when the order enters the manufacturing department to when the finished products are ready for delivery
production time the duration of the manufacturing process
productivity the ratio of outputs produced per unit of input
professional labour costs the salaries of employees who have professional qualifications, and who work directly on producing and delivering a service
professional services firms firms that are staffed by professional staff who provide personal services and serve relatively few customers
profit and loss account a summary of all expenses and revenues, including cost of goods sold (COGS), for the relevant accounting period
profit centre a sub-unit in which the manager is held accountable for the profit of that sub-unit
profit on disposal the profit made when an asset is sold for more than its current book value
profit-sharing plan a plan where cash bonuses are paid to each employee, based on a specified percentage of the company's profit
profit volume (PV) graph a graph that shows the total amount of profit or loss at different sales volumes
profitability index (or **excess present value index**) the present value of cash flows, exclusive of initial investment, divided by the initial investment
program budgeting a form of budgeting where the various programs undertaken by the enterprise are identified, program objectives are developed and budgets are prepared for each program
proration the allocation of underapplied or overapplied overhead between cost of goods sold (COGS), work in process (WIP) and finished goods
pull system production and inventory purchases are pulled through the system, driven by the actual demands of the final customer
purchases budget a budget that is used to determine the quantity and cost of goods that need to be purchased during the budget year

purchasing activities activities that involve the acquisition and management of goods purchased for resale
pure rate variance the difference between actual hourly wage rate and standard hourly wage rate, multiplied by the number of standard hours allowed
push system goods are produced or purchased to meet inventory requirements rather than to meet actual customer demand

Q

qualitative information information relevant to a decision that cannot be expressed easily in numerical terms
quality the degree to which a product or service meets customers' needs and expectations
quality accreditation formal recognition that a series of quality standards set out in the international ISO 9000 series have been met
quality of conformance the degree to which a product meets its formal design specifications
quality of design the degree to which a product's design specifications meet customers' expectations
quantitative information information that can be expressed in numerical terms, such as in dollars
quantity discounts price reductions provided by suppliers when firms order large quantities

R

raw and in process inventory (**RIP account**) a ledger account where movements in both raw material and work in process are recorded under a backflush costing system
raw material inventory the major materials that will be used in production
real dollars a measure of dollars that is adjusted to reflect the dollar's purchasing power
real required rate of return the rate of return that covers investment risk
real-time reporting systems that allow managers access to up-to-date information whenever they require it
realisation rate the final fee charged to the client as a percentage of the billing system fee based on the firm's chargeout rates
reciprocal services services that are provided between support departments
reciprocal services method a method of allocating support department costs that fully recognises the provision of services between support departments
recoupment any asset sold for more than its tax value will be subject to a recoupment which is added to a company's taxable income. The recoupment is limited to cost, so a recoupment is determined as selling price less tax value at the date of sale. If the selling price exceeds cost, then the recoupment is cost less the asset's tax value
regression analysis a statistical technique that can be used to estimate the relationship between a dependent variable (cost) and independent variables (cost drivers)
relative sales value method a method of allocating joint cost to joint products in proportion to their sales value at the split-off point
relevant information information that differs between alternative courses of action, is future-oriented, timely, includes opportunity costs and can be qualitative or quantitative
relevant range the range of activity over which a particular cost behaviour pattern is assumed valid
required rate of return (or **hurdle rate** or **discount rate**) the minimum acceptable rate of return on investments
resale price maintenance when a supplier dictates the minimum price at which a product or service is to be resold by a buyer to the retail or wholesale market
research and development activities activities to identify potential new services or service production processes
research and development (or **R & D**) **costs** all the costs incurred in the development of new products and processes
residual income the amount of profit that remains (as a residual) after subtracting an imputed interest charge
residual value the value of the firm at the end of the forecast period
resource driver a cost driver used to estimate the cost of resources consumed by an activity
resources financial and non-financial means of the organisation, including information, work processes, employees, committed customers and suppliers
responsibility accounting the practice of holding managers responsible for the activities and performance of their area of the business
responsibility accounting system a system in which managers are held responsible for the activities and performance in their area of the business
responsibility centre a sub-unit in an organisation where the manager is held accountable for the sub-unit's activities and performance

retailers businesses that resell goods directly to the public
return on investment (**ROI**) a financial measure calculated as profit divided by invested capital
return on investment (**ROI**) **pricing** the selling price determined by using the required rate of return to calculate the markup on cost
return on sales the percentage of each sales dollar that remains as profit after all expenses are covered, calculated as profit divided by sales revenue
revenue centre a sub-unit in which the manager is held accountable for revenue generated by that sub-unit
reward system processes, practices and systems that are used to provide levels of pay and benefits to employees
rolling (or **continuous**) **budget** a budget that is continually updated by adding a new time period (such as a quarter) and dropping the period just completed
root cause cost drivers the underlying factors that cause activities to be performed and their costs to be incurred

S

safety margin the difference between the budgeted sales revenue and the break-even sales revenue
safety stock the extra inventory kept on hand to cover any above-average usage or demand
sales budget a detailed summary of the estimated sales units and revenues from the organisation's products for the budget period
sales forecasting the process of estimating the composition and level of sales for the coming period
sales mix the relative proportions of each type of product sold by the organisation
sales price variance the difference between actual sales price and budgeted sales price, multiplied by actual sales volume
sales volume variance the difference between actual sales volume and budgeted sales volume, multiplied by budgeted unit contribution margin
scatter diagram a plot of costs at various levels of activity
schedule of cost of goods manufactured schedule detailing the cost of direct materials, direct labour and manufacturing overhead applied to work in process during the period, and showing the changes to the work in process inventory
schedule of cost of goods sold a report showing the cost of goods sold, which is equal to the cost of goods manufactured adjusted for changes in finished goods inventory and under/overapplied overhead
scrapping allowance if an asset is sold for less than its tax value in the normal course of business, then a firm may deduct this allowance from the firm's taxable income. The scrapping allowance is equal to tax value less selling price
segmented profit statement a report of the profits for the major responsibility centres, and for the entire organisation
self-managed work teams teams that have wide responsibilities to manage all aspects of a particular process
selling expenses the costs of marketing and distributing the firm's goods or services
semivariable (or **mixed**) **cost** a cost that consists of both fixed and variable components
sensitivity analysis an approach which examines how a result or outcome may change if there are variations in the predicted data or underlying assumptions
separable processing costs manufacturing costs that are incurred after the split-off point and that can be traced directly to specific products
service level agreement (**SLA**) a contract between two sub-units of an organisation to establish the nature of the service that will be provided by one unit to the other, and the responsibilities of the supplying and buying parties
service organisations organisations that deliver help, utility or care, providing an experience, information or other intellectual content, where the majority of the value is intangible rather than residing in any physical products
service shops organisations that fit between professional and mass service entities in terms of number of customers, staff time and degree of customisation
set-up time the time that it takes to get the machine and materials ready to start producing a product
shared services the concentration of support services that are typically spread across a decentralised organisation, into a separate unit to service multiple internal customers
shareholder value the value that shareholders, or owners, place on a business
shareholder value added (**SVA**) the corporate value of the company, less the debt
shortage (or **stockout**) **costs** the costs of running out of inventory

simple regression a statistical technique that estimates a linear relationship between a dependent variable and only one independent variable
skimming pricing a strategy of setting the initial product price high, and reaping high short-term profits on a new product
social auditing a formal process where organisations measure and report the extent to which they have operated in accordance with their stated shared values and objectives
social performance the impact of an organisation's behaviour on society, including the broader community, employees, customers and suppliers
source document the basic document used to initiate an accounting entry
spare (**excess**) **production capacity** situations in which equipment, labour or other inputs to production are not being utilised, and hence are available for other purposes
split-off point the stage in the production process at which the joint products are identifiable as separate products
spoilage defective products and wasted resources that cannot be recovered by rework or recycling
staff management managers who support the activities of an organisation as a whole, and are only indirectly involved in the operations of a business
standard cost the budgeted cost, based on estimates of the cost of material, labour and overhead resources, that should be used to make one unit of product
standard cost variance the difference between the actual cost and the budgeted or standard cost
standard costing system a system in which all inventories are recorded at standard cost
standard direct labour quantity the number of labour hours needed to manufacture one unit of a product
standard error of the coefficient a measure of the degree to which the estimated value of each coefficient is likely to have been affected by random factors
standard labour rate the total hourly cost of wages, including on-costs
standard material price the total delivered cost of direct material required to produce one unit of a product, after subtracting any quantity discounts
standard material quantity the total amount of direct material required to produce one unit of a product
static budget a detailed budget that relates to one specific planned level of activity
statistical control chart a plot of the standard cost variances across time compared with a statistically determined critical value to highlight the variances that should be investigated
step-down method a method of allocating support department costs that partially recognises services provided by one support department to another
step-fixed cost a cost that remains fixed over a wide range of activity levels, but jumps to a different amount for levels outside that range
strategic alliances formalised cooperative arrangements between two or more parties, involving the sharing of resources and activities to enhance the strategies of all participants
strategic business unit (**SBU**) a profit centre or investment centre that has its own clearly defined strategies and markets
strategic cost reduction challenge the difference between the product-level target cost and the allowable cost
strategic planning long-term planning to achieve the organisation's objectives, usually undertaken by senior managers
strategic processes those processes that focus on achieving the company's business objectives and strategies
strategies the direction that the organisation intends to take over the long term, to meet its mission and achieve its objectives
strategy implementation putting plans into place to implement and support a chosen business strategy
sunk costs costs that have already been incurred and are irrelevant to any future decisions
supplier costs the costs associated with dealing with a particular supplier, including the purchase price of materials, and a range of costs that are triggered by the purchase activity or the supplier
supplier performance index (**SPI**) the ratio of supplier activity costs to the total purchase price
supply chain the interlinked customers and suppliers that work together to convert, distribute and sell goods and services among themselves, leading to a specific end product
supply chain management (**SCM**) the management of key business processes that extend across that supply chain, from the original suppliers to the final customers
supply costs the costs of sourcing and managing incoming parts, assemblies and supplies
support department (or **service department**) a manufacturing department that does not work directly on producing products but is necessary for the manufacturing process to occur
support department cost allocation the process of reassigning all support department costs to the production departments

T

***t*-statistic** a statistic used to test the significance of each individual independent variable in the regression equation
tactical decisions decisions that do not require significant or permanent resource commitments, and can be changed or reversed if better opportunities arise
target cost reduction objective the cost reductions that are achievable, based on a realistic assessment of the ability of the product designers, production engineers and suppliers to remove cost from the product
target costing a system of profit planning and cost management that determines the life cycle cost at which a proposed product must be produced, to generate the firm's desired level of profit, given the product's anticipated selling price
target profit a desired profit level determined by management
target profit margin the return on sales that the business requires to make an acceptable profit on the product
target selling price the anticipated selling price for the product, based on market considerations and the strategic objectives for the product
tax value (or **written-down value**) an asset's cost less depreciation deductions to date
team-based incentive schemes systems where individuals are rewarded when their work team exceeds certain performance targets
theoretical capacity the maximum level of production that can be achieved in a specified period where the plant runs at peak efficiency
theory of constraints an approach to managing costs and improving quality and delivery performance, by focusing on identifying and removing bottlenecks
throughput accounting a method of measuring the effects of bottlenecks and operational decisions using financial measures of throughput, inventory and operating expense
time and material pricing an approach to cost-plus pricing where one charge is determined for the labour used on a job and another charge is determined for the materials
time and motion studies (or **task analysis** or **work measurement**) observation of the steps required and time taken by employees to perform particular activities, in order to estimate a cost function
time-based management (**TBM**) an approach that focuses on compressing the time it takes to undertake all of the business's processes to enhance customer value and reduce costs
time driver any factor that changes the duration of an activity
time sheet a form used to record the amount of labour time spent on each job or activity
timely information information that is available in time to be used in the decision-making process
top-down budgeting the system where senior managers impose budget targets on more junior managers with little or no consultation
total contribution margin the difference between total sales revenue and total variable costs
total cost curve a graph of the relationship between total cost and the quantity produced and sold
total cost of ownership the costs associated with dealing with a particular supplier, including the purchase price of materials, and a range of costs that are triggered by the purchase activity or the supplier
total factor productivity a measure of the ratio of outputs produced to all production inputs
total quality management (**TQM**) a management approach that centres on meeting customer requirements by achieving continuous improvement in products or services
total revenue curve a graph of the relationship between total sales revenue and quantity sold
transfer price an internal selling price used when goods or services are transferred between profit centres and investment centres within a divisionalised organisation
transferred-in costs the costs assigned to partially completed goods transferred from one department or process to the next
triple bottom line (**TBL**) **report** a report that focuses on three aspects of performance: financial (or economic), social and environmental
two-dimensional activity-based costing a costing system that provides information about activities, cost drivers and performance, as well as the costs of cost objects
two-stage cost allocation process the process of allocating overhead costs to products by first assigning overhead costs to production departments, and then applying departmental overhead costs to product

U

unavoidable costs costs that will continue to be incurred no matter which course of action is chosen
uncontrollable cost a cost that a manager cannot control or influence significantly

underapplied overhead the amount by which the total manufacturing overhead applied to production is less than the total of the actual overhead costs incurred
unit contribution margin the difference between the sales price per unit and variable cost per unit
unit level activities activities performed for each unit of product
unit level costs costs relating to activities that are performed for each unit produced

V

value-added activity an activity that provides essential value to the customer, or is essential to the functioning of the business
value (or **activity**) **analysis** a method that classifies activities as value-added or non-value-added
value-based management (**VBM**) a framework for making key business decisions that add economic value to the business
value-based pricing a pricing strategy where customers' perceptions of value guide the price
value chain a set of linked processes or activities that begins with acquiring resources and ends with providing (and supporting) products and services that customers value
value drivers activities or actions that create value for a business
value engineering (**VE**) a systematic approach to analysing the product and process design to eliminate any non-value-added elements to achieve the target cost, while maintaining or increasing customer value
variable cost a cost that changes, in total, in direct proportion to a change in the level of activity
variable cost of goods sold the total amount of direct material, direct labour and variable overhead assigned to the units sold
variable costing only variable costs are assigned to products: direct material, direct labour and variable manufacturing overhead
variable manufacturing overhead costs indirect manufacturing costs that vary in proportion to the level of production (or volume of overhead cost driver)
variable overhead efficiency variance a measure of the difference between actual activity and the standard activity allowed, given the actual output, multiplied by the standard variable overhead rate
variable overhead spending variance a measure of the difference between the actual variable overhead and the standard variable overhead rate multiplied by actual activity
virtual close the ability to close the accounting books at any time
vision the desired future state or aspiration of an organisation
volume-based cost driver (**1**) a cost driver that assumes that costs are driven, or caused, by the volume of production (or sales) (**2**) a measure of, or proxy for, the volume of production

W

waiting time the time between an order being received by manufacturing and production commencing
weighted average cost of capital (**WACC**) the weighted average of the cost of funds from all sources of borrowings and equity
weighted average method a process costing method that averages the cost of opening WIP inventory and current production costs to determine the cost of completed production and closing WIP
weighted average unit contribution margin the average of the products' unit contribution margins, weighted by the sales mix
what-if analysis allows the analyst to specify changes in assumptions in a financial model, and to examine the effect of those changes on the output
wholesalers businesses that resell goods to other businesses for use in their production processes or for resale to the public
work in process inventory the products on which manufacture has begun but is only partially complete at balance date
working capital the excess of current assets over current liabilities

Z

zero-base budgeting the process where all activities in the organisation are initially set to zero. To receive an allocation of resources during the budgeting process, managers must justify each activity in terms of its continued usefulness to the business

Index